PASTORAL LETTERS AND STATEMENTS
of the United States Catholic Bishops

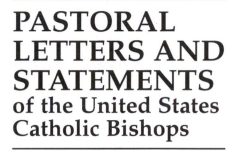

PASTORAL LETTERS AND STATEMENTS
of the United States Catholic Bishops

Patrick W. Carey, Editor

Volume VI
1989-1997

National Conference of Catholic Bishops
United States Catholic Conference
Washington, D.C.

The bishops of the United States have provided religious and moral guidance and leadership to American Catholics since the establishment of the hierarchy in the United States. *Pastoral Letters and Statements of the United States Catholic Bishops, 1989-1997, Volume VI,* is a collection of statements issued by the Catholic hierarchy of the United States during the nine-year period. This collection was initiated by the USCC Office for Publishing and Promotion Services and is authorized for publication by the undersigned.

Monsignor Dennis M. Schnurr
General Secretary
NCCB/USCC

Dust jacket: Detail of a bishop's crosier from the ruins of the Cisterian Abbey, Boyle, Country Roscommon, Ireland; photo by Dan Juday.

First Printing, November 1998

ISBN 1-57455-174-4

I am the good shepherd,
and I know mine
and mine know me,
just as the Father knows me
and I know the Father;
and I will lay down my life
for the sheep.
I have other sheep
that do not belong to this fold.
These also I must lead,
and they will hear my voice.

John 10:14-16

Contents

Appendices

Foreword

"Unless the LORD build the house, they labor in vain who build." These opening words of Psalm 127 contain a profound truth that comes to mind in surveying the nearly decade's worth of activity by the National Conference of Catholic Bishops/United States Catholic Conference, which this sixth volume of *Pastoral Letters and Statements of the United States Catholic Bishops* represents.

The NCCB/USCC, organized in 1966 in accord with the wishes of the Second Vatican Council and as the successor to the National Catholic Welfare Conference, has entered its fourth decade. It is a "house" which the Lord continues to build, enabling the bishops of the United States to support one another and to shepherd the flock given into their care more effectively.

In the *Decree on the Bishops' Pastoral Office in the Church*, the fathers of the Second Vatican Council said that they considered it "supremely opportune everywhere that bishops belonging to the same nation or region form an association to meet together at fixed times. Thus, when the insights of prudence and experience have been shared and views exchanged, there will emerge a holy union of energies in the service of the common good of the church" (*Christus Dominus*, no. 37). With this principle already in operation in the United States, the U.S. bishops were quick to take the necessary additional steps to put into effect the council's solemn wish.

Far from diminishing the creativity of individual dioceses, as some suggested that bishops' conferences might do, this conference helps focus and define issues and offers practical approaches to them. It provides a national and sometimes international resonance to concerns for youth, family life, evangelization, and the pastoral needs of African American and Hispanic Catholics, to mention only a few areas covered by the documents in this volume.

Happily and helpfully, these volumes are not limited to formal "pastoral letters." Thus this newest volume contains, as do previous ones, a variety of types of statements: those issued by the conference's Administrative Committee/Board, statements and resolutions issued by individual committees with authorization by the conference, and statements responding to current events made in accord with general conference policy.

One thing that should strike the reader is the conference's concentration on building up the interior life of the Church. At times, news coverage puts so much emphasis on the conference's consideration of matters which are also on the agenda of secular society that even some

1

Catholics are left with a skewed impression of the bishops' activities and interests.

This volume reflects clearly the bishops' pastoral concern for the spiritual well-being of the Catholic people of the United States. One example is *A Future Full of Hope,* the national strategy for vocations. It has brought focus and a systematic approach to a matter facing individual dioceses and the entire Church in the United States. *Go and Make Disciples: A National Plan and Strategy for Catholic Evangelization in the United States* does the same for this basic duty of the Church and of each Catholic. *The Pastoral Plan for Church Communication,* developed in response to a call for such plans by the Pontifical Council for Social Communications, provides a similar impetus in the important area of communicating the Gospel through contemporary means of communication.

As the contents of this volume show, the conference continues to be characterized by actions and statements in support of Catholic schools. Other matters of substance and concern to every Catholic which find their place on the bishops' agenda are the liturgy, Catholic health care, women's role in the Church, and the role of the laity.

Stewardship—how to encourage our lay people to share their time, talent, and material resources and how best to use these generous gifts when offered—is a subject to which the bishops gave more of a systematic reflection in these years than ever before in the history of the Church in the United States. The resulting pastoral letter is found in this volume.

Nor should the pastoral ministry which the bishops offer one another through the conference be ignored. The conference is a forum for bishops to share their concerns and to be refreshed by prayer and consultation among themselves. In this volume, this aspect is most clearly revealed in documents on the bishops' teaching office and on the bishops' relationship to theologians. The resolution on clergy sexual abuse also shows the bishops' finding in the conference an opportunity for developing the insights to help each other shoulder the burden of dealing with these tragic and disturbing incidents, where they are present.

While news coverage which emphasizes only the bishops' response to public policy issues distorts the record, the U.S. bishops do speak out regularly on a variety of national and international issues.

The previous volumes witness the courage that bishops of past eras had in speaking on public issues, even while some of their fellow citizens tried to make the Catholic faith appear alien to the American way of life. Any reticence bred in the bishops by this anti-Catholicism which pervaded much of U.S. society was obliterated when the Supreme Court made "abortion on demand" not only legal but a "constitutional right." Since that time the bishops have been outspoken in opposition to this massive violation of human rights. As nearly the sole national voice in opposition at the time, the conference's statements were indispensable to guaranteeing that a pro-abortion mentality would not take hold in the United States.

The contents of this volume witness the conference's consistency in the matter of abortion and its presence at the forefront of making the public aware of the horror of all abortion by working to ban partial-birth abortion. During the last decade, the movement to legalize euthanasia gathered force and has been regularly opposed by the bishops, as this volume will also tell the reader. These life issues are discussed with the kind of pastoral sensitivity which helps us in upholding and proclaiming our moral principles (cf. *Nutrition and Hydration: Moral and Pastoral Reflections,* the updated *Ethical and Religious Directives for Catholic Health Care Services,* and *Critical Decisions: Genetic Testing and Its Implications*).

The initial lonely public opposition to abortion gave an impetus to the conference's willingness to look critically at society and its attitudes. This is demonstrated by the substantial pastoral letters which offered critiques of Marxism, the U.S. economy, and our nation's posture vis-à-vis weapons of mass destruction published in the previous volumes. In issuing these letters—and in making any public policy statements—the conference takes the view that the practical application of principles must be made by those with the expertise and legitimate authority to do so. At the same time, the bishops emphasize that these practical decisions must be based on fundamental moral principles.

Some, even some Catholics, question on what basis the bishops offer statements on public policy. When I first addressed the conference as president, I spoke to these questions. Guided by the words of the Second Vatican Council, I identified the role of the bishop in this regard as that of "teacher." Citing *Christus Dominus,* I noted that it describes the teaching office of bishops in three paragraphs. It begins by saying that announcing the Gospel is "a task which is eminent among the chief duties of bishops." After listing a great variety of specific matters about which bishops should teach, the passage concludes by saying that bishops "should set forth the ways by which are to be solved the very grave questions concerning the ownership, increase, and just distribution of material goods, peace and war, and brotherly relations among all peoples" (*Christus Dominus,* no. 12).

In my talk I pointed out that these paragraphs are not a "shopping list of topics" but the expression of a truly Catholic vision that links the eternal with the temporal, the things of this world with those of the next, the love of God with the love of neighbor. Thus, "this passage expresses our vocation to reflect on the Church's theological and moral tradition; to draw from it the lasting principles which are at the foundation of any healthy society; and to persuade our society—where persuasion is needed—to live by those principles."

The bishops are conscious, of course, that exercising their role as teacher in the area of public policy is hindered by society's lack of familiarity with the great tradition of Catholic social teaching. In the hope of doing something about this, the conference issued *A Century of Social Teaching: A Common Heritage, A Continuing Challenge* in advance of the centenary of Pope Leo XIII's encyclical *Rerum Novarum*, the fountainhead of modern Catholic social teaching. The conference's document calls the Catholic people to appropriate this heritage and make it an active part of their church commitment. Another document, *Communities of Salt and Light*, offers a very practical reflection on the social mission of the parish. Both are included here.

One issue that was articulated with a new clarity and urgency in the years covered by this volume is summed up by the title of the relevant document that appears in this volume, *Renewing the Earth: An Invitation to Reflection and Action on Environment in Light of Catholic Social Teaching*. Other documents contained in this volume manifest the concerns of the bishops along a wide spectrum of public policy issues, including Third World debt, food policy, labor issues, violence, the arms trade and landmines, health care, and welfare reform. The U.S. bishops' conference continues to manifest its concern for the well-being of the Church elsewhere in the world especially, during these years of dramatic change, for the Church in Central and Eastern Europe.

Several documents demonstrate the conference's growing "maturity" as the bishops take time to turn to documents now several years old for reassessment and renewal. *Called and Gifted for the Third Millennium; A Decade After "Economic Justice for All": Continuing Principles, Changing Context, New Challenges;* and *The Harvest of Justice Is Sown in Peace* are all rooted in previous documents which are now bearing this new fruit.

Reviewing the contents of this volume, I cannot think of a single issue for which the conference would not be the poorer if it had chosen not to address it. This is not to say that every document exhausts the wisdom of what can be said about its subject. I do contend, however, that given the long view which history provides, the conference comes far closer to reflecting the real needs of Church and society than even we bishops are sometimes aware.

I hope that all readers of this volume and its predecessors will conclude that the Lord is indeed building the house that is the NCCB/USCC, and that the bishops who have been given the privilege of laboring with him are not building in vain.

Most Reverend Anthony M. Pilla
Bishop of Cleveland
President, NCCB/USCC

Preface

From 1989 until the end of 1997, the National Conference of Catholic Bishops/United States Catholic Conference (NCCB/USCC) produced more than 185 statements on a variety of national, international, and ecclesiastical issues. No other national Catholic body in the United States communicates the faith and teachings of the Catholic Church with the authority of the NCCB/USCC. On national and international matters, the NCCB/USCC relates officially to the Holy See and to the Church in other parts of the world through national and regional bishops' conferences. As the Catholic hierarchy of a nation which emerged as one of the world's two superpowers in the aftermath of World War II, the U.S. Catholic bishops assumed a more important role in international ecclesiastical and civil affairs than ever before in its two hundred-year history.

The publication of episcopal statements follows a long tradition of Catholicism in the United States, established in 1791 when, after the first diocesan synod, Bishop John Carroll, the first U.S. Catholic bishop, published a pastoral letter to his priests and people explaining what had been accomplished during the synod and calling upon the faithful to participate in the upbuilding of the Catholic Church in the country.[1]

Periodically throughout the nineteenth century and annually after 1919, the U.S. Catholic bishops published statements and pastoral letters to the American people on a variety of issues. After the Second Vatican Council (1962-1965) and especially after the establishment of the NCCB/USCC in 1966, the bishops and their national committees and administrative units have published numerous documents each year on a wide range of ecclesial, ethical, legislative, and domestic and foreign policy issues.

This sixth volume of *Pastoral Letters and Statements of the United States Catholic Bishops* contains sixty-four episcopal statements, that is, about 35 percent of the 185 that the bishops produced.[2] The number of statements produced about a wide range of issues has, at various times, caused some bishops to ask whether their very productivity has led to individual statements being less effective than they could have been. On the one hand, with no lack of issues having moral and religious implications in American society, many bishops emphasized the responsibility to make those implications clear to their people. Creating a proper balance is still under discussion within the conference at this time.

Of the documents reproduced here, pastoral letters and other statements of official policy require a two-thirds majority vote of the full body of the U.S. Catholic episcopate. Other documents received the approval of the full body with a simple majority. Some of these documents are statements issued by the Administrative Committee/Board or by one of the episcopal committees of the NCCB or USCC. All committees need the approval of the Administrative Board/Committee to issue their statements.

The statements in this volume, like those in the previous three volumes, reflect the U.S. episcopate's attempts to carry out the implications of the Second Vatican Council. It has been said that implementing the directives of an ecumenical council takes a century or more,[3] and the U.S. episcopal statements in this volume are a continuing part of that implementation process. Looked at as a whole, they manifest the bishops' sense of responsibility for the continued renewal of Christian life within the Church and for the moral and social implications of the faith in American culture and in international affairs.

Although united in faith and in a sense of social justice and bound together institutionally and canonically, the 350 bishops within the NCCB have not always agreed among themselves on a number of issues. The statements that they produced generally reflected a working consensus that took into account the range of theological and ecclesiastical opinion. Although the bishops were not as divided as the media made them out to be, their consensus statements are all the more interesting for their being worked out, in some cases, on the anvil of conflicting opinion.

I want to thank Ms. Cynthia Orticio of the USCC's Office for Publishing and Promotion Services for her guidance and support during the preparation of the introduction and the selection process for this volume.

Patrick W. Carey
Editor

Notes

1. "Pastoral Letter," May 28, 1792, in *Pastoral Letters of the United States Catholic Bishops,* ed. Hugh J. Nolan, 5 vols. (Washington, D.C.: United States Catholic Conference, 1983, 1984, 1989), 1:16-27.
2. A full listing of the documents is in *Origins,* the journal where most of the episcopal statements were originally published.
3. Bishop Phillip F. Straling of Reno, "Minutes of the General Meeting, National Conference of Catholic Bishops," Washington, D.C., November 13-16, 1995, p. 29.

Introduction

This introduction sets the historical context for the documents included in this volume. In preparing it, I had access to the minutes of all the national episcopal meetings that took place between 1989 and 1997. The bishops regularly meet in November of each year and also in June.

I have organized this introduction thematically around the various issues that have preoccupied the U.S. bishops during the period. They can be characterized as ecclesial issues; domestic social, economic, environmental, medical-moral, political, and educational issues; and foreign relations issues, primarily international issues of justice and peace. Within this structure I have taken a chronological approach to each of the thematic issues that emerged.

Internal Ecclesial Issues

A primary and overriding concern for the U.S. Catholic bishops during the last decades of the twentieth century was evangelization. Renewed attention to evangelization was one of the aims of the Second Vatican Council. It was the focus of Pope Paul VI's *On Evangelization in the Modern World* (*Evangelii Nuntiandi*, 1975) and of two Roman episcopal synods (1974, 1977), and it has been a central subject for Pope John Paul II. In fact, Pope John Paul II refers to a "new evangelization," and the U.S. bishops have picked up on that phrase in many of their own statements. In general the new evangelization is a renewed effort to proclaim the Gospel in such a way as to transform individual persons and modern society and culture in conformity with the word of God.

The U.S. bishops have focused on evangelization in its personal dimension of conversion to Christ and holiness of life and the social dimension of the transformation of culture and society in line with the Gospel. By the late 1980s and early 1990s, it was becoming clear to the bishops that they needed to focus on this fundamental mission of the Church in the United States.

One of the first major explicit statements on evangelization during this period was *Here I Am, Send Me* (1989, republished here), a title taken from Isaiah 6:8. This statement was a response to a detailed plan for evangelizing African American Catholics. The plan itself had actually been created at the National Black Catholic Congress (May 1987), the first national meeting of Black Catholics since the last Afro-American Catholic Congress in 1894.[1] When introduced on the floor of the bishops' annual meeting, Auxiliary Bishop John Ricard, SSJ, of

Baltimore, chair of the bishops' Committee on Black Catholics (now the Committee on African American Catholics), noted that the statement reflected the committee's "concern for the spiritual and pastoral growth of African American Catholics, which takes on greater urgency in light of the threats to social, economic, and community survival for these Americans."[2] The statement and the detailed plan for evangelizing (the plan is not included in this volume) passed unanimously. The statement called for a renewed diocesan emphasis upon evangelization that was focused on the needs of African Americans. It also recalled two previous episcopal statements on the situation of African Americans in American society: *Brothers and Sisters to Us: U. S. Bishops' Pastoral Letter on Racism in Our Day* (1979)[3] and *What We Have Seen and Heard: A Pastoral Letter on Evangelization from the Black Bishops of the United States* (1984).[4]

Some national surveys indicated that by 1991 there were about 2.5 million African American Catholic laity (i.e., a number larger than many Protestant denominations)[5] and eleven African American Catholic bishops. The focus on evangelization pointed in particular to the maturity of the African American Catholic faith community and its responsibility to participate in the evangelization of other Americans, particularly the unchurched.

In 1990 the bishops returned to the issue of evangelization, this time using the occasion of the fifth centenary of the evangelization of the Americas to call for renewed efforts to evangelize. *Heritage and Hope: Evangelization in the United States* (republished here), using the words of Pope Paul VI, defined evangelization as "bringing the good news [of Jesus Christ] into all strata of humanity, and through its influence transforming humanity from within and making it new." It reflected on the past failures and successes in evangelization, hoping to learn from the past and dedicating new initiatives toward evangelization in the third millennium. It acknowledged the Church's own sins of neglect and racism in the past, focused on the twentieth-century opportunities for personal and social transformation, and called for reconciliation, solidarity, and a renewed commitment to the life of the Gospel in the Americas. The challenges in Catholicism in the United States were acute, as was evident by the presence of over seventeen million inactive Catholics and the traditional reluctance of active Catholics to spread the faith in American culture. The document addressed these issues by calling for a "new evangelization" among Catholics in the United States of all occupations and professions: scholars and teachers, parents and youth, artists and public servants, laborers and mechanics—all had a baptismal responsibility to spread the faith and transform the society in which they lived. It also stressed the Catholic's responsibility to take care of culture and the natural environment, an essential aspect of the broadened concept of evangelization.

In 1992, the quincentenary of the discovery of America, the bishops again explicitly raised the issue of evangelization in two major documents, *Go and Make Disciples: A National Plan and Strategy for Catholic Evangelization in the United States* and *A Time for Remembering, Reconciling, and Recommitting Ourselves as a People* (both documents republished here). The first document recalled the past Catholic experiences of evangelization in the United States, but focused more particularly on the need to reconcile inactive Catholics to the Church, to re-evangelize active Catholics, to deepen the sense of Christian unity among all churches, to invite the unchurched to consider conversion to Christ, and to foster gospel values in society. During a 1992 NCCB meeting, Archbishop Edward A. McCarthy of Miami asserted that the need for evangelization in the United States was clear: 17 million Catholics were inactive; 23 percent of Hispanics had left the Church; a large percentage of professed Catholics ignored the eucharist and other sacraments; vocations continued to decline; and corruption, materialism, consumerism, licentiousness, and social irresponsibility were polluting American society and debilitating the Church.[6] *Go and Make Disciples* clearly distinguished evangelization, a free invitation to conversion, from proselytism, the use of pressure tactics and manipulation to draw peoples to Christ and the Church. The second document focused in particular on evangelization among Native Americans, inculturation of the faith, a more active Native American participation in the Church, and a stronger encouragement of Native American leadership within the Church as a chief form of inculturation and evangelization.

The emphasis on the new evangelization was also clearly the intention in the bishops' 1995 pastoral *Hispanic Presence in the New Evangelization in the United States* (republished here). That document was an episcopal response to "Convocation '95," a national convention of those involved in Hispanic ministries that convened in San Antonio, Tex., in June 1995 to commemorate the fiftieth anniversary of the U.S. bishops' establishment of the national office for ministry to Hispanics. In 1945, because of the insistence and persistence of San Antonio's Archbishop Robert E. Lucey, the National Catholic Welfare Conference, predecessor to the NCCB/USCC, developed the office of Hispanic Affairs primarily to act as an advocate for poor and oppressed Hispanics in the Southwest. Since that time the office increased its attention to Hispanic affairs and broadened its concerns from justice and peace issues to issues of ministry and inculturation.

"Convocation '95" issued a "Statement of Commitment," which called upon the bishops to share with the entire Church the convention's own views of the contributions of Hispanics to the Church. *Hispanic Presence* was the episcopal response. It outlined in particular the relationship between faith and culture and used the Hispanic experience as a model for the new evangelization. During the NCCB floor discussion of the pastoral, Coadjutor Bishop Roberto Gonzales, OFM, of Corpus Christi pointed out the significance of the Hispanic presence in Catholicism in the United States: about one-third of Catholics in the United States were Hispanic; 50 percent of Hispanics were under the age of twenty-five; 20 percent were under ten years of age; 70 percent were native born; and by the year 2020, demographers estimate, the majority of Catholics in the United States would be Hispanic.[7] Thus, the bishops must pay close attention to the Hispanic culture when speaking of the new evangelization.

The Hispanic experience was also highlighted in another 1995 document, *Communion and Mission: A Guide for Bishops and Pastoral Agents on Small Church Communities* (republished here). Small group communities, the document asserted, could be seen as an effective instrument in the new evangelization, and the Hispanic experience of them could be seen as a gift to the entire Church. The statement itself was designed as a tool for use by bishops and others involved in the new evangelization, emphasizing in particular the numerous fruits that result from gathering Catholics within small group communities where they can personally become involved in the new evangelization and participate intimately in building up a common life in grace and service. The document saw small base communities, which were developing and increasing within the Hispanic community, as significant agents for the renewal of the entire Church. The document also provided small group leaders with a series of questions to guide them in evaluating their identity and mission.

In preparation for the Jubilee Year 2000,[8] proclaimed in Pope John Paul II's *Tertio Millennio Adveniente* (1994), the bishops' Subcommittee on the Third Millennium produced in 1997 *Open Wide the Doors to Christ: A Framework for Action to Implement* Tertio Millennio Adveniente (parts of which are republished here). The document outlined a detailed three-year plan of preparation for the jubilee year. The plan focused on continuous conversion of Catholics and other Christians to Christ, preparing for a "new springtime of Christianity."

The emphasis on evangelization was also evident in a number of episcopal statements on catechesis. Since the Second Vatican Council the bishops have produced a *General Catechetical Directory* (1971), "Basic Teachings for Catholic Religious Education" (1972), and *Sharing the Light of Faith, The National Catechetical Directory for Catholics of the United States* (1979). The third and fourth general assemblies of the Roman Synod of Bishops in 1974 and 1977, Pope John Paul II's *On Catechesis in Our Time* (*Catechesi Tradendae*, 1979), and especially the 1985 Synod of Bishops (which proposed the establishment of a catechism for the universal Church) have encouraged a renewed look at the catechetical enterprise. In response to these documents and a general concern about instruction in the faith, the bishops produced in 1990 *Guidelines for Doctrinally Sound Catechetical Materials* (republished here), a document intended as a national guide for publishers of catechetical materials and programs in the United States. The guidelines laid down some general principles for dealing with doctrine in the production of catechetical materials. This document singled out certain doctrines that seemed to need particular emphasis in American life and culture in the early 1990s.

In 1994 the long-awaited English edition of the *Catechism of the Catholic Church* was published in the United States. Pope John Paul II promulgated the original French text in 1992, and the Catechism soon became a major instrument in passing on the faith. The English edition was widely distributed in the United States, selling millions of copies. The role of catechesis in the Church in the United States would continue to be a concern at annual meetings of the NCCB. The bishops periodically examined catechetical materials in the 1990s, and in June 1997 the NCCB Ad Hoc Committee to Oversee the Use of the Catechism outlined what it considered to be some major lacunae and deficiencies in them.[9]

The issue of communicating the faith also involved the question of the Church's use of various print as well as electronic media. In 1997 the bishops published *A Pastoral Plan for Church Communication*,[10] which outlined the way in which the Church could more effectively use media to evangelize and get the Church's message into the public forum. In 1997, too, the USCC Committee on Communications produced a "Resolution on Computer Networking" (republished here), encouraging the use of new forms of media and calling attention to some specific moral and religious concerns about the use of the Internet.

The liturgical life of Catholics in the United States continued to be a central focus of concern at the annual meetings of the U.S. hierarchy. Some of the longest and most tense debates within the conference were on the revisions and translations of liturgical texts. In 1990 the bishops produced *Criteria for the Evaluation of Inclusive Language Translations of Scriptural Texts Proposed for Liturgical Use* (republished here), outlining nine general principles that should guide translators in their translations and bishops in their supervision of public worship in the use of biblical language that is doctrinally sound and appropriately adjusted to the changing connotations of language in American culture. The task, as the document outlined, was to balance theological and doctrinal integrity while developing linguistic and aesthetic beauty in the public discourse of the liturgy. The document described general principles that were intended to help bishops and others distinguish a legitimate translation from one that was imprecise or lacked doctrinal integrity.

The document on inclusive language was published after much committee discussion and after a lengthy floor debate at the NCCB general meeting in 1990. Initiated in 1985, the document was revised seven times in committee before it was presented to the full body of bishops. During the floor discussion it was clear that different theories seemed to be guiding approaches to the translation of texts for liturgical use, giving rise to different preferences within the episcopal body on what should be the principles for judging translations.

At the end of the debate Archbishop Oscar Lipscomb, the chair of the committee that produced the document, responded to the episcopal discussion by saying that "the Church must be willing to change when change is necessary, so long as it remains faithful to the tradition." And, he believed that the document on inclusive language did that. The document passed by a vote of 183 to 35.[11]

Liturgical concerns were also reflected in a 1990 episcopal-sponsored study of the sacrament of penance.[12] The study listed various reasons for the decline of confession, offered anthropological, cultural, and theological analysis of this data, and suggested ways to improve and increase the practice in the future. Emphasizing the absolute secrecy of the seal of confession, moreover, the bishops were outraged by an Oregon prison official's taping of a suspect's confession in 1996. In response, the Archdiocese of Portland filed a lawsuit, and USCC General Counsel prepared legal briefs and protested against this invasion of the free exercise of religion.[13] As in 1978 and 1988,[14] furthermore, the U.S. bishops in 1995 published *Guidelines for the Celebration of the Sacraments with Persons with Disabilities* (republished here). The document offered a series of general principles for giving persons with disabilities access to sacramental celebrations. With the increasing use of cremation within the Catholic Church, the bishops also published *Reflections on the Body, Cremation, and Catholic Funeral Rites*[15] to provide some new directives for funeral rites within a context of a Catholic understanding of the body.

The new evangelization had as one of its intended aims the building up of the ecclesial community. That emphasis upon the communal reality was evident in all of the previous documents and was clear in a number of other documents specifically addressed to that issue. In November 1995, fifteen years after its last statement on the laity,[16] the bishops published *Called and Gifted for the Third Millennium* (republished here), which updated the previous calls to holiness, community, mission and ministry, and Christian maturity "in light of church teaching, pastoral practice, and the changing conditions in the world." It focused, moreover, on the gifts of the laity and their contribution to building up the Christian life in the new millennium.

Three other statements focused on the youth in the Church. In October 1994 the bishops addressed *A Message to Youth: Pathway to*

Hope (republished here), which called young people not only "our future" but also "a special gift to the Church." In *A Letter to College Students* (1995, republished here), the bishops called upon students to live out their Catholic and Christian calling through their devotion to their studies, their exemplary lives on campuses, and their service to the needs of the poor. In 1997, the bishops published *Renewing the Vision: A Framework for Catholic Youth Ministry*,[17] which focused upon ministries to adolescents and called upon all involved with adolescents to use the elements of the new evangelization in their approaches to young people.

The role of women in the Church and in society was one of the most hotly debated issues. The NCCB had long desired to produce a pastoral letter on women's concerns as a means of strengthening the ecclesial community. The proposed pastoral letter was envisioned as a statement that would have an impact similar to that produced by two other pastorals: *The Challenge of Peace* (1983) and *Economic Justice for All* (1986).[18] The general interest in addressing women's issues was evident already in 1972 when the NCCB first established an Ad Hoc Committee on Women in Society and in the Church. In 1983, the committee first proposed to the NCCB that the bishops prepare a pastoral on women's concerns. After the NCCB approved the proposal, the committee established a national commission on women's issues that included a cross section of women scholars and theologians. The commission's task was to hold hearings across the country on women's issues and discuss them prior to preparing a draft of the pastoral.

A first draft of the intended pastoral, "Partners in the Mystery of Redemption: A Pastoral Response to Women's Concerns for Church and Society,"[19] was published in 1988. Before its publication, the world Synod of Bishops met in 1987 to discuss the roles of lay people in Church and society and dealt explicitly with women's participation in the Church. Following that synod, Pope John Paul II published an apostolic exhortation, *The Vocation and the Mission of the Lay Faithful in the Church and in the World (Christifideles Laici*, 1988),[20] which reiterated the synod's perspectives. Six months after the U.S. bishops published their first draft, Pope John Paul II issued his own reflections *On the Dignity and Vocation of Women (Mulieris Dignitatem*, 1988).[21] The proposed U.S. pastoral letter, thus, was surrounded by a flurry of ecclesiastical reflection on women's issues in Church and society.

The first draft of the U.S. pastoral was criticized from various sectors of the Church and returned to the committee for revision. "One in Christ Jesus,"[22] a second draft, was published in 1990 and like the first draft was somewhat descriptive of the diversity of opinions on women's issues.

In 1976, the Vatican had issued *Inter Insigniores* ("A Declaration on the Question of the Admission of Women to the Ministerial Priesthood"),[23] which asserted unequivocally that the ordination of men to the priesthood was a normative part of the tradition which the Church had no authority to change. Although the second draft of the bishops' pastoral acknowledged the complaints and opposition to this church teaching, it quoted the teaching approvingly.

The second draft was never discussed by the NCCB. In October 1990, after the episcopal committee had produced the second draft, the Vatican Secretary of State, Cardinal Agostino Casaroli, at the request of the Congregation for the Doctrine of the Faith which had evaluated the document and sent its appraisal to the NCCB committee, suggested that the U.S. bishops hold a consultation with other national episcopal bodies before they produced their pastoral on women's concerns.

After the consultation took place in Rome on May 28-29, 1991, and in light of this discussion, the NCCB committee produced a third draft, "Called To Be One in Christ Jesus"[24] in March 1992, which was presented at the NCCB meeting in June 1992 and again returned to the committee for final revisions. At that meeting the full body of bishops discussed the document for the first time.

When the draft was presented to the bishops during the June meeting, Bishop Joseph Imesch of Joliet, the chair of the committee, noted that there were divisions on the committee as well as in the full body of bishops. Throughout the process of preparing the pastoral, moreover, various groups had lobbied the committee to abandon the project. The chair asserted that the pastoral should go forward and that the third draft was a middle road between extreme positions in the Church. He and his committee believed that the third draft provided a solid basis for a dialogue on women's issues. It was a tentative and provisional statement.

In the course of the discussion that followed, it was clear that the bishops were divided on whether or not the pastoral should be published and on what they wanted the pastoral to convey to the American people.[25] After much discussion the bishops took a straw vote to continue the process, to revise the current third draft, and to debate and vote on a fourth revised draft during their November meeting.

During the November meeting, after nine years of preparation, the bishops continued to be divided on the contents of the pastoral and on whether or not it should be produced now that it had been revised a number of times to meet the demands of various elements in the Church. After discussing the final draft, the bishops voted by 137 to 110 to publish the pastoral, but since a vote on a pastoral letter required a two-thirds majority (in this case 190 votes), the pastoral did not pass.[26] In effect the bishops decided that the time was not ripe for such a statement since there was very little consensus over so many neuralgic women's issues.

In the course of the discussion, Cardinal Joseph Bernardin offered what he called a compromise proposal for dealing with the pastoral and women's issues in the Church. Like others he saw that there were some philosophical and theological issues underlying the Church's teaching in the pastoral that needed further study, reflection, and dialogue, but there were also some recommendations in the pastoral that needed immediate support and action by the bishops. He suggested, therefore, that the bishops publish the recommended actions and remand to committee for further study the other issues over which the bishops were in disagreement. The motion was amended to include publishing the fourth draft as a committee report and not as a pastoral. The amended motion eventually passed by a vote of 185 to 51.[27]

The decade-long work of the committee did not result in a pastoral letter, but many bishops perceived the necessity of publishing something on the equality and dignity of women in the Church and society and recommending the initiation or continuation of a number of practices in the Church that reinforced women's dignity and leadership. In 1994, therefore, the NCCB published with full episcopal approval *Strengthening the Bonds of Peace* (republished here), which was a general pastoral statement on the equality and leadership of women in the Church. That statement also described what women were already doing in leadership in and for the Church and requested that the provisions in canon law on women's roles in the Church be more widely publicized because they offered opportunities for involvement that were probably not widely known.

The chairman of the NCCB Committee on Women in Society and in the Church, Bishop John Synder of St. Augustine, acknowledged during the episcopal discussion of the draft statement on women that Pope John Paul II's apostolic letter *On Reserving Priestly Ordination to Men Alone* (*Ordinatio Sacerdotalis*, 1994), was the immediate occasion of this statement, but that the document was not about ordination, nor was it about feminism; it was simply a reflection to reaffirm the bishops' belief in the equality of men and women, the need for women's leadership, and the value of diversity of gifts within the Church.[28]

Although a number of bishops, in the debate prior to the vote, pointed out flaws in the document, it underlined some important teachings the bishops believed it was timely to publish. Bishop Michael Pfeifer, OMI, of San Angelo, however, urged that the bishops not only approve the document which collectively admitted that there was sexism in the Church, but also that they do something to eliminate sexist words and actions within the Church. Auxiliary Bishop P. Francis Murphy of Baltimore, moreover, while speaking in favor of the statement, argued that the bishops themselves needed to sit down and discuss feminism and equality because it was obvious from various episcopal debates that the bishops had very different definitions of those terms. The document, therefore, ought to lead to further discussion within the Church and not represent the end of the debate. At the end of the long session the document passed by a vote of 228 to 10.[29]

Strengthening the Bonds of Peace reaffirmed the Church's teaching and practice of ordaining only men. That issue, however, remained a topic of discussion among the bishops as well as among others in the Church. In response to a question (or "dubium") on the definitive nature of the Church's teaching on the ordination issue, the Congregation for the Doctrine of the Faith, in November 1995, responded by reasserting that the Church had no authority to ordain women to the priesthood. In 1996 the Catholic Theological Society of America (CTSA) began preparing a response to the Congregation's "Responsum," and in 1997 the CTSA statement on "Tradition and Women's Ordination" was passed by a vote of the membership present at the June meeting and sent to the NCCB.[30] The theologians' statement questioned whether the "Responsum" settled the question whether the teaching could be considered as set forth infallibly by the Church's ordinary and universal magisterium. In October 1997 the NCCB Committee on Doctrine published a response to the CTSA report (republished here), which took issue with the CTSA statement and outlined again reasons for the Church's declaration against the ordination of women. The response, however, acknowledged the need for continued study, reflection, and discussion among theologians on the Church's teaching because "the theological arguments for the teaching have not yet been fully explored."

Within the Catholic community the bishops also focused upon the lives and ministry of the permanent deacons. In fact, on the twenty-fifth anniversary of the establishment of the permanent diaconate in the United States the bishops issued a "Statement on the Permanent Diaconate,"[31] which indicated that there were 10,324 deacons serving in the Church in 1993, 2,000 men were in formation programs, and 145 of the 185 Latin-rite dioceses in the United States had already established formation programs for deacons. The bishops also sponsored a national study of the permanent diaconate.[32]

The bishops were concerned with vocations to the priesthood and issues of clerical life and spirituality. They were also continuing to monitor the problem of sexual abuse by clergy. Almost everyone in the Catholic Church in the United States was aware of the continuous decline in vocations to the priesthood and religious life in the period after 1965. Bishops repeatedly called attention to the decline at various NCCB general meetings. In 1989, the bishops published a "Statement on Vocations to the Priesthood" (republished here), which was addressed to all levels of parish decision makers. The document called upon all members of the Church to develop a more supportive climate to foster vocations in the young. The episcopal Committee on

Vocations also sponsored two studies[33] on vocations in the 1990s and in 1995 produced a document, *Future Full of Hope: A National Strategy for Vocations to the Priesthood and Religious Life in the Dioceses and Archdioceses of the United States,*[34] which outlined clearly a variety of successful methods for encouraging vocations.

The bishops sought to strengthen the unity of the clergy in the dioceses by emphasizing their co-ministry with the bishop in building up the Church. *United in Service: Reflections on the Presbyteral Council* (1991, republished here) underlined the necessity of cooperation in the task of evangelizing or re-evangelizing the local church. The presbyteral council was a very visible sign of the unity of the sacrament of orders and a way of demonstrating the unity in the priesthood of Christ. During the first days of these diocesan priests' councils in the mid 1960s, the bishops recalled, a number of these councils saw themselves as the loyal opposition and, therefore, confrontation and controversy characterized their proceedings. By the 1990s, the bishops were calling for an attitude of mutual trust to make the structure work for the good of the entire Church.

Numerous complaints of clerical sexual misconduct, particularly with minors, came to public attention in the 1980s and 1990s primarily because of civil suits for damages, and a number of the cases of clerical misconduct were highly publicized in the news media.

The vast implications of sexual abuse became clearly evident to bishops and to the public in 1984 with the case of Fr. Gilbert Gauthe, a multiple sexual offender whose many victims brought suit against him.[35] The revelation of this notorious case also brought to the bishops' attention the medical and psychologically addictive conditions that could cause such behavior. In 1985, the bishops discussed these implications in closed sessions at their annual meetings and began to develop a series of documents to guide bishops in caring for the victims, handling the legal suits, providing medical and psychological help for the offenders, and developing diocesan policies for assisting victims, disciplining the offenders, and constructing ways of detecting signs of this kind of addictive behavior.

Initially the bishops chose to treat the issue confidentially. However, between 1988 and 1997, the conference issued a series of public statements on clerical sexual abuse, which dealt openly with the issue and assured the public that they would swiftly respond to reported cases.

In June 1993 the NCCB established an Ad Hoc Committee on Sexual Abuse. That committee outlined five areas of their focus: (1) pastoral responses to victims and to parishes; (2) emphasis upon the well-being of priests and the prevention of abuse; (3) provision of general resources of information to dioceses; (4) education of church members on the problem; and (5) initiation and support of research that would help not only in the Church but in the wider society. Bishop John Kinney of Bismarck (later bishop of St. Cloud), chair of the committee, acknowledged that up to 1993 the media had given high profile to victims and a relatively low profile to the Church's response to the problem, in part because "many of the Church's efforts were undertaken privately and were not presented to the media." The media rarely acknowledged the bishops' own regret and sorrow over these cases and their sympathy for the pain suffered by all involved.[36] Between 1994 and 1996, the ad hoc committee, which was reauthorized for an additional three years by the conference in 1997, produced three reports, *Restoring Trust*, Vol. I-III.

Of the documents produced on sexual abuse between 1988 and 1997,[37] the "Resolution on Clergy Sex Abuse" (1992, republished here) was the first nationally approved statement of the entire body of bishops. While affirming the goodness, holiness, and dedication of thousands of priests who ministered faithfully to God's people and while respecting the privacy of individuals, the bishops resolved that they would, in each case of sexual abuse, deal openly and candidly with the public, respond promptly to all allegations, relieve alleged offenders if evidence was sufficient, comply with civil law in reporting all incidents, and reach out pastorally to all victims. These public resolutions became the cornerstone of all future statements and policies on sexual abuse of minors in the conference and were used as models by numerous dioceses here and abroad.

While the bishops were aware of many confirmed cases of abuse, they were also warned in 1993 about giving too ready a credence to such charges when Cardinal Joseph Bernardin was, as it was later proven, falsely charged with sexual abuse. The bishops pointed out in a joint statement in support of Bernardin that the damages caused by false charges are not easily repaired.[38] They were also concerned that the media were distorting the problem by focusing on it as if only the Catholic priesthood were affected and not other significant social groups.

The bishops continued to point to the toll such problems take on society in general. Following up on a previous document on domestic violence, the Committee on Marriage and Family Life produced a document on sexual abuse in families, *Walk in the Light: A Pastoral Response to Child Sexual Abuse* (republished here). Relying on scientific information that, among other things, described the characteristics of abusers and abused children, the document made some pastoral and practical suggestions for local communities to deal with abusers and the abused.

In all of the issues the bishops addressed in their pastorals and other statements, they implicitly acknowledged how they saw their own role in Church and society. The NCCB, however, also explicitly addressed specific issues that related to the episcopal role in the Church and in the new evangelization.

During the late 1980s and early 1990s, the NCCB emphasized the teaching role of the bishop. From the publication of *On the Regulation of Birth* (*Humanae Vitae*, 1968) until the 1990s there had been an unprecedented public conflict in the Church over a number of ecclesiastical teachings. Theological dissent in the Church had become a very public matter, and the bishops had to face a new issue for which they had no previous experience. The relationship between bishops and theologians grew strained, and both bodies were forced to create some new instruments for developing cooperation and for resolving theological disputes within the Church. In 1980 the Catholic Theological Society of America formed a joint committee with the Canon Law Society of America to produce a 1983 document laying down guiding principles for cooperation between bishops and theologians and for resolving disputes. The joint committee then presented their document to the NCCB for its approval. That document was discussed, revised, sent to Rome for review, and finally published in June 1989 as *Doctrinal Responsibilities: Approaches to Promoting Cooperation and Resolving Misunderstandings Between Bishops and Theologians* (republished here). The statement focused upon the teaching mission of the Church and the different but complementary roles that bishops and theologians had within the Church. The statement also outlined specific suggestions for implementing cooperation between diocesan bishops and theologians and reaffirmed formal procedures that had been previously established (*On Due Process*;[39] and "Committee on Conciliation and Arbitration"[40]) for resolving conflicts within the Church.

The pastoral concern for sound teaching in the Church, clearly articulated in these documents, came up again in 1996 when the NCCB Committee on Doctrine issued a review of the third edition of theologian Richard McBrien's *Catholicism* because, in the committee's judgment, it posed pastoral problems particularly as a textbook for beginners in theology.[41] The NCCB committee acted when it judged that McBrien's third edition was published without sufficient attention to previous episcopal suggestions for emendations.

The relationship between bishops and theologians was also the focal concern of attempts to implement Pope John Paul II's *On Catholic Universities* (*Ex Corde Ecclesiae*, 1990), an apostolic constitution on the Catholic identity of institutions of higher education. In 1990 the NCCB established a committee of bishops, Catholic university presidents, and consultants to work out ways of implementing the papal document. In December 1993 the bishops on the committee presented a first "Draft Ordinances for Implementing *Ex Corde Ecclesia*,"[42] which underwent further discussion and revision. In 1996 the NCCB approved "*Ex Corde Ecclesiae*: An Application to the United States."[43]

This document sought to confirm and preserve the Catholic identity of these institutions but remanded to future study the issue of greatest contention between the bishops and presidents: the canonical mandate, which is the requirement in canon 812 of the Code of Canon Law that theologians hired at Catholic colleges and universities be granted a mandate to teach by ecclesiastical authority. During the discussion of the draft at the NCCB meeting of November 1995, the following sentence was added: "The mandate of Canon 812 will be the subject of further study by the NCCB."[44]

Although the document received approval by a vote of 224 to 6, it was not fully acceptable to the Congregation for Catholic Education, which reviewed it. In the congregation's view the document lacked "necessary juridical elements" that would help to resolve conflicts; it needed to provide, moreover, more explicit directives for preparing college mission statements; and, most significantly, with reference to the episcopal mandate, which the NCCB put off for further study, the Congregation expressed the "hope that a solution will soon be found [for the question of the mandate] so as to have a full application of the canon incorporated into a second draft of the ordinances."[45] A special subcommittee was immediately formed to deal with these issues.

In November 1991, the bishops also issued *The Teaching Ministry of the Diocesan Bishop: A Pastoral Reflection* (republished here), a document intended to speak more widely than had *Doctrinal Responsibilities* on the overall responsibilities of the bishops for evangelizing culture and for supervising the inculturation of the faith within the country. The document encouraged a positive presentation of Catholic doctrine by the bishops and emphasized the need to discover ways to reaffirm the episcopal teaching office in a culture like that of the United States. The document also paid some attention to the various degrees of acceptance and nonacceptance of church teachings and the various grades of authority attributed to church teachings. In draft form the document had received, as some bishops would complain later,[46] a critique from the Holy See prior to the U.S. bishops' own discussion of it.

As teachers of the faith, the bishops prepared in November 1990 a document, *In Support of Catholic Elementary and Secondary Schools* (republished here), which reaffirmed the episcopal commitment to the continuation of Catholic schooling in the United States, calling the schools the "best and fullest opportunity" to realize the Christian message, community, worship, and service. They outlined the successes of the schools, pointed to studies that confirmed those successes, called upon the need for schools for African American and Hispanic Catholics, among other minorities, and noted some of the fundamental challenges for the schools in the future. They also laid out a series of episcopal commitments to the schools that they hoped would be realized by 1997, the year of the twenty-fifth anniversary of their publication *To Teach as Jesus Did*.[47] Some bishops, too, called for the strengthening of local organizations to foster, promote, and obtain state and foundation funding for the schools.[48] By December 1994, the NCCB had established an office in support of Catholic school parents associations.

The episcopal emphasis upon evangelization and education was reinforced in 1993 when they published *Stewardship: A Disciple's Response* (republished here). That statement emphasized that all Christians and all Catholics were called upon to evangelize and to practice authentic Christian stewardship which leads to evangelization. The bishops created this document as a tool to be used in parishes and in small groups to discuss the most appropriate ways in which Christians could share their financial resources, talents, and time with others. They acknowledged that talk about stewardship was difficult in a society where materialism, individualism, hedonism, and consumerism were rampant, but they insisted that they must speak out on the ideal of stewardship as a way of sharing the gifts that God had bestowed upon individuals for their own good and that of the entire community to which they belonged. The document also reflected the fact that Catholics were apparently not contributing to the Church and their society in proportion to their own improved economic and social status in American society.[49]

Catholic Social Thought: Domestic Issues

The post-Vatican II new evangelization included social and political issues (foreign as well as domestic) that ranged from Catholic care and responsibility for families to matters of justice and peace throughout the world. In the period between 1989 and 1997, the bishops continued to articulate Catholic positions on various topics that were part of the public debate and not purely internal ecclesial concerns. Episcopal involvement in public debates was part of the Church's dialogue with the modern world—a dialogue that involved listening and learning, but also discerning and teaching.

In preparation for the centenary anniversary of Pope Leo XIII's groundbreaking encyclical, *On the Condition of Workers* (*Rerum Novarum,* 1891), the NCCB published *A Century of Social Teaching: A Common Heritage, A Continuing Challenge* (1990, republished here) to summarize and reinforce the social mission of Catholicism in the modern world. The bishops noted that "the social dimensions of our faith have taken on special urgency and clarity over this century," although that dimension of Catholic thought had not been widely known. In their emphasis on social teachings, the U.S. bishops were following a path set by the 1971 world Synod of Bishops in Rome, which called working for justice a constitutive dimension of responding to the Gospel. The NCCB document reasserted the fact that religion was not just personal and private, as so many in American society perceived it, but social. This document called Catholics to a renewed sense of the social mission of the Church and to a reexamination of the Church's social teachings.

In *A Decade After "Economic Justice for All": Continuing Principles, Changing Context, New Challenges* (1995, republished here), commemorating the tenth anniversary of the pastoral letter on economics, the bishops again reminded Catholics and others about the relationship of faith to justice in the economy and asserted that American society was "falling far short" of the standards and principles that were upheld in their previous pastoral. In 1996, moreover, the bishops outlined ten principles in "A Catholic Framework for Economic Life" (republished here) for reflection, judgment, and action.

Episcopal statements since 1986 had been concerned with the macro-issues of economic justice, but the bishops were also concerned that these and other issues of justice were discussed at the local level: in parishes, schools, and universities. In 1993, therefore, they published *Communities of Salt and Light: Reflections on the Social Mission of the Parish* (republished here) to focus Catholic attention on the very specific issue of the social mission of the individual parish because the "parish is where the Church lives." Here they noted the inherent link between evangelization and parish concerns for justice and peace. The parish was the locus of liturgy, prayer, and a social ministry which should foster personal responsibility and common action for changing unjust social structures. The document called parishes to engage in social ministry at the local level and provided some examples of what parishes in various parts of the country were doing to carry out this dimension of the common faith experience. In 1997, the bishops returned to the theme of parish responsibility to the wider world. In *Called to Global Solidarity* (republished here) the bishops tried to counter a growing sense of isolationism in American society by calling upon parishes to refashion the old "mission mentality" that characterized much of Catholic life after World War II. As Catholic and as American, parishes were called to a new global responsibility.

Because the family was the basic unit of society, the bishops tried to focus Catholic social thought on issues that related to the family. In fact, in *Putting Children and Families First: A Challenge for Our Church, Nation, and World* (1991, republished here), the bishops emphasized the priority that family issues should have in economic, religious, and moral concerns. The bishops called upon public figures and all elements in society from education to industry to develop policies that would support children and family life and overcome the various forces that threatened them. Again in 1993, the bishops published a statement, *Follow the Way of Love* (republished here), which anticipated the United Nations' call for an International Year of the Family (1994) and emphasized the multiple ways to increase love in family life in the face of numerous contemporary challenges.

Catholic social thought on labor, its dignity, and its rights and responsibilities had been the subject of papal encyclicals since *Rerum Novarum* (1891) and was the topic of four episcopal statements during this period. Labor Day statements were a regular duty for the episcopal chairmen of the USCC Committee on Domestic Policy. "Freedom, Justice, and the Role of Unions,"[50] a Labor Day address by Auxiliary Bishop Joseph Sullivan of Brooklyn, chair of the USCC Committee on Domestic Policy, reinforced the Church's support for labor unions and called upon those unions to serve the common good. He noted, too, that workers in the United States were measurably worse off in 1989 than they were a decade before, and reminded Americans that workers throughout the world, but especially in Poland, had demonstrated the effectiveness and importance of unions in supporting freedom, justice, and human dignity. In 1994, Auxiliary Bishop John Ricard, SSJ, of Baltimore, also a chair of the Committee on Domestic Policy, prepared another Labor Day statement, "Work: Still the Center of the Social Question,"[51] which asserted that the first priority in any just economy was to find a way to use the talents and energy of all who were willing and able to work. The next year on Labor Day Bishop Sullivan again addressed the dignity of work in "A Shifting, Churning Economy,"[52] which highlighted the problems associated with corporate downsizing, especially the elimination of jobs, the decline in wages, and the increasing dependence upon lower paying jobs. The USCC also sent Bishop Frank Rodimer of Paterson to testify before a Senate subcommittee on labor in support of a bill (Bill S-55) that would have made it illegal for companies to hire permanent replacements of striking workers. Bishop Rodimer's statement (republished here) was a powerful testimony to the rights of labor unions and the good they could generate for the whole of society, despite some of the past as well as present abuses in the unions. They were, he argued, sometimes the only protection against certain destructive corporate tactics; nonetheless they were unfortunately weaker in 1991 than at any previous time in the last forty years.

In the 1990s the bishops also took part in the national debate on welfare reform. Bishop Ricard testified before a Clinton administration committee on welfare reform in 1993 about historic Catholic activity for the general welfare of American citizens and, on the basis of that experience, called for improvements in American welfare programs, articulating seven moral and social principles that the U.S. bishops believed should be followed in any reform of the welfare system.[53] In March 1995 the USCC issued a statement that clearly articulated six

Moral Principles and Policy Priorities for Welfare Reform (republished here), indicating that welfare reform would be a fundamental test of the nation's moral priorities, the first of which should be protection of the poor and children.[54]

A relatively new issue in American society and in Catholic social thought since the 1960s was care and responsibility for the natural environment. In 1991, the bishops prepared *Renewing the Earth: An Invitation to Reflection and Action on Environment in Light of Catholic Social Teaching* (republished here), which referred to the environmental crisis as "a moral challenge." This was the bishops' contribution to the national debate on the issue and their attempt to awaken Catholics and others to the interrelatedness of creation and the development of human beings and human community. While inspiring Catholics and others to consider the religious and ethical dimensions of the environmental crisis, the document outlined the human responsibility to protect, preserve, and distribute equitably the goods of creation. In 1993, Bishop James Malone of Youngstown carried this message of the interrelationship of justice and environmental issues to an international conference on the environment at Ohio State University.[55] He challenged the industrialized nations in particular to "curb consumption."

Throughout the 1990s, as in the previous three decades, the bishops entered into the national debates over a host of issues where medical, moral, legal, scientific, and public policy concerns intersected. Abortion, euthanasia, general health care reform, sexuality, sexual abuse, cultural violence, substance abuse, HIV and AIDS, embryo research, and genetic testing were among the issues that evoked a number of position statements from the NCCB/USCC.

The "life issues," abortion and euthanasia, had a priority for the bishops because, as they saw it, the right to life was the foundation of all other human rights and the primary plank of Catholic moral and social thought. Catholic teaching on abortion, of course, was no secret in American society. The bishops had clearly and unequivocally asserted their opposition to abortion as a violation of the divine gift of life. In at least eleven episcopally sponsored statements and congressional testimonies between 1989 and 1997, the bishops argued against numerous attempts in society to increase or support abortion measures. In 1989, USCC General Counsel argued in *Webster vs. Reproductive Health Services* that the U.S. Supreme Court reconsider and reverse its decision to include abortion "within the right of privacy" in *Roe vs. Wade* (1973).[56] When the Supreme Court upheld Missouri's right to require testing for viability after the twentieth week of gestation in *Webster,* the bishops rejoiced and saw hope in the court's decision to uphold state restrictions on abortion levels. The NCCB Committee on Pro-Life Activities saw the Webster case as a new opportunity to defend life. The committee, while maintaining the bishops' First Amendment right to proclaim Catholic convictions on these public policy issues, also granted that when they entered the arena of public policy debates they were "bound by the same rules as other participants. We must present reasons for our proposals which can be understood and appreciated by people of good will who may not share our faith convictions."[57] That statement expressed the bishops' understanding of their participation in public policy issues and the reason for their numerous published declarations on national issues like abortion.

In November 1989, the bishops again announced in a "Resolution on Abortion" (republished here) their public policy goals relative to the abortion issue and urged public officials, especially Catholics, to support their plan.[58] The bishops, however, did not deal with abortion exclusively from the point of view of public policy. Since 1975 they had focused upon three approaches to abortion: education and pastoral care as well as public policy. By the 1990s the bishops realized that their highest priority in the abortion issue was, they noted in *Faithful for Life: A Moral Reflection* (1995, republished here), "helping to form consciences of our Catholic people." The abortion and euthanasia issues had implications for "our fidelity to God and to one another." The appeals to freedom and choice in these issues were, in the bishops' view, wrongheaded because such appeals separated freedom from life and did not acknowledge that fidelity was the essential link between freedom and life.

Repeatedly the bishops asserted that abortion was a significant part of the culture of death in American society. Public officials who supported abortion were participating in this cultural violence. In "Statement on Partial-Birth Abortion Ban Veto" (1996, republished here), the bishops protested against President Clinton's veto of the ban on partial-birth abortions as another manifestation of public callousness in regard to life issues. In 1997 Cardinal Bernard Law, chair of the Committee on Pro-Life Activities, returned to the issue of partial-birth abortions, which he called "heinous and unnecessary," when he wrote to all U.S. senators urging support of the ban.[59]

As the bishops had opposed abortion so also they opposed premature deliveries of infants with anencephaly.[60] They opposed the view that anencephalic children lacked human rights or at least had lives of less meaning or purpose than others. All human beings, no matter what their physical condition, had dignity and the sacred right to life.

The bishops also rejected violent opposition to abortion providers. A few anti-abortion protesters had, by the late 1980s and early 1990s, turned to violent measures in opposition to abortion providers, even to the extent of justifying the murder of some providers. The bishops were swift to respond that any violence against another person violated the pro-life position. When a Catholic priest in the Archdiocese of Mobile publicly supported the murder of abortion doctors, Archbishop Oscar Lipscomb of Mobile deprived him of his faculties and removed him as pastor. There is a presumption against vigilantism, the archbishop wrote, in the Catholic tradition.[61]

Another life issue that came increasingly to the fore in the 1980s and 1990s was active euthanasia and physician-assisted suicide. The assisted-suicide activities of the Michigan physician Jack Kevorkian was an extreme symptom of a growing campaign in favor of the right to choose one's own death. In this atmosphere, the bishops produced at least seven public statements in opposition to various forms of euthanasia. While they opposed the direct intervention (as in physician-assisted suicide) to end life and rejected the withdrawal of nutrition and hydration necessary to sustain life, they did not oppose, in certain cases, withdrawing or refusing to use what were called extraordinary medical means of preserving life. The bishops published two statements (republished here) outlining their moral positions on these issues: "Statement on Euthanasia" (1991) and *Nutrition and Hydration: Moral and Pastoral Reflections* (1992).

Because the issue of euthanasia and physician-assisted suicide was a public policy as well as a moral issue, the bishops became involved in a number of court cases and legislative battles over correct public policy. In 1989, USCC General Counsel filed an amicus brief in the Nancy Cruzan case that was being tried before the U.S. Supreme Court, arguing for the preservation of a state's responsibility to exercise some regulatory authority in health care and arguing against the creation of an autonomous constitutional right to choose death.[62] In 1994, the General Counsel filed two other amicus briefs, one before the Ninth Circuit Court of Appeals in support of Washington State's ban against physician-assisted suicide and the other before the Second Circuit Court of Appeals in support of the New York State law.[63] In the wake of the 51 to 49 percent passage by initiative in Oregon of the "Death with Dignity Act," the first law in the United States to authorize physician-assisted suicide, USCC General Counsel filed an amicus brief supporting a U.S. District Court decision which overturned the law.[64]

The bishops also became involved in the national debate over health care reform in the United States. That issue became a public policy issue throughout the 1980s, but heated up particularly in the early 1990s, during President Clinton's first term. In four statements the bishops asserted that they were competent to comment on health care issues in the United States because as Catholics they sponsored the second largest health care system in the United States (second only to that of the Veterans Administration); had a long history in the country as health care providers, purchasers, administrators, and subjects; and had a tradition of moral reflection on issues of health. Health care reform was a public policy issue, but it was also an ethical, medical, and social justice concern for the bishops.

The episcopal statements all acknowledged the need for reform, but they were also cautious about some specific proposals for reform because in their view some proposals violated certain ethical and social justice priorities that the bishops had been advocating for years. In 1991, for example, Bishop James Malone, as chair of the USCC Committee on Domestic Policy, criticized an Oregon proposal for health care (Medicaid) rationing because it could lead, among other things, to medical neglect and even to deaths of poor women and children.[65] In a letter to members of the U.S. Congress in 1992, moreover, Bishop Malone outlined the USCC's eight basic criteria for health care reform, asserted that health care was a "basic human right," and called for the development of a national health insurance program.[66] In June 1993, the NCCB issued *A Framework for Comprehensive Health Care Reform: Protecting Human Life, Promoting Human Dignity, Pursuing the Common Good* (republished here), acknowledging that the current health care system served too few and cost too much. It called health care reform an economic and moral imperative and outlined for the public its eight criteria for assessing all proposals for reforming the system.

When he introduced the resolution on health care reform to the entire NCCB, Bishop John Ricard, SSJ, noted that the document reinforced central Catholic concerns, including pro-life concerns. During the discussion there was near unanimous support for the proposed statement, many bishops saying that the document positioned the bishops very well for the upcoming national debate on health care reform that the Clinton administration was initiating.[67]

Because of major administrative changes in American hospitals, particularly the numerous mergers, the bishops were becoming increasingly concerned with the Catholic identity of church-related hospitals and other health care units. In 1994, therefore, the bishops published an updated edition of their *Ethical and Religious Directives for Catholic Health Care Services* (republished here).

The bishops also addressed the moral and spiritual dimensions of human sexuality, emphasizing again respect for life and human dignity. During the twenty-fifth anniversary of *On the Regulation of Birth* (*Humanae Vitae*, 1968), the bishops published "Human Sexuality from God's Perspective" (1993, republished here). That document looked to revelation as the primary source for understanding sexuality, placed human sexuality within the context of marriage and family life, and asserted that there was an urgent need to do so to counter the predominant "secular or pseudo scientific" views of sexuality as a purely pragmatic matter and to oppose the cultural and media violence against human dignity in contemporary forms of sexual promiscuity. In "Reflection on 'The Truth and Meaning of Human Sexuality'" (1996, republished here), the bishops also supported education in human sexuality in the schools as long as that education assisted and complemented the parents' role in educating their children and as long as sexuality was not presented as a "value neutral" arena of human activity. In 1997, moreover, the bishops published *Always Our Children* (republished here), a statement to parents of homosexual children calling them to love their children and not to break off contact with them.

The episcopal concern with sexual promiscuity in the culture was matched by their statements on what they repeatedly called a "culture of violence" against human life and dignity in the United States— manifested in abortion, euthanasia, disregard for the poor and oppressed, capital punishment, and other forms of violence against human persons. In 1992, the Committee on Marriage and Family Life published *When I Call for Help: A Pastoral Response to Domestic Violence Against Women* (republished here), which described very clearly the statistics on domestic violence and addressed female victims, pastors, male abusers, and society at large on the crimes against women. It also provided some practical pastoral suggestions for parishes to recognize and deal with abusive relationships. Alarmed also by the growth of pornography in various media, the Committee on Ecumenical and Interreligious Affairs joined with the Interreligious Affairs Committee of the Synagogue Council of America in calling for societal resistance and a boycotting of those who promoted such degradation of human dignity.[68] The NCCB committee also joined the Synagogue Council in condemning the neo-Nazi-influenced reinterpretations and denials of the existence of the holocaust.[69] In 1996, moreover, after a rash of burnings of African American churches, the NCCB/USCC adopted a statement drawn up by four committees that asserted that the burnings themselves destroyed the illusion that racial and religious bigotry was no longer a problem in the United States. Such burnings were part of the culture of violence against persons and property.[70] After the Oklahoma City bombing of the federal building there, killing 168 persons, Bishop William Skylstad of Spokane, chair of the USCC Committee on Domestic Policy, issued a statement on capital punishment (1997, republished here), calling for justice with mercy and asserting that the execution of Timothy McVeigh, who was convicted of the bombing, "would tragically perpetuate a terrible cycle of violence and further diminish respect for life."[71]

In 1994, the bishops published *Confronting a Culture of Violence: A Catholic Framework for Action* (republished here), which outlined the various forms of violence in the society and called for a conversion in the Catholic community and a general "moral revolution" in society to reverse the trend toward violence. That reversal could be accomplished only by increasing the respect for the dignity of the human person and by a renewed ethic of justice, responsibility, and community.

The dignity of the human person and the sense of community were violated, too, by addictive and destructive substance abuse, a problem the bishops addressed in *New Slavery, New Freedom* (1990, republished here). The document described the psychological, sociological, and physical dependency dimensions of the problem and outlined the terrible social and personal tragedies associated with it before pointing to the religious resources available for responding to the problem.

The HIV/AIDS crisis also brought a response during these years. In 1987, the Administrative Board produced a lengthy statement entitled *The Many Faces of AIDS: A Gospel Response*.[72] In 1989, the full body of bishops produced *Called to Compassion and Responsibility: A Response to the HIV/AIDS Crisis* (republished here), which underlined the ethical and spiritual dimensions of the issue. The 1989 document reiterated the call to compassion that was a part of *Many Faces;* brought Catholics up-to-date on new information that was available on the crisis; pointed out the various medical, scientific, and sociological dimensions of the problem; and focused on the moral, spiritual, and pastoral implications of the crisis.

The draft of *Called to Compassion* asserted that "we must reject the idea that this illness [AIDS] is a direct punishment by God." During the floor debate, the bishops considered an amendment that added "always" or "necessarily" after "is" on the basis that one could not exclude the notion that God may directly punish sin. This amendment elicited a long discussion over whether or not the illness could be related to divine punishment. Those who spoke against the amendment maintained that, as moral leaders, the bishops must oppose the kind of thinking which considered HIV/AIDS a direct punishment by God for certain behaviors. In the end, the amendment was voted down and the original language was preserved.[73] In 1994, the bishops published "Ministry for Those Suffering from HIV/AIDS"[74] to promote understanding of suffering and death in light of the cross and resurrection and to reaffirm their view that discrimination and violence against those suffering from HIV/AIDS was "unjust and immoral."

The bishops also addressed two medical-moral research issues that were receiving much public comment in the 1980s and 1990s: embryo research and genetic testing. A protest was lodged, for example, with the National Institutes of Health Human Embryo Research Panel because some of their proposals involved destroying human life.[75] In 1996 the Committee on Science and Human Values stated very clearly that there was indeed no irreconcilable conflict between religion and science, that both could offer complementary insights on complex topics, but that, as human beings and believers, scientists had to be aware of the moral and spiritual dimensions of their research and of the potential for abuse that existed when moral considerations were ruled out of areas like genetic testing.[76] Theologians, in particular, were encouraged to become acquainted with biotechnical knowledge and methods so that they could aid researchers on the moral and religious dimensions of their research work and goals.

Christian Responsibility for Domestic Politics

Most of the statements the bishops produced on economics as well as those on medical-moral problems involved the bishops in issues of domestic politics. In a number of statements, the bishops called Catholics and others to a Christian responsibility for fostering the common good, a fundamental goal of all domestic politics. Periodically, too, representatives of the NCCB addressed members of the U.S. Congress to express episcopal concerns. In 1990, Archbishop Roger Mahony of Los Angeles and Bishop James Malone of Youngstown called upon members of Congress to put the needs of the poor and vulnerable first in constructing the 1991 federal budget and suggested other ethical priorities to be considered in budgetary decisions.[77]

Since 1975 the conference's Administrative Board had produced every four years a general election-year statement on political responsibility, outlining their positions on important issues in American public life. During this period, the board produced two such statements in 1991[78] and 1995, respectively. *Political Responsibility: Proclaiming the Gospel of Life, Protecting the Least Among Us, and Pursuing the Common Good* (1995, republished here) called all members of the Church and society to become involved in the political process and commented on the Church's distinct role in that process. The statement also listed the various concerns that the bishops had in the political order: e.g., abortion, arms control, capital punishment, discrimination and racism, economic justice, education, euthanasia, family life, food and agriculture and environment, health and AIDS and substance abuse issues, housing, human rights, immigration, mass media, refugees, international affairs, and welfare reform. On each of these issues the bishops' conference articulated its significance and reflected on the direction the country should take on each issue for the sake of the common good.

Every fourth year, moreover, a questionnaire was sent to the major presidential candidates seeking their responses to a variety of issues. Subsequently, the responses were sent to the bishops, many of whom chose to publish them.[79] Each presidential election year, too, USCC General Counsel sent a memorandum to bishops and their advisors about the legal requirements governing political involvement of churches as tax-exempt organizations, warning about the fine line between legitimate political education and illegitimate advocacy for or against particular candidates.[80]

In 1996, Bishop Anthony Pilla of Cleveland, president of the NCCB, addressed the bishops on his own understanding of the relationship of the Church to democracy, upholding the bishops' teaching role within a democracy, underlining their nonpartisan participation within the political process, and emphasizing that their primary concerns were with the religious and ethical dimensions of political issues. The Catholic Church, he asserted, had much to bring to the political debate, particularly in its focus on serving the common good as the primary goal of all political activity.[81]

By the 1990s many within and outside the religious communities were becoming increasingly concerned with political divisiveness in the United States. In 1993 the USCC joined together with the National Council of Churches and the Synagogue Council of America to produce "The Common Good: Old Idea, New Urgency" (republished here). The general purpose of the joint statement was to help focus the national political debate on a renewed sense of the country's general welfare. To do so the three religious bodies drew on their common heritage to bring forth a "fresh and empowering vision of the common good." Concern for the common good was not only a moral imperative but an essential religious calling, the statement asserted. In 1995, when Congress reached an impasse over the federal budget and consequently shut down the government, Archbishop William Keeler of Baltimore, president of the NCCB, reasserted the need to emphasize the common good in politics and criticized the partisan political bickerings and ideological commitments that frustrated any attempts to achieve the common good in society.[82]

The bishops were concerned with Catholic schools and Catholic education in general, as noted earlier, but they were also concerned with public education, not just because most Catholics were enrolled in public schools but because, as they saw it, such education was a necessary part of the common good in American society. In 1990 the Committee for Ecumenical and Interreligious Affairs joined with the Interreligious Affairs Committee of the Synagogue Council of America in a common statement on "Moral Education in the Public Schools" (republished here). The common document noted that there appeared to be a reluctance among public educators to teach values (e.g., honesty, compassion, integrity, tolerance, loyalty, belief in human worth and dignity), and thus these religious leaders felt compelled to speak out on the absolute necessity of moral education in the public schools, calling upon public educators to teach these values because they believed there was a broad consensus on them in society. In 1995, too, the bishops' conference joined the national debate on educational reform when it issued *Principles of Educational Reform in the United States* (republished here), articulating six principles that should guide public education and all proposals for educational reform.

Foreign Relations Issues

The U.S. bishops shared in the collegiality of the worldwide Catholic episcopate. Because of their own involvement in missionary activities in other parts of the world and because of their own financial and material contributions to those in need throughout the world through Catholic Relief Services and other institutions, the U.S. bishops were in a unique position to comment on international affairs. They were sensitive to their own solidarity with their brother bishops and fellow Catholics in other parts of the world, and to their own responsibility to speak out on American foreign policies and issues of international justice and peace.

Periodically, through their representatives the bishops made statements that reinforced the solidarity of Catholics in the United States with Catholics in other parts of the world. In 1989, after Archbishops Roger Mahony, Theodore McCarrick, and Edward O'Meara had visited Vietnam and other parts of Southeast Asia, they published a document intended to strengthen the bonds of solidarity with Vietnamese Catholics and to call for measures to ensure religious liberty and human rights (particularly the right to emigrate).[83]

Since the late 1960s there were a number of statements on American relations with Vietnam. In 1989 the conference published *A Time for Dialogue and Healing: A Pastoral Reflection on United States–Vietnam Relations* (republished here), which was the result of U.S. episcopal visits in Vietnam and consultations with ten Vietnamese bishops. As in 1975, the statement again called for normalizing United States–Vietnam relations, pointing to the improved conditions of religious liberty and other beneficial changes in Vietnam. It also outlined a series of issues that needed to be resolved in Vietnam and other parts of Indochina before normalization could be possible. Its major purpose, however, was to call for healing of the ongoing tragedy in that country.

When the "Iron Curtain" began to fall in 1989, Archbishop John May of St. Louis, representing the NCCB, published a message of solidarity with the Catholic Church in the Ukraine.[84] In 1994 and 1995, other statements of solidarity were published to support Bishop Dom Samuel Ruiz Garcia of San Cristobal de Las Casas in Mexico when he and his diocese came under assault by Mexican authorities.[85]

The USCC testified periodically before Congress on the needs and concerns of refugees from war-torn countries throughout the world. In 1991, USCC representatives appealed to Congress to aid Gulf War Iraqi refugees and refugees fleeing from Haiti, Liberia, and Southeast Asia.[86] The bishops were also concerned about an increasing anti-foreigner sentiment in the United States and the expanding attempts to produce more restrictive immigration legislation in the 1990s. Catholics and all Americans were called to examine their attitudes toward refugee foreigners and the new immigrants, and a "generous and reasonable" immigration policy was urged.[87]

American foreign aid policies also came under the bishops' scrutiny from time to time. In 1991, USCC staff protested against the increasing emphasis in foreign aid bills on military aid to developing nations, an aid which the bishops considered irrelevant to the real needs.[88] Again in 1992, the USCC Committee on International Policy published "American Responsibilities in a Changing World" (republished here), which was an attempt to counteract the growing American isolationism of the 1990s, which was in part occasioned by the fall of the Iron Curtain.[89] The statement reminded Catholics that their Church was global and that it repeatedly received requests for aid and support from churches in other parts of the world. It also encouraged all Americans to support two goals in the changing world of the 1990s: peacemaking and support for sustainable development. In practice these goals meant "progressive nuclear disarmament"[90] and, as the bishops advocated in their *Sowing Weapons of War: A Pastoral Reflection on the Arms Trade and Landmines* (1995, republished here), a radical reduction in the selling of arms.

Since the publication of *The Challenge of Peace* in 1983, the U.S. bishops were repeatedly concerned with peace in various parts of the world. But peace meant more to them than just the absence of war; it meant a primary concern for just economic development and an equitable distribution of the goods of this earth as well as global attempts to secure the end of violence throughout the world.

Third World debt was a concern to the bishops because it hindered any possibilities for genuine peace and economic stability. In 1989, USCC staff testified before Congress on the impact of such a debt and articulated seven principles and suggested actions to relieve the debt.[91] This testimony was followed later that year by a USCC statement on the topic, *Relieving Third World Debt: A Call for Co-responsibility, Justice, and Solidarity* (republished here), which clearly outlined the bishops' ethical and religious perspectives on economic interdependency throughout the world. *Food Policy in a Hungry World: The Links That Bind Us Together* (1989, republished here) underlined the moral connections between agricultural interests in the United States and the distribution of food throughout the world.

On the tenth anniversary of the publication of *The Challenge of Peace* and the thirtieth anniversary of John XXIII's *Peace on Earth (Pacem in Terris)*, the bishops published *The Harvest of Justice Is Sown in Peace* (republished here), reiterating their 1983 concerns for peace but also addressing more particularly the new situation of bloody regional wars, the lethal arms trade, and the recurring need to provide for sustained development in parts of the world that were racked with poverty and violence.

The USCC Committee on International Policy repeatedly from 1989 to 1997 issued policy statements on specific conflicts throughout the world so that their general concerns for peace and justice were translated into ad hoc statements on very particular and timely topics in international policy. Throughout these years they published eleven statements on various problems in the Middle East. In 1978 the USCC had published a statement on peace in the Middle East,[92] and in 1989 they renewed that statement in *Toward Peace in the Middle East: Perspectives, Principles, and Hopes* (republished here). After describing the historical conditions in the region, particularly with regard to the Palestinian peoples, Israel, Lebanon, and the Arab States, the bishops made a series of policy recommendations for the United States. In the course of the next eight years, as in the previous twenty, the troubles in the Middle East would be the source of a series of statements addressed to a variety of issues and events: the debilitating effects of the United Nations' 1991 embargo on Iraq,[93] commendation for President George Bush's attempts to establish peace in the Middle East,[94] a call for more protective legislative measures for selective conscientious objectors (especially in reference to those who refused to support the Gulf War of 1991),[95] protests against the Israeli-Lebanon brutality in the border wars of 1993,[96] welcome for the 1993 peace accord between the Palestinian Liberation Organization and Israel,[97] celebration in 1995 of the West Bank accord which expanded Palestinian autonomy and a call for a repeal of the Palestinian Covenant,[98] a call for reconciliation of religious parties within Lebanon and for its territorial integrity in 1996,[99] a lament for the return to the cycle of terror and counterterror on the Lebanese-Israeli border in May 1996,[100] and a letter to the Iraqi Patriarch, Raphael Bidawid of Baghdad, pledging the U.S. bishops' continued efforts to provide humanitarian aid to the people of Iraq and to advocate peace policies in the Middle East.[101]

The civil war in El Salvador also drew the attention of the U.S. bishops. The killing of four American missionary women in 1980 and six Jesuits in 1989 was especially troubling to Catholics in the United States. A 1990 letter to President Bush outlined the principal points of concern regarding U.S. policy and requested, among other things, the government's help to end the pattern of harassment of the Catholic

Church in El Salvador and to help establish a cease fire in the war-torn country.[102] In 1993 Archbishop John Roach, chair of the USCC Committee on International Policy, commended those El Salvadorans who testified before a United Nations Commission about murders committed in El Salvador.[103]

The bishops also kept a watchful eye on developments in Africa. In 1993, after consulting the bishops in the Southern African Catholic Bishops' Conference, economic sanctions against South Africa, which had been imposed in 1986, were discontinued. It was now believed that "carefully planned and monitored investment designed to advance the prospects for a full, rapid, and peaceful dismantling of apartheid" would assist the South African people in the new situation.[104] In 1994, the slaughter in Rwanda, which included three Rwandan bishops, brought a statement calling for an end to the conflict and international assistance and intervention.[105] Violent civil uprisings in Nigeria in 1996 also evoked a response from the U.S. bishops, who joined the Nigerian bishops in calling for political negotiations and peace.[106]

U.S. bishops followed closely the developments in the Caribbean, especially in Haiti and Cuba. In 1992, the chairman of the USCC Committee on International Policy, Archbishop Roach, sent the general secretary of the Organization of American States a plea to end the embargo on Haiti at the earliest possible moment and requested James Baker, U.S. Secretary of State, to continue humanitarian aid to the Haitian people.[107] Following the appeals of the Haitian bishops, the USCC joined the episcopal conferences of Canada and Latin America in calling for an end of hostilities in Haiti, an end to foreign military interventions, and establishment of democratic procedures that would promote the rule of law and stimulate economic growth.[108] Affairs in Cuba, too, had worsened in 1992, and the Cuban bishops protested the government's increasing abuse of religious liberty for Catholics. Archbishop Roach protested against those abuses to the U.S. secretary of state and criticized American measures like the economic embargo of Cuba, which inflicted suffering on the Cuban people.[109] By 1997, the conference asked President Clinton to authorize direct flights to Cuba for purposes of delivering humanitarian aid. The prohibition of such flights meant that charitable agencies had to take costly measures to deliver humanitarian aid to Cubans by way of third countries.[110]

When the Iron Curtain fell in 1989 there was immediate euphoria about the end of the arms race, the cessation of Cold War hostilities between the superpowers, and the restoration of international peace. In 1990, the USCC Administrative Board seized the day by publishing *The New Moment in Eastern and Central Europe* (republished here), which called the moment a grace-filled advent of a new era, outlined

Catholic responsibilities to help "our brothers and sisters" rebuild their churches, and invited the American people to help revive the countries in the former Soviet Union after the Cold War. The statement, however, pointed to the "fragile nature of the present moment."

After it was published troubles broke out in various parts of the former Soviet Union. The drive for self-determination in places like Lithuania was followed by increased governmental restrictions upon those newly granted freedoms, a situation which was protested in a 1990 letter to the Soviet ambassador.[111]

The greatest crisis and eruption of old civil hostilities broke out in the Balkans, and especially in the former Yugoslavia. During the 1990s statements were issued on the hostilities in the Balkans, calling for an end to the violence and for the peoples of the West to help rebuild those countries.[112] In 1991, the bishops called upon the international community to mediate a political settlement to the "unjust war" against the people of Croatia, asserting the necessity of recognizing the independence of Croatia, Slovenia, and other republics in the former Yugoslavia.[113] The nightmarish hostilities in Bosnia-Herzegovina drew a strong condemnation in 1993. The USCC Administrative Board called for the international community to disarm the aggressors and to end the "ethnic cleansing" in the Balkans, but it was not prepared to recommend a military solution to the problem, except where the use of force could be well defined and limited primarily to disarming aggressors.[114] When some in the United States interpreted statements from the conference as support for military measures to put an end to the hostilities in Bosnia, the Committee on International Policy responded that there had not been a general endorsement of U.S. military intervention in Bosnia but that several stringent moral criteria had been laid down to judge what kind of limited military measures would protect peoples from unjust aggression.[115]

The USCC also prepared statements on other troubled spots throughout the world. In 1991, when President Bush was considering extending most-favored-nation status to China, the conference expressed some serious concerns about China's continued violations of human rights, violations that were clearly documented. Granting China such a status, the conference said, should be conditioned by China's adherence to norms governing human rights and religious liberty.[116] In 1997, the USCC clearly urged Congress to revoke China's favored-nation status because of continued and documented violations of religious liberty, human dignity, and the rights of workers.[117] In 1994, moreover, the USCC joined Anglican, Presbyterian, Methodist, and Catholic religious leaders in the United States and Ireland to call for economic investments in Northern Ireland to provide jobs and to end the unfair economic employment situation, especially for Catholics in Northern Ireland.[118]

These episcopal statements on internal ecclesiastical issues, and foreign as well as domestic issues, were indicative of the post-Vatican II disposition of the U.S. Catholic bishops who saw themselves not only as teachers of faith but also as religious leaders whose faith had implications for the general issues of justice and peace in American society and in the world at large.

Patrick W. Carey
Editor

Notes

1. On the Congress, see *U.S. Catholic Historian* 7 (Spring/Summer 1988): 299-356.
2. "Minutes of the General Meeting, National Conference of Catholic Bishops," Baltimore, Md., November 6-9, 1989. All minutes of the episcopal meetings are located in the Archives of the National Conference of Catholic Bishops, Washington, D.C., and hereafter will be referred to simply as "Minutes NCCB," with place and date of meeting.
3. See Hugh Nolan, ed. *Pastoral Letters of the United States Catholic Bishops*, 5 vols. (Washington, D.C.: United States Catholic Conference, 1983, 1984, 1989), 4:342-355.
4. (Cincinnati, Ohio: St. Anthony Messenger Press, 1984).
5. Seymour P. Lachman and Barry A. Kosmin, "Black Catholics Get Ahead," *New York Times* (September 14, 1991).
6. "Minutes NCCB," Washington, D.C., November 16-19, 1992.
7. "Minutes NCCB," Washington, D.C., November 13-16, 1995.
8. The jubilee year refers to the Hebrew practice of periodically heralding (*jubilee* in Hebrew means ram's horn, a horn which was used to herald) a "year of the Lord's favor" (Is 61:1-2), a time when slaves were freed, lands restored to their original owners, and debts forgiven (Lv 25:10). The Catholic Church has used that practice periodically in announcing special times of grace, repentance, prayers, and pilgrimages.
9. Archbishop Daniel M. Buechlein, OSB, of Indianapolis, chair of the Ad Hoc Committee to Oversee the Use of the Catechism, "Recurring Deficiencies in Catechetical Texts," in NCCB Archives. See also "Minutes NCCB," Kansas City, Mo., June 19-20, 1997.
10. (Washington, D.C.: United States Catholic Conference, 1997).
11. "Minutes NCCB," Washington, D.C., November 12-15, 1990.
12. "Sacrament of Penance Study," *Origins* 19 (February 22, 1990): 613, 615-624.
13. "Destroy Tape of Suspect's Sacramental Confession," *Origins* 26 (June 6, 1996): 270-275, and "Oregon's Taping of Prisoner's Sacramental Confession," *Origins* 26 (December 5, 1996): 413.
14. *Pastoral Letters of the United States Catholic Bishops*, 4:267-276; 5:725-726.
15. (Washington, D.C.: United States Catholic Conference, 1997).

16. "Called and Gifted: The American Catholic Laity," in *Pastoral Letters of the United States Catholic Bishops*, 4:417-424.
17. (Washington, D.C.: United States Catholic Conference, 1997).
18. See *Pastoral Letters of the United States Catholic Bishops*, 4:493-582; 5:371-493. Also published separately by the United States Catholic Conference.
19. *Origins* 17 (April 21, 1988): 757, 759-788.
20. (Washington, D.C.: United States Catholic Conference, 1988).
21. (Washington, D.C.: United States Catholic Conference, 1988).
22. "A Pastoral Response to the Concerns of Women for Church and Society," *Origins* 19 (April 5, 1990): 717, 719-740.
23. "Vatican Declaration: Women in the Ministerial Priesthood," *Origins* 6 (February 3, 1977): 517, 519-524.
24. *Origins* 21 (April 23, 1992): 761, 763-776.
25. "Minutes NCCB," Notre Dame, Ind., June 18-20, 1992.
26. "Minutes NCCB," Washington, D.C., November 16-19, 1992.
27. Ibid. For the "Committee Report on Women's Concerns: One in Christ Jesus (Final Text)," see *Origins* 22 (December 31, 1992): 489, 491-508.
28. "Minutes NCCB," Washington, D.C., November 14-17, 1994.
29. Ibid.
30. The statement was published in *Origins* 27 (June 19, 1997): 74, 76-79.
31. See *Origins* 23 (December 2, 1993): 434.
32. *A National Study on the Permanent Diaconate of the Catholic Church in the United States, 1994-1995* (Washington, D.C.: United States Catholic Conference, 1996). For a summary of the statement, see "National Study of the Diaconate," *Origins* 25 (January 18, 1996): 497, 499-504.
33. For a summary of the results of one of those CARA studies, see "Priestly and Religious Vocations: Survey of Youth and Parents," *Origins* 27 (May 29, 1997): 25-27.
34. The full text is available from the Bishops' Committee on Vocations, 3211 Fourth Street, N.E., Washington, DC 20017-1194. In 1996 the bishops published an abridged version of the same document (Washington, D.C.: NCCB/Committee on Vocations, 1996).
35. For an analysis of the significance of the Gauthe case and the problem of sexual abuse, see Philip Jenkins, *Pedophiles and Priests: Anatomy of a Contemporary Crisis* (New York: Oxford University Press, 1996).
36. "Minutes NCCB," Washington, D.C., November 15-18, 1993; also "Minutes NCCB," Washington, D.C., November 14-17, 1994.
37. Among these are "USCC Pedophilia Statement," *Origins* 17 (February 18, 1988): 624; "Painful Pastoral Question: Sexual Abuse of Minors," *Origins* 22 (August 6, 1992): 177-178; "Brief History: Handling Child Sex Abuse Claims," *Origins* 23 (March 10, 1993): 666-670; "Child Sexual Abuse: Think Tank Recommendations," *Origins* 23 (July 1, 1993): 108-111; "Statement Supporting Cardinal Bernardin," *Origins* 23 (November 25, 1993): 421-422; "Policy Statement on How Dioceses Are Advised to Handle Sex Abuse Cases," *Origins* 23 (March 10, 1994): 669; "Twenty-Eight Suggestions on Sexual Abuse Policies" (excerpted from *Restoring Trust*, Vol. I) *Origins* 24 (December 8, 1994): 443-444; *Walk in the Light: A Pastoral Response to Child Sexual Abuse* (Washington, D.C.: United States Catholic Conference, 1995).
38. "Statement Supporting Cardinal Bernardin," 421-422.

39. Rev. ed. (Washington, D.C.: United States Catholic Conference, 1972).

40. *Pastoral Letters of the United States Catholic Bishops*, 4:330-342.

41. "Review Criticizes New Edition of Father McBrien's *Catholicism*," *Origins* 25 (April 18, 1996): 737, 739-744.

42. *Origins* 23 (December 16, 1993): 474-475; a second draft, "Implementing *Ex Corde Ecclesiae*," was published in *Origins* 24 (December 8, 1994): 445-446.

43. *Origins* 26 (November 28, 1996): 381, 383-384.

44. "Minutes NCCB," Washington, D.C., November 11-14, 1996.

45. "Vatican Observations on United States Bishops' 'Ex Corde Ecclesiae' Application Document," *Origins* 27 (June 12, 1997): 53-55; see also "Vatican Asks Review of Several Aspects of United States 'Ex Corde Ecclesiae' Application," *Origins* 27 (June 5, 1997): 39-40.

46. See, e.g., "Issues in Restructuring the Bishops' Conference," *Origins* 25 (July 13, 1995): 129-134, especially 133.

47. For the document, see *Pastoral Letters of the United States Catholic Bishops*, 3:306-338.

48. "Promoting Choice in Education," *Origins* 24 (December 8, 1994): 444-445.

49. In 1994 Bishop William McManus of Fort Wayne-South Bend cited two responsible research institutions that had clearly demonstrated that the percentage of household income given to parishes and dioceses by Catholic families had dropped. "Minutes NCCB," Washington, D.C., November 14-17, 1994.

50. *Origins* 19 (August 31, 1989): 217-218.

51. *Origins* 24 (September 8, 1994): 229-231.

52. *Origins* 25 (September 7, 1995): 199-200.

53. "Welfare Reform: Jobs and Families," *Origins* 23 (September 9, 1993): 217, 219-220.

54. On this issue, see also "Factors of Genuine Welfare Reform," *Origins* 24 (February 9, 1995): 564-566. In 1995, moreover, Cardinal William Keeler of Baltimore, president of the NCCB, protested against a House bill for welfare reform that would have provided for a family cap and child-exclusion, giving evidence for his assertion that eliminating payments to welfare mothers for numbers of children does not in fact lead to lower birth rates. See "Having Children, Encouraging Abortions," *Origins* 25 (November 16, 1995): 383.

55. "Environmental Degradation and Social Injustice," *Origins* 22 (March 18, 1993): 685, 687-692.

56. "Missouri: Abortion Case Before Supreme Court," *Origins* 18 (March 9, 1989): 645, 647-653.

57. "Webster: Opportunity to Defend Life," *Origins* 19 (April 9, 1989): 213-214.

58. The bishops also protested against proposals to provide for abortions in military hospitals abroad in "Abortions on Request in Military Hospitals?" *Origins* 23 (June 18, 1992): 87; against abortion provisions in the United Nations Population and Development Conference in Cairo, see "Concerns Expressed to Clinton on Cairo Conference," *Origins* 24 (June 9, 1994): 58-59, and "Critique of Cairo Draft Plan," *Origins* 24 (July 21, 1994): 170-171; against proposals to support and export abortions through foreign aid, see "A Letter to Congress," *Origins* 26 (February 13, 1997): 562-563; against President Clinton's ban of partial-birth abortions, see "The

Partial-Birth Abortion Ban Veto," *Origins* 25 (April 25, 1996): 753, 755, and "Letter to the Senate: Partial-Birth Abortions," *Origins* 27 (May 29, 1997): 24-25; and against the *Roe vs. Wade* decision after twenty-five years of experience with the effects of that decision, "Light and Shadows: The Nation 25 Years After 'Roe Vs. Wade,'" *Origins* 27 (November 27, 1997): 410-411.

59. "Letter to the Senate: Partial-Birth Abortions," *Origins* 27 (May 29, 1997): 24-25.

60. "Moral Principles Concerning Infants with Anencephaly," *Origins* 26 (October 10, 1996): 276.

61. "Violence and Homicide Rejected in Pro-Life Cause," *Origins* 24 (September 29, 1994): 273, 275-278.

62. "USCC Brief in Nancy Cruzan Case," *Origins* 19 (October 16, 1989): 345-351.

63. "Brief Asks Reversal of Assisted-Suicide Ruling," *Origins* 24 (September 1, 1994): 214-222. Similar amicus briefs were also filed before the U.S. Supreme Court when the Circuit Court found states' bans unconstitutional. See "A Threat of Unforeseeable Magnitude," *Origins* 25 (March 28, 1996): 671-672, and "Assisted Suicide Issue Moves to Supreme Court," *Origins* 26 (December 12, 1996): 421, 423-429.

64. "USCC-Led Group Opposes Assisted-Suicide Law," *Origins* 25 (February 8, 1996): 553, 555-562. The USCC unsuccessfully urged the U.S. Supreme Court to hear argument in the case before the law's taking effect.

65. "Oregon's Health Plan: Step Toward Medical Neglect?" *Origins* 21 (October 3, 1991): 270-272.

66. "Criteria for Evaluating Health-Care Reform," *Origins* 22 (May 21, 1992): 23-24.

67. "Minutes NCCB," New Orleans, La., June 17-18, 1993.

68. "Joint Statement on Pornography," *Origins* 23 (December 16, 1993): 466.

69. "Joint Statement on Holocaust Revisionism," *Origins* 23 (March 31, 1994): 714.

70. "Church Burnings," *Origins* 26 (July 4, 1996): 109.

71. For another episcopal statement against capital punishment, see "The Church and the Death Penalty," *Origins* 27 (June 26, 1997): 81, 83-85.

72. See *Pastoral Letters of the United States Catholic Bishops*, 5:543-561.

73. "Minutes NCCB," Baltimore, Md., November 6-9, 1989. The entire document was approved by a vote of 219 to 4.

74. *Origins* 24:26 (December 8, 1994): 433, 435.

75. "Embryo Research: Letter to National Health Director," *Origins* 24 (December 15, 1994): 462.

76. *Critical Decisions: Genetic Testing and Its Implications* (Washington, D.C.: United States Catholic Conference, 1996).

77. "Letter to Congress on 1991 Budget," *Origins* 19 (March 27, 1990): 787-788.

78. *Political Responsibility: Revitalizing American Democracy* (Washington, D.C.: United States Catholic Conference, 1991).

79. "USCC Presidential Candidates Questionnaire," *Origins* 22 (October 29, 1992): 341-352; see also "1996 Presidential Candidate Questionnaire," *Origins* 26 (September 26, 1996): 233-237.

80. See, e.g., "Election-Year Action of Tax-Exempt Organizations," *Origins* 22 (August 22, 1992): 179-185, and "Activities of Tax-Exempt Catholic Organizations," *Origins* 25 (March 14, 1996): 643-648.

81. "The Bishops' Non-Partisan Election-Year Agenda," *Origins* 26 (July 18, 1996): 113, 115-119.

82. "A Catholic Appeal: Leadership for the Common Good," *Origins* 25 (November 23, 1995): 393-394.

83. "Archbishops' Report on Southeast Asian Trip," *Origins* 18 (February 2, 1989): 545, 547-548.

84. "Archbishop May Statement," *Origins* 19 (November 23, 1989): 402.

85. "Solidarity Expressed with Mexican Church Leaders," *Origins* 23 (February 3, 1994): 578; "Concern for Chiapas and Its Bishop," *Origins* 24 (March 9, 1995): 625, 627.

86. "Addressing the Needs of Refugees," *Origins* 20 (April 17, 1991): 763-767.

87. "The Injustice of Anti-Foreigner Sentiment," *Origins* 23 (November 25, 1993): 422-423; "Pending Immigration Legislation's Punitive Tone," *Origins* 26 (July 4, 1996): 111-112.

88. "Establishing Foreign Aid Priorities," *Origins* 21 (October 24, 1991): 323-324.

89. The issue of American indifferentism and isolationism was also addressed on the fiftieth anniversary of the atomic bombing of Hiroshima and Nagasaki. See "What a Commitment to Peace Means Today," *Origins* 25 (September 7, 1995): 195-196.

90. "Statement on Strategic Arms Reduction Treaty II," *Origins* 22 (January 21, 1993): 542.

91. "Third World Debt and the Poor," *Origins* 18 (January 4, 1989): 607-612.

92. "Statement on the Middle East: The Pursuit of Peace with Justice," *Pastoral Letters of the United States Catholic Bishops*, 4:276-279.

93. "Letter to the Secretary of State on the Impact of the Embargo of Iraq," *Origins* 21 (August 15, 1991): 174-175; "Letter to Iraq's United Nations Ambassador," ibid., 175-176.

94. "The Cause of Peace in the Middle East," *Origins* 21 (November 7, 1991): 353-354.

95. "After the Gulf War: Issues of Conscience," *Origins* 21 (November 7, 1991): 352.

96. "Statement on Cease-Fire on Israeli-Lebanese Borders," *Origins* 23 (August 12, 1993): 162.

97. "Religious Leaders Welcome Peace Accord," *Origins* 23 (September 23, 1993): 254-255.

98. "Next Steps for Israel and the Palestinians," *Origins* 25 (October 12, 1995): 291-292.

99. "Respecting and Protecting Lebanon's Integrity," *Origins* 25 (February 22, 1996): 592.

100. "Intensified Hostilities in the Middle East," *Origins* 25 (May 2, 1996): 777-778.

101. "Letter of Solidarity to Iraqi Patriarch," *Origins* 27 (November 27, 1997): 412.

102. "Bishops in the White House Meeting Discuss El Salvador," *Origins* 19 (January 4, 1990): 501, 503-504.

103. "Statement on United Nations Truth Commission's Report on El Salvador," *Origins* 22 (April 1, 1993): 718.
104. "Statement on Investing in South Africa," *Origins* 23 (October 21, 1993): 338.
105. "The Unspeakable Horror Visited Upon Rwanda," *Origins* 24 (June 23, 1994): 81, 83-84.
106. "The Violence in Nigeria," *Origins* 25 (January 11, 1996): 495-496.
107. "Crisis in Haiti," *Origins* 21 (January 9, 1992): 499-500.
108. "Urgent Call for Democracy and Dialogue in Haiti," *Origins* 24 (September 22, 1994): 266.
109. "Steps to Lessen Suffering in Cuba," *Origins* 22 (November 19, 1992): 398-399.
110. "President Clinton Asked to Authorize Direct Flights to Cuba," *Origins* 27 (June 19, 1997): 80.
111. "Resolving Lithuania's Crisis Peacefully," *Origins* 19 (April 9, 1990): 785-786.
112. See, e.g., "Statement on the Soviet Union and Yugoslavia," *Origins* 21 (September 26, 1991): 258-259.
113. "Statement on Croatia," *Origins* 21 (November 21, 1991): 380-381.
114. "Humanitarian Nightmare in the Balkans," *Origins* 22 (April 8, 1993): 733, 735-736. See also "On United States Intervention in Bosnia," *Origins* 23 (May 27, 1993): 22-23.
115. "Clarification of Position on Aiding Bosnia," *Origins* 23 (May 27, 1993): 23.
116. "According China Most-Favored-Nation Status," *Origins* 21 (June 27, 1991): 120.
117. "Congress Urged to Revoke China's Trade Status," *Origins* 27 (June 5, 1997): 40-42.
118. "Appeal for Investment and Fair Employment in Northern Ireland," *Origins* 23 (January 27, 1994): 572.

Doctrinal Responsibilities: Approaches to Promoting Cooperation and Resolving Misunderstandings Between Bishops and Theologians

A Pastoral Statement of the National Conference of Catholic Bishops

June 1989

Preface

The present document constitutes a part of the continuing work by the Committee on Doctrine concerning the teaching mission of the Church. While the material was first prepared by a joint committee of the Canon Law Society of America and the Catholic Theological Society of America, with extensive consultation among bishops and scholars, this current text represents a revision drafted by the Committee on Doctrine in the winter of 1986-1987 and then emended in view of suggestions from the Administrative Committee in September 1987 and amendments or suggestions proposed before and during the general meeting of November 1987.[1] After further consultation with the full body of bishops from April through June of 1988 and with the Holy See in 1989, and subsequent revisions, *Doctrinal Responsibilities* has been clarified and strengthened as an instrument for promoting cooperation and for helping to resolve theological questions between bishops and theologians.

The document is in three parts.

I. *The Context of Ecclesial Responsibilities* presents a general statement of the ecclesial framework, the operative principles, and the responsibilities and rights of bishops and theologians. This section does not propose a full, much less a definitive, theological treatment. Rather it speaks in a summary and descriptive way to provide a context for the rest of the report.

II. *Promoting Cooperation and Informal Dialogue* recommends ways in which bishops and theologians can enhance cooperation in their common service of the Gospel and the Church, especially through personal contacts and informal dialogue. This section focuses on positive efforts to promote cooperation and also makes suggestions for actions by which bishops or theologians can screen complaints from third parties so that unnecessary disputes might be avoided.

III. *A Possibility for Formal Doctrinal Dialogue* sets out a suggested procedure designed specifically to deal with doctrinal disputes between bishops and theologians in dioceses. Since the circumstances in the nearly 200 dioceses of the United States vary widely, the approach given here is intended to be flexible and adaptable to local needs.

The recommended structures for promoting cooperation and for resolving doctrinal disputes draw upon experience already acquired by the Church in the United States for building a spirit of collaboration and resolving conflicts. They are designed to address the special problems of disputes of a doctrinal nature. It must be stressed that these guidelines can only serve if they are *adapted* to the particular conditions of a diocese, its history, and its special needs. The document presents a full complement of procedures as something from which bishops and theologians can draw. The adaptability of the procedures to local conditions by mutual consent of bishops and theologians should promote collaboration and conflict resolution. Although this report is concerned with theologians who are members of the Catholic Church, its approach may also prove useful with other theologians in Catholic institutions.

Both bishops and theologians are called to serve the word of God.[2] In the exercise of their office, bishops serve through authoritative teaching.[3] On the basis of scholarly competence illumined by faith,[4] theologians serve through disciplined reflection seeking an understanding of the Gospel for humanity today.[5] As they fulfill their distinctive but complementary duties, both bishops and theologians are sustained by the faith of the Church in God's revelation and by their participation in the Church's life of prayer, especially the sacred liturgy.

Moreover, in a time of philosophical and theological pluralism, much of which is good and enriching, the task of building cooperation between bishops and theologians becomes more urgent than ever so that Catholic doctrine may be effectively taught and intractable disputes avoided. A common commitment of bishops and theologians to the integrity of the word of God and a common sensitivity to the pastoral implications of theological teaching within the Church can make the structures suggested effective both in promoting cooperation and in resolving disputes.

The approach outlined here is offered to bishops and theologians in the United States for their use, though it does not have the status of law. Obviously, when used, these guidelines are to be interpreted in a manner consistent with the *Code of Canon Law*. Likewise they presuppose, as will be indicated in the pages that follow, the teaching of the Second Vatican Council and the subsequent statements of the magisterium on the nature of episcopal office and authority in the Church.

This document is not intended to offer suggestions for handling specific cases of dissent. Neither is it primarily to provide an approach to clarifying Catholic doctrine, although this may be one benefit of the process. Finally it does not in any way presuppose a situation of tension or envisage adversarial relations between bishops and theologians in the United States, as if the rights of one had to be protected against the other. On the contrary, the purpose of this document is to encourage increased communication and collaboration between bishops and theologians, to forestall disputes, and, if such disputes arise, to promote their resolution for the good of the faithful. Its guidelines will be reevaluated and, if necessary, refined in the light of these goals and the experience in using them.

I. The Context of Ecclesial Responsibilities

A. Context and Principles

The ecclesial context is critical for understanding the relationship between bishops and theologians, for encouraging cooperation, and for constructing an adequate approach to prevent or to address disputes related to the Church's teaching.

Before considering the different services which bishops and theologians render to the Church, it is important to recognize what they have in common as members of the body of Christ. In virtue of their faith, baptism, and communion with the Church, bishops and theologians alike—however distinct their ministries, charisms, and authority—are dedicated to the active proclamation of the Gospel and its transformative power for contemporary society. Both participate in the community's experience of faith and both seek to promote greater understanding of the word of God. In their common effort, both recognize the importance of communicating the faith with sensitivity to the cultural pluralism of today's world. Their common fidelity to the word of God permeates the particular responsibilities and rights of bishops and theologians; revelation is the good which both serve in analogous ways according to their distinctive ecclesial roles.[6] Thus, in different ways, rooted in the sacramental life of the Church, theologians and bishops discharge the mission of the Church "to show forth in the world the mystery of the Lord in a faithful though shadowed way, until at last it will be revealed in total splendor."[7]

In his address to leaders of Catholic higher education at Xavier University in New Orleans on September 12, 1987, Pope John Paul II stressed this ecclesial context which bishops and theologians share in common and which helps clarify the right relations between them. These words and the practice of *communio* they embody we make our own:

> Theology is at the service of the whole ecclesial community. The work of theology involves an interaction among the various members of the community of faith. The bishops, united with the Pope, have the mission of authentically teaching the message of Christ; as pastors they are called to sustain the unity in faith and Christian living of the entire People of God. For this they need the assistance of Catholic theologians, who perform an inestimable service to the Church. But theologians also need the charism entrusted by Christ to the bishops and, in the first place, to the Bishop of Rome. The fruits of their work, in order to enrich the lifestream of the ecclesial community, must ultimately be tested and valuated by the Magisterium. In effect, therefore, the ecclesial context of Catholic theology gives it a special character and value, even when theology exists in an academic setting.[8]

Thus, diverse gifts, ministries, and authority exist for the full development of the Church's unity in life and mission. They require an ecclesiological application of shared responsibility, legitimate diversity, and subsidiarity. Upon the bishops devolves the responsibility to encourage this diversity and to unify the various contributions of members of the Church. It is inevitable that misunderstandings about the teaching of the Gospel and the ways of expressing it will arise. In such cases, informal conversation ought to be the first step toward resolution. If this proves unproductive, a reasonable, clear, and fair process must protect fundamental human and sacramental responsibilities and rights of all parties concerned. Any guidelines developed for such cases should encourage that free and responsible theological inquiry in service to the Gospel which is faithful to Catholic tradition, in accord with the teaching authority of bishops, and responsive to the needs of the Church and the world. Similarly, any guidelines should promote the informed judgment of the bishops and hence their freedom to act responsibly as guardians and authoritative teachers of the faith.

Hence, the ultimate goal and importance of these procedures are to foster collaboration between bishops and theologians for the good of the entire Church, recognizing the vocation of theologians to study, clarify, and mediate the truth of the Gospel which the magisterium authoritatively proposes.[9] The recommendations given in sections II and III deal with the diocese. It is advisable that attempts to resolve doctrinal disputes be made first at the local level before an appeal is made to the Holy See. Of course, any bishop or theologian can contact the Holy See directly, but in terms of subsidiarity, every effort should ordinarily be made to initiate the process within the local church.[10]

The terms *magisterium, theologian,* and *responsibilities* and *rights* are frequently used in this report. There is considerable variation in the current use of these words, but for the sake of clarity, the following specific meanings are stipulated here.

Magisterium will be used to refer to the ecclesiastical magisterium, i.e., to the unique teaching authority exercised in the name of Christ by the pope and other bishops united with the pope. Throughout, this document affirms the final pastoral authority of the episcopal office in the Church and the tasks of sanctifying, teaching, and ruling which are conferred by the sacrament of orders.[11] By their ordination and hierarchical communion, bishops are members of the college of bishops and authoritative teachers in their local churches. By virtue of their divine and ecclesial mission and with a discerning awareness of the needs of contemporary society, bishops have the pastoral duty in the name of Christ to proclaim the word of God with authority, to teach the truth of the faith, and to maintain the authentic interpretation of the word of God as it has been handed down in the course of history.[12] For this reason, the *Directory on the Pastoral Ministry of Bishops* stated for every bishop:

> In order that he [the bishop] may be found a faithful minister and supporter of the orthodox faith that has been handed on to him, protecting it from errors and dangers, he must diligently cultivate theological science and daily increase it with new yet proven doctrine.[13]

The term *theologian* in these pages is used to designate the Catholic who seeks to mediate, through the discipline of scholarship, between a living faith and the culture it is called to transform.[14] Thus, within the ecclesial community, theologians fulfill certain specific tasks. Like other Catholics, theologians live lives of faith within the community and in fidelity to the teaching authority of the Church.[15] Grounded in the commitment of their ecclesial faith and trained in the skills of scholarship, theologians systematically explore the nature and foundations of God's revelation and the teaching of the Church. They examine the interrelationships of Christian truths and offer interpretations of God's word in response to the challenges of contemporary society. Though theologians as such share in the Church's mission to serve the Gospel as effectively as possible and do so through their scholarly work, they are not primarily preachers or catechists. Typically, they hold a doctorate or comparable degree in one of the sacred sciences, have had extensive exposure to the Catholic tradition in their particular area of expertise, and are engaged in teaching and research in a seminary, college, or university.

The contribution and cogency of a theologian's work, therefore, depend upon scholarly competence that is rooted in faith and is faithful to the Church's teaching under the guidance of the Holy Spirit.[16] That competence can be assessed from the quality of the evidence theologians adduce and the soundness of the arguments they advance for the sake of Christ's truth. Such competence can be shown, for example, when theologians ask searching and serious questions as they seek to discern and communicate the abiding truth of Christ. The constructive critical quality of theological scholarship does not compromise its fidelity to the Church and its magisterium, but indicates the disciplined reflection characteristic of genuine scholarly investigation.

Responsibilities and rights are used variously in law and ethics. We mean by *right* a moral or legal power to act or to be immune from injury. Responsibilities, and the rights with which they are correlative, have their source in one's human dignity, in one's standing in the Church, or from one's functions within the Catholic community. Commonly the possession of a right is distinguished from its exercise, because the exercise of a right may be circumscribed in order to protect the common good or the rights of others, even though the right itself remains intact. In the Catholic heritage, individual rights are always to be promoted within the context of the common good.[17]

B. The Responsibilities and Rights of Bishops

The guidelines proposed in this document reflect a concern to recognize and foster the responsibilities and rights of both bishops and theologians.[18]

The responsibilities and rights of bishops flow from their pastoral office of teaching, sanctifying, and governing in the Church. These tasks *(munera)* cannot be fully separated one from the other; they form a single pastoral office. Of the responsibilities and rights of bishops which arise from their pastoral task of authoritative teaching, we call attention to the following.

Preeminent among the responsibilities of bishops is preaching the word of God. Bishops are also charged to preserve and protect the truth of faith, i.e., to transmit the authentic Gospel of Christ. Moreover, in the particular church where he serves, the bishop is to teach in the name of Christ and the Church; he is to make the pastoral judgment as to how the faith of the community will be publicly expressed at a given time and place. For that reason, the bishop is called upon to judge whether some opinions endanger or are contrary to faith and the Christian life. But it is also the responsibility of bishops to discharge their office so as to respect the gifts imparted by the Holy Spirit to various members of the Church. It follows that in the exercise of their pastoral role, bishops should encourage theologians to pursue a deeper understanding of the

Gospel and its meaning for contemporary life.[19] In order to encourage theology and to make provisions for the consultation he needs in his teaching, the bishop should select the most suitable candidates for theological studies and should encourage these studies among religious communities and lay men and women within his diocese.

In addition to these responsibilities, certain rights of bishops are rooted in their task as teachers. Thus, the bishops of particular churches have the right to exercise their care for the truth of the Gospel in the Church over which they preside. The bishops teach in the name of Christ and his Church, in union with the head and other members of the episcopal college. What they teach should meet with that religious reception proportionate to the degree of authority with which it is presented.[20]

But bishops also have the right to draw upon the contributions and the gifts of all who share the Church's saving mission, which includes the heralding of the faith.[21] In their particular church communities bishops have the right to the cooperation and support of the priests who form one presbyterate with the bishop. Bishops also have a right to the collaboration of theologians: bishops draw on their scholarly competence and support as well as rely upon them as one necessary resource for their own ongoing theological study. Bishops consult theologians for aid in scrutinizing the signs of the time and in evaluating new issues and questions. Bishops look to theologians for aid in keeping their own formulations of Catholic belief and practice faithful to the word of God. Further, bishops have a right to require in the name of the Church that theologians faithfully discharge their own responsibility for the integrity of the Gospel. Bishops must also have the freedom to teach without interference from civil authority or unwarranted criticism by theologians or others in the Church. Finally, because their solicitude extends to the universal Church, bishops have a right to expect fraternal support from one another.

C. The Responsibilities and Rights of Theologians

The responsibilities and rights of theologians may be grouped according to the ways in which theologians participate in the life of the Church.

As members of the community of faith, theologians share the common responsibility of maintaining the unity and integrity of Catholic faith, reflected in the *sensus fidei*[22] and the documents of tradition in which it is set forth. They must keep in mind the pastoral and missionary effects of their work.[23] Theologians also acknowledge that it is the role of bishops as authoritative teachers in the Church to make pastoral judgments about the soundness of theological teaching so that the integrity of Catholic doctrine and the unity of the faith community may be preserved. In other words, theological teaching always remains subject to testing in the life of the Church and to the teaching of its bishops.

As scholars, theologians discharge their responsibility in fidelity to apostolic faith by meditative appropriation of the faith and by critical inquiry according to the principles of that branch of theology in which their work is done.[24] As they fulfill that responsibility, theological scholars must expect to exchange constructive criticism with other scholars, other Christians, and other interested persons of good will. Fidelity to the faith and to the canons of sound scholarship requires a willingness on the part of members of the theological community to exchange candid judgments on one another's work.

As members of diverse communities, theologians have the responsibility to seek suitable ways of communicating doctrine to people today. They should adapt the communication of their research to the audience of their lectures or publications and take into account the effect their presentation may have. They should use pastoral discretion in dealing with the communications media in order to avoid any harm which might result from premature or inappropriate dissemination of their thought to the theologically untrained.[25]

To the extent that theologians accept more specifically ecclesiastical activities, such as the formation of future priests, they must accept reasonable canonical ordering of their work.

Correlative to the responsibilities of theologians in the life of the Church are certain rights. Paramount among them is lawful freedom of inquiry and expression of scholarly opinion.[26] As they discharge their responsibilities, theologians have the right to moral support from the Church, though they must also expect and even welcome objective criticism of their work.

Closely related to that right is another: the right of the theologian to a good reputation,[27] and, if needed, the defense of that right by appropriate administrative or judicial processes within the Church. In cases of dispute, the theologian has the right to expect access to a fair process, protecting both substantive and procedural rights. In addition, as professional scholars, theologians have the right to employ the usual means of research and publication and to associate freely in private and professional groups.

II. Promoting Cooperation and Informal Dialogue

A. *The Purposes and Climate of Cooperation*

Authoritative teaching and theological inquiry are distinct but inseparable tasks. For this reason, bishops and theologians need to cooperate with one another in accordance with their respective responsibilities to enhance the quality of their diverse service to the Church. This cooperation is intended to realize the ideals of mutual encouragement, support, and assistance which are proposed by Vatican II, as well as to promote the efficacy of the episcopal office, the soundness of theological scholarship, and that unity without which the Church's mission in the world becomes weak and diffuse.[28]

Cooperation between theologians and bishops ought to play a significant, indeed indispensable, role as context and prelude to the employment of formal doctrinal dialogue for resolving doctrinal disputes. Bishops and theologians involved in ongoing collaboration are likely to grow in respect and trust for one another and thus to assist and support their respective service to the Gospel. As they appreciate each other's struggles to be faithful to the demands of the Gospel according to their different functions in the Church, their mutual respect and trust should grow. This may serve to prevent theological disagreements and differences in viewpoint from degenerating to such an extent that formal doctrinal dialogue must be used to resolve the conflict.

Even in cases where formal doctrinal dialogue is employed, structured cooperation will already have established a climate in which all the parties are motivated to act prudently, patiently, and in charity.[29] Regular and meaningful cooperation provides the opportunity for each party to discern and clarify the responsibilities, rights, and interests of the other. Thus, if and when formal doctrinal dialogue is requested, both bishops and theologians can be aware of the necessary distinctions and of the possibilities and limitations of formal procedures used to deal with them.

Cooperation has a long history in the Church. In our own century prior to Vatican II, there were well-established ways for theologians to cooperate with bishops in their tasks of teaching, sanctifying, and governing in the Church. In the 1917 *Code of Canon Law*, theologians (who were, in almost all cases, clerics) were envisaged as members of seminary faculties, as censors of books, as synodal examiners, and as conciliar and curial experts. In the revised *Code of Canon Law* even more cooperative roles for theologians are envisaged, at least by implication.[30]

Bishops do rely upon theologians, explicitly or implicitly. Every bishop has been educated by theologians. So has every priest who cooperates with him in his ministry. Bishops have been encouraged, even charged, to study theology regularly to inform their preaching and to make their exercise of the pastoral office more effective.[31] So the appropriate questions are: How should bishops select theologians for consultation? When do they rely upon them? How is that reliance enacted?

Some bishops have appointed theologians as advisors and vicars for theological affairs or have established boards of theological consultants.[32] The National Conference of Catholic Bishops (NCCB) regularly calls upon theologians to cooperate in its work. While collaborative efforts like these are surely encouraging, much more needs to be done.[33]

Theologians, too, could profit from reinvigorated cooperation. Their relationship to the Church, which is an essential element in their identity and work as Catholic theologians, may take a further vital form in the course of collaboration with bishops. Cooperation would thus enable theologians better to understand and to fulfill their specific responsibilities in the Church.

While the focus of this section of the report is on structured cooperation between bishops and theologians, not all cooperation need or should take place in a formal mode. If bishops and theologians are convinced of the importance of the help they can render one another in carrying out the mission of the Church, they will be determined and creative in seeking ways to work together informally. Without the pressure of a crisis, they may find their conversations deeply nourishing and empowering. Together they need to foster regular and personal ways of contact.

The emergence of an important national issue, the promulgation of a papal document, and the weeks preceding or following a meeting of the NCCB can be occasions for the bishop and theologians of a diocese to discuss materials, proposals, or concerns and to discern their local implications and applications. Further, bishops could invite Catholic faculties of theology to consider and evaluate theological issues which have arisen in the life of the Church. On the other hand, Catholic colleges, universities, and seminaries might make it a practice to invite the bishop to campus events of theological or pastoral significance. Catholic scholars at secular institutions could do the same. In some dioceses, it may be feasible for bishops and theologians to meet regularly for informal exploration of mutual concerns or simply for shared prayer.

B. Implementing Structured Cooperation

1. Suggested Areas of Implementation

Initiation and development of collaboration between bishops and theologians will not always require the establishment of new structures. Most dioceses already have offices, departments, and staffs which assist the bishop in meeting his varied and complex responsibilities. The issues and areas delegated to these offices often have important theological dimensions, e.g., health care, ecumenical relations, adult education, catechetics, liturgy, finances, and family life. It would be a relatively simple matter to invite competent theologians to serve as consultants to these offices or even as part-time staff members.

There are also other questions of concern and interest to both bishops and theologians in which a cooperative approach could yield very desirable results. The importance of these matters will motivate joint efforts to establish the appropriate collaborative structures to deal with them. Just as presbyteral councils and pastoral councils cooperate with their bishops, so ways could be developed for theologians and bishops to bring their expertise and talent to bear on concerns such as:

- The means and efficacy of the local church's proclamation of the Gospel
- Diocesan goals, mission statements, and priorities
- Religious education materials in use or proposed for use in the diocese
- Health care policies and procedures
- Goals and policies of Catholic educational institutions in the diocese
- Policies and guidelines for lectures, conferences, and workshops held in the diocese
- Priorities and policies for the Church's charitable endeavors
- Continuing education for priests, religious, deacons, and catechists
- The theological supports for diocesan statements, position papers, and testimony to be presented at various civic and legal fora
- The theological background for pastoral letters
- Ecumenical relations
- Diocesan employment policies and procedures

Although bishops and theologians teach in very different ways, nevertheless the position of either can become the target of complaints and charges which have no substance or merit. Although the accuser(s) might be well intentioned, these situations are potentially volatile and enervating for everyone involved. In some dioceses, it may prove desirable to the diocesan bishop to establish a procedure which prevents groundless charges from occupying more time and attention than they deserve.

An individual or a small committee recognized by the bishop and the theological community for theological expertise, tact, and pastoral sensitivity could be appointed by the bishop to screen these complaints. All complaints about theological teaching in the diocese could be referred here, after they have been presented to the bishop as well as the theologian in question. The screening task, while respecting and protecting the dignity of the complainant, is to keep a groundless complaint from becoming a dispute which needlessly distracts the bishop and/or the theologian from their more important services to the Church.

Another area that calls for cooperation is the provision contained in canon 812 of the revised *Code of Canon Law*. This requires theologians teaching in institutes of higher learning to have *habeant oportet*, a mandate granted by the competent ecclesiastical authority. It is important that bishops and the theological community work together to formulate a constructive way of ensuring the pursuit of truth in teaching Catholic doctrine, observing church law, and respecting the legitimate concerns of the American system of higher education.

2. Means of Implementation

The first steps toward structured cooperation can be taken by the bishop or by theologians in his diocese. The bishop himself can request the theologians to provide him with the names and areas of expertise of theologians who are willing and competent to offer their services to the local church in a collaborative way. Theologians themselves could also develop such information and offer it to the bishop. Either way, the local church would have more substantial theological expertise available to it.

With a view to appointing a theological advisor, the bishop could also consult widely with theologians inside and outside the diocese. In larger dioceses, this advisor could be of great assistance for theological affairs and serve as the bishop's liaison to the theologians in the diocese. The theological advisor could facilitate contact between the bishop and the theologians. Such a person should not be the bishop's only spokesperson on theological issues, nor substitute for the personal contact of the bishop with theologians.

In large urban centers or wherever there is a sufficient number of theologians, the bishop might well consider establishing a board of theological advisors. Among other functions, the board could serve in cases of dispute as the mediating, screening, or fact-finding body, prior to the initiation of any formal procedures.

Most dioceses in the United States do not have enough theologians to implement structured cooperation very extensively on their own. While this factor presents particular difficulties, it also provides the bishops and theologians of a province or region an opportunity to realize the vision of mutual support and cooperation among dioceses set forth by Vatican II.[34]

The theologians and bishops of a region could come together informally in the ways suggested above. They could also consider ways in which formal and regular cooperation could be established among them. For example, some dioceses have coordinated regional resources to develop more effective tribunals. Efforts have already been made in the United States with a view to sharing the theological and canonical resources of a region. The document *On Due Process* proposed a regional pooling of resources for more effective resolution of doctrinal conflicts.[35] Some state Catholic conferences have established medical-moral commissions.

Granted that the geographical distances involved make such cooperation more difficult to develop and maintain, still the advantages to be gained far outweigh the difficulties involved. Perhaps a demonstration project in a particular region could develop guidelines to facilitate regional structures for cooperation elsewhere.

Structured cooperation between bishops and theologians should, and to some extent already does, exist on the national level.[36] Prospects for developing it further, however, deserve serious consideration.

3. Principles Regarding Theological Consultants

Most theologians hold full-time positions in colleges, universities, or seminaries. As a result, in most instances of structured cooperation their role will be consultative. This means that they will serve in a part-time capacity as consultants or advisors to bishops or to diocesan departments and staffs which assist the bishop in carrying out his service to the Church.

If this form of structured collaboration is to function effectively and to realize the purposes for which it is established, certain principles should be followed.

First, theological consultants should be persons in full accord with the faith of the universal Church and aware of the ways that faith is known and lived in the particular church which they serve as consultants. The bishop is always free to choose his own advisors, but the competence of theologians who serve in any consultative capacity should be recognized by their peers. They should be selected from as many segments as possible on the spectrum of acceptable theological opinion, so that the Church can reap the benefits of the fullest range of theological resources available on particular issues or problems.

Second, there are often advantages to making public the names of consultants and perhaps even the selection process. Unnecessary secrecy can lead to suspicion and mistrust.

Third, whenever possible, consultants should serve for a fixed term. A policy of orderly succession among consultants will foster the benefits of both continuity and freshness of perspective on the issues. It will also realize the ideal of common effort which is at the heart of authentic unity in the Church.

Fourth, everyone involved centrally or marginally in the process should remember that the theological consultant, through faithfulness to the truth of the Gospel and the demands of theological science, serves not only the local bishop, but also the entire local church. Otherwise, the complementary but distinct and irreducible roles of the bishop and the theologian may be confused and the anticipated results of real cooperation may not be fully realized.[37]

C. Cooperation as Aiding Doctrinal Dialogue

As their conversation and collaboration become more common, bishops and theologians are likely to gain a greater sense of the distinct but inseparable services they perform in the one Church through, for example, authoritative teaching and pastoral leadership (on the part of the bishops) and ethical reflection, theological education, and research (on the part of the theologians). This alone should eliminate many misunderstandings between them.[38]

Regular and active cooperation will also establish a mutual personal knowledge and trust between bishops and theologians which can lessen the occasions when formal doctrinal dialogue is required to resolve a dispute. As bishops and theologians come to know each other not merely in official roles but as faithful persons, recourse to formal procedures to resolve conflicts between them should become less and less frequent.

If formal doctrinal dialogue is necessary, however, the mutual knowledge and trust established by previous cooperation will help to ensure that it works to the benefit of everyone involved. The dispute is also less likely to become an arena for an adversary relationship between the bishop and the theologian. Mutual knowledge and trust will help to maintain the unity of love throughout the course of the procedures, when tempers may be short, sensitivities acute, and feelings high. Each will more likely be concerned to protect the other's good name and reputation and to employ the formal doctrinal dialogue so as to preserve and enhance the service each offers to the Church. Both bishops and theologians will be solicitous for the maintenance and exercise of each other's responsibilities and rights.

III. A Possibility for Formal Doctrinal Dialogue

A. Purposes of the Dialogue

Collaboration and structured cooperation help to clarify doctrinal positions. Throughout such contacts there is a presupposition of sound doctrine, a presumption which holds unless it is refuted by contrary evidence. Nevertheless, there may be differences of opinion, disagreements, or questions concerning doctrinal matters. The bishop may have already deemed it necessary to speak or act publicly in an effort to provide pastoral guidance to the faithful. If these differences or actions lead to conflict or dispute, formal doctrinal dialogue may be used, always respecting the differing roles of bishops and theologians in the Church (cf. canons 753, 218).

Such dialogue is not a judicial or administrative proceeding.[39] Its scope is to determine the facts and their theological and pastoral implications, and thereby to resolve any misunderstandings between bishops and theologians. It would precede any judgment which the bishop as authoritative teacher might eventually feel himself obliged to make for the sake of the faith of the Church. A dialogue about doctrine would also ordinarily take place before any consideration of a possible administrative response to a doctrinal matter. This distinction between doctrinal discussion and administrative action is basic. A doctrinal dialogue does not entail new obligations for bishops in their authoritative teaching or for theologians in their scholarly reflection, but offers adaptable means for both to exercise their roles as effectively as possible. By entering such a dialogue no theologian acquires the authority of a bishop, nor is a bishop expected to be a theological scholar. Each would participate according to his or her respective role in the Church, but each also as desiring greater understanding of the question at issue. If a bishop is to make a final determination of his view of a theologian's teaching, his judgment should be well informed and reasonable. While not expected to justify his decision in the manner of a scientific theologian, he should ordinarily present reasons for his judgment. If theologians are to sustain or modify their positions, they should do so through dialogue with bishops as well as with their theological colleagues. For example, if a bishop has questioned the teaching of a theologian, the theologian might request such a dialogue. On the other hand, if a bishop is concerned about the reported opinions of a theologian, he might be the one to request the initiation of formal doctrinal dialogue. In such cases, initiation of a private formal dialogue would serve the unity of the Church far better than public disagreement.

Neither a bishop nor a theologian may be *required* to use this process, and public pressure should not be brought to bear upon their choice. If they choose to do so, the dialogue would proceed through adopting or adapting any of the procedures that follow. A formal dialogue does not imply equality of roles in the Church but a structured pattern for doctrinal discussion.

Briefly stated, the purpose of formal doctrinal dialogue is to determine the nature and gravity of the issue at dispute as well as its pastoral significance and to achieve an agreement between the parties. The process will normally involve meetings, although much can be accomplished by written statements. As a sign of unity and charity, an atmosphere of prayer should mark the dialogue in all its stages.

B. Participants

For the purpose of these guidelines, the dispute in need of resolution is presumed to be between a theologian and a bishop. The theologian or bishop who requests the use of this formal dialogue is termed the *initiating party*. The other partner who agrees to this formal dialogue is termed the *second party*. Several bishops or several theologians may be acting as initiating party or second party.

Other persons may assist the principals in the formal dialogue. These may be involved in regard to one or more of the following functions.

1. *Advice*. Advisors may assist the initiating party or the second party by their advice and counsel. Advisors are selected freely by the party whom they will be serving as advisor.

2. *Expertise*. Experts may be called upon to assist the parties in reaching mutual understanding about their respective positions, to offer an evaluation of the relationship of theological statements with Catholic tradition, and to give advice about the pastoral effect of such teaching. Experts, therefore, should be knowledgeable about the matter under discussion, should be representative of the variety of views within Catholic tradition, and should participate in the process in a manner acceptable to both parties. Normally such experts will themselves be professional theologians or persons versed in pastoral ministry. While the opinion of experts, even if unanimous, is not binding on either of the parties, it should be given serious weight in proceeding with the dialogue and should not be rejected without good reason.

3. *Facilitation*. At the request of both parties, a facilitator may assist at any of the various stages of formal dialogue. The facilitator helps the process to move forward by bringing the principals to a better understanding of what each means, by setting specific questions for them, and by providing at various stages in the dialogue a *state of the question* to clarify what points are truly at issue at that particular moment.

4. *Delegation*. Dialogue is carried out most effectively in a face-to-face exchange, through which each party comes to a more personal appreciation of the other's position. Although this is the preferred method, there may be occasions when either party considers it necessary to delegate another person to assist in the various tasks of formal doctrinal dialogue. A bishop, for example, may choose to participate directly throughout this dialogue or to have his concerns represented by a theologian. In every case, however, the final statement of agreement for each task in the formal dialogue should be signed by the principal parties themselves.

C. Procedures for Formal Doctrinal Dialogue

1. Beginning the Dialogue

Either a theologian or a bishop may request formal doctrinal dialogue. But the decision to begin such a dialogue must be freely agreed upon by both.

a. Direct contact between the two parties:

The initiating party should first have approached the second party in an informal manner to determine whether the apparent dispute may be immediately resolved without formal dialogue. If formal dialogue is needed, the initiating party makes a written request to the second party to enter into formal doctrinal dialogue. The written request outlines the doctrinal points at issue, the manner in which the dispute has arisen, the attempts to resolve the issue which have already been made, the specific request to employ formal doctrinal dialogue to settle the question, and initial suggestions concerning ways to resolve the doctrinal dispute.

b. Indirectly, through a contact person:

A contact person may be appointed within a diocese to process requests for the use of formal doctrinal dialogue. The contact person is appointed by the bishop and should be qualified to evaluate and process such requests, generally acceptable also to the theological community and easily available for contact.

The first function of the contact person would be to determine whether the request for formal dialogue is legitimate. If the request is judged to be inappropriate, the contact person informs the initiating party, indicating the reasons for rejecting the request. If the initiating party then resubmits the request, the contact person submits it to the second party for a response.

If the request at the outset is judged to be appropriate, it is sent to the second party for a response and the initiating party is informed immediately of the date of this action. Rejection of the request by the contact person or submission of the request to the second party for response should normally take place within one month of the receipt of the request by the contact person.

2. The Response

Acknowledgment of a request for formal dialogue ordinarily should be given in writing within two weeks of the receipt of the request, and a formal response within one month of the receipt of the request.

a.   An affirmative response to the request should include an explicit commitment to formal doctrinal dialogue, a statement of the points about which both parties seem at the outset to be in agreement, the points which seem to be in dispute, and initial suggestions concerning ways to resolve the doctrinal dispute.

b. A negative response should explicitly refuse to make use of formal doctrinal dialogue and state the reasons for refusal.

c. If after six weeks from the date on which the formal request was sent to the second party no response has been received by the initiating party, a second request should be sent to the second party. Failure to respond to this second request within two weeks shall be interpreted as refusal to make use of formal doctrinal dialogue.

3. Agreement on Procedure

The written request for dialogue and the response may have already clarified the disagreement and the desired goal in dialogue. Nevertheless, the next step should be a preliminary agreement on the statement of the issues, on the procedures to be followed, and on the goal to be achieved by their formal dialogue.

In determining procedures, the preliminary agreement should address matters such as the following:

a. Level of confidentiality to be respected
b. Participation by other persons and how they are to be selected (see above, B, 1-4)
c. Record keeping and, if appropriate, transcripts
d. Time limits
e. Responsibility for expenses

Good order requires that this preliminary agreement be in writing and signed by both parties. It can be modified at any time by their mutual consent.

4. The Dialogue

Disputes between theologians and members of the ecclesiastical magisterium are usually complex and may involve deep feelings. It is not easy to decide *a priori* on the best or simplest method to resolve the situation. At the beginning it is essential that both parties be committed to the procedure. As the dialogue progresses, the parties may find it helpful to alter by mutual consent the procedures they had agreed upon.

Although disputes may be considerably different, formal doctrinal dialogue proposes primarily to clarify the objective content of what is at issue and to accomplish this through the completion of four tasks:

a. Gathering data
b. Clarifying meaning

    c.   Determining the relationship of the points at issue to Catholic tradition

    d.   Identifying implications in the life of the Church

One of the main instruments for achieving agreement is the formulation of written statements with regard to each of the tasks. These statements, signed by both parties, express points of agreement, clarify reasons for disagreement, and specify further questions to be addressed.

First Task: Gathering the Data. Since doctrinal disputes arise from public utterances or writings, the first task is to agree on what was actually said or written. There may be no disagreement as to the data at all, in which case a statement of agreement should immediately be drawn up and signed by both parties.

If the parties initially disagree about what was said or written, ways should be found to solve this difference of opinion. Examples include:

1. In written matters, copies of the actual materials should be made available to both parties.
2. In spoken matters, tape recordings, written reports, and other trustworthy records, if they exist, should be made available to both parties.
3. If no record exists to settle the question of what was actually said or written, it may be necessary to call upon witnesses.

Adequate access to the record by both parties is essential to effective dialogue. In cases in which a dispute has arisen because of complaints or accusations by other persons, the party accused or complained against has the right of access to the materials sent by the other persons—confidentiality in accord with church law, of course, always being respected. In such situations the burden of proof as to matters of fact rests on those bringing the complaint or accusation.

In determining what was said or written, it is important to specify the pertinent context, such as:

1. The literary genre: newspaper article, theological study, popular religious work, etc.
2. The context of spoken communications: lecture, classroom, seminar, radio or television, etc.
3. The audience addressed
4. The level and extent of publicity

In especially complicated matters the accomplishment of the task of gathering data may very well benefit from a facilitator who can settle factual questions to the satisfaction of both parties. The parties may also make use of advisors or, if necessary, delegates to expedite the process.

This task should be completed with a written statement of agreement, signed by both parties. It specifies the data gathered and the agreement of the parties on the essential points of what was said or written. In some cases agreement on accurate data may itself resolve the dispute and complete the dialogue.

Second Task: Clarifying the Meaning. While completion of the first task may determine clearly what was said or written, questions may still exist about the meaning of the data. Since words may admit of varying interpretations, the parties need to seek a common understanding of the meaning of what was said or written. The result of this effort should be an agreement either on a single meaning of these data or on their possible, differing interpretations.

In reaching this clarification, consideration should be given to various factors, such as:

1. The significance of the words in text and context
2. The broader corpus of the author's work, philosophical and theological perspective, and method
3. The author's intention in presenting the material, whether the position was being advocated, defended, described, etc.
4. The pertinent context of the work at issue as determined in the first task (see above)
5. The degree to which the statement is presented as a personal opinion or as a teaching of the Church

If agreement on meaning is not readily achieved, the parties may find it useful to rely on the advice of others or perhaps to submit the matter to a jointly acceptable facilitator.

This second task should be completed with a written statement of agreement, signed by both parties, expressing as clearly as possible the mutually accepted meaning of what was said or written. The statement may also specify any differing interpretations which remain. In some cases, agreement on the meaning may itself resolve the dispute and complete the dialogue.

Third Task: Determining the Relationship with Catholic Tradition. Every doctrinal dispute will initially involve at least an apparent divergence of opinion about the consonance of a public utterance or writing with Catholic tradition. The completion of the first two tasks may result in the conclusion that the disagreement was unfounded. Nevertheless, the first two tasks may simply serve to clarify the point at issue, that is, the consonance of what was said or written with Catholic tradition.

This stage of the doctrinal inquiry is complex. It is not the same as a final judgment about public teaching that the bishop may make at the end of the entire process. Nor is it a task that can be isolated from the parties themselves; their personal involvement is especially important. It is a learning process in which dialogue should assist both parties to develop a more precise understanding of the fullness of Catholic tradition. Thus, in approaching this task the parties should seek to discover points of agreement, particularly in regard to the questions which must be studied and the appropriate order for addressing those questions.

This stage of dialogue should begin with a written statement by the initiating party outlining the basis on which consonance with Catholic tradition is questioned. The second party should respond to this initial statement in writing. If no agreement is reached, these two documents form the basis for further dialogue.

The term *Catholic tradition* refers to the whole range of church teaching grounded in the word of God, especially in the Scriptures, and received in the Church through the centuries. The magisterium serves the word of God by proposing doctrine in solemn conciliar or papal pronouncements, in ordinary papal and episcopal teaching, and in other activities such as the approval of materials used in the instruction of the faithful and the worship of the Church. Catholic tradition is also reflected and furthered in the *sensus fidelium*, the works of approved authors, and in Catholic life, worship, and belief. Determining the consonance of a theological view with Catholic tradition will demand a careful consideration of the historical context and development of church teaching, an understanding of the hierarchy of truths, an evaluation of the various levels of teaching authority, appreciation of the distinction between the substance of the faith and its expression, and the degree to which the Church has committed itself in this matter.

At this stage in the dialogue the parties may be assisted by a facilitator, by personal advisors, and especially by consultation with theological experts.

This task should be completed with a written statement of agreement, signed by both parties. It specifies the steps taken to complete the task, the resulting points of agreement, and any remaining disagreement. Here, too, the written statement of agreement may suffice to resolve the dispute and complete the dialogue.

Fourth Task: Identifying the Implications for the Life of the Church. The previous tasks have resulted in agreements on the public utterances and writings in question and possibly differing interpretations and disagreements about them. The fourth task is to determine the pastoral implications of these utterances and writings in the life of the Church. While actual or apparent implications precipitate most doctrinal disputes, they are frequently the most difficult to sort out and agree upon. This task requires not merely understanding, but prudence; not just learning, but wisdom. Concern for such implications is a responsibility of both bishops and theologians.

To begin this task, the initiating party should state in writing the nature and extent of the implications. The second party should respond to this statement in writing. If no agreement has been reached, these two documents form the basis for further dialogue on this matter.

A discussion about implications cannot be simply an exchange of personal impressions. It should clarify the criteria used by the parties to assess pastoral life. Conclusions should be based on adequate information required for prudential judgments. This may necessitate gathering additional evidence. The discussion might be assisted by the opinion of persons noted for prudence and experience in pastoral and theological matters. The parties may rely on advisors or may mutually agree on a facilitator to assist in this task.

This task is concluded with a written statement of agreement signed by both parties, specifying the steps taken to determine the implications in the life of the Church and their mutual and individual conclusions. It may include actions agreed upon for the future. This written statement may suffice to resolve the dispute and conclude the dialogue, or even provide for continued review of the issue.

D. Possible Results of Formal Doctrinal Dialogue

Formal doctrinal dialogue may conclude in a variety of ways. It is important to identify the conclusion of the dialogue process and the outcome of the dispute itself. The degree of publicity to be given to the results of the dialogue should be carefully adapted to the particular situation. In every case, even if complete agreement has not been reached, both parties should discuss these matters so that both are aware of proposed actions.

These are some possible results of the dialogue:

1. The theological and pastoral issues may be resolved to the satisfaction of both parties at any stage in the formal dialogue.
2. At the conclusion of the formal dialogue the theological issue may be unresolved, but both parties may agree that the issue may remain so without the need for further action. Agreement to disagree may be a recognition of legitimate pluralism or of a situation in which pastoral responsibility requires no further action.
3. There may be no agreement concerning the theological and pastoral issues nor acceptance of the disagreement as a form of legitimate pluralism. In light of pastoral considerations, various responses on the doctrinal level are then possible. Such responses vary in purpose, intensity, and publicity. They will

also depend on the qualification of the theological issue in question. The following are some possibilities:

a. Call for continued critical theological study.
b. Expand the context of the dialogue to a regional or national level.
c. Restate in a positive fashion authoritative church teaching.
d. Issue a doctrinal *monitum*, i.e., a clear warning of danger to the faith in what is being taught.
e. Declare publicly the apparent error of a position.
f. Classify certain positions as one of the following:

    1. A private position which may be presented by itself, provided it is not represented as official Catholic teaching
    2. A private opinion which, when presented, must be accompanied by other more acceptable positions
    3. Unsuitable for teaching as Catholic doctrine

g. Make an accurate presentation of views to the media.

E. Subsequent Administrative Action

The foregoing procedure has been a doctrinal dialogue. The best response to bad teaching is good teaching. A doctrinal response which convincingly expresses the authoritative teaching of the Church is, therefore, the most desirable response to a doctrinal dispute. Nonetheless, when doctrinal differences begin to affect the common good and doctrinal dialogue has failed to resolve them, administrative action on the part of bishops or canonical recourse on the part of theologians may be appropriate or even necessary.[40]

Administrative procedures do not of themselves resolve doctrinal issues; they are intended primarily to address pastoral situations. The kind and degree of administrative action should be proportionate to the pastoral requirements of the common good and should be no more severe than those requirements demand.

The degree of understanding reached in the doctrinal dialogue should help all parties to appreciate their mutual concern for the good of the Church and will influence the decision about any subsequent action or recourse. In addition, the signed agreements of the formal doctrinal dialogue will provide a valuable record for subsequent action on the part of bishops or recourse on the part of theologians. Differences of responsibility and authority, of course, can become especially apparent at this point. But this should not obscure the fact that doctrinal truth is not decided or assured by juridical decisions alone.

In all cases, bishops and theologians alike should recognize that administrative action is always in service to the truth of a Gospel that is meant to free us to love God and one another.

Afterword

The Church's witness and mission in the world are seriously conditioned by its own internal care for truth and justice. Disputes about doctrines and the manner of their resolution seldom remain purely internal affairs. On the contrary, our understanding and practice of faith today concern Christians and non-Christians alike. Bishops and theologians should all be conscious that unavoidable publicity is a fact of modern life. They should take care that media involvement not render ineffective the opportunity and structure for cooperation and dialogue.

They should be concerned to avoid scandal. The attitude of participants and atmosphere for process should blend civility and charity with restraint and, where necessary, that dimension of confidentiality conducive to trust, understanding, and, perhaps, reconciliation.

We believe that, with the guidance of the Spirit, the many different parts of the body of Christ can be knit together in justice and love and thereby become more truly themselves before God. In seeking clear and equitable ways to resolve disagreements about our faith, we recommit ourselves to being a Church that is one and open, a genuine community of grace sharing the truth freely given to it. Thus we choose again the life that has been offered to us, that there truly may be "one body and one Spirit, as you were also called to the one hope of your call; one Lord, one faith, one baptism, one God and Father of all, who is above all and through all and in all" (Eph 4:4-6).

Notes

1.   In June 1980 an Ad Hoc Committee on Cooperation Between Theologians and the Church's Teaching Authority reported to the Catholic Theological Society of America and recommended that the Catholic Theological Society of America and the Canon Law Society of America jointly form a committee "to develop a proposed set of norms to guide the resolution of difficulties which may arise between theologians and the magisterium in North America" (*Catholic Theological Society of America Proceedings*, 35 [1980]: 331). The two societies agreed and, in September 1980, they formally constituted the Joint Canon Law Society of America–Catholic Theological Society of America Committee on Cooperation Between Theologians and the Ecclesiastical Magisterium.

The committee divided its task into two phases. In the first, the members prepared six background studies and published them for scholarly discussion and criticism as *Cooperation Between Theologians and the Ecclesiastical Magisterium*, ed. Leo J. O'Donovan, SJ (Washington, D.C.: Canon Law Society of America, 1982). In the second phase, the committee worked to develop procedures for cooperation and circulated them for reaction from representative bishops, canonists, and theologians. Further, Bishop James R. Hoffman (Toledo), Bishop John F. Kinney (Bismarck), and Archbishop Daniel E. Pilarczyk (Cincinnati) accepted the committee's invitation to join its meetings and contribute to the formulation of its final document.

The joint committee completed its procedural document, *Doctrinal Responsibilities*, and presented it to the annual meetings of the two societies in June and October 1983, where it received unanimous votes of approval. The societies then presented it to the NCCB, which remitted it to the Committee on Doctrine. After a preliminary review by the committee under the chairmanship of Archbishop John R. Quinn, *Doctrinal Responsibilities* was taken up again in 1986 by the reorganized Committee on Doctrine chaired by Bishop Raymond W. Lessard. This committee accepted the document as a working draft and collaborated with representatives of the Joint Canon Law Society of America/Catholic Theological Society of America Committee to develop it in its present form.

Previous to this entire project, the National Conference of Catholic Bishops had adopted two other procedural documents. In 1972, the conference adopted *On Due Process* (rev. ed., Washington, D.C.: United States Catholic Conference, 1972) as a model for due process in dioceses. In 1979, the conference issued its procedures for conciliation and arbitration, *Committee on Conciliation and Arbitration* (Washington, D.C.: United States Catholic Conference, 1979). However, in contrast with *Doctrinal Responsibilities*, those procedures dealt only with administrative conflicts.

2. Cf. Second Vatican Council, *Dogmatic Constitution on Divine Revelation (Dei Verbum)*, no. 10; Second Vatican Council, *Decree on the Pastoral Office of Bishops in the Church (Christus Dominus)*, no. 12.

3. Second Vatican Council, *Constitution on the Church (Lumen Gentium)*, no. 25.

4. Denziger-Schönmetzer, *Enchiridion Symbolorum Definitionum et Declarationum de Rebus Fidei et Morum*, 3016.

5. Second Vatican Council, *Pastoral Constitution on the Church in the Modern World (Gaudium et Spes)*, no. 62.

6. *Dei Verbum*, no. 10; International Theological Commission, *Theses on the Relationship Between the Ecclesiastical Magisterium and Theology* (Washington, D.C.: United States Catholic Conference, 1977), 2.

7. *Lumen Gentium*, no. 8.

8. John Paul II, "Catholic Higher Education," *Origins* 17:16 (October 1, 1987): 270, no. 7.

9. Cf. *Theses on the Relationship Between the Ecclesiastical Magisterium and Theology*, theses 2 and 4:

Thesis 2
The element common to the tasks of both the magisterium
and theologians, though it is realized in analogous and distinct fashions, is "to preserve the sacred deposit of revelation, to examine it more deeply, to explain, teach and defend
it," for the service of the people of God and for the whole
world's salvation. Above all, this service must defend the
certainty of faith; this is a work done differently by the magisterium and by the ministry of theologians, but it is neither
necessary nor possible to establish a hard and fast separation between them.

Thesis 4
Common to both, although also different in each, is the
manner, at once collegial and personal, in which the task of
both the magisterium and the theologian is carried out. If
the charism of infallibility is promised to "the whole body of
the faithful," to the College of Bishops in communion with
the Successor of Peter, and to the Supreme Pontiff himself,
the head of that College, then it should be put into practice
in a co-responsible, co-operative, and collegial association of
the members of the magisterium and of individual theologians. And this joint effort should also be realised as much
among the members of the magisterium as among the
members of the theological enterprise, and also between the
magisterium on the one hand and the theologians on the
other. It should also preserve the personal and indispensable responsibility of individual theologians, without which
the science of faith would make no progress.

10. Subsidiarity as used in this text was introduced into ecclesiology by Pius
XII in his address to the newly created cardinals of February 20, 1946:

That is why the Apostle of the Gentiles, speaking of
Christians, proclaims they are no more "children tossed to
and fro" by the uncertain drift in the midst of human
society. Our predecessor of happy memory, Pius XI, in his
Encyclical *Quadragesimo Anno* on social order, drew a practical conclusion from this thought when he announced a principle of general application, viz.: that what individual human
beings can do by themselves and by their own forces should
not be taken from them and assigned to the community.

It is a principle that also holds good for smaller communities and those of lower rank in relation to those which
are larger and in a position of superiority. For—as the wise
Pontiff said, developing his thought—every social activity is
of its nature subsidiary (*sussidiaria*); it must serve as a support to members of the social body and never destroy or
absorb them. These are surely enlightened words, valid for

social life in all its grades and *also for the life of the Church without prejudice to its hierarchical structure.*

Now Venerable Brethren, over and against this doctrine and practice of the Church, place in their real significance the tendencies of imperialism. (*Acta Apostolicae Sedis* 38 [1946]: 144-145)

In his letter to the presidents of the episcopal conferences throughout the world, Francis Cardinal Seper, Prefect of the Sacred Congregation for the Doctrine of the Faith, used this same principle in his formulation of the mandate for the recently established doctrinal commissions of these conferences. His Eminence connects this principle with the mind of the Second Vatican Council:

Episcopi opera Commissionis doctrinalis uti possunt in quaestionibus quae territorium Conferentiae seu Coetus Episcopalis tangunt. Ad determinandum vero quaenam negotia ad hanc Sacram Congregationem mittenda sint, prae oculis habeatur "principium subsidiarietatis," ad mentem Concilii Oecumenici Vaticani II, ita nimirum ut ordinarie ipsae Conferentiae seu ipsi Coetus per se expediant ea quae suos territoriales limites non excedunt, neque ob aliam rationem peculiarem Sanctae Sedis interventum requirere videantur. (July 10, 1968, Prot. No. 214/67)

Also see thesis 12 in *Theses on the Relationship Between the Ecclesiastical Magisterium and Theology.*

11. Cf. *Lumen Gentium,* no. 21; *Theses on the Relationship Between the Ecclesiastical Magisterium and Theology,* thesis 6.

12. Cf. *Lumen Gentium,* no. 25; *Dei Verbum,* no. 10.

13. Sacred Congregation for Bishops, *Directory on the Pastoral Ministry of Bishops* (Ottawa: Publication Service of the Canadian Catholic Conference, 1974), part 1, chap. 4, no. 24.

14. *Gaudium et Spes,* nos. 44, 62. From another point of view and concerned more with theology's function *ad intra,* the International Theological Commission recalls the assertion of Pope Paul VI and speaks of the theologians as "in some way mediat[ing] between the magisterium and the People of God" (thesis 5, no. 2). This thesis also recalls the urgent question of culture addressed in *Gaudium et Spes,* no. 62.

15. *Lumen Gentium,* no. 25.

16. *Theses on the Relationship Between the Ecclesiastical Magisterium and Theology,* thesis 6:2.

17. The term *interests* sometimes occurs in discussions of responsibilities and rights. In such cases, it designates other and more elusive factors in a conflict situation. *Interests* relate to particular and concrete concerns involved in the exercise of personal or official discretion. *Interests* arise in the pursuit of one's rights or obligations, or more generally, from the freedom appropriate to all the people of God. Within this ecclesial context, the procedures designed to resolve conflicts must determine facts, the responsi-

bilities and rights of the parties, and the interests of the parties which are at issue.

18. Because those responsibilities and rights have been discussed elsewhere, they are recalled here only schematically to provide the general context for the sections that follow. See, for example, the articles by John P. Boyle, Robert J. Carlson, Jon Nilson, and John A. Alesandro in O'Donovan, *Cooperation Between Theologians and the Ecclesiastical Magisterium.*

19. *Lumen Gentium,* no. 25; *Christus Dominus,* nos. 12, 13, 14; Second Vatican Council, *Decree on the Ministry and Life of Priests (Presbyterorum Ordinis),* no. 19; *Gaudium et Spes,* no. 62; *Theses on the Relationship Between the Ecclesiastical Magisterium and Theology,* thesis 5:1.

20. *Lumen Gentium,* no. 25; canon 753.

21. *Lumen Gentium,* nos. 12-13; Second Vatican Council, *Decree on the Church's Missionary Activity (Ad Gentes),* nos. 10-18.

22. Cf. *Lumen Gentium,* no. 12.

23. *Theses on the Relationship Between the Ecclesiastical Magisterium and Theology,* thesis 3.

24. *Theses on the Relationship Between the Ecclesiastical Magisterium and Theology:*

> Thesis 8
> The difference between the magisterium and the theologians takes on a special character when one considers the freedom proper to them and the critical function that follows from it with regard to the faithful, to the world, and even to one another.
>
> 1. By its nature and institution the magisterium is clearly free in carrying out its task. This freedom carries with it a great responsibility. For that reason, it is often difficult, although necessary, to use it in such a way that it not appear to theologians and to others of the faithful to be arbitrary or excessive. There are some theologians who prize scientific theology too highly, not taking enough account of the fact that respect for the magisterium is one of the specific elements of the science of theology. Besides, contemporary democratic sentiments often give rise to a movement of solidarity against what the magisterium does in carrying out its task of protecting the teaching of faith and morals from any harm. Still, it is necessary, though not easy, to find always a mode of procedure which is both free and forceful, yet not arbitrary or destructive of communion in the Church.
>
> 2. To the freedom of the magisterium there corresponds in its own way the freedom that derives from the true scientific responsibility of theologians. It is not an unlimited freedom, for, besides being bound to the truth, it is also true of theology that "in the use of any freedom, the moral principle of personal and social responsibility must be observed"

(*Dignitatis Humanae*, no. 7). The theologians' task of interpreting the documents of the past and present magisterium, of putting them in the context of the whole of revealed truth, and of finding a better understanding of them by the use of hermeneutics, brings with it a somewhat critical function which obviously should be exercised positively rather than destructively.

25. *Theses on the Relationship Between the Ecclesiastical Magisterium and Theology,* thesis 3:4.
26. Canon 218; *Gaudium et Spes,* no. 62.
27. Canon 220; *Gaudium et Spes,* no. 26.
28. *Lumen Gentium,* nos. 4, 13; *Dei Verbum,* no. 8; *Gaudium et Spes,* no. 44.
29. Second Vatican Council, *Declaration on Religious Freedom (Dignitatis Humanae),* no. 14.
30. Cf. John A. Alesandro, "The Rights and Responsibilities of Theologians: A Canonical Perspective," in O'Donovan, *Cooperation Between Theologians and the Ecclesiastical Magisterium,* 101-102.
31. *Lumen Gentium,* no. 25. See also Bishop John Cummins, "The Changing Relationship Between Bishops and Theologians," *Origins* 12:5 (June 17, 1982): 65-71, and Archbishop James Hickey, "The Bishop as Teacher," *Origins* 12:9 (July 29, 1982): 140-144.
32. "One method I find most helpful is to have the assistance of a personal theologian. . . . We would not think of leading a diocese without someone trained in canon law. How much more then the presence of someone well trained in the authentic theology of the Church?" Hickey, 141-142.
33. See Cummins, 69, for recent instances of cooperation between bishops and theologians; also, *Catholic Theological Society of America Proceedings* 35 (1980): 332-336.
34. *Lumen Gentium,* no. 23; *Christus Dominus,* nos. 6, 36, 37.
35. *On Due Process,* 10.
36. Ibid.
37. See *Theses on the Relationship Between the Ecclesiastical Magisterium and Theology,* 17.
38. "The magisterium and theology have two different tasks to perform. That is why neither can be reduced to the other. Yet they serve the one whole. But precisely on account of this configuration they must remain in consultation with one another." John Paul II, *L'Osservatore Romano* [English edition] 50:662 (December 15, 1980): 17.
39. Cf. *Theses on the Relationship Between the Ecclesiastical Magisterium and Theology,* theses 10, 11, 12 with commentary.
40. On the limits of dialogue, cf. *Theses on the Relationship Between the Ecclesiastical Magisterium and Theology,* thesis 12 with commentary.

Source: Washington, D.C.: United States Catholic Conference, 1989.

A Time for Dialogue and Healing: A Pastoral Reflection on United States–Vietnam Relations

A Statement of the United States Catholic Conference

June 1989

We speak to the complex and troubling issue of U.S.-Vietnamese relations and the broader issues touching Southeast Asia as pastors who know the pain, division, and loss caused by the tragic war in Vietnam. We speak as pastors seeking to bring a word of healing and a hope for constructive dialogue and as teachers of a Gospel of justice and reconciliation. We cannot speak for the Church in Vietnam, but we wish to stand in solidarity with that Church and work with our brother bishops in Vietnam toward a better relationship between our two peoples, a relationship based on respect for the dignity and rights of all peoples.

Vietnam Today: Signs of Some Change

Today, more than a decade since the end of that tragic war, is an appropriate time to reexamine the relationship between Vietnam and the United States. We are convinced that improved relations and increased humanitarian assistance could help all of the Vietnamese people, including the Church. There is recent evidence of significant political and social change within Vietnam. A more pragmatic and less rigid leadership in Vietnam has begun to try to revive a failed economy, not only by adjusting domestic policies, but also in the international trade arena. Catholics and other Christians and non-Christians face fewer restrictions in public expression and practice of their faith. In addition, the new leadership has explicitly invited practicing Catholics and others, who in the past had been excluded, into the economic mainstream. The government of Vietnam has also stated its intention to remove its military forces from Cambodia. Serious problems remain, however. Much more needs to be done to recover from the wounds of war, to develop the economy, and to promote the full human rights and religious liberty of the Vietnamese people. With respect and admiration for the strength and resilience demonstrated by the people of God in Vietnam—our brother bishops, their priests and religious, and the laity—we welcome needed changes and call for a full and genuine respect for the role of the Church by the Vietnamese government, based on the principles of religious liberty for all faiths and the recognition of the important contributions the Church can make to national economic, human, and social development.

Last January, our conference sent a formal episcopal delegation to Vietnam to meet with more than ten bishops and to see firsthand the changing and complex situation of the Church in Vietnam. On their return, the bishops of the delegation reported:

> We came away from our brief but very helpful visit to Vietnam with greater awareness of the enormous needs as well as the great strengths of the people of Vietnam, with renewed appreciation for the great faith of the Catholic community, and with a sense of the modest but real changes during the last two years within Vietnamese society. We also came away with a stronger commitment to build more effective bridges between our two peoples. We seek to work for a new relationship that can help heal the wounds of war in both lands and can begin to help the Vietnamese people to live with greater dignity and hope for a better life. . . .
>
> There are modest and hopeful signs of a new developing relationship between church and state, with the government apparently moving away from past forms of repression and intimidation.
>
> More steps are needed now to realize this promise and to confirm this direction. . . . Vietnam's leaders need to be encouraged to respect more fully the Church's autonomy in selecting seminarians, ordaining priests, transferring pastors, and organizing its own affairs. They should release any remaining priests or religious in detention. Instances of discrimination against Catholics in employment and education need to give way to the genuine freedom promised by the state. Religious materials and books need to be more available both from within Vietnam and from other lands. . . .
>
> We believe the interests of both nations—and the concerns and needs of both peoples—could be much better served by a more normal relationship. . . . We are not naive; genuine differences and problems remain. But, we believe a different approach could more effectively advance the values we seek to uphold and assist people in both countries.

Our conference shares these real concerns and hopes.

The Challenge of Reconciliation

For many years the U.S. government, because of a variety of reasons, has rejected formal diplomatic relations with Vietnam. However, there is recent evidence that this policy is undergoing review and may change. This prospect opens up a unique and important opportunity for the citizens of our country, as well as our Vietnamese population, to participate constructively in increased formal communication with leaders in Vietnam toward betterment of international relations, reconciliation, and welfare of the citizens of Vietnam. This statement addresses some of the ways in which we can make this process both just and fruitful.

It is time to put the tragedy of Vietnam and the United States' role there in proper perspective. In our own country, we have begun to recognize more fully the pain, sacrifice, and needs of those who served in Vietnam and of their families. We sense the pain of families of POWs and MIAs. An essential part of the reconciliation process in our own country must be a continuing and practical recognition of the sacrifices made and burdens borne by those who fought the war and by the families who lost loved ones in that tragic conflict. We stand with the Vietnam veterans and these families in their legitimate claim on our nation's help and understanding. In addition, we recognize the sincerity of many whose consciences called them to protest against our involvement in the Vietnam War. We have lived with the terrible divisions and mistrust wrought by the differing political opinions regarding American participation in the Vietnam War. It has taken much time for us as a people to begin to be able to deal with the intense emotions and conflicting judgments about the Vietnam War. The passage of time, the dedication of healing public memorials, and the maturation of dramatic presentations about the tragedies of Vietnam as they affected Americans—both in Vietnam and at home—have helped us to reflect upon the divisiveness of the past in a way that we might move toward healing in the present and future—a healing that would create an atmosphere in which a sober dialogue concerning humanitarian assistance and religious liberty could prosper.

The Vietnamese in Our Midst

As a result of decades of civil war, international conflict, and their aftermath, over 700,000 Vietnamese have made their home in the United States. We understand and sympathize with their strong feelings and powerful memories of how and why they came here and of those responsible for their personal tragedies and the suffering, not yet ended, of the people of their homeland. We admire the strong faith and the remarkable contributions of the Vietnamese in our midst. They have enriched and strengthened the life of the Church and our whole society. We commend those who minister to them and ask all our people to continue to welcome and to accept our Vietnamese brothers and sisters. We need to address, as best we can, the pressing needs of the

Vietnamese people, here in the United States and in their native land.

As we work toward reconciliation among Americans, it is also time to work toward a better relationship with the people of Vietnam. We understand that bitter memories of past injustices and brutal conflict are hard to put aside, but we are a people redeemed by the divine mercy of God. To Christians the lesson of the Gospels is clear and challenging—enemies are to be forgiven and even loved. As Pope John Paul II said in a special message to Catholics in Vietnam, "The whole Church has her eyes fixed upon you. In her you have a special place." In the same message, the Holy Father noted that the Church has taken a special interest in the rebuilding of the country after so many years of war and ". . . willingly encourages the Catholic movements and international bodies to provide you with unselfish aid."[1] Earlier, Pope Paul VI said, "Let us do everything we can to alleviate the tragedy of these people and to prove to them that our world is not indifferent to the cries of our brethren."[2] We wish to respond generously to this call, but in ways which ensure that governmental and charitable assistance goes to those who are most in need without reference to political or ideological loyalties.

Dialogue: A Tool for Dealing with Serious Needs and Problems

The American people, including the Vietnamese people in our midst, have a list of important issues which require prompt and serious Vietnamese cooperation in resolving. We, as bishops in the United States, share these concerns. Among these are:

1. Most important, full enjoyment by all Vietnamese, whatever their faith, of that essential human right—religious liberty
2. The immediate release of those priests, monks, and ministers from the prisons to the churches or temples and pagodas for their free religious ministry, as well as the early release of those remaining in political reeducational camps or house arrest and the expedited emigration from Vietnam of those who desire to leave
3. The development of a political environment in which all Vietnamese may enjoy basic human rights
4. An accounting of missing U.S. servicemen
5. An end to the Vietnamese military presence in Cambodia
6. More rapid processing of separated families and others eligible to leave Vietnam under the Orderly Departure Program

7.   Expedited emigration of those Amerasian young people who wish to leave, as well as eligible members of their immediate families

Neither the pressing needs of the Vietnamese people nor the concerns of the United States government can be effectively addressed without continuing, intensive, and regular official dialogue. Several voices in the United States Congress have urged the establishment of some kind of official presence in each country in order to seek resolution of these issues, a step which the United States government has opposed thus far. We wish to emphasize that an official presence and an ongoing dialogue do not indicate approval or disapproval of a particular regime, but it is mutually advantageous to establish a formal mechanism by means of which problems may be discussed and, when possible, resolved. We note that the United States government has found it useful to have diplomatic relations with the Soviet Union and its Warsaw Pact allies, as well as with oppressive regimes on other continents. Surely the serious problems we should discuss and seek to resolve with Vietnam merit an appropriate mechanism for dialogue. The level of official U.S. presence during this process should reflect the progress being made in resolving the important human rights, religious liberty, and other issues we have enumerated, which we believe are essential for genuine and long-lasting reconciliation. The representatives of our conference who visited Vietnam on our behalf this year found a Church alive and vital, authentically Vietnamese and truly Catholic, deeply concerned about the many needs and problems of their own country and strongly committed to improving relationships between our two churches and peoples, including explicit support for increased diplomatic and trade relations.

The United States and Vietnam have vital mutual problems to discuss which clearly require this kind of focused attention and candid dialogue. The war's lasting legacy of suffering must be addressed and resolved. A Vietnamese government that says it wishes to end its military presence in Cambodia should be pressed to do so. At the same time, the United States and others in the international community are obligated to develop a framework that will protect the Cambodian people from the return of the genocidal leaders of the Khmer Rouge while permitting the Cambodian people to choose freely their own government. In addition, a Vietnam which may wish to lessen its dependence on the Socialist bloc and to enter the world trading and diplomatic community more fully should be assisted to do so. However, this official dialogue must include, as we have consistently advocated, a constant concern for human and religious rights and a continuing search for justice consistent with the Universal Declaration of Human Rights whose fortieth anniversary was celebrated last year.

The present leadership of Vietnam should also be challenged and encouraged to develop a social, political, and economic environment that will permit their brave and industrious people to realize their full human and spiritual potential.

The whole Vietnamese people, in their homeland, on their way to the free world, in their refugee camps, or abroad, need our support in building a future that will truly promote reconciliation, dialogue, family reunification, and a more open, more livable, and more just Vietnam.

The United States government, for its part, must move beyond hostility and adopt a traditional American response to the needs of desperate and hungry people—whatever the ideology of their leaders. As was poignantly written by a highly decorated American veteran after a recent trip to Vietnam, "Any soldier who has been in combat knows that there comes a time after the battle, when the smoke has blown away and the dust has settled, when you must lean down and give your foe a hand, for in that moment of generosity, the war is truly over."[3]

The Broader Reality in Indochina

We recognize that the relationship between the United States and Vietnam is only one aspect of a broad and complex reality which is the product of more than a millennium of history. There are also the peoples of Cambodia and Laos with their own unique cultures and traditions who, together with the Vietnamese, make up that distinct region known as Indochina.

Cambodia

Cambodia once enjoyed a remarkable culture and ruled much of Indochina, but almost a century of colonialism, the adverse impact of thirty years of warfare on and within Cambodian borders, the genocidal misgovernment of Pol Pot and his followers, and a Vietnamese military occupation have left a scarred and exhausted land and people. Still plagued by guerrilla warfare, an acute shortage of trained and educated people, a crippled economy, and a completely inadequate infrastructure, Cambodia desperately needs peace, freedom from outside interference, a government of its own choosing, freedom of religion for members of all faiths, and generous outside humanitarian and development assistance. Vietnam has now pledged to remove its troops from Cambodia. Thus, the challenge now is to the interested international community, perhaps under the aegis of the UN, to devise means to ensure that the ruthless leaders of the Khmer Rouge do not seize power and that the Cambodian people can peacefully choose their own destiny.

Laos

This small land, like its Indochinese neighbors, suffered from colonial neglect, interminable war, underdeveloped natural and human resources, and interference by stronger neighbors. Now, Laos, too, may soon be free of foreign military forces and, it is hoped, better able to pursue its own political and economic development in an environment of greater human and religious rights. It has, however, an urgent need for increased humanitarian and development aid. Laos will need generous assistance to share in the growth of a stronger regional economy, which peace should bring.

The Regional Challenge

Not only must the countries of Indochina make political concessions in order to find regional security, so must the member countries of the Association of Southeast Asian Nations, especially contiguous Thailand. The delicate balance of regional political and security interests, which can provide an environment in which all the countries of the area can grow and prosper, necessarily requires positive contributions by the Soviet Union and China, as well as the United States. Sincere efforts by all concerned could result in a secure Vietnam free to pursue a better material life for its people, a peaceful Laos and Cambodia free to choose their own destinies, a Thailand with secure and orderly borders, a China hopefully again on the road to reform and confident of its ability to live in peace with its neighbors to the West and South, and an entire Southeast Asian community enjoying an interdependent, productive economy which can fulfill the promise of peace and prosperity for the region. This is not a utopian dream; it is within the grasp of regional and world political leadership, given the political will.

An important objective of this effort must be the end of one of the greatest human tragedies of our time—the hundreds of thousands of refugees who have fled their countries and the millions of other displaced peoples in the region. Those people of Indochina in refugee camps throughout the region, in the chaotic limbo of the camps along the Thai border, in hopeless detention in Hong Kong and elsewhere, as well as the desperate souls in leaky boats on the China Sea and the Gulf of Thailand have the right to expect that all of us, great and small powers alike, who contributed to their tragedy will make every effort to fashion a lasting regional solution.

Conclusion

As pastors, deeply concerned about the pain and costs of the conflict which touched us so profoundly and firmly committed to stand with the Church in Vietnam, we believe it is time to move beyond the legacy of war, to begin to respond to the pressing needs of those affected by that war, and to address better both the problems and possibilities of a new relationship between the American and Vietnamese peoples.

We, therefore, renew the appeal made on December 2, 1975, by leaders of the United States Catholic Conference, the National Council of Churches, and the Synagogue Council of America:

> We seek the normalization of relations between our nations as soon as possible. To this end we urge that the trade embargo be lifted, and that the citizenry support private efforts for the people-to-people aid program for the victims of the war. . . . These voluntary efforts would contribute significantly to healing the wounds of the war.

We believe that it is in the interest of both Americans and Vietnamese—in their homeland and in the diaspora—to seek to turn away from the bitterness of the past and look to a new constructive and realistic relationship—a relationship that allows a normal and spirited official dialogue which can address the political, economic, humanitarian, and human and religious rights problems that have for too long delayed and frustrated the needed reconciliation and healing from the effects of that war which so tragically touched our two peoples.

Notes

1. John Paul II, "Special Message to the People of Vietnam," *Origins* 14:2 (May 24, 1984), no. 18.
2. Paul VI, *Holy Week Statement, 1975.*
3. Frederick Downs Jr., "Vietnam: My Enemy, My Brother," *The Washington Post,* January 31, 1988.

Source: Washington, D.C.: United States Catholic Conference, 1989.

Relieving Third World Debt: A Call for Co-Responsibility, Justice, and Solidarity

A Statement of the USCC Administrative Board

September 1989

The problem of international debt is a clear example of the interdependence which characterizes relations between countries and continents. It is a problem which cannot be solved without mutual understanding and agreement between debtor and creditor nations, without sensitivity to the real circumstances of indebted nations on the part of the creditor agencies, and without a wise and committed policy of growth on the part of the developing nations themselves. Is it merely a rhetorical question to ask how many infants and children die every day in Africa because resources are now being swallowed up in debt repayment? There is no time now to lament policies of the past or those elements in the international financial and economic picture which have led up to the present situation. Now it is the time for a new and courageous international solidarity, a solidarity not based on self-interest but inspired and guided by a true concern for human beings.[1]

Introduction

Three years ago we began our pastoral letter *Economic Justice for All* by stating three fundamental criteria by which we believe an economy should be measured: "Every perspective on economic life that is human, moral, and Christian must be shaped by three questions: What does the economy do *for* people? What does it do *to* people? And how do people *participate* in it?"[2] Among the public policy issues we examined in light of those three questions was what to do about the debt of the developing countries of the Third World, more than 30 percent of which is owed to U.S. commercial banks and the U.S. government.

Those words of the pope in Zambia pose a special challenge for the Church in this country. They challenge us to understand better and act upon the dire consequences of the enormous external debt of poor countries. The Holy Father calls upon us to examine the moral and human aspects of this crisis and to explore how our nation's institutions and policies have contributed to the situation. We are challenged to consider what we can do now to alleviate suffering and pursue justice in confronting a central question of worldwide concern.

As members of the universal Church, united by bonds of faith and common humanity, we must respond to the clear challenge of the Holy Father and the strong and eloquent pastoral appeals of our brother bishops in poor countries as we seek to address the ethical and human dimensions of the debt crisis. Because so much of the money is owed to U.S. banks, we have a special responsibility to serve the universal Church by speaking out. We believe these aspects are too often neglected in public discussion of the debt, dominated as it is by economic, political, and even ideological concerns.

As bishops of the United States, we accept this difficult challenge. We understand both the complexity and urgency of the debt crisis and the central role of our country as a leader in the global economy. We have heard the pleas of our brother bishops, our Catholic missionaries, and church workers in poor countries. During the past year, in preparing this statement we have consulted on this matter with chief executives of U.S. banks, officials of government and international financial institutions, leaders of developing countries, theologians, and other experts and policymakers.

In these brief reflections, we seek to apply Catholic moral principles to this problem in the hope of making a constructive contribution to the broader discussion of the debt question. We draw particularly on the teachings of our Holy Father and the 1987 statement of the Pontifical Commission Justitia et Pax, *At the Service of the Human Community: An Ethical Approach to the International Debt Question.* In addition we are guided by the experience and insight of the Church in many parts of the world. We seek to encourage a sense of true "co-responsibility" and solidarity across the boundaries of geography and economics as we confront this crisis in all its fiscal, human, and ethical dimensions. The tragic fact is that in trying to pay their debts, the neediest countries are sacrificing their future and the lives of millions of their people to contribute capital to the richest countries through debt service and debt payment.

The Human Face of Third World Debt

Since we adopted our pastoral letter on economic justice in November 1986, total Third World debt has increased by more than 30 percent, from just under $1 trillion to more than $1.3 trillion, and the plight of the poor in the debtor countries, by every account, has worsened. The debt is now growing much more slowly, for the most part because the commercial banks are reluctant to lend, but also because many debtors have stopped borrowing in order to pay interest. Nevertheless, most of these countries have not been able to reinvigorate their economies or grow out of their debt burdens.

Though much attention, public and private, has been devoted to this chronic and growing problem, the main focus continues to be the situation of the creditors and the future of the international financial system, not the plight of the debtors. The deepening misery of the victims is obscured by an avalanche of statistics and by the complexity of proposed solutions. One purpose of our reflections is to put a human face on the reality and injustice hidden by the figures, the reports, and the proposals—what the Latin American bishops described to us as "an iron ring around the necks of our people." When we talk about these human consequences of the debt, we are referring to the policies and practices that creditors, governments, and multilateral agencies adopt in order to pay the debt; these policies and practices often result in disaster for human beings.

Although there is considerable debate about how Third World debt grew to such enormous proportions, the facts—and some of the causes—are increasingly clear. The crisis first came to public attention in August 1982, with the prospect of default by Mexico. But the problem began earlier and arose from factors external to most developing countries (e.g., the dramatic rise in oil prices beginning in 1973, preceded by the unilateral decision of the U.S. government in 1971 to suspend redemption of dollars in gold). There was also injudicious lending of "oil money" by Western capital markets for often ill-conceived projects, as well as economic mismanagement and conceptual misjudgment on the part of many debtor countries.

The total debt has grown in the last decade from a little over $400 billion to $1.3 trillion. During the same period, the burdensome debt service, which drains away the debtors' export earnings and impedes their development, was aggravated by considerably higher interest payments, with no significant economic growth or reduction of principal. Moreover, the commercial lenders that encouraged larger and larger loans to eager Third World borrowers in the 1970s are not now lending enough to keep payments current. As a result, many heavily indebted countries are falling behind on servicing their debt.

Scores of suggestions on how to manage this difficult situation have been proposed—by economists, bankers, and government officials; by multilateral institutions such as the World Bank and the International Monetary Fund (IMF); and by agencies and individuals in the nongovernmental development community. Most of these proposals would seek to improve the present financial system by calling on the major actors to act more responsibly in it. Many would involve new multilateral debt management institutions related in some fashion to the World Bank and the IMF. Although there continues to be some discussion of a threat to international financial stability, most observers now agree that banks, by setting up reserves, have taken adequate measures to absorb losses to them that might result from default on the part of any single large debtor.

Few of the proposed remedies, however, address the basic concern of social justice: Why should the poor in debtor countries, who have nothing to say about accruing the debt and have received little or no benefit from it, have to bear the greater burden of its payment? That is the tragedy and the scandal to which we referred in *Economic Justice for All*. Many wealthy people in debtor countries, who often invested the borrowed capital right back in the creditor bank, are minimally affected by the austerity measures adopted in order to repay the debt. Those who are paying it, with poverty, unemployment, misery, sickness, and death, do not owe it and have not been helped by it. *Austerity* simply puts the burden on the poor.

The recent UNICEF annual report *The State of the World's Children 1989* makes the same point concerning the responsibility for payment as explicitly as the pope did in his Zambia speech: ". . . It is children who are bearing the heaviest burden of debt and recession in the 1980s. . . . In most countries the real cost of such cuts (in public services) is being paid, disproportionately, by the poor and by their children. . . ."[3]

The news media have carried dramatic accounts of food riots in Algeria resulting from debt restructuring agreements; of deaths in disturbances in South Jordan caused by price increases entailed in a debt rescheduling with the IMF; of disturbances in the Dominican Republic, in Egypt, in Zambia—all because of food price increases; of a state of siege in Argentina to curb violence provoked by austerity measures; of more than 300 deaths in Venezuela during a week of violence that followed the imposition of similar austerity measures by the new president in order to help service the debt.

Comments from our brother bishops in the developing countries help to highlight the problem:

- The Chilean bishops' conference told us in April 1989: "The payment of the external debt has a most serious effect upon the Chilean population. Just in the last three years it has caused an increase of unemployment that in some sectors is over 50 percent. . . . The Chilean debt has come to be one of the highest in per capita terms (almost $2,000). But the grave sacrifices imposed on the nation have fundamentally been due to the high interest rates. . . ."
- In that same month the bishop of Kumasi, Ghana wrote us that "the debt repayment has affected almost everybody. . . . I do not know what they have gained from the loan anyway. The suffering of the people has become intense and there appears

to be no end to it. . . . Our local currency has been devalued by at least 10,000 percent. . . . Yet the prices of commodities are shooting up all the time. . . ."

- In a letter to President Bush, July 7, 1989, we joined with Mexican bishops to say: ". . . as pastors we are deeply anguished by the devastating effects of the debt on real people, especially the world's poor, who had no voice in creating the debt and received minimal benefit from it. . . . Mexico has taken very responsibly the measures necessary to put its economy in order. But in doing so, the people's standard of living has suffered severely. . . . Still, Mexico . . . has not been able to reduce its debt; on the contrary, the debt has grown. In addition the very effort is strangling the economy. . . ."

- A bishop in the Caribbean wrote us in July 1989: "Catholic social teaching insists that there is an obligation that men and women should have a decent standard of life as a priority before others reap large profits. . . . The saddest thing about those who are suffering as a result of the debts is that they are those who were not responsible for the incurring of the debts. . . ." Two years ago one of his brother bishops wrote: "No reading of Scripture would oblige hungry people to starve themselves and their children simply to honor contractual obligations to repay rich people and institutions."

Debt and Development

Finding a solution to the problem of Third World debt is a prerequisite to any significant progress toward development in the poor regions of the world. The World Bank estimated that in 1988, Third World countries made a net transfer of more than $43 billion to their creditors in the industrialized world to service their massive debt—the fifth consecutive year of such transfers. Unemployment in the debtor countries has increased significantly in the 1980s. Per capita income has fallen to the level of twenty-five years ago in Sub-Saharan Africa. The social and environmental costs are incalculable. Living standards have declined more than 25 percent in Sub-Saharan Africa and 15 percent in Latin America, and both regions are deeper in debt than ever. In these circumstances development is not possible.

In *Economic Justice for All*, we noted the irony that the intensive borrowing which has so damaged these developing countries was a major factor contributing to sustained economic growth in the industrialized countries during the 1970s. In effect they helped us maintain our prosperity after the first "oil shock," when the Organization of Petroleum Exporting Countries (OPEC) quadrupled prices in 1973. But

when OPEC doubled oil prices again in 1979, the industrialized countries responded by tightening their economies, discouraging production growth, dampening demand, and raising many protectionist
barriers to discourage imports.

As a result, the value of the developing countries' exports dropped
sharply just as the interest rates on old and new loans alike, as well as
the prices of manufactured goods they imported, rose even more
sharply. Nevertheless, in just the five years between 1982 and 1987,
Latin American countries alone transferred $150 billion in interest to
the industrialized world—the equivalent of two Marshall Plans—while
their debt grew by more than half that amount, from $330 billion to
$410 billion. If they had not continued to borrow, our own recession in
this country in the early 1980s might have lasted longer.

The seven years since the crisis in Mexico have been marked mainly by crisis management and by an increasing variety of proposed
strategies for dealing with the problem. But none of these has reduced
the debt burden significantly so far; in fact, that burden has increased
sightly. All those with whom we spoke, including bankers, have led us
to believe that there is a growing recognition among creditors of the
relation of the debt problem to broader questions of development and
justice in the global economy and a growing willingness to consider
new approaches, such as debt reduction. We need to take advantage of
what may be a new moment and encourage this growing sentiment.

Varieties of Debt

Debt problems of the various regions of the developing world differ vastly. The *Sub-Saharan African* countries' share is only about one-
tenth of the total, but those debtor countries, many of which inherited
an export-dependent agriculture from the colonial period as their main
economic base and then neglected it, are among the poorest in the
world. More than 80 percent of their debt is owed to governments in
the industrialized world or to the World Bank, the IMF, and the regional lending institutions. These institutions are forbidden by their charters to forgive loans, but there is no such prohibition on creditor governments. They could cancel their share of the African debts, as some
have and as the United States now appears to be considering.

Most *Latin American* and *Asian* debt, however, is owed to commercial banks in the industrialized world. The Asian countries, with the
notable exception of the Philippines, are not having serious difficulty
handling their debt. But Latin American countries, which owe more
than a half trillion dollars to commercial banks, about a third of it to
those in the United States, are hard put to service those huge obligations. Generally speaking, these debtor countries have been unable to

grow economically. They have had to export their primary commodities at falling prices while cutting back on imports, and they have
experienced declining per capita incomes. Already in 1987, as the
United Nations Secretary General told the General Assembly in
September of that year, "after half a decade of difficult adjustment in
their economies, many developing countries are now showing unmistakable signs of debt fatigue."[4]

Responsibility for the debt does not, of course, rest with creditors
alone. Some political and economic leaders, governments, and elites in
the debtor countries have borrowed to excess, failed to adopt sound
economic and social policies, ignored the real needs of their people,
squandered funds on poorly conceived and corruptly or ineptly administered projects, and sent billions of dollars back to the industrialized
world as flight capital. In some cases, economic policies in debtor
countries have still not improved sufficiently; this also adds a burden
on the poor.

The United States, because of its fiscal policies and its continuing,
though diminished, central role in the global economy, has an almost
decisive impact on this process: The persistent U.S. budget deficit of
well over $100 billion requires the United States to borrow heavily to
service its own $2.7 trillion debt. This has impact on interest rates, and
creditor countries or banks that lend to the United States have less to
lend to the Third World. The U.S. trade deficit of nearly $150 billion is
also financed by foreign investors and lenders, and it is unlikely to be
lowered significantly until impoverished debtor countries can reduce
the debt service payments that prevent them from buying U.S. exports.

Up to this point, U.S. proposals on the debt have not responded adequately to the urgency or the magnitude of the problem. They have
been conceived more in the interests of the international financial system than of the poor; nor have broader U.S. interests been taken into
account. The most recent of these proposals, however, put forward by
U.S. Treasury Secretary Nicholas Brady in March 1989, may in fact
decrease the debt because it emphasizes debt reduction as well as new
lending and makes open discussion of debt reduction acceptable in
financial circles. But, at the same time, it firmly rejects creating any
new debt management facility—a solution favored by many lawmak-
ers and others.

Our Assessment of the Debt Situation

It is against the background of this brief history that we seek to examine the debt problem and to recommend some possible directions for
remedial action or, at least, ethical principles to guide the search for solu-

tion. We believe the debt problem, with its human consequences, is economically unsound, politically dangerous, and ethically unacceptable.

The many attempts at *economic* solutions for the commercial debt problem have not brought significant relief to many debtor countries or put an end to the crisis. These proposals have been short term, designed primarily to protect creditors and the financial system. They include increasing reserves against potential default, creating new multilateral institutions and guarantee or insurance programs, and persuading creditors to reduce total debt and/or swap it for some other form of financial relationship, such as an investment in the debtor country. But even this last, often recommended procedure has only converted $30 billion of debt since it began a few years ago. During the same period the aggregate Third World debt increased ten times as much.

The debt impasse also poses a *political* threat to new or revived democratic governments which often have inherited massive obligations from previous undemocratic or oppressive regimes, as in the Philippines and several Latin American countries. The key consideration here is the social cost. The proportion of the population living in poverty in the Southern Hemisphere is growing; malnutrition is increasing; unemployment is rising; income distribution is worsening; social programs (especially education, health care, and transportation) are being cut; and diseases thought to have been eradicated have reappeared.

Although a significant part of the debt accumulation has resulted from unsound financial and economic decisions by debtor governments, some of these governments are now undertaking serious corrective efforts. They are reducing budget deficits, collecting taxes, improving or shutting down wasteful or corrupt state enterprises, and trying to recapture flight capital. Yet in many cases, domestic production has declined, export commodity prices have fallen, and per capita income has dropped to the level of the 1970s. And no relief seems in sight. All of this spells recession, leads Latin Americans in particular to question their leaders' economic strategy and commitment to the common good, and breeds political and social upheaval. Since much of the reason for debt reduction revolves around its benefits for U.S. public policy (e.g., better relations with Latin America, increased democracy and respect for human rights in the hemisphere), government should be willing to pay for these benefits.

Many advocates, especially in the religious community, advance *ethical* arguments for considering the debt, in the aggregate, to be unjust.

- Even though there may have been a contract in the beginning, the debt has increased and become more burdensome over time in ways that were unforeseeable when the contract was made. Neither creditors nor debtors foresaw the extent to which developing country terms of trade would decline, the severity of the world economic recession in the early 1980s, or the unprecedented rise in industrial country interest rates that occurred at the same time. In retrospect, it was unrealistic to expect that the indebted countries could service their large debts no matter what occurred in the global economy, but that is what the original contracts required of them.

- The debt was accrued without participation by or benefit to those (the poor) who suffer most from the austerity measures imposed to service it.
- It has been paid already many times over through the unusually high interest rates.
- Most of the renewed borrowing, beyond the initial loans, has been undertaken almost entirely to service the debt, rather than for genuine development.
- A considerable part of the borrowed funds was expended on dangerous and wasteful armaments or on projects and programs benefiting the elites. In some cases it was simply returned to the industrialized world in the form of foreign investment—what has come to be called *flight capital.*

One does not, however, need to accept the argument that the debt is illegitimate to urge that there be relief from payment, or even forgiveness in whole or in part, in order to lessen the suffering of those most vulnerable to the effects of the debt burden.

Catholic Social Teaching and the Debt

Rooted in the revelation of Scripture, rational reflection on human nature, and historical experience, Catholic social teaching offers a unique perspective for examining this problem. From Pope John XXIII through Pope John Paul II, a major theme of that teaching has been the meaning and implications of increasing global interdependence. The *fact* of interdependence is clear to anyone aware of the economic, social, and political forces at work in our world. Our concern, however, has been the *moral quality* of interdependence—how the rules and relationships of nations and peoples are shaped and how they affect the dignity of the person. In the words of Pope John Paul II, "when . . . interdependence is separated from its ethical requirements, it has *disastrous consequences* for the weakest."[5]

The Third World debt problem exemplifies not only the general meaning of interdependence, but also the truth of Pope John Paul II's judgment about the dynamic of an interdependence devoid of moral direction. As both the Holy Father and others have observed, the human costs of Third World debt are being paid most directly by children. A fundamental ethic of the early Hebrew community was the just treatment of widows and orphans. The moral character of a society was to be measured by how it cared for its most vulnerable. Today, Third World children are the orphans of the debt crisis, and their mothers are the widows. Their malnutrition, poverty, and premature deaths indict the patterns of interdependence within and among nations that have produced the crisis.

How should the fact of interdependence be shaped to meet the demands of human dignity and human rights? The development of Catholic social teaching in the last thirty years has grown steadily in the direction of expanding the standards of justice and charity traditionally applied to domestic (national) societies, so that they also apply to relations among states and peoples across national boundaries. It is recognized that the move from national to international responsibilities involves new elements and that moral responsibilities for social justice are not confined to society within nations.

The basis for this claim lies in the common creation, humanity, and destiny of the human race, which we explored at some length in *Economic Justice for All.* There we spoke of this threefold human bond of creation, covenant, and community that establishes the moral framework for Catholic social teaching.[6] Within this framework the dignity of the person is affirmed, a doctrine of human rights is articulated, the duties of justice and solidarity are asserted, and a moral order for society—locally, nationally, and internationally—is outlined.

Three basic concepts are pertinent to our moral reflection on Third World debt. *First,* Pope John XXIII's notion of the international common good in *Mater et Magistra* maintains that the policy of a nation must now be tested by its impact not only on its own citizens, but also on the welfare of others. For example, "domestic" interest rates in a nation like the United States directly affect the quality of life in other societies. *Second,* the World Synod of Bishops in Rome in 1971 spoke of the need to assess the global economy in the context of international social justice. This was precisely the criterion Pope Paul VI used in *Populorum Progressio,* when he measured patterns of trade relations against the standards of justice. *Third,* Pope John Paul II argued in *Sollicitudo Rei Socialis* (1988) that solidarity is the virtue needed to define properly our relationships in an interdependent global economy.

All three of these views require that the problem of Third World debt be seen in moral perspective. The fact of the debt erodes the international common good. The consequences for the poor in debtor countries of repaying the debt violate minimal standards of social justice because their basic needs go unfulfilled. The failure to find a just and effective method of resolving the debt crisis is not only a technical or political mistake, but also a failure of solidarity.

In the Scriptures, how one deals with debtors is a test case of moral rectitude and spiritual sensitivity. In the Jewish tradition, the institution of the jubilee year in which debts were to be forgiven and land restored was a means of redressing what we today might call "structural injustice" in patterns of ownership. In the New Testament, Jesus uses stories of how debtors are treated as a means of helping people understand God's mercy and the obligation to reflect that mercy in our dealings with others, and in the daily prayer of Christians, we ask God to treat our debts in light of our treatment of others' debts to us.

These biblical images do not provide either a formula for addressing the complexity of international debts or even clear principles for adjudicating a fair resolution of this major institutional question. However, the biblical imagery does provide a starting point, a way to understand creditor-debtor relations, which a purely empirical assessment of the debt problem will never offer. The biblical lessons reject an interpretation of these issues cast purely in terms of economic gain or power over others. Those who are in debt retain their dignity as well as their basic human rights, which make demands upon creditors; debtors cannot be reduced to a situation of abject poverty in order to pay debts.

These themes need to be developed in institutional terms in order to address the problem of Third World debt. The relations are not between individuals but between governments or between governments and commercial banks and multilateral institutions. The Church has used the concepts of justice and solidarity to translate biblical themes into structural categories of moral analysis. These categories go beyond the attitudes that should prevail between debtors and creditors; they examine the justice of the relationship itself as well as the fairness of the mechanisms through which debt is incurred and is to be repaid.

Many voices in the Church, using both biblical and philosophical categories, challenge the legitimacy of the debt in its totality. Using patristic arguments about the purpose of creation and medieval arguments about usury, many contend that because it is clear that the poor of the developing world had no voice in deciding to accumulate the debt and reaped little or no benefit from the money borrowed, their interest should predominate and the debt should not be serviced at all. The argument is not simply a political/economic/factual case that the debt *cannot* be paid; it is a moral claim that the debt *should not* be paid. One Third World bishop wrote to us in July 1989 that "repayment of such debt is now a wholly hypothetical question."

We agree that, in terms of social justice, it may be possible to make the case that the total debt should not be simply accepted as legitimate. At the same time, we believe a moral presumption exists, in personal and social relations, that debts should be paid. But in the case of Third World debt this presumption must be tested against a further series of questions. Like Pope Leo XIII's critique of the wage contract and Pope Paul VI's critique of trading relationships, our analysis questions the justice of the contractual arrangements between Third World governments and their creditors. It is often not a relationship of equal bargaining power, and in some cases (particularly in Latin America), the Third World representatives were hardly representing the interests of their populations. In many cases, the governments were of dubious legitimacy, having come into power through military coups or fraudulent elections. Unequal power does not invalidate contracts *per se*, but these relations do temper judgments on how the contract is to be fulfilled.

Not only the original contract but the record of what has been paid because of very high interest rates must also be included in any assessment of what, if anything, remains to be paid from a moral point of view. Many Third World governments have been serving their debts at significant internal social cost. Authoritarian governments like those of Chile and Romania can repay because democratic resistance is hardly possible in those societies. Other countries such as Algeria, Argentina, Brazil, Mexico, and Venezuela have repaid at great social cost and with marked social unrest and resistance.

Both the nature of the original agreements and the attempts of some debtors to repay them lead us to the conviction that no single principle can govern all the different situations of indebtedness. We believe that in many instances the presumptive obligation to repay should be overridden or modified because of the social costs imposed on the poor. When the social costs erode personal dignity causing hunger, homelessness, sickness, and death, the principles of justice point not toward repayment by the debtors, but toward remission, even if partial, by creditors. Remission in complex cases like this does not mean "forgiveness" for all states. A range of remedies is possible and necessary; a scale of redress is needed to judge different situations. At least partial forgiveness will be a fair response, as we noted in *Economic Justice for All*, or at other times renegotiation of partial rescheduling.

We believe that in the case of some African states, for example, these government-to-government debts should be forgiven, as President Bush now appears willing to consider. The Latin American cases are more complex because of the commercial lenders involved, but at least in some cases simple repayment is neither possible nor, in our view, necessarily demanded by justice. In all cases, the internal record of performance of the debtor government—the soundness of its economic planning and particularly its efforts on behalf of the poor—should be key criteria of how the external debt is adjudicated.

The 1987 statement of the Pontifical Commission Justitia et Pax called for "co-responsibility" by all the major actors in resolving the debt problem. These major actors are governments of creditor countries, governments of debtor countries, commercial lending institutions, and multilateral agencies (the IMF, the World Bank "family," and the regional development banks). Clearly all share the responsibility, and each has a role to play.

Guidelines and Recommendations

We offer the following criteria on how the principles of justice, solidarity, and the common good can be used in contributing to the resolution of Third World debts:

a. The primary objective ought to be to assist in revitalizing the economies of debt-burdened countries and to help poor people participate in their economy and improve their quality of life; in general, the greatest help should be provided for the greatest need.

b. Any debt solution ought to preserve the basic human rights of the people and the autonomy and independence of the debtor nation.

c. Responsibility for the solution ought to be shared equitably by both creditors and debtor countries, especially by the wealthier segments of their societies; the burden should not continue to be borne disproportionately by poor people.

d. The solution should not increase the debt; generally, less money going out of the country is better than more money coming in.

e. Some immediate benefit should be obtained by the debtor country, especially for poor people.

f. Criteria established for adjusting debt should take into account the extent to which those responsible are accountable to their people and how human rights are fostered and protected in the debtor country, what the money was borrowed for, how it was used, what kinds of efforts the country had made or is making to develop as well as repay, and how the debtor nation proposes to reform its economy, including how to deal with capital flight.

g. Any acceptable solution ought to recognize and attempt to relieve external factors beyond the control of the debtor country which tend to aggravate or perpetuate the burden (e.g., interest rates, commodity prices, trade barriers, budget deficits, and geopolitical considerations). The global economy should be managed in the interest of equity and justice; participation of the poor ought to be a central test of the morality of the system.

h.   Proposed solutions ought to enhance the ability of the debtor nation to pursue independent, self-reliant, participatory, sustainable development. This consideration should receive high priority in any judgment as to the country's ability to service a discounted debt (i.e., the amount of debt the country can reasonably be expected to manage fairly).

In our judgment, the debt problem is intimately related to all the other international economic problems, upon whose solution the global common good depends. The debt situation can be seen more as symptom than as disease and should be treated as one manifestation of an international economic system that is becoming increasingly unworkable and inequitable. The challenge, therefore, is not only to correct the present imbalance, but also to address the need for fundamental change in the global economic system itself. It is likewise necessary to ask how much debt relief is actually provided, who pays what share of its cost, and what the conditions for this debt relief are. The debtor country should not be compelled to choose debt service over self-reliant development.

Remedial action has to be looked at from the point of view of both the structure of the system and how the various actors function in it. We doubt that it is enough to suggest that only the way people operate the global economic machinery needs to be changed, or just to propose that the structure of that system be realigned. Although human behavior built the structure, human behavior is now often decisively conditioned and limited by it. Therefore, in our view *both structure and behavior* have to change. The world needs to look deeply into the increasingly complex power relationships in the international financial system as we try to solve these immediate problems. Every banker with whom we have consulted emphasized that the ultimate solution to the debt problem will have to be a political solution, not simply a technical or economic one. Policies of the United States and other governments are central to effective action toward a solution.

We believe that changes in the international economic system are needed in order to increase the prospect for social justice and to avoid crises like the debt problem in the future. But to begin to change the system will probably entail negotiations as substantive and prolonged as those that led to agreement nearly half a century ago at Bretton Woods. It will also require broadening the participation in such negotiations to include the countries of the Third World, which were not represented at Bretton Woods. In addition, it will probably also necessitate a new kind of practical and effective collaboration and solidarity in the Third World—to balance the *de facto* "cartel" of creditors—and to ensure the participation of the poor in its decisions.

Constructive and courageous actions by corporations, banks, labor unions, governments, multilateral agencies, and other major actors in the international economy will be needed if real progress is to be made in alleviating poverty and promoting social justice. Our pastoral letter on economic justice, repeating our earlier letter on war and peace, said that "the major international economic relationships to aid, trade, finance, and investment are interdependent among themselves and illustrate the range of interdependence issues facing U.S. policy. . . . Each relationship offers us the possibility of substantial, positive movement toward increasing social justice in the developing world; in each, regrettably, we fall short."[7]

Conclusion

Although we recognize that the multilateral institutions, other industrialized countries, and the debtor country governments must of course be central participants in any co-responsible effort to reduce Third World debt, we address our remarks in this section to our own government and to the American people. The United States remains a central force in any effective response to this problem. We also know that the Third World's debt is related to our own budget and trade deficits. Real solidarity means that we cannot accept that the world's poor be required to sacrifice in order to sustain the lifestyle of the world's more affluent people.

We want to promote social justice and economic stability in the world; we are disturbed by the growing violence and dehumanization that injustice provokes both in the Third World and in our own inner cities, and we are mindful of the Gospel's call to seek justice for the poor. We are concerned about how the misery caused by the debt crisis assaults human dignity, demeans people created in God's image, and thus affronts the Creator, who bestowed that human dignity on all people.

We look to our government to adopt policies that will help ease the debt of Third World countries owed both to commercial banks and to the government itself. We do so mainly for the moral reasons we have described, but also out of concern for the United States' own interests. Jobs are lost in the United States and farm income decreases as our exports to impoverished debtor countries decline. Bank portfolios lose value as larger reserves are set aside. U.S. security is threatened as desperation rises in debtor countries. Programs to help our own disadvantaged people suffer reduced funding in order to continue high outlays for defense.

Specifically, we ask the president to carry out courageously his decision to exercise his statutory authority to forgive the debt of Sub-Saharan African countries under certain conditions, and we ask the Congress to make funds available if they are required to permit that action to go forward.

We also ask the president and the Congress to take appropriate steps, as Secretary of the Treasury Brady has suggested, to modify banking regulations that may deter commercial banks from pursuing debt reductions that are clearly in the interest of all parties.

Further, we call upon our government to exercise leadership in the World Bank and the IMF to help move those institutions toward lending policies more consistent with equitable development in the Third World. We favor policies less tied to the highly questionable development model of structural adjustment, which often actually worsens the situation of the poor and vulnerable. These programs have further deepened the misery of the poor by stressing export earnings to pay the debt, holding down wages, and cutting public services that are used mainly by poor people. We believe there should be genuine flexibility and a case-by-case approach to different countries with vastly different circumstances rather than the rigid and uniform conditionality to which the IMF and the World Bank seem in fact to be committed.

If restrictions in the charters of the IMF, the World Bank, and the regional banks constitute an obstacle to their participation in effective debt-reduction schemes, U.S. representatives on these institutions' governing boards should be instructed to initiate action to waive or modify them.

We urge our commercial bankers, including the many who are Catholic, to understand and accept co-responsibility for the solution of this urgent and crucial problem. This is not a matter of what is often, but inaccurately, termed "charity," but of justice. Justice is neither sentimental nor optional; it is realistic, and it is obligatory. Co-responsibility is not optional either, and properly interpreted, it entails effective debt relief, which can include at least partial forgiveness of debt. Deciding upon debt relief for developing countries is necessarily a complex and technical matter, but it need not be as drawn out and arduous as it has been in the past. We urge U.S. bankers to place considerations of justice and co-responsibility above those of short-term financial gain or loss. They should use their unique influence as leaders in the world financial community to forge just and lasting solutions to the debt crisis in each of the most affected nations.

Pope John Paul II's exhortation in a private audience with members of the board of the Chase Manhattan Bank on June 19, 1989, is particularly relevant and helpful:

> Your position as business leaders and board members of a prestigious international bank enables you to understand

and to influence the complex, interdependent economic life of today's world. . . . I am thinking in particular of the international debt question, which remains a serious threat to the peace and progress of the human family. The Holy See has . . . urged greater human solidarity and mutual respect based on our common humanity and the common good of all mankind. . . . It is my conviction that the attitudes and decisions of leaders like yourselves do make a profound difference for good or ill in shaping the future of humanity. I am confident that you . . . will not fail to be compassionate as well as responsible stewards of the material goods entrusted to you.[8]

We urge that the pope's words be heard and heeded by leaders in government and business, as well as in banking—indeed by all who in any way can help relieve the tragic burden of the poorer countries' external debt. In short, we call on the four "co-responsibles" identified above (no. 43) to exercise the solidarity described by the pope in Madagascar on May 1, 1989:

When one speaks of solidarity, one sees straight away that institutional cooperation has as its main aim the good of all nations, the proper utilization of their human resources, the development of their capacities, the optimum exploitation of their territory, the acceptance of their particular contribution to the richness of the whole human community, even if this richness cannot be measured in economic terms. . . .

In *Economic Justice for All,* we restated the classic principles of justice:

Commutative justice calls for fundamental fairness in all agreements and exchanges between individuals or private social groups. . . . Distributive justice requires that the allocation of income, wealth, and power in society be evaluated in light of its effects on persons whose basic material needs are unmet. . . . Social justice implies that persons have an obligation to be active and productive participants in the life of society and that society has a duty to enable them to participate in this way.[9]

In our view, the Third World debt crisis violates all three of these forms of justice, and the approaches thus far made or proposed to deal with it fail to offer adequate remedies.

We believe that interdependence is a fact of economic—indeed, of all—life. Solidarity, in the pope's words, is "the correlative response as a moral and social attitude, as a virtue."[10] Co-responsibility is the expression of that virtue relative to, among other things, the problem of Third World debt. Like the Holy Father, we are not interested in assessing blame or assigning guilt; these are descriptions of the past, and there is plenty of both to be shared. Rather, we want to stress responsibility, which looks to the future.

We are aware that even total forgiveness of the indebtedness would not solve the problem, because it would leave the underlying systemic causes of the present crisis—both structural and behavioral—intact. Therefore, we believe that future lending to Third World countries should be designed to benefit *all* the inhabitants equitably.

We desire and urgently plead that considerations of justice, human dignity, and human rights enter centrally into the decisions made about this and other social justice issues. Solving the problem of Third World debt will take time—but not as much, we hope, as the problem itself has taken to develop and be recognized. But while the longer-term systemic change is being pursued, there also needs to be immediate action to assist the victims. Our brother bishops remind us repeatedly that many persons, human beings created in God's image, especially the most vulnerable—women and children—are literally dying of the consequences of the debt. And that is intolerable.

Notes

1. John Paul II, Discourse Given to Members of the Diplomatic Corps (Lusaka, Zambia, May 3, 1989), *L'Osservatore Romano* [English edition] 20 (May 15, 1989).
2. National Conference of Catholic Bishops, *Economic Justice for All* (Washington, D.C.: United States Catholic Conference, 1986), no. 1.
3. UNICEF, *The State of the World's Children 1989* (Oxford: Oxford University Press, 1989), 1, 17.
4. UN General Assembly, A/42/523.
5. John Paul II, *On Social Concern (Sollicitudo Rei Socialis)* (Washington, D.C.: United States Catholic Conference, 1986), no. 17.
6. *Economic Justice for All*, no. 30.
7. Ibid., no. 264.
8. John Paul II, "Message to Representatives of Chase Manhatten Bank," *L'Osservatore Romano* [English edition] 26 (June 19/20, 1989): 15.
9. *Economic Justice for All*, nos. 69-71.
10. *Sollicitudo Rei Socialis*, no. 38.

Source: Washington, D.C.: United States Catholic Conference, 1989.

Statement on Vocations to the Priesthood

*Statement from the NCCB Vocations Committee on the
Occasion of the Bicentennial of the American Hierarchy
Approved by the NCCB Administrative Committee*

October 1989

It is notorious to you all, that the present clergymen are insufficient for the exigencies of the faithful; and that they will be more and more so, as the population of our country increases so rapidly; unless, by providence of our good and merciful God, a constant supply of zealous and able pastors can be formed amongst ourselves; that is, of men accustomed to our climate, and acquainted with the tempers, manners and government of the people to whom they are to dispense the ministry of salvation.[1]

When Bishop John Carroll wrote this first pastoral letter, he could not have imagined the growth that the Catholic Church in the United States would experience in 200 years. This missionary land with only a handful of Catholics and a few priests would grow in the present day to include 54,918,989 Catholics, divided into 33 archdioceses and 155 dioceses being served in more than 19,000 parishes by 34,390 diocesan priests and 18,558 religious order priests.

Religious communities of men and women founded educational institutions at every level, forming the largest private Catholic school system in the world. Add to this 640 Catholic hospitals, 239 child welfare centers, and countless numbers of shelters, nursing homes, soup kitchens, and crisis centers across the nation serving the varied human, social, and religious needs of the newest immigrant and the most established.

In addition, the Catholic Church in the United States has flourished in many ways during this post-Vatican II era. Many dioceses have been blessed with the new ministry of those ordained as permanent deacons, and there is a new and closer working relationship between local bishops and women and men religious in their witness to the good news of love, justice, and peace. And throughout our nation, there is a special grace and blessing present in the movement of lay people today to a deeper awareness of their responsibility to the service of Christ and the Church.[2]

However, we as bishops personally know of many hardships in our dioceses and the religious communities serving among us brought about by the increasing shortage and aging of our priests in the past twenty-five years. It is for that reason that in this statement on vocations we recall Bishop John Carroll's words from that first pastoral letter and focus particularly on the vocation to the ministerial priesthood.

Discerning the Call

We do not believe that God is calling fewer young men to the priesthood. Rather, we fear that some young people, who may live lives that are good and generous in a purely natural way, are not involved enough in the life of the Church or familiar enough with the teaching of the Gospel to be able to hear or appreciate a call to the priesthood. Others are not receiving adequate spiritual direction and encouragement. Unclarified and undisciplined desires can then confuse God's call. This is daunting for a person of faith, especially when the options of our affluent secular world speak with such a clear voice. Such frustrations can delay the commitment to the call indefinitely.

The call of Christ, "Come follow me" (Jn 1:43), is fundamentally a call to holiness. Therefore, it is difficult to respond if a person is not already living a life that is based on a solid faith in Jesus Christ. Lack of faith in Christ may cause a person to hold back or choose other values and so refuse a vocation.

The call to follow Christ is at the beginning of every call to life in the Church and to service in the ministerial priesthood. It is an awareness of being summoned by name, by someone in such a way that it makes the one who calls present to the one called (Ex 3:4-14).

Vocation is expressed in terms of a response, and it is always other directed (Mt 28:18-19)—every authentic vocation is unreserved and permanent. It is faith centered and calls for sacrifice (Lk 9:23-27).[3]

Today, as in days gone by, this message must be shared with our young people. Greater appreciation of this sense of inner vocation to intimate relationship with God is one of the great needs of our time:

> It may help those who are trying to make an initial vocational decision to recognize that vocation call is experienced on at least three levels of life: first, on an inner, unique level in which God invites us to holiness of life; that is, to enter into intimacy with him within the concrete circumstances of our life; second, in a basic state of life, such as marriage, religious life, priesthood or celibate life in the world; third, in specific occupational tasks.[4]

Speaking to the youth of the world on the occasion of International Youth Year, Pope John Paul II said, "If such a call comes into your heart, do not silence it! Let it develop into the maturity of a vocation! Respond to it through prayer and fidelity to the commandments! For 'the harvest is great,' and there is an enormous need for many to be reached by Christ's call 'follow me.'"[5]

As young people experience this closeness with God, they are more willing to live their lives for God. There is great need today for this kind of bold witness. Our young people are ready to be challenged, and we already know "the laborers are few" (Mt 10).

This witness manifests itself through chaste, caring relationships and through a detachment from material things. In this way, our youth "work hard to purify their spirit and sometimes reach the point of making their lives gifts of love to God. They thus become living examples to the people around them, by their very conduct showing the primacy of eternal values over the elusive and sometimes ambiguous values of the society in which they live."[6]

Ministerial Priesthood

In establishing his Church, the Lord Jesus called some of his disciples to serve his community in roles of leadership. In particular, those servant-leaders were charged with overseeing and animating the life of the Church in all her activities: preaching, teaching, evangelization, worship, discipline, and discernment. As the Church grew, she made pastoral adaptations and developed new expressions of her ministries in order to fulfill her mandate of carrying the Gospel "to the ends of the earth" (Acts 1:8). Since the ministry of official leadership is an essential element of the life of the Church, God continues in this day to call individuals to the offices of bishop, presbyter, and deacon.

This ordained ministry is essential for the very life and existence of the Church, irreplaceable by other expressions of service. To the Church's ordained leaders Christ has entrusted in particular the mission of preaching the Gospel. In addition to being empowered to "offer sacrifice and remit sins," priests and bishops participate "in the authority by which Christ himself builds up, sanctifies, and governs his body."[7] Standing in the place of Christ, bishops and their co-workers, the priests, serve to unify and reconcile the Christian community and to confirm and order the other ministries within the community. The ordained ministers of the community receive charisms of leadership and service, thus enabling them competently to exercise authority in the Church.

In encouraging and discerning vocations to priesthood, the Church and her leaders will count among the serious signs of God's call a desire to serve the community; a deep attachment to the word of God and to prayer; regular participation in the liturgical and sacramental life of the Church; profound love for Christ and God's people, especially the poor, with a personal commitment to justice; and a capacity for leadership, enabling the candidate to become a good and zealous pastor.

The Commitment to Celibacy

With the universal Church at Vatican Council II, we want to testify to the goodness, wisdom, and fittingness of calling to priesthood those freely willing to live a celibate lifestyle for the kingdom (Mt 19:12). From the beginning, celibacy has been a valued charism and an especially treasured legacy of the Latin Church for the last millennium. Celibacy was a concrete way in which the radical call to discipleship was lived out. In our contemporary culture with its fascination with sex and fulfillment, the powerful witness of this charism is in no way diminished but, in fact, enhanced. Celibacy remains an effective and faithful witness to radical discipleship in Christ.

The New Testament witness to celibacy is strong and clear. Matthew 19:10-12, Mark 10:29-30, Luke 18:29-30, and 1 Corinthians 7:32-40 link celibacy to apostolic service for the kingdom. Matthew 22:30, Mark 12:25, and Revelation 14:4 link celibacy also to eschatological witness and the reality of the resurrection. Celibacy is always a gift from God. It is a powerful sign when it becomes a way in which Christ is made more personally present to the priest himself and to the community. True, this is an example of sacrifice for the Christian community, but it is not undertaken solely for this purpose. With Christ in the paschal mystery, a mature celibate life expresses the priest's loving self.

For celibacy, in imitation of Jesus, testifies to Christ's all-embracing love and reverence for the Father, and his mission of universal salvation, which Jesus came to carry out in the world for the glory of the Father. Celibacy, as the priest's gift to the Church and to the Lord, empowers priestly ministry in a unique way.

Celibacy is "generative, life giving and life producing, not in a genital, physical sense, but in a genuinely personal sense."[8] Through his celibacy the priest becomes "a man for others." The priest, by renouncing the fatherhood proper to married men, seeks another fatherhood by his ministry to those entrusted to his pastoral care by the Good Shepherd. As the *Decree on the Ministry and Life of Priests* states, this fatherhood is directed to the whole Church and therefore is missionary in character.[9] However, it is normally linked to a particular community in which each member expects attention, care, and love.

Nurturing Vocations

Pope John Paul II, in his 1989 Holy Thursday letter to the Church's 400,000 priests, referred to the laity as a "spiritual seedbed of vocations," adding that "wherever vocations are scarce, the Church must be attentive."

However, for parents who want to encourage vocations, these are difficult days because of the declining number of priests, the loneliness of some, and the conflicting expectations people have for priests today. Because of the requirement of celibacy or because the priesthood is not open to women, some refuse to reflect with their children on a priestly vocation. Indeed, parish priests sometimes say the same thing. Yet interviews with young men studying for the priesthood indicate that the common thread running through their discernment was the encouragement of family and the parish priest.

Parents and priests or religious, as well as those who are charged with the formation of the young, by taking a passive attitude to priestly vocations do young people and the next generation of Catholics a great disservice. In some cases, they stand in the way of God, since it is always the Lord who calls.

Fr. Eugene Hemrick, in his study of seminarians today, found that most of them were associated with the local parish before going to the seminary. They functioned as altar boys, lectors, eucharistic ministers, and taught in the parish religious education program, and yet only 17 percent received any type of encouragement to consider the priesthood from CCD teachers; 35 percent from their Catholic school teachers; 40 percent from a religious sister; 27 percent from a religious brother; and 23 percent from campus ministers.[10]

It is our responsibility as bishops to ask our brother priests and each parish community to nurture vocations and call forth individuals to look specifically at priesthood and religious life. As we continue to call forth the laity to vital roles in our local churches, we cannot forget to call forth priests to gather this community around Christ in the eucharist. This demands an approach which responds to the shortage in the priesthood and the rediscovery of the meaning of religious life, which at the same time keeps in balance the special role of the lay minister.

Research at the national level has revealed several very important factors which encourage vocations to the priesthood and religious life at the parish level:

1. Most seminarians were altar servers and participated in retreats and vocation programs that the parish held for young people.
2. While vocation talks and literature have a moderate influence on men deciding to become priests, the two most influential

factors causing seminarians to become priests are an inner calling and a priest's example.

3. Over half of the seminarians have been involved in church service before entering the seminary. These services have been predominantly in the area of education and the liturgy.

4. Approximately one-fifth of the seminarians have lived a month or more in a rectory or monastery before deciding to enter the seminary.[11]

These factors demand a parish environment that supports general vocation awareness, one which readily provides information and counseling to people interested in the priesthood and religious life. Strong faith communities sensitive to ethnic diversity with good liturgy and happy priests will produce vocations. This is especially true if parish decision makers—parish council, school administrators, religious education coordinators, and youth leaders—have been involved in creating a climate supportive of people deepening themselves in their calling.

Vocation directors and others charged by the local bishop with vocation recruitment, in addition to their work with the individual candidate, should keep in mind the value of meeting with each family to discuss issues, concerns, doubts, and questions concerning the particular candidate's interest in priestly ministry. This is especially true with the Hispanic candidate since, in the Hispanic culture, the family plays such an important role in the discernment process.

Finally, in closing, we turn our thoughts to our Blessed Mother as an example today of vocation fulfilled. Truly, at the foot of the cross when our Lord looked down upon his mother and said, "Woman, there is your son" (Jn 19:26), the Church was to discover in Mary the reality of vocation of all redeemed humanity—"There is your mother" (Jn 19:27). So, Mary as the mother of the beloved disciple, John, becomes herself the disciple par excellence and hence the first type or model of the Church. She gives powerful expression to this vocation in her beautiful Magnificat: "My being proclaims the greatness of the Lord, my spirit finds joy in God my savior" (Lk 1:46-47).

Aided by the Blessed Mother, with us as she was with the apostles in the Upper Room, may we welcome the spirit of courage and boldness, and offer today's world the liberating truth of Christ (Col 1:25ff) through an increase of vocations to the priesthood and religious life.[12]

Notes

1.   Bishop John Carroll, pastoral letter, May 28, 1792, in Hugh J. Nolan, ed., *Pastoral Letters of the United States Catholic Bishops* (Washington, D.C.: United States Catholic Conference, 1984), 1:18.

2.   Second Vatican Council, *Decree on the Apostolate of Lay People (Apostolicam Actuositatem)*, no. 1.

3.   Cardinal Bernard Law, "The Mystery of Vocation" *Vocations and Future Church Leadership* (Washington, D.C.: United States Catholic Conference, 1986), 15-17.

4.   Alfred C. Hughes, *Preparing for Church Ministry* (Denville, N.J.: Dimension Books, 1979), 65.

5.   John Paul II, *Apostolic Letter to the Youth of the World on the Occasion of International Youth Year* (Vatican City: Vatican Polyglot Press, 1985), no. 8, p. 29.

6.   Ibid., p. 26.

7.   Second Vatican Council, *Decree on the Ministry and Life of Priests (Presbyterorum Ordinis)*, no. 2.

8.   Cardinal Joseph Bernardin, "Toward a Spirituality of Marital Intimacy," Address to the 1980 Synod of Bishops, *Origins* 10:18 (October 16, 1980), no. 286.

9.   *Presbyterorum Ordinis*, no. 16.

10.   Eugene Hemrick, "Energizing the Role of Vocation Directors," *National Conference of Diocesan Vocation Directors News* (March-April 1989): 4.

11.   Eugene Hemrick and Dean Hoge, *Seminary Life and Visions of the Priesthood: A National Survey of Seminarians* (Washington, D.C.: National Catholic Educational Association Department of Seminaries, 1987).

12.   Law, 20-21.

Source: *Origins* 19:22 (October 20, 1989): 358-361.

Here I Am, Send Me:
A Conference Response to the Evangelization of African Americans and The National Black Catholic Pastoral Plan

A Statement of the National Conference of Catholic Bishops

November 1989

Introduction

The proclamation of the good news of Jesus Christ is both the privilege and the vocation of the whole Church. All the faithful, by virtue of their baptism, are invited to participate in this grace-filled work, as individuals and as a community of faith. The good news of the Gospel not only transforms those who hear it, but it must also transform those who preach it. "The person who has been evangelized," Pope Paul VI wrote, "goes on to evangelize others."[1] This transforming Gospel, however, goes much farther than personal conversion. The gospel message means the transformation, through holiness, of the heart of society. Again, Pope Paul VI wrote:

> Evangelization would not be complete if it did not take account of the unceasing interplay of the gospel and of man's concrete life, both personal and social. . . . Evangelization involves an explicit message, adapted to the different situations constantly being realized, about the rights and duties of every human being, about family life without which personal growth and development are hardly possible, about life in society, about international life, peace, justice and development—a message especially energetic today about liberation.[2]

We focus on *The National Black Catholic Pastoral Plan* and recommend it to the Church in the United States for three primary reasons: (1) the nature of the plan; (2) the timeliness of the plan within the history of the Church; and (3) the importance of the plan for the African American community.

First, the nature of the plan itself. The plan is the culmination of the National Black Catholic Congress that was held in Washington, D.C.,

May 21-24, 1987. During the two years of planning for the congress, an extensive consultation process took place. U.S. dioceses with a significant number of African American Catholics were requested to conduct a series of "Reflection Days" to discuss issues relating to evangelization of African Americans on the local level. One hundred and seven dioceses participated in the process, developing particular evangelization goals and objectives for the local church. The diocesan goals and objectives were collected from the participants and forwarded to the central planning committee of the congress, where common elements were transformed into a cohesive national evangelization plan. It can truly be said that *The National Black Catholic Pastoral Plan* is the result of a distillation of the dreams and aspirations of the African American community as a whole. The selected representatives to the national congress came with a knowledge and understanding of the local community's ideas and goals. There was an understanding of the need to construct a national plan that would contain essential elements appropriate to local situations.

Second, this pastoral plan comes at a timely moment in the history of the Church in the United States, of this nation, and of the African American community. African American Catholics have become a recognized and articulate component of the Church in the United States. There is a vitality and an enthusiasm in the African American Catholic community that must be channeled and nurtured. No longer simply recipients of the ministry of others, they are called to be full participants in the life and mission of the Church, on both the local and national levels. *The National Black Catholic Pastoral Plan* outlines well-defined goals and objectives, enabling that process. There is, however, a serious concern on the part of many observers regarding the attrition of African American Catholics from the Church. Many do not find the Church culturally relevant and, consequently, they do not feel at home; this results in numerous instances of African American Catholics leaving the Church for Protestant denominations. In addition, unfortunately, the nation and the Church still remain burdened with the problem of racism and its consequences. As a Church, we must bear witness to our multifaceted role as mediator, reconciler, and healer. The actions of the Church in the United States—whereby the African American community becomes an active participant in the Church's work of evangelization—will be a beacon of hope to our society.

Third, this plan is important for the African American community today, which is faced with a variety of social ills: increased poverty, crime, drug addiction, teenage pregnancy, and many other problems that beset all of our society, but which affect to a greater degree the African American community. These social ills, however, can also be seen in a spiritual and religious light: they come within the scope of evangelization, and they cry out for a response from African American Catholics themselves.

This last reason is most certainly not the least. As bishops, we are called upon to guide and teach, to recognize the initiatives inspired by the Holy Spirit, and to be the authentic voice of the Church for her sons and daughters. In approving this plan, we recognize that the Holy Spirit works within the Church, in the midst of God's people. For this reason, we are indeed happy to present to the Church in the United States, *Here I Am, Send Me: A Conference Response to the Evangelization of African Americans and The National Black Catholic Pastoral Plan*. We recommend it to our brothers and sisters in faith because it is a plan for the evangelization of the African American community—those who are within the community of faith and those who find themselves outside of our community of believers. As a plan for evangelization, this document is a challenge to all people, regardless of race, language, or culture. As a commitment to the Gospel and its values of liberation and justice, this plan reaches all the faithful, becoming a blueprint for the building of the kingdom.

Background

In the spring of 1987, African American Catholics from every part of the country—representatives from the major Black Catholic organizations, women and men religious, permanent deacons, priests, and our Black bishops—met in congress in the shadow of the Shrine of the Immaculate Conception in the nation's capital to discuss evangelization within the African American community.

Although this was the first National Black Catholic Congress in this century, it was not the first in the history of the Church in the United States. Between 1889 and 1894, five Black Catholic lay congresses were held in Washington, D.C., Cincinnati, Philadelphia, Chicago, and Baltimore. The reason for the first congress was set forth succinctly in the planning stages: "The Catholics of the Colored race should be the leaven, which would raise up their people not only in the eye of God but before men."[3] The concern for the evangelization of the African American community was central in all the deliberations of these congresses. Ever mindful of their faith and their love for the Church, these congress members made known their concerns for Catholic education, for ending racial segregation in the churches, for improving living conditions, and for broadening job improvements for all African Americans—in a word, the implementation of the Gospel as the source of salvation and liberation.[4]

These congresses were a way for Black Catholic leaders to address the needs of the African American Catholic community—needs that were not being addressed by many Catholics within the Church. As early as the Second Plenary Council of Baltimore in 1866, Archbishop Martin J. Spalding (Baltimore) prophetically stated the necessity of planning for the needs of the freed slaves. He observed that there was "a golden opportunity for reaping a harvest of souls, which neglected may not return."[5] For a variety of reasons, the opportunity for coordinated efforts was never taken. In a way, the Black Catholic lay congresses in the last decade of the nineteenth century opened up a new door of opportunity. This pastoral plan of the twentieth century is the fruit of the work and tears of men and women of faith—White and Black—who labored to make the Church within the African American community a leaven of faith and a sign of reconciliation. If the words of our Black bishops' pastoral letter *What We Have Seen and Heard* ring true: "within the history of every Christian community there comes the time when it reaches adulthood,"[6] then this plan is the foundation charter for mature and concerted action in the evangelization of African American Catholics.

The plan embraces three broad areas: (1) the Catholic identity of African American Catholics; (2) the ministry and leadership within the African American Catholic community; and (3) the responsibility of this community to reach out to the broader society. Within these areas are such issues as culture, family, youth, spirituality, liturgy, ministry, lay leadership, parishes, education, social action, and community development.

The Catholic Identity of African Americans

A people without a history is a people without an understanding of who they are. As our Black bishops observed in their pastoral letter *What We Have Seen and Heard,* "The historical roots of Black America and those of Catholic America are intimately intertwined." Hence, they can issue the challenge: "Now is the time for us who are Black Americans and Black Catholics to reclaim our roots and to shoulder the responsibilities of being both Black and Catholic."[7] On the national and diocesan levels and within each parish, the story of African American Catholics must be told. In many instances, the contributions of African American Catholics to the local church have been forgotten, overlooked, or deliberately set aside. In other instances, little importance is given to the symbolic value that historic monuments, records, artifacts, and photographs may have in encouraging the faith and evangelization of a people, especially a people whose history has so often been denied.

At the same time that African American Catholics are encouraged to discover their past, let them be encouraged to retell their story for the sake of the present. The role of history in evangelization is that it relates the story of faith in the midst of struggle, and the story of hope and perseverance in the midst of opposition. Hence, there are two goals that must be sought on the diocesan and parish levels. First, scholars and local historians should be encouraged and offered incentives to study the past of African American Catholics. Second, African American Catholics must be encouraged to conserve their records and documents; without conservation and preservation of records today, there is no history to be written tomorrow. The efforts of Catholic institutions of higher learning and the activities of diocesan and institutional archives could be of immense help in this area. Finally, occasions such as "Black History Month," the anniversaries of parishes and institutions with African American ties, or the observance of special events in local history should be seen as opportunities to highlight the presence and the contributions of African American Catholics.

The possession of one's history is the first step in an appreciation of one's culture. Commenting on the rights of minorities in his 1989 World Day of Peace Message, Pope John Paul II said, "Another right which must be safeguarded is the right of minorities to preserve and develop their own culture."[8] In a country such as ours, where there is a plurality of cultures and subcultures, it is necessary that the message of evangelization be woven into the cultural environment of each people. This process is called *inculturation*. In his apostolic exhortation *Evangelii Nuntiandi*, Pope Paul VI noted:

> The Kingdom which the Gospel proclaims is lived by men who are profoundly linked to a culture and the building up of the Kingdom cannot avoid borrowing the elements of human culture or cultures. . . . Therefore every effort must be made to ensure a full evangelization of culture or more correctly of cultures. They have to be regenerated by an encounter with the Gospel.[9]

For African American Catholics, this means that elements of their culture should not be foreign to the worship and ministry of the local parish and the local church. Pastors, catechists, religion teachers, and program directors working in parishes with African Americans should familiarize themselves with the major cultural elements arising out of the African American experience, such as their art, music, language, dance, and drama. These elements, with proper thought, can be incorporated into the religious experiences of the African American Catholic community.

The Catholic heritages of recent immigrants and refugees from Africa, Haiti, and the Caribbean are of particular concern when the issue of African American Catholic culture is discussed. These newcomers are often subject to a double prejudice, that of racism and xenophobia (i.e., fear and hatred of anything strange or foreign). The Pontifical Commission on Justice and Peace, in its document *The Church and Racism*, stated:

> The prejudices which these immigrants frequently encounter risk setting into motion reactions which can find their first manifestation in an exaggerated nationalism. . . . Such reactions can subsequently degenerate into xenophobia or even racial hatred. . . . On the other hand, the ostracism and the harassment of which refugees and immigrants are too often the object are deplorable.[10]

The newest arrivals to the United States, whose heritage is both African American and Catholic, demand our special attention. In his September 1987 address to Black Catholics in New Orleans, at the time of his second visit to the United States, Pope John Paul II called attention to the importance of the family and, in particular, the importance of the family in the African American tradition:

> Your faithful Christian families are a source of comfort in the face of the extraordinary pressures affecting society. Today, you must rediscover the spirit of family life, which refuses to be destroyed in the face of even the most oppressive forces. Surely that spirit can be found in exploring your spiritual and cultural heritage.[11]

The family and the home are where we learn who we are. It is the family that teaches us much about ourselves. It is the family that is the first school and the first laboratory for the transmission of culture, the passing on of values, the handing down of traditions, the planting of the seed of faith, and the proclamation of the good news of love and hope. The Church in the African American community begins its evangelization with the Black family, in all its strengths and frailties. The Church must address itself to the needs of the family in this community. We strongly affirm the Church's vision of family life. We also recognize, however, the lived experience of the African American family, which was adversely affected by the conditions of slavery and subsequent social and economic conditions that were not conducive to family life. As our Holy Father remarked, there are family values that have for a long time been present in the African American community that coincide with the family values of the Catholic tradition. These values need to be reactivated and restored. They need to be addressed within the framework of the parish community, using the resources present in the local community.

It is within the framework of the parish that the male role models for African American youths can best be presented. We learn from examples. Youths especially assimilate the values and ideals of adults. Young men need to be challenged by the moral stamina and courage of older men who have not succumbed to the allure of drugs, crime, and sexual immorality.

Throughout its history, the Church has always stressed the importance of character building. Therefore, it is essential that the Church be prepared to provide the resources necessary to enable this work to take place within the framework of the African American community. The hard reality of budgetary constraints, on the one hand, must be confronted with the equally harsh reality of critical human need, on the other. That human need may be a disturbing factor for a Church of the affluent and the upwardly mobile; but for a Church that has made a preferential option for the poor, it presents a challenge. The challenge is one that many local churches must face throughout the country, as the Catholic Church begins to explore viable alternatives. In a question of problems and poverty, persons over poverty, and human potential versus profit loss—which is the dilemma presented to the Church in our inner-city communities—the Church cannot neglect the Gospel or its investment in the future.

The future lies with the children; they are our future. The command of our Savior to go teach all nations (cf. Mt 28:19-20) cannot be carried out if we do not invest in our inner-city Catholic schools, in our youth programs, in our catechetical programs, and in other areas of youth-ministry and youth leadership training facilities. In all of these sectors, the local church has to remain aware of the special needs of minorities and the importance of tailoring activities to the cultural dimensions of African American youth. Again, we call special attention to the Catholic schools that still exist in our inner cities, where African Americans and other minorities comprise much of the enrollment. Pope John Paul II singled out the work of Catholic education when he spoke with Black Catholic leaders in New Orleans:

> The Catholic Church has made a profound contribution to the lives of many members of the Black community in this land through the gift of education received in Catholic schools. Because of the splendid commitment of dioceses and parishes, many of you here today have joined us at the table of unity and faith as a result of the evangelization carried out in these institutions. . . . They are a great gift from God. Keep your Catholic schools strong and active. Their uncompromising Catholic identity and Catholic witness at every level must continue to enrich the Black communities of this nation.[12]

Because many inner-city schools teach a large number of non-Catholic students in addition to Catholic students, this places them in the forefront of evangelization as a "special place in the work of spreading the gospel of Christ."[13] And, as the Holy Father said, these schools must be witnesses of an "uncompromising Catholic identity."

In addition to the schools, most parishes offer a variety of programs for young people, as well as continuing education classes for adults. Of great benefit to both the members of the faith community and to the entire Church would be the institution of courses in Scripture, catechetics, and lay-ministry formation within the African American Catholic community. We applaud those parishes that have already begun this work.

In all of these efforts, the cultural dimension of African Americans can enrich and enhance. The roots of African American Catholic spirituality are to be found in the family. This spirituality has come out of the historical lived experience of the African American community in this country, in Africa, and, for some, in the Caribbean. Moreover, it is rooted in the present-day lived experience of African Americans as they face the problems and demands of today's society. This unique cultural dimension, with its varied expressions, can be woven into the fabric of Catholic worship, in the parish liturgy and in spiritual programs such as days of recollection and retreats. African American spirituality can also find its place in the context of diocesan renewal programs and the RCIA. Whenever parish and diocesan programs are planned, the needs of minority groups—as well as those of the majority—are to be considered.

In their pastoral letter *What We Have Seen and Heard*, our Black bishops pointed out that in the African American religious tradition, the "communal experience of worship has always had a central position."[14] It is there that the cultural richness of the African American community has made and continues to make a remarkable contribution. Their pastoral letter rightly recalls that the liturgical celebration in the parishes of the African American community should be always "authentically Black . . . truly Catholic . . . well prepared and well executed."[15] It is essential that pastors and parish associates working within the African American community become familiar with the richness of African American art and music—as well as the art and music of other Black cultures—so that they may cooperate with their parishioners in making the liturgical celebration an authentic and true representation of the African American Catholic cultural experience. It is also important for the celebrant, the ministers, and the choir to use the opportunities afforded them by the liturgical texts and incorporate the cultural gifts of African Americans into the liturgical service.[16] Finally, no one should ignore the fact that the culture and history of African Americans are rich in diversity and style. The same is especially true of the African American Catholic community.

Ministry and Leadership

Regarding the question of leadership within the context of the African American Catholic community, we recall the statement delivered to the National Conference of Catholic Bishops in 1985, which noted that African American Catholics are not highly visible in our Church. The statement of our African American bishops, delivered by Bishop Joseph Howze, said: "If we are to change our image in the larger Black community, Black Catholics must be visible in many different aspects of church life."[17] It also stated that in order for there to be more visible Black leadership, there first must be "appropriate training, opportunity, and visibility."

We can begin this process by assuring the establishment of Offices of Black Catholic Ministries, with appropriate funding and personnel. The form such pastoral offices may take will vary according to place and local conditions. The competence of many qualified African Americans can also be utilized by appointing them to responsible positions in other diocesan offices. In our country today, African Americans enjoy responsible positions in the government, the judiciary, and the armed services. As we noted in our pastoral letter *Brothers and Sisters to Us:*

> All too often in the very places where Blacks, Hispanics, Native Americans, and Asians are numerous, the Church's officials and representatives . . . are predominantly White. Efforts to achieve racial balance in government, the media, the armed services, and other crucial areas of secular life should not only be supported but surpassed in the institutions and programs of the Catholic Church.[18]

In an age where the media play such an important role in daily life, it is important that the catholic reality of the Church be made evident in the local Church's media, such as the diocesan press and television.

Today, vocations to the religious life, the diocesan priesthood, and the permanent diaconate are a major concern to us all. The efforts made to promote vocations also need to include those elements that will speak to the hearts and minds of African American youth. For example, posters, programs, and other vocation materials could portray African American men and women along with their White counterparts, so as to indicate that God's call to follow in Christ's footsteps is not limited to one racial group. We urge those who plan vocation days and workshops to include African American speakers and facilitators in their programs. Diocesan vocation directors, in particular, need to discover ways to reach out to African American men for service in the Church. Again, this may mean tapping the resources already available in the African American Catholic community. As a preparation for ministry among African American Catholics, diocesan and religious seminaries and permanent diaconate programs could include study modules that highlight the history and the culture of African Americans. Too often, White ministers engaged in pastoral ministry among African Americans come into the community with willing hearts but inadequate formation. The Vatican document *The Church and Racism* states:

> Respect for every person and every race is respect for basic rights, dignity and fundamental equality. This does not mean erasing cultural differences. Instead it is important to educate to a positive appreciation of the complementary diversity of peoples. A well-understood pluralism resolves the problem of closed racism.[19]

A knowledge of the culture and history of African Americans, as well as the many contributions made to the Church in the United States by African American Catholics, may facilitate the respect necessary to combat racial prejudice and hatred.

Finally, in looking at the question of vocations on the diocesan and parish levels, it seems appropriate to point out the importance of the permanent diaconate for the evangelization of African Americans. In his address to Black Catholic leaders in New Orleans, Pope John Paul II made special mention of the Black permanent deacons, saying that their "generous response is a clear indication of the growing maturity of the Black Catholic community. . . ."[20] Our Black bishops also mentioned the permanent diaconate in *What We Have Seen and Heard:*

> In the Black community this unique calling is of special importance because it provides an opportunity for men of competence who have had an experience of life much broader than that of many priests and religious. . . . [They have] access to opportunities for evangelization in places where a priest or religious might find entry difficult. This is particularly true for Black deacons in the Black community where many of the clergy are not Black.[21]

The presence of African American permanent deacons in our society today is a reminder once again that there are African American male role models present in the local church.

At the same time, the presence of African American lay ministers needs to be facilitated through leadership-training programs that will improve the skills and talents among African Americans. These lay leaders can enable the African American parish to become that beacon of hope and seedbed of growth for the entire community. While encouraging self-sufficiency and fiscal responsibility, we also encourage programs of mutual help and shared facilities, particularly the sharing that comes from "networking," whereby the needs of one are covered by the resources of the other.

Outreach

On the parish level, African American Catholics need to share their gifts with the surrounding community. It is essential that parishes take a leadership role in the formation of neighborhood outreach programs within the African American community. In many instances, this role is carried out by Catholic schools, which are towers of strength and stability for the whole community. It can also be carried out by offering African American Catholic young people in the community incentives and encouragement to continue their education beyond the secondary level. The local church, in cooperation with school administrators, can encourage Catholic colleges and universities in the area to increase their minority enrollments and seek better racial balances. If there is a disproportionately low number of African American Catholic students in these institutions, then the question must be asked: What can be done to shift the balance?

African American parishes can also take a leadership role in involving the local church in issues of peace and justice and right-to-life issues. Too often, theoretical conclusions do not come face to face with the actual problems. In the African American parish, however, the abstract is made concrete; the questions receive a name and a reality. The questions and issues that should engage diocesan officials and committees—injustice, institutional racism, abortion, economic oppression, and human exploitation and waste—are confronted daily in the African American parishes. In addition to involving the local church in these areas of peace and justice and right-to-life, leaders within the African American parish can also work with the Black Protestant churches. The African American parish can ill afford to become a symbol of a "closed fortress" or an "enclosed garden." As a beacon of hope and a sign of salvation, the African American parish has to be a center of evangelization, reaching out to all "to bring glad tidings to the poor . . . to proclaim liberty to captives and recovery of sight to the blind, to let the oppressed go free, and to proclaim a year acceptable to the Lord" (Lk 4:18-19).

Conclusion

Pope John Paul II expressed that same challenge of leadership, when he spoke with Black Catholic leaders: "Black Americans must offer their own special solidarity of Christian love to all people who bear the heavy burden of oppression, whatever its physical or moral nature."[22] Earlier in the same address, the pope referred to the vitality of the African American community, calling it "a sign of hope for society." At the end of his conversation with Black Catholic leaders, he spoke of the first Pentecost as a sign of the Church's unity and universality; all nations, peoples, and tongues heard the apostles speak of God's wonders in their own tongue (cf. Acts 2:4f). This expresses both the meaning of evangelization and the mystery of the Church. African American Catholics are a sign of the new Pentecost because their "Black cultural heritage enriches the Church and makes her witness of universality more complete."[23]

May Mary, who is the Mother of all who are reborn in Christ, and who was present at the wonder of that first Pentecost, be with the Church anew as Christ is reborn once more in the African American community in our day.

Notes

1. Paul VI, *On Evangelization in the Modern World (Evangelii Nuntiandi)* (Washington, D.C.: United States Catholic Conference, 1976), no. 24.
2. Ibid., no. 29.
3. *American Catholic Tribune*, May 14, 1888.
4. See *Three Catholic Afro-American Congresses* (New York: Arno Press, 1978), a reprint of the 1893 edition published in Cincinnati by the *American Catholic Tribune*. See especially, "Address of the Congress to Their Catholic Fellow-Citizens of the United States," 66-72.
5. Letter of Archbishop Spalding to Archbishop McCloskey (October 9, 1865), the New York Archdiocesan Archives. Cited by Edward J. Misch, "The American Bishops and the Negro from the Civil War to the Third Plenary Council of Baltimore, 1865-1884" (dissertation, Gregorian University, 1968), 130.
6. Black Bishops of the United States, *What We Have Seen and Heard: A Pastoral Letter on Evangelization from the Black Bishops of the United States* (Cincinnati: St. Anthony Messenger Press, 1984), 1.
7. Ibid., 17.
8. John Paul II, "To Build Peace, Respect Minorities," 1989 World Day of Peace Message, *Origins* 18:29 (December 29, 1988): 465-469.
9. *Evangelii Nuntiandi*, no. 20.
10. Pontifical Commission on Justice and Peace, *The Church and Racism: Towards a More Fraternal Society* (Washington, D.C.: United States Catholic Conference, 1988), no. 14.

11. John Paul II, *Unity in the Work of Service* (Washington, D.C.: United States Catholic Conference, 1987), 53.
12. Ibid., 54-55.
13. Ibid., 55.
14. *What We Have Seen and Heard*, 30.
15. Ibid.
16. See Secretariat of the Bishops' Committee on the Liturgy, *In Spirit and Truth: Black Catholic Reflections on the Order of Mass* (Washington, D.C.: United States Catholic Conference, 1988).
17. "Statement by the Black Bishops of the United States," *Origins* 15:24 (November 28, 1985): 395-399.
18. National Conference of Catholic Bishops, *Brothers and Sisters to Us: U.S. Bishops' Pastoral Letter on Racism in Our Day* (Washington, D.C.: United States Catholic Conference, 1979), 11.
19. *The Church and Racism*, 44.
20. *Unity in the Work of Service*, 52.
21. *What We Have Seen and Heard*, 24.
22. *Unity in the Work of Service*, 54.
23. Ibid., 55.

Source: Washington, D.C.: United States Catholic Conference, 1990.

Food Policy in a Hungry World: The Links That Bind Us Together

A Pastoral Statement of the United States Catholic Conference

November 1989

Introduction

> A world with nearly half a billion hungry people is not one
> in which food security has been achieved. The problem of
> hunger has a special significance for those who read the
> Scriptures and profess the Christian faith. From the Lord's
> command to feed the hungry, to the eucharist we celebrate
> as the bread of life, the fabric of our faith demands that we
> be creatively engaged in sharing the food that sustains life.
> There is no more basic human need. The gospel imperative
> takes on new urgency in a world of abundant harvests
> where hundreds of millions of people face starvation.[1]

These words from our pastoral letter of 1986 on the U.S. economy
present the tragic irony and profound challenge of so much hunger in
the midst of plenty. In these new reflections, we wish to return to this
challenge; to share our concerns as pastors; and to focus on the linkages between food, agriculture, rural concerns, and the broader common good which affects us all wherever we live.

We also wish to offer some values to our nation and the world as
we seek to meet the moral challenges that haunt a hungry world. We
believe that these values can assist both rural and urban people in a
common search for justice for all, but in particular for those people
who produce our food and for the people who are suffering and dying
for the lack of it.

In these reflections, we speak especially to our fellow Catholics—
many deeply involved in these issues as producers, consumers, and
policymakers. But we also want to share these reflections with the
wider religious community and with others who are deeply involved
with these concerns. We invite you to join with us as believers and as
citizens to examine the ethical dimensions of these issues; to study the
complex forces that shape them; and to act to protect the poor and the
hungry, vulnerable farmers, ranchers, farmworkers, and others hurt
by the way the current food system operates.

Many policies and practices, which seem to us to be increasingly inadequate and unjust, pose some basic questions. How, in a world that produces so much food, can so many, like Lazarus, still be left begging for crumbs? Why do millions of people still face starvation every day? Why do so many farm and ranch families here in the United States continue to lose their farms? Why do thousands of farmworkers live in subhuman conditions, while the large agribusiness farms they work on prosper? Why are young people leaving rural America in such numbers? Why are consumers increasingly fearful about the quality and safety of their food and the inadequate stewardship of land and water? How did we develop a "food production and distribution system" that, despite all the knowledge, skill, productivity, and energy of those who participate in it, can still leave so many people hungry, so many hardworking producers in jeopardy, and so many farmworkers without access to decent work conditions or land to farm themselves?

We intend these reflections to contribute to the broader public dialogue about the difficult choices our nation faces in food and agricultural policy at home and abroad. These are not new concerns for the Church. The National Catholic Rural Life Conference has for almost seventy years addressed various aspects of these issues with courage and persistence. Catholic Relief Services has fed the hungry of the world and brought dignity and hope to millions of people in many countries. The Campaign for Human Development and Catholic Charities USA support farmers and farmworkers in their struggle for justice. Other Catholic agencies have also written some detailed policy position papers on the issues of hunger and food systems. Catholic Charities USA, in October 1989, adopted its paper entitled *A Just Food System*, which highlights many of the same concerns we discuss in this paper. These efforts have been enriched and multiplied by the commitment and collaborative efforts we share with our sisters and brothers in other faiths and in the broader community.

We bring to this statement our experience as pastors who serve the poor, the hungry, and those who work the land and produce the food we eat. As bishops, who also serve a community deeply engaged in feeding the hungry through our local Catholic charities, parishes, soup kitchens, and food pantries, we know the reality of hunger and malnutrition in the United States. Through our international relief and development efforts, we see even worse conditions abroad. We also speak on these issues as teachers called to share an important heritage of social thought and values.

Following the adoption of our pastoral letter on the U.S. economy, a special Task Force on Food, Agriculture, and Rural Concerns was established. Its charge was to examine how the various parts of the Church in this country could work together more effectively to improve our ministry and service to rural people and to contribute to the public debate and decisions on food and agriculture.

Last year, the conference of bishops decided to focus more directly on the moral and human dimensions of food and agricultural policy. We did this because of several increasingly alarming trends and problems in this area:

- Hundreds of millions of people malnourished or facing starvation in the developing countries
- Hardworking U.S. farm families leaving the land as a result of public policy choices, private practices, and larger economic forces beyond their influence or control
- Continuing exploitation of farmworkers, rural poverty, homelessness, and inadequate basic services in rural America
- Growing concentration in the ownership of land and other farm resources in the hands of larger farmers and nonfarm investors
- Continuing reliance on what were intended as emergency and short-term ways to deal with the food needs of the poor (e.g., food pantries, soup kitchens), instead of the more permanent and dignified programs
- Increasing malnutrition and hunger here in the world's richest country, where one out of every ten people cannot afford an adequate diet
- An accelerating trade war among the major food producers that threatens the impoverishment of farmers here and abroad
- Continuing damage to land and water resources—and of the environment in general—because of unsound agricultural practices, often stimulated by at least equally unsound policies

We also wish to identify the connection between the problems of food production, distribution, and consumption and what is often called the "farm crisis" in this country. We wish to emphasize that because of this link, farmers, ranchers, and consumers in this country and abroad share responsibility for addressing these problems. In particular, consumers through their daily choices can exercise responsibility and can have some collective impact on the direction and shape of the food system. Consumers' responsibility calls for a conversion to an attentive attitude about how their food consumption choices can affect farmers, farmworkers, the poor, and corporate policies and practices. The fact that starvation is still a brutal reality in a world with the technical capacity to feed everyone touches all of us. Something is basically wrong when hunger still haunts the richest nation on earth, when thousands of family farmers who produce our food cannot sustain their own families and keep their farms, and when public policy seems designed to promote and reward the biggest and richest farmers at the expense of smaller and more moderately sized farms, for which the original farm programs were intended.

These problems are not just rural or domestic. They touch the lives of consumers as well as farmers, inner-city and suburban residents as well as rural communities. These problems certainly raise technical and political questions, but they raise moral questions as well. How do our food and agricultural policies enhance or diminish the life, dignity, and rights of the human person? What is their impact on human life, hungry people, farm families, and the land that sustains us?

We seek to put a human face on what often appears to be abstract issues. Our experience and recent studies suggest that the human face of hunger is often the face of women and of children. That is what UNICEF reports about the Third World, and it is what the Physicians' Task Force on Hunger in America says about our own nation. In considering the fate of those women and children, we fear that the global food system often seems adrift without a moral compass.

Our Teaching, Our Values

Major principles of Scripture and Catholic social teaching provide a framework for assessing present problems and evaluating potential solutions. These principles can help shape a more just food and agriculture system:

- The sacredness of the human person
- The fundamental right to food
- The Christian call to human solidarity
- The Church's preferential option for the poor
- The biblical call for respect for God's creation

First, at the core of Catholic social teaching is the *sacredness of the human person*. Each one of us is created in the image of God. Our dignity is bestowed on us by the love and creative hand of God, and not by our race, creed, ethnic origin, national heritage, sex, or economic status. It is the responsibility of each individual, and of society as a whole, to ensure and protect the life and dignity of every human person by promoting conditions in which human life can flourish and not be undermined, in which people can move toward their ultimate goal of union with God. For us, this means that everyone has a legitimate claim to the goods and services necessary to live a truly human life.

Second, understanding human dignity leads to a commitment to the rights of the human person—the baseline against which the justice of a society can be measured. One such right is the *right to food* to sustain life. People must have access to food sufficient for their normal physical and human development, through either cultivation or purchase; they must be able to grow it, secure it from the waters, or buy it. A world of abundance that cannot assure everyone food sufficient for life is unjust. Food policy deals not with just another commodity to be bought or sold, but with sustenance of life itself.

Third, the human person is not only sacred but social. Although Catholic tradition recognizes and celebrates the person and stresses personal salvation, it also insists that we are fundamentally and ultimately social; we grow and develop in community. This concern of the Church for the social nature of the person leads it to emphasize *community, solidarity, cooperation, and participation* in the decisions that affect people's lives. This emphasis of the Church on the social nature of the person leads it to oppose excessive individualism and unbridled competition as the contemporary norm for economic or social activity.

In *On Social Concern*, Pope John Paul II emphasizes the virtue of solidarity. What is needed, he says, is not simply compassion or charity, but a "firm but persevering determination to commit oneself to the common good. . . ."[2] A commitment to solidarity in the food area would dramatically alter the notion often advanced that the food that sustains life is just one more item in a list of commodities.

This emphasis on the common good, solidarity, participation, and cooperation leads us to be very concerned about the increasing concentration of control of productive land, especially agricultural. The accumulation of economic power that comes with the consolidation of land ownership and the concentration of management, marketing, and distribution through corporate integration of various stages of the food system can threaten the common good and erode accountability to the public. The pattern of farm ownership has a powerful and decisive influence on the quality of social and economic life in rural communities. We believe that widespread ownership of farms coupled with responsible public policy and effective farm management will preserve rural communities and ensure that more people have access to the food which is their right. Ultimately, a pluralistic system with widespread ownership and greater diversity in size and style of farming operations serves the common good more effectively than a highly concentrated one.

Fourth, the Scriptures and our tradition express a *special concern— a preferential option—for the poor.* This is not a new concern. It is a restatement of the lesson of the Scriptures that we will be judged by how we care for the poor and vulnerable, the least among us. How a community treats the powerless and the needy is the measure of its justice. Solidarity does not mean choosing the poor over everyone else, but recognizing that authentic human development cannot be achieved without the inclusion of poor people as full participants in society. This means not only that the poor must have access to enough food, but that the poor must have a real voice in deciding how the food system—and indeed, society itself—should be organized to serve the common good, at home and abroad.

Fifth, by acknowledging that the earth is the Lord's and that God is present in all of creation, we show *respect for God's creation*. Our respect for creation is a demonstration of our reverence for God and respect for life itself. All of creation is a gift we share, "the habitat within which humanity must live," Pope John Paul II said, "which . . . has been given to us in trust."

This is especially true of air, water, and land—resources intimately connected to food production. All of society, of course, must accept the responsibility to care for the earth and its natural resources. The Church has repeatedly condemned the misuse of the earth's resources or their appropriation for selfish purposes as theft of gifts God meant all humanity to share. "The dominion granted . . . by God the Creator is not an absolute power, nor can one speak of a freedom to 'use or misuse,' or to dispose of things as one pleases. . . ."[3] Pope John Paul II has spoken often of what he calls the "social mortgage" on private property. Private property, he emphasizes, has a social purpose; it must be used for the benefit of the human family and preserved for future generations. It is not for the exclusive use of its legal owner, but must serve the common good.

Our Experience Here at Home: Hungry People and Farmers at Risk

The above principles drawn from Catholic social teaching lead us to be very concerned about the problems we see in our own domestic food production and distribution system. Our pastoral letter on the U.S. economy describes the situation this way:

> We are concerned that [the nation's] food system may be in jeopardy as increasing numbers of farm bankruptcies and foreclosures result in increased concentration of land ownership. We are likewise concerned about the increasing damage to natural resources resulting from many modern agricultural practices: the overconsumption of water, the depletion of topsoil, and the pollution of land and water. . . . Our food production system is clearly in need of evaluation and reform.[4]

As pastors serving farmers and farmworkers, we know the tragedy and pain that touch so many of our brothers and sisters with whom we live and work. The loss of a farm, the hard and underpaid labor of the farmworker, the lack of land to own and till—these forces are destroying lives, families, and communities in rural America.

Our parishes are facing these problems every day. We see this statement as a word of support and solidarity and a call to strengthen our pastoral care and witness on behalf of justice in America. We believe much is being done and more needs to be done, working together and ecumenically to make a difference in our local communities and our nation.

But these conditions affect more than rural people. Food and agriculture issues are not just farm and ranch issues; they are not even solely rural issues. Food is a crucial concern in our inner cities as well, where many do not have enough money to buy it, and in other communities, where fears about the quality and safety of our food are growing.

Technological changes, larger economic forces, and government policies alter the shape of food production and the distribution of farm-program benefits among farmers. The drive to increase production has often promoted farming practices that can be cost effective only if the scale of production (i.e., the size of farms and the investment in machinery and other resources) increases. Farms have grown to accommodate the type of technology developed. The result has been increasing concentration in the ownership of farms and more and bigger farm benefits to fewer farmers. Moreover, while the mechanical and chemical technologies have led to a rapid increase in food supplies and made farming easier in some ways, and the emerging biotechnologies will likely have a similar effect, they are not without cost. Some of the costs are economic, but they are increasingly social and environmental as well.

Many of these changes are fueled by government farm policies (e.g., tax, credit, research, and price supports) that stimulate and reward farm expansion. We believe that limited tax dollars should not be spent disproportionately to support these larger farms and thus further ownership concentration. Public policy can be used to promote the diversity of agriculture by protecting and advancing the viability of smaller and more moderately sized farms through the development of technology and public policies more suitable to these farms. It is a matter of public choice. These latter farms have a proven record of economic efficiency, productivity, and resiliency. They contribute to the vitality and diversity of rural communities in a way that a smaller number of large industrialized farms cannot.

Moreover, despite this concentration or perhaps because of it, the average farmer receives a shrinking share of the food dollar. Figures for 1987 indicated that only 25 cents of every food dollar goes to the farmer. In the case of a one-pound loaf of white bread selling, for example, for 61 cents in the grocery store, only 4 cents goes to the wheat farmer. The bulk of the food-dollar benefits goes to the enterprises in the middle: elevator operators, grain companies, railroads, shipping companies, processors, warehouses, retailers, and marketing firms.

An examination of this middle segment of the food system—processing, marketing, and distribution—reveals much the same pattern of concentration as the ownership of farms. A few large grain companies control the bulk of world grain trade. This concentration can seriously distort the price-setting mechanisms of the market. For consumers, too, the concept of a global supermarket in the food industry takes on a more serious tone of realism because of recent mergers and takeovers in the food industry and new global strategies of food product sales. If these trends continue, the control of the food system—quantity, quality, price, availability, and choice—will be concentrated in fewer and fewer hands. Such concentration has serious implications for the fulfillment of the right to food.

In addition, farmers in the industrialized nations also face the uncertainties of external economic forces, both domestic and international, which have at least as much impact on food production as farm price and income-support programs. Interest and exchange rates are especially important. Agriculture relies heavily on the availability of credit, and competition for credit pits not only farmer against farmer but also agriculture against other sectors of the economy for available funds, driving up production costs. Yet, policy continues to favor capital-intensive farming and discriminates against those who lack wealth. And as long as a significant portion of farm income depends on international trade—in 1987 one-third of U.S. crop acres produced for the export market—the value of the dollar in relation to other currencies will play an important role in the distribution of income and in the agricultural sector.

Food trade is also a major area of increased international tension. The United States has become the world's global grain storehouse, its residual supplier. In good times the grain stays stored, and in lean years the United States has been able to help supply large amounts of agricultural products to meet global demand. Playing this role unilaterally in an increasingly complex, interdependent, and competitive international food system has become more destabilizing economically and politically, both for the United States and for other participants in the global food system.

In the 1970s, the United States responded to an increased global demand for food—and the prospect of greater profits from trade—by greatly expanding food production and, as a result, capturing for the time being a significantly larger share of global food trade. In the 1980s, however, as other nations, for much the same reasons, adopted newer technologies and expanded their production capacities, the international food system as a whole has developed a capacity for overproduction. At the same time, reduced income and higher debt service have weakened effective demand for agricultural products in the poorer importing countries, and the strong U.S. dollar (until 1985) pushed up the cost of U.S. farm goods. These factors led to a sharp decrease in the U.S. share of global food trade, from which the United States has only partially recovered. Many farms, especially those with heavy debts, could not sustain this loss, and we are seeing the human consequences in our rural communities.

These problems of the 1980s have moved the world into what is increasingly recognized as a food trade war. Competition for the world food market is most evident between Western Europe and the United States. Both of these economic giants have the technological capacity for overproduction, large national treasuries with which to compete in a subsidy war, strong competitive urges, and politically vocal farm sectors. This competition and the large subsidies it has spawned have been major contributing factors to lower global farm prices.

Thus, the agricultural and macroeconomic policies of both the industrialized and the developing countries have fostered a volatile and contentious world food trading system dominated by the industrialized exporters, to the detriment of agriculture and of development in the Third World. As agricultural policy has become a dependent variable of trade policy, divisions and tensions have grown among nations, among producers of various agricultural commodities, and between farmers and consumers. To the extent that food is grown more by capital and for profit than by people and for people, we can expect further decline in the number of family farms, greater tension among the exporting countries, and increased hunger and malnutrition among the world's poor.

In analyzing our domestic problems, we also wish to draw special attention to the needs of small or minority farmers, farmworkers, and those who are hungry here in our midst in this country. The plight of minority farmers, particularly Black farmers in the South, is too often forgotten or ignored in public policy. While many of these farms are small, they provide a sense of identity and economic stability for many members of our minority populations. The continued loss of farmland owned by Blacks and Hispanics could contribute to further marginalization of minority people. Regrettably, this same situation holds true for many Native American farmers in some parts of our country.

Economic Justice for All also addresses the plight of many farmworkers and migrant laborers who are among those with the lowest pay and least benefits in the labor force and who more often live in squalor and work under unsafe conditions. Regarding their situation, our pastoral letter is clear:

They are not as well protected by law and public policy as
other groups of workers; and their efforts to organize and
bargain collectively have been systematically and vehe-
mently resisted, usually by farmers themselves. Migratory
field workers are particularly susceptible to exploitation.
This is reflected not only in their characteristically low
wages but also in the low standards of housing, health care,
and education made available to these workers and their
families.[5]

Our pastoral letter on the U.S. economy is very explicit in reference
to farmworkers' wages and benefits, calling for guarantees and protections such as minimum wages and benefits and unemployment
compensation to be extended on the same basis as other workers. This
includes legislation and effective implementation of state and federal
protections, particularly in the area of pesticide usage. It also includes
an extension and enforcement of the most basic field labor standards
of potable drinking water and adequate sanitation facilities. Finally,
the provision of decent and affordable housing for farmworkers—
especially migrant farmworkers—who comprise a large number of
rural homeless, needs to be addressed.

In our pastoral letter on the U.S. economy, we state:

Farmworkers have a legitimate right to belong to unions of
their choice and to bargain collectively for just wages and
working conditions. In pursuing that right they are protecting the value of labor in agriculture, a protection that also
applies to farmers who devote their own labor to their farm
operations.[6]

The Church should affirmatively promote the right of farmworkers to
unionize, especially where this right is denied by employers or
through ineffective enforcement of fair labor laws.

Furthermore, targeted health and education programs are the key
to the future of farmworker children if they are to overcome the
myriad equal opportunity barriers that they face. These programs, but
especially education programs, should be tailored to the cultural and
linguistic differences of minority farmworker children.

Finally, the presence of so many hungry people in our midst is
morally intolerable. While there may be disagreements about the
actual statistics of hunger and malnutrition, or about what the changing rates of poverty and infant mortality mean, no one can reasonably
deny that this nation faces a serious problem of hunger. We see evidence every day in our soup kitchens, food pantries, and shelters. We
know that millions of people suffer the ravages of hunger and malnutrition every day here in the United States—especially children,

infants, single working mothers, and the elderly, who are the most vulnerable among us. Our churches, parishes, and charitable institutions feed millions of people every year. Many communities have joined together to start and support impressive and innovative voluntary efforts to meet the needs of the hungry. They have formed food banks, cooperative arrangements to recover unused or unsold food, and creative involvement of churches and other groups in serving the hungry on a regular basis. We applaud and support these necessary efforts. But our own efforts and the response of others cannot substitute for fair and equitable public policy and for action by society, in general, and by government, as the instrument of our common purpose, to end hunger in America and throughout the world.

International Dimensions: Feeding a Hungry World

When we look beyond our own shores, we are struck by the massive human problems that at first seem unrelated to these domestic concerns, but which on closer examination reveal the common bonds that bind together farmers and consumers all over the world.

The *first* reality is the scandal that nearly a billion people lack access to sufficient food because they either cannot grow it or do not have enough income to buy it. We know from UNICEF that 40,000 children die every day from hunger and disease. Malnutrition is on the rise. The UN's Food and Agriculture Organization emphasizes that after two years of poor harvests and the continuing effects of droughts in key world agricultural areas, the poorer nations face increased hunger and starvation as global competition increases for the world's declining stocks of grain. The fact that these stocks are at their lowest levels since the early 1970s seriously threatens world food security: When supplies dwindle and prices rise, who then will decide who lives and who dies?

A *second* pressing problem of the global food system is the inability of many farmers in developing countries to earn a sufficient living from farming, mainly because they do not own land, cannot obtain adequate farm supplies or credit, or face low prices for their products. In the poorer nations of Latin America, Africa, and Asia, the majority of the people live in rural areas and are engaged in farming or farm-related activities, but too many of them cannot earn enough even to survive. Some suffer because land ownership is concentrated in the hands of a few, as in some Latin American countries, or because the land they own is unsuitable for farming. For others, the prices they receive for food products are deliberately held down by governments in order to appease restive and politically sensitive urban populations through a cheap urban food policy. Governments in many developing countries deliberately discourage farm production and depend on imported food. Ironically, many new urban residents have left the land because they could not earn a living in the rural areas and have come to the cities in a desperate search for greater opportunity.

Third, agriculture in many poor countries is devoted increasingly to export markets. This is done for two reasons: first, in part, to pay their burgeoning debts to the industrialized countries, the multilateral financial institutions, and the commercial banks; and second, in part, in order to follow the development model of export-led economic growth urged on them by donors in the industrialized world. These forces have tied poorer nations to the economic fortunes of the more powerful industrial states and subordinated them to the latter's competitive market drives. Over the past decade, the industrialized nations' economic growth has slowed, and competition among them has intensified. This has meant less demand for the products of the developing nations on the part of the developed countries. The result is slower economic growth for the poorer countries, less ability to meet their ever-growing external debt burdens, and still greater problems in feeding their steadily growing populations. It has meant a cruel choice for many poor countries of whether to produce agricultural products for export in order to earn foreign exchange to pay debt, or to grow food to feed their own hungry people. Because of these policies and practices, the ability of poorer countries to be self-reliant in feeding their people—through growing or purchasing food—is in jeopardy. We need to help them in ways that preserve their human dignity and provide the incentives for them to help themselves. We should take care that our own legal immigration policies do not encourage the draining of needed human resources from developing countries.

Stewardship: Protecting the Earth

Just as world food security and international agricultural trade underscore our global interdependence, so, too, does the way farming practices affect the environment we all share. Soil erosion brought on by intensive farming—especially of erodible land—and other destructive practices has depleted much farmland in this country and abroad. In the tropics, it has led to the inexorable expansion of deserts, the reduction of rain forests, and destructive downstream flooding. In some places in the United States, water is depleted at rates exceeding its natural replacement; in other cases, it is also polluted by excessive use of chemicals. In addition, the very real threat of a global warming trend raises serious questions and potential problems for future food production.

Abuse of the environment—of the resources God gave to us to share—harms all of us alive today and threatens future generations.

Global environmental problems, which in part are caused by agriculture, pose an enormous danger to society, as well as a challenge to both science and politics. Yet the environmental costs have rarely been included in the calculation of efficiencies or "economies of scale" in agriculture. Unless more farming practices are developed and adopted that can sustain the earth's capacity to regenerate itself and avoid damaging the environment, the risk of accelerating the damage to our food productive capacity and to society as a whole will grow.

In part, the present environmental crisis reflects the inextricable linkages in the world's food production and distribution system. But, in part, it also reflects the finiteness of the planet's resources. Nevertheless, even though there clearly are limits to land, water, energy, and other natural resources, and although weather—the ultimate variable for food production—is still unpredictable and uncontrollable, the major causes of food insecurity are probably not in these areas. Rather, it is political decisions made in the various capitals of the world that determine who will benefit from the present food and agriculture system and who will not.

Future Directions: Goals and Criteria for Policy

A. A Look Back to the Pastoral on the U.S. Economy

In our economic pastoral, we concluded that what we saw happening in the food sector did not serve the common good of the United States or the world. We suggested three guidelines for the reshaping of U.S. agriculture:

- "First, moderate-sized farms operated by families on a full-time basis should be preserved and their economic viability protected."[7]
- "Second, the opportunity to engage in farming should be protected as a valuable form of work."[8]
- "Third, effective stewardship of our natural resources should be a central consideration in any measures regarding U.S. agriculture."[9]

To these judgments, we would now add a clear reaffirmation that we are linked together—farmers and consumers, rural and urban communities—by the issues of food security. We also affirm that the food crisis is truly global and that the solidarity needed in our own country must extend to our sisters and brothers in all parts of the world.

As pastors, we know the human consequences of these issues. The Church will continue to serve farm families, farmworkers, rural people, and hungry families. But these ministries are not enough. We also are called to address the causes of hunger, to prevent the loss of farms, and to help resolve the broader problems of the food system. This is the arena of public policy.

B. National Goals

In this statement, we do not offer detailed, specific remedies. Rather, we seek to raise questions, suggest moral criteria, and outline directions for public policy. We recognize the complexity of these issues and the difficulty of integrating a variety of goals and meeting the needs of various constituencies that may, at times, seem at cross-purposes. However, the challenge to design an integrated food policy must be undertaken. An effective and responsible U.S. food and agriculture policy should, in our view, be one that

- Enables farmers to produce good quality food at prices consumers can afford and that provide farmers with a fair income
- Promotes food production and distribution that is economically viable and environmentally sustainable
- Increases the opportunities for the widespread distribution and ownership of farmland and other agricultural resources to protect the diversity and resiliency of our farm system and to help revitalize rural communities
- Renews a viable family farming system that discourages the use of land for speculative purposes and helps stem the tide of the loss of smaller and more moderate-sized farms and permits those wishing to enter farming to do so
- Ensures fair compensation, decent working conditions, and legal protections and enforcement for farmworkers
- Provides needed assistance to minority farmers
- Negotiates fair international trade practices that acknowledge the uniqueness of food, safeguard the interests of poorer nations, and lessen tensions among exporting countries
- Seeks to ensure world food security and promote global agricultural development
- Responds effectively to food emergencies

C. Directions for Policy

In light of these principles, we recommend the following general directions for U.S. policy:

- Establish food security as the ultimate goal of food and agricultural policy—ensuring that every human being has access to enough food to maintain a decent human standard of living. Internationally managed global food reserves may be required to achieve this goal.

- Foster an equitable system of land tenure, especially the widespread ownership of land and productive property, which constitutes one of the strongest guarantees of human dignity and democratic freedom. We support a viable family farm system of agriculture in the United States and equitable and workable land reform in developing countries.

- Structure federal commodity and insurance programs so that farmers who depend on their farm for their livelihood can attain an annual income adequate to meet the needs of their families. Farm program benefits should be targeted to these farmers, with special assistance available for limited resource, beginning, and minority farmers.

- Support farming methods and technologies that sustain rather than damage the environment (e.g., crop diversification and rotation, conservation practices, and less reliance on environmentally destructive and life-threatening chemicals and other technologies). The care and protection of natural resources for future generations is of paramount importance.

- Strengthen rural communities by helping rural people participate in building their own economic and social future. The rural dimensions of poverty, poor housing, inadequate health care, and other broader problems deserve serious attention. A commitment to strengthen rural communities, including their physical aspects, should be a key element of agricultural policy. Through increased emphasis on education and job creation, rural citizens should have more opportunities to remain in their home communities if they wish.

- Assure farmworkers fair wages, unemployment compensation, and protections and benefits afforded to all other workers. The right to organize must be assured and defended. Improvements in farmworker housing, health care (including better protection against harmful pesticide exposure), education, and general working conditions are particularly urgent requirements of social justice.

- Encourage and support cooperatives as a way of giving both consumers and producers a measure of economic power and greater participation in the economic enterprise, as has been the policy of the Campaign for Human Development in its ongoing effort to empower the powerless.

- Combat hunger in the United States by strengthening the domestic food assistance programs to ensure that no one in America goes hungry or suffers malnutrition. When the economy fails to provide the jobs and income necessary to prevent hunger and malnutrition, the various local, state, and national food assistance programs must be funded and expanded to provide food to all in need. Emergency programs that do not provide food in a manner that respects human dignity should be challenged and changed.

- Conduct food trade relations with equity and food security as the first priority goals. Food is not just another commodity. Subsidies should not be used as political or economic weapons, and food aid and trade policies should not deepen the dependency of poor importing nations or undercut their ability to grow their own food. Development assistance should foster self-reliance in the poorer nations.

We are aware that these directions for food and agriculture policy cannot be realized without changes in the external economic environment. The problems that we have discussed are often symptoms of deeper underlying problems in the international economy. Fiscal and monetary policies, for example, have to be conceived more intelligently and managed more cooperatively if progress is to be made in these areas. Relief of the excessive debt burdens of poor nations is a matter of urgent and high priority. Moreover, as we have pointed out in two of our pastoral letters, *The Challenge of Peace* and *Economic Justice for All*, expenditures on arms, now approaching $1 trillion per year around the world, represent "a massive distortion of resource allocations."[10]

We shall use these guidelines as general criteria in assessing public policy and legislation in these areas. We ask others to join us in raising these issues and advocating these values in the public debate about food and agricultural policy.

Conclusion

The stark realities of poverty and hunger, the maldistribution of farm benefits, damage to the environment, and the threat of food trade wars challenge the Church and other groups to work together in solidarity for just and practical solutions to the many problems in the global food system. As Pope John Paul II said in Monterey, Calif., during his 1987 pastoral visit to the United States:

> All agree that the situation of the farming community in the United States and in other parts of the world is highly complex, and that simple remedies are not at hand. The Church, on her part, while she can offer no specific technical solu-

tions, does present a social teaching based on the primacy of the human person in every economic and social activity. At every level of the agricultural process, the dignity, rights, and well-being of people must be the central issue. No one person in this process—grower, worker, packer, shipper, retailer, or consumer—is greater than the other in the eyes of God.

Giving voice therefore to the sufferings of many, I appeal to all involved to work together to find appropriate solutions to all farm questions. This can only be done in a community marked by a sincere and effective solidarity—and, where still necessary, reconciliation—among all parties to the agricultural productive process.[11]

We reaffirm and accept our Holy Father's call to solidarity and urge all involved in our country and the broader international community to work together to ensure that a food system that should sustain life is not undermined by the actions or policies of any group or nation. Solidarity requires a new effort to feed the hungry at home and help the hungry abroad.

Solidarity requires new policies that assist small farms, not threaten them. Solidarity requires special care and concern for the land we all share.

Therefore, we call upon our pastors and our people, key Catholic organizations—the National Catholic Rural Life Conference, Catholic Relief Services, the Campaign for Human Development, Catholic Charities USA, and the National Catholic Educational Association among others—and the broader ecumenical and public policy community to join with us in an effort to recommit ourselves in justice to making the elimination of hunger a central focus of our actions and programs. Hope remains alive in every crisis, the hope that a generous and determined people, with God's providential care, can help one another alter the conditions under which we live and make social justice and genuine solidarity the foundation of our life together.

Solidarity is required among both urban and rural people if these problems are to be resolved. These problems know no boundaries; they do not stop at the gates of the cities or the borders of nations. We are all bound one to the other. The response of the United States and of other nations to the challenges posed in the area of food and agriculture will enrich or diminish each of us, no matter where we live or what we do. With God's grace, may we find the will and the ways to remove the obstacles that prevent millions of our sisters and brothers from living in dignity, freed from the threat of hunger and with a share of the goods of the earth, which God has created for the benefit of all.

Notes

1. National Conference of Catholic Bishops, *Economic Justice for All* (Washington, D.C.: United States Catholic Conference, 1986), no. 282.
2. John Paul II, *On Social Concern (Sollicitudo Rei Socialis)* (Washington, D.C.: United States Catholic Conference, 1988), no. 38.
3. *Sollicitudo Rei Socialis,* no. 34.
4. *Economic Justice for All,* no. 217.
5. Ibid., no. 230.
6. Ibid., no. 249.
7. Ibid., no. 233.
8. Ibid., no. 236.
9. Ibid., no. 238.
10. Ibid., no. 289.
11. John Paul II, "Agriculture and the Church's View of Work," homily at Luguna Seca, Monterey, Calif., September 17, 1987, *Origins* 17:18 (October 15, 1987): 310.

Source: Washington, D.C.: United States Catholic Conference, 1989.

Toward Peace in the Middle East:
Perspectives, Principles, and Hopes

A Statement of the National Conference of Catholic Bishops

November 1989

Introduction

As Catholic bishops and as citizens of the United States, we are particularly concerned for the peoples, the nations, and the Church in the Middle East. Christianity is rooted in the soil of the Holy Land, where Jesus Christ was born, lived, taught, died, and rose again. As pastors, we wish to offer solidarity with our brother bishops and support to the Church in the Middle East at a time of trial and difficulty. We sense the fear, hope, vulnerability, and suffering of the diverse peoples of the region—Jewish, Christian, and Muslim. We have a deep and abiding relationship of respect for the Jewish people and support for the notion of Israel. We also feel with new urgency the pain and hopes of the Palestinian people. We have persistently tried to support the Lebanese people in their agony of war and devastation. As citizens of the United States, we also recognize the continuing engagement of our nation with the various Middle East countries and the significant impact of U.S. policy on the region.

We write this statement first and foremost as pastors and religious teachers, deeply concerned about what continuing conflict and violence in the Middle East mean for the people who live there, for all the world, and for people of faith everywhere. Our religious convictions, our traditional teaching, and our ecclesial responsibilities call us to stand with the suffering, to advocate dialogue in place of violence, and to work for genuine justice and peace. In 1973 and in 1978, the United States Catholic Conference issued policy statements on the Middle East, outlining the principles we believed would contribute to a just and lasting peace. In light of a number of important subsequent developments, we seek in this statement to share our own reflections in the hope that they will contribute to a broad and sustained effort to help secure peace, justice, and security for all people in the Middle East. While our title refers to "the Middle East," this statement will focus on two major dimensions of the region: first, the fate of Lebanon; second, the relationship of the Palestinian people, Israel, and the Arab states.

At the outset, we wish to say a word about our hopes and concerns in addressing this complex set of issues, fraught with such power and emotion among peoples of different faiths and convictions. We have sought in these reflections to state our concerns clearly, with balance and restraint, and with genuine respect and appreciation for the strong feelings and deep convictions of others. We believe constructive dialogue does not require silence or avoidance of differences but rather an understanding that people of goodwill can sometimes disagree without undermining fundamental relationships of respect. We hope our reflections will be perceived, understood, and discussed in this context. Our consideration of this statement has been aided by the perspectives of leaders of a number of Jewish, Muslim, and other Christian communities and organizations.

To address the Middle East is to confront a region with a sacred character and a conflicted history. To understand "the Middle East question," it is necessary to probe political, religious, cultural, and moral issues that are woven together in a complex tapestry. Reducing the reality of the Middle East to one dimension—whether it be political, military, religious, ethnic, or economic—inevitably distorts the nature of the problems people and nations face there. This quest for simplification, in turn, leads to proposals that frustrate the task of shaping a just and stable peace in the Middle East.

I. The Religious and Political Significance of the Middle East

The complexity and challenge of the Middle East are related to its unique blend of religious and political history. Because it is the birthplace of Judaism, Christianity, and Islam, the region engages the interests, the hopes, and the passions of people throughout the world. The history and geography of the Middle East are permeated by events, memories, traditions, and texts by which hundreds of millions of believers in every part of the globe, in different ways, define their religious commitments and convictions. The religious communities living in the Middle East today hold in trust the religious legacy and heritage of much of the world's population.

The sacred character and content of Middle East history provide an abiding resource of hope: that the family of Abraham, his descendants in faith, may be able to draw from their religious values and moral principles a common framework for shaping a peaceful future. As Catholic bishops, we believe this hope is well founded; religious conviction and the moral vision that flows from it can provide the motivation and direction for transforming the present conflicts of the Middle East into a stable political community of peace. However, injudicious use of religious convictions can harden political attitudes, raise contingent claims to absolute status, and obscure the fact that both prudence and justice may require political compromise at times.

It is difficult to conceive of this stable and peaceful future for the Middle East apart from the contributions of Judaism, Christianity, and Islam—a contribution that must be shaped and guided by balanced, careful, and prudent resort to each religious tradition.

The religious diversity of the Middle East is matched by its political complexity. There are very few places in the world today where the political and human stakes are as great, and where the danger of military conflict is so high. A distinguishing characteristic of the Middle East is the way in which the political life of the region has direct and often dangerous global implications. At both the regional and the global levels, therefore, the Middle East poses a major moral and political challenge.

The Region. The region, in fact, contains several distinct political conflicts. The 1980s have vividly demonstrated the destructive capacities resident in the Middle East; the carnage of the Iran-Iraq war (including the use of children as foot soldiers and the resurgence of chemical warfare), as well as the devastation of Lebanon, both testify to multiple sources of conflict in the region.

An adequate analysis of the Middle East must be grounded in a recognition of the distinct kinds of conflict that run through the area. At the same time, it is possible to identify a crucial issue that has characterized the history of the Middle East for the last forty years: the Israeli-Arab-Palestinian struggle. Both the moral dimension of the Middle East problem and its direct relationship to the larger issues of world politics are best illustrated by the continuing conflict of Israel, the Arab states, and the Palestinian people.

While the disputes are cast in political terms, it is essential to understand that each of the major parties, particularly the Israelis and Palestinians, sees its political position and objectives as having a moral basis. Political objectives are supported by moral claims on both sides. The moral claims, in turn, are grounded in and supported by historical memories. The depth and the duration of the Israeli-Palestinian conflict have produced contrasting historical memories for both sides. Israelis and Palestinians "remember" and interpret the past very differently. These different memories and interpretations of recent history provide conflicting contexts for discussion of how to pursue peace and justice in the region.

In the Passover Seder, Jews "[preserve] the memory of the land of their forefathers at the heart of their hope."[1] They recall centuries of discrimination in East and West. They remember the Shoah (the Holocaust), which in the words of Pope John Paul II is a "warning, witness, and silent cry to all humanity." At the time of the Holocaust, they found few secure places to flee to or take refuge. Israel represents for the Jewish community the hope of a place of security and safety in a world that has often not provided either for the Jewish people. Israel also represents for Israelis more than a place of security; it is regarded by them as a fulfillment of a religious promise.

Palestinians have ancient ties to the land as well. Some trace their roots to biblical times. Their history includes centuries of living under the rule of others: Byzantium, the Caliphates, the Crusaders, the Ottoman Empire, and the British Mandate. In recent times, their memories include the loss of ancestral lands and hundreds of villages; the displacement of now more than 2 million people, most living as exiles from their native land; the indifference of the world to their plight; and the frustration of their national aspirations.

The politics of the Middle East, shaped by this historical, moral, and religious background, are not politics as usual. The essential stakes in the Israeli-Palestinian conflict are the central values by which nations and peoples define their existence: security, sovereignty, and territory. It is difficult to conceive of a more fundamental definition of political conflict. Without trying to define and describe the essence of the conflict at this point, it is useful to illustrate its intense and unyielding character.

For Israel, one way to describe its policy problem is the relationship of territory to security and survival. How much territory is required to guarantee the security of the state and the survival of its people? The terms of the debate have changed over time, particularly after the 1967 War, but the essential argument—what constitutes "secure borders"—has run through Israel's history as a modern state.

The Israelis live with a sense of political and psychological vulnerability, which outside observers (especially in a country as large and physically protected as the United States) often fail to understand. Surrounded by Arab states (and formally at peace only with Egypt), Israelis see their geographical position as one of persistent vulnerability; they have an overriding sense that there is very little room for error in judging security issues. In addition to threats from other states, Israel has been continuously faced with acts of violence, including some acts of terrorism, by groups aligned with the Palestinian cause.

A result of this history, and the fact of five wars in forty years, is Israel's determination to be secure by amassing military power sufficient to offset the threat of its neighbors. In the minds of the Israelis, both the objectives they seek—security and territory—and their means are morally justified because what is at stake is their survival as a people.

The reason why many in the Middle East and in the world have not been able to identify with Israel's case in all its aspects is not simply the inability to appreciate Israeli psychology. The more substantial reason is that Israel's conception of what is needed for security, particularly after 1967, has run directly counter to Palestinian claims and the territorial integrity of neighboring states.

The problem for the Palestinians has not been security and territory alone, but territory and that sovereignty needed to guarantee security. The Palestinian case—often represented by other Arab voices in the past, but today a case made by Palestinians themselves—is that they have been deprived of territory and denied status as a sovereign state. Palestinians argue that political existence in a world of sovereign states requires recognition of sovereignty; both territory and sovereignty are needed if Palestinians, living inside and outside the Israeli occupied territories, are to realize their political identity.

The Palestinian conception of how much territory is necessary for a viable sovereign state has also changed over time. From an early policy laying claim to all the areas described as Palestine, the Palestinian position today is focused on the West Bank and Gaza. Even with this change, however, it is clear that Israeli and Palestinian positions collide over the same territory. The regional challenge in the Middle East involves the adjudication of legitimate but conflicting claims aimed at breaking the cycle of a violent past.

Global Fears. Success or failure at the regional level has global implications. The Middle East is one of the regions of the world where local conflict has the capacity to engage the superpowers. The political moral problem of the Middle East involves, therefore, not only regional justice, but global security. The threat of proliferation of nuclear weapons, ballistic missiles, and chemical weapons in the Middle East has only intensified the danger that a regional conflict would escalate to international proportions. Indeed, it must also be acknowledged that a continuing source of danger in the Middle East has been and remains the conventional arms trade, fueled by major countries outside the region—including the United States—often for reasons of commercial profit as well as political and military objectives.

A stable peace, based on the just satisfaction of the needs of states and peoples in the region, is required first of all because the citizens of the Middle East have suffered for too long. But peace there is also a requirement for the welfare of the citizens of the world. Regional justice and international security are joined in the Middle East.

II. The National Conference of Catholic Bishops and the Middle East

The Middle East can be analyzed from many perspectives. In this statement, we write as Catholic bishops, in our role as pastors and teachers. This identity shapes our approach to the issues of the Middle East.

We are bound by deep ties of faith to the Holy Land, the land of the Hebrew prophets, the land of Jesus' birth, ministry, passion, death, and resurrection. These ties are the starting point of our reflection. As bishops in the universal Church, we are guided by the continuing engagement of Pope John Paul II with all the major questions of the Middle East. Building on the pastoral concern and policies of his predecessors, the Holy Father consistently seeks to lift up before the international community the human, religious, and moral dimensions of the Middle East.

By this statement, we hope to foster the process described by the Holy Father: "that the Israeli and Palestinian peoples, each loyally accepting the other and their legitimate aspirations, may find a solution that permits each of them to live in a homeland of their own, in freedom, dignity, and security."[2] The statement also responds to Pope John Paul II's determination to protect the Lebanese people and their country: "We cannot resign ourselves to seeing that country deprived of its unity, territorial integrity, sovereignty, and independence. It is a question here of rights which are fundamental and incontestable for every nation."[3]

We are also bound by ties of solidarity with the leaders of the Christian communities in the Middle East, many of whom signed the *Statement by the Heads of the Christian Communities in Jerusalem,* and those whom they serve. We are conscious of the crucial and doubly difficult vocation of the Christians in the Middle East. In almost all situations, they live as a religious minority in a predominantly Islamic world, often under pressures of various kinds as they seek to live their faith. Yet, they also have the possibility and the duty of living their Christianity in an interreligious context, where they can witness to its value and share its resources generously.

In this statement, we express our solidarity with these Christian communities of the Middle East, especially those in Lebanon, and demonstrate our concern through an effort aimed at enhancing the search for peace in their homelands.

We approach the Middle East question conscious of three different relationships, each of which we value highly, all of which are pertinent to the quest for peace in the Middle East.

In the United States, we maintain relationships with both the Jewish and Islamic communities through our interreligious dialogue. Since the Second Vatican Council, Catholic-Jewish dialogue has made major strides. Living with the largest Jewish community in the world, we have enjoyed extensive exchanges and deepening friendship, leading to a fuller understanding of Judaism and our own faith.

Our relationships with Islamic communities in the United States are more recent, but they are expanding rapidly. As in the Catholic-Jewish dialogue, Catholic-Islamic interests range from explicitly religious issues to social questions, among which peace and justice in the Middle East have a special place. Here also the process of dialogue has enhanced our understanding of Islam and deepened our own sense of faith. Islamic-Christian dialogue is facilitated by the climate of respect for the religious convictions of others in the United States.

Finally, as bishops in the United States, we are citizens of and religious leaders in a nation with a critical role in the Middle East. In terms of both the regional and the global significance of the Middle East, the U.S. role is always important and sometimes decisive.

The relationship of the United States with Israel has been a defining element of Middle East politics in the last forty years. The very prominence of the fact, in the Middle East and in the United States itself, often obscures the extensive relationship of the United States with virtually all of the Arab states. This important relationship has been significantly enhanced by the U.S. decision to open political discussions with the Palestine Liberation Organization (PLO) in December of 1988. The United States now has the opportunity to advance the peace process and to use its influence and relationships to foster a more extensive dialogue among Israel, the Palestinian people, and the Arab states.

Public attention and discussion of the Middle East have been renewed because of the *intifada* (i.e., the Palestinian uprising), the continuing tragedy of the hostages in Lebanon, and the devastation occurring within Lebanon. We addressed the question of U.S. policy in the Middle East in 1973 and in 1978. We return to the topic in this statement because we believe that a possibility to build relationships of trust and shape a secure peace exists today in the Middle East.

As often happens in political affairs, a moment of opportunity is partly the product of conflict and suffering: this is surely the case in Lebanon, the West Bank and Gaza, in Israel, as well as in the lives of the hostages. The suffering must be lamented, but the moment of opportunity must be grasped. We are convinced that active, diplomatic engagement by the United States is needed to stimulate a new initiative for peace in the region of the Middle East. Past experience illustrates that sustained U.S. efforts, pursued at the highest level of government, can catalyze a peace process. In this statement, we focus on two aspects of the wider Middle East picture: the fate of Lebanon and the Israeli-Arab-Palestinian question. Our concern is to examine these issues in light of the challenge they pose for the Church in the United States and for U.S. policy.

We address these issues in light of the religious and moral dimensions at the heart of the Middle East. We offer these reflections as a contribution to the Catholic community and to the wider U.S. policy debate on the Middle East.

III. Lebanon: The Tragedy and the Crime

In a region that has long known war, death, and suffering, the case of Lebanon in the last fifteen years still stands out as particularly horrifying. Since 1975, over 100,000 Lebanese have been killed in a nation of 4 million; in recent months, thousands were killed or wounded in the constant shelling that left Beirut devastated and depopulated. The statistics convey some of the horror of the war in Lebanon. The tragedy lies first of all in the loss of human life, but also in the contrast between what Lebanon could have been and could be in the Middle East and what it is. Because the Middle East requires that political and religious convictions be continuously balanced, Lebanon has stood for over forty years as a daring experiment. From the time of the National Pact in 1943, the effort to weave various religious traditions into a form of democratic governance has been pursued with determination in Lebanon. The process had major flaws, and the description of the system was always better than its performance, but the Lebanese experiment in interreligious comity and democratic governance held a unique place in the Middle East. The present disintegration of both the religious and political dimensions of Lebanese society is an incalculable loss for the Middle East. As Pope John Paul II said, in his appeal to the followers of Islam:

> The eyes of the whole world behold a ravaged land, where human life no longer seems to count. The victims are the Lebanese themselves—Moslems and Christians—and day after day the ruins on Lebanese soil become ever more numerous. As children of the God of mercy, who is our creator and guide but also our judge, how can we believers allow ourselves to remain indifferent to a whole people which is dying before our very eyes?[4]

There are several causes that contributed to the terror and tragedy of Lebanon in the 1980s. It is possible to distinguish internal and external reasons for the dissolution of the Lebanese state and society. Typically, Lebanese stress the external elements, and outside observers assign major responsibility to the Lebanese themselves. However the balance is struck, both dimensions are necessary for an understanding of Lebanon in the 1970s and 1980s.

Internally, the description often given of Lebanon is that it has been the scene of what many people perceive to be a "religious war" since 1975. The reality is more complex. It is not possible to understand Lebanon apart from its religious rivalries, but it is not accurate to analyze the Lebanese conflict exclusively through a religious prism. In addition, unfortunately, many groups responsible for violence are identified, or choose to be identified, by a religious label.

The National Compact of 1943, an unwritten agreement formulated by Lebanese Christians and Muslim leaders at the time of independence, sought to achieve a balance of religious freedom and religious participation in Lebanese society for seventeen different religious groups in the country. Part of the agreement was to confirm the assignment of constitutional offices to different religious constituencies: the president was to be a Maronite; the prime minister was to be a Sunni; the speaker of the parliament was to be a Shiite. There was also a system of proportional representation in parliament. The system survived and succeeded to a degree not often acknowledged from the perspective of the 1980s. Its success should not be forgotten amidst the destruction of these past years in Lebanon.

But the system did fail to adapt and to accommodate political changes within key groups in Lebanon. Political and economic reforms were urgently needed, but not undertaken. The failure to address internal reform, the inability of the political leadership (Christian and Muslim) to shape a viable constitutional consensus, and the presence of armed Palestinians opened the way for the Lebanese political, economic, and religious controversy to get caught up in open military conflict, beginning in 1975 and continuing in much intensified form in 1989.

Internal factors alone cannot account for the history of Lebanon since 1975. The external causes of Lebanese conflict are essentially the projection of the major rivalries of the Middle East into Lebanon. The country has become the battleground of the region. The fact that there were Lebanese parties willing to strike deals with the outsiders must be acknowledged, but it does not diminish the point. Lebanon has been devastated from within and without.

In the 1970s, Palestinians were granted refuge and support by the Lebanese. Some Palestinians then tried to construct an autonomous base of operations from Lebanese soil, thereby threatening Lebanon's external relations and helping to shred its internal cohesion. In the early conflict of Lebanese and Palestinians, the Syrians entered Lebanon; they came at the invitation of other Arab states, but they have long ago outlived their welcome.

The limited legitimacy of Syria's initial intervention is exhausted; yet, it still has the capacity to play a positive role in relation to Lebanon. There is no long-term answer to Lebanon's predicament that does not include Syrian military withdrawal.

The other major intervention in Lebanon is that of Israel. The Israeli invasion in 1982, undertaken for Israel's purposes with the support of some Lebanese factions, did not end Israel's involvement in Lebanon. Israeli forces, with the cooperation of some Lebanese, continue to control part of southern Lebanon.

Another tragic and complicating factor is the holding of innocent hostages by groups and states. While the fate of U.S. hostages is understandably most on our minds and in our hearts and those of all Americans, it is no less tragic that hundreds of Lebanese citizens have also been taken hostage. The international community must condemn these unjust and unjustifiable actions and work to bring about the prompt release of all hostages.

Pope John Paul II powerfully described what is at stake in Lebanon in his Angelus Message of August 15, 1989:

> What is happening before everyone's eyes is the responsibility of the whole world. It is a process that is bringing on the destruction of Lebanon.
>
> Truly, we are confronted with a menace to the whole of international life. It is a moral menace, all the more painful because it is a weaker State that endures the violence or the indifference of stronger ones. In fact, the principle according to which it is not lawful to harm the weak, to kill the weak, is valid also in international life. Who so behaves is guilty not only before God, the supreme Judge, but also before the justice of human history.
>
> Moral guilt weighs also on all those who, in such situations, have not defended the weak when they could and should have done so.[5]

What can be done? To ask that question in 1989, after months of slaughter in Beirut, is to be faced with very narrow choices. What is at stake in the first instance is Lebanese life: the lives of women and children who have lived in bunkers and bomb shelters; the lives of the vast majority of ordinary Lebanese who are not terrorists or members of militias, but citizens who have lived and worked in a free-fire zone. At a different level, the stakes are political and cultural; the Lebanese experiment—a multi-religious, multi-ethnic democracy—must be restored. It is important for the Lebanese, and it was a crucial ingredient in the Middle East; it is now mortally threatened. What is at stake today is whether this valuable attempt of bridging both East and West and Christianity and Islam can survive or will ever be tried again.

The significance of what is at stake in Lebanon has been continually stressed by Pope John Paul II. In his letter to the secretary general of the United Nations of May 15, 1989, he said:

> At this point, the very existence of Lebanon is threatened; for many years, this country has been an example of the peaceful coexistence of its citizens, both Christian and Muslim, based on the foundation of the equality of rights, and respect for the principles of a democratic society.[6]

One need not endorse, support, or agree with some things done under the title Christian during the last fifteen years, to be able to say that Christian presence in Lebanon is an anchor for Christian life in the Middle East. What is at stake in Lebanon is not only the Christian presence, but also the way that presence there has sustained Christian hope and life in other countries of the Middle East.

What can be done? If the tragedy of Lebanon involves, in part, what some outside forces have done in the country, the crime against Lebanon is the way other outside forces have failed to provide constructive diplomatic and political support in Lebanon's hour of need. The parties who did intervene in Lebanon had interests there, but little concern for the Lebanese. What is needed are outside parties who have a concern for Lebanon, but are not self-interested parties in the usual sense of the term.

In his September 26, 1989 message to episcopal conferences throughout the world, Pope John Paul II forcefully emphasized the moral imperative that today confronts the international community in its duty to Lebanon:

> To be sure, it is not for the pope to put forward technical solutions; yet, out of concern for the spiritual and material well-being of every person without distinction, I feel that it is my grave duty to insist on certain obligations which are incumbent upon the leaders of nations. Disregard for these obligations could lead quite simply to a breakdown of orderly international relations and, once again, to the handing over of mankind to brute force alone. If rights, duties, and those procedures which international leaders have worked out and subscribed to are scorned with impunity, then relations between peoples will suffer, peace will be threatened, and mankind will end up a hostage to the ambitions and interests of those who hold the most power. For this reason, I have wished to state again and again—and I repeat it once more today on behalf of the whole Church— that international law and those institutions which guarantee it remain indispensable points of reference for defending the equal dignity of peoples and of individuals.[7]

Intervention has hurt the Lebanese, but it is seriously questionable in 1989 whether the Lebanese are capable of moving beyond war and destruction without help. It will take a mix of internal and external forces to reconstruct Lebanon. The reforms that are required—constitutionally, politically, economically, and legally—must be the work of the Lebanese themselves. They must be shaped by a generation of Lebanese political leaders who recognize that the designs of the 1940s will not fit the Middle East of the 1990s and who can command respect and loyalty across religious lines.

Successful internal reform, however, requires a setting in which the Lebanese can discuss, decide, and choose. Hence, immediate Syrian withdrawal from Beirut and ultimate withdrawal of all foreign forces from Lebanon is a necessary condition for lasting peace and democratic progress in Lebanon. At present, the Syrians have little incentive to withdraw from all of Lebanon; a larger international framework must be created that will advocate and create the conditions for Syrian withdrawal and will promise that legitimate Syrian foreign policy concerns will be addressed.

The same logic applies to Israel; it has legitimate security concerns that must be addressed, but not at the expense of Lebanon.

Creating this larger international context is a task in which the United States is an indispensable force, together with the Arab League and France. There is also the widespread conviction that Soviet influence in Syria could be considerable. The imperative is to free Lebanon of all foreign forces and to pursue the task of reconstruction of Lebanese political and economic institutions.

The Arab League, in an effort to help end the violence in Lebanon and provide an opportunity for reform, undertook an initiative in 1989 that led to a new accord adopted in Taif and was followed by the election of a new president of Lebanon. In a document such as this, we cannot fully assess the impact of events unfolding, even as we consider this statement. We call on all the parties in Lebanon, especially the Christians, as well as the United States government, to use recent developments, future opportunities, and any viable process to work toward the objectives we have already outlined: a lasting end to the violence; effective reform and reconciliation; and the final withdrawal of all foreign forces from Lebanon. In addition to necessary political reconstruction, significant economic assistance—both immediate humanitarian aid and longer-term development assistance—will be essential for Lebanon's recovery.

IV. Israel, the Arab States, and the Palestinians: Principles for Policy and Peace

During the last forty years, it is possible to distinguish two levels of the Israeli-Arab-Palestinian question. One level involves Israel and the Arab states; this conflict has been at the forefront of the wars of 1948, 1956, 1967, and 1973. From this history emerged the formula of "land for peace" in UN Resolution 242, which remains the diplomatic guideline for a lasting resolution to the Arab-Israeli conflict. The goal of the formula, exemplified in the Israeli-Egyptian Peace Treaty (1979), would return captured lands in exchange for diplomatic recognition of Israel and an end to the state of belligerency by the Arab states.

A second level of the conflict is the Israeli-Palestinian question. While this issue, increasingly the focus of attention since 1973, is embedded in the larger Arab-Israeli relationship, it has taken on its own life particularly in the light of the *intifada* in the Israeli-occupied territories of the West Bank and Gaza since December 1987.

A. Principles for Policy

The achievement of a lasting and comprehensive peace in the Middle East must address both levels of the problem. There can be no secure peace that does not eventually include full diplomatic relations between the Arab states and Israel. Anything short of this leaves the "legitimacy" of Israel undefined in the policy of the Arab states and reinforces Israel's position that the only road to survival is one requiring vastly superior military power.

Negotiations are essential for both Israel and the Arab states. All have needs that can only be met in the context of a negotiated agreement, supported by other members of the international community. Israel has justifiably sought a clear declaration of its acceptance by its Arab neighbors. The time is long past when this basic element of international life should be affirmed for Israel.

The Arab states need negotiations to address territorial claims resulting from the wars of the last forty years. The bitter disputes about the Golan Heights, the West Bank, and Gaza, which have divided the Middle East for years, must find a negotiated resolution that meets the justifiable claims of the Arab states, the security requirements of Israel, and the long-denied rights of the Palestinian people.

The Israeli-Palestinian question is theoretically distinguishable from the first set of issues, but it cannot be divorced from them. Both principles and public opinion bind the Arab states to make settlement of the Palestinian question an intrinsic part of any settlement with Israel. At the same time, it is clear that the term *Arab-Israeli conflict* is insufficient for defining the specific elements of the Palestinian question.

Unlike the formula adopted in UN Resolution 242, which treated Palestinians as refugees, the situation today—post-Rabat (1974), in light of the *intifada* (1987-1989), and after U.S.-PLO talks (1988-1989)—requires independent recognition of the rights of the Palestinian people and a specific addressing of the issues between Israel and the Palestinians. More than the UN Resolution 242 and 338 approach and the Camp David approach, in which Palestinians are in a secondary role, is needed for framing the Middle East question today.

Addressing both dimensions of the Israel-Arab-Palestinian problem, we recommend the following propositions, rooted in a moral assessment of the problem and related to its political dimensions.

1. *Pope John Paul II's Proposal.* In a series of addresses and statements, Pope John Paul II has framed a basic perspective in light of which diplomatic efforts should proceed toward a settlement of the Israeli-Palestinian question. The Holy Father has expressed the perspective in diverse forms, but with a consistent meaning: the fundamental right of both Israelis and Palestinians to a homeland. On September 11, 1987, while addressing U.S. Jewish leaders in Miami, the pope said:

> Catholics recognize among the elements of the Jewish experience that Jews have a religious attachment to the land, which finds its roots in biblical tradition.
>
> After the tragic extermination of the Shoah, the Jewish people began a new period in their history. They have a right to a homeland, as does any civil nation, according to international law. "For the Jewish people who live in the State of Israel and who preserve in that land such precious testimonies to their history and their faith, we must ask for the desired security and the due tranquility that is the prerogative of every nation and condition of life and of progress for every society."[8]
>
> What has been said about the right to a homeland also applies to the Palestinian people, so many of whom remain homeless and refugees. While all concerned must honestly reflect on the past—Muslims no less than Jews and Christians—it is time to forge those solutions which will lead to a just, complete, and lasting peace in that area. For this peace, I earnestly pray.[9]

The Holy Father reiterated this concern in his Angelus Message of October 24, 1989:

> From the Holy Land, pleas for help and solidarity are arriving from the inhabitants of the West Bank and Gaza. They are the cries of the entire people who are being particularly tried today, and who feel weaker after decades of conflict with another people bound by their history and faith to that same land. One cannot be indifferent to these pleas and to the daily suffering of so many people. To them I should like to express my deepest solidarity, assuring them that the pope continues to make his own their legitimate request to live in peace in a homeland of their own, respecting the right of every other people to enjoy the necessary security and tranquility. Let us pray to Almighty God that he may inspire all those in authority to put an end as soon as possible to so

much suffering, and that peace and harmony may be earnestly sought for that land which is holy for millions of believers: Christians, Jews, and Muslims.

On December 23, 1988, a Vatican press statement reiterated Pope John Paul II's view of the problem: "The supreme pontiff repeated that he is deeply convinced that the two peoples have an identical, fundamental right to have their own homeland in which they live in freedom, dignity, and security in harmony with their neighbors."

The assertion that each party—Israel and the Palestinian people—has a fundamental right to a homeland establishes the framework in moral terms for political negotiations. Because each party has a right to a homeland, the goal of negotiations should be fulfillment of the rights of both. Because the content of the right (territory with a legitimately recognized title to it) cannot be realized without each party accepting limits on its claim (how much territory each possesses), the classical distinction of affirming a right, then setting limits on its meaning and exercise, will have to guide negotiations.

The result of recognizing the same right in both parties, then limiting its extent to allow for fulfillment of both rights should work toward a settlement that achieves three objectives:

- First, it should formalize Israel's existence as a sovereign state in the eyes of the Arab states and the Palestinians.
- Second, it should establish an independent Palestinian homeland with its sovereign status recognized by Israel.
- Third, there must be negotiated limits to the exercise of Palestinian sovereignty so that it is clear that Israel's security is protected.

These general goals should be pursued through a process of negotiations in which appropriate guarantees for the objectives of security, self-determination, sovereignty, and territory for each party are established. We offer these objectives not to limit or predetermine the process or substance of negotiations, but to lay out key needs and requirements that ought to be addressed through good faith and serious negotiations between the parties. These objectives build upon and reflect principles that we have advocated in our statements of 1973 and 1978 and now reaffirm.

2. *Recognition of Israel's Right to Existence within Secure Borders.* Both the UN Resolution 242 and the papal statements require this recognition as a means of resolving the "security-territory" problem for Israel. In our view, this is a foundation stone for a just and stable peace. This issue is so central, as a matter of survival, in Israel's conception of its situation in the Middle East, that it is in everyone's interest for security to be guaranteed politically, strategically, and psychologically for

the Israelis. Secure borders are the means by which a nation's existence can be defended. The affirmation of Israel's right to exist necessarily entails a resolution of the question of secure borders. Resolving the issue, however, will require a disciplined definition of what constitutes adequate security. Israel's security needs must be reconciled with Palestinian needs for self-determination. The resolution of the security-territory issue cannot be based on such an expansive definition of security for Israel that the fundamental rights of other parties (especially the Palestinians and the neighboring states) are preempted.

3. *Recognition of Palestinian Rights*. At the heart of the legitimate rights of the Palestinians is the right to self-determination, including their option for an independent homeland—another foundation stone of a just peace. The right to a homeland for the Palestinians is tied to recognition of other rights:

- Their right to choose their own leadership without intervention by others
- Their right to participate as equals, through representatives selected by Palestinians, in all negotiations affecting their destiny
- The right to a clear, legitimated title to their territory, not dependent on the authority of others

The conclusion that follows from these assertions is as clear as it has been controversial: Palestinian representation in Middle East negotiations, leading to Palestinian territorial and political sovereignty.

To draw this conclusion requires recognizing limits on Palestinian rights: title to a territory of their own means disavowing larger claims to other territory in Israel. Coexistence with Israel requires an understanding that *security* is a mutual term—Palestinians will ensure secure possession of their homeland by being clear in word and deed about Israel's security and territory. There must be limits to the exercise of Palestinian sovereignty, so that it is clear Israel's security is protected. The nature of mutual security requires a willingness by all parties to accept limits on the definition and exercise of their rights. Limits on Israel's definition of its security claims and on Palestinian pursuit of their territorial claims are complementary. Acceptance of limits is crucial to a conception of mutual security between the two peoples. In addition, respect for each other's right to a homeland requires scrupulous observance by both parties of the principle of non-intervention.

It is important to emphasize that the solution of the Palestinian situation cannot rest simply on Israel. All the states in the region, as well as others in the international community, have a responsibility to help address the legitimate aspirations of the Palestinian people and to seek an effective response to their expressed need for territory and sovereignty.

4. *Fulfillment of UN Resolutions 242 and 338.* These two resolutions still embody central principles for any lasting settlement in the Middle East. Other texts help to fill out the picture in light of changed and changing circumstances in the region (e.g., Egyptian-Israeli Peace Treaty [1979]; Fez Summit [1982]; the Arafat Statements [December 1988]), but they do not dispense with UN Resolutions 242 and 338.

The thrust of UN Resolution 242 is to assert the formula of land for peace, to secure acceptance of Israel by the other Middle East states, and to affirm the inadmissibility of the acquisition of territory by war.

5. *Human Rights and Religious Freedom.* This principle is crucial throughout the Middle East. Respect for human rights is a precondition for stable peace; this is a conviction that our episcopal conference has consistently affirmed.[10] The very diversity of the religious communities in the region and the differences among political regimes mean that constant vigilance about religious liberty is required. Moreover, it is critical to emphasize that religious freedom means not only respect for the personal conscience of believers, but also recognition of the rights of religious communities to worship, to establish and maintain churches and educational institutions, and to sponsor social institutions. The Palestinians (Christian and Muslim) and the Israelis (Jewish, Christian, and Muslim) can be an example of religious toleration and pluralism to all the world. In contrast to this hope, we are deeply concerned by the threat posed to Christian and other communities in the Middle East by militant movements that often reject tolerance and pluralism.

Another threat to this principle is the existence of attitudes that deny the human dignity and human rights of persons because of their religion, race, or nationality. Prejudice or bigotry in speech, behavior, and the media against either Jews or Arabs intensifies conflict in the region and inflames discussion of the Middle East in the broader world community. As the Pontifical Justice and Peace Commission said in its November 1988 document, *The Church and Racism: Towards a More Fraternal Society:*

> Amongst the manifestations of systematic racial distrust, specific mention must once again be made of anti-Semitism. . . . Terrorist acts which have Jewish persons or symbols as their target have multiplied in recent years and show the radicalism of such groups.[11]

Anti-Arab prejudice, ethnic hatred, and bigotry also clearly undermine the dignity and rights of Palestinians and other Arab people. Their humanity is assaulted by brutal stereotypes, unfounded generalizations, and other traditional forms of prejudice. The search for peace in the Middle East must be guided by respect for the rights of all and opposition to every form of prejudice that denies the dignity of the human person.

6. *Compensation for Past Losses.* The long and destructive history of the Israeli-Palestinian struggle has left many with just claims for compensation. Both the Palestinians and the Israelis can document these claims, and in our judgment, the claims should be carefully reviewed and met. We are convinced that the achievement of a just political settlement would move many states and other institutions to assist this process legally and financially.

7. *The Status of Jerusalem.* The city of Jerusalem has been a contested issue in the Arab-Israeli-Palestinian question since 1948. Clearly, the ultimate status of the city cannot be settled by unilateral measures.

Here we reaffirm and support the basic principles set forth by the Holy See on several occasions:

- The sacred character of Jerusalem as a heritage for the Abrahamic faiths should be guaranteed.
- Religious freedom of persons and of communities should be safeguarded.
- The rights acquired by the various communities regarding shrines, holy places, educational and social institutions must be ensured.
- The Holy City's special religious status and the shrines proper to each religion should be protected by "an appropriate juridical safeguard" that is internationally respected and guaranteed.

It is useful to recognize that these elements are not fulfilled by simply discussing who has sovereignty in Jerusalem, nor do these elements require any one particular form of jurisdiction or sovereignty. They neither demand nor exclude one civil power exercising sovereignty in the city of Jerusalem.

B. *The* Intifada

The principles just outlined find a specific reference in the Israeli-Palestinian question. It is this aspect of the Middle East that the *intifada* has pushed to the center of the moral and political agenda. For much of the last decade, the Palestinian question has been overshadowed by the Egyptian-Israeli negotiations, the hostage crises, the Iran-Iraq War, the Persian Gulf conflict, and the Lebanese War.

It was precisely when others seemed to ignore them that the Palestinians in the Israeli-occupied territories of the West Bank and Gaza took matters into their own hands. Since December 1987, Palestinians have demanded that Israel, the United States, the Arab states, and the international community pay attention to them again. The *intifada* has been an effort to recast the policy agenda in the Middle East.

There are several possible ways to interpret the significance of this event of the *intifada*. Here, its political, psychological, and human rights significance strike us as important to highlight. Politically, the *intifada* is a statement that, after more than twenty years of military occupation, the Palestinians refuse to accept this status. The essence of the Palestinian claim is that the present political situation in the Israeli-occupied territories rests upon an injustice, a denial of fundamental human rights.

Psychologically, the pressing of their political position through the *intifada* has provided a new sense of political self-determination and solidarity for a whole generation of Palestinians. The central theme that needs to be lifted up and repeated is that the *intifada* is a cry for justice; it is a cry for personal and political identity; it is an expression of the personal and political rights that Palestinians have as human beings worthy of being respected as individuals and as a people.

The scope and duration of the *intifada* have created the strongest challenge yet mounted against Israel's military rule in the West Bank and Gaza since 1967. The government of Israel has recognized the fundamental political challenge posed by the *intifada* and it has responded by attempting to suppress it. The U.S. government's human rights report concisely captures the response. The Israeli government sees the *intifada* not simply as a civil disturbance, but "as a new phase of the forty-year war against Israel and as a threat to the security of the state."[12] Israeli concerns about this security threat coexist with their need to maintain public order in the face of the newly aroused Palestinian resistance.

The measures taken in this "war" have produced the strongest human rights criticism—inside and outside of Israel—in the twenty-two years of occupation.

The U.S. government's *Country Reports on Human Rights Practices for 1988* documents several principal categories of human rights violations, including but not limited to:

- Excessive use of force resulting in many Palestinian deaths
- Physical abuse and beatings of prisoners and of others not directly involved in demonstrations
- Demolition and sealing of homes
- Closing of educational institutions
- Arbitrary arrest, detention, and exile

Of particular concern to us as bishops is the April 1989 *Statement by the Heads of Christian Communities in Jerusalem,* describing their peoples' experience of constant deprivation of their fundamental rights and tragic and unnecessary loss of Palestinian lives, especially among minors:

> In Jerusalem, on the West Bank, and in Gaza our people experience in their daily lives constant deprivation of their fundamental rights because of arbitrary actions deliberately taken by the authorities. Our people are often subjected to unprovoked harassment and hardship.[13]

The precise adjudication of distinct human rights claims is open to continuous review, but the deeper political question—the justice and legitimacy of Palestinian demands for territory and sovereignty—is the fundamental issue posed by the *intifada*. It is precisely the political foundation of the *intifada*, a reality acknowledged both by the Palestinians and the Israelis, that gives it special significance. It is for this reason that the *intifada* is chosen here for attention among the many serious human rights issues in the Middle East.

V. U.S. Policy: Recommendations

We have had U.S. policy in mind throughout this statement since we write as bishops of the United States. The purpose of this section, however, is to draw out more specifically a set of recommendations for U.S. policy in light of the assessment we have made of the Middle East. Our concern here is to relate the moral principles found within this statement to specific choices in the U.S. policy discussion. By definition these specific judgments are open to debate and to amendment in light of changes in the Middle East.

What is not open to debate is the need to move forward in the Middle East peace process. The status quo is untenable for the peoples of the Middle East and the broader world community. The method of progress must be dialogue; it is the tested alternative to violence. Pope John Paul II has described the dynamic of dialogue that can lead to peace:

> I exhort that consideration with sincere good will be given to every positive and constructive gesture that may come from either party. The road of dialogue in the search for peace is certainly arduous and tiring, but each obstacle that is removed can be considered true progress, certainly worthy of inspiring other corresponding gestures and the needed confidence to proceed.[14]

The specific policy recommendations we make in this section are all designed to enhance a movement toward dialogue, promoting confidence among the parties and removing obstacles in the search for a just peace. The recommendations highlight the role of the United States, but the appeal to a broader dialogue involves in the first instance the parties to the conflict in the Middle East. The key to successful political dialogue will be Palestinians willing to discuss secure boundaries and stable political relations with Israel, and Israelis willing to discuss territory and sovereignty with Palestinians. Successful political dialogue will require Arab states to assure Israeli legitimacy and security, and it will require Israeli commitment to land for peace. The Israel-Egypt negotiations of the 1970s provide a model for successful dialogue. They also highlight the essential role of the United States in fostering such negotiations.

Presently, there are several proposals to begin negotiations advocated by different parties. The Israeli government advanced a proposal on May 14, 1989. President Mubarak of Egypt has offered recommendations that build upon the Israeli plans. The Mubarak Plan is a creative initiative, designed to expand upon other initiatives and to transcend both procedural and substantive obstacles. Palestinian representatives and other states have called for an international conference as the forum for Middle East negotiations.

Without entering a discussion of these proposals, our purpose is to urge consideration of them and to reiterate our conviction that dialogue and negotiation are the road to peace in the Middle East.

Dialogue—practical, realistic negotiations—based on a firm commitment to secure a just peace is also a key to the survival of Lebanon. The dialogue required is between Lebanese and Lebanese, about the internal structure and polity of their country. But a diplomatic dialogue of Syrians and Israelis with the Lebanese is needed as well.

The United States is positioned to help break the political impasse in the Middle East. It cannot substitute for others, but it can assist them. Our recommendations are offered to urge more active diplomatic engagement by the United States in the process of seeking and making peace in the Middle East.

A. *The U.S.-Soviet Relationship in the Middle East*

One of the elements that leads us to believe there is a new moment—indeed an open moment—in the Middle East is the possibility for constructive change in the U.S.-Soviet relationship.

For many years, the Soviet Union has been at the margin of Middle East developments. Recent Soviet statements seem to suggest that the Soviet "new thinking" on foreign policy is not satisfied to stay at the margin. At the same time, the tenor and themes of Soviet statements indicate a willingness to play a more constructive role in the region.

It is evident that superpower rivalry in the past forty years has intensified the danger of the Middle East and has made resolution of key issues very difficult. If a shift of orientation allows a more coordinated superpower approach to the region, the change should be welcomed and pursued.

The perspective that should guide the superpowers is one that gives priority to the welfare of the local states and people. It should not be an imposition of superpower views on weaker states.

B. *The United States and Lebanon*

The horror and tragedy of Lebanon demand more systematic attention from the United States than they have received in several years. The United States cannot "solve" the Lebanese problem, but the Lebanese cannot overcome the legacy of a fifteen-year war without outside moral, diplomatic, humanitarian, and economic assistance. The dissolution of Lebanon as a nation could move relentlessly forward; without the diplomatic and humanitarian—but not military— intervention of major outside powers, Lebanon as a sovereign state could pass tragically into history.

Some Lebanese believe the United States is sacrificing Lebanon to larger Middle East policy goals. Whatever the reason for believing this to be the case, the United States must take steps immediately to demonstrate that it is not. The United States should pursue a clear, consistent policy, pressing for the withdrawal of all foreign forces from Lebanon. The United States should also be actively involved in supporting the process of constitutional reform and reconciliation in Lebanon. Finally, the United States should lead and help coordinate an effort of international assistance designed to alleviate the scars of war and to begin a systematic process of rebuilding Lebanese society and the economy.

C. *The United States, the Palestinians, and the* Intifada

The fact of the *intifada* demands—on both moral and political grounds—a more creative and constructive response by the U.S. government.

Human rights violations should be addressed in light of U.S. policy and legislation on human rights. The assessment of the situation found in the *Country Reports on Human Rights Practices for 1988* is a solid beginning and should be taken into account in the implementation of U.S. policy.

As noted above, the *intifada* points beyond human rights questions to the deeper political issue of Palestinian rights to a homeland. In our discussion of principles for policy, we have set forth what we believe is needed to address the security, sovereignty, and territory issues between the Israelis and Palestinians. The United States should (1) continue its political discussions with the Palestinians and raise the level of this exchange and (2) clearly express its support for a Palestinian homeland and Palestinian political rights. At the same time, the U.S. role should be to obtain Palestinian clarification of the December declaration accepting Israel's existence and the terms of UN Resolutions 242 and 338. Such discussions could lead, in turn, to broader diplomatic talks with both Israelis (clarifying their acceptance of 242 and 338) and Palestinians about measures needed to guarantee secure borders for both parties. This can also lead to more specific discussion of how the Palestinians and Israelis would see the measures needed to build trust and confidence between the two peoples.

The United States should continue to press with the Palestinians the principles affirmed by John Paul II: that dialogue is the road to peace in the Middle East, "while excluding any form of recourse to weapons and violence and above all, terrorism and reprisals."[15]

The relevance of this principle extends, in our view, to all parties in the Middle East. The people of the region have too long been subject to the scourge of war, to a repeated pattern of violence, and to acts of terrorism that inevitably strike the innocent and the vulnerable in civilian populations. Such acts of terrorism have neither moral nor political justification and should be condemned without qualification.

D. The United States and Israel

U.S. support for Israel is basically a sound, justified policy in the interests of both nations and can contribute to the progress needed in the Middle East to produce peace for Israel, its Arab neighbors, and the Palestinians. U.S. support for Israel—politically, strategically, and morally—should be continued. This proposition does not conflict with the need for the United States to maintain its own position on a range of issues, at times in opposition to Israel, nor does it conflict with concern for human rights. For example, the United States regards the Israeli settlements in the West Bank as legally problematic and an impediment to peace.

As bishops, we believe that U.S. aid to Israel, as to other states, should have as its purpose the pursuit of peace with justice for all people.

E. The United States and the Arab States

The political settlement of the Middle East requires, as we have said, stable, just relations between Israel and the Arab states, as well as settlement of the Israeli-Palestinian question.

While U.S. relations with the Arab states vary across a spectrum, there is substantial influence with many of the key states. The United States should continue to encourage, persuade, and press Israel's neighbors to normalize relations with Israel, within the context of negotiations for settling the Arab-Israeli-Palestinian conflicts.

The history of four major wars, the needs of the Arab states themselves, and the fact that Israeli willingness to address Palestinian concerns is contingent upon the attitude of Arab states toward Israel—all point to the need to "normalize" the political map of the Middle East.

The history of the Middle East in the past forty years has been marked by failure of the Arab states as well to respond adequately to Palestinian needs and aspirations. Today, there is clearly a consensus of moderate Arab states that is seeking a settlement of the Palestinian question, based on land for peace. The United States should encourage this consensus and press Israel to see and grasp this moment of opportunity.

VI. Conclusion

It is our conviction that a truly open moment for peace exists in the Middle East, and that the United States has an indispensable role to play in the peace process that has moved us to write this statement. As religious leaders, it is our hope and our prayer that this moment will be seized, that our nation will meet its responsibilities to advance the cause of peace. To grasp the open moment, to transform the potential for peace into a real process for peace will require the best efforts of many institutions, communities, and individuals. In this statement, we have found it necessary to probe some of the complexities of the Middle East in order to highlight the moral principles and problems that lie at the heart of the Middle East question.

We believe, however, that even beyond the political and moral intricacy of the Middle East there is a deeper reality that must be recognized and relied upon in the pursuit of a just peace. The deeper reality is the pervasive religious nature of the Middle East: its territory, history, and its peoples have been visited by God in a unique way. The religious foundations of the Middle East have political and moral relevance. The search for peace in the region requires the best resources of reason, but it also should rely upon the faith, prayer, and convictions of the religious traditions that call the Middle East their home.

True peace cannot effectively be built with new policies and guarantees alone. True peace also requires the building of trust between peoples, even when history divides them. Steps are needed now to encourage greater dialogue, to deepen trust, and to build confidence between the diverse peoples of the Middle East. As believers, as people of faith, we find in our three religious traditions the resources for mutual trust and hope; the call to reach across political, religious, ethnic, and geographic boundaries; and the summons to work for peace.

Above all else, the achievement of a just and lasting peace is a grace and gift of God. Although human peacemakers have their essential roles—and are blessed by Muslims, Christians, and Jews—ultimately, peace comes as a work of God in history.

We request the prayers of all believers for peace in the Middle East. In *The Challenge of Peace* (1983), we called on our people for prayer, fasting, and Friday abstinence for the sake of peace. Here, we renew that call with special reference to the Middle East. We also pledge continuing dialogue with our Jewish and Muslim partners and friends. In our three religious traditions, we share two central themes: (1) the capacity for hope in the face of difficulty and danger, and (2) the pursuit of peace in the face of conflict and violence. Let us seek to turn our hopes into true progress toward genuine and lasting peace.

Notes

1. The Holy See, Commission for Religious Relations with the Jews, "Notes on the Correct Way to Present the Jews and Judaism in Preaching and Catechesis of the Roman Catholic Church," *Origins* 15:7 (July 4, 1985): section VI.
2. John Paul II, Angelus Address for First Sunday of Advent, *L'Osservatore Romano* [English edition] 49 (December 5, 1988): 1.
3. John Paul II, "Address to Diplomatics Corps Accredited for the Holy See," *L'Osservatore Romano* [English edition] 7 (February 13, 1989): 2.
4. John Paul II, "Appeal to Followers of Islam," *L'Osservatore Romano* [English edition] 40 (October 2, 1989): 2.
5. John Paul II, Angelus Address for the Assumption, *L'Osservatore Romano* [English edition] 34 (August 21, 1989): 1.
6. John Paul II, "Letter to the United Nations General Secretary (May 15, 1989)," *L'Osservatore Romano* [English edition] 22 (May 29, 1989): 2.
7. John Paul II, "Letter to All Bishops of the Catholic Church Concerning the Situation in Lebanon (27 September 1989)," *L'Osservatore Romano* [English edition] 40 (October 2, 1989): 1.
8. Pius XII, *Redemptionis Anno* (1954).
9. John Paul II, *Unity in the Work of Service* (Washington, D.C.: United States Catholic Conference, 1987), 28-29.
10. National Conference of Catholic Bishops, *A Word of Solidarity, A Call for Justice: A Statement on Religious Freedom in Eastern Europe and the Soviet Union* (Washington, D.C.: United States Catholic Conference, 1988).
11. Pontifical Justice Peace Commission, *The Church and Racism: Towards a More Fraternal Society* (Washington, D.C.: United States Catholic Conference, 1988), no. 15.
12. U.S. Department of State, *Country Reports on Human Rights Practices for 1988* (Washington, D.C.: Government Printing Office, 1989), 1377.
13. Statement by the Heads of the Christian Communities in Jerusalem.

14. John Paul II, "To Build Peace, Respect Minorities," Message for the World Day of Peace (January 1, 1989), *L'Osservatore Romano* [English edition] 51-52 (December 19/26, 1988): 2.

15. John Paul II, Angelus Address for First Sunday of Advent, *L'Osservatore Romano* [English edition] 49 (December 5, 1988): 1.

Source: Washington, D.C.: United States Catholic Conference, 1989.

Called to Compassion and Responsibility: A Response to the HIV/AIDS Crisis

A Statement of the National Conference of Catholic Bishops

November 1989

I. Introduction

1. The Many Faces of AIDS

The *Human Immunodeficiency Virus* (hereafter HIV) continues to spread throughout the world. As a contribution to the nation's response to this complex disease and its devastating consequences, we wish to help turn ignorance into understanding and understanding into action. We, the Catholic bishops of the United States, approach this task from the perspectives of faith and reason: faith which believes that health and sickness, life and death have new meaning in Jesus Christ;[1] and moral reasoning which supports the insights concerning human nature and individual dignity, which we here affirm. We address this statement to the Catholic community and to all people of goodwill. It is our hope that these reflections will stimulate discussion and foster understanding of the ethical and spiritual dimensions of the HIV crisis.

We speak conscious of the interest and discussion occasioned by the release in 1987 of *The Many Faces of AIDS: A Gospel Response by the Administrative Board of the United States Catholic Conference*.[2] As that document itself pointed out, it was "not intended to be the last word on AIDS, but rather a contribution to the current dialogue."[3] Meeting in Collegeville, Minn., in the spring of 1988, our conference of bishops committed itself to issuing a further document.[4]

There are good reasons for doing so. Public discussion concerning HIV has intensified in the last two years, and new facts, fears, and initiatives have emerged. The AIDS crisis has worsened. The need for compassion has grown more urgent. Also, we are mindful of the 1988 *Report of the Presidential Commission on the Human Immunodeficiency Virus Epidemic*,[5] which calls upon religious groups to be of "special assistance," especially by emphasizing "the worth and dignity of every human being."

The Many Faces of AIDS made several important points, which we now reaffirm.

1. AIDS is an illness to which all must respond in a manner consistent with the best medical and scientific information available.
2. As members of the Church and society, we must reach out with compassion to those exposed to or experiencing this disease and must stand in solidarity with them and their families.
3. As bishops, we must offer a clear presentation of Catholic moral teaching concerning human intimacy and sexuality.
4. Discrimination and violence against persons with AIDS and with HIV infection are unjust and immoral.
5. Social realities like poverty and oppression and psychological factors like loneliness and alienation can strongly influence people's decisions to behave in ways which expose them to the AIDS virus.
6. Along with other groups in society, the Church must work to eliminate the harsh realities of poverty and despair.
7. The expression of human sexuality should resemble God's love in being loving, faithful, and committed. Human sexuality in marriage is intrinsically oriented to permanent commitment, love, and openness to new life.
8. The spread of AIDS will not be halted unless people live in accord with authentic human values pertaining to personhood and sexuality.
9. Since AIDS can be transmitted through intravenous drug use, there is need for drug treatment programs, a halt to traffic in illicit drugs, and efforts to eliminate the causes of addiction.
10. Considering the widespread ignorance and misunderstanding about HIV infection and its modes of transmission, educational programs about the medical aspects of the disease and legitimate ways of preventing it are also needed.

2. The Church's Concern

As we enter more deeply into the public dialogue regarding HIV infection, we are conscious of the social responsibility of the Church. In his encyclical letter *On Social Concern,* Pope John Paul II speaks of it in these terms:

> The Church is an "expert in humanity," and this leads her necessarily to extend her religious mission to the various fields in which men and women expend their efforts . . . in line with their dignity as persons. . . . In doing so the Church fulfills her

> mission to evangelize . . . when she proclaims the truth about
> Christ, about herself and about man, applying this truth to a
> concrete situation. The teaching and spreading of her social
> doctrine are part of the Church's evangelizing mission. And
> since it is doctrine aimed at guiding people's behavior, it con-
> sequently gives rise to a commitment of justice, according to
> each individual's role, vocation, and circumstances.[6]

As far as HIV is concerned, moreover, social responsibility has an
important international dimension. The problem is not confined to the
United States and cannot be solved only here. We are deeply conscious
of the devastation this terrible disease is bringing to many other parts
of the world. The United States must play a significant role in responding to the worldwide dimension of the disease.

The Church enters into this conversation in the conviction that
"faith throws a new light on everything, manifests God's design for
man's total vocation, and thus directs the mind to solutions which are
fully human."[7] Indeed, "only God . . . provides a fully adequate
answer to these questions. This he does through what he has revealed
in Christ his Son. . . ."[8]

The 1988 *Report of the Presidential Commission* states: "The term 'AIDS'
is obsolete. 'HIV infection' more correctly defines the problem. The medical, public health, political, and community leadership must focus on the
full course of HIV infection rather than concentrating on later stages of
the disease (ARC and AIDS)."[9]

3. Progress to Date

Real progress has been made in the battle against HIV infection.
For example:

- Dioceses throughout the United States have made significant
  strides in addressing the HIV epidemic. The steps include
  providing care for children with AIDS, opening and maintaining hospices for persons with AIDS, maintaining facilities for
  homeless people, providing pastoral and health care through
  Catholic health facilities, implementing HIV education programs, and publishing documents that address the issue of
  HIV infection and its prevention.
- The medical community has developed therapies that extend
  the lives of people with HIV infection while enhancing their
  quality. New discoveries raise hopes for the eventual cure or
  prevention of the disease.
- The federal government has adopted a more realistic approach
  to this health crisis. The twelve chapters of the *1988 Report of*

the Presidential AIDS Commission contain important recommendations requiring close study and response.[10]

- Numerous volunteer groups and organizations, including those of the homosexual communities, have made significant efforts in caring for those with HIV and have developed new and effective services to help meet the many unmet needs of those who are ill.

Many, though not all, persons with AIDS have many of the following characteristics: young; alienated from family; frightened (of isolation and abandonment, of pain and suffering, of dependency and loss of control); embarrassed and/or guilty; more or less alone; possibly angry; isolated by societal attitudes and a backlash of anger; without financial resources.

4. The Obstacles Remaining

Numerous obstacles to addressing the AIDS problem still remain.

- Self-abusive behavior through drug abuse and sexual promiscuity continues in this country.
- Lack of education about HIV in large segments of the society fosters continued misunderstanding about the epidemic. For example, confusion about how the infection is transmitted generates some unwarranted fear and undue alarm.
- Technology often outpaces ethical reflection; the study of ethics is widely neglected in school curricula.
- People infected with HIV or at risk of infection may not be aware of their situation; others shirk their basic moral obligation to refrain from behavior that can do grave harm to others.
- Public campaigns often promote solutions that are contrary to morality and against human dignity.
- Persons infected with HIV still too often suffer discrimination, disrespect, violence, and inhumane treatment.
- There is a lack of adequate housing, "step-down units," and home health care.
- Federal funding for AIDS care remains insufficient.

5. More to Accomplish

While encouraged by progress in the struggle with HIV, we must not exaggerate it. Where research is concerned, for example, the Fifth International Conference on AIDS held in Montreal in June 1989 noted that even the well-studied AIDS virus known as HIV-1 has not yielded up all its secrets.

HIV infection is transmitted mainly in three ways: through sexual contact (e.g., exchange of blood, semen, and vaginal secretions); through parenteral exposure (needle-sharing for drugs, blood transfusions); and through perinatal exposure (i.e., a mother infected with HIV can transmit the virus to her baby during pregnancy, delivery, or breastfeeding).

Statistics show that AIDS is spreading, with large increases in AIDS cases and deaths projected in the years ahead. As many as 54,000 Americans may die from AIDS during 1991 alone.[11]

More accurate statistical systems to monitor HIV infection are badly needed. Since many people are infected with HIV for long periods before showing symptoms of AIDS, health officials still do not know the current extent of the epidemic. Not only will the lives of many of these infected persons be substantially shortened, all of them also are capable of transmitting the infection and thereby spreading the epidemic.

Furthermore, without better data the nation cannot really know whether current strategies for controlling the spread of the virus are working. Nor will we be able to prepare adequately for future demands for hospital beds and health care services.

As we write, the number of diagnosed AIDS cases in the United States is more than 100,000.

- HIV is increasingly emerging as a problem for minorities and the homeless in inner cities.
- In most parts of the country AIDS remains largely a disease of homosexual men.
- Nearly 20,000 Americans are expected to be afflicted with AIDS in the next four years from transfusions administered before HIV blood screening was begun.
- Higher rates of AIDS among adults have resulted in more cases among newborn children who were infected by their mothers' blood in the womb. No less tragic are AIDS cases among children born to drug-addicted parents.[12]

All this bears out an assertion made at the 1989 Montreal International Conference on AIDS: The HIV epidemic is following an uncontrolled, unstable, volatile, and dynamic course.[13]

It is of critical importance to recognize the shift of the disease to economically disadvantaged populations. In the opinion of the Centers for Disease Control (CDC), AIDS may become predominantly a minority disease. This would be disastrous for African Americans and Hispanics. Though only 12 percent and 8 percent of the U.S. population, respectively, they currently account for a disproportionate 24 percent and 14 percent of the reported U.S. cases of AIDS, according to CDC statistics. The figures are even more striking for women with AIDS, some 52 percent of whom are African American and 20 percent Hispanic, and for children with the disease (80 percent African American or Hispanic).

There is a clear connection between these figures and the fact that, according to the National Institute on Drug Abuse, an estimated 70 percent of the nation's 1.28 million intravenous addicts are African American or Hispanic. Underlying this statistic, of course, are the social and psychological injuries inflicted by poverty and discrimination.

6. Some Basic Facts About HIV and AIDS

While our basic concern as bishops is the moral teaching and pastoral outreach of the Church to those affected in any way by the growing HIV infection across the country, still we must point out the various medical, scientific, and sociological dimensions of the problem. Here we give a brief overview of some of these key issues.

Infection with HIV is followed by incubation and latency periods whose duration varies enormously from individual to individual. It is currently thought that 50 percent will develop full-blown AIDS within 10.8 years, 75 percent within 16 years, and "almost 100 percent in 30 years."[14]

Although people who are HIV-infected do not manifest AIDS symptoms during the subclinical period, they are subject to serious emotional, social, and physical problems. At the point when AIDS is diagnosed, a variety of symptoms emerge: prolonged fevers; rashes; swollen lymph glands; fungi around the nails; oral thrush; shingles; lymphoma; severe psoriasis; cryptococcal meningitis; cancers of the tongue, rectum, and brain; and the illnesses classically associated with the disease, pneumocystis carinii pneumonia and Kaposi's sarcoma (lesions that spread over the body surfaces). These are opportunistic infections that, in various combinations, eventually prove fatal. Also, 75 percent of people with AIDS suffer significant brain damage often leading to dementia.[15]

While the progress of the HIV infection cannot be predicted in every case, there are identifiable stages.

- HIV-positive or antibody-positive: The blood shows antibodies indicating exposure to HIV. At this "seropositive" stage, the individual may remain asymptomatic for five to ten years, but he or she can transmit the virus to others.
- ARC (AIDS-Related Complex): This includes symptoms such as chronic diarrhea, recurrent fevers, weight loss, persistent swelling of the lymph nodes. The term "ARC" has fallen into disfavor, however, because of medical disagreements regarding these symptoms and manifestations.

- AIDS: This refers to the most severe clinical manifestations of the HIV infection. It includes opportunistic infections, as well as the pneumocystis carinii pneumonia and neoplasms such as Kaposi's sarcoma.

7. Three Problems and the Need for Education

HIV/AIDS is not only a biomedical phenomenon but a social reality rooted in human behavior. It is a product of human actions in social contexts. The actions and their circumstances are shaped by larger cultural and social structures.

Associated with this epidemic are at least three widespread problems.

First, there is the public health problem. As applied to HIV/AIDS, the term epidemic is sometimes misunderstood. Typically during an epidemic, new cases of a disease increase dramatically in a short period of time, peak, then decline; there may also be cycles of rise and decline.[16] The following points are important to understanding the HIV/AIDS epidemic.

- AIDS cases lag behind the spread of HIV infection. Typically, years elapse between the time an adult is infected with HIV and the diagnosis of AIDS. Thus, current counts of new AIDS cases do not tell us how widely HIV is spreading.
- A decline in either the spread of HIV infection or new AIDS cases, or both, would not mean that the danger had passed. HIV is already substantially seeded in the U.S. population. It will likely continue to spread, if not in epidemic form, then in a persistent, more stable "endemic" (literally, "dwelling with the people") form.
- The threat of epidemic and endemic disease will be most serious for groups most heavily seeded with HIV infection. These are IV drug users and homosexual and bisexual men who have sex with men, as well as their female sexual partners and offspring.
- AIDS data suggest that the African American and Hispanic populations may be more heavily seeded with HIV infection than other ethnic groups and may be disproportionately threatened by the virus.[17]

The second problem concerns discrimination arising from ignorance and fear.[18] The *1988 Presidential Report* affirms: "Fear and misunderstanding about HIV infection has been the underlying cause of much of the anxiety, hostility, and discrimination shown towards HIV-infected individuals." The result has been a variety of unconscionable deeds: the fire-bombing of a family's home because their sons had AIDS; the exclusion of students from school because they are infected with HIV; the isolation and virtual quarantining of other children in school situations; refusal by physicians and health care workers to care for persons with AIDS; and assertions that a cure for AIDS will never be found because it is God's judgment on its victims.

The third problem is the refusal to discuss publicly the direct link between sexual activity and intravenous drug use on the one hand and HIV/AIDS on the other. Silence about the connection between these forms of behavior and HIV/AIDS is not only intellectually dishonest, but unfair to those at risk.

HIV/AIDS must be opposed with early diagnosis, testing, education, counseling, and persuasion. People must be shown the right thing to do and encouraged to make right choices. The discovery of effective therapies or vaccines, desirable as those are, would not change the need for personal accountability and response. In this respect, the HIV/AIDS epidemic is similar to outbreaks of other, non-fatal diseases transmitted by particular kinds of behavior. For example, gonorrhea and syphilis persist in the United States even though drugs effective against them have been available for forty years. The obvious lesson is that to eradicate some diseases, people must desist from the behavior that spreads them. Given the severity of the HIV/AIDS epidemic, this need is particularly great.

The spread of HIV can be controlled by lasting changes in the way people act. We repeat: People need education and motivation, so that they will choose wisely and well. Providing information that is both accurate and appropriate is a logical and necessary starting point. This requires understanding an intended audience in order to formulate and deliver a persuasive message. Educational programs and public information campaigns cannot rely simply on fear as a motive. They must provide convincing assurances that something can be done to prevent infection—that the changes in behavior that are being recommended are possible and will do some good. These educational programs should be directed to both individuals and groups.

8. The Intent of This Document

In the remainder of this document we issue five calls: to compassion, to integrity, to responsibility, to social justice, and to prayer and conversion. For "the joys and the hopes, the griefs and the anxieties of the people of this age, especially those who are poor or in any way afflicted, these too are the joys and the hopes, the griefs and the anxieties of the followers of Christ."[19]

II. A Call to Compassion

1. Compassion and Human Dignity

Compassion is much more than sympathy. It involves an experience of intimacy by which one participates in another's life. The Latin word *misericordia* expresses the basic idea: The compassionate person has a heart for those in misery. This is not simply the desire to be kind. The truly compassionate individual works at his or her own cost for the others' real good, helping to rescue them from danger as well as alleviate their suffering.

2. The Ministry of Jesus

We learn compassion's meaning from the model of Jesus. His ministry contains many examples. He gives sight to the blind (Mt 20:30-34; Mk 10:46-52; Lk 18:35-43) and makes the crippled walk (Mt 9:2-7; Mk 2:3-5; Lk 5:18-24); he touches and heals lepers (Mt 8:3; Mk 1:41; Lk 5:13); he shares a meal with people considered legally impure (Mt 26:6; 9:10; 11:11; Mk 2:15-16; Lk 5:30); he shames the judges of the adulterous woman and forgives her sin (Jn 8:1-10). With compassion, Jesus breaks through the barriers of sickness and sinfulness in order to encounter and heal the afflicted.

He tells us to do as he did, for "whatever you did for the least brothers of mine, you did for me" (Mt 25:40). We need to bear in mind his warning on this matter.

> When the Son of Man comes in his glory . . . all nations will be assembled before him. . . . Then he will say to those on his left, "Depart from me, you accursed. . . . For I was hungry and you gave me no food, I was thirsty and you gave me no drink, a stranger and you gave me no welcome, naked and you gave me no clothing, ill and in prison, and you did not care for me. . . . What you did not do for one of these least ones you did not do for me." And these will go off to eternal punishment. (Mt 25:31-32, 41-46)

3. The Good Samaritan

The story of the Good Samaritan presents the call to compassion in concrete terms (Lk 10:30-37). Pope John Paul II graphically demonstrated its meaning when in 1987 he embraced a young boy with AIDS at Mission Dolores Basilica in San Francisco. This was a way of saying that in each case AIDS has a human face, a unique personal history. The Holy Father verbalized that message on Christmas Day 1988, in his "*Urbi et Orbi*" blessing. "I think of them all, and to all of them I say, 'Do not lose hope.'" And he added that those with AIDS are "called to face the challenge not only of their sickness but also the mistrust of a fearful society that instinctively turns away from them." On May 4, 1989, he returned to this subject, declaring in a homily in Lusaka that the Church "proclaims a message of hope to those of you who suffer . . . to the sick and dying, especially those with AIDS and those who lack medical care."[20]

In his apostolic letter *On the Christian Meaning of Human Suffering* (1984),[21] Pope John Paul II calls each of us to imitate the Good Samaritan: "Man owes to suffering that unselfish love which stirs in his heart and actions. The person who is a 'neighbor' cannot indifferently pass by the suffering of another."[22]

In his 1987 visit to Mission Dolores Basilica, Pope John Paul II spoke of the meaning of compassion—again, in the specific context of AIDS.

> The love of God is so real that it goes beyond the limits of human language, beyond the grasp of artistic expression, beyond human understanding. And yet it is concretely embodied in God's son, Jesus Christ, and in his Body the Church. . . . God loves you all, without distinction, without limit. He loves those of you who are elderly, who feel the burden of the years. He loves those of you who are sick, those who are suffering from AIDS and from AIDS-Related Complex. He loves the relatives and friends of the sick and those who care for them. He loves us all with an unconditional and everlasting love.[23]

Persons with AIDS are not distant, unfamiliar people, the objects of our mingled pity and aversion. We must keep them present to our consciousness, as individuals and a community, and embrace them with unconditional love. The Gospel demands reverence for life in all circumstances. Compassion—love—toward persons infected with HIV is the only authentic gospel response.

III. A Call to Integrity

1. The Dignity of the Human Person

In his 1980 encyclical *Rich in Mercy*, Pope John Paul II says that compassion and mercy are rooted in the recognition of human dignity and integrity. Authentic compassion and mercy call us to "a whole lifestyle [that] consists in the constant discovery and persevering practice of love as a unifying and also elevating power despite all difficulties of a psychological or social nature."[24]

In praying to the Father "that they may all be one . . . as we are one" (Jn 17:21-22), Jesus revealed something we could not have known by ourselves: There is a likeness between the unity of the divine persons in the Trinity and the unity of human persons with one another. In practical terms, we learn from the model of the Trinity that we become most fully ourselves by giving ourselves to others.[25] An abuse of self is somehow also an act of injustice to others, and, by the same token, the abuse of others is an abuse of self and an abuse of our relationship with God, the Creator and Father of us all.

All human beings are created in God's image and are called to the same end, namely, eternal life in communion with God and one another. For this reason, the greatest commandment is to love the Lord with all one's heart and soul and mind, and the second is like the first: to love one's neighbor as one's self.[26] For people growing daily more mutually dependent and a world in which interdependence is increasing, this is a truth of paramount importance since it provides a transcendent rationale for the pursuit of good human relationships.

2. Human Integrity

God is love (1 Jn 4:9). This means that the inner reality of God is a mystery of relationship. But God has created humankind to share in his divine life (Gn 1:26-27). The basic goodness of humanity is confirmed in Genesis 1:31: "God looked at everything he had made, and he found it very good."

Pope Paul VI in his encyclical *Humanae Vitae* (1968) underscored the importance of the "total vision of man."[27] Yet today this "total vision" is often dismissed or ignored in favor of particular elements or aspects of personhood and limited ideas of human fulfillment.

Fundamentally, we are called to realize the basic goodness of our personhood as God has created it. This is not a prerogative or an obligation only for Christians. Everyone, whether believer or nonbeliever, is obliged to honor the integrity of the human person by respecting himself or herself along with all other persons.[28]

The meaning of sexuality and personhood can only be fully discerned within this framework of human integrity. In God's plan as it existed at the beginning (Gn 1:1, 17) we find the true meaning of our bodies: We see that, in the mystery of creation, man and woman are made to be a gift to each other and for each other. By their very existence as male and female, by the complementarity of their sexuality, and by the responsible exercise of their freedom, man and woman mirror the divine image implanted in them by God.

The Church makes an invaluable contribution to society by pointing out that the full meaning of human integrity is found within the context of redemption and its call in Christ to "live in newness of life" (Rom 6:4).[29] St. Paul reminds us that redemption means, among other things, that we must "respect" our own bodies and the bodies of others and must live always "in holiness and honor." By self-respect and mutual respect we observe God's original plan.

Originally, God endowed our bodies with a harmony which St. Paul speaks of as "mutual care of the members for one another." It corresponds to that authentic "purity of heart" by which man and woman "in the beginning" were able to unite as a community of persons. Now, by redeeming us, Jesus graces us with a new dignity: the Holy Spirit dwelling within us. We are called to live as temples of the Spirit.

All this requires that we understand ourselves, and live, not just naturalistically, as it were—as bundles of bodily drives and instincts—but in a manner that respects the integrity of our personhood, including its spiritual dimension. Through the grace of the Spirit, that can be done.

3. The Challenge of Chastity

Human integrity requires the practice of authentic chastity. Chastity is understood as the virtue by which one person integrates one's sexuality according to the moral demands of one's state in life. It presupposes both self-control and openness to life and interpersonal love, which goes beyond the mere desire for physical pleasure. In particular, desire for union with another must not degenerate into a craving to possess and dominate. Chastity calls us to affirm and respect the value of the person in every situation.

While chastity has special meaning for Christians, it is not a value only for them. All men and women are meant to live authentically integral human lives. Chastity is an expression of this moral goodness in the sexual sphere. It is also a source of that spiritual energy by which, overcoming selfishness and aggressiveness, we are able to act lovingly under the pressure of sexual emotion. Chastity makes a basic contribution to an authentic appreciation for human dignity.

4. Obstacles to Integrity and Chastity

Many factors militate against the practice of chastity today. Our culture tends to tolerate and even foster the exploitation of the human person. People are pressured to seek power and domination, especially over other persons, or else to escape into self-gratification. Television, movies, and popular music spread the message that "Everybody's doing it."

One can scarcely exaggerate the impact this has. Casual sexual encounters and temporary relationships are treated on a par with permanent commitment in marriage. It is taken for granted that fidelity and permanence are not to be expected, and may even be undesirable. Sin is made easy because the reality of sinfulness is denied.

What is sin? It is an act motivated by the deliberate refusal to live according to God's plan. It is a disruption, more or less serious, of the order that should prevail in our relationships with God and with one another. It is the root cause of alienation and disintegration in individual and social life. It is a practical denial of God's presence in oneself and one's neighbor.

5. The Challenge and Call to Youth

A. Hope of the Future

The obstacles to human integrity of which we speak are especially daunting today for young people. Yet the Church sees in the young the hope of the future. As Pope John Paul II said at the youth assembly in Los Angeles in 1987: "The future of the world shines in your eyes. Even now you are helping to shape the future of society."[30]

That underlines how necessary it is that the rest of us help young people live chaste and responsible lives. Youth should be a time of idealism. And most young people do wish to do what is right. They want to be responsible, and they are capable of understanding that authentic integrity, while demanding much of them, offers them rich rewards in individual and communal fulfillment. Adults for their part must actively support young people, not stand by idly while media and other social influences inundate them with amoral and immoral messages.[31]

Integrity and chastity, which we propose here, are virtues that, with God's grace, can be realized by all people of goodwill, by people of any religion and indeed of no religion. But their realization not only presupposes a creation that is good, it presupposes a willingness on society's part to create and sustain a social environment in which individuals truly can know and choose what is right.

Perhaps the most important thing that adults can do in this regard is themselves to be models of upright living. Young people are bewildered by the contradiction between adult preachments about the dangers of drugs and alcohol and adult reliance on the same substances; by adult messages on the theme of sexual responsibility and adult models of extreme irresponsibility in the sexual sphere. This sort of double standard has a debilitating impact on the young.

B. Youth, Sexuality, and Marriage

The sexual dimension of a person is ordered to the establishing and maintaining of honest, committed personal relationships. The Holy See's *Declaration on Certain Questions Concerning Sexual Ethics* affirms that sexuality is not only "one of the principal formative elements in the life of a man or woman" but also "the source of the biological, psychological and spiritual characteristics which . . . considerably influence each individual's progress toward maturity and membership in society."[32]

Sexual intercourse is an expression of maturity achieved within the committed relationship of marriage. Adolescents who engage in sexual intercourse are sometimes misled into believing that they have already arrived at maturity; indeed, many are pressured to have sexual intercourse precisely as a sign that they have reached adulthood. Not only is this a great temptation for them, it fails the test of human integrity.

Sexual intercourse is meant to be both exclusive and committed, and it has these characteristics only in marriage. It should never be regarded as a form of conquest or as a means of paying for attentions. One of the great evils of casual sexual intercourse is that, more often than not, the relationship is exploitative for one or both of the parties.

Nor does sex before marriage really shed light on whether a potential partner is, for example, trustworthy, even-tempered, capable of loving and being loved, caring, affectionate, industrious, considerate, faithful, sensitive, stable, disciplined. It takes time and a variety of different friendships to find a suitable marriage partner. During adolescence, young people should be developing attachments and testing them through companionship. In this process, sexual intercourse is not a research tool for ascertaining compatibility. Rather, it is meant for marriage, to express and complete a compatibility whose existence has already been established by more reliable means.

Sexual intimacy is thus a sign of a special kind of relationship, which has two inseparable aspects: It is unitive (the persons give themselves unreservedly to each other, take permanent and public responsibility for each other, accept the risk of a shared life), and it is procreative (that is, fundamentally related to begetting, bearing, and raising children).

Sexual intercourse is the expression of this special marital relationship. Only in the context of this relationship do genital sex acts have full human meaning. It is marriage that gives intercourse its true meaning.

Once a man and woman are married, they begin a journey that is uniquely theirs. Sexual intercourse forms part of the background against which they grow in love and knowledge of each other. The words of Pope John Paul II in *Familiaris Consortio* are of great importance: "To bear witness to the inestimable value of the indissolubility and fidelity of marriage is one of the most precious and most urgent tasks of Christian couples in our time."[33] Important, too, is what he said to young people in 1987 at the Louisiana Superdome:

> Jesus and His Church hold up . . . God's plan for human love, telling you that sex is a great gift of God that is reserved for marriage. At this point, the voices of the world will try to deceive you with powerful slogans, claiming that you are unrealistic, out of it, backward, even reactionary. But the message of Jesus is clear: Purity means true love and it is the total opposite of selfishness and escape.[34]

C. Youth and HIV

National studies on contraception and teenage pregnancy suggest that young people are not particularly knowledgeable or skillful in dealing with their sexual lives. Moreover, teenage pregnancy is very often related to socioeconomic problems. The experience of poverty is frequently accompanied by fatalism, deprivation, and boredom, while pregnancy holds out the promise of status and a sense of self-worth. These circumstances have at least two implications for the transmission of HIV. First, there is a large group of heterosexually active but relatively immature young people; second, there is little understanding of how to encourage change in their behavior patterns once these are already well established.

This, however, is scarcely a problem only for the poor. Today sexual intercourse seems to be an element in the experience of a majority of young people in our country.[35] For some, apparently, it is no longer linked to marriage or even to permanent relationships. Yet, at the same time, many young men and women feel profound anxiety in their struggles to establish sexual identity and fit sexuality into their lives. This underscores how critically important it is that the moral and religious values we have sketched in speaking of integrity and sexuality be properly taught to the young.

Education in human sexuality that tells young people in effect that abstinence and "safe sex" are equally acceptable options sends a contradictory, confusing message. Nor should education in sexuality be reduced to mere biological facts and processes, unrelated to their ethical significance.

We repeat: Young people need to know the human and religious meanings of personal integrity and chastity. Chastity requires treating the gift of human sexuality with reverence. Chastity is both a human attitude and a spiritual gift that helps overcome selfishness and aggressiveness. It empowers people to act lovingly while avoiding destructive relationships that are superficial and trivializing.[36]

Jesus tells us: "Love one another as I have loved you" (Jn 15:12). His self-giving, life-giving love led him to accept the cross as an unavoidable part of carrying out his redemptive mission. In the name of self-giving love, we too must accept the discipline of sacrifice so as to achieve true happiness and fulfillment for ourselves and others. Casual and permissive sex does not prepare people for faithfulness in marriage or help them appreciate the sanctity and dignity of the human person.

IV. A Call to Responsibility

1. AIDS and Homosexuality

It is a matter of grave concern that, while many homosexual persons may be making changes in specific sexual practices in response to HIV/AIDS, fewer may be choosing to live chaste lives.[37] This further underlines the critical importance of the Church's teaching on homosexuality.

In 1975 the Congregation for the Doctrine of the Faith presented this teaching in its *Declaration on Certain Questions Concerning Sexual Ethics*.[38] The document reiterates the Church's constant teaching regarding the intrinsic immorality of homosexual activity, while recognizing that not every homosexual is "personally responsible" for his or her homosexual orientation.

The teaching was further clarified in 1986 in the Congregation's *Letter to the Bishops of the Catholic Church on the Pastoral Care of Homosexual Persons*. It affirms the Church's view that heterosexuality is normative. While homosexual inclination in itself is not a sin, neither is homosexual activity "a morally acceptable option."[39] This conclusion rests on the vision in Genesis of the God-given complementarity of male and female and the responsibility for the transmission of human life.

HIV and AIDS have had a terrible impact on the homosexual community. The *Report of the Presidential Commission* says, for example, that "Violence against those perceived to carry HIV . . . is a serious problem. The Commission has heard reports in which homosexual men in particular have been victims of random violent acts that are indicative of some persons in society who are not reacting rationally to the epidemic. This type of violence is unacceptable and should be condemned by all Americans."[40] We emphatically condemn such violence. It is entirely contrary to gospel values.

The Church holds that all people, regardless of their sexual orientation, are created in God's image and possess a human dignity which must be respected and protected. Thus we affirmed in *To Live in Christ*

Jesus (1976): "The Christian community should provide them [homosexual persons] with a special degree of pastoral understanding and care."[41] Specific guidelines regarding such pastoral support are found in our 1973 document *Principles to Guide Confessors in Questions of Homosexuality*. It envisages a pastoral approach that urges homosexual persons to form chaste, stable relationships.[42]

2. AIDS and Substance Abuse

As we have stressed, however, HIV/AIDS is by no means exclusively a homosexual problem. Intravenous drug use also plays a large role in the spread of HIV. Nearly 70 percent of the reported cases of heterosexually acquired AIDS in the United States have been associated with IV drug use; almost 75 percent of pediatric AIDS cases have been diagnosed in cities with high seroprevalence rates among IV drug users. These data, combined with the potential for the rapid spread of HIV infection among IV drug users through needle-sharing, define a problem whose solution requires both immediate action and long-term research.

Drugs and HIV are linked in several ways.

1. Direct transmission of HIV occurs through the sharing of hypodermic needles, syringes, and paraphernalia used in "shooting up" drugs.
2. Sexual transmission occurs from infected IV drug users to their sexual partners.
3. Perinatal transmission occurs when women who are IV drug users or the sexual partners of drug users become infected and transmit the virus to their infants during pregnancy, delivery, or breast feeding.[43]

One must also recognize the fact of increased sexual risk and needle-using behavior on the part of persons under the influence of drugs or alcohol. Even with good intentions, abusers may not live up to promises they have made to themselves and others. Those at risk because of their use of alcohol and drugs are called to change their behavior. They merit our special attention and need to be embraced in light of their double burden of illness and addictions.[44]

In evaluating the moral issue here, it is important to see substance abuse as an actual or potential disease for some persons—a disease, however, for which there are treatment and hope. It should not be supposed that a confirmed substance abuser can simply stop, and this assumption—that the addict would stop if he or she really wanted to—can easily become a rationale for not aggressively encouraging treatment. Often, drug or alcohol abuse points to an underlying emotional illness of which it is a symptom rather than the cause. We believe those who suffer from substance abuse should be referred to appropriate treatment programs and should also receive necessary mental health counseling.[45]

While drug abuse is a chronic, progressive, life-threatening disease, addicts can be freed from this form of enslavement. Participation in a treatment program is as an interim step that allows substance abusers to receive comprehensive psychological help and counseling on how to avoid HIV.

As that suggests, drug dependency treatment should always be accompanied by education and counseling about the risk of infection and how to avoid it. Education for intravenous drug users who reject treatment should focus on the risk of repeated exposure to HIV and on the availability of help in conquering their addiction.

In this whole area, education and treatment are of paramount importance. Specific programs suited to particular groups are needed. Persons who have not begun intravenous drug use but are at risk of doing so may be reached through programs in elementary and high schools; those who do not attend school may be reached through health clinics and clinics for sexually transmitted disease, neighborhood and religious groups, day care centers, employers, job-training programs, and street outreach projects; in areas with high rates of drug use, health departments can open storefront AIDS education centers and use mobile vans, with staffing by professionals and "street smart" personnel.

Education and treatment aimed at changing behavior are the best way to control the spread of HIV among intravenous drug users and to prevent passage of the virus to their sexual partners and to children in the womb. Although some argue that distribution of sterile needles should be promoted, we question this approach for both moral and practical reasons:

- More drug use might result while fewer intravenous drug users might seek treatment.
- Poor monitoring could lead to the increased spread of HIV infection through the use of contaminated needles.
- Distribution of sterile needles and syringes would send a message that intravenous drug use can be made safe. But IV drug users mutilate and destroy their veins, introduce infection through contaminated skin, inject substances that often contain lethal impurities, and risk death from overdoses.

A better approach to the drug epidemic would be increased government support for outreach and drug treatment programs.

3. AIDS and the Use of Prophylactics

The "safe sex" approach to preventing HIV/AIDS, though frequently advocated, compromises human sexuality and can lead to promiscuous sexual behavior. We regard this as one of those "quick fixes," which the *Report of the Presidential Commission* says foster "a false sense of security and actually lead to a greater spread of the disease."

Sexual intercourse is appropriate and morally good only when, in the context of heterosexual marriage, it is a celebration of faithful love and is open to new life. The use of prophylactics to prevent the spread of HIV is technically unreliable.[46] Moreover, advocating this approach means, in effect, promoting behavior that is morally unacceptable. Campaigns advocating "safe/safer" sex rest on false assumptions about sexuality and intercourse. Plainly they do nothing to correct the mistaken notion that nonmarital sexual intercourse has the same value and validity as sexual intercourse within marriage.[47]

We fault these programs for another reason as well. Recognizing that casual sex is a threat to health, they consistently advise the use of condoms in order to reduce the danger. This is poor and inadequate advice, given the failure rate of prophylactics and the high risk that an infected person who relies on them will eventually transmit the infection in this way. It is not condom use that is the solution to this health problem but appropriate attitudes and corresponding behavior regarding human sexuality, integrity, and dignity.

By contrast, there is an urgent need for education campaigns in the media, in schools, and in the home that foster a view of human sexuality that is sound from every point of view.[48] At the same time, we are conscious of the powerful relationship between economics—the profit motive—and the promotion of contraceptives, pornography, and the marketing of sex in entertainment. This fact should be taken into account in our education efforts.

V. A Call to Social Justice

1. Continued Research and Care

We urge continued scientific and medical research aimed at finding a cure for HIV as well as treating persons with AIDS. Government agencies should draw up clear educational guidelines on the use and effectiveness of new and emerging drugs (e.g., AZT, azidathymidine).[49] Similarly, government and private agencies should provide the public with information about new methods and drugs.

Social justice also requires that public and private agencies seek creative ways to meet the health and human service needs of those who are HIV-positive. To date, acute general hospitals have borne the primary burden of caring for this population. It is imperative that a continuum of care be developed that allows for the integration of all necessary services within a given community: nutritional services, home health care, ambulatory care, transportation, hospital services, extended and/or skilled nursing care, and hospice services.

Such a system of care will assure the appropriate placement within the continuum of care of persons who are HIV-positive or who have AIDS and will avoid placing an unnecessary and inappropriate burden on any given sector of the provider community. All health and human services for persons who are HIV-positive or who have AIDS should be delivered in a sensitive and nondiscriminatory manner. At the same time, we also recognize the right of surgeons and other medical personnel to adequate protection against HIV.[50]

The health and human services described should be available to all who suffer from the disease including those without the resources to pay.[51]

2. Routine Voluntary Testing and Educational Programs

Broadly based routine voluntary testing and educational programs are needed as a matter of public policy. These voluntary programs should always guarantee anonymity and should be preceded and followed by necessary counseling for individuals diagnosed as HIV-positive or -negative. Counseling should supply information about the disease, the moral aspects involved, immediate emotional support, and information about resources for continuing emotional and spiritual support. It should also underscore, sensitively but forthrightly, the grave moral responsibility of individuals with HIV to inform others who are at risk because of their condition.

3. Immigrants and Refugees

There are special problems associated with HIV testing for immigrants and refugees: For example, false positive test results from other countries may have the effect of excluding people from the United States. In addition, permanent resident aliens may be unjustly deported before their circumstances can be adequately examined. A more flexible and humane government policy seems necessary.

4. The Person with HIV/AIDS as a Handicapped or Disabled Person

A growing body of legislation considers the individual with HIV a handicapped or disabled person. In 1978, in a statement on persons with disabilities, we said: "Defense of the right to life . . . implies the defense of other rights that enable the individual with disabilities to achieve the fullest measure of personal development of which he or she is capable."[52]

Pope John Paul has recently spoken to this same point, defending the inalienable dignity of all human persons and the need especially to protect those "who are vulnerable and most helpless: this is the task which the Catholic Church, in the name of Christ, cannot and will not forsake."[53]

Discrimination against those suffering from HIV or AIDS is a deprivation of their civil liberties. The Church must be an advocate in this area, while also promulgating its own nondiscrimination policies in employment, housing, delivery of medical and dental care, access to public accommodations, schools, nursing homes, and emergency services.

5. Those Who Care for Persons with HIV

The provision of HIV/AIDS services involves some unusual problems. One of these is stress on staff. Many feel a growing and eventually intolerable sense of helplessness as they watch patients, mostly young people, die. In providing services, it is important to take into account how long a particular individual can remain on the front line, as it were, and to provide support systems that help these dedicated people deal with their own grief and anger. We also urge all health facilities to develop practical guidelines to protect physicians, nurses, paramedics, and all other health care workers against contracting HIV and to provide adequate training and supplies for infection control.

Similar guidelines should be developed for the protection of law enforcement and corrections personnel and others in public service who may be at risk.

Dioceses should also develop guidelines not only for preventing infection but also for respite and counseling for health care professionals, volunteers, and pastoral workers, and for family and loved ones who care for HIV-infected persons.

While some have allowed their disapproval of the actions of certain persons with AIDS to interfere with the provision of care to these persons, the *Report of the Presidential Commission* points out that this is a "minority view."[54] Generally speaking, health care workers tirelessly provide quality care to HIV sufferers with compassion and sensitivity.

We applaud and thank them and we encourage all health professionals to rise to the same high level of care and beneficence.

6. Families of Persons with AIDS

The consequences of whether a person with HIV/AIDS lives hopefully or dies in despair are borne not only by that individual but also by his or her entire family.[55] An HIV or AIDS diagnosis may mark the first time the family has had to confront a loved one's drug problem or homosexuality. This sharp encounter with a difficult reality can lead to anger, guilt, sorrow, and even rejection on the part of family members; it can even drive a family into a kind of collective isolation. Families should recognize that Jesus has set for all of us an example of loving kindness to all persons and that he calls us to reconciliation with those from whom we have been estranged.

Catholic communities, especially parishes, should reach out to these families with understanding and practical help—for example, by providing respite time from caring for their sick members. Acceptance and emotional and spiritual support are crucial needs.

Families of HIV patients badly need to talk about what they are experiencing. Although family members usually are ambivalent about disclosing the nature of their relative's disease to outsiders, it is important for them to communicate. The Catholic community should create networks of people prepared to assist such families in this way.

7. The Public Good and Confidentiality

A. Nondiscrimination and Individual Privacy

Our understanding of the common good expresses our vision as a people of the kind of society we want this to be. The common good is, therefore, central to the evaluation of legislative and public policy proposals. Two objectives are fundamental to any adequate understanding of the common good: first, preserving and protecting human dignity while guaranteeing the rights of all; second, caring for all who need help and cannot help themselves.

The appropriate goals of AIDS-related legislation include helping to prevent the transmission of HIV; providing adequate medical care; and protecting civil rights, that is, nondiscrimination in employment, schooling, entertainment, business opportunities, housing, and medical care, along with the protection of privacy.

Dioceses and church-related institutions should also pursue these objectives in appropriate ways through their own policies and practices. Their hiring decisions, for example, should not be based on the fact that particular job applicants are HIV-infected but on other factors such as qualifications, ability to do the work, and moral character.

Individual privacy and liberty are highly valued in our society. Liberty, however, carries with it the obligation not to harm or interfere with others. If HIV-infected persons have rights that others must respect, they also must fulfill their fundamental ethical responsibility to avoid doing harm to others. As the *Report of the Presidential Commission* says, this is "an affirmation of the rights of others."[56]

B. Rights of the Human Person

Framing and implementing public policy frequently requires the balancing of individual and community rights and interests. With respect to HIV/AIDS, it is important to infringe as little as possible, in light of community needs, on individual liberty, privacy, and confidentiality. Other, quite specific, conditions must also be met. For example, respect for persons requires informing people that they are being tested when donating blood; they also have a right to be informed of test results; and both pre- and post-testing counseling should be available.[57]

Although specific exceptions might be made, universal mandatory testing does not seem justified at this time.

C. Disclosure and Confidentiality: General Guidelines

While the presumption should always favor confidentiality, there may be circumstances that warrant disclosure. In deciding for disclosure or confidentiality in a particular case, the following points are relevant.

1. The two main factors in favor of disclosure are (a) the need to prevent the infection of others and (b) the need to provide medical care to the person who is HIV-positive or has AIDS. If disclosure in a particular case will reduce the danger of infection to others or increase the ability to treat the individual effectively, it may be the right course of action if no other effective action is possible.
2. Of primary importance in weighing the individual's interest in and right to confidentiality are (a) the ability to confine the disclosure to those who have the right to know, (b) the likelihood that recipients of the information will use it for proper purposes, and (c) the obligation to maintain patient confidentiality.

VI. A Call to Prayer and Conversion

1. Discover Christ in Those Who Suffer

Our response to persons with AIDS must be such that we discover Christ in them and they in turn are able to encounter Christ in us. Although this response undoubtedly arises in the context of religious faith, even those without faith can and must look beyond suffering to see the human dignity and goodness of those who suffer.

Without condoning self-destructive behavior or denying personal responsibility, we reject the idea that this illness is a direct punishment by God.[58] At the same time, we recognize that suffering and sickness are consequences of original sin, which each of us has confirmed by personal sin.

Even as he permits human suffering, however, God wills to bring out of it some greater good for our sake. Jesus reveals a God who is compassionate and forgiving. Sinners are special objects of his merciful love. And who are the sinners? We have all been touched by original sin, and all of us commit personal sins of our own. The story of the prodigal son (Lk 15:11-32) calls each of us to personal conversion and reform. The prodigal son discovered that the way he had chosen, the way of sin, was leading him to death. His very life hung on the choice to return to his father. And the father's love was so total, so unconditional, that he joyfully welcomed his son home. Mindful of our own misguided and sinful choices, we also must return to God, our Father, who waits to embrace us with open arms.

2. Suffering and Death

Pope John Paul II urges those who suffer never to lose heart. Christ, the innocent Son of God, knew suffering in his own flesh. For us, too, suffering, accepted and lived as Jesus accepted and lived it, can be redemptive.[59]

Faith does not tell us to seek suffering for its own sake, but it does tell us that suffering and death, joined to the suffering and death of Jesus, the Lord of life, lead ultimately to growth, fulfillment, and lasting joy. The experience of suffering can be a vital time in one's life, a time for becoming reconciled both to life and to death and for attaining interior peace.[60]

Finally, suffering and death lead to the resurrection. Death is not the end. Christ gathers up suffering, sin, and death into his triumph. His resurrection means we also have a future which God is preparing for us in the midst of suffering and death, just as Christ's glory was being prepared on the cross.

But suffering has meaning not just for those who suffer. In the case of HIV and AIDS, the entire Christian and human community is called to respond with compassion, love, and support. Any suggestion of assisted suicide or euthanasia as a response offends against human integrity and God's law. Our fundamental task is to assist the suffering and dying, not to terminate their lives.

Every human death somehow mirrors the death of Christ: It is the entrusting of the spirit to him who created us for eternal life.[61] The Christian can be serene in the face of death because of Jesus' promise: "In my Father's house there are many dwelling places. . . . I am going to prepare a place for you" (Jn 14:2).[62] Life and death are not polar opposites but points on a continuum that leads to eternal life.

3. Christian Hope and Joy

Hope is an essential component of the Christian response to suffering and death. Persons with AIDS and their families and loved ones need prayer and spiritual support to sustain them in hope. At the very heart of human life lie profound questions about meaning, identity, individual and communal destiny, transcendence, reconciliation, love, God. This is the context of Pope Paul VI's words concerning Christian hope: "It is indeed in the midst of their distress that our fellow men need to know joy, to hear its song."[63]

The lives of holy men and women offer many examples of hope and joy in the midst of difficulties and sufferings. One thinks of St. Thérèse of Lisieux, a young woman who suffered greatly, and who courageously abandoned herself into the hands of God, entrusting her littleness to him. One thinks of the message of Mother Teresa of Calcutta, who reminds us constantly that love is stronger than hatred, life than death, and that the lives of ordinary people bear witness time and again to the human capacity for extraordinary courage and compassion. Persons with AIDS, she holds, are Jesus among us. Christian hope and joy guard us against the temptation to desert them—and him.

4. Ministry to Persons with HIV/AIDS

The Church offers all its members the rich treasury of grace through its sacramental life. For those who are ill, the Church offers the sacrament of the anointing of the sick, together with the sacrament of penance and the eucharist. These encounters with Christ in forgiveness, healing, and the restoration of the life of grace are profound moments of conversion and renewal. For family members, as well as health care workers, these same sacramental sources of grace provide the inner strength and needed hope that the world cannot give. We encourage all who minister in the Church to bring the full sacramental life of Christ to those who most need to be touched by his healing hand.

We urge daily prayer for those suffering from HIV and AIDS. We also encourage dioceses to provide qualified priests, deacons, religious, and lay people who will communicate the necessary information about HIV/AIDS. Every diocese should have a list of resource persons and support systems for persons with HIV/AIDS and their families. Where appropriate, a diocese should also have a person responsible for coordinating its ministry in this area. Dioceses should likewise develop training programs for those who minister to people affected by AIDS (e.g., eucharistic ministers in hospitals, visitors to the sick, confessors, and counselors). Catholic health facilities should continue to provide local professional leadership in responding to the needs.

5. The Church and Those Who Suffer

In sum, then, in its ministry to and for persons with HIV/AIDS, the Church calls everyone to conversion; offers sacramental reconciliation and human consolation; seeks to assist all those who suffer; proclaims faith's explanations of suffering, sin, and death in the light of the cross and the resurrection; and accompanies those who suffer on their journey of life while helping them face death in the light of Christ. We recall again the words of *Salvifici Doloris:*

> In the messianic program of Christ, which is at the same time the program of the Kingdom of God, suffering is present in the world in order to release love, in order to give birth to works of love towards neighbor, in order to transform the whole of human civilization into a "civilization of love."[64]

We offer this document in response to the need—of the nation; the Church; and countless communities, families, and individuals—to confront the crisis of HIV and AIDS. The crisis continues, but it can be met with understanding, justice, reason, and deep faith.

HIV/AIDS brings with it new anguish and new terrors and anxiety, new trials of pain and endurance, new occasions for compassion. But it cannot change one enduring fact: God's love for us all. We proclaim anew this message: "God so loved the world that he gave his only Son, so that everyone who believes in him should not perish but might have eternal life" (Jn 3:16).

Notes

1. "None of us lives for oneself, and no one dies for oneself. For if we live, we live for the Lord, and if we die, we die for the Lord; so then, whether we live or die, we are the Lord's" (Rom 14:7-8).
2. United States Catholic Conference Administrative Board, *The Many Faces of AIDS: A Gospel Response* (Washington, D.C.: United States Catholic Conference, 1987).
3. Ibid., 6. *The Many Faces of AIDS* treats nine basic topics: (1) gospel values; (2) facts about AIDS; (3) societal responsibilities; (4) health care professionals/institutions; (5) testing; (6) persons with AIDS; (7) public policy; (8) pastoral issues; and (9) prevention of AIDS.
4. See "AIDS Discussion at June Bishops' Meeting," *Origins* 17:43 (April 7, 1988): 726; and "AIDS Statement: Proposal of Cardinal Bernardin Accepted," *Origins* 18:8 (July 7, 1988): 118-120.
5. *Report of the Presidential Commission on the Human Immunodeficiency Virus Epidemic* (Washington, D.C.: The Commission, June 1988).
6. John Paul II, *On Social Concern (Sollicitudo Rei Socialis)* (Washington, D.C.: United States Catholic Conference, 1988), no. 41.
7. Second Vatican Council, *Pastoral Constitution on the Church in the Modern World (Gaudium et Spes)*, no. 11.
8. Ibid., no. 41.
9. 1988 *Report of the Presidential Commission, Executive Summary,* xviii.
10. The chapters of this report are Incidence and Prevalence; Patient Care; Health Care Providers; Basic Research, Vaccine, and Drug Development; The Public Health System; Prevention; Education; Societal Issues; Legal and Ethical Issues; Financing Health Care; The International Response; and Guidance for the Future.
11. HIV and AIDS statistics change rapidly. Here we present only some current data. The Centers for Disease Control (CDC) projects, for example, that by 1992, 20,000 AIDS cases nationally will have been diagnosed in those who had blood transfusions before HIV screening in early 1985. The CDC also reports the alarming statistic that presently there is a 0.2 percent rate of HIV infection among 16,861 college students. The General Accounting Office maintains that AIDS cases are now underreported, with the true toll a third higher than reported. In addition, 2 percent of those infected are under 13 years of age; 58 percent are white; 26 percent are African American; 15 percent are Hispanic; and 1 percent are Asian and Pacific Islanders. As we write, figures for those with AIDS vary slightly (not substantially), depending on the source. See *AIDS: Sexual Behavior and Intravenous Drug Use,* Charles F. Turner, Heather G. Miller, and Lincoln E. Moses, eds. (Washington, D.C.: National Academy Press, 1989).

    - 73 percent are homosexual and bisexual men
    - 17 percent are IV drug users
    - 3 percent are those without a well-defined risk factor
    - 1 percent are children
    - 1.6 percent were infected by blood transfusions
    - 1 percent are hemophiliacs
    - 1 percent are heterosexuals exposed to those in risk categories

12. See "The Epidemiology of AIDS in the U.S.," *Scientific American* 259 (October 1988): 72-81; and "Prevalence of HIV Infection Among Intravenous Drug Users in the United States," *Journal of the American Medical Association* 261 (May 12, 1989): 2677-2684.

13. "Report from Montreal: The Fifth International AIDS Conference," AIDS commentary, ed. Bernard McNamara, M.D., (Los Angeles: Design Alliance to Combat AIDS, 1989). Dr. Jonathan Mann, chief of the World Health Organization's AIDS Campaign, spoke of the epidemic's history in the first eight years during which its existence was known. He indicated that between 5 and 10 million people have been infected worldwide. He said that half were in Africa, 40 percent in America, less than 10 percent in Europe, and only a tiny fraction in Asia and the Pacific Islands. Mann further spoke of a disturbing change, namely, that the epidemic is exploding in countries such as Thailand, where viral infections have multiplied twentyfold among intravenous drug users and more than tenfold among prostitutes. He indicated that in West Africa the epidemic is spreading swiftly in many of this continent's larger cities. As another example, in Brazil, a new urban epidemic of cocaine injection has caused a threefold rise in AIDS infections; and in Spain and Italy, infections originating in drug abuse now account for more than 60 percent of all AIDS cases. By the turn of this century, Mann said, at least 6 million people will have the disease or will have died from it. The startling numbers of homeless people infected with the HIV virus in a number of major American cities reflect the high number of intravenous drug abusers and young homosexual runaway men among the homeless population. At the present time, nowhere in the world is the AIDS epidemic more devastating than in New York City.

14. Researchers indicate that people who were over forty years old when infected are four to eight times as likely to develop AIDS within seven years as people who were under twenty. People who are older progress to AIDS at a significantly greater rate than teenagers or young adults. In addition, Richard P. Keeling, president of the American College Health Association, has recently said: "We are more disturbed than heartened. Because of patterns of sexual activity and drug abuse among college students, it is possible that there could be further significant spread of HIV in this population." See *The New York Times* (May 21, 1989): 16; and *The Washington Post* (May 23, 1989): A5. Although researchers have learned a great deal about how HIV spreads, they are still struggling with some extremely important questions. For example, why are the patterns of AIDS virus infectivity so different in Africa and North America? In Africa, almost all of the cases occur in heterosexuals, affecting men and women equally; in North America, the disease primarily strikes male homosexuals. Recent studies indicate that lack of circumcision alone increased the likelihood of AIDS infection some five- to eightfold, whereas a history of genital ulcers alone increased it four- to fivefold. See "Circumcision May Protect Against the AIDS Virus," *Science* 245 (August 4, 1989): 470-471.

15. William L. Heyward and James W. Curran, "The Epidemiology of AIDS in the U.S.," *Scientific American* 259 (October 1988): 72-81. An additional complication concerns the mysterious mutations of the AIDS virus. Up to now,

researchers have encountered over two hundred. Although there is scientific controversy regarding these mutations, it is clear that the family of human retroviruses is on the increase.

16. Walter J. Smith, SJ, *AIDS: Living and Dying with Hope* (New York: Paulist Press, 1988), 1-16. Two technical terms are frequently used in discussions of epidemic diseases: *incidence* and *prevalence*. Incidence denotes the rate of occurrence of new infections per unit of time (e.g., per year). Thus, an incidence of .03 per year in some group means that new infections occurred in 3 percent of the group during the year in question. Prevalence denotes that proportion of a group that is currently infected. A prevalence of .10 means that 10 percent of the group is currently infected. The retrovirus responsible for AIDS infects and leads to the death of T helper cells, with resultant dysfunction of the immune system. It was originally referred to as *Human T cell Lymphotrophic Virus Type III* (HTLV-III) and more cumbersomely as HTLV-LAV-III *(lymph-adenopathy-associated virus).* Most literature now follows the usage of the International Committee on the Taxonomy of Viruses: *Human Immunodeficiency Virus (HIV).*

17. See National Research Council, *AIDS: Sexual Behavior and Intravenous Drug Use* (Washington, D.C.: National Academy Press, 1989). See also 1:5 in this paper.

18. In their *Statement on AIDS*, the Canadian bishops stated, "We must do all we can to overcome [fear] because there is danger that fear will sap the energies we need to face this disease" (*Origins* 19:2 [May 25, 1989]: 25-27, citation at 25-26).

19. *Gaudium et Spes*, no. 1.

20. John Paul II, "A Meeting with AIDS Victims," Address at Mission Dolores Basilica, San Francisco, Calif. (September 17, 1987), *Origins* 17:18 (October 15, 1987): 313.

21. John Paul II, *On the Christian Meaning of Human Suffering (Salvifici Doloris)* (Washington, D.C.: United States Catholic Conference, 1984), no. 29. The pope emphasized this same point in speaking to the United States Catholic health care leaders in 1987:

> Besides your professional contribution and your human sensitivities toward all affected by this disease, you are called to show the love and compassion of Christ and his Church. As you courageously affirm and implement your moral obligation and social responsibility to help those who suffer, you are, individually and collectively, living out the parable of the Good Samaritan (see Lk 10:30-37). (*Unity in the Work of Service: John Paul II on the Occasion of His Second Pastoral Visit to the United States* [Washington, D.C.: United States Catholic Conference, 1987], 1031)

22. See Karol Wojtyla, *Love and Responsibility* (New York: Farrar, 1981), 202.

> Tenderness . . . springs from awareness of the inner state of another person (and indirectly of that person's external situation, which conditions his inner state) and whoever feels it

> actively seeks to communicate his feeling of close involve-
> ment with the other person and his situation. This closeness
> is the result of an emotional commitment: That sentiment
> enables us to feel close to another "I." . . . Hence also the need
> actively to communicate the feeling of closeness, so that ten-
> derness shows itself in certain outward actions which of their
> very nature reflect their inner approximation to another "I."

23. *Unity in the Work of Service,* 185.
24. John Paul II, *Rich in Mercy (Dives in Misericordia)* (Washington, D.C.: United States Catholic Conference, 1981), no. 14.
25. See *Gaudium et Spes,* especially chapter 2, and John Paul II, *On the Dignity and Vocation of Women (Mulieris Dignitatem)* (Washington, D.C.: United States Catholic Conference, 1988), no. 7.
26. Scripture teaches that love of God cannot be separated from love of neigh-bor: "If there is any other commandment, it is summed up in this saying, 'You shalt love thy neighbor as yourself' "(Rom 13:9-10; 1 Jn 4:20).
27. Paul VI, *On Human Life (Humanae Vitae)* (Washington, D.C.: United States Catholic Conference, 1968), no. 7.
28. John Paul II has addressed this point on various occasions: see *L'Osservatore Romano,* September 10, 1979; September 17, 1979; September 24, 1979; October 1, 1979; October 15, 1979; October 29, 1979; November 5, 1979; November 12, 1979; November 19, 1979; November 26, 1979; December 17, 1979; December 24, 1979; January 7, 1980; January 14, 1980; January 21, 1980; February 4, 1980; February 11, 1980; February 18, 1980; February 25, 1980; March 10, 1980; March 17, 1980; March 31, 1980; April 21, 1980; April 28, 1980; May 5, 1980; May 19, 1980; June 2, 1980; June 23, 1980; June 30, 1980; July 28, 1980; August 4, 1980; August 11, 1980; August 25, 1980; September 1, 1980; September 8, 1980; September 15, 1980; September 22, 1980; September 29, 1980; October 6, 1980; October 13, 1980; October 20, 1980; October 27, 1980; November 3, 1980; November 10, 1980; 17 November 1980; 8 December 1980; 15 December 1980; 29 December 1980; 12 January 1981; 19 January 1981; 2 February 1981; 9 February 1981; 16 February 1981; 23 March 1981; 6 April 1981; and 13 April 1981; and "On Human Sexuality and Personhood," February 20, 1981, cited in James V. Schall, SJ, ed., *Sacred in All Its Forms* (Boston: St. Paul Editions, 1984), 287-290.
29. Cardinal Joseph Ratzinger has spoken to this same point:

> In a society which seems increasingly to downgrade the
> value of chastity, conjugal fidelity and temperance, and to
> be preoccupied sometimes almost exclusively with physical
> health and temporal well-being, the Church's responsibility
> is to give that kind of witness which is proper to her, namely
> an unequivocal witness of effective and unreserved solidar-
> ity with those who are suffering and, at the same time, a wit-
> ness of defense of the dignity of human sexuality which can
> only be realized within the context of moral law. (*Origins*
> 18:8 [July 7, 1988]: 117- 118; citation at 118)

30. John Paul II, "The Los Angeles Youth Assembly and Teleconference," *Origins* 17:16 (October 1, 1987); citation at 275.

31. See Princeton Religion Research Center, "Parents Disturbed by TV Content" and "Dating is Strongest Peer Pressure Among Teens," *Emerging Trends* 11 (1989): 1-3, 5. See also Pontifical Council for Social Communications, *Pornography and Violence in the Communications Media: A Pastoral Response* (Washington, D.C.: United States Catholic Conference, 1989).

32. Congregation for the Doctrine of the Faith, *Declaration on Certain Questions Concerning Sexual Ethics* (Washington, D.C.: United States Catholic Conference, 1976), no. 1.

33. John Paul II, *On the Family (Familiaris Consortio)* (Washington, D.C.: United States Catholic Conference, 1981), no. 20.

34. *Unity in the Work of Service,* 63.

35. See James J. DiGiacomo, "All You Need Is Love," *America* 156 (February 14, 1987): 126-129; and Princeton Religion Research Center, "Dating is Strongest Peer Pressure Among Teens," *Emerging Trends* 11 (1989): 5.

36. See the Pennsylvania Catholic Bishops, *To Love and To Be Loved* (Harrisburg: Pennsylvania Catholic Conference, 1989).

37. "Given the very high background rate of HIV it is clear that relapses from safe sex, however occasional, constitute a threat to the health of gay men in San Francisco and other cities" (Dawn Garcia, "Unsafe Sex Practices," *San Francisco Chronicle* [March 11, 1989]). The article reported on a study by Ron Stall and Maria Ekstrand released in February 1989 by the Center for AIDS Prevention Studies at the University of California-San Francisco, which reported that relapses into "unsafe" sex practices are increasing among gay men. Their study of 453 men showed a decline of 59 percent in high-risk sexual behavior between 1984 and 1987; 15.7 percent of those studied had at least one incident of relapse into "unsafe" sex practices.

38. Congregation for the Doctrine of the Faith, *Declaration on Certain Questions Concerning Sexual Ethics (Persona Humana)* (Washington, D.C.: United States Catholic Conference, 1975), no. 8.

39. Congregation for the Doctrine of the Faith, *Letter to the Bishops of the Catholic Church on the Pastoral Care of Homosexual Persons* (Washington, D.C.: United States Catholic Conference, 1978), no. 3. This document importantly teaches that

> From this multifaceted approach there are numerous advantages to be gained, not the least of which is the realization that a homosexual person, as every human being, deeply needs to be nourished at many different levels simultaneously. The human person, made in the image and likeness of God, can hardly be adequately described by a reductionist reference to his or her sexual orientation. Everyone living on the face of the earth has personal problems and difficulties, but challenges to growth, strengths, talents and gifts as well. Today the Church provides a badly needed context for the care of the human person when she refuses to consider the person as a "heterosexual" or a "homosexual" and insists

that every person has a fundamental identity: the creature of God, and by grace, His child and heir to eternal life. (no. 16)

Homosexual activity has been one of the main transmitters of HIV virus. In this light, it is of critical importance to heed the Church's teaching regarding homosexual activity, which affirms the basic complementarity of the sexes and the intrinsic "spousal significance" of the human body.

40. *Report of the Presidential Commission*, 9-103.
41. *To Live in Christ Jesus*, no. 9.
42. National Confrence of Catholic Bishops, *Principles to Guide Confessors in Questions of Homosexuality* (Washington, D.C.: United States Catholic Conference, 1973): 9, 11:

> The confessor should encourage the person to form stable relationships with persons of both sexes. . . . Two other elements which should be stressed are regular access to spiritual direction and the formation of a stable friendship with at least one person. One of the greatest difficulties for the homosexual is the formation of such a friendship. . . . If a homosexual has progressed under the direction of a confessor, but in the effort to develop a stable relationship with a given person has *occasionally* fallen into a sin of impurity, he should be absolved and instructed to take measures to avoid the elements which lead to sin without breaking off a friendship which has helped him grow as a person. If the relationship, however, has reached a stage where the homosexual is not able to avoid overt actions, he should be admonished to break off the relationship.

43. Don C. Jarlais and Samuel R. Friedman, "AIDS and IV Drug Use," *Science* 245 (August 11, 1989): 578. A correlation between the use of volatile amyl and butyl nitrites (poppers) and the development of Kaposi's sarcoma has also been demonstrated. Although not directly linked to AIDS, alcohol, marijuana, cocaine, and amphetamines have been demonstrated to be immunosuppressant, and their use may accelerate disease progression from HIV infection to AIDS.
44. In 1972, Pope Paul VI pointed out this urgent need: "It is indispensable to mobilize public opinion through clear and precise information on the nature and true and deadly consequences of drug abuse, about those misunderstandings which are circulating on its presumed harmlessness and on its beneficial influences" (*Insegnamenti di Paolo VI* 10 [1972]: 1286). Pope John Paul II has also spoken of this contemporary scourge:

> Neither alarmism nor over-simplification serve to confront drug abuse. Rather, what is effective is an effort to know the individual and understand his interior world; to lead him to the discovery, or rediscovery, of his own dignity as man; to help him to revive and nurture those personal resources that drugs have buried, by reactivating the mechanisms of the

will and directing them toward certain and noble ideals. (John Paul II, "The Evil of Drugs," *The Pope Speaks* 29 [1984]: 356-359; citation at 357)

45. See Philip W. Brickner, M.D., et al., "Recommendations for Control and Prevention of *Human Immunodeficiency Virus* (HIV) Infection in Intravenous Drug Users," *Perspective: Annals of Internal Medicine* 110 (1989): 833-837. Despite the lack of data on the number of female prostitutes, available data suggest that the majority of prostitutes who have become infected with HIV in the United States have not become infected through sexual behavior. Most AIDS cases among women in the United States have occurred in women who use IV drugs. Although it is seldom possible to disentangle completely the effects of sexual transmission from drug-related transmission, the fact that there are relatively few women with HIV infection who are not IV drug users suggests that shared injection equipment—rather than sexual activity—has been the most significant transmission factor among female prostitutes. Medical advances are only just beginning to develop programs for polysubstance abusers.

46. Milton C. Weinstein et al., "Cost Effectiveness Analysis of AIDS Prevention," in Charles F. Turner et al., eds., *AIDS: Sexual Behavior and Intravenous Drug Use* (Washington, D.C.: National Research Council, 1989), 498. See "Can You Rely on Condoms?" *Consumer Reports* 157 (1989): 135-140.

47. See *Gaudium et Spes*, part 2, chapter 1, for a precise presentation of the Church's teaching on the nobility of marriage and the family; also *Familiaris Consortio*.

48. See "National Federation of Catholic Physicians' Guilds Proposed Position Paper: Statement on Prevention of AIDS by Condoms," *Linacre Quarterly* 55 (1988): 12-15; *The Many Faces of AIDS*; and *AIDS: A Catholic Educational Approach* (Washington, D.C.: National Catholic Educational Association, 1988).

49. In August 1989, the National Institutes of Health announced that new studies have found that AZT is effective in slowing the development of AIDS in people who have not yet contracted the disease but who exhibit its earliest signs. The studies also found that people with early symptoms of HIV infection not only can benefit from AZT but also suffer far fewer of the toxic side effects that mark the use of the drug among people with AIDS. This research, conducted by a division of the National Institutes of Health, shows that AZT dramatically slows the multiplication of HIV virus in people with mild symptoms of the disease, such as diarrhea, thrush, or a chronic rash. Until this time, AZT was thought to be effective only in patients with more advanced cases of AIDS. This study, called Protocol 019, has several implications:

   1.   All those who may have been infected with HIV should undergo immediate testing for the virus. This counsel rests on certain clear assumptions: the growing accuracy of the HIV test; increased guarantees of confidentiality; the growth of proper

counseling both before and after the test; the enactment of effective city, state, and federal antidiscrimination laws.

2.   AZT treatment now costs $8,000.00 per person per year, and other drugs and diagnostic tests are needed in the treatment of HIV/AIDS sufferers. It is thus crucial to provide financial and medical resources to assist persons with the HIV disease.

50.   "Ethical Issues Involved in the Growing AIDS Crisis," *Council Report: The Journal of the American Medical Association* 259 (1988). We recall the 1987 determination by the Council on Ethical and Judicial Affairs of the American Medical Association that refusing treatment to the afflicted is unethical. Also, Dr. Edmund Pellegrino, director of the Kennedy Institute of Ethics, has stated: "A medical need in itself constitutes a moral claim on those equipped to help." This echoes John Paul's words to the Catholic Health Association in Phoenix in 1987, when he spoke of "your moral obligation and social responsibility to help those who suffer" from AIDS and said: "You are called to show the love and compassion of Christ and his Church."

51.   The 1988 meeting of the American Medical Association stated: "The Board recommends continued support for adequate funding for all aspects of this epidemic including education, research and patient care" (Proceedings, 210).

52.   National Conference of Catholic Bishops, *Pastoral Statement of the U.S. Catholic Bishops on Persons with Disabilities* (Washington, D.C.: United States Catholic Conference, 1978; revised 1989), no. 10.

53.   Cited in the *Los Angeles Tidings* (May 26, 1989): 1. The *Statement of the Holy See on the International Year of the Disabled* also affirms:

> The first principle . . . is that the disabled person (whether the disability be the result of a congenital handicap, chronic illness or accident, or from mental or physical deficiency, and whatever the severity of the disability) is a fully human subject with the corresponding innate, sacred and inviolable rights. . . . This principle, which stems from the upright conscience of humanity, must be made the inviolable basis of legislation and society. (*Origins* 10:47 [May 7, 1981]; citation at 747)

54.   *Report of the Presidential Commission*, section 7.

55.   See Betty Clare Moffat, *When Someone You Love Has AIDS* (New York: Dell Publications, 1985); Barbara Peabody, *The Screaming Room* (San Diego: Oak Tree Publications, 1986); Walter J. Smith, SJ, *AIDS: Living and Dying with Hope* (New York: Paulist Press, 1988); and William C. Spohn, SJ, "The Moral Dimension of AIDS," *Theological Studies* 49 (1988): 89-109. See also The Catholic Health Association, and the Conference of Major Superiors of Men, *Shadow on the Family: AIDS in Religious Life* (St. Louis: The Catholic Health Association, 1988); and The Catholic Health Association and the Conference of Major Religious Superiors of Men's Institutes, *The Gospel Alive* (St. Louis: The Catholic Health Association, 1988).

56.   *Report of the Presidential Commission*, 9-99.

57. See James Childress, "An Ethical Framework for Assessing Policies to Screen for Antibodies to HIV," *AIDS and Public Policy Journal* 2 (1987): 28-31. It may be appropriate for seminaries and religious communities to screen for the HIV antibody. In regard to candidates for the priesthood, canon 241.1 is pertinent:

> The diocesan bishop is to admit to the major seminary only those who are judged capable of dedicating themselves permanently to the sacred ministries in light of their human, moral, spiritual and intellectual characteristics, their physical and psychological health and their proper motivation. (*Code of Canon Law,* Latin-English Edition, Canon Law Society of America)

The point here is not to automatically exclude a candidate who is HIV-positive but rather to discern carefully this person's present health situation as well as future health prospects and thus to make an overall moral assessment of an individual's capacity to carry out ministerial responsibilities. Canon 642 is relevant in terms of admission to a religious community:

> Superiors are to be vigilant about admitting only those who, besides the required age, have health, suitable character and sufficient qualities of maturity to embrace the particular life of the institute. . . .

58. The 1983 document of the National Conference of Catholic Bishops, *Pastoral Care of the Sick: Rites of Anointing and Viaticum* is instructive to this point: "Although closely linked with the human condition, sickness cannot as a general rule be regarded as a punishment indicted on each individual for personal sins" (*The Rites of the Catholic Church* [New York: Pueblo Publishing Company, 1983]: 593-740; citation at no. 2).

59. John Paul II, "The Cross of Suffering" (July 8, 1980), cited in Schall, op. cit., 106-111; citation at 108. See also John Paul II, "The Mystery of Life and Death" *Origins* 15:25 (December 5, 1985): 415-417.

60. Pope John Paul II has explained: "Suffering has a special value in the eyes of the Church. It is something good, before which the Church bows down in reverence with all the depth of her faith in the redemption. . . ." (*Salvifici Doloris,* nos. 1-8).

61. John Paul II, "Every Human Death: A Reflection of the Death of Christ," *L'Osservatore Romano* [English edition] 15 (April 15, 1985): 3-4; citation at 4.

62. See also John Paul II, "Death and Eternity," *L'Osservatore Romano* [English edition] 45 (November 7, 1988): 5. See also Psalm 27:1-4.

63. Paul VI, *On Christian Joy (Gaudete in Domino)* (Washington, D.C.: United States Catholic Conference, 1975), no. 8.

64. *Salvifici Doloris,* no. 30.

Source: Washington, D.C.: United States Catholic Conference, 1990.

Resolution on Abortion

From the National Conference of Catholic Bishops

November 1989

The decision of the U.S. Supreme Court in *Webster vs. Reproductive Health Services* provides reason to hope that our nation is moving toward a time when unborn children will again enjoy the protection of law. The court recognized states' legitimate interest in protecting pre-natal life and their authority to adopt laws favoring childbirth over abortion. The court indicated that a state's interest in protecting life might well exist throughout pregnancy, not only after viability. We are encouraged by this.

Yet abortion on demand remains our nation's legal policy because the 1973 Supreme Court decisions that legalized abortion throughout pregnancy have not been overturned. Because of those decisions many citizens believe that women have a moral right to abort their unborn children. This has led to erosion of respect for the right to life, which is bestowed by the Creator and cannot legitimately be denied by any nation or court. More than 1.5 million unborn children in the United States continue to die each year by abortion, and increasing numbers of women suffer abortion's physical, emotional, and spiritual pain. Often they suffer alone, deserted by men unwilling to acknowledge their own responsibilities as fathers.

Most Americans believe that abortion should be illegal except in certain limited circumstances; an overwhelming majority agrees that unmarried minors should not obtain abortions without parental knowledge or consent.

Nonetheless, pro-abortion or so-called "pro-choice" groups have mounted a campaign to convince legislators and others that Americans want abortion on demand. These organizations have formed new political arms and have intensified efforts to defeat politicians who do not support permissive abortion.

Because of the critical importance of the issue and the need for a timely response, we wish to reaffirm our conviction that all human life is sacred whether born or unborn. With the Second Vatican Council we declare that "from the moment of conception life must be guarded with the greatest care, while abortion and infanticide are unspeakable crimes."[1]

As leaders of the Catholic community in the United States we acknowledge our right and responsibility to help establish laws and social policies protecting the right to life of unborn children, providing care and services for women and children, and safeguarding human life at every stage and in every circumstance.

At this particular time, abortion has become the fundamental human rights issue for all men and women of goodwill. The duty to respect life in all its stages and especially in the womb is evident when one appreciates the unborn child's membership in our human family and the grave consequences of denying moral or legal status to any class of human beings because of their age or condition of dependency.

We who revere human life as created in the image and likeness of God have all the more reason to take a stand. For us abortion is of overriding concern because it negates two of our most fundamental moral imperatives: respect for innocent life and preferential concern for the weak and defenseless. As we said three years ago in reaffirming our *Pastoral Plan for Pro-Life Activities:* "Because victims of abortion are the most vulnerable and defenseless members of the human family, it is imperative that we, as Christians called to serve the least among us, give urgent attention and priority to this issue. Our concern is intensified by the realization that a policy and practice allowing over 1.5 million abortions annually cannot but diminish respect for life in other areas." No Catholic can responsibly take a "pro-choice" stand when the "choice" in question involves the taking of innocent human life.

We therefore call upon Catholics to commit themselves vigorously to the implementation of all three elements of the pastoral plan—an education and public information effort, pastoral care for pregnant women and their children, and a public policy program in defense of human life in all its stages, especially the unborn. Our long- and short-range public policy goals include:

1. Constitutional protection for the right to life of unborn children to the maximum degree possible
2. Federal and state laws and administrative policies that restrict support for and the practice of abortion
3. Continual refinement and ultimate reversal of Supreme Court and other court decisions that deny the inalienable right to life
4. Supportive legislation to provide morally acceptable alternatives to abortion, and social policy initiatives which provide support to pregnant women for prenatal care and extended support for low-income women and their children

We urge public officials, especially Catholics, to advance these goals in recognition of their moral responsibility to protect the weak and defenseless among us.

Our concern about the national debate on the legal dimension of this vital issue should not distract us from the continuing need within our own community to educate, to form, to encourage people on life issues, most specifically the right to life of the unborn. This right of the unborn to life demands legal protection and we will continue to insist on this. At the same time we recognize, as we rightfully engage in this debate, that we must hear the issues, the struggles, and the anguish of women who face issues in a way that we never will. As we continue to teach clearly and forcefully the moral evil of abortion, we must also—as our pastoral plan suggests—speak to them a word of understanding and encouragement, a word of solidarity and support. Both in word and deed we must inspire the entire community to help carry the burdens of all our sisters in need.

Above all, we ask people to commit themselves to daily prayer and sacrifice so that our nation might soon witness the end of the scourge of abortion. We continue to ask God's merciful assistance, without which we labor in vain. May the patroness of our nation, Mary, the Mother of God, who herself said yes to life, intercede before her Son for the restoration of respect for all human life in our day.

Note

1. Second Vatican Council, *Pastoral Constitution on the Church in the Modern World (Gaudium et Spes)*, no. 51.

Source: *Origins* 19:24 (November 1, 1989): 395-396.

The New Moment in Eastern and Central Europe

A Statement of the Administrative Board
of the United States Catholic Conference

March 1990

"Peoples and individuals aspire to be free. . . ."[1] In churches, synagogues, and mosques; in schools; in parliaments; and in the streets, the people of Eastern and Central Europe and the Soviet Union are demonstrating the truth of these words of Pope John Paul, who throughout his pontificate has worked strenuously for this new moment. Showing an "unquenchable thirst for freedom,"[2] these people have confounded the world by moving with unprecedented speed to begin dismantling the stultifying controls over all aspects of their lives that they have endured for a generation or more. In the area of religion, we are happily witnessing through most of Eastern and Central Europe and in the Soviet Union the removal of the severe restrictions that we deplored just a short time ago in our statement, *A Word of Solidarity, A Call for Justice* (1988).[3] For the first time in decades, these people and nations have new possibilities for restructuring their moral, social, economic, and political life.

These new possibilities are the result of many factors, not the least of which is the more open political climate ushered in by President Mikhail Gorbachev's policies. To the extent that *perestroika* and *glasnost* have created an environment in which these changes could take place, they should be applauded and supported.

But, as important as these and other political and economic factors have been, only a deep yearning for a renewal of society based on truth, justice, freedom, and solidarity can explain what is occurring. At root, we are witnesses to a time of special grace. We see signs of a deeper movement of the Spirit; a reassertion of the transcendent, of a deeper understanding of the full meaning of what it is to be human. In the words of our Holy Father, "Little by little candles have been lit making a veritable path of light, as if to say to those who for years tried to limit man's horizons to this earth that he cannot remain enchained indefinitely."[4]

It is this yearning that is rooted in the human heart that makes religious freedom so indispensable. We are inspired and strengthened by the faithful witness to the Gospel and the courageous moral leadership of so many believers in the face of an abiding intolerance of religion.

Despite severe restrictions and, at times, outright repression, they did not abandon their faith or the Church's essential mission. They have helped preserve a respect for truth, justice, solidarity, and human rights; they have called for nonviolence, dialogue, and national reconciliation. All this has contributed in no small way to the radical—yet largely peaceful— restructuring that has begun in such a dramatic and unexpected manner.

With the Holy Father and our brother and sister believers in Eastern and Central Europe and the Soviet Union, we thank a providential God for the grace-filled time in which we live—for the advent of a new era! At the same time, we cannot but recognize the fragile nature of the present moment. In parts of Eastern Europe, authoritarian regimes or their structures remain in place. Elsewhere, the people have rejected unjust regimes and their discredited ideologies, but they face a monumental task of constructing a new political, economic, social, and moral order. This task may be impeded by nationalistic and ethnic rivalries, anti-Semitism and religious conflicts, social divisions, secularizing trends, and various negative ideologies, not to mention a deep economic crisis. The Church has particular capabilities to ameliorate effectively these dangers. Like other institutions in society, however, in many of these countries the Church faces a long and arduous process of rebirth and rebuilding after years of repression and strict controls.

As Americans, we have a historic opportunity to assist the people of Eastern and Central Europe in addressing these most difficult of problems in ways appropriate to their particular cultures and needs, and which take into account moral considerations, including respect for fundamental human rights. No doubt this will require a major undertaking that will draw on scarce resources. But, with a reordering of national priorities, we will be able to do our part in this region of the world and at the same time give priority to meeting other unmet human and social needs, both at home and in the developing world. Moreover, a revitalized Eastern and Central Europe could become a major new force for development in the less developed nations.

As American Catholics, we have a special duty and responsibility to assist our brother and sister Catholics to rebuild their church. The many groups and organizations that have tirelessly done this for many years are especially deserving of our support. In coming to the aid of our fellow believers, we may also share our own experience in identifying and combating some of the pernicious effects of excessive materialism, consumerism, and individualism that plague our own society, in the hope that some of these may be avoided as new economic and political systems are established in Eastern and Central Europe.

These efforts to help rebuild Eastern and Central Europe should be seen as part of our response to the larger challenge of global solidarity issued by our Holy Father in the encyclical *On Social Concern*: namely, that countries, especially the stronger and richer ones like our own, exercise a heightened sense of moral, political, and economic responsibility toward other nations, with the goal of establishing a new international system based on respect for national autonomy, self-determination, and the equality of all peoples.[5]

We are citizens of one of the handful of nations capable of moving the world beyond the Cold War and its legacies. Consequently, we have a grave human, moral, and political responsibility to ensure that our government takes prudent, but ever more determined steps to replace what our Holy Father has called "the logic of the blocs" with a new vision.[6] This requires that we not be satisfied with the status quo or small achievements, but rather that we seek to fashion a "real international system" that is grounded in solidarity—the path to authentic peace and integral development.[7]

As we help to reshape the political fabric of East-West relations, we must take advantage of the opportunity presented by this new political situation to diminish and ultimately end the military confrontation between East and West. The progress in arms control negotiations over chemical, strategic, and conventional weapons is encouraging, but much deeper cuts than those envisioned in the current strategic nuclear and conventional talks will be necessary.

Near the end of World War II, the American bishops asked: "We have met the challenge of war. Shall we meet the challenge of peace?"[8] Today, in 1988, we are only beginning to meet this challenge of a generation ago. We must not miss this historic opportunity.

We thank God for the momentous developments in Eastern Europe, and we pray that our brothers and sisters there will have the strength and wisdom to construct new, more just societies in a spirit of peace and reconciliation. We pray also that we will do our part to replace the East-West competition with a new partnership for peace and justice—in Europe and in the whole world.

Notes

1. John Paul II, *On Social Concern (Sollicitudo Rei Socialis)* (Washington, D.C.: United States Catholic Conference, 1988), no. 46.
2. John Paul II, "Address to Diplomatic Corps" (Rome, January 13, 1990), *Origins* 19:35 (February 1, 1990): 578.
3. United States Catholic Conference, *A Word of Solidarity, A Call for Justice: A Statement on Religious Freedom in Eastern Europe and the Soviet Union* (Washington, D.C.: United States Catholic Conference, 1988).
4. John Paul II, "Address to Diplomatic Corps," 578.
5. *Sollicitudo Rei Socialis*, no. 39.
6. Ibid., no. 20.

7. Ibid., no. 39.
8. National Catholic Welfare Conference Administrative Board, "A Statement on International Order" (November 16, 1944), in *Pastoral Letters of the United States Catholic Bishops*, ed. Hugh J. Nolan (Washington, D.C.: United States Catholic Conference, 1988), 2:56, no. 1.

Source: Washington, D.C.: United States Catholic Conference, 1990.

Moral Education in the Public Schools

A Joint Statement of the NCCB Committee for Ecumenical and Interreligious Affairs and the Interreligious Affairs Committee of the Synogogue Council of America

June 1990

American public schools feel inhibited about teaching moral values, yet we are losing our children.

Drug addiction, depression, suicide, promiscuity, crime, alienation, AIDS, academic failure, emotional illness, teen pregnancy, alcoholism, intolerance, violence—the litany of problems besetting American youth seems to have no end.

Why?

What have we done—or failed to do—that has brought this plague upon our children? What must we do to fight it?

Obviously there are no simple answers. But from our perspective as religious leaders, these maladies are only symptoms of a deeper and more basic problem: a lack of fundamental values.

These values, like honesty, compassion, integrity, tolerance, loyalty, and belief in human worth and dignity, are embedded in our respective religious traditions and in the civic fabric of our society. They are the very underpinnings of our lives.

There is broad consensus among Americans, regardless of religion and cultural background, concerning these values.

In a world where short-term gratification is pressed upon children by their peers, the media, and many adults, to raise a young person without a basic value system is to cast him or her adrift. Yet we persist in cheating our children of this critically important education—necessary if they are to grow to respect, cherish, and care for themselves and others.

Traditionally the family, the church or synagogue, the school, and the government have worked to educate children in basic values. But in recent years there has been a growing reluctance to teach values in our public educational system out of a fear that children might be indoctrinated with a specific religious belief.

All major religions advocate these values, as do the Constitution and the Bill of Rights, much of the world's greatest literature and ethical business practices as well. We are convinced that even apart from the context of a specific faith, it is possible to teach these shared values.

In fact, public schools do teach values all the time—but they are not necessarily the core moral values. Indeed, by deliberately excluding these shared moral values from the curriculum, the educational system actually undermines them. Children naturally look to the school to provide them with important knowledge. It is all too easy for children to assume that information not taught in school cannot be very important.

To raise a generation without an understanding of values is to assure disaster. Children are the future. The specter of a nation with an amoral citizenry is terrible to contemplate. The damage would be irreversible. If we cannot teach our children values, who will teach their children values?

We recognize that parents have a responsibility to teach values. Indeed, in such a morally apathetic environment, that so many parents have instilled strongly grounded values in their children is testimony to the unique role parents have in shaping their children's lives. (In fact, these children are important resources both as role models to their peers and in values education.)

But in our society parents can use all the help they can get. Therefore, it is urgent that there be a national effort to implement moral public education in our schools, integrated into the total curriculum and corresponding to student needs and community consensus.

There is a groundswell of support from parents, teachers and government, religious and community leaders who are struggling for a renewed moral vision within the public schools grounded in the common bond of humanity that links all races and religions. They realize that our country is more than a land; it is a people—a people historically admired for its biblically based values and religious traditions.

In some parts of the country, major strides have been made in the herculean struggle to develop our schools into moral communities. Many school systems have developed excellent values education programs. We recognize and praise the efforts of these dedicated parents and teachers who have fought the paralyzing fear that prevents values education. Yet substantial, even drastic, systemic change is still necessary if we as a nation are to salvage the moral fiber of our children. To bring about that basic change, we urge that:

1.   Those responsible for schooling at the local, state, and national levels convene the administrators, teachers, parents, students, and citizens to address the moral educational needs of children and young people. We call for state governors and legislative leadership to create committees to promote values education in the public schools.

2.   Public schools introduce moral education into their curricula; that the schools use textbooks, resources, and teaching

methodologies that emphasize basic civic and personal values. (We repeat that this can be done apart from teaching a specific religious faith.) We call on school boards to state clearly the values they will teach and how they will teach them.

3. All faiths work together to bring about systemic change and to encourage the teaching of values in public schools. To facilitate this effort we will strongly recommend a joint commission to meet quarterly to evaluate matters pending in the courts and before the Congress that will affect the promotion of values education in America.

4. Foundations underwrite values education programs in public schools.

5. The media, especially television, promote civic and personal values in their programming.

6. For our part, we will:

> a) Establish within our consultation an ad hoc committee to discuss this issue and make recommendations on the substance of value-based curricula and teaching methodologies. We will assist in providing teaching materials and guides reflecting our shared moral values.
> b) Ask that Catholics and Jews begin a widespread dialogue about moral education in the public schools; we ask that this dialogue take place in state Jewish councils, Catholic conferences, and ministerial associations.
> c) Support educational opportunities to teach values— and values teaching—to parents.
> d) Within our own educational institutions, emphasize anew our commitment to moral values, which come ultimately from divine revelation.

Children are not born with values any more than they are born with math and reading skills. In a nation that spends billions of dollars to influence youth as to which cars to buy and which clothes to wear, it is a national disgrace to fail to teach basic values in the public schools.

Our children need these values. Our society requires them. We, as a nation, can teach them. We must teach them now—before we lose our children.

Source: *Origins* 20:9 (July 19, 1990): 133-136.

Criteria for the Evaluation of Inclusive Language Translations of Scriptural Texts Proposed for Liturgical Use

Practical Principles for the Members of the National Conference of Catholic Bishops to Exercise Their Canonical Responsibility for Approving Translations, Approved by the NCCB

November 1990

Introduction: The Origins and Nature of the Problem

1. Five historical developments have converged to present the Church in the United States today with an important and challenging pastoral concern. First, the introduction of the vernacular into the Church's worship has necessitated English translations of the liturgical books and of Sacred Scripture for use in the liturgy. Second, some segments of American culture have become increasingly sensitive to "exclusive language," i.e., language that seems to exclude the equality and dignity of each person regardless of race, gender, creed, age, or ability.[1] Third, there has been a noticeable loss of the sense of grammatical gender in American usage of the English language. Fourth, English vocabulary itself has changed so that words that once referred to all human beings are increasingly taken as gender-specific and, consequently, exclusive. Fifth, impromptu efforts at inclusive language, while pleasing to some, have often offended others who expect a degree of theological precision and linguistic or aesthetic refinement in the public discourse of the liturgy. Some impromptu efforts may also have unwittingly undermined essentials of Catholic doctrine.

These current issues confront a fundamental conviction of the Church, namely, that the word of God stands at the core of our faith as a basic theological reality to which all human efforts respond and by which they are judged.

2. The bishops of the United States wish to respond to this complex and sensitive issue of language in the English translation of the liturgical books of the Church in general and of Sacred Scripture in particular. New translations of scriptural passages used in the liturgy are being proposed periodically for their approval. Since the promulgation of the 1983 Code of Canon Law, these translations must be

approved by a conference of bishops or by the Apostolic See.[2] The question confronts the bishops: With regard to a concern for inclusive language, how do we distinguish a legitimate translation from one that is imprecise?

3. The recognition of this problem prompted the submission of a *varium* to the National Conference of Catholic Bishops requesting that the bishops' Committee on the Liturgy and the Committee on Doctrine be directed jointly to formulate guidelines that would assist the bishops in making appropriate judgments on the inclusive language translations of biblical texts for liturgical use. These two committees established a Joint Committee on Inclusive Language, which prepared this text.

4. This document, while providing an answer to the question concerning translations of biblical texts for liturgical use, does not attempt to elaborate a complete set of criteria for inclusive language in the liturgy in general, that is, for prayers, hymns, and preaching. These cognate areas will be treated only insofar as they overlap the particular issues being addressed here.

5. This document presents practical principles for the members of the National Conference of Catholic Bishops to exercise their canonical responsibility for approving translations of Scripture proposed for liturgical use. However, just as this document does not deal with all cases of inclusive language in the liturgy, neither is it intended as a theology of translation. The teaching of *Dei Verbum* and the instructions of the Pontifical Biblical Commission prevail in matters of inspiration, inerrancy, and hermeneutics and their relationship with meaning, language, and the mind of the author. While there would be a value in producing a study summarizing these issues, it would distract from the immediate purpose of this document.

6. This document treats the problem indicated above in four parts: general principles; principles for inclusive language lectionary translations; preparation of texts for use in the lectionary; special questions, viz., naming God, the Trinity, Christ, and the Church.

Part One: General Principles

7. There are two general principles for judging translations for liturgical use: the principle of fidelity to the word of God and the principle of respect for the nature of the liturgical assembly. Individual questions, then, must be judged in light of the textual, grammatical, literary, artistic, and dogmatic requirements of the particular scriptural passage and in light of the needs of the liturgical assembly. In cases of conflict or ambiguity, the principle of fidelity to the word of God retains its primacy.

I. Fidelity to the Word of God

The following considerations derive from the principle of fidelity to the word of God.

8. The people of God have the right to hear the word of God integrally proclaimed[3] in fidelity to the meaning of the inspired authors of the sacred text.

9. Biblical translations must always be faithful to the original language and internal truth of the inspired text. It is expected, therefore, that every concept in the original text will be translated within its context.

10. All biblical translations must respect doctrinal principles of revelation, inspiration, and biblical interpretation (hermeneutics), as well as the formal rhetoric intended by the author (e.g., Heb 2:5-18). They must be faithful to Catholic teaching regarding God and divine activity in the world and in human history as it unfolds. "Due attention must be paid both to the customary and characteristic patterns of perception, speech and narrative which prevailed at the age of the sacred writer and to the conventions which the people of his time followed."[4]

II. The Nature of the Liturgical Assembly

The following considerations derive from the nature of the liturgical assembly.

11. Each and every Christian is called to and indeed has a right to full and active participation in worship. This was stated succinctly by the Second Vatican Council: "The Church earnestly desires that all the faithful be led to that full, conscious, and active participation in liturgical celebrations called for by the very nature of the liturgy. Such participation by the Christian people as 'a chosen race, a royal priesthood, a holy nation, God's own people' (1 Pt 2:9, see 2:4-5) is their right and duty by reason of their baptism."[5] An integral part of liturgical participation is hearing the word of Christ, "who speaks when the Scriptures are proclaimed in the Church."[6] Full and active participation in the liturgy demands that the liturgical assembly recognize and accept the transcendent power of God's word.

12. According to the Church's tradition, biblical texts have many liturgical uses. Because their immediate purposes are somewhat different, texts translated for public proclamation in the liturgy may differ in some respects (cf. Part Two) from those translations which are meant solely for academic study, private reading, or *lectio divina*.

13. The language of biblical texts for liturgical use should be suitably and faithfully adapted for proclamation and should facilitate the

full, conscious, and active participation of all members of the Church, women and men, in worship.

Part Two: Principles for Inclusive Language Lectionary Translations

14. The word of God proclaimed to all nations is by nature inclusive, that is, addressed to all peoples, men and women. Consequently, every effort should be made to render the language of biblical translations as inclusively as a faithful translation of the text permits, especially when this concerns the people of God, Israel, and the Christian community.

15. When a biblical translation is meant for liturgical proclamation, it must also take into account those principles that apply to the public communication of the biblical meaning. Inclusive language is one of those principles, since the text is proclaimed in the Christian assembly to women and men who possess equal baptismal dignity and reflects the universal scope of the Church's call to evangelize.

16. The books of the Bible are the product of particular cultures, with their limitations as well as their strengths. Consequently not everything in Scripture will be in harmony with contemporary cultural concerns. The fundamental mystery of incarnational revelation requires the retention of those characteristics that reflect the cultural context within which the word was first received.

17. Language that addresses and refers to the worshiping community ought not use words or phrases that deny the common dignity of all the baptized.

18. Words such as *men, sons, brothers, brethren, forefathers, fraternity,* and *brotherhood,* which were once understood as inclusive generic terms, today are often understood as referring only to males. In addition, although certain uses of *he, his,* and *him* once were generic and included both women and men, in contemporary American usage these terms are often perceived to refer only to males. Their use has become ambiguous and is increasingly seen to exclude women. Therefore, these terms should not be used when the reference is meant to be generic, observing the requirements of nos. 7 and 10.

19. Words such as *adam, anthropos,* and *homo* have often been translated in many English biblical and liturgical texts by the collective terms *man* and *family of man.* Since in the original languages these words actually denote human beings rather than only males, English terms which are not gender-specific, such as *person, people, human family,* and *humans* should be used in translating these words.

20. In narratives and parables the sex of individual persons should be retained. Sometimes, in the synoptic tradition, the gospel writers

select examples or metaphors from a specific gender. Persons of the other sex should not be added merely in a desire for balance. The original references of the narrative or images of the parable should be retained.

Part Three: The Preparation of Texts for Use in the Lectionary

21. The liturgical adaptation of readings for use in the lectionary should be made in light of the norms of the introduction to the *Ordo Lectionum Missae* (1981). Incipits should present the context of the various pericopes. At times, transitions may need to be added when verses have been omitted from pericopes. Nouns may replace pronouns or be added to participial constructions for clarity in proclamation and aural comprehension. Translation should not expand upon the text, but the Church recognizes that in certain circumstances a particular text may be expanded to reflect adequately the intended meaning of the pericope.[7] In all cases, these adaptations must remain faithful to the intent of the original text.[8]

22. Inclusive language adaptations of lectionary texts must be made in light of exegetical and linguistic attention to the individual text within its proper context. Blanket substitutions are inappropriate.

23. Many biblical passages are inconsistent in grammatical person, that is, alternating between second person singular or plural *(you)* and third person singular *(he)*. In order to give such passages a more intelligible consistency, some biblical readings may be translated so as to use either the second person plural *(you)* throughout or the third person plural *(they)* throughout. Changes from the third person singular to the third person plural are allowed in individual cases where the sense of the original text is universal. It should be noted that, at times, either the sense or the poetic structure of a passage may require that the alternation be preserved in the translation.

24. Psalms and canticles have habitually been appropriated by the Church for use in the liturgy, not as readings for proclamation, but as the responsive prayer of the liturgical assembly. Accordingly, adaptations have justifiably been made, principally by the omission of verses that were judged to be inappropriate in a given culture or liturgical context. Thus, the liturgical books allow the adaptation of psalm texts to encourage the full participation of the liturgical assembly.

Part Four: Specific Questions

25. Several specific issues must be addressed in regard to the naming of God, the persons of the Trinity, and the Church, since changes in language can have important doctrinal and theological implications.

I. Naming God in Biblical Translations

26. Great care should be taken in translations of the names of God and in the use of pronouns referring to God. While it would be inappropriate to attribute gender to God as such, the revealed word of God consistently uses a masculine reference for God. It may sometimes be useful, however, to repeat the name of God as used earlier in the text rather than to use the masculine pronoun in every case. But care must be taken that the repetition not become tiresome.

27. The classic translation of the Tetragrammaton (YHWH) as LORD and the translation of *Kyrios* as *Lord* should be used in lectionaries.

28. Feminine imagery in the original language of the biblical texts should not be obscured or replaced by the use of masculine imagery in English translations, e.g., Wisdom literature.

II. Naming Christ in Biblical Translations

29. Christ is the center and focus of all Scripture.[9] The New Testament has interpreted certain texts of the Old Testament in an explicitly christological fashion. Special care should be observed in the translation of these texts so that the christological meaning is not lost. Some examples include the Servant Songs of Isaiah 42 and 53, Psalms 2 and 110, and the Son of Man passage in Daniel 7.

III. Naming the Trinity in Biblical Translations

30. In fidelity to the inspired word of God, the traditional biblical usage for naming the persons of the Trinity as *Father, Son,* and *Holy Spirit* is to be retained. Similarly, in keeping with New Testament usage and the Church's tradition, the feminine pronoun is not to be used to refer to the person of the Holy Spirit.

VI. Naming the Church in Biblical Translations

31. Normally the neuter third person singular or the third person plural pronoun is used when referring to the people of God, Israel, the Church, the body of Christ, etc., unless their antecedents clearly are a masculine or feminine metaphor, for instance, the reference to the Church as the *bride of Christ* or *mother* (cf. Rv 12).

Conclusion

32. These criteria for judging the appropriateness of inclusive language translations of Sacred Scripture are presented while acknowledging that the English language is continually changing. Contemporary translations must reflect developments in American English grammar, syntax, usage, vocabulary, and style. The perceived need for a more inclusive language is part of this development. Such language must not distract hearers from prayer and God's revelation. It must manifest a sense of linguistic refinement. It should not draw attention to itself.

33. While English translations of the Bible have influenced the liturgical and devotional language of Christians, such translations have also shaped and formed the English language itself. This should be true today as it was in the age of the King James and Douay-Rheims translations. Thus, the Church expects for its translations not only accuracy but facility and beauty of expression.

34. Principles of translation when applied to lectionary readings and psalm texts differ in certain respects from those applied to translations of the Bible destined for study or reading (see nos. 22-25 above). Thus, when submitting a new or revised translation of the Bible, an edition of the lectionary, or a liturgical psalter for approval by the National Conference of Catholic Bishops, editors must supply a complete statement of the principles used in the preparation of the submitted text.

35. The authority to adapt the biblical text for use in the lectionary remains with the conference of bishops. These *Criteria for the Evaluation of Inclusive Language Translations of Scriptural Texts Proposed for Liturgical Use* have been developed to assist the members of the National Conference of Catholic Bishops to exercise their responsibility so that all the people of God may be assisted in hearing God's word and keeping it.

Notes

1. Cf. Bishop Members of the Pastoral Team, Canadian Conference of Catholic Bishops, "To Speak as a Christian Community," *Origins* 19:16 (September 1989), 2.
2. Code of Canon Law, canon 825.1.
3. Canon 213.
4. Second Vatican Council, *Dogmatic Constitution on Divine Revelation (Dei Verbum)*, no. 12.
5. Second Vatican Council, *Constitution on the Sacred Liturgy (Sacrosanctum Concilium)*, no. 14.
6. Ibid., no. 7.
7. Secretariat for Christian Unity (Commission for Religious Relations with Judaism), "Guidelines and Suggestions for the Application of No. 4 of the Conciliar Declaration *Nostra Aetate*" *Acta Apostolicae Sedis* 67 (1975): 73-79.

8. Sacred Congregation of Rites (Consilium), instruction *Comme le Prévoit: On the Translation of Liturgical Texts for Celebrations with a Congregation* (January 25, 1969), in *Documents on the Liturgy 1965-1979: Conciliar, Papal and Curial Texts* (Collegeville, Minn.: The Liturgical Press, 1982), 123.
9. Cf. *Dei Verbum*, no. 16.

Source: Washington, D.C.: United States Catholic Conference, 1990.

A Century of Social Teaching:
A Common Heritage,
A Continuing Challenge

*A Pastoral Message of the Catholic Bishops of the United States
on the Hundredth Anniversary of* Rerum Novarum

November 1990

Our faith calls us to work for justice; to serve those in need; to pursue peace; and to defend the life, dignity, and rights of all our sisters and brothers. This is the call of Jesus, the challenge of the prophets, and the living tradition of our Church.

Across this country and around the world, the Church's social ministry is a story of growing vitality and strength, of remarkable compassion, courage, and creativity. It is the everyday reality of providing homeless and hungry people with decent shelter and needed help, of giving pregnant women and their unborn children lifegiving alternatives, of offering refugees welcome, and so much more. It is believers advocating in the public arena for human life wherever it is threatened, for the rights of workers and for economic justice, for peace and freedom around the world, and for "liberty and justice for all" here at home. It is empowering and helping poor and vulnerable people to realize their dignity in inner cities, in rural communities, and in lands far away. It is the everyday commitment of countless people, parishes and programs, local networks and national structures—a tradition of caring service, effective advocacy, and creative action.

At the heart of this commitment is a set of principles, a body of thought, and a call to action known as Catholic social teaching. In 1991, we mark the hundredth anniversary of the first great modern social encyclical, *Rerum Novarum,* and celebrate a century of powerful social teaching. We recall the challenges of that new industrial age and the role of our own James Cardinal Gibbons, who encouraged Pope Leo XIII to issue this groundbreaking encyclical on work and workers. But this celebration is more than an anniversary of an important document; it is a call to share our Catholic social tradition more fully and to explore its continuing challenges for us today. This is a time for renewed reflection on our shared social tradition, a time to strengthen our common and individual commitment to work for real justice and true peace.

Social Mission and Social Teaching

The story of the Church's social mission is both old and new, both a tradition to be shared and a challenge to be fulfilled. The Church's social ministry is:

- *Founded on the life and words of Jesus Christ,* who came "to bring glad tidings to the poor . . . liberty to captives . . . recovery of sight to the blind . . ." (Lk 4:18-19), and who identified himself in the powerful parable of the Last Judgment with the hungry, the homeless, the stranger, "the least of these" (cf. Mt 25:45)
- *Inspired by the passion for justice of the Hebrew prophets* and the scriptural call to care for the weak and to "let justice surge like water" (Am 5:24)
- *Shaped by the social teaching of our Church,* papal encyclicals, conciliar documents, and episcopal statements that, especially over the last century, have explored, expressed, and affirmed the social demands of our faith, insisting that work for justice and peace and care for the poor and vulnerable are the responsibility of every Christian
- *Lived by the people of God,* who seek to build up the kingdom of God, to live our faith in the world and to apply the values of the Scriptures and the teaching of the Church in our own families and parishes, in our work and service, and in local communities, the nation, and the world

The social dimensions of our faith have taken on special urgency and clarity over this last century. Guided by Pope Leo XIII and his successors, by the Second Vatican Council, and by the bishops of the Church, Catholics have been challenged to understand more clearly and act more concretely on the social demands of the Gospel. This tradition calls all members of the Church, rich and poor alike, to work to eliminate the occurrence and effects of poverty, to speak out against injustice, and to shape a more caring society and a more peaceful world.

Together we seek to meet this challenge. Much, however, remains to be done if social doctrine is to become a truly vital and integral part of Catholic life and if we are to meet its challenges in our own lives and social structures. For too many, Catholic social teaching is still an unknown resource. It is sometimes misunderstood as a peripheral aspect rather than as an integral and constitutive element of our faith. The challenge of the 1971 Synod to make working for justice a constitutive dimension of responding to the Gospel should be emphasized in our society, where many see religion as something personal and private. This is tragic since the Catholic social vision offers words of hope, a set of principles and directions for action to a world longing for greater freedom, justice, and peace.

Catholic social teaching is a powerful and liberating message in a world of stark contradictions: a world of inspiring new freedom and lingering oppression, of peaceful change and violent conflict, of remarkable economic progress for some and tragic misery and poverty for many others. Our teaching is a call to conscience, compassion, and creative action in a world confronting the terrible tragedy of widespread abortion, the haunting reality of hunger and homelessness, and the evil of continuing prejudice and poverty. Our teaching lifts up the moral and human dimensions of major public issues, examining "the signs of the times" through the values of the Scriptures, the teaching of the Church, and the experience of the people of God.

Basic Themes

Our Catholic social teaching is more than a set of documents. It is a living tradition of thought and action. The Church's social vision has developed and grown over time, responding to changing circumstances and emerging problems—including developments in human work, new economic questions, war and peace in a nuclear age, and poverty and development in a shrinking world. While the subjects have changed, some basic principles and themes have emerged within this tradition.

A. The Life and Dignity of the Human Person

In the Catholic social vision, the human person is central, the clearest reflection of God among us. Each person possesses a basic dignity that comes from God, not from any human quality or accomplishment, not from race or gender, age or economic status. The test of every institution or policy is whether it enhances or threatens human life and human dignity. We believe people are more important than things.

B. The Rights and Responsibilities of the Human Person

Flowing from our God-given dignity, each person has basic rights and responsibilities. These include the rights to freedom of conscience and religious liberty, to raise a family, to immigrate, to live free from unfair discrimination, and to have a share of earthly goods sufficient for oneself and one's family. People have a fundamental right to life and to those things that make life truly human: food, clothing, housing, health care, education, security, social services, and employment. Corresponding to these rights are duties and responsibilities—to one another, to our families, and to the larger society, to respect the rights of others and to work for the common good.

C. The Call to Family, Community, and Participation

The human person is not only sacred, but social. We realize our dignity and rights in relationship with others, in community. No community is more central than the family; it needs to be supported, not undermined. It is the basic cell of society, and the state has an obligation to support the family. The family has major contributions to make in addressing questions of social justice. It is where we learn and act on our values. What happens in the family is at the basis of a truly human social life. We also have the right and responsibility to participate in and contribute to the broader communities in society. The state and other institutions of political and economic life, with both their limitations and obligations, are instruments to protect the life, dignity, and rights of the person; promote the well-being of our families and communities; and pursue the common good. Catholic social teaching does offer clear guidance on the role of government. When basic human needs are not being met by private initiative, then people must work through their government, at appropriate levels, to meet those needs. A central test of political, legal, and economic institutions is what they do *to* people, what they do *for* people, and how people *participate* in them.

D. The Dignity of Work and the Rights of Workers

Work is more than a way to make a living; it is an expression of our dignity and a form of continuing participation in God's creation. People have the right to decent and productive work, to decent and fair wages, to private property and economic initiative. Workers have the strong support of the Church in forming and joining union and worker associations of their choosing in the exercise of their dignity and rights. These values are at the heart of *Rerum Novarum* and other encyclicals on economic justice. In Catholic teaching, the economy exists to serve people, not the other way around.

E. The Option for the Poor and Vulnerable

Poor and vulnerable people have a special place in Catholic social teaching. A basic moral test of a society is how its most vulnerable members are faring. This is not a new insight; it is the lesson of the parable of the Last Judgment (see Mt 25). Our tradition calls us to put the needs of the poor and vulnerable first. As Christians, we are called to respond to the needs of all our sisters and brothers, but those with the greatest needs require the greatest response. We must seek creative ways to expand the emphasis of our nation's founders on individual rights and freedom by extending democratic ideals to economic life and thus ensure that the basic requirements for life with dignity are accessible to all.

F. Solidarity

We are one human family, whatever our national, racial, ethnic, economic, and ideological differences. We are our brothers' and sisters' keepers (cf. Gn 4:9). In a linked and limited world, our responsibilities to one another cross national and other boundaries. Violent conflict and the denial of dignity and rights to people anywhere on the globe diminish each of us. This emerging theme of solidarity, so strongly articulated by Pope John Paul II, expresses the core of the Church's concern for world peace, global development, environment, and international human rights. It is the contemporary expression of the traditional Catholic image of the *mystical body*. "Loving our neighbor" has global dimensions in an interdependent world.

There are other significant values and principles that also shape and guide the Church's traditional social teaching, but these six themes are central parts of the tradition. We encourage you to read, reflect on, and discuss the documents that make up this tradition.[1] They are a rich resource touching a wide variety of vital, complex, and sometimes controversial concerns. This teaching offers not an alternative social system, but fundamental values that test every system, every nation, and every community. It puts the needs of the poor first. It values persons over things. It emphasizes morality over technology, asking not simply what can we do, but what ought we do. It calls us to measure our lives not by what we have, but by who we are; how we love one another; and how we contribute to the common good, to justice in our community, and to peace in our world.

The Continuing Challenge

This long tradition has led our Church over the last century to support workers and unions actively in the exercise of their rights; to work against racism and bigotry of every kind; to condemn abortion, the arms race, and other threats to human life; and to pursue a more just society and a more peaceful world. These principles are the foundation of the Catholic community's many efforts to serve the poor, immigrants, and other vulnerable people. We know our individual and institutional acts of charity are requirements of the Gospel. They are essential, but not sufficient. Our efforts to feed the hungry, shelter the homeless, welcome the stranger, and serve the poor and vulnerable must be accompanied by concrete efforts to address the causes of human suffering and injustice. We believe advocacy and action to carry out our principles and constructive dialogue about how best to do this both strengthen our Church and enrich our society. We are called to transform our hearts and our social structures, to renew the face of the earth.

Social justice is not something Catholics pursue simply through parish committees and diocesan programs, although these structures can help us to act on our faith. Our social vocation takes flesh in our homes and schools, businesses and unions, offices and factories, colleges and universities, and in community organizations and professional groups. As believers, we are called to bring our values into the marketplace and the political arena, into community and family life, using our everyday opportunities and responsibilities, our voices and votes to defend human life, human dignity, and human rights. We are called to be a leaven, applying Christian values and virtues in every aspect of our lives.

We are also called to weave our social teaching into every dimension of Catholic life, especially worship, education, planning, and evangelization. The Holy Father can teach; bishops can preach; but unless our social doctrine comes alive in personal conversion and common action, it will lack real credibility and effectiveness. We need to build on the experience and commitment of so many parishes where worship consistently reflects the gospel call to continuing conversion, caring service, and creative action. The call to penance and reconciliation must include both the social and the individual dimensions of sin. Our schools and catechetical efforts should regularly share our social teaching. We know that liturgy, religious education, and other apostolates that ignore the social dimensions of our faith are neither faithful to our traditions nor fully Catholic. We also know that parish life that does not reflect the gospel call to charity and justice neglects an essential dimension of pastoral ministry. We cannot celebrate a faith we do not practice. We cannot proclaim a Gospel we do not live. We must work together to ensure that we continue to move together from strong words about charity and justice to effective action, from official statements to creative ministry at every level of the Church's life.

1991—A Celebration and a Call

The hundredth anniversary of *Rerum Novarum* is a unique opportunity to take up these challenges with new urgency and energy. We hope 1991 will be a time of deepening roots, broadening participation, and increasing collaboration on our common social mission. We urge parishes, dioceses, national organizations, and educational and other institutions to use this opportunity to share our social teaching and further integrate it into ongoing efforts. We especially ask that parishes make a major effort to celebrate and share our social teaching during this year, especially from Ascension Thursday to Pentecost Sunday, May 9-19, including May 15, the actual hundredth anniversary of *Rerum Novarum* (or at some other specific time if local circumstances suggest a more appropriate date).

We are very pleased that so many people are already preparing impressive efforts to celebrate this centennial. The creative response of so many demonstrates the vitality, diversity, and unity of the Catholic community in recalling and applying our social teaching.

Conclusion

As we celebrate this century of social teaching, it is important to remember who calls us to this task and why we pursue it. Our work for social justice is first and foremost a work of faith, a profoundly religious task. It is Jesus who calls us to this mission, not any political or ideological agenda. We are called to bring the healing hand of Christ to those in need; the courageous voice of the prophet to those in power; and the gospel message of love, justice, and peace to an often suffering world.

This is not a new challenge. It is the enduring legacy of Pope Leo XIII, who a century ago defended the rights of workers. It is the lasting message of Pope John XXIII, who called for real peace based on genuine respect for human rights. It is the continuing challenge of Pope Paul VI, who declared, "If you want peace, work for justice." It is the commitment of the Second Vatican Council, which declared, "the joys and hopes, the griefs and anxieties" of people of this age, especially those who are poor or afflicted, are "the joys and hopes, the griefs and anxieties of the followers of Christ." And it is the powerful vision of our present Holy Father, Pope John Paul II, who by word and deed calls for a new global solidarity that respects and enhances the dignity of every human person.

Most of all, it is the challenge of our Lord Jesus Christ, who laid out our continuing challenge in the Sermon on the Mount. In 1991, let us explore together what it means to be "poor in spirit" in a consumer society; to comfort those who suffer in our midst; to "show mercy" in an often unforgiving world; to "hunger and thirst for justice" in a nation still challenged by hunger and homelessness, poverty and prejudice; to be "peacemakers" in an often violent and fearful world; and to be the "salt of the earth and the light of the world" in our own time and place.

We hope and pray that, in this centennial year of *Rerum Novarum*, we will become a family of faith evermore committed to the defense of the life, the dignity, and the rights of every human person and a community of genuine solidarity, working every day to build a world of greater justice and peace for all God's children.

Note

1. Among the major topics addressed by these documents are a wide range of economic concerns: the roles of workers and owners; the rights to private property and its limitations; employment and unemployment; economic rights and initiative; debt and development; poverty and wealth; urban and rural concerns. Central concerns include major questions covering human life: abortion, euthanasia, health care, the death penalty, and the violence of war and crime. Also emphasized are issues of discrimination and diversity: racism, ethnic prejudice, cultural pluralism, the dignity and equality of women, and the rights of immigrants and refugees. The teaching also addresses broader questions of religious liberty, political freedom, the common good, the role of the state, subsidiarity and socialization, church-state relations, and political responsibility. A major focus has been the pursuit of peace, disarmament, the use of force and nonviolence, as well as international justice. An emerging issue is the environment.

    For a fuller understanding of Catholic social teaching, see the original documents; an annotated bibliography produced by the U.S. Catholic Conference; or an excellent Vatican document, *Guidelines for the Study and Teaching of the Church's Social Doctrine in the Formation of Priests* (Washington, D.C.: United States Catholic Conference, 1988).

Source: Washington, D.C.: United States Catholic Conference, 1990.

New Slavery, New Freedom

*A Pastoral Message on Substance Abuse from the
United States Catholic Conference*

November 1990

Early this year a young man named David came before a committee
of our conference and told a powerful story of pain, hope, and challenge.

*I used cocaine for a period of twelve years. I lost some very wonderful
jobs, a couple of cars, and lots of money. Eventually, the material things were
gone, and I began chewing through the human beings around me. . . . As I am
sure you can imagine, the combination of drugs and children is uniquely horrible. Even while I was in the midst of using around my children, I had a
strong feeling that this was something that God would not easily forgive. It
felt like the end of the line. . . .*

*I promised myself that I would never lose a marriage because of drug use,
but it happened. And I swore I would never resort to dishonesty to feed my
addiction, but I did. But when it came to being a bad parent, something of my
old values responded with revulsion and disgust. I showed up at my parents'
house with my daughters under each arm and told my folks that there were no
adults in my house, only dope addicts. I felt completely worthless, having violated everything I had ever learned. I entered detox and was referred to a six-
month residential treatment center. It was my fourth stab at sobriety and
something took. I got honest. I got serious. I got clean. That was fourteen
months ago. . . .*

*Those folks who manage to stay clean for a month are really still very sick,
vulnerable people. In that sense, the unconditionally loving arms of the Church
could possibly mean the difference between somebody living or dying. It was
hard to avoid a spiritual dimension in my own recovery. I woke up to a mira-
cle every day that I was clean and crawled into bed each night grateful. . . .*

*Part of the program that I am living each day requires that I take a fear-
less moral inventory of myself and share it with another person. . . . The priest
listened impassively as I described leaving my children parked outside the
crack house on a cold winter's night. He didn't react when I talked about leaving them hungry while I took another hit. When I was finished, I was crying.
I asked how I could ever be forgiven. Each sober breath you draw is an act of
grace, my friend said. You are making amends every day you do not use. I
found enough comfort in what he said to forgive myself. . . .*

*I am not a big believer in the "war on drugs." There is no war, and there
are no sides. There is only addiction and the human and social consequences
that go with it. The Church can do more than mitigate the gravest of those*

problems. In my opinion, by demonstrating a willingness to minister to those afflicted with this disease, the Church becomes better. . . . The Church has the proximity and the people to make a difference in what seems like an insoluble problem. . . .

In today's environment, drug addicts have become almost like lepers. It seems like it is an entirely appropriate place for the Church to serve. Helping people rebuild their lives sounds like noble work to me.

There are many Davids in our midst, people recovering from addiction whose daily courage is a sign of the power of God's healing presence to all of us.

Sadly, there are millions more still caught in the deadly grip of addiction—millions of lives wasted in dependency and despair, lives diminished by fear and hopelessness, lives lost in sickness and violence. The alcohol and drug epidemic sweeping America is not a pretty picture, not for the nation and not for the many communities affected: rich and poor, urban, rural, and suburban; and all races and ethnic groups. Some signs of this crisis are dramatic, such as the drug-related violence and crime we see in our newspapers and on television. Other aspects are hidden in the quiet desperation of families struggling with alcoholism. The fundamental reality is clear: the lives and dignity of so many in our family of faith are being undermined or threatened by the abuse of alcohol and other drugs.

As pastors, we feel the pain and we know the suffering that comes with substance abuse. Many in the Catholic community have recognized the needs of chemically dependent individuals and families and have begun heroic parish, neighborhood, family, and school programs to address this tragic situation. Our Catholic Charities, hospitals, and other social and family agencies also have developed comprehensive programs in prevention, treatment, and rehabilitation.

A number of individual bishops and state Catholic conferences have already addressed this problem, calling their dioceses to new and renewed efforts to expand the pastoral care existing in hundreds of parishes and church agencies and institutions for those suffering from chemical dependency.[1] We applaud their efforts and have built upon their leadership in fashioning this pastoral message. Chemical dependency, however, is a nationwide problem of immense proportions; the entire Catholic community must demonstrate Christ's own love in opening our arms and hearts to those suffering from addiction and in advocating effective, compassionate policies to turn the tide of addiction in this country.

We must look at the harsh realities of addiction as a people of faith who recognize the power of evil to enslave us and the love and power of Jesus Christ to bring us freedom from slavery. We must look at these realities as a people of hope for whom the modern darkness of alcohol and drug addiction can be dispelled by transforming us into a people who walk in the light. We must look at these realities as a people of love strong enough to confront addiction in our own homes or crime in our streets and tender enough to extend a healing touch to those who are enslaved, alone, and broken-hearted, casualties of abuse of alcohol and other drugs.

As people of faith, we are called to share our hope and love with those whose lives are already wounded by this epidemic. We must assure them that this tragic situation can be overcome through proper recovery programs and rehabilitation and that, with the power of God's love, they can create new lives from the brokenness of past weakness and failures. As so many recovering substance abusers know, only when they acknowledge their own powerlessness over chemical dependency and that their lives have become unmanageable can they experience the power that is greater than any drug and the freedom that breaks the shackles of any slavery. What they have learned about the power and freedom of God's grace can enrich the faith of all of us as well.

The Casualties

Substance abuse creates many casualties. One in ten persons in the United States is an alcohol abuser, and one in four is affected by the abuse of alcohol in their own families. More than just a matter of statistics, chemical dependency is a reality in the lives of many members of our own Church—clergy and laity alike. Substance abuse is a critical factor in the painful stories told by millions of individuals and families served by our Catholic Charities and Catholic health agencies and institutions. Many are the children of substance abusers who repeat the patterns of abuse in their own lives, all the while promising themselves, "It'll never happen to me."[2] Others are the co-dependents terrorized in the privacy of even the nicest homes by the erratic and threatening behavior of chemically dependent family members.

Among the casualties are young people with serious drug problems, 55 percent of whom name alcohol as their primary drug. The average starting age for alcohol use is twelve (thirteen for illegal drugs), and 6 percent of high school students are daily users of alcohol. Their second primary drug is marijuana, which has been tried by 50 percent of America's youth.[3] PCP ("angel dust") is currently making a major comeback nationally, especially with urban, minority youth, for whom it is a particularly destructive drug.

Cocaine—especially when smoked as the highly addictive "crack cocaine"—is fast destroying the health and lives of many young people. For many communities, among their younger and older members, cocaine is the newest, most pervasive, and most terrifying form of addiction, drawing down upon its users and traffickers and their families a dreadful combination of quick money, deadly violence, and personal physical and moral disintegration. A smokeable form of methamphetamine—"ice"—is now making inroads, presenting all the problems of crack cocaine with more lasting highs and more bizarre and dangerous psychological effects.

In many ways, the most tragic casualties are the children. Some are placed in foster care as substance abusing parents are no longer capable of providing home or family. Others are born addicted themselves, heirs of the drug slavery destroying their mothers. One estimate is that as many as 375,000 newborns may be damaged annually by drug and alcohol exposure during pregnancy.[4] Abuse of alcohol and other drugs victimizes hundreds of thousands of other children in their own homes when it fuels the gratuitous violence and anger of their parents or their addict friends in patterns of child abuse.

The elders of our communities have fallen victim to substance abuse as well. For many, the most common form of chemical dependence is not the traditional use of alcohol but the newer abuse of prescription drugs, often an escape from the all-too-common isolation and loneliness of old age.

Ultimately, we are all casualties of substance abuse and chemical dependency. Besides the millions of individuals and families personally ruined by abuse of alcohol and other drugs, the economic and social costs are immense. The multibillion dollar "war on drugs" and the drug-related street violence that stalks our communities and kills so many young people are the most visible signs of the severe disease infecting our country. It is estimated that over $100 billion is spent each year on medical treatment for complications arising from untreated alcohol and drug dependency. The annual cost of illegal drug use to the business community is estimated to be an additional $60 billion, more than half of which is in lost productivity.[5]

Reasons for Our Concern

Chemical dependency is a direct assault on the dignity of the human person, a destructive invasion of the lives of individual users, their families, and their communities. Each of us, created in God's own image, is intended to share our Creator's freedom, love, and happiness. People physically, mentally, or emotionally addicted to a drug, in contrast, are clearly dependent, enslaved, and unhappy—a perversion of God's creative plan for us.

Those who abuse alcohol and other drugs often believe that they must have the drug just to feel good, to feel normal, or just to get by. This psychological dependence usually leads to physical dependence, the full-blown "addiction." In both psychological and physical dependence, individuals have great difficulty stopping or even controlling their drug use. Many are so dependent upon their chemical of choice that they are incapable of mature love for those who love and reach out to them.

Chemical dependency then can lead to disorders of the nervous system, physical deterioration, and even death due to drug-related physical problems, accidents while intoxicated, or by suicide—tragically prevalent among drug-using adolescents. The mushrooming growth of AIDS, transmitted by intravenous drug users by the sharing of needles and by sexual contacts, threatens increasing numbers of addicts, their spouses, and their children. At the same time, it is creating a crushing demand on medical and social services in both rural and urban communities.[6]

In many ways, the spiritual symptoms of abuse and addiction reveal most poignantly the human devastation from chemical dependency. Rather than making themselves happy, dependent persons enter a world of lonely isolation, seeing their surroundings as increasingly hostile. Their reality is devoid of a caring God; they feel dominated by forces of evil. To protect their dependency, they lie to themselves and to their loved ones. They deny the evil eroding their bodies, minds, and character, and often blame others for a host of imagined wrongs, including their drug abuse. The chemical abuser's self-worth is often reduced to nothing; and even the possibility of change, recovery, treatment, and rehabilitation is overwhelmed by hopelessness, alienation, and spiritual starvation.

Left alone, most chemically dependent persons will progress more and more deeply into their addictive illness and self-destruction. Blind to their own slavery, they are least able to liberate themselves from it. Their condition cries out for others to recognize the problem and intervene to confront and support them. Responding effectively is the challenging task of family, co-workers, friends, and faith community.

Time for Action

Calming the storm of alcohol and drug abuse raging across our communities will take time and great effort. As people of faith, though, we can and must marshal the combined voices of family, community, and Church in a resounding "no" to drugs; "no" to alcohol abuse; "no" to fear and crime in our streets; and "no" to indifference, neglect, and inaction.

We must begin first in the *family*. The family plays the essential role in prevention. Positive parental role models and stable, loving relationships in the home offer the first and best hope for a drug-free and fulfilling life. This is true in all families—two-parent, single-parent, and multi-generational households—where responsible love often demands heroic efforts of parents and other caretakers. Every family member must help all members, especially the young, to make responsible choices about alcohol and drugs in the larger context of their personal responsibility to use the gifts God has given each of us in service to others.

The family remains the best resource for prevention, early detection, recovery, and treatment of chemical abuse. Families need to be helped to become aware of the early signs of substance abuse and those effective techniques for intervention designed to help individuals suffering from abuse to get into proper treatment or otherwise begin recovery. The family must also be involved in the treatment process and, certainly, in effective follow-up after formal treatment is completed and the recovering alcoholic or addict returns to the community.

Community responses begin by acknowledging that substance abuse is widespread—from our poorest to our most affluent neighborhoods. We must confront the indifference, cynicism, and even racism that imply that as long as the most brutal aspects of this crisis are confined to a few neighborhoods, it does not touch us or call for our action. Problems with abuse of alcohol and other drugs are pervasive, costly, and will have profound economic, social, and political consequences for years to come.

Specifically, we must insist that our communities recognize that they have a severe problem and that public denial only worsens it. We must call for comprehensive educational programs at all levels in all schools, as well as in the broader community, for example, in parent and neighborhood groups. Our stand against substance abuse is a stand *for* human life and dignity. Therefore, we must not let our fear and frustration turn us to means inconsistent with our values, such as the use of the death penalty for drug-related crimes.[7] Furthermore, the widespread use of handguns and automatic weapons in connection with drug commerce reinforces our repeated "call for effective and courageous action to control handguns, leading to their eventual elimination from our society."[8]

When we call for more police protection and swift punishment for violent crime, we must urge and be willing to pay for adequate federal, state, and local resources for prevention, treatment, and rehabilitation for all substance abusers as well. Not doing so will cost far more in the future than appropriate programs now. Good programs do exist in many communities already, but they must be supported and strengthened. Let us build on their hard work and caring service. Businesses, too, should promote drug-free workplaces and employee assistance programs that include counseling and treatment. Finally, we must address the underlying problems that contribute to the allure of these substances and promote an illegal economy based on drug trafficking—lack of employment, poverty, inadequate education, lack of purpose and meaning, poor housing, and powerlessness.

Our *church* response to drug and alcohol dependency must draw upon all our spiritual, pastoral, social, and institutional resources. Across this nation, Catholics are already deeply involved in works of education, health care, human services, and pastoral ministry to those affected by chemical abuse. Many people in our dioceses are confronting substance abuse—in their own lives and in their families and communities—and their efforts need to be supported and affirmed. But more is needed.

Our *parishes* should pray regularly for those suffering with substance abuse, those involved in recovery, treatment, prevention, and enforcement, as well as for their families. Homilies should present the realities of substance abuse in the context of our responsibilities to one another and the power of God to enable personal change. Every parish should be reminded that chemical dependency tears at the fabric not just of family and community but of our faith community as well. Whenever some are tormented by chemical dependency, we all suffer. Specific parish initiatives exist across the country and span a wide variety of responses:

1. Our parishes can offer individuals and families struggling with substance abuse the abundant resources of personal and communal prayer, the power of God's word in the Scriptures, and the rich treasure of our sacramental life. They can experience healing and strengthening for life without addiction in the sacrament of reconciliation and know the loving presence of Christ Jesus in the celebration of the eucharist in the midst of a supportive faith community.

2. An alcohol and drug awareness effort should develop educational, informational, preventive, and advocacy programs of service to the entire community. *Wherever possible, our parishes should offer adult education programs on a regular basis to make this knowledge available to as many families as possible.* Parishes are also ideal locations for formation of parent groups to share information and concerns about substance abuse and to develop education and training resources for parental guidance in youth development.

3. Parish facilities also could be made available to self-help groups such as Alcoholics Anonymous (AA), Narcotics Anonymous (NA), Al-Anon, Alateen, Adult Children of Alcoholics, and NAR-Anon. The Twelve-Step Program, the centerpiece of these powerful groups, has a profoundly spiri-

tual foundation based on trust in God. Our parishes ought to be places of hospitality and support for those confronting and recovering from substance abuse.

4. Parish schools and religious education programs should include an appropriate substance-abuse curriculum, with maximum appropriate parental involvement and collaboration with other schools and community educational efforts. Teachers and other professionals should be trained to present this curriculum. These efforts should stress the importance of family and the dignity, self-esteem, and responsibility of individuals.

5. Pastors and all parish and school professionals should learn to recognize early signs of abuse of alcohol and other drugs. They are often the first persons contacted by individuals and families in crisis, and they should familiarize themselves with available community resources and respond by making appropriate referrals. We are blessed in this country with some excellent treatment centers, and parishes should be prepared to help people in need to find appropriate assistance. Parishes should also advocate on behalf of the many persons who encounter obstacles when searching for appropriate and affordable treatment or other recovery programs. Parishes also should reach out to families where alcohol and drug abuse is already identified and to the children of those families, who are likely to continue substance abuse in their own lives.

6. Parishes can help people in the process of recovery, including those who return to the community after treatment. They can provide supportive services to spouses and children during this time when persons in recovery are rebuilding their lives, seeking new jobs, learning employment and social skills, and reentering the community.

7. Where possible, parish efforts should be joined to those of other churches, ecclesial communities, and other religiously sponsored programs for prevention, treatment, rehabilitation, and advocacy. Parish functions and activities need to model responsible use of alcohol. They should also support and work with local community organizations committed to the common struggle against substance abuse and its causes.

All parish efforts should flow from the faith-filled acknowledgment of our own sinfulness and from the healing power of the risen Christ mediated through the church community. We who have experienced the tender compassion of a loving God should graciously share it with others wounded by dependency and addiction.

When parishes welcome recovering alcoholics and addicts and families wrestling with this disease, they are calling people into the healing and grace-filled dynamic of penance, forgiveness, and reconciliation. Such parishes will find their celebration of the Lord's death and rising in the eucharist enriched by the pattern of death and resurrection fleshed out in the one-day-at-a-time recovery of those affected by addiction. Faith, hope, and love shared with people wounded by dependency will be returned in the renewed commitment of those who are so welcomed into our parish families.

As dioceses, we must also bring to bear the wealth of our diverse gifts and resources to confront chemical dependency. Days designated for diocesan-wide prayer for alcoholics, addicts, and their families and special petitions in the Prayers of the Faithful during the liturgical year can be combined with specific actions on the part of diocesan offices and agencies.

Each diocese should have a clear substance abuse policy. Catholic Charities,[9] social services, youth services, education offices, and health care institutions and agencies should continue and expand education, prevention, treatment, and rehabilitation programs. They also should explore and develop new responses to community needs for prevention, treatment, rehabilitation, and advocacy. High priority should be given to:

- Outreach programs to the poor and to minority communities
- Promotion of drug-free workplaces
- Expansion of services in conjunction with parishes
- Provision of child care for those families where parents are attending recovery groups or undergoing treatment
- Model employee assistance programs in dioceses and in all church institutions that will include counseling and treatment for substance abuse

As a national conference and in our state Catholic conferences, we are concerned that government at all levels exercise its responsibility for the coordination and provision of essential services to combat substance abuse. We commit ourselves to ongoing advocacy efforts to promote public policy and to enact legislation to ensure access to adequate, affordable, and appropriate treatment and services for all those in need. No persons suffering from chemical dependency should be denied access to the treatment that could free them and their families from this slavery. Especially, no pregnant woman or mother should be denied the care that can ensure the health of her children and promote the integrity of her family. We will urge legislators and other public officials to allocate sufficient funds for prevention and treatment to accomplish these goals.

We are often reminded of the vivid impact, especially on youth, of television programs, films, and recordings that present the use of alcohol and other drugs as attractive and harmless. We note, too, that some in the entertainment media have taken first steps to reverse such trends. As we applaud this beginning, we encourage the entertainment industry to do all it can to convince young people to avoid substance abuse.

Regarding efforts by our government to reduce the supply of drugs, particularly in the countries of Latin America, we will work with the Church in those countries in assessing U.S. policy there, in formulating appropriate criteria for judging U.S. programs there, and in advocating common directions for the future. We share the deep concern of the Church in the region over the increasing militarization of the U.S. drug program. Such programs may prove not only ineffective but counterproductive, potentially involving increasing U.S. military commitment within these countries. Rather than short-term, often futile, programs of crop eradication, which may do more harm to the peasant farmer and to a fragile environment than to the drug criminals, we favor effective programs of international cooperation for genuine economic development and other strategies to overcome the impact of drugs within both societies.

Conclusion

As a believing community, we try to confront chemical dependency with both the honesty to recognize its power for human destruction and the faith that we can prevail with the grace and power of God. Christ comes into our hearts and our lives whenever any one of us takes the bold steps to see addiction for the slavery it is, to act to prevent its spread, and to reach out to those suffering from its devastating power.

To every sister or brother challenging addiction in daily recovery, we extend our prayerful admiration and concern. To every family struggling to confront and heal chemical dependency in its members, we pledge the solidarity, support, and service of this faith community. The Church is called to serve, to reach out, to help rebuild lives, and to support individuals, families, and communities in the fight against the slavery of drug and alcohol abuse. This is a noble calling worthy of our most generous and dynamic response.

We ask your prayers and personal involvement in bringing the gospel message of hope and love to the terrible challenge of chemical dependency in our nation. Let us together extend the healing hand of Christ to one another and to all those suffering from substance abuse in our midst.

Notes

1.   New Jersey Bishops, "Pastoral Statement on Substance Abuse," *Origins* 18:6 (June 23, 1988): 94-96; James Cardinal Hickey, "Confronting a New Slavery: Pastoral Reflections on Washington's Substance Abuse Crisis," *Origins* 19:5 (June 15, 1989): 78-88; New York State Catholic Conference, "Chemical Dependency: A Challenge for the Church," *Origins* 19:16 (September 21, 1989): 268-272.

2.   Claudia Black, Ph.D., MSW, *It Will Never Happen to Me!* (Denver: M.A.C. Printing and Publications Division, 1982).

3.   "Chemical Dependency: A Challenge for the Church," 3.

4.   Study based on a survey of thirty-six hospitals by the National Association for Perinatal Addiction Research and Education (NAPARE, August 1988).

5.   The White House Conference for a Drug Free America, *Final Report* (Washington, D.C., June 1988), 85.

6.   See our discussion of HIV/AIDS in National Conference of Catholic Bishops, *Called to Compassion and Responsibility: A Response to the HIV/AIDS Crisis* (Washington, D.C.: United States Catholic Conference, 1989).

7.   United States Catholic Conference, *U.S. Bishops' Statement on Capital Punishment* (Washington, D.C.: United States Catholic Conference, 1980).

8.   USCC Committee on Social Development and World Peace, *Handgun Violence: A Threat to Life* (Washington, D.C.: United States Catholic Conference, 1975), no. 8.

9.   See "Addiction and Recovery: A Look at What Catholic Charities Agencies Can Do to Bring an End to Substance Abuse," in *Charities USA* 17:3 (May/June 1990).

Source: Washington, D.C.: United States Catholic Conference, 1990.

Heritage and Hope:
Evangelization in the United States

*Pastoral Letter of the National Conference of Catholic Bishops on the
Fifth Centenary of Evangelization in the Americas*

November 1990

Introduction

As we observe the five hundredth anniversary of the encounter between Europe and the Americas, we join with our fellow citizens in the United States, Canada, Latin America, and many European nations in commemorating an event that reshaped the course of world history. Although we share this event with many throughout the world, our primary concern in this letter is with our own land, the United States of America. As pastors and teachers of the people of God, we wish to call attention to the crucial role that evangelization has played in forming the present civilization of our continent. Evangelization, as Pope Paul VI has said, "means bringing the Good News [of Jesus Christ] into all strata of humanity, and through its influence transforming humanity from within and making it new."[1]

It is that process of transformation that we highlight as we observe the quincentenary, the change that results from men and women hearing the proclamation of the good news that, in Christ, God is reconciling the world and bringing to light a kingdom of righteousness, peace, and joy. We recall the history of that process on our own continent, rejoicing in its successes and lamenting and learning from its failures. As Pope John Paul II has indicated, the Church wishes to approach the quincentenary "with the humility of truth, without triumphalism or false modesty, but looking only at the truth, in order to give thanks to God for its successes and to draw from its errors motives for projecting herself, renewed, towards the future."[2] As Church, we often have been unconscious and insensitive to the mistreatment of our Native American brothers and sisters and have at times reflected the racism of the dominant culture of which we have been a part. In this quincentennial year, we extend our apology to the native peoples and pledge ourselves to work with them to ensure their rights, their religious freedom, and the preservation of their cultural heritage.

Mindful of the valuable contribution of other Christians in bringing the Gospel to our hemisphere, we, nevertheless, focus in this statement on the legacy of Catholics. We wish to gain from an examination

of our past a firm sense of our identity as an evangelized and evangelizing Church.

But beyond that we wish to speak to the present, to look at the
challenges we face here and now. We wish, as well, to look to the
future to see how to continue the work of evangelization and to promote what Pope John Paul II has described as "a new evangelization:
new in its ardor, its methods, its expression."[3]

We challenge all those who hear our message to respond, to be
part of the process by which the word of God takes root and bears fruit
that nourishes every part of life. The story of the Americas is our story,
not only in the sense that there have been millions of Christians who
have populated this hemisphere, but also in the sense that, as the
Second Vatican Council has taught, there is nothing genuinely human
that does not touch the followers of Christ. All the joys, the hopes, the
griefs, and the anxieties that make up the story of the last half millennium are our heritage as Catholics and as members of the American
community.[4]

The Drama of Evangelization

Human history is the drama of humanity's search for God and
God's loving revelation. God has made women and men, placing deep
within their souls a hunger for the divine. God has established within
creation signs that manifest the Creator's love. In the great event of the
Incarnation, that drama reached its high point. "And the Word became
flesh and made his dwelling among us" (Jn 1:14). Christ is "the true
light which enlightens everyone" (Jn 1:9) who comes into the world.
He is the fullness of the Godhead from whom we have all received
grace and truth (cf. Jn 1:14). To spread the good news of his coming,
Jesus called to himself a people and sent them forth as witnesses of the
great things that they had seen and heard (cf. Acts 4:20). Compelled by
the love of Christ they went forth to the ends of the earth to proclaim
the message of Jesus. The Church, as the people of God, stands on that
"foundation of the apostles and prophets" (Eph 2:20). The Spirit also
has been at work outside the visible Church, scattering among the
nations what the church fathers of the second and third centuries
called the "seeds of the word," inspiring men and women through
their discoveries, their aspirations, their sufferings, and their joys.

Human beings have responded in various ways to God's loving
revelation, often cooperating with God's grace and also, in their weakness, falling short of the invitation to abundant life. At times the seeds
of the word sown on good ground have been choked by the cares of
this world. The struggle to allow the word to blossom in our lives is an
acute one that was no less arduous in the past than today. The failures,

which often have tragic consequences, are, likewise, not new but part of our heritage as imperfect yet graced daughters and sons of God.

The fundamental unity of the human race stems from the fact that it has been made in God's image and likeness. "Christ's Gospel of love and redemption transcends national boundaries, cultural differences, and divisions among peoples. It cannot be considered foreign anywhere on earth; nor can it be considered identical with any particular culture or heritage."[5]

The faith, however, finds expression in the particular values, customs, and cultural institutions of those who respond to God's revelation. This means that both the message and the people to whom it is addressed must be viewed with respect and dignity.[6] The story of the coming of faith to our hemisphere must begin, then, not with the landing of the first missionaries, but centuries before with the history of the Native American peoples.

Migrating across this great continent, the peoples settled over thousands of miles from the mountains of the Pacific Northwest to the tropical swamps of the Southeast, developing distinct languages and cultures and carefully planned social systems to meet the demanding needs of a vast, challenging environment. The Creator walked with the first Americans, giving them a realization of the sacredness of creation, manifested in their rites of chant, dance, and other rituals. The sun dance and the vision quest spoke of their understanding of the importance of prayer and spiritual growth. The sweatlodge, the traditions of fasting and keeping silence illustrated an understanding of the values of self-humiliation and deprivation for the sake of something greater. Their respect for unborn life, for the elderly, and for children told of a refined sense of the value of life. The prayers, practices, and sacred celebrations showed the wonder and awe with which the native peoples carried out their stewardship of the earth.

The encounter with the Europeans was a harsh and painful one for the indigenous peoples. The introduction of diseases to which the Native Americans had no immunities led to the death of millions.[7] Added to that were the cultural oppression, the injustices, the disrespect for native ways and traditions that must be acknowledged and lamented.[8] The great waves of European colonization were accompanied by destruction of Native American civilization, the violent usurpation of their lands, and the brutalization of their inhabitants. Many of those associated with the colonization of the land failed to see in the natives the workings of the same God that they espoused. Confronted with a vastly different culture, European Christians were challenged to reexamine how their own culture shaped their faith. Often they failed to distinguish between what was crucial to the Gospel and what were matters of cultural preference. That failure brought with it catastrophic consequences for the native peoples who were at times forced to become European at the same time they became Christian.

Yet, that is not the whole picture. The effort to portray the history of the encounter as a totally negative experience in which only violence and exploitation of the native peoples was present is not an accurate interpretation of the past. The notion, traditionally known as the "black legend," that Catholic Spain was uniquely cruel and violent in the administration of its colonies is simply untrue. Spanish monarchs, through the *Patronato Real,* financed the ministries of thousands of missionaries and made extensive efforts to support the Church's efforts in the newly encountered lands. Also through Spain many of the cultural refinements and scientific advances of Renaissance Europe were brought to the Americas.

There was, in fact, a deeply positive aspect of the encounter of European and American cultures. Through the work of many who came in obedience to Christ's command to spread the Gospel, and through the efforts of those who responded to the word—the Native Americans and peoples of the new race that resulted from the mingling of the European and American peoples—the Gospel did in fact take root. The encounter engendered an unprecedented missionary effort on the part of European Christians that was to reshape the map of the Church. It represented a widening of the frontiers of humanity and a vigorous effort on the part of the Church to bring about the universality that Christ desired for his message. It cannot be denied that the interdependence of the cross and the crown that occurred during the first missionary campaigns brought with it contradictions and injustices. But neither can it be denied that the expansion of Christianity into our hemisphere brought to the peoples of this land the gift of the Christian faith with its power of humanization and salvation, dignity and fraternity, justice and love.

From the earliest days there were Catholic missionaries who exercised a humanizing presence in the midst of colonization. Many of the missionaries made an effort at adapting the forms and symbols of Christianity to the customs of the indigenous American peoples. They learned the languages, the ceremonies, and the traditions of the native peoples, attempting to show how Christianity complemented their beliefs and challenged those things in their culture that conflicted with Christ's message. They labored for the spiritual and material welfare of those to whom they ministered.

Perhaps the most significant moral problem the Church faced in the Americas was that of human dignity and slavery. Some spoke out energetically for the rights of native peoples and against the mistreatment of imported slaves. Bartolomé de las Casas, a Dominican bishop and friend of the Columbus family, was a tireless defender of Indian rights. While for a time he advocated the practice of importing African peoples to replace the Indian slaves, he soon repented upon suffering profound moral anguish. As bishop of Chiapas he ordered the denial of absolution to those who persisted in holding slaves. This mandate earned him the opposition of so many in his diocese that he resigned as bishop. Las Casas went on to become one of the earliest opponents of the enslavement of peoples of any race.

Las Casas inspired the work of the Spanish theologians Francisco de Vitoria and Francisco Suarez, who were pioneers in the creation of a philosophy of universal human rights based on the dignity of the person. Spanish rulers like Charles I responded to the call for reform and instituted new laws to protect the rights of natives. The pontiffs also responded, condemning any efforts at the enslavement of the native population. Pope Paul III, in 1537, issued his bull *Sublimis Deus* in which he "denounced those that held that the inhabitants of the West Indies and the southern continents . . . should be treated like irrational animals and used exclusively for our profit and service." He declared that "Indians, as well as any other peoples which Christianity will come to know in the future, must not be deprived of their freedom and their possessions . . . even if they are not Christians and that, on the contrary, they must be left to enjoy their freedom and their possessions." Later Urban VIII declared that anyone who kept Indian slaves would incur excommunication.[9]

Stories of Evangelization

For 500 years the Gospel of Jesus Christ informed the lives of the Americas attempting to complete and fulfill that which was good in both the native and immigrant cultures and confront what was not. The stories of the many evangelizers—men and women, clergy, religious, and lay—who strove to spread the good news are numerous and varied. In what follows we tell only a few of those stories, not necessarily the most important, but ones that illustrate the range and depth of the evangelizing process in our history. It is not intended to be a list of the most famous or the best but of significant voices that can inspire us today.

Christopher Columbus

The year 1992 marks the half millennium of the voyage of Christopher Columbus. He was the son of a Europe freshly astir, reaching out for new resources and new trade routes to the East. It was also a Europe in which missionary fervor ran high. Spain's Ferdinand and Isabella, as Pope Alexander VI wrote in 1493, "for a long time had intended to seek out and discover certain islands and mainlands, remote and unknown and not hitherto discovered by others, to the end that [they] might bring to them the worship of our Redeemer and the profession of the Catholic faith.[10] On October 12, 1492, Columbus planted the cross on the soil of the Americas. He named the land San Salvador—Holy Savior—and thus began the process of bringing Christianity to the hemisphere.

Columbus had close ties to the Franciscan order and was influenced by ideas on missions, then current among the friars, that spoke of a new age of the Holy Spirit that was about to dawn, marked by the activities of zealous missionaries who would bring the Gospel to non-believers throughout the world.[11] On his second voyage, instructed by the Catholic rulers to "in every way and manner that you can, procure and work on inducing the dwellers of these islands and mainland to convert to our holy catholic faith," he was accompanied by a group of religious men, the first of the missioners, whom Pope John Paul II has called "the architects of that admirable action of evangelization."[12]

The exploitation and eventual extermination of the Arawaks that followed Columbus's landing, encouraged in no small part by his own reports, was inexcusable. Much has been written on the motivations and character of Columbus that reveals the workings of a complex man whose journeys to America were motivated by forces ranging from self-interest to piety. In him, as in the whole experience of the encounter between Europeans and peoples of the Americas, diverse motivations were at work.

Complex as well was the process by which the word of God became part of the lives of the peoples who would come to be known as Americans. Human weakness coexisted with virtue, openness with prejudice, charity with injustice. Through it all the seeds of the word variously sown brought forth the fruits of the Gospel. Over the centuries thousands of men and women sought to bring the good news of Jesus to their times, healing the sick, educating the ignorant, and witnessing to their culture of the presence of Christ. There were clergy, religious, and laity from different races and from different times but all motivated by a common desire to evangelize.

Early Spanish Missionaries

Spain surpassed all other colonial powers in its comprehensive efforts to bring the Gospel to America. The hundreds of missionaries who came to the new land shared a concern for applying the Gospel to all of life. Struggling with soldiers and other colonists whose self-interest was greater than any care for the native peoples and with limited understanding of the integrity of native cultures, the missionaries often took part in the destruction of valuable aspects of Native American life. But they also strove to serve the needs of the native population, combining their preaching of the faith with large-scale efforts at improving health care, engineering, agriculture, and education through an elaborate mission system.

Those efforts came early in the history of our land. In 1565, secular priest Francisco Lopez de Mendoza Grajales dedicated the first Catholic parish in what is now the United States in St. Augustine, Fla., and began work among the Timucuan Indians of Florida. Nuestra Señora de la Soledad, the first hospital in North America, opened its doors in 1599 in St. Augustine. The friars' advocacy of the rights of the native peoples was so strong that on two notable occasions during the latter half of the seventeenth century two governors of Florida were removed from office and imprisoned by the Crown for their acts against the Indians.[13] In 1599, Franciscan friars with the colonizing expedition of Juan de Oñate established churches in northern New Mexico to serve the new communities of settlers as well as to provide Native American converts with improved education, nutrition, agriculture, and shelter. Another Franciscan, the Venerable Antonio Margil, worked during the early eighteenth century in Texas, founding missions in the region of present-day San Antonio. He established the first church in Louisiana and walked barefoot from there to Guatemala in an extraordinary journey that resulted in the conversion of 60,000 Indians to the faith.

Eusebio Francisco Kino, the seventeenth-century Jesuit missionary to Sonora and Arizona, set the stage for the conversion and transformation of tens of thousands of desert-dwelling Native Americans. He opened overland routes to distant California and inspired the creation of the Pious Fund of the Californias. His unwavering love for his people is still recognized by generations of pilgrims to his grave in Sonora, where he died in 1711. The upper California coast was the venue for the work of one of the most indefatigable of Franciscan missionaries, Blessed Fray Junípero Serra. Between 1769 and 1784, he founded nine of California's famous twenty-one missions, stretching from San Diego to the Great Bay of San Francisco. Serra's zeal for the conversion of souls has carried into our times as special inspiration for priestly vocations.

Juan Diego and Hispanic Americans:
The Story of Our Lady of Guadalupe

That process by which Christianity became not the religion of the invader but the prized possession of the native peoples and of the many peoples of mixed Spanish and Native American descent is perhaps best symbolized in the story of Our Lady of Guadalupe. According to the long-established tradition, the Indian peasant Juan Diego recounted his vision of the Virgin Mary appearing to him in

Tepeyac in 1531. He told of how she appeared on the site of a shrine to the virgin mother goddess, Tonantzin, venerated by the native peoples. As one greater than the sun god, Mary appeared to hide the sun whose rays shone around her. As one greater than the moon goddess, she seemed to stand on the moon itself. Yet she appeared not as a war-like goddess, but as a young mestiza. She wore a little black band that indicated she was an expectant mother. She was beautiful and comforting, promising protection and liberation to Juan Diego in a time of great loss and hardship. She enabled him and the native people to endure, in the light of faith, suffering, deplorable injustice, and humiliation. As one of his own she directed him to another that was greater than she: to her son Jesus, to the Christ in whom all the fullness of the Godhead dwells. When she parted, she left on his cloak an image of herself—Mary, the Mother of God, the symbol of the Church, the one through whom Christ has come into the world, imaged on native cloth, grown on the Mexican hillsides and formed by the hands of the people of that land. The devotion to Our Lady of Guadalupe that followed (recently advanced by the Church's beatification of Juan Diego) illustrates vividly how the Gospel was able to find forms of expression that came from the cultures of those to whom it was addressed. The contributions of Native Americans and Hispanics who have followed in Juan Diego's footsteps have enriched many and enabled us all more deeply to understand and express the message of Christ.[14]

Andrew White and the Maryland Jesuits

It was not only in the Spanish dominion that missions blossomed. The English Jesuits were part of the early efforts of the second Lord Baltimore to found a colony in the Chesapeake Bay area. Jesuit missionary Andrew White and two other missionaries journeyed on Baltimore's ships, the *Ark* and the *Dove*, in 1633. White wrote of the enterprise: "The first and most important design of the Most Illustrious Baron . . . is not to think so much of planting fruits and trees in a land so fruitful, as of sowing the seeds of Religion and piety. . . . Who can doubt that by one such glorious work as this many thousands of souls will be brought to Christ?"[15] White composed a catechism in Piscataway, as well as a grammar and dictionary. The missionaries had great success with the Anacostians and Piscataways despite the persecution of Catholic missionaries by Protestants from Virginia and the decline of the missions in ensuing decades.

The Catholic presence in Maryland was to become an enduring part of the history of that land. With it came religious toleration that briefly marked Maryland as the first colony where citizens had the freedom to practice the religion of their choice without suffering the persecutions of the state.

The Evangelizers in New France
and Marie of the Incarnation

In New France as well the Gospel accompanied settlement and exploration. The great valleys of the St. Lawrence and Mississippi rivers formed the centers of the French presence in North America. French Jesuit missionaries Pierre Baird and Ennemond Mass began their work at Port Royal, Nova Scotia, in 1608. From there they brought the Gospel to Native Americans throughout northern New England. Father Baird celebrated the first Mass in New England on November 1, 1611, on an island off the coast of Maine. To the west, Jacques Marquette combined a zeal for exploration with efforts to evangelize. After four years of mission work in the upper Great Lakes area he joined explorer Louis Joliet on a 2,500-mile canoe trip down the Mississippi. He founded the mission of the Immaculate Conception of the Blessed Virgin at Kaskaskia on the banks of the Illinois River in 1674.

An important part of that evangelization was a concern for the education of the young. During the 1650s, Marie of the Incarnation was part of a small group of Ursuline sisters who had come from France to work with the children of Native Americans and French colonists. Their schools for girls were among the earliest efforts by women's communities to evangelize native peoples in North America. Marie left the comforts of family and home in Europe to go to the frontier settlement of Quebec. After risking her life in a three-month Atlantic crossing, she told of her encounters with the people she had come to serve: "thanks to the goodness of God, our vocation and our love for the natives has never diminished. I carry them in my heart and try very gently through my prayers to win them for heaven. There is always in my soul a constant desire to give my life for their salvation."[16]

In fact martyrdom was an awful reality for some of the earliest evangelizers. Not all of the native peoples welcomed the missionaries or saw in Christianity a faith and way of life that complemented their own. Brave Franciscan Friar Juan de Padilla, who had accompanied the Coronado expedition, was martyred probably near Quivira in the Kansas prairie in 1542 where he was dwelling with the native peoples. He thus became the first martyr in North America. Spanish Dominican friars, Fathers Luis Cancer and Diego de Tolosa and Brother Fuentes were killed in Florida in the area of Tampa Bay in 1549. Jesuit Juan Bautista Segura lost his life in Virginia in 1571. Six other Jesuits, who were later known as North American Martyrs, gave up their lives in the spread of the Gospel. Among them was St. Isaac Jogues, who zealously served the Huron nation and was killed by a neighboring tribe in 1646 in what is now Auriesville, New York.

Blessed Kateri Tekakwitha

The word that was brought by the early missionaries to the Native American peoples yielded rich fruit that was nowhere more evident than in the life of Blessed Kateri Tekakwitha. Kateri was born in 1656 in the Indian village of Ossernenon (in the area that is now upstate New York). Orphaned as a child, she came to the Christian faith at age twenty through the ministry of a French Jesuit. Her new faith brought upon her abuse and ostracism from her family and tribe. A year later she fled her village, walking 200 miles in the snow to a Christian Indian village near Montreal to receive the eucharist for the first time. There she became known for a life of great charity as she shared her faith and worked for the benefit of her new community until her death in 1680 at the age of twenty-four.

Evangelization and the African Americans

The coming of the Gospel to America involved not only the European and American peoples but also those of the other great continent that made up the Atlantic world: Africa. Around the time of Columbus's first voyage, Europe was also taking new interest in Africa. The need for laborers in the American colonies gave rise during the next century to the slave trade that linked the three continents during the colonial period. During much of that time, Africans made up a significant part of the populations of the colonies.

As was the case with Native Americans, there were many followers of Christ who, unwilling to acknowledge the image of God in the Africans, enslaved and treated them like chattel. The injustice done to the African peoples was profound and deplorable.

Despite the oppression, there were those evangelizers who sought to serve their African American brothers and sisters. Alonso de Sandoval worked tirelessly during the first half of the seventeenth century, evangelizing slaves en route from Africa to the West Indies. His writings were among the first warnings to Europeans of the horrors of the slave trade. Through his example, Jesuit St. Peter Claver began his work as a priest and physician that resulted in the conversion of over 300,000 slaves to Christianity.

The Gospel took root and bore fruit among the African American people. Peruvian mulatto St. Martín de Porres, of Spanish father and African mother, has become a source of inspiration for African Americans and Catholics of many countries and races, because of his holiness and his dedicated service to the poor, the sick, and orphaned children. In Florida, former slave Francisco Menendez was successful in his efforts to found the first town of free Blacks in what is now the United States, Gracia Real de Santa Teresa de Mose. In early nineteenth-century New York, the saintly Pierre Toussaint worked to evangelize and minister to fellow Haitians and Blacks, French refugees, the homeless, and the sick of all races and conditions. African American Catholic women also played a significant role in the life of the Church in the United States. Mother Mary Elizabeth Lange became the foundress of the Oblate Sisters of Providence, the first congregation of African American women religious, in 1829. The Oblate Sisters worked to evangelize and educate African Americans, operating schools and orphanages in Maryland. In 1842, Henriette Delille and Juliette Gaudin began the Holy Family Sisters in New Orleans, ministering to the sick and poor among the African American community and bringing the good news to the needy.

St. Elizabeth Seton

One of the great resources of the Catholic Church in the United States has been her converts. Among them none is more noteworthy than the first person born in the United States to attain sainthood, Elizabeth Seton. Born in 1774 in New York, she was raised as a devout Anglican. A wife and mother of five children, she was received into the Catholic Church after the death of her husband. Writing to a non-Catholic friend afterward, she said of her new life: "As to my manner of life, every day increases my interest in it. And for that religion you think folly, madness, bigotry, superstition, etc., I find it a source of every consolation."[17] Her love of the Gospel and interest in the education of children led her to open a school for girls in Baltimore in 1808. With the encouragement of Archbishop John Carroll of Baltimore she formed a women's community to instruct poor children. The Sisters of Charity were the first religious community founded in the United States, and their work was at the vanguard of the parochial school movement.

Pierre DeSmet and the Northwest

Expansion into the American West brought whole new waves of missionary endeavor to the Pacific Coast. For many years the leaders of various Native American tribes had asked that the "Black Robe" come to teach them about "the place where abides the Great Spirit." Finally, in 1840, Fr. Pierre Jean DeSmet, a Belgian Jesuit missionary, traveled from St. Louis to present-day western Wyoming where he was met by 1,800 Native Americans who were members of the Flathead, Nez Percé, and Pen d'Oreille tribes. Later, together with Fr. Modest Demers and Francis Blanchet, he began an extensive evangelization program for the entire Northwest including Idaho, Oregon, and Washington. Considered a most loved and trusted friend of the

Northern nations, DeSmet was frequently called on by the U.S. government to write treaties of peace. His successful missionary work marked one of the most imaginative evangelization efforts in the history of the Church in the United States.

Félix Varela

The ability of evangelizers to adapt to new situations is an important part of the story of the Gospel in our hemisphere. That quality is well illustrated in the life of Félix Varela. Varela was born in 1788 in Cuba. For the first thirty-five years of his life he strove to spread the good news in his native land through his teaching and writing in areas of philosophy and politics. His involvement with the early movement to achieve greater Cuban national autonomy forced him to flee the Spanish dominion for his life when he became the center of a movement to introduce a new form of government to Cuba. As an exile from his own land, he arrived in New York City in 1823 and there found ways to continue his lifelong work of evangelization. His remarkable career as a priest and journalist extended for thirty years. He became vicar general of the diocese of New York and ministered to immigrant Irish. He edited *El Habanero,* a magazine for Cuban exiles, and became involved in the early efforts among U.S. Catholics to produce religious journals in English and Spanish. Throughout his life he was a tireless champion of human freedom and of the compatibility of Catholicism with free democratic society.

Isaac Hecker

The question of how the Gospel becomes incarnate in a specific culture is one that U.S. Catholics struggled with long after the colonial period. During the nineteenth century there were few who gave themselves as fully to an examination of how Catholicism should address the culture of the United States as Isaac Hecker. In 1858, he founded the first society of North American priests, the Missionary Society of St. Paul the Apostle. While a young man at the Transcendentalist commune Brook Farm in West Roxbury, Mass., he came to believe that Catholicism would have great appeal to many non-Catholics searching for a religion that could fulfill their spiritual aspirations and the demands of their reason. He believed that Catholicism was the religion best suited for the new republic and that Catholics were gifted by their tradition with the tools to build a more just society. His conviction led him to develop new means for evangelizing, utilizing mass market magazine and book publishing media, along with innovative public lectures to reach non-Catholics. His vision of the evangelization of American culture became the inspiration for many, including James

Cardinal Gibbons, archbishop of Baltimore, and Monsignor John J. Burke, CSP, the first general secretary of the National Catholic Welfare Conference (now the National Conference of Catholic Bishops).

St. Philippine Rose Duchesne and Blessed Katharine Drexel

In the course of 500 years, many inspired by the Gospel have chosen service to the less fortunate over a life of comfort. Of those, few are more relevant to our present day than St. Philippine Rose Duchesne and Blessed Katharine Drexel.

Philippine Rose Duchesne was born in 1769 into an upper-class family in Grenoble, France. Her father was a prominent lawyer and member of parliament. She grew up in privileged surroundings in the family's palatial home on the Grande Rue. Yet her desire to serve Christ and the poor caused her to join the Visitation Sisters at the age of nineteen. Forced to leave the convent by the anticlerical forces of the French Revolution, she returned to Grenoble where she did charitable work until she was able to join the newly founded Society of the Sacred Heart in 1804. Under her leadership a group journeyed to America in 1818 to work with young girls. Over the next thirty-four years she was involved with the establishment of six schools along the Mississippi. One of her last years was spent living among the Potawatomi Indians in Kansas.

Born in 1858, Katharine Drexel was the daughter of wealthy investment banker Francis Drexel of Philadelphia. She abandoned her life of luxury to work with two groups of Americans that had suffered greatly: African Americans and Native Americans. She donated large sums of her own money to found schools on Indian reservations to educate children and to train teachers. In 1891, after a time with the Sisters of Mercy, she founded the Sisters of the Blessed Sacrament for Indians and Colored People. She established sixty-three schools over her long career, among which was the school that became Xavier University in New Orleans, the first Catholic university in the United States for African Americans.

St. John Neumann

Economic, political, and religious disruptions in Europe during the nineteenth century occasioned the immigration of thousands of Catholics—Armenians, Czechs, Germans, Irish, Italians, Lithuanians, and Poles, among others—who were followed by faithful pastors and religious. Settling in the inner cities and on the distant frontiers, they laid the foundations for a growing Catholic Church.

St. John Nepomucene Neumann, himself an immigrant seminarian from Bohemia, was ordained for work among the German-speaking immigrants of New York. After zealous work as a diocesan priest and then as a Redemptorist, he continued his apostolate as bishop of Philadelphia serving immigrant communities and establishing parochial schools until his death in 1860.

St. Frances Xavier Cabrini

The growth of cities during the late nineteenth century in the United States created special needs for evangelization. New immigrants crowded into large metropolitan areas that had few structures to meet the needs of the newly arrived. Frances Xavier Cabrini, an Italian-born foundress of the Missionary Sisters of the Sacred Heart, came to New York in 1889 where she worked among Italian immigrants, establishing orphanages, schools, adult classes in Christian doctrine, and the Columbus Hospital. Her work spread to other U.S. cities, reaching thousands.

The Twentieth Century

The work of evangelization has continued into our own century. Each generation has tested the resolve and inventiveness of those who tried to spread the good news. The call of the Gospel to penetrate every aspect of human life has been heard by many in our day. Here we can only note the worthy efforts of persons like Dorothy Day and Peter Maurin to evangelize the social milieu by working for the dignity of the poor. Others, such as Christopher founder Fr. James G. Keller, attempted to spread the Gospel to the marketplace by encouraging Catholics to witness to their faith by their actions. Evangelists, especially Frank Sheed and Archbishop Fulton J. Sheen, used the new media of mass communications to reach many with the message of Christ. Some like Thomas Merton, through a life led in seclusion from the world, nevertheless reached thousands through their writings. Still others, among them Fr. Thomas Price and Fr. James Anthony Walsh, founders of Maryknoll, engaged in the creation of new missionary societies to spread the word. Leaders, including Glenmary founder William Howard Bishop, strove to bring the good news to the rural poor of the United States. Some, especially Sr. Thea Bowman, who through her efforts as an educator and liturgist worked to evangelize African Americans and make their gifts better known and appreciated, played a significant role in the ongoing evangelization of our culture. During the 1930s, in Houston, Tex., Sr. Benitia Vermeersch founded the Missionary Catechists of Divine Providence, the first religious community of Mexican American women, to meet the needs of Hispanics in their language and culture. Since its foundation in 1905 by Fr. Francis Clement Kelley, the Catholic Church Extension Society has been a vital source of energy in evangelizing America's poor rural missions. Movements like the Grail, headed in this country by Lydwine van Kersbergen and Joan Overboss, strove to reach out especially to women to bring a fresh vision of discipleship to today's world. The healing message of the Gospel also reached the area of interracial relations as witnessed by the work of people like Catherine de Hueck Doherty, foundress of the Friendship House movement. All of these twentieth-century evangelizers were able to embody a part of the message of salvation and incarnate it in their world in a manner fit for their day.

In addition to those who have become widely known for their work, there have been millions who have passed down the faith from one generation to another within the family. The meteoric growth of the Church in our country is due, in large part, to the massive immigration of Catholic faithful of both Latin and Eastern Rites, who kept their faith and in turn passed it on to their children. With the faith have come the distinctive ethnic cultures in which it was nourished, cultures that in many aspects have been shaped by centuries of Christian faith. The stories of those family evangelizers—those parents and children, those grandparents and godparents—need to be remembered and told in this time of commemoration. Every family, every parish, every ethnic and regional group in the Church has its own special memories that can be sources of hope and inspiration for a new generation of believers.

Recommitment Through Evangelization

Reflecting on our past, we can with new self-awareness address the challenges of our present day. Recently, the Church has experienced a heightened awareness of the importance of evangelization in its life and mission. It has sought to answer the questions: What has happened to the hidden energy of the good news that so moved Christians of the past? And to what extent and in what way is that evangelical force capable of really transforming our world today?[18]

We proclaim good news that is, first of all, the revelation that God the Almighty Creator is the loving Father of each of us, who ". . . so loved the world that he gave his only Son, so that everyone who believes in him might not perish but might have eternal life" (Jn 3:16). The foundation, center, and summit of the good news is the proclamation that in Jesus Christ salvation is offered as a gift of God's grace and mercy. We are each called to respond personally to that grace and mercy of Christ. We are challenged to experience a total interior renewal, a profound change of mind and heart that leads to a life lived in the spirit of the beatitudes. Christ's salvation exceeds the limits of this world and is fulfilled in union with God forever in heaven. The good news reveals that Christ has sent his Holy Spirit among us, that he has given us the Church through which we are called to relate to him personally, to experience and live out the way of life of his kingdom, to celebrate the eucharist, to receive instruction, guidance, and sacramental graces that will fulfill our search for God and bring us to eternal happiness with him.

Through both Scripture and tradition Jesus has enriched his Church with the fullness of his teachings.[19] The good news reaches every part of human activity. It proclaims the rights and responsibilities of each human being. It addresses family life and life in society, calling us to strive for peace and justice and for the authentic advancement of humanity.[20] It speaks of the dignity of work, of all human endeavors that are destined to complement the creating action of God in order to serve the human community. It challenges us to transform every aspect of the workplace in light of the Gospel. Evangelization means embracing the good news. It means a conversion of hearts that begins with our own, whether we are clergy, religious, or laity.

It involves reaching out with the compassion of Christ to the alienated of our Church, reconciling the great number of people who have been lured from the Lord by contemporary materialism, secularism, and hedonism and offended by failures and insensitivity of their Christian communities. It includes reaching out to the unchurched and to those who do not share the fullness of our blessings as members of the Church of the Lord Jesus.

When we speak of evangelization we are speaking of challenging not only individuals but society at large to change. We are speaking of God's power to transform cultures, to renew political, economic, ecclesial, and human relationships.

Today, five centuries after the coming of the Gospel to America, our land is still in need of the transforming power of Jesus. The year 1992 presents an opportunity for Catholics of the United States to reflect on the needs of the present in light of the inspiring examples given by evangelizers of past ages and to recommit ourselves to the task of evangelizing our continent. As Pope John Paul II has urged us, now is not the time to be paralyzed by the wrongs of the past or to look back nostalgically to a golden age but to "learn from the mistakes of the past and . . . work together for reconciliation and healing. . . ."[21]

A major aspect of that healing must include efforts at reconciliation with Native Americans and African Americans, *mestizos* and *mulattos*, for whom the encounter that we commemorate was, and continues to be, so painful.

Yet the healing of which we speak is not only from the effects of repression and racism, but indeed a healing from the effects of sin in all its many facets. Christ has come that we—in our individual and social lives—might have abundant lives, free from bondage to evil.

The Challenges and Opportunities for Today's Evangelizers

The 1992 world in which the modern evangelist serves presents vastly different challenges and opportunities from those of Columbus's day. There are serious problems confronting the evangelizer of today. Not the least of these are problems within our own household of faith. Among our Catholic brothers and sisters there are over 17 million inactive persons. Many are poorly instructed and indifferent about the faith. Proselytism by avid non-Catholic churches draws away large numbers, especially Hispanics.[22] Only 2 percent of Catholics, when polled, say that they are personally involved in efforts of evangelization, and only one in three parishes has any evangelization program. The number of priests and religious has declined. Disturbingly, in a recent survey, only 49 percent of Catholics polled said they placed a high value on helping those in need, a consistently lower percentage than for other Christian groups.[23]

Beyond those special problems within our own community, there are tumultuous forces affecting society at large and creating a crucial need for the healing power of the Gospel. Public policy in many areas of education, health, and social services reflects values in conflict with the Gospel. Efforts to redirect resources to human needs, such as those outlined by the U.S. bishops' *Economic Justice for All: Pastoral Letter on Catholic Social Teaching and the U.S. Economy,*[24] meet with resistance in many quarters.

Our public educational system many times fails to develop in students adequate awareness of the moral and ethical responsibilities of their chosen vocations. An atmosphere of selfish manipulation and greed has in some areas displaced a concept of service in the public good as is witnessed by the debacles of massive frauds on Wall Street and in federal government agencies.

The modern-day communication system of the press and the electronic media sometimes abandons its role as responsible educator by polluting our culture, obscuring the good news by heralding the bad news: the confusing, divisive, impoverishing message of secularism. By advertising material possessiveness and by preempting family communication and interpersonal dialogue, our media at times leave in their wake lonely and despondent people. The arts at times fall prey to the same temptations, appealing to the prurient and the base, rather than to the dignity of women and men.

The structure of family life has been changing dramatically, often with traumatic effects on the spouses, the children, the society, and the community of faith.

Without the Gospel, modern life with its immediacy, efficiency, and speed, its constant changes and congestion at times has resulted in misery, increasing violence, controversy, and tension. Humanity is suffering from confusion, self-doubt, and uncertainty about fundamental values. Pragmatism, materialism, consumerism are the creeds of the age. There is a declining sense of moral values; there is fear, hopelessness, and a growing lack of respect for law and for life.

The evangelizer is faced with the problem of indifference to matters of religion. Relativism makes many wonder why they should hold any truths as sacred. With those forces of our age has come the growth of an extreme form of individualism that sees no need for the faith community or for the necessity of comparing one's own insights with those offered by tradition.

Signs of Hope

Despite the obstacles and serious problems confronting us, U.S. Catholics possess the resources and strengths for effective evangelization to respond to the present challenges, perhaps to a degree never before enjoyed. Today Catholics make up 28 percent of the U.S. population, making Catholics by far the largest denomination in the country. By the middle of the next century, Catholics presumably will comprise a larger part of the populace than all other Christian denominations for the first time in our history. Today Catholics are present in all income and educational levels in our society, including the highest. A higher percentage of Catholics than in the general population is currently in college, suggesting that gains in income, education, and influence are likely. Our youth is increasingly Catholic. A third of all U.S. teenagers are Catholic, and 29 percent of U.S. citizens under the age of thirty are Catholic.

From the earliest days, Catholic schools have been a source of strength both for Catholics and for the larger community, including minorities. Today Catholic elementary and secondary schools are places where learning in service to God and to humanity continues to take place, forming our young people religiously and intellectually and preparing them to meet the challenges of tomorrow. To that network of schools are added over 250 Catholic colleges and universities that strive to provide religious, moral, and intellectual development for their students. Outside of the schools, effective catechetical programs assist our children, youth, and adults to grow in their faith.

For nearly five centuries, Catholics have played a leading role in health care in our nation. From the earliest hospital in St. Augustine, to the expansive efforts of women religious in the nineteenth century, to the sophisticated centers of today, Catholics have been witnessing to the Gospel by caring for the sick and testifying to the compassion of our Lord and to the worth of human life.

Many Catholics now play leading roles in the cultural, economic, and political life of the nation. They are in a singular position to influence the course of our nation as never before. Through decisions and actions imbued with gospel values, they can work together with others of good will to build a society of compassion, justice, and liberty for all.

But beyond those material advantages, Catholicism possesses certain strengths, which are well suited for meeting the spiritual longings of our contemporary culture. Prescient observers of U.S. Catholicism in the past have commented on its ability to provide our society with much needed influences. Orestes Brownson, writing in the last century, believed that it was in the United States that the proper blend of individual liberty and order was to be worked out. He argued that U.S. citizens, with their penchant for freedom and their great appreciation for individual liberty, needed to learn from Catholicism the values of tradition that functioned to pass on through history the shared wisdom and cumulative experience of humanity. Without some appreciation of the past, people are left to rediscover for themselves the right and prudent behavior in every new situation—a burden that few can bear. It is essential, he argued, that people recognize the organic bond that ties them to one another and to the countless generations that have preceded them.[25]

John Courtney Murray, in our own century, led the way in exploring the implications of the U.S. proposition of ordered freedom for the Church. Part of his program was his effort to promote Catholic involvement in culture-forming acts of engagement with society that would transform it according to Christian values.[26] Both Brownson and Murray believed that Catholicism was a comprehensive tradition that combined in it a balanced and healthful appreciation for the individual and the community, for change and continuity. It was that comprehensive nature, that wisdom, that tacit dimension of moral knowledge that a people could learn by being exposed to Catholic thought. In an encounter with the living tradition of the Church, a tradition both self-confirming and self-renewing, U.S. citizens could learn important lessons.

Many in our own time, from all ends of the theological and political spectra, have been calling for new formulations of the relationship between the public and the private. There is a fresh concern for the common good, a new quest for ways of conserving the wisdom of the past and blending it with the innovations of the present, and an awareness of the insufficiency of present solutions. Many are searching for new ways to speak of values and virtue. In such a climate U.S. Catholicism, the embodiment of the dynamic tradition of the apostles lived in a land committed to freedom and human dignity, has much to offer.

Dating back at least to the very time of the first encounters between the peoples of this hemisphere and Europe, Catholics have sought to make visible the connection between individual conversion of heart and the society's responsibility to seek the common good. The Church in our country has developed a tradition of insisting that the relation between faith and the pursuit of a more just social order is constitutive of the Gospel call. As the Church throughout the world observes the hundredth anniversary of Pope Leo XIII's encyclical *Rerum Novarum*, the Church in this country recalls its own strong tradition. Since 1919, the time of the U.S. bishops' *Program of Social Reconstruction*,[27] U.S. Catholics have addressed the moral dimensions of public policy, engaging issues of war and peace, of economic justice, of the fundamental rights of the unborn, of women, of workers, of minorities, of refugees, and of all who suffer discrimination.[28]

The cultural richness of our Catholic heritage also can contribute to our present situation as we announce the good news to the people of the Americas. The Catholic Church in the United States is made up of diverse cultures and peoples. Each of them is a special gift. Hispanics, African Americans, Native Americans, Asians, and Europeans join the many other cultures from the world over that have all played a part in the formation of our U.S. Catholic community. As they all express the one faith through their unique cultural gifts, the whole Church is enriched. The Church is in this sense an instrument for guarding and restoring unity in the human family. Our nation, like our Church, has prided itself on its diversity. "E pluribus unum" is a motto that today is as important as ever to hold, not as a denial of the uniqueness of individual cultures, but as a commitment to the dignity of each people and to the peaceful collaboration among persons of different cultural backgrounds who, rejoicing in their uniqueness, affirm together a common identity as people of the United States.

The Church often has been a great patroness of the arts in the West. Religious inspirations lie behind many of the masterpieces of visual, musical, and literary arts on our continent. In an age in which the relationship of art to goodness, truth, and beauty has often been obscured, Christians can promote an integrated vision that can enkindle again a sense of wholeness and provide the background for works of beauty and of depth. Art can be a valuable resource for spiritual renewal.

As those who have been evangelized, we have a responsibility to care not only for other persons but for the creation. The growing concern in our nation for ecology, for preserving the natural riches of the earth, is a sign of hope. They point, as does Native American spirituality, to God the Creator and confirm our belief that humanity shares in God's creative and caring role in creation. The Incarnation should stir us to a new concern for the earth. Too often since the dawn of the industrial age, our planet has been despoiled out of ignorance, carelessness, and greed. We have now the resources to correct serious problems that unchecked could disturb the delicate balance of life in our hemisphere and in our world. As Pope John Paul II has emphasized: "The ecological crisis reveals the *urgent moral need for a new solidarity,* especially in relations between the developing nations and those that are highly industrialized."[29] We are part of a worldwide Church renewed in identity and mission by the Second Vatican Council and by the leadership of extraordinary pontiffs. The Church is a sign of the transcendence of the human person and of the solidarity of the human race. We believe in a God who, in Christ, forged a bond of unbreakable solidarity with every human being. In proclaiming that solidarity throughout our land and, indeed throughout the world, the Church calls the citizens of our country to be mindful of their linkage with their sisters and brothers throughout the world, especially with those who share this continent.

We have a sacramental system that speaks to the spiritual needs of those searching for God. We have the *Rite of Christian Initiation of Adults,*[30] which enables inquirers who have received the seeds of the word to come to know the living God in a community of faith. We also have a rich tradition of spirituality reaching back to apostolic times and containing some of the greatest achievements of the spirit that history has seen. Most important, we have the eucharist, our ultimate expression of worship and praise.

One of our greatest strengths is a renewed sense of the vocation of the lay person in the Church and in the world. As the Second Vatican Council reminded us, each of us is called by baptism and confirmation to share in the saving mission of our Lord Jesus and his Church. Through parishes, through Catholic organizations, through pastoral plans such as the *National Pastoral Plan for Hispanic Ministry*[31] and the *National Black Catholic Pastoral Plan,*[32] through renewal movements, through the family, and through the marketplace lay men and women are increasingly aware of the importance of bearing witness to God's kingdom. By work, however exalted or humble, believers participate in transforming the world. By the presence of God's people in the whole range of social, cultural, intellectual, political, and economic life, our society is benefited and enriched.[33]

The importance of the Christian family as a source of strength is, in this moment in the history of our culture, hard to overstate. The family's role is to perform a service of love and life. The love between husband and wife in marriage embraces all members of the family and forms a community of persons united in heart and soul. There life is handed on from generation to generation.

The family forms an evangelizing community where the Gospel is received and put into practice, where prayer is learned and shared, where all the members, by word and by the love they have for one another, bear witness to the good news of salvation. In contemporary U.S. society, where the stability of the family has been undermined by divorce, disrespect for life, and a culture of hedonism, families centered on Christ can be sources of healing for many.

In our parish communities throughout the nation, the faithful are brought into a living relationship with Christ. They are nourished spiritually by the proclaiming, celebrating, and witnessing of the good news. In these local communities of God's people, the work of prayer goes on continually, giving to our lives a sacred rhythm and grounding. The parish is a family of families in which faith is nourished and expressed. In the parish the faith is transmitted, passed from the universal community of faith, as the authentic teaching of the apostles. There the task of building up a living community serving the needs of individuals and families is undertaken. Parishes can be evangelizing centers, reaching out to the alienated and the unchurched, bringing people together to work for social justice, and providing all with opportunities for friendship and spiritual encouragement. Those gifts enable us to build communities of mutual love and care that stand in stark contrast to the often exploitative relationships of the society around us.

Beyond that, we have a new appreciation for the sacred Scriptures, which, together with tradition, form one sacred deposit of the word of God.[34] St. Jerome reminded us that ignorance of the Scriptures is ignorance of Christ. Catholics today, inspired by the Second Vatican Council, which looked for a new surge of spiritual vitality from intensified veneration of God's word, are meeting together to study the Scriptures. They are praying in their homes with the Scriptures and teaching their children to value them.[35]

A special sign of hope in our day is the dedicated clergy and religious who are committed to the service of God and people. Using their gifts of orders, grace, and nature, they labor to form Christ in God's people. The clergy, as servant leaders, proclaim and celebrate in worship the mysteries of our faith. By their love and leadership, they guide the people to the kingdom. The permanent deacons, numbering over 10,000 in our country, evangelize through the ministry of the word and of charity. Vowed witnesses to the Gospel, the religious, by their lives of prayer and service, animate the living of the faith throughout the land.

A Call to the Civilization of Love

America for these 500 years has stood as a sign of hope for many peoples. The moment calls for Christians, faithful to the Gospel, to realize the hope that a people renewed by the saving presence of Christ may help build a better society. May the new evangelization stimulate holiness, integrity, and tireless activity to promote the dignity of all human life, thus witnessing more fully to the presence of the kingdom of God in our midst. May we all, through a fresh commitment to the Gospel, engage in a new *discovery*, a new creation of a world still being sought: a community of faith, a culture of solidarity, a civilization of love. The future is struggling to be born as the word of God entreats men and women to respond more fully to its message. It is one in which a "new inspired synthesis of the spiritual and temporal, of the ancient and modern" might be brought forth.[36]

All of the people of God must do their part in this new evangelization. Scholars and teachers, in reverence for the truth, should see their work as contributing to the good of humanity in the light of the Gospel. Parents, in their trying but immeasurably important task, should work to build the *domestic church* in which faith and virtue are nurtured. The young, who have a special vocation to hope, should spread among their peers the message of light and life that is in Christ. Artists, who toil to create works of beauty and meaning, should view their art as a medium through which others may see something of the transcendent. Public servants, who struggle in an environment of utilitarianism, should spread the justice of Christ's kingdom by their way of life. Laborers and mechanics, those working in commerce and law, those who care for the sick, and those who engage in scientific research: the Gospel calls them all to a special witness in our society. It calls each of us to incarnate the good news of Christ in the midst of our labors.

We are each called to become salt and light for the world, and at times, a sign of contradiction that challenges and transforms the world according to the mind of Christ. While we are not called to impose our religious beliefs on others, we are compelled to give the example of lives of faith, goodness, and service. On issues of fundamental moral importance, it is at times necessary to challenge publicly the conscience of society—as did our sisters and brothers in other ages—to uphold those basic human values that advance fundamental human rights and promote the spiritual aspirations of every person.

It is our hope that during 1992 and thereafter, our nation will give special attention to the condition of Native Americans. We encourage all Americans to better understand the role of native peoples in our history and to respond to the just grievances of our Native American brothers and sisters.

We hope that this will be a graced time for rejecting all forms of racism. The negative consequences of slavery are still painfully felt in both the African American culture of today and throughout society in the Americas. We acknowledge and lament this and pledge ourselves during the quincentennial year to redress those injustices.

The Church in this country is truly multicultural. Our many peoples, each in their uniqueness, are gifts of God. May we at this time renew our appreciation of this as we welcome the new immigrants to our land, many of whom come to our shores with a vibrant Catholic faith. Asians, Europeans, Africans, and citizens of the Americas each enrich our faith community.

It is our hope that during this time, we recognize and give thanks for the birth of the Hispanic people, a beautiful fruit of the coming together of diverse peoples and cultures. Theirs was indeed a painful birth, but the result was five centuries of transformation affecting both Church and society. The Hispanic presence is now more evident than ever as we move into the second half millennium of the Gospel in America.

We wish to strive for a new reconciliation in the spirit of the Gospel among all Americans and to recognize more fully our solidarity with the nations of this hemisphere. Evangelization is unfinished if exploitation of the weak, of minorities, and of peoples of the third world countries still exists. The quincentenary calls us to a new commitment as Christians to right the evils of the past and the present and to be forceful advocates of the peace and justice proclaimed by the Gospel. May we stand with our sisters and brothers of Latin America in their struggles for dignity, freedom, and peace with justice.

May the Church in the United States also not forget its commitment to the universal dimension of evangelization. May we continue as a Church to share our human and material resources with those evangelizers of other lands who strive to bring the Gospel to their peoples.[37] With Pope Paul VI, may we say as we witness a growing number of Catholics proclaiming their faith: "We cannot but experience a great inner joy when we see so many pastors, religious, and lay people, fired with their mission to evangelize, seeking ever more suitable ways of proclaiming the Gospel effectively."[38]

Observance of the Quincentenary in the United States

The bishops of the United States join with our brother bishops in the hemisphere in urging our people to respond to the challenge of the Vicar of Christ that the five-hundredth anniversary year be one of a new commitment to living and sharing, in private and public life, the Gospel of Jesus Christ. We bishops of the United States call the attention of the faithful to the significance, the potential of this year of grace. We invite our dioceses, parishes, universities, schools, movements, and organizations to make the observance of the quincentenary a priority. Specifically we suggest observing the event by focusing on three dimensions:

1. **The historical dimension.** A fresh effort to remember our past in stories, in song, in writing, whether at the popular or scholarly level, is an important part of the observance. Together we should strive to answer the questions: Who are we as American Catholic people? What do we believe in and stand for? Where did we come from, and what forces helped make us who we are? What can we learn from our mistakes and our successes?

2. **The observance dimension.** Observances to commemorate the social and civic aspects of the quincentenary will be planned by various groups throughout the country in 1992. We call on Catholics to bring to those observances the unique perspective we have presented here. In particular, we urge Catholics to develop observances such as prayer services, pilgrimages, pageants, and festivals that focus attention on the issues we have raised. Our observances should include times of mourning over the injustices of the past and vital efforts at reconciliation with our Native American brothers and sisters through prayer and social action.

3. **The evangelization dimension.** This is the heart of the quincentenary observance for the Catholic community and as such should be pursued with great vigor. We wish to see this new evangelization promoted in two phases. In phase one, we call upon all to become increasingly aware of the need for being evangelized afresh, for bringing the light of Christ to our own lives and to those of our families and faith communities. During phase two, we urge reaching out to alienated Catholics, the unchurched, and society at large with the good news.

Most appropriately, the quincentenary may be observed by the celebration of the eucharist. The bishops have prepared, with the approval of the Holy See, the text of a special liturgy of thanksgiving for the occasion. In addition, we urge that other services be held to worship the Lord and to thank him for his blessings upon the people of the hemisphere over these 500 years, to atone for our failures, and to ask his continued blessings especially on our evangelization efforts and on peace initiatives in the hemisphere.

We also will be part of a convocation of all the bishops of the hemisphere to reconsecrate the hemisphere to the Lord and to recommit ourselves and our people to evangelization, to justice and peace, and to responding to the needs of the poor.

Conclusion:
A Renewed Presence of Jesus in Our Land

We as the Church are an enduring presence of the Gospel of Jesus, which came to our hemisphere 500 years ago. Jesus is the first evangelizer, and we are called upon to continue his mission. The life of the Church, the charity we live, and the sacred bread and cup we share only acquire their full meaning when they give witness, when they inspire imitation and conversion, when they become the preaching and proclamation of the good news.[39]

The world is calling for evangelizers to speak to it of a God whom they know and serve. It is in need of new vocations to the priesthood and to the religious life. It is calling for evangelizers who give witness in the world. What is more, our age expects of all believers simplicity of life, a spirit of prayer, charity toward all, obedience and humility, detachment and sacrifice. Without these marks of holiness, the evangelists will have difficulty touching the hearts of modern people. Their activity risks being vain and sterile. The 1992 evangelizers come with a commitment of ever-increasing love for those whom they are evangelizing. They say with the apostle Paul: "With such affection for you, we were determined to share with you not only the Gospel of God, but our very selves as well, so dearly beloved had you become to us" (1 Thes 2:8). They come with the fervor of the saints, the fervor that urges them to proclaim with joy the good news that they have come to know through the Lord's mercy. To proclaim the good news is the evangelizers' duty. It is the right of every person to receive freely and without coercion the proclamation of the good news of salvation in the integrity of one's own conscience. Men and women may be able to gain salvation in ways other than through our proclaiming it to them. But we must ask: Can we gain salvation if through negligence or fear or shame—what St. Paul called blushing for the Gospel—we fail to proclaim it? (cf. Rom 1:16).

At this graced historic moment, we bishops address the laity, religious, and clergy with the words of Pope Paul VI:

> Let us therefore preserve our fervor of spirit. Let us preserve the delightful and comforting joy of evangelizing, even when it is in tears that we must sow. May it mean for us— as it did for John the Baptist, for Peter and Paul, for the other Apostles and for a multitude of splendid evangelizers all through the Church's history—an interior enthusiasm that nobody and nothing can quench. May it be the great joy of our consecrated lives. And may the world of our time, which is searching, sometimes with anguish, sometimes with hope, be enabled to receive the Good News not from evangelizers who are dejected, discouraged, impatient or

anxious, but from ministers of the Gospel whose lives glow
with fervor, who have first received the joy of Christ, and
who are willing to risk their lives so that the Kingdom may
be proclaimed and the Church established in the midst of
the world.[40]

We entrust our observance of the quincentennial year, our commitment to giving birth with new fervor to the life of the Gospel in our
hemisphere, to Our Lady of Guadalupe, Patroness of the Americas.
She truly was the first Christ-bearer; by her maternal intercession, may
her faithful sons and daughters be renewed and discover afresh the joy
and splendor and promise of being bearers of the good news.

Father,
let the light of your truth
guide us to your kingdom
through a world filled with lights
contrary to your own.
Christian is our name and the gospel
we glory in.
May your love make us what you have
called us to be.
We ask this through Christ our Lord.[41]
Amen.

Notes

1. Paul VI, *On Evangelization in the Modern World (Evangelii Nuntiandi)*
    (Washington, D.C.: United States Catholic Conference, 1975), no. 18.
2. John Paul II, "Building a New Latin America," *Origins* 14:20 (November
    1, 1984), 308.
3. Cf. ibid., 307.
4. Cf. Second Vatican Council, *Pastoral Constitution on the Church in the
    Modern World (Gaudium et Spes)* (Washington, D.C.: United States Catholic
    Conference, 1965), no. 1.
5. National Conference of Catholic Bishops, *Statement of the U.S. Catholic
    Bishops on American Indians* (Washington, D.C.: United States Catholic
    Conference, 1977), 6.
6. *Evangelii Nuntiandi*, no. 4.
7. Cf. Alfred Crosby, *The Columbian Exchange* (Westport, Conn.: Greenwood
    Press, 1972).
8. John Paul II, "Meeting with Native Americans," in *Unity in the Work of
    Service* (Washington, D.C.: United States Catholic Conference, 1987), 109.
9. Cf. Pontifical Commission Justitia et Pax, *The Church and Racism: Towards
    a More Fraternal Society* (Washington, D.C.: United States Catholic
    Conference, 1988), 11.

10. Alexander VI, *Inter Caetera*, in John Tracy Ellis, ed., *Documents of American Catholic History* (Wilmington, Del.: Michael Glazier, 1987), 1:1.

11. Cf. Delano C. West, "Medieval Ideas of Apocalyptic Mission and the Early Franciscans in Mexico," *The Americas* 45 (January 1989): 293-313; Leonard I. Sweet, "Christopher Columbus and the Millennial Vision of the New World," *Catholic Historical Review* 72 (July and October 1986): 369-382 and 715-716.

12. John Paul II, "The Beloved Land of Columbus," Address on Arrival in the Dominican Republic (January 25, 1979), *L'Osservatore Romano* [English edition] 6 (February 5, 1979): 8.

13. Cf. Michael V. Gannon, "Defense of Native American and Franciscan Rights in the Florida Missions" (typescript).

14. See *Gaudium et Spes*, no. 58.

15. "Narrative of a Voyage to Maryland (1634)," in Robert Emmett Curran, ed., *American Jesuit Spirituality* (New York: Paulist Press, 1988), 47.

16. "Relation of 1654," in Irene Mahony, ed., *Marie of the Incarnation* (New York: Paulist Press, 1989), 139.

17. To Julia Scott, July 24, 1817, in A. Melville and E. Kelly, eds., *Elizabeth Seton* (New York: Paulist Press, 1987), 61.

18. Cf. *Evangelii Nuntiandi*, no. 4.

19. Cf. Second Vatican Council, *Constitution on the Church* (*Lumen Gentium*) (Washington, D.C.: United States Catholic Conference, 1964), no. 8.

20. See *Evangelii Nuntiandi*, nos. 25-39.

21. "Meeting with Native Americans," 110.

22. *Proselytism* here is meant to convey important attitudes and behavior in the practice of Christian witness. Proselytism embraces whatever violates the right of the person, Christian or non-Christian, to be free from external coercion in religious matters, or in the proclamation of the Gospel, whatever does not conform to the ways God draws free persons to himself in response to his call to serve in spirit and in truth. Cf. Second Vatican Council, *Decree on the Church's Missionary Activity* (*Ad Gentes Divinitus*) nos. 6, 15; and World Council of Churches, "Joint Action for Mission," World Council of Churches, 3d Assembly, New Delhi, India (1961), *The New Delhi Report* (New York: Association Press, 1962), 29.

23. George Gallup Jr. and James Castelli, *The American Catholic People* (Garden City, N.Y.: Doubleday, 1987), 1-9.

24. National Conference of Catholic Bishops, *Economic Justice for All: Pastoral Letter on Catholic Social Teaching and the U.S. Economy* (Washington, D.C.: United States Catholic Conference, 1986).

25. Cf. Orestes Brownson, *The American Republic* (New York: P. O'Shea, 1865).

26. Cf. John Courtney Murray, *We Hold These Truths* (Garden City, N.Y.: Doubleday, 1964).

27. National Catholic War Council, Program of Social Reconstruction (1919) in *Pastoral Letters of the United States Catholic Bishops* (Washington, D.C.: United States Catholic Conference, 1984), 1: 255-271.

28. See United States Catholic Conference, *A Century of Social Teaching: A Common Heritage, A Continuing Challenge* (Washington, D.C.: United States Catholic Conference, 1990).

29. John Paul II, *The Ecological Crisis: A Common Responsibility* (Washington, D.C.: United States Catholic Conference, 1990), no. 10.
30. International Commission on English in the Liturgy, *Rite of Christian Initiation of Adults* (Washington, D.C.: United States Catholic Conference, 1988).
31. National Conference of Catholic Bishops, *National Pastoral Plan for Hispanic Ministry* (Washington, D.C.: United States Catholic Conference, 1988).
32. See National Conference of Catholic Bishops, *Here I Am, Send Me: A Conference Response to the Evangelization of African American Catholics* and *"The National Black Catholic Pastoral Plan"* (Washington, D.C.: United States Catholic Conference, 1990).
33. See *Lumen Gentium,* no. 31.
34. Cf. Second Vatican Council, *Constitution on Divine Revelation (Dei Verbum)* (Washington, D.C.: United States Catholic Conference, 1965), no. 10.
35. Cf. ibid., no. 26.
36. Paul VI, "Homily Delivered in St. Peter's Basilica," July 4, 1964.
37. See National Conference of Catholic Bishops, *To the Ends of the Earth: A Pastoral Statement on World Mission* (Washington, D.C.: United States Catholic Conference, 1986).
38. *Evangelii Nuntiandi,* no. 73.
39. Cf. ibid., no. 15.
40. Ibid., no. 80.
41. Alternative Opening Prayer, Fifteenth Sunday in Ordinary Time, *The Sacramentary: The Roman Missal Revised by the Decree of the Second Vatican Ecumenical Council and Published by the Authority of Pope Paul VI,* English trans. prepared by ICEL (New York: Catholic Book Publishing, 1985), 304.

Source: Washington, D.C.: United States Catholic Conference, 1991.

In Support of Catholic Elementary and Secondary Schools

A Statement of the United States Catholic Conference

November 1990

Our Conviction

The year 1997 will mark the twenty-fifth anniversary of our pastoral letter, *To Teach As Jesus Did*. Now, in 1990, seven years before that anniversary, we wish to commit ourselves to certain seven-year goals as a sign of our affirmation of the principles laid down in that pastoral. It is our deep conviction that Catholic schools must exist for the good of the Church. Our concern for the importance of Catholic schools is set in the context of the responsibility we have by our episcopal office to ensure total Catholic education in all its phases for all ages.

In 1972 we stated: "Of the educational programs available to the Catholic community, Catholic schools afford the fullest and best opportunity to realize the threefold purpose [message, community, and service] of Christian education among children and young people."[1] In our National Catechetical Directory, *Sharing the Light of Faith*, we included worship among the purposes of Christian education, and now speak about the fourfold purpose of Catholic schools.[2]

We are encouraged that our statements are reflective of the teachings of our Holy Father, Pope John Paul II, and of the official documents from the Holy See. Speaking to Catholic educators in New Orleans in 1987, the Holy Father said:

> The presence of the Church in the field of education is wonderfully manifested in the vast and dynamic network of schools and educational programs extending from the preschool through the adult years. *The entire ecclesial community—bishops, priests, religious, the laity—the Church in all her parts, is called to value ever more deeply the importance of this task and mission, and to continue to give it full and enthusiastic support* [emphasis in the original].[3]

Further in the same address, the Holy Father said:

> As an institution the Catholic school has to be judged extremely favorably if we apply the sound criterion: "You

> will know them by their deeds" (Mt 7:16). . . . The heroic sac-
> rifices of generations of Catholic parents in building up and
> supporting parochial and diocesan schools must never be
> forgotten. Rising costs may call for new approaches, new
> forms of partnership and sharing, new uses of financial
> resources. But I am sure that all concerned will face the chal-
> lenge of Catholic schools with courage and dedication, and
> not doubt the value of the sacrifices to be made.[4]

In 1977, the Sacred Congregation for Catholic Education wrote that "the Church is absolutely convinced that the educational aims of the Catholic school in the world of today perform an essential and unique service for the Church herself."[5]

A decade later, the same congregation issued *The Religious Dimension of Education in a Catholic School.* If anything, the congregation in 1988 was more insistent on the role of the school in the Church: "The Congregation offers enthusiastic encouragement to those dioceses and Religious Congregations who wish to establish new schools. Such things as film clubs and sports groups are not enough; not even classes in catechism instruction are sufficient. What is needed is a school."[6]

In 1983, the bishops of the United States recognized the impor-tance and the role of Catholic education in the formation of Hispanic youth:

> Catholic educators in the United States have a long record of
> excellence and dedication to the instruction and formation of
> millions of Catholic faithful. Now they must turn their skills
> to responding to the educational needs of Hispanics. . . .[7]

In 1984, ten of our brother bishops of African American ancestry also wrote about the need for Catholic schools in *What We Have Seen and Heard: A Pastoral Letter on Evangelization from the Black Bishops of the United States.* They reaffirmed that

> Today the Catholic school still represents for many in the
> Black community, especially in the urban areas, an opportu-
> nity for quality education and character development. . . .
> The Catholic school has been and remains one of the chief
> vehicles of evangelization within the Black community. We
> cannot overemphasize the tremendous importance of
> parochial schools for the Black community. We even dare to
> suggest that the efforts made to support them and to insure
> their continuation are a touchstone of the local church's sin-
> cerity in the evangelization of the Black community.[8]

In *To Teach As Jesus Did,* we called upon parents, educators, and pastors "to ensure the continuance and improvement of Catholic schools."[9] And we pointed to specific areas of concern: greater fiscal responsibility, quality education for the disadvantaged, and the need to look at alternative models. Much progress has been made. More needs to be done. We encourage our parents and pastors who presently are shouldering the onerous task of educating our youth in Catholic schools. In our day, it is more important than ever that they give their active support to Catholic schools.

We reaffirm our commitment to Catholic schools. We invite the whole Catholic community to address with us these and other issues of concern.

Our Successes and Challenges

In this new decade, there is good news about Catholic schools and there are challenges.

Research has shown that Catholic schools directly impact the future lives of their students. Graduates of Catholic schools are more closely bonded to the Church, more deeply committed to adult religious practices, happier, and more supportive of religious perspectives on women and have more confidence in other people, more benign images of God, and a greater awareness of the responsibility for moral decision making. They give in a committed fashion more contributions to the Catholic Church.[10]

Research by the United States Department of Education over the last decade has found that Catholic school students consistently outscore students in the public schools in reading, mathematics, and science. They are especially effective in educating minority and low-income students, much more so than the public schools or other private schools.[11]

There are also some serious challenges facing Catholic schools. Costs have increased 500 percent in the last twenty years, over twice the Consumer Price Index. Fewer than 200 Catholic schools have opened since 1966, and only thirty of those were in the ten largest (arch)dioceses. In the last ten years, the percentage of potential Catholic students attending Catholic schools has dropped from 33 percent for elementary schools to 27 percent and from 22 percent for secondary schools to 19 percent. Much of this decline is due to shifting demographics and would be reversed if parishes and clusters of parishes opened schools where Catholic families now live. In many wealthy suburban areas, some parents perceive that the free public schools are better than Catholic schools in spite of the research to the contrary. Other parents perceive that the public schools offer their children a broader cultural experience and, as a result, they opt for the public school education.

There are some dioceses that do not have education boards or commissions connected to their schools but, rather, operate with the traditional parish governance structure. There is, therefore, a lack of consistency in the relationship of the Catholic laity to the schools. Dioceses should be encouraged to study patterns of school governance and financial development with the goal of enhancing the role of parents and other interested laity, e.g., alumni, grandparents, and parishioners.

In 1972, we declared that we were well aware of the problems which face Catholic schools in the United States. We also said that we wished "to make our position clear. For our part, as bishops, we reaffirm our conviction that Catholic schools . . . are the most effective means available to the Church for the education of children and young people."[12]

Therefore, we called "upon all members of the Catholic community to do everything in their power to maintain and strengthen Catholic schools" which embrace the fourfold purposes of Catholic education.[13]

We will not waver from that conviction.

Our Future Goals for 1997

By the twenty-fifth anniversary of *To Teach As Jesus Did* in 1997, we commit ourselves unequivocally to the following goals:

1. That Catholic schools will continue to provide high-quality education for all their students in a context infused with gospel values.
2. That serious efforts will be made to ensure that Catholic schools are available for Catholic parents who wish to send their children to them.
3. That new initiatives will be launched to secure sufficient financial assistance from both private and public sectors for Catholic parents to exercise this right.
4. That the salaries and benefits of Catholic school teachers and administrators will reflect our teaching as expressed in *Economic Justice for All.*

In order to accomplish these interrelated goals, we commit ourselves to the following initial actions.

Stewardship

We will teach clearly, consistently, and continuously that we are all stewards of the mysteries of God and disciples of Jesus Christ. This will include an understanding that God has given us gifts which are to be shared with others in the practical application of discipleship and stewardship to which all are called. We will invite all Catholics to share in the apostolate of Catholic education, realizing that financial support is a means of responding to God's call to stewardship.

Development

We commit ourselves to the establishment of diocesan educational development offices or similar initiatives that will be concerned with soliciting funds from other sources and wisely investing the money. These development efforts should include some form of endowment for Catholic schools established in accordance with diocesan guidelines. We would hope that these efforts would be in place by the fall of 1995.

Recognizing that some dioceses may need assistance in establishing and fostering their development efforts, we will open a national development office by January 1992. In addition to its educational efforts, this office will be charged with the responsibility to ensure ethical practices in the Church's development efforts. Furthermore, we challenge our successful business and community leaders to join us in supporting Catholic schools. Recognizing that there are a number of corporations which limit their charitable contributions to national projects, it is our intention to convene a group of diocesan bishops and chief executive officers from the business community to consider funding national efforts on behalf of Catholic schools.

Ensuring Parental Rights

In union with the Holy Father, we have consistently taught that parents are the first and foremost educators of their children. Almost seventy years ago, we assisted the Sisters of the Holy Names of Jesus and Mary to bring suit against one state that sought to encroach on these rights of parents. In *Pierce v. Society of Sisters*, the Supreme Court of the United States recognized that choosing the education most appropriate for the child was both the right and responsibility of parents. In 1983, in *Mueller v. Allen*, the court held that states could constitutionally assist parents in defraying the costs associated with those educational choices. The time has come for all citizens of the United States, especially those who govern in their name, to fortify this right and promote this responsibility.

Recognizing that Catholic schools are a significant part of education in the United States, we call on all citizens to join with us in supporting federal and state legislative efforts to provide financial assistance to all parents which will ensure that they can afford to choose the type of schooling they desire for their children. For our part, we are so convinced that the Catholic community needs to enter seriously into both national and state educational discussions that we are taking immediate steps to educate all citizens of the United States about the importance of assuring that all parents have a meaningful choice of schools.

Recognizing the long-term nature of convincing the nation that parents should have not only a choice in selecting educational opportunities for their children, but also financial support to exercise that choice, we are taking immediate steps to accomplish this end.

We support and encourage the formation of diocesan, state, and national organizations of Catholic school parents. To assist in this effort, we will provide, through outside funding obtained by the General Secretary, two million dollars in seed money for a national office, which will provide assistance to diocesan and state groups and found a national parent organization.

Furthermore, from this seed money, we will fund one additional staff position in the Department of Education; the sole responsibility of this person will be to work with diocesan superintendents of schools and parent representatives to establish a national communications network. We will also fund one additional staff position in the Office of Government Liaison; this person's sole responsibility will be to work on educational issues.

Strategic Plan

Because of our long-term commitment to Catholic schools, we are instructing our Committee on Education to develop a strategic plan for Catholic schools to be presented for our consideration no later than 1995.

Conclusion

We want to acknowledge that today's children and youth are our future. Catholic schools have provided and will continue to provide an excellent total education. In doing so, they have also fostered the improvement of all of education in the United States. Many of the reforms being suggested for public education (school-based management, greater parental involvement, values education, increased homework, more rigorous courses, and even school uniforms) have long been associated with the success of Catholic schools. Our inner-city Catholic schools have been especially prominent in providing quality education for the most disadvantaged to improve their future status in society. Our Church and our nation have been enriched because of the quality of education provided in Catholic schools over the last three hundred years. We express our deep and prayerful thanks to the religious, priests, and laity who formed this ministry. Now we are called to sustain and expand this vitally important ministry of the Church.

Notes

1. National Conference of Catholic Bishops, *Basic Teachings for Catholic Religious Education* (Washington, D.C.: United States Catholic Conference, 1973), 2-3.
2. National Conference of Catholic Bishops, *National Catechetical Directory, Sharing the Light of Faith* (Washington, D.C.: United States Catholic Conference, 1979), no. 215.
3. John Paul II, "Address to Teachers," *Origins* 17:17 (September 1987), no. 279.
4. Ibid., no. 15.
5. Sacred Congregation for Catholic Education, *The Catholic School* (Washington, D.C.: United States Catholic Conference, 1977), 15.1.
6. Sacred Congregation for Catholic Education, *The Religious Dimension of Education in a Catholic School* (Washington, D.C.: United States Catholic Conference, 1988), no. 41.
7. National Conference of Catholic Bishops, *The Hispanic Presence: Challenge and Commitment* (Washington, D.C.: United States Catholic Conference, 1983), 181.
8. Black Bishops of the United States, *What We Have Seen and Heard: A Pastoral Letter on Evangelization from the Black Bishops of the United States* (Cincinnati, Ohio: St. Anthony Messenger Press, 1984).
9. National Conference of Catholic Bishops, *To Teach as Jesus Did* (Washington, D.C.: United States Catholic Conference, 1972), no. 119.
10. National Opinion Research Center [NORC], *General Social Survey 1988* (Chicago, Ill.: NORC, 1989).
11. U.S. Department of Education, Office for Educational Research and Improvement, *National Assessment of Educational Progress Studies* (Washington, D.C.: Government Printing Office.)
12. *To Teach as Jesus Did*, no. 118.
13. Ibid.

Source: Washington, D.C.: United States Catholic Conference, 1990.

Guidelines for Doctrinally Sound
Catechetical Materials

Guidelines Approved by the National Conference of Catholic Bishops

November 1990

Preface

As shepherds of the people of God, and by reason of their unique teaching office, bishops have the responsibility of preserving the deposit of faith and ensuring that it is passed on so that the faith of individuals and the community becomes "living, conscious and active, through the light of instruction."[1] According to the *Decree on the Bishops' Pastoral Office in the Church* of Vatican II, this responsibility implies the use of publications and "various other media of communication" that are helpful in proclaiming the Gospel of Christ.[2]

From time to time, the National Conference of Catholic Bishops issues pastoral letters and statements on specific issues of national concern, but it is individual bishops who must provide guidance and oversee catechetical programs and materials in their dioceses. Diocesan bishops, acting alone, are not in a position, however, to influence publishers outside their jurisdiction. And for their part, publishers have on occasion asked for national norms and standard criteria that can help them in presenting the Church's doctrine on faith and morals while taking into account "the natural disposition, ability, age, and circumstances of life" of their audiences.[3] Accordingly, the NCCB/USCC adopted as one of its objectives for the years 1988-90:

> To support the catechetical ministry of the Church in the United States by developing policy guidelines for the creation of doctrinally sound textbooks and by providing for their implementation.

The Division of Catechesis/Religious Education of the USCC's Department of Education was given the assignment to implement this objective. The plan of action called for the formation of a task force chaired by Bishop John Leibrecht of Springfield-Cape Girardeau. Included among its eighteen members were Bishop Donald Wuerl of Pittsburgh and Auxiliary Bishop Robert Banks of Boston. The task force members brought varied professional and personal experiences to the work and were generally representative of the geographic, cultural, and social profile of the Church in the United States.

The task force met between June 1988 and May 1990. Evolving through several drafts, the guidelines benefitted from consultations with publishers of catechetical materials, members of the NCCB Committee on Doctrine, and members of the NCCB Committee on the Liturgy. The task force submitted its work to the USCC Committee on Education, which after amending it presented it for adoption to the full body of bishops. The bishops, after making several recommendations for text improvements, approved the document at their meeting of November 14, 1990.

Introduction

Since the Second Vatican Council, the Church has experienced a remarkable renewal in catechesis. This renewal has been encouraged and guided by the *General Catechetical Directory* (GCD; 1971); the third and the fourth general assemblies of the Synod of Bishops (1974, 1977); Paul VI's apostolic exhortation *Evangelization in the Modern World* (1975); John Paul II's *Catechesis in Our Time* (1979); and in the United States, by *Sharing the Light of Faith: National Catechetical Directory for Catholics of the United States* (1979). In 1985, the Extraordinary Synod of Bishops proposed a *Catechism for the Universal Church* that will offer a presentation of doctrine, inspired by Scripture and the liturgy, and "suited to the present life of Christians."[4] In recent years, the ongoing effort toward renewal of catechesis in the United States has been nowhere more evident than in the area of religion textbooks and catechetical materials. Each year many new materials for children, youth, and adults appear on the market. Publishing companies, with admirable dedication and zeal, make significant investments in researching, testing, editing, and marketing catechetical tools. They employ writers and editors with the finest credentials, and they seek the guidance of theologians, biblical scholars, specialists in pastoral liturgy, professional educators, and catechetical experts. Most of these materials advance and enrich the Church's catechetical mission, but their diversity and quantity present a new challenge. The faithful expect the bishops—and we recognize it as our responsibility—to assure them that these materials express the teaching of the Church as faithfully as possible.

The traditional way for bishops to exercise supervision in this ecclesial process is through the granting of an *imprimatur* to catechetical works. The 1983 *Code of Canon Law* directs that "catechisms and other writings dealing with catechetical formation or their translations need the approval of the local ordinary for their publication" (canon 827.1). The Code further states that it "is the responsibility of the diocesan bishop to issue norms concerning catechetics and to make provision that suitable instruments for catechesis are available" (canon 775.1). It is with this latter directive in mind that the National Conference of Catholic Bishops, with due regard for the responsibility and prerogatives of the local ordinary, responding to the desire of publishers for guidance and concerns of the faithful, outlines a number of principles and offers a series of guidelines.

These guidelines are intended to provide direction to the publishers, particularly in the area of Catholic doctrine regarding both faith and morals. Based on the major catechetical documents of the Church and the teachings of Vatican II, they highlight essential components of the documents that relate to doctrinal soundness in catechetical materials. *Doctrinal soundness* implies, first of all, a complete and correct presentation of church teaching, with proper attention to its organic unity. In the context of catechesis, doctrinal soundness also requires that church teaching be presented clearly and in a manner that can be readily understood. Language and images must be adapted to the capacity of the learners in accord with their age levels and cultural backgrounds.

Catechesis is a pastoral ministry "which leads both communities and individual members of the faithful to maturity of faith."[5] John Paul II reminds us that early in the Church's history

> the name of *catechesis* was given to the whole of the efforts within the Church to make disciples, to help people believe that Jesus is the Son of God, so that believing they might have life in his name, and to educate and instruct them in this life and thus build up the body of Christ."[6]

Thus it is part of the mission of the Church and a significant concern of the bishops that catechesis be provided for all members of the Catholic community.

The faith that the Church seeks to strengthen is the free acceptance of the mystery of God and the divine plan of salvation offered in revelation to all peoples. The act of faith has two aspects that by their nature are inseparable. Faith includes both the firm adherence given by a person "under the influence of grace to God revealing himself (the faith *by which* one believes) [and] the content of revelation and of the Christian message (the faith *which* one believes)."[7] This latter aspect has a communal dimension insofar as it is handed on by the Church and shared by the Catholic faithful. These guidelines pertain chiefly to the Christian message as it is dealt with in catechetical materials.

Catechetical Materials

Catechetical materials are intended as effective instruments for teaching the fullness of the Christian message found in the word of God and in the teachings of the Church. They include many kinds of resources: printed and audiovisual materials, and textbooks and programs that utilize such learning strategies as role playing, crafts, and other supportive educational activities. They are prepared for groups and persons of diverse interests, needs, ages, and abilities. Although the National Catechetical Directory recognizes that catechists are more important than their tools, it acknowledges that "good tools in the hands of skilled catechists can do much to foster growth in faith."[8]

Dimensions of Catechesis

Catechesis nurtures the faith of individuals and communities by integrating four fundamental tasks: (1) proclaiming Christ's message; (2) participating in efforts to develop community; (3) leading people to worship and prayer; and (4) motivating them to Christian living and service.[9] Catechetical materials aid this process. First, catechesis, a form of ministry of the word, supposes that the hearer has embraced the Christian message as a salvific reality. It is the purpose of catechesis and, by extension, of catechetical materials to motivate the faithful to respond to the message in an informed way, both personally and in community. Catechesis takes place within the Church, and catechetical materials reflect the beliefs, values, and practices of the Christian community.

Second, catechetical materials develop community by keeping traditions alive and recommending activities that build up the Church, making it a "community of believers [striving to be] of one heart and one mind" (Acts 4:32).

Third, the Church, from its earliest days, has recognized that liturgy and catechesis are supportive of one another. Catechetical materials can be expected, therefore, to explain how liturgical celebrations deepen the community's knowledge of the faith and to "promote an active, conscious, genuine participation in the liturgy of the Church."[10] Sound catechetical materials provide examples of ways that the Christian community prays together, with particular emphasis on forms of devotional prayer inspired by and directed toward the liturgy itself.[11]

Fourth, in calling upon Christians to serve others, catechetical materials should explain clearly the Church's moral teaching. They should emphasize the twofold responsibility of individuals and communities to strive for holiness and to witness to Christian values. This includes respect for life, service to others, and working to bring about peace and justice in society.[12]

In short, catechetical materials should present the story of salvation and the Church's beliefs according to the principles of doctrinally sound catechesis that we describe below.

Principles and Criteria of Doctrinally Sound Catechetical Materials

The first principle of doctrinal soundness is that the Christian message be both *authentic* and *complete*. For expressions of faith and moral teachings to be authentic, they must be in harmony with the doctrine and traditions of the Catholic Church, which are safeguarded by the bishops who teach with a unique authority. For completeness, the message of salvation, which is made up of several parts that are closely interrelated, must, in due course, be presented in its entirety, with an eye to leading individuals and communities to maturity of faith. Completeness also implies that individual parts be presented in a balanced way, according to the capacity of the learners and in the context of a particular doctrine.

The second principle in determining the doctrinal soundness of catechetical materials is the recognition that the mystery of faith is *incarnate* and *dynamic*. The mystery of the divine plan for human salvation, revealed in the person of Jesus Christ and made known in the Sacred Scriptures, continues as a dynamic force in the world through the power of the Holy Spirit until finally all things are made subject to Christ and the kingdom is handed over to the Father "so that God may be all in all" (1 Cor 15:28). God's creative power is mediated in the concrete experiences of life, in personal development, in human relationships, in culture, in social life, in science and technology, and in "signs of the times." The *National Catechetical Directory* refers to the Scriptures, the teaching life and witness of the Church, the Church's liturgical life, and life experiences of various kinds as "signs of God's saving activity" in the world.[13] These biblical, ecclesial, liturgical, and natural signs should inform the content and spirit of all catechetical materials.

From these two basic principles flow several criteria that describe doctrinally sound catechetical materials.

First, a holistic approach to catechesis reflects the progressive, step-by-step initiation of the believer into the church community, and the lifelong conversion that is required of individuals and communities if they are to mature in faith. Catechetical materials should relate to the age, ability, and experience of those being catechized. The principal form of catechesis is catechesis of adults, for adults are those "who have the greatest responsibilities and the capacity to live the Christian message in its fully developed form."[14] Catechesis for children and other age groups is always necessary and should in some way lay the foundation for adult catechesis.[15]

Second, proper expression of our faith highlights the centrality of fundamental doctrines of the Christian tradition. Both the *General Catechetical Directory* and the *National Catechetical Directory* offer valuable guidance in this regard, as will a *Catechism for the Universal Church*. The trinitarian structure of the Apostles' Creed and the Nicene Creed is an example that offers helpful guidance in ordering the hierarchy of truths. In presenting the Christian message, catechetical materials take into account the developmental nature of the learner and the particular circumstances of the local church community, but they cannot be selective as to content and emphasis in ways that compromise the authentic and complete teaching of the Church.[16]

Third, authentic catechesis recognizes that Christian faith needs to be incarnated in all cultures; accordingly, it is expressed in diverse ways that witness to the catholicity of the Church without endangering its unity. John Paul II has stated, "The Gospel of Christ is at home in every people. It enriches, uplifts and purifies every culture."[17] Catechetical materials not only alert the faithful to the full meaning of catholicity and the cultural dimensions of the Christian faith experience, but they also facilitate the assimilation of the gospel message, using language, customs, and symbols familiar to those being taught.

Fourth, the fruit of effective catechesis is unity "among all who hold and teach the Catholic faith that comes to us from the apostles."[18] The common faith is shared and celebrated most perfectly in the eucharist. Biblical, creedal, and prayer formulas are also essential to the unity of the faith community. There is "one Lord, one faith, one baptism; one God and Father of all, who is over all and through all and in all" (Eph 4:5). For believers to share their faith, they must have common experiences and a shared language in which to express and celebrate it. Some common expression of faith is essential to the unity of the believing community. Without a shared language, the faithful cannot profess and celebrate their faith in communion with one another. Catechetical materials, taken as a whole, need to promote a healthy and vital Catholic identity in such a way that the believer hears the message clearly, lives it with conviction, and shares it courageously with others.

In the NCCB document *Basic Teachings for Catholic Religious Education*, the bishops of the United States expressed a desire for an informed laity, people of faith who know their religion and can give an account of it.[19] But now, as then, this means a Church transformed by the gospel message, for Christians who bring the Gospel into their daily lives; for faithful men and women whose zeal for peace and justice, joy and simplicity, witness to Christ's continuing presence in the world while we await his return in glory, when every tear will be wiped away and death will be no more. It is our hope that these

Guidelines for Doctrinally Sound Catechetical Materials will contribute to these goals.

I. Guidelines for Doctrinally Sound Catechetical Materials

The following guidelines are based on major catechetical documents of the Church; the constitutions, decrees, and declarations of Vatican II; recent papal encyclicals and apostolic exhortations; and the pastoral letters of the U.S. bishops. The guidelines, even taken as a whole, are not a synthesis of the gospel message nor an exhaustive list of Catholic beliefs. They are not intended to supplant—and in fact should be studied in conjunction with—the outline of the "Principal Elements of the Christian Message for Catechesis"[20] and any exposition of doctrine found in a future *Catechism for the Universal Church.*

The guidelines differ from the *National Catechetical Directory* and our earlier document *Basic Teachings for Catholic Religious Education* in two ways: First, they incorporate teachings and principles stated in recent papal encyclicals and in pastoral letters issued by the National Conference of Catholic Bishops; second, they single out certain doctrines that seem to need particular emphasis in the life and culture of the United States at this time. The guidelines take into account a hierarchy of truths of faith insofar as they give priority to the foundational mysteries in the creed, but they do not prescribe a particular order in which the truths are to be presented.[21] The guidelines are intended to present church teachings in a positive and meaningful way so that authors, editors, and publishers of catechetical materials can better assist the faithful to integrate the truth of Catholic doctrine and moral teachings into their lives.

General Doctrinal Content

Doctrinally sound catechetical materials:

1. Help the baptized, as members of the Church founded by Christ, appreciate Catholic tradition, grounded in the Scriptures and celebrated in the divine liturgy, in such a personal way that it becomes part of their very identity.

2. Present the teaching of the Church in a full and balanced way that includes everything necessary for an accurate understanding of a particular doctrine and express it in a manner appropriate to the audience and purpose of a given catechetical text.

3. Situate the teachings of the Church in the context of God's saving plan and relate them to one another so that they can be seen as

parts of an organic whole and not simply as isolated and fragmented truths.[22]

4. Describe the many ways that God has spoken and continues to speak in the lives of human beings and how the fullness of revelation is made known in Christ (Heb 1:1-2).[23]

5. Explain the inspired Scriptures according to the mind of the Church, while not neglecting the contributions of modern biblical scholarship in the use of various methods of interpretation, including historical-critical and literary methods.[24]

6. Are sensitive to distinctions between faith and theology, church doctrine and theological opinion, acknowledging that the same revealed truth can be explained in different ways. However, every explanation must be compatible with Catholic tradition.[25]

7. Reflect the wisdom and continuing relevance of the church fathers and incorporate a sense of history that recognizes doctrinal development and provides background for understanding change in church policy and practice.

8. Explain the documents of the Second Vatican Council as an authoritative and valid expression of the deposit of faith as contained in Holy Scripture and the living tradition of the Church.[26]

9. Present the uniqueness and preeminence of the Christian message without rejecting anything that is true and holy in non-Christian religions, show a high regard for all religions that witness to the mystery of divine presence, the dignity of human beings, and high moral standards.[27]

Father, Son, and Holy Spirit

Doctrinally sound catechetical materials:

10. Are trinitarian and christocentric in scope and spirit, clearly presenting the mystery of creation, redemption, and sanctification in God's plan of salvation.[28]

11. Help Christians contemplate with eyes of faith the communal life of the Holy Trinity and know that, through grace, we share in God's divine nature.[29]

12. Arouse a sense of wonder and praise for God's world and providence by presenting creation, not as an abstract principle or as an event standing by itself, but as the origin of all things and the beginning of the mystery of salvation in Jesus Christ.[30]

13. Focus on the heart of the Christian message: salvation from sin and death through the person and work of Jesus, with special emphasis on the paschal mystery—his passion, death, and resurrection.

14. Emphasize the work and person of Jesus Christ as the key and chief point of Christian reference in reading the Scriptures.[31]

15. Present Jesus as true God, who came into the world for us and for our salvation, and as true man who thinks with a human mind, acts with a human will, loves with a human heart,[32] highlighting the uniqueness of his divine mission so that he appears as more than a great prophet and moral teacher.

16. Describe how the Holy Spirit continues Christ's work in the world, in the Church, and in the lives of believers.[33]

17. Maintain the traditional language, grounded in the Scriptures, that speaks of the Holy Trinity as Father, Son, and Spirit and apply, where appropriate, the principles of inclusive language approved by the NCCB.[34]

Church

Doctrinally sound catechetical materials:

18. Recognize that the Church, a community of believers, is a mystery, a sign of the kingdom, a community of divine origin, that cannot be totally understood or fully defined in human terms.[35]

19. Teach that the Church's unique relationship with Christ makes it both sign and instrument of God's union with humanity, the means for the forgiveness of sin as well as a means of unity for human beings among themselves.[36]

20. Emphasize the missionary nature of the Church and the call of individual Christians to proclaim the Gospel wherever there are people to be evangelized, at home and abroad.[37]

21. Nourish and teach the faith and, because there is often a need for initial evangelization, aim at opening the heart and arousing the beginning of faith so that individuals will respond to the word of God and Jesus' call to discipleship.[38]

22. Emphasize that Jesus Christ gave the apostles a special mission to teach and that today this teaching authority is exercised by the pope and bishops, who are successors of St. Peter and the apostles.

23. Highlight the history and distinctive tradition of the Church of Rome and the special charism of the pope as successor of St. Peter in guiding and teaching the universal Church and assuring the authentic teaching of the Gospel.

24. Explain what it means when the Church professes to be "one, holy, catholic and apostolic."[39]

25. Show how the Church of Christ is manifest at the local level in the diocesan church and the parish, gathered in the Holy Spirit through the Gospel and the eucharist.[40]

26. Present the Church as a community with a legitimate diversity in expressing its shared faith according to different ages, cultures, gifts, and abilities.

27. Foster understanding and unity by accurately presenting the traditions and practices of the Catholic churches of the East.[41]

28. Are sensitive in dealing with other Christian churches and ecclesial communities, taking into account how they differ from the Catholic tradition while at the same time showing how much is held in common.[42]

29. Foster ecumenism as a means toward unity and communion among all Christians and recognize that division in the Church and among Christians is contrary to the will of Christ.[43]

30. Integrate the history of the Jews in the work of salvation so that, on the one hand, Judaism does not appear marginal and unimportant and, on the other hand, the Church and Judaism do not appear as parallel ways of salvation.[44]

31. Explain the pastoral role and authority of the magisterium—the bishops united with the pope—in defining and teaching religious truth.

32. Emphasize that individuals reach their full potential and work out their salvation only in community—the human community and the community that is the Church.[45]

33. Support the family as the basic unit of society and underline its role as "domestic church" in living the Gospel.[46]

Mary and the Saints

Doctrinally sound catechetical materials:

34. Explain the sacramental meaning of "communion of saints," linking it to the eucharist, which, bringing the faithful together to share the "holy gifts," is the primary source and sign of church unity.

35. Explain the biblical basis for the liturgical cult of Mary as mother of God and disciple *par excellence* and describe her singular role in the life of Christ and the story of salvation.[47]

36. Foster Marian devotions and explain the Church's particular beliefs about Mary (e.g., the immaculate conception, virgin birth, and assumption).[48]

37. Explain the Church's teaching on angels and its veneration of saints, who intercede for us and are role models in following Christ.[49]

Liturgy and Sacraments

Doctrinally sound catechetical materials:

38. Present the sacraments as constitutive of Christian life and worship, as unique ways of meeting Christ, and not simply as channels of grace.

39. Emphasize God's saving and transforming presence in the sacraments. In the eucharist, Christ is present not only in the person of

the priest but in the assembly and in the word and, uniquely, in the eucharistic species of bread and wine that become the body and blood of Christ.[50]

40. Link the eucharist to Christ's sacrifice on the cross, explaining it as a sacrament of his presence in the Church and as a meal of communal solidarity that is a sign of the heavenly banquet to which the faithful are called.[51]

41. Call attention to the special significance of Sunday as the day of the Lord's resurrection, emphasizing active participation in Sunday Mass as an expression of community prayer and spiritual renewal.

42. Explain the liturgical year, with special attention to the seasons of Advent-Christmas, Lent-Easter.[52]

43. Promote active participation in the liturgy of the Church, not only by explaining the rites and symbols, but also by fostering a spirit of praise, thanksgiving, and repentance, and by nurturing a sense of community and reverence.[53]

44. Explain the Catholic heritage of popular devotions and sacramentals so that they serve as a means "to help people advance towards knowledge of the mystery of Christ and his message."[54]

45. Embody the norms and guidelines for liturgy and sacramental practice found in the *praenotanda* of the revised rites, with special attention to those that preface the sacraments of initiation.

46. Assist pastors, parents, and catechists to inaugurate children into the sacraments of penance and eucharist by providing for their proper initial preparation according to Catholic pastoral practice as presented by the magisterium.

47. Promote lifelong conversion and an understanding of the need for reconciliation that leads to a renewed appreciation of the sacrament of penance.

48. Establish the foundations for vocational choices—to the married life, the single life, the priesthood, the diaconate, and to the vowed life of poverty, chastity, and obedience—in the framework of one's baptismal commitment and the call to serve.

49. Respect the essential difference between the ministerial priesthood and the common priesthood, between the ministries conferred by the sacrament of orders and the call to service derived from the sacraments of baptism and confirmation.[55]

50. Foster vocations to the priesthood and religious life in appropriate ways at every age level.

Life of Grace and Moral Issues

Doctrinally sound catechetical materials:

51. Teach that from the beginning, God called human beings to holiness, but from the very dawn of history, humans abused their free-

dom and set themselves against God so that "sin entered the world" (Rom 5:12), and that this "original sin" is transmitted to every human being.[56]

52. Introduce prayer as a way of deepening one's relationship with God and explain the ends of prayer so that a spirit of adoration, thanksgiving, petition, and contrition permeates the daily lives of Christians.[57]

53. Promote the continual formation of right Catholic conscience based on Christ's role in one's life; his ideals, precepts, and examples found in Scripture; and the magisterial teaching of the Church.[58]

54. Cultivate the moral life of Christians by inculcating virtue and nurture a sense of responsibility that goes beyond external observance of laws and precepts.

55. Discuss the reality and effects of personal sins, whereby an individual, acting knowingly and deliberately, violates the moral law, harms one's self, one's neighbor, and offends God.[59]

56. Make it clear that the dignity of the human person and sanctity of life are grounded in one's relation to the triune God, and that individuals are valued not because of their status in society, their productivity, or as consumers, but in themselves as being made in God's image.[60]

57. Go beyond economic and political concerns in describing ecological and environmental issues and define human accountability for the created universe in moral and spiritual terms.[61]

58. Present a consistent ethic of life that, fostering respect for individual dignity and personal rights, highlights the rights of the unborn, the aged, and those with disabilities and explains the evils of abortion and euthanasia.

59. Explain the specifics of Christian morality, as taught by the magisterium of the Church, in the framework of the universal call to holiness and discipleship; the Ten Commandments; the Sermon on the Mount, especially the Beatitudes; and Christ's discourse at the Last Supper.[62]

60. Include the responsibilities of Catholic living, traditionally expressed in the precepts of the Church.

61. Present Catholic teaching on justice, peace, mercy, and social issues as integral to the gospel message and the Church's prophetic mission.[63]

62. Explain that the Church's teaching on the "option for the poor" means that while Christians are called to respond to the needs of everyone, they must give their greatest attention to individuals and communities with greatest needs.[64]

63. State the Church's position on moral and social issues of urgent concern in contemporary society, for example, the developing role of women in the Church and in society, racism, and other forms of discrimination.

64. Present human sexuality in positive terms of life, love, and self-discipline, explain the responsibilities of a chaste Christian life, and teach that love between husband and wife must be exclusive and open to new life.[65]

65. Link personal morality to social issues and professional ethics and challenge the faithful to make responsible moral decisions guided by the Church's teaching.[66]

66. Teach that all legitimate authority comes from God and that governments exist to serve the people, to protect human rights, and secure basic justice for all members of society.[67]

67. Teach that though sin abounds in the world, grace is even more abundant because of the salvific work of Christ.[68]

Death, Judgment, and Eternity

Doctrinally sound catechetical materials:

68. Explain the coming of Christ "in glory" in the context of the Church's overall teaching on eschatology and final judgment.[69]

69. Teach, on the subject of the last things, that everyone has an awesome responsibility for his or her eternal destiny and present, in the light of Christian hope, death, judgment, purgatory, heaven, or hell.[70]

II. Guidelines for Presenting Sound Doctrine

A second set of guidelines—no less important than the first if catechesis is to be effective—is based on pastoral principles and practical concerns. They are reminders that catechetical materials must take into account the community for whom they are intended, the conditions in which they live, and the ways in which they learn.[71] Publishers are encouraged to provide catechetical materials that take into consideration the needs of Hispanic communities and other ethnic and culturally diverse groups that comprise the Church in the United States. No single text or program can address the many cultures and social groups that make up society in the United States, but all catechetical materials must take this diversity into account. Effective catechesis, as we have noted above, requires that the Church's teaching be presented correctly and in its entirety, and it is equally important to present it in ways that are attractive, appealing, and understandable by the individuals and communities to whom it is directed.

To present sound doctrine effectively, catechetical materials:

70. Take into account the experience and background of those being catechized and suggest ways that the Christian message illumines their life.[72]

71. Must be based on accepted learning theory, established peda-gogical principles, and practical learning strategies.[73]

72. Use language and images appropriate to the age level and developmental stages and special needs of those being catechized.[74]

73. Integrate biblical themes and scriptural references in the pres-entation of doctrine and moral teaching and encourage a hands-on familiarity with the Bible.[75]

74. Challenge Catholics to critique and transform contemporary values and behaviors in light of the Gospel and the Church's teaching.

75. Maintain a judicious balance between personal expression and memorization, emphasizing that it is important both for the commu-nity and themselves that individuals commit to memory selected bib-lical passages, essential prayers, liturgical responses, key doctrinal ideas, and lists of moral responsibilities.[76]

76. Provide for a variety of shared prayer forms and experiences that lead to an active participation in the liturgical life of the Church and private prayer.[77]

77. Continually hold before their intended audience the ideal of living a life based on the teachings of the Gospel.

78. Include suggestions for service to the community that is appro-priate to the age and abilities of the persons who are being catechized.

79. Stress the importance of the local church community for Christian living, so that every Catholic contributes to building up the spirit of the parish family and sees its ministries as part of the Church's universal mission.

80. Are sensitive to the appropriate use of inclusive language in the text and avoid racial, ethnic, and gender stereotypes in pictures.[78]

81. Reflect the catholicity of the Church in art and graphics by pre-senting the diverse customs and religious practices of racial, ethnic, cultural, and family groups.[79]

82. Assist catechists by including easy-to-understand instructions regarding scope, sequence, and use of texts.

83. Suggest a variety of strategies, activities, and auxiliary resources that can enrich instruction, deepen understanding, and facil-itate the integration of doctrine and life.

84. Include material that can be used in the home to aid parents in communicating church teaching and nurturing the faith life of the fam-ily.

85. Instruct teachers and catechists on how to respond to the needs of persons with disabilities and individuals with special needs.[80]

86. Help teachers and catechists distinguish between church doc-trine and the opinions and interpretations of theologians.[81]

87. Help develop the catechists' own faith life, experience of prayer, and mature commitment to the Church and motivate them toward ongoing enrichment.

Notes

1. Second Vatican Council, *Decree on the Pastoral Office of Bishops in the Church (Christus Dominus)*, no. 14.
2. Ibid., no. 13.
3. Ibid., no. 14.
4. Extraordinary Synod of Bishops, *A Message to the People of God and The Final Report, Rome, 1985* (Washington, D.C.: United States Catholic Conference, 1986).
5. Congregation for the Clergy, *General Catechetical Directory* (Washington, D.C.: United States Catholic Conference, 1971), no. 21.
6. John Paul II, *On Catechesis in Our Time (Catechesi Tradendae)* (Washington, D.C.: United States Catholic Conference, 1979), no. 1.
7. *General Catechetical Directory*, no. 36.
8. United States Catholic Conference, *Sharing the Light of Faith: National Catechetical Directory for Catholics in the United States* (Washington, D.C.: United States Catholic Conference, 1979), no. 249.
9. Ibid., no. 213.
10. Ibid., no. 36.
11. Second Vatican Council, *Constitution on the Sacred Liturgy (Sacrosanctum Concilium)*, no. 13.
12. *National Catechetical Directory*, no. 38.
13. Ibid., no. 42.
14. *Catechesi Tradendae*, no. 43.
15. *General Catechetical Directory*, no. 20; *National Catechetical Directory*, no. 321.
16. *General Catechetical Directory*, no. 46; *National Catechetical Directory*, no. 47.
17. John Paul II, "Address to Native Americans" (September 14, 1988), *Origins* 17:17 (October 8, 1988): 297-298.
18. Eucharistic Prayer I, *The Sacramentary: The Roman Missal Revised by the Decree of the Second Vatican Ecumenical Council and Published by the Authority of Pope Paul VI*, English translation prepared by ICEL (New York: Catholic Book Publishing Co., 1985), 542.
19. United States Catholic Conference, *Basic Teachings for Catholic Religious Education* (Washington, D.C.: United States Catholic Conference, 1972), 2-3.
20. *National Catechetical Directory*, chapter 5.
21. *General Catechetical Directory*, no. 46.
22. Ibid., no. 39.
23. *Catechesi Tradendae*, nos. 20, 52.
24. *The Historical Truth of the Gospels (The 1964 Instruction of the Biblical Commission)* (Glen Rock, N.J.: Paulist Press, 1964).
25. *National Catechetical Directory*, no. 16.
26. Synod of Bishops (Second Extraordinary), *A Message to the People of God and The Final Report* (Washington, D.C.: United States Catholic Conference, 1985).
27. Second Vatican Council, *Declaration on the Relationship of the Church to Non-Christian Religions (Nostra Aetate)*, no. 2.
28. *National Catechetical Directory*, no. 47.
29. *General Catechetical Directory*, no. 47.
30. *General Catechetical Directory*, no. 51; *National Catechetical Directory*, no. 85.

31. The Pontifical Council for Promoting Christian Unity, *Notes on the Correct Way to Present the Jews and Judaism in Preaching and Catechesis in the Roman Catholic Church* (Washington, D.C.: United States Catholic Conference, 1985), II, 5, 6.
32. *National Catechetical Directory,* no. 89.
33. Ibid., no. 92.
34. See National Conference of Catholic Bishops, *Criteria for the Evaluation of Inclusive Language Translations of Scriptural Texts Proposed for Liturgical Use* (Washington, D.C.: United States Catholic Conference, 1990).
35. *National Catechetical Directory,* no. 63.
36. Ibid.
37. Ibid., nos. 71, 74e.
38. *Catechesi Tradendae,* no. 19.
39. *National Catechetical Directory,* nos. 72, 74i, ii.
40. *Christus Dominus,* no. 11; Second Vatican Council, *Dogmatic Constitution on the Church (Lumen Gentium),* no. 26.
41. *National Catechetical Directory,* nos. 73, 74g.
42. Ibid., no. 76.
43. Second Vatican Council, *Decree on Ecumenism (Unitatis Redintegratio),* no. 1.
44. *Notes on the Correct Way,* I, 7.
45. National Conference of Catholic Bishops, *Economic Justice for All* (Washington, D.C.: United States Catholic Conference, 1986), nos. 63, 65, and *passim.*
46. John Paul II, *On the Family (Familiaris Consortio)* (Washington, D.C.: United States Catholic Conference, 1981), no. 12.
47. *Lumen Gentium,* nos. 66, 67.
48. *General Catechetical Directory,* no. 68; *National Catechetical Directory,* no. 106.
49. *General Catechetical Directory,* no. 68.
50. *Sacrosanctum Concilium,* no. 7.
51. *Sacrosanctum Concilium,* nos. 7, 47; *Gaudium et Spes,* no. 38.
52. *National Catechetical Directory,* no. 144c.
53. Ibid., no. 36.
54. *Catechesi Tradendae,* no. 54.
55. John Paul II, *The Vocation and Mission of the Lay Faithful in the Church and in the World (Christifideles Laici)* (Washington, D.C.: United States Catholic Conference, 1988), nos. 22, 23.
56. *Gaudium et Spes,* no. 13.
57. *National Catechetical Directory,* no. 140.
58. Ibid., no. 190.
59. *General Catechetical Directory,* no. 62.
60. *Economic Justice for All,* nos. 28, 48.
61. John Paul II, *On Social Concern (Sollicitudo Rei Socialis)* (Washington, D.C.: United States Catholic Conference, 1987), no. 38.
62. *National Catechetical Directory,* no. 105.
63. Ibid., no. 170.
64. *Economic Justice for All,* nos. 86-87.
65. *Familiaris Consortio,* no. 29.
66. *National Catechetical Directory,* nos. 38, 170.
67. *Economic Justice for All,* no. 122.
68. *National Catechetical Directory,* no. 98.

69. Ibid., no. 110.
70. Ibid., no. 109; *General Catechetical Directory*, no. 69.
71. *General Catechetical Directory*, foreword.
72. *National Catechetical Directory*, no. 176e.
73. Ibid., no. 175.
74. Ibid., nos. 177-188.
75. Ibid., no. 60a.
76. *Catechesi Tradendae*, no. 55; *National Catechetical Directory*, no. 176e.
77. Ibid., nos. 145, 264.
78. Ibid., no. 264.
79. Ibid., nos. 194, 264.
80. Ibid., nos. 195, 196, 264.
81. Ibid., no. 264.

Source: Washington, D.C.: United States Catholic Conference, 1990.

Testimony on the Permanent Replacement of Strikers

Testimony by Bishop Frank Rodimer Before the Senate Committee on Labor on Behalf of the United States Catholic Conference

March 1991

Thank you, Mr. Chairman, for this opportunity to testify in support of S. 55, which would outlaw the practice of hiring permanent replacements to take the jobs of workers who go on strike. I am Bishop Frank Rodimer, bishop of the Diocese of Paterson, N.J., and a member of the U.S. Catholic Conference, the public policy agency of the nation's Roman Catholic bishops. I am here today to represent the bishops' conference at the request of Bishop James Malone, who chairs the bishops' Committee on Domestic Social Policy. That committee voted at its January meeting to give general support for this legislation.

It is especially appropriate for the conference of Catholic bishops to speak out on this issue at this time. This year the Church around the world is celebrating the hundredth anniversary of *Rerum Novarum,* the first papal encyclical on modern Catholic social teaching. The English title of the encyclical is "On the Condition of Workers," and in his letter Pope Leo XIII pointed out that workers' associations should be protected by the state since they can be beneficial not just for the workers they represent but for the stability of society. That theme is a constant in our social teaching—from Pope Leo in 1891 to Pope John Paul II in 1991. In his encyclical "On Human Work" in 1981, the present Holy Father wrote that unions are "an indispensable element of social life, especially in modern industrialized countries."

The role of unions in promoting the dignity of work and of workers is very important in Catholic teaching. In the words of Pope John Paul II, through labor unions workers can "not only have more, but be more." Rooted in the basic human right to freedom of association, the right to organize unions and to bargain collectively remains essential in order to prevent the exploitation of workers and to defend the human person as more than just a factor in production. For one hundred years the Church has called on governments to respect and defend labor unions in their essential roles in the struggle for justice in the workplace and as building blocks for freedom and democracy.

In the U.S. bishops' 1986 pastoral letter *Economic Justice for All,* we pointed out that "the way power is distributed in a free-market economy frequently gives employers greater power than employees in the negotiation of labor contracts. Such unequal power may press workers into a choice between an inadequate wage and no wage at all." The letter goes on to reiterate the benefits to workers and society of strong and effective labor unions and opposes efforts to break existing unions and prevent workers from organizing. The letter concludes, "U.S. labor-law reform is needed to meet these problems as well as to provide more timely and effective remedies for unfair labor practices."

Mr. Chairman, an essential tool for unions in pursuing the just rights of their members is the possibility of a strike; without the threat of a strike, unions would be next to powerless to resist unjust demands by employers. Without the right to strike, workers come to the bargaining table at a serious disadvantage, facing employers who are holding most of the cards. This relative weakness of workers in a market economy is the reason that Catholic teaching supports the legitimacy of the resort to a strike when this is the only available means to obtain justice. The right to strike has not always been used wisely nor are unions above criticism; but neither the corruption that has plagued some—not all—unions nor the violence associated with some—not all—strikes can justify the denial or the erosion of workers' basic rights.

One of the major documents of the Second Vatican Council, the *Pastoral Constitution on the Church in the Modern World*, includes a strong affirmation of the moral and practical value of unions. It says:

> Among the basic rights of the human person is to be numbered the right of freely founding unions for working people. . . . Included is the right of freely taking part in the activity of these unions without risk of reprisal.

Mr. Chairman, I am not a labor lawyer, but I have been a pastor for many years and have observed labor-management relations in New Jersey over that time. I can tell you from my own observation what economists and lawyers and business analysts will tell you. There is no question that labor unions in this country are weaker today than at any time in my memory. At the same time, the people over at the Department of Labor tell us that average real wages are dropping, and the census takers have found that the gap between the rich and the poor in this country is an ever-widening chasm. It now takes two earners to support most families with children, even with a lower standard of living than their parents had. In our pastoral letter on economic justice, we bishops made the connection between these harsh realities and the declining percentage of union representation in this country.

In the midst of these troubling conditions, there is a new and dangerous development that is further weakening labor unions and endangering the very right to organize. Forty years ago, when I became a priest, it would have been unthinkable for an employer in my community to respond to a strike by hiring permanent replacements. I am told that because of a Supreme Court decision in 1938 it would have been legal to do so, but in those days employers knew better. Labor unions represented a large proportion of workers, and union values permeated the community. In those days, solidarity was not the name of a union in Poland but a working principle in American communities.

However, economic restructuring and social change have undermined the cohesiveness of our communities, and devotion to the common good is often sacrificed in pursuit of personal gain. The painful recessions of the 1970s and the relentless individualism of the 1980s have left many without either the financial cushion or the community connections to ride out strikes or prolonged unemployment. In such an atmosphere, some employers feel free to use strikes as an opportunity to get rid of the union and collective bargaining and their union workforce. I know many employers who wouldn't do this, but unfortunately there are those that have done so and others that are open to it.

The results have been predictable and damaging. Not only have unions been weakened in their ability to defend the rights of workers, but communities have experienced savage struggles, with neighborhoods in turmoil, families divided, and workers without hope. The promise of permanent employment made to the replacement workers becomes an impediment to settling the strike, and negotiations are stymied. The victims are the original workers and their families, who often have no place else to go, and even the replacement workers, who are later discharged when the business closes because of the damage of a prolonged strike. In some places, whole communities suffer wounds that won't heal for generations.

As Cardinal John O'Connor, archbishop of New York, said in his testimony before this subcommittee last December 11:

> It is useless to speak glowingly in either legal or moral terms about the right to strike as a last resort or even the right to unionize if either party, management or labor, bargains in bad faith or, in the case of management, with the foreknowledge of being able to permanently replace workers who strike on the primary basis of the strike itself. In my judgment, this can make a charade of collective bargaining and a mockery of the right to strike.

When employers are allowed to offer permanent jobs to strikebreakers, strikers lose their jobs. It's that simple. If workers lose their jobs, what does it mean to have a right to strike? If there's no effective right to strike, what does it mean to have a right to organize?

Human dignity is clearly threatened in our country. The evidence is visible on our streets and in our shelters, where a growing number of people are forced to live even though they work every day. In our cities and in our rural areas throughout this country working people are homeless because their wages have fallen so far below the cost of housing. Recent immigrants and single mothers, newcomers to the labor force and those least likely to have union representation, are mired in poverty.

In previous generations labor unions were the bridge to economic and social participation for newcomers, and union wages gave the kind of security families needed to raise children and build communities. While some argue that unions are outdated, we believe workers need them now more than ever.

In the words of Msgr. John A. Ryan, first director of the Social Action Department of the National Catholic Welfare Conference, the forerunner of the present-day national bishops' conference:

> Effective labor unions are still by far the most powerful force in society for the protection of the laborer's rights and the improvement of his or her condition. No amount of employer benevolence, no diffusion of a sympathetic attitude on the part of the public, no increase in beneficial legislation, can adequately supply for the lack of organization among the workers themselves.

The right to strike without fear of reprisal is fundamental to a democratic society. The continued weakening of worker organizations is a serious threat to our social fabric. I think we have to decide whether we will be a country where workers' rights are totally dependent on the goodwill of employers or whether we will be a country where the dignity of work and the rights of workers are protected by the law of the land.

Source: *Origins* 20:43 (April 4, 1991): 697-700.

Statement on Euthanasia

A Statement of the NCCB Administrative Committee

September 1991

Current efforts to legalize euthanasia place our society at a critical juncture. These efforts have received growing public attention due to new publications giving advice on methods of suicide and some highly publicized instances in which family members or physicians killed terminally ill persons or helped them kill themselves.

Proposals such as those in the Pacific Northwest, spearheaded by the Hemlock Society, aim to change state laws against homicide and assisted suicide to allow physicians to provide drug overdoses or lethal injections to their terminally ill patients.

Those who advocate euthanasia have capitalized on people's confusion, ambivalence, and even fear about the use of modern life-prolonging technologies. Further, borrowing language from the abortion debate, they insist that the "right to choose" must prevail over all other considerations. Being able to choose the time and manner of one's death, without regard to what is chosen, is presented as the ultimate freedom. A decision to take one's life or to allow a physician to kill a suffering patient, however, is very different from a decision to refuse extraordinary or disproportionately burdensome treatment.

As Catholic leaders and moral teachers, we believe that life is the most basic gift of a loving God—a gift over which we have stewardship but not absolute dominion. Our tradition, declaring a moral obligation to care for our own life and health and to seek such care from others, recognizes that we are not morally obligated to use all available medical procedures in every set of circumstances. But that tradition clearly and strongly affirms that as a responsible steward of life one must never directly intend to cause one's own death or the death of an innocent victim by action or omission. As the Second Vatican Council declared, "Euthanasia and willful suicide" are "offenses against life itself" which "poison civilization"; they "debase the perpetrators more than the victims and militate against the honor of the Creator."[1]

As the Vatican Congregation for the Doctrine of the Faith has said, "Nothing and no one can in any way permit the killing of an innocent human being, whether a fetus or an embryo, an infant or an adult, an old person or one suffering from an incurable disease or a person who is dying." Moreover, we have no right "to ask for this act of killing" for ourselves or for those entrusted to our care; "nor can any authority legitimately recommend or permit such an action." We are dealing here with "a violation of the divine law, an offense against the dignity of the human person, a crime against life and an attack on humanity."[2]

Legalizing euthanasia would also violate American convictions about human rights and equality. The Declaration of Independence proclaims our inalienable rights to "life, liberty, and the pursuit of happiness." If our right to life itself is diminished in value, our other rights will have no meaning. To destroy the boundary between healing and killing would mark a radical departure from longstanding legal and medical traditions of our country, posing a threat of unforeseeable magnitude to vulnerable members of our society. Those who represent the interests of elderly citizens, persons with disabilities, and persons with AIDS or other terminal illnesses are justifiably alarmed when some hasten to confer on them the "freedom" to be killed.

We call on Catholics and on all persons of goodwill to reject proposals to legalize euthanasia. We urge families to discuss issues surrounding the care of terminally ill loved ones in light of sound moral principles and the demands of human dignity, so that patients need not feel helpless or abandoned in the face of complex decisions about their future. And we urge health care professionals, legislators, and all involved in this debate to seek solutions to the problems of terminally ill patients and their families that respect the inherent worth of all human beings, especially those most in need of our love and assistance.

Notes

1. Second Vatican Council, *Pastoral Constitution on the Church in the Modern World (Gaudium et Spes)*, no. 27.
2. Congregation for the Doctrine of the Faith, *Declaration on Euthanasia* (Washington, D.C.: United States Catholic Conference, 1980).

Source: *Origins* 21:6 (September 26, 1991): 257-258.

United in Service: Reflections on the Presbyteral Council

A Statement of the National Conference of Catholic Bishops

November 1991

Introduction

> The Second Vatican Council, which so explicitly highlighted the collegiality of the episcopate in the Church, also gave a new form to the life of priestly communities, joined together by a special bond of brotherhood and united to the bishop of the respective local church. The whole priestly life and ministry serve to deepen and strengthen that bond, and a particular responsibility for the various tasks involved by this life and ministry is taken on by the priests' councils, which . . . should be functioning in every diocese.[1]

These words of Pope John Paul II set the tone for this reflection on the presbyteral council. A bond of brotherhood exists between priests and bishops. They are united in service by the sacrament of orders, through which they share in different degrees the priesthood of Christ. The presbyteral council, uniting priests and the diocesan bishop, is a visible expression of this sacramental bond. It represents the presbyterate and aids the diocesan bishop in the governance of the diocese. Priests and bishops cannot remain in isolation from each other and expect to respond adequately to the pastoral needs of the people of God.

Presbyterorum Ordinis of the Second Vatican Council recommended such a council. The *motu proprio Ecclesiae Sanctae* (1966) and the *Code of Canon Law* (1983) mandated that there be a council of priests in each diocese. According to Pope John Paul II, the diocesan bishop should establish a presbyteral council "to seek and obtain counsel and suggestions from his priests, as well as insights into many serious diocesan problems and help in solving them."[2]

The presbyteral council is not just another administrative structure in the Church. Rather it is an expression of the profound sacramental communion that exists between the bishop and his priests. They are united as co-workers and friends in the same ministerial priesthood. The presbyteral council is both the senate of the bishop and a body representative of the presbyterate.

It is appropriate to study the presbyteral council because of its great value in the life of the Church throughout the world. The purpose of these reflections is manifold: to explain the nature and operation of the presbyteral council; to offer encouragement to all priests and bishops who are members of a council to manifest brotherhood; to elicit support for the council from other members of the diocese; and to suggest ways in which the presbyteral council can function more effectively for the good of the Church. It is also hoped that this document, based upon the experience of presbyteral councils in many dioceses and developed in consultation with priests, theologians, and canonists, will stimulate further examination of the presbyteral council. Our audience, therefore, includes bishops, priests, and other members of the Christian faithful who share in the life and growth of the local church.

This study is divided into four chapters. Chapter 1 presents the historical context of the presbyteral council with special emphasis on the scriptural and patristic background. Chapter 2 discusses the theology of the priesthood as the underpinning of the presbyteral council. Chapter 3 gives the canonical dimensions of the council, and chapter 4 offers some practical observations.

Chapter 1: The Historical Context

The presbyteral council has an intriguing and complex historical background. The first part of this chapter will treat the recent history of this form of collaboration among priests and the diocesan bishop. The chapter then will deal with the origins and subsequent development of the presbyteral council.

I. The Renewal of the Presbyteral Council

Within the context of the *Dogmatic Constitution on the Church (Lumen Gentium)* and the *Pastoral Constitution on the Church in the Modern World (Gaudium et Spes)*, the Second Vatican Council (1962-1965) devoted two specific conciliar decrees to a discussion of the ministerial priesthood: the *Decree on Priestly Formation (Optatam Totius)* and the *Decree on the Ministry and Life of Priests (Presbyterorum Ordinis)*. Other documents also discussed priestly ministry.

The council viewed the ministerial priesthood as an ecclesial reality and analyzed it in terms of its biblical, historical, sacramental, and pastoral dimensions. Priests and bishops share in the one priesthood of Christ in a unique way. Both are necessary elements in the conciliar definition of a diocese, "that portion of God's people which is entrusted

to a bishop to be shepherded by him with the cooperation of the presbytery."[3]

In addition to references to the cathedral chapter and to diocesan
consultors,[4] the council also instituted another collegial body, the senate or council of priests. The latter is heir to the presbyteral colleges of
the New Testament and patristic times and emphasizes collaboration
and communication between priests and the diocesan bishop in the
governance of a diocese.

Presbyterorum Ordinis, no. 7 clearly stated the purpose of the presbyteral council.

> Therefore, on account of this communion in the same priest-
> hood and ministry, the bishop should regard priests as his
> brothers and friends. . . . He should gladly listen to them,
> indeed consult with them, and have discussions with them
> about those matters which concern the necessities of pas-
> toral work and the welfare of the diocese. In order to put
> these ideals into effect, a group or senate of priests repre-
> senting the presbytery should be established. It is to operate
> in a manner adapted to modern circumstances and needs
> and have a form and norms to be determined by law. By its
> counsel, this body will be able to give effective assistance to
> the bishop in his government of the diocese.

Pope Paul VI issued the *motu proprio Ecclesiae Sanctae* (August 6,
1966) which required that each diocese have a presbyteral council and
set down norms for its establishment and operation. The Congregation
for the Clergy published a circular letter on April 11, 1970, which
offered suggestions for implementing the provisions of *Ecclesiae
Sanctae* relative to the presbyteral council.

In the years immediately following the Second Vatican Council,
many dioceses in the United States established presbyteral councils.
By the end of 1966, there were forty-five councils in the United States,
and a year later 135 were in place. At present, all dioceses have presbyteral councils. In 1968, a number of presbyteral councils in the
United States formed the National Federation of Priests' Councils.

In the 1960s and 1970s, priests in some of the larger dioceses in the
United States formed their own "associations," which were independent of the presbyteral council and of the diocesan bishop. The popularity of these groups, often controversial and confrontational, waned
with the establishment of presbyteral councils.

Finally, a most important statement from the Church on the presbyteral council is the 1983 *Code of Canon Law* (canons 495-501). These
canons, which will later be examined in detail, reaffirm the importance
of the presbyteral council in the governance of the diocese and prescribe universal norms regarding its nature and function.

II. The Origins of the Presbyteral Council

A few observations are in order before beginning the historical survey. First, what follows is only a broad overview of the history of the presbyteral council and not an exhaustive treatment. Second, the scriptural and patristic texts do not give a detailed description of how the presbyteral council functioned in the early Church. Third, the presbyteral council differed from place to place because of the diversity in structures among the churches. Fourth, contemporary theological ideas or canonical norms should not be applied anachronistically to earlier historical periods.

New Testament authors indicate that ecclesial leaders often acted together as a group. At the conclusion of the Council of Jerusalem, for example, "It was decided by the apostles and presbyters, along with the whole Jerusalem Church, that representatives be chosen from among their number and sent to Antioch along with Paul and Barnabas" (Acts 15:22).[5]

Patristic authors, furthermore, indicate that in the early centuries the bishop and his priests worked closely together. Such authors include Ignatius of Antioch, Hippolytus of Rome, and Cyprian of Carthage.

Ignatius of Antioch (ca. 110). On his way to martyrdom in Rome, Ignatius wrote letters to several churches. For him the Church was organized hierarchically in a threefold structure of bishop, priest, and deacon, without which "no Church is worthy of the name."[6] He insisted on the authority of the bishop: "The bishop is to preside in the place of God."[7] But Ignatius did not neglect the presbyterate; thirteen times in these seven letters he referred to it. The priests formed a college which was subordinate to the bishop, but which shared the pastoral governance of the community with him. Although Ignatius did not indicate in detail the relationship between the bishop and presbyters, his use of the term *synedrion* for the senate of presbyters[8] suggests that the presbyters were actively involved with the bishop in the leadership of the local church.

Ignatius emphasized the need for harmony among his ministers. He compared the presbyters to a finely woven spiritual crown.[9] They are related to the bishop as strings to a harp.[10] In speaking of the bishop, Ignatius often added "and with his presbyters." Obedience is owed both to the bishop and to the presbyters. "It is necessary, then, and such is your practice, that you do nothing without the bishop, but be subject also to the presbytery as representing the apostles of Jesus Christ, our hope."[11]

The Apostolic Tradition of Hippolytus of Rome (ca. 215). This document attests to church practice in third-century Rome. At the ordination of priests, the bishop put his hand on the head of the candidate and the other presbyters also touched him. "On a presbyter, the presbyters alone shall lay on hands, because of the common and like spirit of their order."[12]

The special charism of the presbyter was to offer counsel to the bishop. The ordination ritual for priests stated: "God, the Father of our Lord Jesus Christ, look upon this your servant, and grant him the Spirit of grace and counsel of the presbyterate, that he may sustain and govern your chosen people with a pure heart."[13] The presbyters, then, primarily functioned as a council for the bishop, but they also governed and instructed the Church. Little is said of their liturgical duties.

Deacons were distinct from presbyters. At the ordination of deacons, only the bishop laid on hands because the deacon "is not being ordained to the priesthood" and "does not share in the counsel of the presbyterate."[14]

Although the bishop was in a position of authority over the presbyters, he was also considered part of the presbyterate. Until the middle of the third century, the bishops of Rome were referred to as presbyters in many inscriptions.

Cyprian of Carthage (d. 258). Cyprian, one of the great defenders of episcopal authority, summarized his vision of the episcopacy in the following familiar text: "Whence you ought to know that the bishop is in the Church and the Church is in the bishop, and if there is anyone who is not with the bishop, he is not in the Church."[15] Yet Cyprian was also an outspoken advocate of consultation. He wrote to his presbyters and deacons: "From the beginning of my episcopacy, I decided to do nothing on my own private opinion, without your advice and without the consent of the people."[16] Cyprian took this pledge seriously, and throughout his episcopate he consulted regularly with the clergy and the laity. Convinced that "a bishop must not only teach but learn,"[17] he gave many reasons for consultation: mutual love, honor, reverence, and, above all, the contribution it makes in ensuring the unity of the Church.

The presbyters of Carthage had an active voice in what Cyprian called "a common council," which discussed serious issues facing the community. To his presbyters and deacons he wrote: "For this is fitting to the respect and to the discipline and to the life itself of all of us, that we bishops, assembled with the presbyters in the presence of the people who stand steadfast, . . . be able to dispose of all matters according to the religious obligation of a common council."[18] Cyprian made clear that the presbyters should not act in opposition to the bishop, but he welcomed their advice and collaboration. In his letters he referred to the presence of presbyteral colleges in Rome, Spain, and throughout North Africa.

III. The Decline of the Presbyteral Council

By the third century it was clear that the bishop was the head of the college of presbyters and was conscious of his special authority within the college. Yet bishops also encouraged consultation with the presbyters and valued their advice. In the pre-Nicene period, presbyters performed almost no liturgical rituals when the bishop was present. During the persecution of Decius, Cyprian allowed presbyters to celebrate the eucharist with the assistance of a deacon.[19] As the Church grew, presbyters more and more began to take care of liturgical functions with the exception of ordination and, in the Latin rite, confirmation.

The Edict of Milan (313) was a decisive event in the decline of the presbyteral college. This edict of toleration issued by the co-emperors, Constantine and Licinius, abrogated laws prejudicial to Christians, returned confiscated church property, and allowed Christians to form legal corporations and to worship publicly. As a result the number of Christians greatly increased, new churches were built, and the Church spread in the cities and in rural areas. Bishops sent presbyters to form new communities often far from the episcopal residence.

Because of the dispersal of the presbyters, the sacramental and pastoral aspects of their life increased. On the other hand, their role as counselors of the bishop was greatly reduced.

Those presbyters, physically separated from their colleagues and from the bishop, concentrated on the pastoral needs of their own communities. Their identity became less defined as members of the group of presbyters and more as individual pastors. The title *sacerdos*, previously reserved only for the bishop, was now also applied to the presbyter. Bishops, for their part, depended less on the corporate counsel of the presbyterate and began to operate with more limited consultation.

The presbyters who remained with the bishop continued to assist him in an advisory capacity and to work with him in pastoral and administrative duties. This group eventually became the cathedral chapter, the historical heir to the old presbyteral college. The cathedral chapter reached its highest period of influence between the twelfth and the fourteenth centuries. It became a corporate body with precise legal rights and duties. The canons of the cathedral were clerics who publicly celebrated the divine office, acted as advisers to the bishop, and governed the diocese when it was vacant.

The Council of Trent (1545-1563) modified the authority of the cathedral chapter, and the 1917 *Code of Canon Law* thoroughly revised the entire law concerning cathedral chapters. It also gave legal recognition to the diocesan consultors as another form of governance. The 1983 *Code of Canon Law* significantly revised the section on cathedral chapters; the thirty-two canons of the 1917 Code (canons 391-422) were reduced to eight (canons 503-510). The advisory responsibilities of the cathedral chapter were eliminated, unless the episcopal conference determine otherwise (canon 502.3). Thus, the function of the chapter is now mostly liturgical. In some European dioceses, however, the statutory role of the cathedral chapter is affected by concordats and other arrangements with the government.

In the United States cathedral chapters were never formally established. A cathedral chapter was instituted in New Orleans in 1793 before that area became part of the United States. The first episcopal council—a college of consultors—was established in the Diocese of Mobile, Ala., in 1835. The First Plenary Council of Baltimore (1852) encouraged the bishop to appoint consultors and, by the time of the Second Plenary Council of Baltimore (1866), most of the larger dioceses had consultors.

Subsequently, as we have seen, the Second Vatican Council and the *Code of Canon Law* restored the presbyteral council to an important place in the life of the local church. Other factors, in addition to the theological ones taught by the Second Vatican Council, contributed to the recent restoration of the presbyteral council. Increased technological advances in communication and transportation brought priests and the bishop into closer contact. Furthermore, the complexity of life—both secular and religious—made the fraternal cooperation between priests and the bishop in the form of the presbyteral council an effective way to provide proper pastoral care for the local church.

Chapter 2: The Theological Foundation

The presbyteral council is a manifestation of a theological reality and not simply a canonical entity. The purpose of the presbyteral council, representative of the priests, is to aid the bishop in the pastoral governance of the diocese for the common good of the local church. The theological basis of the presbyteral council rests on the fact that priests and the diocesan bishop are in a distinctive and indeed unique sacramental communion, since they participate in the same ministerial priesthood. The presbyteral council is an expression of this communion.

I. The Ordained Ministry

All members of the Christian faithful "share a common dignity from their rebirth in Christ."[20] All the baptized share in the priesthood of Christ and in the mission of the Church. They all possess the same grace, hope, and salvation. Sharing a common dignity, all Christians are called to holiness and contribute to the building up of the body of Christ. "Priests are brothers . . . with all those who have been reborn at the baptismal font."[21] Along with this fundamental equality there also exists a variety of gifts and ministries in the Christian community (Rom 12:6-8 and 1 Cor 12:4-11).

Within the community of faith in which all the baptized participate in the priesthood of Christ, there is a difference between the ordained and the rest of the faithful. The Second Vatican Council clearly acknowledged that difference: "The common priesthood of the faithful and the ministerial or hierarchical priesthood, although they differ in essence and not simply in degree, are nonetheless interrelated. Each of them in its own particular way shares in the one priesthood of Christ."[22] The council did not elaborate the difference between the ordained and the non-ordained, but it did recall that the ministerial priesthood is not just an extension or development of baptism. It belongs to a different category.

The sacramental reality of the ministerial priesthood can be properly understood only in the relationship of Christ to the Church. The Second Vatican Council makes clear that priests are empowered by the Lord himself. Priests are "instruments of Christ, the eternal priest";[23] "ministers of Jesus Christ among the nations";[24] and "ministers of the head."[25] In addition, priests "represent Christ";[26] "assume the person of Christ himself";[27] "act in the person of Christ the head";[28] and "act as Christ's ministers."[29]

The call and commission of priests comes from the Lord himself. Priests are ministers of Christ; they receive their sacred authority from Christ through the Church. Their ministry is to serve the Church *in persona Christi capitis ecclesiae.* The traditional adage *in persona Christi* identifies the ordained priest with the person of Christ. The Synod of 1971 observed that "only a priest is able to act in the person of Christ in presiding over and effecting the sacrificial banquet wherein the people of God are associated with Christ's offering."[30]

Ordination to the priesthood confers a unique participation in the mediatorship of Christ. Priestly ministers continue Christ's function as mediator. The sacrament of orders "configures the ordained minister to Christ the priest."[31]

Priestly ministry expresses itself in service. Just as Jesus was "one who serves" (Lk 22:27), priests minister most effectively to people when they help the body of the faithful carry out their part in the mission of Christ. The Spirit calls a person to serve, as a priest, as a sacrament of Christ who is head and shepherd of the Church. The ministry of leadership is designed to foster unity and love in the community and to encourage believers to embrace the redemptive mission of Christ.

This concept of service is found in St. Paul: "And to some, his gift was that they should be apostles; to some, prophets; to some, evangelists; to some, pastors and teachers; so that the saints together make a unity in the work of service, building up the body of Christ" (Eph 4:11-12). In a similar vein, Pope John Paul II has observed that priests participate in the priesthood "not because we are worthy, but because Christ loves us and has entrusted to us this particular ministry of service."[32]

The sanctifying, teaching, and governing mission of priests begins with and is supported by faith in the risen Lord. Priests are consecrated and commissioned to perform many duties within the Christian community, above all (a) to preach the saving message of the Gospel to all; (b) to celebrate the sacraments and especially to preside at the eucharistic sacrifice; and (c) to shepherd the faithful by gathering them together as a family and by overseeing and coordinating as well as calling forth their gifts. This act of leadership includes taking care of their pastoral needs by instruction, administration, consolation, reconciliation, and direction, and being of service to humanity through a ministry of peace and justice.

The Second Vatican Council stressed the idea of sacerdotal fraternity. "All priests, together with the bishop, so share in the one and the same priesthood and ministry of Christ that the very unity of their consecration and ministry require their hierarchical communion with the order of bishops."[33] This relationship is hierarchical in the sense that only the bishop possesses the fullness of the sacrament of orders.[34] It is a communion because it is a spiritual and organic bond between priests and the bishop that has its foundation in their participation in the life of the triune God and the reception of the sacrament of orders. There exists among priests a fellowship, a unity that is more than just political or social. This unifying force is the supernatural relationship that comes from ordination.

The episcopacy is not an office or honor beyond the priesthood; it is the fullness of the priesthood. It is the responsibility of the diocesan bishop to proclaim the Gospel; to promote the unity of faith, love, and discipline; and to celebrate the sacraments. As a member of the college of bishops, the bishop is also entrusted with responsibility for the whole Church.[35] This responsibility is not one of jurisdiction, but one of service to the entire Christian community.

Bishops are successors of the apostles, and priests are "collaborators with the episcopal order."[36] "Priests, to the degree of their authority and in the name of the bishop, exercise the office of Christ the head and the shepherd."[37]

II. The One Presbyterate

There is only one priesthood of Jesus Christ, which is shared by priests and the bishop and, in a different way, by all the faithful. Priests and bishop form one corporate body. Therefore, as the 1985 Synod of

Bishops said, "friendly relations and full trust must exist between bishops and their priests."[38] Priests with the diocesan bishop and under his leadership constitute the presbyterium.[39] "The priestly office, inasmuch as it is connected with the episcopal order, shares in the authority by which Christ himself builds up, sanctifies, and rules his body."[40] The concept of communion *(koinonia)* is central to understanding the relationship among priests and the diocesan bishop.

In the New Testament, communion is used in two senses. In the primary sense, it means a profound, spiritual participation of individuals in the life of the risen Lord. Baptism establishes a "vertical" relationship or fellowship with God. In a related sense, communion refers to the bond of union or "horizontal" relationship with our fellow believers that exists because of our union with God. Participation in the risen Lord is the basis of our communion with one another. Our communion with one another is the sacrament or sign of our participation in the risen Lord. Believers in local churches are united, and the communion of local churches throughout the world, joined in faith and charity, is the universal Church.

Communion in the local church is intimately connected to the eucharist and to the bishop. The eucharist is "the source and summit of the Christian life."[41] At the eucharist we are united to Christ and to one another. The bishop, for his part, is the "visible principle and foundation of unity" in the local church.[42] Priests are in communion with their bishop, and a bishop is in communion with his priests.

The Second Vatican Council used several expressions to describe the communion between priests and the bishop. It referred to priests as "prudent collaborators with the episcopal order"[43] and as brothers, sons, and friends of the bishop.[44] Priests are not simply vicars, agents, or proxies of the bishop but his collaborators.[45]

In one significant passage, the council referred to priests as the bishop's "necessary helpers and counselors in the ministry and in the task of teaching, sanctifying, and nourishing the people of God."[46] The word *necessary* suggests that consultation with priests is required for the sake of the Church. An essential unity exists between episcopal and presbyteral ministry, and both have the responsibility of working together. "Where there is one communion," writes St. Ambrose, "there should also be common judgment and harmonious consent."[47]

The collaboration between priests and the bishop is shaped by communion, which manifests itself in authority and partnership. The bishop is to regard priests as friends and collaborators, to be willing to listen to them and to consult with them on pastoral matters. Priests, for their part, should respect the bishop as possessing special authority in the Church and cooperate with him in obedience. Cooperation is necessary especially in view of the theological reality of the presbyterate, the complexity of life today, and the demands made on ecclesial ministers.

Communion between priests and the diocesan bishop is expressed liturgically in a special way when priests concelebrate with their bishop. Priests present at priestly ordinations are invited to impose hands on the candidates. At every Mass priests acknowledge union with the local bishop and with the bishop of Rome.

Such communion is expressed functionally when priests and the bishop meet to discuss pastoral matters[48] and, of course, in the presbyteral council. Mutual exchanges between priests and bishop "should be carried out," as the 1971 Synod of Bishops reminded us, "in a spirit of faith, mutual charity, filial and friendly confidence, and constant and patient dialogue."[49]

III. The Presbyteral Council

The presbyteral council is a concrete expression of cooperation among priests and the diocesan bishop. The 1971 Synod of Bishops affirmed that "the council of priests, which is of its nature something diocesan, is an institutional manifestation of the brotherhood among priests, which has its basis in the sacrament of orders."[50]

Part of the priestly vocation is to work with other priests and with the bishop. By ordination "all priests are united among themselves in an intimate sacramental brotherhood."[51] Because they share the same priesthood, priests have a mission to the wider Church and "must have at heart the care of all the churches."[52] They also have a special relationship with members of their own diocesan presbyterate. Diocesan and religious priests in the same diocese can legitimately expect that "in a brotherly attitude and in sincere, friendly dialogue, he [the bishop] converses with them about their work and also about matters pertaining to the life of the whole diocese, so that the entire presbytery has the feeling that it is carrying the burden of a particular church along with the bishop."[53]

The presbyteral council is a sign of priestly communion, being a privileged place of communication and collaboration between the presbyterate and the diocesan bishop. The circular letter from the Congregation for the Clergy (1970) affirmed that the council is "a special consultative organ because by its nature and its procedural process it is pre-eminent among other organs of the same kind."[541] It is not a substitute for the bishop but, as a consultative body, the presbyteral council can be an effective force within a diocese.

In *Redemptoris Hominis* Pope John Paul II said that a "spirit of collaboration and shared responsibility" characterizes presbyteral councils.[55] The pope also has observed that an encouraging sign of the mutual support among priests "is the development of presbyteral councils committed to the solidarity of priests with one another and with their bishop in the mission of the universal Church."[56]

Chapter 3: The Canonical Perspective

The theological understanding of the Church and of the priesthood found in the Second Vatican Council is reflected in the law regarding the presbyteral council. The 1983 *Code of Canon Law* provides universal norms regarding the nature and function of the presbyteral council. John Paul II, in promulgating the revised code, said that the code "fully corresponds to the nature of the Church, especially as it is proposed by the teaching of the Second Vatican Council in general and in a particular way by its ecclesiological teaching."[57]

I. Establishment of the Presbyteral Council

Canon 495:

1. A presbyteral council is to be established in each diocase, that is, a body of priests who are to be like a senate of the bishop, representing the presbyterate; this council is to aid the bishop in the governance of the diocese according to the norm of law, in order that the pastoral welfare of the portion of the people of God entrusted to him may be promoted as effectively as possible.

2. In apostolic vicariates and prefectures the vicar or the perfect is to establish a council of at least three missionary presbyters whose opinion is to be heard in more serious matters, even by letter.

Canon 496:

The presbyteral council is to have its own statutes approved by the diocesan bishop, in light of the norms issued by the conference of bishops.[58]

The diocesan bishop is required to establish a presbyteral council (canon 495.1). The council represents the entire presbyterate of the diocese and functions like a senate to the bishop, aiding him in providing proper pastoral care for the people of God. Thus, the presbyteral council has a relationship to the bishop, to the presbyterate, and to the particular church.

The presbyteral council is described in law as a body of priests. Only the bishop and priests, since they have a unique relationship rooted in the sacrament of priestly ordination, may be members of the presbyteral council. The presbyterate necessarily includes the person of the bishop, since he is the fullness of the priesthood in the local church. *Lumen Gentium* stated that "priests, prudent collaborators with the episcopal order and its aid and instrument, constitute one presbyterate with the bishop."[59] Canon 495.1 calls the presbyteral council a *coetus sacerdotum*. The use of the term *sacerdos* and not *presbyter* emphasizes the unity of priestly ministry shared by the episcopacy and the presbyterate.

Deacons are not members of the presbyteral council because, even though they share in the sacrament of orders, they are not ordained to the priesthood.[60] Although some presbyteral councils in the past have included deacons as a recognition of the valuable ministry they perform in the Church, this is not envisioned in the present law.

The statutes of the presbyteral council, which may be drafted by the council members themselves, are to be drawn up "in light of the norms issued by the conference of bishops" (canon 496). However, since the National Conference of Catholic Bishops has not as yet established such norms, the statutes are to be in conformity with the *Code of Canon Law* and all applicable universal and particular law (cf. canon 94). The diocesan bishop must give formal approval to the statutes before they go into effect (canon 496). Subsequent changes in the statutes also require the bishop's approval.

II. Membership of the Presbyteral Council

Canon 497:
With regard to the designation of the members of the presbyteral council:

1. About half the members are to be freely elected by the priests themselves according to the norm of the following canons as well as the council's statutes.

2. Some priests, according to the council's statutes, ought to be ex-officio members, that is, members of the council in virtue of their office.

3. The diocesan bishop is free to name some others.

Canon 498:
1. The following have the right to both active and passive vote in constituting the presbyteral council:

—.01. All secular priests incardinated in the diocese;

—.02. Secular priests not incardinated in the diocese, and priests who are members of an institute of consecrated life or a society of apostolic life, who live in the diocese and exercise some office for the good of the diocese.

2. To the extent the statutes provide for it, the same right of election can be extended to other priests who have a domicile or quasi-domicile in the diocese.

Canon 499:
The manner of electing members of the presbyteral council is to be determined in the statutes in such a way that, insofar as it is possible, the priests of the presbyterate

are represented, taking into account especially the diversity
of ministries and various regions of the diocese.

There are three categories of members: elected, ex officio, and
appointees of the bishop. At least half the members are to be freely
elected by the priests themselves (canon 497.1). Canon 498.1 cites two
categories of priests who by right can be elected to the presbyteral
council and can vote in elections: (a) all secular priests incardinated in
the diocese, whether or not they are actually residing in the diocese
and (b) other secular and religious priests not incardinated but now
resident in the diocese and exercising some office for the good of the
diocese. The statutes may allow other priests to be eligible for membership in the council if they have a domicile or quasi-domicile in the
diocese (canon 498.2). Although the code does not require it, an effort
should be made to encourage religious priests to participate in the
council. They belong to the local church and have a responsibility to
share in its life and mission.

The statutes are to determine precisely how members are to be
elected. Canon 499 specifies to some extent, without being exhaustive,
the general norm of representation given in canon 495.1. Thus, canon
499 says that in the selection of priests to represent the presbyterate,
special, but not exclusive, consideration be given to the diversity of
ministries and to the various regions of the diocese. It is important to
note that every member of the presbyteral council represents the
whole presbyterate and not a particular group of constituents.

Some priests ought to be ex officio members, and the statutes
should indicate this (canon 497.2). The code does not specify which
officeholders should be members, though some dioceses have included,
for example, auxiliary bishops and episcopal vicars.

Finally, the bishop can appoint members (canon 497.3). The only
restriction is that the bishop may not appoint so many members that
half the members are not elected by the priests.

The code does not specify a minimum or maximum number of
members. Since the diocesan bishop selects members of the college of
consultors from the membership of the presbyteral council (canon
502.1) and since there must be at least six consultors, it would seem
that six is the minimum number of members in the presbyteral council as well. The statutes should indicate how many members will be on
the council, which will depend to a great extent on the size of the diocese. The council should not be too large if it is to be effective.

The term of office for members of the presbyteral council is to be
determined by the statutes in such a way that the council in whole or
in part is renewed within a five-year period (canon 501.1). The statutes
may include terms of different lengths and terms which begin at different times.

III. Authority of the Presbyteral Council

Canon 500:
1. It pertains to the diocesan bishop to convoke the presbyteral council, to preside over it and to determine the questions to be treated by it or to receive proposals from its members.
2. The presbyteral council enjoys only a consultative vote; the bishop is to listen to it in matters of greater moment, but he needs its consent only in cases expressly defined by law.
3. The presbyteral council is never able to act without the diocesan bishop, who alone can divulge what was determined in keeping with Sec. 2.

The ultimate responsibility for the welfare of the diocese pertains to the bishop. By definition the presbyteral council is a representative, consultative group with the express purpose of helping the diocesan bishop in the governance of the diocese. It is the right of the diocesan bishop to convoke the presbyteral council, preside over it, and determine what it will discuss (canon 500.1). In some dioceses the bishop is both the president of the presbyteral council and the one who chairs the meetings. In other dioceses the bishop "presides," but the members elect officers who run the council under the authority of the bishop.

However the council is structured, it is the duty of the bishop to see that the council functions properly. It is neither the sole possession of the bishop nor of the priests, but a joint venture. Its purpose is thwarted if it is dominated by either. At the same time, it can be said that the bishop is critical to the effectiveness of the council. Although the bishop by himself cannot make the council a success, without his wise direction, support, and collaboration, and without his presence and participation, it cannot flourish.

The primary criterion is always the good of the Church. The council acts only with the diocesan bishop, because the bishop is the head of the council. The bishop alone has the right to make public those matters on which he has formally consulted the council (canon 500.3). Members of the council are expected to give their opinions sincerely, and, if the diocesan bishop so decides in certain serious matters, they are bound to maintain secrecy (canon 127.3).

"The presbyteral council enjoys only a consultative vote" (canon 500.2). The phrase "only consultative" (*tantum consultativum*) should not be interpreted as "just consultative," conveying the idea that it is of little value. The task of the presbyteral council is not simply to affirm predetermined decisions of the bishop, but to assist the bishop by offering him counsel.

Canon 127.2.2 indicates the importance of consultation:

> If counsel is required, the action of the superior is invalid if the superior does not listen to those persons; although in no way obliged to accede to their recommendation, even if it be unanimous, nevertheless the superior should not act contrary to it, especially when there is a consensus, unless there be a reason which, in the superior's judgment, is overriding.

Consultation is a form of collaboration and coresponsibility. In the seventeenth century, Suarez (d. 1617) considered consultation a reasonable and prudent way to seek the truth, since "the bringing together of many opinions contributes greatly to the discovery of truth."[61] Pope Benedict XIV (d. 1758) likewise saw the value in the bishop receiving counsel from the cathedral chapter. "Although the bishop is not bound to follow it, he is instructed by reasons his counselors give him, and he is taught, lest he act precipitately or thoughtlessly."[62]

Consultation may be cumbersome and burdensome at times, but it allows an administrator to make a well-informed decision. Collaborative decision making through consultation is designed to produce a decision that is balanced, reasonable, equitable, and practical. At times it may be useful for the bishop and priests to consult with specialists who have experience or expertise on specific matters.

Canon 500.2 states that the diocesan bishop is to listen to the council "in matters of greater moment, but he needs its consent only in cases expressly defined by law."

The *Directory on the Pastoral Ministry of Bishops* provides examples of "matters of greater moment" in a diocese. These include

> the holiness of life, sacred sciences and other needs of the priests, or the sanctification and religious instructions of the faithful, or the government of the diocese in general. . . . It is the task of this council, among other things, to seek out clear and distinctly defined aims of the manifold ministries in the diocese, to propose matters that are more urgent, to indicate methods of acting, to assist whatever the Spirit frequently stirs up through individuals or groups, to foster the spiritual life, in order to attain the necessary unity more easily. They ought, finally, to deal with equal distribution of funds for the support of clerics, and also with the erection, suppression and restoration of parishes.[63]

Canon law prescribes several instances when the diocesan bishop must consult the presbyteral council. Consultation is required when the bishop decides the following matters:

1.   The advisability of a diocesan synod (canon 461.1)

2. The erection, modification, division, or suppression of parishes (canon 515.2; canon 813)
3. The determination of the use of offerings of the faithful made on the occasion of parish services and placed in a general parish fund (canon 531)
4. The appropriateness of parish councils (canon 536.1)
5. The granting of permission to build a church (canon 1215.2)
6. The granting of permission for a church to be converted to secular purposes for reasons other than its poor condition (canon 1222.2)
7. The imposition of a tax for the needs of the diocese on public juridic persons subject to the bishop; also the imposition of an extraordinary and moderate tax for very grave needs on other juridic persons and on physical persons (canon 1263)

The diocesan bishop can determine other cases requiring consultation with the presbyteral council and can establish them as the particular law of the diocese.

Canon law gives another example of the competency of the presbyteral council in canon 1742.1. It states that the presbyteral council is to choose a group of pastors from persons proposed by the bishop. The bishop, during the process of removing pastors, is to discuss the matter with two pastors from this group.

IV. Cessation of the Presbyteral Council

Canon 501:

1. Members of the presbyteral council are to be designated for a term determined in the statutes in such a way that the full council or some part of it is renewed within a five-year period.

2. When the see is vacant the presbyteral council ceases and its functions are fulfilled by the college of consultors; within a year of taking possession of the diocese the bishop must establish the presbyteral council anew.

3. If the presbyteral council is no longer fulfilling the function committed to it for the good of the diocese or is gravely abusing it, the diocesan bishop can dissolve it after consulting with the metropolitan or, if it is a question of the metropolitan see itself, with the suffragan senior by promotion, but the bishop must establish it anew within a year.

Because the presbyteral council is a consultative body to the bishop, it ceases to exist when the diocesan bishop dies, retires, or is transferred. The college of consultors takes over its functions. The new bishop must re-establish the presbyteral council within a year after he takes office (canon 501.2). The diocesan bishop, after consulting with the metropolitan, can dissolve the presbyteral council if it is "no longer fulfilling the function committed to it for the good of the diocese or is gravely abusing it" (canon 501.3), but he must establish a new one within one year.

V. The Presbyteral Council and Other Consultative Bodies

At the diocesan level, there are a number of consultative bodies. The presbyteral council, the college of consultors (canon 502), and the finance council (canons 492-494) are mandated by law. The college of consultors and the finance council have a deliberative vote by law under certain circumstances. The diocesan pastoral council (canon 511) and the episcopal council (canon 473.4) are not mandated by law but are often desirable for the good of the Church. Other consultative bodies may also be established at the discretion of the diocesan bishop.

Three bodies that share many common concerns are the presbyteral council, the college of consultors, and the diocesan pastoral council. In those dioceses that have a diocesan pastoral council, collaboration with the presbyteral council and the college of consultors is necessary for good pastoral order.

The presbyteral council has as its task "to aid the bishop in the governance of the diocese . . . in order that the pastoral welfare . . . may be promoted as effectively as possible" (canon 495.1). The council is obligatory in the diocese, its only members are priests and bishops, and the diocesan bishop presides over it.

The college of consultors, whose members are chosen by the diocesan bishop from the presbyteral council (canon 502.1), is also involved in diocesan governance. The college of consultors is required in a diocese, its members are priests chosen from the presbyteral council, and the diocesan bishop presides over it. It is "responsible for the functions determined in the law" (canon 502.1). Some of these functions prescribed in the universal law are election of the diocesan administrator when the see becomes vacant (canon 421.1); fulfillment of special duties when a see is impeded or vacant (canons 272; 413.2; 419; 422; 485; 501.2; 1018.1,2); advice concerning the appointment and removal of the finance officer (canon 494.1-2); advice in the more important acts of administration (canon 1277); consent for acts of extraordinary administration (canon 1277); and consent for alienation of certain ecclesiastical property (canon 1292.1).

The diocesan pastoral council has a general charge: "to investigate . . . all those things that pertain to pastoral works, to ponder them and to propose practical conclusions about them" (canon 511). The *Directory on the Pastoral Ministry of Bishops* indicates that the pastoral council, by study and reflection, enables "the diocesan community to plan its pastoral program systematically and to fulfill it effectively."[64] The *Code of Canon Law* does not require each diocese to have a pastoral council, but it does strongly recommend it if pastoral circumstances call for it. Its members include clergy, religious, and laity, and the diocesan bishop presides over it (canons 512; 514.1).

These three bodies need careful coordination in the diocese if they are to be effective. However, the *Code of Canon Law* gives no comprehensive guidelines to assist the bishop in his responsibility for coordinating them as well as other consultative bodies in the diocese. The diocesan pastoral council, when present in a diocese, is useful for discovering the major and urgent issues facing the diocese and for discerning what the faithful are thinking. It provides a good forum to plan policy. The bishop might assemble the college of consultors, since it is a relatively small group, to discuss some delicate issue or an urgent problem that needs an immediate response. Finally, the bishop might consult the presbyteral council for several reasons: first, to seek counsel concerning the pastoral governance of the diocese, and second, to encourage and to be encouraged by his priests, to listen to their concerns, and to be solicitous about their spiritual and material welfare.

Bishops differ in the ways they coordinate the presbyteral council and the diocesan pastoral council. Some dioceses use a two-tiered administrative approach: (a) the presbyteral council and the diocesan pastoral council work together in creating and developing policies and programs, and (b) diocesan agencies with the help of the deans, consultors, and the episcopal council, where it exists, implement them. Other dioceses have a coordinating office that acts as a secretariat for the presbyteral council and the diocesan pastoral council. The secretariat keeps abreast of what each group is working on and informs the bishop of its activities.

In conclusion, we have seen that the canons give more general than specific norms regarding the presbyteral council. Most of the procedural details are determined by particular law in each diocese with the approval of the diocesan bishop. For example, the law does not give the precise method of electing members to the council, the number of members, the frequency of meetings, the organizational structure of offices, the publicizing of the council's decisions, and the relationship with other consultative bodies and with the presbyterate at large. Because of this flexibility, each diocese must work out many details, taking into account the unique character and special needs of the local church.

Chapter 4: The Practical Aspects

The presbyteral council seeks to express the communion of the priests and the diocesan bishop in a concrete, effective way. The presbyteral council is a human organization and, hence, is subject to continual development. The bond between priests and the diocesan bishop in the presbyteral council is strengthened by charity, prayer, and cooperation; such cooperation, based on shared faith and exercised in charity, is a sign of Christ's continued love for his Church. On the other hand, excessive bureaucracy, lack of commitment, inadequate procedures, and refusal to dialogue can hamper the effectiveness.

Some common elements exist in all presbyteral councils, but councils can function in a variety of ways. The size, location, history, and cultural situation of the diocese all influence the presbyteral council. This chapter presupposes the historical, theological, and canonical background given earlier. It presents some observations concerning the practical operation of the presbyteral council. It is hoped that presbyteral councils use these ideas to evaluate their own effectiveness and to develop improved procedures.

I. Trust

The effectiveness of the presbyteral council demands trust between the bishop and the council, among the members of the council, and between the council and the presbyterate.

The collaboration of priests and the diocesan bishop working for the welfare of the diocese through the presbyteral council is linked to their primary priestly obligation: the proclamation of the Gospel of Christ to all people.[65] The importance of the work of the council requires that all participants strive to develop an attitude of trust.

When the presbyteral council meets in an atmosphere of trust it becomes a valuable element in the decision-making process of the bishop. Because decision making is a process that involves several individuals, a variety of abilities, and many stages, trust is vital to the process.

Trust between the bishop and the presbyteral council. At times it may be difficult for the bishop to use the consultative process with his priests and for priests to share the sense of responsibility which weighs upon the bishop. Positive experiences with the presbyteral council, characterized by mutual respect, dialogue, and the free exchange of opinions, serve to strengthen the trust between the bishop and the council and to convince the participants of the value of the council.

The diocesan bishop as head of the presbyterate should actively participate in and preside at the meetings of the presbyteral council. Since the council is necessarily dependent on the bishop for the way it functions, it is incumbent upon the bishop to convey his trust in the council and his willingness to collaborate with it for the good of the Church. He should welcome and actively seek its advice. It is essential that he communicate clearly his need for the assistance of the council. A council that knows that the bishop will listen to it is likely to work with greater enthusiasm. The bishop should not be reluctant to state his own perspective and to encourage others to do the same.

The presbyteral council must not view itself as the "loyal opposition" or the "minority party." The language of confrontation, power tactics, and intimidation are out of place in the council. Similarly, the council must avoid a passive posture whereby it fails to express the concerns and experiences of priests.

Trust among the members of the presbyteral council. Many of the issues a presbyteral council addresses are complex; council members will have differing understandings about them. It is, therefore, important for members to encourage each other's diverse gifts for the good of the whole Church. A collective discussion of ideas raises a wide variety of approaches which can enrich diocesan pastoral programs and foster creativity. If the council's work is to be beneficial, it is necessary that all parties engaged in it practice humility, charity, and patience.

When members of the presbyteral council speak honestly and thoughtfully to one another, the council can be a forum for dialogue, mutual support, and mutual challenge. It can also provide an opportunity for intellectual and spiritual growth. The reading of background material, the study of theological positions, and the discussion of plans and policies can be a kind of continuing education for the participants.

Trust between the presbyteral council and the rest of the presbyterate. Members of the council must strive to discover the experiences and concerns of the other priests of the diocese. A newsletter and occasional meetings with groups of priests can keep open the channels of communication. The presbyteral council should carefully consider the ways it consults with other priests in the diocese.

It is critical that the presbyterate elect those priests as representatives to the council who have the requisite spirituality, interest, energy, and commitment. In order to ensure a genuinely representative body, it may be advisable to nominate candidates according to geographic location, type of ministry, age, ethnic and racial background, and diocesan or religious affiliation. The diocesan bishop should exercise care in making appointments to the presbyteral council: After studying the roster of those elected, he may wish to appoint others who will reflect experiences not yet represented on the council.

The presbyteral council is not the only way priests cooperate with the bishop, and it is not meant to relieve other priests of their responsibility. The presbyterate also corporately manifests its spirit of unity and contributes to the good of the diocese through convocations,

regional meetings, workshops, retreats, and task forces. The presbyteral council, while not necessarily responsible for all these events, can
provide help in preparing them and in supporting them.

II. Participation

Full participation is required for a productive presbyteral council.

A productive presbyteral council exhibits a high degree of participation and commitment on the part of its members. Experience has
shown that members of the presbyteral council are positive about their
participation when they feel that the council is important in the life of
the diocese and that their contributions are taken seriously. It is necessary, therefore, to encourage meaningful consultation and an open
exchange of ideas.

Some priests have an ambivalent attitude toward the presbyteral
council and are unwilling to participate in it. In theory they grant that
the presbyteral council has some spiritual and practical values in view
of the many demands made on today's ministers. Yet they are not fully
convinced that the presbyteral council is an effective pastoral instrument. Many reasons have been suggested to explain this negative attitude: that the bishop uses the council to affirm what he has already
decided; that a consultative body has little significant impact on the
decision-making process; that priests have been so conditioned to a
spirit of individualism that they are uneasy with the collegial style of
the council; that the council might deprive other priests of their independence; that all problems should be referred directly to the diocesan
bishop for a solution; and that speaking candidly to the bishop at the
meeting of the presbyteral council could be held against a priest.

No easy answer can be given to all these concerns. In instances
where the presbyteral council is mired in apathy an evaluation is
urgently needed to determine the cause of the difficulty and to suggest
steps to remedy it. Several questions should be asked. Is the council in
harmony with the theological and canonical principles that determine
its character? Are there organizational problems? Do the priests and
the bishop demand more from the council than it can give? Does the
council require more energy and time from the priests and the bishop
than they think it deserves? Are some members apathetic and unprepared? Do the members use the council simply as a forum to bring up
old, controversial topics? Are there personality conflicts within the
council that impede communication?

Council members must hold themselves accountable to the bishop,
to one another, and to the presbyterate. One way to do this is to evaluate the council's performance periodically; perhaps the above questions could be included in such an evaluation. A self-study can help
prevent complacency, since it identifies the major accomplishments of

the presbyteral council and specifies those areas that need improvement.

III. Agenda

The agenda, with input from many sources, needs to address issues of substance.

The diocesan bishop has the right to determine the agenda of the presbyteral council and to receive proposals from its members (canon 500.1). Agenda items—dealing with substantial issues—are to be generated from the bishop himself, council members, other priests, diocesan departments, lay organizations, and religious groups. The statutes should specify how the agenda is to be drawn up and indicate specific ways various segments of the diocese can be encouraged to suggest matters for the agenda. The council is to interest itself in the concerns not only of the local church, but of the Church in the United States and, indeed, of the universal Church. A genuine ecclesial spirituality helps priests broaden their vision beyond their own parish or particular ministry to the wider Church.

The agenda, with appropriate background material, is to be distributed before the meeting to allow the members sufficient time to study the material and to consult with others. It is helpful if the agenda distinguishes between action items and information items.

Canon law does not prescribe restrictions concerning items to be discussed by the presbyteral council. That decision is left to the discretion of the bishop. However, the *Code of Canon Law*, as we saw ear-lier, says that matters of greater moment and certain cases defined by the law are to be brought before the presbyteral council (canon 500.2).

In the early days of presbyteral councils much time was spent on discussion of such issues as clerical salaries, health insurance, pension plans, stipends, sabbatical programs, alternate living situations, and the seniority system. The presbyteral council, however, should not concentrate solely or even primarily on the personal needs of priests.

The council needs to be interested in the varied facets of diocesan life for which the bishop and priests are responsible. Thus any matter dealing with the pastoral governance and welfare of the diocese may be on the agenda, even though it may also be discussed by other consultative bodies in the diocese. The council should be concerned with administrative and pastoral policies affecting parishes and other institutions in the diocese; this would include, for example, such topics as evangelization, catechetics, justice and peace, liturgy, ecumenism, vocations, parishes, and schools.

Yet it is right for the presbyteral council also to be concerned with the spiritual and material needs of the presbyterate. Some presbyteral councils have been successful in developing programs for alcoholic rehabilitation, counseling services, and the care of sick and aged priests. At times the presbyteral council may look for ways to affirm the exceptional work done by priests, perhaps by sponsoring awards dinners, by organizing anniversary celebrations at which the accomplishments of individual priests are recognized, or by encouraging the diocesan paper to write articles about those priests. The diocesan bishop and the presbyteral council will provide the strongest affirmation for priests by listening carefully to their concerns and experiences and by trying to channel these elements into pastoral action.

IV. Preparation

Careful preparation facilitates the operation of the presbyteral council.

An effective presbyteral council does not happen by accident. It is the result of careful planning, a committed membership, prudent leadership, and conscientious preparation for meetings. Members should thoroughly study the agenda before the meeting, discuss it with their brother priests and others, and be ready to exchange ideas with the council members. Such preparation—by both the diocesan bishop and his priests—helps to avoid rambling discussions and arbitrary decisions.

Some presbyteral councils have both standing and ad hoc committees and find them useful in working on complex issues. A committee, composed of council members and perhaps others, makes recommendations to the full council, and thereby contributes to the efficiency and productivity of the council. Experience indicates, however, that these committees work best when they receive clear responsibilities and when they are regularly held accountable for these responsibilities by the leadership of the presbyteral council.

V. Procedures

Proper procedures contribute to the success of the presbyteral council.

All meetings of the presbyteral council should include prayer and be conducted in a prayerful atmosphere. For the council, in meeting to build up the kingdom of God, is a group of individuals who share the same gospel values and who collaborate in carrying out the work of the Lord.

The meetings should be run professionally. Disorganized meetings promote apathy and give the impression that the council does not take its responsibilities seriously. Chairing the meeting requires specific skills, and the one who chairs the council must try to develop those skills. Minutes of the meeting should be taken, distributed to members, and approved. Finally, the diocesan bishop should normally inform the presbyterate of any action taken by the council.

Many councils have found that diocesan offices and agencies offer important resources for the work of the presbyteral council. In such instances, the council works with the bishop to establish appropriate lines of communication.

The presbyteral council must have a clear understanding of its role in the decision-making process of the bishop. The council seeks information; evaluates that information; encourages those affected by the final decision to have a voice in the process; discusses the matter with the bishop; and makes a recommendation to the bishop. The council, after studying the alternatives and the consequences of any proposed action, should make recommendations that are well thought out and feasible. The presbyteral council is ordinarily not expected to implement its recommendations; the bishop usually oversees that responsibility through diocesan agencies and offices.

VI. Consensus

The presbyteral council seeks consensus in its deliberations.

It often happens, when consultation and discussion are well done, that a consensus emerges that clearly indicates what recommendations should be made. The council should strive for this kind of consensus through dialogue.

Canon law does not stipulate how a presbyteral council is to arrive at its recommendations. Current practice varies among councils: balloting, parliamentary procedure, or a discernment process. The observation concerning the presbyteral council in the 1971 Synod of Bishops council is apropos: "The activity of this council cannot be fully shaped by law. Its effectiveness depends especially on a repeated effort to listen to the opinions of all in order to reach a consensus with the bishop, to whom it belongs to make a final decision."[66]

Conclusion

This reflection has reviewed the historical, theological, canonical, and practical dimensions of the presbyteral council. It has focused on the idea of communion, which primarily refers to participation in the life of God through Christ in the Holy Spirit. Because of incorporation in Christ, Christians are united and the Church itself is rightly called a communion. Ecclesial authority is at the service of this communion and the purpose of all forms of ministry in the Church is to foster communion. The presbyteral council, sharing in the responsibility of the bishop as it does, makes an important contribution to communion in the local church.

The ideas and suggestions made here are intended to improve the effectiveness of the council in the local church and to stimulate further study. It may be useful for the diocesan bishop to organize a forum or workshop for priests to discuss this document. The presbyteral council needs continual evaluation and renewal if it is to serve the needs of an ever-changing society and Church.

As a sign of unity in ministry, the presbyteral council enables the diocesan bishop and his priests to work collaboratively in preaching the saving truth of the Gospel. Presbyteral councils have developed much in the years since the Second Vatican Council. Priests and bishops are to be commended for their generosity, enthusiasm, and dedication in this particular priestly apostolate. The bond that unites bishops and priests is rooted in the mystery of Christ and sustained by it. The Second Vatican Council says it clearly.

> By sacred ordination and by the mission they receive from their bishops, priests are promoted to the service of Christ, the teacher, the priest and the king. They share in his ministry of unceasingly building up the church on earth into the people of God, the body of Christ and the temple of the Holy Spirit.[67]

Notes

1. John Paul II, "Letter to Priests" (April 9, 1979), *Origins* 8:44 (April 19, 1979): 697.
2. John Paul II, Address to the bishops of Northeast Brazil during ad limina visit (September 17, 1990), *The Pope Speaks* 35:6 (November 1, 1990): 409
3. Second Vatican Council, *Decree on the Pastoral Office of Bishops in the Church (Christus Dominus)*, no. 11.
4. *Christus Dominus*, no. 27.
5. See also Acts 6:2, 6; 11:30; 15:2, 4, 6, 23; 16:4; 20:17; 21:18; Phil 1:1; 1 Thes 5:12-13; Ti 1:5; 1 Pt 5:1-3.
6. Ignatius of Antioch, *Letter to the Trallians*, no. 3, 1.
7. Ignatius of Antioch, *Letter to the Magnesians*, no. 6, 1.
8. Ignatius of Antioch, *Trallians*, no. 3, 1; *Letter to the Philadelphians*, no. 8, 1.
9. Ignatius of Antioch, *Magnesians*, no. 13, 1.
10. Ignatius of Antioch, *Letter to the Ephesians*, no. 4, 1.
11. Ignatius of Antioch, *Trallians*, no. 2, 2.
12. Hippolytus of Rome, *The Apostolic Tradition*, no. 8.
13. Ibid., no. 7.
14. Ibid., no. 8.
15. Cyprian, Letter 66, *To Florentius Puppian*, no. 8.
16. Cyprian, Letter 14, *To the Priests and Deacons*, no. 4.
17. Cyprian, Letter 74, *To Pompey*, no. 10.
18. Cyprian, Letter 19, *To Priests and Deacons*, no. 2.
19. Cyprian, Letter 5, *To Priests and Deacons*, no. 2.

20. Second Vatican Council, *Dogmatic Constitution on the Church (Lumen Gentium)*, no. 32.
21. Second Vatican Council, *Decree on the Ministry and Life of Priests (Presbyterorum Ordinis)*, no. 9.
22. *Lumen Gentium*, no. 10.
23. *Presbyterorum Ordinis*, no. 12.
24. Ibid., no. 2.
25. Ibid., no. 12.
26. Second Vatican Council, *Decree on the Church's Missionary Activity (Ad Gentes)*, no. 39.
27. *Presbyterorum Ordinis*, no. 12.
28. Ibid., no. 2.
29. Ibid., no. 5.
30. Synod of Bishops, *The Ministerial Priesthood and Justice in the World* (Washington, D.C.: United States Catholic Conference, 1971), 14.
31. Ibid. Pope John Paul II at the Synod of Bishops (1990) noted the unique character of the ministerial priesthood when he referred to "the specific ontology which unites the priesthood to Christ, the high priest and good shepherd" (*Origins* 20:23 [November 15, 1990]: 379).
32. John Paul II, "Address to Priests" (Miami, September 10, 1987) *Origins* 17:15 (September 24, 1987): 234.
33. *Presbyterorum Ordinis*, no. 7.
34. *Lumen Gentium*, nos. 28, 41; *Christus Dominus*, no. 15.
35. *Lumen Gentium*, no. 23.
36. *Presbyterorum Ordinis*, no. 2.
37. *Presbyterorum Ordinis*, no. 6.
38. Synod of Bishops, *A Message to the People of God and The Final Report* (Washington, D.C.: United States Catholic Conference, 1986), 20.
39. *Lumen Gentium*, no. 28.
40. *Presbyterorum Ordinis*, no. 2.
41. *Lumen Gentium*, no. 11.
42. *Lumen Gentium*, no. 23.
43. *Christus Dominus*, no. 28; *Lumen Gentium*, no. 28.
44. *Lumen Gentium*, no. 28; *Presbyterorum Ordinis*, no. 7.
45. *Ad Gentes*, no. 39.
46. *Presbyterorum Ordinis*, no. 7.
47. Cyprian, Letter 13, *To Candidianus*, no. 8.
48. *Christus Dominus*, no. 28.
49. Synod of Bishops, *The Ministerial Priesthood* (Washington, D.C.: United States Catholic Conference, 1986), 26.
50. Ibid.
51. *Presbyterorum Ordinis*, no. 8.
52. Ibid., no. 10.
53. Congregation for Bishops, *Directory on the Pastoral Ministry of Bishops* (Ottawa: Canadian Catholic Conference, 1974), no. 111.
54. Congregation for the Clergy, "Circular Letter on Priests' Councils," *Canon Law Digest* 7:388, no. 9.
55. John Paul II, "Redemptor Hominis," *Origins* 8:40 (March 22, 1979): 629.
56. "Address to Priests" (Miami), 237.

57. John Paul II, "Sacrae Disciplinae Leges," *Acta Apostolicae Sedis* 75:2 (1983): xi.

58. The translation of these canons is taken from the translation prepared by the Canon Law Society of America, *Code of Canon Law: Latin-English Edition* (Washington: Canon Law Society of America, 1983).

59. *Lumen Gentium,* no. 28.

60. *Lumen Gentium,* no. 29; *Christus Dominus,* no. 15.

61. F. Suarez, *De Legibus,* XIII, chap. 1, no. 6, in *R. P. Francisci Suarez Opera Omnia,* ed. M. André (Paris: Ludovicum Vivès, 1856).

62. Benedict XIV, *De Synodo Diocesano,* XIII, chap. 1, no. 6, in *Benedicti XIV Pont. Opt. Max., olim Prosperi Cardinalis de Lambertinis, opera omnia,* ed. Joseph Silvestro (Prati: Typographia Aldina, 1839-1847).

63. *Directory on the Pastoral Ministry of Bishops,* no. 203c.

64. Ibid., no. 204.

65. *Lumen Gentium,* no. 25; *Presbyterorum Ordinis,* no. 4.

66. "The Ministerial Priesthood," 26.

67. *Presbyterorum Ordinis,* no. 1.

Source: *Origins* 21:26 (December 5, 1991): 409-421.

The Teaching Ministry of the Diocesan Bishop: A Pastoral Reflection

A Statement of the National Conference of Catholic Bishops

November 1991

Preface

In 1985, in response to requests received from bishops, the Committee on Doctrine began work on a document which would address a number of issues facing the bishops of the United States in the exercise of their teaching office. Among others, concerns included the understanding of the teaching office, some of its canonical dimensions, the difficulties confronting bishops as authoritative teachers in the United States today, and the response of bishops to difficulties posed by dissent to church teaching. In 1988, during the National Conference of Catholic Bishops' discussion of our earlier document "Doctrinal Responsibilities," some bishops requested that additional reflections on the relationship between bishops and theologians become part of the committee's work on the teaching office of the bishops.

While all these issues are related to the teaching office of the bishop, each of them presents a different kind of doctrinal or pastoral challenge to the bishop as teacher. To treat them together, in the judgment of the committee, would require a document of some length. A subcommittee was formed to consider the issues and to draft the document. Its work was regularly reviewed by the Committee on Doctrine.

In May 1991 a draft of the document was sent to all bishops and to a selected group of theologians for comment. Comments were also sought from the Congregation for the Doctrine of the Faith. In light of the many suggestions and comments submitted to the Committee on Doctrine, the text was revised into its present form.

"The Teaching Ministry of the Diocesan Bishop: A Pastoral Reflection" is the result of this process. It is presented as a self-reflection by bishops on their teaching office within the context of the Church in the United States today. It is conceived of as first and foremost a document by bishops for bishops. In its two chapters the document invites bishops to reflect anew on the theological and ecclesial significance of their teaching office and offers some insights on the pastoral context within which bishops are called to exercise that office today. In addressing some of the issues facing bishops, the document makes certain pastoral suggestions which the Committee on Doctrine believes will be of assistance to the bishops.

To the extent that the issues engaged in this document are also of interest or concern to other members of the Church, the text offers ample food for reflection. Certainly all who are engaged in preaching or teaching the Gospel will find within the document doctrinal and pastoral orientations for fulfilling their responsibilities within the Church. In particular, priests, deacons, catechists, and theologians will find set forth here an understanding of the bishop's teaching office which directly touches upon their own service to the truth of the Gospel.

Chapter 1 presents the teaching of the Church on the teaching office of the bishops, both as a college with and under the pope and as authoritative teachers in the particular churches entrusted to their pastoral care. The basis of these doctrinal reflections is sacred Scripture and tradition, with special emphasis on the documents of the Second Vatican Council, particularly *Dei Verbum*, the constitution on revelation, and *Lumen Gentium*, the constitution on the Church. Chapter 2 offers reflections, principally of a pastoral nature, on the cultural and ecclesial context within which bishops in the United States must exercise their teaching ministry today. It includes a presentation of the various levels of church teaching, the response appropriate to each level, and the bishop's responsibility in instances of deficient reception of that teaching. It concludes with some reflections on characteristics of episcopal teaching that seem particularly appropriate at the present moment.

It has been the conviction of the Committee on Doctrine throughout the process of writing this document that the best response to insufficient, defective, or erroneous teaching is the positive, effective, consistent, and forthright teaching of the doctrine of the Church by bishops. It is the hope of the committee that these reflections will help and encourage bishops in the fulfillment of their teaching ministry. It is also our hope that they will be taken to heart by all members of the Church, for in various ways they participate in its teaching mission.

Chapter 1: The Episcopal Teaching Office

Part A: Teaching and the College of Bishops

1. The Teaching Office Within the Church

The eternal Word of God made flesh, Jesus Christ, sent his Holy Spirit from the Father in order to reveal to us the Father's will to draw all men and women to himself.[1] By this revelation God gives us himself in love and invites us to a relationship of love and friendship with him.

Beyond the revelation of his presence in created things, God has spoken to human beings in words and deeds from the first moments of human existence. Even after the fall of our first parents, God continued to reveal his love by the care he lavished upon the human race. With the call of Abraham God chose a people for himself, to be the means by which he would disclose his true nature as the one God. Through Moses and the prophets he continued to instruct Israel in the way of truth and planted within them the seed of hope for the fullness of redemption.[2]

Finally, "in these last days God has spoken to us through a son" (Heb 1:1-2). In Jesus Christ, the Son of God, the Father has brought to completion the revelation of himself. Jesus is God's final word to us and God's ultimate deed of salvation. In the words and deeds of Jesus, in his signs and miracles, and above all in his death and resurrection and the sending of his Spirit, the Father has disclosed the fullness of his love and shown us the way to eternal life. For this reason Christians believe that in Jesus Christ revelation has received its definitive form and that no new public revelation will occur until the Lord Jesus is manifested in glory.[3]

The truth about God and his plan of salvation for the human race revealed in Jesus Christ is valid for all time. That is why we call it the Gospel, the good news. Precisely because the Gospel has this definitive character, God has also provided for its preservation and its transmission to all succeeding human generations by entrusting this Gospel to the apostles. By the command of Christ (Mt 28:20), the apostles handed on what they had received from Christ himself. In their preaching, by the example of their own lives, and in the dispositions they made for the nascent Church, the apostles imparted the saving truth of Jesus Christ to others. Under the guidance of the Holy Spirit, this message of salvation in Christ was faithfully preserved as a living tradition in the teaching, life, and worship of the Church and committed to writing in the books of the New Testament.[4] The Spirit guides the Church's progress in understanding what the apostles handed on "through contemplation and study by believers, through . . . the spiritual things which they experience and through the preaching of those who, on succeeding to the office of the bishop, receive the sure charism of truth."[5]

For just as the apostles received an authoritative teaching office from Christ himself, they, in turn, appointed others, the bishops, to succeed them, in order that the Gospel might forever be preserved in its entirety and might be lived in all its integrity in the Church.

As the New Testament bears witness to the unfolding of the teaching mission of the Church, it is clear that the apostles understood themselves to be acting in the name and by the authority of Christ himself. The Acts of the Apostles tell us that after the death and resurrection of Jesus, the apostles, with Peter as their head, received from Jesus and carried out the task of proclamation in a preeminent and normative way. It was to their teaching that the newly baptized devoted themselves (Acts 2:42). This was the group that "with great power gave their testimony to the resurrection of the Lord Jesus" (Acts 4:33). The fulfillment of their responsibility for the proclamation of the Gospel was so primary for the Twelve that they knew it was not right for them to give up preaching the word of God even to serve the physical needs of those around them (Acts 6:2).

Further, it was the apostles, acting as a collegial body, who exercised normative oversight of teaching. Thus we see the Twelve, together with James and the elders in Jerusalem, considering and confirming the validity of the Gospel preached to the gentiles by Paul and Barnabas (Acts 15; see Gal 2:1-10). Paul, whose apostolic ministry was reflected in a variety of ways in the New Testament, nevertheless saw his own apostolic calling as involving both normative teaching and judgment. He could summarize his apostolic care for the original tradition with: "So we preach and so you believed" (1 Cor 15:11). He could also judge the alternative doctrine preached in Galatia as "a perversion of the Gospel of Christ" and, as such, condemn it (Gal 1:6-9).

Beyond proclamation and normative judgment, the New Testament witnesses to a prophetic dimension to the apostolic teaching office. The working out of the implications of the Gospel for Christian life in the world, as well as its applications to new situations, are also essential components of caring for the Gospel. Paul's advice on marriage (1 Cor 7:1-7) and his teaching on virginity (1 Cor 7:25-35) are examples of this concern that the Gospel and its values inform the lived experience of believers. The later books of the New Testament give evidence of the adaptation of the gospel message by apostolic authority to the situation in which the expectation of the parousia had largely receded.

While the New Testament picture may be complex, it is clear that the apostles and, within that wider group, the Twelve, obviously exercised from the beginning the ministry of normative teaching which was established by Christ. While there were others who were not apostles but who enjoyed a particular charism of teaching, the apostolic office included from the beginning the essential task of authoritative teacher in the Church.

In the ministry of normatively teaching, judging, and applying the Gospel, the college of bishops is successor to the college of the apostles. The Church believes that the college of bishops is destined to perdure precisely because the Gospel must be proclaimed as the saving truth until the end of time. The teaching authority and ministry, to which the contemporary Church applies the term *magisterium*,[6] takes its origin and its purpose from this mission of announcing the Gospel and caring for its truth. This ministry "will continue to the end of the world (see Mt 28:20), since the Gospel which is to be handed on by them is for all time the principle of all life for the Church. For this reason the apostles, within this hierarchically structured society, took care to arrange for the appointment of successors."[7]

However one reconstructs the early decades and the evolution of the episcopate, the body of those charged by office with the governance and teaching of the Church succeeds to the teaching position held by the apostolic college, which Cyprian in the third century called "the college of their fellow bishops."[8] There are some elements in the original apostolic charism—such as being eyewitnesses to the risen Lord—that episcopal consecration cannot transmit. But the college of bishops inherits the teaching office which the apostolic college once carried. Thus the Second Vatican Council repeatedly taught: "However, the order of bishops, which succeeds the college of apostles in teaching authority and pastoral government, and indeed in which the apostolic body continues to exist without interruption, is also the subject of supreme and full power over the universal Church, provided it remains united with its head, the Roman pontiff, and never without its head."[9] Bishops as such, in union with the Roman pontiff, have the duty both to see that God's self-revelation in Christ is given voice in every culture and to safeguard the authenticity of any representation of this revelation. In this ministry they summon the Christian community to respond in living faith, the graced and appropriate response to this proclamation.

Revealed truth is grasped precisely as revealed only when its content is seen as salvific. So one can never understand the teaching of the Church about the episcopal office unless this teaching is perceived as saving knowledge. The pragmatic reduction of the bishops to necessary functionaries, to characteristic figures in the Church over its history—some good, some bad, some mediocre, but of proven necessity for good government—may allow Catholics to accept this ministry as a variation of the common human need for organization and authority. It will never allow them to understand its distinctively Christian dimensions or its salvific import within the body of Christ. Such a reduction would admit that the episcopate is useful without perceiving why it is actually part of the saving work of God in history.

The primary question for any Catholic teaching always involves salvation. How, then, does the doctrine of the Church on the episcopate touch upon eternal life? What salvific difference does it make?

2. The Character and Necessity of the Teaching Office

The proclamation of the Gospel over centuries and within diverse cultures has continually demanded its transposition into diverse languages and conceptual structures. The introduction of Hellenistic philosophical terms, for example, enabled the Church to deepen and expand its understanding of the Gospel and to evangelize the Greco-Roman world. The Nicene Creed does not read like the New Testament nor should it be expected to. The critical question for the Church was not whether a creed literally repeated the New Testament, but whether it was true to the New Testament. The teaching of Vatican I on the relationship between faith and reason, *Dei Filius,* does not read like the Epistle to the Romans, but the concern of the Church in the nineteenth century was to safeguard the doctrine asserted by Romans that God can be known from created reality. Nor does Vatican II speak the same language as sacred Scripture or Vatican I. If the Church did not ceaselessly transpose the Gospel into contemporary idiom, it could not teach. The inculturation of the Gospel demands its translation into new languages, new images or concepts, and new modes of living and worship. Faith, the acceptance of God's self-revelation in Jesus Christ as absolute, is not a static reality. This acceptance, made possible by the transforming Spirit and the Church's preaching of the Gospel, bears all the marks of a living reality. Faith can develop, but it can also decline.

There is no contact with the past that does not inevitably involve some transposition. Even the literal and fundamentalistic repetition of scriptural words cannot shelter a first-century document from a twentieth-century translation and transposition. To repeat *justice* from Romans can be misleading in a culture in which this word is given a very different meaning. Of course, there will be classic texts and privileged formulas in which the faith of the Church is perennially expressed and handed on to a new generation. These constitute an indispensable part of the historical continuity of the Church, but even these normative texts need continual explanation as they are read or repeated in later centuries.[10]

Every effort to evangelize another culture will, then, inescapably introduce the message of the Gospel into another way of understanding and articulation. But the development of doctrine is not an effect simply of inculturation. Within a single culture new questions arise for the whole Church, further implications are perceived and new applications demanded. All of these necessitate a growth in the understanding of what has been handed down. As the social and cultural situation of believers changes, so is it necessary to situate this timeless revelation within the modes of a new civilization. As questions, implications, and applications arise, it is necessary to understand revelation at a deeper level. But in doing this, Christian individuals and groups risk being exposed to partial or false articulations of the faith. Absolute claims of truth and of the obedience of faith for such false or partial articulations lie at the very core of heterodoxy and sectarianism. How, then, may one discriminate between authentic Christian doctrine and error?

If the common faith of the Church is to survive from one generation to the next, the Church must possess the internal resources to distinguish for the entire community what is true from what is false in these translations and developments of the gospel message. The Church must be able to formulate a judgment in such a way that authentic faith can be continuously offered in a contemporary idiom. This judgment is part of the teaching ministry of the college of bishops. It is a necessary condition that the word of God be continued in its authentic meaning into every culture and into every century.

Such a ministry entails a twofold responsibility before God: In the name of Christ and the Church, the magisterium must declare authoritatively the faith of the Church; it must also judge whether what is presented as the content of faith is accurate.

These two responsibilities, intrinsic to episcopal teaching, distinguish such *teaching* from the more ordinary American use of this term. Like teachers all over the world, the bishops are entrusted with the communication of knowledge and the evoking of virtues. Thus they foster "the surpassing knowledge of my Lord Jesus Christ" (Phil 3:8) and those habits of Christian life by which this revelation can be grasped and realized in daily living. But in addition to this knowledge and these virtues, there are two other dimensions to *teacher* when predicated of the college of bishops: The bishops are to determine authoritatively the correct interpretation of the Scripture and tradition committed to the Church as no other teachers do about the subject matter committed to them; and they are to judge for the Church the accuracy of the presentation of this revelation by others.

These basic responsibilities of their teaching ministry engage the bishops in five interrelated functions. By the mandate and in the name of Christ, the bishops are charged with (1) the proclamation of the Gospel to the world; (2) the fostering of the Gospel within the habits and life of the Christian community; (3) the prophetic application of the Gospel to new issues; (4) the normative interpretation of the meaning of the Gospel; (5) the authoritative judgment of the interpretations advanced by others.

At the heart of all of the normative teaching of the Church is the indwelling Spirit. Only the Holy Spirit can make possible a ministry to the world that asks for faith and offers genuine hope. Only the indwelling Holy Spirit, then, can make the ministry of the college of bishops possible. Without this ministry empowered by the Spirit, the Church could not ask human beings to respond in faith to the word of salvation.

The pope and the bishops are empowered to teach not by their personal gifts, but by the Holy Spirit given in ordination. Only within the command of Christ to preach the Gospel—with all of the continual challenge to interpretation and application inherent in that command—can this ministry of the bishops be understood. The bishops are called to embody and to effect the Church's consistent witness to Christ in their care for orthodoxy. The magisterium is to continue and to serve the presence of the teaching Christ. Although the bishops must use the disciplines of theology and philosophy as well as personal religious insights in their teaching, they are to teach finally not theology, not philosophy, and not their personal religious insights, but the unchanging faith of the Church as it is to be understood and lived today.

To articulate effectively the faith of the Church, the pope and the bishops must be personally well informed about this life in faith of the people of God. It is not enough for bishops of the Church to examine their consciences, to pray, to consult advisers, and to recall what was once learned in early theological studies—though all of these are obviously essential. To teach well the bishops themselves must know the Scriptures and be knowledgeable in Catholic theology. There is an inescapable element of study and scholarship demanded by episcopal ministry.

Bishops also need to know the faith of the Christian community, how believers throughout the ages, graced by the Holy Spirit, have understood and appropriated the truth that has been handed on, the *sensus fidelium*. Episcopal ordination does not of itself confer the knowledge that can be gained only by close contact with the life of faith of the Christian community. The personal study of the bishops and their fidelity to the Catholic tradition permit them to fulfill this official responsibility of speaking authoritatively to the Church for the Church.

At ecumenical councils from Nicea through Vatican II the bishops have usually drawn on the specialized knowledge of scholars and have taken into account the sense of the faithful. So likewise popes, before issuing dogmatic definitions such as those of the immaculate conception (1854) and the assumption (1950), have consulted their fellow bishops and have sought out the opinions of theologians and the corporate beliefs of the people of God. In ascertaining the *sensus fidelium*, the beliefs of God's people throughout the history of the Church until the present time must be taken into account. These practices are based on the conviction that when the pastors and the faithful are of one mind concerning the content of revelation "the universal body of the faithful, who have received the anointing of the Holy One (cf. 1 Jn 2:20, 27), cannot be mistaken in belief."[11]

On another level, in several recent pastoral letters that present the social doctrine of the Church with prudential applications to contemporary issues, the National Conference of Catholic Bishops has made fruitful use of official teaching documents, theological research, and the counsel of knowledgeable lay persons. Because of the particular nature of those documents, dealing as they do with contingent social issues, it seemed appropriate to publish successive drafts and revise them in the light of additional insights.

Generally speaking, then, individual bishops and groups of bishops, in teaching the faith and in applying it to concrete situations, draw on the resources of the Holy See, confer with their fellow bishops, consult theological experts, and seek out the sense of the faithful. In the last analysis, however, the authority of the teaching does not stem from prior consultation. By virtue of his ordination and on condition that he remains in hierarchical communion with the college and its head, the bishop of Rome, the diocesan bishop teaches with personal authority. His relationship of communion with the pope and the other bishops gives assurance that his teaching is consonant with the "faith that comes from the apostles."[12]

3. The Teaching Ministry as Grace and Vocation

The teaching office of the bishops is part of God's gracious gift to the Church so that this community of human beings may continue in radical fidelity to the teaching Christ. This fidelity makes possible the meaning and witness of the whole Church, and the preservation and proclamation of this meaning weighs upon the bishops as a profound responsibility.

There are bishops because God cares for what is taught in the Church; there is a Church with its teaching ministry because Christ's presence and mission continue in our own time in the community formed by the Holy Spirit. There is a mission of the Son of God and of the Holy Spirit to all human life because God wills to be with us both in our historical, tangible lives and in the depths of human subjectivity. In short, there are bishops, called into this service to the Church, so that the triune God may be with the people of God and be continually manifested to the world through the Church. The teaching ministry of the bishops derives its existence and its meaning only as the servant of the self-communication and the self-revelation of the Father in Christ and through the Holy Spirit.

Accordingly, Ignatius of Antioch could write to the Ephesians in the first decade of the second century: "I am taking this opportunity to exhort you to live in harmony with the mind of God. Surely, Jesus Christ, our inseparable life, for his part is the mind of the Father, just as the bishops, though appointed throughout this vast wide earth, represent for their part the mind of Jesus Christ. Hence it is proper for you to act in agreement with the mind of the bishop."[13] The authoritative teaching ministry of the bishops is charged with this sacred responsibility: that the Church keep faith until the end of time with the Gospel, i.e., with what the Father through the Spirit has done, is doing, and will do in Jesus Christ. The care of the bishops is that the Church remain faithful to the truth of Christ. "To this mystery we owe our faith," wrote Ignatius of Antioch to the Magnesians, "and because of it we submit to sufferings to prove ourselves disciples of Jesus Christ, our only teacher."[14]

Confronting both the massive demands of the sacred responsibility that is his and the problematic situation in which he is called upon to exercise this ministry, the bishop must bear in mind that he engages in this service to the Church because of the call of Christ and by the consecration of the Holy Spirit: "The bishops, accordingly, through the Holy Spirit who has been given to them, have been made true and authentic (authentici) teachers of the faith, pontiffs and pastors."[15] This ministry to the Church and to the world is religious, not simply because its subject is religious, but because the call to this service is the call of God. God wills the grace of divine revelation and its indefectible word to be given to the world over the centuries. And from the beginning, the call of Christ is to ordinary human beings for a mission that is beyond their powers.

Bishops are sacramentally ordained to care for this mission to which the Church has been summoned, "the never-ending work of Christ, the eternal pastor."[16] Whatever be the difficulties the bishop must encounter or the sense of profound inadequacy he must carry to the accomplishment of his task, the source of his strength and the definition of his office lie with God.

The episcopate, then, must be seen as both a grace and a vocation. The episcopate is essentially a religious vocation, a call within the Church rather than a role or a career whose meaning would be intelligible outside of this context. It is also a grace, a gift of God, one realization of that outpouring of the Spirit to a world that Christ would not leave orphan.[17]

4. Collegiality and Communion

The individual bishop has a unique and authoritative role in teaching the faith of the Catholic Church in the particular church that is given to his care. The teaching office of the bishop is a constitutive element of each of the particular churches that make up the universal Church. Even as he fulfills his irreplaceable function as teacher for the local church, however, the bishop embodies that special dynamic of ecclesial communion which finds its expression in the college of bishops.

As the bishops draw upon the faith of the Church, so they draw upon one another for the verification of their teaching. In our age of almost instant communication, the unity of the bishops' teaching can be greatly enhanced. Individual bishops have greater and more rapid access to their brother bishops as well as to the Holy See in the process of discernment and discussion. The unity of teaching can be thus greatly enriched by the capacities for communication in our own age. This development, however, can be harmful if it leads bishops to abdicate their own inherent teaching authority in a concession toward an excessive centralization or to defer to the statements of a regional body without personal commitment or assent. If teaching is done only at the regional or universal level, the Church may be weakened by its loss of the varied contributions of individual bishops and the churches they serve.

The college of bishops should be of immense support to the teaching of the individual bishop. A manifest continuity in Catholic teaching results when the position of one bishop is confirmed by the teaching of his brother bishops. Moral unity in teaching has been normally a sign of its authority.

The primary realization of the college of bishops is, of course, the entire episcopate of the world together with the successor of Peter, whether that fullness of collegiality be expressed through an ecumenical council or "dispersed throughout the world, but maintaining the bond of communion among themselves and with the successor of Peter."[18] Throughout the long history of the Church, other manifestations of joint episcopal teaching have arisen. One of its earliest and principal expressions was soon defined by regional circumstances: "Various churches, founded in various places by the apostles and by their successors, have in the course of time become joined together into several groups, organically united."[19] New questions were raised as the Church became established in diverse regions of the world, when it came into contact with new civilizations and cultures. Differences about critical issues of faith arose within the believing community, either about the common meaning that held the community together or about a mode of expression by which this would be communicated. It fell to the bishops in synods and particular councils not only to decide what was and is the content of the true faith, but also what verbal expression might best preserve this truth and serve its communication within the community.

In the course of time the Church came to recognize that "bishops in communion with the head and members of the college whether as individuals or gathered in conferences of bishops or in particular councils are authentic teachers and instructors of the faith for the faithful entrusted to their care" (canon 753). The ancient canons of Nicea and of Chalcedon had dictated that the bishops of a region meet twice a year for the discussion of doctrinal and pastoral issues.[20] The Second Vatican Council noted that modern episcopal conferences were brought into being by that divine providence which from the origin of the Church had led particular churches to join together in a multiplicity of associations. Just as this providence lay at the origin and character of the ancient patriarchates, so "in a similar way episcopal conferences can today make a manifold and fruitful contribution to the concrete application of the spirit of collegiality."[21] The council defined these episcopal conferences as "a kind of assembly in which the bishops of some nation or region discharge their pastoral office in collaboration, the better to promote the good which the Church offers to people, and especially through forms and methods of apostolate carefully designed to meet contemporary conditions."[22]

This collegial spirit, whether in its fullest form of the entire college of bishops with the pope as its head or in one of its partial forms of particular councils or national conferences, inspires structures within which the individual bishop carries out the mandate of his office.[23]

Part B: *The Diocesan Bishop as Teacher*

Section 1: Teaching Role of the Individual Diocesan Bishop

1. Context of the Teaching of the Diocesan Bishop. In the light of the teaching obligations of the Church and the service given to this responsibility by the college of bishops, the role and function of the individual bishop can be seen more clearly. A bishop's teaching and his individual witness are authoritative only when he teaches in communion with the college of bishops under the primacy of the pope.

In the ministry of the bishop, continuity is absolutely essential both to credible witness and to teaching. The individual diocesan bishop finds continuity with the gospel message in his unity with the pope and the college of bishops throughout the ages. Paul himself thought such communion essential "to make sure that the course I am pursuing is not in vain" (Gal 2:2). Unlike Paul, however, the teaching of the individual bishop does not result from a personal revelation. It issues from his relationship with the whole Church, whose faith he articulates. When he maintains this relationship of communion, it in turn gives the individual bishop the assurance he needs to proclaim authoritatively the truth of salvation in ways appropriate to his times. In this sense, the teaching of each bishop takes on its particular importance: He teaches as the authoritative voice of the local church in which the universal Church is rendered present in a particular place. Thus the bishop's voice echoes the teaching of the entire Church.

Thus the diocesan bishop shares in the protection of the Spirit that accompanies the ordinary magisterium of the Church. His teaching makes it possible for the faithful to hear the truth of Christ and to maintain a single communion with their brothers and sisters both with the Church of their own times and with prior generations back to the apostolic Church. He does this in his personal teaching and preaching, his encouragement of the teaching of others, and his care for the accuracy with which the content of Catholic faith is represented.

2. Preaching the Faith. Repeatedly and solemnly, the Church has insisted that the teaching of the bishop finds its most significant expression in his preaching of the Gospel.[24] In this ministry the bishops realize the nature of their teaching office in its purest form as the public voice for the faith *(fidei praecones)*. As bishops they share in the authority of Christ *(doctores authentici seu auctoritate Christi praediti)*. In this ministry they invite others into the community of disciples. They also offer to those persons committed to their pastoral care a growing understanding of the faith that should be believed and lived. Such an increase in the understanding of faith will inevitably lead to a richer spirituality for which the bishop also is a teacher and guide in his diocese. The teaching of the bishop, in whatever form it takes, draws from "the treasury of revelation things new and old (see Mt 13:52), they make it bear fruit and they vigilantly ward off errors that are threatening their flock (see 2 Tm 4:1-4)."[25] The bishop, then, is charged with fostering the truth of the revelation of Christ, either directly or through those commissioned to work with him in this ministry. His primary concern is that the Church's faith remain true to what God has done in Christ, that it not be distorted in its rearticulations and explanations. He must also be concerned that the faith not be abstract. Doctrinal principles concerning social affairs or moral conduct, for example, must be applied to the concrete circumstances of his diocese.[26] The bishop must show this concern for teaching primarily in his own ministry to the word, especially in his preaching.

3. Encouragement and Supervision of the Trustworthy Presentation of the Faith. The original term for the bishop, *episkopos*, is literally translated "overseer," and in the Pauline letters this supervisory task was given great emphasis. Every bishop coming out of the tradition of the primitive Christian community must accept as his own the final charge given to Timothy: "O Timothy, guard what has been entrusted to you" (1 Tm 6:20). This same care for the supervision of authentic doctrine permeated the early Church of the fathers. "Be watchful," wrote Ignatius of Antioch to Polycarp, "because you have received a spirit that does not slumber."[27] Just as the Church's faith had been the original impetus behind both preaching and theology, so its fidelity demanded that it evaluate the accuracy of new developments and understandings. For this reason, it is the duty of the bishop "to supervise the entire ministry of the word in regard to the flock committed to his care."[28] He does this both by seeing that those who preach the Gospel are well prepared for this ministry and by correcting those who preach false doctrine. In this way, the bishop aids the Church to realize the promise of Christ: "If you continue in my word, you are truly my disciples, and you will know the truth and the truth will make you free" (Jn 8:31-32).

As indicated previously, these judgments about the authenticity of doctrine are not made by the individual bishop in isolation. He is a teacher of the faith, but the verification of his teaching stems from his communion with the pope and his fellow bishops and with the faith of the whole Church. In this union, each bishop has the duty to teach the faith in his diocese, conscious that his doctrine is not simply his own (Jn 7:16). In this union, each bishop has the responsibility to supervise the proclamation of the faith in his diocese, conscious that to render judgment he must be in communion with the college so as to secure its collective wisdom and support. Obviously it is important for him to invite the assistance of theologians.[29]

Supervision should not carry an overtone that is predominantly negative. Even when correction is necessary, it can be constructive. The letters to Timothy were meant to encourage his teaching: "Preach the word, be urgent in season and out of season, convince, rebuke and exhort, be unfailing in patience and in teaching" (2 Tm 4:2). This encouragement given to Timothy is akin to the more general encouragement given in the early decades of the Church to those possessing charismata within the Church: "Having gifts that differ according to the grace given to us, let us use them: if prophecy, in proportion to our faith; if service, in our serving; he who teaches, in his teaching; he who exhorts in his exhortation" (Rom 12:6-8). The diocesan bishop is similarly charged to encourage and support these gifts of teaching, exhortation, service, and prophecy as well as the various theological disciplines—all of which in their turn surround and support his teaching in the name of Christ and the Church.

The teaching ministry of the diocesan bishop, then, serves the revelation of God, either directly in his own activity or in the encouragement he gives for its accurate presentation by others "so that the whole of Christian doctrine is imparted to all" (canon 386). His ministry shares in the Church's prophetic ministry to the Gospel, a service for which the Holy Spirit empowers the bishop to fulfill this enormous responsibility. The life and future of the Church to no small extent depend upon his care for this mission.

Section 2: The Diocesan Bishop as Moderator of the Ministry of the Word

For the sake of the community, the Church chooses and ordains those who will carry out this ministry of teaching in its name. Bishops, who have the fullness of the sacrament of order, have the responsibility to teach not only as witnesses of the faith of the community, but by the authority that comes to them from Christ himself. This charge the bishops cannot morally evade, but they can share it with others. In fact, the nature of the Church and of the task itself necessitates that it be shared widely.

1. *Priests and Deacons of the Diocese.* First among those who assist the bishops in their ministry of teaching are those ordained for this very purpose, the priests. Both religious and diocesan priests are designated by the Church to cooperate with the bishop and in this way to speak in the name of the Church.[30] Like the bishop, the priest is so configured to Christ through ordination that he is "able to act in the person of Christ, the head."[31] As pastors and teachers officially sent by the bishop they preach the Gospel. "In the individual local congregations of the faithful in a certain sense they make the bishop present, and they are united with him in a spirit of trust and generosity; and in accordance with their position they undertake his duties and his concern and carry these out with daily dedication."[32] As is true for the bishops, the principal task and embodiment of the teaching ministry of priests lies in their preaching of the Gospel.[33] The priest must share the bishop's concern for the authentic teaching of the faith and morals. He is called to exhibit that concern by his manner of preaching, teaching, and counseling. He needs to ensure that those entrusted to his care receive sound teaching and moral guidance in parish religious education programs and other forms of pastoral ministry.

The restoration of the permanent diaconate in the Latin Church, and its re-emphasis in the Eastern churches, has renewed an order of sacramental ministers. They, along with transitional deacons, assist the teaching office of the bishops by proclaiming the word to the faithful, instructing and exhorting the people.[34]

2. *Shared Teaching Ministries.* Also joined with the bishop in his ministry are those religious and laity who are appointed to be teachers of the faith. By the call of the bishop, these Christians share his responsibility and cooperate in his teaching office. This ministry includes schoolteachers of religion and catechists, who actively serve the word not only by virtue of their baptism and confirmation, but also in the name of the Church because of their designation by the bishop (canon 759).

The bishop's care for the selection of those who exercise this ministry as well as for their formation, training, and religious education is but one of the ways in which he both teaches and exercises pastoral supervision over the ministry of the word in his diocese. *The Code of Canon Law,* following the teaching of the Second Vatican Council, places a particular emphasis on this responsibility of the diocesan bishop to supervise preaching (canons 386.1, 756.2), catechesis (canons 773, 775), religious instruction in schools (canons 804.2, 805), and the explanations of the faith through the social means of communication (canon 823).

One important way in which the bishop exercises his supervisory function in these areas is through the approval of texts. Catechisms require the imprimatur for publication. Other catechetical materials or "books which treat questions of sacred Scripture, theology, canon law, Church history or which deal with religious or moral disciplines cannot be employed as the textbooks on which instruction is based in elementary, middle or higher schools unless they are published with the approval of the competent ecclesiastical authority or subsequently approved by it" (canon 827.2). Canon 827.3 recommends that books dealing with the above subject matter be submitted for judgment even if they are not used as textbooks.

What is asked from all religious educators is the presentation of the faith of the Church to those who seek the truth of salvation from the Church. This fundamental concern is reflected in its legislation: "The mystery of Christ is to be expounded completely and faithfully in the ministry of the word, which ought to be based upon sacred Scripture, tradition, liturgy, the magisterium and the life of the Church" (canon 760). The object of all of these distinct activities is the mystery of Christ himself. The purpose of this ministry is that all may come to believe in him and to live lives that are a realization of his word. The sources from which this self-revelation of God is drawn are Scripture and the living tradition of the Church, especially as these have been articulated in the teaching of the magisterium. It is essential that what is taught be faithful to the reality of Christ as it is contained in these sources. Those who are called into such a pastoral ministry offer their efforts for the continuation into their own times of the apostolic tradition of the Church.

Not all teaching in the Church is by designation of the bishop. Much teaching in the Church comes out of the general mission given in baptism and confirmation and by the charismatic gifts of the Spirit.[35] Such teaching, e.g., the instruction of children by parents as the primary educators in the faith,[36] is neither a participation in the mission of the clergy nor a participation in the responsibility of the bishop, although like all teaching in the Church it is subject to his guidance. This kind of teaching in the Church—but not in the name of the Church—has been recognized and fostered from the earliest times because it is crucial to the life of the Church. Because this document is dealing with the teaching mission of the diocesan bishop, its concentration would be dissipated by attempting to give an adequate description of the nature and diversity of other forms of teaching in the Church. Let it suffice to note here that these are both present and essential to the Church.

In exercising his teaching mission and office, the individual bishop is called upon to assess not only his own teaching but also that which is done in his name and with his authority—as well as any teaching which presents the doctrine of the Church. Thus the bishop's supervision, both to encourage and to correct, extends in one form or another to all presentations of Catholic faith. His is an overarching responsibility to see that the Christian faith is accurately presented to the faithful and to the world. In every case the bishop is called to encourage and to evaluate the accurate presentation of Catholic doctrine. In all of the legislation of the Church which bears upon the bishops' supervision of doctrine, the care of the Church is that the mystery of Christ be presented in all of its fullness and in fidelity to the apostolic tradition of the Christian community.

Section 3: Bishops and Theologians

1. *Collaboration Between Bishops and Theologians.* From its earliest centuries the Church has experienced the need for that systematic reflection upon its faith that is called *theology.* The term itself has passed through a variety of related meanings. Only after the Church passed into its second millennium did *theology* come to be understood as it is today, i.e., as an intellectual discipline, a systematic investigation, an organized body of knowledge. As cultural matrices have changed, so have the structure and expectations of theology. Over various centuries, emphases have been placed upon different aspects of the general theological enterprise. A theme that runs through this diversity and provides a unity of purpose within its pluralism is the classic definition of Anselm, faith seeking understanding.[37] Theology is neither preaching nor catechetics; it is a faith-inspired, disciplined reflection upon the realities which both preaching and catechetics present.

The effort of Catholic theology is multiple: to discover and express what is and has been believed in the life of the Christian community, to inquire into the events which constitute its grounding data, and to explore creatively the reality which faith presents to the reflecting Christian mind and its relationship to human culture in general.[38] Catholic theology is both the recovery of the inexhaustible tradition out of which it comes and the discovery of new meanings, new dimensions of truth, new realizations in its mediation between its foundational faith and culture. Catholic theology also purifies statements, howsoever true, from misunderstandings, misleading expressions, irrationality and excessive dependence upon the metaphors and myths of a particular culture. A vital theology mediates between faith and culture in a dialogue which brings out of both their inherent religious challenge, promise, and depth.

The Church encourages theology and theologians because "the service of doctrine, implying as it does the believer's search for an understanding of the faith, i.e., theology, is . . . something indispensable for the Church."[39] Such understanding will always be inadequate and incomplete, but some understanding is ineluctably present even in the most rudimentary faith. Theology, in the usual, professional sense of that word, is a continuation on a more scholarly and systematic level of the fundamental "obedience of faith" which initiates all Christian life. Faith functions as foundational experience for the reflections of theology, and theology has in turn enabled Christians to purify and deepen their understanding of the faith, "religion using theology and theology using religion."[40]

The Church cannot exist without the office of bishop nor thrive without the sound scholarship of the theologian. Bishops and theologians are in a collaborative relationship.[41] Bishops benefit from the work of theologians, while theologians gain a deeper understanding of revelation under the guidance of the magisterium. The ministry of bishops and the service rendered by theologians entail a mutual respect and support.

Both bishops and theologians teach, but they teach in different ways. Bishops teach as pastors in the name of Christ and the Church. Theologians can be designated to share in this ministry when they receive the canonical mandate to teach.[42] But there is only one authoritative ecclesiastical magisterium that can call for the obedience of faith or religious assent of mind and will, and this pertains to the office of bishops. Their authority comes from Christ through sacramental ordination and hierarchical communion. The value of theologians' work stems from their adherence to the doctrine of the Church and from their scholarly competence. The responsibility of bishops, here as elsewhere, is to see that what is being presented as Catholic faith is accurately such. Both bishops and theologians serve the word of God with its salvific truth and the community of the Church which adheres to it.[43]

The bishop is to teach the faith of the Church, its basic understanding of the Gospel of Christ; the theologian is to teach theology, the disciplined extension of this understanding through philosophic, scientific, and cultural concepts or methods. Faith and theology are never in fact separated. For theology is a reflection upon the faith the bishop proclaims, and much of the teaching of the faith by bishops derives its conceptual and linguistic forms from the work of theologians. Nevertheless, it is one thing to teach the faith and another to do theological inquiry and discussion. The bishop as a bishop, i.e., precisely because of the commission he receives from Christ in episcopal ordination, is entitled to be heard as the authoritative teacher in the particular church of which he is pastor and as a member of the college of bishops. The theologian gains credibility according to the importance of the issues he explores and the strength of his arguments.

"Even when collaboration takes place under the best conditions, the possibility cannot be excluded that tensions may arise between the theologian and the magisterium."[44] A theologian's fundamental commitments to the truth and to communion with the Church, to further scholarly inquiry and dialogue, and to openness to the possibility of correction or revision of an opinion are indispensable when such tensions do arise, for it is precisely these commitments which prevent tensions from becoming hostilities. The perspective presented by the *Instruction on the Ecclesial Vocation of the Theologian*, nos. 25-31, deserves particular emphasis in this regard. Theologians "who might have serious difficulties, for reasons which appear to [them] well-founded, in accepting a non-irreformable magisterial teaching"[45] deserve special pastoral attention from the bishop in view of the important service they render to the bishop in his teaching office. But they must also seek in peace and charity to be in harmony with the bishop, and they must recognize that all Catholic theology is done within the Church, not apart from it. It was for this reason, namely, that cooperation between bishops and theologians be fostered and that problems not become intractable nor disputes become dissent, that the bishops of the United States in June of 1989 approved *Doctrinal Responsibilities: An Approach for Promoting Cooperation and Resolving Disputes Between Bishops and Theologians.*[46]

   2. Freedom of Theological Inquiry. "Theological science responds to the invitation of truth as it seeks to understand the faith. It thereby aids the people of God in fulfilling the apostle's command (cf. 1 Pt 3:15) to give an accounting for their hope to those who ask it" (*Instruction*, no. 6). There is within the Church a lawful freedom of scholarly inquiry, debate, and speculation that ultimately serves the magisterium and the Church at large.[47] Within the framework of acceptance of church teaching there is broad freedom for exploration and critique. The underlying assumptions and explicit formulations of doctrine are subject to investigation, to questions about their meaning or their doctrinal and pastoral implications, to comparison with other doctrines, to the study of their historical and ecclesial context, to translation into diverse cultural categories, and to correlation with knowledge from other branches of human and scientific inquiry.[48] Such critical analyses, or probing for context and meaning, or even persistent questioning of the presuppositions, assertions, and formulations of magisterial statements enable the Church to achieve greater clarity in its teaching, to apply it in an appropriate manner to Christian life, to respond to new problems and possibilities as they arise, and to proclaim the essential truth of the Gospel in a manner that is appropriately adapted to the requirements of a culture or to the needs of the times.[49] Scholars carry on this work as believing members of the Church, faithful to its magisterium. They are also bound by the methodological requirements of their particular theological discipline, and they are subject to the critique of their peers.[50] The vitality of Catholic theology and its fidelity to sacred Scripture, tradition, and the magisterium are strengthened by the vigorous exercise of peer review, critique, and dialogue within the theological disciplines. These necessary functions in theological discourse cannot be suspended or eliminated without debilitating consequences for theology itself.

Acceptance of church teaching, far from limiting scholarly investigation, actually fosters it, for the acceptance itself establishes a fundamental conviction on the basis of which one can confidently address further questions a particular doctrine may pose.

3. *Forums for Theological Discussion.* The Church has in its long history attempted to preserve an arena for the discussions among theologians and for theological investigation that ranges freely over many subjects and even challenges through careful argument the teaching of the Church to achieve greater accuracy and depth. In such a discussion, prolonged perhaps over many years, the worth of a private theological opinion is tested. Such testing is a crucial function of theologians themselves as they review, analyze, and criticize one another's ideas and writings. It is here, in the first instance, that an individual's ideas and opinions ought to stand or fall. Theological faculties, Catholic universities, professional societies, learned journals, books, and monographs have been the customary setting for such discussion.

Given the collaborative relationship between the magisterium and theology, bishops themselves ought to foster dialogue between themselves and theologians. Whether this occurs on a diocesan or regional level, such dialogues ought to encourage theological discussion of the many issues facing the Church and its mission in today's world. Such dialogues could provide a forum for discussion of issues which may be of particular importance for the life of the Church or of issues over which theologians may be in disagreement among themselves. Such dialogues could invite the participation of the distinct schools and perspectives in theology, thereby assuring a hearing for a variety of views. Such forums could also provide an opportunity for theologians to present to bishops persistent difficulties they may have with the content, argumentation, or presentation of the teaching of the magisterium.[51] Diocesan or regional dialogues between bishops and theologians give expression to their collaborative relationship in the service of the truth of the Gospel, foster trust, and provide the bishops with an effective means of theological consultation.

Chapter 2: Pastoral Observations on the Teaching Office of the Diocesan Bishop

Introduction

The bishop teaches the doctrine of the Church in response to the vocation and grace he has received from Christ, in whose name he summons the members of the Church to faith. He teaches in communion with the pope and the college of bishops, a bond which authenticates his teaching in the name of Christ. Because the authority and authenticity of the bishop's teaching comes from Christ, his teaching calls for acceptance on the part of the faithful. These are fundamental truths about episcopal office in the Church, valid for all time and in every particular church where there is a bishop in communion with the pope and his brother bishops.

The individual diocesan bishop, however, exercises his ministry also in a particular time and in a particular place, and the characteristics and contingent realities of a time and place determine in part the pastoral context within which he must fulfill his office of teaching. This chapter intends to address some of the realities of our present day which may have a profound impact on the effectiveness of episcopal teaching. Any attempt to describe a pastoral context as rich and divergent as that of the contemporary United States must be selective. The issues addressed in this chapter have been chosen because of their timeliness or because of requests received from bishops.

Section 1: Cultural Factors

While the Catholic Church in the United States is itself multiethnic, multicultural, and multiracial, the Church lives its life within the context of that culture which predominates in the nation. This culture presents many resources which support the teaching ministry of the bishop. Yet these same dimensions of the culture may present significant challenges to that teaching.

From the time of de Tocqueville to the latest Gallup Poll, American culture has displayed a persistent religious dimension. Historically, the colonization of North America was driven at least in part by religious factors such as the desire to spread the Gospel or the desire for freedom from religious persecution. The explicit acknowledgment of God-given human rights in the founding documents of the United States, and particularly of the right of religious freedom, has had a profound impact on the life and culture of our nation. While this religious dimension may at times seem to be reduced to a kind of civil religion, there is a fundamental concern for religious belief and practice and for ethical norms for the conduct of public affairs. American culture remains open to public dialogue of a religious and ethical nature.

This religious dimension of the culture is a great asset for the teaching ministry of the bishop. His ability to comment on public affairs, to testify about legislation or public policy, to reaffirm publicly basic beliefs about God and the dignity of the human person are but some of the ways in which this aspect of the culture provides a platform for the public presentation of the teaching of the Church.

The revolution in human communication brought about by the technological developments of our era enhances the bishop's ability to proclaim the Gospel and to bring its light to bear upon issues of ecclesial and public life. The media provide the bishop with direct access to the members of the local church as well as to the entire population of an area. While the effect of direct and immediate communication with thousands of people may not be fully understood or may be difficult to evaluate, the ready access to these technologies in our society means that the bishop can reach people in unprecedented numbers and more frequently than ever before.

Further, American culture has consistently appealed to a core of stable values and ideals. Given the pragmatic character of the nation, these values and ideals are not so much the product of ideological commitments as they are the expression of the need to find common ground on which to build communities and a society out of the diverse nationalities which make up the American population. Some of these may seem to be almost contradictory. So, for example, a basic respect for the autonomy and privacy of individuals coexists with a spontaneous willingness to help others in need. A basic respect for laws, institutions, and authority coexists with a strong assertion of the right to question them, to demand accountability from them, and to be free to change them.

The cultural patterns of building community, of respecting the individuality of members of the community, and of responding cooperatively to leadership in the community have had a beneficial impact on the development of the Church in the United States, particularly on the parochial level. At the same time, the pragmatic nature of American community building and the expectation of the right to question authority within that community are elements in the American culture which may obscure the spiritual nature of ecclesial communion. Consequently, when he teaches, the bishop may find a willingness to accept his teaching authority and even the teaching itself coexisting with the assertion of a right to question his teaching by many of the members of the local church.

As is true in any culture, the factors which support the teaching office of the bishop may also present it with significant challenges. The religious freedom and pluralism of American society may lead to a relativizing of religious commitments, particularly with regard to the doctrine of the Church. Church teaching may encounter a cultural attitude which sees church doctrine as a matter of private opinion only, to be accepted or rejected according to the dispositions or interests of individuals.

The practice within the communications media of juxtaposing differences of opinion without regard to their inherent value, or of emphasizing situations of conflict, or of characterizing and labeling issues internal to the life of the Church in much the same manner as political or social issues are characterized and labeled can have serious consequences for the faithful's ability to accept or to understand church teaching. Such methods may also foster the kind of religious indifference mentioned above.

Finally, the cultural factors of pragmatism and individualism may lead to a view that reduces authority within the Church to a set of practical arrangements necessary for any society or to a bias against all teaching proposed in an authoritative way. The value attached to the right to question authority may become an attitude of antecedent suspicion toward every exercise of authority. This latter attitude may become visible particularly when the bishop may have to correct teaching that is erroneous or inaccurate.

The predominant culture of the United States provides an atmosphere of freedom and openness in which the bishop can exercise his teaching office straightforwardly. As a matter of fact, careful attention to the very cultural dynamics which sometimes create difficulties for the reception of church teaching may enable the bishop to find ways to teach church doctrine effectively.

Section 2: Reception of Church Teaching

Church teaching is presented with varying degrees of magisterial authority. Corresponding to these differentiations are gradations in the kind of response which the teaching calls forth from the faithful. Before considering this matter in detail, however, it seems appropriate to recall the ecclesial context within which such discussion takes place.

1. The Ecclesial Dimension

In the creed we affirm our belief in the triune God and the salvific actions attributed to each of the persons of the Trinity. Rooted in this faith, the believer also affirms *credo in ecclesiam*, i.e., a living communion with and commitment to the Church which is the creation of Christ and the Spirit. To "believe in the Church" means to believe that the Holy Spirit is so intimately united with and active in the Church that the living witness to the Gospel of salvation is found there. There is, then, an ecclesial dimension essential to Christian faith and church teaching because the Church itself was founded by Christ to proclaim and to live the paschal mystery until he comes in glory.

The fidelity of the Church's living witness is more than a matter of human integrity or of discernible historical continuity. It comes about through the guidance of the Holy Spirit who was promised by Christ to the Church, which is "the pillar and foundation of truth" (1 Tm 3:15). Thus the dynamic presence of the Spirit stands behind the Church's fidelity to the teaching of Christ. The "Spirit of truth" guides the Church to the full possession of the truth of the Gospel (Jn 14:17, 26; 15:26; 16:13). It is this assistance of the Spirit that grounds the indefectibility of the Church, the apostolic authority of the teaching office, and the assent of individuals to magisterial teaching.

That guidance, therefore, is much broader than merely its guarantee of infallible statements. An unforeseen development after the definition of papal infallibility was the increasing persuasion, present even today, that the infallibility of a teaching is the sole reason or principal ground for its religious reception. An equally unforeseen effect of the Second Vatican Council's broader discussion of the teaching ministry of the Church, however, has been the reduction by some Catholics of all non-definitive teaching of the magisterium to the level of one theological opinion among others. Both of these positions present a sadly truncated view of what the abiding presence of the Spirit of truth means for the life of the Church.

Finally, in our present context, *credo in ecclesiam* embraces that aspect of the apostolicity of the Church which is continually manifested in the college of bishops under the leadership of the pope. Believers are called to devote themselves to the apostolic tradition the bishops teach, just as the original communities devoted themselves to the teaching of the apostles (Acts 2:42). Authoritative teaching by the bishops is one of the principal exercises of apostolic office in the Church and therefore carries with it a claim of credibility and the expectation of acceptance on the part of the faithful.

The conviction expressed by *credo in ecclesiam* results in an attitude of fundamental trust. One trusts the Church in its search for the adequate expression, interpretation, and application of the truth of Christ. This trust is expressed in a determination to be one with the Church and "to preserve the unity of the Spirit through the bond of peace" (Eph 4:3). The conviction of faith and the bond of trust enable the believer to accept church teaching even when its expression seems limited or partial. Some may see in such limitations a reason to doubt the Church or to mistrust its authority, but the fact of the matter is that to expect the Church to move through history without significant limitations is to presume that it could exist apart from human life with its inadequacy and imperfection.

Belief in the Church includes the fundamental conviction that its teachings are a unique and reliable guide to life according to the Gospel. It is the fidelity of the community gathered around the resurrected Christ and standing firm on the rock upon which it was built (Mt 7:24-29; 16:18) that bears witness to the presence of the Spirit who sustains this community, keeps it faithful to the Gospel, and continually urges it to draw out the essentials and implications of that Gospel for its teaching and life.

The magisterium is able to ask for, and the Catholic faithful are able to give, true assent to the authoritative teaching of the Church not only because of the rationale presented in proposing doctrine, but—crucially—because of a reliance based in faith on the Spirit's governance as well as the recognition that the doctrinal and moral guidance of the Church is ultimately guaranteed by God. The specific form of acceptance of individual doctrines varies with their source and authority; equally varied are the terms used to describe that acceptance.

The reception which a bishop seeks from his hearers is not mere passive submission. He seeks a genuine response of faith in revealed truth, and he looks to them to be faithful disciples in their response to other authoritative teachings. True reception results in faithful reflection on his teaching, personal assimilation by the hearer, and sincere application to life. "Blessed are those who hear the word of God and observe it" (Lk 11:28). The bishop hopes to stir up in his hearers the Holy Spirit which is already in them from baptism, and he hopes by his teaching to bring the light of faith to their own experience as Christians. The appropriate response to his teaching, the teaching of the Church, is a living response which transforms the hearers' minds, hearts, and lives.

2. Faith: Assent to Revealed Truth

The assent given to revealed truth definitively taught by the magisterium is, properly, the assent of faith. The acceptance of such infallible teaching of the Church is an act of faith in the strict sense because the self-revelation of God is expressed in that teaching. "In response to God's revelation our duty is 'the obedience of faith' (see Rom 16:26; compare Rom 1:5; 2 Cor 10:5-6). By this, a human being makes a total and free self-commitment to God, offering 'the full submission (obsequium) of intellect and will to God as he reveals,'[52] and willingly assenting to the revelation he gives."[53] The Church, through its magisterium, has been entrusted with the task of authoritatively interpreting what is contained in revelation, so that "all that is proposed for belief as being divinely revealed is drawn from the one deposit of faith."[54] In some cases these doctrines have been explicitly defined; in others, they are universally considered to be an essential and irreformable element of the one Catholic faith.

Doctrine definitively taught by the Church as revealed can engage the response of faith precisely because of its intrinsic relationship to the word of God and its authoritative claim. The Church infallibly teaches doctrines of this kind as truths contained explicitly or implicitly in the word of God as attested by Scripture and apostolic tradition. The Second Vatican Council expressed church teaching about infallibility in this way: "This infallibility, however, with which the divine Redeemer willed his Church to be endowed in defining doctrine concerning faith or morals, extends just as far as the deposit of divine revelation that is to be guarded as sacred and faithfully expounded."[55]

3. Firm Assent: Acceptance of Definitive, Nonrevealed Truth

Besides the guarantee of infallibility for the Church's teaching of what is contained in the deposit of faith, this gift of infallibility also extends to matters of faith and morals that, "even though not revealed in themselves, are required to safeguard the integrity of the deposit of faith, to explain it rightly and to define it effectively."[56] When it proposes infallible teaching of this second order, the magisterium requires the acceptance of its teaching as true and the rejection of whatever is contrary to it as objectively false. Such teaching is to be accepted by the faithful, not indeed by an act of divine faith (which is due solely to the contents of revelation), but by firm assent. To hold the contrary of such teaching is error.[57] Such assent is not merely an act of deference to the ecclesiastical authority, but is rather the only personal response that is adequate to the truth expressed in this teaching.[58]

4. *Obsequium Religiosum:* Acceptance of Nondefinitive Teaching

The magisterium does not always teach definitively. Often "not intending to act definitively," it "teaches a doctrine to aid a better understanding of revelation and to make explicit its contents, or to recall how some teaching is in conformity with the truths of faith or finally to guard against ideas that are incompatible with these truths."[59] In such cases the appropriate response is technically called *religiosum voluntatus et intellectus obsequium.*[60]

This Latin expression is not easy to translate into English. Nevertheless, the reality intended is reasonably clear. The Latin phrase means religious submission of the will and intellect. Negatively, "the response cannot be simply exterior or disciplinary."[61] Positively, it involves a disposition of will and intellect to accept the teaching of the magisterium, a faith-inspired acceptance of teaching in virtue of the authority of the speaker and the connection of the content with truths of faith. It is a response "under the impulse of obedience to the faith."[62]

The specific form of acceptance may vary according to "the authorita-tiveness of the interventions which become clear from the nature of the documents, the insistence with which the teaching is repeated and the very way in which it is expressed."[63]

Considered as an inner attitude or disposition, religious *obsequium* should result in acceptance of nondefinitive teaching. Such acceptance derives from a fundamental Christian desire to be one with the Church both in its teaching and in its searching for the adequate translation, interpretation, and application of the truth of revelation to the modern world. It is a response that is grounded in the bond of communion and is a concrete expression of the Pauline exhortation to strive "to pre-serve the unity of the Spirit through the bond of peace" (Eph 4:3). A response to church teaching that undermines the Church's unity fails to qualify as *obsequium religiosum*.

Further, the response of *obsequium religiosum* acknowledges the Spirit's assistance to the Church not just in moments of infallible teach-ing, but also in the day-to-day applications of the Gospel and in the whole Church's historical and developing understanding of that Gospel. The Spirit is with the Church both in its proclamation and in its search for further meaning of the truth. In the course of this search the papal or episcopal magisterium, especially when treating complex new questions, for the sake of the good of the people of God may issue a statement which, though reflecting a prudent pastoral judgment at a particular stage of development, is not proposed as definitive teaching.

The ordinary, nondefinitive teaching of individual popes and bishops may contain assertions that fall short of the full truth of the Gospel and may be in need of development and amplification. Interventions in the prudential order may even be in need of correc-tion.[64] Even if such teaching contains limitations, the Catholic trusts that the Spirit will guide the Church in a process of discernment in its life, prayer, and theological reflection that will lead to a fuller under-standing and improvement of the teaching. Over time this process has revealed that defective teaching or even explicitly erroneous teaching by individual bishops has never had the signs of universality, continu-ity, and consistency with the Gospel that mark the sound and lasting teaching of the Church.

In proposing ordinary, nondefinitive teaching, bishops rightly expect Catholics to give religious acceptance, i.e., one that is morally certain, excluding a prudent doubt about what is taught. Moral certi-tude is sufficient basis for giving true intellectual assent to nondefini-tive teaching. At times, however, professional theologians or other competent persons may conclude that the search has not been com-pleted or that what has been asserted is still imperfect, and their acceptance will be qualified accordingly. Still "the willingness to submit loyally to the teaching of the magisterium on matters per se not irreformable must be the rule."[65]

This understanding of the nature and foundation of acceptance of nondefinitive teaching is particularly important when that doctrinal or moral guidance is perceived as a "hard teaching" (Jn 6:60)—a matter which may cause personal difficulty or challenge accepted cultural patterns. There may be many factors at play creating this perception. But a reception that is colored by an overarching expectation that the teaching will in fact be reformed precisely because it is difficult or in the name of keeping up with the times does not recognize the Spirit's directing the Church toward a clearer sense of the mystery of Christ and a greater consistency in and fidelity to the Gospel's demands on Christian life.

There is diversity and differentiation in the magisterial teaching of the Church. The Catholic, then, does not accept all the statements of the ordinary magisterium as if they were credal affirmations demanding the response of faith nor as if they were simply particular theological opinions now in favor with those in authority.[66] The Catholic receives even the ordinary, nondefinitive teaching of the magisterium with that reverence, openness, and acceptance due the teaching authority of the Church in virtue of the assistance of the Holy Spirit promised it by Christ, that is, with *religiosum voluntatis et intellectus obsequium.*[67]

Section 3: Deficient Reception

The Church is animated by the Spirit, who elicits, purifies, and strengthens the free assent of its members. Whether this acceptance be the absolute commitment of faith or the firm assent to definitive teaching of nonrevealed truth or the reverent submission (*obsequium*) to nondefinitive authoritative teaching, the assent of the people of God forms that consensus which lies at the heart of this community of faith and makes possible its collective ministry to the world. To deal with this subject, however, as well as to respond to current questions in the Church, the foregoing reflections on the acceptance of church teaching must be complemented by a consideration of its opposite: nonacceptance.

When he teaches, the bishop today, as in certain critical periods of the past, can meet with various kinds of resistance. Nonacceptance ought initially to stimulate the bishop to clarify church teaching, to respond to questions about it, and to be persuasive in his presentation of it. At the same time, those who find themselves in the position of not accepting church teaching also have an obligation to study, reflect, discuss, and pray over the matter, and to avoid any weakening of the faith of another by challenging that teaching.

Nevertheless, persistent nonacceptance can indicate a serious problem that will need to be addressed. Any rejection of authoritative church teaching is a serious matter. Yet even here one must distinguish among fundamentally different kinds of rejection of church teaching. These distinctions will now be taken up in order to clarify their nature and to suggest pastoral responses on the part of the bishop.

1. Rejection of Definitive Teaching

A. Heresy. In answer to the mandate of the risen Lord, the Christian community has been concerned from its beginnings to proclaim to the world the Gospel of Christ as the word of God (1 Thes 2:4, 13). Such a mission demands not only that the Gospel not be falsified, but that its proclamation not be fragmented into discordant voices. Contradictory positions would negate the truth of what this community proclaims and undermine the credibility of its call for faith.

The rejection of divisions that would discredit the Gospel or scatter the community that bears witness to it runs like a leitmotif through the Pauline letters. It finds perhaps its strongest statement in the anathema pronounced in the Letter to the Galatians: "But even if we, or an angel from heaven, should preach to you a Gospel other than the one that we preached to you, let him be accursed" (Gal 1:8). The pastoral letters reflect these same concerns within the growing Church and urge the importance of unity and continuity in teaching. Repeatedly Christians are warned against the alien instruction and influence of anyone who departs from the apostolic preaching, i.e., "whoever teaches something different and does not agree with the sound words of our Lord Jesus Christ and the religious teaching" (1 Tm 6:3; cf. 1:3-7).

These frequent warnings against altering or falsifying the Gospel persisted in the early fathers of the Church. Ignatius of Antioch, for example, wrote against those who held aloof from the eucharist and from prayer "because they do not confess that the eucharist is the flesh of our savior, Jesus Christ."[68] The Didache warns against "those who have changed and now teach another" doctrine.[69] Polycarp censured Christians who deny the humanity of Jesus and who repudiate belief in the resurrection of the dead and a final judgment.[70] On the essentials of the Gospel the Church, to be itself, cannot compromise. For this is the meaning and the truth that are indispensable for the communion of faith. Whatever form this insistence has taken over the centuries, the undeviating determination of the Church is to preserve the revelation of what God has done for us in Christ Jesus. This is the Gospel of Christ, the good news.

The Church bears the same responsibility for the integrity of the Gospel today that it has throughout the centuries since the time of Christ. It receives the Gospel as once preached by the apostles, explored in its implications by the fathers of the Church and theologians, realized in its promise by the holiness of countless saints and the worship of the community, and defined in its meaning over the centuries by the magisterium in ecumenical councils and solemn judgments of the Roman pontiffs. The Church in our own time must be faithful to this teaching and continuous with this historical community.

Throughout its history, the Church has experienced successive contradictions of the Gospel. The most destructive denial within the Christian community has been designated by a very specific term, *heresy*. According to canon law, heresy is "the obstinate postbaptismal denial of some truth which must be believed with divine and catholic faith or it is likewise an obstinate doubt about the same" (canon 751).[71] Hence nonacceptance of magisterial teaching is heresy only if it is in regard to matters of faith in the strict sense, i.e., revealed truths definitively taught by the Church as such, and it is formal only if it is an obstinate refusal by members of the Church to accept such teaching when adequately informed of its divine and catholic character.

The Church has been deliberately careful in its description of something so serious, so harmful to its identity. Unfortunately, in the context of intrachurch polemics, *heresy* is often used rather loosely to designate any form of nonacceptance of church teaching or any proposal of novel theological opinions or pastoral practices. To use the technical term *heresy* in such a broad way would be erroneous and unjust. The canonical determination whether a teaching is heresy or not must be reserved to the bishops or the Holy See.

When such heresy is determined to be present, the bishop must counteract it by defending the Catholic faith. He may wish to begin a conversation with those involved in the hope of persuading them to turn from their error. The bishop may have recourse to the medicinal use of additional sanctions provided for in law. Those who formally commit heresy knowingly place themselves outside the communion of the Church (canon 1364).[72] If the matter becomes public, the bishop may also have to issue a public warning that the positions taken are heretical and incompatible with membership in the Catholic community.

B. Error: The Rejection of Definitively Taught Nonrevealed Truth. The rejection of definitive nonrevealed truth or the holding of opinions contrary to such teaching constitutes error. In practice, when this has occurred, the magisterium has responded by declaring that the proposed opinion is erroneous or false, with the expectation that such an opinion will be withdrawn. In some cases the declaration may state the judgment that a particular position endangers definitively taught truth and may not be taught or held. In cases where Catholics continue to hold or teach such opinions, despite the authoritative judgment that the opinions are erroneous and despite being admonished by proper authority, they may be liable to administrative measures or penalties.[73]

2. Nonacceptance of Nondefinitive Teaching

Apart from rejection of definitive teaching through heresy and error, there is a broad range of responses that in one way or another represent nonacceptance or rejection of the nondefinitive teaching of the magisterium. Such responses may occur for a variety of reasons and may be expressed in different ways. Some responses may be quite individual and private, while others may be public and even serve as the organizational focus of certain groups within the Church. Such nonacceptance can be harmful to the Church when it affects preaching, teaching, worship, and counseling—the ordinary means by which the Church's teaching is communicated. Each of them presents a challenge and an opportunity for the diocesan bishop as teacher.

A. Withholding of Assent. Perhaps a more common experience of nonacceptance in the Church today is the withholding of assent to what is identified as nondefinitive teaching. This lack of assent may take different forms. It may be a pastoral minister's silence about various teachings, or an individual's ignoring of an authoritative teaching of the Church or the entertaining of persistent doubt about a particular teaching while taking no steps to resolve the doubt. It may involve the refusal to admit that a particular teaching applies to an individual's life or even the reinterpretation of a teaching in opposition to its original significance. Assent may be withheld because a person chooses to be guided more by individual subjective experience than by authoritative teaching. It may even occur in Catholics who allow a certain doctrinal imbalance to permeate their faith, placing an exaggerated emphasis on the importance of one particular area of teaching while, at the same time, diminishing the significance of other areas of Catholic doctrine.

These manifestations of the withholding of assent to church teaching should not be confused with acceptance of the teaching of the Church but failure to put it into practice. For example, the failure to conform in one's individual actions with a moral norm taught by the Church may constitute sin. Such failure may even be habitual in some cases and disclose an attachment to wrongdoing over a period of time. A person may even experience or express a strong resistance to a call to conversion away from such a moral disorder. But this moral failure is not the same as the withholding of assent from church teaching or even dissent, which is the subject of these reflections.

While these manifestations of nonacceptance may fall short of outright rejection, nevertheless they remain nonacceptance, the withholding of the *religiosum voluntatis et intellectus obsequium* due to the ordinary magisterium of the Church. They may occur for a number of reasons. Our culture frequently entertains a deep-seated suspicion of all forms of authority, particularly when authority attempts to give

guidance about ultimate values. Perhaps the inability to bring together the teaching of the Church and the ethos expressed in economic,
political, and social life lies at the root of nonacceptance in particular
instances. Ignorance or misunderstanding of the true meaning of a
particular doctrine may also be at work in some cases.

B. *Private Dissent*. Quite distinct from the withholding of assent is
the private, individual judgment that conclusively rejects the ordinary,
nondefinitive teaching of the Church. Such a judgment constitutes private dissent and is not consistent with that *religiosum voluntatis et intellectus obsequium* due to church teaching. Even though dissent of this
kind remains private, nevertheless it is unacceptable. It may have serious consequences for the individual Catholic's life of faith. To the
extent that it affects a person's participation in the life and mission of
the Church, it may also harm the Church.

Fortunately, in many instances of the withholding of assent or
even of private dissent, the factors that lead to nonacceptance may be
resolved by a variety of means that are at the disposal of the local
church. Clarification, dialogue, education, pastoral counseling, and
moral or spiritual formation are effective tools for countering these
kinds of nonacceptance. Retreats, parish missions, marriage preparation and enrichment programs, the Catholic press, personal outreach
on the part of clergy and laity as well as the sacrament of penance offer
opportunities to address many of these issues. The diocesan bishop
can effectively address many occurrences of nonacceptance by his own
preaching and teaching as well as by encouraging those pastoral programs that facilitate patient, persistent, and understanding dialogue
with individuals or groups.

When it becomes clear that a situation of this kind is prevalent or
widespread in the local church, particularly if it concerns a particular
teaching or area of Catholic life, the bishop may well decide to use the
mass media or to issue a pastoral letter or other statement to present
the teaching of the Church in an appropriate fashion. Teaching in this
way can be even more effective if it acknowledges the doubts and difficulties that are present and casts the light of faith on them.

C. *Public Dissent*. Sometimes the nonacceptance of nondefinitive
teaching passes beyond the nature of a "difficulty" and becomes a
judgment that an authoritative teaching is false. This, of course, is
quite different from a critical judgment about the adequacy of expression or the conceptual limitations of a particular teaching.[74] The
Instruction on the Ecclesial Vocation of the Theologian restricts the meaning of the word *dissent* to "public opposition to the magisterium of the
Church, which must be distinguished from the situation of personal
difficulties."[75] This should be noted because in American usage the
term *dissent* is used more broadly to include even the private expression of rejection of reformable magisterial teaching. In that broader

usage the term has connotations of individual liberty and rights associated with the Enlightenment and American intellectual, political,
and religious history, ideas that are very much a part of the culture and
society of the United States with its long-standing admiration and
defense of a "right of dissent" covering both private and public disagreements. For our purposes, in the following we will distinguish
between private and public dissent. We understand *public dissent* in the
same sense that the instruction uses the word *dissent*, namely, public
opposition to the magisterium of the Church.

Before offering our reflections on pastoral responses to such dissent,
it may be useful to call attention to the meaning of the word *public* as it
is used in this specific context. Obviously, *public opposition* does not
encompass the private denial of teaching on the part of an individual.

More important, however, it does not seem appropriate to apply
the term *public* to the professional discussions that occur among theologians within the confines of scholarly meetings and dialogues or to
the scholarly publication of views. Such forums for the exchange of
views among theologians are invaluable for the refinement of positions that comes through peer critique of evidence, methodology, and
scholarship. They serve the advancement of truth itself. Even if the
views expressed in such forums are critical of or in disagreement with
the ordinary, nondefinitive teaching of the magisterium, the magisterium itself may benefit from an understanding of objections to its
teaching, and from the refinement and development of authoritative
teaching that may result from such scholarly exchanges.[76] These considerations presume that theologians and scholars are willing to take
the necessary steps to overcome their difficulties and abide by an
authoritative intervention on the part of the magisterium should it
consider one necessary.

When, however, a judgment rejecting magisterial teaching is widely
disseminated in the public forum (dissent in the proper sense as formulated by the instruction), such as may occur through popular religious journals or through books intended for mass distribution or
through the press and electronic media, then a situation of public dissent is at hand.

Public dissent can take a number of forms. It may be expressed in
words or in behavior. It may come from an individual Catholic as a private person or from a public figure in the arena of theology, business,
politics, culture, or the arts. It is of particular concern when the person
who publicly dissents is also involved in the public life of the Church
through teaching, preaching, or writing. In its most extreme form, public dissent involves not merely the contradiction of the teaching of the
Church, but the advocacy of an alternative position as the correct interpretation of beliefs or as reliable guidance for the lives of Catholics.

3. Doctrinal and Pastoral Responses of the Magisterium to Public Dissent

When any type of public dissent occurs, it places special demands and burdens on the bishop. It presents a situation that requires of the bishop a genuine act of discernment, grounded in prayer, reflection, counsel, and time.

First, the bishop must consider the issue at hand. If there is uncertainty whether a proposed position does, in fact, constitute dissent, the procedures for formal doctrinal dialogue which were suggested in our document "Doctrinal Responsibilities" may assist the bishop in clarifying the issue.[77]

Second, the bishop must consider the gravity of the teaching that is being rejected. The degree of theological certitude it enjoys, the emphasis, frequency, or constancy of its being taught, and the level of magisterium that is teaching it are all relevant considerations.

Third, the bishop must consider the context within which an individual or group may be rejecting a teaching. If the denial takes place within a much broader context of assent to church teaching, the bishop may wish to institute a dialogue with those dissenting to ascertain the basis and motives of their dissent. If the denial is part of a broader pattern of dissent from church teaching, possibly involving the public advocacy of alternative positions, then the issue of ecclesial allegiance and magisterial authority in general may be at stake and might require a different response from the bishop. "As bishops we must be especially responsive to our role as authentic teachers of the faith when opinions at variance with the Church's teaching are proposed as a basis for pastoral practice."[78]

Fourth, the bishop must consider the effect of this dissent on the Church at large. Dissent that is expressed in such a way that it disrupts ecclesial communion, or that leads to divisiveness and a partisan spirit, or that disregards the community's right to hear sound doctrine or its genuine religious sensibilities, or that affects moral values cannot be tolerated, especially if it is protracted.

Fifth, the bishop must consider the forum in which dissent has been expressed. It is one thing, for example, to write an article expressing dissent in a scholarly theological journal and subject oneself to criticism and correction from one's theological peers; it is quite another thing to use the mass media to express one's dissent from church teaching.

Sixth, the bishop must consider the public position in the Church of those who are expressing dissenting views. Preachers and catechists as well as teachers of theology appointed by the competent authority to teach in the name of the Church are bound to present faithfully what the Church teaches. As defined above, public dissent expressed by such persons, especially when it occurs in the course of performing the duties of their office, cannot be reconciled with the responsibilities that these positions entail.

Finally, the disposition toward the teaching authority of the bishop on the part of those who are dissenting must be taken into consideration. If an individual or group dissents, but retains the disposition to abide by a final judgment of the magisterium on an issue, the possibility of *obsequium religiosum* remains. On the other hand, if dissent is expressed in absolute terms and there are no signs of docility toward the Church, that possibility may well be foreclosed. In that case the bishop may initiate the process leading to the possible imposition of a canonical penalty (canon 1371.1).

Bishops cannot be indifferent to the public denial or the contradiction of church teaching, especially by those whose position confers public influence. Public dissent, especially in the form of advocacy for alternative positions, seriously impairs the Church as a communion of faith and witness. In this regard, as noted by Pope John Paul II in his address to the American bishops in 1987, such dissent poses a very significant challenge to the teaching office of bishops.[79]

Bishops must deal with dissent in an authoritative and candid manner. Dissent is never acceptable, but in some cases it may be accompanied by evidences of good faith and competence, viz., prayer, study, serious and objective grounds, consultation, fidelity, reverence for the Church and the Church's magisterium, the signs of the Spirit (Gal 5:22-23), and the willingness to discuss the issues. Nevertheless the leadership in the Church cannot evade an authoritative decision; the final pastoral judgment about individual cases of dissent, about teaching that contradicts that of the ordinary magisterium, lies with the bishops, whose office entails this responsibility.

In order to execute his responsibilities, the bishop has the duty to make such a judgment and may legitimately expect that his decision will be accepted in obedience or at least in reverential silence for the good of the Church. It may not be a matter directly of the content of faith, but it does involve that *obsequium* which comes out of faith, namely, such confidence of the presence of God in the Church that one responds to the call for obedience or silence. One is not asked to make an act of faith in what is taught; one is asked to submit in obedience, with the internal sense that the mystery of God is present in this reception and that truth is great and it will prevail.

The bishop may be persuaded that such a demand for silence is not the best response to the situation and that his responsibilities can be fulfilled in some other ways. These might range from restating in a positive fashion the authoritative teaching of the Church to insisting that a particular position be presented in such a way that its relationship to the teaching of the magisterium is clear or to issuing a doctrinal *monitum*—a clear warning of danger to the faith in what is being publicly taught to the contrary.[80]

The truth proclaimed by the magisterium should normally engage the sense of the faith that is present among Catholics of goodwill. Yet the reception of nondefinitive teaching may be significantly limited by ignorance, prejudice, and poor or no teaching as well as by disagreement and contestation among the faithful. This may be a sign that the issue would benefit from clarification or from comprehensive restatement and persuasive teaching by the magisterium.

Decisions about public dissent lie within the responsibility of the bishops. In facing the often difficult and delicate situation posed by public dissent, the bishops recognize that they are called by God to foster both that unity of the body of Christ and that progress in the systematic reflection upon the Gospel which mark the Church as a communion of love and wisdom.

4. Some Special Considerations

A. Public Presentation of the Teaching of the Church. What is true of the personal assent of every Catholic applies even more to one engaged in preaching or teaching. The Church can be seriously hurt by widespread and open contradiction of its teaching: "Hard sayings" can be undermined, leadership weakened, factions encouraged, religious skepticism advanced, and responsible ecclesial discernment reduced to individual private opinions. The Church as a community loses something of its ability to speak to the world.

Even conscientious questioning does not excuse one from faithfully and effectively presenting the doctrine of the Church—especially when one is performing a ministry in its name. The people of God have a right to hear Catholic teaching, and no member of the Church has the right to ignore the existence of that doctrine because of personal opinions to the contrary. The faithful also have a right to communion in a united faith and witness, and this touches precisely on the ministry of the magisterium. The voice of the magisterium must not then be relegated to one opinion out of many. It speaks with an authority and a responsibility of office to the entire Church in a way that no theologian can. Even if one finds an alternative position compelling, one is still obliged in conscience to present the doctrine of the magisterium with the authority which it possesses, to probe it for the truth that it contains, and to safeguard official church teaching by the reverence and reluctance with which any disagreement is voiced.

B. Dissent and the Media. Our age is characterized both by popular interest in theological debate and by the realities of modern mass media. Serious and well-informed religious journalism serves to communicate information and perspective about theological and ecclesial issues to the general public. It is a commendable use of the means of communication in the service of society. Yet the media can also be used as a platform by those who dissent from church teaching. This can sometimes pose a genuine threat to scholarly interchange, can create pressures and difficulties that challenge the entire Church, and may require the intervention of the bishop. The creation of the impression of widespread conflict, its facile categorization in terms adopted from political discussion, and the implicit or explicit assumption that the dissenting view is of equal validity with the teaching of the magisterium are the unhappy consequences of carrying on theological discussions of great pastoral import in the mass media.[81] The ensuing pressures for instantaneous responses from church authorities usually serve only to strengthen the perception of conflict or to confirm prejudices about the repressive nature of ecclesial authority.

Theologians should be aware that discussions proper to their professional circles may often become known to a wider public through inaccurate or misleading reports in the media. When this occurs, they should take whatever steps may be available to them to correct any mistaken impressions. They should also underscore the difference between personal theological opinion and the authoritative teaching of the Church.

The appropriate ways in which theological discussion can profitably occur should continue to be the object of dialogue between bishops and theologians. But given the complexities of many theological issues, there is no warrant for publicizing dissenting theological views through the media, where scant attention will be paid to the nuance required by the issues themselves and by informed theological discussion.

Section 4: Observations on Characteristics of Effective Teaching

Throughout, this document has encouraged the positive presentation of Catholic doctrine by the bishops as the most effective way of countering difficulties presented by the culture. Effective teaching is also the best response to situations of theological dissent. The truth of the doctrine of the Church, taught in a manner that is accommodated to the needs of the faithful, bears within itself a claim on their assent. But to be effective, a bishop's teaching must have certain characteristics. Among those that seem particularly important today are insightfulness, humility, courage, persuasiveness, and charity.

1. Insightfulness

If a bishop is to transmit the salvific truth of the mysteries of faith, he must first make that truth his own. Through pastoral experience, study, reflection, and judgment, through prayer, dialogue, and consultation, the bishop comes to a deeper personal appropriation of the meaning of the teaching of the Church. We call this *insightfulness*. The achievement of this true insight brings with it a liberation from distortion or partiality in his own understanding of the faith. It enables the bishop to relate one truth of the faith to others and to judge correctly its place in the hierarchy of salvific truths.

Insightfulness gives the bishop's act of teaching an especially communicative power as he presents to others the faith of the Church. It makes possible faith's accommodation to the culture and mindset of the people, while preserving the inner logic of the truth itself. When joined with the bishop's understanding of the historical moment in which he teaches and with his charism to discern the needs of the people, insight's grasp of essential meaning provides the bishop with a firm basis for deciding on appropriate courses of action in fulfilling his teaching ministry. Insight into the faith of the Church is crucial in assuring the correctness of the bishop's judgments about the orthodoxy of others who teach. The quality of insightful teaching reinforces the many suggestions this document has already made about the bishop's need to make time for study and reflection, to collaborate with other bishops, and to consult with experts.

2. Humility

The bishop teaches what he himself has received from the Church. His teaching is in service to the word of God and the tradition of the Church. His acts of teaching are an essential part of his ministry, his service to the people of God, modeled on the service of Jesus Christ. Episcopal teaching, then, precisely because it is in the service of God and of God's people, has that character of humility that ought to qualify all ministry in the Church.

Humility, as it applies to episcopal teaching, also means that the bishop is aware that the mystery of God and the teaching of the Church transcend even the most careful and sustained human effort to find expression in words. The bishop will be conscious of the limitations of his own words to convey the essential truth of the faith. In nondefinitive teaching, the bishop recognizes that he may be proclaiming and applying to the life of his particular church a teaching that may need to be more developed in the future and which, nevertheless, he proposes as authoritative guidance for his people. In all his acts of teaching, the bishop understands himself as performing an act of service, modeled on the service of Jesus Christ, who invites his followers to "learn from me, for I am gentle and humble of heart" (Mt 12:29).

3. Courage

Courageous and forthright proclamation of the saving truth of the Gospel has been a characteristic of apostolic office from the very beginning (Acts 4:29-31). The right and the power to speak openly and with boldness *(parresia)* of the redemption accomplished in Christ is a gift of the Spirit to the apostles and their successors. Episcopal ordination confers on the bishop the right—and its corresponding duty—to be the principal spokesman for the faith in the local church. Part of the grace of ordination is the power, the charism, to bear courageous witness to the faith (2 Tm 1:6-8; 4:1-4). This charism is manifest in the teaching of the bishop in a variety of ways. In confessing his faith before the community of faith, the bishop expresses the belief that unites the community and strengthens the individual members in their own witness. In speaking out on moral issues in society, the bishop may serve as its conscience, naming the evils and injustices that many would prefer to tolerate or ignore. In confronting those who would relegate the Gospel to the private sphere, or dismiss its message from significant areas of human life, or relativize its values and demands, the bishop bears witness to the truth that alone can redeem and set free. Courageous preaching and teaching may exact a price from the bishop in terms of stress, hostility, and ridicule. In every age the Church has seen bishops pay the ultimate price of their lives for the bold proclamation of the Gospel. Yet the courage to teach in the name of Christ and the Church gives the bishop's teaching an eloquence beyond his words and skills and makes it effective.

4. Persuasiveness

The persuasiveness of the bishop's teaching arises from a number of factors. It is not only the bishop's communication skills, but above all the constancy of his teaching itself that constitutes an ongoing call to faith and practice. The grounding of teaching in revelation and tradition, its convincing articulation, its visible functioning as a guiding principle for the internal life of the local church, its implementation in diocesan and parochial programs, its ability to grapple with and respond to the lived faith experience of the faithful so as to elicit acceptance—these are but some of the elements which give the teaching office of the bishop a persuasive force. They are tangible expressions of the bishop's own faith and prayer life. They constitute his witness, in word and deed, to the apostolic faith of the Church and to the way of life that flows from it. Ultimately, it is the congruity of the bishop's teaching with revelation itself that enables the faithful to hear a call to faith in the teaching of the bishop.

5. Charity

Above all, the teaching of the bishop is characterized by charity. When the bishop instructs his local church, he carries out for his own people the exhortation of Paul to the Ephesians: "Living the truth in love, we should grow in every way into him who is the head, Christ" (Eph 4:15). The proclamation of the faith has its purpose fulfilled when the hearer, accepting the salvific truth of the Gospel, is united with God in love. This same love of God impels the Church and its members to share the light of faith with everyone. Charity must especially suffuse the response of the bishop, and indeed all of the faithful, when the teaching of the Church encounters resistance and rejection. While the truth must be forthrightly proclaimed, this should be done with charity and civility.

Conclusion

The broad range of these considerations—from reception to dissent, from collaboration to the witness that is a bishop's alone to give—is in itself an indication of how the complexity of modern life and of American society affects the teaching ministry of the bishop. Still the bishop must teach, for that is his vocation and his grace. The care and concern to do so effectively may place many demands on the bishop's time and energy, even to the point of delegating other matters to his collaborators. "A bishop has a personal responsibility to teach the faith of the Church. He himself therefore needs time to read, study and prayerfully assimilate the contents of the Church's tradition and magisterium. . . . Administrative and social engagements, however unavoidable, must be harmonized with more basic tasks. Bishops also need to practice a subsidiarity which leaves ample room for the cooperation of priests and qualified laypersons in activities not strictly related to their pastoral office."[82]

Collaboration, in all of its dimensions, is a key element in the effective exercise of the bishop's teaching ministry. To the extent that collaboration frees the bishop to spend adequate time on his teaching ministry, it contributes to his exercise of this office. To the extent that the bishop seeks the collaboration of qualified theological advisers, he will be able to teach more effectively. To the extent that the bishop in his teaching collaborates and consults with the members of the college of bishops and its head, he will give clear expression to the apostolic faith of the Church.

The teaching ministry of the diocesan bishop is a unique responsibility in the Church. When it is done with care and with the assistance of all the means at his disposal, the articulation of the faith may be a responsibility whose fulfillment brings with it an experience of evangelical joy, both for the bishop himself and for the Church entrusted to his service.

Notes

1. Second Vatican Council, *Dogmatic Constitution on Divine Revelation (Dei Verbum)*, no. 2.
2. See *Dei Verbum*, no. 3.
3. See *Dei Verbum*, no. 4.
4. See *Dei Verbum*, no. 8.
5. *Dei Verbum*, no. 8.
6. "By *ecclesiastical magisterium* is meant the task of teaching that by Christ's institution is proper to the college of bishops or to individual bishops linked in hierarchical communion with the supreme pontiff," International Theological Commission, *Theses on the Relationship Between the Ecclesiastical Magisterium and Theology* (Washington, D.C.: United States Catholic Conference, 1977), thesis 1. *Authentic* in the phrase *authentic magisterium* is a transliteration from the Latin and means *authoritative*. *Extraordinary magisterium* means that teaching office when exercised solemnly to define doctrine, either by an ecumenical council or by the pope speaking *ex cathedra* to the universal Church. All other exercises of the magisterium are called *ordinary*. When all of the bishops, together with the pope, in the ordinary exercise of their authority teach the same doctrine, one speaks of the *universal and ordinary magisterium*. The conditions under which the universal and ordinary magisterium can teach infallibly have been indicated by *Lumen Gentium*, no. 25.
7. Second Vatican Council, *Dogmatic Constitution on the Church (Lumen Gentium)*, no. 20.
8. Cyprian, Letter 55, *To Antonian of Numidia*, no. 21 (in *S. Thasci Caecili Cypriani Opera omnia*, ed. Wilhelm A. R. von Hartel [Vindobona: C. Geroldi, 1871], 3:639). Cyprian uses the same concept in Letter 68, *To Stephen*, no. 1, in Hartel, 3:744.
9. *Lumen Gentium*, no. 22.
10. Cf. Paul VI, *Mysterium Fidei* (September 3, 1965), *Acta Apostolicae Sedis* 57 (1965): 758:

> And so the rule of language which the Church has established through the long labor of centuries, with the help of the Holy Spirit, and which she has confirmed with the authority of the councils and which has more than once been the watchword and banner of orthodox faith, is to be religiously preserved, and no one may presume to change it at his own pleasure or under the pretext of new knowledge. Who would ever tolerate that the dogmatic formulas used by the ecumenical councils for the mysteries of the Holy Trinity and the incarnation be judged as no longer appropriate for men of our times and let others be substituted for them? In the same way, it cannot be tolerated that any indi-

vidual should on his own authority take something away from the formulas which were used by the Council of Trent to propose the eucharistic mystery for our belief. These formulas—like the others that the Church used to propose the dogmas of faith—express concepts that are not tied to a certain specific form of human culture or to a certain level of scientific progress or to one or another theological school. Instead they set forth what the human mind grasps of reality through necessary and universal experience and what it expresses in apt and exact words, whether it be in ordinary or more refined language. For this reason, these formulas are adapted to all men of all times and all places.

But also see Congregation for the Doctrine of the Faith, *Declaration in Defense of the Catholic Doctrine on the Church Against Some Present-day Errors (Mysterium Ecclesiae)* (Washington, D.C.: United States Catholic Conference, 1973), where the language used to express Catholic doctrine is acknowledged as historically conditioned. The nature of such language must "be taken into account in order that these pronouncements may be properly interpreted" *Origins* 3:7 (July 19, 1973): 110. Additional observations on the interpretation of church teaching may be found in Congregation for the Doctrine of the Faith, *Instruction on the Ecclesial Vocation of the Theologian (Donum Veritatis)* (Washington, D.C.: United States Catholic Conference, 1990), nos. 10, 24, 30, 34.

11. *Lumen Gentium*, no. 12.
12. Eucharistic Prayer I, *The Sacramentary: The Roman Missal Revised by the Decree of the Second Vatican Ecumenical Council and Published by the Authority of Pope Paul VI*, English trans. prepared by ICEL (New York: Catholic Book Publishing Co., 1985), 542.
13. Ignatius of Antioch, *Epistle to the Ephesians*, 3-4, trans. and ed. James A. Kleist, "The Epistles of St. Clement of Rome and St. Ignatius of Antioch," *Ancient Christian Writers I*, ed. Quasten and Plume (Westminster, Md.: Newman, 1946), 61. See also *Epistle to the Trallians*, 2, p. 75, and *Epistle to the Philadelphians*, 2, pp. 85-86; 7, pp. 87-88 *et passim*.
14. Ignatius of Antioch, *Epistle to the Magnesians*, 9.
15. Second Vatican Council, *Decree on the Pastoral Office of Bishops in the Church (Christus Dominus)*, no. 2.
16. Ibid.
17. What is said here about the teaching authority of diocesan bishops applies with necessary modifications to coadjutor, auxiliary, and retired bishops. They too are members of the episcopal college and share in its teaching office by reason of their ordination as bishops (*Lumen Gentium*, no. 38). Although coadjutor and auxiliary bishops do not have charge of a diocese, they have been commissioned to assist the diocesan bishop in his teaching ministry.
18. *Lumen Gentium*, no. 25; canon 749.2.
19. *Lumen Gentium*, no. 23.
20. Nicea, canon 5; Chalcedon, canon 19, in *Conciliorum Oecumenicorum Decreta*, ed. Instituto per le scienze religiose, J. Alberigo et al. (Bologna: Instituto per le scienze religiose, 1973), 8 and 96.

21. *Lumen Gentium,* no. 23.
22. *Christus Dominus,* no. 38.1.
23. Episcopal collegiality in reference to conferences of bishops is at present under study by the Holy See at the request of the 1985 extraordinary Synod of Bishops.
24. See Council of Trent, ses. V, canon 2, no. 9. and ses. XXIV, canon 4: "It is the desire of the council that the office of preaching, which particularly belongs to the bishop, be exercised as often as possible for the salvation of the people" (*Christus Dominus,* no. 12):

    In discharging their obligation to teach, they should proclaim to humanity the Gospel of Christ. This stands out among the most important duties of bishops. With the courage imparted by the Spirit, they should call people to faith or strengthen them in living faith. To them they must expound the mystery of Christ in its entirety. This involves those truths ignorance of which is ignorance of Christ. They must likewise point out the way divinely revealed for giving glory to God and thereby attaining eternal happiness.

    See also *Lumen Gentium,* no. 25. For the Church's insistence upon this duty of the bishop, see Sacred Congregation for Bishops, *Directory on the Pastoral Ministry of Bishops* (Ottawa: Publication Service of the Canadian Catholic Conference, 1974), nos. 55-64.
25. *Lumen Gentium,* no. 25.
26. See *Directory on the Pastoral Ministry of Bishops,* no. 56.
27. Ignatius of Antioch, *To Polycarp,* no. 1.3.
28. *Directory on the Pastoral Ministry of Bishops,* no. 65; canons 386.1, 756.2.
29. *Directory on the Pastoral Ministry of Bishops,* no. 63.
30. *Christus Dominus,* nos. 28-30, 34, 35.
31. *Presbyterorum Ordinis,* no. 2; *Lumen Gentium,* no. 28.
32. *Lumen Gentium,* no. 28; see *Presbyterorum Ordinis,* no. 4, especially footnote 4.
33. *Presbyterorum Ordinis,* no. 4.
34. See *Lumen Gentium,* no. 29.
35. *Lumen Gentium,* nos. 11, 12.
36. See John Paul II, *On the Family (Familiaris Consortio)* (Washington, D.C.: United States Catholic Conference, 1982), nos. 51-53.
37. "Neque enim quaero intelligere ut credam, sed credo ut intelligam," Anselm, *Proslogion,* 1, in J. P. Migne, *Patrologiae cursus completus, series latinae* [hereafter, PL] (Paris, 1841-1864), 158:227c. See Anselm, *Cur Deus homo* I, 2, in PL 158:364a.
38. See *Instruction on the Ecclesial Vocation of the Theologian,* no. 10.
39. *Instruction on the Ecclesial Vocation of the Theologian,* no. 1.
40. John Henry Newman, *An Essay in Aid of a Grammar of Assent,* part 1, chap. 5, ed. and intro. I. T. Ker (Oxford: Clarendon Press, 1985), 98.
41. See *Instruction on the Ecclesial Vocation of the Theologian,* nos. 21ff.
42. Canon 812; *Instruction on the Ecclesial Vocation of the Theologian,* no. 22.
43. See *Instruction on the Ecclesial Vocation of the Theologian,* no. 21.
44. Ibid., no. 25.
45. Ibid., no. 28.

46. National Conference of Catholic Bishops, *Doctrinal Responsibilities: An Approach for Promoting Cooperation and Resolving Disputes Between Bishops and Theologians* (Washington, D.C.: United States Catholic Conference, 1989).
47. Second Vatican Council, *Pastoral Constitution on the Church in the Modern World (Gaudium et Spes)*, nos. 10, 62; canon 218.
48. *Gaudium et Spes*, nos. 44, 62; cf. *Instruction on the Ecclesial Vocation of the Theologian*, no. 10.
49. See *Instruction on the Ecclesial Vocation of the Theologian*, no. 24.
50. See *Instruction on the Ecclesial Vocation of the Theologian*, nos. 9, 11; *Doctrinal Responsibilities*, 5.
51. See *Instruction on the Ecclesial Vocation of the Theologian*, no. 30.
52. Denziger-Schönmetzer, *Enchiridion Symbolorum, Definitionum et Declarationum de Rebus Fidei et Morum*, 3008.
53. *Dei Verbum*, no. 5.
54. Ibid., no. 10.
55. *Lumen Gentium*, no. 25. An example of revealed truth which calls for the assent of faith is the doctrine of the resurrection of Jesus from the dead.
56. *Relatio* of Bishop Vincent Gasser, 84th general congregation (July 11, 1870), First Vatican Council, in J. D. Mansi, *Sacrorum Conciliorum Nova et Amplissima Collectio* (Arnhem and Leipzig, 1927), 52:1226. Gasser was speaking on behalf of the *deputatio de fide*.
57. See *Mysterium Ecclesiae, Acta Apostolicae Sedis* 65 (1973): 401; *Instruction on the Ecclesial Vocation of the Theologian*, nos. 16 and 23.
58. An example of definitive, nonrevealed truth which calls for firm assent is the natural immortality of the human soul.
59. *Instruction on the Ecclesial Vocation of the Theologian*, no. 23.
60. *Lumen Gentium*, no. 25; canon 752; *Instruction on the Ecclesial Vocation of the Theologian*, no. 23.
61. *Instruction on the Ecclesial Vocation of the Theologian*, no. 23.
62. Ibid.
63. Ibid.; cf. *Lumen Gentium*, no. 25.
64. "When it comes to the question of interventions in the prudential order, it could happen that some magisterial documents might not be free from all deficiencies. Bishops and their advisers have not always taken into immediate consideration every aspect or the entire complexity of a question. . . . The theologian knows that some judgments of the magisterium could be justified at the time in which they were made, because while the pronouncements contained true assertions and others which were not sure, both types were inextricably connected. Only time has permitted discernment, and after deeper study, the attainment of true doctrinal progress" (*Instruction on the Ecclesial Vocation of the Theologian*, no. 24).
65. Ibid.
66. See Ibid., nos. 33 and 34, where this attitude is addressed in detail.
67. *Lumen Gentium*, no. 25. An example of teaching which is nondefinitive and calls for *obsequium religiosum* is the teaching of the instruction *Donum Vitae* against such practices as artificial insemination, surrogate motherhood, and *in vitro* fertilization.
68. Ignatius of Antioch, *Letter to the Smyraeans*, no. 7, 1.

69. *The Didache or Teaching of the Twelve Apostles,* no. 11.
70. Polycarp, *Letter to the Philippians,* no. 7.
71. Latin text: "Dicitur Haeresis, pertinax, post receptum baptismum, alicuius veritatis fide divina et catholica credendae denegatio, aut de eadem pertinax dubitatio." See also Denziger-Schönmetzer, 3011, and *Lumen Gentium,* no. 25. While the canonical crime of heresy involves subjective guilt, *heresy* is not always understood only in this sense. *Material heresy* is also of great concern to the Church and bishops. Church teachers are concerned not simply with the guilt of those who deny church teaching, but more so about the truth and goodness of the faith. Some may teach contrary to defined teachings of the Church without being aware of this. One may criticize such works as involving heresy without accusing the authors of being formal and deliberate heretics.
72. Canon 1364.1: "With due regard for canon 194.1, no. 2, an apostate from the faith, a heretic or a schismatic incurs automatic *(latae sententiae)* excommunication and if a cleric, he can also be punished by the penalties mentioned in canon 1336.1, nos. 1, 2, and 3:

    > 2. If long-lasting contumacy or the seriousness of scandal warrants it, other penalties can be added, including dismissal from the clerical state.

73. See canon 1371: "The following are to be punished with a just penalty: 1. besides those mentioned in canon 1364.1, a person who teaches a doctrine condemned by the Roman pontiff or by an ecumenical council or who pertinaciously rejects the doctrine mentioned in canon 752 and who does not make a retraction after having been admonished by the Apostolic See or by the ordinary."
74. See pp. 43-44, above.
75. *Instruction on the Ecclesial Vocation of the Theologian,* no. 33.
76. See ibid., nos. 29, 30.
77. *Doctrinal Responsibilities,* 16-23.
78. John Paul II to the bishops of the United States (September 16, 1987), in *Origins* 17:16 (October 1, 1987): 261.
79. See ibid.
80. See *Doctrinal Responsibilities,* 22-23.
81. See *Instruction on the Ecclesial Vocation of the Theologian,* especially nos. 32 and 39.
82. John Paul II, ad limina address to Philippine bishops (April 24, 1990), in *L'Osservatore Romano* [English edition], 18 (April 30, 1990): 9-10.

Source: *Origins* 21:30 (January 2, 1992): 473-492.

Putting Children and Families First:
A Challenge for Our Church,
Nation, and World

A Statement of the United States Catholic Conference

November 1991

I. Introduction: Children Within a Family Perspective

Our nation is failing many of our children. Our world is a hostile and dangerous place for millions of children. As pastors in a community deeply committed to serving children and their families, and as teachers of a faith that celebrates the gift of children, we seek to call attention to this crisis and to fashion a response that builds on the values of our faith, the experience of our community, and the love and compassion of our people. We seek to shape a society—and a world—with a clear priority for families and children in need and to contribute to the development of policies that help families protect their children's lives and overcome the moral, social, and economic forces that threaten their future.

We focus on the situation of our children for several reasons:

- **Our children are a test of both our humanity and our faith.** As Pope John Paul II said in *Familiaris Consortio,* "In the Christian view, our treatment of children becomes a measure of our fidelity to the Lord himself."
- **Our children are hurting,** in the United States and around the world. They are among the most vulnerable members of the human family. The lives, dignity, rights, and hopes of literally millions of children are at risk.
- **Our children are our future**—they will be the leaders, the believers, the parents, the citizens of tomorrow. In responding to their needs today, we shape a better future for all.
- **Our children are our present.** Our children bring us special gifts, today, not just tomorrow. They are the sign of God's continual gift to the world. Thus, we need to respect them and place their rights as a priority in our society and our Church.
- **Parents need support and help** in meeting the challenges of raising children in the face of the cultural, economic, and moral pressures of our day. No institution can substitute for

the committed love, daily sacrifice, and hard work of parents in caring for their children. But every institution should support parents in their essential tasks. Our Church must be an ally and advocate for parents as they struggle to meet their children's needs at home and in an often hostile world where powerful economic and social forces can overwhelm the love and care of a family.

Our purpose is to share the facts of a society failing its children and a world neglecting children, and to explore the moral dimensions, human consequences, and religious meaning of these failures. We invite the Catholic community and the broader society to respond to this urgent moral challenge and to suggest some basic values and directions for our families, nation, and world in meeting it. We urge a reordering of priorities—personal, ecclesial, and societal—to focus more on the needs and potential of our children. This message is a call for conversion and action—a spiritual and social reawakening to the moral and human costs of neglecting our children and families.

In these reflections, we build on our past efforts, especially our statements on family, human life, and social justice. We focus on children, not as unconnected individuals, but as members of families. Every family has a mission "to guard, reveal, and communicate love," and children are at the center of that mission. We address the needs of children from a family perspective.

If society seeks to help children, it has to support families, since children's lives are nurtured or neglected, enhanced or diminished by the quality of family life.

II. The Realities

Childhood should be a happy, secure, and safe time of growth and development. For many children, it is. We are learning more and more about the remarkable human, moral, and spiritual development of young people. They are resilient, adaptive, and resourceful. But for far too many of our children all over the world, childhood is an often dangerous and overwhelming struggle.

A. *Children in the United States*

We ask you to consider these sad facts of our national life:

- Every year 1.6 million of our children are destroyed by legalized abortion even before they are born. They are denied their most basic right, the right to life itself.

- Children are the poorest members of our society—one out of five children grows up poor in the richest nation on earth. Among our youngest children, a fourth are poor. Children are nearly twice as likely to be poor as any other group. Among children, the younger you are, the more likely you are to be poor in America. And poverty means children miss the basics—the food, housing, and health care they need to grow and develop. They are deprived in a way that hurts and distorts their lives.
- Forty thousand children born each year in the United States do not live to see their first birthday. Sixty-seven newborn babies die each day in our land. Our infant mortality rate puts us last among twenty western nations.
- The United States has the highest divorce rate, the highest teenage pregnancy rate, the highest child poverty rate, and the highest abortion rate in the western world.
- An estimated 5.5 million U.S. children under twelve are hungry; another 6 million are underfed.
- The rate of teenage suicide has tripled in thirty years.
- More than 2.5 million children suffer physical, emotional, or sexual abuse or neglect in one year in the United States.
- More teenage boys die of gunshot wounds than from all natural causes combined.
- More than 25 percent of our teenagers drop out of school; SAT scores have declined 70 points since 1963.
- More than 8 million children are in families without health insurance.
- Mothers and children make up an increasing proportion of the homeless in our land.

Children need a secure and stable **family life.** However, families today are facing enormous pressures and significant change:

- Many parents, regardless of income, struggle to meet the emotional, spiritual, and physical needs of their children in the face of powerful moral, economic, and social pressures that make their task more difficult.
- Divorce has quadrupled in thirty years to touch almost half of all marriages. Half of all noncustodial parents do not see their children in the first year after divorce. Three-quarters of these parents have no contact with their children after ten years.
- Most families need two incomes to meet their economic needs. More than half of mothers with children under six are in the paid workforce.

- Almost a fourth of our children are growing up in single-parent families, most of them headed by women who are more likely to live in poverty.
- More middle-class families are experiencing greater difficulty affording a home, obtaining quality health care, and paying for their children's education, especially college.
- Families face diverse challenges in raising children: the reality of crime and violence, the allure of materialism and consumerism, continuing prejudice and intolerance, media that often belittle family values, and public policy and corporate practices that too often ignore the family responsibilities of parents.

These pressures are exacerbated by prejudice and discrimination. African American, Asian American, Hispanic, and Native American families have remarkable strengths often unappreciated by others. Against pervasive discrimination, the family in these communities has been both a refuge and a launching pad; however, minority children still face very significant obstacles. Forty-three percent of African American children grow up in poverty. A majority of these children are in single-parent families. The poverty rate for Hispanic children (32 percent) is growing more rapidly than for any other group. In addition, discrimination against women means that they still earn significantly less than men; this often has devastating consequences for children in families headed by women.

However, common stereotypes are often misleading. Only one out of ten poor children is a Black child living in a female-headed family on welfare in a central city. Most poor children are White; most are from working families; and the child poverty rate in rural America is higher than for the nation as a whole.

Changes in economic life, personal values, and American culture have combined to leave children vulnerable. Joblessness and declines in real wages have squeezed many families. Anti-family welfare, tax, health, and workplace policies have undermined children's lives. The national failure to invest adequately in programs that clearly work (e.g., Head Start, WIC, Child Health Services) has left many families without the help they need. Broader cultural and social forces, including the media, have also undermined family values and the importance of children. We are faced with a pattern of national neglect that seriously shortchanges our children. We have neither a comprehensive family policy nor a consistent concern for children. And the youngest members of our society are paying a huge price for our neglect.

B. Children in the World

Across the globe—and especially in the poorest countries—the picture is even more stark and discouraging:

- Millions of children are dying—from starvation, disease, poverty, and military conflict. According to UNICEF, forty thousand children die *every day* from malnutrition and related diseases.
- Wars have killed nearly 2 million children in the last fifteen years; more than twice that number have been physically disabled; and it is not possible to even estimate the number who have been traumatized as a result of these conflicts.
- Seven million children are growing up in refugee camps because of war and natural disasters; a slightly larger number have been uprooted from their homes in their own countries. More than five thousand refugee children without parents have been resettled over the last decade by our Church here in the United States; while, unfortunately, other undocumented children without their parents who have entered the United States are held in detention under terrible conditions.
- Approximately 80 million children work in often monotonous, repetitive, and dangerous jobs; in some countries these exploited children earn wages of five to seven cents an hour.
- Fifteen percent of the world's 2 billion children under fifteen years of age live under what UNICEF terms "especially difficult circumstances." Millions, for example, live in the streets of the exploding Third World cities, resorting to theft, drug trafficking, prostitution, and other desperate measures to survive.
- Children's futures are undermined by war, injustice, and denial of human rights around the world. For example, children pay the highest price for apartheid in South Africa, violence in Central America, repression in China, and war in the Persian Gulf and Croatia.
- Sickness ravages poor families. Diseases long banished or generally unknown in the industrialized world—measles, malaria, sleeping sickness—kill hundreds of thousands annually. And now we see the worldwide consequences of AIDS, which will produce an estimated 10 million orphans in this decade in Africa alone.

As in our own nation, poverty around the world falls most heavily and directly on women and children. They are the most likely to suffer from the chronic hunger which results from poverty and powerlessness. Their future is mortgaged to flawed "development" which increases a nation's gross national product, but worsens its distribution, helping the rich at the expense of the poor. It is women and children who suffer most when the elites of poor nations invest abroad rather than at home, and when foreign aid from more affluent nations is reduced. And they are the first victims of the cuts in social services made by developing countries to "adjust" their economies in order to pay their burdensome debts. As we pointed out in our statement on the external debt, children are literally dying of the consequences of that debt.

The sheer magnitude of these national and international statistics can obscure and overwhelm the human dimensions of this crisis. Imagine the loss and despair of a parent watching a child die of hunger. Consider the pain of a parent who cannot provide a home for a child. These realities are not abstract issues, but human tragedies and moral challenges. We believe that behind each of these numbers is a sister or brother, a child of God. The tragic fate of too many children is not simply an economic or social problem, but a sign of moral failure and a religious test.

III. The Moral and Religious Dimension

In the Catholic community, we draw on three basic resources to shape our response to this moral challenge: the Scriptures, Catholic teaching, and our experience in serving children and their families.

A. The Lessons of Scripture

In the Bible, children are both a blessing from God and a test of the community's values. The ancient Hebrews believed children were a sign of God's favor (Gn 15:1-6). Our fathers and mothers in faith prayed for children, and God answered their pleas (Gn 15:1-6; 1 Sm 1:9-21). But the Scriptures also record terrible sins against the young. Children were the victims of abuse (Ps 10:18; 94:6; Jb 22:9). Orphans were especially vulnerable and became objects of God's special care. God and his covenant upheld the rights of abandoned children (Ps 68:5; Jer 49:11), provided for their support (Dt 24:19-22), and demanded their protection (Ex 22:22-24).

Holiness and justice are to be found in those who are ready to give wholehearted, generous support to the vulnerable children: "To the fatherless be as a father, and help their mother as a husband would . . ." (Sir 4:10). "Religion that is pure and undefiled before God . . . is this," the Letter of James declares, "to care for orphans and widows in their affliction . . ." (Jas 1:27).

Under the covenant, care of orphans and widows, like that of aliens and the poor, was the responsibility of both families and the whole society. The prophets inveighed against the people for their failure to do justice "by advancing the claim of the fatherless" (Jer 5:28) and by exploiting widows and orphans (Ez 22:7). Indeed, God's continued presence among the people depended on doing justice to the oppressed:

> Only if you thoroughly reform your ways and your deeds;
> if each of you deals justly with his neighbor, if you no longer
> oppress the resident alien, the orphan, and the widow; . . .
> will I remain with you in this place, in the land which I gave
> your fathers long ago and forever. (Jer 7:4-7)

In the New Testament we read how Jesus came into the world as a vulnerable and homeless child. We also hear of God's love for us and the frequent reference to children in the parables. For example, in explaining the goodness of God, Jesus says, "Which one of you would hand his son a stone when he asks for a loaf of bread, or a snake when he asks for a fish? If you then, who are wicked, know how to give good gifts to your children, how much more will your heavenly Father give good things to those who ask him" (Mt 7:7-11).

Jesus welcomed and blessed children (Mt 19:12-15) and called his disciples to act as children in receiving the word of God. Jesus tells his disciples: "Whoever receives one child . . . in my name, receives me; and whoever receives me, receives not me but the One who sent me" (Mk 9:36-37). This parallels the story of the last judgment, where we learn that in serving "the least among us," we serve the Lord; this parable insists that our judgment depends on our response to the hungry, the thirsty, the naked (Mt 25). In our day the "orphans and widows" are poor children and single parents; the "least of these" are hungry and homeless children; unwanted, unborn children; crack babies; and children with AIDS.

The Scriptures call on believers to stand up for the poor and vulnerable. "Speak out for those who cannot speak for themselves, for the rights of the destitute, open your mouth, decree what is just, defend the needy and the poor" (Prv 31:8-9). And, the early Church was called in the First Letter of John to put love of God into action, ". . . We should love one another. . . . If someone who has worldly means sees a brother in need and refuses him compassion, how can the love of God remain in him? Children, let us love not in word or speech but in deed and truth" (1 Jn 3:11-17).

B. The Teaching of the Church

1. Traditional Social Teaching

The biblical call to speak for those who cannot speak for themselves and to make Christian love real and active has taken explicit shape over the last century in the traditional social teaching of our Church. This tradition and its key principles shape and guide our response to the moral challenge of our children. These principles include the life and dignity of the human person, human rights and responsibilities, the call to family and community, the dignity of work, the option for the poor and vulnerable, and the principle of solidarity. These principles take on increasing urgency and relevance as they are so clearly violated in the lives of so many children. Applying Catholic social teaching today requires a priority focus on children.

2. Teaching on Family

We also share a more specific ecclesial heritage of teaching on children and families. Through children, God shares with women and men a special participation in creation.[1] If we are to protect and nurture this gift of children, we must have strong families.[2]

The physical, psychological, moral, and spiritual health of children is intimately linked to the health of families. In Christian terms, the family is sacred and holy, a "community of life and love," which prepares, nourishes, and sustains the youngest members of the Church in their task of building up the kingdom of God.[3] In social terms, families are the "first and vital cell of society," the building block of community.[4]

Our family perspective demands that the rights of children are directly linked to the rights and responsibilities of families. These rights were outlined in the Holy See's *Charter of Family Rights*. They include the right to found a family, to a stable marriage, to bear and educate children in one's faith, to social and economic security, to decent housing, to protect children from harm, and to immigrate.[5]

These rights are linked to the responsibilities of families, including four fundamental tasks:

- *Families form children in a loving community.* Each member of the family shares in the responsibility to build this unique community of love. Children contribute to this community through their gift of love, respect, and obedience toward their parents. Parents, in turn, nurture their children in self-giving love, mutual respect, and discipline. In these ways, families challenge the exaggerated individualism and selfishness that so distort our society.
- *Families serve the life and dignity of children.* Men and women joined in marriage share in God's love and power as Creator by their free and responsible cooperation in transmitting the gift of human life through the moral exercise of the gift of human sexuality. This participation in God's creative activity

involves both bringing children into the world and taking part in their upbringing and education. Parents are the first and most important educators of their children. Responsible parenthood is a cornerstone of the Church's teaching on family and a healthy society.

- *Families bring children to participate in the development of society.* Parents help children grow in moral and spiritual maturity and also help to build a caring and just society. Through families, children should come to identify with the most needy in the community, especially poor and suffering children, and should develop a lifelong commitment to respond through service of the poor and disadvantaged and through action for justice and peace in their own communities and the world.
- *Families enable children to share in the life and mission of the Church.* In the family, parents communicate the Gospel to their children, and children as well as parents learn to live it in their daily lives. Parents have a responsibility, through word and example, to help make prayer and the sacraments an integral part of their children's lives. The Gospel of Jesus and the life of faith are enormous gifts to our children, offering meaning, direction, and discipline in a world that often lacks them. Parents instill in their children a commitment to loving service of others, helping them to discover in every person the image of God.

These tasks of families are shared with others, especially extended families, parishes, and other networks of family support. An African proverb suggests, "It takes a whole village to raise a child." In our society it takes grandparents and godparents, friends and relatives, teachers and pastors, and many others. We recognize and support the diverse sources of strength and help for families.

3. Society: Protector and Promoter of Children and Families

Social institutions increasingly share many of the family's responsibilities toward children, but they can never take the place of families. Rather, social institutions—government at all levels, employers, religious institutions, schools, media, community organizations—should enter into creative partnerships with families so that families can fulfill their responsibilities toward children. As we said in *Economic Justice for All,* "Economic and social policies as well as the organization of work should be continually evaluated in light of their impact on the strength and stability of family life."

These themes are reinforced by the message of Pope John Paul II's encyclical *Centesimus Annus,* which emphasizes the continuing value of Catholic social teaching. The pope calls the family "the sanctuary of life" and says:

> In order to overcome today's widespread individualistic mentality, what is required is *a concrete commitment to solidarity and charity*, beginning in the family. . . . It is urgent therefore to promote not only family policies, but also those social policies which have the family as their principal object, policies which assist the family by providing adequate resources and efficient means of support, both for bringing up children and for looking after the elderly. . . . [6]

The Holy Father also insists that the strengths and efficiency of a market economy like our own need to be harmonized with the needs and rights of families, especially the poor and workers, and he warns against overly bureaucratic responses to family needs.

C. The Experience of the Catholic Community

For decades, even centuries, the Catholic community has been deeply involved in meeting the human, pastoral, and educational needs of children and their families. In 1727 the Ursuline Sisters founded the first Catholic home for abandoned children in New Orleans. Presently, millions of families are served by Catholic Charities, which offers help in meeting basic needs, providing foster care and adoption, family counseling and alternatives to abortion. Hungry and homeless children are assisted in our shelters, by our soup kitchens and our parish-based food pantries. Our elementary and secondary schools offer educational opportunities to millions of children. Through parish religious education and adult education programs, we provide ongoing programs of marriage preparation and enrichment, natural family planning, family ministry, youth ministry, and parenting skills.

Our national and state conferences of Catholic bishops, Catholic Charities, arch/diocesan ministerial offices, and other organizations are deeply involved in advocacy for children and families. We also provide ongoing programs of family ministry and marriage preparation and enrichment. The Campaign for Human Development helps to empower families in their search for justice. Around the world, missionaries, Catholic Relief Services, Holy Childhood Association, and our immigration and refugee programs offer hope and help to desperate children and families.

Because of our long and continued involvement with children and families, the concerns on which we now focus are neither new nor abstract, but rather evidence of real, continuing, and perhaps worsening conditions for children. We bring not only our values to this concern, but also broad experience and expertise in caring for children and their families. No institution is more deeply involved in serving the needs of children than our community of faith. We bring not only deep conviction, but also vast experience to the challenge of meeting the needs of children.

IV. The Moral Challenge

Believers, as heirs of this religious tradition, cannot confront the tragic situation of so many children and turn away. As family members and citizens we must measure our choices as individuals, as a nation, and as a global community for their impact on children and families.

Within our *families*, we need to teach—by word and example, by our priorities and our lives—the values that help our children grow to be responsible, faithful, caring, and disciplined. Our love, our values, and our faith are passed on not only by what we say, but also by how we live. Parents, especially, show love for their children by providing for their emotional and spiritual needs, as well as their material needs. This occurs, for example, when parents spend time with their children, when they discipline and guide them, when they show affection, and when they teach their children to pray and grow in faith.

In our *churches* we need to help families in their essential roles, offering both support and challenge. This requires liturgy and pastoral care responsive to children and families, first-rate religious education, schools, and other vital ministries. We can prepare people for marriage and help families learn the skills of parenting. We need to lift up the vocation of marriage and family life and offer to people the resources of our spiritual and sacramental heritage in effective and creative ways: through education, family life movements, family retreats, outreach to families in distress, support groups, youth programs, counseling, and the timeless spiritual resources of prayer, liturgy, and meditation.

As a *nation*, we need to make children and families our first priority; to invest in their future; to combat the forces—cultural, economic, and moral—which hurt children and destroy families; to manage our economy, shape our government, and direct our institutions to support and not undermine our families. In our society, we need to resist the trends toward excessive individualism, materialism, and the quest for personal pleasure above all else. Real happiness and satisfaction come from who we are and how we care for one another rather than from what we have. Our news and entertainment media, despite some laudable efforts, too often attack family values, undermine moral principles, and expose children to violence and to sexual themes on a daily basis. Fundamental values of integrity, compassion, respect for others, and honesty must be encouraged and reinforced by the culture at large.

In an *interdependent world*, we need to see clearly how children pay the price for global poverty and indifference, for official corruption, for far too much debt and not enough development, for a global economy dominated by the industrial countries which further impoverishes the poor. We need to understand and act on the links between the children we see dying on the nightly news and the economic and political structures that bring poverty and hunger to millions.

As believers and citizens, we need—each of us—to use our values, voices, and votes to hold our public officials accountable and to shape a society that puts our children first.

V. Criteria for National Policy

The most important work to help our children is done quietly—in our homes and neighborhoods, our parishes and community organizations. No government can love a child and no policy can substitute for a family's care, but clearly families can be helped or hurt in their irreplaceable roles. Government can either support or undermine families as they cope with the moral, social, and economic stresses of caring for children.

There has been an unfortunate, unnecessary, and unreal polarization in discussions of the best way to help families. Some emphasize the primary role of moral values and personal responsibility, the sacrifices to be made and the personal behaviors to be avoided, but they often ignore or de-emphasize the broader forces which hurt families, e.g., the impact of economics, discrimination, and anti-family policies. Others emphasize the social and economic forces that undermine families and the responsibility of government to meet human needs, but they often neglect the importance of basic values and personal responsibility.

The undeniable fact is that our children's future is shaped both by the values of their parents and the policies of our nation. Families are undermined by parental irresponsibility *and* discrimination and poverty. Children's lives are enriched by their parents' sacrifices and by economic policies that help mothers and fathers meet the demands of parenthood. It is time to move beyond rigid ideologies and political posturing to focus on the real needs of families. We believe parental responsibility *and* broader social responsibility, changed behavior *and* changed policies are complementary requirements to help families.

Our nation must move beyond partisan and ideological rhetoric to help shape a new consensus that supports families in their essential roles and insists that public policy support families, especially poor and vulnerable children. We will continue to advocate policies, programs, and priorities which meet these basic criteria:

1. *Put children and families first.* Analyze every policy and program—diocesan, parish, domestic, and international—for its impact on children and families; look at every proposal from a family perspective. Poor and vulnerable children have first claim on our common efforts.

2. *Help; don't hurt.* Insist that economic, tax, education, welfare, immigration and refugee, and human service policies support families rather than undermine families; that programs encourage self-help rather than promote dependency.

3. *Those with the greatest need require the greatest response.* This is the "option for the poor" in action. While every family needs support, poor families and families facing discrimination carry the greatest burdens and require the most help. With limited resources, we need to focus assistance on those with the greatest needs.

4. *Empower families. Help families meet their responsibilities to their children.* Families need to be empowered to make the choices that meet their diverse needs—in education, child care, health, work, and other areas. Tax, workplace, divorce, and welfare policies must help families stay together and care for their children.

5. *Fight economic and social forces which threaten children and family life.* Poverty; joblessness; lack of access to affordable health care, child care, and decent housing; and discrimination are among the greatest threats to families and children. Efforts to overcome poverty, provide decent jobs, and promote equal opportunity are pro-family priorities.

6. *Build on the strengths of families; reward responsibility and sacrifice for children.* Policy must recognize the resiliency and capacity for self-help of families and reward members of families who avoid destructive behavior.

7. *Recognize that foreign policy is increasingly children's policy.* Global poverty, armed conflict, and systematic injustice threaten the lives of millions of children and their families. Children will pay a terrible price for indifference toward international, economic policy and neglect of human rights.

These criteria have led our conference to support a wide variety of pro-family initiatives at both the national and international level:

- Family and medical leave
- Pro-life legislation and alternatives to abortion

- Broad-based child care which allows for religious and cultural values
- An increase in the minimum wage and Earned Income Tax Credit
- Pro-family welfare reform
- Proposals for choice in education
- Civil rights laws
- Laws prohibiting housing discrimination against families with children
- Family-based immigration
- Asylum and refugee policy
- New federal budget priorities
- Increased access to health care and decent housing
- Support for substance abuse programs
- Broader proposals for economic justice and family support
- Reform of U.S. foreign assistance programs

VI. Directions for National Policy

In fashioning national policy, our society must recognize a serious problem both in our national and personal priorities. Our society neglects the needs of poor children. When our nation makes a commitment, it can make a difference. Decades ago poverty haunted large numbers of our elderly citizens. As a society we decided this was intolerable and put in place Social Security, Medicare, and other measures to protect the dignity of the elderly—with an impressive drop in poverty among their population. Now, our children are more likely to be poor, but our government spends less on children's needs. Cuts in federal expenditures have come disproportionately in programs serving children. Children don't vote; they don't contribute to political campaigns, and therefore, they are more likely to be ignored by governments and policy makers. Money alone will not solve the problems of poor families, but there is no substitute for wise and thoughtful investment in meeting the needs of America's children. We need to invest now, because the children are suffering now; and if we do not invest now, we will all suffer later.

At the same time, national policy should reinforce basic moral values while recognizing the diversity of America's families. The problems of American families stem from the misplaced priorities of our federal government, of some parents, and of society at large. Studies indicate that parents spend 40 percent less time with their children today than they did just twenty years ago. The absence of many fathers is a particularly serious problem—not only economically but socially as well. Public policy ought to reward parents who take their responsibilities seriously and encourage more responsible behavior in those who do not. The policies of our nation should neither exaggerate nor ignore the changes in family life. They must recognize both the diversity of families and the fact that, in general, stable, loving two-parent families offer the best chance for children.

Traditional moral values are not relics of a bygone age. Rather, they are the best guides to a productive future for our children and health for our society. A case in point is the often confused discussion of the best way to confront the AIDS crisis and its growing impact on young people. We continue to insist that our response should combine both compassion for those who live with AIDS and responsibility in avoiding behaviors which put people at risk. Instead of promoting the illusion of *safe sex,* we need to warn our children and society of the dangers of sexual promiscuity and drug abuse. Our moral convictions about expressing human sexuality within marriage now represent not only appropriate moral guidance, but also wise health counsel. Responsibility, unselfishness, concern for others, fidelity in marriage, and commitment to children are the building blocks of a creative and satisfying life and a just and decent society. They ought to be recognized in our public policies, encouraged in our media, and supported by our community institutions. In our society, we need to develop incentives and rewards for policies and behaviors that serve the needs of children and disincentives for those actions and policies which threaten or hurt children.

There is growing consensus in this area. A series of studies, reports, and a bipartisan commission have documented the needs of children and the failures of our society to meet those needs. And increasingly, experts and organizations including marriage and family counselors have shown signs of rethinking the positive values of stable marriage, the human costs of easy divorce laws, the social costs of excessive individualism, and the consequences of economic pressures on families.

We welcome and support renewed efforts of the helping professions to promote the reconciliation of spouses as a viable alternative to divorce. We acknowledge the significant changes in family life; we affirm the major contributions of women in the workforce; and we support and applaud the often heroic efforts of single-parent families. We also emphasize the value of parents staying together and sacrificing to raise children. Children generally do best when they have the love and support—personal and material—of both their parents.

Many single-parent families overcome huge economic and social obstacles, but others are overwhelmed by these forces. Government efforts need to help families stay together and overcome the many pressures that pull families apart. We owe special help to those parents—mothers or fathers—who face family life alone, knowing how discrimination and other forces make a difficult job even tougher. This is especially true when single parenthood is combined with poverty, as it often is.

A. Protecting the Lives of Children

1. Unborn Children

From conception, unborn children are most at risk from this nation's anti-life policy of abortion on demand. The ultimate example of powerlessness is to be destroyed before birth. And a terrible sign of national failure is the implicit suggestion to many women—especially poor women—that they must choose between life for their unborn child and a decent future for themselves and for their families. We need to shape a society where economic and social forces do not leave women facing fundamental questions of life and death alone and isolated without the support of a caring community. We reiterate our strong opposition to abortion and government funding for abortion. We will continue through education to expose the realities of abortion, to promote life-giving alternatives to abortion, and to provide the loving choice of adoption and caring support for pregnant women and mothers and children, especially the poor.

Unborn children are also at risk from AIDS and substance abuse, both of which call for expanded national efforts at education and prevention, the provision of prenatal and other health care, and treatment and rehabilitation of abusers of alcohol and other drugs.

2. Abuse and Neglect

Children are hurt and killed by violence within families. Families are destroyed by verbal, physical, and sexual abuse. These brutal and tragic realities threaten the lives and welfare of millions of children and women. They require education, treatment, and prevention. The family must be a place of safety, not of danger. And society must act to protect children and women from family violence and sexual abuse. Physical and sexual abuse of children constitutes a terrible betrayal of trust, a threat to their emotional and physical health, and a challenge for every institution that serves children. Child pornography represents a particularly terrible threat to children. They serve as subjects in the production of pornography and sex objects for those who make use of pornographic materials. This illegal and immoral use of children for sexual purposes and profit must be confronted and stopped. Pornography demeans women, degrades our society, and destroys the love at the center of human sexuality. We need effective, constitutional remedies which protect children, women, and all of society.

Growing violent abuse and neglect of infants and children have led to families where children are not only rejected but also endangered and to the phenomenon of the "no parent" family. These sad realities have created widespread strains on our child welfare system, including lack of adequate foster homes, inadequate support services, a shortage of trained personnel, inappropriate placements, and a serious absence of preventive services. System-wide reform is called for, including special attention to families where there is substance abuse and families in which children have serious emotional problems. The primary goal of reform should be preserving families, wherever possible, through long-term, home-based services and programs designed to meet individual family needs before children's safety is jeopardized. We need far more coordination in the provision of family services, emphasizing prevention and replacing fragmented individual programs with concern for the whole family.

We also support policies which assist families who choose to adopt children or provide loving foster care for children at risk. Special efforts are needed to help minority and older children and children with disabilities find loving and supportive homes. Creative public policy and private action are needed to help every child find a home where his or her unique needs can be met.

B. Economic Help for Families

1. Poverty and Families

Poverty is not merely the lack of adequate financial resources. It often entails a more profound kind of deprivation; a denial of full participation in the economic, social, and political life of society; and an inability to influence decisions that affect one's life. It means being powerless in a way that assaults not only one's pocketbook but also one's fundamental human dignity.

Many children are poor because they were born to young parents who are unmarried and are not equipped to support them, but many others are poor because their parents are casualties of economic forces beyond their control: recession, industrial restructuring, erosion of real wages, unemployment, and discrimination in hiring and promotion. Staggering increases in the costs of essentials such as rent and medical care have meant that even full-time work is no guarantee against poverty. Moreover, the holes in the safety net have gotten larger, making it much harder for families to recover from a layoff or extensive medical bills.

2. Decent Jobs at Decent Wages

Despite the long uninterrupted period of economic expansion in the 1980s, child poverty increased significantly in this nation. Clearly, economic growth alone is not sufficient to solve the problem, and the recent recession has already cost 2 million Americans their jobs. As we wrote in our 1986 pastoral letter on the U.S. economy, targeted economic policies are necessary to create sufficient jobs at adequate wages to support families in dignity. Decent jobs at decent wages—what used to be called a "family wage"—are the most important economic assets for families. Periodic increases in the minimum wage to reflect inflation would be a useful step in this direction.

Too many of our young people come to adulthood without goals or the skills needed in the world of work. All too often some succumb to the allure of crime or to the despair of a life without direction or accomplishment. Greater public and private efforts are needed to introduce young people to the challenges and rewards of meaningful work. Communities, in partnership with the public sector, should offer the kinds of training, apprenticeships, and service opportunities that will prepare young people to use their talents and energy in positive ways. National policies should ensure that all those who can work in fact have the opportunity to contribute to the common good by their labor.

3. Changing Tax Policy to Help Families

The 1986 tax reform law and later expansion of the Earned Income Tax Credit have lightened some of the federal tax burden of poverty-level families with children, but the tax code needs further reform to bring fairness to the treatment of families, especially to those raising children on modest incomes. The current tax code fails to reflect the real costs of raising children and offers inadequate help to families with children.

We welcome proposals to reform the tax code to help families cope with the high cost of raising children. These proposals, which have drawn bipartisan support, would allow middle-income families with children to keep more of what they earn and would help lift low-income families out of poverty. Such proposals deserve serious consideration and general support in light of the current bias against children in our tax laws, especially those in low- and moderate-income families. As one commentator pointed out recently, taxpayers in America today can receive a bigger tax break for breeding racehorses than for raising children. We continue to support an expanded Earned Income Tax Credit to assist poor, working families. This pro-work, pro-family provision needs to be enhanced and supported as an important contribution to tax fairness.

4. Help for Poor Children

Children's lives are diminished every day in this nation because of the low level of welfare benefits. Misleading stereotypes of welfare families and misguided budget priorities are largely responsible for the failure of both federal and state governments to protect children from hunger, homelessness, and deprivation. We reiterate our call for a minimum national welfare benefit that will permit children and their parents to live in dignity. A decent society will not balance its budget on the backs of poor children. Sadly, the fiscal difficulties in many of our states has meant disproportionate cuts and unfair burdens for poor families.

Some aspects of welfare are anti-family. For example, in many states, unemployed fathers must leave the home so that the children can get welfare assistance beyond an initial six-month period. We have frequently called for true welfare reform that would be both pro-family and pro-child. No family should have to separate as a condition of receiving assistance.

At a time when most mothers of young children are employed at least part-time, our society sometimes loses sight of the value of parental care of young children. As preschoolers in day care becomes the norm, we fear the work of mothers in the home is becoming devalued, since it does not offer the economic rewards or recognition of other work.

Our conference strongly supports effective voluntary programs to equip parents with education and job skills. We oppose compulsory and poorly designed efforts to require them to hand over to others the daily care of their preschool children. The fact that children are poor and in need of government aid does not take away their basic human right to be cared for by their parents if that is their family's choice.

C. Helping Families at Work

1. Family-Friendly Policies

Families need workplace policies that promote responsive child care arrangements; flexible employment terms and conditions for parents; and family and medical leave for parents of newborns, sick children, and aging parents. Increasing corporate efforts in this area are a major sign of hope for employees who are also members of families. Public policy should ensure and promote these family-friendly workplace arrangements, adequate public funding of broad-based and inclusive child care and other essential services needed by families, especially poor families. In our own structures and institutions, we need to move toward personnel policies that more fully reflect our commitment to family life.

For seven years our conference has called for a law to protect people who have to take time away from their jobs to handle serious family responsibilities. Parents should not have to worry about losing their jobs when they welcome a new child, nurse a sick spouse, or comfort a dying parent.

Passage of a family leave bill would not only protect the jobs of parents whose employers might otherwise penalize them for taking time for family responsibilities, but it would also send a message that the nation sees children as a real priority for all of society.

2. Child Labor

Another aspect of children's vulnerability to economic exploitation is new signs of child labor abuse. This abuse accompanies changes in industrial and agricultural patterns, in increasing pools of immigrants, in the dramatic increase in families living below the poverty line, and in the disregard for this nation's long-established laws designed to protect children. Improved child labor law enforcement must be combined with adequate family economic support so that families do not depend on exploitation of children for economic survival.

D. Families and Discrimination

1. Race

Racial and ethnic discrimination hurts many families, limiting the income and future of African American, Asian American, Hispanic, and Native American families. Black children are twice as likely to be poor as White children. Minority children are also more likely to lack health care, to live in substandard housing, and to attend inadequate schools. Equal opportunity in education, affirmative action in employment, and nondiscrimination in housing are essential steps to ensure a productive and just future for children in minority families.

2. Gender

The lives of children are clearly bound with the lives and welfare of women in multiple ways. Discrimination against women continues to be a major contributor to children's poverty. Measures to combat economic discrimination against women—whether working in or outside the home—deserve strong support. Family decisions about parents' job choices should not be dictated by economic pressures which require both parents to work full-time outside the home or should not be frustrated by discrimination which limits women's opportunity. Public policy and private action should encourage a range of possibilities, so that parents are able to work at home or are able to use job-sharing, flex time, and other means to better meet their obligations both as workers and as parents to their children.

Mothers who work outside the home to support their children often still struggle to balance work and family responsibilities and are confronted with continuing discrimination. As a group, women are still often relegated to jobs where low wages and few opportunities for advancement are common. Even in other occupations, some women experience continuing discrimination and sexual harassment, making it difficult to support their children with dignity. In *Economic Justice for All* we called for attention to proposals to correct the disparities in men's and women's wages, and we have supported legislation to protect women from discrimination in hiring and promotions. A society that discriminates against women impoverishes its children.

E. Meeting Children's Basic Needs

Children need the love, acceptance, and support of a family that cares for them. But families need to be able to meet basic physical and social needs to help their children grow and develop.

1. Education

Adequate preschool, primary, and secondary education is essential to full development of our children. Nevertheless, several factors combine to produce increasing numbers of school dropouts, unskilled citizens, and functionally illiterate adults. Inadequate education is one of the surest predictors of poverty, contributing strongly to intergenerational cycles of poverty. Programs that work—Head Start for preschoolers, education for children with disabilities, and vocational training—must be made available to every child who needs them.

Society at large is increasingly recognizing the effectiveness of Catholic schools in meeting the educational needs of children, including poor and minority children. Families must be given genuine choice in education—selecting the public, parochial, or private school that best serves their family's needs. Parents have the primary right and responsibility for the education of children. For this reason, our nation needs education policies that respect parental choice such as vouchers and tax credits. We also need creative policies that will improve poor quality schools, increase parental and family involvement, and encourage teacher excellence in education. All schools need to support and affirm parents in their roles as the primary educators of their children—reinforcing basic values, discipline, honesty, character, citizenship, and concern for others.

2. Food and Hunger

The continuing reality of hungry children in our midst is a dismaying sign of failure. We see signs of this failure in our food pantries, soup kitchens, parishes, and schools. New investment and improvements are needed in basic nutritional programs, such as food stamps, to ensure that no child goes hungry in America. An urgent priority is the Women, Infant, and Children (WIC) program, that still does not reach all expectant mothers, infants, and young children in need.

3. Health Care

The lack of basic health care—and factors tied directly to poverty—have been documented in the tragic reality that poor children are twice as likely as other children to have physical or mental disabilities or other chronic health conditions that impair daily activity. Our nation's continuing failure to guarantee access to quality health care for all people exacts its most painful toll in the preventable sickness, disability, and deaths of our infants and children. Beginning with our children and their mothers, we must extend access to quality health care to all our people. Quality and accessible prenatal care is essential for healthy children. There can be no excuse for the failure to ensure adequate health care and nutrition for pregnant women. Nothing would make a greater contribution to reducing infant mortality than progress in this area.

4. Housing

Many families cannot find or afford decent housing, or must spend so much of their income for shelter that they forego other necessities, such as food and medicine. National policy has neglected the housing needs of families—with serious consequences for children who are growing up in shelters or in overcrowded or substandard housing. We support housing policies which seek to preserve and increase the supply of affordable housing and help families pay for it. We urge national and local governments as well as community groups to work together in bringing about housing, planning, and zoning policies that reflect the needs for affordable housing for families. We also continue to call for efforts to eliminate housing discrimination, especially against families with children.

5. Families with Persons with Disabilities

Children with disabilities are fortunate indeed when they are born into or adopted by families that recognize that the spark of life is valuable, despite what impairments may accompany that gift. However, most disabled children are born into families who have no prior experience with such challenges.

Families with disabled children need and deserve extra support and encouragement from society, their communities, and the Church.

Government at all levels must do more to ensure that children receive the medical, educational, rehabilitation, and social services they need to grow up to realize their full human potential. For example, the conference has pressed for several years for reform of the Supplemental Security Income (SSI) Program to make benefits available to the many disabled children whose requests for assistance had been denied. Recent court decisions and legislative action setting more reasonable criteria and requiring outreach should be implemented as soon as possible.

Parents with disabilities are sometimes prevented from providing adequately for their children. Job discrimination, physical barriers in public transportation and work sites, and lack of rehabilitative services all contribute to the isolation and segregation of disabled parents and their children. The Americans with Disabilities Act of 1990 has been called the most significant civil rights legislation since 1964. For the first time it was required that employment, transportation, public accommodations, and telecommunications be made fully accessible to disabled persons. All Americans need to work together to see the new law fully and properly implemented to benefit children and adults with disabling conditions.

F. Divorce and Child Support

It is also time for society to reconsider the consequences of permissive divorce, particularly in the case of couples with children. All of us have a stake in strong, stable families; yet, as a society, we do too little to help couples stay together and work things out during the inevitable times of stress and conflict. While many single parents struggle heroically to provide the love and care that normally require two parents, who can doubt that growing up in a secure environment with both parents generally gives children a head start?

In the United States today, one million children see their parents divorce each year. Another million children are born annually to single parents. Social and economic realities now confirm values which the churches have long taught—that the economic, emotional, and spiritual well-being of children is significantly diminished by divorce and out-of-wedlock birth, and that the negative consequences for children's futures, the lives of women, and for society at large are numerous and pervasive.

The facts are that family structure remains an important predictor of economic standing in society, and two-parent families generally are the most effective units for raising children. Public policy must be designed to help families stay together, to enhance their capacity for child-rearing and for passing on moral and social values to their children, and to reinforce parental responsibilities.

As a Church, we need to reinvigorate our pastoral ministry to families, being a companion to parents whose marriages are strained, offering hope and practical assistance to them in times of trouble, and helping them strengthen their marriage for their children, of course, but also for themselves.

While keeping families together is our goal, we recognize the widespread tragedy of divorce and the realities of violence and destructive behavior within some families. We are not advocating that people remain in relationships which seriously endanger or harm members of a family. We do advocate that laws recognize the frequently devastating consequences of divorce on children.

In the area of divorce law, society should

1. Embrace a "children first" principle that focuses on adequate property and income to meet the needs of the children and their custodial parent before resolving disposition of marital and individual property
2. Take into account the impact of motherhood on a woman's earning capacity as well as the per capita expenses of the household with women and children
3. Introduce "braking" mechanisms that encourage, for example, resolution of matters involving a child's future before settling questions of property and maintenance

Our nation also needs tough new rules for establishing and collecting child support from absent parents and for closing the gap between what can reasonably be collected and the actual costs of raising children. Effective means must be found to ensure that absent parents provide for their children's needs.

Among the possibilities that should be considered are

1. Establishment of minimum child-support awards based on the number of children and the absent parent's income
2. Automatic wage withholding, not only on new cases as required by law, but on existing child support orders
3. Possible registration of social security numbers of both parents on birth certificates
4. More vigorous efforts by state agencies to establish paternity of children born out-of-wedlock. Perhaps most important, states must invest more resources to locate and collect support from runaway parents who frequently move across state lines to escape their responsibilities.

While much is appropriately said about how the lives of women and children are bound so closely together, we wish to say a specific word about the importance of fathers. A crucial measure of a man is the manner in which he cares for his family—whether children see his love, respect, and care for their mother; and whether he is involved in their daily care, emotional support, spiritual growth, education, and development. For too many women, the care of children is a lonely commitment lacking the full and active participation of fathers. In these cases, children lose vital emotional support, and fathers miss one of the richest and most challenging human experiences. Parenting should be a partnership of love and mutual support—fully involving both mother and father.

G. Broader Cultural Forces

There are broader cultural and societal forces that contribute to the neglect of children. An ethic of excessive individualism, a culture of consumerism, and a preoccupation with material progress have contributed to a situation where sacrifice for others and concern for the common good are neglected virtues.

In our society children are too often considered a liability, rather than the sacred promise of the future. Sadly, some young couples are fearful or indifferent to the joys and responsibilities of bringing children into the world and could miss one of the most enriching and creative dimensions of human life. In many families—rich, poor, and in-between—children miss the emotional, intellectual, and spiritual support they desperately need to thrive.

A particularly influential force is the communications media. Too often this powerful cultural force seems less an ally and more an adversary in sharing basic values and helping shape healthy children. With notable exceptions, our children are often exposed to pervasive violence; casual sex; and racial, ethnic, and sexual stereotypes in music, film, and television. We hope media could increasingly reinforce basic values of honesty, compassion, respect for others, and fairness, rather than simply send messages that diminish and distort human life and love. Changed policies in our nation must be matched by changed values in our society at large.

VII. International Dimensions

Internationally, the needs are no less urgent and the problems are, if anything, more intractable. The cheap labor of children helps debt-ridden Third World countries pay their creditors. The intensification of local conflicts through the international arms trade and, until recently, the competing strategies of superpowers, displaces children and diverts public spending from meeting their basic needs. And adjustment programs conceived in macroeconomic terms by donor governments and international development institutions bring increased suffering to families and children who are already the victims of ill-conceived development policies.

But our actions for children abroad are likely to be less direct and our prescriptions less detailed. We do not—and should not—control the internal policies of Third World governments. Yet the United States, representing nearly one-third of the world's economic powers, cannot escape a heavy responsibility to those who do not benefit from the global economy, especially, in our view, its least responsible victims—the millions of desperate Third World children.

The fate of children, however, cannot be separated from the fate of their societies. As long as so many nations languish in poverty, the fate of many children will be grim. To overcome the legacy of neglect and mismanagement, indifference, and corruption will require new policies in our nation, in other affluent societies, and in the poor countries themselves.

The UN World Summit on Children and its Convention on the Rights of the Child outlined a constructive agenda for action. The promises made at that summit must be kept. The basic human rights of children must be respected and promoted, and their basic needs must be met. The agenda is long and comprehensive:

- Shelter and relief for refugees and the homeless
- Food aid for disaster victims
- Medical treatment for the sick
- Maternal and child health programs
- Basic education and child care
- Improved nutrition
- The elimination of child labor, children in military service, and other exploitative practices

But more fundamental reforms are necessary. Foreign policy, military policy, and international economic policy are also children's policies. Advocates for children need to be deeply involved in designing, implementing, and assessing international policy since the international economic system and the policies and practices that support and perpetuate it are taking the future of so many children hostage.

As recent papal encyclicals have pointed out, we need a new vision of solidarity in which poor children are seen not as remote issues or abstract problems, but as our sons and daughters, members of a global human family. We especially need to be their advocates here in the United States where global economic policy is so often made.

U.S. economic policy touches four key international economic relationships—trade, aid, finance, and investment.

- We need an *international trading system* that helps poor children by allocating the benefits of trade more equitably and ensures that poor countries receive fair prices for their exports. The exploitation of child labor for competitive advantage is essentially wrong; nor does it lead to authentic development. Unbridled competition is not an adequate or acceptable rationale for a trade policy; neither is selfish protectionism that simply restricts imports from the developing world.
- We need a *foreign aid program* that gives greater priority to the basic needs of families and children in the developing countries than to the national security or competitive advantage of the United States or the military appetites of Third World governments. Development must be understood and promoted in terms of helping poor people improve the quality of their lives and build for their future, rather than merely increasing the quantity of their possessions and their nation's military arsenal.
- We need a *global financial system* that looks at the human consequences of the massive external debt of the developing countries and realistically attempts to relieve it through a genuine sharing of responsibility among creditors and debtors. We cannot approach this problem as no more than a question of exchange rates, inflation, and debt service. This results in policies in the debtor countries that further punish children and others by reducing housing, education, transportation, and other public services. It also often deprives them of food in order to increase the export of agricultural products that will earn the foreign exchange required to pay external debts.
- And we need an *increase in both foreign and domestic investment* in developing countries which neither creates dependency nor enriches investors at the expense of poor families. Business firms in the United States and elsewhere have demonstrated many times that there is no intrinsic contradiction between the pursuit of reasonable profit and the realization of social and economic justice. It is neither moral nor necessary to invest in enterprises that injure or exploit natural resources or people, especially children.

There are other important priorities. We are required to address the continuing danger for children that comes with the still unresolved conflicts in the Middle East, Central America, and other parts of the world. The anti-child and anti-family coercive population and abortion policies of some societies deserve our continued opposition. We cannot ignore the pervasive discrimination against women in some parts of the world which jeopardizes the lives of female infants and deprives girls of a promising future. Finally, the continuing human costs of the lethal international arms trade which robs children of opportunity and assistance require our active resistance as well. Our work for peace is a work for the children of the world since children pay a huge price for warfare. Catholic Relief Services and the UN report the terrible suffering of children in Iraq in the aftermath of the Persian Gulf War. Our conference has joined with others in advocating the restructuring of economic sanctions to pursue regional security and effective arms control without putting at risk the vulnerable children of Iraq.

Environmental concerns touch our children. The United Nations' 1990 report on "Children and the Environment" puts this point very succinctly: "What do we owe these children—our children and our grandchildren? We owe them a planet fit to live on and capable of sustaining the future."

We also need to recognize fully the family dimensions of refugee and immigration policies, seeking to keep families together and to respect the rights and dignity of families driven from their homes by violence, oppression, or injustice.

In the international arena, as in the national, we need policies and programs aimed not only at solving problems, but also even more at preventing them. Preventive medicine is almost always less costly than other treatment, but foresight is also harder and less clear than hindsight. But we now know more clearly from experience how debt burdens accumulate, what kinds of investments create or perpetuate dependency, what sorts of development assistance programs work or do not work, and how trade practices harm working people and the poor here and abroad.

In our hearts, we know something is wrong as we watch children die on the nightly news. We need to link those heartbreaking pictures of hunger and desperation to the structures of debt and development, conflict and violence which contribute—directly or indirectly—to the death of those children. We can no longer remain indifferent. We need to respond not only with sadness and contributions, but with concrete commitment to seek change in the way the world treats children. Foreign policy is frequently children's policy, and people who care for children need to be deeply involved in assessing the consequences of economic policy and military action for its impact on children. We need to see and hear more clearly the stories of our missionaries and Catholic Relief Services who share with us the terrible consequences of violence, poverty, debt, and injustice on the lives of children. We need to see Jesus in the hungry and helpless children who haunt our world.

VIII. A Call to Action

We are approaching the third millennium. Can we summon the will and the ways to make our families, our nation, and our world welcoming and decent places for our children? We hope the Catholic community will become a persistent, informed, and committed voice for children and families, urging all American institutions from neighborhood associations to the federal government to put our children first. Let us find life-giving and loving alternatives to the despair of abortion. Let us insist that by the year 2000 we will finally eliminate poverty among children in this affluent society, and we will have a world where children will no longer die of hunger. Let us support all families in their struggle to offer their children the values, help, and hope they need. Let us seek to break the cycle of poverty and destructive behavior which leaves so many children imprisoned.

1992 is an election year. While others are campaigning for public office, let us campaign for children. Let us insist that the needs of our children, all children, but especially unborn children and poor children, take first place in the dialogue over the values and vision that ought to guide our nation. Let us also campaign within our Church to develop a genuine family perspective in our own policies and programs and in our ministries and services. As bishops we pledge to keep these concerns before our conference through our various committees and our offices so that we, too, move beyond rhetoric to action of behalf of our children.

We call on the institutions of Catholic life to join with us in continuing to reach out and support children and their parents. A great deal is already being done—in thousands of parishes and schools, in Catholic Charities and diocesan programs. Let us build on this solid foundation to assess all our efforts from a family perspective and become even more effective sources of help and advocacy for children and families. In the months and years to come, let us with even greater urgency and commitment focus our pastoral care, direct our services, and lift our voices to enhance the life and dignity of all children, especially poor children.

It is not only poor children, however, who are vulnerable and in need of our concrete commitment. *All* children need our active concern. The children of affluence, too, can experience poverty, a spiritual and moral poverty according to Robert Coles, noted author and psychiatrist, and others. These children—indeed, all children—need parents who care enough about them to give them time, one of the surest measures of human love. They also need appropriate discipline, i.e., loving limits in which they can grow into mature men and women, who themselves are full of care for the next generation. And when parents are unable to fully meet their children's needs, other adults must demonstrate that children belong to a larger, loving community, and society at large must act to protect the life, dignity, and rights of all God's children.

In closing, we would like to say a special word to parents—a word of appreciation, gratitude, and hope. We recognize the joy and hope and occasional sadness and hurt that come with the difficult and exhilarating responsibility of being a good mother or father. Children challenge, but they also educate. They can open our eyes to new depths of spiritual and religious insight. They test our patience, touch our hearts, and fill our lives. We appreciate the sacrifice, care, and hard work that make a parent the clearest example of God's love in our midst.

IX. Conclusion

For generations, the Catholic community has reached out to children—to welcome them into our faith, to teach them, to serve their spiritual growth, and to offer food, shelter, and help at times of need. We have defended their right to life itself and their right to live with dignity, to realize the bright promise and opportunity of childhood. Now we renew this commitment and build on it. We seek to bring new hope and concrete help to a generation of children at risk. We seek to measure our ministry, our nation, and our world for the manner in which we protect the lives, dignity, and rights of all God's children.

This is a work of faith: a commitment of a community that believes that we are judged by our response to those most in need—poor and vulnerable children.

This is a work of hope: a commitment to the future, to the children who will shape the Church, the nation, and the world of tomorrow.

This is a work of love: a commitment to reach out and care for the children in our midst and around the world who desperately need our help.

Two thousand years ago, Jesus said, "Let the children come to me" (Lk 18:16). Today, as his followers, we say let us put our children first; let us shape our families, churches, nation, and world to care for our most precious gift—our children.

Notes

1. Second Vatican Council, *Pastoral Constitution on the Church in the Modern World* (*Gaudium et Spes*), no. 50.
2. We define family here as "an intimate community of persons bound together by blood, marriage, or adoption for the whole of life. In our Catholic tradition, the family proceeds from marriage—an intimate, exclusive, permanent, and faithful partnership of husband and wife. This definition is intentionally normative and recognizes that the Church's

normative approach is not shared by all (NCCB Ad Hoc Committee on Marriage and Family Life, *A Family Perspective in Church and Society: A Manual for All Pastoral Leaders* [Washington, D.C.: United States Catholic Conference, 1988], 19).

3.   John Paul II, *On the Family (Familiaris Consortio)* (Washington, D.C.: United States Catholic Conference, 1981), nos. 17, 50.

4.   Second Vatican Council, *Decree on the Apostolate of the Laity (Apostolicam Actuositatem)*, no. 11.

5.   *Familiaris Consortio*, no. 46.

6.   John Paul II, *On the Hundredth Anniversary of Rerum Novarum (Centesimus Annus)* (Washington, D.C.: United States Catholic Conference, 1991), no. 49.

Source: Washington, D.C.: United States Catholic Conference, 1992.

Renewing the Earth:
An Invitation to Reflection
and Action on Environment in Light
of Catholic Social Teaching

A Pastoral Statement of the United States Catholic Conference

November 1991

Faced with the widespread destruction of the environment, people everywhere are coming to understand that we cannot continue to use the goods of the earth as we have in the past. ... A new *ecological awareness* is beginning to emerge. ... The ecological crisis is a moral issue.[1]

I. Signs of the Times

At its core, the environmental crisis is a moral challenge. It calls us to examine how we use and share the goods of the earth, what we pass on to future generations, and how we live in harmony with God's creation.

The effects of environmental degradation surround us: the smog in our cities; chemicals in our water and on our food; eroded topsoil blowing in the wind; the loss of valuable wetlands; radioactive and toxic waste lacking adequate disposal sites; threats to the health of industrial and farm workers. The problems, however, reach far beyond our own neighborhoods and workplaces. Our problems are the world's problems and burdens for generations to come. Poisoned water crosses borders freely. Acid rain pours on countries that do not create it. Greenhouse gases and chlorofluorocarbons affect the earth's atmosphere for many decades, regardless of where they are produced or used.

Opinions vary about the causes and the seriousness of environmental problems. Still, we can experience their effects in polluted air and water; in oil and wastes on our beaches; in the loss of farmland, wetlands, and forests; and in the decline of rivers and lakes. Scientists identify several other less visible but particularly urgent problems currently being debated by the scientific community, including depletion of the ozone layer, deforestation, the extinction of species, the generation and disposal of toxic and nuclear waste, and global warming. These important issues are being explored by scientists, and they require urgent attention and action. We are not scientists, but as pastors we call on experts, citizens, and policymakers to continue to explore the serious environmental, ethical, and human dimensions of these ecological challenges.

Environmental issues are also linked to other basic problems. As eminent scientist Dr. Thomas F. Malone reported, humanity faces problems in five interrelated fields: environment, energy, economics, equity, and ethics. To ensure the survival of a healthy planet, then, we must not only establish a sustainable economy but must also labor for justice both within and among nations. We must seek a society where economic life and environmental commitment work together to protect and to enhance life on this planet.

A. Aims of This Statement

With these pastoral reflections, we hope to add a distinctive and constructive voice to the ecological dialogue already underway in our nation and in our Church. These are beginning reflections for us, not final conclusions. We want to stimulate dialogue, particularly with the scientific community. We know these are not simple matters. We speak as pastors, offering our thoughts on a global problem that many people also recognize as a moral and religious crisis as well. In speaking out at this time, we have six goals:

1. To highlight the ethical dimensions of the environmental crisis
2. To link questions of ecology and poverty, environment and development
3. To stand with working men and women and poor and disadvantaged persons, whose lives are often impacted by ecological abuse and tradeoffs between environment and development
4. To promote a vision of a just and sustainable world community
5. To invite the Catholic community and men and women of goodwill to reflect more deeply on the religious dimensions of this topic
6. To begin a broader conversation on the potential contribution of the Church to environmental questions

Above all, we seek to explore the links between concern for the person and for the earth, between natural ecology and social ecology. The web of life is one. Our mistreatment of the natural world diminishes our own dignity and sacredness, not only because we are destroying resources that future generations of humans need, but because we are engaging in actions that contradict what it means to be human. Our tradition calls us to protect the life and dignity of the human person, and it is increasingly clear that this task cannot be separated from the care and defense of all of creation.

B. Justice and the Environment

The whole human race suffers as a result of environmental blight, and generations yet unborn will bear the cost for our failure to act today. But in most countries today, including our own, it is the poor and the powerless who most directly bear the burden of current environmental carelessness. Their lands and neighborhoods are more likely to be polluted or to host toxic waste dumps, their water to be undrinkable, their children to be harmed. Too often, the structure of sacrifice involved in environmental remedies seems to exact a high price from the poor and from workers. Small farmers, industrial workers, lumberjacks, watermen, rubber-tappers, for example, shoulder much of the weight of economic adjustment. Caught in a spiral of poverty and environmental degradation, poor people suffer acutely from the loss of soil fertility, pollution of rivers and urban streets, and the destruction of forest resources. Overcrowding and unequal land distribution often force them to overwork the soil, clear the forests, or migrate to marginal land. Their efforts to eke out a bare existence adds in its own way to environmental degradation and not infrequently to disaster for themselves and others who are equally poor.

Sustainable economic policies, that is, practices that reduce current stresses on natural systems and are consistent with sound environmental policy in the long term, must be put into effect. At the same time, the world economy must come to include hundreds of millions of poor families who live at the edge of survival.

C. Catholic Responses

In the face of these challenges, a new spirit of responsibility for the earth has begun to grow. Essential laws are being passed; vital anti-pollution efforts are underway; public concern is growing.

American Catholics are an integral part of this new awareness and action. In many small ways, we are learning more, caring more, and doing more about the environment and the threats to it. As a community of faith, we are also seeking to understand more clearly the ethical and religious dimensions of this challenge. This pastoral message, building on the previous statements and actions of individual bishops, dioceses, state conferences, and the episcopal conferences of other nations, as well as on the reflections and research of theologians, scientists, and environmentalists, is an effort to help that understanding. A distinctively Catholic contribution to contemporary environmental awareness arises from our understanding of human beings as part of nature, although not limited to it. Catholics look to nature, in natural theology, for indications of God's existence and purpose. In elaborating a natural moral law, we look to natural processes themselves for norms for human behavior. With such limits in mind, Pope John Paul II in *Centesimus Annus* urged that in addition to protecting natural systems and other species, we *"safeguard the moral conditions for an authentic 'human ecology'"* in urban planning, work environments, and family life.[2] Nature is not, in Catholic teaching, merely a field to exploit at will or a museum piece to be preserved at all costs. We are not gods, but stewards of the earth.

We recognize with appreciation the efforts of other Christian churches and people of other faiths on behalf of the planet. We accept our common religious responsibility to shape an ethic of care for the earth.

Our own Campaign for Human Development supports a wide variety of local environmental efforts. Among them are the following projects:

- In Washington state, a farm worker organization tries to reduce pesticides in the apple industry.
- In rural Mississippi, a community coalition seeks to secure greater access to drinkable water.
- In Jersey City, forty local parishes and congregations seek the removal of chromium wastes from the building site for 600 affordable homes they have sponsored.
- In Oakland, Calif., immigrant Asian women try to monitor the exposure of electronics workers to hazardous chemicals.
- In our nation's capital, victims of radiation released from government nuclear programs lobby for medical treatment of their injuries.

Across our nation, the National Catholic Rural Life Conference continues to urge greater respect for the land; to advocate sustainable agricultural practices; to combat soil loss and water pollution; to promote a fair living for those who work the land; and to assist religious communities and local churches in the management of the farms, forests, and wetlands they hold.

In addition, Catholic Relief Services (CRS) furthers the Church's commitment to proper use of technology in its rural development projects, which aim at sustainable agriculture and community-based development in other countries. To help reverse the cycle of poverty and environmental decline in the Third World, CRS assists projects such as these.

- In the highlands of Peru, fifty-four communities have been able to increase agricultural production by readopting sustainable farming methods used by their pre-Inca ancestors that help crops resist drought and frost damage.

- In Bangladesh, a local organization has developed a program to process the toxins from waste water using an aquatic surface plant, duckweed, so that river-dwellers are protected from water-borne diseases.
- In Madagascar, where overcrowding has caused serious deforestation, the government and local groups are training transient farmers to grow crops in productive but environmentally safe ways.
- In Egypt, two communities have established a waste water collection and disposal system, benefiting 3,500 families.

D. A Call to Reflection and Action

Grateful for the gift of creation and contrite in the face of the deteriorating condition of the natural world, we invite Catholics and men and women of goodwill in every walk of life to consider with us the moral issues raised by the environmental crisis.

We ask the Catholic community: How are we called to care for God's creation? How may we apply our social teaching, with its emphasis on the life and dignity of the human person, to the challenge of protecting the earth, our common home? What can we in the Catholic community offer to the environmental movement, and what can we learn from it? How can we encourage a serious dialogue in the Catholic community—in our parishes, schools, colleges, universities, and other settings—on the significant ethical dimensions of the environmental crisis?

To other people of goodwill across this country, we say: How do we proceed to frame a common and workable environmental ethic? What steps can we take to devise a sustainable and just economy? What can we do to link more firmly in the public mind both the commitment to justice and duties to the environment? How can we recognize and confront the possible conflicts between environment and jobs, and work for the common good and solutions that value both people and the earth? How do we secure protection for all God's creatures, including the poor and the unborn? How can the United States, as a nation, act responsibly about this ever more global problem? And how, in working for a sustainable global economy, do we fulfill our obligations in justice to the poor of the Third World?

These are matters of powerful urgency and major consequence. They constitute an exceptional call to conversion. As individuals, as institutions, as a people, we need a change of heart to preserve and protect the planet for our children and for generations yet unborn.

II. The Biblical Vision of God's Good Earth

Biblical studies are deepening our understanding of the creation story and its meaning for our developing views of the natural world.

A. *The Witness of the Hebrew Scriptures*

Christian responsibility for the environment begins with appreciation of the goodness of all God's creation. In the beginning, "God looked at everything he had made, and he found it very good" (Gn 1:31). The heavens and the earth, the sun and the moon, the earth and the sea, fish and birds, animals and humans—all are good. God's wisdom and power were present in every aspect of the unfolding of creation (see Prv 8:22-31).

It is no wonder that when God's people were filled with the spirit of prayer, they invited all creation to join their praise of God's goodness:

> Let the earth bless the Lord;
>   praise and exalt him above all forever.
> Mountains and hills, bless the Lord;
>   praise and exalt him above all forever.
> Everything growing from the earth, bless the Lord;
>   praise and exalt him above all forever.
> You springs, bless the Lord;
>   praise and exalt him above all forever.
> Seas and rivers, bless the Lord;
>   praise and exalt him above all forever.
> You dolphins and all water creatures, bless the Lord;
>   praise and exalt him above all forever.
> All you birds of the air, bless the Lord;
>   praise and exalt him above all forever.
> All you beasts, wild and tame, bless the Lord;
>   praise and exalt him above all forever. (Dn 3:74-81)

The earth, the Bible reminds us, is a gift to all creatures, to "all living beings—all mortal creatures that are on earth" (Gn 9:16-17).

People share the earth with other creatures. But humans, made in the image and likeness of God, are called in a special way to "cultivate and care for it" (Gn 2:15). Men and women, therefore, bear a unique responsibility under God: to safeguard the created world and by their creative labor even to enhance it. Safeguarding creation requires us to live responsibly within it, rather than manage creation as though we are outside it. The human family is charged with preserving the beauty, diversity, and integrity of nature, as well as with fostering its productivity. Yet, God alone is sovereign over the whole earth. "The Lord's are the earth and its fullness; the world and those who dwell in it" (Ps

24:1). Like the patriarch Noah, humanity stands responsible for ensuring that all nature can continue to thrive as God intended. After the flood, God made a lasting covenant with Noah, his descendants, and "every living creature." We are not free, therefore, to use created things capriciously.

Humanity's arrogance and acquisitiveness, however, led time and again to our growing alienation from nature (see Gn 3-4, 6-9, 11ff). In the Bible's account of Noah, the world's new beginning was marked by the estrangement of humans from nature. The sins of humankind laid waste the land. Hosea, for example, cries out:

> There is no fidelity, no mercy,
>   no knowledge of God in the land.
> False swearing, lying, murder, stealing and adultery!
>   in their lawlessness, bloodshed follows bloodshed.
> Therefore, the land mourns,
>   and everything that dwells in it languishes:
> The beasts of the field, the birds of the air,
>   and even the fish of the sea perish. (Hos 4:1b-3)

In the biblical vision, therefore, injustice results in suffering for all creation.

To curb the abuse of the land and of fellow humans, ancient Israel set out legal protections aimed at restoring the original balance between land and people (see Lv 25). Every seventh year, the land and people were to rest; nature would be restored by human restraint. And every seventh day, the Sabbath rest gave relief from unremitting toil to workers and beasts alike. It invited the whole community to taste the goodness of God in creation. In worship, moreover, the Sabbath continues to remind us of our dependence on God as his creatures, and so of our kinship with all that God has made. But people did not honor the law. A few went on accumulating land, many were dispossessed, and the land itself became exhausted. God then sent his prophets to call the people back to their responsibility. Again the people hardened their hearts; they had compassion for neither the land nor its people. The prophets promised judgment for the evil done the people of the land, but they also foresaw a day of restoration, when the harmony between humanity and the natural world would be renewed (see Is 32:15b-20).

B. The Gospel Message

Jesus came proclaiming a jubilee (see Lk 4:16-22) in which humanity, and with us all creation, was to be liberated (see Rom 8:18-25). He taught about salvation, however, with a countryman's knowledge of the land. God's grace was like wheat growing in the night (see Mk

4:26-29); divine love like a shepherd seeking a lost sheep (see Lk 15:4-7). In the birds of the air and the lilies of the field, Jesus found reason for his disciples to give up the ceaseless quest for material security and advantage and to trust in God (see Mt 6:25-33). Jesus himself is the Good Shepherd, who gives his life for his flock (see Jn 10). His Father is a vineyard worker, who trims vines so that they may bear more abundant fruit (see Jn 15:1-8). These familiar images, though they speak directly to humanity's encounter with God, at the same time reveal that the fundamental relation between humanity and nature is one of caring for creation.

The new covenant made in Jesus' blood overcomes all hostility and restores the order of love. Just as in his person Christ has destroyed the hostility that divided people from one another, so he has overcome the opposition between humanity and nature. For he is the firstborn of a new creation and gives his Spirit to renew the whole earth (see Col 2:18; Ps 104:30). The fruits of that Spirit—joy, peace, patience, kindness, goodness, trustfulness, gentleness, and self-control (see Gal 5:22)— mark us as Christ's own people. As they incline us to "serve one another through love" (Gal 5:13), they may also dispose us to live carefully on the earth, with respect for all God's creatures. Our Christian way of life, as saints like Benedict, Hildegard, and Francis showed us, is a road to community with all creation.

III. Catholic Social Teaching and Environmental Ethics

The tradition of Catholic social teaching offers a developing and distinctive perspective on environmental issues. We believe that the following themes drawn from this tradition are integral dimensions of ecological responsibility:

- *A God-centered and sacramental view of the universe,* which grounds human accountability for the fate of the earth
- A consistent *respect for human life,* which extends to respect for all creation
- A worldview affirming the ethical significance *of global interdependence and the common good*
- *An ethic of solidarity* promoting cooperation and a just structure of sharing in the world community
- An understanding of *the universal purpose of created things,* which requires equitable use of the earth's resources
- *An option for the poor,* which gives passion to the quest for an equitable and sustainable world

- A conception of *authentic development,* which offers a direction for progress that respects human dignity and the limits of material growth

Although Catholic social teaching does not offer a complete environmental ethic, we are confident that this developing tradition can serve as the basis for Catholic engagement and dialogue with science, the environmental movement, and other communities of faith and goodwill.

A. A Sacramental Universe

The whole universe is God's dwelling. Earth, a very small, uniquely blessed corner of that universe, gifted with unique natural blessings, is humanity's home, and humans are never so much at home as when God dwells with them. In the beginning, the first man and woman walked with God in the cool of the day. Throughout history, people have continued to meet the Creator on mountaintops, in vast deserts, and alongside waterfalls and gently flowing springs. In storms and earthquakes, they found expressions of divine power. In the cycle of the seasons and the courses of the stars, they have discerned signs of God's fidelity and wisdom. We still share, though dimly, in that sense of God's presence in nature. But as heirs and victims of the industrial revolution, students of science and the beneficiaries of technology, urban-dwellers and jet-commuters, twentieth-century Americans have also grown estranged from the natural scale and rhythms of life on earth.

For many people, the environmental movement has reawakened appreciation of the truth that, through the created gifts of nature, men and women encounter their Creator. The Christian vision of a sacramental universe—a world that discloses the Creator's presence by visible and tangible signs—can contribute to making the earth a home for the human family once again. Pope John Paul II has called for Christians to respect and protect the environment, so that through nature people can "contemplate the mystery of the greatness and love of God."

Reverence for the Creator present and active in nature, moreover, may serve as ground for environmental responsibility. For the very plants and animals, mountains and oceans, which in their loveliness and sublimity lift our minds to God, by their fragility and perishing likewise cry out, "We have not made ourselves." God brings them into being and sustains them in existence. It is to the Creator of the universe, then, that we are accountable for what we do or fail to do to preserve and care for the earth and all its creatures. For "the LORD'S are the earth and its fullness; the world and those who dwell in it" (Ps 24:1). Dwelling in the presence of God, we begin to experience ourselves as part of creation, as stewards within it, not separate from it. As faithful stewards, fullness of life comes from living responsibly within God's creation.

Stewardship implies that we must both care for creation according to standards that are not of our own making and at the same time be resourceful in finding ways to make the earth flourish. It is a difficult balance, requiring both a sense of limits and a spirit of experimentation. Even as we rejoice in earth's goodness and in the beauty of nature, stewardship places upon us responsibility for the well-being of all God's creatures.

B. Respect for Life

Respect for nature and respect for human life are inextricably related. "Respect for life, and above all for the dignity of the human person," Pope John Paul II has written, extends also to the rest of creation.[3] Other species, ecosystems, and even distinctive landscapes give glory to God. The covenant given to Noah was a promise to all the earth.

> See, I am establishing my covenant with you and your descendants after you and with every living creature that was with you: all the birds, and the various tame and wild animals that were with you and came out of the ark. (Gn 9:9-10)

The diversity of life manifests God's glory. Every creature shares a bit of the divine beauty. Because the divine goodness could not be represented by one creature alone, Aquinas tells us, God "produced many and diverse creatures, so that what was wanting to one in representation of the divine goodness might be supplied by another . . . hence the whole universe together participates in the divine goodness more perfectly, and represents it better than any single creature whatever."[4] The wonderful variety of the natural world is, therefore, part of the divine plan and, as such, invites our respect. Accordingly, it is appropriate that we treat other creatures and the natural world not just as means to human fulfillment but also as God's creatures, possessing an independent value, worthy of our respect and care.

By preserving natural environments, by protecting endangered species, by laboring to make human environments compatible with local ecology, by employing appropriate technology, and by carefully evaluating technological innovations as we adopt them, we exhibit respect for creation and reverence for the Creator.

C. The Planetary Common Good

In 1963, Pope John XXIII, in the letter *Pacem in Terris,* emphasized the world's growing interdependence. He saw problems emerging, which the traditional political mechanisms could no longer address, and he extended the traditional principle of the common good from the nation-state to the world community. Ecological concern has now heightened our awareness of just how interdependent our world is. Some of the gravest environmental problems are clearly global. In this shrinking world, everyone is affected and everyone is responsible, although those most responsible are often the least affected. The universal common good can serve as a foundation for a global environmental ethic.

In many of his statements, Pope John Paul II has recognized the need for such an ethic. For example, in *The Ecological Crisis: A Common Responsibility,* his 1990 World Day of Peace Message, he wrote,

> Today the ecological crisis has assumed such proportions as to be the responsibility of everyone. . . . Its various aspects demonstrate the need for concerted efforts aimed at establishing the duties and obligations that belong to individuals, peoples, states and the international community.[5]

Governments have particular responsibility in this area. In *Centesimus Annus,* the pope insists that the state has the task of providing "for the defense and preservation of common good such as the natural and human environments, which cannot be safeguarded simply by market forces."[6]

D. A New Solidarity

In the Catholic tradition, the universal common good is specified by the duty of solidarity, "*a firm and persevering determination* to commit oneself to the *common good,*" a willingness "to 'lose oneself' for the sake of the other[s] instead of exploiting [them]."[7] In the face of "the structures of sin," moreover, solidarity requires sacrifices of our own self-interest for the good of others and of the earth we share. Solidarity places special obligations upon the industrial democracies, including the United States. "The ecological crisis," Pope John Paul II has written, "reveals the *urgent moral need for a new solidarity,* especially in relations between the developing nations and those that are highly industrialized."[8] Only with equitable and sustainable development can poor nations curb continuing environmental degradation and avoid the destructive effects of the kind of overdevelopment that has used natural resources irresponsibly.

E. Universal Purpose of Created Things

God has given the fruit of the earth to sustain the entire human family "without excluding or favoring anyone." Human work has enhanced the productive capacity of the earth and in our time is, as Pope John Paul II has said, "increasingly important as the productive factor both of non-material and of material wealth."[9] But a great many people, in the Third World as well as in our own inner cities and rural areas, are still deprived of the means of livelihood. In moving toward an environmentally sustainable economy, we are obligated to work for a just economic system which equitably shares the bounty of the earth and of human enterprise with all peoples. Created things belong not to the few, but to the entire human family.

F. Option for the Poor

The ecological problem is intimately connected to justice for the poor. "The goods of the earth, which in the divine plan should be a common patrimony," Pope John Paul II has reminded us, "often risk becoming the monopoly of a few who often spoil it and, sometimes, destroy it, thereby creating a loss for all humanity."[10]

The poor of the earth offer a special test of our solidarity. The painful adjustments we have to undertake in our own economies for the sake of the environment must not diminish our sensitivity to the needs of the poor at home and abroad. The option for the poor embedded in the Gospel and the Church's teaching makes us aware that the poor suffer most directly from environmental decline and have the least access to relief from their suffering. Indigenous peoples die with their forests and grasslands. In Bhopal and Chernobyl, it was the urban poor and working people who suffered the most immediate and intense contamination. Nature will truly enjoy its second spring only when humanity has compassion for its own weakest members.

A related and vital concern is the Church's constant commitment to the dignity of work and the rights of workers. Environmental progress cannot come at the expense of workers and their rights. Solutions must be found that do not force us to choose between a decent environment and a decent life for workers.

We recognize the potential conflicts in this area and will work for greater understanding, communication, and common ground between workers and environmentalists. Clearly, workers cannot be asked to make sacrifices to improve the environment without concrete support from the broader community. Where jobs are lost, society must help in the process of economic conversion, so that not only the earth but also workers and their families are protected.

G. Authentic Development

Unrestrained economic development is not the answer to improving the lives of the poor. Catholic social teaching has never accepted material growth as a model of development. A *"mere accumulation* of goods and services, even for the benefit of the majority," as Pope John Paul II has said, "is not enough for the realization of human happiness."[11] He has also warned that in a desire "to have and to enjoy rather than to be and to grow," humanity "consumes the resources of the earth, subjecting it without restraint . . . as if it did not have its own requisites and God-given purposes."

Authentic development supports moderation and even austerity in the use of material resources. It also encourages a balanced view of human progress consistent with respect for nature. Furthermore, it invites the development of alternative visions of the good society and the use of economic models with richer standards of well-being than material productivity alone. Authentic development also requires affluent nations to seek ways to reduce and restructure their overconsumption of natural resources. Finally, authentic development also entails encouraging the proper use of both agricultural and industrial technologies, so that development does not merely mean technological advancement for its own sake but rather that technology benefits people and enhances the land.

H. Consumption and Population

In public discussions, two areas are particularly cited as requiring greater care and judgment on the part of human beings. The first is *consumption of resources.* The second is *growth in world population.* Regrettably, advantaged groups often seem more intent on curbing Third World births than on restraining the even more voracious consumerism of the developed world. We believe this compounds injustice and increases disrespect for the life of the weakest among us. For example, it is not so much population growth, but the desperate efforts of debtor countries to pay their foreign debt by exporting products to affluent industrial countries that drives poor peasants off their land and up eroding hillsides, where in the effort to survive, they also destroy the environment.

Consumption in developed nations remains the single greatest source of global environmental destruction. A child born in the United States, for example, puts a far heavier burden on the world's resources than one born in a poor developing country. By one estimate, each American uses twenty-eight times the energy of a person living in a developing country. Advanced societies, and our own in particular, have barely begun to make efforts at reducing their consumption of resources and the enormous waste and pollution that result from it. We in the developed world, therefore, are obligated to address our own wasteful and destructive use of resources as a matter of top priority.

The key factor, though not the only one, in dealing with population problems is sustainable social and economic development. Technological fixes do not really work. Only when an economy distributes resources so as to allow the poor an equitable stake in society and some hope for the future do couples see responsible parenthood as good for their families. In particular, prenatal care, education, good nutrition, and health care for women, children, and families promise to improve family welfare and contribute to stabilizing population. Supporting such equitable social development, moreover, may well be the best contribution affluent societies, like the United States, can make to relieving ecological pressures in less developed nations.

At the same time, it must be acknowledged that rapid population growth presents special problems and challenges that must be addressed in order to avoid damage done to the environment and to social development. In the words of Pope Paul VI, "It is not to be denied that accelerated demographic increases too frequently add difficulties to plans for development because the population is increased more rapidly than available resources."[12] In *Sollicitudo Rei Socialis,* Pope John Paul II has likewise noted, "One cannot deny the existence, especially in the southern hemisphere, of a demographic problem which creates difficulties for development."[13] He has gone on to make connections among population size, development, and the environment. There is "a greater realization of the limits of available resources," he commented, "and of the need to respect the integrity and the cycles of nature and to take them into account when planning for development."[14] Even though it is possible to feed a growing population, the ecological costs of doing so ought to be taken into account. To eliminate hunger from the planet, the world community needs to reform the institutional and political structures that restrict the access of people to food.

Thus, the Church addresses population issues in the context of its teaching on human life, of just development, of care for the environment, and of respect for the freedom of married couples to decide voluntarily on the number and spacing of births. In keeping with these values, and out of respect for cultural norms, it continues to oppose coercive methods of population control and programs that bias decisions through incentives or disincentives. Respect for nature ought to encourage policies that promote natural family planning and true responsible parenthood rather than coercive population control programs or incentives for birth control that violate cultural and religious norms and Catholic teaching.

Finally, we are charged with restoring the integrity of all creation. We must care for all God's creatures, especially the most vulnerable.

How, then, can we protect endangered species and at the same time be callous to the unborn, the elderly, or disabled persons? Is not abortion also a sin against creation? If we turn our backs on our own unborn children, can we truly expect that nature will receive respectful treatment at our hands? The care of the earth will not be advanced by the destruction of human life at any stage of development. As Pope John Paul II has said, "protecting the environment is first of all the right to live and the protection of life."[15]

I. A Web of Life

These themes drawn from Catholic social teaching are linked to our efforts to share this teaching in other contexts, especially in our pastoral letters on peace and economic justice and in our statements on food and agriculture. Clearly, war represents a serious threat to the environment, as the darkened skies and oil-soaked beaches of Kuwait clearly remind us. The pursuit of peace—lasting peace based on justice—ought to be an environmental priority because the earth itself bears the wounds and scars of war. Likewise, our efforts to defend the dignity and rights of the poor and of workers, to use the strength of our market economy to meet basic human needs, and to press for greater national and global economic justice are clearly linked to efforts to preserve and sustain the earth. These are not distinct and separate issues but complementary challenges. We need to help build bridges among the peace, justice, and environmental agendas and constituencies.

IV. Theological and Pastoral Concerns

Today's crises in global ecology demand concerted and creative thought and effort on the part of all of us: scientists, political leaders, business people, workers, lawyers, farmers, communicators, and citizens generally. As moral teachers, we intend to lift up the moral and ethical dimensions of these issues. We find much to affirm in and learn from the environmental movement: its devotion to nature, its recognition of limits and connections, its urgent appeal for sustainable and ecologically sound policies. We share considerable common ground in the concern for the earth, and we have much work to do together. But there may also be some areas of potential confusion and conflict with some who share this common concern for the earth. We offer some brief comments on three of these concerns in the hope that they will contribute to a constructive dialogue on how we can best work together.

A. The Creator and Creation

Nature shares in God's goodness, and contemplation of its beauty and richness raises our hearts and minds to God. St. Paul hinted at a theology of creation when he proclaimed to the Athenians, the Creator who "made from one the whole human race to dwell on the entire surface of the earth, and he fixed and ordered the seasons and the boundaries of their regions, so that people might seek God, even perhaps grope for him, though indeed he is not far from any of us" (Acts 17:26-27). Through the centuries, Catholic theologians and philosophers, like St. Paul before them, continue to search for God in reasoning about the created world.

Our Catholic faith continues to affirm the goodness of the natural world. The sacramental life of the Church depends on created goods: water, oil, bread, and wine. Likewise, the western mystical tradition has taught Christians how to find God dwelling in created things and laboring and loving through them.

Nonetheless, Christian theology also affirms the limits of all God's creatures. God, the source of all that is, is actively present in all creation, but God also surpasses all created things. We profess the ancient faith of God's people.

> Hear O Israel! The LORD our God is LORD alone! You shall love the LORD your God with all your heart, with all your soul, with all your mind, and with all your strength. (Dt 6:4-5; Mk 12:29-30)

An ordered love for creation, therefore, is ecological without being ecocentric. We can and must care for the earth without mistaking it for the ultimate object of our devotion. A Christian love of the natural world, as St. Francis showed us, can restrain grasping and wanton human behavior and help mightily to preserve and nurture all that God has made. We believe that faith in a good and loving God is a compelling source of passionate and enduring care for all creation.

B. Human Reason and Invention

Guided by the Spirit of God, the future of the earth lies in human hands. To maintain landscapes in integrity, to safeguard endangered species, to preserve remaining wilderness, to ensure the feeding of a hungry world will require much human decision, social cooperation, experimentation, and invention. To restore the purity of air and water, to halt the loss of farmland, to sustain ecological diversity in plant and animal life, concerted human action will be needed over many decades. To avert further depletion of the ozone layer, to check the production of greenhouse gases, and to redress the effects of global warming will require unprecedented collaboration and commitment among the nations of the earth. Even as humanity's mistakes are at the root of earth's travail today, human talents and invention can and must assist in its rebirth and contribute to human development.

Incontestably, people need to exhibit greater respect for nature than they have for some centuries, but we will also need to apply human reason to find remedies for nature's ills. Scientific research and technological innovation must accompany religious and moral responses to environmental challenges. Reverence for nature must be combined with scientific learning. In a Catholic worldview, there is no necessary clash between an environmentally responsible morality and an active application of human reason and science. Problematic uses of technology provide no excuse to retreat into prescientific attitudes toward nature. The ecological crisis heightens our awareness of the need for new approaches to scientific research and technology. Many indigenous technologies can teach us much. Such technologies are more compatible with the ecosystem, are more available to poor persons, and are more sustainable for the entire community.

C. Christian Love

At the heart of the Christian life lies the love of neighbor. The ecological crisis, as Pope John Paul II has urged, challenges us to extend our love to future generations and to the flourishing of all earth's creatures. But neither our duties to future generations nor our tending of the garden entrusted to our care ought to diminish our love for the present members of the human family, especially the poor and the disadvantaged. Both impoverished peoples and an imperiled planet demand our committed service.

Christian love draws us to serve the weak and vulnerable among us. We are called to feed the hungry, to give drink to the thirsty, to clothe the naked, to shelter the homeless. We are also summoned to restore the land; to provide clean, safe water to drink and unpolluted air to breathe; to preserve endangered species; to protect wild places; and to help the poor help themselves. We ought to remember that Francis of Assisi, the patron saint of the environmental movement, tamed wolves and preached to the birds only after a long novitiate in which he ministered to outcasts and lepers.

Christian love forbids choosing between people and the planet. It urges us to work for an equitable and sustainable future in which all peoples can share in the bounty of the earth and in which the earth itself is protected from predatory use. The common good invites regions of the country to share burdens equitably in such areas as toxic and nuclear waste disposal and water distribution and to work together to reduce and eliminate waste which threatens health and environmental quality. It also invites us to explore alternatives in which our poor brothers and sisters will share with the rest of us in the banquet of life, at the same time that we preserve and restore the earth, which sustains us.

V. God's Stewards and Co-Creators

As others have pointed out, we are the first generation to see our planet from space—to see so clearly its beauty, limits, and fragility. Modern communication technology helps us to see more clearly than ever the impact of carelessness, ignorance, greed, neglect, and war on the earth.

Today, humanity is at a crossroads. Having read the signs of the times, we can either ignore the harm we see and witness further damage, or we can take up our responsibilities to the Creator and creation with renewed courage and commitment.

The task set before us is unprecedented, intricate, complex. No single solution will be adequate to the task. To live in balance with the finite resources of the planet, we need an unfamiliar blend of restraint and innovation. We shall be required to be genuine stewards of nature and thereby co-creators of a new human world. This will require both new attitudes and new actions.

A. New Attitudes

For believers, our faith is tested by our concern and care for creation. Within our tradition are important resources and values that can help us assess problems and shape constructive solutions. In addition to the themes we have already outlined from our social teaching, the traditional virtues of prudence, humility, and temperance are indispensable elements of a new environmental ethic. Recognition of the reality of sin and failure as well as the opportunity for forgiveness and reconciliation can help us face up to our environmental responsibilities. A new sense of the limits and risks of fallible human judgments ought to mark the decisions of policy makers as they act on complicated global issues with necessarily imperfect knowledge. Finally, as we face the challenging years ahead, we must all rely on the preeminent Christian virtues of faith, hope, and love to sustain us and direct us.

There are hopeful signs: public concern is growing; some public policy is shifting; and private behavior is beginning to change. From broader participation in recycling to negotiating international treaties, people are searching for ways to make a difference on behalf of the environment.

More people seem ready to recognize that the industrialized world's overconsumption has contributed the largest share to the degradation of the global environment. Also encouraging is the growing conviction that development is more qualitative than quantitative, that it consists more in improving the quality of life than in increasing consumption. What is now needed is the will to make the changes in public policy, as well as in lifestyle, that will be needed to arrest, reverse, and prevent environmental decay and to pursue the goal of sustainable, equitable development for all. The overarching moral issue is to achieve during the twenty-first century a just and sustainable world. From a scientific point of view, this seems possible. But the new order can only be achieved through the persevering exercise of moral responsibility on the part of individuals, voluntary organizations, governments, and transnational agencies.

In the Catholic community, as we have pointed out, there are many signs of increased discussion, awareness, and action on environment. We have offered these reflections in the hope that they will contribute to a broader dialogue in our Church and society about the moral dimensions of ecology and about the links between social justice and ecology, between environment and development. We offer these reflections not to endorse a particular policy agenda nor to step onto some current bandwagon, but to meet our responsibilities as pastors and teachers who see the terrible consequences of environmental neglect and who believe our faith calls us to help shape a creative and effective response.

B. New Actions

This statement is only a first step in fashioning an ongoing response to this challenge. We invite the Catholic community to join with us and others of goodwill in a continuing effort to understand and act on the moral and ethical dimensions of the environmental crisis:

- We ask *scientists, environmentalists, economists, and other experts* to continue to help us understand the challenges we face and the steps we need to take. Faith is not a substitute for facts; the more we know about the problems we face, the better we can respond.
- We invite *teachers and educators* to emphasize, in their classrooms and curricula, a love for God's creation, a respect for nature, and a commitment to practices and behavior that bring these attitudes into the daily lives of their students and themselves.
- We remind *parents* that they are the first and principal teachers of children. It is from parents that children will learn love of the earth and delight in nature. It is at home that they develop

the habits of self-control, concern, and care that lie at the heart of environmental morality.

- We call on *theologians, scripture scholars, and ethicists* to help explore, deepen, and advance the insights of our Catholic tradition and its relation to the environment and other religious perspectives on these matters. We especially call upon Catholic scholars to explore the relationship between this tradition's emphasis upon the dignity of the human person and our responsibility to care for all of God's creation.

- We ask *business leaders and representatives of workers* to make the protection of our common environment a central concern in their activities and to collaborate for the common good and the protection of the earth. We especially encourage pastors and parish leaders to give greater attention to the extent and urgency of the environmental crisis in preaching, teaching, pastoral outreach, and action, at the parish level and through ecumenical cooperation in the local community.

- We ask the *members of our Church* to examine our lifestyles, behaviors, and policies—individually and institutionally—to see how we contribute to the destruction or neglect of the environment and how we might assist in its protection and restoration. We also urge celebrants and liturgy committees to incorporate themes into prayer and worship that emphasize our responsibility to protect all of God's creation and to organize prayerful celebrations of creation on feast days honoring St. Francis and St. Isidore.

- We ask *environmental advocates* to join us in building bridges between the quest for justice and the pursuit of peace and concern for the earth. We ask that the poor and vulnerable at home and abroad be accorded a special and urgent priority in all efforts to care for our environment.

- We urge *policy makers and public officials* to focus more directly on the ethical dimensions of environmental policy and on its relation to development, to seek the common good, and to resist short-term pressures in order to meet our long-term responsibility to future generations. At the very minimum, we need food and energy policies that are socially just, environmentally benign, and economically efficient.

- As *citizens*, each of us needs to participate in this debate over how our nation best protects our ecological heritage, limits pollution, allocates environmental costs, and plans for the future. We need to use our voices and votes to shape a nation more committed to the universal common good and an ethic of environmental solidarity.

All of us need both a spiritual and a practical vision of stewardship and co-creation that guides our choices as consumers, citizens, and workers. We need, in the now familiar phrase, to "think globally and act locally," finding the ways in our own situation to express a broader ethic of genuine solidarity.

C. Call to Conversion

The environmental crisis of our own day constitutes an exceptional call to conversion. As individuals, as institutions, as a people, we need a change of heart to save the planet for our children and generations yet unborn. So vast are the problems, so intertwined with our economy and way of life, that nothing but a wholehearted and ever more profound turning to God, the maker of heaven and earth, will allow us to carry out our responsibilities as faithful stewards of God's creation.

Only when believers look to values of the Scriptures, honestly admit their limitations and failings, and commit themselves to common action on behalf of the land and the wretched of the earth will we be ready to participate fully in resolving this crisis.

D. A Word of Hope

A just and sustainable society and world are not an optional ideal, but a moral and practical necessity. Without justice, a sustainable economy will be beyond reach. Without an ecologically responsible world economy, justice will be unachievable. To accomplish either is an enormous task; together they seem overwhelming. But "all things are possible" to those who hope in God (Mk 10:27). Hope is the virtue at the heart of a Christian environmental ethic. Hope gives us the courage, direction, and energy required for this arduous common endeavor.

In the bleak years of Britain's industrial revolution, Gerard Manley Hopkins wrote of urban decay wrought by industry and of Christian hope for nature's revival. His words capture the condition of today's world as it awaits redemption from ecological neglect:

> And all is seared with trade; bleared, smeared with toil;
> And wears man's smudge and shares man's smell: the soil
> Is bare now, nor can foot feel, being shod.
>
> And for all this, nature is never spent:
> There lives the dearest freshness deep down things;
> . . . .
>
> Because the Holy Ghost over the bent
> World broods with warm breast and with ah! bright wings.[16]

Saving the planet will demand long and sometimes sacrificial commitment. It will require continual revision of our political habits, restructuring economic institutions, reshaping society, and nurturing global community. But we can proceed with hope because, as at the dawn of creation, so today the Holy Spirit breathes new life into all earth's creatures. Today, we pray with new conviction and concern for all God's creation:

> Send forth thy Spirit, Lord,
> and renew the face of the earth.

Notes

1. John Paul II, *The Ecological Crisis: A Common Responsibility,* Message of Pope John Paul II for the celebration of the World Day of Peace, January 1, 1990 (Washington, D.C.: United States Catholic Conference, 1990), nos. 1, 15.
2. John Paul II, *On the Hundredth Anniversary of Rerum Novarum (Centesimus Annus)* (Washington, D.C.: United States Catholic Conference, 1991), no. 38.
3. *The Ecological Crisis: A Common Responsibility,* no. 7.
4. St. Thomas, *Summa Theologica,* I, q. 47, art. 1.
5. *The Ecological Crisis: A Common Responsibility,* no. 15.
6. *Centesimus Annus,* no. 40.
7. John Paul II, *On Social Concern (Sollicitudo Rei Socialis)* (Washington, D.C.: United States Catholic Conference, 1987), no. 38.
8. *The Ecological Crisis: A Common Responsibility,* no. 10.
9. *Centesimus Annus,* no. 31.
10. John Paul II, "Creation is an Example of Divine Goodness," Address at a Conference Marking the Presentation of the Second Edition of the St. Francis "Canticle of the Creatures" International Award for the Environment (October 25, 1991), *L'Osservatore Romano* [English edition] 45 (November 11, 1991): 2.
11. *Sollicitudo Rei Socialis,* no. 28.
12. Paul VI, *On the Development of Peoples (Populorum Progressio)* (Washington, D.C.: United States Catholic Conference, 1967), no. 37.
13. *Sollicitudo Rei Socialis,* no. 25.
14. Ibid., no. 26.
15. John Paul II, "Homily at Cuiaba, Mato Grosso, Brazil" (October 16, 1991), *Origins* 21:21 (October 31, 1991): 336.
16. Gerard Manley Hopkins, "God's Grandeur" in *Poems of Gerard Manley Hopkins* (New York: Oxford University Press, 1967).

Source: Washington, D.C.: United States Catholic Conference, 1992.

1992: A Time for Remembering, Reconciling, and Recommitting Ourselves as a People

Statement of the National Conference of Catholic Bishops on Native Americans

November 1991

Introduction

The fifth centenary of the coming of Europeans to this land is both a challenge and an opportunity, a time for looking back at where we have been and looking ahead to where we should be as a people and a nation. No specific aspect of this observance challenges us more than the situation of Native Americans in our midst—their past treatment, their current condition, and their future aspirations.

As we prepare for the historic year of 1992, with both its opportunity for dialogue and its significant controversy, the Catholic community is blessed, enriched, and profoundly challenged by the faith of Native Americans in our midst. We ask the Catholic community to join us in seeking new understanding and awareness of their situation and in committing our Church to new advocacy and action with our Native American brothers and sisters on issues of social justice and pastoral life which touch their lives.

In this effort, we build on our reflections of a year ago regarding the fifth centenary, *Heritage and Hope.*[1] In these additional comments, we do not offer a comprehensive historical perspective but rather our reflections as pastors and teachers on the successes, failures, and hopes that shape the relationship between our Church and Native Americans.

We seek to speak not only to Native Americans, but to the whole Church in this land. We speak as pastors, not only about important issues but first and foremost about a people—about our brothers and sisters whose dignity, culture, and faith have too often been diminished and not adequately respected and protected by our civil society or our religious institutions. We seek to recognize and respond to the strengths of traditional Native American culture and spirituality, the pastoral and human needs of native peoples, the many pastoral efforts already underway, and the continuing moral challenge of pursuing justice in the face of continuing discrimination.

419

In our letter on the fifth centenary, *Heritage and Hope,* we sought to emphasize the ongoing challenge of evangelization, calling for continuing conversion to Jesus Christ and his values rather than emphasize a celebration of past events. We consider this historic year a time for sharing the Gospel with new energy and exploring its continuing demands. This fifth centenary should be a time for remembering, reconciling, and recommitting ourselves as a Church to the development of the people whose ancestors were here long before the first Europeans came to these shores five hundred years ago.

I. A Time for Remembering

In this centennial year we recall the suffering of native peoples that followed the arrival of explorers and wave after wave of immigrants. We have spoken clearly about some of these failures in our letter on the fifth centenary. We repeat these strong words to remind ourselves of lessons which must be learned and commitments which must be kept as a part of this observance:

> As Church, we often have been unconscious and insensitive to the mistreatment of our Native American brothers and sisters and have at times reflected the racism of the dominant culture of which we have been a part. In this quincentennial year, we extend our apology to our native peoples and pledge ourselves to work with them to ensure their rights, their religious freedom, and the preservation of their cultural heritage.[1]

In this letter, we point out that the coming of religious faith in this land began not five hundred years ago, but centuries before in the prayers, chants, dance, and other sacred celebrations of native people.

We also acknowledge that the encounter with the Europeans was often a "harsh and painful one" for native peoples, and we lament the diseases, death, destruction, injustices, and disrespect for native ways and traditions which came with it. We recognize that:

> Often they [European Christians] failed to distinguish between what was crucial to the Gospel and what were matters of cultural preference. That failure brought with it catastrophic consequences for the native peoples, who were at times forced to become European at the same time they became Christian.
>
> Yet that is not the whole picture. The effort to portray the history of the encounter as a totally negative experience in which only violence and exploitation of the native peoples was present is not an accurate interpretation of the past. [3]

Convinced of the saving truth of the Gospel and grateful for the sacrifices, care, and concern of many missionaries for native people, we point out that "the expansion of Christianity into our hemisphere brought to the peoples of this land the gift of the Christian faith with its power of humanization and salvation, dignity and fraternity, justice and love."[4]

We bishops urge that in 1992 our nation should give renewed attention to the condition of Native Americans:

> We encourage all Americans to better understand the role of native peoples in our history and to respond to the just grievances of our Native American brothers and sisters. We hope that this will be a graced time for rejecting all forms of racism.[5]

Now in these pastoral reflections we seek to offer some direction in realizing this hope. It is not enough for us simply to repeat strong words. The challenge of this historic year is not simply to look back, but also to look around at the current situation of native peoples and to look ahead to future challenges for our Church and society in responding to the aspirations and needs of Native Americans.

II. A Time for Reconciliation

We have also called for "new reconciliation in the spirit of the Gospel among all Americans and to recognize more fully our solidarity."[6] The challenge of reconciliation in Jesus Christ requires greater awareness and understanding, increased dialogue and interaction, and a commitment to mutual respect and justice among diverse peoples. Most Americans know almost nothing about the lives and history of the first Americans. Our religious organizations, schools, and other educational efforts must tell the truth about how Native Americans have been treated and how they have endured in this land. History can be healing if we will face up to its lessons.

All of us need to examine our own perceptions of Native Americans—how much they are shaped by stereotypes, distorted media portrayals, or ignorance. We fear that prejudice and insensitivity toward native peoples is deeply rooted in our culture and in our local churches. Our conference has consistently condemned racism of every kind, and we renew our call for increased efforts to overcome prejudice and discrimination as they touch our Native American brothers and sisters.

This reconciliation should also reflect the realities of Native American life today, in our nation and our Church. The Native American community now includes almost two million Indians,

Eskimos, and Aleuts, including a number of Hispanic people who also identify themselves as Indians. Native Americans are both citizens of the United States and members of their tribes, pueblos, or nations. Native Americans are among the fastest growing populations in our country. They constitute a vital, diverse, and growing community.

Native Americans are present in every state. The largest number are found in Oklahoma where many tribes were relocated. While a majority of Native Americans live in the Western part of the United States, North Carolina has the fifth largest Indian population in the country. Only Oklahoma, California, Arizona, and New Mexico have larger populations. Moreover, well over a third of all Native Americans now reside in large cities. Native American people are an integral part of many of our metropolitan areas, especially in the Midwest and West.

One in four Native Americans is poor. Many struggle with the realities of inadequate housing, joblessness, and health problems including the disease of alcoholism. While significant numbers of Native Americans have become lawyers, doctors, artists, and other professionals, many others live with dashed hopes and bleak futures as a result of discrimination, lack of opportunity, and economic powerlessness.

Within our family of faith we are very blessed to have significant numbers of Native American Catholics, now numbering more than a quarter of a million. Our Church is blessed with two Native American bishops, more than two dozen priests, many deacons, ninety sisters and brothers, and many lay leaders.

There are a variety of significant initiatives focused on the pastoral life and needs of Native American Catholics:

- For more than a century, the Bureau of Catholic Indian Missions has through the generosity of U.S. Catholics served the pastoral and spiritual needs of Native American Catholics providing for Native American ministries providing more than $3 million annually.
- The Tekakwitha Conference provides an important voice and gathering place for those who serve the Native American Catholic community.
- Many dioceses have undertaken creative efforts, and religious communities have established ministries to serve the needs of Native American Catholics.
- Our own national conference of bishops has previously developed and adopted a major statement on the Church and American Indians outlining pastoral priorities and a social justice agenda that still are valid today.[7]

- Several dioceses and state Catholic conferences have also made justice for Native Americans a major ecclesial priority.

In this task of reconciliation, the persistence and vitality of Catholic faith in the Native American community is an irreplaceable asset. We are one family united in faith, citizenship, and humanity. However, the Native American Catholic community faces three special and related challenges.

A. Inculturation

The Church is called to bring the saving word of the Gospel to every people and culture. Our goal must be an authentic inculturation of Catholic faith within the Native American community through a vital liturgical life, continuing educational efforts, and creative pastoral ministry which demonstrate deep respect for native culture and spiritualities and which enhance fidelity to the Catholic faith.

This is not an easy or simple task. Authentic inculturation moves in three integral steps: (1) The culture which the word of God encounters is challenged and purified by that word; (2) the best of the culture is enhanced by the truth of the Gospel; (3) the Church is enriched by respecting the culture which the Gospel embraces and which in turn embraces the Gospel.

This task of inculturation is not an unprecedented or new challenge, but it remains an essential step toward an authentic Catholic Native American community within the structure and bonds of the universal Church. As Pope John Paul II has said:

> When the Church enters into contact with cultures, the Church must welcome all that is compatible with the Gospel in these traditions of the peoples in order to bring the richness of Christ to them and to be enriched herself by the manifold wisdom of the nations of the earth.[8]

In liturgical, pastoral, and spiritual life, we seek a genuine reconciliation between the essential traditions of Catholic faith and the best of the traditions of Native American life, each respecting, shaping, and enriching the other. Native American Catholics are called to be both true Catholic believers and authentic Native Americans. Far from being incompatible, these two traditions—the Catholic way and the native way—enrich each other and the whole Church.

Our challenge is to make sure that a truly Catholic religious culture interfaces with truly Native American cultures. A highly secularized society can overshadow a Catholic and Native American sense of mystery when encountering God, the created world, and human life.

We call on liturgists, theologians, and pastoral leaders to help us address these real issues as we shape a Native American expression of faith that is authentically Catholic and deeply Native American. It is our responsibility as bishops to encourage and supervise the presentation of the faith in liturgy and catechetics which safeguard Catholic tradition and native ways.

B. Participation

This challenge will require an ongoing effort to increase the participation of Native Americans in the life of the Church. We need to hear clearly the voice of Catholic Native Americans. We need their leadership in the dialogue that can take place between Native American traditionalists and the Church. We welcome their gifts and contributions. We need their active participation in the ministries and life of the Church. We ask their advice about the ways the whole Catholic community can best respond to the realities of injustice and ignorance and their impact on native peoples. We advocate full opportunities for native people and we seek new partnerships with them in building the body of Christ within the Native American community.

C. Pastoral Leadership

We especially need to call forth and support the leadership of Native Americans—as priests, religious, and lay leaders. We are already blessed with many faithful and creative leaders, but more are needed to preach the Gospel and serve the needs of the Native American communities. We continue to welcome the generosity and commitment of many non-Native Americans who serve this community, but we look forward to the time when Native American bishops, priests, deacons, sisters, brothers, and lay leaders will increasingly shape and carry out the work of the Church in the Native American community and in the larger Catholic community. All those who serve within the Native American Catholic community should be well trained in Catholic theology and Native American culture and ways.

We pray that the blessings of the past and the hard work of the present will yield an even more vibrant and faithful Catholic Native American community. We strongly support the impressive efforts underway to train and prepare Native Americans for leadership in the priesthood, diaconate, religious life, and lay ministries.

In all these efforts we will build on our past and current pastoral ministries, educational commitments, and spiritual care within the Native American community. We acknowledge the failure and misguided direction of some past efforts, but we also recognize the enormous contributions of Indian schools, parishes, and ministries in meeting the needs of the Native American community and developing leaders from among their number. More authentic inculturation, increased participation, and stronger pastoral leadership will strengthen the faith of not only our Native American sisters and brothers, but our entire family of faith in the United States.

III. A Time for Recommitment

A. Public Advocacy

As we seek to respond to these ecclesial challenges, we also recommit ourselves to stand with native peoples in their search for greater justice in our society. We seek to be advocates with native leaders in this effort, not simply advocates for their needs. Together we must call our nation to greater responsiveness to the needs and rights of native people. We recognize that there are groups working for justice and cultural recognition for native peoples at regional and global levels. We encourage these efforts to build bridges among the indigenous people in the Americas and throughout the world.

We once again commit ourselves as the National Conference of Catholic Bishops to recognize and act upon the Native American dimensions of our ongoing advocacy regarding health, housing, employment, education, poverty, and other national issues. No group is touched more directly by federal policy than Native Americans. We must be alert and active regarding federal policies which support or undermine Native American lives, dignity, and rights. As a Church committed to a "preferential option for the poor and vulnerable," we recognize that Native Americans are often the most poor and vulnerable in our midst. We shall actively support initiatives to meet housing, health, and employment needs of native people, with a priority for measures that increase self-sufficiency and economic empowerment.

B. Respecting Treaty Rights

We also renew our commitment to press for justice in the prompt and fair adjudication of treaty rights. These treaties for which Native American tribes gave up their homelands, keeping only a fraction of what they originally inhabited, are of prime concern to their descendants. In some important ways they are now receiving some greater recognition of their rights, but agencies of government and courts do not always recognize the complexities of tribal autonomy within the territories of sovereign states. Native Americans have the right to be self-determining, to decide the ways their land and natural resources on those lands are used for the benefit of their people and for the broader common good.

C. Ongoing Support for Native American Communities

Our Campaign for Human Development has supported the quest for justice and self-help among native peoples. In its brief history, CHD has provided almost $3.5 million to support more than one hundred projects focused on stewardship of Indian land and resources, restoration of tribal recognition and rights, cultural preservation, and increased accountability for tribal education, welfare, and legal systems. We support continued efforts to empower and assist Native Americans in their search for justice. We also renew our support for the Bureau of Catholic Indian Missions and its essential work of evangelization and pastoral care within the Native American community. The American Board of Catholic Missions and the Catholic Church Extension Society also supply valuable assistance and help to the Native American Catholic community. Their support for the Church's work is a crucial resource building a vibrant Catholic faith within our dioceses and parishes which serve native people.

IV. A Call to Action

The Catholic community and our bishops' conference are called in this historic year to join together in renewed efforts to address several important areas which affect our Native American brothers and sisters. We call on the relevant committees of our conference of Catholic bishops to integrate the needs and contributions of native Catholics into their ongoing agenda. Significant work has been done in approving translations of eucharistic prayers, in public policy, in pastoral and social justice efforts, but more is required. Questions of Native American inculturation need to be further addressed by our liturgy and pastoral practices committees; advocacy and empowerment by our domestic policy and the Campaign for Human Development committees; pastoral leadership by our Committees on Vocations, Priestly Life and Ministry, Priestly Formation, and Permanent Diaconate; Indian education by our education committee. We also propose for consideration the establishment of an ad hoc NCCB Committee on Native American Catholics to help oversee this effort and to coordinate our conference's response to this statement.

Finally, we ask all believers to join with us in making this centennial year a time of continuing conversion and reflection on the demands of the Gospel now as we seek to bring greater respect and justice to our ministry among Native Americans. As we said a year ago: "Evangelization is unfinished if exploitation of the weak, of minorities still exists. The quincentenary calls us to a new commitment as Christians to right the evils of the past and the present, and to be forceful advocates of the peace and justice proclaimed by the Gospel. . . . Our observances should include times of mourning over the injustices of the past and vital efforts at reconciliation with our Native American brothers and sisters through prayer and social action."[9] This historic year calls us to both reflection and action concerning the most effective ways we can seek justice and build up the body of Christ within the Native American community.

We recognize that Hispanic and African Americans share with native peoples the reality of discrimination and the challenge of achieving full acceptance in our society and Church. A significant number of Hispanic people share roots and cultural ties with native peoples, as do some African Americans. These ties of solidarity and common struggle can help these communities work together to assist the Church in recognizing diversity as a strength and gift. Native, Hispanic, and African American members of our communities are called to be leaders and allies in the task of shaping a truly "Catholic" community—open to all God's children.

Conclusion

When he came to our land four years ago, Pope John Paul II affirmed and challenged Native American Catholics as he still challenges all of us in this fifth centenary year:

> I encourage you as native people to preserve and keep alive your cultures, your languages, the values and customs which have served you well in the past and which provide a solid foundation for the future. . . . "Your encounter with the Gospel has not only enriched you; it has enriched the Church. We are well aware that this has not taken place without its difficulties and, occasionally, its blunders. However . . . the Gospel does not destroy what is best in you. On the contrary, it enriches the spiritual qualities and gifts that are distinctive of your cultures. . . ."
>
> Here I wish to urge the local churches to be truly "catholic" in their outreach to native peoples and to show respect and honor for their culture and all their worthy traditions. . . . All consciences must be challenged. There are real injustices to be addressed and biased attitudes to be challenged.[10]

Solidarity with the Native American community is a special challenge for our Church in this fifth centenary year. We ask the intercession of Blessed Kateri Tekakwitha and Blessed Juan Diego as we seek
to recognize the burdens of history and meet the challenges of today.
We hope and pray that 1992 will be a time for remembering, for genuine reconciliation, and recommitment to work for greater justice for
the descendants of the first Americans.

Notes

1. National Conference of Catholic Bishops, *Heritage and Hope: Evangelization in the United States* (Washington, D.C.: United States Catholic Conference, 1991).
2. Ibid., introduction.
3. Ibid., 6.
4. Ibid., 7.
5. Ibid., 42.
6. Ibid., 43.
7. Statement of the U.S. Catholic bishops on American Indians, "The Church and the American Indians: Towards Dialogue and Respect," *Origins* 6:48 (May 19, 1977): 766-770.
8. John Paul II, Discourse to the Pontifical Council for Cultures (January 17, 1987), *L'Osservatore Romano* [English edition] 6 (February 9, 1987): 11.
9. *Heritage and Hope*, 45.
10. John Paul II, "Address to Native Americans" (September 14, 1988), *Origins* 17:17 (October 8, 1988): 297-298.

Source: Washington, D.C.: United States Catholic Conference, 1992.

Nutrition and Hydration: Moral and Pastoral Reflections

A Statement of the NCCB Committee for Pro-Life Activities

April 1992

Introduction

Modern medical technology seems to confront us with many questions not faced even a decade ago. Corresponding changes in medical practice have benefited many but have also prompted fears by some that they will be aggressively treated against their will or denied the kind of care that is their due as human persons with inherent dignity. Current debates about life-sustaining treatment suggest that our society's moral reflection is having difficulty keeping pace with its technological progress.

A religious view of life has an important contribution to make to these modern debates. Our Catholic tradition has developed a rich body of thought on these questions, which affirms a duty to preserve human life but recognizes limits to that duty.

Our first goal in making this statement is to reaffirm some basic principles of our moral tradition, to assist Catholics and others in making treatment decisions in accord with respect for God's gift of life.

These principles do not provide clear and final answers to all moral questions that arise as individuals make difficult decisions. Catholic theologians may differ on how best to apply moral principles to some questions not explicitly resolved by the Church's teaching authority. Likewise, we understand that those who must make serious health care decisions for themselves or for others face a complexity of issues, circumstances, thoughts, and emotions in each unique case.

This is the case with some questions involving the medically assisted provision of nutrition and hydration to helpless patients—those who are seriously ill, disabled, or persistently unconscious. These questions have been made more urgent by widely publicized court cases and the public debate to which they have given rise.

Our second purpose in issuing this statement, then, is to provide some clarification of the moral issues involved in decisions about medically assisted nutrition and hydration. We are fully aware that such guidance is not necessarily final, because there are many unresolved medical and ethical questions related to these issues, and the continuing development of medical technology will necessitate ongoing reflection. But these decisions already confront patients, families, and health care personnel every day. They arise whenever competent patients make decisions about medically assisted nutrition and hydration for their own present situation, when they consider signing an advance directive such as a "living will" or health care proxy document, and when families or other proxy decision makers make decisions about those entrusted to their care. We offer guidance to those who, facing these issues, might be confused by opinions that at times threaten to deny the inherent dignity of human life. We therefore address our reflections first to those who share our Judeo-Christian traditions, and second to others concerned about the dignity and value of human life who seek guidance in making their own moral decisions.

Moral Principles

The Judeo-Christian moral tradition celebrates life as the gift of a loving God, and respects the life of each human being because each is made in the image and likeness of God. As Christians we also believe we are redeemed by Christ and called to share eternal life with him. From these roots the Catholic tradition has developed a distinctive approach to fostering and sustaining human life. Our Church views life as a sacred trust, a gift over which we are given stewardship and not absolute dominion. The Church thus opposes all direct attacks on innocent life. As conscientious stewards we have a duty to preserve life, while recognizing certain limits to that duty:

1. Because human life is the foundation for all other human goods, it has a special value and significance. Life is "the first right of the human person" and "the condition of all the others."[1]

2. All crimes against life, including "euthanasia or willful suicide," must be opposed.[2] Euthanasia is "an action or an omission which of itself or by intention causes death, in order that all suffering may in this way be eliminated." Its terms of reference are to be found "in the intention of the will and in the methods used."[3] Thus defined, euthanasia is an attack on life which no one has a right to make or request, and which no government or other human authority can legitimately recommend or permit. Although individual guilt may be reduced or absent because of suffering or emotional factors that cloud the conscience, this does not change the objective wrongfulness of the act. It should also be recognized that an apparent plea for death may really be a plea for help and love.

3. Suffering is a fact of human life, and has special significance for the Christian as an opportunity to share in Christ's redemptive suffering. Nevertheless there is nothing wrong in trying to relieve someone's suffering; in fact, it is a positive good to do so, as long as one

does not intentionally cause death or interfere with other moral and religious duties.[4]

4. Everyone has the duty to care for his or her own life and health and to seek necessary medical care from others, but this does not mean that all possible remedies must be used in all circumstances. One is not obliged to use either "extraordinary" means or "disproportionate" means of preserving life—that is, means which are understood as offering no reasonable hope of benefit or as involving excessive burdens. Decisions regarding such means are complex and should ordinarily be made by the patient in consultation with his or her family, chaplain or pastor, and physician when that is possible.[5]

5. In the final stage of dying one is not obliged to prolong the life of a patient by every possible means: "When inevitable death is imminent in spite of the means used, it is permitted in conscience to take the decision to refuse forms of treatment that would only secure a precarious and burdensome prolongation of life, so long as the normal care due to the sick person in similar cases is not interrupted."[6]

6. While affirming life as a gift of God, the Church recognizes that death is unavoidable and that it can open the door to eternal life. Thus, "without in any way hastening the hour of death," the dying person should accept its reality and prepare for it emotionally and spiritually.[7]

7. Decisions regarding human life must respect the demands of justice, viewing each human being as our neighbor and avoiding all discrimination based on age or dependency.[8] A human being has "a unique dignity and an independent value, from the moment of conception and in every stage of development, whatever his or her physical condition." In particular, "the disabled person (whether the disability be the result of a congenital handicap, chronic illness or accident, or from mental or physical deficiency, and whatever the severity of the disability) is a fully human subject, with the corresponding innate, sacred and inviolable rights." First among these is "the fundamental and inalienable right to life."[9]

8. The dignity and value of the human person, which lie at the foundation of the Church's teaching on the right to life, also provide a basis for any just social order. Not only to become more Christian, but to become more truly human, society should protect the right to life through its laws and other policies.[10]

While these principles grow out of a specific religious tradition, they appeal to a common respect for the dignity of the human person. We commend them to all people of goodwill.

Questions About Medically Assisted
Nutrition and Hydration

In what follows we apply these well-established moral principles to the difficult issue of providing medically assisted nutrition and hydration to persons who are seriously ill, disabled, or persistently unconscious. We recognize the complexity involved in applying these principles to individual cases and acknowledge that, at this time and on this particular issue, our applications do not have the same authority as the principles themselves.

1. Is the withholding or withdrawing of medically assisted nutrition and hydration always a direct killing?

In answering this question one should avoid two extremes.

First, it is wrong to say that this could not be a matter of killing simply because it involves an omission rather than a positive action. In fact a deliberate omission may be an effective and certain way to kill, especially to kill someone weakened by illness. Catholic teaching condemns as euthanasia "an action *or an omission* which of itself or by intention causes death, in order that all suffering may in this way be eliminated." Thus "euthanasia includes not only active mercy killing but also the omission of treatment when the purpose of the omission is to kill the patient."[11]

Second, we should not assume that *all* or *most* decisions to withhold or withdraw medically assisted nutrition and hydration are attempts to cause death. To be sure, any patient will die if all nutrition and hydration are withheld.[12] But sometimes other causes are at work—for example, the patient may be imminently dying, whether feeding takes place or not, from an already existing terminal condition. At other times, although the shortening of the patient's life is one foreseeable result of an omission, the real *purpose* of the omission was to relieve the patient of a particular procedure that was of limited usefulness to the patient or unreasonably burdensome for the patient and the patient's family or caregivers. This kind of decision should not be equated with a decision to kill or with suicide.

The harsh reality is that some who propose withdrawal of nutrition and hydration from certain patients do directly *intend* to bring about a patient's death, and would even prefer a change in the law to allow for what they see as more "quick and painless" means to cause death.[13] In other words, nutrition and hydration (whether orally administered or medically assisted) are sometimes withdrawn not because a patient is dying, but precisely because a patient is not dying (or not dying quickly) and someone believes it would be better if he or she did, generally because the patient is perceived as having an unacceptably low "quality of life" or as imposing burdens on others.[14]

When deciding whether to withhold or withdraw medically assisted nutrition and hydration, or other forms of life support, we are called by our moral tradition to ask ourselves: What will my decision do for this patient? And what am I trying to achieve by doing it? We must be sure that it is not our intent to cause the patient's death—either for its own sake or as a means to achieving some other goal such as the relief of suffering.

2. Is medically assisted nutrition and hydration a form of "treatment" or "care"?

Catholic teaching provides that a person in the final stages of dying need not accept "forms of treatment that would only secure a precarious and burdensome prolongation of life," but should still receive "the normal care due to the sick person in similar cases."[15] All patients deserve to receive normal care out of respect for their inherent dignity as persons. As Pope John Paul II has said, a decision to forgo "purely experimental or ineffective interventions" does not "dispense from the valid therapeutic task of sustaining life or from assistance with the normal means of sustaining life. Science, even when it is unable to heal, can and should care for and assist the sick."[16] But the teaching of the Church has not resolved the question whether medically assisted nutrition and hydration should always be seen as a form of normal care.[17]

Almost everyone agrees that oral feeding, when it can be accepted and assimilated by a patient, is a form of care owed to all helpless people. Christians should be especially sensitive to this obligation, because giving food and drink to those in need is an important expression of Christian love and concern (Mt 10:42 and 25:35; Mk 9:41). But our obligations become less clear when adequate nutrition and hydration require the skills of trained medical personnel and the use of technologies that may be perceived as very burdensome—that is, as intrusive, painful, or repugnant. Such factors vary from one type of feeding procedure to another, and from one patient to another, making it difficult to classify all feeding procedures as either "care" or "treatment."

Perhaps this dilemma should be viewed in a broader context. Even medical "treatments" are morally obligatory when they are "ordinary" means—that is, if they provide a reasonable hope of benefit and do not involve excessive burdens. Therefore, we believe people should make decisions in light of a simple and fundamental insight: *Out of respect for the dignity of the human person, we are obliged to preserve our own lives, and help others preserve theirs, by the use of means that have a reasonable hope of sustaining life without imposing unreasonable burdens on those we seek to help, that is, on the patient and his or her family and community.*

We must therefore address the question of benefits and burdens next, recognizing that a full moral analysis is only possible when one knows the effects of a given procedure on a particular patient.

3. What are the benefits of medically assisted nutrition and hydration?

According to international codes of medical ethics, a physician will see a medical procedure as appropriate "if in his or her judgment it offers hope of saving life, reestablishing health or alleviating suffering."[18]

Nutrition and hydration, whether provided in the usual way or with medical assistance, do not by themselves remedy pathological conditions, except those caused by dietary deficiencies. But patients benefit from them in several ways. First, for all patients who can assimilate them, suitable food and fluids sustain life, and providing them normally expresses loving concern and solidarity with the helpless. Second, for patients being treated with the hope of a cure, appropriate food and fluids are an important element of sound health care. Third, even for patients who are imminently dying and incurable, food and fluids can prevent the suffering that may arise from dehydration, hunger, and thirst.

The benefit of sustaining and fostering life is fundamental, because life is our first gift from a loving God and the condition for receiving his other gifts. But sometimes even food and fluids are no longer effective in providing this benefit, because a patient has entered the final stage of a terminal condition. At such times we should make the dying person as comfortable as possible and provide nursing care and proper hygiene as well as companionship and appropriate spiritual aid. Such a person may lose all desire for food and drink and even be unable to ingest them. Initiating medically assisted feeding or intravenous fluids in this case may increase the patient's discomfort while providing no real benefit; ice chips or sips of water may instead be appropriate to provide comfort and counteract the adverse effects of dehydration.[19] Even in the case of the imminently dying patient, of course, any action or omission that of itself or by intention causes death is to be absolutely rejected.

As Christians who trust in the promise of eternal life, we recognize that death does not have the final word. Accordingly, we need not always prevent death until the last possible moment; but we should never intentionally cause death or abandon the dying person as though he or she were unworthy of care and respect.

4. What are the burdens of medically assisted nutrition and hydration?

Our tradition does not demand heroic measures in fulfilling the obligation to sustain life. A person may legitimately refuse even procedures that effectively prolong life, if he or she believes they would impose excessively grave burdens on himself or herself, or on his or her family and community. Catholic theologians have traditionally viewed medical treatment as excessively burdensome if it is "too painful, too damaging to the patient's bodily self and functioning, too psychologically repugnant to the patient, too restrictive to the patient's liberty and preferred activities, too suppressive of the patient's mental life, or too expensive."[20]

Because assessment of these burdens necessarily involves some subjective judgments, a conscious and competent patient is generally the best judge of whether a particular burden or risk is too grave to be tolerated in his or her own case. But because of the serious consequences of withdrawing all nutrition and hydration, patients and those helping them make decisions should assess such burdens or risks with special care.

Here we offer some brief reflections and cautions regarding the kinds of burdens sometimes associated with medically assisted nutrition and hydration.

Physical risks and burdens. The risks and objective complications of medically assisted nutrition and hydration will depend on the procedure used and the condition of the patient. In a given case a feeding procedure may become harmful or even life-threatening. (These medical data are discussed at length in an appendix to this paper.)

If the risks and burdens of a particular feeding procedure are deemed serious enough to warrant withdrawing it, we should not automatically deprive the patient of all nutrition and hydration but should ask whether another procedure is feasible that would be less burdensome. We say this because some helpless patients, including some in a "persistent vegetative state," receive tube feedings not because they cannot swallow food at all but because the tube feeding is less costly and difficult for health care personnel.[21]

Moreover, because burdens are assessed in relation to benefits, we should ask whether the risks and discomfort of a feeding procedure are really excessive as compared with the adverse effects of dehydration or malnutrition.

Psychological burdens on the patient. Many people see feeding tubes as frightening or even as bodily violations. Assessments of such burdens are necessarily subjective; they should not be dismissed on that account, but we offer some practical cautions to help prevent abuse.

First, in keeping with our moral teaching against the intentional causing of death by omission, one should distinguish between repugnance to a particular procedure and repugnance to life itself. The latter may occur when a patient views a life of helplessness and dependency on others as itself a heavy burden, leading him or her to wish or even to pray for death. Especially in our achievement-oriented society, the burden of living in such a condition may seem to outweigh any possible benefit of medical treatment and even lead a person to despair. But we should not assume that the burdens in such a case always outweigh the benefits; for the sufferer, given good counseling and spiritual support, may be brought again to appreciate the precious gift of life.

Second, our tradition recognizes that when treatment decisions are made, "account will have to be taken of the *reasonable* wishes of the patient and the patient's family, as also of the advice of the doctors who are specially competent in the matter."[22] The word "reasonable" is important here. Good health care providers will try to help patients assess psychological burdens with full information and without undue fear of unfamiliar procedures.[23] A well-trained and compassionate hospital chaplain can provide valuable personal and spiritual support to patients and families facing these difficult situations.

Third, we should not assume that a feeding procedure is inherently repugnant to all patients without specific evidence. In contrast to Americans' general distaste for the idea of being supported by "tubes and machines," some studies indicate surprisingly favorable views of medically assisted nutrition and hydration among patients and families with actual experience of such procedures.[24]

Economic and other burdens on caregivers. While some balk at the idea, in principle cost can be a valid factor in decisions about life support. For example, money spent on expensive treatment for one family member may be money otherwise needed for food, housing, and other necessities for the rest of the family. Here, also, we offer some cautions.

First, particularly when a form of treatment "carries a risk or is burdensome" on other grounds, a critically ill person may have a legitimate and altruistic desire "not to impose excessive expense on the family or the community."[25] Even for altruistic reasons a patient should not directly intend his or her own death by malnutrition or dehydration, but may accept an earlier death as a consequence of his or her refusal of an unreasonably expensive treatment. Decisions *by others* to deny an incompetent patient medically assisted nutrition and hydration for reasons of cost raise additional concerns about justice to the individual patient, who could wrongly be deprived of life itself to serve the less fundamental needs of others.

Second, we do not think individual decisions about medically assisted nutrition and hydration should be determined by macro-economic concerns such as national budget priorities and the high cost of health care. These social problems are serious, but it is by no means established that they require depriving chronically ill and helpless patients of effective and easily tolerated measures that they need to survive.[26]

Third, tube feeding alone is generally not very expensive and may cost no more than oral feeding.[27] What is seen by many as a grave financial and emotional burden on caregivers is the total long-term care of severely debilitated patients, who may survive for many years with no life support except medically assisted nutrition and hydration and nursing care.

The difficulties families may face in this regard, and their need for improved financial and other assistance from the rest of society, should not be underestimated. While caring for a helpless loved one can provide many intangible benefits to family members and bring them closer together, the responsibilities of care can also strain even close and loving family relationships; complex medical decisions must be made under emotionally difficult circumstances not easily appreciated by those who have never faced such situations.

Even here, however, we must try to think through carefully what we intend by withdrawing medically assisted nutrition and hydration. Are we deliberately trying to make sure that the patient dies, in order to relieve caregivers of the financial and emotional burdens that will fall upon them if the patient survives? Are we really implementing a decision to withdraw all other forms of care, precisely because the patient offers so little response to the efforts of caregivers? Decisions like these seem to reach beyond the weighing of burdens and benefits of medically assisted nutrition and hydration as such.

In the context of official church teaching, it is not yet clear to what extent we may assess the burden of a patient's total care rather than the burden of a particular treatment when we seek to refuse "burdensome" life support. On a practical level, those seeking to make good decisions might assure themselves of their own intentions by asking: Does my decision aim at relieving the patient of a particularly grave burden imposed by medically assisted nutrition and hydration? Or does it aim to avoid the total burden of caring for the patient? If so, does it achieve this aim by deliberately bringing about his or her death?

Rather than leaving families to confront such dilemmas alone, society and government should improve their assistance to families whose financial and emotional resources are strained by long-term care of loved ones.[28]

5. What role should "quality of life" play in our decisions?

Financial and emotional burdens are willingly endured by most families to raise their children or to care for mentally aware but weak and elderly family members. It is sometimes argued that we need not endure comparable burdens to feed and care for persons with severe mental and physical disabilities, because their low "quality of life" makes it unnecessary or pointless to preserve their lives.[29]

But this argument—even when it seems motivated by a humanitarian concern to reduce suffering and hardship—ignores the equal dignity and sanctity of all human life. Its key assumption—that people with disabilities necessarily enjoy life less than others or lack the potential to lead meaningful lives—is also mistaken.[30] Where suffering does exist, society's response should not be to neglect or eliminate the lives of people with disabilities, but to help correct their inadequate living conditions.[31] Very often the worst threat to a good "quality of life" for these people is not the disability itself, but the prejudicial attitudes of others—attitudes based on the idea that a life with serious disabilities is not worth living.[32]

This being said, our moral tradition allows for three ways in which the "quality of life" of a seriously ill patient *is* relevant to treatment decisions.

1. Consistent with respect for the inherent sanctity of life, we should relieve needless suffering and support morally acceptable ways of improving each patient's quality of life.[33]

2. One may legitimately refuse a treatment because it would itself create an impairment imposing *new* serious burdens or risks on the patient. This decision to avoid the new burdens or risks created by a treatment is not the same as directly intending to end life in order to avoid the burden of living in a disabled state.[34]

3. Sometimes a disabling condition may directly influence the benefits and burdens of a specific treatment for a particular patient. For example, a confused or demented patient may find medically assisted nutrition and hydration more frightening and burdensome than other patients do because he or she cannot understand what it is. The patient may even repeatedly pull out feeding tubes, requiring burdensome physical restraints if this form of feeding is to be continued. In such cases, ways of alleviating such special burdens should be explored before concluding that they justify withholding all food and fluids needed to sustain life.

These humane considerations are quite different from a "quality of life" ethic that would judge individuals with disabilities or limited potential as not worthy of care or respect. It is one thing to withhold a procedure because it would impose new disabilities on a patient, and quite another thing to say that patients who already have such disabilities should not have their lives preserved. A means considered ordinary or proportionate for other patients should not be considered extraordinary or disproportionate for severely impaired patients solely because of a judgment that their lives are not worth living.

In short, while considerations regarding a person's quality of life have some validity in weighing the burdens and benefits of medical treatment, at the present time in our society judgments about the quality of life are sometimes used to promote euthanasia. The Church must emphasize the sanctity of life of each person as a fundamental principle in all moral decision making.

6. Do persistently unconscious patients represent a special case?

Even Catholics who accept the same basic moral principles may strongly disagree on how to apply them to patients who appear to be persistently unconscious—that is, those who are in a permanent coma or a "persistent vegetative state" (PVS).[35] Some moral questions in this area have not been explicitly resolved by the Church's teaching authority.

On some points there is wide agreement among Catholic theologians.

1. An unconscious patient must be treated as a living human person with inherent dignity and value. Direct killing of such a patient is as morally reprehensible as the direct killing of anyone else. Even the medical terminology used to describe these patients as "vegetative" unfortunately tends to obscure this vitally important point, inviting speculation that a patient in this state is a "vegetable" or a subhuman animal.[36]

2. The area of legitimate controversy does not concern patients with conditions like mental retardation, senility, dementia, or even temporary unconsciousness. Where serious disagreement begins is with the patient who has been diagnosed as completely and permanently unconscious after careful testing over a period of weeks or months.

Some moral theologians argue that a particular form of care or treatment is morally obligatory only when its benefits outweigh its burdens to a patient or the care providers. In weighing burdens, they say, the total burden of a procedure and the consequent requirements of care must be taken into account. If no benefit can be demonstrated, the procedure, whatever its burdens, cannot be obligatory. These moralists also hold that the chief criterion to determine the benefit of a procedure cannot be merely that it prolongs physical life, since physical life is not an absolute good but is relative to the spiritual good of the person. They assert that the spiritual good of the person is union with God, which can be advanced only by human acts, i.e., conscious, free acts. Since the best current medical opinion holds that persons in the persistent vegetative state (PVS) are incapable now or in the future of conscious, free human acts, these moralists conclude that, when careful diagnosis verifies this condition, it is not obligatory to prolong life by such interventions as a respirator, antibiotics, or medically assisted hydration and nutrition. To decide to omit non-obligatory care, therefore, is not to intend the patient's death, but only to avoid the burden of the procedure. Hence, though foreseen, the patient's death is to be attributed to the patient's pathological condition and not to the omission of care. Therefore, these theologians conclude, while it is always wrong directly to intend or cause the death of such patients, the natural dying process which would have occurred without these interventions may be permitted to proceed.

While this rationale is convincing to some, it is not theologically conclusive and we are not persuaded by it. In fact, other theologians argue cogently that theological inquiry could lead one to a more carefully limited conclusion.

These moral theologians argue that while particular treatments can be judged useless or burdensome, it is morally questionable and would create a dangerous precedent to imply that any human life is not a positive good or "benefit." They emphasize that while life is not the highest good, it is always and everywhere a basic good of the human person and not merely a means to other goods. They further assert that if the "burden" one is trying to relieve by discontinuing medically assisted nutrition and hydration is the burden of remaining alive in the allegedly undignified condition of PVS, such a decision is unacceptable, because one's intent is only achieved by deliberately ensuring the patient's death from malnutrition or dehydration. Finally, these moralists suggest that PVS is best seen as an extreme form of mental and physical disability—one whose causes, nature, and prognosis are as yet imperfectly understood—and not as a terminal illness or fatal pathology from which patients should generally be allowed to die. Because the patient's life can often be sustained indefinitely by medically assisted nutrition and hydration that is not unreasonably risky or burdensome for that patient, they say, we are not dealing here with a case where "inevitable death is imminent in spite of the means used."[37] Rather, because the patient will die in a few days if medically assisted nutrition and hydration are discontinued,[38] but can often live a long time if they are provided, the inherent dignity and worth of the human person obligates us to provide this patient with care and support.

Further complicating this debate is a disagreement over what responsible Catholics should do in the absence of a final resolution of this question. Some point to our moral tradition of probabilism, which would allow individuals to follow the appropriate moral analysis that they find persuasive. Others point to the principle that in cases where one might risk unjustly depriving someone of life, we should take the safer course.

In the face of the uncertainties and unresolved medical and theological issues, it is important to defend and preserve important values. On the one hand, there is a concern that patients and families should not be subjected to unnecessary burdens, ineffective treatments, and indignities when death is approaching. On the other hand, it is important to ensure that the inherent dignity of human persons, even those who are persistently unconscious, is respected, and that no one is deprived of nutrition and hydration with the intent of bringing on his or her death.

It is not easy to arrive at a single answer to some of the real and personal dilemmas involved in this issue. In study, prayer, and compassion, we continue to reflect on this issue and hope to discover additional information that will lead to its ultimate resolution.

In the meantime, at a practical level, we are concerned that withdrawal of all life support, including nutrition and hydration, not be viewed as appropriate or automatically indicated for the entire class of PVS patients simply because of a judgment that they are beyond the reach of medical treatment that would restore consciousness. We note the current absence of conclusive scientific data on the causes and implications of different degrees of brain damage, on the PVS patient's ability to experience pain, and on the reliability of prognoses for many such patients.[39] We do know that many of these patients have a good prognosis for long-term survival when given medically assisted nutrition and hydration, and a certain prognosis for death otherwise—and we know that many in our society view such an early death as a positive good for a patient in this condition. Therefore we are gravely concerned about current attitudes and policy trends in our society that would too easily dismiss patients without apparent mental faculties as non-persons or as undeserving of human care and concern. In this climate, even legitimate moral arguments intended to have a careful and limited application can easily be misinterpreted, broadened, and abused by others to erode respect for the lives of some of our society's most helpless members.

In light of these concerns, it is our considered judgment that while legitimate Catholic moral debate continues, decisions about these patients should be guided by a presumption in favor of medically assisted nutrition and hydration. A decision to discontinue such measures should be made in light of a careful assessment of the burdens and benefits of nutrition and hydration for the individual patient and his or her family and community. Such measures must not be withdrawn in order to cause death, but they may be withdrawn if they offer no reasonable hope of sustaining life or pose excessive risks or burdens. We also believe that social and health care policies should be carefully framed so that these patients are not routinely classified as "terminal" or as prime candidates for the discontinuance of even minimal means of life support.

7. Who should make decisions about medically assisted nutrition and hydration?

"Who decides?" In our society many believe this is the most important or even the only important question regarding this issue, and many understand it in terms of who has *legal* status to decide. Our Catholic tradition is more concerned with the principles for good *moral* decision making, which apply to everyone involved in a decision. Some general observations are appropriate here.

A competent patient is the primary decision maker about his or her own health care and is in the best situation to judge how the benefits and burdens of a particular procedure will be experienced. Ideally the patient will act with the advice of loved ones, of health care personnel who have expert knowledge of medical aspects of the case, and of pastoral counselors who can help explore the moral issues and spiritual values involved. A patient may wish to make known his or her general wishes about life support in advance; such expressions cannot have the weight of a fully informed decision made in the actual circumstances of an illness, but can help guide others in the event of a later state of incompetency.[40] Morally even the patient making decisions for himself or herself is bound by norms that prohibit the directly intended causing of death through action or omission and by the distinction between ordinary and extraordinary means.

When a patient is not competent to make his or her own decisions, a proxy decision maker who shares the patient's moral convictions, such as a family member or guardian, may be designated to represent the patient's interests and interpret his or her wishes. Here, too, moral limits remain relevant—that is, morally the proxy may not deliberately cause a patient's death or refuse what is clearly ordinary means, even if he or she believes the patient would have made such a decision.

Health care personnel should generally follow the reasonable wishes of patient or family, but must also consult their own consciences when participating in these decisions. A physician or nurse told to participate in a course of action that he or she views as clearly immoral has a right and responsibility either to refuse to participate in this course of action or to withdraw from the case, and he or she should be given the opportunity to express the reasons for such refusal in the appropriate forum. Social and legal policies must protect such rights of conscience.

Finally, because these are matters of life and death for human persons, society as a whole has a legitimate interest in responsible decision making.[41]

Conclusion

In this document we reaffirm moral principles that provide a basis for responsible discussion of the morality of life support. We also offer tentative guidance on how to apply these principles to the difficult issue of medically assisted nutrition and hydration.

We reject any omission of nutrition and hydration intended to cause a patient's death. We hold for a presumption in favor of providing medically assisted nutrition and hydration to patients who need it, which presumption would yield in cases where such procedures have no medically reasonable hope of sustaining life or pose excessive risks or burdens. Recognizing that judgments about the benefits and burdens of medically assisted nutrition and hydration in individual cases have a subjective element and are generally best made by the patient directly involved, we also affirm a legitimate role for families' love and guidance, health care professionals' ethical concerns, and society's interest in preserving life and protecting the helpless. In rejecting broadly permissive policies on withdrawal of nutrition and hydration from vulnerable patients, we must also help ensure that the burdens of caring for the helpless are more equitably shared throughout our society.

We recognize that this document is our first word, not our last word, on some of the complex questions involved in this subject. We urge Catholics and others concerned about the dignity of the human person to study these reflections and participate in the continuing public discussion of how best to address the needs of the helpless in our society.

Appendix: Technical Aspects of Medically Assisted Nutrition and Hydration

Procedures for providing nourishment and fluids to patients who cannot swallow food orally are either "parenteral" (bypassing the digestive tract) or "enteral" (using the digestive tract).

Parenteral or intravenous feeding is generally considered "more hazardous and more expensive" than enteral feeding.[42] It can be subdivided into peripheral intravenous feeding (using a needle inserted into a peripheral vein) and central intravenous feeding, also known as total parenteral feeding or hyperalimentation (using a larger needle inserted into a central vein near the heart). Peripheral intravenous lines can provide fluids and electrolytes as well as some nutrients; they can maintain fluid balance and prevent dehydration, but cannot provide adequate nutrition in the long-term.[43] Total parenteral feeding can provide a more adequate nutritional balance, but poses significant risks to the patient and may involve costs an order of magnitude higher than other methods of tube feeding. It is no longer considered experimental and has become "a mainstay for helping critically ill patients to survive acute illnesses where the prognosis had previously been nearly hopeless," but its feasibility for lifelong maintenance of patients without a functioning gastrointestinal tract has been questioned.[44]

Because of the limited usefulness of peripheral intravenous feeding and the special burdens of total parenteral feeding—and because few patients so completely lack a digestive system that they must depend on these measures for their sole source of nutrition—enteral tube feeding is the focus of the current debate over medically assisted nutrition and hydration. Such methods are used when a patient has a functioning digestive system but is unable or unwilling to ingest food orally and/or to swallow. The most common routes for enteral tube feeding are nasogastric (introducing a thin plastic tube through the nasal cavity to reach into the stomach), gastrostomy (surgical insertion of a tube through the abdominal wall into the stomach), and jejunostomy (surgical insertion of a tube through the abdominal wall into the small intestine).[45] These methods are the primary focus of this document.

Each method of enteral tube feeding has potential side effects. For example, nasogastric tubes must be inserted and monitored carefully so that they will not introduce food or fluids into the lungs. They may also irritate sensitive tissues and create discomfort; confused or angry patients may sometimes try to remove them; and efforts to restrain a patient to prevent this can impose additional discomfort and other burdens. On the positive side, insertion of these tubes requires no surgery and only a modicum of training.[46]

Gastrostomy and jejunostomy tubes are better tolerated by many patients in need of long-term feeding. Their most serious physical burdens arise from the fact that their insertion requires surgery using local or general anesthesia, which involves some risk of infection and other complications. Once the surgical procedure is completed, these tubes can often be maintained without serious pain or medical complications, and confused patients do not often attempt to remove them.[47]

Notes

1. Congregation for the Doctrine of the Faith, *Declaration on Procured Abortion* (Washington, D.C.: United States Catholic Conference, 1974), no. 11.
2. Second Vatican Council, *Pastoral Constitution on the Church in the Modern World (Gaudium et Spes)*, no. 27. Suicide must be distinguished from "that sacrifice of one's life whereby for a higher cause, such as God's glory, the salvation of souls or the service of one's brethren, a person offers his or her own life or puts it in danger," Congregation for the Doctrine of the Faith, *Declaration on Euthanasia* (Washington, D.C.: United States Catholic Conference, 1980), part 1.
3. *Declaration on Euthanasia,* part 2.
4. See *Declaration on Euthanasia,* part 3; United States Catholic Conference, *Ethical and Religious Directives for Catholic Health Facilities* (Washington, D.C.: United States Catholic Conference, 1971), directive 29.
5. *Declaration on Euthanasia,* part 4.
6. Ibid.
7. Ibid., Conclusion.
8 *Gaudium et Spes,* no. 27; *Declaration on Procured Abortion,* no. 12.
9. Vatican Statement on the International Year of Disabled Persons (March 4, 1981), section 1, no. 1, and section 2, no. 1 in *Origins* 10:47 (May 7, 1981): 747-748.
10. *Declaration on Euthanasia,* Introduction; *Declaration on Procured Abortion,* nos. 10-11, 21; Congregation for the Doctrine of the Faith, *Instruction on Respect for Human Life in Its Origin* (Boston: St. Paul Editions, 1987), part 3.

11. Archbishop John Roach, "Life-Support Removal: No Easy Answers," *Catholic Bulletin* (March 7, 1991): 1 (citing Biomedical Ethics Commission of the Archdiocese of St. Paul-Minneapolis).

12. "If all fluids and nutrition are withdrawn from any patient, regardless of the condition, he or she will die—inevitably and invariably. Death may come in a few days or take up to two weeks. Rarely in medicine is an earlier death for the patient so certain," Ronald E. Cranford, M.D., "Patients with Permanent Loss of Consciousness,"in *By No Extraordinary Means*, ed. Joanne Lynn (Bloomington, Ind.: Indiana University Press, 1986), 191.

13. See the arguments made by a judge in the Elizabeth Bouvia case and by the attorneys in the Hector Rodas case, among others. See *Bouvia v. Superior Court*, 225 Cal. Rptr. 297, 307-308 (1986) (Compton, J., concurring); *Complaint for the Declaratory Relief in Rodas Case, Issues in Law and Medicine* 2 (1987): 499-501, quoted verbatim from *Rodas v. Erkenbrack*, no. 87 ev. 142 (Mesa County, Colo., filed Jan. 30, 1987).

14. As one medical ethicist observes, interest in a broadly permissive policy for removing nutrition and hydration has grown "because a denial of nutrition may in a long run become the only effective way to make certain that a large number of biologically tenacious patients actually die." Daniel Callahan, "On Feeding the Dying," *Hastings Center Report* 13 (October 1983): 22.

15. Alfred O'Rahilly, *Moral Principles* (Cork, Ireland: Cork University Press, 1948), no. 5.

16. Address to a Human Pre-Leukemia Conference, November 15, 1985: *Acta Apostolicae Sedis* 78 (1986): 361. Also see his October 21, 1985 address to a study group of the Pontifical Academy of Sciences: "Even when the sick are incurable, they are never untreatable; whatever their condition, appropriate care should be provided for them," *Acta Apostolicae Sedis* 78 (1986): 314; *Origins* 15:25 (December 5, 1985): 416.

17. Some groups advising the Holy See have ventured opinions on this point, but these do not have the force of official church teaching. For example, in 1985 a study group of the Pontifical Academy of Sciences concluded: "If a patient is in a permanent, irreversible coma, as far as can be foreseen, treatment is not required, but all care should be lavished on him, including feeding," Pontifical Academy of Sciences, "The Artificial Prolongation of Life," *Origins* 15:25 (December 5, 1985): 415. Since comatose patients cannot generally take food orally, the statement evidently refers to medically assisted feeding. Similar statements are found in Pontifical Council Cor Unum, *Question of Ethics Regarding the Fatally Ill and the Dying* (Vatican City: Vatican Press, 1981), 9; "Ne Eutanasia Ne Accanimento Terapeutico," *La Civiltà Cattolica* 3280 (February 21, 1987): 324.

18. World Medical Association, *Declaration of Helsinki* (1975), II.1.

19. See Joyce V. Zerwekh, "The Dehydration Question," *Nursing* (January 1983): 47-51.

20. See William E. May et al., "Feeding and Hydrating the Permanently Unconscious and Other Vulnerable Persons," *Issues in Law and Medicine* 3 (Winter 1987): 208.

21. Ronald E. Cranford, "The Persistent Vegetative State: The Medical Reality (Getting the Facts Straight)," *Hastings Center Report* 18 (February/March 1988): 31.

22. *Declaration on Euthanasia*, part 4 (emphasis added).

23. Current ethical guidelines for nurses, while generally defending patient autonomy, reflect this concern: "Obligations to prevent harm and bring benefit . . . require that nurses seek to understand the patient's reasons for refusal. . . . Nurses should make every effort to correct inaccurate views, to modify superficially held beliefs and overly dramatic gestures, and to restore hope where there is reason to hope," American Nurses' Association Committee on Ethics, "Guidelines on Withdrawing or Withholding Food and Fluids," *BioLaw* 2 (October 1988): U1124-1125.

24. In one such study, "70 percent of patients and families were 100 percent willing to undergo intensive care again to achieve even one month of survival"; "age, severity of critical illness, length of stay, and charges for intensive care did not influence willingness to undergo intensive care," Danis et al., "Patients' and Families' Preferences for Medical Intensive Care," *Journal of the American Medical Association* 260 (August 12, 1988): 797. In another study, out of thirty-three people who had close relatives in a "persistent vegetative state," twenty-nine agreed with the initial decision to initiate tube feeding and twenty-five strongly agreed that such feeding should be continued, although none of those surveyed had made the decision to initiate it. See Tresch et al., "Patients in a Persistent Vegetative State: Attitudes and Reactions of Family Members," *Journal of the American Geriatrics Society* 39 (January 1991): 17-21.

25. *Declaration on Euthanasia*, part 4.

26. "In striving to contain medical care costs, it is important to avoid discriminating against the critically ill and dying, to shun invidious comparisons of the economic value of various individuals to society, and to refuse to abandon patients and hasten death to save money," Hastings Center, *Guidelines on the Termination of Life-Sustaining Treatment and Care of the Dying* (Briar Cliff Manor, N.Y.: Hastings Center, 1987), 120.

27. A possible exception is total parenteral feeding, which requires carefully prepared sterile formulas and more intensive daily monitoring. Ironically, some current health care policies may exert economic pressure in favor of TPN because it is easier to obtain third-party reimbursement. Families may pay more for other forms of feeding because some insurance companies do *not* see them as "medical treatment." See U.S. Congress, Office of Technology Assessment, *Life-Sustaining Technologies and the Elderly*, OTA-BA-306 (Washington, D.C.: Government Printing Office, July 1987), 286.

28. "One can never claim that one wishes to bring comfort to a family by suppressing one of its members. The respect, the dedication, the time and the means required for the care of handicapped persons, even of those whose mental faculties are gravely affected, is the price that a society should generously pay in order to remain truly human," *Vatican Statement*, section II, no. 1 in *Origins*, p. 748 (see no. 9 above). The Holy See acknowledges that society as a whole should willingly assume these burdens, not leave them on the shoulders of individuals and families.

29. For example, see P. Singer, "Sanctity of Life or Quality of Life?" *Pediatrics* 72 (July 1983): 128-129. On the use and misuse of the term "quality of life," see Cardinal John O'Connor, "Who Will Care for the AIDS Victims?" *Origins* 19:33 (January 18, 1990): 544-548. Some Catholic theologians agree that a low "quality of life" justifies withdrawal of medically assisted feeding only from patients diagnosed as permanently unconscious. This argument is discussed separately in section 6 below.

30. See David Milne, "Urges MDs to Get Birth Defects Patient's Own Story," *Medical Tribune* (December 12, 1979): 6.

31. United States Catholic Conference, *Pastoral Statement of the U.S. Catholic Bishops on Persons with Disabilities* (Washington, D.C.: United States Catholic Conference, 1978).

32. Some patients with disabilities ask for death because all their efforts to build a life of self-respect are thwarted; a "right to die" is the first right for which they receive enthusiastic support from the able-bodied. See Paul K. Longmore, "Elizabeth Bouvia, Assisted Suicide and Social Prejudice," *Issues in Law and Medicine* 3 (Fall 1987): 141-168.

33. "Quality of life must be sought, in so far as it is possible, by proportionate and appropriate treatment, but it presupposes life and the right to life for everyone, without discrimination and abandonment," John Paul II, Address of April 14, 1988 to the Eleventh European Congress of Perinatal Medicine, *Acta Apostolicae Sedis* 80 (1988): 1426; *The Pope Speaks* 33 (1988): 264-265.

34. See Archbishop Roger Mahony, "Two Statements on the Bouvia Case," *Linacre Quarterly* 55 (February 1988): 85-87.

35. Coma and persistent vegetative state are not the same. Coma, strictly speaking, is generally not a long-term condition, for within a few weeks a comatose patient usually dies, recovers, or reaches the plateau of a persistent vegetative state. "Coma implies the absence of both arousal and content. In terms of observable behavior, the comatose patient appears to be asleep, but unlike the sleeping patient, he cannot be aroused from this state. . . . The patient in the vegetative state appears awake but shows no evidence of content, either confused or appropriate. He often has sleep-wake cycles but cannot demonstrate an awareness either of himself or his environment," Levy, "The Comatose Patient,"in *The Clinical Neurosciences*, ed. R. Rosenberg (New York: Churchill Livingstone, 1983), 1:956.

36. While his pejorative connotation was surely not intended by those coining the phrase, we invite the medical profession to consider a less discriminatory term for this diagnostic state.

37. O'Rahilly, no. 5.

38. Because patients need nutritional support to live during the weeks or months of observation required for responsible assessment of PVS, the cases discussed here involve decisions about discontinuing such support rather than initiating it.

39. One recent scientific study of recovery rates followed up 84 patients with a firm diagnosis of PVS. Of these patients, "41 percent became conscious by six months, 52 percent regained consciousness by one year, and 58 percent recovered consciousness within the three-year follow-up interval." The study was unable to identify "predictors of recovery from the vegetative state," that is,

there is no established test by which physicians can tell in advance which PVS patients will ultimately wake up. The data "do not exclude the possibility of vegetative patients regaining consciousness after the second year," though this "must be regarded as a rare event," H. S. Levin, C. Saydjari, et al., "Vegetative State After Closed-Head Injury: A Traumatic Coma Data Bank Report," *Archives of Neurology* 48 (June 1991): 580-585.

40. Some Catholic moralists, using the concept of a "virtual intention," note that a person may give spiritual significance to his or her later suffering during incompetency by deciding in advance to join these sufferings with those of Christ for the redemption of others.

41. See NCCB Committee for Pro-Life Activities, "Guidelines for Legislation on Life-Sustaining Treatment" (November 10, 1984), *Origins* 14:32 (January 24, 1985): 526-528; "Statement on the Uniform Rights of the Terminally Ill Act" (June 1986), *Origins* 16:12 (September 4, 1986): 222-224; United States Catholic Conference, Brief as *Amicus Curiae* in Support of Petitioners, "*Cruzan v. Director of Missouri Department of Health v. McCanse*," U.S. Supreme Court, No. 88-1503, *Origins* 19:21 (October 26, 1989): 345-351.

42. David Major, M.D., "The Medical Procedures for Providing Food and Water: Indications and Effects,"in *By No Extraordinary Means,* ed. Joanne Lynn (Bloomington, Ind.: Indiana University Press, 1986), 27.

43. Peripheral veins (e.g., those found in an arm or leg) will eventually collapse after a period of intravenous feeding and will collapse much faster if complex nutrients such as proteins are included in the formula. See U.S. Congress, Office of Technology Assessment, *Life-Sustaining Technologies and the Elderly,* OTA-BA-306 (Washington, D.C.: U.S. Government Printing Office, July 1987), 283-284.

44. Major, 22, 24-25. Also see OTA, 284-286.

45. See Major, 22, 25-26.

46. Major, 22; OTA, 282-283; Ross Laboratories, *Tube Feedings: Clinical Applications* (1982), 28-30.

47. Major, 22; OTA, 282. Many ethicists observe that there is no morally significant difference in principle between withdrawing a life-sustaining procedure and failing to initiate it. However, surgically implanting a feeding tube and maintaining it once implanted may involve a different proportion of benefit to burden, because the transient risks of the initial surgical procedure will not continue or recur during routine maintenance of the tube.

Source: Washington, D.C.: United States Catholic Conference, 1992.

When I Call for Help:
A Pastoral Response to
Domestic Violence Against Women

*A Statement of the Committee on Marriage and
Family Life and the Committee on Women in Society and
in the Church Affirmed by the NCCB Administrative Committee*

September 1992

- She told the psychotherapist that she was living in the doghouse because her husband locked her out when he was in a rage.
- He told the abuse counselor in group therapy that after the first couple of beatings, he didn't have to beat her up again. All he had to do was raise his fist.

Introduction

As pastors of the Church in the United States, we join bishops in other countries, notably Canada and New Zealand, in stating as clearly and strongly as we can that violence against women, in the home or outside the home, is *never* justified. Violence in any form—physical, sexual, psychological, or verbal—is sinful; many times, it is a crime as well.

Abuse is a topic that no one likes to think about. But, because it exists in our parishes, dioceses, and neighborhoods, we present this statement as an initial step in what we hope will become a continuing effort in the Church in the United States to combat domestic violence against women. This statement is our response to the repeated requests of many women and men around the United States to address the issue.

We write out of our desire to offer the Church's resources to both the women who are battered and the men who abuse. Both groups need Jesus' strength and healing. We also write out of an awareness that times of economic distress such as the present, when wage earners lose their jobs or are threatened with their loss, often are marked by an increase in domestic violence.

Though we focus here on violence against women, we are not implying that violence against men or against youths or violence against the elderly or the unborn is any less vicious. In fact, violence against any person is contrary to Jesus' gospel message to "love one another as I have loved you." When violence toward women is tolerated, it helps to set the stage for violent acts against other groups as well.

Violence against women in the home has particularly serious repercussions. When the woman is a mother and the violence takes place in front of her children, the stage is set for a cycle of violence that may be continued from generation to generation.

Domestic violence counselors teach that violence is learned behavior. In many cases, men who become abusive and the women who are abused grew up in homes where violence occurred. In such a situation, a child can grow up believing that violence is acceptable behavior; boys learn that this is a way to be powerful. Abuse counselors say that a child raised in a home with physical abuse is a thousand times more likely to use violence in his own family. At the same time, 25 percent of men who grow up in an abusive home choose not to use violence.

We agree with the bishops of Quebec, Canada, in calling on the Christian community to "join forces with and complement the work of those associations and groups that are already involved in preventing and fighting this form of violence."[1]

We also agree with the Canadian church leaders, who stated that when men abuse women, they "reflect a lack of understanding in our society about how men and women ought to relate to each other. They violate the basic Christian values of justice, equality, respect, dignity, and peace; they go against the call to practical kindness, gentleness, faithfulness, mutual support, and to love one another as ourselves."[2]

Those We Are Addressing

Recognizing the seriousness of the problem, we are addressing this statement to several audiences:

- First, to women who are victims of violence and who may need the Church's help to break out of their pain and isolation
- To pastors, parish personnel, and educators who often are a first line of defense for women who are suffering abuse
- To men, especially to those men who as abusers may not know how to break out of the cycle of violence—or who realize that it is possible to do so
- To society, which slowly is recognizing the extent of domestic violence against women

NOTE: This is not meant to be an all-inclusive statement on violence against women. Because violence has many dimensions and ramifications, this statement is intended to be an introduction along with some practical pastoral suggestions of what parishes can do now.

Domestic Violence in the United States

An estimated 3 to 4 million women in the United States are battered each year by their husbands or partners.

Approximately 37 percent of obstetric patients—of every race, class, and educational background—report being physically abused while pregnant.

More than 50 percent of the women murdered in the United States are killed by their partner or ex-partner.

In 1987, 375,000 abused women and children were served by shelters and safe houses, but shelters can accept only about 60 percent of those who need help.

Dimensions of the Problem

"Evidence collected over the last twenty years indicates that physical and sexual violence against women is an enormous problem. The high prevalence of violence against women brings them into regular contact with physicians; at least one in five women seen in emergency departments has symptoms relating to abuse."[3] Domestic violence is the most common form of violence in our society and the least reported crime.

What is *abuse*? It is any kind of behavior that one person uses to control another through fear and intimidation. It includes emotional and psychological abuse, battering, and sexual assault. Abuse is not limited to a single group. Cutting across racial and economic backgrounds, it occurs in families from every ethnic, economic, religious, and educational background.[4]

Because violence usually occurs in the privacy of people's homes, it often is shrouded in silence. People outside the family hesitate to interfere, even when they suspect abuse is occurring. Traditionally, the abuse of a wife by her husband has been considered "not only a family matter but virtually a husband's prerogative."[5] Even today, some people—mistakenly—argue that intervention by outside sources endangers the concept of the sanctity of the home.

Yet, "abuse, assault, or murder are not less serious because they occur within the family. . . . Violence, whether committed against family members or strangers, is antithetical to the Judeo-Christian messages of love and respect for the human person."[6]

As we have said, "a woman's dignity is destroyed in a particularly vicious and heinous way when she is treated violently. It shocks us to learn that currently one woman in four will be sexually assaulted in her lifetime."[7]

Why Men Batter

Some psychiatric opinion holds that in a very small percentage of cases a psychophysical disorder may trigger violent behavior. However, in the majority of cases, other reasons can explain men's abusive behavior. Men who abuse women convince themselves that they have a right to do so. They may believe that violence is a way to dissipate tension and to solve problems—a view that society often supports. Battering and other forms of abuse occur in a society saturated with violence, where violence is glorified in books, in movies, and on television. Often, violence is portrayed as an appropriate way for people to respond to threatening situations.

Abusive men tend to be extremely jealous, possessive, and easily angered. For example, they may fly into a rage because their spouse called her mother too often or because she didn't take the car in for servicing. Many try to isolate their wives by limiting their contact with family and friends.

Often, abusive men have low self-esteem and feel vulnerable and powerless. They are "more likely to have witnessed or experienced violence in childhood, to abuse alcohol, to be sexually assaultive to their wives, and to be at risk for violence against children."[8] Typically, they deny that the abuse is happening, or they insist that it happens rarely. Many try to pin the blame for their abusive behavior on someone or something other than themselves—their wives, the job, and so forth. Alcohol is an especially serious presence in many domestic-violence incidents. Alcohol and drugs lessen inhibitions and can heighten anger, impair judgment, desensitize, and increase the amount of force being used.

Many abusive men hold a view of women as inferior. Their conversation and language reveal their attitudes toward a woman's place in society. Many believe that men are meant to dominate and control women.

Why Women Stay

No answer fully explains why women stay with their abusers. Psychiatrists report that abusive relationships usually start out like other relationships; initially, they are loving and rewarding to both parties. Down the road, when the first violent act occurs, the woman is likely to be incredulous and willing to believe her spouse when he apologizes and promises that he will never repeat the abuse.

As time goes by and the abuse is repeated, many women come to believe they somehow are to blame for their husband's or partner's actions; that if they just acted differently, the abuse would not occur. In time, as their self-esteem plummets, they feel trapped in the abusive relationship, especially if they have children and no other means of support.

Many abused women are isolated and alone with their pain. Even if they would like to seek help, they do not know where to go. In addition, many women are deeply ashamed to admit what is happening. They may believe that they are responsible for the success or failure of the marriage. Accordingly, many women are ashamed to admit that the man they married and with whom they have children, the one they love, is the one who is terrorizing them. "Violence at home typically leaves no place in which defenses can be let down."[9]

Finally, many battered wives are vulnerable economically. They may not believe that they can support themselves, much less their children. Accordingly, they do not see how they can escape. The result is that they become passive, anxious, and depressed. Most are unable to visualize a different future for themselves.

Over time, abuse escalates, though it may not always involve ongoing physical violence. Often, the threat of physical abuse is enough to terrorize women. For some victims, the final outcome of abuse is murder.

Toward a Church Response to Domestic Violence

Scriptural Teaching

A theme throughout Scripture, beginning with Genesis, is that women and men are created in God's image. As John Paul II has said, "Both man and woman are human beings to an equal degree."[10] In the New Testament, Jesus consistently reached out to those on the fringes of society, those without power or authority, those with no one to speak on their behalf. He taught that all women and men are individuals worthy of respect and dignity.

Jesus unfailingly respected the human dignity of women. John Paul II reminds us that "Christ's way of acting, the Gospel of his words and deeds, is a consistent protest against whatever offends the dignity of women."[11] Jesus went out of his way to help the most vulnerable women. Think of the woman with the hemorrhage (see Mk 5:25-34) or the woman caught in adultery (see Jn 8:1-11). By his actions toward women in need, Jesus set an example for us today. Like him, we are called to find ways to help those most vulnerable women in our midst. We also need to find ways to help the men who want to break out of the pattern of abuse.

As a Church, one of the most worrying aspects of the abuse practiced against women is the use of biblical texts, taken out of context, to support abusive behavior. Counselors report that both abused women and their batterers use scripture passages to justify their behavior.

Abused women say, "I can't leave this relationship. The Bible says it would be wrong." Abusive men say, "The Bible says my wife should be submissive to me." They take the biblical text and distort it to support their right to batter.

As bishops, we condemn the use of the Bible to condone abusive behavior. A correct reading of the Scriptures leads people to a relationship based on mutuality and love. Again, John Paul II describes it accurately: "In the 'unity of the two,' man and woman are called from the beginning not only to exist 'side by side' or 'together,' but they are also called to exist mutually one for the other."[12]

Even where the Bible uses traditional language to support the social order common in the day, the image presented is never one that condones the use of abuse to control another person. In Ephesians 5:21-33, for instance, which discusses relationships within the family, the general principle laid down is one of mutual submission between husband and wife. The passage holds out the image to husbands that they are to love their wives as they love their own body, as Christ loves the Church. Can you imagine Jesus battering his Church?

What We Can Do to Help

Presented here are some practical suggestions to implement in your parish and diocese.

For Abused Women

- Begin to believe that you are not alone. Women have reached for help and found a way to a new life for themselves and their children.
- Talk in confidence to someone you trust: a relative, a friend, a parish priest, a deacon, a sister, a lay minister. Though it is distressing to talk about intimate family matters, trust them with the truth about yourself.
- If you must stay in the situation at least for now, set up a safety plan of action for when you think another episode of abuse is near. This includes hiding a car key somewhere outside the house; keeping a small amount of money in a safe place; locating somewhere to go in an emergency. When you fear another episode of violence is near, leave the house at once and do not return until you think it is likely to be over.
- Check out the resources in your area that offer help to battered women and their children. Your doctor or local librarian can

refer you to the appropriate groups. Your diocesan Catholic Charities Office or Family Life Office can help. Catholic Charities Offices often have qualified counselors on staff and can provide emergency assistance and other kinds of help.

- The telephone book lists shelters for abused women in your area. 911 is the universal number to call the police.

For Men Who Abuse

- Have the courage to look honestly at your actions in the home and especially toward your wife. Begin to believe that you can change your behavior if you choose to do so.
- Acknowledge the fact that abuse is your problem; it's not your wife's problem. Do not look for excuses to batter.
- Be willing to reach out for help. Talk to someone you trust who can help you look at what is going on. Contact Catholic Charities or shelters in your area for the name of a program for abusers.
- Keep in mind that the Church is available to help you. Part of the mission Jesus trusted to us is to offer healing when it is needed. Contact your parish.
- Find alternative ways to act when you become frustrated or angry. Talk to other men who have overcome abusive behavior. Find out what they did and how they did it.

For Pastors and Pastoral Staff

- Make your parish a safe place where abused women and men who batter can come for help.
- Learn as much as you can about domestic violence. Be alert for the signs of abuse among parish women.
- Join in the national observance of October as "Domestic Violence Awareness Month." Dedicate at least one weekend that month to educate parishioners about abuse and its likely presence in your parish.
- Make sure that parish homilies address domestic violence. If abused women do not hear anything about abuse, they think no one cares. Describe what abuse is so that women begin to recognize and name what is happening to them.
- If you suspect abuse, ask direct questions. Ask the woman if she is being hit or hurt at home. Carefully evaluate her response. Some women do not realize they are being abused, or they lie to protect their spouses.
- In talking to an abused person, be careful of your language. Don't say anything that will bolster her belief that it is her

fault and that she must change her behavior. The victim is not to blame. The abuser must be accountable for his behavior.

- In marriage-preparation education sessions, check couples' patterns of handling disagreements and their families' problem-solving patterns. Suggest postponing marriage if you identify signs of abuse or potential abuse.
- In baptismal-preparation programs, be alert that the arrival of a child and its attendant stress may trigger violent behavior.
- Keep an updated list of resources for abused women in your area.
- Have an action plan in place to follow if an abused woman calls on you for help. Build a relationship with police and domestic-violence agencies. Find a safe place for abused women.

For Educators and Catechists

- Make sure all teachers and catechists receive training in how to recognize abuse.
- Insist that teaching and texts be free of sexual stereotyping. Battering thrives on sexism.
- Try to include shelters for abused women and children on lists of service for confirmation classes and other service groups.
- Include information about domestic violence in human-sexuality and family-life classes.
- Sponsor parish workshops on domestic violence.

Ultimately, abused women must make their own decisions about staying or leaving. It is important to be honest with women about the risks involved. *Remember:* Women are at a most dangerous point when they attempt to leave their abusers. Research indicates that "women who leave their batterers are at a 75 percent greater risk of being killed by the batterer than those who stay."[13]

For Liturgy Committees

- In parish reconciliation services, identify violence against women as a sin.
- Include intercessions for victims of abuse, for the men who abuse women, and for those who help both victims and abusers.
- Strive to use inclusive language in liturgical celebrations, as authorized.

For Commissions on Women and Other Women's Groups

- Include a list of names and telephone numbers of parish contacts in parish bulletins and directories for abused women to call.
- Work to see that women as well as men are represented in parish leadership positions (e.g., on parish finance and pastoral councils).
- Offer free meeting space to support groups for abused women and for men who abuse.
- Spearhead education in your parish/diocese on crimes of violence against women.
- Look for resource people in your parish who can offer their expertise.

A Conclusion and a Prayer

This statement has addressed the problem of violence against women in their homes. Such violence has repercussions on all residing there, even to the extent of setting up a situation for repeating violence in successive generations. Accordingly, we encourage all parents and all educators and catechists to teach children from the earliest ages that abuse is not appropriate behavior. As pastors of the Church, we are dedicated to encouraging all that nurtures and strengthens family life.

One of the sources of healing we have in our lives as Christians is prayer. The psalms in particular capture the depth and range of human anguish and hope and reassure us of God's help. Psalm 31 may be an especially apt prayer for women who are dealing with abusive situations. With all of you we pray:

> Have pity on me, O LORD, for I am in distress;
>   with sorrow my eye is consumed;
>   my soul also, and my body. . . .
>   I am like a dish that is broken. . . .
> But my trust is in you, O LORD;
>   I say, "You are my God." (Ps 31:10-15)

Notes

1. Social Affairs Committee, Assembly of Quebec Bishops, *A Heritage of Violence: A Pastoral Reflection on Conjugal Violence* (Montreal: L'Assemblée des évêques du Québec, 1989).
2. Canadian Church Leaders, "Violence Against Women," testimony given by an ecumenical coalition to the Canadian Panel on Violence Against Women, *Origins* 21:47 (April 30, 1992): 789-790.

3. Council on Scientific Affairs, American Medical Association, "Violence Against Women: Relevance for Medical Practitioners," *Journal of the American Medical Association* 267 (June 17, 1992): 3184-3189.
4. The Women's Commission, *A Pastoral Response to Domestic Violence* (Richmond, Va.: Catholic Diocese of Richmond, n.d.).
5. Commission on Women in Church and Society, *A Pastoral Response to Domestic Violence Against Women* (Buffalo, N.Y.: Catholic Diocese of Buffalo, n.d.).
6. United States Catholic Conference, *Violence in the Family: A National Concern, A Church Concern* (Washington, D.C.: United States Catholic Conference, 1979).
7. National Conference of Catholic Bishops, *Called to Be One in Christ Jesus,* third draft (Washington, D.C.: United States Catholic Conference, 1992), 46.
8. Council on Scientific Affairs, "Violence Against Women."
9. Ibid.
10. John Paul II, *On the Dignity and Vocation of Women (Mulieris Dignitatem)* (Vatican City: Polyglot Press, 1989), nos. 6, 7.
11. Ibid., no. 15.
12. Ibid., no. 7.
13. National Coalition Against Domestic Violence, 1990.

Source: Washington, D.C.: United States Catholic Conference, 1992.

American Responsibilities in a Changing World

A Statement of the USCC Committee on International Policy

October 1992

"At his gate there lay a poor man called Lazarus" (Lk 16:20).

We are living at a turning point in world history. The Cold War is over, the Iron Curtain is no more. The East-West rivalry has ended, and some lasting conflicts in Central America, Africa, and Asia appear to be coming to an end.

Only months ago, people greeted these changes with relief and expectation. But in a short time some of our hope has turned into fear and confusion. These are days of contrasts and contradictions in world affairs and growing problems at home. The hopes generated by the march of freedom in 1989 and 1991 gave way in 1992 to new realities of ethnic conflict and violence.

New opportunities for cooperation and progress are being undermined by old hatreds, and continuing problems of debt and underdevelopment loom even more ominously over the world's poor. People are losing hope that this new world of freedom will lead to a better future.

While the nations of Western Europe struggle along the road to economic and political integration, the breakup of Yugoslavia has resulted in a horrendous war which international authorities have seemed helpless to prevent or restrain. Still other conflicts threaten to break out in Eastern Europe and Central Asia.

In Africa, wars, internal oppression, and natural disasters have once again led to masses of starving refugees whose need strains international humanitarian agencies to the limit. After hopeful beginnings, peacemaking in Cambodia and Central America is making only slow progress. The path toward racial justice in South Africa is slowed by continuing violence and conflict. Persecution of religious believers and ethnic minorities continues in China.

The international institutions forged at the end of World War II sometimes seem too weak, underfunded, and conflicted to meet the challenges of this new world. Regional organizations often appear even less capable of affecting events.

The Temptation to Withdraw

For decades the Catholic Church has championed the unity of the human family, the interdependence of peoples, and the need for solidarity across national and regional boundaries. So we have welcomed the advances in communications, technology, economics, and other secular forces which have brought people into ever closer contact with one another.

We must acknowledge, however, that some aspects of interdependence bring danger rather than promise. Drugs harvested in the Andes show up on the streets of our cities. A coup in Haiti sends refugees to our shores. Peacekeeping in far-off places proves more costly than anticipated. Economic decisions in other lands cost American workers their jobs. The temptation to withdraw, to build new walls, and even to lash out against foreigners is great.

At the same time, we face many long-neglected problems at home. After the Cold War, Americans naturally desired to address domestic needs with new vigor: to reduce poverty among our children, to build housing for the homeless, to retrain and hire workers, to improve our children's education, and to provide adequate health care for all our people. The riots in Los Angeles this past summer demonstrate that our need for healing and action is urgent and pressing. Indeed, justice, like charity, does begin at home.

Out of an understandable desire and clear need to face neglected problems at home, then, many Americans may be tempted to shut out international problems and to shun global responsibilities. Yet as pastors in a universal Church, we appeal to the American people not to turn away from the cries of a still suffering world beyond our shores.

We urge U.S. Catholics at this pivotal moment to renew their commitment to the good of the whole human family. As we approach the third millennium, we call on our leaders and fellow citizens to demonstrate creativity and determination in building the institutions which will assure the world community a more just, peaceful, and sustainable future.

The Global Church and Human Family

Each day, appeals from the Church around the world reach our conference: to aid the victims of famine in Africa, to heal the casualties of war, to assist refugees fleeing violence and oppression, to defend the victims of aggression in the Balkans, to work for justice and peace in the Middle East, to strengthen the fragile peace, to support reconstruction in Central America, and to appeal for religious liberty in China.

Today more than ever our world needs an ethic of solidarity and a vision of the global common good. This is a moment that requires boldness and vision on the part of political leaders—and of citizens. Our country still has a vital role to play in building a more just and peaceful world community.

United with our brothers and sisters in faith and in solidarity with the human family, we urge American Catholics and all our fellow citizens to take up the urgent challenges of a new world:

- The strengthening of peacemaking and peacekeeping institutions
- Social and economic development in the poorest nations
- Support for refugees and migrants fleeing oppression and seeking a new life
- Collaboration on global environmental protection and restoration
- The protection of human rights and the advancement of democracy
- Help for economic and political transformation in Eastern Europe and the Commonwealth of Independent States
- Restraint on the arms trade

We urge our fellow citizens to insist that those who seek to lead us address these global concerns with the seriousness and imagination they deserve.

The debates of this election season should reflect the challenges to global responsibility presented the United States in a changed but still dangerous world; and the decisions citizens make should take into account the leading role our country is still called to exercise in international affairs.

The Universal Common Good

Nearly thirty years ago Pope John XXIII, in his encyclical *Pacem in Terris,* recognized the inability of the international system at that time to meet the increasingly global problems of the world community. He identified our duty to create arrangements to promote global human community through the pursuit of what he called "the universal common good."

Two major priorities are especially vital in pursuing this global common good:

1. *Peacemaking.* The last several months have revealed both the potential and the limits of existing international institutions to meet world problems. First in Cambodia and then in El Salvador, the United

Nations moved warring parties toward compromise and committed personnel and resources to help bring about peace.

But in the former Yugoslavia both the United Nations and the European Community have thus far failed to stop a savagely destructive war against a civilian population. Governments and international organizations, as U.N. Secretary General Boutros Boutros-Ghali has lamented, have been even slower to respond to the human catastrophe brought on by the civil war and anarchy in Somalia. While the community of nations has sought to act in concert in these cases, it has failed to stop the violence. Even international efforts to supply humanitarian assistance to the victims of conflict have been held hostage by the warring parties.

The need to strengthen peacekeeping and peacemaking institutions, both through the United Nations and through regional groupings, is a central priority for our time. We encourage diplomats and international civil servants to devise proposals for improving conflict-resolution mechanisms and strengthening the peacekeeping and peacemaking capacities of the world community. We urge our own government and political leaders to contribute to and receive such proposals in a constructive spirit, and to provide the financial and technical resources along with personnel to help make them truly effective.

2. *Sustainable Development.* The U.N. Conference on Environment and Development, held last June in Rio de Janeiro, highlighted for all the world the connection between environmental integrity and equitable development for the poor nations of the world. The preservation of the earth's ecology demands finding ways for the poor to improve their lives without placing further stress on fragile ecological systems.

The Earth Summit in Rio made considerable strides in ecological understanding; but much more must be done, particularly in augmenting the opportunities for sustainable development in poor countries. Effective support for sustainable development represents a major challenge for U.S. leadership in the world.

At the same time, wars and natural disasters have created the necessity of greater development assistance in Central America, Southeast Asia, and in most of sub-Saharan Africa. With the end of the Cold War and with the prospect of peace in the Middle East, the time is right to rethink foreign aid and to redirect it from security to development and from geopolitical concerns to human needs. Development assistance has been a shrinking part of U.S. foreign aid in recent years and now is even more vulnerable. Rather than abandoning foreign aid, we need to redirect U.S. foreign assistance toward a more effective effort to help poor people improve the quality of their lives.

In *Centesimus Annus,* Pope John Paul II urged, "It will be necessary above all to abandon a mentality in which the poor—as individuals, as peoples—are considered a burden, as irksome intruders."[1] The poor majority of the world are our sisters and brothers. The common good demands that redesigned foreign-aid programs focus once again on their lives, development, and dignity.

Call to Solidarity

On many fronts, we face today what the late Pope Paul VI called "a crisis of solidarity." In the encyclical letter *Populorum Progressio*, Pope Paul identified "a duty of solidarity" binding developed nations to underdeveloped ones. He anticipated "the day when," through generous initiatives, "the poor man Lazarus can sit down at the same table with the rich man."[2] Since that time the story of Lazarus (Lk 16:19-31) has become central to the Church's interpretation of the crisis of solidarity in world affairs.

Time and again Pope John Paul II has turned to the story of Lazarus to warn against indifference to the suffering and aspiration of peoples in the developing nations. In his visits to the United States, the Holy Father has explicitly urged American Catholics to take this parable into account in shaping our national response to developing nations.

An especially acute symptom of this crisis of solidarity is the world refugee emergency. In the Balkans, Europe is experiencing the largest forced displacement of people since World War II. Two and one-half million people have been forced to abandon their homes; one million of these have fled their country. The Gulf War produced one of the largest one-year movements of people on record. In Africa, war, drought, and famine threaten to add still millions more to the ranks of the world's homeless wanderers. Mozambique alone has 2.5 million internally displaced, and over 1.5 million have sought refuge in other countries.

Closer to our own shores, since the 1991 coup in Haiti over 37,000 people, whom our government has not for the most part recognized as refugees, have fled the island by boat. The Haitian people and particularly would-be Haitian refugees remain a test of solidarity for our people. We ought not turn our backs.

Refugees, displaced people, and migrants are another sign of our time. In the short term, international efforts deserve generous support from our government, particularly to meet problems in Croatia and Bosnia and Herzegovina and in Somalia.

In the long-term, political leaders, with the backing of their people, must develop improved means to protect and care for the uprooted, whether they are driven from their homes by fear, hunger, or need. Movement is "the last refuge of liberty." The world community must secure that refuge.

A New Moment

An opportunity like the present one comes once every two or three generations. Choices made and policies set in the months and years immediately ahead may well determine whether or not the peoples of the world can meet the challenges of the twenty-first century. In this new moment, it is urgent that American Catholics, as citizens of a powerful democracy and members of a universal Church, reject the temptation to isolationism or indifference and take up the challenge of pursuing peace and securing justice both in our nation and in a new world.

The people of far-off lands are not abstract problems, but sisters and brothers. We are called to protect their lives, to preserve their dignity, and to defend their rights. Our future in this shrinking world depends not only on our national achievements, but also on global progress.

The interests of our nation and the values of our faith are best served by consistent commitment and generous investment in shaping a more just and peaceful world, especially for the poor and vulnerable.

Building peace, securing democracy, confronting poverty and despair, and protecting human rights are not only moral imperatives, but also wise national priorities. They can shape a world that will be a safer, more secure, and more just home for all of us.

Mindful that those who work for peace will be called God's children, we pray for the community of faith, for our fellow citizens, and our political leaders: "Give peace, Lord, to those who wait for you; listen to the prayers of your servants and guide us in the way of justice."[3]

Notes

1. John Paul II, *On the Hundredth Anniversary of Rerum Novarum (Centesimus Annus)* (Washington, D.C.: United States Catholic Conference, 1991), no. 28.
2. Paul VI, *On the Development of Peoples (Populorum Progressio)* (Washington, D.C.: United States Catholic Conference, 1967), no. 47.
3. Entrance Antiphon, Mass for Peace and Justice, *The Sacramentary: The Roman Missal Revised by the Decree of the Second Vatican Ecumenical Council and Published by the Authority of Pope Paul VI*, English trans. prepared by ICEL (New York: Catholic Book Publishing Co., 1985), 902.

Source: *Origins* 22:20 (October 29, 1992): 337-341.

Go and Make Disciples: A National Plan and Strategy for Catholic Evangelization in the United States

A Statement of the National Conference of Catholic Bishops

November 1992

> Go, therefore, and make disciples of all nations, baptizing them in the name of the Father, and of the Son, and of the holy Spirit, teaching them to observe all that I have commanded you. And behold, I am with you always, until the end of the age. —Mt 28:19-20

> I have come to set the earth on fire, and how I wish it were already blazing.—Lk 12:49

Jesus set the world on fire, and that blaze goes on even today. Here is Bartimaeus, blind and begging on the roadside; he hears of Jesus and, no matter what, will not stop shouting until Jesus stops to heal him. Once healed, he follows Jesus (Mk 10:46-52). Or the unnamed centurion, not even a Jew, whose servant is dying. "I am not worthy," he says. Jesus' command saves the servant's life. And the depth of the centurion's faith astonishes even Jesus (Lk 7:2-9). The woman of Samaria goes to get water; after she meets Jesus and feels his kindness, she opens her soul and her pain to him. Not only does she believe—she must tell others as well (Jn 4:7-42). Or Jesus' friends, the family of Mary, Martha, and Lazarus: the sisters would often welcome Jesus into their house; and when Lazarus died, Jesus wept, but then put his tears aside, and raised him. "This caused many to believe" (Lk 10:38-45; Jn 11:1-45). Each of these people, touched by Christ Jesus, responded to him and so became part of the story of salvation.

We have heard these and so many other gospel stories of Jesus Sunday after Sunday at church, in our own reading and sharing of Scriptures, in the words mothers and fathers tell their children, in the private meditation of our prayer, in the celebration of the sacraments. We have become, through the power and truth of these stories, and through the free gift of grace, disciples of Jesus.

We have heard them, and they will not let us rest. They burn, and they still set us ablaze!

Part I: A Vision of Catholic Evangelization

Introduction

We present to you, our Catholic sisters and brothers, this plan and strategy of evangelization because the fire of Jesus burns even today. We, your brothers and your bishops, profess our faith in Christ Jesus, in the revelation that he is and the kingdom that he proclaimed, and in the Church he founded. We proclaim that, through our faith, the stories of Christ continue and that our lives, as believers, are part of the story of salvation.

We say it about ourselves as bishops: God has touched our lives in Jesus, bestowed his Spirit, given us salvation and hope, and called us to live in witness to his love.

We know this is true of you as well: you have received the Spirit of Christ Jesus, which brings salvation and hope; your lives are a witness of faith. Whether you were baptized as a child or joined the Church as an adult, you have a story of faith. Whether you sincerely live your faith in quiet or have a great public ministry, you have a story of faith. Whether you have a grade-school knowledge of the catechism or have a theological degree, you have a story of faith.

We all have—and are—stories of faith, for through the Spirit, the Gospel of Jesus Christ takes hold of us in the proclamation of his word, and Jesus touches us in the celebration of his sacraments. When this genuinely happens, we are all set ablaze by his love.

We can understand evangelization in light of these stories of faith: namely, how we have been changed by the power of Christ's word and sacraments and how we have an essential role in sharing that faith through our daily lives as believers. Looked at this way, evangelization is what we are all about! Being involved in the story of salvation is what faith is all about! Evangelization is the essential mission of the Church.[1]

As we begin this plan and strategy, we turn in prayer to the Holy Spirit, that we may receive the guidance we need to set the hearts of Catholics in the United States on fire with a desire to bring the Gospel of Jesus, in its fullness, to all the people of our land.

What Is Evangelization?

The simplest way to say what evangelization means is to follow Pope Paul VI, whose message *On Evangelization in the Modern World* has inspired so much recent thought and activity. We can rephrase his words by saying that evangelizing means bringing the good news of Jesus into every human situation and seeking to convert individuals and society by the divine power of the Gospel itself.[2] Its essence is the proclamation of salvation in Jesus Christ and the response of a person in faith, both being the work of the Spirit of God.

Evangelization must always be directly connected to the Lord Jesus Christ. "There is no true evangelization if the name, the teaching, the promises, the Kingdom and the mystery of Jesus of Nazareth, the Son of God are not proclaimed."[3]

Conversion

Conversion is the change of our lives that comes about through the power of the Holy Spirit. All who accept the Gospel undergo change as we continually put on the mind of Christ by rejecting sin and becoming more faithful disciples in his Church. Unless we undergo conversion, we have not truly accepted the Gospel.

We know that people experience conversion in many ways. Some experience a sudden, shattering insight that brings rapid transformation. Some experience a gradual growth over many years. Others undergo conversion as they take part in the Rite of Christian Initiation of Adults—the normal way adults become members of the Church today. Many experience conversion through the ordinary relationships of family and friends. Others have experienced it through the formation received from Catholic schools and religious education programs. Still others have experienced ongoing conversion in renewals, ecumenical encounters, retreats, parish missions, or through some of the great spiritual movements that have blessed church life today.

This is crucial: we must be converted—and we must continue to be converted! We must let the Holy Spirit change our lives! We must respond to Jesus Christ. And we must be open to the transforming power of the Holy Spirit who will continue to convert us as we follow Christ. If our faith is alive, it will be aroused again and again as we mature as disciples.

We can only share what we have received; we can hold on to our faith only if it continues to grow. "But if salt loses its taste," Jesus asked, "with what can it be seasoned?" (Mt 5:13).

Individuals and Society

The continuing story of salvation in Christ involves each of us one by one as well as society itself. How else could it be? Conversion speaks of the change of heart that, as members of the Church, each one must undergo. The Gospel speaks across time and space to each human being, each mind, each heart. It asks us what we think about our lives, how we hope, whom we love, and what we live for. If faith is not transforming each heart and life, it is dead.

But faith is not something that only happens to each of us individually or privately, within ourselves. The Gospel also speaks to society itself, with its values, goals, and systems. The Gospel must overflow from each heart until the presence of God transforms all human existence. Sometimes this means that, as believers, we must confront the world as did the prophets of old, pointing out the claims of God to societies that are blind to God. More often, however, this means that we must let our faith shine on the world around us, radiating the love of Jesus by the everyday way we speak, think, and act.

The fruit of evangelization is changed lives and a changed world—holiness and justice, spirituality and peace. The validity of our having accepted the Gospel does not only come from what we feel or what we know; it comes also from the way we serve others, especially the poorest, the most marginal, the most hurting, the most defenseless, the least loved. An evangelization that stays inside ourselves is not an evangelization into the good news of Jesus Christ.

The Force of the Gospel Itself

Evangelization happens when the word of Jesus speaks to people's hearts and minds. Needing no trickery or manipulation, evangelization can happen only when people accept the Gospel freely, as the "good news" it is meant to be, because of the power of the gospel message and the accompanying grace of God.

Our message of faith proclaims an eternally faithful God, creating all in love and sustaining all with gracious care. We proclaim that God, whose love is unconditional, offers us divine life even in the face of our sin, failures, and inadequacies. We believe in a God who became one of us in Jesus, God's Son, whose death and resurrection bring us salvation. We believe that the risen Christ sends his own Spirit upon us when we respond to him in faith and repentance, making us his people, the Church, and giving us the power of new life and guiding us to our eternal destiny.

This gospel message gives us a different vision of what life is about. We see a pattern of love, hope, and meaning because the intimate relationship with God in which we were created, lost through sin, has been restored by Jesus, whose death has destroyed our death and whose resurrection gives us the promise of eternal life (Rom 5:12-21). We do not see a world of blind forces ruled by chance, but a universe created to share God's life; we know that following Jesus means we begin to share God's life here and now. We do not view life's purpose as the gathering of power or riches, but as the gracious invitation to live for God and others in love. We do not calculate what we think is possible, but know the Spirit of God always makes new things possible, even the renewal of humanity. We do not merely look for many years of contented life, but for an unending life of happiness with God. In our faith, we discover God's eternal plan, from creation's first moment to creation's fulfillment in heaven, giving meaning to our human lives.

This vision we share is the power of the good news. As it compels us, we believe it can compel, by its beauty and truth, all who sincerely seek God. How different our world would be if everyone could accept the good news of Jesus and share the vision of faith!

Other Implications

Evangelization, then, has both an inward and an outward direction. *Inwardly,* it calls for our continued receiving of the Gospel of Jesus Christ, our ongoing conversion both individually and as Church. It nurtures us, makes us grow, and renews us in holiness as God's people. *Outwardly,* evangelization addresses those who have not heard the Gospel or, having heard it, have stopped practicing their faith, and those who seek the fullness of faith. It calls us to work for full communion among all who confess Jesus, but do not yet realize the unity for which Christ prayed. Pope John Paul II, in his encyclical on missionary activity, summed up the three objectives of mission: to proclaim the Gospel to all people; to help bring about the reconversion of those who have received the Gospel but live it only nominally; and to deepen the Gospel in the lives of believers.[4]

We know that the word *evangelization* sometimes raises uncomfortable images for Catholics—especially in the culture of the United States, where evangelism has sometimes meant only an individual response to enthusiastic preaching or a style of mass religion or contrived ways to recruit new members or, at its worst, a way to play on people's needs. Still, we use the word *evangelization* because its root meaning is *Gospel* (good news) and because it calls us, even if uncomfortably, to live the faith of our baptism more openly and share it more freely.

We want to make it clear that evangelization means something special for us as Catholics. We can see what it means by looking at what happens to evangelized people. Not only are they related to Jesus by accepting his Gospel and receiving his Spirit; even more, their lives are changed by becoming disciples, that is, participants in the Church, celebrating God's love in worship and serving others as Jesus did.[5]

Some might think of evangelization solely in terms of Jesus and our relationship with him. Yet our relationship with Jesus is found in our relationship with the community of Jesus—the Church. The way to Christ is through the community in which he lives. Did not Jesus say, "I am with you always" (Mt 28:20) and "Whatever you did for one of these least" brothers and sisters of mine, "you did for me"? (Mt 25:40). Did not the Jesus who met Paul on the road to Damascus say that he lived in his persecuted followers, the Church? (Acts 9:5). Jesus is present in and among his disciples, the people of God.

Evangelization, then, has different implications depending on our relationship to Jesus and his Church. For those of us who practice and live our Catholic faith, it is a call to ongoing growth and renewed conversion. For those who have accepted it only in name, it is a call to reevangelization. For those who have stopped practicing their faith, it is a call to reconciliation. For children, it is a call to be formed into disciples through the family's faith life and religious education. For other Christians, it is an invitation to know the fullness of our message. For those who have no faith, it is a call to conversion to know Christ Jesus and thus experience a change to new life with Christ and his Church.

Why We Evangelize

We must evangelize because the Lord Jesus commanded us to. He gave the Church the unending task of evangelizing as a restless power, to stir and to stimulate all its actions until all nations have heard his good news and until every person has become his disciple (Mt 28:18-20).

The Lord commanded us to evangelize because salvation is offered to every person in him. More than a holy figure or a prophet, Jesus is God's Word (Jn 1:1, 14), God's "very imprint" (Heb 1:3), the power and wisdom of God (1 Cor 1:24). He is our savior. Becoming like us and accepting our human nature (Phil 2:7), he addresses in himself, in his death and resurrection, the brokenness of our lives. He suffers through our sin; he feels our pain; he knows the thirst of our death; he accepts the limits of our human life so that he might bring us beyond those limits. "He humbled himself, becoming obedient to death, even death on a cross. Because of this, God greatly exalted him! . . ." (Phil 2:8-9). Taking on our death as savior, Jesus was raised to life. In Christ, all can come to know that the sin, the coldness, the indifference, the despair, and the doubt of our lives are overcome by God's taking on our human nature and leading us to new life. In him, and him alone, is the promise of resurrection and new life.

We evangelize because people must be brought to the salvation Jesus the Lord offers in and through the Church. While we acknowledge that the grace of God is mysteriously present in all lives, people all too often resist this grace. They refuse change and repentance. We evangelize so that the salvation of Christ Jesus, which transforms our human lives even now, will bring as many as possible to the promised life of unending happiness in heaven.

Jesus commanded us to evangelize, too, in order to bring enlightenment and lift people from error. The Lord Jesus, "the way and the truth and the life" (Jn 14:6), came to us as a teacher, opening for us the wisdom that not only leads to life eternal but also leads to a human fulfillment that reflects the dignity and mystery of our nature. Unless people know the grandeur for which they are made, they cannot reach fulfillment and their lives will be incomplete. Nor will they know that they are called into interpersonal union with God and with each other. The intimate union that Jesus revealed in his life, being one with the Father (Jn 14:10) and rejoicing in the Holy Spirit (Lk 10:21), can envelop our lives. This is the union in which Jesus wishes all to share (Jn 17:21), a union whose realization brings great peace to people, families, societies, and the world. Evangelization opens us to Christ's wisdom and personal union with God and others.

The Lord gave us a message that is unique. All faiths are not merely different versions of the same thing. To know Christ Jesus and belong to his Church is not the same as believing anything and belonging to any community. Pope John Paul II has pointed out, "While acknowledging that God loves all people and grants them the possibility of being saved (cf. 1 Tm 2:4), the Church believes that God has established Christ as the one mediator and that she herself has been established as the universal sacrament of salvation."[6] The unique claim of our message does not negate the sincerity and faith of others; likewise, the sincerity and faith of others do not take away from the clarity and truth of our message. As Pope John Paul II reminds us, "It is necessary to keep these two truths together, namely, the real possibility of salvation in Christ for all humankind and the necessity of the Church for salvation. Both these truths help us to understand the one mystery of salvation."[7]

Finally, the Lord gave us yet another reason to evangelize: our love for every person, whatever his or her situation, language, physical, mental, or social condition. Because we have experienced the love of Christ, we want to share it. The gifts God has given to us are not gifts for ourselves. Like the large catch of fish (Lk 5:6) or the overflowing measure of flour (Lk 6:38), our faith makes our hearts abound with a love-filled desire to bring all people to Jesus' Gospel and to the table of the eucharist. As Jesus wanted to gather all Jerusalem, "like a hen gathers her young" (Mt 23:37), so also do we want to gather all people into God's kingdom, proclaiming the Gospel "even to the ends of the earth" (Acts 1:8).

How Evangelization Happens

The Holy Spirit is the fire of Jesus. The Spirit, the first gift of the risen Christ to his people (Jn 20:22), gives us both the ability to receive the Gospel of Jesus and, in response, the power to proclaim it. Without the Holy Spirit, evangelization simply cannot occur.[8] The Spirit brings about evangelization in the life of the Church and in the Church's sharing the Gospel with others.

In the Life of the Church

We cannot really talk about the "ordinary" life of the Church because all of it is the graced gift of the Holy Spirit. Yet there are familiar ways by which evangelization happens: by the way we live God's love in our daily life; by the love, example, and support people give each other; and by the ways parents pass faith on to their children; in our life as Church, through the proclamation of the word and the wholehearted celebration of the saving deeds of Jesus; in renewal efforts of local and national scope; in the care we show to those most in need; in the ways we go about our work, share with our neighbors, and treat the stranger. In daily life, family members evangelize each other, men and women their future spouses, and workers their fellow employees by the simple lives of faith they lead. Through the ordinary patterns of our Catholic life, the Holy Spirit brings about conversion and a new life in Christ.

Here, there are two elements at work: *witness,* which is the simple living of the faith; and *sharing,* which is spreading the good news of Jesus in an explicit way.

Certainly, our families, parishes, associations, schools, hospitals, charitable works, and institutions give powerful witness to the faith. But do they share it? Does their living faith lead to the conversion of minds and hearts to Jesus Christ? Does the fire of the Holy Spirit blaze in them? This plan and strategy wants to make Catholics in the United States, individually and as a Church, better sharers of God's good news.

In Sharing the Gospel with Others

The Holy Spirit also evangelizes through our attempts to reach those who have given up the practice of their Catholic faith for one reason or another and those who have no family of faith. Many in our Catholic community know family members, friends, and neighbors who do not have or practice faith.

Millions of Catholics no longer practice their faith. Although many of them may say they are Catholic, they no longer worship with the community and thereby deprive themselves of the gifts of word and sacrament. Some were never formed in the faith after their childhood. Some have drifted away because of one or another issue. Some feel alienated from the Church because of the way they perceive the Church or its teaching. Some have left because they were mistreated by church representatives.

As a community of faith, we want to welcome these people to become alive in the good news of Jesus, to make their lives more fully a part of the ongoing story of salvation and to let Christ touch, heal, and reconcile them through the Holy Spirit. We want to let our inactive brothers and sisters know that they always have a place in the Church and that we are hurt by their absence—as they are. We want to show our regret for any misunderstandings or mistreatment. And we want to help them see that, however they feel about the Church, we want to talk with them, share with them, and accept them as brothers and sisters. Every Catholic can be a minister of welcome, reconciliation, and understanding to those who have stopped practicing the faith.

Our plan also asks Catholics to reach out to those who do not belong to a faith community and to invite them to consider the power of the Gospel of Jesus, which the riches of the Catholic Church can bring into their lives. Perhaps this may seem the most difficult of all the tasks evangelization asks of us. Yet if we have once seen the joy of those received into the Church at Easter, if we have ever experienced the growth of those going through the Rite of Christian Initiation of Adults, if we have ever seen someone thrilled with the Gospel for the first time in his or her life, we know that this is, in truth, one of the sweetest gifts of the Spirit.

The Holy Spirit, through the ecumenical movement, is calling churches and ecclesial communities into ever deeper communion through dialogue and cooperation. We look forward with great eagerness to the day when all are members of one family. While recognizing that the life of other Christian communions can truly bring about a life of grace, we nevertheless cannot ignore all that still divides us. Our love for all who confess Christ and our desire for unity compel us to share the fullness of revealed truth God has entrusted to the Catholic Church and to learn from them expressions of the truths of faith that other churches and ecclesial communities share with the Catholic Church.

Those who have not received the Gospel deserve honor and respect for following God as their consciences direct them. They are related to the people of God in a variety of ways. First are the Jews, the chosen people, to whom the covenants and promises were made and who, in view of the divine choice, are a people most dear to God.

People of other non-Christian religions also have the right to hear the Gospel, as missionaries have brought it over the centuries. God's plan of salvation also includes the Muslims who profess the faith of Abraham and, together with us, adore the one, merciful God. Then there are those who through no fault of their own do not know the Gospel of Christ or his Church but nevertheless seek God with sincere heart and seek to do God's will as they know it. Interreligious dialogue presents an opportunity to learn about other religious traditions and to explain our own. Such dialogue, however, must never be a camouflage for proselytizing. Rather, it should be approached with utmost respect and sensitivity. Catholics earnestly share their faith in Jesus Christ, which gives meaning to their lives, praying for that good day, known to God alone, when all peoples will address the Lord in a single voice and serve God with one accord (Zeph 3:9; Is 66:23; Ps 65:4; Rom 11:11-32).

Our Goals

We, your brothers and your bishops in the faith, propose three goals as part of this plan and strategy for Catholic evangelization in the United States. In addition, we pledge ourselves to work for the accomplishment of these goals, which spring from our understanding of evangelization and how it happens. None of these goals is presented by itself; taken together, they challenge us to the full scope of Catholic evangelization.

Goal I: To bring about in all Catholics such an enthusiasm for their faith that, in living their faith in Jesus, they freely share it with others.

Clearly, unless we continue to be evangelized ourselves, with renewed enthusiasm for our faith and our Church, we cannot evangelize others. Priority must be given to continued and renewed formation in the faith as the basis of our deepening personal relationship with Jesus.

We are aware that many Catholics tend to keep their faith to themselves or to manifest it only around other Catholics. Perhaps our heritage as immigrants and our acknowledgment of religious pluralism make us shy in showing forth our faith. Certainly, there has also been a decline in the public practice of our faith in recent decades. For many, the fire of faith burns cooler than it should.

Yet we have no reason to be shy about the heritage of our Catholic faith. We have God's own word, formed through God's revelation to the Jewish people and the disciples' testimony of God's deeds in Jesus, in the Sacred Scriptures. This word is the light by which we live and see. We have the sacraments, especially the eucharist, Jesus bequeathed to his disciples, means of holiness and growth, healing and salvation. These sacraments join us with God at life's most touching points and bring us into unity with each other. This heritage of word and sacrament has brought about, in every generation of our twenty centuries of Catholic life, a path of holiness, a profoundly moral way of life, a variety of spiritual journeys, and countless saints. It brings Christ's faithful followers to eternal life.

This heritage, our Church, is apostolic, coming as it does from the testimony of the apostles; our unbroken unity with the bishop of Rome reveals our continuity with the faith of Peter and Paul. It is catholic, for our heritage is given not only for us but for all, for the world, as the hope of all humanity one day united in love. It is holy, because its source is Christ who is holy and insists that every believer also be a disciple. And our heritage is one, binding us in every continent into one community because we are bound in nothing less than the reality of Jesus through his Spirit.

Our joy in this heritage calls us to offer it as a legacy, a treasure God would bestow on everyone who, touched by the Spirit, begins to respond to God's call. The tools that have been developed over time and the *Catechism of the Catholic Church* will help us pass on this legacy to others.

This first goal calls us to an enthusiasm for all that God has given us in our Catholic faith. It also fosters ongoing conversion within the Catholic Church which, as an institution and a community of people, it continually needs.

Goal II: To invite all people in the United States, whatever their social or cultural background, to hear the message of salvation in Jesus Christ so they may come to join us in the fullness of the Catholic faith.

Catholics should continually share the Gospel with those who have no church community, with those who have given up active participation in the Catholic Church, as well as welcoming those seeking full communion with the Catholic Church. People can know they are invited to experience Jesus Christ in our Church only if they are really and effectively asked and adequate provisions are made for their full participation. We want our Catholic brothers and sisters to effectively ask and to really invite.

At the same time, we Catholics cannot proselytize—that is, manipulate or pressure anyone to join our Church. Such tactics contradict the good news we announce and undermine the spirit of invitation that should characterize all true evangelization.

Goal III: To foster gospel values in our society, promoting the dignity of the human person, the importance of the family, and the common good of our society, so that our nation may continue to be transformed by the saving power of Jesus Christ.

When the story of Jesus is truly our story, when we have caught his fire, when his good news shapes our lives individually, as families and households, and as a Church, his influence will be felt far beyond our Church. Pope Paul VI taught us that evangelization transforms culture, that the Gospel affects and at times upsets the "criteria of judgment, determining values, points of interest, lines of thought, sources of inspiration and models of life" that make up our cultural world.[9]

Not only must each of us live the Gospel personally in the Church, but our faith must touch the values of the United States, affirming what is good, courageously challenging what is not. Catholics applaud our nation's instinctual religiousness, its prizing of freedom and religious liberty, its openness to new immigrants and its inspiring idealism. If our society were less open, indeed, we might not be free to evangelize in the first place. On the other hand, our country can be faulted for its materialism, sexism, racism, consumerism, its individualism run wild, its ethic of selfishness, its ignoring of the poor and weak, its disregard of human life, and its endless chase of empty fads and immediate pleasures.

Seeing both the ideals and the faults of our nation, we Catholics need to recognize how much our Catholic faith, for all it has received from American culture, still has to bring to life in our country. On the level of truth, we have a profound and consistent moral teaching based upon the dignity and destiny of every person created by God. On the practical level, we have the witness of American Catholics serving those most in need, educationally, socially, materially, and spiritually.

This goal calls for results not only in the way we evaluate things but also in the way we carry good news through the practical works of justice, charity, and peace which alone can fully authenticate our message. With Pope John Paul II, we affirm that "to teach and spread her social doctrine pertains to the Church's evangelizing mission and is an essential part of the Christian message, since this doctrine points out the direct consequences of that message in the life of society and situates daily work and struggles for justice in the context of bearing witness to Christ the savior."[10]

Why We Are Issuing the Plan Now

Since the turn of this century, the Holy Spirit has inspired great events to further evangelization in the Church. A new appreciation of the Scriptures and the mystery of our sharing in the body of Christ, the Church, flowered into the Second Vatican Council which was called so that the face of Jesus might radiate more fully upon all.[11] This council brought a renewed sense of faith and worship, a commitment to ecumenical unity, an affirmation of the call to holiness that each one has, and a new emphasis on evangelization. This council has changed the way we live our Catholic faith. Following the council in 1974, bishops from all over the world met in Rome to reflect on evangelization; their reflections were expressed by Pope Paul VI in his apostolic exhortation *On Evangelization in the Modern World.* Pope John Paul II has developed further the awareness of evangelization. Recognizing the need from his global travels, he called for a "new evangelization" in 1983 and called for lay people to become involved in evangelization.[12] In 1991, the pope published his eighth encyclical, *Redemptoris Missio, On the Permanent Validity of the Church's Missionary Mandate.* The Holy Father's powerful words call us to a renewed commitment to mission and evangelization as we come to the final decade of this millennium: "I sense that the moment has come to commit all of the Church's energies to a new evangelization. . . ."[13]

We bishops have dealt with the importance of evangelization in our statements. A wide consultation among Hispanic Catholics resulted in the publication of the *National Pastoral Plan for Hispanic Ministry*[14] to address issues relevant to the many Hispanic peoples entering and enriching our nation. Likewise, our African American brothers and sisters have worked on a pastoral plan entitled *Here I Am, Send Me: A Conference Response to the Evangelization of African Americans and "The National Black Catholic Pastoral Plan,"*[15] that speaks from their cultural uniqueness and is a gift to all of us. In our own recent pastoral statement, *Heritage and Hope: Evangelization in the United States,*[16] we explored the meaning of the five hundredth anniversary (1492-1992) of Christopher Columbus's voyage to the New World. While all Christians deeply regret the disease, death, exploitation, and cultural devastation European settlement brought, we rejoice that missionaries carried the light of Christ and were the first to raise their voices against oppression. That first evangelization planted the faith that we now seek to nurture.

All this movement and all these documents call us to reexamine our hearts and recommit our wills to the pursuit of evangelization; they motivate us to issue this plan to make evangelization a natural and normal part of Catholic life and to give evangelizers the tools and support they need to carry out this ministry today.

Led in the Spirit

One day Jesus left Galilee and went to the River Jordan where he saw his kinsman, John the Baptist, calling people to repentance and renewal. He stepped forth from the crowd and approached John for baptism. John hesitated, recognizing the uniqueness of Jesus. When Jesus insisted, John plunged him into the water. At that point, people heard a voice from the clouds; John saw the Spirit come upon Jesus who was being revealed at this moment by God as the "Chosen One" (see Mt 3:13-17 and Jn 1:29-34).

The Spirit drove Jesus out into the desert (Mk 1:12) and, after a while, into a ministry that began with Jesus addressing simple fishermen and small groups of people in his homeland. The Spirit led Jesus on a journey through Palestine to Jerusalem where his message came to challenge the whole world.

Jesus was led by the Spirit of God to a life of preaching and service, to the giving of himself in sacrifice. Jesus Christ sends that same Spirit upon everyone who is baptized in his name. For we have all gone down into the water of Christ and have all been anointed to bring good news and be true disciples (cf. Rom 6:3-4). We have all received his Spirit. This is not a spirit of timidity or fear, but a bold spirit of life, truth, joy, and grace.

We, bishops and Catholic people, are all led by this same Spirit who would stir up the faithful in our land to bring about a new and powerful evangelization. With Jesus, we undertake this journey, knowing that he is with us and his Spirit can never fail.

Jesus came to set this fire upon the earth, until all is ablaze in the love of God. We pray this fire will come upon us as disciples as we, led by the Spirit, carry out Christ's great commission to go and make disciples of all the nations.

Part II: Goals and Strategies

Not long after Jesus was raised from the dead, a small group huddled together in a secluded room. Suddenly, the building shook, a great wind encircled them, and flames of fire, like tongues, appeared around the group (Acts 2:1-4).

We see, in the midst of this small group, two people whose lives still guide us in the work of evangelization. We see a woman, Mary, now middle-aged, who, over thirty years before, was overshadowed by the Holy Spirit and became the mother of Jesus (Lk 1:26-38). God used the faith of this Jewish woman, her cooperation with God's way, to bring Jesus into the world. So Mary, long devoutly loved by Christians as the Mother of Jesus and Mother of God, also is a model of true discipleship and evangelization. With Mary's example and prayer, we grow as disciples, ever faithful to Jesus and ever wanting to reveal him.

We also see a former fisherman, now called Peter, whom Jesus chose to give as a leader to the disciples (Mt 16:13-16). Though weak enough to deny his friend Jesus (Mk 14:66-72), he is yet empowered to proclaim the faith of Jesus as Messiah (Acts 2:14ff). He would proclaim that message until he died in testimony for the faith (Jn 21:18-19). Jesus made Peter the "rock" of the Church and his faithfulness to the Lord, in spite of his weakness, strengthens us disciples today.

Two people, Mary and Peter, encircled by the other disciples, receive in the tongues of flame at Pentecost a confirmation of their discipleship, of their involvement in the story of Jesus, of their role in spreading God's good news (Acts 2:1-14).

This is the fire of the Holy Spirit from whom all evangelization springs. May the Spirit that came upon Mary and filled the apostles also come upon us as we present the apostolic parts of our plan.

How to Use This Plan and Strategy

Our hope, upon issuing this plan and strategy, is that it will lead Catholics to action. The goals, though broad, speak of the way we live our faith. The objectives, which follow each goal, expand those goals into several separate parts. The suggested strategies elaborate in more detail some of the ways of working at the objectives and goals.

We envision groups of Catholics reading this plan together, discussing its implications, and being stimulated by the range of suggested strategies. We see these groups seeking to do things, both within and beyond their own Catholic communities, in ways that make sense for their locale and situation. This document should generate discussion about action: the possibilities and activities present in every Catholic parish and institution.

Parish councils and parish evangelization teams should be able to use this plan and strategy to sharpen a parish's mission and develop concrete, suitable evangelizing activities. People who work in unchurched or marginalized areas will carry out this plan and strategy in less structured settings than those who work in large suburban parishes. Youth groups will read the document from their special situation in life and think about how to reach peers in convincing ways. On college campuses, students and campus ministers can form groups to see what the goals of this document mean on today's campuses. Catholics who share the same workplace may form a group that supports their own faith, strengthens them to invite people with whom they work, and also explores how their faith bears upon their occupation.

Individuals, too, should be led beyond insight and reflection into a range of actions that can be done in the home, the workplace, the neighborhood, and the civic setting. Each one's personal gifts and unique setting call for unique approaches in sharing faith.

Our presentation can only suggest the richness of this ministry. In fact, at the end of this plan we explicitly invite additional responses to the objectives we are setting forth. We look for innovative responses, far exceeding the suggested strategies we offer in this plan. The ministry of evangelization does not consist in following a recipe but in letting the Spirit open our hearts to God's word so that we can live and proclaim God's word to others. So, let the Spirit work!

The Context of the Goals

These goals are addressed to *all Catholics* in our country: to every diocese and every parish; to every Catholic person and to every family; to the ordained, religious women and men, and the laity; to the professional religious worker and ordinary parishioner; to large national organizations of Catholics and to every parish committee; to institutions like our Catholic colleges, high schools, and grade schools as well as to associations of the faithful. Although everyone will pursue these goals with different gifts, no one can claim exemption from them.

These goals are meaningless unless they are steeped in *prayer*. Without prayer, the good news of Jesus Christ cannot be understood, spread, or accepted. These goals can be accomplished only by opening our hearts to God, who gives to his children everything they seek (Mt 7:11), who responds when we knock, and who answers when we persevere in asking (Mt 7:7-8). At Mass, in the Liturgy of the Hours, in prayer groups and individual prayer and devotions, we must ask unceasingly for the grace to evangelize. The moment we stop praying for the grace to spread the good news of Jesus will be the moment when we lose the power to evangelize.

These goals also are issued in accord with the ministry of evangelization that belongs to the *whole Catholic Church*. This plan, the product of our reflection in the United States, adapts to our situation the missionary goals of Christ's Church throughout the world. They are offered in union with all Catholics everywhere, with their bishops, and the Holy Father, the vicar of Christ, the bishop of Rome, the city of the apostles Peter and Paul. Unless evangelization is done in the context of this universal Catholic community, it is incomplete.[17] We urge this spirit upon our Catholic brothers and sisters.

These goals must bear upon our *everyday life,* in the family and the workplace, in our neighborhoods and associations, in the way we live. Catholics will be able to affect people in everyday life long before they are invited to a parish or to a formal religious event. All evangelization planning basically strives to make more possible the kind of everyday exchange between believers and unbelievers, which is the thrust of evangelization.

The *parish* is the most fitting location for carrying out these goals because the parish is where most Catholics experience the Church. It has, on the local level, the same commitments as the universal Church, with the celebration of God's word and eucharist as its center of worship. Evangelization inevitably involves the parish community for, ultimately, we are inviting people to our eucharist, to the table of the Lord. When an individual evangelizes, one to one, he or she should have the good news and the eucharistic table as the ultimate focus.

These goals assume that an evangelizing spirit will touch every dimension of Catholic parish life. Welcome, acceptance, the invitation to conversion and renewal, reconciliation and peace, beginning with our worship, must characterize the whole tenor of our parishes. Every element of the parish must respond to the evangelical imperative— priests and religious, lay persons, staff, ministers, organizations, social clubs, parochial schools, and parish religious education programs. Otherwise, evangelization will be something a few people in the parish see as their ministry—rather than the reason for the parish's existence and the objective of every ministry in the parish. The spirit of conversion, highlighted in the liturgy and particularly in the Rite of Christian Initiation of Adults, should radiate through the action of all Catholics so that the call to conversion is experienced and celebrated as part of our way of life.

Evangelization in the parish should be seen as a *collaborative* effort that springs from a partnership between the clergy and the laity. Priests have a special leadership role in carrying out this plan, but they should not feel isolated, overburdened, or frustrated in implementing it. Indeed, we even hope an increase in evangelizing will attract more people to the priesthood and religious life. The goals and strategies of our plan are not meant to be an added burden on already overworked pastoral staffs, as if evangelization were merely another program to be done. Rather, they should help parishes see the evangelizing potential of their current activities, even as they stretch parishes to develop new activities from a renewed spiritual energy.

These goals also call for a *consistency:* evangelization must affect the attitude of our Catholic life from top to bottom. We cannot call for renewal only on the parish level; we cannot proclaim mercy only for part of the year; we cannot welcome only some people. Everywhere Americans see Catholics and Catholic institutions they should sense the spirit of evangelization.

These goals, finally, will be carried out in the midst of a culture that will make them difficult to achieve. This difficulty will be, in part, a problem of communication because people may prefer stereotypes of the Catholic Church to a true picture of our faith. Another part of the difficulty will be social, because people will see the Catholic Church only as an organization of a certain economic class or educational level rather than as a richly varied and inviting community. Also, a superficial pluralism makes it hard for people to discuss faith seriously in our society. But most difficult of all will be the moral issues, which make the good news hard to hear by people whose values are contrary to the Gospel and who must experience change in order to hear the message of life we proclaim.

A Concluding Prayer

As we present this plan to our brother and sister Catholics in the United States, we pray that, through the Holy Spirit, it may be a means of bringing renewal to our Church and new life to all who search for God. We have felt the hunger of our nation for God and the Gospel of Jesus as we have developed this plan and strategy. As this plan is read, studied, and implemented, may it help all Catholics know the hunger for faith in today's society.

We pray that our Catholic people will be set ablaze with a desire to live their faith fully and share it freely with others. May their eagerness to share the faith bring a transformation to our nation and, with missionary dedication, even to the whole world. We ask God to open the heart of every Catholic, to see the need for the Gospel in each life, in our nation and on our planet.

We ask Mary, the one through whom Jesus entered our world, to guide us in presenting Jesus to those who live in our land. May her prayers help us to share in her courage and faithfulness. May they lead us to imitate her discipleship, her turning to Jesus, her love for God and for all. May the compassion that Mary has always reflected be present in our hearts.

We also pray that, like the disciples walking that Easter morning to Emmaus, all Catholics may feel their hearts burning through the presence of Jesus. As those two disciples felt the presence of Jesus in their journey, we ask that the ministry of evangelizing help believers feel anew the presence of Jesus and help others discover his gracious presence.

We pray that the fire of Jesus enkindled in us by God's Spirit may lead more and more people in our land to become disciples, formed in the image of Christ our Savior.

Notes

1. Paul VI, *On Evangelization in the Modern World (Evangelii Nuntiandi)* (Washington, D.C.: United States Catholic Conference, 1976), no. 14.
2. Ibid., no. 18.
3. Ibid., no. 22.
4. John Paul II, *On the Permanent Validity of the Church's Missionary Mandate (Redemptoris Missio)* (Washington, D.C.: United States Catholic Conference, 1990), no. 33.
5. *Evangelii Nuntiandi*, no. 24.
6. *Redemptoris Missio*, no. 9.
7. Ibid., no. 9.
8. *Evangelii Nuntiandi*, no. 75.
9. Ibid., no. 19.
10. John Paul II, *On the Hundredth Anniversary of Rerum Novarum (Centesimus Annus)* (Washington, D.C.: United States Catholic Conference, 1991), no. 5.
11. Second Vatican Council, *Dogmatic Constitution on the Church (Lumen Gentium)*, no. 1.
12. John Paul II, *On the Vocation and Mission of the Lay Faithful in the Church and in the World (Christifideles Laici)* (Washington, D.C.: United States Catholic Conference, 1989), nos. 17 and 34.
13. *Redemptoris Missio*, no. 3.
14. National Conference of Catholic Bishops, *National Pastoral Plan for Hispanic Ministry* (Washington, D.C.: United States Catholic Conference, 1988).
15. National Conference of Catholic Bishops, *Here I Am, Send Me: A Conference Response to the Evangelization of African Americans and The National Black*

Catholic Pastoral Plan (Washington, D.C.: United States Catholic Conference, 1990).

16. National Conference of Catholic Bishops, *Heritage and Hope: Evangelization in the United States* (Washington, D.C.: United States Catholic Conference, 1991).

17. *Evangelii Nuntiandi,* no. 60.

Source: Washington, D.C.: United States Catholic Conference, 1993.

Resolution on Clergy Sex Abuse

A Resolution of the National Conference of Catholic Bishops

November 1992

Gathered in general assembly, we the members of the National Conference of Catholic Bishops express our profound concern for all those who have been victims of sexual abuse, particularly when that abuse has been committed by a member of the clergy.

The president of our conference, at the close of our assembly last June, spoke clearly and eloquently to this subject with our assent. We reaffirm that statement here and recognize that policies to address the grave issues presented by this problem are in place throughout our country.

In the course of our assembly this week, we have reflected—once again and more deeply—upon the pain, anguish, and sense of alienation felt by victims.

At the same time, we affirm the thousands of good, holy, and dedicated priests who minister faithfully to God's people.

We pledge ourselves to one another to return to our dioceses and there to examine carefully and prayerfully our response to sexual abuse; to assure ourselves that our response is appropriate and effective; and to be certain that our people are aware of and confident in that response.

Among the elements to be considered for ongoing response, we continue to recommend the following:

- Respond promptly to all allegations of abuse where there is reasonable belief that abuse has occurred.
- If such an allegation is supported by sufficient evidence, relieve the alleged offender promptly of his ministerial duties and refer him for appropriate medical evaluation and intervention.
- Comply with the obligations of civil law as regards reporting of the incident and cooperating with the investigation.
- Reach out to the victims and their families and communicate our sincere commitment to their spiritual and emotional well-being.
- Within the confines of respect for the privacy of the individuals involved, deal as openly as possible with members of the community.

In these days of our assembly we are reminded again that all our actions should show our Church as a living, caring, and healing Church. We pledge again our care and concern for all victims of abuse, wherever and however it occurs. We commit ourselves anew to bring the healing ministry of our Church to our people, to dialogue and pray with all who have suffered, and to foster opportunities for reconciliation.

Source: *Origins* 22:25 (December 3, 1992): 418.

Stewardship: A Disciple's Response

A Pastoral Letter on Stewardship from the
National Conference of Catholic Bishops

November 1992

As each one has received a gift, use it to serve one another
as good stewards of God's varied grace.
—1 Pt 4:10

Introduction

Three convictions in particular underlie what we say in this pastoral letter:

1. Mature disciples make a conscious, firm decision, carried out
    in action, to be followers of Jesus Christ no matter the cost to
    themselves.
2. Beginning in conversion, change of mind and heart, this commitment is expressed not in a single action, nor even in a number of actions over a period of time, but in an entire way of life.
    It means committing one's very self to the Lord.
3. Stewardship is an expression of discipleship, with the power
    to change how we understand and live out our lives. Disciples
    who practice stewardship recognize God as the origin of life,
    the giver of freedom, the source of all they have and are and
    will be. They are deeply aware of the truth that "the Lord's are
    the earth and its fullness; the world and those who dwell in it"
    (Ps 24:1). They know themselves to be recipients and caretakers of God's many gifts. They are grateful for what they have
    received and eager to cultivate their gifts out of love for God
    and one another.

The Challenge

In some ways it may be harder to be a Christian steward today
than at times in the past. Although religious faith is a strong force in the
lives of many Americans, our country's dominant secular culture often
contradicts the values of the Judeo-Christian tradition. This is a culture
in which destructive "isms"—materialism, relativism, hedonism, individualism, consumerism—exercise seductive, powerful influences.

486

There is a strong tendency to privatize faith, to push it to the margins of society, confining it to people's hearts or, at best, their homes, while excluding it from the marketplace of ideas where social policy is formed and men and women acquire their view of life and its meaning.

The Choice

Christians are part of this culture, influenced by it in many ways.

In recent decades many Catholics in particular have entered into the mainstream of American society. This has been a remarkable achievement. Often, though, this process also has widened the "split" between faith and life which Vatican II saw as one of "the more serious errors of our age."[1] Thus American Catholicism itself has taken on some of the less attractive values of the secular culture.

For example, although religious people often speak about community, individualism infects the religious experience of many persons. Parishes, dioceses, and church institutions appear impersonal and alienating in the eyes of many. Evangelization is not the priority it should be. How to use people's gifts and charisms, how to empower the laity, how to recognize the role of women, how to affirm racial, cultural, and ethnic minorities, how to overcome poverty and oppression—these and countless other issues remain vexing questions, as well as opportunities.

Also, while many Catholics are generous in giving of themselves and their resources to the Church, others do not respond to the needs in proportion to what they possess. The result now is a lack of resources which seriously hampers the Church's ability to carry out its mission and obstructs people's growth as disciples.

This pastoral letter recognizes the importance of church support, including the sharing of time, talent, and treasure. But it stipulates church support in its broader context—what it means to be a disciple of Jesus Christ.

This also is the context of stewardship. Generous sharing of resources, including money, is central to its practice, and the church support is a necessary part of this. Essentially, it means helping the Church's mission with money, time, personal resources of all kinds. This sharing is not an option for Catholics who understand what membership in the Church involves. It is a serious duty. It is a consequence of the faith which Catholics profess and celebrate. This pastoral letter initiates a long-term, continuing process encouraging people to examine and interiorize stewardship's implications. At the start of this process it is important to lay out a comprehensive view of stewardship—a vision of a sharing, generous, accountable way of life rooted in Christian discipleship—which people can take to heart and apply to the circumstances of their lives. Concentrating on one specific obligation of stewardship, even one as important as church support, could make it harder—even impossible—for people to grasp the vision. It could imply that when the bishops get serious about stewardship, what they really mean is simply giving money.

The Vision

Jesus' invitation to follow him is addressed to people of every time and condition. Here and now it is addressed to us—Catholic citizens of a wealthy, powerful nation facing many questions about its identity and role in the waning years of a troubled century, members of a community of faith blessed with many human and material resources yet often uncertain about how to sustain and use them.

As bishops, we wish to present a vision that suits the needs and problems of the Church in our country today and speaks to those who practice Christian stewardship in their particular circumstances.

What we say here is directed to ourselves as much as to you who read these words. As bishops, we recognize our obligation to be models of stewardship in all aspects of our lives. We must be stewards in our prayer and worship, in how we fulfill our pastoral duties, in our custody of the Church's doctrine, spiritual resources, personnel, and funds, in our lifestyle and use of time, and even in such matters as the attention we give to personal health and recreation.

As we ask you to respond to the challenge of stewardship, we pray that we also will be open to the grace to respond. We pray that the Holy Spirit, whose gracious action conforms us to Jesus Christ and to the Church, will enlighten us all and help us to renew our commitment as the Lord's disciples and as stewards of his bountiful gifts.

The Plan of the Pastoral Letter

The pastoral letter proceeds according to the following plan.

I. *The Call.* Stewardship is part of discipleship. But Christian discipleship begins with vocation, the call to follow Jesus and imitate his way of life. The letter therefore begins with vocation. Then it presents a very general overview of stewardship, considered in the context of discipleship, noting that people first of all are stewards of the personal vocations they receive from God. Discipleship and the practice of stewardship constitute a way of life that is both privileged and challenging.

II. *Jesus' Way.* Next, the pastoral letter focuses more closely on the idea of stewardship, relying on the teaching and life of Jesus to probe its meaning. It considers the implications for disciples of Jesus engaged in stewardship. One of these is that all are called to evangelize, to share the good news with others. And what is the reward to which good stewards can look forward? The answer is perfect fulfillment in God's kingdom—a kingdom already present, real but imperfect, in this world, which Jesus' disciples help bring to its full reality by the practice of stewardship.

III. *Living as a Steward.* Having reflected in general terms upon Christian life considered from the point of view of discipleship and stewardship, the letter turns to the content of this way of life. It considers the content of life in relation to two human activities that are fundamental to the Christian vocation. The first is collaborating with God in the work of creation. The second is cooperating with God in the work of redemption. Both lie at the very heart of Christian stewardship in its deepest meaning.

IV. *Stewards of the Church.* The pastoral letter next considers the community of faith, the people of God, which is formed by the new covenant in and through Christ. Each member of the Church shares in responsibility for its mission; each is called to practice stewardship of the Church. Christians also are called to look outward and to place themselves at the service of the entire human community, especially those who are most in need. The eucharist is both the sign and the agent of this expansive communion of charity.

V. *The Christian Steward.* The letter closes with a brief portrait or profile of the Christian steward, drawn from the New Testament. In a special way, the Blessed Virgin is the model of Christian discipleship and of the practice of Christian stewardship as it is understood here. Do we also wish to be disciples of Jesus Christ and to live in this way?

Who is a Christian disciple? One who responds to Christ's call, follows Jesus, and shapes his or her life in imitation of Christ's. Who is a Christian steward? One who receives God's gifts gratefully, cherishes and tends them in a responsible and accountable manner, shares them in justice and love with others, and returns them with increase to the Lord.

Genesis tells us that God placed the first human beings in a garden to practice stewardship there—"to cultivate and care for it" (Gn 2:15). The world remains a kind of garden (or workshop, as some would prefer to say) entrusted to the care of men and women for God's glory and the service of humankind. In its simplest yet deepest sense, this is the Christian stewardship of which the pastoral letter speaks.

I. The Call

As our concept of stewardship continues to evolve after twelve years of marriage, we are grateful for the people who have challenged us from the beginning to embrace fully Christ's teachings. They weren't always telling us the things we wanted to hear, but we feel blessed that we were able to work through the initial frustrations of committing the best

portion of our time, talent, and treasure to the Church. It's
difficult to separate ourselves from the demands and possessions of the world, but there's a tremendous amount of
peace that comes from every decision we make for Christ
and his will for us. We can't overstate the powerful impact
the lifestyle has had on our marriage and three children.
—Tom and LaNell Lilly, Owensboro, Ky.

The Disciple's Vocation

The Christian vocation is essentially a call to be a disciple of Jesus.
Stewardship is part of that. Even more to the point, however,
Christians are called to be good stewards of the personal vocations
they receive. Each of us must discern, accept, and live out joyfully and
generously the commitments, responsibilities, and roles to which God
calls him or her. The account of the calling of the first disciples, near
the beginning of John's Gospel, sheds light on these matters.

John the Baptist is standing with two of his disciples—Andrew
and, according to tradition, the future evangelist John—when Jesus
passes by. "Behold," John the Baptist exclaims, "the Lamb of God!"
Wondering at these words, his companions follow Christ.

"What are you looking for?" Jesus asks them. "Rabbi," they say,
"where are you staying?" "Come and you will see." They spend the day
with him, enthralled by his words and by the power of his personality.

Deeply moved by this experience, Andrew seeks out his brother
Simon and brings him to Jesus. The Lord greets him: "You will be
called Kephas"—Rock. The next day, encountering Philip, Jesus tells
him: "Follow me." Philip finds his friend Nathanael and, challenging
his skepticism, introduces him to the Lord. Soon Nathanael too is convinced: "Rabbi, you are the Son of God; you are the King of Israel."

This fast-paced narrative at the beginning of John's Gospel (see
Jn 1:35-50) teaches a number of lessons. For our purposes, two stand
out.

One is the personal nature of a call from Jesus Christ. He does not
summon disciples as a faceless crowd but as unique individuals.
"How do you know me?" Nathanael asks. "Before Philip called you,"
Jesus answers, "I saw you under the fig tree." He knows people's personal histories, their strengths and weaknesses, their destinies; he has
a purpose in mind for each one.

This purpose is individual vocation. "Only in the unfolding of the
history of our lives and its events," says Pope John Paul II, "is the eternal plan for God revealed to each of us."[2] Every human life, every personal vocation, is unique.

And yet the vocations of all Christians do have elements in common. One of these is the call to be a disciple. In fact, we might say that

to be disciples—to follow Christ and try to live his life as our own—*is* the common vocation of Christians; discipleship in this sense *is* Christian life.

The other lesson that John's narrative makes clear is that people do not hear the Lord's call in isolation from one another. Other disciples help mediate their vocations to them, and they in turn are meant to mediate the Lord's call to others. Vocations are communicated, discerned, accepted, and lived out within a community of faith which is a community of disciples;[3] its members try to help one another hear the Lord's voice and respond.

Responding to the Call

Jesus not only calls people to him but also forms them and sends them out in his service (cf. Mt 10:55ff; Mk 6:7ff; Lk 9:1ff). Being sent on a mission is a consequence of being a disciple. Whoever wants to follow Christ will have much work to do on his behalf—announcing the good news and serving others as Jesus did.

Jesus' call is urgent. He does not tell people to follow him at some time in the future but here and now—at *this* moment, in *these* circumstances. There can be no delay. "Go and proclaim the kingdom of God. . . . No one who sets a hand to the plow and looks to what was left behind is fit for the kingdom of God" (Lk 9:60, 62).

But a person can say no to Christ. Consider the wealthy and good young man who approaches Jesus asking how to lead an even better life. Sell your goods, Jesus tells him; give to the poor, and follow me. "When the young man heard this statement, he went away sad, for he had many possessions" (Mt 19:22).

Attachment to possessions is always more or less a problem, both for individuals and for the community of faith. In *The Long Loneliness*, written years after she became a Catholic, Dorothy Day recalls the "scandal" of encountering a worldly Church—or, more properly, the worldliness of some Catholics: "businesslike priests . . . collective wealth . . . lack of sense of responsibility for the poor." She concludes: "There was plenty of charity but too little justice."[4]

The Call to Stewardship

Becoming a disciple of Jesus Christ leads naturally to the practice of stewardship. These linked realities, discipleship and stewardship, then make up the fabric of a Christian life in which each day is lived in an intimate, personal relationship with the Lord. This Christ-centered way of living has its beginning in baptism, the sacrament of faith. As Vatican II remarks, all Christians are "bound to show forth, by the example of their lives and by the witness of their speech," that new life of faith which begins in baptism and is strengthened by the power of the Holy Spirit in confirmation.[5] Faith joins individuals and the community of Jesus' followers in intimacy with their Lord and leads them to live as his disciples. Union with Christ gives rise to a sense of solidarity and common cause between the disciples and the Lord and also among the disciples themselves.

Refracted through the prisms of countless individual vocations, this way of life embodies and expresses the one mission of Christ: to do God's will, to proclaim the good news of salvation, to heal the afflicted, to care for one's sisters and brothers, to give life—life to the full—as Jesus did.

Following Jesus is the work of a lifetime. At every step forward, one is challenged to go further in accepting and loving God's will. Being a disciple is not just something else to do, alongside many other things suitable for Christians, it is a total way of life and requires continuing conversion.

Stewardship plays an important role in the lives of people who seek to follow Christ. In particular, as we have said, Christians must be stewards of their personal vocations, for it is these that show how, according to the circumstances of their individual lives, God wants them to cherish and serve a broad range of interests and concerns: life and health, along with their own intellectual and spiritual well-being and that of others; material goods and resources; the natural environment; the cultural heritage of humankind—indeed, the whole rich panoply of human goods, both those already realized and those whose realization depends upon the present generation or upon generations yet to come. Catholics have a duty, too, to be stewards of their Church: that community of disciples, that body of Christ, of which they, individually and together, are the members, and in which "if one part suffers, all the parts suffer with it; if one part is honored, all the parts share its joy" (1 Cor 12:26).

The Cost of Discipleship

The way of discipleship is privileged beyond any other. Jesus says: "I came so that they might have life and have it more abundantly" (Jn 10:10). But discipleship is not an easy way. "If you wish to come after me," Jesus also says, "you must deny yourself and take up your cross daily and follow me. For if you wish to save your life you will lose it, but if you lose your life for my sake you will save it" (Lk 9:23-24).

The Lord's way is not a way of comfortable living or of what Dietrich Bonhoeffer, in *The Cost of Discipleship*, scornfully calls "cheap grace." This is not real grace but an illusion. It is what happens when people approach the following of Christ as a way to pleasant experiences and feeling good. Bonhoeffer contrasts this with "costly" grace. It is costly because it calls us to follow *Jesus Christ*. It is costly because it requires a disciple for Jesus' sake to put aside the craving for domination, possession, and control, and grace because it confers true liberation and eternal life. It is costly, finally, because it condemns sin, and grace because it justifies the sinner. But all this is very general. To understand and practice this way of life, people need models to imitate. These exist in abundance in the holy women and men who have gone before us in the faith; while our supreme source of guidance is found in the person and teaching of Jesus. Let us reflect on what he tells us about stewardship.

II. Jesus' Way

> Our parents are an inspiration to us as we look back on their lives of giving themselves for each other and for others. Had it not been for their lives of stewardship and giving, we would not perhaps have the faith we have today; and we want to pass that faith and love on to our children, grandchildren, and others. And then our thoughts are turned to the ultimate sacrifice that Christ made for us. He did so, not because he had to, but because of his great love for us. And to think, all he asks in return is for us to love him and others! But it would mean little to tell someone we love them if we did not try to show that love in a concrete way.
> —Paul and Bettie Eck, Wichita, Kans.

The Example of Jesus

Jesus is the supreme teacher of Christian stewardship, as he is of every other aspect of Christian life; and in Jesus' teaching and life self-emptying is fundamental. Now, it might seem that self-emptying has little to do with stewardship, but in Jesus' case that is not so. His self-emptying is not sterile self-denial for its own sake; rather, in setting aside self, he is filled with the Father's will, and he is fulfilled in just this way: "My food is to do the will of the one who sent me and to finish his work" (Jn 4:34).

Jesus' mission is to restore to good order the created household of God which sin has disrupted. He not only perfectly accomplishes this task, but also, in calling disciples, empowers them to collaborate with him in the work of redemption for themselves and on behalf of others.

In describing the resulting way of life, Jesus does not waste time proposing lofty but unrealistic ideals; he tells his followers how they are expected to live. The beatitudes and the rest of the Sermon on the Mount prescribe the lifestyle of a Christian disciple (cf. Mt 5:3–7:27).

Although it does not suit worldly tastes, "the wisdom of this world is foolishness in the eyes of God" (1 Cor 3:19). One does well to live in this way. "Everyone who listens to these words of mine and acts on them will be like a wise man who built his house on a rock. . . . Everyone who listens to these words of mine but does not act on them will be like a fool who built his house on sand" (Mt 7:24, 26).

The Image of the Steward

Jesus sometimes describes a disciple's life in terms of stewardship (cf. Mt 25:14-30; Lk 12:42-48), not because being a steward is the whole of it but because this role sheds a certain light on it. An *oikonomos* or steward is one to whom the owner of a household turns over responsibility for caring for the property, managing affairs, making resources yield as much as possible, and sharing the resources with others. The position involves trust and accountability.

A parable near the end of Matthew's Gospel (cf. Mt 25:14-30) gives insight into Jesus' thinking about stewards and stewardship. It is the story of "a man who was going on a journey," and who left his wealth in silver pieces to be tended by three servants.

Two of them respond wisely by investing the money and making a handsome profit. Upon returning, the master commends them warmly and rewards them richly. But the third behaves foolishly, with anxious pettiness, squirreling away the master's wealth and earning nothing; he is rebuked and punished.

The silver pieces of this story stand for a great deal besides money. All temporal and spiritual goods are created by and come from God. That is true of everything human beings have: spiritual gifts like faith, hope, and love; talents of body and brain; cherished relationships with family and friends; material goods; the achievements of human genius and skill; the world itself. One day God will require an accounting of the use each person has made of the particular portion of these goods entrusted to him or her.

Each will be measured by the standard of his or her individual vocation. Each has received a different "sum"—a unique mix of talents, opportunities, challenges, weaknesses and strengths, potential modes of services and response—on which the master expects a return. He will judge individuals according to what they have done with what they were given.

St. Ignatius of Loyola begins his *Spiritual Exercises* with a classic statement of the "first principle and foundation" permeating this way of life. "Human beings," he writes, "were created to praise, reverence and serve God our Lord, and by this means to save their souls. The other things on the face of the earth are created for them to help them in attaining the end for which they are created. Hence they are to make use of these things in as far as they help them in the attainment of their end, and they must rid themselves of them in as far as they provide a hindrance to them. . . . Our one desire and choice should be what is more conducive to the end for which we are created."[6] St. Ignatius, fervently committed to the apostolate as he was, understood that the right use of things includes and requires that they be used to serve others.

What does all this say to busy people immersed in practical affairs? Is it advice only for those whose vocations lead them to withdraw from the world? Not as Jesus sees it: "But seek first the kingdom of God and his righteousness, and all these things will be given you besides" (Mt 6:33).

The Steward's Reward

People trying to live as stewards reasonably wonder what reward they will receive. This is not selfishness but an expression of Christian hope. Peter raises the question when he says to Jesus, "We have given up everything and followed you" (Mk 10:28).

Christ's response is more than Peter or any other disciple could reasonably hope or bargain for: "There is no one who has given up house or brothers or sisters or mother or father or children or lands for my sake and for the sake of the gospel who will not receive a hundred times more now in this present age: houses and brothers and sisters and mothers and children and lands, with persecutions, and eternal life in the age to come" (Mk 10:29-30).

That is to say: Giving up means receiving more, including more responsibility as a steward; among the consequences of living this way will be persecution; and even though discipleship and stewardship set the necessary terms of Christian life in this world, they have their ultimate reward in another life.

Start, though, with the here and now. To be a Christian disciple is a rewarding way of life, a way of companionship with Jesus, and the practice of stewardship as a part of it is itself a source of deep joy. Those who live this way are happy people who have found the meaning and purpose of living.

For a long time religious believers—to say nothing of those who do not believe—have struggled with the question of what value to assign human activity. One solution is to consider it a means to an end: do good here and now for the sake of a reward in heaven. Another solution passes over the question of an afterlife; do good here and now for the sake of making this a better world.

Vatican Council II points to a third solution. It recognizes that human activity is valuable both for what it accomplishes here and now and also for its relationship to the hereafter. But, more important, it stresses not only the discontinuity between here and now and here-after, but also the astonishing fact of continuity.

God's kingdom already is present in history, imperfect but real.[7] To be sure, it will come to fulfillment by God's power, on his terms, in his own good time. And yet, by their worthy deeds in this life, people also make a limited but real human contribution to building up the kingdom. They do so with an eye to present happiness and also to the perfect fulfillment which the kingdom—and themselves as part of it—will enjoy in the life to come. The Council, therefore, teaches that the purpose of the human vocation to "earthly service" of one's fellow human beings is precisely to "make ready the material of the celestial realm."[8]

In Christ, God has entered fully into human life and history. For one who is Christ's disciple there is no dichotomy, and surely no con-tradiction, between building the kingdom and serving human pur-poses as a steward does. These are aspects of one and the same reality—the reality called the Christian life.

God's kingdom is not an earthly kingdom, subject to decline and decay; it is the everlasting kingdom of the life to come. But that "life to come" is in continuity with this present life through the human goods, the worthy human purposes, which people foster now. And after peo-ple have done their best, God will perfect human goods and bring about the final fulfillment of human persons. "The throne of God and of the Lamb will be in it, and his servants will worship him. They will look upon his face, and his name will be on their foreheads. Night will be no more, nor will they need light from lamp or sun, for the Lord God shall give them light, and they shall reign forever and ever" (Rv 22:3-5).

III. Living as a Steward

I have learned to share because I want to, not because I need to. There are no controls, no strings attached, and no guaran-tee when we give unconditionally. That doesn't mean that in retrospect I haven't questioned my decisions; it simply means that I've tried to look at it as a growth experience, always keeping in mind the life of Jesus Christ. I personally see stewardship as a nurturing process. It is, in a sense, an invitation to reassess our priorities. It is ongoing and often painful, but most of all it brings a personal sense of happiness and peace of mind as I continue my journey through life.
—Jim Hogan, Green Bay, Wis.

Creation and Stewardship

Although it would be a mistake to think that stewardship by itself includes the whole of Christian life, in probing the Christian meaning of stewardship one confronts an astonishing fact: God wishes human beings to be his collaborators in the work of creation, redemption, and sanctification; and such collaboration involves stewardship in its most profound sense. We exercise such stewardship, furthermore, not merely by our own power but by the power of the Spirit of truth, whom Jesus promises to his followers (cf. Jn 14:16-17), and whom we see at work at the first Pentecost inspiring the apostles to commence that proclamation of the good news which has continued to this day (cf. Acts 2:14).

The great story told in Scripture, the story of God's love for humankind, begins with God at work as Creator, maker of all that is: "In the beginning, when God created the heavens and the earth . . ." (Gn 1:1). Among God's creatures are human persons: "The Lord God formed man out of the clay of the ground and blew into his nostrils the breath of life" (Gn 2:7). God not only creates human beings, however, but bestows on them the divine image and likeness (cf. Gn 1:26). As part of this resemblance to God, people are called to cooperate with the Creator in continuing the divine work.[9] Stewardship of creation is one expression of this. The divine mandate to our first parents makes that clear. "Be fertile and multiply; fill the earth and subdue it. Have dominion over the fish of the sea, the birds of the air, and all the living things that move on the earth" (Gn 1:28). Subduing and exercising dominion do not mean abusing the earth. Rather, as the second creation story explains, God settled humankind upon earth to be its steward—"to cultivate and care for it" (Gn 2:15).

This human activity of cultivating and caring has a generic name: work. It is not a punishment for or a consequence of sin. True, sin does painfully skew the experience of work: "By the sweat of your face shall you get bread to eat" (Gn 3:19). But, even so, God's mandate to humankind to collaborate with him in the task of creating—the command to work—comes *before* the fall. Work is a fundamental aspect of the human vocation. It is necessary for human happiness and fulfillment. It is intrinsic to responsible stewardship of the world.

So, as Vatican II observes, far from imagining that the products of human effort are "in opposition to God's power, and that the rational creature exists as a kind of rival to the Creator," Christians see human achievements as "a sign of God's greatness and the flowering of his own mysterious design."[10] While it is lived out by individual women and men in countless ways corresponding to their personal vocations, human cooperation with God's work of creation in general takes several forms.

Collaborators in Creation

One of these is a profound reverence for the great gift of life, their own lives and the lives of others, along with readiness to spend themselves in serving all that preserves and enhances life.

This reverence and readiness begin with opening one's eyes to how precious a gift life really is—and that is not easy, in view of our tendency to take the gift for granted. "Do any human beings ever realize life while they live it?—every, every minute?" demands Emily in *Our Town*. And the stage manager replies, "No. The saints and poets, maybe—they do some."[11] Yet it is necessary to make the effort. For Vatican II speaks of the "surpassing ministry of safeguarding life" and declares that "from the moment of its conception life must be guarded with the greatest care."[12]

Partly too, stewardship of the world is expressed by jubilant appreciation of nature, whose God-given beauty not even exploitation and abuse have destroyed.

> And for all this, nature is never spent;
>   There lives the dearest freshness deep down things;
> And though the last lights off the black West went
>   Oh, morning, at the brown brink eastward, springs—
> Because the Holy Ghost over the bent
>   World broods with warm breast and with ah! bright
>   wings.[13]

Beyond simply appreciating natural beauty, there is the active stewardship of ecological concern. Ecological stewardship means cultivating a heightened sense of human interdependence and solidarity. It therefore calls for renewed efforts to address what Pope John Paul II calls "the structural forms of poverty" existing in this country and on the international level.[14] And it underlines the need to reduce military spending and do away with war and weapons of war.

Especially this form of stewardship requires that many people adopt simpler lifestyles. This is true not only of affluent persons and societies, but also of those who may not be affluent as that term is commonly understood yet do enjoy access to superfluous material goods and comforts. Within the Church, for example, it is important to avoid even the appearance of consumerism and luxury, and this obligation begins with us bishops. As Pope John Paul II says, "simplicity, moderation, and discipline, as well as a spirit of sacrifice, must become a part of everyday life, lest all suffer the negative consequences of the careless habits of a few."[15]

At the same time, life as a Christian steward also requires continued involvement in the human vocation to cultivate material creation.

This productivity embraces art, scholarship, science, and technology, as well as business and trade, physical labor, skilled work of all kinds, and serving others. So-called ordinary work offers at least as many opportunities as do supposedly more glamorous occupations. A woman who works at a supermarket checkout counter writes: "I feel that my job consists of a lot more than ringing up orders, taking people's money, and bagging their groceries. . . . By doing my job well I know I have a chance to do God's work too. Because of this, I try to make each of my customers feel special. While I'm serving them, they become the most important people in my life."[16]

Redemption and Stewardship

Everyone has some natural responsibility for a portion of the world and an obligation in caring for it to acknowledge God's dominion. But there are also those who might be called stewards by grace. Baptism makes Christians stewards of this kind, able to act explicitly on God's behalf in cultivating and serving the portion of the world entrusted to their care. We find the perfect model of such stewardship in the Lord. "For in him all the fullness was pleased to dwell, and through him to reconcile all things for him, making peace by the blood of his cross" (Col 1:19-20); and finally it will be he who "hands over the kingdom to his God and Father" (1 Cor 15:24).

Although Jesus is the unique priest and mediator, his disciples share in his priestly work. Baptism makes them "a royal priesthood" (1 Pt 2:9) called to offer up the world and all that is in it—especially themselves—to the Lord of all. In exercising this office, they most fully realize the meaning of our Christian stewardship. Part of what is involved here for Catholics is a stewardship of time, which should include setting aside periods for family prayer, for the reading of Scripture, for visits to the blessed sacrament, and for attendance at Mass during the week whenever this is possible.

Participation in Christ's redemptive activity extends even, though certainly not only, to the use people make of experiences that otherwise might seem the least promising: deprivation, loss, pain. "Now I rejoice in my sufferings for your sake," St. Paul says, "and in my flesh I am filling up what is lacking in the afflictions of Christ on behalf of his body, which is the church" (Col 1:24). Here also one looks to Jesus to lead the way. For one's estimate of suffering, as Pope John Paul II points out, is transformed by discovering its "salvific meaning" when united with the suffering of Christ.[17]

Penance also belongs to this aspect of Christian life. Today as in the past, the Church commends what Pope Paul VI called the "traditional triad" of prayer, fasting, and almsgiving,[18] while also encouraging Catholics to adopt penitential practices of their own choice that suit their particular circumstances.

Through penance voluntarily accepted one gradually becomes liberated from those obstacles to Christian discipleship which a secularized culture exalting individual gratification places in one's way. These obstacles include not just the quest for pleasure but avarice, a craving for the illusion of absolute dominion and control, valuing creatures without reference to their Creator, excessive individualism, and ultimately the fear of death unrelieved by hope for eternal life.

These are consequences of sin—sin which threatens the way of life of Christian stewardship and the identity of Christians as disciples of the Lord. "Let us master this great and simple truth," Cardinal Newman once said, "that all rich materials and productions of this world, being God's property, are intended for God's service; and sin only, nothing but sin, turns them to a different purpose."[19]

Sin causes people to turn in on themselves; to become grasping and exploitative toward possessions and other people; to grow accustomed to conducting relationships not by the standards of generous stewardship but by the calculus of self-interest: "What's in it for me?" Constantly, Christians must beg God for the grace of conversion: the grace to know who they are, to whom they belong, how they are to live—the grace to repent and change and grow, the grace to become good disciples and stewards.

But if they do accept God's grace and, repenting, struggle to change, God will respond like the father of the prodigal son. "Filled with compassion" at seeing his repentant child approaching after a long and painful separation, this loving parent "ran to his son, embraced him and kissed him" even before the boy could stammer out the words of sorrow he had rehearsed (Lk 15:20). God's love is always there. The Spirit of wisdom and courage helps people seek pardon and be mindful, in the face of all their forgetting, that the most important work of their lives is to be Jesus' disciples.

Thus, the stewardship of disciples is not reducible only to one task or another. It involves embracing, cultivating, enjoying, sharing—and sometimes also giving up—the goods of human life. Christians live this way in the confidence that comes from faith: for they know that the human goods they cherish and cultivate will be perfected—and they themselves will be fulfilled—in that kingdom, already present, which Christ will bring to perfection and one day hand over to the Father.

IV. Stewards of the Church

When I began to provide dental treatment for persons with AIDS, I knew HIV-positive people desperately needed this service, but I did not know how much I needed them. Time and again, reaching out to serve and heal, I have found myself served and healed. Their courage, compassion, wisdom, and faith have changed my life. I have faced my own mortality, and I rejoice in the daily gift of life. My love for people has taken on new dimensions. I hug and kiss my wife and family more than ever and see them as beautiful gifts from God. My ministry as a deacon has become dynamic, and I regard my profession as a vital part of it.
—Dr. Anthony M. Giambalvo, Rockville Centre, N.Y.

The new covenant in and through Christ—the reconciliation he effects between humankind and God—forms a community: the new people of God, the body of Christ, the Church. The unity of this people is itself a precious good, to be cherished, preserved, and built up by lives of love. The Epistle to the Ephesians exhorts Christians to "live in a manner worthy of the call you have received, with all humility and gentleness, with patience, bearing with one another through love, striving to preserve the unity of the spirit through the bond of peace: one body and one Spirit, as you were also called to the one hope of your call; one Lord, one faith, one baptism; one God and Father of all" (Eph 4:1-6).

Because its individual members do collectively make up the body of Christ, that body's health and well-being are the responsibility of the members—the personal responsibility of each one of us. We all are stewards of the Church. As "to each individual the manifestation of the Spirit is given for some benefit" (1 Cor 12:17), so stewardship in an ecclesial setting means cherishing and fostering the gifts of all, while using one's own gifts to serve the community of faith. The rich tradition of tithing set forth in the Old Testament is an expression of this. (See, for example, Dt 14:22; Lv 27:30.) Those who set their hearts upon spiritual gifts must "seek to have an abundance for building up the church" (1 Cor 14:12).

But how is the Church built up? In a sense there are as many answers to the question as there are individual members with individual vocations. But the overarching answer for all is this: through personal participation in and support of the Church's mission of proclaiming and teaching, serving, and sanctifying.

The participation takes different forms according to people's different gifts and offices, but there is a fundamental obligation arising from the sacrament of baptism:[20] that people place their gifts, their resources—their selves—at God's service in and through the Church.

Here also Jesus is the model. Even though his perfect self-emptying is unique, it is within the power of disciples, and a duty, that they be generous stewards of the Church, giving freely of their time, talent, and treasure. "Consider this," Paul says, addressing not only the Christians of Corinth but all of us. "Whoever sows sparingly will also reap sparingly, and whoever sows bountifully will also reap bountifully. . . . God loves a cheerful giver" (2 Cor 9:6-7).

Evangelization and Stewardship

In various ways, then, stewardship of the Church leads people to share in the work of evangelization or proclaiming the good news, in the work of catechesis or transmitting and strengthening the faith, and in work of justice and mercy on behalf of persons in need. Stewardship requires support for the Church's institutions and programs for these purposes. But, according to their opportunities and circumstances, members of the Church also should engage in such activities personally and on their own initiative.

Parents, for instance, have work of great importance to do in the domestic church, the home. Within the family, they must teach their children the truths of the faith and pray with them; share Christian values with them in the face of pressures to conform to the hostile values of a secularized society; and initiate them into the practice of stewardship itself, in all its dimensions, contrary to today's widespread consumerism and individualism. This may require adjusting the family's own patterns of consumption and its lifestyle, including the use of television and other media which sometimes preach values in conflict with the mind of Christ. Above all, it requires that parents themselves be models of stewardship, especially by their selfless service to one another, to their children, and to church and community needs.

Parishes, too, must be, or become, true communities of faith within which this Christian way of life is learned and practiced. Sound business practice is a fundamental of good stewardship, and stewardship as it relates to church finances must include the most stringent ethical, legal, and fiscal standards. That requires several things: pastors and parish staff must be open, consultative, collegial, and accountable in the conduct of affairs. And parishioners must accept responsibility for their parishes and contribute generously—both money and personal service—to their programs and projects. The success or failure of parish programs, the vitality of parish life or its absence, the ability or inability of a parish to render needed services to its members and the community depend upon all.

We, therefore, urge the Catholics of every parish in our land to ponder the words of St. Paul: "Now as you excel in every respect, in faith, discourse, knowledge, all earnestness, and in the love we have for you, may you excel in this gracious act also" (2 Cor 8:7). Only by living as generous stewards of these local Christian communities, their parishes, can the Catholics of the United States hope to make them the vital sources of faith-filled Christian dynamism they are meant to be.

At the same time, stewardship in and for the parish should not be narrowly parochial. For the diocese is not merely an administrative structure but instead joins communities called parishes into a "local church" and unites its people in faith, worship, and service. The same spirit of personal responsibility in which a Catholic approaches his or her parish should extend to the diocese and be expressed in essentially the same ways: generous material support and self-giving. As in the case of the parish, too, lay Catholics ought to have an active role in the oversight of the stewardship of pastoral leaders and administrators at the diocesan level. At the present time, it seems clear that many Catholics need to develop a better understanding of the financial needs of the Church at the diocesan level. Indeed, the spirit and practice of stewardship should extend to other local churches and to the universal Church—to the Christian community and to one's sisters and brothers in Christ everywhere—and be expressed in deeds of service and mutual support. For some, this will mean direct personal participation in evangelization and mission work, for others generous giving to the collections established for these purposes and other worthy programs.

Every member of the Church is called to evangelize, and the practice of authentic Christian stewardship inevitably leads to evangelization. As stewards of the mysteries of God (cf. 1 Cor 4:1), people desire to tell others about them and about the light they shed on human life, to share the gifts and graces they have received from God, especially knowledge of Christ Jesus, "who became for us wisdom from God, as well as righteousness, sanctification, and redemption" (1 Cor 1:30). Human beings, says Pope Paul VI, "have the right to know the riches of the mystery of Christ. It is in these . . . that the whole human family can find in the most comprehensive form and beyond all their expectations everything for which they have been groping."[21]

Solidarity and Stewardship

While the unity arising from the covenant assumes and requires human solidarity, it also goes beyond it, producing spiritual fruit insofar as it is founded on union with the Lord. "I am the vine, you are the branches," Jesus says. "Whoever remains in me and I in him will bear much fruit" (Jn 15:5). As Simone Weil remarks, "A single piece of bread given to a hungry man is enough to save a soul—if it is given in the right way."

In this world, however, solidarity encounters many obstacles on both the individual and social levels. It is essential that Jesus' disciples do what can be done to remove them.

The most basic and pervasive obstacle is sheer selfish lack of love, a lack which people must acknowledge and seek to correct when they find it in their own hearts and lives. For the absence of charity from the lives of disciples of Jesus in itself is self-defeating and hypocritical. "If anyone says, 'I love God,' but hates his brother, he is a liar" (1 Jn 4:20).

Extreme disparities in wealth and power also block unity and communion. Such disparities exist today between person and person, social class and social class, nation and nation. They are contrary to that virtue of solidarity, grounded in charity, which Pope John Paul II commends as the basis of a world order embodying "a new model of the unity of the human race" whose "supreme model" is the intimate life of the Trinity itself.[22] Familiarity with the Church's growing body of social doctrine is necessary in order to grasp and respond to the practical requirements of discipleship and stewardship in light of the complex realities of today's national and international socioeconomic life.

Social justice, which the pastoral letter *Economic Justice for All* calls a kind of contributive justice, is a particular aspect of the virtue of solidarity. Encompassing the duty of "all who are able to create the goods, services, and other nonmaterial or spiritual values necessary for the welfare of the whole community," it gives moral as well as economic content to the concept of productivity. Thus productivity "cannot be measured solely by its output of goods and services." Rather, "patterns of productivity must . . . be measured in light of their impact on the fulfillment of basic needs, employment levels, patterns of discrimination, environmental impact, and sense of community."[23]

Finally, and most poignantly, solidarity is obstructed by the persistence of religious conflicts and divisions, including those that sunder even followers of Christ. Christians remain tragically far from realizing Jesus' priestly prayer "that they may all be one, as you, Father, are in me and I in you" (Jn 17:21).

As all this suggests, our individual lives as disciples and stewards must be seen in relation to God's larger purposes. From the outset of his covenanting, God had it in mind to make many one. He promised Abram: "I will make of you a great nation, and I will bless you; I will make your name great, so that you will be a blessing. . . . All the communities of the earth shall find blessing in you" (Gn 12:2-3). In Jesus, the kingdom of God is inaugurated—a kingdom open to all. Those who enter into Jesus' new covenant find themselves growing in a union of minds and hearts with others who also have responded to God's call. They find their hearts and minds expanding to embrace all men and women, especially those in need, in a communion of mercy and love.

Eucharistic Stewardship

The eucharist is the great sign and agent of this expansive communion of charity. "Because the loaf of bread is one, we, though many, are one body, for we all partake of the one loaf" (1 Cor 10:17). Here people enjoy a unique union with Christ and, in him, with one another. Here his love—indeed, his very self—flows into his disciples and, through them and their practice of stewardship, to the entire human race. Here Jesus renews his covenant-forming act of perfect fidelity to God, while also making it possible for us to cooperate. In the eucharist, Christians reaffirm their participation in the new covenant; they give thanks to God for blessings received; and they strengthen their bonds of commitment to one another as members of the covenant community Jesus forms.

And what do Christians bring to the eucharistic celebration and join there with Jesus' offering? Their lives as Christian disciples; their personal vocations and the stewardship they have exercised regarding them; their individual contributions to the great work of restoring all things in Christ. Disciples give thanks to God for gifts received and strive to share them with others. That is why, as Vatican II says of the eucharist, "if this celebration is to be sincere and thorough, it must lead to various works of charity and mutual help, as well as to missionary activity and to different forms of Christian witness."[24]

More than that, the eucharist is the sign and agent of that heavenly communion in which we shall together share, enjoying the fruits of stewardship "freed of stain, burnished and transfigured."[25] It is not only the promise but the commencement of the heavenly banquet where human lives are perfectly fulfilled.

We have Jesus' word for it: "Whoever eats this bread will live forever; and the bread that I will give is my flesh for the life of the world" (Jn 6:51). The glory and the boast of Christian stewards lie in mirroring, however poorly, the stewardship of Jesus Christ, who gave and still gives all he has and is, in order to be faithful to God's will and carry through to completion his redemptive stewardship of human beings and their world.

V. The Christian Steward

It was sixteen years ago, but it seems like only yesterday. I was suddenly confronted with serious surgery, which I never thought would happen to me. It always happened to others. The memory is still there, and I recall vividly the days before the surgery. I really received the grace to ask myself, "What do I own, and what owns me?" When you are wheeled into a surgery room, it really doesn't matter

who you are or what you possess. What counts is the confidence in a competent surgical staff and a good and gracious God. I know that my whole understanding and appreciation of the gifts and resources I possess took on new meaning. It is amazing how a divine economy of life and health provides a unique perspective of what really matters.
—Most Rev. Thomas J. Murphy, Archbishop of Seattle

While the New Testament does not provide a rounded portrait of the Christian steward all in one place, elements of such a portrait are present throughout its pages.

In the Gospel, Jesus speaks of the "faithful and prudent steward" as one whom a householder sets over other members of the household in order to "distribute the food allowance at the proper time" (Lk 12:42; cf. Mt 24:25). Evidently, good stewards understand that they are to share with others what they have received, that this must be done in a timely way, and that God will hold them accountable for how well or badly they do it. For if a steward wastes the owner's goods and mistreats the other household members, "that servant's master will come on an unexpected day and at an unknown hour and will punish him severely and assign him a place with the unfaithful" (Lk 12:46).

In the lives of disciples, however, something else must come before the practice of stewardship. They need a flash of insight—a certain way of seeing—by which they view the world and their relationship to it in a fresh, new light. "The world is charged with the grandeur of God," Gerard Manley Hopkins exclaims; more than anything else, it may be this glimpse of the divine grandeur in all that is that sets people on the path of Christian stewardship.

Not only in material creation do people discern God present and active, but also, and especially, in the human heart.

"Do not be deceived . . . all good giving and every perfect gift is from above" (Jas 1:17), and this is true above all where spiritual gifts are concerned. Various as they are, "one and the same Spirit produces all of these" (1 Cor 12:11)—including the gift of discernment itself, which leads men and women to say: "We have not received the spirit of the world but the Spirit that is from God, so that we may understand the things freely given us by God" (1 Cor 2:12). So it is that people have the power to live as stewards, striving to realize the ideal set forth by Paul: "Whether you eat or drink, or whatever you do, do everything for the glory of God" (1 Cor 10:31).

Christian stewards are conscientious and faithful. After all, the first requirement of a steward is to be "found trustworthy" (1 Cor 4:2). In the present case, moreover, stewardship is a uniquely solemn trust. If Christians understand it and strive to live it to the full, they grasp the fact that they are no less than "God's co-workers" (1 Cor 3:9), with their own particular share in his creative, redemptive, and sanctifying work. In this light, stewards are fully conscious of their accountability. They neither live nor die as their own masters; rather, "if we live, we live for the Lord, and if we die, we die for the Lord; so then, whether we live or die, we are the Lord's" (Rom 14:8).

Christian stewards are generous out of love as well as duty. They dare not fail in charity and what it entails, and the New Testament is filled with warnings to those who might be tempted to substitute some counterfeit for authentic love. For example: "If someone who has worldly means sees a brother in need and refuses him compassion, how can the love of God remain in him?" (1 Jn 3:17). Or this: "Come now, you rich, weep and wail over your impending miseries. Your wealth has rotted away, your clothes have become moth-eaten, your gold and silver have corroded, and that corrosion will be a testimony against you; it will devour your flesh like a fire. You have stored up treasure for the last days" (Jas 5:1-3).

What, then, are Christians to do? Of course people's lives as stewards take countless forms, according to their unique vocations and circumstances. Still, the fundamental pattern in every case is simple and changeless: "Serve one another through love . . . bear one another's burdens, and so you will fulfill the law of Christ" (Gal 5:13, 6:2). This includes being stewards of the Church, for, as we are quite specifically told, "the Church of the living God" is "the household of God" (1 Tm 3:15), and it is essential to practice stewardship there.

The life of a Christian steward, lived in imitation of the life of Christ, is challenging, even difficult in many ways; but both here and hereafter it is charged with intense joy. Like Paul, the good steward is able to say, "I am filled with encouragement, I am overflowing with joy all the more because of all our affliction" (2 Cor 7:4). Women and men who seek to live in this way learn that "all things work for good for those who love God" (Rom 8:28). It is part of their personal experience that God is "rich in mercy [and] we are his handiwork, created in Christ Jesus for the good works that God has prepared in advance, that we should live in them" (Eph 2:4, 10). They readily cry out from the heart: "Rejoice in the Lord always! I shall say it again: Rejoice!" (Phil 4:4). They look forward in hope to hearing the Master's words addressed to those who have lived as disciples faithful in their practice of stewardship should: "Come, you who are blessed by my Father. Inherit the kingdom prepared for you from the foundation of the world" (Mt 25:34).

After Jesus, it is the Blessed Virgin Mary who by her example most perfectly teaches the meaning of discipleship and stewardship in all their fullest sense. All of their essential elements are found in her life: she was called and gifted by God; she responded generously, creatively, and prudently; she understood her divinely assigned role as "handmaid" in terms of service and fidelity (see Lk 1:26-56).

As mother of God, her stewardship consisted of her maternal service and devotion to Jesus, from infancy to adulthood, up to the agonizing hours of Jesus' death (Jn 19:25). As mother of the Church, her stewardship is clearly articulated in the closing chapter of the Second Vatican Council's *Constitution on the Church (Lumen Gentium)*.[26] Pope John Paul II observes: "Mary is one of the first who 'believed,' and precisely with her faith as Spouse and Mother she wishes to act upon all those who entrust themselves to her as children."[27]

In light of all this, it only remains for all of us to ask ourselves this question: Do we also wish to be disciples of Jesus Christ? The Spirit is ready to show us the way—a way of which stewardship is a part.

Genesis, telling the story of creation, says God looked upon what had been made and found it good; and seeing the world's goodness, God entrusted it to human beings. "The Lord God planted a garden" and placed there human persons "to cultivate and care for it" (Gn 2:18, 15). Now, as then and always, it is a central part of the human vocation that we be good stewards of what we have received—this garden, this divine human workshop, the world and all that is in it—setting minds and hearts and hands to the task of creating and redeeming in cooperation with our God, Creator and Lord of all.

Notes

1.   Second Vatican Council, *Pastoral Constitution on the Church in the Modern World (Gaudium et Spes)*, no. 43.
2.   John Paul II, *The Vocation and Mission of the Lay Faithful in the Church and in the World (Christifideles Laici)* (Washington, D.C.: United States Catholic Conference, 1989), no. 58.
3.   Cf. John Paul II, *Redeemer of Man (Redemptor Hominis)* (Washington, D.C.: United States Catholic Conference, 1979), no. 21.
4.   Dorothy Day, *The Long Loneliness* (New York: Doubleday/Image Books, 1959), 140.
5.   Second Vatican Council, *Decree on the Church's Missionary Activity (Ad Gentes)*, no. 11.
6.   Ignatius of Loyola, *Spiritual Exercises*, ed. G. Ganss (St. Louis, Mo.: Institute for Jesuit Sources, 1992), no. 23 (alt.).
7.   Cf. Mt 10:7; Second Vatican Council, *Dogmatic Constitution on the Church (Lumen Gentium)*, no. 48; *Gaudium et Spes*, no. 39.
8.   *Gaudium et Spes*, no. 38.
9.   Cf. John Paul II, *On Human Work (Laborem Exercens)* (Washington, D.C.: United States Catholic Conference, 1981), no. 25.
10. *Gaudium et Spes*, no. 34.
11. Thornton Wilder, *Our Town* (New York: Harper and Row, 1958), 100.
12. *Gaudium et Spes*, no. 51.
13. Gerard Manley Hopkins, "God's Grandeur," *Poems of Gerard Manley Hopkins* (New York: Oxford University Press, 1967).

14. John Paul II, "Peace with God, Peace with All Creation," *Origins* 19:28 (December 14, 1989): 465-468.
15. Ibid.
16. Maxine F. Dennis, *Of Human Hands* (Minneapolis and Chicago: Augsburg Fortress/ACTA Publications, 1991), 49.
17. John Paul II, *On the Christian Meaning of Human Suffering (Salvifici Doloris)* (Washington, D.C.: United States Catholic Conference, 1984), no. 27.
18. Paul VI, *Paenitemini (On Christian Penance)*, *Acta Apostolicae Sedis* 58 (1966): 177-198.
19. "Offerings for the Sanctuary" in *Parochial and Plain Sermons* (San Francisco: Ignatius Press, 1987), 1368.
20. Cf. *Christifidelis Laici*, no. 15.
21. Paul VI, *On Evangelization in the Modern World (Evangelii Nuntiandi)* (Washington, D.C.: United States Catholic Conference, 1975), no. 53.
22. John Paul II, *On Social Concern (Sollicitudo Rei Socialis)* (Washington, D.C.: United States Catholic Conference, 1988), no. 40.
23. National Conference of Catholic Bishops, *Economic Justice for All* (Washington, D.C.: United States Catholic Conference, 1986), no. 71.
24. Second Vatican Council, *Decree on the Ministry and Life of Priests (Presbyterorum Ordinis)*, no. 6.
25. *Gaudium et Spes*, no. 39.
26. *Lumen Gentium*, nos. 52-69.
27. John Paul II, *The Mother of the Redeemer (Redemptoris Mater)* (Washington, D.C.: United States Catholic Conference, 1987), no. 46.

Source: Washington, D.C.: United States Catholic Conference, 1993.

The Common Good:
Old Idea, New Urgency

*A Joint Statement of the General Secretary of the United States Catholic
Conference, Msgr. Robert Lynch, with Rev. Joan Brown Campbell, General
Secretary of the National Council of Churches, and Rabbi Henry
Michelman, Executive Vice President of the Synagogue Council of America*

June 1993

In holy and infinite love, God has created us for community and
has called us to covenants of justice and the common good.

The word of God is addressed to communities, to cities, to nations,
to the whole family of nations, so that all earth's peoples may become
one people.

The will of God is forsaken whenever a nation fails to nurture and
sustain the dignity and rights of all its people.

The Renewal of Promise

As Jews and Christians standing on the common ground of faith
in one holy and loving God, we commit ourselves to the renewal of
our nation's general welfare and its promise to all our people.

We seek to articulate a fresh and empowering vision of the common good, a vision which inspires public action to meet the basic
human needs of all our sisters and brothers. We judge this moment
especially to be filled with great promise for such renewal of the
national bond, which extends to every person in our land. The return
of our national confidence must quicken our responsiveness not only
to our budget deficits but more profoundly to our growing social
deficits. It is these that have most dramatically rent the fabric of life for
our people.

Too often, genuine focus on the common good has been missing
from our national dialogue, lost in a confusing clash of individual aspirations and narrow appeals. The common good is frequently diminished and sometimes destroyed by powerful currents in our national
life, including

- Social forces such as excessive individualism, materialism,
  and consumerism, which suggest that we are what we have

510

and which permit us to remain indifferent to those who are most in need of our active concern

- Economic forces in cities, suburbs, and rural communities which condemn 20 percent of our children to poverty, which tolerate the lack of decent work for millions, which foster a growing chasm between haves and have-nots, and which promote the choice of short-term gains over long-term investment
- Cultural forces such as irresponsible sexual behavior, the plagues of sexism and ageism, and escalating crime and violence which corrode human lives and deplete human resources, undercut family and community life, and threaten our moral integrity
- Political forces which, dominated by special interests, too often promote narrow causes with little regard for broader national interests
- The forces of racism, which leave us vulnerable to the bitter consequences of discrimination, intolerance, and polarization

The common good is an old idea with a new urgency. It is an imperative to put the welfare of the whole ahead of our own narrow interests. It is an imperative which we fervently hope will guide our people and leaders at this new moment. It is an imperative for a national embrace of responsibility and sacrifice, of compassion and caring as building blocks for meaningful lives and for a healthy society. We believe we can and must do better.

A Heritage for the Common Good

Jews and Christians share a common heritage in Hebrew Scripture, which proclaims that God's covenant of righteousness is devoted to the creation and preservation of community. Beyond this shared heritage, we celebrate a rich diversity of societal visions in our several faith traditions.

Judaism has ever taught a vision of moral solidarity and social justice that transcends and transforms individual conduct. The Exodus experience yet promises a future of liberation, a new and alternative community grounded in equity and uniquely marked by active compassion for the poor and the dispossessed. The towering imperatives of Leviticus 19 continue to demand that a holy people find its most worthy guidelines for action in imitation of the deeds of God. A holy people empowers the poor, extends legal protections to all regardless of rank or status, demands that the marketplace be girded with honesty, and responds with active concern and respect to the disabled. It is out of the encounter with the divine that the people recognize their responsibility not only to God but to each other.

Christian Orthodoxy, in its Eastern and Oriental expressions, holds a vision of the commonweal which is rooted in the power of a radiant tradition, of a profound historical consciousness of human solidarity throughout all generations. God's gift of salvation is radically social, compassionate, even cosmic, binding the faithful in loving kinship with the whole creation. The incarnation is the revelation of true humanity in the oneness of all life and death, all joy and suffering, all despair and hope. At the center of Orthodox life is the liturgy with its vivifying disclosure that authentic selfhood is experienced only in communion. True personhood requires the disavowal of egoistic individualism. The Orthodox Church is called to energetically pursue harmony with public institutions in order to promote the welfare of all the people.

For centuries the social teachings of Roman Catholicism have offered a rather explicit interpretation of the common good as a normative principle. In scholastic moral theology, papal encyclicals, the Second Vatican Council, and pastoral letters, the common good has been a guiding principle for Catholic involvement in politics, economics, human relations, and international affairs. The U.S. Catholic bishops' 1986 pastoral letter *Economic Justice for All* set forth these imperatives:

1. "Human dignity can be realized and protected only in community . . . and requires a [broad] commitment to the common good."
2. "The common good demands justice for all, the protection of the human rights of all."
3. "The obligation to provide justice for all means that the poor have the single most urgent economic claim on the conscience of the nation."
4. "As individuals and as a nation, therefore, we are called to make a fundamental option for the poor."
5. The prime purpose of this special commitment to the poor is to enable them to become active participants in the life of society.

Pope John Paul II has identified the virtue of solidarity as "a firm and persevering determination to commit oneself to the common good" *(On Social Concern [Sollicitudo Rei Socialis])*.

The reforming spirit of Protestantism generated covenantal visions of commonwealth, social contract, and republican government founded upon natural rights and common consent. In Europe and later on this continent Protestant theology has addressed itself not only to the life of the Church but to the society as well. A century ago the Protestant Social Gospel arose in protest against the weakness and corruption of government in the face of the inhumanities of uncontrolled industrialization, urbanization, and monopoly capital. This attack upon "the superpersonal forces of evil" sprang from a conception of social salvation grounded in a recovery of the biblical image of the kingdom of God, a realm requiring economic democracy as well as political democracy.

Matthew's Gospel provided a basic text. The ethical and moral questions of judgment are addressed to nations as well as to individuals. Nations, too, must answer whether they have responded compassionately to people who were hungry, thirsty, naked, sick, prisoners, or strangers (Mt 25:31-46).

Prophets of the Social Gospel sought common ground among the divided Churches for the sake of social justice and became founders of the modern ecumenical movement.

African American Protestants have conceived the Church as the prime community-nurturing and community-building institution. They have exalted the highest ethical and spiritual qualities of nationhood inspired by a vision of the beloved community. Consistently they have called our nation to fidelity to its historic covenant of unity in diversity. While sharing some of White America's Protestant history, African American Churches—nurtured in the biblical affirmation of freedom and separated from White society even after the abolition of slavery—became the dominant social institutions in segregated American society.

The civil rights movement of the twentieth century was born in the thousands of worshiping communities throughout the nation. The 1963 rally at the foot of the Lincoln Memorial was, for the African American Churches, confirmation of their long commitment to social justice, political and economic freedom, and the rights of individuals in a pluralistic society. The experience and affirmations of African American Churches currently have increasing influence within the community of Churches which seeks both social justice and personal piety.

These communitarian visions of our several faith traditions testify to the shared conviction that our faithfulness will generate action for the common good. Such visions, which emerge from classical philosophy as well as from Western political ethics, have been enhanced by commitment to the common good. But all too often our lack of active fidelity to our own teaching has obstructed the common good. We acknowledge the complicity of our religious institutions in the brokenness of our society and our world.

The pursuit of the common good is therefore not simply an agenda for public policy, but also a necessary guide for wise choices in our families, Churches, synagogues, businesses, unions, and communities. The religious community is called to proclaim these values and to support its members as they work in every aspect of ministry for moral, spiritual, and community renewal. In worship, spiritual formation, pastoral care, and advocacy we seek to build real community and promote the values which strengthen the commonweal.

Justice and the Common Good

To grapple with social justice requires a diligent quest for the meaning of justice itself. For Jews and Christians, our primary conception of justice comes from the very character of a holy and loving God:

- Justice is human action that joins God's active involvement in human history.
- Justice is the structure of human rights and responsibilities that best expresses God's covenant love in society.
- Justice and love are indispensable partners in the structures of society—political, legal, economic, social.

Justice is equity—not arithmetical equality; but fairness in all relationships of persons and groups; fairness that condemns inequalities of opportunity; fairness with a special commitment toward the poor, the weak, the marginalized, and the oppressed.

The indivisibility of justice and love is sealed by the Hebrew word at the heart of biblical testimony to the will of God: *Shalom*—the potential of mutual welfare, health, wholeness, harmony, and ultimately peace—is God's gift in the community and in all its relationships. That potential must be actualized by human beings as both children and partners of God.

Advocacy for the Common Good

It is in the service of and guided by the vision of God's *shalom* that our various communities have been led to ministries of service and vocations of public advocacy in the past. Acting individually and sometimes together we have sought to provide food, shelter, child care, counseling, jobs programs, health clinics, elderly and disabled services, solace, succor, and strength to neighbors in need. The involvement of our own vast networks of volunteers has taught us much about the extent of need in our society and of the dignity of those in need.

Together religious institutions have historically witnessed to the whole nation as a part of the exercise of religious freedom. Though such efforts must now be intensified, they cannot substitute for just public policy reflective of the common good. That is why people of faith now have come to call for the establishment of policies, programs, and governmental action that seek to secure justice and promote the general welfare. This religiously motivated commitment to the common good does not mean that we always find full unity in applying these principles on specific and complex matters of public policy. Rather, in the notion of *shalom* we find a common calling to action and advocacy which will be shared not only within but beyond our own communities.

We believe men and women of goodwill throughout the country share this vision of a holistic approach to social welfare as a matter of human rights as well as human need.

But our vision must extend far beyond a view of human rights that tends to focus exclusively on individual civil and political liberties. Rather, we must include as well claims to economic and social rights among our people and responsibilities to one another and to society to advance the dignity and well-being of all.

Without such a comprehensive ideal of human rights and responsibilities, the common good is obstructed, forestalling public policies urgently needed for the promotion of the general welfare. Corporately we understand our vocation to be to:

- Speak out for those who cannot speak for the rights of all the destitute.
- Speak out, judge righteously, and defend the rights of the poor and needy (Prv 31:4-9).

Renewal of the Debate

Making common appeal to the biblical foundation of creation, covenant, and community, we offer a provisional public theology of the common good, whose moral core is social justice, human dignity, and human rights. We believe that this appeal will strike a deep and responsive chord not only within people of faith but among many persons throughout our society. For everywhere such persons share in the recognition that

- Millions of our children enter life with deficient prenatal care and continue their precarious development with inadequate health care, nutrition, education, and family support. Child care continues to be costly, scanty, and of uneven quality. Family life itself has been ravaged by economic, moral, and social pressures, lack of affordable services for children and the elderly, and a profound sense of social insecurity.
- Millions of our disadvantaged young adults are seemingly trapped in a life without a future in which dropping out of school, unemployment, inadequate job training, teenage pregnancy, street violence, drugs, and welfare dependency provide a dehumanizing struggle for survival.

- Millions of working adults have suffered declining real income and lack of health coverage at a time when even those with insurance have seen family budgets impelled by escalating health care costs. At least 10 million adults remain unemployed. In the past decade, homelessness has become the fate of perhaps a million or more Americans, including tens of thousands of families.
- Millions of disabled persons and elderly persons, mostly single women, are living in poverty. Most older Americans are without adequate resources to cope with long-term care, chronic or catastrophic illness, and disability.

Government must always seek the general welfare of the people and pursue the common good. But government alone cannot address so large a question. Rather, in our democracy individuals and institutions from every sector of the society need to view their rights within the context of their responsibilities. The voluntary capacity and history of America's institutions provide a rich legacy upon which we must draw. Our history as a people has given evidence of this remarkable tradition.

In partnership with government we must call anew upon our traditions of community care and concern. Governmental programs must supplement and undergird but not supplant the efforts of individuals and families to participate fully in the social, cultural, and economic life of our land.

No less must institutions find appropriate partnerships with government to shoulder democracy's responsibility to its citizens so that they may enjoy the blessings of liberty. Each institution must examine its own purposes and capacity for such involvement.

As people of faith we will be guided by Scripture's injunction to heed the cry of the widowed and orphaned, the afflicted and the homeless. In infant voices, in the sighs of the discontented, and in the plaintive voice of the stranger at the gate we find the imperative to action and advocacy.

We do not in these reflections make specific reference to the continuing need of our nation to pursue the common good on a global basis or to protect God's creation and preserve our environment. These vital matters are ongoing priorities for our religious bodies, but not the focus of these reflections.

We seek to contribute to a fresh debate over the renewal of the general welfare. We do not offer specific policy proposals, but rather basic values and general directions, coupled with a sense of urgency. Our faith communities must continue to strengthen our ongoing efforts to engage our constituencies in study, dialogue, and action in pursuit of the common good. Let then the leaders of our nation heed this call and pursue its directions with urgency and creativity.

A Call to Commitment

The challenge of pursuing the common good is both concrete and complex. Not fitting the partisan categories of our day, such a pursuit calls upon our national leaders to join us to affirm old values and pursue new policies. Through such a process we will all be expected to exercise more personal responsibility and broader social responsibility. We are now being asked to embrace greater restraint and discipline in our lives and more compassion within the broader society.

More than anything else, the call to the common good is a reminder that we are one human family, whatever our differences of race, gender, ethnicity, or economic status.

In our vision of the common good, a crucial moral test is how the weakest are faring. We give special priority to the poor and vulnerable since those with the greatest needs and burdens have first claim on our common efforts. In protecting the lives and promoting the dignity of the poor and vulnerable, we strengthen all of society.

To this task, the religious community brings strong values; deep convictions; extensive experience in meeting human needs; and enduring relationships across national, racial, ethnic, and political lines. Moreover we bring 100 million adherents who are both people of faith and participants in this democracy.

We also bring an agenda that we believe is at the heart of building real community and pursuing the common good in our nation, an agenda which is of compelling importance to believers and nonbelievers alike:

- *Priority for the poor.* In all debate over economic policy, poor children and their families must be of paramount concern. Our nation must offer concrete economic opportunity and wise investment to secure the future of the most powerless in our midst and our future as well.
- *Focus on basic human dignity and needs.* The absence of decent work and housing, of an equitable and effective system of education, and especially of affordable and universal health care, undermines the well-being of millions. The search for the common good must prevail over the powerful defenders of the status quo in these crucial tests for community.
- *Genuine reform of the welfare system.* True welfare reform attacks poverty, not the poor. We call for policy changes which will empower the poor to move beyond privation and dependency toward economic independence. Even as the religious community strengthens our own profound involvement in efforts to help those in need, we seek proactive policy reform

to offer opportunity for decent work to support families and to combat poverty.

- *Respect for diversity.* Discrimination still weakens our nations and diminishes each of us. We need to forge a national consensus that racism, anti-Semitism, and all other forms of discrimination have no place in our society.
- *New politics of community.* We must grow beyond polarization and gridlock as we seek to evaluate each new policy proposal by the manner in which it enhances the pursuit of the common good. We urge that partisanship yield now to the renewed will of our American community; that we can no longer tolerate a society which closes its eyes to the well-being of all of its people.
- *A commitment to empowerment.* As we advocate reshaping national policy and restructuring our national agenda, we continue to believe that there is no substitute for the efforts of families, neighborhoods, churches, synagogues, and other organizations to help individuals meet their local needs. These mediating institutions do often exercise far more creativity and effectiveness than distant bureaucracies and impersonal agencies.

Our call therefore is for full and active partnership, people and government, government and people, to bring to bear both justice and loving kindness in responding to the needs of our people.

Our agenda derives from the values inherent within our faiths, not from any partisan political positions.

Our agenda reflects our common convictions about the moral measure of community.

Our pursuit of the common good, therefore, is a reflection of who we are, what we believe, and what we have experienced. We assert that the common ground that we have found in pursuing the common good is not only a moral imperative, but an essential religious calling.

Source: *Origins* 23:6 (June 24, 1993): 81-86.

A Framework for Comprehensive Health Care Reform: Protecting Human Life, Promoting Human Dignity, Pursuing the Common Good

A Resolution of the Catholic Bishops of the United States

June 1993

Introduction

Our nation's health care system serves too few and costs too much. A major national debate on how to assure access for all, restrain costs, and increase quality is moving to the center of American public life. This resolution is addressed to the Catholic community and the leaders of our nation. We seek to outline the values, criteria, and priorities that are guiding our conference's participation in this vital dialogue. We hope to offer a constructive and distinctive contribution reflecting the Catholic community's strong convictions and broad experience in health care.

The debate and decisions will not be easy. They will touch every family and business, every community and parish. Health care reform represents an effort to redirect one-seventh of our national economy and to reshape our society's response to a basic human need. It is not only an economic challenge, it is a moral imperative.

The Catholic community has much at stake and much to contribute to this vital national dialogue. For decades, we have advocated sweeping reform. In communities across our land, we serve the sick and pick up the pieces of a failing system. We are pastors, teachers, and leaders of a community deeply committed to comprehensive health reform. Our urgency for reform reflects both on our traditional principles and everyday experience.

A Tradition of Teaching

Our approach to health care is shaped by a simple but fundamental principle: "Every person has a right to adequate health care. This right flows from the sanctity of human life and the dignity that belongs to all human persons, who are made in the image of God." Health care is more than a commodity; it is a basic *human right*, an essential safeguard of human life and dignity. We believe our people's health care should not depend on where they work, how much their parents earn, or where they live. Our constant teaching that each human life must be protected and human dignity promoted leads us to insist that all people have a right to health care. This right is explicitly affirmed in *Pacem in Terris* and is the foundation of our advocacy for health care reform. When millions of Americans are without health coverage, when rising costs threaten the coverage of millions more, when infant mortality remains shockingly high, the right to health care is seriously undermined and our health care system is in need of fundamental reform.

Our call for health care reform is rooted in the biblical call to heal the sick and to serve "the least of these," the priorities of social justice and the principle of the common good. The existing patterns of health care in the United States do not meet the minimal standard of social justice and the common good. The substantial inequity of our health care system can no longer be ignored or explained away. The principle defect is that more than 35 million persons do not have guaranteed access to basic health care. Others have access, but their coverage is too limited or too costly to offer health security for their families. High health care costs contribute to a declining standard of living for many American families. The current health care system is so inequitable, and the disparities between rich and poor and those with access and those without are so great that it is clearly unjust.

The burdens of this system are not shared equally. One out of three Hispanics and one of five African Americans are uninsured. The health care in our inner cities and some rural communities leads to Third World rates of infant mortality. The virtue of *solidarity* and our teaching on the *option for the poor* and the vulnerable require us to measure our health system in terms of how it affects the weak and disadvantaged. In seeking the fundamental changes that are necessary, we focus especially on the impact of national health policies on the poor and the vulnerable.

The traditional value of *stewardship* also contributes to our call for reform. It is predicted that health care costs will more than double between 1980 and 2000. Our nation pays far more for health care than other industrialized countries and that strains the private economy and leaves too few resources for housing, education, and other economic and social needs. Stewardship demands that we address the duplication, waste, and other factors that make our system so expensive.

For three-quarters of a century, the Catholic bishops of the United States have called for national action to assure decent health care for all Americans. We seek to bring a *moral perspective* in an intensely political debate; we offer an ethical framework in an arena dominated by powerful economic interests.

A Community of Caring

The Catholic community, in states, cities, and towns all across our country, brings not only strong convictions, but also broad experience as providers and purchasers of health care. The Church has been involved in the delivery of health care services since the early days of this nation. Catholic health care facilities are now the largest network of nonprofit hospitals and nursing homes in the United States, serving more than 20 million people in a single year.

As pastors, we see the strains and stresses related to inadequate health care, the human consequences of a failing system. In approximately 600 Catholic hospitals and 1,500 long-term and specialized-care settings, in our parishes and schools, in Catholic Charities shelters and services, in Campaign for Human Development–funded groups, we see the consequences of failed and confused policy: families without insurance, the sick without options, children without care, the plight of real people behind the statistics. We seek to offer a *human perspective* in an often overly technical discussion.

Our Experience as Employers

Catholic dioceses, parishes, schools, agencies, and hospitals are major purchasers of insurance and health care. The rapidly escalating costs of coverage are impacting almost every diocese, agency, parish, and school. The increasing resources we spend on health care are dollars that do not fund much-needed ministry, services, and personnel. We know well the fiscal consequences of the rising health costs which are hurting our economy and diverting precious resources.

A Capacity for Advocacy

Our community also brings to this debate expertise and credibility rooted in our experience and values; a history and record of active support for health care reform that goes back decades; active ministry in inner-city, suburban, and rural communities; an institutional presence in every state and congressional district. We are a very diverse community of believers and citizens who could make a big difference in the health care debate.

The Catholic Health Association (CHA), which serves Catholic-sponsored health care facilities, has developed a comprehensive framework for a reformed health care system. This plan reflects the experience and expertise of Catholic leaders who are deeply involved in meeting the health care needs of the nation. We welcome CHA's impressive initiative in developing this plan, which includes important values and policy directions to help guide the debate and decisions in the months ahead.

Health care reform is an issue that unites the Catholic community. We need to continue to work together to help make the case for comprehensive reform, share our values and experience, and urge our representatives to adopt health care reform that will protect the life and dignity of all. We offer a potential constituency of conscience in the midst of a debate too often dominated by special interests and partisan needs. The debate over national health care reform will test both our Church and our country.

Criteria for Reform

Applying our experience and principles to the choices before the nation, our bishops' conference strongly supports comprehensive reform that will ensure a decent level of health care for all without regard to their ability to pay. This will require concerted action by federal and other levels of government and by the diverse providers and consumers of health care. We believe government, an instrument of our common purpose called to pursue the common good, has an essential role to play in assuring that the rights of all people to adequate health care are respected.

We believe reform of the health care system which is truly fundamental and enduring must be rooted in values that reflect the essential dignity of each person, ensure that basic human rights are protected, and recognize the unique needs and claims of the poor. We commend to the leaders of our nation the following criteria for reform:

- *Respect for Life.* Whether it preserves and enhances the sanctity and dignity of human life from conception to natural death.
- *Priority Concern for the Poor.* Whether it gives special priority to meeting the most pressing health care needs of the poor and underserved, ensuring that they receive quality health services.
- *Universal Access.* Whether it provides ready universal access to comprehensive health care for every person living in the United States.
- *Comprehensive Benefits.* Whether it provides comprehensive benefits sufficient to maintain and promote good health; to provide preventive care; to treat disease, injury, and disability appropriately; and to care for persons who are chronically ill or dying.
- *Pluralism.* Whether it allows and encourages the involvement of the public and private sectors, including the voluntary, religious, and nonprofit sectors, in the delivery of care and serv-

ices; and whether it ensures respect for religious and ethical values in the delivery of health care for consumers and for individual and institutional providers.

- *Quality.* Whether it promotes the development of processes and standards that will help to achieve quality and equity in health services, in the training of providers, and in the informed participation of consumers in decision making on health care.

- *Cost Containment and Controls.* Whether it creates effective cost containment measures that reduce waste, inefficiency, and unnecessary care; measures that control rising costs of competition, commercialism, and administration; and measures that provide incentives to individuals and providers for effective and economical use of limited resources.

- *Equitable Financing.* Whether it assures society's obligation to finance universal access to comprehensive health care in an equitable fashion, based on ability to pay; and whether proposed cost-sharing arrangements are designed to avoid creating barriers to effective care for the poor and vulnerable.

Key Policy Priorities

We hope Catholics and others will use these criteria to assess proposals for reform. In applying these criteria, we have chosen to focus our advocacy on several essential priorities:

Priority Concern for the Poor/Universal Access: We look at health care reform from the bottom up, how it touches the unserved and underserved. Genuine health care reform must especially focus on the basic health needs of the poor (i.e., those who are unable through private resources, employer support, or public aid to provide payment for health care services, or those unable to gain access to health care because of limited resources, inadequate education, or discrimination).

When there is a question of allocating scarce resources, the vulnerable and the poor have a compelling claim to first consideration. Special attention must be given to ensuring that those who have suffered from inaccessible and inadequate health care (e.g., in central cities, isolated rural areas, and migrant camps) are first brought back into an effective system of quality care. Therefore, we will strongly support measures to ensure true universal access and rapid steps to improve the health care of the poor and unserved. Universal access must not be significantly postponed, since coverage delayed may well be coverage denied. We do not support a two-tiered health system since separate health care coverage for the poor usually results in poor health care. Linking the health care of poor and working-class families to the health care of those with greater resources is probably the best assurance of comprehensive benefits and quality care.

Respect for Human Life and Human Dignity: Real health care reform must protect and enhance human life and human dignity. Every member of the human family has the right to life and to the means that are suitable for the full development of life. This is why we insist that every human being has the right to quality health services, regardless of age, income, illness, or condition of life. Government statistics on infant mortality are evidence that lack of access and inadequate care are literally matters of life and death. The needs of the frail elderly, the unborn child, the person living with AIDS, and the undocumented immigrant must be addressed by health care reform.

Neither the violence of abortion and euthanasia nor the growing advocacy for assisted suicide is consistent with respect for human life. When destructive practices such as abortion or euthanasia seek acceptance as aspects of "health care" alongside genuine elements of the healing art, the very meaning of health care is distorted and threatened. A consistent concern for human dignity is strongly demonstrated by providing access to quality care from the prenatal period throughout infancy and childhood, into adult life, and at the end of life when care is possible even if cure is not. Therefore, we are convinced it would be a moral tragedy, a serious policy misjudgment, and a major political mistake to burden health care reform with abortion coverage that most Americans oppose and the federal government has not funded for the last seventeen years. Consequently, we continue to oppose unequivocally the inclusion of abortion as a health care benefit, as do three out of four Americans.[1]

As long-time advocates of health care reform, we appeal to the leaders of the nation to avoid a divisive and polarizing dispute which could jeopardize passage of national health reform. We strongly believe it would be morally wrong and counterproductive to compel individuals, institutions, or states to pay for or participate in procedures that fundamentally violate basic moral principles and the consciences of millions of Americans. The common good is not advanced when advocates of so-called choice compel taxpayers to fund what we and many others are convinced is the destruction of human life.

Pursuing the Common Good and Preserving Pluralism: We fear the cause of real reform can be undermined by special interest conflict and the resistance of powerful forces who have a major stake in maintaining the *status quo.* It also can be thwarted by unnecessary partisan political combat. We believe the debate can be advanced by a continuing focus on the common good and a healthy respect for genuine pluralism. A reformed system must encourage the creative and renewed involvement of both the public and private sectors, including voluntary, religious, and nonprofit providers of care. It must also respect the religious and ethical values of both individuals and institutions involved in the health care system. We are deeply concerned that Catholic and other institutions with strong moral foundations may face increasing economic and regulatory pressures to compromise their moral principles and to participate in practices inconsistent with their commitment to human life. The Catholic community is strongly committed to continuing to meet the health needs of the nation in a framework of genuine reform, which respects the essential role and values of religiously affiliated providers of health care.

Restraining Costs: We have the best health care technology in the world, but tens of millions have little or no access to it and the costs of the system are straining our nation, our economy, our families, and our Church to the breaking point. We insist that any acceptable plan must include effective mechanisms to restrain rising health care costs. By bringing health care cost inflation down, we could cut the federal deficit, improve economic competitiveness, and help stem the decline in living standards for many working families. Without cost containment, we cannot hope to make health care affordable and direct scarce national resources to other pressing problems that, in turn, worsen health problems (e.g., inadequate housing, poverty, joblessness, and poor education).

Conclusion

The Catholic bishops' conference will continue to work with our people and others for reform of the U.S. health care system, especially on these key priorities. In our view, the best measure of any proposed health care initiative is the extent to which it combines universal access to comprehensive quality health care with cost control, while ensuring quality care for the poor and preserving human life and dignity.

We welcome the signs that our nation and our leaders are beginning to face up to the challenge of reform. We will assess the Clinton administration's plan and the alternatives to it on the basis of our criteria and experience. We will be active and involved participants in this vital national debate.

New public policy is essential to address the health care crisis, but it is not sufficient. Each of us must examine how we contribute to this crisis—how our own attitudes and behavior demonstrate a lack of respect for our own health and the dignity of all. Are we prepared to make the changes, address the neglect, accept the sacrifices, and practice the discipline that can lead to better health care for all Americans? In our own lives and in this vital health care debate, we are all called to protect human life, promote human dignity, and pursue the common good. In particular, we call on all Catholics involved in the health care system to play leadership roles in shaping health care reform that respects human life and enhances human dignity.

Now is the time for real health care reform. It is a matter of fundamental justice. For so many, it is literally a matter of life and death, of lives cut short and dignity denied. We urge our national leaders to look beyond special interest claims and partisan differences to unite our nation in a new commitment to meeting the health care needs of our people, especially the poor, and vulnerable. This is a major political task, a significant policy challenge, and a moral imperative.

Note

1.   CBS News Poll, "Priorities on Health Care and Its Costs," *New York Times* (April 6, 1993): A20.

Source: Washington, D.C.: United States Catholic Conference, 1993.

Human Sexuality from God's Perspective

Statement of the NCCB Committee for Pro-Life Activities on the Twenty-Fifth Anniversary of Humanae Vitae

August 1993

"If you choose, you can keep the commandments, and to act faithfully is a matter of your own choice. He has placed before you fire and water; stretch out your hand for whichever you choose. Before each person are life and death, and whichever one chooses will be given" (Sir 15:15-17, NRSV).

It is clear in the Scriptures that God looks at the world and human life differently from human beings with their limited vision. His comprehensive view encompasses the whole of the human family and all the ages and all eternity. He willed to share with women and men a unique role in his creative generativity which makes human sexuality unique in all creation. It is this uniqueness, revealed to us by God in the gradual unfolding of his salvific plan, that Pope Paul VI invoked in his prophetic encyclical *Humanae Vitae (On Human Life)* published twenty-five years ago.[1]

Due to our world's increasing technological ability to prevent conception, many today view human sexuality in a purely pragmatic way. They believe that we are simply sexual beings who instinctively seek to be sexually active. From a physiological and psychological point of view, sexual intercourse is looked on as solely a natural response to human instinct and human need. Science is often called upon to help people divorce sexual activity from the prospect of unwanted pregnancy and free them from religious teachings which are thought to inhibit freedom. This is a secular perspective about human sexuality which has become pervasive and dominant in our culture. But it is a very limited perspective, a perspective devoid of God's revelation about the uniqueness of human life, a perspective unmindful of the data gathered from our observations about the true nature of human sexuality.

This is why, in the face of growing opposition to the Church's teaching about human sexuality, Pope Paul VI issued *Humanae Vitae* twenty-five years ago. He understood then, as the Church understands today, the responsibility to keep God's revelation as part of the equation in viewing human sexuality. It is not just instinct, human desire, or need which must be considered in human sexual activity.

One must understand human life and the human spirit, which transcends biology and humanistic philosophy. Human sexual activity cannot be separated from the nature and dignity of human life and the process by which that life is transmitted.

And so this year we commemorate the twenty-fifth anniversary of *Humanae Vitae*, in which Pope Paul VI reaffirmed the Church's teaching on the sanctity of marriage and the responsible transmission of human life. Pope Paul based his encyclical on the natural law as illumined by divine revelation and consistently taught by the Church. Expanding on this teaching, especially as expressed in the Second Vatican Council's *Pastoral Constitution on the Church in the Modern World (Gaudium et Spes)*, he presented a dignified and unified vision of marriage, sexuality, and family life. On this twenty-fifth anniversary we wish to reaffirm the teaching of *Humanae Vitae* as the authentic and constant teaching of the magisterium.

Paul VI spoke of marriage as "the wise institution of the Creator to realize in mankind his design of love."[2] In this way he set the context in which we might better understand and appreciate the love that exists between husband and wife, the love that exists between parent and child. He set the context too for understanding the dignity of human sexual activity as one of the ways in which married couples express their love for one another.

God's love is total. It is permanent. His love is an unlimited gift of himself to us, his children. As Catholic Christians, this understanding of God's love serves as the foundation of our teachings on marriage as a sacrament. In marriage, spouses live a true communion of persons in the Lord. The sign value of marital love lies precisely in its ability to mirror God's love. Marriage is therefore a vocation, a real path to union with God.

Conjugal Love

In *Humanae Vitae*, Pope Paul recognized conjugal love as eminently human, but rooted in God's love for his people. He saw it as the dynamic element in every marriage, bringing permanence to the marriage and enabling the couple to make wise, generous, and responsible decisions about the spacing of births and the size of their family. *Humanae Vitae* provides a positive and dignified understanding of sexuality as a gift from God which ennobles, enriches, and reconciles married couples. Through sexual union, couples strengthen their marital relationship and participate in a special way in God's creation of new life. From this follows the profound meaning of a life of intimacy—that communion of two persons who must be open to each other in a mutual self-donation that reaches its apex in the loving union that bears fruit in children.

Sexuality, then, is not merely a matter of biology nor is it simply a source of personal pleasure. Rather, it concerns, as Pope John Paul II reminds us in the apostolic exhortation *Familiaris Consorti (On the Family)*, "the innermost being of the human person as such. It is realized in a truly human way only if it is an integral part of the love by which a man and woman commit themselves totally to one another until death."[3]

Spouses are called to celebrate their conjugal love by becoming one flesh in the Lord and to see their sexual intimacy in the context of God's creative role and the nature of marriage itself. By remaining open to life each time they come together in the conjugal embrace, by preserving "the two meanings of the conjugal act: the unitive meaning and the procreative meaning,"[4] married couples reverence the presence of God in their union. In truth, the Church teaches that there are two aspects of marital intercourse—the strengthening of interpersonal unity between the spouses and the procreation of new life. These two goods are inseparable—not in the sense that both must be achieved in every act of conjugal intimacy, but in the sense that one may not deliberately act against either good in any act of conjugal intimacy.

Responsible Parenthood

Complementing its teaching on conjugal love, Paul VI reaffirmed the Church's tradition that responsible parenthood flows from the intimate communion that is at the heart of the meaning of marriage. Too often childbearing is characterized as burdensome, risky, destructive of personal aspirations, and dangerous for a world thought by some to be already overpopulated. But in reality married couples also experience a profound desire to share their life and love by cooperating with God in creating new life and building a family.

The teaching of *Humanae Vitae* reminds us that parenthood is a privilege as well as a responsibility. Couples are able to associate themselves in the deepest and closest way with God in the work of procreation. They are able, in John Paul II's words, "to serve life, to actualize in history the original blessing of the Creator—that of transmitting by procreation the divine image from person to person."[5] Today it is especially important to remember that each child is a unique and unrepeatable person and a testimony to the love of his or her parents as well as a testimony to the love of God. Too often the personal joys of parenthood and the promise that children hold for the future are overlooked or denigrated. All who follow Christ must see each child as a creature of God endowed with inestimable dignity who is called to accomplish his or her human destiny and to take an active role in the Church's missionary vocation.

Responsible parenthood, then, implies a positive openness to life. It is a decision that couples make mutually and prayerfully, confident that God's grace will complement their generosity. Couples should make decisions about spacing births and the size of their families free of coercion or pressure. Taking into account their mutual responsibilities to God, themselves, their family, and the society of which they are a part, in a correct hierarchy of values a couple may responsibly decide to delay childbearing. Or a husband or wife may conclude that they are unable to have more children. In the formation of their consciences, however, the couple must be well-instructed in and guided "by objective standards . . . that preserve the full sense of mutual self-giving and human procreation in the context of true love."[6]

We recognize the problems and difficulties couples face in making decisions about parenthood. Concerns about economic stability, employment, health care, education of children, or fulfilling existing responsibilities must be taken into account; and these concerns may suggest the avoidance, at least for the time being, of another birth. But we also recognize that unsubstantiated claims about population growth and cultural attitudes that diminish the value of the child may induce fear of having more than one or two children. These pressures compromise the freedom of the couple. We recall the teaching of the Second Vatican Council that "children are really the supreme gift of marriage and contribute very substantially to the welfare of their parents."[7] We also recognize that for some couples, despite their intense desire, childbearing does not occur. At the same time, "those merit special mention who with a gallant heart, and with wise and common deliberation, undertake to bring up suitably even a relatively large family."[8]

Negative Influences

Studies of marriage and family life in the United States chronicle an increase in nonmarital cohabitation, out-of-wedlock pregnancy, abortion, and divorce. To some degree, these phenomena reflect the state of confusion many people experience with regard to the meaning of human sexuality. For others, it is a clear rejection of moral principles and a trivialization of sex itself. They also reflect an exaggerated individualism and a flight from intimacy and commitment. At the same time, we are keenly aware of an increase in the incidence of sexual abuse, sexual exploitation, and sexual violence. All this has profound and destructive effects not only on individual persons but on society as well. The family is universally recognized as the basic unit of society, and the well-being of society depends on the stability and vitality of the family. When a society permits sexual behavior to be torn from its moorings in human love and marriage, when it treats sex as a mechanism for personal pleasure, it encourages a destructive mentality and diminishes the value of personal commitment and of human life itself. To a large degree this is the situation in our nation today.

Natural Family Planning

As we reflect on the teaching of *Humanae Vitae*, we recognize the advances in natural family planning and the efforts of scientists, pastors, and married couples committed to "instilling conviction and offering practical help to those who wish to live out their parenthood in a truly responsible way."[9] With proper instruction, married couples can readily understand the cycle of fertility, and they are able to plan and space births in a way that is both consistent with God's law and supportive of their own intimacy and unity. Natural family planning, as Pope John Paul II reminds us, "involves accepting dialogue, reciprocal respect, shared responsibility, and self-control."[10] And as Paul VI noted in *Humanae Vitae*, its benefits to married couples are many:

> It demands continual effort, yet, thanks to its beneficent influence, husband and wife fully develop their personalities, being enriched with spiritual values. Such discipline bestows upon family life fruits of serenity and peace, and facilitates the solution of other problems; it favors attention for one's partner, helps both parties to drive out selfishness, the enemy of true love, and deepens their sense of responsibility. By its means, parents acquire the capacity of having a deeper and more efficacious influence in the education of their offspring. (no. 21)

Natural family planning gives couples a richer appreciation of human sexuality and of their own marital relationship, and it strengthens their openness to childbearing.

Conclusion

Humanae Vitae represents a call to celebrate and reverence God's vision of human sexuality. It reminded us that we are stewards of God's gifts of marital love and procreation. It sounded a prophetic message for people to live chastely, to welcome children and protect families and never to treat human life as a commodity. Ultimately, it challenged the people of God to grow in Christian maturity.

Realizing that twenty-five years represents the coming of a new generation, it is our hope that the new generation might read *Humanae Vitae* and hear its gentle and loving message. In the face of a society that has lost sight of the profound meaning of marital intimacy, a society that has separated sexuality from married love and intimacy from procreation, it is important to call everyone to listen once again to the wisdom of *Humanae Vitae* and to make the Church's teaching the foundation for a renewed understanding of marriage and family life.

Recalling the teachings expressed in *Humanae Vitae*, we renew our commitment to respect for human life. We rededicate ourselves to increase our efforts to expand Christian education, pastoral programs for engaged and married couples, and natural family planning services. We will work to dispel the sexual confusions of our age and strive to help our brothers and sisters respect the "laws written by God" in our very nature, laws which we "must observe with intelligence and love."[11]

In our pastoral efforts and in support of the Church's consistent teaching as presented in *Humanae Vitae*, on this twenty-fifth anniversary we pledge ourselves to "work ardently and incessantly for the safeguarding and the holiness of marriage, so that it may always be lived in its entire human and Christian fullness."[12]

Notes

1. Paul VI, *On the Regulation of Birth (Humanae Vitae)* (Washington, D.C.: United States Catholic Conference, 1968).
2. *Humanae Vitae*, no. 8.
3. John Paul II, *On the Family (Familiaris Consortio)* (Washington, D.C.: United States Catholic Conference, 1982), no. 11.
4. *Humanae Vitae*, no. 12.
5. *Familiaris Consortio*, no. 28.
6. Second Vatican Council, *Pastoral Constitution on the Church in the Modern World (Gaudium et Spes)*, no. 51.
7. *Gaudium et Spes*, no. 50.
8. Ibid.
9. *Familiaris Consortio*, no. 35.
10. Ibid., no. 32.
11. *Humanae Vitae*, no. 31.
12. Ibid., no. 30.

Source: *Origins* 23:10 (August 12, 1993): 164-166.

Communities of Salt and Light: Reflections on the Social Mission of the Parish

A Statement of the National Conference of Catholic Bishops

November 1993

> You are the salt of the earth. But if salt loses its taste, with
> what can it be seasoned? It is no longer good for anything
> but to be thrown out and trampled underfoot. You are the
> light of the world. . . . Your light must shine before others,
> that they may see your good deeds and glorify your heav-
> enly Father. (Mt 5:13-16)

Introduction

The parish is where the Church lives. Parishes are communities of
faith, of action, and of hope. They are where the Gospel is proclaimed
and celebrated, where believers are formed and sent to renew the
earth. Parishes are the home of the Christian community; they are the
heart of our Church. Parishes are the place where God's people meet
Jesus in word and sacrament and come in touch with the source of the
Church's life.

One of the most encouraging signs of the Gospel at work in our
midst is the vitality and quality of social justice ministries in our
parishes. Across the country, countless local communities of faith are
serving those in need, working for justice, and sharing our social
teaching as never before. Millions of parishioners are applying the
Gospel and church teaching in their own families, work, and communities. More and more, the social justice dimensions of our faith are
moving from the fringes of parishes to become an integral part of local
Catholic life.

We welcome and applaud this growing recognition of and action
on the social mission of the parish. We offer these brief reflections to
affirm and support pastors and parish leaders in this essential task and
to encourage all parishes to take up this challenge with renewed commitment, creativity, and urgency.

In the past decade, we have written major pastoral letters on peace
and economic justice and issued pastoral statements on a number of
important issues touching human life and human dignity. But until

now, we have not specifically addressed the crucial role of parishes in the Church's social ministry. We offer these words of support, encouragement, and challenge at this time because we are convinced that the local parish is the most important ecclesial setting for sharing and acting on our Catholic social heritage. We hope that these reflections can help pastors, parish staffs, parish councils, social concerns committees, and other parishioners strengthen the social justice dimensions of their own parish life. This focus on the social mission of the parish complements and strengthens the call to evangelization found in our statement *Go and Make Disciples: A National Plan and Strategy for Catholic Evangelization in the United States.*

We offer a framework for integration rather than a specific model or new national program. We seek to affirm and encourage local parish commitment and creativity in social ministry. We know pastors and parish leaders do not need another program to carry forward or more expectations to meet. We see the parish dimensions of social ministry not as an added burden, but as a part of what keeps a parish alive and makes it truly Catholic. Effective social ministry helps the parish not only do more, but be more—more of a reflection of the Gospel, more of a worshiping and evangelizing people, more of a faithful community. It is an essential part of parish life.

This is not a new message, but it takes on new urgency in light of the increasing clarity and strength of Catholic social teaching and the signs of declining respect for human life and human dignity in society. We preach a Gospel of justice and peace in a rapidly changing world and troubled nation. Our faith is tested by the violence, injustice, and moral confusion that surround us. In this relatively affluent nation, a fourth of our children under six grow up in poverty.[1] Each year in our nation, 1.6 million children are destroyed before birth by abortion.[2] And every day, 40,000 children die from hunger and its consequences around the world.[3] In our streets and neighborhoods, violence destroys the hopes, dreams, and lives of too many children. In our local communities, too many cannot find decent work, housing, health care, or education. In our families, parents struggle to raise children with dignity, hope, and basic values.

Our faith stands in marked contrast to these grim realities. At a time of rampant individualism, we stand for family and community. At a time of intense consumerism, we insist it is not what we have, but how we treat one another that counts. In an age that does not value permanence or hard work in relationships, we believe marriage is forever and children are a blessing, not a burden. At a time of growing isolation, we remind our nation of its responsibility to the broader world, to pursue peace, to welcome immigrants, to protect the lives of hurting children and refugees. At a time when the rich are getting richer and the poor are getting poorer, we insist the moral test of our society is how we treat and care for the weakest among us.

In these challenging days, we believe that the Catholic community needs to be more than ever a source of clear moral vision and effective action. We are called to be the "salt of the earth" and "light of the world" in the words of the Scriptures (cf. Mt 5:13-16). This task belongs to every believer and every parish. It cannot be assigned to a few or simply delegated to diocesan or national structures. The pursuit of justice and peace is an essential part of what makes a parish Catholic.

In urban neighborhoods, in suburban communities, and in rural areas, parishes serve as anchors of hope and communities of caring, help families meet their own needs and reach out to others, and serve as centers of community life and networks of assistance.

The Roots of Parish Social Mission

The roots of this call to justice and charity are in the Scriptures, especially in the Hebrew prophets and the life and words of Jesus. Parish social ministry has clear biblical roots.

In the Gospel according to Luke, Jesus began his public life by reading a passage from Isaiah that introduced his ministry and the mission of every parish. The parish must proclaim the transcendent message of the Gospel and help

- Bring "good news to the poor" in a society where millions lack the necessities of life
- Bring "liberty to captives" when so many are enslaved by poverty, addiction, ignorance, discrimination, violence, or disabling conditions
- Bring "new sight to the blind" in a culture where the excessive pursuit of power or pleasure can spiritually blind us to the dignity and rights of others
- "Set the downtrodden free" in communities where crime, racism, family disintegration, and economic and moral forces leave people without real hope (cf. Lk 4:18)

Our parish communities are measured by how they serve "the least of these" in our parish and beyond its boundaries—the hungry, the homeless, the sick, those in prison, the stranger (cf. Mt 25:31). Our local families of faith are called to "hunger and thirst for justice" and to be "peacemakers" in our own communities (cf. Mt 5:6, 9). A parish cannot really proclaim the Gospel if its message is not reflected in its own community life. The biblical call to charity, justice, and peace claims not only each believer, but also each community where believers gather for worship, formation, and pastoral care.

Over the last century, these biblical mandates have been explored and expressed in a special way in Catholic social teaching. The central message is simple: our faith is profoundly social. We cannot be called truly "Catholic" unless we hear and heed the Church's call to serve those in need and work for justice and peace. We cannot call ourselves followers of Jesus unless we take up his mission of bringing "good news to the poor, liberty to captives, and new sight to the blind" (cf. Lk 4:18).

The Church teaches that social justice is an integral part of evangelization, a constitutive dimension of preaching the Gospel, and an essential part of the Church's mission. The links between justice and evangelization are strong and vital. We cannot proclaim a Gospel we do not live, and we cannot carry out a real social ministry without knowing the Lord and hearing his call to justice and peace. Parish communities must show by their deeds of love and justice that the Gospel they proclaim is fulfilled in their actions. This tradition is not empty theory; it challenges our priorities as a nation, our choices as a Church, our values as parishes. It has led the Church to stand with the poor and vulnerable against the strong and powerful. It brings occasional controversy and conflict, but it also brings life and vitality to the people of God. It is a sign of our faithfulness to the Gospel.

The center of the Church's social teaching is the life, dignity, and rights of the human person. We are called in a special way to serve the poor and vulnerable; to build bridges of solidarity among peoples of differing races and nations, language and ability, gender and culture. Family life and work have special places in Catholic social teaching; the rights of the unborn, families, workers, immigrants, and the poor deserve special protection. Our tradition also calls us to show our respect for the Creator by our care for creation and our commitment to work for environmental justice. This vital tradition is an essential resource for parish life. It offers a framework and direction for our social ministry, calling us to concrete works of charity, justice, and peacemaking.[4]

The Social Mission of the Parish:
A Framework of Integration

In responding to the Scriptures and the principles of Catholic social teaching, parishes are not called to an extra or added dimension of our faith, but to a central demand of Catholic life and evangelization. We recognize the sometimes overwhelming demands on parish leadership and resources. We know it is easier to write about these challenges than to carry them out day by day. But we believe the

Church's social mission is an essential measure of every parish community, and it needs more attention and support within our parishes.

Our parishes are enormously diverse—in where and who they serve, in structures and resources, in their members and leaders. This diversity is reflected in how parishes shape their social ministry. The depth and range of activity are most impressive. Across our country, parishioners offer their time, their money, and their leadership to a wide variety of efforts to meet needs and change structures. Parishes are deeply involved in meeting their members' needs, serving the hungry and homeless, welcoming the stranger and immigrant, reaching out to troubled families, advocating for just public policies, organizing for safer and better communities, and working creatively for a more peaceful world. Our communities and ministries have been greatly enriched and nourished by the faith and wisdom of parishioners who experience injustice and all those who work for greater justice.

There has been tremendous growth of education, outreach, advocacy, and organizing in parishes. From homeless shelters to prayer services, from food pantries to legislative networks, from global education programs to neighborhood organizing, parishes are responding. But in some parishes the social justice dimensions of parish life are still neglected, underdeveloped, or touch only a few parishioners.

We have much to learn from those parishes that are leading the way in making social ministry an integral part of parish ministry and evangelization. We need to build local communities of faith where our social teaching is central, not fringe; where social ministry is integral, not optional; where it is the work of every believer, not just the mission of a few committed people and committees.

For too many parishioners, our social teaching is an unknown tradition. In too many parishes, social ministry is a task for a few, not a challenge for the entire parish community. We believe we are just beginning to realize our potential as a community of faith committed to serve those in need and to work for greater justice.

The parishes that are leaders in this area see social ministry not as a specialized ministry, but as an integral part of the entire parish. They weave the Catholic social mission into every aspect of parish life—worship, formation, and action. They follow a strategy of integration and collaboration, which keeps social ministry from becoming isolated or neglected.

A framework of integration might include the following elements.

Anchoring Social Ministry: Prayer and Worship

The most important setting for the Church's social teaching is not in a food pantry or in a legislative committee room, but in prayer and worship, especially gathered around the altar for the eucharist. It is in the liturgy that we find the fundamental direction, motivation, and strength for social ministry. Social ministry not genuinely rooted in prayer can easily burn itself out. On the other hand, worship that does not reflect the Lord's call to conversion, service, and justice can become pious ritual and empty of the Gospel.

We support new efforts to integrate liturgy and justice, to make clear that we are one people united in faith, worship, and works of charity and justice. We need to be a Church that helps believers recognize Jesus in the breaking of the bread and those without bread. Eucharist, penance, confirmation, and the other sacraments have essential social dimensions that ought to be appropriately reflected in how we celebrate, preach, and pray. Those who plan and preside at our worship can help the parish community understand more clearly the spiritual and scriptural roots of our pursuit of justice without distorting or imposing on the liturgy.

Our social ministry must be anchored in prayer, where we uncover the depths of God's call to seek justice and pursue peace. In personal prayer, the reading of the Scriptures, and quiet reflection on the Christian vocation, we discover the social mission of every believer. In serving those in need, we serve the Lord. In seeking justice and peace, we witness to the reign of God in our midst. In prayer, we find the reasons, the strength, and the call to follow Jesus in the ways of charity, justice, and peace.

Parishioners at St. John the Baptist in Silver Spring, Md., try to reflect their concern for the poor during each Sunday liturgy. Parishioners bring donations of food to Mass which are included in the offertory and later distributed through a food pantry. Regular preaching on the Gospel's call for justice and peace, as well as consistent prayers for those in need during the general intercessions, help St. John's parish community connect its social mission with worship.

The consistent life ethic is the theme around which social ministry is organized at St. Isaac Jogues Parish in Orlando, Fla. The parish respect life coordinator works with other parish leaders on activities and advocacy in such areas as pro-life, aging, disabilities, and social justice. Together, they try to root their work in prayer and in the common theme of the dignity of human life. In November, they sponsor a Consistent Life Ethic Prayer Service, to which they invite members of the parish and members of other nearby churches. In January, they sponsor a prayer service that focuses on nonviolence—before and after birth. On St. Francis Day, they sponsor a blessing of animals.

"We hope these events are opportunities for conversion," says parishioner Deborah Shearer. "In addition to times of prayer, they are opportunities for education on the full meaning of respect for life."

Sharing the Message: Preaching and Education

We are called to share our social teaching more effectively in our parishes than we have. Our social doctrine is an integral part of our faith; we need to pass it on clearly, creatively, and consistently. It is a remarkable spiritual, intellectual, and pastoral resource that has been too little known or appreciated even in our own community.

Preaching that reflects the social dimensions of the Gospel is indispensable. Priests should not and need not impose an agenda on the liturgy to preach about justice. Rather, we urge those who preach not to ignore the regular opportunities provided by the liturgy to connect our faith and our everyday lives, to share biblical values on justice and peace. Week after week, day after day, the lectionary calls the community to reflect on the scriptural message of justice and peace. The pulpit is not a partisan rostrum and to try to make it one would be a mistake, but preaching that ignores the social dimensions of our faith does not truly reflect the Gospel of Jesus Christ.

Our social doctrine must also be an essential part of the curriculum and life of our schools, religious education programs, sacramental preparation, and Christian initiation activities. We need to share and celebrate our common social heritage as Catholics, developing materials and training tools that ensure that we are sharing our social teaching in every educational ministry of our parishes. Every parish should regularly assess how well our social teaching is shared in its formation and educational ministries.

Young people learn firsthand about the social mission of the Church at St. Mary's Parish in Richmond, Va. Beginning in junior high school, every religious education class selects a single social issue on which to focus both direct service and advocacy during the school year. Last year the class, whose issue was homelessness, served food at a homeless shelter and assisted with a parish-sponsored sheltering program. They also wrote to their state legislators encouraging increased funding for homeless programs and a state Earned Income Tax Credit (EITC) to help the working poor.

Supporting the "Salt of the Earth": Family, Work, Citizenship

Our parishes are clearly called to help people live their faith in the world, helping them to understand and act on the social dimensions of the Gospel in their everyday lives. National statements, diocesan structures, or parish committees can be useful, but they are no substitute for the everyday choices and commitments of believers—acting as parents, workers, students, owners, investors, advocates, policy makers, and citizens.

For example, parishes are called to support their members in

- Building and sustaining marriages of quality, fidelity, equality, and permanence in an age that does not value commitment or hard work in relationships
- Raising families with gospel values in a culture where materialism, selfishness, and prejudice still shape so much of our lives
- Being a good neighbor; welcoming newcomers and immigrants; treating people of different races, ethnic groups, and nationalities with respect and kindness
- Seeing themselves as evangelizers who recognize the unbreakable link between spreading the Gospel and work for social justice
- Bringing Christian values and virtues into the marketplace
- Treating co-workers, customers, and competitors with respect and fairness, demonstrating economic initiative, and practicing justice
- Bringing integrity and excellence to public service and community responsibilities, seeking the common good, respecting human life, and promoting human dignity
- Providing leadership in unions, community groups, professional associations, and political organizations at a time of rising cynicism and indifference

In short, our parishes need to encourage, support, and sustain lay people in living their faith in the family, neighborhood, marketplace, and public arena. It is lay women and men, placing their gifts at the service of others (cf. 1 Pt 4:10), who will be God's primary instruments in renewing the earth by their leadership and faithfulness in the community. The most challenging work for justice is not done in church committees, but in the secular world of work, family life, and citizenship.

"In this situation, what does love—the commitment to others and the needy among us—require?" This kind of question might be posed by one of eighteen vocation reflection groups sponsored by St. Martha's Parish in Akron, Ohio. Open to all in the community, the groups are organized by occupation—lawyers, educators, counselors, journalists, and others—as well as one general group for those who do not fit in the other seventeen. They meet monthly to reflect on their work and to discuss how they can apply their beliefs and values in their workplaces. Fr. Norman Douglas, pastor of St. Martha's, helps lay facilitators from each group plan each meeting. Occasional workshops and panels provide in-service educational credits.

During Sunday liturgies, Fr. Douglas also tries to acknowledge how people's work life is related to ministry. For example, when the readings focus on Jesus as healer, those involved in health care occupations are invited to stand after communion for a special blessing. "We try to infuse the spirituality of all of life into what is already going on in the parish," explains Fr. Douglas. "We focus on practical spirituality lived out in the real world."

Serving the "Least of These": Outreach and Charity

Parishes are called to reach out to the hurting, the poor, and the vulnerable in our midst in concrete acts of charity. Just as the Gospel tells us our lives will be judged by our response to the "least of these," so too our parishes should be measured by our help for the hungry, the homeless, the troubled, and the alienated—in our own community and beyond. This is an area of creativity and initiative with a wide array of programs, partnerships with Catholic Charities, and common effort with other churches. Thousands of food pantries, hundreds of shelters, and uncounted outreach programs for poor families, refugees, the elderly, and others in need are an integral part of parish life. The parish is the most significant place where new immigrants and refugees are welcomed into our Church and community. A Church that teaches an option for the poor must reflect that option in our service of those in need. Parish efforts to meet human needs also provide valuable experience, expertise, and credibility in advocating for public policy to address the forces that leave people in need of our charity.

Catholic teaching calls us to serve those in need and to change the structures that deny people their dignity and rights as children of God. Service and action, charity and justice are complementary components of parish social ministry. Neither alone is sufficient; both are essential signs of the Gospel at work. A parish serious about social ministry will offer opportunities to serve those in need and to advocate for justice and peace. These are not competing priorities, but two dimensions of the same fundamental mission to protect the life and dignity of the human person.

St. Augustine's Parish in Spokane, Wash., combines service to those in need in the local community with international outreach. When Catholic Charities purchased the former Shriners Hospital, the parish social concerns committee mobilized volunteers to sort through the beds, wheelchairs, and other medical equipment that it contained and ship it to West Africa for use in a children's hospital in Ghana. What was not shipped was auctioned, with proceeds of the auction used to convert the hospital structure into apartments for single parents and their children.

Queen of the Most Holy Rosary Parish on Long Island, N.Y., had a well-established outreach program that offered food, clothing, and financial assistance for rent and other needs. Many who sought help wanted to work, but could not find jobs. Many lacked training and education, and some had been in jail.

With support from Catholic Charities of Rockville Centre, parishioners established a job training and referral service. Volunteers help the unemployed identify training programs and jobs through local papers and other employment services. Parishioners identify jobs in their own companies or odd jobs at home. A parishioner with a background in personnel helps with resumes and interviewing skills. Clients with little work experience are offered volunteer opportunities at the parish. Recently, the local Department of Labor set up an outreach site at the parish.

"We're acting on church teaching about the dignity of work," explains Louise Sandberg, coordinator of outreach for the parish. "We're happy that so many people have gotten jobs."

Advocating for Justice: Legislative Action

Parishes need to promote a revived sense of political responsibility calling Catholics to be informed and active citizens, participating in the debate over the values and vision that guide our communities and nation. Parishes as local institutions have special opportunities to develop leaders, to promote citizenship, and to provide forums for discussion and action on public issues. Religious leaders need to act in public affairs with a certain modesty, knowing that faith is not a substitute for facts, that values must be applied in real and complex situations, and that people of common faith and goodwill can disagree on specifics. But parishioners are called to use their talents, the resources of our faith, and the opportunities of this democracy to shape a society more respectful of the life, dignity, and rights of the human person. Parishes can help lift up the moral and human dimension of public issues, calling people to informed participation in the political process.

The voices of parishioners need to be heard on behalf of vulnerable children—born and unborn—on behalf of those who suffer discrimination and injustice, on behalf of those without health care or housing, on behalf of our land and water, our communities and neighborhoods. Parishioners need to bring our values and vision into the debates about a changing world and shifting national priorities. Parishes and parishioners are finding diverse ways to be political without being partisan, joining legislative networks, community organizations, and other advocacy groups. In election years, parishes offer nonpartisan voter registration, education, and forums to involve and inform their members. This kind of genuine political responsibility strengthens local communities as it enriches the witness of our parishes.

Parishioners at Corpus Christi Parish in Roseville, Minn., are expanding their social ministry to include legislative action. They have set up a parish phone tree with more than thirty members who call or write their elected representatives on policy issues affecting children and the poor. As a part of "Voices for Justice," the legislative network of the Archdiocese of St. Paul-Minneapolis, they receive regular "action alerts" on state and federal issues.

At each Mass one recent Sunday, the parish advocacy group spoke in support of a proposal to provide state financing and child care for welfare mothers to complete their education. Postcards were made available in the church vestibule, and over 400 parishioners wrote to their legislators in support of the program.

"We think social justice is an integral part of living our faith," explains parishioner Nonnie Andre. "We need to make the system work for all people. We can't just stand back and say we wish it would work. We need to make it work. We need to be the voices for those who have no voice in legislative decisions."

Creating Community: Organizing for Justice

Many parishes are joining with other churches and groups to rebuild a sense of community in their own neighborhoods and towns. Parish leaders are taking the time to listen to the concerns of their members and are organizing to act on those concerns. These kinds of church-based and community organizations are making a difference on housing, crime, education, and economic issues in local communities. Parish participation in such community efforts develops leaders, provides concrete handles to deal with key issues, and builds the capacity of the parish to act on our values.

The Campaign for Human Development has provided vital resources to many self-help organizations empowering the poor to seek greater justice. Parish support and participation in these organizations help put Catholic social teaching into action and to revitalize local communities.

In the south Phoenix, Ariz., neighborhood where St. Catherine Parish is located, gangs ruled the streets and drive-by shootings were terrorizing the community. St. Catherine's parishioners decided they had to do something. They contacted an organizer from the Valley Interfaith Project, which is funded by the Campaign for Human Development, and conducted a six-month series of meetings focused on the problems in the neighborhood and the need for community organization and concern. Parish leaders approached other community leaders and developed a six-point plan with the police and local schools to take back their neighborhood. Street violence was reduced, and the number of parents participating in school events went from twenty to two hundred. Plans are underway with the city of Phoenix to build a multicultural recreation center in the community. And St.

Catherine is now working with other churches in Phoenix on wider issues of justice.

Building Solidarity: Beyond Parish Boundaries

Parishes are called to be communities of solidarity. Catholic social teaching more than anything else insists that we are one family; it calls us to overcome barriers of race, religion, ethnicity, gender, economic status, and nationality. We are one in Christ Jesus (cf. Gal 3:28)—beyond our differences and boundaries.

Parishes need to be bridge-builders, reminding us that we are part of a universal Church with ties of faith and humanity to sisters and brothers all over the world. Programs of parish twinning, support for Catholic Relief Services, mission efforts, migration and refugee activities, and other global ministries are signs of solidarity in a shrinking and suffering world. Advocacy on human rights, development and peace through legislative networks, and other efforts are also signs of a faith without boundaries and a parish serious about its social responsibilities. A key test of a parish's "catholicity" is its willingness to go beyond its boundaries to serve those in need and work for global justice and peace. Working with others for common goals across religious, racial, ethnic, and other lines is another sign of solidarity in action.

At Our Lady of the Miraculous Medal Parish in Los Angeles, Calif., Catholic Relief Service's Operation Rice Bowl helps parishioners learn about human needs around the globe and offers them an opportunity to act to address those needs. Throughout their Lenten observances—at Masses, in the bulletin, during their Soup Night—information is provided about the international relief programs funded by Operation Rice Bowl (ORB) and the importance of support for this program by U.S. parishes. Families are encouraged to use ORB materials in their own Lenten programs of prayer, fasting, and almsgiving. To supplement the money raised through individual gifts, parishioners sell bread from a local "Justice Bakery." A portion of the proceeds from these sales is kept by the parish and contributed to Operation Rice Bowl programs.

We hope these seven elements of the social mission of parishes can serve as a framework for planning and assessing parish social ministry. The more practical resources that accompany these reflections may offer some help and assistance in meeting these challenges. National and diocesan structures have materials, resources, and personnel to help parishes assess and strengthen their social ministry.

Lessons Learned

Many parishes have found their community life enriched and strengthened by a serious effort to integrate more fully the social justice dimensions of our faith. They have also learned some lessons.

Rooting Social Ministry in Faith

Parish social action should flow clearly from our faith. It is Jesus who calls us to this task. Social ministry is an expression of who we are and what we believe; it must be anchored in the Scriptures and church teaching. With the eyes of faith, we see every "crack baby" or person with AIDS, every Haitian refugee or Salvadoran immigrant, every victim of unjust discrimination, and every person combating addiction as a child of God, a sister or brother, as Jesus in disguise. These are not simply social problems, economic troubles, or political issues. They are moral tragedies and religious tests. Parish social ministry is first and foremost a work of faith.

The social mission of the parish begins in the Gospel's call to conversion: to change our hearts and our lives; to follow in the path of charity, justice, and peace. The parish is the place we should regularly hear the call to conversion and find help in answering the Lord's call to express our faith in concrete acts of charity and justice.

Respecting Diversity

We are a very diverse community of faith—racially, ethnically, economically, and ideologically. This diversity should be respected, reflected, and celebrated in our social ministry. For example, what works in a predominately African American parish in an urban neighborhood may not be appropriate for a largely White suburban or rural congregation. The issues, approaches, and structures may differ, but our common values unite us. Social justice coalitions across racial, ethnic, and geographic lines can be an impressive sign of the unity of the body of Christ.

Leadership: Pastors, Councils, Committees, and Educators

While pursuing social justice is a task for every believer, strengthening parish social ministry depends on the skill and commitment of particular parish leaders. Pastors and parish priests have special responsibilities to support integral social ministry. By their preaching, participation, and priorities, they indicate what is important and what is not. They can make it clear that social justice is a mission of the whole parish, not a preoccupation of a few. They are called to teach the authentic social doctrine of the universal Church.

Other parish staff members and leaders play crucial roles in shaping the quality of parish social ministry. Parish councils in their important planning and advisory functions can help place social ministry in the center of parish life. Councils can be a means of collaboration and integration, bringing together liturgy, formation, outreach, and action into a sense of common mission. Councils can play a valuable role in assessing current efforts, setting priorities for the future, and building bridges between parish ministries.

Many parishes have special committees focused on social concerns. These structures can play crucial roles in helping the parish community act on the social justice dimensions of its overall mission. Some parishes have staff members who coordinate social ministry efforts. This is a promising development. These committees and coordinators best serve parishes by facilitating and enabling the participation of the parish community, rather than simply doing the work on behalf of the parish.

Educators in parish schools, religious education, and formation efforts have special responsibility to share our tradition of social justice as an integral part of our faith. They shape the leaders of the future and by their teaching and example share the social dimensions of our Catholic faith.

Creative and competent leaders—clerical and lay, professional and volunteer—are indispensable for effective parish social ministry. They deserve more assistance, encouragement, financial support, and tools to help them fulfill these demanding roles. Leadership development efforts and ongoing training help parishes strengthen their social ministry capacity.

St. Rose of Lima in Gaithersburg, Md., is a parish in a middle-class suburb of Washington, D.C. During the early 1980s, when the federal tax code was overhauled, members of St. Rose proposed sharing their new tax benefit with those in less comfortable circumstances. They set up an annual Social Action Fund drive to which parishioners may contribute their tax savings or any amount they choose. Patterned after the Campaign for Human Development, the fund provides annual grants to community groups working to change the root causes of neighborhood poverty. Grants totaling over $150,000 have been awarded over the past ten years.

Links to Diocesan Structures

No parish functions totally by itself. Parish leaders often look to other parishes and diocesan social justice structures for help in fulfilling these responsibilities. Almost all dioceses have social justice structures that offer resources and training for parishes. These structures are diverse including justice and peace commissions, social action offices, CHD funding and education efforts, rural life offices, and parish social ministry programs of Catholic Charities. Other diocesan groups also offer opportunities for service and action for parishes, for example, Councils of Catholic Women, St. Vincent De Paul Society, Ladies of Charity, ecumenical advocacy and outreach efforts. Many dioceses offer specific "handles" for parish action—legislative networks, work on specific issues or needs, convening parish leaders, providing educational programs, coordinating outreach, and so forth. For the most part, parishes cannot go it alone in this area. It is just as clear that diocesan social action can only be effective if it builds parish capacity. Good ties between diocesan and parish efforts are indispensable.

Practicing What We Preach

We also need to try to practice in our own parishes what we preach to others about justice and participation. Too often we are better at talking about justice than demonstrating it, more committed to these values in the abstract than in our everyday ministry. We acknowledge this not to minimize our common efforts, but to acknowledge how far we have yet to go before we fully close the gap between our principles and our performance.

Sensitive, competent, and compassionate pastoral care is an expression of justice. Parish plans and priorities—as well as the use of parish facilities—that reflect the social mission of the Church are expressions of justice. Investing parish resources in social justice and empowering the poor are also expressions of justice. Just personnel policies, fair wages, and equal opportunity efforts are expressions of justice. Respecting and responding to the cultural and ethnic diversity of the communities we serve is an expression of justice. Recognizing the contributions and welcoming the participation of all members of the parish whatever their race, gender, ethnic background, nationality, or disability—these are integral elements of parishes seeking justice.

Some Difficulties and Dangers

In reflecting on the social mission of the parish, the opportunities seem clear. So do some of the difficulties. One danger is the tendency to isolate social ministry, to confine it to the margins of parish life. Another is for social action leaders to isolate themselves, treating the parish as a target rather than a community to be served and empowered.

Another danger is potential partisanship, the temptation to try to use the parish for inappropriate political objectives. We need to make sure our faith shapes our political action, not the other way around. We cannot forget that we pursue the kingdom of God, not some earthly vision or ideological cause.

A significant challenge is to avoid divisiveness; to emphasize the common ground among social service and social action, education and advocacy, pro-life and social justice, economic development and environmental commitment. We need to work together to reflect a comprehensive concern for the human person in our parish.

Another danger is to try to do too much on too many issues, without clear priorities and an effective plan of action. Not everyone can do everything, but the parish should be a sign of unity in pursuing a consistent concern for human life and human dignity.

The final and most serious danger is for parish leaders to act as if the social ministry of the Church was the responsibility of someone else. Every believer is called to serve those in need, to work for justice, and to pursue peace. Every parish has the mission to help its members act on their faith in the world.

A Final Word of Appreciation, Support, and Challenge

We close these brief reflections with a word of support and encouragement for pastors and parish leaders. The social ministry of the Church is not just another burden, another set of expectations to feel bad about, though in these demanding days it may sometimes seem that way.

The social ministry is already a part of your ministry and leadership. We hope these reflections help you and those you work with to explore how best to carry out this part of your parish's mission. What is strong already? What can be further developed? What needs greater attention? How, given limited time and resources and other obligations, can our parish better share and act on the social justice demands of the Gospel?

The Catholic community has been making steady progress in this area. We seek to build on and share these achievements. We know from experience that parishes that strengthen their social ministry enrich every aspect of their parish, bringing increased life and vitality, greater richness, and community to their entire family of faith.

We offer our gratitude and admiration to those who are leading and helping our parishes act on their social mission. We pledge our support to those who pursue this important challenge with new commitment and energy.

In the Gospel, we read how John the Baptist's followers came to Jesus and asked, "Are you the one who is to come, or should we look for another?" Jesus responded in this way: "Go and tell John what you hear and see: The blind regain their sight, the lame walk, lepers are cleansed, the deaf hear, the dead are raised, and the poor have the good news proclaimed to them" (Mt 11:3-5).

These are still the signs of Christ among us—parishes across our country who in their own ways are caring for the sick, opening eyes and ears, helping life overcome death, and preaching the good news to the poor.

Today, more than ever, our parishes are called to be communities of "salt" and "light"; to help believers live their faith in their families, communities, work, and world. We need parishes that will not "lose their flavor" nor put their "light under a basket." We seek to build evangelizing communities of faith, justice, and solidarity, where all believers are challenged to bring God's love, justice, and peace to a world in desperate need of the seasoning of the Gospel and the light of Catholic teaching.

Notes

1. U.S. Department of Commerce, Bureau of the Census, 1990.
2. New York: Allan Guttmacher Institute, 1991.
3. UNICEF, *The State of the World's Children* (New York, N.Y.: UNICEF, 1992).
4. For a more extensive treatment of Catholic social teaching, see United States Catholic Conference, *A Century of Social Teaching: A Common Heritage, A Continuing Challenge* (Washington, D.C.: United States Catholic Conference, 1990).

Source: Washington, D.C.: United States Catholic Conference, 1994.

The Harvest of Justice Is Sown in Peace

A Reflection of the National Conference of Catholic Bishops on the Tenth Anniversary of "The Challenge of Peace"

November 1993

The harvest of justice is sown in peace for those who cultivate peace.
—Jas 3:18

Introduction: The Call to Peacemaking in a New World

A decade ago, with our pastoral letter *The Challenge of Peace: God's Promise and Our Response,* our conference of bishops sought to offer a word of hope in a time of fear, a call to peacemaking in the midst of "cold war," a **No** to a nuclear arms race that threatened the human family.

The response to *The Challenge of Peace* was far greater than any of us could have anticipated. While not everyone received this letter with the same enthusiasm and some criticisms were heard from various parts of the Church and of society, the pastoral letter strengthened our Church, engaged our people, and contributed to a renewed focus on the moral dimension of nuclear arms and broader issues of war and peace. Among us bishops, the pastoral helped unite our efforts to preach the gospel message of justice and peace. The process of writing the pastoral was also an example of how church teaching can be enhanced by consultation and discussion. The letter led to spirited debate and constructive dialogue in our dioceses and parishes and has been widely used in schools, colleges and universities, the armed forces, and research institutes.

Now, ten years after *The Challenge of Peace,* we renew our call to peacemaking in a dramatically different world. The "challenge of peace" today is different, but no less urgent. Although the nuclear threat is not as imminent, international injustice, bloody regional wars, and a lethal conventional arms trade are continuing signs that the world is still marked by pervasive violence and conflict.

In these anniversary reflections we seek

- To build on the foundations of our 1983 pastoral
- To reflect on its continuing lessons and unfinished agenda

- To explore the new challenges of peacemaking and solidarity
- To call the community of faith to the continuing task of peace-making in this new situation

Thus, we do not offer a new pastoral letter that revisits the choices of the past, but a reflection on the challenges of the present and future, especially what peacemaking and solidarity require of believers and citizens today.

Some major tasks identified ten years ago need to be addressed, including a comprehensive test-ban treaty, effective action to halt nuclear proliferation, and greater progress toward nuclear disarmament. In 1993, however, the challenges of peace also involve renewing and reshaping our national commitment to the world community, building effective institutions of peace and alleviating injustice and oppression which contribute to conflict.

As with the peace pastoral, in these reflections we restate universally binding moral and religious principles. We also seek conscientiously to appeal these principles to what, in our judgment, are crucial issues facing our nation and world. Given the nature of these issues, many people who share our values may and will disagree with our specific applications and judgments. We hope that our effort to apply our principles to specific problems will contribute to the public debate on the moral dimension of U.S. foreign policy and will support the many people in our country who are working to build a more peaceful world.

Among the major challenges peacemakers face in this new era are:

The human toll of violence. At home and abroad, we see the terrible human and moral costs of violence. In regional wars, in crime and terrorism, in ecological devastation and economic injustice, in abortion and renewed dependence on capital punishment, we see the tragic consequences of a growing lack of respect for human life. We cannot really be peacemakers around the world unless we seek to protect the lives and dignity of the vulnerable in our midst. We must stand up for human life wherever it is threatened. This is the essence of our consistent life ethic and the starting point for genuine peacemaking.

The illusion and moral danger of isolationism. After the Cold War, there has emerged an understandable but dangerous temptation to turn inward, to focus only on domestic needs and to ignore global responsibilities. This is not an option for believers in a universal Church or for citizens in a powerful nation. In a world where 40,000 children die every day from hunger and its consequences; where ethnic cleansing and systematic rape are used as weapons of war; and where people are still denied life, dignity, and fundamental rights, we cannot remain silent or indifferent. Nor can we simply turn to military force to solve the world's problems or to right every wrong.

This new era calls for engaged and creative U.S. leadership in foreign affairs that can resist the dangers of both isolationism and unwise intervention. We seek a U.S. foreign policy which reflects our best traditions and which seeks effective collaboration with the community of nations to resist violence and achieve justice in peace.

Structure of solidarity. Wherever freedom, opportunity, truth, and hope are denied, the seeds of conflict will grow. Our country, in this ever-shrinking world, should reformulate its policies and programs to address the still-widening gap between the rich and the desperately poor. Generous and targeted assistance, sustainable development, economic empowerment of the poor, and support for human rights and democracy are essential works of peace. We cannot abandon our programs of foreign aid; rather, we must reshape them, shifting from a focus on security assistance to a priority of development aid for the poor. "A leadership role among nations," Pope John Paul II tells us, "can only be justified by the possibility and willingness to contribute widely and generously to the common good."[1]

Peacemaking institutions. The world must find the will and the ways to pursue justice, contain conflict, and replace violence and war with peaceful and effective means to address injustices and resolve disputes. Through the United Nations and regional organizations, our nation must be positively engaged in devising new tools for preserving the peace, finding ways to prevent and police conflicts, to protect basic rights, to promote integral human development, and to preserve the environment.

The vocation of peacemaking. Part of the legacy of *The Challenge of Peace* is the call to strengthen peacemaking as an essential dimension of our faith, reminding us that Jesus called us to be peacemakers. Our biblical heritage and our body of tradition make the vocation of peacemaking mandatory. Authentic prayer, worship, and sacramental life challenge us to conversion of our hearts and summon us to works of peace. These concerns are obviously not ours alone, but are the work of the entire community of faith and of all people of goodwill. A decade ago, our letter sought to be a catalyst and resource for the larger national debate on the moral dimensions of war and peace. Today, we hope these reflections may serve as a call to consider the challenges of peacemaking and solidarity in a very different but still dangerous world.

I. Theology, Spirituality, and Ethics for Peacemaking

An often neglected aspect of *The Challenge of Peace* is the spirituality and ethics of peacemaking. At the heart of our faith lies "the God of peace" (Rom 15:33), who desires peace for all people far and near

(Ps 85; Is 57:19). That desire has been fulfilled in Christ in whom humanity has been redeemed and reconciled. In our day, the Holy Spirit continues to call us to seek peace with one another, so that in our peacemaking we may prepare for the coming of the reign of God, a kingdom of true justice, love, and peace. God created the human family as one and calls it to unity. The renewed unity we experience in Christ is to be lived out in every possible way. We are to do all we can to live at peace with everyone (Rom 12:18). Given the effects of sin, our efforts to live in peace with one another depend on our openness to God's healing grace and the unifying power of Christ's redemption.

Change of mind and heart, of word and action are essential to those who would work for peace (Rom 12:2). This conversion to the God of peace has two dimensions. On the one hand, in imitation of Christ we must be humble, gentle, and patient. On the other, we are called to be strong and active in our peacemaking, loving our enemies and doing good generously as God does (Lk 6:35-36, 38), filled with eagerness to spread the Gospel of peace (Eph 6:15).

Likewise, discovering God's peace, which exceeds all understanding, in prayer is essential to peacemaking (Phil 4:7). The peace given in prayer draws us into God, quieting our anxieties, challenging our old values, and deepening wells of new energy. It arouses in us a compassionate love for all humanity and gives us heart to persevere beyond frustration, suffering, and defeat. We should never forget that peace is not merely something that we ourselves as creatures do and can accomplish, but it is, in the ultimate analysis, a gift and a grace from God.

By its nature, the gift of peace is not restricted to moments of prayer. It seeks to penetrate the corners of everyday life and to transform the world. But, to do so, it needs to be complemented in other ways. It requires other peaceable virtues, a practical vision of a peaceful world, and an ethic to guide peacemakers in times of conflict.

A. Virtues and a Vision for Peacemakers

1. Peaceable Virtues

True peacemaking can be a matter of policy only if it is first a matter of the heart. In the absence of repentance and forgiveness, no peace can endure; without a spirit of courageous charity, justice cannot be won. We can take inspiration from the early Christian communities. Paul called on the Corinthians, even in the most trying circumstances, to pursue peace and bless their persecutors, never repaying evil for evil, but overcoming evil with good (Rom 12:14, 17, 21).

Amid the violence of contemporary culture and in response to the growing contempt for human life, the Church must seek to foster communities where peaceable virtues can take root and be nourished. We need to nurture among ourselves *faith and hope* to strengthen our spirits by placing our trust in God, rather than in ourselves; *courage and compassion* that move us to action; *humility and kindness* so that we can put the needs and interests of others ahead of our own; *patience and perseverance* to endure the long struggle of justice; and *civility and charity* so that we can treat others with respect and love.

"The goal of peace, so desired by everyone," as Pope John Paul has written, "will certainly be achieved through the putting into effect of social and international justice, but also through the practice of the virtues which favor togetherness and which teach us to live in unity."[2]

2. A Vision of Peace

A practical complement to the virtues of peacemaking is a clear vision of a peaceful world. Thirty years ago Pope John XXIII laid out before us a visionary framework for peace in his encyclical letter *Pacem in Terris (Peace on Earth)*, which retains its freshness today. *Pacem in Terris* proposed a political order in service of the common good, defined in terms of the defense and promotion of human rights. In a prophetic insight, anticipating the globalization of our problems, Pope John called for new forms of political authority adequate to satisfy the needs of the universal common good.

Peace does not consist merely in the absence of war, but rather in sharing the goodness of life together. In keeping with Pope John's teaching, the Church's positive vision of a peaceful world includes:

a.   The primacy of the global common good for political life
b.   The role of social and economic development in securing the conditions for a just and lasting peace
c.   The moral imperative of solidarity between affluent, industrial nations and poor, developing ones

a. *The universal common good.* A key element in Pope John's conception of a peaceful world is a global order oriented to the full development of all peoples, with governments committed to the rights of citizens, and a framework of authority which enables the world community to address fundamental problems that individual governments fail to resolve. In this framework, sovereignty is in the service of people. All political authority has as its end the promotion of the common good, particularly the defense of human rights. When a government clearly fails in this task or itself becomes a central impediment to the realization of those rights, the world community has a right and a duty to act where the lives and the fundamental rights of large numbers of people are at serious risk.

b. *The responsibility for development.* A second element consists of the right to and the duty of development for all peoples. In the words of Pope John Paul II, "Just as there is a collective responsibility for avoiding war, so too there is a collective responsibility for promoting development." Development, the Holy Father reasoned, will contribute to a more just world in which the occasions for resorting to arms will be greatly reduced:

> [It] must not be forgotten that at the root of war there are usually real and serious grievances: injustices suffered, legitimate aspirations frustrated, poverty and the exploitation of multitudes of desperate people who see no real possibility of improving their lot by peaceful means.[3]

Development not only serves the interest of justice, but also contributes greatly to a lasting peace.

c. *Human solidarity.* A third imperative is to further the unity of the human family. Solidarity requires that we think and act in terms of our obligations as members of a global community, despite differences of race, religion, or nationality. We are responsible for actively promoting the dignity of the world's poor through global economic reform, development assistance, and institutions designed to meet the needs of the hungry, refugees, and the victims of war. Solidarity, Pope John Paul II reminds us, contributes to peace by providing "a firm and persevering determination" to seek the good of all. "Peace," he declares, will be "the fruit of solidarity."[4]

B. Two Traditions: Nonviolence and Just War

An essential component of a spirituality for peacemaking is an ethic for dealing with conflict in a sinful world. The Christian tradition possesses two ways to address conflict: nonviolence and just war. They both share the common goal: to diminish violence in this world. For as we wrote in *The Challenge of Peace*, "The Christian has no choice but to defend peace. . . . This is an inalienable obligation. It is the *how* of defending peace which offers moral options."[5] We take up this dual tradition again, recognizing, on the one hand, the success of nonviolent methods in recent history, and, on the other, the increasing disorder of the post-Cold War world with its pressures for limited military engagement and humanitarian intervention.

Throughout history there has been a shifting relation between the two streams of the tradition which always remain in tension. Like Christians before us who have sought to read the signs of the times in light of this dual tradition, we today struggle to assess the lessons of the nonviolent revolutions in Eastern Europe in 1989 and the former

Soviet Union in 1991, on the one hand, and of the conflicts in Central America, the Persian Gulf, Bosnia, Somalia, Lebanon, Cambodia, and Northern Ireland on the other.

The devastation wrought by these recent wars reinforces and strengthens for us the strong presumption against the use of force, which is shared by both traditions. Overall, the wars fought in the last fifty years show a dramatic rise in the proportion of noncombatant casualties. This fact points to the need for clear moral restraints both in avoiding war and in limiting its consequences. The high level of civilian deaths raises serious moral questions about the political choices and military doctrines which have had such tragic results over the last half century. The presumption against the use of force has also been strengthened by the examples of the effectiveness of nonviolence in some places in Eastern Europe and elsewhere.

Our conference's approach, as outlined in *The Challenge of Peace,* can be summarized in this way:

1.   In situations of conflict, our constant commitment ought to be, as far as possible, to strive for justice through nonviolent means.
2.   But, when sustained attempts at nonviolent action fail to protect the innocent against fundamental injustice, then legitimate political authorities are permitted as a last resort to employ limited force to rescue the innocent and establish justice.

Despite areas of convergence between a nonviolent ethic and a just war ethic, however, we acknowledge the diverse perspectives within our Church on the validity of the use of force. Many believe just war thinking remains valid because it recognizes that force may be necessary in a sinful world, even as it restrains war by placing strict moral limits on when, why, and how this force may be used. Other object in principle to the use of force, and these principled objections to the just war tradition are sometimes joined with other criticisms that just war criteria have been ineffective in preventing unjust acts of war in recent decades and that these criteria cannot be satisfied under the conditions of modern warfare.

Likewise, there are diverse points of view within the Catholic community on the moral meaning and efficacy of a total commitment to nonviolence in an unjust world. Clearly some believe that a full commitment to nonviolence best reflects the gospel commitment to peace. Others argue that such an approach ignores the reality of grave evil in the world and avoids the moral responsibility to actively resist and confront injustice with military force if other means fail. Both the just war and nonviolent traditions offer significant moral insight, but continue to face difficult tests in a world marked by so much violence and injustice. Acknowledging this diversity of opinion, we reaffirm the

Church's traditional teaching on the ethical conditions for the use of force by public authority.

Ten years after our pastoral letter, recent events raise new questions and concerns which need to be addressed.

1. Nonviolence: New Importance

As *The Challenge of Peace* observed, "The vision of Christian nonviolence is not passive about injustice and the defense of the rights of others."[6] It ought not be confused with popular notions of nonresisting pacifism. For it consists of a commitment to resist manifest injustice and public evil with means other than force. These include dialogue, negotiations, protests, strikes, boycotts, civil disobedience, and civilian resistance. Although nonviolence has often been regarded as simply a personal option or vocation, recent history suggests that in some circumstances it can be an effective public undertaking as well. Dramatic political transitions in places as diverse as the Philippines and Eastern Europe demonstrate the power of nonviolent action, even against dictatorial and totalitarian regimes. Writing about the events of 1989, Pope John Paul II said,

> It seemed that the European order resulting from the Second World War . . . could only be overturned by another war. Instead, it has been overcome by the nonviolent commitment of people who, while always refusing to yield to the force of power, succeeded time after time in finding effective ways of bearing witness to the truth.[7]

These nonviolent revolutions challenge us to find ways to take into full account the power of organized, active nonviolence. What is the real potential power of serious nonviolent strategies and tactics—and their limits? What are the ethical requirements when organized nonviolence fails to overcome evil and when totalitarian powers inflict massive injustice on an entire people? What are the responsibilities of and limits on the international community?

One must ask, in light of recent history, whether nonviolence should be restricted to personal commitments or whether it also should have a place in the public order with the tradition of justified and limited war. National leaders bear a moral obligation to see that nonviolent alternatives are seriously considered for dealing with conflicts. New styles of preventative diplomacy and conflict resolution ought to be explored, tried, improved, and supported. As a nation, we should promote research, education, and training in nonviolent means of resisting evil. Nonviolent strategies need greater attention in international affairs.

Such obligations do not detract from a state's right and duty to defend against aggression as a last resort. They do, however, raise the threshold for the recourse to force by establishing institutions which promote nonviolent solutions of disputes and nurturing political commitment to such efforts. In some future conflicts, strikes and people power could be more effective than guns and bullets.

2. Just War: New Questions

The just war tradition consists of a body of ethical reflection on the justifiable use of force. In the interest of overcoming injustice, reducing violence, and preventing its expansion, the tradition aims at:

    a.   Clarifying when force may be used
    b.   Limiting the resort to force
    c.   Restraining damage done by military forces during war

The just war tradition begins with a strong presumption against the use of force and then establishes the conditions when this presumption may be overridden for the sake of preserving the kind of peace which protects human dignity and human rights.

In a disordered world, where peaceful resolution of conflicts sometimes fails, the just war tradition provides an important moral framework for restraining and regulating the limited use of force by governments and international organizations. Since the just war tradition is often misunderstood or selectively applied, we summarize its major components, which are drawn from traditional Catholic teaching.

First, whether lethal force may be used is governed by the following criteria:

- *Just cause:* Force may be used only to correct a grave, public evil, i.e., aggression or massive violation of the basic rights of whole populations
- *Comparative justice:* While there may be rights and wrongs on all sides of a conflict, to override the presumption against the use of force the injustice suffered by one party must significantly outweigh that suffered by the other
- *Legitimate authority:* Only duly constituted public authorities may use deadly force or wage war
- *Right intention:* Force may be used only in a truly just cause and solely for that purpose
- *Probability of success:* Arms may not be used in a futile cause or in a case where disproportionate measures are required to achieve success

- *Proportionality:* The overall destruction expected from the use of force must be outweighed by the good to be achieved
- *Last resort:* Force may be used only after all peaceful alternatives have been seriously tried and exhausted

These criteria *(jus ad bellum)*, taken as a whole, must be satisfied in order to override the strong presumption against the use of force.

Second, the just war tradition seeks also to curb the violence of war through restraint on armed combat between the contending parties by imposing the following moral standards *(jus in bello)* for the conduct of armed conflict:

- *Noncombatant immunity:* Civilians may not be the object of direct attack, and military personnel must take due care to avoid and minimize indirect harm to civilians
- *Proportionality:* In the conduct of hostilities, efforts must be made to attain military objectives with no more force than is militarily necessary and to avoid disproportionate collateral damage to civilian life and property
- *Right intention:* Even in the midst of conflict, the aim of political and military leaders must be peace with justice, so that acts of vengeance and indiscriminate violence, whether by individuals, military units, or governments, are forbidden

During the last decade, there has been increasing focus on the moral questions raised by the just war tradition and its application to specific uses of force. We welcome this renewed attention and hope our own efforts have contributed to this dialogue. We also recognize that the application of these principles requires the exercise of the virtue of prudence; people of goodwill may differ on specific conclusions. The just war tradition is not a weapon to be used to justify a political conclusion or a set of mechanical criteria that automatically yields a simple answer, but a way of moral reasoning to discern the ethical limits of action. Policy makers, advocates, and opponents of the use of force need to be careful not to apply the tradition selectively, simply to justify their own positions. Likewise, any application of just war principles depends on the availability of accurate information not easily obtained in the pressured political context in which such choices must be made.

The just war tradition has attained growing influence on political deliberations on the use of force and in some forms of military training. Just war norms helped shape public debate prior to the Gulf War. In addition, the military's call for civilian leaders to define carefully objectives for the use of force is in keeping with the spirit of the tradition. At the same time, some contemporary strategies and practices seem to raise serious questions when seen in the light of strict just war analysis.

For example, strategies calling for use of overwhelming and decisive force can raise issues of proportionality and discrimination. Strategies and tactics that lead to avoidable casualties are inconsistent with the underlying intention of the just war tradition of limiting the destructiveness of armed conflict. Efforts to reduce the risk to a nation's own forces must be limited by careful judgments of military necessity so as not to neglect the rights of civilians and armed adversaries.

In light of the preeminent place of air power in today's military doctrine, more reflection is needed on how traditional ethical restraints should be applied to the use of air forces. For example, the targeting of civilian infrastructure, which afflicts ordinary citizens long after hostilities have ceased, can amount to making war on noncombatants rather than against opposing armies. Fifty years after Coventry, Dresden, Hamburg, Hiroshima, and Nagasaki, ways must be found to apply standards of proportionality and noncombatant immunity in a meaningful way to air warfare.

Moral reflection on the use of force calls for a spirit of moderation rare in contemporary political culture. The increasing violence of our society, its growing insensitivity to the sacredness of life, and the glorification of the technology of destruction in popular culture could inevitably impair our society's ability to apply just war criteria honestly and effectively in time of crisis.

In the absence of a commitment of respect for life and a culture of restraint, it will not be easy to apply the just war tradition, not just as a set of ideas, but as a system of effective social constraints on the use of force. There is need for greater public understanding of just war criteria and greater efforts to apply just war restraints in political decision making and military planning, training and command systems, and public debate.

Ten years after *The Challenge of Peace*, given the neglect of peaceable virtues and the destructiveness of today's weaponry, serious questions still remain about whether modern war in all its savagery can meet the hard tests set by the just war tradition. Important work needs to be done in refining, clarifying, and applying the just war tradition to the choices facing our decision makers in this still violent and dangerous world.

C. The Centrality of Conscience

The task of peacemaking requires both just structures and a properly formed conscience. Our policies and structure of peace will reflect the integrity of the individuals who design and participate in them.

For people of faith, this commitment involves a lifelong task of reflecting on Sacred Scripture, cultivating virtues, understanding and applying wisely the Church's teaching on peace, and praying for guidance. We are grateful for all that has been done in the past decade by so many to help form consciences, and we are aware of how much more we can and must do to better translate our moral reflections on war and peace into informed commitments of conscience.

In this statement, just as in our pastoral letter of ten years ago, we state some universally applicable moral principles that are binding on all persons. For example, it is immoral for a commander to issue or for a soldier to obey a command to intentionally kill noncombatants in war. Concrete applications of universal principles—such as our call to reject the first use of nuclear weapons and the targeting of nonnuclear states, and our call for nuclear disarmament—are judgments about which Catholics may disagree. As we said in the peace pastoral, we "do not presume or pretend that clear answers exist to many of the personal, professional, and financial choices" facing those in the military and defense industries. "We seek as moral teachers and pastors to be available to all who confront these questions of personal and vocational choice."[8] We hope that they will evaluate seriously the moral basis for our specific judgments and the implications for their work. And we will continue to improve our own efforts to offer our support and guidance to these and others who struggle on a daily basis to integrate their faith and their work.

There is also a need to define further the proper relationship between the authority of the state and the conscience of the individual on matters of war and peace. In 1983, we restated our long-standing position on military service:

> A citizen may not casually disregard his country's conscientious decision to call its citizens to acts of "legitimate defense." Moreover, the role of Christian citizens in the armed forces is a service to the common good and an exercise of the virtue of patriotism, so long as they fulfill this role within defined moral norms.[9]

"At the same time," we note, "no state may demand blind obedience." We repeat our support both for legal protection for those who conscientiously refuse to participate in any war (conscientious objectors) and for those who cannot, in good conscience, serve in specific conflicts they consider unjust or in branches of the service (e.g., the strategic nuclear forces) which would require them to perform actions contrary to deeply held moral convictions about indiscriminate killing (selective conscientious objection).[10]

> As we hold individuals in high esteem who conscientiously
> serve in the armed forces, so also we should regard consci-
> entious objection and selective conscientious objection as
> positive indicators within the Church of a sound moral
> awareness and respect for human life.[11]

There is a need to improve the legal and practical protection which
this country rightly affords conscientious objectors and, in accord with
the just war tradition, to provide similar legal protection for selective
conscientious objectors.[12] Selective conscientious objection poses complex, substantive, and procedural problems, which must be worked
out by moralists, lawyers, and civil servants in a way that respects the
rights of conscience without undermining the military's ability to
defend the common good.[13] Given the particular problems that arise
in the context of an all-volunteer military, individual objectors must
exercise their rights in a responsible way, and there must be reliable
procedures to verify the validity of their claims. Especially in cases
where military service is compulsory, it is appropriate for the government to require alternative service to the community; this may be in or
outside a military setting, depending on the abilities and conscience of
the particular individual.[14]

II. The Challenges of Peace in a New World: An Agenda for Peacemaking

Peacemaking is both a personal and a social and political challenge: How do we live lives of love, truth, justice, and freedom, and
how do we advance these values through structures that shape our
world? International peace is not achieved simply by proclaiming
peaceful ideals; it also requires building the structure of peace.

The Cold War subjected the world to "structures of sin."[15] It divided
the world into blocs sustained by rigid ideologies. Its hallmarks
included a massive denial of human rights by dictatorial regimes, an
insane arms race, and proxy wars fought mainly in the developing
world.[16] The challenge today is to build a new international order that
will be more just and more peaceful than the one it replaces.

The millions and millions of people killed just in this century in
war or by repressive regimes are ample proof that we must chart a new
path to peace and justice. Pope John Paul II outlined this challenge this
year in Denver:

> The international community ought to establish more effec-
> tive structures for maintaining and promoting justice and
> peace. This implies that a concept of strategic interest should
> evolve which is based on the full development of people—

out of poverty and toward a more dignified existence, out of injustice and exploitation toward fuller respect for the human person and the defense of universal human rights.[17]

As we consider a new vision of the international community, five areas deserve special attention:

1. Strengthening global institutions
2. Securing human rights
3. Assuring sustainable and equitable development
4. Restraining nationalism and eliminating religious violence
5. Building cooperative security

A. Strengthening Global Institutions

Catholic social teaching has long advocated a more integrated international system to serve the cause of human rights, to reduce war between and within states, and to help transform political and economic interdependence into moral solidarity that reflects the common good. At this moment in history, we wish to affirm the positive duty of political leaders and citizens to support the development, reform, and restructuring of regional and global political and legal institutions, especially the United Nations.

The United Nations should be at the center of the new international order. As Pope John XXIII observed in *Pacem in Terris*, a worldwide public authority is necessary, not to limit or replace the authority of states, but rather to address fundamental problems that nations alone, no matter how powerful, cannot be expected to solve.[18] Just as the United Nations should not be asked to solve problems it has neither the competence nor the resources to solve, neither should it be prevented from taking the bold steps necessary to fulfill the promise of its charter to save "succeeding generations from the scourge of war." Perhaps no challenge is more urgent or more complex than that of improving the United Nations' ability to reduce conflict in the world. Preventative diplomacy; peace-building after war, as in Cambodia and El Salvador; and peacekeeping all deserve special support and attention.[19]

The United States should play a constructive role in making the United Nations and other international institutions more effective, responsible, and responsive. Effective multilateral institutions can relieve the United States of the burden, or the temptation, of becoming by itself the world's police force. Effective institutions, however, require the United States and other countries to make a sustained commitment of significant financial, material, and political resources and to nurture a spirit of shared sacrifice and collaboration. At a minimum, the United States must pay in full its UN assessments. All nations,

including the United States, will have to accept the legitimate authority of these institutions; decision-making processes will have to be
more truly democratic; decisions will have to be applied more consistently; and these institutions will have to have the capacity to enforce
international law. For example, the international system could be
strengthened if the United States and other nations could move
toward accepting the compulsory jurisdiction of the International
Court of Justice.

The United Nations system has its own responsibility and obligation to bring to an end the waste of material and human resources that
seems to afflict the system today. It has a task of reforming its own
structures, to see to it that the end of its activities is not the continuation of bureaucracy but a service to the building up of peace and the
common good.

It is not enough, however, to pursue the common good of humanity through multilateral governmental institutions. If a healthy nation-
state requires a strong civic society, so also a healthy international system requires strong nongovernmental groups. These transnational
actors—human rights groups, humanitarian aid organizations, businesses, labor unions, the media, religious bodies, and many others—can
build bridges of understanding and respect between cultures and can
contribute to positive social change and a sense of global community.

We have no illusions about the daunting task of constructing a
more viable international order, nor do we have any doubts that it
must go forward if the twenty-first century is to be less violent and
more humane than the twentieth.

B. Securing Human Rights

The future of international peace hinges more than ever on the initiatives we are willing to take and the sacrifices we are willing to make
for justice both within and among nations. An indispensable condition
for a just and peaceful world order is the promotion and defense of
human rights. In our religious tradition and international law, human
rights include the spectrum of civil, political, social, cultural, and economic rights. Promotion of the full complement of human rights and
religious liberty has been and remains a central priority for our conference. Explicit recognition of these rights, as Pope John Paul II has
reminded us, provides "an authentic and solid foundation" for the
reforms of emerging democracies.[20]

Over the past four decades, some progress has been made by the
international community and nongovernmental organizations in
advancing the rights of oppressed peoples on every continent. In the
years ahead, the maintenance of peace and the progress of authentic
democracy in the world will require enhancing the priority in U.S.

foreign policy of human rights, especially of the poor, women, and vulnerable children, and improving international arrangements for their enforcement.

We continue to be concerned about violations of human rights in many parts of the world. Religious liberty is too often denied or threatened in many countries, including China, some former Soviet Republics, Vietnam, Sudan, Cuba, and parts of the former Yugoslavia. In several African countries, especially Zaire, Angola, and Nigeria, political leaders have impeded progress toward democracy. The people of East Timor are denied human rights and self-determination. Even as the Middle East struggles toward a just peace, human rights continue to be a serious problem there. In Latin America, most notably in Brazil, death squads murder children, and in East Asia, the tourist trade makes young people victims of sexual exploitation. And on every continent, indigenous peoples have suffered egregious violations of their basic rights. There can be no true peace where governments, insurgencies, or criminal elements deny people of any age their rights and dignity as human beings.

Finally, we strongly condemn once again the horrible evil of ethnic cleansing in the Balkans.[21] We are dismayed that the world community has been so ineffective in preventing this scourge and that it shows such reluctance to assist the victims in a sustained and resourceful way. Every effort must be taken to prevent the spread or repetition of this injustice in the months and years ahead. The destruction of people because of their religion, race, ethnicity, or nationality is a crime against humanity which must be banished forever.

A world marked by true respect for the life, dignity, and rights of the human person will be a world at peace. The defense of human rights must be a consistent and persistent priority for the United States and for a world seeking peace.

C. Assuring Sustainable and Equitable Development

Recent years have witnessed a continual deterioration of the economies of many developing nations, "reaching intolerable extremes of misery."[22] Virtually all authorities agree that the disparity of income and wealth between North and South, as well as within countries, including our own, has grown. The goal established by the United Nations in 1960 (the "Decade of Development") to lessen the gap between the poor nations and the rich nations has never been achieved. In fact, the gap has widened in each of the decades since 1960. In 1960, the richest fifth of the world's population held more than two-thirds of the world's wealth. Today, less than one-fifth of the world's people have more than four-fifths of global wealth, but the poorest billion have less than one-fiftieth. The most affluent fifth control 80 percent of world trade, savings, and investment. In a world where almost one billion people exist barely on the margins of human life in absolute poverty, more than half of the earth's food is consumed by the rich nations.

Every day a half billion people go hungry; three times that number are chronically ill. Half the world's population does not have safe water. A third are unemployed or underemployed and at least that many lack shelter. Almost twenty million, mainly women and children, are refugees, and twenty-four million more are displaced within their own countries. A quarter of a million children die every week from hunger, disease, violence, or neglect.

As Pope John Paul II has pointed out, "The collapse of the communist system in so many countries certainly removes an obstacle to facing these problems [in the Third World] in an appropriate and realistic way, but it is not enough to bring about their solution."[23] These problems grew while the West spent billions of dollars to defend against communism, but, ironically, they seem harder to address without their Cold War connection. For example, it has become increasingly difficult to secure funds to support many foreign assistance programs.

One of the disturbing signs of the times is a reduced priority given and growing indifference to the world's poor. From the perspective of faith, the modern world is more and more illustrative of the story of the rich man and Lazarus, with an ever-widening gap between the world's haves and have-nots.[24] "When the West gives the impression of abandoning itself to forms of growing and selfish isolation," Pope John Paul II warns, "then we are up against not only a betrayal of humanity's legitimate expectations—a betrayal that is a harbinger of unforeseeable consequences—but also a real desertion of a moral obligation."[25]

Perhaps the growing awareness of the planet-wide ecological crisis may offer a new opportunity to overcome "the temptation to close in upon [ourselves]" and to neglect "the responsibilities following from [a] superior position in the community of nations."[26] For as the leaders of the world recognized at the Earth Summit in 1992, our common future on earth requires a new covenant between North and South, between rich nations and poor for sustainable global development.

Sustainable development goes beyond "economic growth," which has been synonymous with the concept of development since the early 1960s. Rather, sustainable development is concerned with preserving the planet's ecological heritage, addressing the rampant poverty in the poorest nations, redirecting development in terms of quality rather than quantity in the industrial world, creating environmentally sensitive technologies, and keeping population growth at sustainable levels through programs of development and education that respect cultural, religious, and family values.

Such a sustainable future demands heightened commitment by the United States and others to Third World development. Authentic development by poorer nations will not only help safeguard the earth's resources for all peoples and reduce pollution and environmental degradation, but will also lessen the impact of population growth or decline on the environment and the overall development process.

Only major changes in the international economic order will stop the flow of wealth from the poor to the rich. Arrangements of trade should ensure that poor countries obtain fair prices for their products and access to our markets. Foreign aid should focus more on empowering the poor to improve the quality of their lives than in shoring up the international economic system or pursuing national interest or competitive advantage. The financial system should try to mitigate the human consequences of the massive external debt of the developing countries. Both foreign and domestic investment in the developing countries should increase in ways that neither create nor perpetuate dependency; and environmentally designed technology needs to be shared with Third World countries and developed in ways appropriate to newly emerging economies.

Even with these changes, foreign assistance must remain an important component of a just international economic order. Development assistance has been a shrinking part of U.S. foreign aid in recent years. Compared to other industrialized nations, we continue to rank near the bottom in terms of the share of our economy devoted to development assistance. Rather than abandon foreign aid at a time of growing isolationist sentiments, we need to redirect U.S. foreign assistance toward a more effective effort to help poor people improve the quality of their lives. In this effort, "it will be necessary above all," as Pope John Paul II has written, "to abandon a mentality in which the poor—as individuals and as peoples—are considered a burden, as irksome intruders trying to consume what others have produced."[27] Rather, we must find new ways to empower the world's poor, especially women, to take control of their own lives so as to lead lives of dignity, not deprivation and dependency.

The redesign of U.S. foreign aid and of aid by the international lending institutions ought to focus primarily on eliminating poverty. As we said in our pastoral letter, *Economic Justice for All*, a major test of all policies is their impact on the poor. Currently over half of all U.S. foreign aid is given for military and security purposes. Funding for development, especially for the poorest nations, can and should be realized through transfers from such economic security assistance and military aid to genuine development assistance. Foreign aid is more than an optional form of largesse. It is a fundamental obligation of solidarity on the part of those who enjoy a plentiful share of earth's riches to promote the rightful development of those who have barely enough to survive.

In addition, the movement toward peace in the Middle East and Central America and efforts to promote democracy in Haiti will require programs of concerted economic assistance to succeed. If the gains of recent months are to be lasting, these areas, which have drawn so much U.S. attention in times of conflict, must receive high priority along with the nations of Eastern Europe and the former Soviet Union, as recipients of U.S. foreign aid. As we responded to violent conflict, now let us support the development which can help secure the fragile works of peace.

D. Restraining Nationalism and Eliminating Religious Violence

One of the most disturbing threats to peace in the post-Cold War world has been the spread of conflicts rooted in national, ethnic, racial, and religious differences. While the end of the Cold War may bring new hope for ending some of these conflicts, others continue their bloody logic largely unaffected by recent events and still others, frozen by the Cold War, have erupted with a new and deadly fury, fueled by the dangerous virus of extreme nationalism.

We are especially concerned about the religious dimension of some of these conflicts. Every child murdered, every woman raped, every town "cleansed," every hatred uttered in the name of religion is a crime against God and a scandal for religious believers. Religious violence and nationalism deny what we profess in faith: We are all created in the image of the same God and destined for the same eternal salvation. "No Christian can knowingly foster or support structures and attitudes that unjustly divide individuals or groups."[28]

Some would respond to conflicts with a religious dimension by marginalizing religion in society; by destroying the link between religion, culture, and national identity; and even by repressing so-called fundamentalist movements, especially in the Islamic world. This would be to misinterpret the nature of these conflicts and devalue the positive role of religion in society. In most so-called religious conflicts, political, economic, and ideological factors, rather than religious antagonisms, are the predominant causes of tension and violence. Instances of religion being the principal cause of conflict are extremely rare.

From Central America and Eastern Europe to South Africa and the Philippines, authentic religious belief, rather than being a cause of conflict, has been a powerful moral force for nonviolent human liberation. This moral power is often rooted in the close identification of religious belief with a particular history, culture, language, and nationality. Religious nationalism and religious conflict, while potentially serious problems, are best confronted by an increase, not a disparagement of authentic religious behavior.

In conflicts in which ethnic, religious, and nationalist factors are present, certain values take on special importance:

1. *Self-determination.* Ethnic conflicts often center on competing claims of self-determination which have enormous appeal because they express a yearning for freedom, usually in the face of injustice and political turmoil. Nevertheless, movements for self-determination can also fuel an aggressive nationalism that can lead to division and civil war. Our own experience exemplifies this ambivalent nature of self-determination. Our nation was founded in the name of self-determination, yet many Americans are understandably uneasy about the disintegration and bloody conflicts sometimes associated with secessionist movements.

Self-determination, understood as full political independence, should neither be dismissed as always harmful or unworkable nor embraced as an absolute right or a panacea in the face of injustice. Rather, efforts to find more creative ways to uphold the fundamental values embodied in self-determination claims are called for; peoples have a right to participate in shaping their cultural, religious, economic, and political identities. Self-determination does not necessarily entail secession or full political independence; it can be realized through effective protection of basic human rights, especially minority rights, a degree of political and cultural autonomy, and other arrangements, such as a federal or confederal system of government. While full political independence may be morally right and politically appropriate in some cases, it is essential that any new state meet the fundamental purpose of sovereignty: the commitment and capacity to create a just and stable political order and to contribute to the international common good. As claims to self-determination grow, the international community needs to devise more detailed moral, legal, and political norms for evaluating such claims and for protecting the legitimate right of peoples to self-governance.

2. *Respect for minority rights.* Nationalist conflicts often arise out of injustice and, in turn, can create new forms of injustice. Militant nationalism is less likely to flourish where there is a commitment to fundamental human rights—civil, political, economic, social, and cultural. Full respect for freedom of religion and minority rights is especially crucial. Governments have an affirmative obligation to protect the right of minorities to preserve and develop their religious and cultural identities. At the same time, minorities must respect the rights of others and show a firm willingness to contribute to the common good of the nation in which they live.

3. *Unity out of diversity.* Self-determination and human rights must be firmly linked to a commitment to tolerance and solidarity. Today,

when few nations have truly homogeneous populations, increasing diversity can strain the integrity of both majority and minority cultures. Insistence on ethnic purity or efforts to eliminate cultural and ethnic diversity through aggressive assimilation into an overwhelming, homogeneous culture are not solutions to a difficult problem. Rather, the solution lies in striving toward unity while maintaining diversity. Ways must be found to celebrate religious, cultural, and national identities at the same time that diverse peoples participate more fully in promoting the national and international common good.

4. *Dialogue and reconciliation.* Precisely because of their intractable and explosive nature, ethnic conflicts can be resolved only through political dialogue and negotiation. War and violence are unacceptable means for resolving ethnic conflicts; they serve only to exacerbate them. Nor are political solutions alone sufficient. Also needed is the commitment to reconciliation that is at the heart of the Christian and other religious traditions. For religious believers can imagine what some would dismiss as unrealistic: that even the most intense hatreds can be overcome by love, that free human beings can break historic cycles of violence and injustice, and that deeply divided peoples can learn to live together in peace.

We address these questions of religious, ethnic, and national strife aware of our own failings as a Church and as a nation in fully respecting the rights of minorities, in embracing diversity, and in avoiding excessive nationalism. No nation, including ours, has solved all racial religious and ethnic conflicts or is free of nationalist excesses. We, like others around the world, struggle to distinguish between love of country, which is patriotism, and idolatry of one's nation, which is a form of blasphemy.

Finally, since the liberation of Eastern Europe and the former Soviet Union ended the Cold War, it is both just and wise that Americans work with the people of this region to overcome the disillusionment, hardship, and instability that fuel the ethnic and nationalist conflicts there. We applaud and encourage the contributions and sacrifices many are making to help these nations succeed in their transition to democracy. We encourage far greater attention to the positive and essential role that religion has played and continues to play in building just and peaceful societies there and elsewhere in the world.

E. Building Cooperative Security: Special Problems

Earlier, we addressed the need to strengthen our international institutions, especially the United Nations, in order to end the scourge of war. There are a number of special problems of international security that also must be addressed as part of any cooperative security framework, including

1. The urgency of stopping nuclear proliferation and of promoting further progress toward nuclear disarmament
2. The need for general global demilitarization
3. The legitimacy and scope of economic sanctions
4. The requirements and risks of humanitarian intervention
5. The issue of global responses to regional conflicts

1. Unfinished Business: Nuclear Disarmament and Proliferation

Our 1983 pastoral letter focused special attention on the morality of nuclear weapons at a time of widespread fear of nuclear war. Only ten years later, the threat of global nuclear war may seem more remote than at any time in the nuclear age, but we may be facing a different but still dangerous period in which the use of nuclear weapons remains a significant threat. We cannot address questions of war and peace today, therefore, without acknowledging that the nuclear question remains of vital political and moral significance.

The end of the Cold War has changed the nuclear question in three ways. First, nuclear weapons are still an integral component of U.S. security policies, but they are no longer at the center of these policies or of international relations. In 1983, a dominant concern was the ethics of nuclear weapons. Today, this concern, while still critically important, must be considered in the context of a more fundamental question of the ethical foundations of political order: How do we achieve *Pacem in Terris's* vision of a just and stable political order, so that nations will no longer rely on nuclear weapons for their security? Second, we have new opportunities to take steps toward progressive nuclear disarmament. In 1983, the first task was to stop the growth of already bloated nuclear arsenals; today, the moral task is to proceed with deep cuts and ultimately to abolish these weapons entirely. Third, the threat of global nuclear war has been replaced by a threat of global nuclear proliferation. In addition to the declared nuclear powers, a number of other countries have or could very quickly deploy nuclear weapons, and still other nations, or even terrorist groups, might seek to obtain or develop nuclear weapons. Just as the nuclear powers must prevent nuclear war, so also they, with the rest of the international community, bear a heavy moral responsibility to stop the spread of nuclear, biological, and chemical weapons.

a. *The moral judgment on deterrence.* In 1983, we judged that nuclear deterrence may be morally acceptable as long as it is limited to deterring nuclear use by others; sufficiency, not nuclear superiority, is its goal; and it is used as a step on the way toward progressive disarmament.[29]

Some believe that this judgment remains valid, since significant progress has been made in reducing nuclear weapons, including the most destabilizing ones, while at least some of those that remain are still necessary to deter existing nuclear threats. Others point to the end of the Soviet threat and the apparent unwillingness of the nuclear powers to accept the need to eliminate nuclear weapons as reasons for abandoning our strictly conditioned moral acceptance of nuclear deterrence. They also cite the double standard inherent in nonproliferation efforts: What is the moral basis for asking other nations to forego nuclear weapons if we continue to judge our own deterrent to be morally necessary?

We believe our judgment of 1983 that nuclear deterrence is morally acceptable only under certain strict conditions remains a useful guide for evaluating the continued moral status of nuclear weapons in a post-Cold War world. It is useful because it acknowledges the fundamental moral dilemmas still posed by nuclear weapons, and it reflects the progress toward fulfilling the conditions we elaborated in 1983. At the same time, it highlights the new prospects—and thus the added moral urgency—of making even more dramatic progress in arms control and disarmament as the only basis for the continued moral legitimacy of deterrence.

b. *A post-Cold War agenda for nuclear disarmament.* While significant progress has been made in recent years, we believe additional steps are needed if nuclear policies and priorities are to keep up with the dramatic changes in world politics and if our nation is to move away from relying on nuclear deterrence as a basis for its security. Present challenges include the following:

- *The role of nuclear weapons:* We must continue to say **No** to the very idea of nuclear war. A minimal nuclear deterrent may be justified only to deter the use of nuclear weapons. The United States should commit itself never to use nuclear weapons first, should unequivocally reject proposals to use nuclear weapons to deter any nonnuclear threats, and should reinforce the fragile barrier against the use of these weapons. Indeed, we abhor any use of nuclear weapons.

- *Arms control and disarmament:* Nuclear deterrence may be justified only as a step on the way toward progressive disarmament. The end of the Cold War, according to the Holy See, "challenge[s] the world community to adopt a post-nuclear form of security. That security lies in the abolition of nuclear weapons and the strengthening of international law."[30] A first step toward this goal would be prompt ratification and implementation of the START I and START II treaties. Even once these treaties are fully implemented, there will still be more than 10,000 nuclear weapons in the world, containing explosive power hundreds of thousands times greater than the bombs dropped on Hiroshima and Nagasaki. Therefore, much deeper cuts are both possible and necessary. The eventual elimination of nuclear weapons is more than a moral ideal; it should be a policy goal.

The negotiation of a verifiable comprehensive test ban treaty would not only demonstrate our commitment to this goal, but would improve our moral credibility in urging nonnuclear nations to forego the development of nuclear weapons. We, therefore, support a halt to nuclear testing as our nation pursues an effective global test ban and renewal of the Non-Proliferation Treaty. Also, steps must be taken to reduce the threat of nuclear terrorism. We must reverse the spread of nuclear technologies and materials. We welcome, therefore, U.S. efforts to achieve a global ban on the production of fissionable materials for use in nuclear weapons. Finally, one should not underestimate the role of the International Atomic Energy Agency as a forum for the discussion of these issues and as a force encouraging nations to take the steps necessary in this area.

- *Cooperative security and a just international order:* The nuclear powers may justify, and then only temporarily, their nuclear deterrents only if they use their power and resources to lead in the construction of a more just and stable international order. An essential part of this international order must be a collective security framework that reverses the proliferation of nuclear weapons, guarantees the security of nonnuclear states, and ultimately seeks to make nuclear weapons and war itself obsolete. The United States and other nations should also make the investments necessary to help ensure the development of stable, democratic governments in nations which have nuclear weapons or might seek to obtain them.

An active commitment by the United States to nuclear disarmament and the strengthening of collective security is the only moral basis for temporarily retaining our deterrent and our insistence that other nations forego these weapons. We advocate disarmament by example: careful but clear steps to reduce and end our dependence on weapons of mass destruction.

In our five-year report on *The Challenge of Peace,* we said: "To contain the nuclear danger of our time is itself an awesome undertaking. To reshape the political fabric of an increasingly interdependent world is an even larger and more complicated challenge."[31] Now, on this tenth anniversary, we must be engaged in the difficult task of envisioning a future rooted in peace, with new institutions for resolving differences between nations, new global structures of mediation and conflict-resolution, and a world order that has moved beyond nuclear weapons once and for all. We are committed to join in this struggle, to bring the gospel message of justice and peace to this vital work.

2. Demilitarization

Each year, our nation spends about $275 billion on the military; the entire world spends nearly $1 trillion. The end of the Cold War has led to a welcome decline in U.S. and world military expenditures, but still excessive levels of such spending remain, in the words of Pope John Paul II, a "serious disorder" in a world where millions of people lack even the necessities of life.[32]

According to the Holy Father, the moral judgment about the arms trade "is even more severe."[33] At present there are more than forty regional conflicts, almost all of these fueled by a seemingly limitless arms trade. Recent wars in Central America, Iraq, Somalia, Angola, and Afghanistan provide ample evidence that weapons not only exacerbate conflicts and fuel regional arms races, but, as with Iraq, are often turned against those who supply them. Moreover, the recipients are often irresponsible or repressive regimes whose military ambitions rob their people of their right to human development and sentence them to increasing misery. Our experience over the past decade reinforces the judgment of the Second Vatican Council: ". . . The arms race is one of the greatest curses on the human race and the harm it inflicts on the poor is more than can be endured."[34]

What is especially discouraging is that our country, as well as other permanent members of the U.N. Security Council, each of which have accepted a special responsibility for international peace, are the major participants—some would say profiteers—in this lethal trade. We are faced with a paradoxical situation in which modest defense reductions at home seem to encourage the export of militarism abroad. Defense spending is cut while weapons continue to be supplied to others without effective restraints. It is a matter of concern when the desire to protect jobs in the defense industry overshadows the interests of international peace and stability.

As the world's largest supplier of weapons, the United States bears great responsibility for curbing the arms trade by taking concrete actions to reduce its own predominant role in this trade.[35] The human consequences of unemployment and economic disruption caused by defense cuts must be addressed concretely through economic development and conversion programs, a stronger nonmilitary economy, and other programs to assist those who lose their jobs. Jobs at home cannot justify exporting the means of war abroad.

Neither jobs nor profits justify military spending beyond the minimum necessary for legitimate national security and international peacekeeping obligations. The end of the Cold War still provides an opportunity to reduce substantially military spending. Prudence requires that this reduction take into account emerging threats to world peace. Prudence also dictates that we use the unparalleled opportunities at hand to find alternative ways to respond to new dangers as we redirect resources to meet nonmilitary threats to international security. Diverting scarce resources from military to human development is not only a just and compassionate policy, but it is also a wise long-term investment in global peace and national security.

3. Economic Sanctions

In the aftermath of the Cold War, comprehensive economic sanctions have become a more common form of international pressure. In the case of Iraq and the former Yugoslavia, our bishops' conference has supported sanctions as a means of combating aggression short of military intervention; in the case of South Africa, we have supported less onerous sanctions to encourage the dismantling of apartheid and adopted a policy of divestment to renounce complicity in this immoral regime and to stand in solidarity with those who were seeking to end it. In other cases, we have not been convinced that comprehensive sanctions were helpful, and in still others, we have not taken a position. In each case, we have consulted closely with the Church in the country affected and have been guided by its judgment.

Our record on sanctions reflects an inherent dilemma involved in this form of pressure. We hear the cries of innocent people in Serbia, Haiti, Iraq, Cuba, and elsewhere who have lost their jobs, who can no longer afford what food is available, whose health is deteriorating, and whose political leaders remain recalcitrant and as strong as ever. We take very seriously the charge that sanctions can be counterproductive and sometimes unjustifiably harm the innocent. Yet, sanctions can offer a nonmilitary alternative to the terrible options of war or indifference when confronted with aggression or injustice.

While much more study, reflection, and public debate over the moral dimension of comprehensive sanctions is needed, we offer the following tentative criteria as a contribution to this discussion.

First, concerns about the limited effectiveness of sanctions and the harms caused to civilian populations require that comprehensive sanctions be considered only in response to aggression or grave and ongoing injustice, after less coercive measures have been tried, and with clear and reasonable conditions set for their removal.

Second, the harm caused by sanctions should be proportionate to the good likely to be achieved; sanctions should avoid grave and irreversible harm to the civilian population. Therefore, sanctions should be targeted as much as possible against those directly responsible for the injustice, distinguishing between the government and the people. Selective sanctions which target offending individuals and institutions are usually preferable, therefore, to complete embargoes. Embargoes, when employed, must make provision for the fundamental human needs of the civilian population. The denial of basic needs may not be used as a weapon.

Third, the consent to sanctions by substantial portions of the affected population is morally relevant. While this consent may mitigate concerns about suffering caused by sanctions, however, it does not eliminate the need for humanitarian exemptions.

Finally, sanctions should always be part of a broader process of diplomacy aimed at finding an effective political solution to the injustice.

The troubling moral problems posed by the suffering caused by sanctions and the limits to their effectiveness counsel that this blunt instrument be used sparingly and with restraint. Economic sanctions may be acceptable, but only if less coercive means fail, as an alternative to war, and as a means of upholding fundamental international norms.

4. Humanitarian Intervention

In recent years, we hear increasing calls for humanitarian intervention, that is, the forceful, direct intervention by one or more states or international organizations in the internal affairs of other states for essentially humanitarian purposes. The internal chaos, repression, and widespread loss of life in countries such as Haiti, Bosnia, Liberia, Iraq, Somalia, Sudan, and now Burundi, have all raised the difficult moral, political, and legal questions that surround these calls to intervene in the affairs of sovereign states to protect human life and basic human rights.

Pope John Paul II, citing the "conscience of humanity and international humanitarian law," has been outspoken in urging that "humanitarian intervention be obligatory where the survival of populations and entire ethnic groups is seriously compromised. This is a duty for nations and the international community."[36] He elaborated on this right and duty of humanitarian intervention in his 1993 annual address to the diplomatic corps:

> Once the possibilities afforded by diplomatic negotiations and the procedures provided for by international agreements and organizations have been put into effect, and that [sic], nevertheless, populations are succumbing to the attacks of an unjust aggressor, states no longer have a "right to indifference." It seems clear that their duty is to disarm this aggressor, if all other means have proved ineffective. The principles of the sovereignty of states and of non-interference in their internal affairs—which retain all their

value—cannot constitute a screen behind which torture and murder may be carried out.[37]

The Holy Father's appeal for humanitarian intervention reflects several concerns. First, human life, human rights, and the welfare of the human community are at the center of Catholic moral reflection on the social and political order. Geography and political divisions do not alter the fact that we are all one human family, and indifference to the suffering of members of that family is not a moral option.

Second, sovereignty and nonintervention into the life of another state have long been sanctioned by Catholic social principles, but have never been seen as absolutes. Therefore, the principles of sovereignty and nonintervention may be overridden by forceful means in exceptional circumstances, notably in the cases of genocide or when whole populations are threatened by aggression or anarchy.

Third, nonmilitary forms of intervention should take priority over those requiring the use of force. Humanitarian aid programs, combined with political and economic sanctions, arms embargoes, and diplomatic initiatives may save lives without requiring military intervention. In this context, we affirm the responsibility, which must be respected, of humanitarian relief organizations to aid civilians in war zones and their right of access to vulnerable populations. In the longer run, the international community's first commitment must be to address the root causes of these conflicts, to support the spread of democratic and just political and economic orders, to develop the capacity to prevent conflicts, and to settle them promptly and peacefully when they erupt.

Fourth, military intervention may sometimes be justified to ensure that starving children can be fed or that whole populations will not be slaughtered. They represent St. Augustine's classic case: love may require force to protect the innocent. The just war tradition reminds us, however, that military force, even when there is just cause, must remain an exceptional option that conforms strictly to just war norms and norms of international policing. The particular difficulties involved in meeting criteria of success and proportionality in cases of humanitarian intervention deserve careful scrutiny and further examination. Intervention should also remain limited to achieving clearly deemed humanitarian objectives and to establishing conditions necessary for a just and stable peace. We must be wary that the outstretched hand of peace is not turned into an iron fist of war.

Finally, a right to intervene must be judged in relation to the broader effort to strengthen international law and the international community. Principles of sovereignty and nonintervention remain crucial to maintaining international peace and the integrity of nations, especially the weaker ones. The exceptional cases when humanitarian concerns may justify overriding these principles must be more clearly defined in international law, political philosophy, and ethics. Moreover, effective mechanisms must be developed to ensure that humanitarian intervention is an authentic act of international solidarity and not a cloak for great power dominance, as it sometimes has been in the past. Multilateral interventions, under the auspices of the United Nations, are preferable because they enhance the legitimacy of these actions and can protect against abuse.

If these considerations are taken into account, humanitarian intervention need not open the door to new forms of imperialism or endless wars of altruism, but could be an exceptional means to ensure that governments fulfill the purposes of sovereignty and meet the needs of their people, as the world urgently searches for effective nonviolent means to confront injustice and political disorder.

5. Global Responses to Regional Conflicts

Today's threats to peace tend to be more regional than global, more rooted in geographic, tribal, national, and ethnic conflict than in ideological disputes. Though regional, however, they call for a continuing response from the United States and the international community. Without attempting to reiterate our concerns about pressing problems in countries as diverse as Bosnia, East Timor, China, Peru, and Northern Ireland, the following reflections on Africa, Asia, Central America and the Caribbean, and the Middle East highlight the importance of resolving regional and internal conflicts and developing mechanisms for peace building at the local and regional levels.

Africa. The African continent continues to be wracked by conflict and neglected by U.S. foreign policy. While progress has been made toward reconciliation in some Cold War conflicts, like that in Mozambique, elsewhere fighting continues. Since 1960, not a day has passed without armed conflict. In Sudan, no end is in sight to a lengthy civil war in which government troops have massacred Christians, starved them by siege, forced some into slavery, and coerced many into religious conversion. In Somalia, United Nations forces have not yet succeeded in establishing the peaceful conditions which will permit relief work to continue unimpeded and civil life to be restored. In South Africa, a long-awaited transition to nonracial democracy is marred by intergroup violence. In Zaire, troops still loyal to the old dictatorship hamper progress toward a renewal of democratic government, while in Burundi age-old tribal animosities have again brought bloodshed and dislocations.

Asia. In some parts of this important region the Church is struggling, frequently against official opposition, to win the freedom to openly proclaim the Gospel. We especially support the persistent efforts of our brother bishops in China and Vietnam to demonstrate that genuine religious liberty can improve national harmony, reduce international tensions, and contribute to the common good.

We renew our commitments in our pastoral reflection of 1989, *A Time for Dialogue and Healing,* including "our wish to work with our brother bishops in Vietnam toward a better understanding between our two peoples," and our call for "full and genuine respect for the role of the Church by the Vietnamese government," and for the United States and the broader international community to assist Vietnam "to enter the world trading and diplomatic community."

Central America and the Caribbean. For much of the last decade, Central America preoccupied our nation and this conference. Thankfully, the guns of war have mostly fallen silent as a result of dialogue, negotiation, and a return to democratic decision making. Sadly, the United States, which invested so much in the armed conflict in the region, seems almost indifferent now to the need for significant investment in its development and reconstruction. If the countries of the region are not to return to cycles of violence and repression, continued U.S. involvement and aid will be needed for some time to come. Greater sensitivity on the part of the World Bank and the International Monetary Fund to the impact of their decisions on the abilities of countries to rebuild is also much needed.

We stand with our brother bishops in Cuba in their courageous declaration *Love Hopes All Things.*[38] We support their call for greater religious and political freedom and direct humanitarian assistance, especially food and medicine, from our nation and others at this time of deprivation for their long-suffering people. We hope with them that substantial, improved performance by the Cuban authorities with regard to human rights and religious liberty could lead to progressively greater opportunities for trade and dialogue between our two nations and within Cuban society. We stand in solidarity with the Church and people of Cuba in their hopes for greater freedom and opportunity.

For all too long the people of Haiti have suffered from grinding poverty, denial of human rights, predatory government, indiscriminate violence, and the indifference of outsiders. Today we must accompany the Haitian people as they travel the long road toward democracy and civil peace. To enjoy the fruits of peace, all parties will have to respect basic human rights and commit themselves to restraint and reconciliation. Once the rule of law is established, the Haitian people will need the support of the United States and of the international community for years to come in the development of their island. Much needs to be done in order to institutionalize democratic political processes that will lead to justice for all Haitians.

Middle East. We give thanks to God for the interim agreement between Israel and the Palestine Liberation Organization. It is an his-

toric opening to a new era for which the whole world has been longing for many years. We applaud the courage, the imagination, and the
spirit of compromise that has been shown in negotiating this major
advance toward peace in the Holy Land. The agreement is an historic
beginning, which must be carried out fully, supported actively, and
expanded upon quickly. We support full autonomy for the West Bank,
and a true homeland for the Palestinians, and look forward to a final
settlement that will protect the rights and security of all people, including Israelis and Palestinians.

To succeed, the interim Israeli-Palestinian accord on Gaza and
Jericho as well as eventual Palestinian self-rule on the West Bank will
require serious support from the international community, especially
from the United States. Aid and technical support are needed for
building up the autonomous Palestinian territories and for reconstruction of Lebanon. As the U.S. has been generous in supporting Israel's
security, so now it should be unstinting in helping to build peace for
the region.

A lasting settlement in the region must include a resolution of the
status of Jerusalem that retracts its unique role as a city holy to Jews,
Muslims, and Christians alike. Any settlement must include full recognition of the rights of all believers in the Holy Land and their unimpeded access to the holy places.[39]

We hope that a resolution of the Israeli-Palestinian issue will be the
impetus for tangible progress toward development and disarmament,
peace and security in regional negotiations. Lebanon, which has
suffered so much until now and which still needs to reacquire its full
sovereignty from all its neighbors, is in special need of peace and
reconstruction. The people of Iraq also deserve relief from their present oppressive situation. The new era must bring comprehensive steps
toward a just peace for the whole region.

These and other conflicts show the need for early and vigorous
responses by the international community to support reconciliation
processes whether they are supervised by domestic leaders or outside
mediators. During the Cold War, the United States gave substantial
support to rebel groups and client governments to prevent the spread
of communism. Therefore, it bears a special responsibility in this new
era to provide assistance to overcome the legacy of apartheid, civil
war, and autocratic rule and to bolster civilian groups eager for peace
and the rebirth of democracy.

In these regions and throughout the world, violence and repression have led to a refugee crisis of tragic proportions. The United
States and other nations cannot close their eyes or their doors to the
tide of suffering humanity. Our laws and policies should reflect our
historic openness to victims of war and oppression. Welcoming
refugees is an essential part of peacemaking.

F. Shaping Responsible U.S. Leadership in the World

The preeminence of U.S. influence and power in the world is an undisputed fact. This fact is of great moral significance, first, because American values and actions can bring tremendous good or much suffering to people around the world; and second, because with power and influence comes a responsibility to contribute to the universal common good.

Our nation needs to offer hope for a better future for millions here at home, but, in the face of the world's enormous needs, Pope John Paul II reminds us that a turn to "selfish isolation" would not only be "a betrayal of humanity's legitimate expectations . . . but also a real desertion of a moral obligation."[40]

Building peace, combating poverty and despair, and protecting freedom and human rights are not only moral imperatives, but also wise national priorities. They can shape a world that will be a safer, more secure, and more just home for all of us. Responsible international engagement is based on the conviction that our national interests and the interests of the international community, our common good and the global common good are intertwined.

For these reasons, the leaders and people of the United States are called to take up the vocation to peacemaking with new urgency and commitment. Accepting, though not exaggerating, the lessons of recent history, acknowledging the limits of U.S. influence and humbly confessing past excesses and failures, we are called to commit ourselves firmly to joining with other nations in building a new kind of world, one that is more peaceful, just, and respectful of the life and dignity of the human person. Having paid such a price in the lives of their young and spent so much of their national treasure on the wars of this century, it is both wise and understandable that Americans are reluctant to commit themselves also to serve as the world's police force. As a permanent member of the UN Security Council and the strongest military power in the world, however, the U.S. has a special responsibility to work with other nations to find cooperative ways to promote international peace. As Pope John Paul II said this year in Denver, "Together with millions of people around the globe I share the profound hope that in the present international situation the United States will spare no effort in advancing authentic freedom and in fostering human rights and solidarity."[41]

As our nation helps shape a new world, we must be aware of the values we are contributing to this new order. The best of America's values and actions continue to inspire other peoples' struggles for justice and freedom and contribute to building a more just and peaceful world. Of special significance have been our democratic ideals, which have inspired the spread of democracy and political transformations in many parts of the world. Our society's excessive individualism and materialism, pervasive violence, and tendency to denigrate moral and religious values, however, can be harmful. A practical materialism and a militant secular mentality undermine cultural and moral values here and abroad, generate expectations that cannot and should not necessarily be fulfilled, and inhibit efforts to strengthen international order.

What the United States can offer the world—and what the world desperately needs—is creative engagement, a willingness to collaborate and a commitment to values that can build up the global community. "Liberty and justice for all" is not only a profound national pledge; it is also a worthy goal for a world leader.

III. Concluding Commitments: Blessed Are the Peacemakers

A. A Renewed Commitment

Ten years after *The Challenge of Peace,* we renew our commitment to peacemaking. We are still at a beginning, not an end. On the fifth anniversary of our pastoral letter, we said we must work "to broaden, strengthen, and deepen the Church's work for peace." We are still called to build a peacemaking Church that constantly prays and teaches, speaks and acts for peace. Once again we ask our parishes and people to join with us in:

- *Regular prayer for peace.* Every liturgy is a call to and celebration of peace. The cause of peace should be constantly reflected in our prayers of petition. The scriptural call to peacemaking should be a constant source for prayer and preaching.
- *Sharing the gospel call to peace and the Church's teaching on peace.* In our schools and seminaries, our religious education and formation efforts, our colleges and universities, we need to continue and intensify our efforts to integrate Catholic teaching on justice, nonviolence, and peace into the curriculum and broader life of our educational endeavors. Education is a work of peace.
- *Speaking and acting for peace.* In our advocacy and citizenship efforts, we are called to use the resources of our faith and the opportunities of our democracy to help shape a U.S. foreign policy clearly committed to human life and human rights. Through legislative networks and broader participation in the political process, Catholics can take our principles of peacemaking into the public arena, where they can help shape an active and constructive U.S. role in the world.

In these reflections, we outline an agenda for action, which will guide the conference's future advocacy. We will work for:

- Creative, engaged, and responsible U.S. leadership that rejects the illusion of isolationism and avoids the dangers of unwise intervention
- A reshaped foreign aid program designed to combat poverty with sustainable development and the economic development of the poor, especially women
- Substantive changes in the international economic order to stop the movement of wealth from the poor to the rich
- A commitment to strengthening and improving the capacity of the United Nations and other multilateral institutions to promote human development, democracy, human rights, and peace
- Accelerated progress toward a nuclear test ban, eliminating nuclear weapons, preventing nuclear proliferation, restraining the arms trade, and encouraging worldwide demilitarization
- Legal protection for selective conscientious objectors and improved protection for conscientious objectors
- Prudent use of economic sanctions as an alternative to war and means to enforce fundamental international norms
- Clarification of the right and duty of humanitarian intervention in exceptional cases, by means consistent with Catholic teaching on nonviolence and just war, when the survival of whole populations is threatened

The Catholic community in the United States is already a very active and involved part of both the universal Church and a nation with clear global responsibilities. Day by day, we seek to build a more just and peaceful world through the work of Catholic Relief Services, our migration refugee programs, missionary efforts, advocacy on international issues, and existing aid programs to the churches in Eastern Europe, Latin America, and the Middle East. In these anniversary reflections we call on the leaders of these impressive programs to explore together ways of building upon and strengthening our community's efforts to help those in need and to work for justice around the world. Our international education, outreach, and advocacy efforts need to continue to help shape a Church and nation more clearly committed to solidarity and global responsibility.

B. A Call to Conversion and Hope

In our pastoral of ten years ago, we outlined a call to conversion, reflection, and peacemaking: "Peacemaking is not an optional commitment. It is a requirement of our faith. We are called to be peacemakers, not by some movement of the moment, but by our Lord Jesus."[42]

Now ten years later Jesus calls us to be peacemakers in a very different world. In these anniversary reflections, we have focused less on particular weapons and wars and more on a broader context of violence which still pervades our communities, our country, and our world. This violence is one of the saddest "signs of our times." We see the violence of abortion accepted as normal by too many Americans. We fear our society is becoming accustomed to children dying in our streets and in villages half a world away. We may be growing indifferent to entertainment saturated with blood and death, to nightly television images of deadly warfare, racial hatred, and ethnic cleansing. The pervasiveness of violence deadens our response to the human suffering and the moral damage it causes.

Our age seems to seek quick and decisive solutions to difficult problems, to turn to violence rather than to embark on the painful and complicated search for less deadly, more lasting solutions which require sacrifice, patience, and time. We observe signs of this tragic trend in our domestic life where abortion is seen as a solution to difficult pregnancies, where capital punishment is embraced as a response to rising crime, and where euthanasia is advocated in the face of the burdens of age and illness.

In global affairs, we see similar temptations. Age-old antagonisms are fought out in bloody warfare; terrorism is seen as a means of revenge and advancing a cause; and military force is too often employed as the principal means to redress injustice or to safeguard interests.

It is time to clearly recognize that in the end violence is not a solution, but more often the problem. As we reaffirm the Church's teachings on war and peace, we insist that the world community must urgently search for effective ways to move beyond the violence of war and terrorism to settle scores or to defend what is precious. We need new policies, new structures, new attitudes to resolve disputes and address injustice.

As our Holy Father has said:

> No, never again war, which destroys the lives of innocent people, teaches how to kill, throws into upheaval even the lives of those who do the killing and leaves behind a trail of resentment and hatred, thus making it all the more difficult to find a just solution of the very problems which provoked the war. Just as the time has finally come when in individual states a system of private vendetta and reprisal has given way to the rule of law, so too a similar step forward is now urgently needed in the international community.[43]

Some will find this goal a pious hope or utopian dream. No doubt, finding ways to move the world beyond war will be a complex, demanding, and difficult struggle. But it is a task that must be pursued by all who take faith seriously, and honestly assess the human, social, and moral costs of continuing conflict and bloodshed. As history's bloodiest century ends, there should be no question that, in the words of Pope John Paul II, we must "proceed resolutely toward outlawing war completely and come to cultivate peace as a supreme good to which all programs and all strategies must be subordinated."[44]

At its heart, today's call to peacemaking is a call to conversion, to change our hearts, to reject violence, to love our enemies. We will not fashion new policies until we repudiate old thinking. Ten years ago, in addressing the seemingly intractable dynamic of the Cold War, our pastoral letter suggested:

> To believe we are condemned in the future only to what has been the past of United States-Soviet relations is to underestimate both our human potential for creative diplomacy and God's action in our midst which can open the way to changes we could barely imagine.[45]

Changes we could barely imagine ten years ago have taken place before our eyes. Without violence, the hope, courage, and power of ordinary people have brought down walls, restored freedoms, toppled governments, and changed the world.

For believers, hope is not a matter of optimism but a resource for action, a source of strength in demanding causes. For peacemakers, hope is the indispensable virtue. This hope, together with our response to the call to conversion, must be rooted in God's promises and nourished by prayer and penance, including fasting and Friday abstinence.[46]

C. Witnesses to Peacemaking

In our faith, we find the reason for hope and witnesses for genuine peacemaking. In the Scriptures, in the life of Jesus, and in the teaching of his Church are the principles we need to follow as peacemakers.

We also find examples in the witness of peacemakers across the globe. Pope John Paul II has been a consistent voice for peace and justice in a world lacking both. We watched with awe the courage and faithfulness of solidarity and other movements for freedom in Eastern Europe. We have seen the leadership and sacrifice of church leaders in Central America who stand with the poor and suffering, who call for dialogue and reconciliation to replace repression and war. We cannot forget the scenes of people in the Philippines confronting guns and tanks with rosaries and flowers. Our call to peacemaking does not have the drama and dangers these peacemakers and so many others have faced. But each of us is called in our own way to work for peace with justice in our own families and communities, our nation and world.

As pastors, we especially seek to support lay men and women who are called to serve the cause of peace by breaking down barriers of alienation and creating bonds of friendship and love in their personal and family lives, in their daily commitments as members of our armed forces, diplomats, researchers, advocates, workers, scientists, and public officials. We also seek to encourage preachers, teachers, chaplains, and all believers to share the scriptural call to peace, the teachings of the Church, and the message of our pastoral. We urge all Catholics to join with us in finding ways to be true peacemakers as citizens of a powerful nation and shrinking world.

D. Concluding Word

In this anniversary statement, we have shared more challenges than answers, offered more pastoral reflections than policy prescriptions. This approach reflects our conviction that the most fundamental task is for our community of faith to understand and act on two fundamental ideas. The first is drawn from the beatitudes: "Blessed are the peacemakers, they will be called children of God." The second is the familiar call of Pope Paul VI: "If you want peace, work for justice." These two deceptively simple statements outline the key elements of our mission: To be a Christian is to be a peacemaker and to pursue peace is to work for justice.

The Challenge of Peace contributed to greater prayer, reflection, discussion, and action for peace on the part of many. We hope these anniversary reflections will help renew and revitalize discussion in the Catholic community and contribute to the dialogue in the broader community on the moral dimensions of foreign affairs. Our peacemaking vocation is not a passing priority, a cause for one decade, but an essential part of our mission to proclaim the Gospel and renew the earth. As followers of the Prince of Peace, we work for a world where the promise of the Apostle James is realized for all God's children: "The harvest of justice is sown in peace for those who cultivate peace" (Jas 3:18).

Notes

1. John Paul II, *On Social Concern (Sollicitudo Rei Socialis)* (Washington, D.C.: United States Catholic Conference, 1987), no. 23.
2. Ibid., no. 39.
3. John Paul II, *On the Hundredth Anniversary of Rerum Novarum (Centesimus Annus)* (Washington, D.C.: United States Catholic Conference, 1991), no. 52.

4. *Sollicitudo Rei Socialis*, nos. 38, 39.
5. National Conference of Catholic Bishops, *The Challenge of Peace: God's Promise and Our Response* (Washington, D.C.: United States Catholic Conference, 1983), no. 73.
6. Ibid., no. 116.
7. *Centesimus Annus*, no. 23.
8. *The Challenge of Peace*, no. 318.
9. Ibid., no. 232.
10. National Conference of Catholic Bishops, *Human Life in Our Day* (Washington, D.C.: United States Catholic Conference, 1968), nos. 143-153.
11. United States Catholic Conference, "Declaration on Conscientious Objection and Selective Conscientious Objection," *In the Name of Peace: Collective Statements of the United States Catholic Bishops on War and Peace, 1919-1980* (Washington, D.C.: United States Catholic Conference, 1983).
12. Archbishop John Roach, "Letter to Secretary of Defense Richard Cheney" (October 23, 1991), *Origins* 21:22 (November 7, 1991): 352.
13. "Declaration on Conscientious Objection and Selective Conscientious Objection."
14. Cf. Second Vatican Council, *Pastoral Constitution on the Church in the Modern World (Gaudium et Spes)*, nos. 79, 80.
15. *Sollicitudo Rei Socialis*, no. 36.
16. Ibid., nos. 20-22, 36; *Centesimus Annus*, no. 18.
17. John Paul II, "Remarks at Welcoming Ceremonies and at Regis College," *Origins* 23:11 (August 26, 1993): 188.
18. John XXIII, *Peace on Earth (Pacem in Terris)* (Washington, D.C.: United States Catholic Conference, 1963), no. 140.
19. Of the many proposals being considered, special attention should be given the UN Secretary General's wide-ranging blueprint for strengthening the United Nation's ability to keep and build peace through collective security: *An Agenda for Peace* (New York: United Nations, 1992). See also UN Association of the USA Global Policy Project, *Partners for Peace: Strengthening Collective Security for the 21st Century* (New York: UNA-USA Publications, 1992).
20. *Centesimus Annus*, no. 47.
21. See, e.g., Archbishop John R. Roach, "Letter to Secretary of State Warren Christopher" (May 11, 1993), *Origins* 23:2 (May 27, 1993): 22; USCC Administrative Board, "War in the Balkans: Moral Challenges, Policy Choices" (March 25, 1993), *Origins* 22:43 (April 8, 1993): 733; National Conference of Catholic Bishops, "Statement on Croatia" (November 11, 1991), *Origins* 21:24 (November 21, 1991): 380-381; USCC Administrative Board, "Statement on the Soviet Union and Yugoslavia" (September 12, 1991), *Origins* 21:16 (September 26, 1991): 258.
22. Fourth General Conference of Latin American Bishops, *Santo Domingo Conclusions: New Evangelization, Human Development, Christian Culture* (Washington, D.C.: United States Catholic Conference, 1993), no. 179.
23. *Centesimus Annus*, no. 42.
24. *Sollicitudo Rei Socialis*, nos. 14-17.
25. Ibid.
26. Ibid.

27. *Centesimus Annus,* no. 28.
28. John Paul II, "To Build Peace, Respect Minorities," 1989 World Day of Peace Message, *Origins* 18:29 (December 29, 1988): 469.
29. *The Challenge of Peace,* nos. 186-188.
30. Archbishop Renato Martino, "Address to the United Nations Committee on Disarmament," *Origins* 23:21 (November 4, 1993): 382.
31. NCCB Ad Hoc Committee on the Moral Evaluation of Deterrence, *A Report on The Challenge of Peace and Policy Developments 1983-1988* (Washington D.C.: United States Catholic Conference, 1988), no. 129.
32. *Sollicitudo Rei Socialis,* no. 24.
33. Ibid., no. 24.
34. *Gaudium et Spes,* no. 81.
35. According to the Congressional Research Service, the United States has been "the predominant arms supplier . . . since the Cold War's end," responsible for close to 57 percent of the arms trade in 1992. Congressional Research Service, *Conventional Arms Transfers to the Third World, 1985-1992* (Washington, D.C.: Congressional Research Service, 1993).
36. John Paul II, "Address to the International Conference on Nutrition," *Origins* 22:28 (December 24, 1992): 475.
37. John Paul II, "Address to the Diplomatic Corps" (January 16, 1993), *Origins* 22:34 (February 4, 1993): 587.
38. Statement of the Cuban Bishops, "Love Hopes All Things" (September 8, 1993), *Origins* 23:16 (September 30, 1993): 273.
39. National Conference of Catholic Bishops, *Toward Peace in the Middle East: Perspectives, Principles, and Hopes* (Washington, D.C.: United States Catholic Conference, 1989).
40. *Sollicitudo Rei Socialis,* no. 23.
41. "Remarks at Welcoming Ceremonies and at Regis College," 188.
42. *The Challenge of Peace,* no. 333.
43. *Centesimus Annus,* no. 52; n. 104.
44. "Address to the Diplomatic Corps," 531.
45. *The Challenge of Peace,* no. 258.
46. Ibid., nos. 297-299; *Toward Peace in the Middle East,* 43.

Source: Washington, D.C.: United States Catholic Conference, 1994.

Follow the Way of Love

*A Pastoral Message of the National Conference of Catholic Bishops
to Families on the Occasion of the United Nations
1994 International Year of the Family*

November 1993

Foreword

The family exists at the heart of all societies. It is the first and most basic community to which every person belongs. There is nothing more fundamental to our vitality as a society and as a Church. For, in the words of Pope John Paul II, "The future of humanity passes by way of the family."[1]

Thus, it is fitting that the United Nations has drawn attention to the condition of family life throughout the world. By designating 1994 the International Year of the Family, it has invited everyone—especially families—to deepen their understanding of family life, to identify matters important to the family's well-being, and to take action that will strengthen families.

This message of the United States Catholic bishops to families takes as a starting point the International Year and its theme, *Family: Resources and Responsibilities in a Changing World.* It invites families to examine the quality of their lives. It asks them to reflect on their strengths as well as their weaknesses; on their resources as well as their needs.

The message shares with families a vision of their great calling that is rooted in Christ's teaching and developed in the life of his believing community. It urges families to seek the healing, strength, and meaning that Christ offers through his Church. It pledges the support of the Church so that families might recognize their resources and carry out their responsibilities in a changing world.

This message stands within the tradition of teaching on marriage and family expressed through our Holy Father, the Second Vatican Council, and the National Conference of Catholic Bishops. Of necessity, it deals with only a few of the issues relevant to family life today. It offers a limited pastoral treatment of them consistent with the vocation of every Christian to *follow the way of love, even as Christ loved you* (cf. Eph 5:2).

The message is addressed primarily to Christian families but is intended also for all who can use it toward strengthening their families.

Pastors and church ministers are encouraged to help families receive this message and use it.

Families Are a Sign of God's Presence

Ways of Loving

When people talk about life in a family, they speak of love with its abiding peace, its searing pain, its moments of joy and disappointment, its heroic struggle and ordinary routines.

"Family is where someone loves you no matter what," a teenager declares.

"Family doesn't mean just mom, dad, and kids, but grandparents, aunts, uncles, and others," explains a Hispanic woman.

"In a family you don't have to look very far to find your cross," a father observes.

"My child asks me such mystical questions," reports a young mother. "I learn so much."

"My teenagers were very sensitive to me during my divorce. God was there for me," a single parent recalls.

The story of family life is a story about love—shared, nurtured, and sometimes rejected or lost. In every family God is revealed uniquely and personally, for God is love and those who live in love live in God and God dwells in them (cf. 1 Jn 4:16).

And so our message is one that springs from love and that offers you a reflection on love: how it is experienced in a family, how it is challenged today, how it grows and enriches others, and how it needs the support of the whole Church.

We write to you as pastors and teachers in the Church, but we come to you as family members also. We are sons and brothers and uncles. We have known the commitment and sacrifices of a mother and father, the warmth of a family's care, the happiness and pain that are part of loving.

Some of us lived in single-parent families; others were adopted children. Some of us grew up in alcoholic homes. We came from affluence and from families where money was scarce.

Some of us have felt the hurt of racial discrimination or cultural prejudice. Some have lived for many generations in this country. Others are recent immigrants.

With our families, we celebrate the birth of a baby or a loved one's success. We rejoice at weddings and anniversaries of family members even as we grieve at an untimely death or the breakup of a married couple.

Knowing your many joys and struggles, we value your witness of fidelity in marriage and in family life. We rejoice with you in your happiness. We walk with you in your sorrow.

The Way of Love

Our ministry as pastors and teachers is enriched by our family experience. In addition, our vocation of leadership connects us to all families. It gives us the responsibility of opening up God's truth about human existence and of sharing with you the saving resources which the Lord has entrusted to the Church.

With our Holy Father, we consider it a privilege to undertake "the mission of proclaiming with joy and conviction the good news about the family."[2]

Yes, there is good news to tell. You may occasionally catch a glimpse of it in the news media and in conversation with neighbors or fellow workers. But the full story is to be found in God's word. The First Letter of John puts it succinctly:

> In this way the love of God was revealed to us: God sent his only Son into the world that we might have life through him. In this is love: not that we have loved God, but that he loved us. . . . Beloved, if God so loved us, we also must love one another. (1 Jn 4:9-11)

Thus, the basic vocation of every person, whether married or living a celibate life, is the same: *follow the way of love, even as Christ loved you* (cf. Eph 5:2). The Lord issues this call to your family and to every family regardless of its condition or circumstances.

Love brought you to life as a family. Love sustains you through good and bad times. When our Church teaches that the family is an "intimate community of life and love," it identifies something perhaps you already know and offers you a vision toward which to grow.

What you do in your family to create a community of love, to help each other to grow, and to serve those in need is critical, not only for your own sanctification but for the strength of society and our Church. It is a participation in the work of the Lord, a sharing in the mission of the Church. It is holy.

You Are the Church in Your Home

Baptism brings all Christians into union with God. Your family life is sacred because family relationships confirm and deepen this union and allow the Lord to work through you. The profound and the ordinary moments of daily life—mealtimes, workdays, vacations, expressions of love and intimacy, household chores, caring for a sick child or elderly parent, and even conflicts over things like how to celebrate holidays, discipline children, or spend money—all are the threads from which you can weave a pattern of holiness.

Jesus promised to be where two or three are gathered in his name (cf. Mt 18:20). We give the name *church* to the people whom the Lord gathers, who strive to follow his way of love, and through whose lives his saving presence is made known.

A family is our first community and the most basic way in which the Lord gathers us, forms us, and acts in the world. The early Church expressed this truth by calling the Christian family a domestic church or church of the home.

This marvelous teaching was underemphasized for centuries but reintroduced by the Second Vatican Council. Today we are still uncovering its rich treasure.

The point of the teaching is simple, yet profound. As Christian families, you not only belong to the Church, but your daily life is a true expression of the Church.

Your domestic church is not complete by itself, of course. It should be united with and supported by parishes and other communities within the larger Church. Christ has called you and joined you to himself in and through the sacraments. Therefore, you share in one and the same mission that he gives to the whole Church.

You carry out the mission of the church of the home in ordinary ways when

- You **believe** in God and that God cares about you. It is God to whom you turn in times of trouble. It is God to whom you give thanks when all goes well.
- You **love** and never give up believing in the value of another person. Before young ones hear the word of God preached from the pulpit, they form a picture of God drawn from their earliest experiences of being loved by parents, grandparents, godparents, and other family members.
- You **foster intimacy,** beginning with the physical and spiritual union of the spouses and extending in appropriate ways to the whole family. To be able to share yourself—good and bad qualities—within a family and to be accepted there is indispensable to forming a close relationship with the Lord.
- You **evangelize** by professing faith in God, acting in accord with gospel values, and setting an example of Christian living for your children and for others. And your children, by their spontaneous and genuine spirituality, will often surprise you into recognizing God's presence.

- You **educate**. As the primary teachers of your children, you impart knowledge of the faith and help them to acquire values necessary for Christian living. Your example is the most effective way to teach. Sometimes they listen and learn; sometimes they teach you new ways of believing and understanding. Your wisdom and theirs come from the same Spirit.

- You **pray together,** thanking God for blessings, reaching for strength, asking for guidance in crisis and doubt. You know as you gather—restless toddlers, searching teenagers, harried adults—that God answers all prayers, but sometimes in surprising ways.

- You **serve one another,** often sacrificing your own wants, for the other's good. You struggle to take up your cross and carry it with love. Your "deaths" and "risings" become compelling signs of Jesus' own life, death, and resurrection.

- You **forgive and seek reconciliation.** Over and over, you let go of old hurts and grudges to make peace with one another. And family members come to believe that, no matter what, they are still loved by you and by God.

- You **celebrate** life—birthdays and weddings, births and deaths, a first day of school and a graduation, rites of passage into adulthood, new jobs, old friends, family reunions, surprise visits, holy days and holidays. You come together when tragedy strikes and in joyful celebration of the sacraments. As you gather for a meal, you break bread and share stories, becoming more fully the community of love Jesus calls us to be.

- You **welcome** the stranger, the lonely one, the grieving person into your home. You give drink to the thirsty and food to the hungry. The Gospel assures us that when we do this, they are strangers no more, but Christ.

- You **act justly** in your community when you treat others with respect, stand against discrimination and racism, and work to overcome hunger, poverty, homelessness, illiteracy.

- You **affirm life** as a precious gift from God. You oppose whatever destroys life, such as abortion, euthanasia, unjust war, capital punishment, neighborhood and domestic violence, poverty and racism. Within your family, when you shun violent words and actions and look for peaceful ways to resolve conflict, you become a voice for life, forming peacemakers for the next generation.

- You **raise up vocations** to the priesthood and religious life as you encourage your children to listen for God's call and respond to God's grace. This is especially fostered through

family prayer, involvement in parish life, and by the way you
speak of priests, sisters, brothers, and permanent deacons.

No domestic church does all this perfectly. But neither does any
parish or diocesan church. All members of the Church struggle daily
to become more faithful disciples of Christ.

We need to enable families to recognize that they are a domestic
church. There may be families who do not understand or believe they
are a domestic church. Maybe they feel overwhelmed by this calling or
unable to carry out its responsibilities. Perhaps they consider their
family too "broken" to be used for the Lord's purposes. But remember,
a family is holy not because it is perfect but because God's grace is at
work in it, helping it to set out anew everyday on the way of love.

Like the whole Church, every Christian family rests on a firm
foundation, namely, Christ's promise to be faithful to those he has chosen. When a man and a woman pledge themselves to each other in the
sacrament of matrimony, they join in Christ's promise and become a
living sign of his union with the Church (cf. Eph 5:32).

Therefore, a committed, permanent, faithful relationship of husband and wife is the root of a family. It strengthens all the members,
provides best for the needs of children, and causes the church of the
home to be an effective sign of Christ in the world.

Wherever a family exists and love still moves through its members, grace is present. Nothing—not even divorce or death—can place
limits upon God's gracious love.

And so we recognize the courage and determination of families
with one parent raising the children. Somehow you fulfill your call to
create a good home, care for your children, hold down a job, and
undertake responsibilities in the neighborhood and church. You reflect
the power of faith, the strength of love, and the certainty that God does
not abandon us when circumstances leave you alone in parenting.

Those who try to blend two sets of children into one family face a
special challenge to accept differences and to love unconditionally.
They offer us a practical example of peacemaking.

Families arising from an interreligious marriage give witness to
the universality of God's love which overcomes all division. When
family members respect one another's different religious beliefs and
practices, they testify to our deeper unity as a human family called to
live in peace with one another.

We share the pain of couples who struggle without success to conceive a child. We admire and encourage families who adopt a child,
become foster parents, or care for an elderly or disabled relative in
their homes.

We offer our heartfelt sympathy and support to those parents who grieve at the death of a child due to illness, stillbirth, or the violence so prevalent in our society today.

We honor all families who, in the face of obstacles, remain faithful to Christ's way of love. The church of the home can live and grow in every family.

In our pastoral ministry, we have listened to many families: to husbands and wives, to estranged spouses, to abused and abandoned spouses, to single parents, and to children. We know that all families long for the peace, the acceptance, a sense of purpose, and the reconciliation that the term *church of the home* suggests. We believe that with prayer; hard work; understanding; commitment; the support of other families, parish priests, deacons and their wives, and religious and lay pastoral ministers; and especially with God's grace, the church of the home is built in ordinary homes, in your family.

Families Are Challenged by Change and Complexity

Living in Today's Society

We know you face obstacles as you try to maintain strong family ties and to follow your calling as a church of the home. The rapid pace of social change; the religious, ethnic, and cultural diversity of our society; the revolution of values within our culture; the intrusion of mass media; the impact of political and economic conditions: all these place families under considerable stress.

Some family pressures are due to broad social forces over which a family has little control. But other pressures are caused by personal choices, sometimes involving human weakness and sinful behavior.

Divorce, a serious contemporary problem, takes a heavy toll on family life. Spouses and children are affected most immediately, but so too are grandparents, other relatives, and friends that make up the extended family. Divorce can create in young people a fear of and a reluctance to make lifelong commitments. It often pushes families into poverty and contributes to other social ills.

Families are burdened also by the economic demands of providing housing, health care, child care when needed, education, and proper care for sick or elderly members. Unemployment or the fear of losing a job haunts many families.

Child and spouse abuse are touching the lives of more families. So, too, is the tragedy of AIDS. Families struggle with alcoholism, crime and gang violence in their neighborhoods, substance abuse, and suicide among youth. In a never-ending stream, communications media bring images and messages into your homes that may contradict your values and exert a negative influence on your children.

Some families face multiple burdens of poverty, racism, religious and cultural discrimination. New immigrant families can feel unwelcome in our communities and caught in a conflict between cultures.

Not all families experience these pressures to the same degree. Some are damaged by forces beyond their control. Many more, however, continue with prayerful determination and trust in God. All deserve our compassion and support—those who persevere also our gratitude as they show us the very faithfulness of God.

Pressure is brought to bear on families not only by outside forces but by those ordinary and inevitable tensions which arise from within. Daily you discover how different temperaments and opposing points of view can create hard feelings and even lasting bitterness. Human weakness and sinfulness often make it difficult to accept differences.

Recall how the wayward son swallowed his pride and returned home to find a forgiving father awaiting him and a family celebrating his arrival (cf. Lk 15:11-32). In the same way, all of us who suffer broken relationships are called to make peace, to reestablish trust, and to repledge love.

This can be an especially painful task for parents. What if your child becomes addicted to drugs, or harms others through drunken driving, or chooses friends you consider a bad influence? What if your adult child leaves the Church or makes other choices that cause you pain? Is it still possible to maintain a loving relationship without approving the child's behavior? How much can you accept before you compromise your own integrity?

It's not possible in this message to give complete answers to these questions and to the many others you confront. But what we can do, as your pastors and teachers, is to shed the light of Sacred Scripture and our Catholic tradition on a few key issues which you face.

In the next few pages we would like to discuss with you four challenges in family life. They are living faithfully, giving life, growing in mutuality, and taking time. They make a claim on your resources and responsibilities as a church of the home. They point out how you can *follow the way of love, even as Christ loved you* (cf. Eph 5:2).

Living Faithfully

The Sacred Scripture passage that many couples choose for their wedding ceremony is a marvelous blueprint for loving.

> Love is patient, love is kind. It is not jealous, [love] is not
> pompous, it is not inflated, it is not rude, it does not seek its
> own interests, it is not quick-tempered, it does not brood

over injury, it does not rejoice over wrongdoing, but rejoices
with the truth. It bears all things, believes all things, hopes
all things, endures all things. Love never fails. (1 Cor 13:4-8)

These words of St. Paul are worth daily meditation not only for
their insight into the true shape of love but for strengthening our wills
to follow this way of love. The love that he describes flourishes in
faithful, stable relationships. This applies, first and foremost, to a marriage. It is true also for the entire family.

When a woman and a man vow to be true in good times and in
bad they are confirming a decision to love one another. But, as married
couples have taught us, this decision to love is one we have to make
over and over again, when it feels good and when it does not. It is a
decision to look for, act on, and pray for the good of the people we say
we love. It is a pledge of fidelity.

Our world today needs living witnesses to fidelity. These are the
most convincing signs of the love that Christ has for every human
being. Couples who are living faithful lives of mutual love and support—though not without difficulties—have the gratitude of the
whole Church.

You know the value of a loving and life-giving marriage. Indeed,
your marriage is a gift to all of us. A wonderful way to share this gift,
as well as to reinvigorate your own commitment, would be to help
engaged couples prepare for the sacrament of matrimony. We invite
you to become part of this important ministry through a parish or
diocesan program.

Couples who are finding it hard to stay married deserve our
prayers and assistance. The Church can offer them the counsel of other
married couples and the assurance that, with God's grace, it is possible to live their vocation.

Newly married couples, when you find yourselves in a crisis, do
not conclude that divorce is inevitable. All of us—family members,
friends, communities of faith—should feel responsible for helping you
to recognize that divorce is not inevitable and is certainly not your
only option.

An enduring marriage is more than simply endurance. It is a
process of growth into an intimate friendship and a deepening peace.
So we urge all couples: renew your commitment regularly, seek enrichment often, and ask for pastoral and professional help when needed.

To live faithfully in a marriage requires humility, trust, compromise, communication, and a sense of humor. It is a give-and-take experience, involving hurt and forgiveness, failure and sacrifice. The very
same thing is true of fidelity in other family relationships.

Children who care for parents stricken with Alzheimer's disease,
parents who stand by their adult children even when they seem to

reject the family's values, a grandparent who helps to raise the children when parents are unable, a single parent who goes to great lengths to raise and nurture the children without the benefit of the other parent: all these are living faithful lives. They enflesh the words of Ruth, who refused to forsake her widowed mother-in-law, Naomi, and instead vowed, "wherever you go I will go" (Ru 1:16).

Your faithful love in a marriage and family is tested by change. It can also be strengthened and brought to maturity through change. The challenge is to remain open to the Lord's gracious, healing presence and to see change as an opportunity for growth.

Some changes in a family come unexpectedly, like a major illness, a job transfer, or loss of employment. Others fit more naturally into the flow of life, such as the birth of a child, the arrival of teenage years, or adult children leaving home. Regardless, though, every change brings with it a measure of stress and uncertainty. For many, it is like a dark night of the soul.

In these moments, dare to hope that you will rise to new experiences of love, entering into the very mystery of Christ's own dying and rising.

Maybe your family is trying to cope with a difficult loss or change. Perhaps you are torn by a conflict or trapped in an unhealthy pattern of relationships. If this is so, please seek God's help and the support of the Church.

The Church's treasures of prayer and worship, learning and service, contemplation and spiritual guidance are always available to you. The grace of the sacrament of matrimony and the power of the commitment that you have made to one another are continuing wellsprings of strength.

A marriage between a Christian and a follower of another religion, while not a sacrament, is a holy state instituted by God. It too is a divine gift with sustaining spiritual power.

Also, do not hesitate to seek professional assistance. Counseling, for example, can help you to identify the personal resources you already have and to use them more effectively.

Giving Life

St. Thomas Aquinas taught that love diffuses itself, that is, it wells up and spills over into every aspect of our lives.

When a man and a woman marry they pledge a love which is, in the words of Pope Paul VI, *creative of life.*[3] For a "couple, while giving themselves to one another, give not just themselves but also the reality of their children, who are a living reflection of their love. . . ."[4]

Welcoming a child, through birth or adoption, is an act of faith as well as an act of love. Being open to new life signals trust in the God who ultimately creates and sustains all life. It is also the beginning of a lifetime commitment: nurturing, teaching, disciplining, and, finally, letting go of a child—as he or she follows a new and perhaps uncharted way of love. Parenthood is indeed a Christian call and responsibility. It is the experience of acting as God's instruments in giving life to sons and daughters in various ways; but equally, it is an experience of being formed by God through your children.

The life that you give as parents is not restricted just to your off-spring. The children of other families need your guidance, as do other parents who can benefit from your hard-earned experience. Likewise, you cannot raise your own children alone. All families—even those with two parents—need a wider circle of aunts and uncles, grandparents, godparents, and other faith-filled families.

There are so many ways in which families can give life, especially in a society that devalues life through such actions as abortion and euthanasia. For instance, your family can ask: how have we been blessed as a family? What values and beliefs do we want to hand on to future generations? What strengths and resources do we possess that we could share with others? What traditions and rituals have enriched our lives? Could they benefit other families?

Each generation of a family is challenged to leave the world a more beautiful and beneficial place than it inherited. You can do this, for example, when you deliberately pass on your wisdom and the faith of the Church, providing countercultural messages about poverty, consumerism, sexuality, and racial justice—to name a few.

You also give life as a family by doing such simple things as taking a grandparent out of a nursing home for a ride, bringing a meal to a sick neighbor, helping to build homes for poor people, working in a soup kitchen, recycling your goods, working to improve the schools, or joining political action on behalf of those treated unjustly.

Such activity builds stronger family bonds. It enriches both the receiver and the giver. It releases the "formidable energies" present in families for building a better society.[5] The value of your witness which Christian families offer cannot be overestimated. As a family becomes a community of faith and love, it simultaneously becomes a center of evangelization.

Growing in Mutuality

At the basis of all relationships in a family is our fundamental equality as persons created in God's image. The creation narratives in the Book of Genesis teach this fundamental truth: "both man and woman are human beings to an equal degree, both are created in God's image."[6]

And St. Paul describes the "new creation" made possible in Christ:

> For all of you who were baptized into Christ have clothed
> yourselves with Christ. There is neither Jew nor Greek, there
> is neither slave nor free person, there is not male and female;
> for you are all one in Christ Jesus. (Gal 3:27-28)

Marriage is the partnership of a man and woman equal in dignity and value. This does not imply sameness in roles or expectations. There are important physical and psychological traits which result in differing skills and perspectives. Nor does the equality of persons mean that two spouses will have identical gifts or character or roles.

Rather, a couple who accepts their equality as sons and daughters in the Lord will honor and cherish one another. They will respect and value each other's gifts and uniqueness. They will "be subordinate to one another out of reverence for Christ" (Eph 5:21).

Our competitive culture tends to promote aggressiveness and struggles for power. These are a common part of life, especially in the workplace. It is all too easy for couples to bring an unhealthy competitive spirit to their relationship. The Gospel demands that all of us critically examine such attitudes. Marriage must never become a struggle for control.

For, unlike other relationships, marriage is a vowed covenant with unique dimensions. In this partnership, mutual submission—not dominance by either partner—is the key to genuine joy. Our attitude should be the same as Jesus, "who, though he was in the form of God, did not regard equality with God something to be grasped. Rather, he emptied himself . . ." (Phil 2:6-7).

True equality, understood as mutuality, is not measuring out tasks (who prepares the meals, who supervises homework, and so forth) or maintaining an orderly schedule. It thrives at a much deeper level where the power of the Spirit resides. Here, the grace of the vowed life not only makes the shedding of willfulness possible, but also leads to a joyful willingness.

Mutuality is really about sharing power and exercising responsibility for a purpose larger than ourselves. How household duties are distributed should follow from understanding what it takes to build a life together, as well as the individual skills and interests you bring to your common life.

Our experience as pastors shows us that genuine marital intimacy and true friendship are unlikely without mutuality. One spouse alone is not the keeper of love's flame. Both of you are co-creators of your relationship. Nowhere is this more vividly portrayed than in your decisions about having children. The Church promotes natural family planning for many reasons, among which are that "it favors attention for one's partner, helps both parties to drive out selfishness, the enemy of true love, and deepens their sense of responsibility."[7]

Agreeing that you are equal might be easier than changing your behavior or accepting joint responsibility for your relationship. It takes hard work to really understand another's feelings or to practice shared decision making on important matters.

Sharing feelings and a willingness to be vulnerable can be difficult, particularly for those of us raised in the "strong and silent" tradition. Men in all walks of life seem to have been influenced by this unwritten norm.

Moreover, some women have learned to fear conflict and may remain passive in the face of it. Women who accept their own self-worth are more able to express their beliefs, ideas, and feelings, even such painful ones as anger.

Flexible roles may appear difficult if your families of origin did not model them. Each family (couple) must decide what is best for them in a spirit of respect and mutuality. Especially when both spouses are employed, household duties need to be shared.

We urge you to take advantage of programs sponsored by your parish, diocese, or other organizations in your community that teach communication and conflict resolution to couples and to parents. Also there are worthwhile programs that lead women and men to a spiritual understanding of their behaviors, to appreciate how they influence each other, and to move beyond gender stereotypes.

We urge you to join with other couples and families who are making a conscious effort to follow Christ's way of love. You can find help for this through the Christian Family Movement (CFM), Marriage Encounter, Teams of Our Lady, the New Families Movement, and your diocesan family life office—to name just a few.

When children are born, both mother and father are important in nurturing and forming them. More and more, fathers have been discovering how their involvement in parenting enriches both their children and themselves. This is a hopeful development.

We urge men to interpret their traditional role as "provider" for a family in more than an economic sense. Physical care of children, discipline, training in religious values and practices, helping with school work and other activities: all these and more can be provided by fathers as well as mothers.

There is a lesson to be learned from the way in which many cultures place children at the center of family life. Children in the family share equal dignity as persons with the adults. They too are part of the covenant of mutuality. Parents can demonstrate this by treating children with respect, giving them responsibilities, listening seriously to their thoughts and feelings.

Bringing children into decision-making discussions, especially when the decisions could alter the pattern of family life, has precedent in our tradition. We read in the Rule of St. Benedict that the abbot is to consult with all members of the monastery, even the youngest (who often were children), when their lives were likely to be affected. Rather than undermining authority, this strengthens it in love.

Elders enrich the life of their families. They, too, should be cherished, not merely tolerated, for they are "a witness to the past and a source of wisdom for the young and for the future."[8] Grandparents, we encourage you to continue your lives of caring, especially for the youngest generation, and to find additional ways of demonstrating love for your children and grandchildren.

The pattern of mutuality within a household is closely allied with the virtue of humility. And humility is forged in prayer: husbands and wives praying with and for each other, parents praying with and for their children. This is the heart of ministry within the church of the home.

Taking Time

We are struck by the incredible busyness of family life that can take its toll on loving relationships. Daily we observe families overwhelmed by the demands of work, business travel, household tasks, getting to and from school, keeping appointments with doctors, civic responsibilities, and volunteering.

Both men and women can get caught up in long hours and weekends at their place of work. Balancing home and work responsibilities is a shared obligation for spouses. It is a critical issue facing families today. Where choices exist, hours on the job need to be weighed against their impact on family life.

To thrive, love requires attention, communication, and time—to share a story or confide a need, to play a game, to tell a joke, to watch and cheer on—time to be present to another's failure or success, confusion, despair, or moment of decision.

Spending time together builds intimacy, increases understanding, and creates memories between husband and wife, parent and child, brothers and sisters, grandparents and younger family members. It is hard to imagine how a family can live faithfully, be life-giving, and grow in mutuality without deliberately choosing to spend time together.

It is especially important for couples to have some time alone. Spending time away from children and other adults provides opportunities to grow in understanding and rekindles the fire of love that is often left unattended as children, job, and other commitments claim time and energy.

So, each of us needs to ask: to what am I giving my precious time? What are my priorities? Do television, sports, making money, shopping, getting ahead on the job, volunteering in the church or community swallow up time that could be better spent with those I love?

We challenge you to examine the priorities you have for your family. Compare them with how you actually spend your time. See what individual pursuits could be given up or replaced with family activities. We urge you to take time to be together:

- Making shared meals a priority (even if you gather at a fast food restaurant)
- Praying and worshiping together, especially at the Sunday eucharist and in family prayers, such as the rosary
- Building family traditions and rituals
- Taking part in retreats and family education programs

Watching television together and discussing the values being promoted on programs can be time well spent as a family.

Time given to solitude is also time well spent. When we enter into a genuine sabbath experience, alone with God, we can understand more fully who we are—as distinguished from what we do—and can receive what Jesus offers when he invites us to "come to me . . . and I will refresh you" (Mt 11:28).

Families Are Supported in the Church

An Invitation

Earlier in our message we affirmed the ancient insight that the Christian family is a church of the home. This understanding has guided and informed all we have written. We know that, in the everyday moments of your family lives, you proclaim God's word, communicate with God in prayer, and serve the needs of others. The graced experience you have as a Christian family in your domestic church should be shared more extensively with all of us.

We encourage you to help the Church by speaking to us, but more importantly to other families, about how you are trying to follow the way of love. Tell us how you work to stay married, how your family has overcome obstacles, how you have made time for each other, sought enrichment opportunities or professional help with your problems. Share with us how you have come to understand your vocation as a spouse or parent. Speak to us of your pain over broken promises and relationships. Give witness to your belief in God's mercy as you move toward reconciliation both with your family and with the Church. Help us to appreciate the symbols and traditions with which you celebrate and worship. Let us glimpse how you are trying to live a more simple lifestyle, serve the needy, build justice and peace in your community. Tell us what kinds of support you expect from the larger Church.

In 1994 (The International Year of the Family) Catholic News Service will provide a forum, through its syndicated "Faith Alive" series, for families to tell their stories.

Your words and deeds will lend strength to our exhortations.

Our Pledge

At other times we have urged all institutions of society to forge partnerships with families. We now promise to do our part to develop such a partnership within the Church. Specifically, as the National Conference of Catholic Bishops, we pledge:

- To welcome dialogue between our conference and families by asking the Committee on Marriage and Family to find ways of listening to families' reflections on this message
- To continue our support for families organizing to help one another, e.g., in the responsibilities of parenthood, in the process of grieving and healing after a significant loss, in taking action to serve the poor and remedy injustice, in forming communities of families who walk the way of love together
- To request theologians and pastoral leaders, especially at the national level, to develop resources that will strengthen the unity of marriage and deepen everyone's understanding of the value and role of Christian family as a domestic church
- To study in greater depth how to improve our marriage preparation efforts and how to strengthen and enrich marriages, using the spiritual and pastoral resources of the Church, and to focus particularly on those stages in a marriage when there is the greatest likelihood of divorce
- To include more deliberately within the scope of our pastoral care an attentiveness to single-parent families, families in a second marriage, grandparents raising children, interracial families, interfaith families, and persons who are widowed or divorced
- To broaden our efforts to welcome families from ethnically and racially diverse groups
- To advocate with national organizations, publishers, educators, and other experts for resources that will assist parents in the role of forming the morals and faith of their children
- To continue our national advocacy for public policy and legislation that will promote family stability and the welfare of children and those who are most vulnerable—the unborn, the disabled, and the frail and sick elderly

In general, we wish to initiate or improve things that are within our competence as a national body so that our belief about you, a church of the home, will bear fruit. We bishops need you to infuse the whole Church with your vitality, your understanding, your loving intimacy, your hospitality. We need you, whose faith and discipleship are nurtured within the church of the home, to join more fully with us in proclaiming Christ to the world.

Some Challenges

We acknowledge that official structures sometimes make it difficult to have dialogue with families and to create a partnership with you. Therefore, as bishops in our individual dioceses, we recognize these challenges:

- To urge our diocesan agencies and parishes to create ways for families to communicate with church leadership about their needs and their strengths
- To see that our parishes, schools, institutions, and diocesan agencies examine the extent to which their policies and programs help or hinder family growth and enable families to meet their responsibilities
- To give serious consideration to changing those policies and programs that are no longer responsive to contemporary family needs or make it difficult for families to assume their rightful place as a church of the home.

A Concluding Word

We have expressed in various ways throughout our message how deeply we care about strengthening family life for the well-being of the world and the Church and, indeed, for the sake of every man, woman, and child. Now, as a means of emphasizing, we offer these reflections:

- *Married couples:* The grace of the sacrament of matrimony and the spiritual power of your vows are available to you daily. Call upon these realities to strengthen you in your vocation.
- *Parents:* Not only do your children need discipline and love, they need the example of adults whose behavior demonstrates their caring. Put your children first in making decisions about family life.
- *Children and youth:* You have the right to expect love, guidance, discipline, and respect from your parents and elders. And, in turn, you should obey and respect them while you share with them your love, your experience of God, your fears and hope. You should help your parents and elders in their needs and

accompany them in the way of holiness. Pray for them as they do for you.

- *Spouses who are separated:* The road to healing, reconciliation, and rebuilding of your relationship can be a slow, painful one. If you are willing to begin that journey, the Church has many resources like pastoral counseling, Retrouvaille, and The Third Option program, which can assist you.

- *Divorced and widowed persons:* Relationships and circumstances within your family may have changed, but God's love for you is ever present and does not come to an end. Grasp the hands of those who reach out to you in loving concern. Extend your own hand to others whom you meet on the road to healing and reconciliation. There is a home for you within our parishes and communities of faith.

- *Single parents:* To be faced with all the responsibilities of parenting by yourself is a challenge that touches the very core of your life. We bishops express our solidarity with you. We urge all parishes and Christian communities to welcome you, to help you find what you need for a good family life, and to offer the loving friendship that is a mark of our Christian tradition.

- *Families:* Join with other families in communities of mutual support. Spiritual growth, insight into problems, help in times of trouble, and lasting friendships can flow from such experiences.

- There is no shame in seeking help for family problems, whether it be in the form of counseling, educational programs, or support groups.

- Christian life includes obligations beyond the family circle. For children to learn the true meaning of abundant life in Christ (cf. Jn 10:10), they need to know the joy of contributing to the common good: in the home, in the neighborhood, in the Church, and in society. Duty is an anchor in what seems an ocean of chaos.

If all the members of the Church are to follow Christ's way of love, it is essential that we continue speaking with, listening to, and learning from each other. We are the one body of Christ: the Church in the home, in the small community, in the parish, in the diocese, in a universal communion. We share one Lord, one faith, one baptism. We are one family in Christ!

We bishops prayerfully entrust all families to Mary, the mother of Jesus and mother of the Church. We ask St. Joseph to guide you in all the ways of faithfulness.

Notes

1. John Paul II, *On the Family (Familiaris Consortio)* (Washington, D.C.: United States Catholic Conference, 1981), no. 86.
2. Ibid.
3. Paul VI, *On the Regulation of Birth (Humanae Vitae)* (Washington, D.C.: United States Catholic Conference, 1968), no. 9.
4. *Familiaris Consortio,* no. 14.
5. Ibid.
6. John Paul II, *On the Dignity and Vocation of Women (Mulieris Dignitatem)* (Washington, D.C.: United States Catholic Conference, 1988), no. 6.
7. *Humanae Vitae,* no. 21.
8. *Familiaris Consortio,* no. 27.

Source: Washington, D.C.: United States Catholic Conference, 1994.

A Message to Youth: Pathway to Hope

*A Statement of the NCCB Committee on the Laity
and the Subcommittee on Youth*

October 1994

Dear young people,

In you, we see the face of God. You are the young Church of today and our hope for the future. You are a mosaic of life reflecting the diversity of our nation and Church. You are truly a gift, and we praise and thank God for you. You are a special gift to the Church and to the world!

We bishops write to you as teachers and pastors because of the one faith which we share with you. We have great confidence in you because of who you are today and what you can become tomorrow. We see and hear how you put your beliefs into action by standing up for the sacredness of human life and the dignity of the individual, by working with the poor and reaching out to those who struggle through life. We see you as leaders among both your peers and the parish community. From the times we have been together, we vividly recall your enthusiasm and energy and your support for us and the priests, deacons, religious, and lay people who work with you.

In this letter, we want to talk about three aspects of life: who you are, where you belong, and the challenges and opportunities you will face.

Who Am I? Gifted and Loved—Made in the Image and Likeness of God

You are made in the image and likeness of God. You are loved by God and others! Listen to the words of the psalmist: "Truly you have formed my inmost being; you knit me in my mother's womb. I give you thanks that I am fearfully, wonderfully made; wonderful are your works" (Ps 139:13-14).

The teenage years present many challenges—you know this well. At times you can feel pressure from parents and school to be the perfect athlete, the perfect student, the perfect son or daughter, the perfect musician. Some of you feel the pressure from peers to wear the right clothes, buy the right things, or join the right group. Others face challenges such as alcohol, drugs, loneliness, despair, or physical/sexual abuse. Racism and prejudice can close the door and harden the hearts of many. Poverty and inadequate education can dim the light of your future.

We know, too, that many of you work hard to keep your priorities in order. We commit ourselves to helping you meet the difficult challenges and ask you to look to Jesus Christ to give meaning to the struggles and pain in your life. The good news of the Gospel is that God loves you unconditionally. You don't need to be anyone other than yourself. Those who truly love you accept you for who you are and will challenge you to be a better person.

We also realize that adolescence is a time for examining your moral and religious beliefs and for the reaffirmation of your baptismal commitment. Many of you have grown stronger in faith through this searching, while some of you continue to grapple with your faith. Know that we support you through the many youth activities sponsored by the diocese, the parishes, and the schools and pray for you daily at liturgy as you struggle to grow in faith and to embrace a Christian lifestyle.

God, our Father, invites you to discover the meaning of life centered in Jesus Christ. This conviction provides a foundation for your life. It gives you values and beliefs that can keep your dreams alive as you face the many challenges of life. Look to Jesus and his values: honesty, generosity, compassion, chastity, kindness, tolerance, justice, respect for all life, and peacemaking. These are the gospel values which will bring you true happiness and manifest God's love for the world.

Where Do I Belong? Your Family and the Catholic Community

Two communities that can help you through life are your family and your parish. They are two ways of being part of the body of Christ. Friends also play a significant role in your life. Friends provide affirmation, companionship, and a listening ear. A true friend is willing to challenge you to be a person of integrity.

Your family is an important relationship in your life where you should find nourishment and unconditional love. Enjoy the time with your family, as you do with your friends. Get to know your parents, brothers, and sisters as "friends," not just as family. Invite your friends to be part of your family.

Sadly, for some people, the family is not what it should be. There are many hurting families that need our love, support, and prayers. We know that your relationship to your family can be difficult at times. Many adolescents desire some independence from their families, while others do not receive the guidance and support that they need from their parents. While you seek independence, please don't cut yourself off from the love and care of your family.

Your parish community can also be a place where you find wisdom, direction, and support. The parish reaffirms the values taught by your family and instills other values. Your parish should be a place where you are welcomed, grow in Jesus Christ, and minister side by side with the adults of the community. You know the truth when you hear it. You know God's love when you experience it. In your parish community, you will hear God's word and sense God's presence. We encourage you to invite other young people to hear God's word and sense God's presence in our Catholic communities. Through you, they can meet Jesus, their brother.

We invite you to experience parish life by celebrating the eucharist and the other sacraments, especially the sacrament of reconciliation; by being active participants in the liturgy as lectors, eucharistic ministers, acolytes, and liturgical musicians; by working with parish service and social outreach programs; by attending religious education sessions; and by participating in parish youth ministry activities, especially retreats. Teenage years can be filled with questions and doubts. Participating in these parish programs and activities can help you cope with these questions and concerns.

A most important aspect of your faith development is the knowledge you will gain by reading the Bible and studying the teachings and tradition of the Church. Read the Bible—it is the story of God's love for us and our response to that love.

Your parish should have programs for you that recognize your special talents and role in the life of the Church. You bring to the parish community youthfulness, energy, vitality, hopefulness, and vision. Don't be afraid to share these wonderful traits and talents, and don't be discouraged if you don't always get the welcome you'd like to get. Sadly, we must admit that not all of our parishes make young people feel welcome, but this is part of your mission—to help parish leaders see how you can be a wonderful presence and resource for the parish.

If you live in an area touched by violence or similar problems, your parish should be a safe haven for you and advocate for your needs, assuring a measure of hope. In all parishes, you can find excellent role models and mentors—they can walk the journey with you, listen to you, and give you guidance.

What Am I to Do with My Life?
Be Disciples of Jesus Christ!

As a baptized member of the Church, Jesus Christ calls you to follow in his footsteps and make a difference in the world today. You *can* make a difference! See how God's grace has worked in people like Mother Teresa, Pope John Paul II, Archbishop Oscar Romero, Martin Luther King, Elizabeth Ann Seton, and people in your own family or community and how it has inspired them to do great things by living the Christian life. In the words of our Holy Father: "Offer your youthful energies and your talents to building a civilization of Christian love . . . commit yourself to the struggle for justice, solidarity, and peace."[1]

You can make a difference *now*, and some of you already do—at home, in school, with your friends, and at after-school jobs. You can do this by treating all people justly and with respect; by being a voice for the voiceless, especially the unborn; by being a peaceful person in your language and actions; by sharing your time, talent, and money with your family and those in need; by being a friend to those who are lonely or shunned; by being a healer and reconciler when conflicts arise; by helping friends do the right thing; and by valuing people who are different from you—people of different cultures, people who are disabled, people who think differently from you. When you do these things you will make the world—your family, school, community—a better place, a place where Jesus Christ dwells. We're not saying it will be easy. You may be misunderstood and ridiculed at times, but you will never be alone. Christ and the Christian community walk with you.

We invite you to know Jesus Christ as a companion and friend, teacher and savior, and to discover what he has to offer as you live your life today. See in Jesus Christ the one God-man whose life gives meaning to the joys and sufferings of millions of people over thousands of years. See in Jesus Christ the one who can help you live your life to the fullest! "I came so that you may have life and have it more abundantly" (Jn 10:10).

Remember, you can make the world a better place. As the Lord told Jeremiah, "You are not too young!" (Jer 1:7). Take up our Holy Father's challenge to go out into the streets and, like the apostles, preach the gospel message of Christ. We promise that we will walk with you as Jesus does. We will work with you for justice and peace in your schools, in your families, and with your friends. We will stand by you in the future in carrying out your vocation as parents, priests and religious, teachers, homemakers, factory and construction workers, managers, nurses, or whatever God calls you to be in this world. We end our message with the words of our Holy Father: "For me, I'll make my own the words of St. Paul. I have great confidence in you, I have great pride in you; I am filled with encouragement, I am overflowing with joy (cf. 2 Cor 7:4). So much depends on you."[2]

Notes

1.   John Paul II, Homily at Immaculate Conception Cathedral, Denver, *Origins* 23:11 (August 26, 1993): 193.
2.   John Paul II, Homily at Cherry Creek State Park, *Origins* 23:11 (August 26, 1993): 179.

Source: Washington, D.C.: United States Catholic Conference, 1995.

Strengthening the Bonds of Peace

A Pastoral Reflection of the National Conference of Catholic Bishops on Women in the Church and in Society

November 1994

Earlier this year the Holy Father issued the apostolic letter *Ordinatio Sacerdotalis*, reaffirming the teaching and practice that priestly ordination is restricted to men. We bishops recognize this clear reaffirmation of Catholic teaching as a pastoral service to the whole Church, and we accept that it be definitively held by all the faithful.[1] This letter also reiterated the "necessary and irreplaceable" role of women in the Church.

Some people received the letter with joy and peace. Others found acceptance difficult. We encourage all our brothers and sisters, through prayer, study, and dialogue, to accept and seek to understand more fully the teaching that *Ordinatio Sacerdotalis* reaffirms.

This brief reflection reaches out to all. It is an invitation to strengthen the bonds of peace and cultivate the unity that the Spirit gives (Eph 4:3). For certainly all can agree that peace is a blessing we long for—peace in our hearts, in our homes, in our Church, and in our world.

Peace, we know, is more than the absence of conflict. Peace comes about when we, as members of Christ's Church, respect the dignity of each person, when we welcome the gifts and competencies of all people, when we respect differences, and when we work together to build the reign of God. We will work to bring about this peaceful climate where we can assess and respond to challenges of all kinds.

We can begin by embracing three principles. First, in the words of Pope Paul VI: "If you want peace, work for justice."[2] Second, peacemaking needs to focus on the present and future. We know that people have suffered greatly in the past—for example, from racism and sexism—but we know that these evils must not continue to hold people hostage. As Christians, we look toward the future. Third, in the world at large we have seen that honest, open, sustained dialogue is indispensable for bringing about genuine peace. We believe this same kind of dialogue is necessary in the Church. We offer this message, then, as one moment in a developing dialogue, with the hope that all women and men of the Church will receive it as such and continue as participants in what can be a sacred conversation for all of us.

As characteristics for that dialogue we draw on the wisdom of Pope Paul VI. In his first encyclical, *Ecclesiam Suam,* he said that dialogue, which he spoke of as spiritual communication, is marked by (1) clear, understandable language; (2) meekness, a virtue that makes our dialogue peaceful and patient; (3) trust between speaker and the listener; and (4) sensitivity to the situation and needs of the hearer.[3]

With Pope Paul VI's words in mind, we consider these points: leadership in the Church, equality of women and men, and diversity of gifts. Confident that the Holy Spirit will guide us in the way of peace and justice, we invite all women and men in the Church to join in this dialogue.

Leadership

Strengthened by the teaching reaffirmed in *Ordinatio Sacerdotalis,* we need to look at alternative ways in which women can exercise leadership in the Church. We welcome this leadership, which in some ways is already a reality, and we commit ourselves to enhancing the participation of women in every possible aspect of church life. We are especially concerned that women from different ethnic groups be drawn more fully into this participation.

Today, throughout the world, women hold positions of exacting leadership, as heads of government, judges, research doctors, symphony conductors, and business executives. They serve as presidents at Catholic colleges and universities and as administrators and faculty members at Catholic colleges and seminaries. They are also chief executives of Catholic hospitals and executive directors of Catholic Charities. An increasing number of Catholic theologians are women. Some women serve the diocesan churches as school superintendents and chancellors, as archivists and members of marriage tribunals. More and more women have responsible national positions in the Catholic Church.

Locally, we can see in our parishes the scope of women's leadership: in various liturgical ministries, including altar servers and proclaiming the word before the assembly; in pastoral ministry and administration; in religious education and teaching in schools; in peace and justice activities; in outreach to the homebound and the hospitalized. One recent study shows that 85 percent of non-ordained ministerial positions in parishes are now held by women.[4]

We know that women's gifts have tremendously improved the quality of parish ministry. Looking to the future, we especially want to encourage women to pursue studies in Scripture, theology, and canon law, not only that the Church may benefit from their skills in these areas but that they themselves may benefit from their own scholarly efforts.

An important issue for women is how to have a voice in the governance of the Church to which they belong and which they serve with love and generosity. This can be achieved in at least two ways that are consistent with church teaching: through consultation and through cooperation in the exercise of authority.[5]

As recently as July 1994, Pope John Paul II reiterated the need for the consultative expertise of women, saying: "Qualified women can make a great contribution of wisdom and moderation, courage and dedication, spirituality and fervor for the good of the Church."[6] We need to seek ways to honor this call at every level of the Church, from the parish to the diocese to the national offices that are involved in drafting official church documents for our conference of bishops. As a specific example of this consultative role, we cite the participation of women in the development of pastoral and missionary statements, as called for in the apostolic exhortation on the laity, *Christifideles Laici.*[7]

Consultation is already occurring in a number of ways, of course. Parish and diocesan pastoral and finance councils are vehicles for engaging the gifts of lay women and men as important decisions are crafted. While final decision making rests with the pastor, the *Code of Canon Law* urges consultation even in areas not strictly required. We encourage such consultation. We note, too, that commissions on women, now present in many dioceses, allow for women's concerns to be expressed and their expertise to be utilized.

Second, the *Code of Canon Law*, while situating the foundation of jurisdiction in the sacrament of holy orders, nevertheless allows for the possibility of lay women and men cooperating in the exercise of this power in accord with the norm of law (canon 129). This may be a graced moment in the life of the Church that enables us to take a fresh and deeper look at the relationship between jurisdiction and ordained ministry, and thus gain a better understanding of legislative, executive, and judicial acts within the Church.[8] We strongly urge that the studies which are underway on this issue be pursued; and we urge canonists to make widely known the provisions in the *Code of Canon Law* for the participation of women in the life and mission of the Church.[9]

Change occurs through knowledge and understanding. While all change is not progress, a thoroughly informed laity can only benefit the Church as it seeks to promote dialogue inside and outside the Church. To enhance the dialogue, we invite ecclesiologists and other theologians to join with us to explore new and creative ways in which women can participate in church leadership.

Leadership involves servanthood; we learn this from the example of the head of the Church, Jesus Christ. What does it mean for leaders—ordained and lay—to model this truth? Obviously it will mean rejecting authoritarian conduct. But it will also mean giving time and energy to fostering community life where men and women are called forth and accepted as vital collaborators in the work of evangelization, social justice, teaching, administration, and governance. The collaboration of women and men as equal partners in this servant leadership is a "sign of that interpersonal communion of love which constitutes the mystical, intimate life of God, One in Three."[10]

We welcome, too, women's leadership in more traditional areas, e.g., in advocacy for church and societal policies that support just remuneration for women; in establishing a "family wage" to increase the possibility that at least one parent can remain at home during the child's early years; in pro-life efforts that seek justice for the unborn and compassion and assistance for pregnant women in difficult circumstances; in advocating quality child care for employed women; in action to stem the tide of domestic violence against women; in adherence to a family perspective in institutions, programs, and policies of Church and society. Furthermore, we encourage men to join women in these efforts which are needed for strengthening the family, the parish, and the civic community.

We pledge our partnership in all these endeavors. In no way should these commitments be construed as "ecclesial political correctness"; they are theologically correct. They are rooted in our baptism and in our understanding of the Holy Spirit who works in the Church to build it up through the gifts of its members.

Having looked at women's leadership in the Church, we now turn to two realities that make this leadership possible: the equality of men and women and the diversity of gifts among God's people.

Equality

We reaffirm the fundamental equality of women and men who, created in the image of God, "are called to participate in the same divine beatitude [and] . . . therefore enjoy an equal dignity."[11] What we said of marriage and family life in our pastoral message *Follow the Way of Love* applies to other expressions of church life as well. In that message we pointed out that equality does not imply sameness in roles or expectations, nor does it mean that two spouses will have identical gifts or character. Rather, they will respect each other's gifts and identity. In this "domestic church" we see a spirit and practice of mutuality, a sharing of power and exercising of responsibility for a purpose larger than oneself, that is, for God's purpose.

The domestic church reminds us that all women and men must take seriously the need to listen to one another, to try to understand one another, including an appreciation of the different forms of authority. These lessons of the domestic church, especially concerning relationships, should be reflected in the experience and behavior of the gathered Church. For example, the pastor of a parish has the authority of office, while the lay man or woman will often have a particular competence or knowledge, a specific authority that complements the pastor's. The challenge is for all authority to be exercised for the well-being of the community and the effectiveness of the Church's mission.

To meet such a challenge requires a mature spirituality that understands and practices the virtue of humility. We admit that humility is often misunderstood, and we are sensitive to women's concerns that it not be misused to justify the suppression of women's voices. We stress that all of us are called to "be subordinate to one another out of reverence for Christ" (Eph 5:21). Humility must be practiced mutually by all the faithful, ordained and lay. This mutuality is rooted in an authentic respect for the dignity of each person and our call to belong to one another in the body of Christ.

We can say with certainty that discrimination against women contradicts the will of Christ. We are painfully aware that sexism, defined as "unjust discrimination based on sex,"[12] is still present in some members of the Church. We reject sexism and pledge renewed efforts to guard against it in church teaching and practice. We further reject extreme positions on women's issues which impede dialogue and divide the Church. We commit ourselves to make sure that our words and actions express our belief in the equality of all women and men.

Diversity of Gifts

In St. Paul's Letter to the Ephesians we read, "Grace was given to each of us according to the measure of Christ's gift . . . some as apostles, others as prophets, others as evangelists, others as pastors and teachers, to equip the holy ones for the work of ministry, for building up the body of Christ, until we all attain to the unity of faith and knowledge of the Son of God . . . to the extent of the full stature of Christ" (Eph 4:7, 11-13).

The Church better fulfills its mission when the gifts of *all* its members are engaged as fully as possible. Women are essential in ministry both within the Church and to the world. The diversity of women's gifts and talents should be celebrated. Different voices, different experiences and perspectives, and different methodologies help the Gospel to be proclaimed and received with freshness. The majority of women exercise their gifts in the home, in the workplace, and in civic leadership. In addition, many are now trained and skilled in spiritual direction, in the leadership of prayer groups, and in the study of Scripture. They are educated and formed for pastoral ministry in parishes. Some are psychologists who are also trained in theology. These gifts are essential in a world where the inner peace of so many has been shattered. Spouses in troubled marriages, families affected by abortion, adult children from dysfunctional families, lonely youth, people of all ages who feel isolated and alienated—all need healing.

Countless men and women long for help in the ways of prayer. They seek to be in touch with God in the depths of their souls. We see so many women engaged in meeting these spiritual needs, and we thank God for these gifts to the Church.

We are grateful, too, that many women possess leadership and organizational skills which, although often underutilized in the past, are now coming to the fore. We urge pastors to recognize and to continue to call forth the distinct contributions that women can make to the Church and to the world. Diversity of gifts in the service of Christ is not to be feared or suppressed but recognized as a sign of the Church's vitality and ongoing renewal.

Concluding Words: The True Face of the Church

In *Ordinatio Sacerdotalis* Pope John Paul II emphasizes that "[the role of women] is of capital importance . . . for the rediscovery by believers of the true face of the Church."[13] We have seen that the true face of the Church appears only when and if we recognize the equal dignity of men and women and consistently act on that recognition. It is this face, shaped through the centuries, that is visible to the world. From the beginning, women have been essential to this visage: from Mary, the mother of Jesus, and the women of the early Church, through the martyrs, through the doctors of the Church—St. Teresa of Avila and St. Catherine of Siena—to the women closer to our own time, such as St. Elizabeth Seton, Blessed Kateri Tekakwitha, Dorothy Day, Mother Teresa, and Sr. Thea Bowman, who have graced the Church in both traditional and new ways.

Still, the face of the Church reveals the pain that many women experience. At times this pain results from the flawed behavior of human beings—clergy and lay—when we attempt to dominate each other. Women also experience pain because of persistent sexism. At times this sexism is unconscious, the result of inadequate reflection. A Church that is deepening its consciousness of itself, that is trying to project the image of Christ to the world, will understand the need for ongoing, prayerful reflection in this area.

One example of the need for ongoing reflection concerns the use of language. While inclusive language is becoming a concern in many areas of the world, it has a particular importance in the English-speaking world, especially in North America. Our conference of bishops continues to be engaged in the study of scriptural, doctrinal, and liturgical translations, a highly technical and complex task. Moreover, since the Holy Father has indicated that catechetical and pastoral materials that evolve from the *Catechism of the Catholic Church* could reflect the culture, language, and idiom of a given country, we urge that catechetical and religious materials and hymnals, as well as our daily language and prayer, honor the concerns that shape a more inclusive language, while taking care to ensure that they do not become a source of division, anger, and hurt. This can be accomplished if our conversation within the Church is "full of faith, of charity, of good works, [and is] intimate, and familiar."[14]

For many years a dialogue among women and between women and men took place in the Church in the United States, as we tried to write a pastoral letter that would capture the vast range of concerns expressed by women. The pastoral letter was not approved, but the concluding recommendations were sent to the Executive Committee of the National Conference of Catholic Bishops for action by various conference committees. We bishops pledge ourselves anew, through our committee structure, to continue the dialogue in a spirit of partnership and mutual trust and to implement the recommendations where possible.

To be committed to honest dialogue is no easy task. As Pope Paul VI noted, "In the dialogue one discovers how different are the ways which lead to the light of faith, and how it is possible to make them converge on the same goal. Even if these ways are divergent, they can become complementary by forcing our reasoning process out of the worn paths and by obliging it to deepen its research, to find fresh expressions."[15] As we search together for truth, it is critical that we draw upon the insights of contemporary scholarship in a wide variety of disciplines—Scripture, anthropology, history, women's studies, and systematic theology.

We pray that others will join us as we listen to one another and learn. For our part we take as our own the words of Pope Paul VI: "The dialogue will make us wise; it will make us teachers."[16] Once again, we urge the Church at all levels to establish structures to hear and respond to the concerns of women.

Pope John Paul II has chosen "Women: Educators for Peace" as the theme for the 1995 World Day of Peace, pointing out what women have done, and continue to do, on behalf of peace. While we know that conflict and disagreement often mark the road to peace, we also know that women's energy is a positive force for the good of Church and society. With our Holy Father, we thank God for our sister peacemakers and pray that God will guide us all in the ways of patience, love, unity, justice, and peace.

Notes

1. John Paul II, *Reserving Priestly Ordination to Men Alone (Ordinatio Sacerdotalis)* (Washington, D.C.: United States Catholic Conference, 1994).
2. Paul VI, "Message of His Holiness Pope Paul VI for the Celebration of the Day of Peace (January 1, 1972)," *Origins* 1:29 (January 6, 1972): 490-491.
3. Paul VI, "Paths of the Church," *(Ecclesiam Suam), The Pope Speaks* 10 (1964): 28, no. 81.
4. Philip Murnion, *New Parish Ministers* (New York: National Pastoral Life Center, 1992).
5. Canon 129 states: (1) In accord with the prescriptions of law, those who have received sacred orders are capable of the power of governance, which exists in the Church by divine institution and is also called the power of jurisdiction; (2) Lay members of the Christian faithful can cooperate in the exercise of this power in accord with the norm of law.
6. Catholic News Service, July 13, 1994.
7. John Paul II, *The Vocation and the Mission of the Lay Faithful in the Church and in the World (Christifideles Laici)* (Washington, D.C.: United States Catholic Conference, 1988), no. 51.
8. See *Code of Canon Law,* canon 135.
9. The Committee on Canonical Affairs, National Conference of Catholic Bishops, is currently sponsoring such a study.
10. *Christifideles Laici,* no. 52.
11. *Catechism of the Catholic Church* (Washington, D.C.: United States Catholic Conference, 1994), no. 1934.
12. NCCB Ad Hoc Committee for a Pastoral Response to Women's Concerns, *One in Christ Jesus: Toward a Pastoral Response to the Concerns of Women for Church and Society,* committee report (Washington, D.C.: United States Catholic Conference, 1992), no. 12.
13. Congregation for the Doctrine of the Faith, *Declaration on the Admission of Women to the Ministerial Priesthood (Inter Insigniores), Acta Apostolicae Sedis* 69 (1977): 115-116, no. 6. Quoted in *Ordinatio Sacerdotalis,* no. 3. English trans. of *Inter Insigniores* in *Origins* 6:33 (February 3, 1977): 517-524.
14. *Ecclesiam Suam,* no. 113.
15. Ibid., no. 83.
16. Ibid.

Source: Washington, D.C.: United States Catholic Conference, 1995.

Ethical and Religious Directives for Catholic Health Care Services

A Statement of the National Conference of Catholic Bishops

November 1994

Preamble

Health care in the United States is marked by extraordinary change. Not only is there continuing change in clinical practice due to technological advances, but the health care system in the United States is being challenged by both institutional and social factors as well. At the same time, there are a number of developments within the Catholic Church affecting the ecclesial mission of health care. Among these are significant changes in religious orders and congregations, the increased involvement of lay men and women, a heightened awareness of the Church's social role in the world, and developments in moral theology since the Second Vatican Council. A contemporary understanding of the Catholic health care ministry must take into account the new challenges presented by transitions both in the Church and in American society.

Throughout the centuries, with the aid of other sciences, a body of moral principles has emerged that expresses the Church's teaching on medical and moral matters and has proven to be pertinent and applicable to the ever-changing circumstances of health care and its delivery. In response to today's challenges, these same moral principles of Catholic teaching provide the rationale and direction for this revision of the *Ethical and Religious Directives for Catholic Health Care Services.*

These directives presuppose our statement *Health and Health Care* published in 1981.[1] There we presented the theological principles that guide the Church's vision of health care, called for all Catholics to share in the healing mission of the Church, expressed our full commitment to the health care ministry, and offered encouragement to all those who are involved in it. Now, with American health care facing even more dramatic changes, we reaffirm the Church's commitment to health care ministry and the distinctive Catholic identity of the Church's institutional health care services.[2] The purpose of these *Ethical and Religious Directives* then is twofold: first, to reaffirm the ethical standards of behavior in health care that flow from the Church's teaching about the dignity of the human person; second, to provide authoritative guidance on certain moral issues that face Catholic health care today.

The *Ethical and Religious Directives* are concerned primarily with institutionally based Catholic health care services. They address the sponsors, trustees, administrators, chaplains, physicians, health care personnel, and patients or residents of these institutions and services. Since they express the Church's moral teaching, these directives also will be helpful to Catholic professionals engaged in health care services in other settings. The moral teachings that we profess here flow principally from the natural law, understood in the light of the revelation Christ has entrusted to his Church. From this source the Church has derived its understanding of the nature of the human person, of human acts, and of the goals that shape human activity.

The directives have been refined through an extensive process of consultation with bishops, theologians, sponsors, administrators, physicians, and other health care providers. While providing standards and guidance, the directives do not cover in detail all of the complex issues that confront Catholic health care today. Moreover, the directives will be reviewed periodically by the National Conference of Catholic Bishops, in the light of authoritative church teaching, in order to address new insights from theological and medical research or new requirements of public policy.

The directives begin with a general introduction that presents a theological basis for the Catholic health care ministry. Each of the six parts that follow is divided into two sections. The first section is in expository form; it serves as an introduction and provides the context in which concrete issues can be discussed from the perspective of the Catholic faith. The second section is in prescriptive form; the directives promote and protect the truths of the Catholic faith as those truths are brought to bear on concrete issues in health care.

General Introduction

The Church has always sought to embody our Savior's concern for the sick. The gospel accounts of Jesus' ministry draw special attention to his acts of healing: he cleansed a man with leprosy (Mt 8:1-4; Mk 1:40-42); he gave sight to two people who were blind (Mt 20:29-34; Mk 10:46-52); he enabled one who was mute to speak (Lk 11:14); he cured a woman who was hemorrhaging (Mt 9:20-22; Mk 5:25-34); and he brought a young girl back to life (Mt 9:18, 23-25; Mk 5:35-42). Indeed, the Gospels are replete with examples of how the Lord cured every kind of ailment and disease (Mt 9:35). In the account of Matthew, Jesus' mission fulfilled the prophecy of Isaiah: "He took away our infirmities and bore our diseases" (Mt 8:17; cf. Is 53:4).

Jesus' healing mission went further than caring only for physical affliction. He touched people at the deepest level of their existence; he sought their physical, mental, and spiritual healing (Jn 6:35; 11:25-27). He "came so that they might have life and have it more abundantly" (Jn 10:10).

The mystery of Christ casts light on every facet of Catholic health care: to see Christian love as the animating principle of health care; to see healing and compassion as a continuation of Christ's mission; to see suffering as a participation in the redemptive power of Christ's passion, death, and resurrection; and to see death, transformed by the resurrection, as an opportunity for a final act of communion with Christ.

For the Christian, our encounter with suffering and death can take on a positive and distinctive meaning through the redemptive power of Jesus' suffering and death. As St. Paul says, we are "always carrying about in the body the dying of Jesus, so that the life of Jesus may also be manifested in our body" (2 Cor 4:10). This truth does not lessen the pain and fear, but gives confidence and grace for bearing suffering rather than being overwhelmed by it. Catholic health care ministry bears witness to the truth that, for those who are in Christ, suffering and death are the birth pangs of the new creation. "God himself will always be with them. He will wipe every tear from their eyes and there shall be no more death or mourning, wailing or pain, for the old order has passed away" (Rev 21:3-4).

In faithful imitation of Jesus Christ, the Church has served the sick, suffering, and dying in various ways throughout history. The zealous service of individuals and communities has provided shelter for the traveler; infirmaries for the sick; and homes for children, adults, and the elderly.[3] In the United States, the many religious communities as well as dioceses that sponsor and staff this country's Catholic health care institutions and services have established an effective Catholic presence in health care. Modeling their efforts on the gospel parable of the Good Samaritan, these communities of women and men have exemplified authentic neighborliness to those in need (Lk 10:25-37). The Church seeks to ensure that the service offered in the past will be continued into the future.

While many religious communities continue their commitment to the health care ministry, lay Catholics increasingly have stepped forward to collaborate in this ministry. Inspired by the example of Christ and mandated by the Second Vatican Council, lay faithful are invited to a broader and more intense field of ministries than in the past.[4] By virtue of their baptism, lay faithful are called to participate actively in the Church's life and mission.[5] Their participation and leadership in the health care ministry, through new forms of sponsorship and governance of institutional Catholic health care, are essential for the Church to continue her ministry of healing and compassion. They are joined in the Church's health care mission by many men and women who are not Catholic.

Catholic health care expresses the healing ministry of Christ in a specific way within the local Church. Here the diocesan bishop exercises responsibilities that are rooted in his office as pastor, teacher, and priest. As the center of unity in the diocese and coordinator of ministries in the local Church, the diocesan bishop fosters the mission of Catholic health care in a way that promotes collaboration among health care leaders, providers, medical professionals, theologians, and other specialists. As pastor, the diocesan bishop is in a unique position to encourage the faithful to greater responsibility in the healing ministry of the Church. As teacher, the diocesan bishop ensures the moral and religious identity of the health care ministry in whatever setting it is carried out in the diocese. As priest, the diocesan bishop oversees the sacramental care of the sick. These responsibilities will require that Catholic health care providers and the diocesan bishop engage in ongoing communication on ethical and pastoral matters that require his attention.

In a time of new medical discoveries, rapid technological developments, and social change, what is new can either be an opportunity for genuine advance in human culture, or it can lead to policies and actions that are contrary to the true dignity and vocation of the human person. In consultation with medical professionals, church leaders review these developments, judge them according to the principles of right reason and the ultimate standard of revealed truth, and offer authoritative teaching and guidance about the moral and pastoral responsibilities entailed by the Christian faith.[6] While the Church cannot furnish a ready answer to every moral dilemma, there are many questions about which she provides normative guidance and direction. In the absence of a determination by the magisterium, but never contrary to church teaching, the guidance of approved authors can offer appropriate guidance for ethical decision making.

Created in God's image and likeness, the human family shares in the dominion that Christ manifested in his healing ministry. This sharing involves a stewardship over all material creation (Gn 1:26) that should neither abuse nor squander nature's resources. Through science the human race comes to understand God's wonderful work; and through technology it must conserve, protect, and perfect nature in harmony with God's purposes. Health care professionals pursue a special vocation to share in carrying forth God's life-giving and healing work.

The dialogue between medical science and Christian faith has for its primary purpose the common good of all human persons. It presupposes that science and faith do not contradict each other. Both are grounded in respect for truth and freedom. As new knowledge and new technologies expand, each person must form a correct conscience based on the moral norms for proper health care.

Part One: The Social Responsibility of Catholic Health Care Services

Introduction

Their embrace of Christ's healing mission has led institutionally based Catholic health care services in the United States to become an integral part of the nation's health care system. Today, this complex health care system confronts a range of economic, technological, social, and moral challenges. The response of Catholic health care institutions and services to these challenges is guided by normative principles that inform the Church's healing ministry.

First, Catholic health care ministry is rooted in a commitment to promote and defend human dignity; this is the foundation of its concern to respect the sacredness of every human life from the moment of conception until death. The first right of the human person, the right to life, entails a right to the means for the proper development of life, such as adequate health care.[7]

Second, the biblical mandate to care for the poor requires us to express this in concrete action at all levels of Catholic health care. This mandate prompts us to work to ensure that our country's health care delivery system provides adequate health care for the poor. In Catholic institutions, particular attention should be given to the health care needs of the poor, the uninsured, and the underinsured.[8]

Third, Catholic health care ministry seeks to contribute to the common good. The common good is realized when economic, political, and social conditions ensure protection for the fundamental rights of all individuals and enable all to fulfill their common purpose and reach their common goals.[9]

Fourth, Catholic health care ministry exercises responsible stewardship of available health care resources. A just health care system will be concerned both with promoting equity of care—to assure that the right of each person to basic health care is respected—and with promoting the good health of all in the community. The responsible stewardship of health care resources can be accomplished best in dialogue with people from all levels of society, in accordance with the principle of subsidiarity and with respect for the moral principles that guide institutions and persons.

Fifth, within a pluralistic society, Catholic health care services will encounter requests for medical procedures contrary to the moral teachings of the Church. Catholic health care does not offend the rights of individual conscience by refusing to provide or permit medical procedures that are judged morally wrong by the teaching authority of the Church.

Directives

1. A Catholic institutional health care service is a community that provides health care to those in need of it. This service must be animated by the Gospel of Jesus Christ and guided by the moral tradition of the Church.

2. Catholic health care should be marked by a spirit of mutual respect among care-givers which disposes them to deal with those it serves and their families with the compassion of Christ, sensitive to their vulnerability at a time of special need.

3. In accord with its mission, Catholic health care should distinguish itself by service to and advocacy for those people whose social condition puts them at the margins of our society and makes them particularly vulnerable to discrimination: the poor; the uninsured, and the underinsured; children and the unborn; single parents; the elderly; those with incurable diseases and chemical dependencies; racial minorities; immigrants and refugees. In particular, the person with mental or physical disabilities, regardless of the cause or severity, must be treated as a unique person of incomparable worth, with the same right to life and to adequate health care as all other persons.

4. A Catholic health care institution, especially a teaching hospital, will promote medical research consistent with its mission of providing health care and with concern for the responsible stewardship of health care resources. Such medical research must adhere to Catholic moral principles.

5. Catholic health care services must adopt these directives as policy, require adherence to them within the institution as a condition for medical privileges and employment, and provide appropriate instruction regarding the directives for administration, medical and nursing staff, and other personnel.

6. A Catholic health care organization should be a responsible steward of the health care resources available to it. Collaboration with other health care providers, in ways that do not compromise Catholic social and moral teaching, can be an effective means of such stewardship.[10]

7. A Catholic health care institution must treat its employees respectfully and justly. This responsibility includes equal employment opportunities for anyone qualified for the task, irrespective of a person's race, sex, age, national origin, or disability; a workplace that promotes employee participation; a

work environment that ensures employee safety and well-being; just compensation and benefits; and recognition of the rights of employees to organize and bargain collectively without prejudice to the common good.

8. Catholic health care institutions have a unique relationship to both the Church and the wider community they serve. Because of the ecclesial nature of this relationship, the relevant requirements of canon law will be observed with regard to the foundation of a new Catholic health care institution; the substantial revision of the mission of an institution; and the sale, sponsorship transfer, or the closure of an existing institution.

9. Employees of a Catholic health care institution must respect and uphold the religious mission of the institution and adhere to these directives. They should maintain professional standards and promote the institution's commitment to human dignity and the common good.

Part Two: The Pastoral and Spiritual Responsibility of Catholic Health Care

Introduction

The dignity of human life flows from creation in the image of God (Gn 1:26), from redemption by Jesus Christ (Eph 1:10; 1 Tm 2:4-6), and from our common destiny to share a life with God beyond all corruption (1 Cor 15:42-57). Catholic health care has the responsibility to treat those in need in a way that respects the human dignity and eternal destiny of all. The words of Christ have provided inspiration for Catholic health care: "I was ill and you cared for me" (Mt 25:36). The care provided assists those in need to experience their own dignity and value, especially when these are obscured by the burdens of illness or the anxiety of imminent death.

Since a Catholic health care institution is a community of healing and compassion, the care offered is not limited to the treatment of a disease or bodily ailment but embraces the physical, psychological, social, and spiritual dimensions of the human person. The medical expertise offered through Catholic health care is combined with other forms of care to promote health and relieve human suffering. For this reason, Catholic health care extends to the spiritual nature of the person. "Without health of the spirit, high technology focused strictly on the body offers limited hope for healing the whole person."[11] Directed to spiritual needs that are often appreciated more deeply during times of illness, pastoral care is an integral part of Catholic health care. Pastoral care encompasses the full range of spiritual services, including a listening presence; help in dealing with powerlessness, pain, and alienation; and assistance in recognizing and responding to God's will with greater joy and peace. It should be acknowledged, of course, that technological advances in medicine have reduced the length of hospital stays dramatically. It follows, therefore, that the pastoral care of patients, especially administration of the sacraments, will be provided more often than not at the parish level, both before and after one's hospitalization. For this reason, it is essential that there be very cordial and cooperative relationships between the personnel of pastoral care departments and the local clergy and ministers of care.

Priests, deacons, religious, and laity exercise diverse but complementary roles in this pastoral care. Since many areas of pastoral care call upon the creative response of these pastoral care-givers to the particular needs of patients or residents, the following directives address only a limited number of specific pastoral activities.

Directives

10. A Catholic health care organization should provide pastoral care to minister to the religious and spiritual needs of all those it serves. Pastoral care personnel—clergy, religious, and lay alike—should have appropriate professional preparation, including an understanding of these directives.

11. Pastoral care personnel should work in close collaboration with local parishes and community clergy. Appropriate pastoral services and/or referrals should be available to all in keeping with their religious beliefs or affiliation.

12. For Catholic patients or residents, provision for the sacraments is an especially important part of Catholic health care ministry. Every effort should be made to have priests assigned to hospitals and health care institutions to celebrate the eucharist and provide the sacraments to patients and staff.

13. Particular care should be taken to provide and to publicize opportunities for patients or residents to receive the sacrament of penance.

14. Properly prepared lay Catholics can be appointed to serve as extraordinary ministers of holy communion, in accordance with canon law and the policies of the local diocese. They should assist pastoral care personnel—clergy, religious, and laity—by providing supportive visits, advising patients regarding the availability of priests for the sacrament of penance, and distributing holy communion to the faithful who request it.

15. Responsive to a patient's desires and condition, all involved in pastoral care should facilitate the availability of priests to pro-

vide the sacrament of anointing of the sick, recognizing that through this sacrament Christ provides grace and support to those who are seriously ill or weakened by advanced age. Normally, the sacrament is celebrated when the sick person is fully conscious. It may be conferred upon the sick who have lost consciousness or the use of reason, if there is reason to believe that they would have asked for the sacrament while in control of their faculties.

16. All Catholics who are capable of receiving communion should receive viaticum when they are in danger of death, while still in full possession of their faculties.[12]

17. Except in cases of emergency (i.e., danger of death), any request for baptism made by adults or for infants should be referred to the chaplain of the institution. Newly born infants in danger of death, including those miscarried, should be baptized if this is possible.[13] In case of emergency, if a priest or a deacon is not available, anyone can validly baptize.[14] In the case of emergency baptism, the chaplain or the director of pastoral care is to be notified.

18. When a Catholic who has been baptized but not yet confirmed is in danger of death, any priest may confirm the person.[15]

19. A record of the conferral of baptism or confirmation should be sent to the parish in which the institution is located and posted in its baptism/confirmation registers.

20. Catholic discipline generally reserves the reception of the sacraments to Catholics. In accord with canon 844.3, Catholic ministers may administer the sacraments of eucharist, penance, and anointing of the sick to members of the Oriental churches that do not have full communion with the Catholic Church, or of other Churches that in the judgment of the Holy See are in the same condition as the Oriental churches, if such persons ask for the sacraments on their own and are properly disposed.

   With regard to other Christians not in full communion with the Catholic Church, when the danger of death or other grave necessity is present, the four conditions of canon 844.4, also must be present, namely, they cannot approach a minister of their own community; they ask for the sacraments on their own; they manifest Catholic faith in these sacraments; and they are properly disposed. The diocesan bishop has the responsibility to oversee this pastoral practice.

21. The appointment of priests and deacons to the pastoral care staff of a Catholic institution must have the explicit approval or confirmation of the local bishop in collaboration with the administration of the institution. The appointment of the

director of the pastoral care staff should be made in consultation with the diocesan bishop.

22. For the sake of appropriate ecumenical and interfaith relations, a diocesan policy should be developed with regard to the appointment of non-Catholic members to the pastoral care staff of a Catholic health care institution. The director of pastoral care at a Catholic institution should be a Catholic; any exception to this norm should be approved by the diocesan bishop.

Part Three: The Professional–Patient Relationship

Introduction

A person in need of health care and the professional health care provider who accepts that person as a patient enter into a relationship that requires, among other things, mutual respect, trust, honesty, and appropriate confidentiality. The resulting free exchange of information must avoid manipulation, intimidation, or condescension. Such a relationship enables the patient to disclose personal information needed for effective care and permits the health care provider to use his or her professional competence most effectively to maintain or restore the patient's health. Neither the health care professional nor the patient acts independently of the other; both participate in the healing process.

Today, a patient often receives health care from a team of providers, especially in the setting of the modern acute-care hospital. But the resulting multiplication of relationships does not alter the personal character of the interaction between health care providers and the patient. The relationship of the person seeking health care and the professionals providing that care is an important part of the foundation on which diagnosis and care are provided. Diagnosis and care, therefore, entail a series of decisions with ethical as well as medical dimensions. The health care professional has the knowledge and experience to pursue the goals of healing, the maintenance of health, and the compassionate care of the dying, taking into account the patient's convictions and spiritual needs and the moral responsibilities of all concerned. The person in need of health care depends on the skill of the health care provider to assist in preserving life and promoting health of body, mind, and spirit. The patient, in turn, has a responsibility to use these physical and mental resources in the service of moral and spiritual goals to the best of his or her ability.

When the health care professional and the patient use institutional Catholic health care, they also accept its public commitment to the Church's understanding of and witness to the dignity of the human person. The Church's moral teaching on health care nurtures a truly interpersonal professional-patient relationship. This professional-patient relationship is never separated, then, from the Catholic identity of the health care institution. The faith that inspires Catholic health care guides medical decisions in ways that fully respect the dignity of the person and the relationship with the health care professional.

Directives

23. The inherent dignity of the human person must be respected and protected regardless of the nature of the person's health problem or social status. The respect for human dignity extends to all persons who are served by Catholic health care.

24. In compliance with federal law, a Catholic health care institution will make available to patients information about their rights, under the laws of their state, to make an advance directive for their medical treatment. The institution, however, will not honor an advance directive that is contrary to Catholic teaching. If the advance directive conflicts with Catholic teaching, an explanation should be provided as to why the directive cannot be honored.

25. Each person may identify in advance a representative to make health care decisions as his or her surrogate in the event that the person loses the capacity to make health care decisions. Decisions by the designated surrogate should be faithful to Catholic moral principles and to the person's intentions and values, or if the person's intentions are unknown, to the person's best interests. In the event that an advance directive is not executed, those who are in a position to know best the patient's wishes—usually family members and loved ones—should participate in the treatment decisions for the person who has lost the capacity to make health care decisions.

26. The free and informed consent of the person or the person's surrogate is required for medical treatments and procedures, except in an emergency situation when consent cannot be obtained and there is no indication that the patient would refuse consent to the treatment.

27. Free and informed consent requires that the person or the person's surrogate receive all reasonable information about the essential nature of the proposed treatment and its benefits; its risks, side effects, consequences, and cost; and any reasonable and morally legitimate alternatives, including no treatment at all.

28. Each person or the person's surrogate should have access to medical and moral information and counseling so as to be able

to form his or her conscience. The free and informed health care decision of the person or the person's surrogate is to be followed so long as it does not contradict Catholic principles.

29. All persons served by Catholic health care have the right and duty to protect and preserve their bodily and functional integrity.[16] The functional integrity of the person may be sacrificed to maintain the health or life of the person when no other morally permissible means is available.[17]

30. The transplantation of organs from living donors is morally permissible when such a donation will not sacrifice or seriously impair any essential bodily function and the anticipated benefit to the recipient is proportionate to the harm done to the donor. Furthermore, the freedom of the prospective donor must be respected, and economic advantages should not accrue to the donor.

31. No one should be the subject of medical or genetic experimentation, even if it is therapeutic, unless the person or surrogate first has given free and informed consent. In instances of non-therapeutic experimentation, the surrogate can give this consent only if the experiment entails no significant risk to the person's well-being. Moreover, the greater the person's incompetency and vulnerability, the greater the reasons must be to perform any medical experimentation, especially nontherapeutic.

32. While every person is obliged to use ordinary means to preserve his or her health, no person should be obliged to submit to a health care procedure that the person has judged, with a free and informed conscience, not to provide a reasonable hope of benefit without imposing excessive risks and burdens on the patient or excessive expense to family or community.[18]

33. The well-being of the whole person must be taken into account in deciding about any therapeutic intervention or use of technology. Therapeutic procedures that are likely to cause harm or undesirable side effects can be justified only by a proportionate benefit to the patient.

34. Health care providers are to respect each person's privacy and confidentiality regarding information related to the person's diagnosis, treatment, and care.

35. Health care professionals should be educated to recognize the symptoms of abuse and violence and are obliged to report cases of abuse to the proper authorities in accordance with local statutes.

36. Compassionate and understanding care should be given to a person who is the victim of sexual assault. Health care providers should cooperate with law enforcement officials, offer the person psychological and spiritual support and accu-

rate medical information. A female who has been raped should be able to defend herself against a potential conception from the sexual assault. If, after appropriate testing, there is no evidence that conception has occurred already, she may be treated with medications that would prevent ovulation, sperm capacitation, or fertilization. It is not permissible, however, to initiate or to recommend treatments that have as their purpose or direct effect the removal, destruction, or interference with the implantation of a fertilized ovum.[19]

37. An ethics committee or some alternate form of ethical consultation should be available to assist by advising on particular ethical situations, by offering educational opportunities, and by reviewing and recommending policies. To these ends, there should be appropriate standards for medical ethical consultation within a particular diocese that will respect the diocesan bishop's pastoral responsibility as well as assist members of ethics committees to be familiar with Catholic medical ethics and, in particular, these directives.

Part Four: Issues in Care for the Beginning of Life

Introduction

The Church's commitment to human dignity inspires an abiding concern for the sanctity of human life from its very beginning, and with the dignity of marriage and of the marriage act by which human life is transmitted. The Church cannot approve medical practices that undermine the biological, psychological, and moral bonds on which the strength of marriage and the family depends.

Catholic health care ministry witnesses to the sanctity of life "from the moment of conception until death."[20] The Church's defense of life encompasses the unborn and the care of women and their children during and after pregnancy. The Church's commitment to life is seen in its willingness to collaborate with others to alleviate the causes of the high infant mortality rate and to provide adequate health care to mothers and their children before and after birth.

The Church has the deepest respect for the family, for the marriage covenant, and for the love that binds a married couple together. This includes respect for the marriage act by which husband and wife express their love and cooperate with God in the creation of a new human being. The Second Vatican Council affirms:

> This love is an eminently human one. . . . It involves the good of the whole person. . . . The actions within marriage

by which the couple are united intimately and chastely are noble and worthy ones. Expressed in a manner which is truly human, these actions signify and promote that mutual self-giving by which spouses enrich each other with a joyful and a thankful will.[21]

Marriage and conjugal love are by their nature ordained toward the begetting and educating of children. Children are really the supreme gift of marriage and contribute very substantially to the welfare of their parents. . . . Parents should regard as their proper mission the task of transmitting human life and educating those to whom it has been transmitted. . . . They are thereby cooperators with the love of God the Creator, and are, so to speak, the interpreters of that love.[22]

For legitimate reasons of responsible parenthood, married couples may limit the number of their children by natural means. The Church cannot approve contraceptive interventions that "either in anticipation of the marital act, or in its accomplishment or in the development of its natural consequences, have the purpose, whether as an end or a means, to render procreation impossible."[23] Such interventions violate "the inseparable connection, willed by God . . . between the two meanings of the conjugal act: the unitive and procreative meaning."[24]

With the advance of the biological and medical sciences, society has at its disposal new technologies for responding to the problem of infertility. While we rejoice in the potential for good inherent in many of these technologies, we cannot assume that what is technically possible is always morally right. Reproductive technologies that substitute for the marriage act are not consistent with human dignity. Just as the marriage act is joined naturally to procreation, so procreation is joined naturally to the marriage act. As Pope John XXIII observed:

The transmission of human life is entrusted by nature to a personal and conscious act and as such is subject to all the holy laws of God: the immutable and inviolable laws which must be recognized and observed. For this reason, one cannot use means and follow methods which could be licit in the transmission of the life of plants and animals.[25]

Because the moral law is rooted in the whole of human nature, human persons, through intelligent reflection on their own spiritual destiny, can discover and cooperate in the plan of the Creator.[26]

Directives

38. When the marital act of sexual intercourse is not able to attain its procreative purpose, assistance that does not separate the unitive and procreative ends of the act, and does not substitute for the marital act itself, may be used to help married couples conceive.[27]

39. Those techniques of assisted conception that respect the unitive and procreative meanings of sexual intercourse and do not involve the destruction of human embryos, or their deliberate generation in such numbers that it is clearly envisaged that all cannot implant and some are simply being used to maximize the chances of others implanting, may be used as therapies for infertility.

40. Heterologous fertilization (that is, any technique used to achieve conception by the use of gametes coming from at least one donor other than the spouses) is prohibited because it is contrary to the covenant of marriage, the unity of the spouses, and the dignity proper to parents and the child.[28]

41. Homologous artificial fertilization (that is, any technique used to achieve conception using the gametes of the two spouses joined in marriage) is prohibited when it separates procreation from the marital act in its unitive significance (e.g., any technique used to achieve extra-corporeal conception).[29]

42. Because of the dignity of the child and of marriage, and because of the uniqueness of the mother–child relationship, participation in contracts or arrangements for surrogate motherhood is not permitted. Moreover, the commercialization of such surrogacy denigrates the dignity of women, especially the poor.[30]

43. A Catholic health care institution that provides treatment for infertility should offer not only technical assistance to infertile couples but also should help couples pursue other solutions (e.g., counseling, adoption).

44. A Catholic health care institution should provide prenatal, obstetric, and postnatal services for mothers and their children in a manner consonant with its mission.

45. Abortion (that is, the directly intended termination of pregnancy before viability or the directly intended destruction of a viable fetus) is never permitted. Every procedure whose sole immediate effect is the termination of pregnancy before viability is an abortion, which, in its moral context, includes the interval between conception and implantation of the embryo. Catholic health care institutions are not to provide abortion services, even based upon the principle of material coopera-

tion. In this context, Catholic health care institutions need to be concerned about the danger of scandal in any association with abortion providers.

46. Catholic health care providers should be ready to offer compassionate physical, psychological, moral, and spiritual care to those persons who have suffered from the trauma of abortion.

47. Operations, treatments, and medications that have as their direct purpose the cure of a proportionately serious pathological condition of a pregnant woman are permitted when they cannot be safely postponed until the unborn child is viable, even if they will result in the death of the unborn child.

48. In case of extrauterine pregnancy, no intervention is morally licit which constitutes a direct abortion.[31]

49. For a proportionate reason, labor may be induced after the fetus is viable.

50. Prenatal diagnosis is permitted when the procedure does not threaten the life or physical integrity of the unborn child or the mother and does not subject them to disproportionate risks; when the diagnosis can provide information to guide preventative care for the mother or pre- or postnatal care for the child; and when the parents, or at least the mother, give free and informed consent. Prenatal diagnosis is not permitted when undertaken with the intention of aborting an unborn child with a serious defect.[32]

51. Nontherapeutic experiments on a living embryo or fetus are not permitted, even with the consent of the parents. Therapeutic experiments are permitted for a proportionate reason with the free and informed consent of the parents or, if the father cannot be contacted, at least of the mother. Medical research that will not harm the life or physical integrity of an unborn child is permitted with parental consent.[33]

52. Catholic health institutions may not promote or condone contraceptive practices but should provide, for married couples and the medical staff who counsel them, instruction both about the Church's teaching on responsible parenthood and in methods of natural family planning.

53. Direct sterilization of either men or women, whether permanent or temporary, is not permitted in a Catholic health care institution. Procedures that induce sterility are permitted when their direct effect is the cure or alleviation of a present and serious pathology and a simpler treatment is not available.[34]

54. Genetic counseling may be provided in order to promote responsible parenthood and to prepare for the proper treatment and care of children with genetic defects, in accordance

with Catholic moral teaching and the intrinsic rights and obligations of married couples regarding the transmission of life.

Part Five: Issues in Care for the Dying

Introduction

Christ's redemption and saving grace embrace the whole person, especially in his or her illness, suffering, and death.[35] The Catholic health care ministry faces the reality of death with the confidence of faith. In the face of death—for many, a time when hope seems lost—the Church witnesses to her belief that God has created each person for eternal life.[36]

Above all, as a witness to its faith, a Catholic health care institution will be a community of respect, love, and support to patients or residents and their families as they face the reality of death. What is hardest to face is the process of dying itself, especially the dependency, the helplessness, and the pain that so often accompany terminal illness. One of the primary purposes of medicine in caring for the dying is the relief of pain and the suffering caused by it. Effective management of pain in all its forms is critical in the appropriate care of the dying.

The truth that life is a precious gift from God has profound implications for the question of stewardship over human life. We are not the owners of our lives and, hence, do not have absolute power over life. We have a duty to preserve our life and to use it for the glory of God, but the duty to preserve life is not absolute, for we may reject life-prolonging procedures that are insufficiently beneficial or excessively burdensome. Suicide and euthanasia are never morally acceptable options.

The task of medicine is to care even when it cannot cure. Physicians and their patients must evaluate the use of the technology at their disposal. Reflection on the innate dignity of human life in all its dimensions and on the purpose of medical care is indispensable for formulating a true moral judgment about the use of technology to maintain life. The use of life-sustaining technology is judged in light of the Christian meaning of life, suffering, and death. Only in this way are two extremes avoided: on the one hand, an insistence on useless or burdensome technology even when a patient may legitimately wish to forgo it and, on the other hand, the withdrawal of technology with the intention of causing death.[37]

Some state Catholic conferences, individual bishops, and the NCCB Committee on Pro-Life Activities have addressed the moral issues concerning medically assisted hydration and nutrition. The bishops are guided by the Church's teaching forbidding euthanasia, which is ". . . an action or an omission which of itself or by intention causes death, in order that all suffering may in this way be eliminated."[38] These statements agree that hydration and nutrition are not morally obligatory either when they bring no comfort to a person who is imminently dying or when they cannot be assimilated by a person's body. The NCCB Committee on Pro-Life Activities report, in addition, points out the necessary distinctions between questions already resolved by the magisterium and those requiring further reflection, as, for example, the morality of withdrawing medically assisted hydration and nutrition from a person who is in the condition which is recognized by physicians as the "persistent vegetative state" (PVS).[39]

Directives

55. Catholic health care institutions offering care to persons in danger of death from illness, accident, advanced age, or similar condition should provide them with appropriate opportunities to prepare for death. Persons in danger of death should be provided with whatever information is necessary to help them understand their condition and have the opportunity to discuss their condition with their family members and care providers. They should also be offered the appropriate medical information that would make it possible to address the morally legitimate choices available to them. They should be provided the spiritual support as well as the opportunity to receive the sacraments in order to prepare well for death.

56. A person has a moral obligation to use ordinary or proportionate means of preserving his or her life. Proportionate means are those that in the judgment of the patient offer a reasonable hope of benefit and do not entail an excessive burden or impose excessive expense on the family or the community.[40]

57. A person may forgo extraordinary or disproportionate means of preserving life. Disproportionate means are those that in the patient's judgment do not offer a reasonable hope of benefit or entail an excessive burden, or impose excessive expense on the family or the community.[41]

58. There should be a presumption in favor of providing nutrition and hydration to all patients, including patients who require medically assisted nutrition and hydration, as long as this is of sufficient benefit to outweigh the burdens involved to the patient.

59. The free and informed judgment made by a competent adult patient concerning the use or withdrawal of life-sustaining procedures should always be respected and normally complied with, unless it is contrary to Catholic moral teaching.

60. Euthanasia is an action or omission that of itself or by intention causes death in order to alleviate suffering. Catholic health care institutions may never condone or participate in euthanasia or assisted suicide in any way. Dying patients who request euthanasia should receive loving care, psychological and spiritual support, and appropriate remedies for pain and other symptoms so that they can live with dignity until the time of natural death.[42]

61. Patients should be kept as free of pain as possible so that they may die comfortably and with dignity, and in the place where they wish to die. Since a person has the right to prepare for his or her death while fully conscious, he or she should not be deprived of consciousness without a compelling reason. Medicines capable of alleviating or suppressing pain may be given to a dying person, even if this therapy may indirectly shorten the person's life so long as the intent is not to hasten death. Patients experiencing suffering that cannot be alleviated should be helped to appreciate the Christian understanding of redemptive suffering.

62. The determination of death should be made by the physician or competent medical authority in accordance with responsible and commonly accepted scientific criteria.

63. Catholic health care institutions should encourage and provide the means whereby those who wish to do so may arrange for the donation of their organs and bodily tissue, for ethically legitimate purposes, so that they may be used for donation and research after death.

64. Such organs should not be removed until it has been medically determined that the patient has died. In order to prevent any conflict of interest, the physician who determines death should not be a member of the transplant team.

65. The use of tissue or organs from an infant may be permitted after death has been determined and with the informed consent of the parents or guardians.

66. Catholic health care institutions should not make use of human tissue obtained by direct abortions even for research and therapeutic purposes.[43]

Part Six: Forming New Partnerships with Health Care Organizations and Providers

Introduction

Until recently, most health care providers enjoyed a degree of independence from one another. In ever-increasing ways, Catholic health care providers have become involved with other health care organizations and providers. For instance, many Catholic health care systems and institutions share in the joint purchase of technology and services with other local facilities or physicians' groups. Another phenomenon is the growing number of Catholic health care systems and institutions joining or co-sponsoring integrated delivery networks or managed care organizations in order to contract with insurers and other health care payers. In some instances, Catholic health care systems sponsor a health care plan or health maintenance organization. In many dioceses, new partnerships will result in a decrease in the number of health care providers, at times leaving the Catholic institution as the sole provider of health care services. At whatever level, new partnerships forge a variety of interwoven relationships: between the various institutional partners, between health care providers and the community, between physicians and health care services, and between health care services and payers.

On the one hand, new partnerships can be viewed as opportunities for Catholic health care institutions and services to witness to their religious and ethical commitments and so influence the healing profession. For example, new partnerships can help to implement the Church's social teaching. New partnerships can be opportunities to realign the local delivery system in order to provide a continuum of health care to the community; they can witness to a responsible stewardship of limited health care resources; and they can be opportunities to provide to poor and vulnerable persons a more equitable access to basic care.

On the other hand, new partnerships can pose serious challenges to the viability of the identity of Catholic health care institutions and services and their ability to implement these directives in a consistent way, especially when partnerships are formed with those who do not share Catholic moral principles. The risk of scandal cannot be underestimated when partnerships are not built upon common values and moral principles. Partnership opportunities for some Catholic health care providers may even threaten the continued existence of other Catholic institutions and services, particularly when partnerships are driven by financial considerations alone. Because of the potential dangers involved in the new partnerships that are emerging, an increased collaboration among Catholic-sponsored health care institutions is essential and should be sought before other forms of partnerships.

The significant challenges that new partnerships may pose, however, do not necessarily preclude their possibility on moral grounds. The potential dangers require that new partnerships undergo systematic and objective moral analysis, which takes into account the various factors that often pressure institutions and services into new partnerships that can diminish the autonomy and ministry of the Catholic partner. The following directives are offered to assist institutionally based Catholic health care services in this process of analysis. To this end, the National Conference of Catholic Bishops has established the Ad Hoc Committee on Health Care Issues and the Church as a resource for bishops and health care leaders. An appendix at the end of the directives offers a clarification of the terms relative to the principles governing cooperation and their application to concrete situations.

Directives

67. Decisions that may lead to serious consequences for the identity or reputation of Catholic health care services, or entail the high risk of scandal, should be made in consultation with the diocesan bishop or his health care liaison.

68. Any partnership that will affect the mission or religious and ethical identity of Catholic health care institutional services must respect church teaching and discipline. Diocesan bishops and other church authorities should be involved as such partnerships are developed, and the diocesan bishop should give the appropriate authorization before they are completed. The diocesan bishop's approval is required for partnerships sponsored by institutions subject to his governing authority; for partnerships sponsored by religious institutes of pontifical right, his *nihil obstat* should be obtained.

69. When a Catholic health care institution is participating in a partnership that may be involved in activities judged morally wrong by the Church, the Catholic institution should limit its involvement in accord with the moral principles governing cooperation.

70. The possibility of scandal (e.g., generating a confusion about Catholic moral teaching) is an important factor that should be considered when applying the principles governing cooperation. Cooperation, which in all other respects is morally appropriate, may be refused because of the scandal that would be caused in the circumstances.

Conclusion

Sickness speaks to us of our limitations and human frailty. It can take the form of infirmity resulting from the simple passing of years or injury from the exuberance of youthful energy. It can be temporary or chronic, debilitating, and even terminal. Yet the follower of Jesus faces illness and the consequences of the human condition aware that our Lord always shows compassion toward the infirm.

Jesus not only taught his disciples to be compassionate, but he also told them who should be the special object of their compassion. The parable of the feast with its humble guests was preceded by the instruction: "When you hold a banquet, invite the poor, the crippled, the lame, the blind" (Lk 14:13). These were people whom Jesus healed and loved.

Catholic health care is a response to the challenge of Jesus to go and do likewise. Catholic health care services rejoice in the challenge to be Christ's healing compassion in the world and see their ministry not only as an effort to restore and preserve health but also as a spiritual service and a sign of that final healing which will one day bring about the new creation that is the ultimate fruit of Jesus' ministry and God's love for us.

Appendix: The Principles Governing Cooperation

The principles governing cooperation differentiate the action of the wrongdoer from the action of the cooperator through two major distinctions. The first is between formal and material cooperation. If the cooperator intends the object of the wrongdoer's activity, then the cooperation is formal and, therefore, morally wrong. Since intention is not simply an explicit act of the will, formal cooperation can also be implicit. Implicit formal cooperation is attributed when, even though the cooperator denies intending the wrongdoer's object, no other explanation can distinguish the cooperator's object from the wrongdoer's object. If the cooperator does not intend the object of the wrongdoer's activity, the cooperation is material and can be morally licit.

The second distinction deals with the object of the action and is expressed by immediate and mediate material cooperation. Material cooperation is immediate when the object of the cooperator is the same as the object of the wrongdoer. Immediate material cooperation is wrong, except in some instances of duress. The matter of duress distinguishes immediate material cooperation from implicit formal cooperation. But immediate material cooperation—without duress—is equivalent to implicit formal cooperation and, therefore, is morally wrong. When the object of the cooperator's action remains distinguishable from that of the wrongdoer's, material cooperation is mediate and can be morally licit.

Moral theologians recommend two other considerations for the proper evaluation of material cooperation. First, the object of material cooperation should be as distant as possible from the wrongdoer's act. Second, any act of material cooperation requires a proportionately grave reason.

Prudence guides those involved in cooperation to estimate questions of intention, duress, distance, necessity, and gravity. In making a judgment about cooperation, it is essential that the possibility of scandal should be eliminated. Appropriate consideration should also be given to the Church's prophetic responsibility.

Notes

1. USCC Office of Domestic Social Development, *Health and Health Care: A Pastoral Letter of the American Catholic Bishops* (Washington, D.C.: United States Catholic Conference, 1981).
2. Health care services under Catholic auspices are carried out in a variety of institutional settings (e.g., hospitals, clinics, outpatient facilities, urgent care centers, hospices, nursing homes, and parishes). Depending on the context, these directives will employ the terms "institution" and/or "services" in order to encompass the variety of settings in which Catholic health care is provided.
3. *Health and Health Care*, 5.
4. Second Vatican Council, *Decree on the Apostolate of the Laity (Apostolicam Actuositatem)*, no. 1.
5. John Paul II, *On the Vocation and the Mission of the Lay Faithful in the Church and in the World (Christifideles Laici)* (Washington, D.C.: United States Catholic Conference, 1988), no. 29.
6. As examples, see Congregation for the Doctrine of the Faith, *Declaration on Abortion* (Washington, D.C.: United States Catholic Conference, 1974); Congregation for the Doctrine of the Faith, *Declaration on Euthanasia* (Washington, D.C.: United States Catholic Conference, 1980); Congregation for the Doctrine of the Faith, *Instruction on Respect for Human Life in its Origin and on the Dignity of Procreation: Replies to Certain Questions of the Day (Donum Vitae)* (Washington, D.C.: United States Catholic Conference, 1987).
7. John XXIII, *Peace on Earth (Pacem in Terris)* (Washington, D.C.: United States Catholic Conference, 1963), no. 11; *Health and Health Care*, 5, 17-18; *Catechism of the Catholic Church* (Washington, D.C.: United States Catholic Conference, 1994), no. 2211.
8. John Paul II, *On Social Concern (Sollicitudo Rei Socialis)* (Washington, D.C.: United States Catholic Conference, 1988), no. 43.
9. National Conference of Catholic Bishops, *Economic Justice for All: Pastoral Letter on Catholic Social Teaching and the U.S. Economy* (Washington, D.C.: United States Catholic Conference, 1986), no. 80.

10. The duty of responsible stewardship demands responsible collaboration. But in collaborative efforts, Catholic institutionally based health care services must be attentive to occasions when the policies and practices of other institutions are not compatible with the Church's authoritative moral teaching. At such times, Catholic health care institutions should determine whether or to what degree collaboration would be morally permissible. To make that judgment, the governing boards of Catholic institutions should adhere to the moral principles on cooperation. See part 6.

11. *Health and Health Care,* 12.

12. Cf. *Code of Canon Law,* canons 921-923.

13. Cf. ibid., canons 867.2, and 871.

14. To confer baptism in an emergency, one must have the proper intention (to do what the Church intends by baptism) and pour water on the head of the person to be baptized, meanwhile pronouncing the words: "I baptize you in the name of the Father, and of the Son, and of the Holy Spirit."

15. Cf. canon 883.3.

16. For example, while the donation of a kidney represents loss of biological integrity, such a donation does not compromise functional integrity since human beings are capable of functioning with only one kidney.

17. Cf. directive 53.

18. *Declaration on Euthanasia,* part 4; cf. also directives 56-57.

19. It is recommended that a sexually assaulted woman be advised of the ethical restrictions that prevent Catholic hospitals from using abortifacient procedures; cf. Pennsylvania Catholic Conference, "Guidelines for Catholic Hospitals Treating Victims of Sexual Assault," *Origins* 22:47 (May 6, 1993): 810.

20. John Paul II, "Address of October 29, 1983 to the 35th General Assembly of the World Medical Association," *Acta Apostolicae Sedis* 76 (1984): 390.

21. Second Vatican Council, *Pastoral Constitution on the Church in the Modern World (Gaudium et Spes),* no. 49.

22. Ibid., no. 50.

23. Paul VI, *On the Regulation of Birth (Humanae Vitae)* (Washington, D.C.: United States Catholic Conference, 1968), no. 14.

24. Ibid., no. 12.

25. John XXIII, *On Christianity and Social Progress (Mater et Magistra)* (Washington, D.C.: United States Catholic Conference, 1961), no. 193, quoted in Congregation for the Doctrine of the Faith, *Instruction on Respect for Human Life in Its Origin and on the Dignity of Procreation: Replies to Certain Questions of the Day (Donum Vitae)* (Washington, D.C.: United States Catholic Conference, 1987), no. 4.

26. John Paul II, *The Splendor of Truth (Veritatis Splendor)* (Washington, D.C.: United States Catholic Conference, 1993), no. 50.

27. "Homologous artificial insemination within marriage cannot be admitted except for those cases in which the technical means is not a substitute for the conjugal act but serves to facilitate and to help so that the act attains its natural purpose," *Donum Vitae,* part 2, B, no. 6; cf. also part 1, no. 1, and part 1, no. 6.

28. Ibid., part 2, A, no. 2.

29. "Artificial insemination as a substitute for the conjugal act is prohibited by reason of the voluntarily achieved dissociation of the two meanings of the conjugal act. Masturbation, through which the sperm is normally obtained, is another sign of this dissociation: even when it is done for the purpose of procreation, the act remains deprived of its unitive meaning: 'It lacks the sexual relationship called for by the moral order, namely, the relationship which realizes the full sense of mutual self-giving and human procreation in the context of true love'" (*Donum Vitae*, part 2, B, no. 6).

30. Ibid., part 2, A, no. 3.

31. Cf. directive 45.

32. *Donum Vitae*, part 1, no. 2.

33. Cf. ibid., no. 4.

34. Cf. Congregation for the Doctrine of the Faith, "Responses on Uterine Isolation and Related Matters" (July 31, 1993), *Origins* 24:12 (September 1, 1994): 211-212.

35. John Paul II, *On the Christian Meaning of Human Suffering (Salvifici Doloris)* (Washington, D.C.: United States Catholic Conference, 1984), nos. 25-27.

36. National Conference of Catholic Bishops, *Order of Christian Funerals* (Collegeville, Minn.: The Liturgical Press, 1989), no. 1.

37. *Declaration on Euthanasia*.

38. Ibid., part 2, p. 4.

39. NCCB Committee for Pro-Life Activities, *Nutrition and Hydration: Moral and Pastoral Reflections* (Washington, D.C.: United States Catholic Conference, 1992). On the importance of consulting authoritative teaching in the formation of conscience and in taking moral decisions, see *Veritatis Splendor*, nos. 63-64.

40. *Declaration on Euthanasia*, part 4.

41. Ibid.

42. Cf. ibid.

43. *Donum Vitae*, part 1, no. 4.

Source: Washington, D.C.: United States Catholic Conference, 1995.

Confronting a Culture of Violence: A Catholic Framework for Action

A Pastoral Message of the National Conference of Catholic Bishops

November 1994

"Choose life, then, that you and your descendants may live." (Dt 30:19)
"If you want peace, work for justice." (Pope Paul VI)
"Blessed are the peacemakers." (Mt 5:9)

I. Introduction

Our families are torn by violence. Our communities are destroyed by violence. Our faith is tested by violence. We have an obligation to respond.

Violence—in our homes, our schools and streets, our nation and world—is destroying the lives, dignity, and hopes of millions of our sisters and brothers. Fear of violence is paralyzing and polarizing our communities. The celebration of violence in much of our media, music, and even video games is poisoning our children.

Beyond the violence in our streets is the violence in our hearts. Hostility, hatred, despair, and indifference are at the heart of a growing culture of violence. Verbal violence in our families, communications, and talk shows contributes to this culture of violence. Pornography assaults the dignity of women and contributes to violence against them. Our social fabric is being torn apart by a culture of violence that leaves children dead on our streets and families afraid in our homes. Our society seems to be growing numb to human loss and suffering. A nation born in a commitment to "life, liberty, and the pursuit of happiness" is haunted by death, imprisoned by fear, and caught up in the elusive pursuit of protection rather than happiness. A world moving beyond the Cold War is caught up in bloody ethnic, tribal, and political conflict.

It doesn't have to be this way. It wasn't always this way. We can turn away from violence; we can build communities of greater peace. It begins with a clear conviction: respect for life. Respect for life is not just a slogan or a program; it is a fundamental moral principle flowing from our teaching on the dignity of the human person. It is an approach to life that values people over things. Respect for life must guide the choices we make as individuals and as a society: what we do and won't do, what we value and consume, whom we admire and whose example we follow, what we support and what we oppose. Respect for human life is the starting point for confronting a culture of violence.

The Catholic community cannot ignore the moral and human costs of so much violence in our midst. These brief reflections are a call to conversion and a framework for action. They propose neither a sweeping plan nor specific programs. They recognize the impressive efforts already underway in dioceses, parishes, and schools. They offer a word of support and gratitude for those already engaged in these efforts. We believe the Catholic community brings strong convictions and vital experience which enrich the national dialogue on how best to overcome the violence that is tearing our nation apart.

We know these reflections are not enough. Words cannot stop weapons; statements will not contain hatred. Yet commitment and conversion can change us and together we can change our culture and communities. Person by person, family by family, neighborhood by neighborhood, we must take back our communities from the evil and fear that come with so much violence. We believe our faith in Jesus Christ gives us the values, vision, and hope that can bring an important measure of peace to our hearts, our homes, and our streets.

II. A Culture of Violence

Decades ago, the Kerner Commission called violence "as American as apple pie."[1] Sadly, this provocative statement has proved prophetic. No nation on earth, except those in the midst of war, has as much violent behavior as we do—in our homes, on our televisions, and in our streets:

- While crime statistics vary year to year, we face far higher rates of murder, assault, rape, and other violent crimes than other societies. One estimate is that crime costs us $674 billion a year. Violent crime quadrupled from 161 reported crimes per 100,000 in 1960 to 758 in 1992.[2]
- The most violent place in America is not in our streets, but in our homes. More than 50 percent of the women murdered in the United States are killed by their partner or ex-partner. Millions of children are victims of family violence.[3]
- The number of guns has also quadrupled from 54 million in 1950 to 201 million in 1990. Between 1979 and 1991, nearly 50,000 American children and teenagers were killed by guns, matching the number of Americans who died in battle in Vietnam. It is now estimated 13 American children die every

day from guns. Gunshots cause one out of four deaths among American teenagers.[4]

- Our entertainment media too often exaggerate and even celebrate violence. Children see 8,000 murders and 100,000 other acts of violence on television before they leave elementary school.[5]
- We must never forget that the violence of abortion has destroyed more than 30 million unborn children since 1972.[6]

Behind these numbers are individual human tragedies, lives lost, families destroyed, children without real hope.

Violence in our culture is fed by multiple forces—the disintegration of family life, media influences, growing substance abuse, the availability of so many weapons, and the rise of gangs and increasing youth violence. No one response can address these diverse sources. Traditional liberal or conservative approaches cannot effectively confront them. We have to address simultaneously declining family life and the increasing availability of deadly weapons, the lure of gangs and the slavery of addiction, the absence of real opportunity, budget cuts adversely affecting the poor, and the loss of moral values.

While many communities are touched by crime and the fear that comes with it, violence especially ravages poor communities. Young people are particularly threatened by violence. In some communities, teens talk of "if" they grow up, instead of "when" they grow up, planning their funerals instead of their futures. Between 1985 and 1992, the annual number of youth killed by guns grew from 2,500 to 5,326.[7]

Increasingly, our society looks to violent measures to deal with some of our most difficult social problems—millions of abortions to address problem pregnancies, advocacy of euthanasia and assisted suicide to cope with the burdens of age and illness, and increased reliance on the death penalty to deal with crime. We are tragically turning to violence in the search for quick and easy answers to complex human problems. A society which destroys its children, abandons its old, and relies on vengeance fails fundamental moral tests. Violence is not the solution; it is the most clear sign of our failures. We are losing our respect for human life. How do we teach the young to curb their violence when we embrace it as the solution to social problems?

We cannot teach that killing is wrong by killing. We have reached the point in one very visible case where a jury has urged the execution of the person who murdered the physician who was destroying unborn children. This cycle of violence diminishes all of us—especially our children. For our part, we oppose both the violence of abortion and the use of violence to oppose abortion. We are clear in our total repudiation of any effort to advocate or carry out murder in the name of the pro-life cause. Such acts cannot be justified. They deny the fundamental value of each human life and do irreparable harm to genuine pro-life witness. Just as clearly, a nation destroying more than one and a half million unborn children every year contributes to the pervasive culture of violence in our nation. We must affirm and protect all life, especially the most vulnerable in our midst.

Likewise, we cannot ignore the underlying cultural values that help to create the environment where violence grows: a denial of right and wrong, education that ignores fundamental values, an abandonment of personal responsibility, an excessive and selfish focus on our individual desires, a diminishing sense of obligation to our children and neighbors, a misplaced priority on acquisitions, and media glorification of violence and sexual irresponsibility. In short, we often fail to value life and cherish human beings above possessions, power, and pleasure.

Less obvious and less visible is the slow-motion violence of discrimination and poverty, hunger and hopelessness, addiction and self-destructive behavior. The deterioration of family life and the loss of community leave too many without moral direction and personal roots. Grinding poverty and powerlessness leave too many without a stake in society and a place in our community. Economic, social, and moral forces can tear apart communities and families not as quickly, but just as surely, as bullets and knives. Lives sometimes are diminished and threatened not only in the streets of our cities, but also by decisions made in the halls of government, the boardrooms of corporations, and the courts of our land. An ethic of respect for life should be a central measure of all our institutions—community, economic, political, and legal.

This growing culture of violence reflected in some aspects of our public life and entertainment media must be confronted. But it is not just our policies and programming that must change; it is our hearts. We must condemn not only the killing but also the abuse in our homes, the anger in our hearts, and the glorification of violence in movies and music. It is time, in the words of Deuteronomy (30:19), to "choose life, then, that you and your descendants may live. . . ." We must join with Pope John Paul II to "proclaim, with all the conviction of my faith in Christ and with an awareness of my mission, that violence is evil, that violence is unacceptable as a solution to problems, that violence is unworthy. . . . Violence is a lie, for it goes against the truth of our faith, the truth of our humanity."[8]

Around the globe, we are seeing the promises of a new world lost in deadly conflict and renewed war. In Bosnia, Rwanda, Haiti, Sudan, and so many other places, the world too often has watched as sisters and brothers were killed because of their religion, race, tribe, or political position. The post-Cold War world has become a tumult of savage attacks on the innocent. Unprepared for this disorder and confused about what to do to resolve ancient rivalries, the international community has too often stood by indecisively as hundreds of thousands of men, women, and children have been slaughtered and millions more have been maimed, raped, and driven from their homes. Peacekeeping and peacemaking are the most urgent priorities for a new world.

Not all violence is deadly. It begins with anger, intolerance, impatience, unfair judgments, and aggression. It is often reenacted in our language, our entertainment, our driving, our competitive behavior, and the way we treat our environment. These acts and attitudes are not the same as abusive behavior or physical attacks, but they create a climate where violence prospers and peace suffers. We are also experiencing the polarization of public life and militarization of politics with increased reliance on "attack" ads, "war" rooms, and intense partisan combat in place of the search for the common good and common ground.

Fundamentally, our society needs a moral revolution to replace a culture of violence with a renewed ethic of justice, responsibility, and community. New policies and programs, while necessary, cannot substitute for a recovery of the old values of right and wrong, respect and responsibility, love and justice. God's wisdom, love, and commandments can show us the way to live, heal, and reconcile. "Thou shalt not kill, Thou shalt not steal" are more than words to be recited; they are imperatives for the common good. Our faith challenges each of us to examine how we can contribute to an ethic which cherishes life, puts people before things, and values kindness and compassion over anger and vengeance. A growing sense of national fear and failure must be replaced by a new commitment to solidarity and the common good.

III. Catholic Tradition, Presence, and Potential

In this task, the Catholic community has much at stake and much to contribute. What we believe, where we are, and how we live out our faith can make a great difference in the struggle against violence. We see the loss of lives. We serve the victims. We feel the fear. We must confront this growing culture of violence with a commitment to life, a vision of hope, and a call to action. Our assets in this challenge include:

- The *example and teaching* of Jesus Christ
- The *biblical values* of respect for life, peace, justice, and community
- *Our teaching* on human life and human dignity, on right and wrong, on family and work, on justice and peace, on rights and responsibilities
- *Our tradition* of prayer, sacraments, and contemplation which can lead to a disarmament of the heart

- A *commitment to marriage and family life,* to support responsible parenthood and to help parents teach their children the values to live full lives
- A *presence* in most neighborhoods—our parishes and schools, hospitals and social services are sources of life and hope in places of violence and fear
- An *ethical framework* which calls us to practice and promote virtue, responsibility, forgiveness, generosity, concern for others, social justice, and economic fairness
- A *capacity for advocacy* that cuts across the false choices in national debate—jails or jobs, personal or social responsibility, better values or better policies
- A *consistent ethic of life* which remains the surest foundation for our life together

Across our land, parishioners and priests, men and women religious, educators and social workers, parents and community leaders are hard at work trying to offer hope in place of fear, to fight violence with programs of peace, to strengthen families and weaken gangs.

Here are a few examples of ongoing efforts in dioceses and parishes to deal with violence in their communities:

- In Los Angeles, the Church through its "Hope in Youth" initiative works with others to combat gang violence with youth opportunities and economic development.
- In Boston, the Ten Point Coalition is an ecumenical group of clergy and lay leaders working to mobilize the Christian community around issues affecting African American youth—especially those at risk.
- The Diocese of Cleveland coordinated an interfaith, gun turn-in program that took more than 1,500 weapons off the streets.
- In Chicago, youth outreach efforts include conflict management; workshops on violence, drugs, and health; and positive alternatives to violence. A business training program called "Something Good for the Hood" was created by St. Sabina's Parish to teach youth and young adults responsibility and work skills.
- In Saginaw, the Office of Black Catholic Concerns uses a multimedia approach—marches, TV, radio, PSAs—with gang members to help them refocus their lives and reconnect with Church and community.
- The Toledo Diocese, in cooperation with the local YMCA, involves elementary schools in "conflict resolution and peer mediation" to heighten the awareness of the root causes of violence and address them.

- The Dioceses of Palm Beach and Billings offered the program *Building a Sacred Bridge of Reconciliation*, which challenges traditional attitudes about women that contribute to domestic abuse. The program is sponsored by the National Council of Catholic Women.
- Catholic parishes joined in the Greater Bridgeport Interfaith Action, which successfully passed a ban on assault weapons later upheld by the courts.
- In Phoenix, the social action office has made available to parents suggestions for responsible TV viewing and ways to approach local stations regarding antiviolence themes.
- In Jackson, Miss., Catholic Charities sponsors a shelter for battered families which serves 350 women and children each year from seven rural counties providing transitional housing, legal assistance, and individual and group counseling.
- Little Friends for Peace, in the Washington, D.C. area, is an organization dedicated to teaching nonviolent skills to young children through playful skill-building activities.
- The Diocese of Pittsburgh has joined a community-wide program for young people at risk providing viable alternatives to gangs through educational, recreational, and employment opportunities.

In parishes and schools, human service agencies, and family life and youth programs, our community of faith offers alternatives to violence, a commitment to education, and a source of hope and help in places of fear and failure. Now is the time for all of us to follow their leadership, to build on their example, to place our facilities at the service of the community. Our young people, especially, need support and challenge, discipline and opportunities to use their talents and carry out their responsibilities in a world of conflicting values and often dangerous choices.

IV. A Framework for Action

Much is being done, but more is required. Our community is called to reorganize its priorities and recommit its resources to confront the violence in our midst. This challenge will have many dimensions including:

- The call to *pray* for peace in our hearts and our world
- The ability to *listen*—to hear the pain, anger, and frustration that come with and from violence

- The duty to *examine* our own attitudes and actions for how they contribute to or diminish violence in our society
- The call to help people *confront* the violence in their hearts and lives
- The capacity to *build on existing efforts* and the strengths of our community: the work of parishes, schools, Catholic Charities, the Campaign for Human Development, and so forth
- Efforts to *hold major institutions accountable,* including government, the media, and the criminal justice system
- An *advocacy* strategy which moves beyond the often empty rhetoric of national debate, including
  —confronting the violence of *abortion*
  —curbing the easy availability of *deadly weapons*
- Supporting community approaches to *crime prevention and law enforcement,* including community policing, neighborhood partnerships with police, and greater citizen involvement
- Pursuing swift and effective *justice* without vengeance
- Support for efforts to attack *root causes* of crime and violence—including poverty, substance abuse, lack of opportunity, racism, and family disintegration
- Promoting more *personal responsibility* and broader social responsibility in our policies and programs
- *Building bridges* and promoting solidarity across racial and economic lines
- Pursuing *economic justice,* especially employment
- Working for legislation that *empowers parents* to choose and afford schools that reflect their values
- Overcoming the tragedy of *family violence* and confronting all forms of violence against women
- Promoting education, research, and training in *nonviolence*
- Responding to *victims* of violence, hearing their anguish and defending their dignity;
- *Strengthening families* by putting the needs of children and families first in our national priorities
- Continuing to work for *global disarmament,* including curbs on arms sales and a ban on the export of landmines

Unless we are able to cut through divisive rhetoric and false claims that suggest that more prisons are the only answer, more brutality the cure, or more violence the solution, we will not succeed. Our criminal justice system is failing. Too often, it does not offer security to society, just penalties and rehabilitation to offenders, or respect and restitution to victims. Clearly, those who commit crimes must be swiftly apprehended, justly tried, appropriately punished, and held to proper restitution. However, correctional facilities must do more than confine criminals; they must rehabilitate persons and help rebuild lives. The vast majority of those in prison return to society. We must ensure that incarceration does not simply warehouse those who commit crimes but helps them overcome the behaviors, attitudes, and actions that led to criminal activity. The answer is not simply constructing more and more prisons but also constructing a society where every person has the opportunity to participate in economic and social life with dignity and responsibility. People must answer for their actions. Those who harm others must pay the price, but all our institutions must also be held accountable for how they promote or undermine greater responsibility and justice.

Bumper sticker solutions—"three strikes and you're out," "two years and you're off," "one more child and your benefits are cut"—are no substitute for less appealing but more effective efforts to fight crime and strengthen families. Our nation needs to focus its energies and resources on helping communities combat crime and helping families overcome destructive moral and economic pressures, discrimination, and dependency. Our policies must help people escape poverty and discrimination and leave behind lives of addiction, self-destruction, and crime. We need both to hold people accountable *and* offer them concrete help and hope for a better future.

We also need to encourage a commitment to civility and respect in public life and communications—in the news media, politics, and even ecclesial dialogue. The search for the common good is not advanced by partisan gamesmanship, challenging other people's motives, or personal attacks. The focus on the sensational, the search for conflict, and the assumption of bad will are not the basis for dialogue and hurt the search for common ground.

The culture of violence also has worldwide dimensions. As the only world superpower, as the world's greatest consumer, and as the largest arms exporter, the United States has a special obligation to seek peace and promote justice through creative and responsible world leadership. We renew our commitment expressed in *The Harvest of Justice Is Sown in Peace* to work against the violence that threatens life in so many lands. Our nation must be engaged in devising new tools for promoting peace: finding ways to prevent and police conflicts, to protect basic rights, to promote integral human development, and to preserve the environment. The United States must move from leadership in supplying arms to leadership in providing resources, technology, and knowledge and for replacing conflict with peaceful progress. Rather than restrain the further development of the United Nations, the United States should help improve it by developing tools for preventing conflict, mediating disputes, and rescuing vulnerable populations from internal as well as external aggression. Catholic international education, outreach, and advocacy efforts need to continue to help shape a Church and nation more clearly committed to global responsibility and the pursuit of peace in a still violent world.

Perhaps the greatest challenge is the call for all of us to examine our own lives, to identify how we can choose generosity over selfishness, and choose a real commitment to family and community over individual acquisition and ambition. In many small ways, each of us can help overcome violence by dealing with it on our block; providing for the emotional, physical, and spiritual needs of our children; dealing with our own abusive behavior; or even treating fellow motorists with courtesy. Violence is overcome day by day, choice by choice, person by person. All of us must make a contribution.

We believe our ongoing *Catholic Campaign for Children and Families* is an important voice against violence and should focus with new priority and renewed urgency on how violence of every kind undermines the lives and dignity of families and children. As we carry this campaign forward, we will work for private action and public policy which help curb the violence in our land. Above all, the Church must be Church—a community of faith reaching out to affirm and protect life, teaching right from wrong, educating the young, serving the hurting, healing the wounds, building community, praying and working for peace.

V. We Can Be More Than We Are

The Catholic community is in a position to respond to violence and the threat of violence in our society with new commitment and creativity. More of the same is not sufficient. Business as usual is not enough. Our faith and facilities can be beacons of hope and safety for those seeking refuge from violent streets and abusive homes. People can become peacemakers in their homes and communities. Parishes can organize mentoring programs for teen parents. The Church can be the first point of referral for spousal abuse. We can incorporate ways to handle family conflict in our religious education and sacramental preparation programs. We can work for public policies that confront violence, build community, and promote responsibility. Finally, we can join with other churches in developing a community-wide strategy for making our neighborhoods more safe, welcoming, and peaceful. Here is a possible outline for action:

Worship and preaching: Parishes can invite parishioners to begin meetings and events with prayers for peace and an end to violence. The Sunday eucharistic celebration provides many opportunities for prayer and reflection on these themes, especially during the penitential rite and general intercessions. The homily can be a powerful means of promoting the scriptural call to peacemaking and to deepen our own relationship with Jesus, the source of true peace. The priest, adding a few words of his own as introduction, may wish to reinforce the significance of the rite of peace. Special penance services can be held, especially during Advent and Lent, to call us away from aggressive and violent behavior to that of peacemaking. We ask our preachers to consider how their preaching can be a call to peacemaking and a voice against violence in our families, neighborhoods, and the broader community.

Education: Our Catholic schools are a very significant bulwark against violence. They continue to offer moral and ethical foundations, discipline, and safety for millions of children. Schools can encourage dialogue between parents and youth, can teach basic values and conflict resolution, and can provide after-school programs (especially between the hours of 4:00 p.m. and 7:00 p.m.) for neighborhood youth. Just as clearly, our parish religious education programs can provide the values and support that can help people, especially young people, choose life and reject violence. Our schools and parish religious education programs can be vital safe havens for youth at risk.

Young adult and adult education programs in parishes can provide classes and learning experiences in parenting, conflict resolution, and spiritual development. Small-group faith sharing can provide opportunities for adults to share their experiences and learn from others. We can form our consciences, strengthen our commitment, and exercise our free will in ways that promote justice and resist violence.

Family ministry: The family is the key to the development of positive values, including peacemaking. Families need to talk about how violence affects each member, the family itself, and their neighborhood and to discuss ways of responding in a nonviolent manner. So much violent behavior has its roots in the deterioration of family life. Families that are experiencing domestic violence should search out helping organizations to assist them in overcoming this burden. Families can also use the evening dinner prayer or a prayer at other times to pray for peace within the family and community and within each individual. Family life ministry can provide parenting education, support groups, and marriage preparation programs that encourage faithful, healthy, and peaceful relationships. They also can offer media literacy resources to help parents take back control of their own television sets.

Youth ministry plays a unique role within the parish by providing young people with a community of peers and adults who affirm, support, and challenge them. Youth programs can provide a safe and healthy place where young people can gather rather than hanging out on the street corner or at the local shopping mall. While some sports programs can contribute to violent behavior, well-directed athletic programs that teach sportsmanship and promote cooperation can have a positive influence on our young people. Retreats—such a powerful experience for teens—can be developed around the theme of peacemaking and conflict resolution. Parishes can offer leadership training programs to develop positive life skills around Christian values. Music, which plays such a significant role in the life of youth, should be used as an instrument to discuss peacemaking and nonviolent behavior. Parish and school youth programs can offer real alternatives to gang membership.

Outreach: Working with their local Catholic Charities agencies, parishes can support and make use of shelters and hotlines for abused family members providing financial support and volunteer assistance. The remarkable response to our statement on violence against women, *When I Call for Help,* has yielded many models of education and outreach. Parish groups can also organize recreational programs for at-risk youth, child care and emergency pregnancy centers, and mentoring programs for youth and beginning families.

Advocacy: Parish and diocesan representatives and other groups can meet with media representatives to bring pressure against excessive violence and pornography. Legislative networks can advocate for public policies that prevent and combat crime, restrict dangerous weapons, promote safe communities, eliminate the death penalty, help lift people out of the "hellish cycle of poverty," and confront the violence of abortion.

Building community: Parishes can participate in wider community efforts to combat crime and work on local housing and education issues, enact spousal abuse laws, and create economic opportunities and viable alternatives to violence. Supporting the Campaign for Human Development in its funding of local self-help groups is an excellent way to help build and empower communities in their battle against violence.

Global solidarity: Through twinning relationships, through support of Catholic Relief Services' Operation Rice Bowl, and through advocacy on United States international policies, parishes can work against reliance on violence to resolve conflicts and for human rights and sustainable development throughout the world.

African American and Hispanic Catholic ministries: Continuing to provide exceptional leadership, these ministries bring together diverse groups across racial and ethnic lines to work against racism and violence and provide opportunities for young people.

Dioceses can support the efforts of parishes by supporting and sharing successful antiviolence models. We can also organize diocesewide efforts such as visits to local media outlets, coordinated social services, convocations, and training. As Church, we must continue our commitment to examine our own policies and practices to eliminate any form of abuse within our own church community wherever it may exist. Diocesan leadership can help our local communities of faith come together to resist violence and promote practical steps to make our neighborhoods more just and more peaceful places. We can work with other religious bodies and community groups to make common cause against violence. Our struggle against violence will be an integral part of an interfaith initiative, the Common Ground for the Common Good. Working with other religious groups, we will seek to advance the common good by overcoming the violence that hurts us all.

We recognize that this reflection is less an outline of solutions and more a call to action. We believe the most effective response to this problem is one that builds on the resources of the local community. To promote and support these local efforts, the committees of our conference who have expressed a special interest in this initiative (African American Catholics, Campaign for Human Development, Communications, Domestic Social Policy, Education, Hispanic Affairs, Laity, Marriage and Family Life, Pro-Life, Women in Society and in the Church, and Youth) will continue to work together to collect effective models and resources and make them available to parishes and dioceses.

We hope that Catholics and Catholic organizations at all levels will join us and respond to this call. Each of us can make a difference. For our part, the NCCB/USCC will in the weeks and months to come:

- Gather and disseminate resources and models for parish and diocesan efforts.
- Intensify our advocacy on national policies that address violence, including strengthening families, violence in the media, the availability of drugs and dangerous weapons, the violence of abortion and the use of the death penalty, and other economic and social policies that attack the root causes of violence.

We can demonstrate our common commitment in a visible way by focusing on the moral and human costs of violence between January 15 and January 22. January 15 is the birthday of Dr. Martin Luther King Jr., a powerful voice for nonviolence and peace. January 22 is the anniversary of the Supreme Court decision legalizing the destruction of unborn children, a terrible sign of the violence in our society. In the days between these two anniversaries, we ask Catholic dioceses, parishes, families, and organizations to join us in prayer, reflection, and action to confront the culture of violence in our midst. The theme of peacemaking is especially appropriate at this time of year when Christian Churches pray and gather to reflect on the challenge of unity within the body of Christ and the human family.

VI. Conclusion

Above all, we must come to understand that violence is unacceptable. We must learn again the lesson of Pope Paul VI, "If you want peace, work for justice."[9] We oppose lawlessness of every kind. Society cannot tolerate an ethic that uses violence to make a point, settle grievances, or help us get what we want. But the path to a more peaceful future is found in a rediscovery of personal responsibility, respect for human life and human dignity, and a recommitment to social justice. The best antidote to violence is hope. People with a stake in society do not destroy communities. Both individuals *and* institutions should be held accountable for how they attack or enhance the common good. It is not only the "down and out" who must be held accountable but also the "rich and famous." Our society needs both more personal responsibility and broader social responsibility to overcome the plague of violence in our land and the lack of peace in our hearts. Finally, we must realize that peace is most fundamentally a gift from God. It is futile to suggest that we can end all violence and bring about full peace merely by our own efforts. This is why we urge the Catholic community to join all our antiviolence efforts with constant and heartfelt prayer to Almighty God through Jesus, the Prince of Peace.

We close these reflections with a word of support and appreciation for those on the "front lines"—parents, pastors, parish leaders, youth workers, catechists and teachers, prison chaplains, men and women religious. At a time when heroes seem scarce, these people are real heroes and heroines, committing their lives to the service of others, standing against a tide of violence with values of peace and a commitment to justice. We commend peace officers who daily confront violence with fairness and courage and we support those who minister to them and their families. We also offer a word of encouragement to parents who daily confront the cultural messages that influence their children in a way that is so contradictory to basic values of decency, honesty, respect for life, and justice.

We believe silence and indifference are not options for a community of faith in the midst of such pain, but we recognize words cannot halt violence. We hope this message has helped to outline the moral challenge, affirm the efforts already underway, share the framework we have as Catholics, and call our community to both conversion and action.

The nation has been transfixed by the terrible tragedy of the five-year-old dropped to his death by two children in Chicago because he wouldn't steal candy. We must get beyond our fear and frustration, our indifference and ideological blinders, to hear his grandmother's cry at his funeral: "We hope somebody, somewhere, somehow, will do something about the conditions which are causing our children to kill each other."[10] We can be the "somebody." Now can be the time.

Let 1995 and the years that follow be a time when the Catholic community brings new energy and creativity to the vocation of peacemaking—within our families, within our neighborhoods, within our country, and within the world community. Let us embrace the challenge of John Paul II in his message to young people, when he calls them and all of us to be "communicators of hope and workers for peace."[11] Let us hear and act with new urgency on the words of Jesus: "Blessed are the peacemakers; they shall be called children of God" (Mt 5:9).

Notes

1. Report of the National Advisory Commission on Civil Disorders (Washington,. D.C.), 1968.
2. Based on reports of the U.S. Department of Justice and Department of Commerce, 1993.
3. "Violence Against Women: Relevance for Medical Practitioners," *Journal of the American Medical Association* 267 (June 17, 1992): 3184-3189.
4. The National Center for Health Statistics, unpublished data for 1991.
5. American Psychological Association, 1992.
6. Alan Guttmacher Institute, "Facts in Brief—Abortion in the United States," August 1994 (New York: Alan Guttmacher Institute, 1994).
7. The National Center for Health Statistics, unpublished data for 1991.
8. Pope John Paul II, "An Appeal for Peace and Reconciliation," Address at Drogheda, Ireland (September 29, 1979), *L'Osservatore Romano* [English edition] 41 (October 8, 1979): 8.
9. Paul VI, "Message of His Holiness Pope Paul VI for the Celebration of the Day of Peace," *Origins* 1:29 (January 6, 1972): 490-491.
10. *The Baltimore Sun*, October 21, 1994.
11. John Paul II, "Message to the Youth of the World on the Occasion of the IX and X World Youth Days," in *Come Home to Christ: World Youth Day '94 Resource Manual* (Washington, D.C.: United States Catholic Conference, 1994), 8; cf. Mt 5:9.

Source: Washington, D.C.: United States Catholic Conference, 1994.

Moral Principles and Policy Priorities for Welfare Reform

A Statement of the Administrative Board of the
United States Catholic Conference

March 1995

Introduction

At this moment in the life of our nation in which we Americans struggle to find a balance between the needs of our poor and the demands of fiscal accountability for our future economic health, we want to present once again the principles of Catholic social teaching in order to provide a context for national discussion. We focus on the question of welfare reform, although our concerns extend equally to critical issues of human life, budget priorities, housing, the rights of immigrants, and health care reform.

Our nation faces fundamental choices on welfare reform. This debate and these decisions will be a test of our nation's values and our commitment to the "least among us." Our people and leaders share many similar goals, including reducing illegitimacy and dependency, promoting work, and empowering families. Congress must sort through fiscal, political, and ideological pressures to fashion real reform which reflects our nation's best values and offers genuine help and opportunity to our poorest families. We pray this debate will advance the common good, not further divide our people along economic, racial, ethnic, and ideological lines.

As the Administrative Board of the United States Catholic Bishops' Conference, we offer these reflections as a contribution to this important debate. Our purpose is not to make any partisan point, but to share our principles and experience in the hope that they will help lift up the moral dimensions and human consequences of this debate. As religious teachers, we draw our directions from consistent Catholic moral principles, not ideological or political agendas. The values that guide our approach to welfare reform are not new:

- Respect for human life and human dignity
- The importance of the family and the value of work
- An option for the poor and the call to participation
- The principles of subsidiarity and solidarity

However, these principles take on special urgency when a fifth of our children are growing up poor in the richest nation on earth and 30 million Americans of all ages live in poverty. Lack of opportunity, poverty, and dependency are destroying millions of families, harming countless children.

As pastors, we also seek to share our community's experiences in serving those in need. Poor families are not an abstract issue for us; they are sisters and brothers. They have names and faces. They are in our shelters and soup kitchens, our parishes and Catholic Charities agencies. As the largest nonpublic provider of human services to poor families, the Catholic community knows all too well the failures and abuses of the current system, the potential and limitations of private and religious charity, and the ways in which lives are diminished and dignity denied by widespread dependency and poverty in our land.

No institution in American life is more committed to the basic moral values of marriage, family, responsibility, work, sexual restraint, and sacrifice for children than our Church. We preach, teach, and promote these values every day in our parishes, schools, and outreach efforts. We also are committed to the values of justice, charity, and solidarity with the poor and vulnerable. We believe our society needs both more personal responsibility and broader social responsibility, better values and better policies to reduce poverty and dependency in the United States.

The Urgency of Reform

We strongly support genuine welfare reform that strengthens families, encourages productive work, and protects vulnerable children. We are not defenders of the welfare status quo, which sometimes relies on bureaucratic approaches, discourages work, and breaks up families. However, we oppose abandonment of the federal government's necessary role in helping families overcome poverty and meet their children's basic needs.

It is worth recalling that many of us are or have been the beneficiaries of government assistance—direct and indirect—but many are rightly frustrated by the current welfare system:

- Recipients who find their dignity undermined and their needs poorly addressed
- Taxpayers who fear their dollars encourage dependency rather than empowerment
- Providers who spend more time checking for fraud than helping families

- Public officials who have responsibility without adequate resources, accountability without sufficient authority

The status quo is unacceptable. It is children who pay the greatest price for the failures of the current system. Genuine welfare reform is a moral imperative and urgent national priority.

An Agenda for Reform

Welfare reform needs to be comprehensive in analysis but targeted and flexible in its implementation. We seek a new approach that promotes greater responsibility and offers more concrete help to families in leaving poverty behind through productive work and other assistance. Increased accountability and incentives should be tailored to a particular family's needs and circumstances, not "one-size-fits-all" requirements. Top-down reform with rigid national rules cannot meet the needs of a population as diverse as poor families. However, simply shifting responsibility without adequate resources, standards, and accountability could leave America's poor children worse off. Genuine welfare reform should rely on incentives more than harsh penalties; for example, denying needed benefits for children born to mothers on welfare can hurt the children and pressure their mothers toward abortion and sterilization.

More specifically, we will advocate for welfare reform which:

A. Protects Human Life and Human Dignity

We believe a fundamental criterion for all public policy, including welfare reform, is protection of human life and human dignity. In states across the country, our state Catholic conferences have stood against proposals that deny benefits to children because of their mother's age or dependence on welfare. These provisions, whatever their intentions, are likely to encourage abortion, especially in those states that pay for abortions but not for assistance to these children. In seeking to change the behavior of parents, these provisions hurt children, and some unborn children will pay with their lives.

Our Church works every day against sexual irresponsibility and the out-of-wedlock births which come with it. We do not believe teenagers should be encouraged to set up their own households. However, legislation offering increased flexibility to states should not restrict assistance in ways we, and most observers, believe will encourage abortions. We are working with Catholic Charities USA and other national pro-life groups in opposing these provisions and in proposing alternatives that provide assistance in ways that safeguard children but do not reinforce inappropriate or morally destructive behavior.

For us, this is a matter of moral consistency. Our faith requires us to protect the lives and dignity of the vulnerable children, whether they are born or unborn. We cannot support policies which are likely to lead to more abortions. Every child is precious to us. We recognize that human life is also threatened and diminished by the failures of the current welfare system and our broader culture. Children thrown from windows, found in Dumpsters, and abused in their homes are tragic symptoms of culture in disarray and a welfare system in urgent need of real reform. It is worth noting that it is not just low-income families that sometimes engage in destructive behavior. Personal irresponsibility, family disintegration, and loss of moral values touch not just the "down and out," but also the "rich and famous" and the rest of us.

B. Strengthens Family Life

Welfare reform should affirm the importance of marriage, strong intact families, personal responsibility, self-discipline, sacrifice, and basic morality. It should help mothers and fathers meet the social, economic, educational, and moral needs of their children. We support a children's tax credit (which includes poor families), a strengthened Earned Income Credit, and stronger child support enforcement to help meet the economic needs of America's families. We also support policies to keep families together and fathers involved, including new efforts to discourage parenthood outside of marriage, an end to marriage penalties in our tax code, and a halt to welfare policies that discourage marriage and discriminate against two-parent families. Our society must discourage adolescent sexual activity and teen pregnancy with at least as much urgency and persistence as we bring to discouraging smoking and substance abuse among our young.

C. Encourages and Rewards Work

Those who can work ought to work. Employment is the expected means to support a family and make a contribution to the common good. Too often welfare discourages work by eliminating health and child care benefits for those who leave the welfare rolls for the labor market. Real reform will offer education, training, and transitional help to those who exchange a welfare check for a paycheck. The challenge is to ensure that reform leads to productive work with wages and benefits that permit a family to live in dignity. Rigid rules and arbitrary timelines are no substitute for real jobs at decent wages and the tax policies that can help keep families off welfare.

D. Preserves a Safety Net for the Vulnerable

For those who cannot work, or whose "work" is raising our youngest children, the nation has built a system of income, nutrition, and other supports. Society has a responsibility to help meet the needs of those who cannot care for themselves, especially young children. AFDC, food stamps, and other entitlement programs provide essential support for poor children. We will support more effective and responsive federal-state-community partnerships, but we cannot support "reform" that will make it more difficult for poor children to grow into productive individuals. We cannot support reform that destroys the structures, ends entitlements, and eliminates resources that have provided an essential safety net for vulnerable children or permits states to reduce their commitment in this area. Also, we cannot support punitive approaches that target immigrants, even legal residents, and take away the minimal benefits that they now receive.

E. Builds Public/Private Partnerships to Overcome Poverty

As advocates of both subsidiarity and solidarity, we believe a reformed welfare system should rely more fully on the skill and responsiveness of community institutions and increased involvement and creativity of states. However, private and religious efforts to serve those in need are being severely stretched. They cannot—and should not—be seen as a substitute for wise public policy that promotes effective public-private partnerships.

Overcoming poverty and dependency will require more creative, responsive, and effective action in both the public and private sectors. Overly bureaucratic programs must give way to more community, local, and family initiatives more responsive to individual needs, potential, and problems. Mediating institutions can serve people with greater effectiveness, efficiency, and dignity. We are not opposed to carefully designed block grant initiatives in some areas if they come with adequate resources, accountability, and safeguards for poor families. States can shape programs to meet their local realities, but poverty has national dimensions and consequences that require federal commitment and national standards, safeguards, and protections. The nation needs to reform its welfare system, not abandon the federal government's role and responsibilities in fighting poverty. At the same time, private service providers should not be burdened with the enforcement of immigration laws.

F. Invests in Human Dignity

In the long run, real welfare reform will save money, but in the short run it will require new investments in a family tax credit, education, training, WIC, work, and child support. Recent state experiences support the reality that moving people off welfare will be neither easy nor inexpensive. Our everyday experience in helping families leave welfare suggests that hope, opportunity, and investment are essential to this transition. The social contract we seek will offer training, education, jobs, and other concrete assistance in exchange for the persistent commitment and effort of persons trying to leave poverty. Simply cutting resources and transferring responsibility is not genuine reform. We must resist the temptation to see poor women, minority families, or immigrants as either passive victims or easy scapegoats for our society's social and economic difficulties.

Conclusion

For the Catholic community, the measure of welfare reform is whether it will enhance the lives and dignity of poor children and their families. The goal of reform ought to be to promote decent work and reduce dependency, not simply cut budgets and programs. The target of reform ought to be poverty, not poor families. We believe our society will be measured by how "the least of these" are faring. Welfare reform will be a clear test of our nation's moral priorities and our commitment to seek the common good. We hope the welfare reform debate will be a time for civil and sustained dialogue, more focused on the needs and potential of poor families than on the search for partisan advantage. This debate could set an important framework for how our nation addresses not only welfare, but also other human needs. We hope these reflections will contribute to this kind of debate and will encourage Catholics to bring their voices and values to this important national dialogue, which will say so much about what kind of society we are and will become.

Source: Washington, D.C.: United States Catholic Conference, 1995.

Communion and Mission: A Guide for Bishops and Pastoral Leaders on Small Church Communities

A Statement from the U.S. Bishops' Committee on Hispanic Affairs
Approved by the NCCB Administrative Committee

March 1995

Preface

Communion and Mission: A Guide for Bishops and Pastoral Leaders on Small Church Communities is designed as a tool for bishops and their pastoral ministers involved in the new evangelization. Given the uniqueness of the relationship between faith and culture in the diverse communities that comprise our Church in the United States, this statement seeks to shed light on the potential that small church communities can have in the efforts to promote the new evangelization, particularly in meeting the challenge of making evangelization new in its ardor, methodology, and expression.

In response to the popularity of small church communities in many Hispanic and non-Hispanic communities, the Bishops' Committee on Hispanic Affairs has developed *Communion and Mission* after several drafts and over several years. The recommendations of experienced pastoral ministers, as well as the theological context and the relationship of small communities to parish life, have been major variables in developing a statement that responds to the many pastoral challenges faced by the Church today.

Small church communities have been present in our country for many years, but in different forms and at times separated from the parish community. Perhaps this occurred because there has been little ecclesial information developed in the United States as to how to foster them, respond to their presence, or work with them in our parish communities. In recent years, however, small church communities have developed significantly. Several books and articles have been published that show how they are established and how they function within the parish community. In addition, there are well-organized diocesan, regional, and national gatherings of small church communities every year. In some dioceses, small church communities are also part of the diocesan structure and are vital to the evangelization process.

Given the diversity of the Church, small church communities are different by nature. They respond to the pastoral needs and realities of the communities of faith that form them. *Communion and Mission* underscores the common elements that are important in preserving and strengthening the Catholic identity of these communities, as well as in fostering their identity.

Communion and Mission: A Guide for Bishops and Pastoral Leaders on Small Church Communities and the accompanying bilingual discussion guide and video, *Comunidad,* can be excellent resources for the new evangelization.

Small Church Communities:
A Source of Hope for the Church

Since Pentecost, the Spirit has guided the Church in each age so that it can credibly proclaim the good news of Jesus Christ. In our time, and under the inspiration of the Spirit, a new ecclesial reality is emerging—that of small church communities—through which we can see the creative grace of God at work. Small church communities are a source of great hope for the whole Church. Steadfast, active church communities linked with the larger parish community should be encouraged and promoted. These small communities are the responsibility of the bishop, who is called to be a living sign of unity in the particular Church entrusted to his care. At this historical juncture, the Bishop's Committee on Hispanic Affairs offers the following reflections to assist the diocesan bishops and their collaborators as they offer leadership and guidance to the small church communities in their dioceses.

Among Hispanics, small church communities are becoming an important and useful vehicle for the new evangelization to which the Church is being called.[1] They are a place in which the religious and cultural identity of Hispanics is affirmed. In addition, the Christian household is a privileged place in which persons relate a faith journey, find nurturing support, and focus on missionary efforts. The strong sense of family which Hispanics retain in their daily living is strengthened in the small church communities.

When solidly rooted in Scripture, church tradition, and Hispanic religiosity, small church communities constitute a new moment in the Church's self-understanding, epitomizing the celebration and proclamation of the Church. These gatherings of the people of God are integrally linked to the parish, and through it, to the diocesan and universal Church.

Today's active communities are works in progress. They have yet to reach their full potential to become authentic community centers of evangelization. This great potential exists, however, since small church communities already engage in personal relationships of faith through fellowship, evangelization, liturgy, mission, and service.

Hispanics and Small Church Communities

For Hispanics, a predominant Catholic presence in the United States,[2] the Catholic faith is closely linked with cultural manifestations of their identity. Small church communities help to affirm the Hispanics' faith-cultural identity on a personal level and provoke a communal evangelical mission. In this way Hispanics continue to contribute as a religious force to the Church and society.

Through small church communities, Latino Catholics are finding a way to preserve and share the rich cultural and faith expressions and family values that help them face the challenges of a rapidly changing world. Small church communities strengthen Hispanic religiosity—a homespun spirituality that enables them to take responsibility for their Christian way of living. The Church respects this emerging spirituality as a reflection of Hispanic cultural and spiritual identity and recognizes that an attack against this identity is an attack against their Catholicity.

Small communities fortify a centuries-old tradition of faith. Affirmed and strengthened in their identity as Catholics, Hispanics can better serve the larger community. Yet, while small communities serve to preserve a vibrant faith, they are not simply warehouses of religious and cultural traditions. They are truly the expression of an emerging spirituality.

In the last few years, they have made significant strides in the religious, educational, political, economic, and social areas of our society. Hispanics are more visible in church leadership as bishops, theologians, and lay leaders. They have become a visible presence in this country's political, economic, and educational systems. Nevertheless, they still rank among the poorest Americans on the economic scale. They are represented disproportionately in the numbers of high school dropouts, pregnant teenagers, and persons in prison.

While many Latinos have not yet found a home in our society, they have generally found one in the Church, especially in small church communities. Many Hispanic Catholics are more comfortable with small communities where people know one another and can interact with their priests and ministers on a personal level. Hispanics look to these communities for a credible experience of evangelization, where the Gospel is preached and truly lived in daily life.

Communion and Mission

The origin of the Church lies in the mission of Jesus Christ, the Incarnate Son. In him and through him, the life of the Trinity is communicated. The community of disciples saw themselves sent by God into history with the mission of Christ in the power of the Spirit.[3] Thus, the small faith communities model is taken from the Church's foundation, the primary community *par excellence*—the Trinity. As Church, the small communities are "a people made one with the unity of the Father, the Son, and the Holy Spirit."[4] At the heart of this unity is the Church's mission of bringing the promises of God to fulfillment.

Since the beginning, the Church has recognized itself as communitarian (Acts 2:42). A small church community, by nature, is a communion with a mission. This belief is grounded in the truth that the mystery of God and the mystery of salvation are inseparable. God's self-emptying love, which draws us into life with the Trinity, is lived out in his saving deeds among us. It is a way of living the mystery that is the Church. As groups with a mission, small church communities realize the trinitarian relationships and God's saving activity among us.

The Triune God invites us to communion. Jesus Christ incarnates this invitation, initiating the reign of God among us. Some reject this invitation, while those who accept it share in God's glory.[5] Small church communities respond to this invitation through their efforts to form authentic communion as Church and through their mission of fostering the reign of God. The Spirit enlightens them so that they can understand Jesus' message. This Spirit reveals to them the true identity of Christ and empowers them for the mission. Since this communion also invites them to include others, giving preference always to the rejected, marginalized, abandoned, and forgotten, the Church is renewed in its self-expression as communion for all. This basic sense of communion enables the Church to authenticate itself by seeing itself in a new light.

Partaking of life in the Triune God has dramatic consequences. It means entering, in the most profound sense, into God's saving project for a new humanity. Living in communion with the Triune God calls members of these communities to enter into a life of love and communion with all their brothers and sisters. In this sense, small communities—communally and prophetically—live out the call as artisans of the coming reign of God.

Integral evangelization is at the core of the faith life of the small communities:

> There is no gap between love of neighbor and the desire for justice. . . . The evil inequities and oppression of every kind which afflict millions of men and women today openly con-

tradict Christ's Gospel and cannot leave the conscience of any Christian indifferent.

The Church, in her docility to the Spirit, goes forward faithfully along the paths to authentic liberation. . . . But a vast number of Christians, from the time of the Apostles onwards, have committed their powers and their lives to liberation from every form of oppression and to the promotion of human dignity. The experience of the saints and the example of so many works of service to one's neighbor are an incentive and a beacon for the liberating undertakings that are needed today.[6]

In their efforts to bring God's providential plan to fulfillment, small communities are confronting obstacles to communion with God and with one another, dictating a re-ordering of life at all levels. They work to triumph over the social, political, economic, racial, gender, and environmental relationships that humanity creates as tools for destruction and death. This struggle against the obstacles that are contemporary society's idols of death serves to renew the small communities, which are not set up for themselves, but for mission.[7]

Small church communities should not be isolated from the rest of the Church's life. The Church is not simply a community of communities. It is an organic whole that expresses itself in ways such as small communities. While these structures are local and particular, their reality is universal and truly Catholic. So is their thrust. As realizations of the mystery of the Church, small church communities do not exist separately from the apostolic ministry of the bishops. Small communities ultimately attest to the faithfulness of God's relationship with us and with our world.

Characteristics of Small Church Communities

The following constitutive elements are common to many authentic small church communities throughout the country. These characteristics can serve as a guide in working with newly formed church communities or in getting to know those communities already in place. It is our sincere hope that by supporting all church communities, they will continue to mature and bear fruit.

1. Composition

Small church communities allow their members to relate to one another at a personal level, sharing in their common journeys of faith. Their small size reflects an attempt at a qualitative, rather than quantitative, approach to faith development. This allows greater emphasis on a person's lived experience as seen through the lens of church tradition, sacred Scripture, and the Hispanic history of suffering and hope.

The smallness of the group allows for concentration of church life and mission. It is not an effort for separation from the parish. The strength of the small groups comes from a concerted effort to delve more deeply into Christian life on a more personal level, while at the same time remaining intimately linked to the Church's universal mission. In a small group the experience of God's daily effect on life stands at the center of the group's activities. Knowing firsthand the needs of its members allows participants to experience a sense of belonging and interconnectedness with their co-journeyers. The small gathering enables a more direct faith formation and personal sharing of stories of God's saving deeds.

2. *Communitarian Life*

In a society plagued by individualism, separatism, and a general disregard for the well-being of others, small church communities reinforce the communitarian nature of church life. By calling their members to make the connection between faith and daily life, small ecclesial communities can credibly live out the Church's preferential option for the poor through their close links with the homeless, the poor, and those suffering at the bottom of the unjust social pyramid.

The essence of church life in the Christian community is to become one with the Trinity through communion with one another. Living in community is to live in communion with the Triune God. God is present where there is authentic communion. A life of communion and love with our brothers and sisters is the path to divine life.

The sharing of faith stories reinforces the experience that Christian life is communitarian. Reading and meditating upon the sacred Scriptures in community helps us to understand the meaning of Scripture with the mind of the Church, thus avoiding individualistic and erroneous interpretations. This leads to a renewed link with the Christian tradition and a deeper understanding of the Church as *koinonia* (Acts 2:42-44; 2 Cor 13:13).

Through a communitarian life, all members are challenged to a shared vision of the life and work of Jesus Christ and the call to imitate him with a view of service to the world. The group aims for authentic community, which is centered on life with God and the mission of bringing the world to full unity in him. Although the Christian community is called to be of one mind (Acts 2:46), differences and conflicts are bound to arise. Living in community, however, calls all to deal creatively with tensions in obedience to the unfolding plan of God. Overcoming difficulties brings new life and depth to each member of the community.

The communitarian life of small church communities invites its members to full life and growth in God. These communities are not simply associations for intimate self-disclosure and emotional support. They promote their members' growth through the experiences and processes in which they discover and accept their God-given vocation. In keeping with the mission of the Church, they become artisans of their own destiny.

In communities people come together to authenticate their interactions and to share in the struggles of their journeys. The communitarian lifestyle, however, poses challenges for its members. In our busy society, small groupings become reflective environs, raising the question of God's saving deeds in our lives and our world. The challenge of living in community is to enlarge a person's vision of God's saving plan without undermining one's development and growth. Individuals can feel accepted, welcomed, and invited to maturity.

The community does not close in on itself, but rather integrates families of grandparents, parents, sisters, and brothers. It promotes strong interpersonal relationships based on faith, love, and unity. Members share their daily lives, their basic problems, their joys, and their struggles. All feel welcomed there—integrated and co-responsible—with a fundamental equality, even if there is a diversity of function. Members of the community demonstrate a mutual, profound, caring, loving, and committed partnership that brings them together in solidarity.

Small ecclesial communities can avoid the trap of being self-serving through a grounding in their mission and through interconnection with other levels of Church. The communitarian aspect strongly emphasizes this unity as an essential element of being Church. This unity forms a bridge with other communities, allowing the mission of God to flourish.

The communion that God desires does not end with the small church community. It reaches out to other levels of church life, including the parish, the diocese, the region, and the universal Church. Small ecclesial communities are in communion with these other elements, as well as with their legitimate pastors. They participate in a strong *pastoral de conjunto*.[8]

3. Ecclesial Role

Small church communities are a communion of God's people living out the mission of Jesus Christ in the power of the Spirit. In these communities, new and effective ways of living the mystery of the Church are being formed. This phenomenon challenges us to look at ourselves as Church. Since it is still too early to know where this movement of the Spirit will lead us, we can only point to the reality and offer constructive direction.

The numbers of small church communities emerging within parishes indicate that parishes are providing pastoral leadership and fostering credible structures. For this we are grateful to their pastors and pastoral leaders and to God who gives the growth. Other parishes could also benefit greatly from the presence of small church communities. Without parish support and proper leadership, small groups could arise but lose direction. Furthermore, fundamentalist groups could easily move in to fill a vacuum.

Small church communities must not be seen in isolation. They are not another Church, but part of the one Church. Their major contribution is the new expression of Christian life. They offer the Church a new inner life. Small communities are not a new movement in the Church. Nor are they simply neighborhood subgroups of the parish structure. They are the Church itself. They are a smaller expression of the universal Church. As such, the Church is developing new structures to allow this inner life to flourish. As communities of faith and mission, they give witness to a renewal of the Church's inner life. Where this will lead depends on the Spirit.

Pope John Paul II has called for new parish structures for the Christian faithful. He calls for "adaptation of parish structures according to the full flexibility granted by canon law . . . in promoting participation of the lay faithful," and sees small communities as "true expressions of ecclesial communion" when united with their pastors.[9] These vibrant small communities allow Catholics to regain their universal momentum at a local level.

Small church communities understand their ecclesial nature as they strive to balance their inner life with their missionary thrust. Without this effort they run the risk of losing their credibility as ecclesial communities. Evangelization in all its dimensions enables the communities to blossom and remain on the path of constant renewal in faithfulness to Christ.

4. Prophetic Mission

Our God is a God of life. As prophet, Jesus announced and initiated God's life as the rule of his coming reign among us. Small communities are called to make as their own Jesus' prophetic vision of the coming reign. Like Jesus, they must stand in solidarity with all who suffer. Thus, it is important that these communities study the Church's social teachings and remain open to living in solidarity with the poor. As small prophetic communities, they exist in the concrete realities of daily life, announcing the reign of God's new life.

In their commitment to fostering the reign of the Triune God, small church communities experience the mystery of God and the mystery of salvation as inseparable. As prophetic communities their task is to examine human reality from the perspective of God's purposes so that their efforts are connected to God's designs for a new humanity.

Small church communities critically investigate the root causes of the idols of death, which are the obstacles to God's plan. They also interpret the signs of the times from the view of the mission of Jesus. Therefore, when small communities discuss, plan, and focus on what direction to take, they begin and end with their commitment to the task of the coming reign of God. In this way, these church communities become faithful to Christ's mission by refusing to give idols of death a place in history. As prophetic communities, they confront sin as an annihilation of communion with God and with one another.

Since God's plan for us is communion, small church communities are seen as countercultural in a society torn by division. The profound alienation felt in today's society is tied to the root cause of sin masquerading itself in the form of injustice, marginalization, abuse, abortion, drugs, and violence. The communities' task of integral evangelization is to view people in all of the dimensions affecting their lives: spiritual, political, cultural, economic, social, educational, and environmental, among others. In this way they can proclaim Christ as true Lord of all creation.

Bonding together under the banner of the God of life, small communities can critically examine the prevailing culture. They support an alternative way of life in a materialistic and consumption-driven society. The tendencies toward individualism and separatism and the disregard for the good of others are challenged by the presence of prophetic communities. Small communities invite and help people to be different in society, calling them to a conversion to the ways of God. This leads to communion.

As prophetic church communities, these groups attest to the possibilities of a new life with the Triune God, bearing witness from the very place where the Gospel is lived. They profess communally that God is for us. Small communities affirm the faithfulness and truthfulness of God's relationship with us and with our world. For this reason, we can call them communities of hope. As such, they proclaim that the God of life is victorious over all the forces of destruction that threaten true communion between sisters and brothers, among themselves, and with the Triune God.

Latinos resonate with the prophetic dimension of small church communities because they have often lived as strangers in their own land. Yet, they have remained united by a profound faith and hope in the providence of God. In spite of historical obstacles, faith is at the center of their lives. Hispanics are experiencing a reawakening of cultural identity which is, at the same time, a rebirth of faith identity. Small faith communities affirm what is inherently good about being an Hispanic Catholic, while at the same time challenging members to grow in light of the Church's universal mission.

5. Liturgical Life

The life of the Church is directed to the worship and praise of the living God. Worship and praise are, therefore, an essential part of living in small church communities. In this worship, the eucharist is the heart of their life and their essential link with the unity of the whole Church. Life in service to the reign of God is connected intimately with praise of God. The eucharist celebrates the paschal mystery—the communion of God with his people—and anticipates the table of the new humanity where all will be one in Christ (Jn 17). It is the summit toward which all is focused and the source of all new life.[10] The eucharistic life of the small communities is inseparable from their commitment to partake in the mission of God's saving plan. The members bring to the eucharist their lives as Christians to offer as a part of worship. They become renewed in their commitment to begin again as agents of the reign of God.

These small assemblies gather as a people of praise and lift up to God key moments in their common journey of joys and struggles. They celebrate in prayers of thanksgiving and petition. While they share in personal devotions, community prayer unites the group with the prayerful chorus of the whole Church. As assemblies of praise, they are centers for celebrating the gift of faith and the promise of new life.

In light of their evangelical mission, it is important for small worshiping communities to develop prayer lifestyles and forms of communal reflection in keeping with the Church's tradition and practice. In so doing, the Bible is primary among their sources. Special sensitivity must be given to the inclusion of the faith traditions and customs of all the members present. Inculturation is indispensable in order to make the people's faith expressions a part of their prayer life. In this way, people touch the mystery of faith in their own language and through their own symbols. They are thus led to a renewed commitment to Christian living.

Hispanics tend to view all of life as sacred and have generally developed a profound sense of the divine in daily living. This is evident in their popular religiosity. Unfortunately, liturgical celebrations reflecting the Hispanic life of faith and other events that are dear to them, such as Guadalupe celebrations, *posadas,* processions, and *quinceañeras,* are often not incorporated into the worship life of the parish. In small communities, Hispanics find support to retrieve this sense of popular piety and to reaffirm the values contained in these celebrations. As a people of praise, Latinos have a profound sense of celebration, or *fiesta,* and view life as a victory of grace over sin. Fiesta celebrates a moment of God's presence among us and anticipates the joy of the coming reign of God.

6. *Missionary Thrust*

As the Father has sent me, so I send you (Jn 17:18). Small church communities are fundamentally missionary agents of the reign of God. The Second Vatican Council stressed the notion of the Church as missionary to the world. In more recent times, Pope John Paul II emphasized the right of all peoples to hear the good news and called the Church to a new evangelization in preparation for the third millennium of faith.

Small church communities engage in evangelization as an ongoing process, with life in a missionary community calling the members to constant conversion. This implies an encounter with Christ and an openness to allowing the reign of God to penetrate and guide one's whole life. To remain faithful to any evangelization effort, missionary church communities need to make solidarity with the poor a priority. This helps the community endure and retain sight of its ultimate goal of communion and mission. A community matures by being missionary; otherwise, it becomes self-serving and self-destructive.

Missionary communities assess how best to concretely live out their evangelical mission by critically studying the causes of alienation, emptiness, and suffering. They question why society supports obstacles to God's plan. As missionary church communities, they challenge the causes of individualism, separatism, and death-dealing ideologies that masquerade as being for the good of others. Small church communities protest all that attacks the coming reign of God. They plan as a group, within the framework of a *pastoral de conjunto,* to more effectively respond to the needs of the people with whom they live. Their efforts attest to God's activity to eradicate sin and death and form a communion where all are brothers and sisters in union with the Triune God.

7. *Ministerial Role*

Small church communities are ministerial because they are made up of baptized persons who are called to be collaborators in the priesthood of Jesus Christ.

> Christ, the high priest and unique mediator, has made of the Church "a kingdom of priests for his God and Father" (Rev 1:6; cf. Rev 5:9-10; 1 Pt 2:5, 9). The whole community of

> believers is, as such, priestly. The faithful exercise their bap-
> tismal priesthood through their participation, each accord-
> ing to his proper vocation, in Christ's mission as priest,
> prophet, and king. Through the sacraments of Baptism and
> Confirmation the faithful are "consecrated to be . . . a holy
> priesthood" (LG, nos. 10, 1).[11]

Through the Church God calls forth its ministers and forms them into ministerial communities. They exercise their role by linking the new evangelization with efforts to manifest among us the saving work of Jesus Christ, the high priest. Seen from this perspective, communities call their members to assume their rightful role in the mission of the whole Church. In this way, the laity will move from seeing themselves as simply father's helpers to seeing themselves as responsible collaborators in the life and mission of the ministerial community. The more the faithful fulfill their work in the home, the parish, the neighborhood, and the world, the more they make present the saving work of Christ, the high priest.

While all members belong to the ministerial community through baptism, confirmation, and eucharist, not everything that the community does is considered ministry. The community engages in authentic ministry when its members' activities are carried out for the sake of the reign of God and in the name of the Church. Ministry is directly tied to the saving work of Christ. For this reason, communities should offer their members proper and adequate training and formation. Ministries will flourish and new ones will emerge as long as members creatively collaborate with their pastors, so that all ministry is done in the name of the Church.

> A rapidly growing phenomenon in the young churches . . .
> is that of "ecclesial basic communities". . . . They . . . become
> leaven of Christian life, of care for the poor and neglected,
> and of commitment to the transformation of society. Within
> them, the individual Christian experiences community and
> therefore senses that he or she is playing an active role and
> is encouraged to share in the common task. Thus, these com-
> munities become means of evangelization and of the initial
> proclamation of the Gospel and a source of new ministries.[12]

In affirmation of the hierarchical nature of the Church, small communities foster a discipleship in solidarity and equal responsibility. According to their proper call and mission, all ministers have the duty to make present the vision and work of Jesus Christ, the priest, prophet, and king.[13]

Ministry is a call, a vocation. Small church communities call their members to promote vocations for all the church ministries. Members involved in ministerial activity are not volunteers who simply help the Church or the clergy, but are responsible disciples participating in the ministry of Christ, the high priest.

Conclusion

The elements outlined above are not an exhaustive list of the characteristics of small church communities. Others will emerge as these communities continue to bear fruit. We single these out simply to highlight certain characteristics of church life that will bind us as one Church. In these basic elements we see factors that renew the Church in a way that makes all of us more credible and at the same time faithful to the Lord. We offer guidance to help small church communities mature as an integral part of the universal Church, especially in light of the new evangelization.

Ultimately, communion and mission are a gift of the Triune God. It is the Father who offers us this gift in the person of Jesus Christ and by the power of the Spirit. It is the Triune God who brings into life these small communities and who sustains them. It is this Spirit of the living God who again calls the Church to credibility in communion and mission, bearing witness to God's faithfulness to us and to our world. As Mary was present at Pentecost with the original church community, may she, model of faithful discipleship, continue to challenge and inspire the small ecclesial communities to bear much fruit.

Notes

1. The experience of small communities among Hispanics/Latinos in the United States is different from the Latin American experience of *comunidades de base*. In the United States, Hispanic Catholics are a minority in a Protestant country, often experiencing cultural and linguistic alienation. Since U.S. Hispanics have forged intimate ties between their identity and their faith expressions, small church communities serve to affirm their faith and cultural identity.

   The rich Latin American experience of small base communities called for in Medellín, Puebla, and Santo Domingo will continue to enrich the discussion and formation of the Church in the Americas. Furthermore, the experience of Hispanic Catholics in small church communities can be a help to others in this country in the formation of these communities.

2. National Conference of Catholic Bishops, *The Hispanic Presence: Challenge and Commitment* (Washington, D.C.: United States Catholic Conference, 1984); National Conference of Catholic Bishops, *National Pastoral Plan for Hispanic Ministry* (Washington, D.C.: United States Catholic Conference, 1988).

3.   Second Vatican Council, *Dogmatic Constitution on the Church (Lumen Gentium)*, nos. 2-4; Eph 2:18.
4.   The expression is from St. Cyprian's *De Oratione Dominica* 23: PL 4, 553, and is quoted in *Lumen Gentium*, no. 4.
5.   "He came to what was his own, but his own people did not accept him. But to those who did accept him he gave power to become children of God . . ." (Jn 1:11-12).
6.   Congregation for the Doctrine of the Faith, *Instruction on Christian Freedom and Liberation* (Vatican City: Vatican Polyglot Press, 1986), no. 57.
7.   Paul VI, *On Evangelization in the Modern World (Evangelii Nuntiandi)* (Washington, D.C.: United States Catholic Conference, 1975). In no. 58, Paul VI calls the small communities to be in solidarity with the Church's life, nourished by its teachings and united with its pastors.
8.   *National Pastoral Plan for Hispanic Ministry*, 9-17.
9.   John Paul II, *The Vocation and Mission of the Lay Faithful in the Church and in the World (Christifideles Laici)* (Washington, D.C.: United States Catholic Conference, 1988), no. 26.
10.   Second Vatican Council, *Constitution on the Sacred Liturgy (Sacrosanctum Concilium)*, no. 10.
11.   *Catechism of the Catholic Church* (Washington, D.C.: United States Catholic Conference, 1994), no. 1546.
12.   John Paul II, *On the Permanent Validity of the Church's Missionary Mandate (Redemptoris Missio)* (Washington, D.C.: United States Catholic Conference, 1990), no. 51.
13.   *Catechism of the Catholic Church*, no. 1268.

Source: Washington, D.C.: United States Catholic Conference, 1995.

Faithful for Life: A Moral Reflection

A Statement of the National Conference of Catholic Bishops

June 1995

A man on his way from Jerusalem to Jericho was beaten, robbed, and dumped by the side of the road to die. Three travelers later saw him lying there. The first and the second were his own countrymen, and in fact, one was a priest and the other a Levite. Each one crossed the road to avoid the victim and hurried on his way. The third man was a foreigner, almost as unwelcome as the bandits themselves. He was the only one who stopped, gave the victim first aid, carried him to the nearest inn (where he himself would not have been welcome to stay), and lodged him there at his own expense to convalesce (Lk 10:29-37).

This was the story told by Jesus when asked: "Who is my neighbor?" The Samaritan befriended the Jew in a way that the Jew's countrymen failed to do. Jesus tells us that the Samaritan did his duty, while the first to see the victim did not. To be a neighbor, the victim did not need to be kin or countryman or someone to whom the rescuer had made a commitment. Anyone lying helpless in that ditch was neighbor.

We are all journeying down from Jerusalem to Jericho, and this story haunts us, for it flatly contradicts the strong persuasion so widely held today that our loyalties and our obligations are owed only to those of our choice. On the contrary, we owe fidelity to those we choose and, beyond them, to others we do not choose. It is *we* who have been chosen to go out of our way for them.

The charity of Christ and the unsettling imperatives of his Gospel compel us as Catholic bishops to speak on behalf of neighbors whose lives are devalued: the faceless poor, the hungry children, the neglected elderly.

Human lives have stood in jeopardy for various reasons in our country and throughout the world, and our witness over the years has taken many forms and defended many victims. Beginning as early as 1840, the Catholic bishops of the United States have spoken out on myriad subjects that concern our fidelity to one another. Alcohol and drug abuse, racial justice, the welfare of working men and women and persons with disabilities, civil freedoms, capital punishment, adolescent pregnancy, and world peace are just a few of these.

Of particularly grave concern at this time, however, are abortion and euthanasia. We choose now to speak about these concerns because each places human life itself at stake, and each has broad implications for our fidelity to God and to one another.

At the very heart of our respect for human life is a special and persistent advocacy for those who depend on others for survival itself. Those most dependent lie on the opposite extremities of their life's journey, near the start and near the finish. Because they are helpless to provide for themselves, they are utterly at the mercy of those closest to them. Many are welcomed by those to whose care they have been entrusted. Others are not so welcomed.

Since the legal floodgates were opened in 1973 by the U.S. Supreme Court's decision in *Roe v. Wade,* an abortion mentality has swept across our land and throughout our culture. The language and the mindset of abortion—presented in terms of unlimited choice, privacy, and autonomy—pervade our entertainment, our news, our public policies, and even our private lives. Wrapped so appealingly in the language of self-determination, cloaked so powerfully in the mantle of federal authority, is it any wonder that the logic of *Roe* has been extended to apply beyond the unborn? Is it any wonder that it appears so explicitly in our public and private conversations about euthanasia?

Over the past year, in the midst of our reflections on the crises of abortion and euthanasia in our country, we were blessed with the papal encyclical, *The Gospel of Life (Evangelium Vitae).* Speaking to every country, the Holy Father reminded us that the modern phenomena of abortion and euthanasia highlight a crying need to respect, protect, love, and serve human life.[1] Here we reflect upon these issues in the context of the alarming trend to advance abortion and euthanasia in the name of freedom. But it is a freedom gone wrong.

As disciples of Christ, as bishops in his Church, our first concern for human life has to be for those who are unwanted—with fatal results—by their parents or their children, or by society itself. Such as these fall victim to the ultimate abuse of abortion or euthanasia. As human beings we are outraged at the cruel injustice of these acts of deliberate killing. And our Christian faith gives an even sharper edge to our consciences in this matter, compelling us to call for courage and unconditional love in defense of those who are helpless.

The Fraying of Fidelity

Faithful to a long tradition, the Second Vatican Council denounced abortion and euthanasia as "disgraceful" and "unspeakable crimes."[2] Yet such practices, proved through centuries of experience to be wrong and destructive of human life and human dignity, are in our day expounded upon in schoolrooms, prescribed by physicians, condoned by public figures, protected by courts, subsidized by legislatures, and even advertised in the Yellow Pages. How has it come to pass that the elimination of one's child or one's parent, acts of desperation wrought in every age, are now described as sensible and even attractive alternatives? And is it not unthinkable that people who call themselves Christians sometimes fit in so well among a people that tolerates the killing of its unborn children and elders?

It is for good reason that many find the roots of this disdain for life in the breakdown of the family. The family has a special role to play throughout the life of its members, for it is within the family that neighboring begins—or does not. The family is the first haven where those who are dependent—by being too young or too old, too disabled or too sick to care for themselves—find their closest and surest support. For this reason it can be called the "sanctuary of life."[3] At the heart of this sanctuary is fidelity—unwavering loyalty both to those we choose and to those who have been given to us. The unraveling of that fidelity in our time leaves dependents to become lawful victims of their guardians.

This same shift towards the self has altered our society's views on marriage and divorce. Men and women find it increasingly difficult to make permanent commitments to each other. Marriage, even for many who plan to parent, is seen as optional. At the same time, the grounds for divorce, restricted at first to adultery and desertion, have continually expanded in our society to include general incompatibility, finally giving way to groundless or "no fault" divorce. The outcome of groundless divorce has been increasingly more divorce and the disabling of marriage itself as an institution in society.

Christian marriage is the union of a man and a woman bound by the same transforming fidelity which Christ has for his Church: for better or for worse. When a people lose confidence in fidelity between husbands and wives, it is an easy leap to imagine that other fidelities— of parents to children, and of adult children to their elder parents—no longer need to be permanent, for-better-or-for-worse obligations. When a family lives in fidelity it is a place of refuge and dignity, a place where each member is accepted, respected, and honored precisely because he or she is a person; and if any member is in greater need, the care which he or she receives is all the more intense and attentive.[4] If it becomes each one only for himself or herself, then instead of being the source, school, and standard for fidelity to neighbor, the family can become the scene of its harshest violations. The home becomes the place where, when you knock, they no longer have to let you in.

Freedom Versus Commitment

This decay of inviolable trust has had pervasive effects. The view of human life as the pursuit of individual satisfaction, not to be curtailed by faithful duty, is a belief powerfully expounded in the United States in the fields of education, entertainment, information, and politics. As servants of Christ's Gospel, however, we are convinced that such a view of human life is profoundly mistaken.[5]

As the Gospel tells us, human beings find fulfillment in pursuing what is authentically good for the human person as created by God. The pursuit of disordered desires masquerading as "interests" easily leads to violence or greed or self-indulgence or loneliness. Our true needs include virtues that human beings sometimes lack the wisdom or the audacity to desire: steadfast friendship, clear thought, patience, candor, compassion, self-control. These are the sinews and ligaments of love.

It is not good for anyone to be alone (Gn 2:18). We find our fulfillment as committed individuals bound in kinship, friendship, and fellowship to our families, our neighbors, and then beyond them to strangers and even to enemies. Without community, we wither.

Many of the critical moments in our lives require that we rise to meet responsibilities given to us, not chosen by us. This is true of our obligation to be stewards of the world's resources. It is equally true of the obligations which bind us in love to our families. We are bound to our children, not because we chose them, but because we were given them: simply because they are our children, our very near neighbors.

Many in our society today seem to live by the belief that human beings find their ultimate sense and fulfillment in unlimited individual freedom. Unlimited personal choice is celebrated as the prerequisite for every satisfying human experience, even within the family. Yet such an individualistic concept of freedom severs the true meaning of freedom from its moorings and distorts social life. It extols a society in which individuals stand side by side, but have no bonds holding them together. Yet between life itself and freedom there is an inseparable bond, a link. And that link is love or fidelity.[6]

To live in fidelity we have to rearrange our lives, yield control, and forfeit some choices. To evade the full burden of putting ourselves at the disposal of those we belong to, to allot them only the slack in our own agendas and not what they require, is to practice desertion by other means.

Violation of Life and Trust

Abortion, and now euthanasia, have become socially accepted acts because many have been persuaded that people unfairly lose their freedom when others make claims on them that pose burdens and obligations. In the course of a very few years many people have come to think of an unplanned baby as an unwanted baby, and of an undesired baby as an undesirable one. The prescribed social remedy has been to put an end to the baby's life before he or she can make a claim on yours. Some even believe that a parent or a spouse who has lost the capacity to fend for herself or himself, or is too old or sick to be a good companion, or for whom the cost of care is hard to bear, should be helped to die. It is cruelly ironic that the thought of eliminating one's child or one's parent could be considered an acceptable, even altruistic, action.

To be sure, no one should be blind to the problems that women may face in regard to pregnancy. A decision to have an abortion is often tragic and painful for the mother. At times it is the father who pressures her to abort their child, or who indirectly encourages her to such a decision by leaving her to face the problems of pregnancy alone. Parents and friends may exert such pressure. A teenager, pregnant and deserted, may feel that she cannot give up her baby in adoption because she does not feel sure that the child will be well cared for. A mother may be persuaded that her child who is disabled would be "condemned" to live a "defective" life. But none of these circumstances, however serious and tragic, gives the parent a right to kill his or her child before or after birth.[7]

The same kinds of seemingly altruistic claims are sometimes made in regard to the very old. The old and the sick can be persuaded that their lives have become too burdensome both to themselves and to their care givers—that they have lives "not worth living." But those who would remove, through killing, the disability, pain, or depression of the young or the elderly often act with a conflict of interest they do not see—that it is *not* the lives of those they care for that are unbearably burdened, but their own lives.

The most obvious victims of abortion and euthanasia are, of course, those who die. But desperate acts leave many casualties. Absolute personal autonomy, pushed to its insanely logical limit, has fueled the abortion movement, resulting in the deaths of more than 30,000,000 unborn children since 1973 in the United States of America. It has also harmed tens of millions of women who are relegated to the "tender mercies" of a $500 million a year abortion industry. Youngsters who learn that their parents destroyed or were ready to destroy a child for one reason or another—wrong gender, wrong father, wrong time, wrong health, wrong economy—can and do fear that their own claim on their parents' love and care might go terminally wrong. If a parent destroys one child in the womb, will she or he be able to retain a no-matter-what loyalty towards other children in the family?

The same can now be asked of adult children and their parents. In a climate in which euthanasia is accepted, will adults be able to provide their infirm parents with the unconditional loyalty they themselves once needed to survive as children?

Distorted Fidelities

Today, when many people fear being treated as an object without dignity at the end of their lives, doctors and families confronting an imminent death can be tempted in two directions. They may resort to aggressive but useless procedures as proof of their faithfulness to the dying patient, who may not want or be able to withstand such demanding procedures. This treatment, when used to cure or to sustain, would be benevolent. But when needlessly imposed on someone who is inevitably and imminently dying, it can cause unnecessary hardship on the patient and other burdens on whoever is responsible for his or her care.

Frustrated by the anguish and complexity of such dilemmas, doctors and families may also be tempted to a total denial of fidelity: the violation of life known as euthanasia. For once we have convinced ourselves that every human ailment simply *must* have a cure, the undeniable fact of incurable illness tempts many to consider "curing" life itself. And the euthanasia movement has convinced many patients that their only "escape" from the pain and indignities of illness and over-treatment is a medically assisted suicide.

This second and more grave violation, that of "assisting" the vulnerable patient by extinguishing his or her life, wears the garb of caring and compassion. But it knows nothing of the Christian understanding of compassion, of "suffering with" our loved ones and alleviating their fears as they confront the shadows at the end of life. It shies away from the search for real solutions to a patient's problems, choosing instead to convince the patient that he or she *is* the problem—a problem solved only by his or her extinction. As Pope John Paul II has reminded us, true compassion leads to sharing another's pain; it does not kill the person whose suffering we cannot bear.[8]

Efforts to legalize such killing are based not just on an uncritical love of freedom—for the "freedom" to kill oneself is not promoted equally for all who encounter problems in life—but on a lack of regard for the perduring worth and dignity of sick and disabled people. The truth is that our young and able-bodied citizens support euthanasia for their elders far more strongly than do the old and the frail themselves.

That any sick person may be convinced that his or her "assisted suicide" is the responsible, perhaps even expected, solution for a painful illness is an indictment against a society with too little love for some of its most vulnerable members. The sick and the elderly may be required to defend their lives at the very moment in which they are the weakest.

A genuine respect for life abhors euthanasia and assisted suicide as attacks on life. At the same time, it does not require us to impose the burdens of over-treatment on persons near death. Once the dying process has begun, the services due from care givers must often change. Even though healing is no longer attainable, the physician is still urgently needed to help family members provide their loved one with a peaceful death. The capacity to manage pain, and to offer a comforting presence to patients we cannot cure, is essential to the health care profession and is among its duties to patients. A love which accepts life as a gift also accepts the given limits on our lives; it never abandons those who are close to death.

A Christian Fidelity

People of wholesome spirit and genuine fidelity do not easily turn from life-giving to abortion or euthanasia. These are not the wayward gestures of the innocent; they are the forlorn acts of a society which has forgotten or rejected fidelity to its own. They are signs of a need for conversion.

The Spirit once spoke to the ancient Church in Laodicea and could speak the same words to us today:

> You keep saying, "I am so rich and secure that I want for nothing." Little do you realize how wretched you are, how pitiable and poor, how blind and naked! Take my advice. Buy from me gold refined by fire if you would be truly rich. Buy white garments in which to be clothed, if the shame of nakedness is to be covered. Buy ointment to smear on your eyes, if you would see once more. (Rev 3:17-18)

When we turn a blind eye and a deaf ear toward those who are so helpless they cannot even appeal for help, we sustain an injury even more grievous than theirs. This is one of the insights that has most helped Christians focus their faith in this often violent world.[9] By closing ourselves off to the needs of others we most surely deprive ourselves of life.

The Lord Jesus gave up his life that we may have life, and have it more abundantly (Jn 10:10). The life he forfeited to violence, the mortal life we all share in this world and which each of us will yield up someday, is a temporary life. It is our only pathway to the life that

Jesus entered through his death and resurrection. The transformed and eternal life which he makes possible for us—forever, but starting here and now—is the ultimate life.

The Lord did not say: "Love your neighbor and hate your enemy." Our love must be of another kind: "Love one another as I have loved you." His gift was not to love those who are deserving of it, and to withhold love from those who are not. This would be an act of mere justice. No, he gave us his own Spirit, empowering us to love as he loves regardless of who deserves what. This is fidelity (Jn 13:34-35; 1 Jn 2:7-8; Mt 5:20-48; 1 Jn 4:9-21; Rom 5:6-11; 1 Jn 3:16).

Like many Americans, we Catholics can be tempted to lose our faith in the virtue of fidelity. But we can scarcely live up to our baptismal fidelity unless we are faithfully committed to persons in need, for better or for worse.

Civil Protest

Our public statements on abortion and euthanasia have often responded to events in the legislative and social order. This has unfortunately fed a misunderstanding, both within the Church and without, that we look only to laws and government to assure society of justice. Quite the contrary. Helping to inform the consciences of our Catholic people is our first priority. To them we say: our obligation in Christ is to speak the truth to your mind, your sensibility, and your moral judgment, no matter what the civil and criminal laws may be. The violations of human life wrought upon the most helpless are not merely illicit; they are, from a Christian perspective, betrayals of trust.

But we are also citizens, and we share the right—indeed, the duty—of all citizens to insist that the laws and policies of the United States be faithful to our founders' conviction that the foremost "unalienable right" conferred by our Creator on all of us is life itself. When disadvantaged or disenfranchised people have their pursuit of happiness, their liberty, and even their lives threatened by their nearest neighbors, we are bound to stand up for them and with them.

Years ago in our nation, African Americans were declared "property" and not "a portion of this people."[10] So their servitude, their enslavement, was then elevated to the stature of a constitutional right. More recently, the Nazis classified the mentally ill and physically disabled as "useless eaters," and Jews, Slavs, and Gypsies were called "subhuman." So they were exterminated. Is it any different today when the law treats unborn children as "non-persons" and those who are senile are seen as possessing insufficient "quality of life" to go on living? How can we not hear in our time echoes of those other times, never to be forgotten, when some were considered less than human and others said to have lives "not worth living"?

As bishops, as Catholics, as citizens, we speak against the injustice of destroying children by abortion and eliminating elderly or impaired people by euthanasia. And we speak against the ultimate disgrace of doing these deeds under the sanction of law.

Christ has charged us with a special care for the widow and the orphan, the refugee and the pauper, the sick and the disabled, the accused and the outcast. Those who serve as public leaders have a special responsibility to make courageous choices in support of life, especially through legislative measures[11]—measures that protect the unborn, the elderly, and the enfeebled who are so mortally threatened today.

What Then Shall We Do?

As Christians, we know our true calling is to find Christ's way, not simply to get our way. If we fail to keep faith with one another, we fail in our loyalty to the Lord himself.

Sometimes we Catholics are slow to admit that fidelity to the Gospel is alien, even hostile, to many selfish understandings prevalent in society today. Many today regard Jesus' call to irrevocable commitment as a hard saying, an "ideal" but not an imperative. Yet this gospel teaching and ancient discipline requires Catholics to take a courageous, even if lonely, stand. It also requires that we apply our beliefs to all our ministries with conviction and intensity.

Within our dioceses the Catholic community is served by a wide variety of agencies that influence and pass on our shared understanding of familial fidelity. Each addresses the protection of human life from its own specialized perspective, witnessing always to the ultimate obligations of open-ended fidelity.

When pregnant women and girls don't know where to turn, thousands of committed Catholics in our dioceses—and others to be sure—are there both to sustain and to challenge them. Ten to 15 million people each year, including many experiencing distressed pregnancies, turn to Catholic Charities for social and emergency services. Across this nation there are more than 3,000 emergency pregnancy centers that offer assistance for prenatal care and related needs, as well as numerous programs of reconciliation and healing to help women and men deal with the emotional and spiritual aftermath of abortion. When families are caught in a bewildering health crisis, our health care professionals and facilities offer them committed service. Our schools and religious education programs offer young people authentic education in chastity to provide them with a more generous and responsible perspective than society offers. When terrifying moral questions confront families in life-threatening crises, we seek to offer competent and compassionate counsel to them. When those who adhere to a belief in the sacredness of life express that belief publicly by their words, public witness, and peaceful protest, we bishops are heard among them—as we have been heard on workers' rights, civil rights, and in the struggle for peace—urging prayerful, non-violent, and even exemplary witness that respects every single human life.

We repeat together what we have stated individually: no woman in need with a child, born or unborn, whether she is Catholic or not, should feel herself without help. We pledge the heart and hands of the Church to help mothers and fathers in need to find pregnancy counseling, pre- and postnatal care, housing and material support, and adoption services.

In preaching Christ's Gospel, all of us must speak these things aloud. Abortion and euthanasia are crimes and betrayals which, repeatedly and consistently over the ages, the Church has condemned as contrary to Catholic faith. The deliberate decision to deprive an innocent human being of his or her life is always morally wrong; it can never be a licit means to a good end.[12] In speaking about this basic teaching, we must also make known from every pulpit the Church's sincere and open welcome to those who seek reconciliation with the Lord and peace with his Church. But let us be clear: No person who subverts this teaching privately or publicly speaks in the name of Catholicism. Nor can anyone who seeks to promote the cause of life through hatred or violence have any part with us.

Who Is This Neighbor?

We are called to be neighbors to everyone, and to "show special favor to those who are poorest, most alone, and most in need. In helping the hungry, the thirsty, the foreigner, the naked, the sick, the imprisoned—as well as the unborn baby and the old person who is suffering or near death—we have the opportunity to serve Jesus. He himself said: 'As you did it to one of the least of these my brethren, you did it to me.'"[13]

When God inquired after the missing Abel, Cain asked, "Am I my brother's keeper?" "Your brother's blood," the Lord rejoined, "is crying out to me from the ground" (Gn 4:9-10). This prompted early Christian writers to list similar deeds that "cried to heaven for vengeance." They included violating resident foreigners, mistreating widows and orphans, and cheating laborers of their wages. What gave each of these sins voice before God was not only the exploitation of the vulnerable by the powerful, but the misuse of the helpless by those who should have been their protectors.

Cain's response also makes one think of modern refusals to accept responsibility for our brothers and sisters. Often we see a lack of solidarity towards our society's weakest members—the old, the sick, immigrants, children—and an indifference toward the world's peoples even when basic values such as survival, freedom, and peace are involved.[14]

Jesus has shown us that his Father's only desire for sinners is forgiveness and restoration, for those who will accept it. Our cry to heaven over violations of trust must include an appeal for the forgiveness and salvation of any who have failed to be their brother's or sister's keeper. Abortion and euthanasia are betrayals of fidelity for which we Catholics should show a special dismay, while showing a specifically Christian compassion for those involved.

Fellow disciples of Jesus Christ, we are called to be a welcoming community to all—both those we choose and those who are sent to us. Abraham offered hospitality to three strangers who emerged from the wilderness. Mary offered life and birth to a Child sent by God, and Joseph offered a home to them both. St. Martin of Tours shared his winter cloak with a shivering beggar, and St. Francis of Assisi kissed the open sores of a leper. They all realized the same thing: It was the Lord! When we take another into our keeping, it is not just our brother or our sister. When we go out of our way to help, it is not just our neighbor we serve. We serve the Lord of life, and we become truly alive ourselves.

The Samaritan who was making his perilous way from Jerusalem to Jericho had every reason to be preoccupied with his own endangerment and survival. But the sight of a stranger in more urgent need made that stranger a neighbor! It is often when we feel most at a loss that we encounter the Lord, who comes in the guise of a stranger. At such times he comes as if his very life depends upon our welcome; but it is our lives, not his, that most depend upon it.

As Pope John Paul II has said in his encyclical letter *The Gospel of Life (Evangelium Vitae)*: "*A great prayer for life is urgently needed,* a prayer which will rise up throughout the world."[15] And so we take his prayer as our own and invite all to pray:

> O Mary,
> bright dawn of the new world,
> Mother of the living,
> to you do we entrust the *cause of life*:
> Look down, O Mother,
> upon the vast numbers
> of babies not allowed to be born,
> of the poor whose lives are made difficult,
> of men and women
> who are victims of brutal violence,

of the elderly and the sick killed
by indifference or out of misguided mercy.
Grant that all who believe in your Son
may *proclaim the Gospel of life*
with honesty and love
to the people of our time.
Obtain for them the grace
to *accept that Gospel*
as a gift ever new,
the joy of *celebrating* it with gratitude
throughout their lives
and the courage to *bear witness to it*
resolutely, in order to build,
together with all people of good will,
the civilization of truth and love,
to the praise and glory of God,
the Creator and lover of life.[16]

Notes

1. John Paul II, *The Gospel of Life (Evangelium Vitae)* (Washington, D.C.: United States Catholic Conference, 1995), no. 5.
2. Second Vatican Council, *Pastoral Constitution on the Church in the Modern World (Gaudium et Spes)*, nos. 27, 51.
3. *Evangelium Vitae*, no. 11.
4. Ibid., no. 92.
5. John Paul II, *The Splendor of Truth (Veritatis Splendor)* (Washington, D.C.: United States Catholic Conference, 1993), nos. 84-87.
6. *Evangelium Vitae*, nos. 20, 76, 96.
7. Ibid., nos. 58-59.
8. Ibid., no. 66.
9. *Gaudium et Spes*, no. 27.
10. *Dred Scott v. Sandford*, 1857.
11. *Evangelium Vitae*, no. 90.
12. Ibid., no. 57.
13. Ibid., no. 87.
14. Ibid., no. 9.
15. Ibid., no. 100.
16. Ibid., no. 105.

Source: Washington, D.C.: United States Catholic Conference, 1995.

Sowing Weapons of War: A Pastoral Reflection on the Arms Trade and Landmines

A Statement of the National Conference of Catholic Bishops

June 1995

The arms trade is a scandal.[1] That weapons of war are bought and sold almost as if they were simply another commodity like appliances or industrial machinery is a serious moral disorder in todays world.[2] The predominant role of our own country in sustaining and even promoting the arms trade, sometimes for economic reasons, is a moral challenge for our nation. Jobs at home cannot justify exporting the means of war abroad.

In too many cases, the global arms trade has brought not security, but aggression, repression, and long-term instability. Starving Somali children, destroyed Angolan villages, Cambodian lands rendered uninhabitable by landmines, and seemingly endless conflict in Afghanistan are the fruits of this deadly trade. "By their fruits you will know them" (Mt 7:20).

These attacks on life led the Holy Father in his recent encyclical *The Gospel of Life (Evangelium Vitae)* to condemn "the violence inherent not only in wars as such but in the scandalous arms trade, which spawns the many armed conflicts which stain our world with blood."[3] These realities moved the African bishops last year to appeal to those in the North to "stop arms sales to groups locked in conflict in Africa."[4] This suffering impelled Cardinal Vinko Puljic of Sarajevo to tell Americans that more weapons will lead to "more destruction, to complete cataclysm" in Bosnia-Herzegovina.[5] Our own relief workers and missionaries, whose lives are often at risk, can recite an endless litany of horrors brought about by this deadly trade.

In response to these appeals and the recent Vatican reflection on the arms trade,[6] we renew our call for our nation and the international community to undertake more serious efforts to control and radically reduce the trade in arms. The arms trade is an integral part of the "culture of violence" we deplored a year ago.[7] Just as we seek to stop the proliferation of arms in our streets, we, too, must stop the proliferation of arms around the world. Curbing the arms trade is now an essential part of the peacemaking vocation we outlined in *The Challenge of Peace* more than a decade ago.

The Free Market in Arms

The decline in arms transfers, as well as global military spending, since the end of the Cold War is a welcome development. Weapons exports remain excessive, however, and the transfer of increasingly sophisticated weapons technology has contributed to a proliferation of arms industries around the world, creating, in turn, new suppliers of still more weapons. Regrettably, as global arms transfers have declined, the United States dominance of this lethal trade has increased dramatically. With aggressive government support, the United States now supplies half the world's arms exports and controls more than 70 percent of the Third World market.[8] The desire to protect jobs and maintain the defense industry has led to a paradoxical situation in which modest reductions in military spending at home seem to encourage the export of weapons abroad.

Too often, arms are sent around the world with insufficient attention to how they threaten peace, development, and human rights. The three dozen regional conflicts around the world are fueled, widened, and prolonged by easy access to weapons, with civilians most often the victims. The glut of arms inhibits relief and development work and vastly complicates the international community's peacekeeping and peacemaking efforts. The developing countries could save an estimated 10 million lives a year if they diverted half their military expenditures to health care.[9] Yet the United States and other developed countries reap healthy profits from sending three-quarters of their arms exports to these countries, thereby contributing to the squandering of scarce resources, often by irresponsible and unrepresentative governments. At a time when our country is increasingly reluctant to share its economic resources in support of sustainable economic development, we remain all too ready to share our weapons in support of military development. Less military assistance, reduced arms sales, and more development assistance respond to the most pressing human needs of poorer countries.

Moral Responsibility and the Arms Trade

Pope John Paul II has said, "The arms-producing countries should consider their moral responsibility, especially concerning their trade with developing countries."[10] The threats to peace, human rights, and development posed by the arms trade demonstrate that no arms transfer is morally neutral. Arms exports may sometimes be legitimate, but they must meet moral principles, which include the following:[11]

1. *The duty to avoid war and promote peace.* The United States, like other nations, can reduce the demand for weapons by doing everything possible to avoid war, rooting out the causes of violence, and affirmatively promoting international justice and peace. It is in light of a determined no to war and yes to peace that the morality of U.S. arms transfers must be weighed.

2. *The right of legitimate defense.* U.S. arms transfers may be justified only by the need to support another nation's right and duty of legitimate defense. Arms transfers subvert the principle of public defense when they expose people to attacks by their own government, the destructiveness of protracted conflict, or intimidation by armed groups that governments are unable or unwilling to control. In some cases, as Pope John Paul II has pointed out, defense of the innocent requires that when "populations are succumbing to the attacks of an unjust aggressor, states [have a] . . . duty to disarm this aggressor, if all other means have proved ineffective."[12]

3. *The principle of sufficiency.* This principle permits the United States to transfer only those arms necessary for legitimate defense. The excessive accumulation of arms or their indiscriminate transfer is unacceptable. Arms sales are not justified by the fact that others will supply weapons if we do not.

4. *The inadequacy of economic justifications for arms transfers.* Economic considerations, such as protecting jobs and profits or promoting economic competitiveness, of themselves, do not justify arms transfers.

Policies for Curbing the Arms Trade

While the stated objectives of U.S. policy often conform to these criteria, our government has often not been diligent in strictly applying its own standards for restraining arms sales, nor has it committed itself to reducing its growing dominance of the world's arms market. The United States needs to put its energies into building peace, not supplying arms. While other nations are also involved in this deadly commerce, the United States should become a leader in multilateral and independent approaches to reduce the arms trade. The following are some specific initiatives that would help redirect U.S. arms trade policies:

1. *Strict controls on U.S. arms transfers.* Together with other countries, the United States should strictly enforce existing controls, strengthen them where necessary, and seek to reduce substantially its weapons transfers. Continued high levels of

U.S. military aid, government subsidies, and other efforts to promote arms sales abroad should be ended. Proposals, such as the Code of Conduct on Arms Transfers, that would bring greater openness and accountability to arms transfer decisions deserve support.

2. *Corporate responsibility.* Government controls do not absolve those involved in the arms industry of moral responsibility for their decisions to sell arms. They have a moral obligation not only to ensure strict compliance with export controls, but also to avoid sales that will probably be used for illegitimate purposes or that will threaten stability and peace.

3. *Nonmilitary ways to protect jobs.* The sometimes dramatic effects of defense cuts on local economies should be dealt with through economic development and conversion programs, efforts to strengthen the nonmilitary economy, and programs to assist the unemployed.

4. *International controls.* Since no single country is responsible for the proliferation of arms and no one country alone can stop it, strict national regulations of arms transfers must be combined with legally binding international norms, with strict verification measures, for all arms transfers. The UN Register of Conventional Arms, the Nuclear Non-Proliferation Treaty, and other multilateral efforts to control the proliferation of weapons deserve widespread support.

5. *Improved cooperative security.* International controls will only be effective and the demand for weapons will only be reduced if there is a strengthening of international mechanisms of cooperative security, including conventional and nuclear arms control agreements. It is particularly appropriate as we commemorate the fiftieth anniversary of the United Nations that the United States does its share and encourages other nations to do their share in providing the financial, political, and other support necessary for the United Nations to fulfill its mandate to reduce and resolve conflicts in the world.

Banning Landmines: An Urgent Task

Finally, we would like to add our voice to the appeals of Pope John Paul II and the growing movement to control and eventually ban antipersonnel landmines. The Holy Father has issued "a vigorous appeal for the definitive cessation of the manufacture and use of those arms called 'antipersonnel mines.' . . . In fact, they continue to kill and to cause irreparable damage well after the end of hostilities, giving rise to severe mutilations in adults and, above all, in children."[13] Some 100 million of these hidden killers are strewn around the world, killing an estimated 500 people per week, most of whom are civilians. In Cambodia, one of every 236 people is an amputee because of mine blasts.[14] While landmines can be used responsibly for legitimate defense, they are often indiscriminate in use, especially in the intrastate conflicts that are so prevalent today. Moreover, landmines are indiscriminate in time because, as the Pontifical Council for Justice and Peace has pointed out, they cause "unacceptable damage to civilian populations long after the cessation of hostilities."[15] From Cambodia to Angola, large areas have been rendered uninhabitable, preventing refugees from returning to their homes, inhibiting postwar reconstruction, and producing an ongoing threat to innocent life.

The United States should lead an international effort to reduce and ultimately ban the use of antipersonnel landmines, just as was done with chemical and biological weapons. The current moratorium on U.S. exports of landmines is commendable; it should be made permanent and should be extended globally. The United States should also take steps, such as those called for in legislation now before Congress, to further restrict its own use of landmines, while it pursues with urgency and persistence international agreements to restrict use globally. The decision to ratify the Conventional Weapons Convention and to seek to strengthen it during its review this year is welcome. Finally, our government should continue to take a leadership role in developing an international effort on the costly and time-consuming process of demining, so important to the protection of innocent life and reconstruction in so many war-torn countries.

Conclusion

Landmines are symptomatic of a wider problem noted by Pope John Paul II in his 1987 encyclical, *On Social Concern (Sollicitudo Rei Socialis)*, that "arms of whatever origin circulate with almost total freedom all over the world."[16] That our own country should be the leader in this deadly market in arms is a source of shame, not pride. As a nation, we should seek to market our ideals, not our weapons. We must "seek peace and pursue it" (Ps 34:15). In the name of peace, development, and human rights, we need an ethic of responsibility and a policy of effective restraint to control the trade in arms.

We urge Catholics involved in decisions to transfer arms to reflect on the moral implications of their decisions. Acting on the biblical injunction to "beat swords into plowshares," we call on our dioceses and parishes to encourage Catholics to press for an abolition of landmines and a reversal of current arms trade policies. As Christians, we believe we are called to build an authentic peace that is based on respect for human dignity and a commitment to the common good, not on the balance of weapons. Spreading weapons of war around the world undermines our efforts to build this authentic peace.

Notes

1. John Paul II, *The Gospel of Life (Evangelium Vitae)* (Washington, D.C.: United States Catholic Conference, 1995), no. 10.
2. John Paul II, *On Social Concern (Sollicitudo Rei Socialis)* (Washington, D.C.: United States Catholic Conference, 1987), no. 24.
3. *Evangelium Vitae*, no. 10.
4. "Final Message of the Special Assembly of the Synod of Bishops for Africa," *Origins* 24:1 (May 19, 1994): 8.
5. Cardinal Vinko Puljic, "Address at the Center for Strategic and International Studies" (March 30, 1995), *Catholic News Service* (April 3, 1995), 7.
6. Pontifical Council for Justice and Peace, "The International Arms Trade: An Ethical Reflection," *Origins* 24:8 (July 7, 1994): 142-151.
7. National Conference of Catholic Bishops, *Confronting a Culture of Violence: A Catholic Framework for Action* (Washington, D.C.: United States Catholic Conference, 1994).
8. Based on 1993 figures. See U.S. Arms Control and Disarmament Agency, *World Military Expenditures and Arms Transfers, 1993-1994* (Washington, D.C.: U.S. Government Printing Office, 1995); Richard F. Grimmett, *Conventional Arms Transfers to the Third World, 1986-1993* (Washington, D.C.: Congressional Research Service, 1994).
9. R. L. Sivard, *World Military and Social Expenditures 1993* (Washington, D.C.: World Priorities, 1993), 5.
10. John Paul II, "Address to Pax Christi International," *L'Osservatore Romano* [English edition] 26 (June 28, 1995): 9.
11. These criteria are based on two documents: National Conference of Catholic Bishops, *The Harvest of Justice Is Sown in Peace: A Reflection on the Tenth Anniversary of the Challenge of Peace* (Washington, D.C.: United States Catholic Conference, 1994), 14; Pontifical Council for Justice and Peace, "The International Arms Trade: An Ethical Reflection," *Origins* 24:8 (July 7, 1994): 141ff.
12. John Paul II, "Address to Diplomatic Corps," *Origins* 22:34 (February 4, 1993): 587.
13. John Paul II, "Address to Pax Christi International," *L'Osservatore Romano* [English edition] 26 (June 28, 1995): 9.
14. U.S. State Department, *Hidden Killers: The Global Landmine Crisis* (Washington, D.C.: U.S. Government Printing Office, 1994), v, 18.
15. Pontifical Council for Justice and Peace, "The International Arms Trade: An Ethical Reflection," *Origins* 24:8 (July 7, 1994): 149.
16. John Paul II, *On Social Concern (Sollicitudo Rei Socialis)* (Washington, D.C.: United States Catholic Conference, 1987), no. 24.

Source: Washington, D.C.: United States Catholic Conference, 1995.

Guidelines for the Celebration of the Sacraments with Persons with Disabilities

A Statement of the National Conference of Catholic Bishops

June 1995

It is essential that all forms of the liturgy be completely accessible to persons with disabilities, since these forms are the essence of the spiritual tie that binds the Christian community together. To exclude members of the parish from these celebrations of the life of the Church, even by passive omission, is to deny the reality of that community. Accessibility involves far more than physical alterations to parish buildings. Realistic provision must be made for persons with disabilities to participate fully in the eucharist and other liturgical celebrations such as the sacraments of reconciliation, confirmation, and anointing of the sick.
—*Pastoral Statement of U.S. Catholic Bishops on Persons with Disabilities,* November 1978; revised 1989

Preface

Catholics with disabilities, as well as those who minister to or with them, often point out that pastoral practice with regard to the celebration of the sacraments varies greatly from diocese to diocese, even from parish to parish. Inconsistencies arise in such areas as the provision of sign language interpreters for persons who are deaf, in the accessibility of church facilities for persons with mobility problems, and in the availability of catechetical programs for persons with developmental and mental disabilities. Pastoral inconsistencies may occur in other areas as well.

The inconsistencies in pastoral practice often arise from distinct yet overlapping causes. Some result from a misunderstanding about the nature of disabilities. Others arise from an uncertainty about the appropriate application of church law towards persons with disabilities. Others are born out of fear or misunderstanding. Still others are the result of a studied and honest acceptance of the realistic limitations of a parish's or diocese's available resources.

These guidelines were developed to address many of the concerns raised by priests, pastoral ministers, other concerned Catholics, persons with disabilities, their advocates, and their families for greater consistency in pastoral practice in the celebration of the sacraments throughout the country. With this objective in view, the guidelines draw upon the Church's ritual books, its canonical tradition, and its experience in ministering to or with persons with disabilities in order to dispel any misunderstandings that may impede sound pastoral practice in the celebration of the sacraments. It is our hope that the guidelines will complement diocesan policies already in existence.

The bishops of the United States offer the *Guidelines for the Celebration of the Sacraments with Persons with Disabilities* in order to give a more concrete expression to our longstanding concern for "realistic provision" for the means of access to full sacramental participation for Catholic persons with disabilities. While they do not address every conceivable situation that may arise in pastoral practice, the guidelines present a set of general principles to provide access to the sacraments for persons with disabilities. Diocesan staff, pastoral leaders, catechists, parishioners, health care workers, and all those who minister to or with Catholics with disabilities are invited and encouraged to reflect upon and accept these guidelines in their continuing effort to bring Christ's healing message and call to justice to the world.

I. General Principles

1. By reason of their baptism, all Catholics are equal in dignity in the sight of God and have the same divine calling.
2. Catholics with disabilities have a right to participate in the sacraments as full functioning members of the local ecclesial community (cf. canon 213). Ministers are not to refuse the sacraments to those who ask for them at appropriate times, who are properly disposed, and who are not prohibited by law from receiving them (cf. canon 843.1).
3. Parish sacramental celebrations should be accessible to persons with disabilities and open to their full, active and conscious participation, according to their capacity. Pastoral ministers should not presume to know the needs of persons with disabilities, but rather they should consult with them or their advocates before making determinations about the accessibility of a parish's facilities and the availability of its programs, policies, and ministries. These adaptations are an ordinary part of the liturgical life of the parish. While full accessibility may not always be possible for every parish, it is desirable that at least one fully accessible community be available in a given area. Parishes may, in fact, decide to collaborate in the provision of services to persons with disabilities.

4. Since the parish is the center of the Christian experience for most Catholics, pastoral ministers should make every effort to determine the presence of all Catholics with disabilities who reside within a parish's boundaries. Special effort should be made to welcome those parishioners with disabilities who live in institutions or group homes and are unable to frequent their parish churches or participate in parish activities. However, pastoral ministers should remember that many persons with disabilities still reside with their families. Pastoral visitation, the parish census, and the diverse forms of parish and diocesan social communication are just a few of the many ways in which the pastoral staff can work towards the inclusion of all parishioners in the parish's sacramental life.

5. In accord with canon 777.4, pastors are responsible to be as inclusive as possible in providing evangelization, catechetical formation, and sacramental preparation for parishioners with disabilities. Persons with disabilities, their advocates and their families, as well as those knowledgeable in serving disabled persons can make a most valuable contribution to these programs. Parish catechetical and sacramental preparation programs may need to be adapted for some parishioners with disabilities. Further, parishes should encourage persons with disabilities to participate in all levels of pastoral ministry (e.g., as care ministers, catechists, etc.). Dioceses are encouraged to establish appropriate support services for pastors to facilitate the evangelization, catechetical formation, and sacramental preparation for parishioners with disabilities.

6. The creation of a fully accessible parish reaches beyond mere physical accommodation to encompass the attitudes of all parishioners towards persons with disabilities. Pastoral ministers are encouraged to develop specific programs aimed at forming a community of believers known for its joyful inclusion of all of God's people around the table of the Lord.

7. In the course of making pastoral decisions, it is inevitable that pastoral care workers will encounter difficult cases. Dioceses are encouraged to establish appropriate policies for handling such cases which respect the procedural and substantive rights of all involved, and which ensure the necessary provision of consultation.

II. Particular Sacraments

Baptism

8. Through the sacrament of baptism the faithful are incorporated into Christ and into his Church. They are formed into God's people and obtain forgiveness of all their sins. They become a new creation and are called, rightly, the children of God.[1]

9. Because it is the sacrament of universal salvation, baptism is to be made available to all who freely ask for it, are properly disposed, and are not prohibited by law from receiving it. Baptism may be deferred only when there is no reason for hoping that the person will be brought up in the Catholic religion (canon 868.1.2). Disability, of itself, is never a reason for deferring baptism. Persons who lack the use of reason are to be baptized provided at least one parent or guardian consents to it (canons 868.1.1 and 852).

10. So that baptism may be seen as a sacrament of the Church's faith and of admittance into the people of God, it should be celebrated ordinarily in the parish church on a Sunday or, if possible, at the Easter Vigil (canons 856 and 857). The Church, made present in the local community, has an important role to play in the baptism of all of its members. Before and after the celebration of the sacrament, the baptized have the right to the love and help of the community.[2]

11. Either personally or through others, the pastor is to see to it that the parents of an infant who is disabled, or those who take the place of the parents, are properly instructed as to the meaning of the sacrament of baptism and the obligations attached to it. If possible, either the pastor or a member of the parish community should visit with the family, offering them the strength and support of the community which rejoices at the gift of new life, and which promises to nurture the faith of its newest member. It is recommended that preparation programs for baptism gather several families together so that they may commonly be formed by pastoral direction and prayer, and so that they may be strengthened by mutual support (canon 851.2).

12. If the person to be baptized is of catechetical age, the Rite of Christian Initiation may be adapted according to need (cf. canons 851.1 and 852.1).

13. A sponsor is to be chosen who will assist the newly baptized in Christian initiation. Sponsors have a special role in fostering the faith life of the baptized person. As such, they are to be

chosen and prepared accordingly. Persons with disabilities may be sponsors for these sacraments of initiation.

Confirmation

14. Those who have been baptized continue on the path of Christian initiation through the sacrament of confirmation. In this way, they receive the Holy Spirit, conforming them more perfectly to Christ and strengthening them so that they may bear witness to Christ for the building up of his body in faith and love.[3]

15. Parents, those who care for persons with disabilities, and shepherds of souls—especially pastors—are to see to it that the faithful who have been baptized are properly instructed to receive the sacrament of confirmation and to approach it at the appropriate time (cf. canon 890). The diocesan bishop is obliged to see that the sacrament of confirmation is conferred on his subjects who properly and reasonably request it (canon 885.1).

16. All baptized, unconfirmed Catholics who possess the use of reason may receive the sacrament of confirmation if they are suitably instructed, properly disposed, and able to renew their baptismal promises (canon 889). Persons who because of developmental or mental disabilities may never attain the use of reason are to be encouraged either directly or, if necessary, through their parents or guardian, to receive the sacrament of confirmation at the appropriate time.

17. Confirmation is to be conferred on the faithful between the age of discretion (which is about the age of seven) and eighteen years of age, within the limits determined by the diocesan bishop, or when there is a danger of death, or in the judgment of the minister a grave cause urges otherwise.

18. A sponsor for the one to be confirmed should be present. The sponsor assists the confirmed person on the continuing path of Christian initiation (cf. canon 892). For this reason, it is desirable that the one who undertook the role of sponsor at baptism be the sponsor for confirmation (canon 893.2).

Eucharist

19. The eucharist is the most august sacrament, in which Christ the Lord himself is contained, offered, and received, and by which the Church constantly lives and grows. It is the summit and the source of all Christian worship and life, signifying and effecting the unity of the people of God, providing spiritual nourishment for the recipient, and achieving the building up

of the Body of Christ. The celebration of the eucharist is the center of the entire Christian life (canon 897).

20. Parents, those who take the place of parents, and pastors are to see to it that children who have reached the use of reason are correctly prepared and are nourished by the eucharist as early as possible. Pastors are to be vigilant lest any children come to the holy banquet who have not reached the use of reason or whom they judge are not sufficiently disposed (canon 914). It is important to note, however, that the criterion for reception of holy communion is the same for persons with developmental and mental disabilities as for all persons, namely, that the person be able to distinguish the body of Christ from ordinary food, even if this recognition is evidenced through manner, gesture, or reverential silence rather than verbally. Pastors are encouraged to consult with parents, those who take the place of parents, diocesan personnel involved with disability issues, psychologists, religious educators, and other experts in making their judgment. If it is determined that a parishioner who is disabled is not ready to receive the sacrament, great care is to be taken in explaining the reasons for this decision. Cases of doubt should be resolved in favor of the right of the baptized person to receive the sacrament. The existence of a disability is not considered in and of itself as disqualifying a person from receiving the eucharist.

21. Eucharistic celebrations are often enhanced by the exercise of the diverse forms of ministry open to the laity. In choosing those who will be invited to use their gifts in service to the parish community, the parish pastoral staff should be mindful of extending Christ's welcoming invitation to qualified parishioners with disabilities.

Reconciliation

22. In the sacrament of reconciliation, the Christian faithful obtain from the mercy of God pardon for their sins. At the same time, they are reconciled with the Church, which they have wounded by their sins and which works for their conversion by charity, example, and prayer.[4]

23. Only those who have the use of reason are capable of committing serious sin. Nevertheless, even young children and persons with mental disabilities often are conscious of committing acts that are sinful to some degree and may experience a sense of guilt and sorrow. As long as the individual is capable of having a sense of contrition for having committed sin, even if he or she cannot describe the sin precisely in words, the

person may receive sacramental absolution. Those with profound mental disabilities, who cannot experience even minimal contrition, may be invited to participate in penitential services with the rest of the community to the extent of their ability.

24. Catholics who are deaf should have the opportunity to confess to a priest able to communicate with them in sign language, if sign language is their primary means of communication. They may also confess through an approved sign language interpreter of their choice (canon 990). The interpreter is strictly bound to respect the seal of confession (canons 983.2 and 1388.2). When no priest with signing skills is available, nor sign language interpreter requested, Catholics who are deaf should be permitted to make their confession in writing. The written materials are to be returned to the penitent or otherwise properly destroyed.

25. In the case of individuals with poor communication skills, sorrow for sin is to be accepted even if this repentance is expressed through some gesture rather than verbally. In posing questions and in the assignment of penances the confessor is to proceed with prudence and discretion, mindful that he is at once judge and healer, minister of justice as well as of mercy (canons 978.1; 979; 981).

Anointing of the Sick

26. Through the anointing of the sick, the Church commends to the suffering and glorified Lord the faithful who are seriously ill, so that they may be relieved of their suffering and be saved (canon 998).

27. Those who have the care of souls and those who are close to the sick are to see to it that the faithful who are in danger due to sickness or old age are supported by the sacrament of anointing at the appropriate time (canon 1001).

28. Since disability does not necessarily indicate an illness, Catholics with disabilities should receive the sacrament of anointing on the same basis and under the same circumstances as any other member of the Christian faithful (cf. canon 1004).

29. The anointing of the sick may be conferred if the recipient has sufficient use of reason to be strengthened by the sacrament, or if the sick person has lost the use of reason and would have asked for the sacrament while in control of his or her faculties.[5] If there is doubt as to whether the sick person has attained the use of reason, the sacrament is to be conferred (canon 1005). Persons with disabilities may at times be served

best through inclusion in communal celebrations of the sacrament of anointing (cf. canon 1002).

Holy Orders

30. By divine institution, some among the Christian faithful are constituted sacred ministers through the sacrament of orders. They are consecrated and deputed to shepherd the people of God, each in accord with his own grade of orders, by fulfilling in the person of Christ the functions of teaching, sanctifying, and governing (canon 1008).
31. The existence of a physical disability is not considered in and of itself as disqualifying a person from holy orders. However, candidates for ordination must possess the necessary spiritual, physical, intellectual, emotional, and psychological qualities and abilities to fulfill the ministerial functions of the order they receive (canons 1029 and 1041.1). The proper bishop or competent major superior makes the judgment that candidates are suited for the ministry of the Church (canons 241.1; 1025.2; 1051.1). Cases are to be decided on an individual basis and in light of pastoral judgment and the opinions of diocesan personnel and other experts involved with disability issues.
32. Diocesan vocations offices and offices for ministry with persons with disabilities should provide counseling and informational resources for men with disabilities who are discerning a vocation to serve the Church through one of the ordained ministries.
33. In preparation for responsible leadership in ordained ministry, the diocesan bishop or major superior is to see to it that the formation of all students in the seminary provides for their service to the disabled community, and for their possible ministry to or with persons with disabilities. Formation personnel should consult with parents, psychologists, religious educators, and other experts in the adaptation of programs for ministerial formation.

Marriage

34. By the sacrament of marriage, Christians signify and share in the mystery of the unity and fruitful love which exists between Christ and his Church. They help each other to attain holiness in their married life and in the rearing and education of their children.[6]
35. All persons not prohibited by law can contract marriage (canon 1058).

36. The local ordinary should make the necessary provisions to ensure the inclusion of persons with disabilities in marriage preparation programs. Through this preparation all couples may become predisposed toward holiness and to the duties of their new state. In developing diocesan policies, the local ordinary should consult with men and women of proven experience and skill in understanding the emotional, physical, spiritual, and psychological needs of persons with disabilities (canons 1063.2 and 1064). The inclusion of persons with disabilities in sponsoring couple programs is an especially effective way of supporting both the needs and the gifts of couples preparing for marriage.

37. For matrimonial consent to be valid, it is necessary that the contracting parties possess a sufficient use of reason; that they be free of any grave lack of discretion affecting their judgment about the rights and duties to which they are committing themselves; and that they be capable of assuming the essential obligations of the married state (canon 1095). It is also necessary that the parties understand that marriage is a permanent union and is ordered to the good of the spouses and the procreation and education of children (canon 1096). Pastors and other clergy are to decide cases on an individual basis and in light of pastoral judgment based upon consultation with diocesan personnel involved with disability issues, and canonical, medical, and other experts. Medical and canonical opinions should be sought in determining the presence of any impediments to marriage. It should be noted, however, that paraplegia in itself does not always imply impotence, nor the permanence of such a condition, and it is not in itself an impediment. In case of doubt with regard to impotence, marriage may not be impeded (canon 1084.2).

38. Catholics who are deaf are to be offered the opportunity to express their matrimonial consent in sign language, if sign language is their primary means of communication (canon 1104.2). Marriage may also be contracted through a sign language interpreter whose trustworthiness has been certified by the pastor (canon 1106).

39. Pastoral care for married persons extends throughout the married couples' lives. By their care and example, the entire ecclesial community bears witness to the fact that the matrimonial state may be maintained in a Christian spirit and make progress toward perfection. Special care is to be taken to include parishioners with disabilities in parish programs aimed at assisting and nourishing married couples in leading holier and fuller lives within their families (canon 1063.4).

These guidelines are presented to all who are involved in pastoral ministry with persons with disabilities. They reaffirm the determination expressed by the bishops of the United States on the tenth anniversary of the pastoral statement on persons with disabilities "to promote accessibility of mind and heart, so that all persons with disabilities may be welcomed at worship and at every level of service as full members of the body of Christ."

Notes

1. General Introduction, *Rite of Christian Initiation of Adults: The Roman Ritual Revised by the Decree of the Second Vatican Ecumenical Council and Published by the Authority of Pope Paul VI*, English trans. prepared by ICEL (New York: Catholic Book Publishing Co., 1988), no. 1.
2. Cf. *Rite of Baptism for Children: The Roman Ritual Revised by the Decree of the Second Vatican Ecumenical Council and Published by the Authority of Pope Paul VI*, English trans. prepared by ICEL (New York: Catholic Book Publishing Co., 1970), nos. 4, 10.
3. *Rite of Confirmation: The Roman Pontifical Revised by the Decree of the Second Vatican Ecumenical Council and Published by the Authority of Pope Paul VI*, English trans. prepared by ICEL (Washington, D.C.: United States Catholic Conference, 1977), nos. 1–2.
4. Second Vatican Council, *Constitution on the Church (Lumen Gentium)*, no. 11.
5. *Pastoral Care of the Sick: Rites of Anointing and Viaticum: The Roman Ritual Revised by the Decree of the Second Vatican Ecumenical Council and Published by the Authority of Pope Paul VI*, English trans. prepared by ICEL (New York: Catholic Book Publishing Co., 1983), nos. 12, 14.
6. *Rite of Marriage: The Roman Ritual Revised by the Decree of the Second Vatican Ecumenical Council and Published by the Authority of Pope Paul VI*, English trans. prepared by ICEL (New York: Catholic Book Publishing Co., 1970), no. 1.

Source: Washington, D.C.: United States Catholic Conference, 1995.

Political Responsibility: Proclaiming the Gospel of Life, Protecting the Least Among Us, and Pursuing the Common Good

Reflections on the 1996 Elections by the Administrative Board of the United States Catholic Conference

September 1995

Pope John Paul II's Challenges for America

Pope John Paul II's visit to the United States in the fall of 1995 was a powerful call to American Catholics to use our freedom in the service of truth, to protect human life and human dignity, and to stand up for unborn children, poor families, and immigrants. The Holy Father's words are a powerful call to genuine political responsibility. We begin these reflections by citing just a few of the challenges he raised in those remarkable few days in our land.

> It is vital for the human family that . . . America keeps compassion, generosity, and concern for others at the very heart of its efforts. . . . It is my prayerful hope that America will persevere in its own best traditions of openness and opportunity. . . . The same spirit of creative generosity will help you to meet the needs of your own poor and disadvantaged. They too have a role to play in building a society truly worthy of the human person—a society in which none are so poor that they have nothing to give and none are so rich that they have nothing to receive. . . . America will continue to be a land of promise as long as it remains a land of freedom and justice for all.[1]

> True patriotism never seeks to advance the well-being of one's own nation at the expense of others. . . . The answer to the fear which darkens human existence at the end of the twentieth century is the common effort to build the civilization of love, founded on the universal values of peace, solidarity, justice, and liberty.[2]

> Is present-day America becoming less sensitive, less caring toward the poor, the weak, the stranger, the needy? It must

not! . . . When the unborn child—the "stranger in the womb"—is declared to be beyond the protection of society, not only are America's deepest traditions radically undermined and endangered, but a moral blight is brought upon society. I am also thinking of threats to the elderly, the severely handicapped, and all those who do not seem to have any social usefulness. . . . Both as Americans and as followers of Christ, American Catholics must be committed to the defense of life in all its stages and in every condition.[3]

In practical terms, this truth tells us that there can be no life worthy of the human person without a culture—and a legal system—that honors and defends marriage and the family . . . . The truth which Christ reveals . . . challenges us to be involved. It gives us the courage to see Christ in our neighbor and to serve him there. We ought to invite others to come to us by stretching out a helping hand to those in need, by welcoming the newcomer, by speaking words of comfort to the afflicted.[4]

The basic question before a democratic society is: "How ought we to live together?" Can the biblical wisdom which played such a formative part in the very founding of your country be excluded from that debate? Would not doing so mean that tens of millions of Americans could no longer offer the contribution of their deepest convictions to the formation of public policy? . . . Every generation of Americans needs to know that freedom consists not in doing what we like but in having the right to do what we ought.[5]

Democracy needs wisdom. Democracy needs virtue. . . . Democracy stands or falls with the truths and values which it embodies and promotes. Democracy serves what is true and right when it safeguards the dignity of every human person, when it respects inviolable and inalienable human rights, when it makes the common good the end and criterion regulating all public and social life.[6]

1. Politics: Citizenship and Cynicism

Elections are a time for debate and decisions on the leaders, policies, and values that will guide our nation. For the last five presidential elections, the administrative board of our bishops' conference has issued a statement on political responsibility to encourage broad participation in the electoral process, outline the role of the Church in public life, and raise the moral and human dimensions of key issues for discussion in the coming campaigns.

We update and reissue this statement, convinced that the 1996 elections will be a time for important choices for our nation. American public life is too often overshadowed by widespread public cynicism and frustration. Many citizens simply don't vote. Many Americans seem disinterested or disenchanted with politics. This alienation is a dangerous trend, threatening to undermine our democratic traditions.

There are a variety of causes for this decline of political life. Some problems are structural, such as unnecessary barriers to voter registration, but others are more subtle. Too many candidates and political professionals engage more in tactical combat than civil debate, seeking to reduce support for an opponent rather than gather support for their own cause. The news media sometimes seem more interested in tactics and "who's ahead" than in issues and character. And many citizens are too often preoccupied by narrow self-interest, indifferent to public life or unconvinced that politics makes any difference. The result is elections without full public participation, campaigns with little substance, and widespread public cynicism and alienation.

It doesn't have to be this way. Public life should be a place of civil debate and broad public participation. However, many people see politics as part of the problem, not part of the solution. Some Americans believe our representatives are more interested in contributors than constituents, spending more of their energies looking for campaign funds than the common good. Sound bites and symbols, war rooms and attack ads are replacing civil debate and the search for the common good. Too much of public life reflects our fears more than our hopes, dividing us by age, race, region, and class. Too often the voices that set the agenda of public life are not those who seek the common good, but those who seek to divide us. The politics of money and polarization may help fund raising and ratings, but it is a bad way to build community.

For example, in the ongoing family values and welfare debates we are offered false choices between responsibility and compassion, between greater involvement of community structures and federal investment in fighting poverty. Some advocates say that we need only better values (more time with children, more sexual restraint, more personal responsibility, a greater focus on moral values). Others say we need only better policies (more jobs, a higher minimum wage, better child care, decent health care, and better housing). Our ongoing Catholic Campaign for Children and Families seeks to move beyond the limited perspectives of both right and left to advocate new policies that reflect our best values.

There is also a growing temptation to blame our sense of economic insecurity and moral decline not on cultural disarray or the failures of political and economic leadership, but on too much compassion. To listen to some, our nation is in trouble because of too many immigrants and welfare mothers; not enough birth control, abortions, prisons, and executions; and too much foreign aid and affirmative action. Our problems are far more fundamental. They cannot be blamed only on people who are poor and powerless. The "rich and famous" and the rest of us have at least as much responsibility as the "least among us."

These political trends diminish genuine public debate and increase cynicism, feeding frustration that "politics as usual" responds to elite and powerful constituencies more than ordinary citizens and the common good. We share these concerns not to cast blame, but to advance and strengthen our democracy. Public service is both a vocation and a public trust. We gratefully acknowledge the sacrifice, hard work, and commitment of those who serve our nation and communities. We regret public attitudes that dismiss the legitimate role of government and ridicule public officials in misguided frustration with all politics. We need more, not less public participation—not only in electoral politics, but also in issue advocacy, legislative networks, and community organizations, which give important vitality and substance to public life.

As the nation prepares for the 1996 elections, we need to examine our own political behavior and take steps to build public confidence and participation in the political process. We ask candidates to trust the American people enough to share their values and vision with us without resorting to empty rhetoric or polarizing tactics. We urge the news media to cover campaigns in ways that tell us more than who's ahead or whose commercials are more clever. The nation needs more thorough and unbiased coverage of the positions and qualifications of the candidates and the major issues facing the nation.

And, most importantly, as citizens we need to face our own public responsibilities: to register and vote; to understand issues and assess candidates' positions and qualifications; and to join with others in advocating for the common good. Together, we can make this election an opportunity for informed debate and clear choices about the future.

Rediscovery of the Common Good

The key to a renewal of public life is reorienting politics to reflect better the search for the common good (i.e., reconciling diverse interests for the well-being of the whole human family) and a clear commitment to the dignity of every person. If politics ignores this fundamental task, it can easily become little more than an arena for partisan gamesmanship, the search for power for its own sake, or interest group conflict. Pope John Paul II has warmly praised democratic values but warned against a "crisis within democracies," which "seem at times to have lost the ability to make decisions aimed at the common good."[7]

In an age of powerful political action committees and justifiable public concern about campaign financing, the Holy Father issued a warning which we should take to heart: "Certain demands which arise within society are sometimes not examined in accordance with criteria of justice and morality, but rather on the basis of the electoral or financial power of the groups promoting them. With time, such distortions of political conduct create distrust and apathy, with a subsequent decline in the political participation and civic spirit of the general population, which feels abused and disillusioned." The pope deplores the "growing inability to situate particular interests within the framework of a coherent vision of the common good" which "demands a correct understanding of the dignity and the rights of the person." He calls on us to "give democracy an authentic and solid foundation through the explicit recognition of [human] rights."[8]

Pope John Paul II is even more insistent in his recent encyclical *The Gospel of Life (Evangelium Vitae)*:

> The value of democracy stands or falls with the values which it embodies and promotes. Of course, values such as the dignity of every human person, respect for inviolable and inalienable human rights, and the adoption of the "common good" as the end and criterion regulating political life are certainly fundamental and not to be ignored.[9]

The Holy Father goes on to point out:

> The Gospel of life is for the whole of human society. To be actively pro-life is to contribute to the renewal of society through the promotion of the common good. It is impossible to further the common good without acknowledging and defending the right to life, upon which all the other inalienable rights of individuals are founded and from which they develop. A society lacks solid foundations when, on the one hand, it asserts values such as the dignity of the person, justice and peace, but then, on the other hand, radically acts to the contrary by allowing or tolerating a variety of ways in which human life is devalued and violated, especially where it is weak or marginalized. . . . There can be no true democracy without a recognition of every person's dignity and without respect for his or her rights.[10]

American political life must refocus on the search for the common good over the pursuit of partisan advantage, private gain, or special interest agendas.

Questions for 1996

The continuing challenge to seek the common good is not an abstract ideal for us, but an urgent task for this election year. We face many important issues. The United States is blessed with extraordinary freedom, resources, and strength. We have accomplished much together in our economic, social, and political life. However, we confront important decisions on how to respond to urgent national problems and dramatic global change. A number of critical questions need to be addressed in the coming campaign:

- How can our nation best respond to the haunting needs of vulnerable children in our midst? We live in a society where 1.5 million unborn children die each year through legalized abortion. We live in a rich nation where more than a fourth of our preschoolers grow up poor. We live in a world where almost 35,000 children die every day from hunger and the diseases associated with malnutrition. The lives and dignity of vulnerable children—born and unborn—remain central questions for 1996.

- How can our nation bring together the strength of a powerful market economy and just public policies to confront continuing poverty and dependency, joblessness and declining real income for many families, and growing hostility toward immigrants and refugees?

- How can our society best combat continuing prejudice and discrimination, overcome the divisions among our people, provide full opportunity for all people, and heal the open wounds of racism and sexism?

- How can our society better support families in their irreplaceable moral role and social duties, offering real choices and help in finding and affording decent education, housing, and health care? How can we help parents raise their children with sound moral values, a sense of hope, and an ethic of responsibility for themselves and others?

- How can our nation respond creatively to dramatic international changes and pursue the values of justice and peace in a world often marked by too much violence and not enough development, too many violations of human rights and not enough respect for human life?

- How can we find fair ways to invest in our human needs, protect the environment, deal with our global responsibilities, and meet our fiscal and moral obligations to future generations without spending resources we don't have and running up deficits in the future? How can we fairly allocate scarce public resources and share the blessings and burdens of citizenship without increasing debt for our children?

- What are the appropriate responsibilities and limitations of free markets, government, voluntary organizations, and families? How can these essential elements of society work together to increase productivity, unleash creativity, restrain excesses, combat injustice, and pursue the common good?

- And perhaps most fundamentally, how can we resist what Pope John Paul II calls a growing "culture of violence"? Why does it seem that our nation is turning to violence to solve some of our most difficult problems—to abortion to deal with unplanned pregnancies, to the death penalty to combat crime, to euthanasia and assisted suicide to deal with the burdens of age and illness?

We raise these questions not to exhaust the possibilities, but to suggest key concerns and issues for the campaigns ahead. We believe every proposal, policy, or political platform should be measured by how it touches the human person; whether it enhances or diminishes human life, human dignity, and human rights; and how it advances the common good.

The common good is shaped by the moral convictions, personal virtue, and active commitment of every person. The renewal of democracy is not simply a task for others, but for each of us. It is the traditional virtue of citizenship that will renew American democracy. In bringing the virtues and values we seek to uphold in our personal lives into the public arena, we strengthen public life and build a better society.

A Religious Call to Political Responsibility

While it is increasingly acknowledged that major public issues have clear moral dimensions and religious values have significant public consequences, there is often confusion and controversy over the participation of religious groups in public life.

The religious community has important responsibilities in political life. We believe our nation is enriched and our traditions of pluralism enhanced when religious groups join with others in the debate over the policies and vision that ought to guide our nation. Our Constitution protects the right of religious bodies to speak out without governmental interference, endorsement, or sanction. Religious groups should expect neither favoritism nor discrimination in their public roles. The national debate is not enhanced by ignoring or ruling out the contributions of citizens because their convictions are grounded in religious belief.

We welcome the growing discussion of the role of moral values in public life and religious groups in the public square. We recognize that religious voices in public life must persuade, not just proclaim, and that the test of our witness is not only how strongly we believe, but how effectively we persuade and translate our beliefs into action.

The challenge for our Church is to be principled without being ideological, to be political without being partisan, to be civil without being soft, to be involved without being used. Our moral framework does not easily fit the categories of right or left, Republican or Democrat. We are called to measure every party and movement by how its agenda touches human life and human dignity. For example, we stand with various religious and other groups to protect the unborn and defend the family; we also insist that a test of public advocacy is how public policies touch the poor and the weak. A key question is where are "the least among us" in any national agenda?

We also work with a variety of groups to defend the poor and to seek greater economic justice. At the same time, we ask some of those who claim to stand for the weak why they protect the eggs of endangered species but fail to defend the lives of unborn children. A key criterion is consistency; we are called to stand up for human life whenever it is threatened, to stand with the weak and vulnerable whatever their age or condition.

As advocates of both subsidiarity and solidarity,[11] we also welcome the dialogue over how public and private sectors, government and community institutions can work together for the common good. What are the responsibilities and limitations of business and labor, churches and charities, and the various levels of government in protecting human life, enhancing human dignity, and pursuing social justice? Our tradition and experience teach us that markets have both advantages and limitations, that government is neither the solution nor the enemy, that private charities have essential roles, but cannot substitute for just public policies. How these sectors complement and restrain one another is a major issue for 1996.

As leaders of the Catholic community, we join these debates to share our experience in serving the poor and vulnerable and to add our values to the national dialogue over our nation's future. What we seek is not a religious interest group, but a community of conscience within the larger society, testing public life on these central values. Our starting point and objectives are neither partisan nor ideological, but are focused on the fundamental dignity of the human person, which cuts across the political categories of our day.

The Catholic community is very diverse. We are Democrats, Republicans, and Independents. We come from differing ideological and political persuasions. But we are all called to a common commitment to ensure that political life serves the common good and the human person. Our call to political responsibility is neither a partisan nor a sectarian appeal, but a call to reinvigorate the democratic process as a place for debate about what kind of society we want to be, about what values and priorities should guide our nation.

This kind of political responsibility does not involve religious leaders telling people how to vote or religious tests for candidates. These would be, in our view, pastorally inappropriate, theologically unsound, and politically unwise. Rather, we seek to lift up the moral and human dimensions of public issues for our own community and for the broader society. We encourage people to use their voices and votes to enrich the democratic life of our nation and to act on their values in the political arena. We hope American Catholics, as both believers and citizens, will use the resources of our faith and the opportunities of this democracy to help shape a society more respectful of the life, dignity, and rights of the human person, especially the poor and vulnerable.

In the Catholic tradition, citizenship is a virtue; participation in the political process is an obligation. We are not a sect fleeing the world, but a community of faith called to renew the earth. The 1996 elections provide new opportunities to replace the politics of polarization and false choices with the politics of participation and the common good.

Our community of faith brings two major assets. The first is *a consistent set of principles*. Our religious teaching provides a moral framework that can guide policy choices. Our community of faith does not rely on focus groups or polls to chart our directions; we advocate a consistent commitment to the human person. We draw our principles from Catholic teaching and tradition, not partisan platforms or ideological agendas. We stand with the unborn and the undocumented when many politicians seem to be abandoning them. We defend children in the womb and on welfare. We oppose the violence of abortion and the vengeance of capital punishment. We oppose assault weapons on our streets and condoms in our schools. Our agenda is sometimes countercultural, but it reflects our consistent concern for human life.

Secondly, we bring *broad experience in serving those in need*. The Catholic community educates the young, cares for the sick, shelters the homeless, feeds the hungry, assists needy families, welcomes refugees, and serves the elderly. People who are poor and vulnerable, the elderly, and immigrants are not abstract issues for us. They are in our parishes and schools, our shelters and soup kitchens, our hospitals and charitable agencies.[12] On many of the most vital issues facing our nation, we have practical expertise and day-to-day experience that can contribute to the debate.

Our task is to bring together our values, experience, and community in an effective public witness. The test of the 1996 elections will be how our choices touch the weak and vulnerable. Catholics need to share our values, raise our voices, and use our votes to shape a society more respectful of human life, human dignity, and human rights. We encourage parishes, dioceses, schools, and other Catholic institutions to encourage active participation by voter registration and voter education efforts that are genuinely nonpartisan. A number of dioceses have established nonpartisan political responsibility guidelines, which promote voter registration efforts, nonpartisan candidate forums, and questionnaires on the issues of human life, social justice, and peace. These efforts seek to promote genuine citizenship and a more active and informed participation in the political process. This kind of religious political responsibility can strengthen our nation and renew our Church.

In the sections that follow we outline traditional Catholic teaching on the Church in the public order and some important issues addressed by our conference.

2. The Church and the Political Order

It is appropriate in this context to offer our own reflections on the role of the Church in the political order. Christians believe that Jesus' commandment to love one's neighbor should extend beyond individual relationships to infuse and transform all human relations from the family to the entire human community. Jesus came to "bring good news to the poor . . . to proclaim liberty to captives and recovery of sight to the blind . . . and to let the oppressed go free . . ." (Lk 4:18). He called us to feed the hungry, clothe the naked, care for the sick and afflicted, and comfort the victims of injustice (cf. Mt 25:35–41). His example and words require individual acts of charity and concern from each of us. Yet they also require understanding and action on a broader scale in pursuit of peace and in opposition to poverty, hunger, and injustice. Such action necessarily involves the institutions and structures of society, the economy, and politics.

The Church, the people of God, is itself an expression of this love and is required by the Gospel and its long tradition to promote and defend human rights and human dignity. In his recent encyclical *The Gospel of Life*,[13] Pope John Paul II quotes with new urgency the message of the Second Vatican Council:

> Whatever is opposed to life itself, such as any type of murder, genocide, abortion, euthanasia, or willful self-destruction; whatever violates the integrity of the human person, such as mutilation, torments inflicted on body or mind, attempts to coerce the will itself; whatever insults human dignity, such as subhuman living conditions, arbitrary imprisonment, deportation, slavery, prostitution, the selling of women and children; as well as disgraceful working con-

ditions, where people are treated as mere instruments of
gain rather than as free and responsible persons; all these
things and others like them are infamies indeed. They poison human society, and they do more harm to those who
practice them than to those who suffer from the injury.
Moreover, they are a supreme dishonor to the Creator.[14]

This view of the Church's ministry and mission requires the
Church to relate positively to the political order, since social injustice
and the denial of human rights can often be remedied only through
governmental action. In today's world, concern for human life, social
justice, and peace necessarily requires persons and organizations to
participate in the political process in accordance with their own
responsibilities and roles.

Christian responsibility in the area of human rights includes two
complementary pastoral actions: the affirmation and promotion of
human rights and the denunciation and condemnation of violations of
these rights. In addition, it is the Church's role as a community of faith
to call attention to the moral and religious dimension of secular issues,
to keep alive the values of the Gospel as a norm for social and political
life, and to point out the demands of the Christian faith for a just transformation of society. Such a ministry on the part of every individual as
well as the organizational Church inevitably involves political consequences and touches upon public affairs. As Pope John Paul II suggests, "as a firm and persevering determination to commit oneself to
the common good, solidarity also needs to be practiced through participation in social and political life."[15]

The Responsibility of All Members of the Church

The Church's responsibility in this area falls on all its members. As
citizens, we are all called to become informed, active, and responsible
participants in the political process. It is the laity who are primarily
responsible for activity in political affairs, since they have the major
responsibility for renewal of the temporal order. In the words of the
Second Vatican Council:

The laity, by their very vocation, seek the kingdom of God
by engaging in temporal affairs and by ordering them
according to the plan of God. . . . They live in the ordinary
circumstances of family and social life, from which the very
web of their existence is woven. . . . They are called there by
God so that by exercising their proper function and being
led by the spirit of the Gospel, they can work for the sanctification of the world from within, in the manner of leaven.[16]

The hierarchy also has a distinct and weighty responsibility in this area. As teachers and pastors, they must provide norms for the formation of conscience of the faithful, support efforts to gain greater peace and justice, and provide guidance and even leadership when human rights are in jeopardy. Drawing on their own experience and exercising their distinctive roles within the Christian community, bishops, clergy, religious, and laity should join together in common witness and effective action to bring about the Church's vision of a well-ordered society based on truth, justice, charity, and freedom.

The Distinct Role of the Church

The Church's role in the political order includes the following:

- Educating the faithful regarding the teachings of the Church and their responsibilities
- Analyzing issues for their social and moral dimensions
- Measuring public policy against gospel values
- Participating with other concerned parties in debate over public policy
- Speaking out with courage, skill, and concern on public issues involving human rights, social justice, and the life of the Church in society

Unfortunately, our efforts in this area are sometimes misunderstood. The Church's participation in public affairs is not a threat to the political process nor to genuine pluralism, but an affirmation of their importance. The Church recognizes the legitimate autonomy of government and the right of all, including the Church itself, to be heard in the formulation of public policy. As the Second Vatican Council declared:

> By preaching the truth of the Gospel and shedding light on all areas of human activity through her teaching and the example of the faithful, she [the Church] shows respect for the political freedom and responsibility of citizens and fosters these values.
> . . . She also has the right to pass moral judgments, even on matters touching the political order, whenever basic personal rights or the salvation of souls make such judgments necessary.[17]

A proper understanding of the role of the Church will not confuse its mission with that of government but, rather, see its ministry as advocating the critical values of human rights and social justice. It is the role of Christian communities to analyze the situation in their own country, to reflect upon the meaning of the Gospel, and to draw norms of judgment and plans of action from the teaching of the Church and their own experience.[18] As Pope John Paul II has pointed out, "The social message of the Gospel must not be considered a theory, but above all else a basis and motivation for action. . . . Today, more than ever, the Church is aware that her social message will gain credibility more immediately from the witness of actions than as a result of its internal logic and consistency."[19]

The application of gospel values to real situations is an essential work of the Christian community. Christians believe the Gospel is the measure of human realities. However, specific political proposals do not in themselves constitute the Gospel. Christians and Christian organizations must certainly participate in public debate over alternative policies and legislative proposals, yet it is critical that the nature of their participation not be misunderstood.

We bishops specifically do not seek the formation of a religious voting bloc; nor do we wish to instruct persons on how they should vote by endorsing or opposing candidates. We do, however, have a right and a responsibility as teachers to analyze the moral dimensions of the major issues of our day. We urge citizens to avoid choosing candidates simply on the basis of narrow self-interest. We hope that voters will examine the positions of candidates on the full range of issues, as well as their personal integrity, philosophy, and performance. We are convinced that a consistent ethic of life should be the moral framework from which we address all issues in the political arena. In this consistent ethic, we address a spectrum of issues, seeking to protect human life and promote human dignity from the inception of life to its final moment.

As bishops, we seek to promote a greater understanding of the important link between faith and politics and to express our belief that our nation is enriched when its citizens and social groups approach public affairs from positions grounded in moral conviction and religious belief. As religious leaders and pastors, our intention is to reflect our concern that politics receive its rightful importance and attention and that it become an effective forum for the achievement of the common good. For, in the words of John Paul II, "An important challenge for the Christian is that of political life. In the state, citizens have a right and duty to share in the political life. For a nation can insure the common good of all the dreams and aspirations of its different members only to the extent that all citizens in full liberty and with complete responsibility make their contributions willingly and selflessly for the good of all."[20]

3. Principles and Issues

Without reference to political candidates, parties, or platforms, we wish to offer a listing of some principles and issues which we believe are important in the national debate during 1996. These brief summaries are not intended to indicate in any depth the details of the positions we have taken in past statements on these matters. For a fuller discussion of our point of view, we refer the reader to the documents listed after each summary.

A Tradition of Concern

These concerns are rooted in a tradition of social teaching which has taken on increasing importance and urgency over the last century. In a statement on the one hundredth anniversary of Pope Leo XIII's encyclical *On the Condition of Workers (Rerum Novarum)*,[21] our conference outlined six basic principles that are at the heart of these issues:

1. *The life and dignity of the human person.* In the Catholic social vision, the human person is central, the clearest reflection of God among us. Each person possesses a basic dignity that comes from God, not from any human quality or accomplishment, not from race or gender, age or economic status. The test of every institution or policy is whether it enhances or threatens human life and human dignity. We believe people are more important than things.

2. *Human rights and responsibilities.* Our dignity is protected when human rights are respected—the right to life and to those things which make life truly human: religious liberty, decent work, housing, health care, education, and the right to raise and provide for a family with dignity.

3. *The call to family and community.* The human person is not only sacred, but social. We realize our dignity and achieve our rights in relationship with others in our families and communities. No community is more central than the family—the basic cell of society.

4. *The dignity of work and the rights of workers.* Work is more than a way to make a living; it is a vocation, participation in creation. Workers have basic rights—to decent work, to just wages, to form and join unions, and to economic initiative, among others. The economy exists for the human person, not the other way around.

5. *The option for the poor.* People who are poor and vulnerable have a special place in Catholic teaching. The Scriptures tell us

we will be judged by our response to the "least of these." We need to put the needs of people who are poor first.

6. *Solidarity.* As Pope John Paul II reminds us, we are one human family despite differences of nationality or race; the poor are not a burden, but our sisters and brothers. Loving our neighbor has global dimensions in the 1990s.

The issues that follow are not the concerns of Catholics alone; in every case we are joined with others in advocating these concerns. They represent a broad range of topics on which we bishops of the United States have already expressed ourselves and are recalled here to emphasize their special relevance in a period of national debate and decision.

Abortion

Human life is a gift from God which all of us are called to protect, nurture, and sustain. The right to life, the most basic of all human rights, must be protected by law. Abortion has become the fundamental human rights issue of our day because it is the deliberate destruction of a human being before birth.

The United States, avowedly a defender of the weak, has one of the highest legal abortion rates and the most extreme abortion policy of any industrialized western nation in the world. There are now more than 1.5 million abortions every year in the United States, over 4,400 a day, with well over 95 percent performed for economic or social reasons. Thousands of unborn children are killed each year in the final months of pregnancy.

We support policies and laws that encourage childbirth over abortion, and urge government and the private sector to provide programs that assist pregnant women and their children, especially those who are poor. We support efforts to prohibit domestic and foreign abortion funding, as well as efforts to protect states from having to fund abortions contrary to their own laws. We reject the 1973 Supreme Court abortion decisions which deny legal protection to unborn children, and we support efforts to prohibit or restrict abortion legislatively and to provide constitutional protection for unborn human life. Laws and policies on medical research, health care, and related issues must respect and protect human life from the moment of conception. (*Documentation on the Right to Life and Abortion,* 1974, 1976, 1981; *Pastoral Plan for Pro-Life Activities: A Reaffirmation,* 1985; *Resolution on Abortion,* 1989, 1995; *Faithful for Life: A Moral Reflection,* 1995.)

Arms Control, Arms Trade, and Disarmament

While some progress has been made in recent years, additional steps are needed if nuclear policies and priorities are to keep up with the dramatic changes in world politics. An active commitment by the United States to progressive nuclear disarmament and the strengthening of collective security is the only moral basis for our deterrent and our insistence that other nations forego these weapons. Ratification and implementation of the arms treaty are essential, but much deeper cuts in nuclear arms are both possible and necessary. We support the current moratorium on nuclear testing as our nation pursues an effective global test ban.

The end of the Cold War still provides an opportunity to substantially reduce military spending. Diverting scarce resources from military to human development is not only a just and compassionate policy, but also a wise long-term investment in global and national security. Concern for jobs cannot justify military spending beyond the minimum necessary for legitimate national security and international peacekeeping obligations.

Neither can jobs at home justify exporting the means of war abroad. The United States has a special responsibility to undertake more serious efforts to control and significantly reduce its disproportional role in the scandalous global trade in arms. The unemployment and economic disruption caused by defense cuts must be addressed concretely through economic development and adjustment programs, a stronger non-military economy, and other programs to assist those affected. The United States should take a leadership role in reducing reliance on, ending export of, and ultimately banning antipersonnel landmines, which kill some 26,000 civilians each year. (*The Challenge of Peace: God's Promise and Our Response*, 1983; *A Report on the Challenge of Peace and Policy Developments 1983-1988*, 1989; *The Harvest of Justice Is Sown in Peace*, 1993; *Confronting a Culture of Violence*, 1995.)

Capital Punishment

The Church's commitment to the value and dignity of human life leads us to oppose the use of the death penalty. We believe that a return to the use of the death penalty is further eroding respect for life in our society. We do not question society's right to protect itself, but we believe that there are better approaches to protecting our people from violent crimes. The application of the death penalty has been discriminatory toward the poor, the indigent, and racial minorities. Our society should reject the death penalty and seek methods of dealing with violent crime that are more consistent with the gospel visions of respect for life and Christ's message of healing love. This principle is set forth in the new *Catechism of the Catholic Church*: "If bloodless means are sufficient to defend human lives against an aggressor and to protect public order and the safety of persons, public authority must limit itself to such means, because they better correspond to the concrete conditions of the common good and are more in conformity to the dignity of the human person." (*Community and Crime,* 1978; *U.S. Bishops' Statement on Capital Punishment,* 1980; *Confronting a Culture of Violence,* 1995.)

Communications

The telecommunications industry has undergone a significant transformation with the advent of new technologies and changing governmental policies and regulations. The battle for ratings and a singular emphasis on profits have too often replaced the commitment to legitimate public interest standards. We are deeply concerned about the glorification of violence and exploitation of sexuality in some television programming, movies, and other newer media. Since the deregulation of the industry that began in the early 1980s, the amount of time and resources the industry has devoted to issues of community importance has declined.

Three principles must be maintained: (1) the communications industry, considering its widespread influence, needs to operate in the public interest as well as its own ownership interests; (2) citizens must be able to participate effectively in defining and enforcing services in the public interest; and (3) fairness and diversity must be assured in ownership, employment, and public access of these services.

We support requirements for the telecommunications industry to air more educational and informational children's programs and to curtail violence and commercialization during children's television programming. We strongly advocate measures that will lead to the improvement of moral standards in the media and an increase in values-based programming.

We also support reasonable and constitutionally acceptable regulations that prohibit the distribution of obscene material and restrict the distribution of indecent material over the electronic media, so that this material is not accessible to minors. We oppose advertising and public service announcements that have the effect of impinging on the right of parents to teach their children about responsible sexuality. (*Statements and testimony by the USCC Department of Communications before Congress and the Federal Communications Commission.*)

Discrimination and Racism

Discrimination based on sex, race, ethnicity, or age continues to exist in our nation. Signs of increased racial hostility poison our society. Such discrimination constitutes a grave injustice and an affront to human dignity. It must be aggressively resisted by every individual and rooted out of every social institution and structure. Discrimination on the basis of race, sex, or other arbitrary standards can never be justified. Where the effects of past discrimination persist, society has the obligation to take positive steps to overcome the legacy of injustice. We support judiciously administered affirmative action programs as tools to overcome discrimination and its continuing effects.

Racism is a particularly serious form of discrimination. Despite significant strides in eliminating racial prejudices in our country, there remains an urgent need for continued reconciliation in this area and continued commitment to move forward to overcome more subtle but still destructive forms of discrimination and intolerance. Racism is not merely one sin among many. It is a radical evil dividing the human family. (*Brothers and Sisters to Us,* 1989.)

The Economy

Our pastoral letter *Economic Justice for All* insists that every economic decision and institution should be judged in light of whether it protects or undermines the dignity of the human person. The economy must be at the service of all people, especially the poor. Society as a whole, acting through private and government institutions, has the moral responsibility to enhance human dignity and protect human rights.

The most urgent priority for domestic economic policy is to create jobs with adequate pay and decent working conditions. High levels of unemployment and underemployment are morally unacceptable in a nation with our economic capacity. The minimum wage should be raised to help workers and their families live decent lives. We reaffirm the Church's traditional teaching in support of the right of all workers to organize and bargain collectively and to exercise these rights without reprisal.

The fact that so many people are poor in a nation as wealthy as ours is a social and moral scandal that must not be ignored. The disproportionate impact of poverty on children, women, and members of racial and ethnic minorities must be addressed through just policies on employment, taxes, welfare, and family life. Wage discrimination against women and other economic consequences of sexism must be overcome. Vigorous efforts are needed to overcome barriers to equal employment and pay for women and minorities. Dealing with poverty is not a luxury to which our nation can attend when it finds the time and resources. Rather, it is a moral imperative of the highest priority.

In the area of tax policies, we support effective incentives for charitable giving, an earned income tax credit that ensures that working families will not have to raise their children in poverty, and a tax code that reflects traditional Catholic teaching that tax rates should reflect a person's ability to pay.

It is essential that all aspects of international economic policy—trade, aid, finance, and investment—reflect basic moral principles and promote the global common good. The United States has a moral obligation to take the lead in helping to alleviate poverty through sustainable development, supporting programs that emphasize greater participation of the poor in grassroots development rather than large-scale government projects. We have a humanitarian obligation to support victims of war and natural disaster. We also support long-term development initiatives for poor countries undergoing transition from civil war or authoritarian regimes. We continue to emphasize human development over military assistance in the priorities of U.S. foreign aid programs. We must reform foreign assistance, not abandon it. (*Economic Justice for All*, 1986; *Relieving Third World Debt*, 1989; *Putting Children and Families First*, 1992; *The Harvest of Justice Is Sown in Peace*, 1993.)

Education

All persons of whatever race, sex, condition, or age, by virtue of their dignity as human beings, have an inalienable right to a quality education. The provision of a quality education, which helps prepare each person to address the complex challenges of our society and world, is a lifelong process and is the responsibility of all members of our civic society. We advocate public policies that provide for the following:

- Adequate public and private funding to make a quality education available for all citizens and residents of the United States in an orderly and respectful environment
- The development and implementation of a form of moral education integrated into the total public school curriculum that responds to student needs and is respectful of the variety of beliefs found in our nation
- Government and voluntary action to reduce inequalities of educational opportunity by improving the opportunities available to educationally, economically, and socially disadvantaged persons

- Orderly compliance with legal requirements for racially integrated schools and additional voluntary efforts to increase racial and ethnic integration in public, private, and religious schools
- Equitable tax support for education of pupils in public, private, and religious schools to implement the natural right of parental freedom of choice in the education of their children
- Salaries and benefits of teachers and administrators that reflect the principles of economic justice
- The principle that private and religious school students and professional staff have the right and opportunity for equitable participation in all government programs to improve education, especially those which address the needs of the educationally, economically, and socially disadvantaged

(*To Teach As Jesus Did,* 1972; *Sharing the Light of Faith: National Catechetical Directory,* 1979; *Value and Virtue: Moral Education in the Public School,* 1988; *Economic Justice for All,* 1986; *In Support of Catholic Elementary and Secondary Schools,* 1990; *Principles for Educational Reform in the United States,* 1995.)

Environmental Justice

Pope John Paul II has called the environmental crisis fundamentally a "moral" challenge. The whole human race suffers as a result of environmental blight, and generations yet unborn will bear the cost for our failure to act today. What is needed is the will to make changes in policy and lifestyles, to arrest, reverse, and prevent environmental decay, and to pursue the goal of sustainable, equitable development for all. Our call to environmental justice includes supporting policies that

- Promote sustainable economic practices that reduce the current stress on natural systems, remain consistent with sound environmental practices, and establish common ground between the needs of workers and the environment
- Place the needs of the poor as a priority through a more just and more equitable sharing of the earth's resources
- Foster environmental justice and the elimination of discriminatory practices, which place a disproportionate burden on poor people and communities of color
- Promote policies which ensure a fair balance between public and private costs of environmental protection
- Seek alternative agricultural and energy sources that rely less on chemical-intensive agricultural practices and nonrenewable energy resources

- Sustain and enhance the biological and ecological diversity of God's creation

(*Renewing the Earth*, 1992; *Economic Justice for All*, 1986.)

Euthanasia

We affirm public policies that respect the life and dignity of those who are dying: legal safeguards against direct killing by action or omission, policies that enable mentally or physically disabled patients to receive the same basic care accorded others, and funding policies to ease burdens on families whose members are in need of long-term care. We reject any law or social policy that sanctions suicide or assisted suicide or any deliberate and direct hastening of death for seriously ill patients. (*Pastoral Statement of U.S. Catholic Bishops on Persons with Disabilities*, 1989; *Guidelines for Legislation on Life-Sustaining Treatment*, 1984; *Statement on Uniform Rights of the Terminally Ill Act*, 1986; NCCB *Administrative Committee Statement on Euthanasia*, 1991; *Faithful for Life: A Moral Reflection*, 1995.)

Families and Children

We urge a reordering of priorities to focus more on the needs and potential of the nation's children. If society seeks to help children, it has to support families, since children's lives are nurtured or neglected, enhanced or diminished by the quality of family life. The undeniable fact is that our children's future is shaped both by the values of their parents and the policies of our nation. Our nation must move beyond partisan and ideological rhetoric to support families in their essential roles and insist that public policy protect poor and vulnerable children.

We continue to advocate policies and priorities which meet these basic criteria:

1. *Put children and families first.* Analyze every policy and program for its impact on children and families.
2. *Help; don't hurt.* Insist that policies support families rather than undermine them; encourage self-help rather than promote dependency.
3. *Those with the greatest need require the greatest response.* While every family needs support, poor families and families facing discrimination carry the greatest burdens and require the most help.

4. *Empower families.* Help families meet their responsibilities to their children in education, child care, health, and other areas. Tax, workplace, divorce, and welfare policies must help families stay together and care for their children.
5. *Fight economic and social forces that threaten children and family life.* Efforts to overcome poverty, provide decent jobs, and promote equal opportunity are pro-family priorities.
6. *Build on the strengths of families.* Reward responsibility and sacrifice for children.
7. *Recognize that foreign policy is increasingly children's policy.* Global poverty, armed conflict, and systematic injustice threaten the lives of millions of children and their families around the world.

(*Putting Children and Families First*, 1992; *A Family Perspective in Church and Society*, 1988.)

Food and Agriculture

In a world where 800 million people, half of them children, are starving or malnourished, we support food and agriculture policy that makes food security for all people its first priority. U.S. agriculture policy should

- Offer farmers the opportunity to make a decent living while providing safe and affordable food to consumers
- Work to keep farmers on the land and encourage broad-based ownership of farmland by targeting farm programs to small and moderate-sized farms
- Ensure that farmworkers receive a just wage and are provided with decent housing and safe working conditions
- Continue to provide food aid to the poorest countries and the neediest people

Ensuring adequate nutrition for low-income pregnant women, children, the elderly, and the unemployed continues to be a cornerstone of food security at home. We support food stamps, WIC, school lunches, and other federal programs that provide for the nutrition needs of low-income people. International food and development aid should be focused on the neediest people and poorest countries in ways that contribute to economic and human development and promote self-reliance. International agricultural policy should emphasize equitable distribution of benefits and broader participation in land ownership and should help other nations move toward food self-sufficiency.

We support food and agriculture policy that promotes food security not only for the present but for future generations. As such, we urge policies that support sustainable agriculture and careful stewardship of the earth and its natural resources. (*Economic Justice for All*, 1986; *Food Policy in a Hungry World*, 1989; *Putting Children and Families First*, 1992; *The Harvest of Justice Is Sown in Peace*, 1993.)

Health, AIDS, and Substance Abuse

Our nation's health care system still serves too few and costs too much. Decent health care is an essential safeguard of human life. We believe reform of the health care system must be rooted in values that respect the essential dignity of each person, ensure that human life is protected, and recognize the unique needs of the poor. Our criteria for reform include respect for life, priority concern for the poor, universal coverage, pluralism, cost containment and controls, and equitable financing.

Genuine health care reform is a matter of fundamental justice. We urge national leaders to look beyond special interest claims and partisan differences to unite our nation in a new commitment to meeting the health care needs of our people.

The continuing crisis of AIDS within our society requires policies that emphasize continuing research, routine voluntary testing, compassionate care, responsible education, effective support for persons with AIDS and their families, and respect for the dignity and rights of persons with AIDS.

Substance abuse is a nationwide problem of immense proportions. Our conference advocates effective, compassionate policies to turn the tide of addiction in this country, including public policy and funding to ensure access to adequate, affordable, and appropriate treatment and services for all those in need, especially pregnant women. (*A Framework for Comprehensive Health Care Reform*, 1993; *Called to Compassion and Responsibility: A Response to the HIV/AIDS Crisis*, 1989; *New Slavery, New Freedom: A Pastoral Message on Substance Abuse*, 1990.)

Housing

Housing is being seriously neglected as a priority of national concern, governmental action, and federal investment. Shelters cannot substitute for real housing for low-income families and poor individuals. The major goals for national housing policy should include the following:

- *Preservation.* Effective policies to help preserve, maintain, and improve low-cost, decent housing.

- *Production.* Creative, cost-effective, and flexible programs that will increase the supply of quality housing for low-income families, the elderly, and other vulnerable people.
- *Participation.* Active and sustained involvement and empowerment of the homeless, tenants, neighborhood residents, and housing consumers, building on American traditions of home ownership, self-help, and neighborhood participation.
- *Opportunity.* Stronger efforts to combat discrimination in housing.

(*Homelessness and Housing,* 1988.)

Human Rights

Respect for fundamental human rights is necessary if nations are to serve human dignity and the common good, including civil, political, social, and economic rights. Religious freedom, a cornerstone for human rights, is a priority concern for us given the extent of its suppression or disregard in many parts of the world, including China, East Timor, Vietnam, Cuba, Sudan, and parts of the Middle East. We condemn once again the evil of "ethnic cleansing," which requires effective action by the international community to banish it forever. The destruction of people because of their religion, race, ethnicity, or nationality is a crime against humanity.

With respect to international human rights, there is a pressing need for the United States to pursue a double task: (1) to strengthen and expand international mechanisms by which human rights can be protected and promoted; and (2) to give greater weight to the human rights dimensions of U.S. foreign policy. Therefore, we support U.S. ratification of the International Covenant on Civil and Political Rights as well as the Convention on Race and Torture, and we support ratification of the remaining Covenant on Economic, Social, and Cultural Rights, and other sound mechanisms to implement the UN Declaration of Human Rights. Further, the United States has a responsibility to use its power and influence consistently and creatively in the effective service of human rights throughout the world. (*The Harvest of Justice Is Sown in Peace,* 1993.)

Immigration

Catholic tradition defends basic human rights, including the right to work. The United States bishops support a generous U.S. immigration policy and a U.S. commitment to providing temporary safe haven for those in need. The bishops have expressed concern at the surge of anti-immigrant sentiment reflected in California's Proposition 187 and proposals to restrict immigration and deny nearly all basic social services to immigrants. The U.S. bishops have reaffirmed several basic immigration principles. First, persons fleeing persecution have a special standing and thus require special consideration as emigrants. Second, workers have the right to live and work without exploitation. Third, family reunification remains an appropriate basis for just immigration policy. Fourth, every effort should be made to encourage and enable highly skilled and educated persons to remain in or return to their homelands. Fifth, efforts to stem migration that do not effectively address its root causes are not only ineffectual, but permit the continuation of the political, social, and economic inequities that cause it. These principles, including a particular pledge of solidarity with the undocumented, form the core of Catholic priorities regarding U.S. immigration policy. (*One Family Under God*, 1995.)

International Affairs and the United Nations

Building peace, combating poverty and despair, and protecting freedom and human rights are not only moral imperatives, but also wise national priorities. They can shape a world that will be a safer, more secure, and more just home for all of us. The U.S. Catholic Conference urges

- Creative, engaged, and responsible U.S. leadership that rejects the illusion of isolationism and avoids the dangers of unwise intervention
- A reshaped foreign aid program designed to combat poverty with sustainable development and economic opportunities for the poor
- Accelerated progress toward a nuclear test ban, preventing nuclear proliferation, eliminating nuclear weapons, and restraining the conventional arms trade
- Legal protection for selective conscientious objectors and improved protection for conscientious objectors
- Review of economic sanctions as an alternative to war and a means to enforce fundamental international norms, in light of the suffering they inflict on innocent people
- Clarification of the right and duty of humanitarian intervention in exceptional cases, by means consistent with Catholic teaching when the survival of whole populations is threatened

Political leaders and citizens have a positive duty to support the development, reform, and restructuring of regional and global political and legal institutions, especially the United Nations. As Pope John

XXIII observed in *Peace on Earth (Pacem in Terris)*, a worldwide public authority is necessary, not to limit or replace the authority of states, but rather to address fundamental problems that nations alone, no matter how powerful, cannot be expected to solve. The United States should play a constructive role in making the United Nations and other international institutions more effective, responsible, and responsive. At a minimum, the United States must pay in full its UN assessments. Preventive diplomacy, peace-building after war, and peacekeeping all deserve special support and attention. (*The Harvest of Justice Is Sown in Peace*, 1993.)

Refugees

In response to what Pope John Paul II has called "perhaps the greatest tragedy of all the human tragedies of our time," the Catholic community operates the largest refugee resettlement system in the United States and is deeply concerned for the fate of the millions of oppressed and dispossessed persons in the world today. As the number of refugees has doubled over the last decade and continues to grow and as the post-Cold War world has also seen an even greater growth in the numbers of internally displaced persons in refugee-like circumstances, the United States must continue to take the lead in bringing an adequate response from the international community. Refugee resettlement of those in particularly difficult situations who cannot return home remains one important component of the U.S. response. In addressing this problem, special attention must be paid to unaccompanied refugee children, single women and women head of families, the disabled, and religious minorities. U.S. policy must respect and seek to ensure the preservation of temporary asylum for all refugees and assistance at levels adequate to ensure the safety and dignity of the world's 40 million refugees and displaced persons. Where voluntary return home is a possibility, this should be encouraged and provided adequate material support. (*One Family Under God*, 1995.)

Regional Concerns: Eastern Europe, Middle East, Latin America, and Africa

The USCC is concerned about human rights and regional conflicts throughout the world, but four areas are of particular concern, in part due to the involvement of the Church, the substantial influence of U.S. policy, and the region's importance for international order: Eastern Europe, the Middle East, Latin America, and Africa.

Eastern and Central Europe

The advent of a new era in Central and Eastern Europe has created radically new opportunities and challenges, both for the nations of that region and for a new, more just international order. U.S. policy should continue to promote religious liberty and human rights and press for necessary political and economic changes where authoritarian regimes or their structures remain in place or reappear. We support a major undertaking by the United States to assist the emerging democracies of the region in their monumental task of constructing a new political, economic, social, and moral order. This should include support for peaceful, democratic, and negotiated efforts for peoples to realize their legitimate aspirations for self-determination in ways compatible with greater stability and justice in the region.

A special tragedy and moral challenge has arisen in the Balkans. The United States and the international community must do more to bring about a just and lasting resolution to the war in the Balkans. Any political solution should avoid, as far as possible, the partition of Bosnia-Herzegovina and other countries of the region along ethnic lines and should continue to insist on the equal rights and equal legitimacy of all ethnic, religious, and national groups there. The international community has a right and duty to intervene, including with the limited use of force, to protect vulnerable civilian populations, to enable relief supplies to get through, and to implement a peace settlement. UN peacekeeping and humanitarian protection should be strengthened so that it can more effectively prevent "ethnic cleansing" and meet its commitments to humanitarian protection. While we do not believe this is a religious conflict, any crime committed in the name of religion is a crime against religion. (*War in the Balkans: Moral Challenges, Policy Choices*, 1993; *The New Moment in Eastern and Central Europe*, March 1990; *The Harvest of Justice Is Sown in Peace*, 1993.)

The Middle East

Israel, Jordan, and the Palestinians. We have worked for, prayed for, and supported the peace process in the Middle East. Peace comes slowly to this troubled region of the world. The peace agreements between Israel and the PLO and between Jordan and Israel have been welcome steps toward peace in the region. A great deal remains to be accomplished between Israel and the Palestinians. We continue to support

- Full support of Israel's right to exist within secure borders
- Recognition of Palestinian rights, the right to self-determination, including their option for an independent homeland
- Fulfillment of UN resolutions 242 and 338 on the Middle East

The parties ought to be scrupulous in fulfilling their stated obligations to one another and in their observance of human rights. The international community ought to be generous with aid to preserve and foster the peace, especially in helping establish the basic humanitarian services to the Palestinian people.

Jerusalem. Our conference has particular concern for the holy city of Jerusalem, a city sacred to Jews, Christians, and Muslims. Special care must be taken to guarantee the rights of the three Abrahamic faiths in Jerusalem, including the rights of the living religious communities in the city. Access to the holy places and religious liberty in the city ought to be guaranteed internationally.

Lebanon. The world must not forget Lebanon. We strongly support a permanent end to violence, effective reform and reconciliation, and the final withdrawal of all foreign forces from Lebanon, as well as significant economic assistance for Lebanon's recovery. (*Toward Peace in the Middle East*, 1989.)

Latin America and the Caribbean

The ties between the churches of Latin America and the United States continue to be strong and enduring. For two decades, issues of human rights, religious liberty, economic justice, and armed violence have been priorities for our conference. We remain concerned about the slow process of economic recovery and have continuing concerns about human rights in Central America and the Caribbean. Nicaragua, El Salvador, Haiti, and Panama continue to need sustained U.S. assistance and attention to protect human rights, promote development, and foster democratic values.

The Church in Cuba has called for greater dialogue within Cuba and between Cuba and the United States. Our priorities remain support for the aspirations of the Cuban people for greater religious liberty, democracy, and economic freedom. We support efforts to provide humanitarian and medical assistance to the Cuban people and to link relaxation of the embargo to concrete steps toward democracy, human rights, and religious liberty.

Mexico has assumed a more significant place in U.S. foreign and economic policy. Continued U.S.-Mexican cooperation is essential in the areas of trade, migration, narcotics control, and environmental protection, as well as concern for human rights. Mexico's troubled democracy and the peace process in Chiapas need the encouragement of the United States.

In other parts of Latin America, U.S. policy should continue to promote democracy, respect for human rights, religious liberty, and demilitarization. Debt and development remain central issues for the future of Latin America. U.S. policy must also address the broader forces at work in much of Latin America—poverty, debt, lack of development, and the drug trade—which diminish respect for the lives, dignity, and rights of so many people. (*USCC Statement on Central America, 1987; The Harvest of Justice Is Sown in Peace,* 1993.)

Africa

The African continent has been plagued with armed conflict, often of long-term duration, that has resulted in millions of displaced persons, tens of thousands maimed both physically and mentally, and untold devastation of human life and physical resources. Ethnic and civil conflicts in Rwanda and Burundi continue to rise, potentially escalating to the proportions of 1993-94 when more than a million civilians were brutally massacred, while the civil conflicts in Liberia and the Sudan continue to rage out of control. These conflicts have created tremendous refugee problems in neighboring countries and a pressing need for an international response to violence and human rights violations occurring in these and other countries of the African continent. The difficult transition to democracy in many countries requires the diplomatic assistance of the United States. And in the aftermath of the UN withdrawal from Somalia, the international community must continue to guard against an escalation of violence. Our conference remains concerned that too many African countries engage in arms races they can ill afford, often with the encouragement of the more powerful nations. More steps are necessary to curb the arms trade, not only in Africa but throughout the world.

We welcome the first free and democratically elected government of South Africa. We renew our call for dioceses and religious bodies, the U.S. government, business, investors, and all interested parties to use every available and practical means to ensure the success of nonracial democracy in south Africa. (*Economic Justice for All,* 1986; *The Harvest of Justice Is Sown in Peace,* 1993; *Statements on South Africa,* 1993, 1994.)

Violence

Violence in our culture is fed by multiple forces—the disintegration of family life, media influences, growing substance abuse, the availability of so many weapons, and the rise of gangs. Traditional liberal or conservative approaches by themselves cannot effectively overcome this plague. In confronting a culture of violence, our Church calls for

- Opposing the violence of abortion
- Curbing the easy availability of deadly weapons
- Supporting community approaches to crime prevention and law enforcement

- Pursuing swift and effective justice without vengeance and effective reform of our criminal justice system
- Attacking the root causes of violence, including poverty, substance abuse, lack of opportunity, racism, and family disintegration
- Promoting more personal responsibility and broader social responsibility in our policies and programs
- Overcoming the tragedy of family violence and confronting all forms of violence against women
- Continuing to work for global disarmament, including curbs on arms sales and a ban on landmines

(*Confronting a Culture of Violence,* 1995.)

Welfare Reform

The Catholic community brings strong convictions and broad experience to welfare reform. We support genuine welfare reform that strengthens families, encourages productive work, and protects vulnerable children—born and unborn. We are not defenders of the welfare status quo; however, we oppose abandonment of the federal government's essential role in helping families overcome poverty and meet their children's basic needs.

Welfare reform needs to be comprehensive in analysis, but targeted and flexible in its implementation. We seek a new approach which promotes greater responsibility and offers more concrete help to families in leaving poverty behind through productive work and other assistance. We advocate for welfare reform which

- Protects human life and human dignity (we, therefore, oppose family cap and child exclusion measures which encourage abortion without addressing the fundamental contributors to illegitimacy)
- Strengthens family life
- Encourages and rewards work
- Preserves a safety net for the vulnerable
- Builds public/private partnerships to overcome poverty
- Invests in human dignity and poor families

For the Catholic community, the measure of welfare reform is whether it will enhance the lives and dignity of poor children and their families. The target of reform ought to be poverty, not poor families. The goal of reform is reducing poverty and dependency, not cutting resources and programs. (*Moral Principles and Policy Priorities for Welfare Reform,* 1995.)

This is not an exclusive listing of the issues that concern us. For example, we have great concern for the elderly, especially those who lack adequate nutrition, medical care, and housing, and who are victims of abuse. As Pope John Paul II has said, the Church cannot remain insensitive to whatever serves true human welfare any more than it can remain indifferent to whatever threatens it.[22] Thus, we are advocates on many other social justice concerns, such as the civil and political rights of the elderly and persons with disabling conditions and the reform of our criminal justice system.

4. Conclusion

In summary, we believe that the Church has a proper role and responsibility in public affairs flowing from its gospel mandate and its respect for the dignity of the human person. We hope these reflections will contribute to a renewed political vitality in our land, both in terms of citizen participation in the electoral process and the integrity and accountability of those who seek and hold public office.

We urge all citizens to use their franchise by registering to vote and going to the polls. We encourage them to get information from the campaigns as well as from the media coverage of those campaigns and to take stands on the candidates and the issues. If this campaign year is to engage the values of the American people, the campaigners and voters alike must share the responsibility for making it happen. We urge each person to become involved in the campaign or party of their choice, to learn about the issues, and to inform their conscience.

We urge Christians to provide courageous leadership in promoting a spirit of responsible political involvement and a commitment to the common good. In the elections of 1996, we urge our fellow believers to proclaim the "Gospel of life," to protect "the least among us," and to pursue the common good.

Notes

1. John Paul II, Arrival Statement, Newark, *Origins* 25:18 (October 19, 1995): 301.
2. John Paul II, "Address at the United Nations," *Origins* 25:18 (October 19, 1995): 299-300.
3. John Paul II, "Homily at Giants Stadium," East Rutherford, N.J., *Origins* 25:18 (October 19, 1995): 304.
4. John Paul II, "Homily at Aqueduct Racetrack," Brooklyn, N.Y., *Origins* 25:18 (October 19, 1995): 305.
5. John Paul II, "Homily at Camden Yards," Baltimore, *Origins* 25:18 (October 19, 1995): 313.

6. John Paul II, Departure Statement, Baltimore, *Origins* 25:18 (October 19, 1995): 318.
7. John Paul II, *On the Hundredth Anniversary of Rerum Novarum (Centesimus Annus)* (Washington, D.C.: United States Catholic Conference, 1991), no. 47.
8. Ibid.
9. John Paul II, *The Gospel of Life (Evangelium Vitae)* (Washington, D.C.: United States Catholic Conference, 1995), no. 70.
10. Ibid., no. 101.
11. In Catholic social teaching, subsidiarity and solidarity are elements of the common good. Subsidiarity helps to establish the autonomy of groups and to specify the correct relationships that ought to exist between different organizations and associations within society. Solidarity is a firm and persevering determination to commit oneself to the common good.
12. The Catholic community has a national network present in virtually every part of the nation. It includes almost 20,000 parishes, 8,300 schools, 231 colleges and universities, 900 hospitals and health care facilities, and 1,400 Catholic Charities agencies. The Catholic community is the largest non-public provider of education, health care, and human services in the United States.
13. *Evangelium Vitae*, no. 3.
14. Second Vatican Council, *Pastoral Constitution on the Church in the Modern World (Gaudium et Spes)*, no. 27.
15. *Evangelium Vitae*, no. 93.
16. Second Vatican Council, *Dogmatic Constitution on the Church (Lumen Gentium)*, no. 31.
17. *Gaudium et Spes*, no. 76.
18. Paul VI, *A Call to Action (Octogesima Adveniens)* (Washington, D.C.: United States Catholic Conference, 1971), no. 4.
19. *Centesimus Annus*, no. 57.
20. John Paul II, Address in Nairobi, Kenya, *Origins* 10:2 (May 29, 1980): 28.
21. United States Catholic Conference, *A Century of Social Teaching: A Common Heritage, A Continuing Challenge* (Washington, D.C.: United States Catholic Conference, 1990), 4-7.
22. John Paul II, *The Redeemer of Man (Redemptor Hominis)* (Washington, D.C.: United States Catholic Conference, 1979), no. 13.

Source: Washington, D.C.: United States Catholic Conference, 1995.

Walk in the Light: A Pastoral Response to Child Sexual Abuse

A Statement by the Bishops' Committees on Women in Society and in the Church and Marriage and Family Affirmed by the NCCB Administrative Committee

September 1995

Part I: Introduction

> Here, then, is the message we heard from him [Christ] and announce to you: that God is light; and in him there is no darkness. . . . If we walk in the light, as he is in the light, we have fellowship with one another. . . . (1 Jn 1:5-7)

In our 1992 statement *When I Call for Help,* we spoke out to condemn domestic violence against women and stated unequivocally that neither the Scriptures nor the Church condoned abusive situations. Now we speak out against another kind of violence: child sexual abuse, particularly in a home or family setting.

Child sexual abuse is the exploitation of a child for the sexual gratification of an adult. It may range from exhibitionism and fondling to intercourse and the use of children in pornographic materials.[1] Child sexual abuse over the centuries has been cloaked in a conspiracy of silence because the abuse often occurs in the home and the victims are children. People tend to think that certain authority figures, such as parents, stepparents, teachers, or clergy, are above reproach; that "pillars of the community" could not abuse children. Abusive behavior often hides behind the masks of love and trust.

While the true incidence of child sexual abuse remains unknown, it is nonetheless significant.[2] We state firmly and clearly that any act of child sexual abuse is morally evil. It is *never* justified.

Why Speak Now?

As the tragedy of child sexual abuse has come to light, we as pastors believe it is important to speak on this delicate and difficult issue, to offer a word of hope, and to help families touched by this tragedy. Priests and parish staff tell of sexually abused people approaching them with their experiences; many more may hesitate to come forth out of embarrassment and fear. Parish staff also tell of the tragedy that happens when family members become aware of sexual abuse but keep silent. We know, however, that when sexual abuse is acknowledged and dealt with, many people can and do move forward to form healthy relationships. We know, too, that some abusers can learn to change their behavior.

We are compelled to speak even knowing that the Church carries a heavy burden of responsibility in the area of sexual abuse. Some ordained ministers and religious brothers and sisters, as well as lay employees and volunteers, have sexually abused children and adolescents. We are acutely aware of the havoc and suffering caused by this abuse and we are committed to dealing with these situations responsibly and in all humility. The National Conference of Catholic Bishops has established an ad hoc committee on sexual abuse by clergy to help church leaders take appropriate action. Each diocese has developed comprehensive policies concerning sexual abuse, which often apply to employees and volunteers, as well as to clergy and religious. We are fully committed to preventing child sexual abuse and to restoring victims to health.[3]

We speak, too, as citizens of a nation and a world that decries the exploitation of girls. While we recognize that sexual abuse of boys is significant—some studies estimate it at 20 to 25 percent of all child victims[4]—the overwhelming number of sexual abuse victims are girls. We are especially alarmed at the large number of victims who are girls under age 12.[5] We join the United Nations, the International Catholic Child Bureau, and other groups in drawing attention to the vulnerability of girls throughout the world, including the United States of America.

To Whom Do We Speak?

- To adults who were sexually abused as children
- To young people who are, or have been, sexually abused, and to their families
- To abusers and potential abusers who act out the impulse to sexually abuse those they are committed to love and protect
- To priests, parish ministers, youth workers, women's commissions and councils, educators, and other church leaders who can assist those who abuse and are abused
- To people of all faiths who are concerned about families in crisis
- To all of society, which is coming to recognize the terrible toll of child sexual abuse and the need to take action against it

What We Hope to Do

We realize that emotional and spiritual healing can occur only when issues can be openly addressed. In this statement, we seek to bring the tragedy of child sexual abuse into the light, to give people needed information, and to offer the spiritual, sacramental, and social resources of the Church so that the healing process may begin. As with *When I Call for Help,* we intend this statement to be an introduction— along with some practical suggestions—to what parishes and dioceses and committed people of all faiths can do about child sexual abuse now.

Part II: Dimensions of Child Sexual Abuse

Those Who Are Abused

Sexual abuse occurs in all racial and cultural groups; in rural, suburban, and urban areas; and at all socioeconomic and educational levels. Authorities believe that many cases go unreported because they involve family or friends.

Reported victims of sexual abuse are most often children of school age. However, evidence indicates that sexual abuse may begin at an even younger age. At least one major treatment center reported in 1993 that 25 percent of its patients are five years old or younger.[6]

Sexual abuse usually takes place in secret and is kept secret because the abuser fears discovery. Sexual abuse is often more difficult for a child to acknowledge than physical or emotional abuse, and the sexually abused child may feel more isolated. Children often blame themselves for the abuse; therefore it is important to reassure the child that he or she is not responsible. The adult, not the child, is responsible for violating the boundaries that the child could not maintain alone.

Profile of an Abuser

Abusers come from all walks of life, all economic backgrounds, and all ethnic groups. Men commit 90 percent of sexual abuse, and 70 to 90 percent is committed by persons the child knows. Family members make up one-third to one-half of the perpetrators against girls and 10 to 20 percent of the perpetrators against boys.[7]

It is impossible to reliably identify potential sex abusers. Various studies indicate that they may be more likely to abuse drugs and alcohol; may have been abused as children or have witnessed abuse; have low self-esteem; consider a sexual relationship with a child easier and less threatening than with an adult; maintain rigid expectations of roles within the family and view anyone outside the family with suspicion; rationalize their actions; and do not consider their abuse to be morally offensive. Some sex abusers, however, display none of these characteristics, while others display only a few. Others may display many characteristics and never even contemplate abuse of children.[8]

One Scenario of Abuse

The process of abuse is complex and varied. Typically it unfolds over time. In preadolescent and younger children it often begins as a "special" game between the child and the abuser, something no one else is "privileged" to share. Most often the sex abuser is in a position of authority over the child, someone the child loves and trusts.

At the outset, abusers may try to explain their actions. They may tell a preadolescent youth curious about sex, "This is your sex education." When a child is upset, the abuser may say, "This will help you feel better." Children do not understand what is happening and often go along willingly, especially at first.

When fondling progresses to more intimate sexual encounters, abusers often tell the child, "This is our secret, just between you and me." Sometimes there is a threat of punishment or injury to others if the child tells anyone. Then, when feelings of shame and guilt surface, children are isolated. They are too terrified to seek help. Revealing a "family secret" to the outside world is unthinkable.

Signs of Sexual Abuse

Sexual abuse may be indicated by certain physical and behavioral signs as well as by indirect comments made by the child. There are several clues to look for when one suspects the possibility of child sexual abuse. Physical signs include irritation, pain or injury to the genital area, and genital or urinary infection. A child may withdraw or show a sudden, unexplained change in behavior. Other signs may be nervous, aggressive, hostile, or disruptive behavior toward adults, especially parents. A child may manifest eating or sleep disturbances, including nightmares or insomnia. One should also be alert to knowledge or actions of a sexual nature that are not age-appropriate. One sign alone may not be a positive indication, since any of these signs can point to other conditions as well. However, if a number of signs are present, the possibility of sexual abuse should be considered and appropriate action taken, including seeking medical evaluation.

Effects of Sexual Abuse on Children and Adults

The degree of harm a child experiences as a result of sexual abuse depends upon various factors, including the nature of the act, the age of the child, and the child's general environment.[9] Sexual abuse may result in physical harm such as cuts, disfigurement, and deformity. Mental harm may include a poor self-image; pervasive feelings of guilt; feelings of isolation that lead to social withdrawal; inability to trust or to maintain friendships; inappropriate sexual behavior; inability to relate sexually with spouses; and symptoms of posttraumatic stress syndrome, such as flashbacks, addiction to alcohol or drugs, and depression. As one expert notes, "While child sexual abuse may not always lead to permanent injury, one should assume that all sexual abuse experiences are potentially harmful."[10] We know, too, that the cycle of abuse, unless broken, may continue in succeeding generations.

Effects on Faith and Spirituality

We are concerned about the effects of sexual abuse on the overall development of abused children and adult survivors; as pastors, we are particularly concerned about spiritual development and religious practice. Children, for instance, usually base their image of God—who God is and how God acts—on the adults they meet in their families and parishes. When the person who abuses them sexually is also their parent or another trusted adult, children may find it difficult to imagine, much less develop, a relationship with a loving God. This difficulty may be intensified if the abuser is perceived as active in the Church. Children may feel angry at God and act with hostility toward those who are God's ministers. Some may be terrified of God, because of distorted images of God embedded in their early experiences. Many are unable to pray, and they reject their religious faith.

Survivors of sexual abuse may find that feelings of rage, betrayal, and guilt make spiritual growth difficult. Survivors may find themselves prone to self-hate and self-destructiveness. Since they do not love themselves, they cannot believe that anyone else, including God, can love them. They may ask angrily: "Where was God in all this? Why didn't God help me?"

Healing, Forgiveness, and Repentance

Scripture reminds us that Jesus extends his healing power in the most desperate circumstances. Recall, for example, the story of Jairus's daughter, whom Jesus restored to life (Lk 8:41-56).

In that seemingly hopeless situation, Jesus reached out to the girl, enkindled that spark of life, and returned her to the community. His solicitude was very human. Give her something to eat, he told the onlookers, when she began to walk about the room.

Survivors of sexual abuse call out for healing. They long to be free from the heavy burden carried within them. Abusers, too, seek healing, after they come to acknowledge and grieve the terrible pain they have inflicted.

Healing for Those Who Have Been Abused

Today, Jesus continues to restore the human spirit through the prayer and sacramental life of the Church. The eucharist, a sign of God's love for us, is a celebration of ongoing healing and reconciliation. Many people have received peace and strength from healing services or from praying with a group for "healing of memories." In addition, the sacrament of reconciliation provides an opportunity to turn people and past events over to God, realizing that his love can bring good out of evil. As the Letter to the Romans assures us, "We know that all things work for good for those who love God" (8:28).

As part of the healing process, we realize that forgiveness is one of the biggest issues that survivors struggle with. Forgiveness is rarely easy, but for survivors of sexual abuse it can seem impossible.

Forgiveness is both a gift and a process—a gift from God and a process that involves the work of human minds and hearts. The process, often a long one, begins with a survivor acknowledging the abuse, dealing with feelings that may have been long suppressed, and developing a positive self-identity. We caution against rushing the process. We cannot push the survivor to forgive just because we, the Christian community, feel uncomfortable dealing with the issue. Rather, we need to stand with the survivor, to show the same gentle, loving, patient concern that Jesus showed to those who were hurting.

Forgiveness is not forgetting, nor does forgiveness consist in excusing the abuse or in absolving the abuser, which only God can do. We again stress that the abuse is not the survivor's fault, but we realize that some survivors struggle with having done things that were perhaps painful and destructive but which were a means of coping with the abuse. We encourage survivors to be gentle with themselves in letting go of inappropriate self-blame for the abuse.

For the Abuser

In regard to abusers, we must remember that justice plays a role in the forgiveness process. Imitating Christ, the Christian community reaches out to the abuser while clearly holding him or her accountable. Some in the Christian community may believe that, in releasing the abuser from his or her suffering, they are being charitable and

Christlike. In order to be healed, however, the abuser must recognize the harm done. We emphasize that the community, including the family, needs to call the abuser to accountability. We need to say: "Abusive behavior is wrong and we hold you accountable for it. We will stand by you as you suffer the consequences of your behavior, but we expect you to acknowledge the harm done and to ask for forgiveness."

Part III: Responding

In the Gospels we see that Jesus healed in different ways. He offered physical healing as well as a deeper, spiritual healing. His words, spoken in truth and love, also brought healing, even when they made his listeners uncomfortable. He responded to those who sought healing for themselves, as well as those who interceded for others.

Like Jesus, the Church reaches out to offer healing and reconciliation to people who seem to be without hope. Desiring to restore wholeness to the victims/survivors of sexual abuse and to their families, and wanting to break the cycle of abuse, we seek to:

- Offer physical safety and help for sexual abuse victims/survivors
- Bring about spiritual and emotional healing, forgiveness, and reconciliation for victims/survivors and their families, recognizing that it is not always possible to keep the family together
- Raise awareness about the issue by our preaching and teaching
- Offer help and support for abusers, while holding them accountable for their actions
- Promote the education of pastors and church workers about the issue and encourage them to provide appropriate assistance

We do not minimize the complicated nature of sexual abuse or the task involved in prevention, intervention, and support of people seeking to surmount the past. We believe, however, that parishes can play a crucial role in this process through the liturgy and sacraments, education, and support of empathetic and knowledgeable parishioners. A survivor attests to this, writing that she found God revealed in the liturgies of her parish community. She says:

> As I walked the dirt roads of Calvary . . . I knew that Jesus, like me, experienced all of the same brutal pain I was experiencing. I knew this Jesus the church elevated during the eucharist was indeed a human Jesus . . . and in the midst of the assembly I experienced his healing and compassionate love.[11]

What Can We Do Together?

As a community of Christians we have the means to shatter the walls of loneliness, shame, and fear that isolate those who are sexually abused and those who have survived abuse. They need us, and we need to hear their stories of pain, endurance, and courage. We also need to let abusers know that while we hold them accountable for their behavior, they can be forgiven.

Some practical suggestions for developing simple action plans at the local level:

For Parishes (Many of These Suggestions Can Be Adapted for Use by Dioceses)

- Create an atmosphere of welcome, trust, and safety in your parish that encourages people to come forward: the abused, abusers, and all those affected by abuse, such as mothers who suspect that a friend or family member is abusing their child, as well as family members who may be in a position to offer support and security to the abused person.
- Establish a procedure to respond when someone approaches a staff member about sexual abuse. Have available a list of referral agencies and resources to give to people who request help. Become familiar with state reporting requirements as well as diocesan policies concerning sexual abuse.
- Develop a network of people with expertise in dealing with sexual abuse. Regularly publish a contact's name and phone number in your Sunday bulletin.
- Mention of sexual abuse within a homily, when appropriate, lets people know that the preacher is aware of the issue. This sometimes opens the door for people to seek assistance.
- Many abused persons and abusers turn to their parishes to find healing and reconciliation. Abused persons need justice and compassion; abusers need accountability, repentance, and support. A prayer service or special liturgical ceremony can help people as they set out on renewed lives.
- Develop programs to teach people about sexual abuse issues. For children, programs should discuss appropriate and inappropriate behavior and include suggestions on where to go if they think they are being abused. Programs for parents should help them to talk with their children about their bodies and the right to privacy, as well as about personal safety and self-protective strategies.

- Raise the questions of violence and the roles of men and women within the family as part of marriage preparation. Delicately introduce questions about how each prospective spouse was treated growing up, how their parents treated each other, and how they expect to act toward their spouse and their children.
- Promote the use of language in parish programs and materials that reflects the equal dignity of women.
- Share information and resources with other parishes and dioceses that are also trying to address sexual abuse issues.

For Those Who Are, or Have Been, Sexually Abused and Their Families

- Look on your parish as a source of support, strength, and assistance. In particular, locate one adult within the parish with whom you can talk about your experiences.
- Realize that you are not alone; many others, men and women, have also experienced abuse. If possible, find a parish or community support group for those who have been abused. Such groups can help survivors of sexual abuse learn how to find healing and courage to build a new, hope-filled life.
- Once the healing process is underway join in parish and/or community activities to combat sexual abuse. Reaching out to others can help the healing process.

A Word to Children

Although we have not addressed this statement to children, our hearts go out to them. Perhaps an adult in their lives who truly cares for them could share the following words with them:

> Dear children, when Jesus walked on the earth he loved little children. Our Holy Father has said, "How important children are in the eyes of Jesus!" Jesus treated children with kindness and respect. He understood when they were hurting. Like Jesus, we care when you hurt, especially when a grown-up has caused your hurt. We know that you are God's very special gift. God loves you, and we love you. You are our hope for the future.

Conclusion

In this statement we have spoken out against the tragedy of child sexual abuse. We have described this abuse and its effects on children and adults. Our statement has emphasized the need for healing and forgiveness, as well as the need to hold the abuser accountable, and has offered some practical suggestions for dealing with sexual abuse. In offering this statement we acknowledge our moral responsibility to put children first, to protect the most vulnerable members of our society.

We know that sexual abuse raises many more issues—moral, legal, psychological, and others—that are not discussed here. They need to be addressed with understanding, compassion, and justice. We hope that communities of faith, accepting their moral obligation to children, will formulate their own responses. We would like to hear from them to learn how they are dealing with survivors, abusers, their families, and their friends. Working together and trusting in the Spirit's wisdom and guidance, we can confront the evil of child sexual abuse, break through the darkness, and walk in the light.

Notes

1. *Fact Sheet No. 19* (Chicago: National Committee for the Prevention of Child Abuse, 1992).

2. According to the *Fifty-State Survey of Child Abuse and Neglect,* an aggregation of state data collected by the National Committee for the Prevention of Child Abuse, in 1993 about 15 percent of all *substantiated* cases of child abuse and neglect concerned sexual abuse, representing approximately 150,000 children. According to David Finkelhor, Ph.D., co-director of the Family Research Laboratory at the University of New Hampshire, the true scope of the problem is better reflected in retrospective surveys of adults. Considerable evidence exists to show that at least 20 percent of American women and 5 to 10 percent of American men experienced some form of sexual abuse as children. See D. Finkelhor, "Current Information on the Scope and Nature of Child Sexual Abuse" in *The Future of Children,* vol. 4, no. 2 (Los Altos, Calif.: The David and Lucile Packard Foundation, 1994), 31-53.

3. Statement of the General Counsel of the National Conference of Catholic Bishops/United States Catholic Conference, February 18, 1988. See also National Conference of Catholic Bishops, *Restoring Trust: A Pastoral Response to Sexual Abuse* (unpublished resource materials for bishops, November 14, 1994).

4. *Basic Facts About Child Sexual Abuse* (Chicago: National Committee for the Prevention of Child Abuse, 1988).

5. U.S. Department of Justice, *Child Rape Victims* (Washington, D.C.: U.S. Government Printing Office, 1992).

6. R. Summit, "The Child Sexual Abuse Accommodation Syndrome," *Child Abuse and Neglect* 7 (1993): 177-193.

7. Finkelhor, 31.
8. For an extended discussion of some of these characteristics, as well as an analysis of recidivism, see Judith V. Becker, "Offenders: Characteristics and Treatments," in *The Future of Children*, 176-197.
9. *Fact Sheet No. 19.*
10. Ibid.
11. *Project Benjamin Handbook* (Milwaukee: Archdiocese of Milwaukee, 1990), 58.

Source: Washington, D.C.: United States Catholic Conference, 1995.

Principles for Educational Reform in the United States

A Statement of the USCC Committee on Education
Approved by the Administrative Board

September 1995

A. Introduction

As citizens and as teachers, the Catholic bishops of the United States have a great interest in and a responsibility to contribute to the public discussion of issues that affect the nation's common good. We feel the strong need to address a critical aspect of the common good which is the topic of great concern in our nation: the ability of our nation to provide a quality education, one that effects a person's intellectual, moral, spiritual, and physical development, to all our children, whether they attend a public, private, or religious school. Since our children are the nation's future, we need to stress that the provision of a quality education for all children is the responsibility of all members of our civic community.

The issue is clear. The academic performance of our nation's students in reading, math, and science still lags behind students in other industrial nations; significant numbers of students are retained in grades or drop out of school completely; often even those who graduate lack the basic skills needed to obtain a productive and rewarding job or to succeed in college.[1] All too often, especially for the most vulnerable children, the educational experience is not filled with hope and nurturing but fear and failure. In addition, there is evidence that we are losing our young people to a variety of personal and social problems that can be traced, at least in part, to a fundamental lack of education in basic religious, moral, and civic values.

We wish to make a positive and lasting contribution to the discussion that is currently taking place on the national, state, and local levels of our nation as to how best to produce true, comprehensive, and lasting educational reform. We seek to outline some basic principles that should guide our nation's approach toward addressing the urgent needs of all our nation's children. In doing this, we draw upon the long and successful history of our Church in the area of education at all levels and in all types of settings.

The Catholic Church has consistently held that one of its primary functions is the education of young people. In the United States, the

Church can proudly point to a positive and productive record of serving the educational needs of our nation's young people almost from the nation's first days. Today Catholic elementary and secondary schools are educating almost 3 million children nationwide. Many of these children are minorities, suffer economic and social hardship in inner-city urban centers, and are often not members of the Catholic faith. Independent research on Catholic schools consistently points to their success in educating students to the highest standards of scholarship and moral and social responsibility, often under pressing economic conditions. We believe that our nation can learn much from what we do and how we approach this most important endeavor.

B. Principles for Educational Reform

We wish to make one thing absolutely clear, our concern for educational reform does not limit itself to what happens in Catholic schools. We have a sincere concern for what happens to all children, including those enrolled in public and private schools as well. We have a deep concern that all children will be provided with a means to attain a quality education that will prepare them to be good citizens, lead productive lives, and be socially and morally responsible. In addition, educational reform efforts will impact on the professional lives of all educators, whether they work in public, private, or religious schools, and we seek to address their needs and concerns.

We wish to present some underlying principles which should guide comprehensive educational reform in our country. At the same time we recognize that any substantive vision or framework of educational reform will have specific implications for federal, state, and local legislative and administrative action to implement these principles. As educators, we offer these ideas for discussion by all concerned parties, and we stand ready to cooperate in designing and effecting necessary implementation efforts.

1. *All persons have the right to a quality education.* We believe that:

- All persons have an inalienable right to a quality education "in virtue of their dignity as human persons" and that all have a right to an education responsive to their responsibility to "develop harmoniously their physical, moral, and intellectual qualities."[2]
- A quality education can be attained only in an orderly, just, and nonviolent environment.
- The attainment of a quality education is a lifelong process, and all members of society have a responsibility to work to ensure

that quality educational opportunities are available to individuals of all ages and all personal, cultural, and economic conditions.

- No single model or means of education is appropriate to the needs and desires of all persons. Therefore, our nation should make available the broadest variety of quality educational opportunities for each individual to choose from, including public, private, and religious models.

2. *Parental rights and responsibilities are primary in education.* We believe that:

- Parents are the first and foremost educators of their children.
- Parental rights are natural and inalienable and should not be limited to the economically privileged.
- While recognizing the primary role of parents in the education of children, there are educational duties and responsibilities vested in civil and religious authority in order to better provide for the common good of all people.
- Parents have the right to choose the kind of education best suited to the needs of their children, and they should not be burdened economically for choosing a private or religious school in the exercise of this fundamental right.
- Often parents will need assistance in providing a quality education for their children. The state and private agencies, including the Church, should provide this assistance which should include information on the full range of educational options available and, where necessary, economic assistance to access those options.
- Parents are responsible to be involved actively in the decisions affecting the education of their children.
- Parents are responsible to be knowledgeable about the full range of ways they can assist in educating their children.
- Parents are responsible to enter into cooperative relationships with those delegated with educating their children.

3. *Students are the central focus of all education.* We believe that:

- The true needs of children are to be the basis for all decisions related to their ongoing education.
- Children can learn and master a challenging curriculum.
- The academic curriculum should be based on high standards and take into account the unique needs of each student.
- Each student should be provided with an environment that is conducive to learning and that is orderly and respectful of

each individual, regardless of the student's social, cultural, or personal condition.

- All students should be provided with the professional and material resources appropriate to a learning process that will prepare them to live and work in the challenging world of the twenty-first century.
- The educational program should help students develop to the fullest their physical, social, spiritual, moral, and intellectual qualities.
- Students who are especially at risk intellectually or personally should be provided special attention and support by parents and teachers so that they may progress appropriately.
- Student academic progress should be assessed on a regular basis, through the use of a variety of approaches, in order to determine if appropriate academic outcomes are being attained.

4. *Quality teaching is essential to the learning process.* We believe that:

- Teachers should be academically prepared to teach and be dedicated to the needs of their students.
- Teachers should understand that they are role models for their students in pursuing their intellectual and moral maturity.
- Principals are the "master teachers" and should possess the qualifications necessary to provide professional, academic, moral, and personal leadership in the school.
- Teacher certification programs should allow for sufficient flexibility to open the teaching profession to individuals with academic potential displayed in other professions.
- Regular, ongoing programs of professional development should be an essential part of every educational program. These programs should address the needs of both the teachers and students and contain procedures for assessment of the impact they have in the teaching and learning situation.
- Teachers should be actively and regularly involved in the curriculum and professional development planning process.
- Teachers and administrators, including boards of education, are responsible to be available to parents and collaborate with them in all decisions relating to the education of their students.
- Regular and ongoing programs aimed at assessing and assisting teachers in the performance of their professional activities should be an integral part of the school life in order to ensure the presence of a quality teaching and learning situation for all

students. Teachers and system and local administrators should play an active role in planning such programs.

5. *True quality education must address the moral and spiritual needs of students.* We believe that:

- The goal of all education is to foster the development of the total person. Educational policy decision makers, including boards of education and system administrators, need to provide students with opportunities for moral and spiritual formation to complement their intellectual and physical development. This formation should be respectful of the variety of beliefs found in our nation; it should be integrated into the public school's total curriculum and correspond to both student needs and community consensus.
- Even in our pluralistic society, with its many varied beliefs, it is possible to reach consensus and teach these shared values and still avoid teaching a specific religious faith.
- The development of this public moral vision will require the active involvement of the total community, both civic and religious.
- While maintaining a commitment to the First Amendment, our society's attitude toward religion should not be so theoretically neutral as to be anti-religious in practice.

6. *Government has a responsibility to provide adequate resources for the attainment of a quality education for all children, and these education policy decisions are best made at the level closest to the actual teaching and learning situation.* We believe that:

- Government at all levels, acting in partnership with parents, has a responsibility to provide adequate professional and material resources to assist all children to attain a quality education and to safeguard their health and safety. This includes, but is not limited to, textbooks, transportation, appropriate health and safety services, economic assistance to those in need, and adequate information to make informed decisions.
- Education policy decisions should foster diversity and flexibility in the delivery of quality educational services to all children.
- There is a need to review all existing regulations affecting education to determine if they are truly necessary to attain the goal of providing a quality education to all children.
- All educational personnel are responsible to be accountable to those they serve: students, parents, and the community.

- Since children and parents do not surrender their rights to receive and choose an education because of their economic status, the equitable financing of education must be a primary goal of education policy at all levels. This will require a thorough review of all current education financing systems.
- Governments at all levels should advocate policies that foster educational, social, and economic justice for all people.
- Since no single educational approach serves all educational needs, policy decisions should allow for the existence of alternative educational systems including, but not limited to, charter schools; magnet schools; and public, private, and religious school choice programs, provided they offer quality programs and do not teach or practice intolerance or advocate illegal activity.
- Government and private agencies should foster comprehensive studies to evaluate the effectiveness of alternative educational delivery systems.
- There is a need to take advantage of the potential resources to be found among business, civic, cultural, educational, and religious groups in our society to improve the overall quality of our nation's educational systems.
- When services that are aimed at improving the educational environment—especially for those most at risk—are available to students and teachers in public schools, these services should also be available to students and teachers in private and religious schools. These individuals should not be penalized for choosing to enroll or work in these schools since they also serve the common good of our nation.

C. Conclusion

We believe that the issue of providing a quality education to all of our children is of the utmost importance to the future well-being of our nation and our children. We come to this issue as advocates for all children, whether they are educated in a public, private, or religious setting.

We are encouraged by the collaboration shown among the president, governors, and federal legislators in developing the eight national educational goals that we hope will help prepare our young people to live productively in the complicated world of the twenty-first century.

Now we call upon all of our partners, at all levels of the educational community—whether public, private, or religious—to join in a collaborative and constructive dialogue on how best we can pool our strengths and work toward the attainment of this critically important common goal.

We believe that the challenges we face in this endeavor can only be met and overcome if we join together, put aside all that might potentially divide us, and seek to serve our common public goal of providing all of our young people, but especially the poor and the vulnerable, with a quality education that will provide them with the knowledge and skills to live happy, productive, and rewarding lives.

We offer these principles as our contribution to the present discussion concerning education, and we stand ready to cooperate with others in a common effort to design and effect true and comprehensive national educational reform.

Notes

1.   National Commission on Children, *Beyond Rhetoric: A New American Agenda for Children and Families: Final Report of the National Commission on Children* (Washington, D.C.: The Commission, 1991), pp. 179-182.
2.   Second Vatican Council, *Declaration on Christian Education (Gravissimum Educationis)*, no. 1.

Source: Washington, D.C.: United States Catholic Conference, 1995.

Called and Gifted for the Third Millennium

*A Statement of the National Conference of Catholic Bishops
on the Thirtieth Anniversary of the* Decree on the Apostolate of the Laity
and the Fifteenth Anniversary of Called and Gifted

November 1995

[The Lord] sends them on the Church's apostolate, an apostolate that is one yet has different forms and methods, an
apostolate that must all the time be adapting itself to the
needs of the moment. . . .
—*Decree on the Apostolate of the Laity,* no. 33

A Prayer

God of love and mercy,
you call us to be your people,
you gift us with your abundant grace.
Make us a holy people, radiating the fullness of your love.
Form us into a community, a people who care, expressing your com-
passion.
Remind us day after day of our baptismal call to serve,
with joy and courage.
Teach us how to grow in wisdom and grace and joy in your presence.
Through Jesus and in your Spirit, we make this prayer.

Introduction

What is the Spirit saying to the world today through the Church in
the United States, particularly through the lives of lay men and
women?

In 1980 we bishops listened to the message of that same Holy
Spirit. In our pastoral statement *Called and Gifted,* we acknowledged
and reflected upon the ways lay men and women were answering the
Lord's call and employing their gifts to take an active and responsible
part in the mission of the Church.

Now, fifteen years after *Called and Gifted,* we take that statement's
four "calls"—to holiness, to community, to mission and ministry, and
to adulthood/Christian maturity—and update them in light of church

teaching, pastoral practice, and changing conditions in the world. We also identify several challenges and suggest questions for individual and group reflection.

In *Called and Gifted* we addressed the whole Church but focused on the laity, inviting them to respond with "next words." In consultation, structured dialogue, correspondence, and reports, they did so with honesty and integrity.

Now, with the benefit of fifteen additional years of consulting the laity, we again address the whole Church, with a focus on the vocation and mission of lay persons. Moreover, we invite all members of the Church—lay men and women in secular life or consecrated life and the ordained—to continue the dialogue with one another and with us.

In this statement we look back with gratitude upon the Second Vatican Council and prepare in hope for the third millennium. We believe that the Church's path into a new millennium is marked by a faithful listening to the Spirit in the midst of God's people.

The Call to Holiness

> Life according to the Spirit, whose fruit is holiness (cf. Rom 6:22; Gal 5:22) stirs up every baptized person and requires each to follow and imitate Jesus Christ, in embracing the beatitudes, in listening and meditating on the Word of God, in conscious and active participation in the liturgical and sacramental life of the Church, in personal prayer, in family or in community, in the hunger and thirst for justice, in the practice of the commandment of love in all circumstances of life and service to the brethren, especially the least, the poor and the suffering.
> —*Christifideles Laici*, no. 16

The Witness of Holy Lives

During the last fifteen years the Christian lay faithful have contributed greatly to the spiritual heritage of the Church, enlarging our understanding of what it means to be called to holiness, that is, to be called to "ever more intimate union with Christ."[1] Their union with Christ is evident in a deepened awareness of the spiritual dimensions of life.

St. Paul wrote to his friend, co-worker, and co-disciple St. Timothy that the value of spirituality is immeasurable because it holds promise for our present life and life hereafter (see 1 Tm 4:8).

We have heard the testimony of many lay persons who have discovered the wisdom of St. Paul's words and who understand that we all share in the one vocation to holiness. They know in their hearts the teaching of the Second Vatican Council: "The forms and tasks of life are many, but holiness is one—that sanctity which is cultivated by all who act under God's Spirit."[2]

While spirituality is more and more an explicit aspect of Christian life, "spiritual sight" or insight is not sufficient in itself. The call to holiness requires effort and commitment to live the beatitudes. We have seen this active spirituality in the lives of countless lay persons and have listened to their stories.

How one experiences the challenges and joys of life in the Spirit is deeply shaped by the concrete realities of one's life. The most frequently mentioned place where lay people encounter Christ is in Christian marriage and family life. We believe that Christian marriage is vocation, sacrament, covenant relationship, and mission. In the sacrament of marriage Christ is made present in a special way to spouses, family members, and the overall society. The Christian family is a sign and means of unity and solidarity in our world. The intimacy of marriage, parents' all-encompassing care of children, the struggle of single-parent families, single persons' relationships with their family members and friends, the battle with addictions, the challenges of caring for aging family members with dignity and love, the acceptance of loss—these are recognized as means of grace.

The laity also speak of the parish as a place where they experience the living God. In the sacraments (especially the eucharist), in counseling and spiritual guidance, and in study and prayer groups people come to know the power of the Spirit. Some have described being away from the Church for years, and one day crossing the threshold of a parish in search of "something" they can't always identify. There they find Christ's love visible in worship, in the sacrament of reconciliation, in a caring community, and in service to the poor. And they are encouraged to return, again and again.

In their work—teaching, cosmetology, medicine, the arts, house painting, real estate—laity discover both meaning and a sense of mission, relating their work to their spiritual life. Their work paths, no matter how diverse, often help them to move beyond self-absorption toward active caring for others.

For lay persons of all ages nature reveals the wonder of God. Older people confined to their homes meditate on the changing seasons; they see that God makes all things new (see Rv 21:5). Children observe the ways of nature and the universe and see the Creator at work. Youth are moved to care for the environment and to set an example of stewardship. Prayers of praise rise from these men, women, and children, echoing the psalmist: "Let the rivers clap their hands, the mountains shout with them for joy" (Ps 98:8).

A common thread in the laity's accounts of their spiritual lives is the primacy of relationships. The bonds of family and friendship, of neighborhood and parish are vital to lay women and men. These relationships help them form ever deeper bonds of unity with Jesus Christ.

Formed in Suffering

Often people can go the extra mile for others because they have been spiritually formed through suffering. For Christians suffering is both hope and challenge.

St. Paul writes: "We know that affliction makes for endurance, and endurance for tested virtue, and tested virtue for hope" (Rom 5:3-4). The laity of our Church are moved to act on behalf of those in need because they have come to know Christ in the depths of their own suffering. Some have been betrayed by their marriage partners. Others, many of whom are women, have endured physical and emotional abuse. Children have had to adjust to divorced and separated parents. And parents have known helplessness as their children leave the Church, become addicted to drugs, or accept an ethic of casual sex. Even others have experienced prejudice or discrimination because of their language or racial background. As people have lost their jobs, their homes, or their loved ones, they have also found the abundance of God's mercy; they know the hope of which St. Paul speaks.

In the darkness that surrounds them they discover the light of Christ and the truth that "the way of perfection passes by way of the Cross."[3] They are ready to help others along the way and in so doing become signs of hope.

As we enter the third millennium, we may well see more collective suffering. As Americans we tend to believe that effective planning can reduce, or even eliminate, certain kinds of suffering. Experience sometimes points to the contrary. New strains of disease, persistent economic instability, large movements of displaced persons, and a multiplicity of wars are already a reality and may increase. On a smaller scale, civil discourse is quickly disappearing while calumny and detraction are on the rise. Too often angry words, sometimes rooted in prejudice, lead to violent acts, shattering whole communities.

How can the Church meet such challenges with realistic hope? Church leaders can continue to speak out and to take action against social injustice, which is the cause of so much suffering. Another way is for the entire Church, especially its leaders, both ordained and lay, to recognize our own implication in the suffering of others and to ask for forgiveness when that is required. In preparation for the third millennium, our Holy Father has set an example by calling the Church to repent of "past errors and instances of infidelity, inconsistency and slowness to act."[4] We bishops seek to follow his example.

The witness of the laity also gives hope. Their presence within the web of society can be a source of solace and strength in the face of enormous human need. The laity are "the front lines of the Church's life . . . they ought to have an ever clearer consciousness not only of belonging to the Church, but of being the Church . . . that is to say, the community of the faithful on earth under the leadership of the Pope, the common head, and of the bishops in communion with him. They are the Church."[5]

Beyond acts of holy compassion—blessed as they are—the laity are called to confront unjust elements in various social systems. They are called by God to apply Christian principles to government, medical research, social services, education, the media—in short, to all those human institutions that exist to help human persons realize their inherent dignity.

For Generous Service

Generosity is surely a sign of holiness. During the past fifteen years thousands of lay men and women have given generously of their time and energy in a variety of ways. Their service in domestic and foreign missions is particularly notable. We rejoice especially in the large number of young adults who devote one or more years to church or public service. Their stories of selfless compassion stand in sharp contrast to prevalent images of private achievement and acquisition. Their stories are living examples of responding to the Holy Father's call for young people to be signs of hope. They are not caught up in materialism, as some charge the young are, but are coming to know that Christ shows himself in a special way in the poor and in the vulnerable.

While not everyone may be called to this exact form of service, we all—clergy and laity alike—can be motivated by such example to examine our daily behavior and choices about what we buy, what entertainment and recreation we choose, and what other comforts we seek—in short, how we use our material resources.

In Simplicity of Life

The human family is facing major choices regarding lifestyle. As economic and ecological issues are increasingly intertwined, we see more clearly that the earth's resources are not limitless. Industrialized nations consume more and more of what God created for all to enjoy, while developing nations can scarcely support their populations.

What is to be done? Biblical teachings about the essential goodness of creation, the human person's responsibility for the stewardship of God's gifts, and the thoroughly changed heart are important resources to draw upon as we try to establish an economy that is just, sustainable, and ecologically responsible. In addition, the Church's tradition of simplicity, embodied in the original charisms of religious orders, merits serious reflection and dialogue as a means of addressing the imbalance.

Challenges for the Future

Because the laity's call to holiness is a vocation in every sense of the word, it makes demands and poses challenges. Many challenges are embedded in the call to holiness on this eve of a new era, but we have raised up three as particularly apt for our time: (1) to make an explicit connection between holiness and active service, especially to the poor and vulnerable; (2) to recognize that human suffering—so much a part of the laity's life—can be the catalyst for them to carry forth the Church's healing ministry in diverse ways; (3) to reappropriate the Church's tradition of a simple lifestyle in light of the pressing need for justice, as well as preserving the earth for ourselves and for generations to come.

The laity's call to holiness is a gift from the Holy Spirit. Their response is a gift to the Church and to the world.

The Call to Community

> From the communion that Christians experience in Christ there immediately flows the communion which they experience with one another: all are branches of a single vine, namely, Christ.
> —*Christifideles Laici,* no. 18

Christian Community in Family and Parish

The renewed outpouring of the Spirit of Pentecost in our times has stimulated a great desire for experiences of deeper Christian community. This was true when we issued *Called and Gifted* in 1980 and it has become even more obvious in the years since then. We note, for example, the growth of faith-sharing groups, study and support groups, lay associations and movements, as well as the increasing number of lay persons joining secular institutes, pious associations, and third orders.

Above all, people long for community in their families and in their parishes. Both are basic and essential to living a fully Christian life. Both communities—the domestic church and the parish church—are challenged: to live faithfully, particularly when changes occur upsetting comfortable patterns; to be life-giving by welcoming and caring for children and by reaching out in service to the needy; and to grow in mutuality, i.e., the realization of our equality as persons created in God's image. By living with these challenges and humbly engaging them, vital Christian communities can be forged.

Beyond the intimate community of family life, the parish is for most Catholics their foremost experience of Christian community, enabling them to express their faith, grow in unity with God and others, and continue the saving mission of Christ. We have seen a welcome renewal in all aspects of parish life and ministry, due in large measure to an informed and committed laity often encouraged by their pastors and priests imbued with the spirit of Vatican II. In addition, the increase of people from different racial and ethnic cultures has been challenging parishes, dioceses, and communities not only to spread a larger, more welcoming table, but also to learn how diversity builds up the body of Christ. African American congregations have discovered much of their worship heritage and have enriched Catholic liturgical life. "All of us have been given to drink of the one Spirit. Now the body is not one member, it is many" (1 Cor 12:13-14).

Small Communities of Faith

A new and promising development, often occurring in the context of parish renewal, has been the formation of small church communities which testify to "the creative grace of God at work" and are "a source of great hope for the whole Church."[6] The mobility of our population, the stresses of the society in which we live, and often the size of parishes are factors leading people to want to participate in the Church's life and ministry on a smaller scale.

Small church communities take shape in various ways. Sometimes people are drawn to them through a parish renewal process or through one of the lay movements and associations, which often provide for their members the experience of Christian community. The Rite of Christian Initiation of Adults (RCIA) can lead members of a parish to become a small community which invites and catechizes those who are considering joining the Church. Still other small communities are organized in neighborhoods or are rooted in various natural groupings that may exist within a parish.

Small church communities not only foster the faith of individuals; they are living cells that build up the body of Christ. They are to be signs and instruments of unity. As basic units of the parish, they serve to increase the corporate life and mission of the parish by sharing in its life generously with their talents and support.

Drawing upon the thorough discussion of small communities which took place at the 1987 synod on the vocation and mission of the lay faithful, Pope John Paul II has urged local ecclesiastical authorities to foster these "living" communities, for they are "where the faithful can communicate the word of God and express it in service and love to one another; these communities are true expressions of ecclesial communion and centers of evangelization, in communion with their pastors."[7]

In all cases, authentic small Christian communities are characterized by obedience to the word of God, common prayer, a commitment of time to one another for building personal relationships, meaningful participation in the life of their local parish, some form of apostolic mission to the wider society, an adherence to the Catholic faith, and an explicit relationship of communion with the Church.

The growing Hispanic/Latino and Asian presence in our country, as well as the influence of other ethnic groups, has been a creative impetus in the formation of small Christian communities. As our Church becomes increasingly multicultural, these small communities can enable lay people from different backgrounds to come to know one another in a trusting way, creating bonds of solidarity, a commitment to mission, and new lay leaders.

Challenges for the Future

1. Pastoral leaders should feel challenged to serve the laity by helping them develop and sustain small Christian communities—including those based on careers and professions. Laity, too, should take a leadership role, working with their pastors to develop these faith communities, bringing their own gifts and wisdom acquired from family and work to renew our Church. In no case, however, should small church communities forget their rootedness in the family—the first and most basic form of the Church—or sever their links to the larger faith community present in the parish and diocese.

2. The laity are called to participate in a "new evangelization." This means sharing the good news of Jesus personally through the witness of our lives. Moreover, the new evangelization is "directed not only to persons but also to entire portions of populations in the variety of their situations, surroundings and cultures."[8] Its purpose is to challenge, through the power of the Gospel, those values, judgments, patterns of behavior, sources of inspiration, and models of life that are inconsistent with the word of God and the plan of salvation[9] and to affirm the ways God is working in the world today.

3. Small church communities offer an important and unique means of formation for the new evangelization. They strengthen their members to persevere in their faith and mission, providing both inspiration and practical support. To be involved in

the new evangelization, however, requires that members of such communities be as ready for engagement with the world outside their community as they are for deepening their relationships within it. If the small community is to be a true expression of the mystery of the Church, then it must be "a communion of God's people living out the mission of Jesus Christ in the power of the Spirit."[10]

The Call to Mission and Ministry

> The ministries which exist and are at work at this time in the Church are all, even in their variety of forms, a participation in Jesus Christ's own ministry as the Good Shepherd who lays down his life for the sheep, the humble servant who gives himself without reserve for the salvation of all.
> —*Christifideles Laici*, no. 21

Participation in the Church's Life and Mission as the Sacrament of Christ in the World

Through the sacraments of baptism, confirmation, and eucharist every Christian is called to participate actively and co-responsibly in the Church's mission of salvation in the world. Moreover, in those same sacraments, the Holy Spirit pours out gifts which make it possible for every Christian man and woman to assume different ministries and forms of service that complement one another and are for the good of all.[11]

Everyone has a responsibility to answer the call to mission and to develop the gifts she or he has been given by sharing them in the family, the workplace, the civic community, and the parish or diocese. A parallel responsibility exists within the Church's leadership "to acknowledge and foster the ministries, the offices, and the roles of the lay faithful that find their foundation in the sacraments of baptism and confirmation, indeed, for a good many of them in the sacrament of matrimony."[12]

The Holy Father teaches that any ministries, offices, and roles undertaken by lay persons are to be exercised "in conformity to their specific lay vocation."[13] This, according to the Second Vatican Council, is that "the laity . . . make the Church present and operative in those places and circumstances where only through them can she become the salt of the earth."[14] A striking example is found in family life where, according to Pope John Paul II, the work "of evangelization carried out by Christian parents is original and irreplaceable."[15]

Today Christian Churches must communicate the importance of the laity's witness and service within the family and within the professional, social, political, and cultural life of society. An effective parish or congregation will help its members make the connections between worship and work, between liturgy and life in the family, community, and workplace. For this reason, church ministers—especially clergy—are called to strengthen and equip lay people to be witnesses to Christ, acting in the power of him who is the Good Shepherd and humble servant of all. We can make common cause with all Christian Churches around this endeavor.

Lay Ministry in the Church

When *Called and Gifted* was published, we were just beginning to experience the tide of professionally prepared lay men and women offering their talents and charisms in the service of the Church. These persons are often called ecclesial lay ministers.

Over the past fifteen years, we have seen great numbers of lay people become involved in the liturgy as cantors and music directors, readers, eucharistic ministers, and altar servers. Furthermore, in some places laity are responsible for leading Sunday worship in the absence of a priest. Men and women of all ages engage in these ministries, which in turn can be a means of spiritual and religious formation for them. As people study the Scriptures that they will proclaim, coordinate musical texts with liturgical seasons, or study eucharistic theology, they are touched in mind and spirit. Being steeped in word and sacrament is a classic means of transforming the human spirit; the grace of this moment is the transformation of so many laity.

The lay faithful are engaged in ministries of other kinds that are also formative. They share the faith of the Church through teaching young people as well as adults; they serve in peace and justice networks, in soup kitchens and shelters, in marriage preparation, in bereavement programs, and in ministry to the separated and divorced. All these actions, when performed in the name of Jesus and enacted under the aegis of the Church, are forms of ministry. Recent research indicates that at least half of our parishes have lay people or vowed religious in pastoral staff positions. In some instances the daily pastoral leadership of a parish has been entrusted to a lay person, in the absence of a resident pastor. Indeed, the pastoral needs of this moment are being ably and generously served by many kinds of ecclesial lay ministers.

Lay ministry is a reality beyond the parish as well. Many church institutions, from colleges and school systems to marriage tribunals, from social services and health care providers to houses of formation, benefit from the expertise and dedication of Catholic women and men exercising their designated ministry. The Church's mission is being carried forward and far by all these lay ministers who tirelessly serve the Church and God's people. We join pastors and parishioners in expressing gratitude for this development.

Ecclesial lay ministers speak of their work, their service, as a calling, not merely a job. They believe God has called them to their ministry, and often the parish priest is the means of discerning the call.

Challenges for the Future

We, and all pastoral leaders, feel challenged:

1. To develop and commit the resources necessary to help laity, both paid staff and volunteers, prepare for church ministry. Lay ministers have often invested in their own education and preparation for ministry and they need church support.
2. To practice justice in the workplace and to provide a living wage. It is often difficult for lay ministers to support themselves and their families.
3. To incorporate minority lay ministers into ecclesial leadership.
4. To ensure that the Church becomes an exemplary steward of all its human resources.

With the entire Church we give thanks that the Church has been blessed with many laity who feel called to ecclesial ministry, even as we continue to work and pray for vocations to the priesthood, diaconate, and consecrated life. We also recognize that God is blessing the Church with lay vocations to ministry.

Finally, we urge Catholic laity to bring Christ's peace and justice to the world by working energetically to reclaim national concern for the common good.

One challenge undergirds all of the above. It is the need to foster respectful collaboration, leading to mutual support in ministry, between clergy and laity for the sake of Christ's Church and its mission to the world. This is a huge task requiring changes in patterns of reflection, behavior, and expectation among laity and clergy alike. As an episcopal conference, we will expand our study and dialogue concerning lay ministry in order to understand better the critical issues and find effective ways to address them. The new evangelization will become a reality only if ordained and lay members of Christ's faithful understand their roles and ministries as complementary, and their purposes joined to the one mission and ministry of Jesus Christ. His prayer at the Last Supper must be our prayer, "That all may be one." Collaboration in ministry is a way to realize that unity.

The Call to Christian Maturity

> The gospel image of the vine and the branches reveals to us
> another fundamental aspect of the lay faithful's life and mis-
> sion: the call to growth and a continual process of matura-
> tion, of always bearing much fruit.
> —*Christifideles Laici*, no. 57

Holiness, community, and ministry are facets of Christian life that come to full expression only by means of development and growth toward Christian maturity. This fourth call of our reflection on the laity is, in its entirety, a major challenge as the Church enters the new millennium. For the laity, the challenge is woven throughout the "web of their existence."[16]

Certainly the ordinary dynamics of life—caring for a family, job responsibilities, exercising the duties of citizenship—demand growth in maturity. But we draw particular attention to certain attitudes and behaviors that signal new levels of maturity needed among Catholic lay men and women in the third millennium.

Caring for Children

Mature persons actively care for future generations. Christian maturity requires that all of us, lay and ordained, provide the best catechesis possible for children and youth. In the past we have pledged our support to parents and families as they seek to undertake their responsibility as primary educators of their children. We renew that pledge. The revitalization of youth ministry, which has been taking place since Pope John Paul II's visit to Denver and World Youth Day in 1993, is a marvelous sign of how adults can care for young people.

We realize, though, that these are troubled and trying times and many children lack the stable presence of family. The Church's social teaching regarding the common good suggests the need for all adults to become conscious of their responsibilities for the young people who are part of their worlds, especially the disabled and the unborn who are among the most vulnerable.

Mature persons of faith can foster the natural resilience in children and youth who live in stressful circumstances. A grandparent, an older sibling, a teacher, librarian, coach, or neighbor—each one can take the time to listen to a child or to a youth and to stir up hope in them. It is often these informal but compassionate contacts that help children and youth discover meaning in their lives and gain energy to press forward.

A major challenge for the third millennium is to bring our Catholic tradition to life in the hearts, minds, and spirits of new generations. No one does this alone; God's grace is the context and the means. All are called to the task of handing on the faith of our mothers and fathers, of the martyrs and saints.

Religious and Theological Education

In the last fifteen years many of the lay faithful have moved beyond the learning laboratories of ordinary life to more systematic education in theology, Scripture, spiritual life, religious studies, and spiritual direction. This development has been beneficial to growing numbers of lay women and men who, in turn, have helped the whole Church understand and communicate the truths of our faith in new ways.

We urge that theological education and formation be extended to more lay persons. In *Strengthening the Bonds of Peace*, we specifically encouraged women to pursue studies in Scripture, theology, and canon law. Now we similarly encourage lay men, so that the Church— and they themselves—may benefit from these scholarly efforts. Innovative ways must be found to bring the best of the Catholic intellectual and spiritual tradition to more laity. Print and electronic media, computer networks, and mentoring programs offer exciting possibilities. The Church needs a well-educated, inquiring, and vocal laity if the new evangelization is to achieve its full potential.

Respect for Differences

Another sign of Christian maturity is respect for differences. This respect, rooted in humility, understands that unity does not require uniformity. The Catholic tradition welcomes diversity as an enrichment, not a threat. At the same time we recognize that some differences are rooted in culture and custom while others reside at the level of essential beliefs and teachings. Even at this level growth and understanding are possible and indeed necessary.

In his encyclical letter *Ut Unum Sint,* the pope rejoices in a renewed awareness of other Christians as "brothers and sisters" instead of "enemies." At this moment in history when Christian solidarity on behalf of human need is so urgent, a mature Catholic laity will search for common ground with Christians and other people of goodwill, not stand behind impregnable walls. We realize that we cannot hold on to this common ground without civility. As we said in *Strengthening the Bonds of Peace*, we must strive for dialogue that is clear, sensitive, patient, and built on trust.

Participation

We consider lay participation in church life at all levels a gift of the Holy Spirit, given for the common good. Laity can and should exercise responsible participation both individually and in groups, not only at the invitation of church leadership but by their own initiative.

Too numerous to mention by name are all those instances in which lay persons have organized educational, advocacy, or charitable efforts which have helped the Church be a more credible and effective witness to the Gospel in public life. In addition, the Church's mission is carried out with creativity and generosity by the many lay movements and associations which have been established for various spiritual and apostolic purposes. These groups play such an essential role in the Christian formation of individuals as well as in the Christian transformation of society that the Church acknowledges and guarantees in law the right of lay persons to form associations (canon 215).

We bishops are grateful particularly for the participation of laity in the development of the pastoral letters on peace, on the economy, and in a number of other statements on the family, on women, and on the religious response to violence. Their knowledge and expertise, as well as their constructive inquiry, helped create a mature dialogue with church teaching that enriched our final products. The challenge is to keep that dialogue alive.

The competence of the lay faithful is evident in their participation in the various councils of church governance. The *Code of Canon Law* requires finance councils in parishes and dioceses. Furthermore, it encourages the establishment of pastoral councils both for dioceses and parishes (canons 511-514, 536-537). Because we believe that they can enrich the life of the Church, we strongly encourage efforts to establish them where they do not exist.

Our conference of bishops benefits from the National Advisory Council, composed mostly of laity, who forward to us their reactions to proposed pastoral documents and other initiatives.

These various councils, at all levels of church leadership, are opportunities for the Church to listen to the wisdom of the laity. So, too, are diocesan synods and pastoral planning processes, which bring together all segments of the Church for mature deliberation about what priorities a diocesan Church should pursue. The challenge is to nurture the growth and development of these various consultative bodies.

We call on all pastoral leaders to strengthen the structures of participation in church life, so that we might listen to one another, grow in understanding, and deepen our experience of dialogue.

Living with Mystery

An embrace of the paschal mystery frees the Christian disciple to live fully despite ambiguity or turmoil. As Christians we recognize the truth of St. Paul's insight: "Now we see indistinctly, as in a mirror; then we shall see face to face" (1 Cor 13:12). When we embrace our lives, with all their unresolved, mysterious ways, then we are led into the divine embrace of the Mystery that lies at the heart of life. We realize that we are called to be faithful, not necessarily successful. We know that one person might plant the seed, another water it, but God makes it grow (cf. 1 Cor 3:6). It is at this juncture, perhaps more than any other, that the ordained and lay members of the Church can sustain each another in the path of fidelity to our Lord Jesus Christ.

Offering encouragement is a concrete way of helping someone be faithful to a vocation. The laity and the ordained need to pray for one another and to offer mutual support. Furthermore, the Church's pastoral ministry can be more effective if we become true collaborators, mindful of our weaknesses, but grateful for our gifts. Collaboration challenges us to understand that we are, in reality, joined in Christ's body, that we are not separate but interdependent.

For our part we bishops cannot imagine ourselves entering a new millennium, embarked upon a new evangelization, unless we walk side by side with our lay sisters and brothers. For together we stand at the threshold of a "great venture, both challenging and wonderful . . . re-evangelization so much needed by the present world."[17]

Reflecting on the last fifteen years we see how much we have to be grateful for in the lives and witness of the lay faithful. Looking ahead, we envision what might be. For the vision to take flesh, however, we need to commit ourselves anew, bishops and people, to prayer and dialogue, to reflection and action.

Notes

1. *Catechism of the Catholic Church* (Washington, D.C.: United States Catholic Conference, 1994), no. 2014.
2. Second Vatican Council, *Dogmatic Constitution on the Church (Lumen Gentium)*, no. 41.
3. *Catechism of the Catholic Church*, no. 2015.
4. John Paul II, *On the Coming of the Third Millennium (Tertio Millennio Adveniente)* (Washington, D.C.: United States Catholic Conference, 1995), no. 33.
5. John Paul II, *The Vocation and Mission of the Lay Faithful in the Church and in the World (Christifideles Laici)* (Washington, D.C.: United States Catholic Conference, 1988), no. 9; quoted in *Catechism of the Catholic Church*, no. 899.

6. NCCB Committee on Hispanic Affairs, *Communion and Mission: A Guide for Bishops and Pastoral Leaders on Small Church Communities* (Washington, D.C.: United States Catholic Conference, 1995), 1.
7. *Christifideles Laici,* no. 26.
8. *Christifideles Laici,* no. 34.
9. Cf. Paul VI, *On Evangelization in the Modern World (Evangelii Nuntiandi)* (Washington, D.C.: United States Catholic Conference, 1975), no. 19.
10. *Communion and Mission,* 8.
11. Cf. *Christifideles Laici,* no. 20.
12. Ibid., no. 23.
13. Ibid.
14. *Lumen Gentium,* no. 33.
15. John Paul II, *On the Family (Familiaris Consortio)* (Washington, D.C.: United States Catholic Conference, 1981), no. 53.
16. *Lumen Gentium,* no. 31.
17. *Christifideles Laici,* no. 64.

Source: Washington, D.C.: United States Catholic Conference, 1995.

A Decade After "Economic Justice for All": Continuing Principles, Changing Context, New Challenges

A Pastoral Message of the National Conference of Catholic Bishops on the Tenth Anniversary of the Economic Pastoral

November 1995

> The challenge of this pastoral letter is not merely to think differently, but also to act differently. A renewal of economic life depends on the conscious choices and commitments of individual believers who practice their faith in the world. . . . This letter calls us to conversion and common action, to new forms of stewardship, service, and citizenship. The completion of a letter such as this is but the beginning of a long process of *education, discussion, and action.*
> —*Economic Justice for All* (nos. 25, 27, 28)

Introduction

Almost ten years ago our bishops conference adopted the pastoral letter *Economic Justice for All.* This letter was an effort to proclaim the Gospel of Jesus Christ in the midst of our complex and powerful economy. Our pastoral letter insisted that the measure of our economy is not only what it produces, but also how it touches human life, whether it protects or undermines the dignity of the human person, and how it promotes the common good. We emphasized that economic decisions have human consequences and moral content; they help or hurt people, strengthen or weaken family life, advance or diminish the quality of justice in our land. Our letter was not an economic blueprint, but a moral challenge and a call to action. We called for a "New American Experiment" of participation and collaboration for the common good that has yet to be really tried in our land.

Ten years after *Economic Justice for All,* the nation needs to hear its message once again and respond to its continuing challenges. At a time of great national debate, the Catholic community must continue to speak for poor children and working families. Our nation must reduce its deficits, reform welfare, reshape its foreign assistance, and reorder national priorities. However, the fundamental moral measure of these policy choices is how they touch the poor in our midst, especially children and families who struggle against economic, social, and moral pressures that leave them poor and powerless. Poor children, workers, and families may not have the most powerful lobbies, but they have the greatest needs. We welcome a broad debate on economic life, but we cannot support a retreat in the fight against poverty and economic injustice.

Therefore, at this time of national choices, we ask the Catholic community's help in assessing how far we have come and where we need to go to realize the promise of our nation and to be faithful to our Catholic teaching on economic life. Much has changed in this decade—in our economy and our world, our churches and our communities. But much remains the same—there is still too much poverty and not enough economic opportunity for all our people.

In this anniversary message, we renew our call to greater economic justice in an economy with remarkable strength and creativity, but with too little economic growth distributed too inequitably. The power and productivity of the U.S. economy sometimes seem to be leading to three nations living side by side:

- One is prospering and producing in a new information age, coping well with new economic challenges.
- A second is squeezed by declining real incomes and global economic competition. They wonder whether they will keep their jobs and health insurance, whether they can afford college education or Catholic schools for their children.
- A third community is growing more discouraged and despairing. Called an American underclass, their children are growing up desperately poor in the richest nation on earth. Their question at the end of the month is whether they can afford the rent or groceries or heat.

As people of faith, we believe we are one family, not competing classes. We are sisters and brothers, not economic units or statistics. We must come together around the values of our faith to shape economic policies that protect human life, promote strong families, expand a stable middle class, create decent jobs, and reduce the level of poverty and need in our society. We need to strengthen our sense of community and our pursuit of the common good. A decade after the pastoral, it remains clear that the moral test of our society is how the poor, the weak, and the vulnerable are faring. And by this standard we are falling far short.

We believe the best way to prepare for this anniversary is not to develop a major new document, but to offer an urgent call to renewed Catholic dialogue and action in pursuit of a more just, productive, and human economy. As we mark this anniversary, we ask the Catholic community in its ongoing activities to

- *Look back* at the economic justice letter and its major themes
- *Look around* at the U.S. economy a decade later, noting progress and continuing problems
- *Look ahead* at future challenges in light of our developing Catholic teaching

A Look Back

The economic justice pastoral was an enormous undertaking. Years in preparation, it generated wide discussion, occasional controversy, and much activity. But it produced remarkable consensus and unity—all but nine bishops voted for the final letter. The process of consultation, listening, and dialogue strengthened the letter and enriched the Church. In parishes, schools, universities, think tanks, and a wide variety of ad hoc efforts, the Church's teaching was shared and discussed and its implications debated. In the years after the pastoral, nine of every ten dioceses conducted education sessions in parishes; 60 percent strengthened legislative advocacy; more than half held sessions with businesses, labor, or farm representatives; and a majority assessed their personnel policies.

While much of the news coverage focused on policy directions, the heart of the letter remains its scriptural roots and Catholic principles. The greatest contribution of our economic justice pastoral was to remind us that the pursuit of economic justice is a work of faith and an imperative of the Gospel. For some Catholics this message was an affirmation of long-held principle. For others, it was a jarring exposure to part of the Catholic tradition they had never encountered. The call to economic justice is not a political preference or ideological choice, but a response to the Scriptures and a requirement of Catholic teaching.

We hope this anniversary period will be a time of increased focus on economic justice in our parishes, institutions, families, and society. A brief resolution cannot communicate the full substance of the letter, but its central message might be summarized in this way:

- The economy exists to serve the human person, not the other way around.
- Economic life should be shaped by moral principles and ethical norms.
- Economic choices should be measured by whether they enhance or threaten human life, human dignity, and human rights.

- A fundamental concern must be support for the family and the well-being of children.
- The moral measure of any economy is how the weakest are faring.

In the last decade, the Church has continued to share and apply its social doctrine. Pope John Paul II continues to be a powerful voice for solidarity and justice in a world often lacking both. His defense of the poor, workers, family life, and the victims of injustice is a constant theme of his travels and teaching. In his 1991 encyclical, *Centesimus Annus,* our Holy Father offered a sweeping moral analysis of the economic and global challenges of our times, reaffirming the principles of our tradition, and developing new themes. This encyclical offers particular challenges for U.S. Catholics. While it recognizes the vital contributions of democratic values and market economics, it insists that these be guided by the common good and be at the service of human dignity and human rights. He reviewed the failed, empty promises of communism, as he warned against a capitalism that neglects the human and moral dimensions of economic life. The *Catechism of the Catholic Church* reaffirms the Church's teaching that economic life must be directed to the service of persons and be subject to the limits of the moral order and the demands of social justice.

Our own conference has sought to apply Catholic principles in a variety of statements and initiatives that build on our economic pastoral. Our reflections on children and families, environmental justice, international responsibility, stewardship, welfare, health care, and violence in our land offer examples of our commitment to continuing education and advocacy on issues of economic justice.

Our economic justice pastoral and the broader Catholic social teaching that shaped it are complex and nuanced. They do not lend themselves to simple ideological identification. Some in our own community welcome the traditions teaching on private property, the limits of the state, the advantages of free markets, and the condemnation of communism, but resist the focus on the poor, the defense of labor unions, the recognition of the moral limits of markets, and the responsibilities of government. Others welcome the teaching on the "option for the poor," the duties of government to protect the weak, the warnings against unbridled capitalism, but seem to ignore the centrality of family, the emphasis on economic initiative, and the warnings against the bureaucratic excesses of a "social assistance" state. Our social tradition is a moral framework, not a partisan platform or ideological tool. It challenges both right and left, labor and management to focus on the dignity of the human person and the common good rather than their own political or economic interests.

In the words of *Centesimus Annus*, we promote *"a society of free work, of enterprise and of participation.* Such a society is not directed against the market, but demands that the market be appropriately controlled by the forces of society and by the State, so as to guarantee that the basic needs of the whole of society are satisfied."[1]

A Look Around

In this brief message, we do not offer an overall assessment of our economy, but we need to acknowledge that some things have changed and some have not. As reported in the *Statistical Abstract of the United States:*

- Americans living in poverty have increased from 33 million to almost 37 million, even though our economy has been growing in recent years. Economic forces, family disintegration, and government action and inaction have combined to leave more than a fifth of our children growing up poor in one of the richest nations on earth.
- Joblessness, hunger, and homelessness still haunt our nation. Millions of people are actively looking for work and cannot find it. Over the past ten years there has been a sharp increase in the percentage of people who work full-time but cannot lift their family out of poverty. At present this represents 18 percent of all workers.
- The poor and the middle class face growing economic insecurity. Wages are stagnating despite recent gains in productivity, and companies seeking to cut costs are turning to part-time and temporary workers, often at the expense of family income.
- In the past ten years, some 234,000 family farms have been lost, and the overall poverty rate for farmers continues to hover around 20 percent.
- Some rural towns are disappearing, and agricultural land and food processing have become increasingly concentrated in fewer and fewer hands.
- Discrimination, lack of jobs, poor education, and other factors have left African Americans and Hispanics far more likely to be jobless and poor.
- Forty-four percent of African American children and 36 percent of Hispanic children are growing up poor.
- Over the past 15 years, the gap between rich and poor in America has grown wider. In 1993, it is reported the highest earning 20 percent of households saw their income increase by

about $10,000. In contrast, the 20 percent of households at the bottom of the income range saw their income decrease by $1,200. At a time of modest economic growth, many families are experiencing declining real wages.

- Family and social factors continue to contribute to poverty and economic stress. It is reported that a child born to a mother who is married, with a high school diploma, whose husband works or has a job herself has an 8 percent chance of growing up in poverty. A child born to a mother who is not married, without a high school education, and without a job in the family has an 80 percent chance of growing up in poverty. Clearly, the disintegration of families, the absence of fathers, high divorce rates, the failures of education, and the reality of joblessness are crucial factors in our economic problems. And just as clearly, strong families contribute to the economic, social, and moral health of our nation.

- The nation continues to pile up debt, burdening both our economy and our children. Government deficits, corporate speculation, and excessive consumerism contribute to an ethic of "buy now—pay later" that violates principles of stewardship and responsibility. The gross federal debt has grown from $1.8 trillion in 1985 to $4.7 trillion in 1994.

- Economic issues are increasingly global issues with growing foreign competition, interdependence, and trade. In a post-Cold War world, much has changed, but for many it is still a world of too much poverty and not enough development. The number of chronically hungry people has risen from 500 million in 1985 to 800 million in 1995. Almost 1.3 billion people, many of them children, live in desperate poverty around the world.

Our current economy is marked by considerable paradox. Profits and productivity grow, while many worker's real income and sense of security decline. Parents, of even modest means, wonder whether their children will live as well as they do.

Some businesses cut jobs and prosper while their workers pay the price for downsizing. Government seems to pile up debt, cut programs, and feed public cynicism all at once. At a time of diminishing government help for poor workers and families, congressional spending for new weapons exceeds the Pentagon's request, justified more by employment needs than defense criteria. We seem a very long way from "economic justice for all."

There is no consensus on what explains these trends. The decline of manufacturing jobs, rapid technological change, the globalization of the economy, the diminished influence of labor and trade unions, the erosion of the minimum wage, and the costs of health insurance all have contributed to the declining real family income. A growing income gap is fed by economic decisions that put profits ahead of people and lead to inadequate wages, reduced benefits, fewer jobs, and less job security. Meanwhile, individual choices and immoral behavior that contribute to increasing out-of-wedlock births, violence, drug use, and the changing family structure are having a significant impact on both families and the economy. We know poverty and economic injustice result from discrimination *and* destructive personal behavior, from unwise decisions of corporations *and* the unresponsive behavior of the public sector.

Our Catholic tradition speaks to these concerns. Ten years after *Economic Justice for All,* our community's greatest challenge is to encourage those with economic power to shape their decisions by how they affect the stability of families and the opportunities of people who are poor, while at the same time calling on all individuals to make personal choices that strengthen their families and contribute to the common good.

A Look Ahead: Questions for the Future

As we observe this anniversary, we wish to encourage lively dialogue and principled action on a wide variety of issues and concerns, including

- How can our nation work together to overcome the scandal of so much poverty in our midst, especially among our children?
- How can our Church take a leadership role in calling those in positions of power to promote economic growth, job security, decent wages, and greater opportunities?
- How can our community shape the priorities of our culture to promote greater personal responsibility and better economic choices?
- What are the moral responsibilities and limitations of markets, the state, and the voluntary sector? How can business, labor, various levels of government, and mediating structures like churches, charities, and voluntary groups work together to overcome economic injustice and exploitation in our communities?
- How can the dignity and rights of workers be protected and enhanced in an economy where increasing competition, frequent downsizing, and less unionization have left many workers at risk?

- How can U.S. workers and enterprises survive and thrive in a world where other nations compete by offering their workers subsistence wages and minimal benefits?
- How can our nation's economic power in the world be used to build a more just global economy? How can trade and development policies offer hope to a still hungry and suffering world?
- How can we address the enormous economic pressures that undermine families and the family factors (e.g., absent fathers, teenage mothers, high rates of divorce) that leave so many children poor? How can we support families in their essential moral, social, and economic roles?
- How can our society make concern for "the least among us" and the common good the central consideration in the development of budget, environmental, and other national policies?
- How can we assess our own work ethic, productivity, consumption, and lifestyles in light of the needs of a hungry world?
- How can the nation address the diverse social and economic forces that leave both inner-city and rural communities as places of disproportionate poverty and discouragement?
- How can we address the racial discord that exists in our nation today?
- How can we overcome the growing racial and ethnic distance between different communities and the continuing impact of discrimination in economic life?
- How can the Church practice in its own life and institutions what it preaches to others about economic justice, human dignity, and the rights of workers?

There are many more questions that could be raised, but these are examples of issues where Catholics can apply the Church's teaching, share our experience, and voice our hopes in civil dialogue and principled action on economic justice. In addressing these and other questions, we believe the Catholic community can be a bridge builder in several ways. Our community crosses lines of class and race, politics and ideology. Catholics are at the center and fringes of U.S. economic life. We are CEOs and senators, union leaders and small-business owners, migrant farm workers, and homeless children. Ten years after the pastoral, we need to help our Church renew its sense of solidarity and our society rediscover a sense of national community, pursuing the common good rather than our own narrow economic and other interests.

In addition, our tradition emphasizes both rights *and* responsibilities, promotes increased charity *and* insists on greater justice, and advocates greater personal responsibility *and* broader social responsibility. We recognize the vital roles *and* limits of markets, government, and voluntary groups. We hope in this anniversary year we can get beyond some of the false choices and ideological polarization in the economic debate and join in a renewed search for the common good.

We can be the advocates of a renewed social contract between employers and employees, between recipients and providers of assistance, between investors and managers that seeks long-term progress over short-term gains, that offers respect and security in exchange for responsibility and hard work, and that protects the vulnerable, especially our children.

A Call to Renewed Commitment

We hope that this anniversary period can be a time of prayer and reflection, discussion and dialogue, advocacy and action. Economic justice begins in our homes and families, in our individual choices and household priorities. Unless we teach our children basic values of honesty, compassion, and initiative they will not be equipped to deal with the "counter values" of selfishness, consumerism, and materialism so prevalent in our society.

We urge Catholic publications to refocus on economic issues and their moral and human implications. We also urge Catholic educational institutions to redouble their efforts to share our teaching, to help their students develop concern for the poor and for justice, and to contribute to the common good by their research and educational activities. We urge national and diocesan organizations to integrate themes of economic justice in their ongoing meetings, publications, advocacy, and other activities. And most especially, we encourage Catholic parishes to continue to weave our teaching on economic life into their prayer and preaching, their education and formation, their outreach and advocacy.

We do not ask Catholic communities to set aside their ongoing ministry to focus on economic justice. Rather, we ask leaders to further integrate these principles and tasks into the worship, formation, and service they offer on a daily basis. The pursuit of economic justice is not an option or add-on for Catholics; it is part of who we are and what we believe.

The Catholic community will continue to carry out the message of the pastoral in many different ways—in the service and advocacy of Catholic Charities, the relief and development efforts of Catholic Relief Services, the empowerment and education of the Campaign for Human Development, to cite a few.

Through our own national conference, our state and diocesan structures, the Catholic community is to continue to educate and advocate for children and families on issues ranging from real welfare reform to school choice, the rights of workers to sustainable development. We need to strengthen and build on these and other impressive efforts.

However, it has always been clear that the pursuit of greater economic justice is not carried out primarily by the statements of religious bodies, but in the broader marketplace—where investments are made, contracts are negotiated, products are created, workers are hired, and policies are set. The search for economic justice is also carried forward in the public square. In this election year, while others are campaigning for office, let us campaign for the poor and vulnerable and for greater economic justice. Let us ask those who seek to lead and represent us how they will govern and vote on key issues of human life, human dignity, and economic justice. And let us as citizens and believers continue to advocate for people who are poor and vulnerable in our communities, nation, and world.

We renew our pastoral's call for believers to shape their choices in the marketplace and public arena according to the values of the Scriptures and the moral principles of the Catholic Church. Whatever our economic status, political identification, or ideological preferences, we are called as Catholics to work for an economy more respectful of human life and human dignity. In our work and citizenship, our economic, political, and personal choices, we must reach out to "the least among us" and seek the common good.

We may differ on specifics and priorities, but let us come together—across economic, ideological, and ethnic lines—to work for a society and economy offering more justice and opportunity, especially for the poor. Differences over how to move forward will give rise to legitimate debate, but indifference to the need to build a more just and open economy is not an option for Catholics. Every Christian is called to follow Jesus in his mission—and ours—of bringing "good news to the poor, new sight to the blind, liberty to captives and to set the downtrodden free" (Lk 4:18). That was the call of our pastoral letter almost ten years ago and still is our task today.

Note

1.   John Paul II, *On the Hundredth Anniversary of Rerum Novarum (Centesimus Annus)* (Washington, D.C.: United States Catholic Conference, 1991), no. 35.

Source: Washington, D.C.: United States Catholic Conference, 1995.

The Hispanic Presence in the New Evangelization in the United States

A Pastoral Statement of the National Conference of Catholic Bishops on the Occasion of the Fiftieth Anniversary of the Establishment of a National Office for Hispanic Ministry

November 1995

"At this moment of grace we recognize the Hispanic[1] community among us as a blessing from God." With this declaration we began our pastoral letter on the Hispanic presence in our Church twelve years ago.[2] Today, at the dawn of a third millennium of Christian history, we wish to reaffirm and expand on this conviction. We affirm that the Hispanic presence in our Church constitutes a providential gift from the Lord in our commitment to that new evangelization to which we are called at this moment of history.

We see the present moment as a time of great opportunity. True, this century has seen some of the greatest offenses ever against human dignity. This has been the century of global wars, genocides, and totalitarian regimes. All yearn for a new beginning, a new hope, a new confidence that the thirst for liberty is not a vain illusion and that the search for the truth that sets us free is not an empty dream. This yearning provides us with the opportunity to proclaim Jesus Christ as the only answer to the questions that torment the human heart. Led by our Holy Father, Pope John Paul II, the Church responds to this challenge by the joyful proposal of the Gospel of life as the basis for a culture truly responsive to all human needs, spiritual and material. The Gospel of life proclaims that human rights have their origin in the Creator's wisdom, that liberty is inseparable from the truths of which we are not the authors, and that a peace founded on authentic solidarity between men and women of different racial and ethnic origins can be secure.

Many around the world still see the United States as the land of hope for liberty and justice. Yet, our country has not been spared from the advances made by the "culture of death" described by the Holy Father, in which the weak are abandoned to the manipulations of the powerful. Still, when we look at the future we are not afraid. We know Jesus Christ, who has conquered sin and death, is the Lord of the Church guiding her at every moment, providing her with the wisdom to interpret the signs of the times and the spiritual resources to respond to the challenges of the moment.

We consider the Hispanic presence in our country a great resource given to us by the Lord himself for our struggle against the culture of death. In our pastoral letter of twelve years ago, we referred to the Hispanic presence as *prophetic*. We called upon our Hispanic brothers and sisters to share with us the prophetic witness of an identity forged by the Catholic faith. This summer, more than five hundred Catholic leaders in Hispanic ministry who gathered in San Antonio exercised their prophetic role. Clergy, religious, and laity from 110 dioceses of our country came together from June 23 to June 25 to celebrate the fiftieth anniversary of the establishment by our conference of a national office for Hispanic ministry. At the end of their gathering, called Convocation '95, they issued a "Statement of Commitment"[3] to the new evangelization in our country. Our statement today is our enthusiastic response to this Statement of Commitment.

We address this statement, however, not only to the participants of Convocation '95. We write to the entire Church in our country, calling all to the blessing offered to us by our Hispanic brothers and sisters' commitment to the new evangelization. There is but one Catholic Church in the United States, as it is everywhere around the world. Evangelization is always the task of the entire Church. Our Church has been truly blessed by the presence of a great variety of cultures, races, and ethnic backgrounds, all contributing to the richness of our ecclesial life. The commitment of our Hispanic Catholics is a gift to all of us, and by welcoming it, we commit ourselves to work together for the spread of the Gospel.

In this statement we do not intend to discuss all the aspects of the new evangelization. This discussion can be found in our 1993 statement *Go and Make Disciples*. Neither do we intend this statement to contain a discussion of the ministry to Hispanics, its history, its characteristics, and its goals. We reaffirm what we said in our pastoral letter on the Hispanic presence and urge all to implement the *National Pastoral Plan for Hispanic Ministry,* published on January 18, 1988. This pastoral plan is the fruit of the encuentro process, which engaged Hispanics from all regions and walks of life in formulating goals and objectives.

Instead, in this statement we wish to respond to what happened in Convocation '95. We see this statement as a dialogue with those who offered their "Statement of Commitment" to the new evangelization. The new evangelization must be based on a dialogue engaging all segments of our Catholic community, seeking the contribution of their experiences of faith, and learning from the witness of all. The participants at Convocation '95 recognized this when they wrote: "We will look for ways to share with the entire Church in the United States the progress brought about in Hispanic ministry."[4] It is in this spirit of dialogue that we offer now our thoughts on what we believe can be the most important contribution of our Hispanic Catholics to the new evangelization, namely, the experience of how faith in Christ generates a culture that protects, sustains, and promotes human dignity. It is in this area, the area of the relation between faith and culture, where the contribution of our Hispanic faithful can be truly prophetic and providential.

In his message to the participants in Convocation '95, our Holy Father Pope John Paul II recognized the importance of the Hispanic contribution in the area of faith and culture. His Holiness expressed the wish that "by drawing on its rich history and experience, the Hispanic community can offer a unique contribution to the dialogue between faith and culture in American society today, and thus open new paths for the spread of the Gospel in the Third Millennium."[5] *We believe this to be the most important contribution of Hispanic Catholics to the new evangelization in the United States.* Therefore, we welcome the commitment by the participants in Convocation '95 to "share with our Catholic brothers and sisters in the United States what a faith incarnate in culture is."[6]

Faith and Culture

The relationship between faith and culture is at the heart of the new evangelization. The word *culture* comes from the Latin verb *colere*, which means to cultivate the ground. Eventually, the expression *cultura animi*, the culture of souls, came to designate the personal formative process of the individual. When the process of personal formation is understood in intellectual terms, a "cultured person" is someone who simply knows a lot. However, personal formation is a process with intellectual, affective, ethical, and practical components. It touches on everything that is characteristically human. Culture is what shapes the human being as specifically human. The Second Vatican Council sees culture as the cultivation of "natural goods and values"[7] through which we reach full human maturity[8] by means of the dominion over the world which develops the resources of creation. Culture thus designates the perfection of the human person, the construction of a just social order, and the service of others.[9] The document of Puebla defines culture as "the specific way in which human beings belonging to a given people cultivate their relationship with nature, with each other, and with God in order to arrive at 'an authentic and full humanity.'"[10] As such, culture designates the style of life that characterizes different peoples. Thus it is appropriate to speak of a plurality of cultures.

The new evangelization is aimed in a special way at those to whom the Gospel has already been proclaimed but for whom it has not become a lived experience of reality in all its dimensions. The Gospel enlightens us as to what is true and false, right and wrong, desirable and undesirable. It informs and transforms our experience of nature, of the passage of time, of work and rest, of other people, of the purpose of life and the meaning of death. *These are the experiences that characterize a culture.* The Gospel, therefore, touches the foundation of all cultures. Although addressed to each person, the invitation to follow Jesus Christ has a necessary cultural dimension. Without it the Gospel becomes an abstract system of ideas and values that can be manipulated to excuse individual and social sin. The new evangelization is intended to bridge the gap between faith and culture by showing that *a faith that does not generate culture is a sterile faith.*

The common and absolutely essential point of departure of all authentic human cultures is the *recognition of human personhood as valuable for its own sake,* as the Second Vatican Council affirms.[11] That is, the human person may never be reduced to an "instrument" to achieve a purpose, no matter how good the purpose may be. The human person, each single human person regardless of circumstances, must be recognized and respected as such unconditionally. All authentic human cultures depend on this fact. *To say that the Gospel has a necessary cultural dimension is to say that it will promote the recognition, the affirmation, and the development of all human persons as such.* The Gospel thus compels the quest for freedom, personal growth, care for the weak and needy, and liberation from alienating economic, political, and religious structures of individual and social life.

Preferential Option for the Poor

On March 9, 1983, when Pope John Paul II said to the bishops of Latin America and the Caribbean that the present moment required an evangelization new in ardor, expression, and methods, he was building precisely on this process of renewal carried out by the Church in Latin America after the Second Vatican Council.[12] Central to this process is the recognition that a successful evangelization occurs only when faith shapes culture. That is, evangelization is inseparable from the affirmation and defense of the dignity of all human persons. However, because the Gospel touches the foundations of cultures, this truth about human dignity is meant to become incarnate in the culture. It is meant to affect those *social structures* through which the human person exercises dominion over the goods of nature and the distribution of the fruits of their development. These structures must be at the service of the human person, recognized and affirmed as valuable for his or her own sake. In order to judge whether this is or is not the case, it is necessary to embrace the experience of those who have no other claim to respect than their own identity as persons, *joining them in their quest for justice.* This experience becomes a criterion for interpretation of the demands of the Gospel in particular social situations.[13] In Latin America this solidarity was given a name: the "preferential option for the poor."

The Statement of Commitment issued by Convocation '95 reminds us of this criterion when it recognizes that a sign of a culture formed by the Gospel is the existence of a *preferential option for the poor* in society. Hence the commitment to "give witness to how the preferential option for the poor, an essential aspect of the Catholic faith, becomes a cultural reality."[14] *We welcome this commitment and recognize it as the contribution to the Church in our country of the last decades of ecclesial reflection and practice in the Church in Latin America.*

The Statement of Commitment correctly understands this term as "the affirmation of the dignity of the human person as created by God with no other purpose than the good of its own existence."[15] Thus the participants express a commitment to "struggle against all attempts to instrumentalize the human person, valuing only its possible contribution to the material progress of society."[16]

The Centrality of Christ

In order to understand the deepest reason for the link between the preferential option for the poor and the impact of faith on culture, we must remember that communion with Jesus Christ involves a stand with respect to life in this world in all its dimensions. Through faith and the sacraments, we enter into the relationship between Jesus Christ and the Father. We acquire a vision of reality and an experience of nature, others, and God consistent with this relationship made possible by the gift of the Spirit of God. This vision and this experience define an outlook or *stand* with respect to reality that is oriented towards the consummation of God's plan for creation at the end of time. Thus we begin to live now, on this earth, the life of the kingdom of God which will be fully manifested at the end of time. It is this outlook or stand that is expressed culturally through social structures, especially those pertaining to work and leisure. The Statement of Commitment issued by Convocation '95 expresses it this way: "We shall seek ways to show that our efforts on behalf of social justice are the result of our faith in Jesus Christ, the Lord, the center of history and the universe. In the truth about Jesus Christ, true God and true man, we discover what the human person is in all its dimensions: individual, social, material, and spiritual."[17]

The Gospel is not a system of concepts to be taught by a teacher to a pupil and adapted to different circumstances. The Gospel is the proclamation of the person of Jesus Christ, of his mission, teachings, and promises. Jesus Christ is not an idea, but a concrete, specific, historical individual: the Son of God who became the Son of Mary. This individual, and he alone, is the Savior. There is no liberation of any kind without him. He became the "Poor One" in whom we experience solidarity with the poor. He is the Redeemer, the Second Person of the Holy Trinity in whom all were predestined to reach their fulfillment as human persons by faith and the sacramental incorporation into his saving death and resurrection. Without this proclamation of Jesus Christ and his worship through faith and the sacraments there is no true evangelization.[18]

Therefore, we wish to emphasize the importance of the commitment of the participants of Convocation '95 to the renewal of our "liturgical, sacramental, and catechetical life,"[19] to the promotion of vocations to the sacramental ministries of priesthood and diaconate, as well as to lay and religious vocations. We especially welcome the commitment to an adequate doctrinal and pastoral formation process based on Sacred Scripture and the new *Catechism of the Catholic Church*, as well as its insistence on the need for prayer and the popular expression of our religious beliefs.

Witness to Hope

The liturgical, sacramental, and catechetical life of the Church aims at introducing us into a personal relationship with Jesus Christ. Through this union with him, we experience the power of God's love, which is stronger than the power of sin and death. We experience the redemption of our personal and collective history by a love greater than all the evil in the world. This love conveys to us an experience of the horror of sin precisely as it awakens us to the reality of redemption and true freedom. Thus it gives rise to a hope which "will not leave us disappointed" (cf. Rom 5:5). Evangelization is the proclamation of this hope rooted in Jesus Christ and committing us to the struggle against the power of sin in our lives. It is this hope, and not a utopian dream, that sustains our struggle for liberation and justice in the world, our preferential option for the poor.

The Church is the people of God formed by the Holy Spirit into the body of Christ. The Church is the place of *communio* or interpersonal communion of faith and love with the Lord and among believers. The life of the Church is the proclamation, beginning, and anticipation of the kingdom of God. The Church evangelizes when its members proclaim the word of God, catechize, worship in the liturgy, serve the need of others, and give witness to their faith by the lives they lead. *The impact of faith on cultures, such as the preferential option for the poor, must be understood as the consequence of this way of life.*

The Culture of Death

In our country, the modern technological, functional mentality creates a world of replaceable individuals incapable of authentic solidarity. In its place, society is grouped by artificial arrangements created by powerful interests. The common ground is an increasingly dull, sterile, consumer conformism—visible especially among so many of our young people—created by artificial needs promoted by the media to support powerful economic interests. Pope John Paul II has called this a "culture of death." In the Holy Father's words, "this culture is actively fostered by powerful cultural, economic, and political currents which encourage an idea of society excessively concerned with efficiency. . . . A life which would require greater acceptance, love, and care is considered useless, or held to be an intolerable burden, and is therefore rejected in one way or another. . . ."[20] In such a culture, "society becomes a mass of individuals placed side by side, but without any mutual bonds."[21] The new evangelization, therefore, requires the Church to provide refuge and sustenance for ongoing growth to those rescued from the loneliness of modern life. It requires the promotion of a culture of life based on the Gospel of life.

The Culture of Life

Hence the importance for the new evangelization in our country of the commitment by the participants in Convocation '95 to "defend the value of each human life from the first moment of conception to natural death."[22] The struggle against abortion and euthanasia is an integral part of the new evangelization, as well as the struggle against capital punishment, contraception, drugs, and the arms trade. Our defense of life requires "solidarity with all who defend the victims of the culture of death in our country, overcoming all racial or ethnic hostility, seeking to be an authentic leaven of unity, and struggling against racism and discrimination which denies access to the necessary resources to escape the poverty in which a large part of our Hispanic population is still immersed."[23]

Specifically, the Statement of Commitment calls for the recognition of the "right to a dignified work, a just salary, decent housing, an education that respects our cultural origins, and the access to health care programs worthy of the value of each human being, regardless of age."[24] Convocation '95 also identified as particularly urgent the defense of the family, the promotion of the dignity of women, and the care of the elderly and the terminally ill. Of particular importance to our Hispanic brothers and sisters is the need to reject immigration policies destructive of families, seeking instead immigration policies free from all racist motivations and selfish fears. In the same spirit, we have frequently denounced the unjust treatment of migrant agricultural workers.

To say all of this is not to reduce evangelization and the mission of the Church to the improvement of life in this world.[25] *Evangelii Nuntiandi* insists on the profound link between the invitation to faith in Christ and the promotion of social justice. The link between them is part of the very mystery of faith being proclaimed through evangelization. It is rooted in the relation between creation and redemption.[26] In *Redemptoris Missio,* John Paul II confirms this teaching and expands it in terms of the *prophetic mission* of the Church at the service of the poor.[27] The Holy Father talks of the Church's solidarity with the poor as a sign of redemption. The Church, he says, is the Church of the poor.[28] The Holy Father refers specifically to the example of the Church in Latin America, where the preferential option for the poor has been recognized as an integral part of the Church's mission. Indeed, this is one of the great insights central to the Latin American ecclesial experience, as articulated in the great declarations of Medellín and Puebla and reaffirmed in Santo Domingo. We welcome the importance given to it by our Hispanic Catholics in the Statement of Commitment of Convocation '95. We see this as an example of how Hispanic Catholics are a "logical bridge between the Church in the United States and the Church in Latin America,"[29] as the Statement of Commitment declares.

The Blessing of the Hispanic Presence

With the Holy Father, we recognize the Hispanic presence in our Church as a blessing, a privileged opportunity to work for a culture that reflects the truth about the human person revealed in the truth about Jesus Christ. As Pope John Paul II wrote to Convocation '95, "From the dawn of evangelization in the New World, the name of Jesus Christ and the liberating power of the Gospel have taken root among the Spanish-speaking peoples of the Americas. The preaching and evangelical witness of the first missionaries bore fruit in lives of holiness and in the growth of a new culture marked by deep faith and authentic Christian values. Today this living heritage continues to be a source of enrichment for the Church in the United States as it faces the challenge of proclaiming the Good News of our salvation and of building up the Body of Christ in the context of an ethnically diverse society."[30]

In our pastoral letter *The Hispanic Presence, Challenge and Commitment,* published in 1983, and in the *National Pastoral Plan for Hispanic Ministry* of 1987, we have already highlighted the Hispanic contribution to the life of the Church in the United States. The fact is that *the future of the Church in the United States will be greatly affected by what happens to Hispanic Catholics,* who constitute a large percentage of its members. The contribution of Hispanic Catholics in the United States to the new evangelization and the future of our Church will depend on the Church's presence in the Hispanic community.

When we speak of the Hispanic presence, it is important to realize we are speaking about a complex, varied, and dynamic reality. The Statement of Commitment of Convocation '95 correctly underlines "the importance of a Hispanic presence in the communications media, in order to present an adequate image of the reality of our communities, their real needs, and their contributions to the life of the Church and society."[31] The participants ask the Church that its programs of education and religious formation in schools, universities, institutes, and seminaries reflect the true significance of the Hispanic presence.

In a way, a new Hispanic American identity is still in the process of being forged in the United States as people from different Latin American cultures come together, discover what they have in common, and interrelate with the dominant North American culture. This new Hispanic American identity will take its place next to all the other expressions of the Hispanic identity, all having a common origin.

The majority of Hispanic people were born here, and their ancestors have been in our country for a long time, some including many generations. Convocation '95 provided the participants with the opportunity to reflect on the origins of the Hispanic presence in our land long before the settlement of the first thirteen English colonies. Today the vast majority of Hispanics are engaged in a struggle similar to that of all previous American immigrant groups, namely, care for the family, work, health, and education. Their needs are obviously different from the needs of those recently arrived. Different responses to different needs are required. In this regard, we agree with the need to "search for ways in which Hispanics who have achieved success in society will contribute with their talents so that [their] experience of faith and culture will assist the Church in the evangelization of the professional world."[32]

The experience of living in the United States is bringing the people of Latin American descent to recognize what they have in common. As the Statement of Commitment says: Hispanics are "the fruit of an inculturation of the Catholic faith which constitutes the basis of our Hispanic identity."[33] This inculturation of the faith has generated similar attitudes about personal and social life that unite Hispanics despite their differences.

Traditional Hispanic cultures preserve many experiences of self, nature, others, and God, which characterize this inculturation of the faith. We have in mind similar attitudes such as openness of spirit; a welcoming disposition to what is unexpected, new, and unplanned;

simplicity; a recognition that a need for companionship and support is not a weakness, but a necessary part of personal growth; creative fidelity and determination to honor promises given; a sense of honor and respect for self and others; patience and willingness to follow the rhythms of nature; a sense of walking together toward a common destiny; a truly creative imagination capable of rising above immediate appearances in order to reach the inner core of reality; a love for home, land, and an extended view of family; a trust in divine providence; and an awareness that what is proper and right is more worthy of sacrifice than immediate satisfaction, that persons are more important than things, personal relations more fulfilling than material success, and serenity more valuable than life in the fast lane. All of this is combined with a joyful resignation born of the awareness that life is greater than any temporary frustration. These similar attitudes, characteristic of an Hispanic *ethos,* are the fruit of the inculturation of the Catholic faith through the tremendous encounter with Iberian, Native American, and African spiritualities at the origin of the history of Hispanics. *The Hispanic ethos is historically inseparable from the Catholic faith. Indeed, sometimes fear and opposition to the Hispanic presence is motivated more by anti-Catholicism than by anything else.*

Of course Hispanics are not the only people who possess these qualities! These are truly attributes of all who are authentically human. Moreover, as with all that is human, these attitudes can also be corrupted by sin and can hide the reality of prejudice and selfishness. Still, with the Holy Father we are convinced that the presence in our Church of such large numbers of Hispanics can be understood spiritually as a *providential opportunity* for all of us to rediscover qualities necessary for our service to society in the name of the liberating Gospel of Jesus Christ. These qualities are not merely folkloric stereotypes. Behind them lies a definite, courageous stand originating in the Catholic faith and sustained throughout the vicissitudes of what is often a very harsh and difficult life.

Prophetic Presence

In our pastoral letter on the Hispanic presence and in the *National Pastoral Plan for Hispanic Ministry,* we referred to the Hispanic presence as *prophetic.* This prophetic presence is due above all to those aspects of the Hispanic ethos arising from its Catholic origins. As prophetic, we believe that the Hispanic presence provides the Church in our country an opportunity to recall its mission to preserve and foster a Catholic identity in the midst of an often hostile culture.

For most of its history, the Catholic Church in the United States sought to convince American society of the patriotism of the Catholic people and their adherence to the fundamental and "self-evident truths" mentioned in our Declaration of Independence. Although anti-Catholicism still remains in our country, much of this effort achieved some success, especially after the Second Vatican Council's *Declaration on Religious Liberty*. At the present time, however, the influence of secularism has led to a debate about the proper interpretation of the American founding principles. Some of the interpretations being proposed—and even adopted in judicial decisions—are absolutely incompatible with our faith. In order to participate in the current debate and assist our country to be faithful to the truths and values upon which it claims to be founded, it is necessary for us as Catholics to appreciate the relationship between faith and culture. The Hispanic presence is prophetic because it is the bearer of traditions flowing from an authentic inculturation of the Catholic faith.[34] Our efforts to help Hispanics preserve and grow in their faith will put us in a position to better understand those currents of thought and practice in our society that undermine the faith of all Catholics.

The Church in the United States began as a Church of poor immigrants who struggled against discrimination in order to obtain their share of the American dream. Yet many times anti-Catholicism excluded them from participation in society. Ironically, in the name of freedom, freedom was denied; in the name of tolerance, tolerance was denied and doors were closed. *We believe this is again increasingly the case,* going even beyond Catholicism to all expressions of biblical faith different from the secularist ethos seeking cultural dominance in our society.

In the past, the Catholic Church created a space within American society where the Catholic people could be nourished and supported in the faith while being cared for in their needs. This was accompanied by a relentless effort to show that Catholics were as fully committed to freedom, pluralism, and democracy as anyone else in the country. As a result of this effort, most of our Catholic immigrants were assimilated into the American mainstream. This was possible because of the commitment of the American people to the rights of the human person based on the unsurpassable dignity of each human being created by God. Of course there were differences of opinion concerning those rights and their ultimate origin and meaning, but a common discourse about this was possible, based on the biblical Jewish and Christian experiences of life and on the great tradition about a natural law grasped by all human beings, regardless of their different beliefs concerning religion.

In the present cultural crisis, this common discourse is not always possible. The crucial and key concepts upon which this discussion was based are the same—concepts such as rights, persons, justice, liberty, and happiness—but the experiences to which these concepts point can no longer be assumed to be the same for all. Of course we must continue the dialogue upon which our future as one nation depends, pursued serenely and with respect for all, but we must always try to understand the experiences at the roots of the concepts being debated. Most important of all, we must *retrieve the cultural dimension of the experiences at the root of Catholic life.* This is a crucial part of the new evangelization, and the large Hispanic presence in our midst constitutes for us a providential resource for this task. That is why we have stated that *the most important contribution of Hispanic Catholics to the new evangelization in our country lies in the area of faith and culture.*

Prophetic Warning

The Hispanic presence is also a prophetic warning to the Church in the United States. For if Hispanic Catholics are not welcomed warmly and offered a home where they can experience our Church as their Church, the resulting loss of their Catholic identity will be a serious blow to the Church in our country. We will have missed an opportunity to be truly Catholic while the culture of death, prevalent in our society, seeks to impose its way on us all.

As the call for a new evangelization in Latin America demonstrates, we cannot take for granted the Catholic faith of Hispanic Catholics. Hispanics do not consider themselves a chosen people protected in any special way from infidelity to the Gospel. Nor do they present themselves as living exemplars of faith. To pretend to do so is an intolerable and dangerous romanticism. A disposition to the faith is not itself faith; a strong religiosity is not identical to the ecclesial-sacramental life in Christ; appreciation of the values of personalism, family, and community are not enough for a moral life in Christ. The devastation of Hispanic families by drugs, alcohol, and licentiousness is well documented. So is the plight of so many Hispanic women who are victims of deeply ingrained *machista* attitudes, as the women attending Convocation '95 strongly reminded us. Although racism, poverty, immigrant bashing, and prejudiced discrimination are still a fact of life for many Hispanics, these vices are present also in the Hispanic communities. The commitment to struggle against these ills by embracing a preferential option for the poor is a commitment by Hispanics to other Hispanics as well.

Yet through it all, there remains a precious gift in our midst brought to us by our Hispanic brothers and sisters: a sense of the sacred, a particular and deep sensitivity to the beauty of creation festively celebrated, a sense of pride in *la hispanidad*, a capacity for profound emotions of devotion to others, a great delicacy in human contacts, and a thirst for the transcendent and divine expressed in powerful Catholic symbols. We believe with the participants of Convocation '95 that the importance of this "cultural Catholicism" should not be underestimated. It is truly a blessing, and it is upon these experiences of a faith becoming culture that the new evangelization in our country must be based.

The Star of Evangelization

In this task we commend ourselves once again to the Queen of the Americas, Our Lady of Guadalupe, as we seek to respond to the call to a new evangelization. It was in the womb of Mary that the Word became flesh. This mystery of the incarnation is the basis for our belief in the mystery of faith becoming culture. Mary's *Magnificat* is the canticle of our preferential option of love for the poor. She is the woman, pursued by the dragon, in whose companionship the people of God, her children, are protected from the culture of death. It is Mary who prevents us from detaching our Lord from the flesh and turning him into an abstract, remote figure. Through her, the Lord becomes a concrete, tangible presence redeeming all aspects of our life, our companion and the goal of our pilgrimage to the definitive manifestation of the kingdom of God. As we welcome the commitment of our brothers and sisters in Convocation '95, we commend them and ourselves to her, Santa Maria, the Star of all Evangelization.

Notes

1. For this document, "Hispanic" is synonymous with Latin American, Latino, Mexican American, Spanish American, and Chicano; it includes all Spanish-speaking persons in the United States.
2. National Conference of Catholic Bishops, *The Hispanic Presence: Challenge and Commitment* (Washington, D.C.: United States Catholic Conference, 1983).
3. Statement of Commitment, Convocation '95, June 25, 1995.
4. Statement of Commitment, no. 9.
5. Letter of May 8, 1995, from Archbishop G. B. Re to Bishop Roberto González, chairman, NCCB Committee on Hispanic Affairs, Prot. No. 370.479.
6. Statement of Commitment, no. 3.
7. Second Vatican Council, *Pastoral Constitution on the Church in the Modern World (Gaudium et Spes)*, no. 53.
8. *Gaudium et Spes*, no. 57.
9. Cf. *Gaudium et Spes*, nos. 55 and 57.
10. *La Evangelización en el Presente y en el Futuro de América Latina* (Puebla: CELAM, 1979), no. 386.
11. Cf. *Gaudium et Spes*, no. 24.
12. Cf. *Acta Apostolicae Sedis* 75 (1983): 771-779.

13. Congregation for the Doctrine of the Faith, *Instruction on Certain Aspects of Liberation Theology* (Washington, D.C.: United States Catholic Conference, 1984), sec. VIII, nos. 1-9.
14. Statement of Commitment, no. 4.
15. Ibid.
16. Ibid.
17. Ibid., no. 8.
18. Cf. Paul VI, *On Evangelization in the Modern World (Evangelii Nuntiandi)* (Washington, D.C.: United States Catholic Conference, 1995), no. 22.
19. Statement of Commitment, no. 8.
20. Cf. John Paul II, *The Gospel of Life (Evangelium Vitae)* (Washington, D.C.: United States Catholic Conference, 1995), no. 12.
21. Cf. ibid., no. 20.
22. Statement of Commitment, no. 5.
23. Ibid.
24. Ibid.
25. Congregation for the Doctrine of the Faith, *Instruction on Certain Aspects of Liberation Theology,* sec. VI, no. 3.
26. Cf. *Evangelii Nuntiandi,* no. 31.
27. John Paul II, *On the Permanent Validity of the Church's Missionary Mandate (Redemptoris Missio)* (Washington, D.C.: United States Catholic Conference, 1990), no. 43.
28. Ibid., no. 60.
29. Statement of Commitment, no. 10.
30. Cf. letter of May 8, 1995, to Bishop Roberto González.
31. Statement of Commitment, no. 6.
32. Ibid.
33. Ibid., no. 3.
34. National Conference of Catholic Bishops, *Hispanic Ministry: Three Major Documents* (Washington, D.C.: United States Catholic Conference, 1995).

Source: Washington, D.C.: United States Catholic Conference, 1996.

A Letter to College Students

A Letter from the Catholic Bishops of the United States

November 1995

Dear College Students,

We write to you as your co-workers in Christ, and we congratulate you on all you have done to arrive at this point in your life. Already you are leaders, because in a very real sense you have begun to lead, especially if you are an older student with family and work responsibilities.

Your college years are a very significant time for you. In these few years you will greatly expand your knowledge and your skills. At the same time, you will be making many important choices—about vocations, relationships, and careers.

These years will also provide a wonderful opportunity for you to grow in your faith, a faith that is rooted in your own personal relationship with Jesus and nourished by prayer, reading the Scriptures, and participating in the sacraments. As you grow in faith, you will recognize the important responsibility of sharing your faith with others.

We realize that foremost among the many priorities in your life is the time devoted to study. Your study is not unrelated to your life of faith. Through your exploration of history, language, science, and art, you can also deepen your faith and your understanding of our religious tradition. In the future, what you study now can help transform business, academia, culture, and the mass media into places where the Spirit of God truly lives and works. And there is always the possibility of a career of ministry and leadership in the Church.

But you do not have to wait. Think of the impact you as a Catholic college student can have even now on others who may not know the rich tradition of Catholicism. Working with students of other faiths and religious traditions on campus, you can make important contributions toward peace and justice, reminding the whole academic community of the presence of those whom society neglects or marginalizes. By your involvement as a Catholic, you can help others see the face of Christ in the faces of the poor.

It is a fact of campus life and life everywhere that many people today experience a deep sense of uncertainty and confusion. It seems that for some the world is filled with questions and even discouragement. While we have to admit that the future, as always, is uncertain, we also have to recognize that it is full of possibilities. And as

Catholics, we have the added certainty and hope that comes from our faith in the victory of Jesus' death and resurrection. You can be witnesses of that hope for everyone you meet, sharing with them the hope that is based on the Gospel and the abiding presence of the Spirit. By your care and concern, you can also reassure other people that they are really loved and that Christ's love is always present for them.

There are many specific ways that you can minister on campus to create a climate of hope and a community of welcome. Begin by inviting your friends and neighbors to join you at Sunday Mass, the most important celebration of the Catholic community. It is easier for them to respond to the prompting of the Spirit when someone else is willing to go with them. Also, offer to be a reader, server, eucharistic minister, cantor, or musician, according to your gifts.

Strengthen your own spirituality by searching for answers and by becoming more knowledgeable about your faith. Start with the Scriptures, God speaking to us. Then the *Catechism of the Catholic Church* is a wonderful reference that can help to answer both your questions and those others might have. And campus ministers, with their special training, want to help you with your questions, spiritual growth, and religious identity.

There are so many other ways to serve. Volunteer to help out in the local community or improve the quality of life on campus by becoming involved in peer ministry or by tutoring your fellow students. Working together with campus ministers, you can organize or participate in small prayer or faith groups in your residence hall or local community. By your efforts on behalf of life, you can remind others that a lived Christian faith begins with a profound respect for human life from conception to natural death. By simplifying your lifestyle, you can be a reminder that our resources are not without limit and ought to be used wisely.

Jesus commissioned us to be his witnesses by the testimony of our lives when he said, "You will receive power when the Holy Spirit comes upon you, and you will be my witnesses in Jerusalem, throughout Judea and Samaria, and to the ends of the earth" (Acts 1:8). We bishops of the United States enumerated in our pastoral letter on campus ministry of 1985, *Empowered by the Spirit*, six ways in which the Church on campus can be a faithful witness to the message of the Gospel: forming the faith community, appropriating the faith, forming the Christian conscience, educating for justice, facilitating personal development, and developing leaders for the future.

Since 1985, many campus ministries have reported increased student involvement in liturgy, community service, retreat opportunities, and justice concerns. Now as the Church approaches the two-thousand-year mark in its history, we challenge you to reflect, using these categories from *Empowered by the Spirit*, on the ways in which you have revealed the Church on campus to be a faithful witness to the truth of the Gospel, a "servant community, dedicated to social justice, and a more effective sign and instrument of the kingdom of peace and justice in the world." This will be especially challenging for you who do not have the help of an organized campus ministry program.

You have so many gifts to offer the Church: your faith, your desire to serve, your spiritual hunger, your vitality, your optimism and idealism, your talents and skills. We can all learn from you, so we ask you to expand your leadership role in witnessing to the Gospel on campus. We promise you our prayerful support and encourage your future involvement in the mission of the Church through a parish faith community. We look forward to working more closely with you to make the Church ever more effective in announcing the reign of God. We ask for your prayers for us in our work of shepherding the Church.

Source: Washington, D.C.: United States Catholic Conference, 1996.

Critical Decisions: Genetic Testing and Its Implications

A Statement of the NCCB Committee on Science and Human Values
Approved by the Administrative Committee

March 1996

- Mrs. Smith undergoes prenatal testing and discovers that her unborn child has a large defect in the closure of the brain or spinal cord.
- Optimum Insurance asks all applicants for individual health care policies to undergo testing for the gene that predisposes to hypertension.
- Optimum Airlines alerts its employees that testing for sickle-cell trait is now available.
- Optimum Pharmaceuticals develops a therapy for depression and offers a test to detect the relevant genetic profile.
- The Supreme Court allows testing to identify those at increased risk for Alzheimer's disease, on the grounds that people have a right to this information in planning their future.
- The state of Maryland denies a marriage license to two people with mild mental retardation; testing shows they may pass severe retardation to their children, raising health care costs.

These situations, though fictional, are not fanciful. Several are present reality, and the rest could happen in a decade or two. Genetic testing—and genetic counseling on how to deal with the results of tests—will certainly grow at a rapid rate, creating a burgeoning challenge for pastors and Catholic health care providers. Obviously, the Church cannot offer a credible opinion on the quality or reliability of these tests; that is the province of the scientific and medical communities. However, genetic testing raises and will continue to raise moral issues for the individual, for the family, for racial or ethnic groups, and for society as a whole. The Church has a responsibility to offer insights based on its venerable tradition and current experience, not only to inform consciences and assist in the formation of wise public policy, but also to keep tradition vital.

Most often genetic tests show no disease, relieving anxiety. Moreover, the Catholic Church welcomes testing when it functions as an extension of sound medical practice. Catholics have served the sick for many centuries, and the Church is one of the major providers of health care in the world; naturally, it applauds every medical advance that promises healing without violating moral law. Pope John Paul II told the World Medical Association in 1983:

> A strictly therapeutic intervention whose explicit objective is the healing of various maladies such as those stemming from chromosomal defects will, in principle, be considered desirable, provided it is directed to the true promotion of the personal well-being of the individual. . . . Such an intervention would indeed fall within the logic of the Christian moral tradition.

Genetic testing can assist sound decision-making in a wide range of situations. It is most commonly employed to detect problems with newborns. Moreover, millions of Americans are hospitalized every year because of hereditary disease and congenital defects. To the extent that genetic testing sets the stage for a cure or effective therapy, it is a blessing.

Testing has legitimate uses even in the delicate arena of human reproduction. Young couples considering marriage may want to know whether one or both partners carry a gene associated with mental retardation, cystic fibrosis, breast cancer, or some other heritable condition. While such testing carries risk, it can be considered an act of prudence, whether the couple subsequently decides to marry or not.

More and more frequently, expectant mothers are undergoing amniocentesis, chorionic villus sampling, and other tests to detect genetic anomalies in their unborn children. The most detailed Catholic teaching on this and related subjects appears in a 1987 statement from the Vatican Congregation for the Doctrine of the Faith called *The Gift of Life (Donum Vitae)*. It asks: "Is prenatal diagnosis morally licit? If prenatal diagnosis respects the life and integrity of the embryo and the human fetus and is directed toward its safeguarding or healing as an individual, then the answer is affirmative."[1] The Holy Father builds on this declaration in his recent encyclical *The Gospel of Life (Evangelium Vitae)*, holding that prenatal diagnostic techniques are morally permissible "when they do not involve disproportionate risks for the child and the mother, and are meant to make possible early therapy or even to favor a serene and informed acceptance of the child not yet born."[2]

However, some prenatal testing poses significant risks to the unborn child, especially when performed on embryos before selection for implantation in the womb. Disturbing test results can also tempt individuals to make decisions not in accord with sound morality. The Holy Father goes on to note:

> But since the possibilities of prenatal therapy are today still
> limited, it not infrequently happens that these techniques
> are used with a eugenic intention which accepts selective
> abortion in order to prevent the birth of children affected by
> various types of anomalies. Such an attitude is shameful and
> utterly reprehensible, since it presumes to measure the
> value of a human life only within the parameters of "nor-
> mality" and physical well-being, thus opening the way to
> legitimizing infanticide and euthanasia.[3]

The Church condemns and will never cease condemning the taking of innocent unborn life, surely the saddest aggression of our violent time.

Other uses of genetic testing, though perhaps not clearly sinful,
invite serious moral reflection. Current therapies, by and large,
manipulate a single gene or gene product. Science has not identified
the multiple genes that may help determine high intelligence, a strong
heart, immunity to cancer, a sunny personality, forcefulness of character, or other complex traits. Within ten years or less, however, the
Human Genome Initiative will have decoded the physical structure of
all 100,000 of our genes. Decades, perhaps centuries, of research and
experiment may be needed to develop sophisticated technology from
this data. Even then, some traits may turn out to have no significant
genetic component, while others may spring from so complex a combination of genes, environment, and experience that they remain
beyond the reach of empirical analysis.

Nevertheless, the rate of discovery for genes that cause disease or
influence physical and mental traits is accelerating rapidly. Within one
or two generations, human beings may be able both to change significantly an individual's genetic makeup through somatic cell therapy
and to affect heredity through germline therapy. As time passes, we
will learn more about our amazing diversity and our uniqueness.
Unfortunately, we will also have the capacity to make finer distinctions among people and to discriminate accordingly. A predisposition
to colon cancer is already detectable. If someone tests positive, should
this information be available to insurance companies, whose financial
success depends on minimizing risk? Potential employers? Potential
marriage partners? What if the existence of a gene predisposing to
homosexuality is confirmed? Who should have access to test results?
These simple examples illustrate the enormous potential for abuse.

The Church's knowledge of the human heart springs from 2,000
years of moral reflection based ultimately on divine revelation.
However, Catholic theology and the Catholic moral tradition mostly
predate the development of genetic technologies, which offer new
challenges. In an address to the Pontifical Academy for Life in
November 1995, Pope John Paul II said:

> Indeed, the biomedical sciences are currently experiencing a period of rapid and marvelous growth, especially with regard to new discoveries in the areas of genetics. . . . But if scientific research is to be directed toward respect for personal dignity and support of human life, its scientific validity according to the rules of each discipline is not enough. It must also qualify positively from the ethical point of view, and this presupposes that from the outset it endeavors to promote the true good of human beings as individuals and as a community. This happens when efforts are made to eliminate the causes of disease by putting real prevention into practice, or whenever more effective therapies are sought for the treatment of serious illnesses.

Clearly, the scientific community cannot shoulder the whole burden of bringing ethics to bear. Catholic clergy and laity must become knowledgeable about emerging biotechnologies if they are to help people make the critical decisions they will inevitably face. Both the Church and the scientific community, we believe, can benefit from the effort to harmonize scientific advance with religious insight. Genetic testing is an important tool, but many will suffer if wisdom and sound morality do not guide its use.

Notes

1. Congregation for the Doctrine of the Faith, *Instruction on Respect for Human Life in Its Origin and on the Dignity of Procreation: Replies to Certain Questions of the Day (Donum Vitae)* (Washington, D.C.: United States Catholic Conference, 1987), sec. 1, no. 2.
2. John Paul II, *The Gospel of Life (Evangelium Vitae)* (Washington, D.C.: United States Catholic Conference, 1995), no. 63.
3. Ibid.

Source: Washington, D.C.: United States Catholic Conference, 1996.

Reflection on "The Truth and Meaning of Human Sexuality"

A Letter of Bishop Robert Banks and Bishop Joseph Charron
Approved by the USCC Administrative Board

March 1996

The Truth and Meaning of Human Sexuality: Guidelines for Education Within the Family issued by the Pontifical Council for the Family serves only to enhance and not undermine the 1990 National Conference of Catholic Bishops/U.S. Catholic Conference document *Human Sexuality: A Catholic Perspective for Education and Lifelong Learning.* We wish to address in this brief analysis the complementarity of both documents, focusing on the role of the Church, school, and religious education programs vis-à-vis parental rights and obligations.

When *Human Sexuality* was published by the U.S. bishops, it was in response to the Congregation for Catholic Education's document *Educational Guidance in Human Love,* which requested that "these guidelines, therefore, should be adapted by the respective episcopates to the pastoral necessities of each local Church."[1] This 1983 Vatican document concludes:

> The Congregation for Catholic Education turns to episcopal conferences so that they promote the union of parents, of Christian communities and of educators for convergent action in such an important sector for the future of young people and the good of society. The congregation makes this invitation to assume this educational commitment in reciprocal trust and with the highest regard for rights and specific competencies, with a complete Christian formation in view.[2]

Thus, drawing on a variety of Vatican and NCCB/USCC sources, especially the Congregation for Catholic Education's *Educational Guidance in Human Love* (1983), Pope John Paul's *Familiaris Consortio* (1981), the Congregation for the Doctrine of the Faith's *Declaration on Certain Questions Concerning Sexual Ethics* (1975), Vatican II's Declaration on Christian Education (1965), and the conference's *Sharing the Light of Faith,* the U.S. bishops in this country wrote their document "to guide our diocesan leaders in their service to parents, parishes, and other church-related institutions as they design and implement programs of formal instruction in human sexuality from a Catholic perspective."[3] While clearly affirming the Catholic educational tradition that parents have the primary responsibility of educating their children in matters of human sexuality, as in all things, *Human Sexuality* notes that:

> Others, however, play vital auxiliary roles in the process by which children and adolescents come to understand their sexuality and its expression. Here, we seek a delicate balance between seeing the proper education of our Catholic young people as primarily and ultimately the responsibility of one's parents.[4]

This approach, which sees the Church, schools, and religious education programs as assisting, complementing, and supporting parents in the education of their children, now finds further expression and clarification in the Pontifical Council for the Family's recent contribution.

The two documents *Human Sexuality* and *The Truth and Meaning of Human Sexuality* complement one another and affirm both the gift of human sexuality and role of the parent as primary educator. The two documents differ somewhat in tone and in audience focus. While *Human Sexuality* is addressed to diocesan leaders and lays out general principles, the pontifical council's document is written primarily to parents and centers on the problems that can and have arisen in this area. In doing so, the pontifical council provides some welcome warnings in regards to the dual problems of sexually permissive cultures and of poorly done, values-neutral, overly explicit sex education programs. The Pontifical Council for the Family sounds a clarion call for parents not to shirk their God-given responsibility to educate their own children in matters of love and sexuality as well as to be vigilant concerning school-based or institutional programs designed to assist them in this task.

Previously *Human Sexuality* stated:

> Diocesan leaders are encouraged to assist parents whose children are enrolled in school to become actively involved in the formation, implementation, and evaluation of programs for education in human sexuality. Exercising their role as parents, they need the support and assistance of the Church as they work to ensure that schools respect the values of the family and their faith tradition.[5]

The strong warnings of the pontifical council can be misunderstood or misinterpreted as condemning all institutional programs. While the pontifical council cautions against poorly done sexuality instruction and while it rightly defends both the innocence and modesty of children, it would be incorrect to interpret this document as opposed to well-done Catholic-based sexuality education programs or as a negation of the orthodox efforts of the Vatican's Congregation for Catholic Education and the NCCB/USCC. "Other educators can assist [parents] in this task, but they can only take the place of parents for serious reasons of physical or moral incapacity."[6] It further states:

> For parents by themselves are not capable of satisfying every requirement of the whole process of raising children, especially in matters concerning their schooling and the entire gamut of socialization. Subsidiarity thus complements paternal and maternal love and confirms its fundamental nature, inasmuch as all other participants in the process of education are only able to carry out their responsibilities in the name of the parents, with their consent and, to a certain degree, with their authorization.[7]

The Truth and Meaning of Human Sexuality raises rightful cautions concerning parental responsibility as well as respect for the innocence and modesty of children and is a welcome guidance to the Church in this challenging area. It is important to underscore that the document from the pontifical council does not lend support to those categorically opposed to church or school assistance in sexuality education. *The Truth and Meaning of Human Sexuality* does not contradict or negate the core doctrinal and religious education content of Human Sexuality, but only enhances it.

Notes

1. Congregation for Catholic Education, *Educational Guidance in Human Love* (Washington, D.C.: United States Catholic Conference, 1983), no. 3.
2. Ibid., no. 111.
3. Pontifical Council for the Family, *The Truth and Meaning of Human Sexuality: Guidelines for Education Within the Family* (Washington, D.C.: United States Catholic Conference, 1996), no. 2.
4. Ibid., no. 3.
5. Ibid., no. 76.
6. Ibid., no. 23.
7. Ibid.

Source: *Origins* 26:5 (June 20, 1996): 78-79.

Statement on Partial-Birth Abortion Ban Veto

A Statement of Bishop Anthony Pilla, NCCB/USCC President,
Issued with the Concurrence of the U.S. Bishops

June 1996

Just over a year ago, Pope John Paul II urged Catholics and all people of goodwill to stand up for human life. With an unmistakable note of urgency, he spoke of a growing "culture of death." This culture, he warned, claims to advance human freedom but "ends up by becoming the freedom of 'the strong' against the weak, who have no choice but to submit."

Was the pope unduly pessimistic in assessing our society at the end of the twentieth century? On the contrary, events of the past few months have shown how accurate he was.

Two federal courts ruled this year to exclude seriously ill people from the protection of laws against assisted suicide. Such people, the courts said, have a "right" to receive lethal drugs from their physicians so they can kill themselves. Such rulings devalue the lives of people most in need of compassion and care. We must do all we can to help bring about their reversal.

During this same period, the president of the United States has acted to extend the logic of our Supreme Court's gravely erroneous abortion decisions. He contends that the U.S. Constitution forbids any meaningful legal protection for children who are almost completely born alive and indeed that it should forbid such protection. The president is defending partial-birth abortion, a particularly heinous and violent way of killing an infant during the process of birth.

Congress voted to stop this shameful practice. However, because the president vetoed the bill, partial-birth abortion—more truly seen as a form of infanticide—continues in our country. We urge the Congress of the United States to override the president's veto of the Partial-Birth Abortion Ban Act.

Catholic parishes across the nation have begun to provide parishioners with information about partial-birth abortion. We will encourage Catholics and other people of goodwill to urge their senators and representatives to override the president's veto.

On July 11, Churches nationwide will conduct a day of prayer and fasting for life. We will pray that our country rejects partial-birth abortion. We will pray that the lives of all may be respected, protected, and nurtured—including the lives of innocent unborn children and those now threatened in the final stages of life. It will be our prayer that the culture of death be transformed by a culture of life, by a civilization of love.

We are not unaware of or indifferent to the serious challenges that confront women with difficult pregnancies. Although we can never experience firsthand the hardships and pressures they may face, we hold out our hands and our hearts—with the support of the spiritual, social, medical, legal, and financial resources available to us—to help women facing a crisis due to pregnancy.

To those who have had abortions, we say with Pope John Paul: We are "aware of the many factors which may have influenced your decision" and do not doubt that it may have been "painful and even shattering." Without ever condoning abortion, which remains terribly wrong, we encourage women and men who have been involved in abortion not to give up hope. The Church continues to offer her healing ministry, which has helped many thousands of women, men, and families to deal with the aftermath of abortion.

We also admire and support the many women who, facing what may seem insurmountable difficulties, nonetheless decide to give their children the one gift no one else can give—the gift of life.

We urge Catholics and others to study and discuss these pressing issues of life and death, and to stand up for life. At the same time, we know that the final outcome of this struggle lies in the hands of an infinitely loving God. As Pope John Paul II reminds us: "There is certainly an enormous disparity between the powerful resources available to the forces promoting the 'culture of death' and the means at the disposal of those working for a 'culture of life and love.' But we know that we can rely on the help of God, for whom nothing is impossible."[1]

Note

1.   John Paul II, *The Gospel of Life (Evangelium Vitae)* (Washington, D.C.: United States Catholic Conference, 1995), no. 100.

Source: *Origins* 26:7 (July 4, 1996): 110.

Moral Principles Concerning Infants with Anencephaly

A Statement of the NCCB Committee on Doctrine
Approved by the Administrative Committee

September 1996

Anencephaly is a congenital anomaly characterized by failure of development of the cerebral hemispheres and overlying skull and scalp, exposing the brain stem. This condition exists in varying degrees of severity. Most infants who have anencephaly do not survive for more than a few days after birth. Modern medical techniques usually can determine this condition with a high degree of certainty before birth. When anencephaly is detected, some physicians recommend that the pregnancy be terminated in order to free the mother from the psychological anxiety and possible physical complications throughout the remainder of the pregnancy.

According to the well-established teaching of the Catholic Church, the rights of a mother and her unborn child deserve equal protection because they are based on the dignity of the human person whatever the condition of that person. Consequently, it can never be morally justified directly to cause the death of an innocent person no matter the age or condition of that person.

Some have attempted to argue that anencephalic children may be prematurely delivered, even when this would be inappropriate for other children. This argument is based on the opinion that because of their apparent lack of cognitive function and in view of the probable brevity of their lives, these infants are not the subject of human rights or at least have lives of less meaning or purpose than others. Doubts about the human dignity of the anencephalic infant, however, have no solid ground, and the benefit of any doubt must be in the child's favor. As a general rule, conditions of the human body, regardless of severity, in no way compromise human dignity or human rights.

The *Ethical and Religious Directives for Catholic Health Care Services*, directive 45, states:

> Abortion (that is, the directly intended termination of pregnancy before viability or the directly intended destruction of a viable fetus) is never permitted. Every procedure whose sole immediate effect is the termination of pregnancy before viability is an abortion, which, in its moral context, includes

the interval between conception and implantation of the embryo.

The phrase *sole immediate effect* is further explained by directive 47 which states:

> Operations, treatments, and medications that have as their direct purpose the cure of a proportionately serious patholog- ical condition of a pregnant woman are permitted when they cannot be safely postponed until the unborn child is viable, even if they will result in the death of the unborn child.

In other words, it is permitted to treat directly a pathology of the mother even when this has the unintended side effect of causing the death of her child, if this pathology left untreated would have life-threatening effects on both mother and child, but it is not permitted to terminate or gravely risk the child's life as a *means* of treating or protecting the mother.

Hence, it is clear that before "viability" it is never permitted to terminate the gestation of an anencephalic child as the "means" of avoiding psychological or physical risks to the mother. Nor is such termination permitted after "viability" if early delivery endangers the child's life due to complications of prematurity. In such cases it cannot reasonably be maintained that such a termination is simply a side effect of the treatment of a pathology of the mother.[1] Anencephaly is not a pathology of the mother, but of the child, and terminating her pregnancy cannot be a treatment of a pathology she does not have. Only if the complications of the pregnancy result in a life-threatening pathology of the mother may the treatment of this pathology be permitted even at a risk to the child, and then only if the child's death is not a means to treating the mother.

The fact that the life of a child suffering from anencephaly will probably be brief cannot excuse directly causing death before "viability" or gravely endangering the child's life after "viability" as a result of the complications of prematurity.

The anencephalic child, during his or her probably brief life after birth, should be given the comfort and palliative care appropriate to all the dying. This failing life need not be further troubled by using extraordinary means to prolong it.[2] It is most commendable for parents to wish to donate the organs of an anencephalic child for transplants that may assist other children, but this may never be permitted before the donor child is certainly dead.

The profound and personal suffering of the parents of an anencephalic child gives us cause for concern and calls for compassionate pastoral and medical care as the parents prepare for the pain and emptiness that the certain death of their newborn child will bring. The mother who carries to term a child who will soon die deserves our every possible support. The baptism of the child assures the parents of the child's eternal happiness, and the provision of Christian burial of the deceased infant gives witness to the Church's unconditional respect for human life and the recognition that in the face of every human being is an encounter with God.

Notes

1. This is described in directive 47 of National Conference of Catholic Bishops, *Ethical and Religious Directives for Catholic Health Care Services* (Washington, D.C.: United States Catholic Conference, 1995).
2. See *Ethical and Religious Directives,* directives 57 and 58.

Source: *Origins* 26:17 (October 10, 1996): 276.

A Catholic Framework for Economic Life

A Statement of the U.S. Catholic Bishops

November 1996

As followers of Jesus Christ and participants in a powerful economy, Catholics in the United States are called to work for greater economic justice in the face of persistent poverty, growing income gaps, and increasing discussion of economic issues in the United States and around the world. We urge Catholics to use the following ethical framework for economic life as principles for reflection, criteria for judgment, and directions for action. These principles are drawn directly from Catholic teaching on economic life:

1. The economy exists for the person, not the person for the economy.
2. All economic life should be shaped by moral principles. Economic choices and institutions must be judged by how they protect or undermine the life and dignity of the human person, support the family, and serve the common good.
3. A fundamental moral measure of any economy is how the poor and vulnerable are faring.
4. All people have a right to life and to secure the basic necessities of life (e.g., food, clothing, shelter, education, health care, safe environment, economic security).
5. All people have the right to economic initiative, to productive work, to just wages and benefits, to decent working conditions, as well as to organize and join unions or other associations.
6. All people, to the extent they are able, have a corresponding duty to work, a responsibility to provide for the needs of their families, and an obligation to contribute to the broader society.
7. In economic life, free markets have both clear advantages and limits; government has essential responsibilities and limitations; voluntary groups have irreplaceable roles, but cannot substitute for the proper working of the market and the just policies of the state.
8. Society has a moral obligation, including governmental action where necessary, to assure opportunity, meet basic human needs, and pursue justice in economic life.

9. Workers, owners, managers, stockholders, and consumers are moral agents in economic life. By our choices, initiative, creativity, and investment, we enhance or diminish economic opportunity, community life, and social justice.
10. The global economy has moral dimensions and human consequences. Decisions on investment, trade, aid, and development should protect human life and promote human rights, especially for those most in need wherever they might live on this globe.

According to Pope John Paul II, the Catholic tradition calls for a "society of work, enterprise and participation" which "is not directed against the market, but demands that the market be appropriately controlled by the forces of society and by the state to assure that the basic needs of the whole society are satisfied."[1] All of economic life should recognize the fact that we are all God's children and members of one human family, called to exercise a clear priority for "the least among us."

The sources for this framework include the *Catechism of the Catholic Church*, recent papal encyclicals, the pastoral letter *Economic Justice for All*, and other statements of the U.S. Catholic bishops. They reflect the Church's teaching on the dignity, rights, and duties of the human person; the option for the poor; the common good; subsidiarity and solidarity.

Note

1. John Paul II, *On the Hundredth Anniversary of Rerum Novarum (Centesimus Annus)* (Washington, D.C.: United States Catholic Conference, 1991), no. 35.

Source: Washington, D.C.: United States Catholic Conference, 1996.

The Bishop's Pastoral Role in Catholic Health Care Ministry

A Statement of the NCCB Administrative Committee

March 1997

Catholic health care participates in the apostolic activity of the local church because it is an expression of the healing ministry of Christ. Speaking to Catholic health care officials during his 1987 visit to the United States, Pope John Paul II said, "Your health care ministry . . . is one of the most vital apostolates of the ecclesial community and one of the most significant services which the Catholic Church offers to society in the name of Jesus Christ."[1] The Church enjoys a grace-filled tradition in the provision of quality health care in the United States.

The Gospel Context of Health Care

The Catholic Church is involved in health care because it believes that care of the sick is an important part of Christ's mandate of service. The gospel accounts of Jesus' ministry chronicle his acts of healing. The Gospels are filled with examples of Jesus curing many kinds of ailment and illness. In one account, our Lord's mission is described as the fulfillment of the prophecy of Isaiah, "He took away our infirmities and bore our diseases" (Mt 8:17; cf. Is 53:4).

Since the principal work of Christ was our redemption from sin and death, the healing that he brought us went beyond caring only for physical afflictions. His compassion for the poor, the sick, and the needy fit within his larger mission of redemption and salvation. Christ touched people at the deepest level of their being. As the source of physical, mental, and spiritual healing and well-being, he described his work as bringing life in abundance.

Christians see care for the sick and maintenance of health within the context of Christ's example. Hence, to understand the significant role of the Catholic Church in health care throughout the centuries, one needs to look at the faith of those who have attempted to imitate the love, compassion, and healing of Jesus. It is nothing less than Christian love that animates health care within the Church. The work of healing and the acts of compassion that envelop it are seen as a continuation of Christ's mission that is enabled by his lifegiving grace. It is out of this context of faith, hope, and love that the Catholic health care ministry came into existence.

Historically, religious communities of women have taken the lead in this country in the development of Catholic health care ministry. While there are many health care organizations sponsored by individual dioceses, religious communities of men, or other associations of the faithful, the vast majority of Catholic health institutions are sponsored and directed by communities of women religious who have made this ministry an integral part of their religious apostolate. In diocesan churches all over this country, health care ministry has been initiated and continues to be nurtured and sustained by the commitment in faith of women religious. Their efforts have resulted in an extraordinary array of health care organizations that reflect and embody the care of the Church and the love of Christ for the sick.

Challenges and Opportunities

The Catholic health care ministry in the United States stands at a critical moment in its history. Some of the changes contributing to this critical moment are the fact that the delivery of health care is not as frequently centered in the hospital; the development of integrated delivery networks; the shift of risk from insurers to providers through managed care and capitation; the increase in institutional partnerships; and staff reductions in order to achieve cost savings.

How Catholic health care organizations can best be structured to respond to these developments and to future needs is the challenge of the moment. Regularly, market pressures drive Catholic health sponsors and other leaders to reassess and even significantly to restructure their organizations in an effort to remain a part—an important part—of today's health care delivery.

This is not only a time of challenge but also a moment of opportunity for Catholic health care. In the words of a recent resource document of our Ad Hoc Committee on Health Care Issues and the Church, "The Responsibility of the Diocesan Bishop for Strengthening the Health Ministry" (1996), as diocesan bishops we should embrace the opportunity to "initiate and coordinate cooperation among acute-care facilities, nursing, rehabilitation and long-term services, health clinics, Catholic Charities, social service agencies, parishes, schools and religious education programs."

Responsibility of the Bishop

Catholic health care, as an expression of the healing ministry of Jesus Christ, participates as an ecclesial ministry in the apostolic mission of the Church in the same way that other ministries do. The varied and complex structures that are employed to deliver such ministry are a special concern of the religious institutes, sponsors, boards, and other leaders who conduct this corporate ministry. But this ministry necessarily also involves the diocesan bishop, who has a responsibility for the local church and the exercise of all ministry within it. The bishop has the right to exercise his authority over all apostolates in his diocese, including that of health care, in accordance with the code of canon law and any particular law that he may legitimately enact. Sponsors of apostolates, including health care facilities, must give due recognition to the lawful authority and role of the bishop. This is the teaching of the Second Vatican Council and the universal law of the Church.[2]

There are a variety of ways in which the pastoral role of the diocesan bishop can be expressed in health care ministry. The bishop, as principal teacher, elicits openness and receptivity to the splendor of truth by proclaiming the Church's teaching and by ensuring the moral and doctrinal integrity of Catholic health care.[3] As sanctifier, the bishop exercises his ministry by ensuring the celebration of the sacraments for the sick in health care settings throughout the diocese and in the parishes.[4] The bishop as pastor governs the particular church in ways that seek appropriately to coordinate the healing ministries in the interest of the common good.[5]

In the area of pastoral governance, the bishop's responsibilities vary according to the canonical status of the health care organization, the canonical status of the sponsor, and the canonical issues involved. In regard to all Catholic institutions within the diocese, it is the bishop's responsibility to ensure doctrinal and moral integrity in the witness and practice of each institution. It is the responsibility of the diocesan bishop, in cooperation with religious and other sponsors and all involved in the ministry of health care, to ensure that the Catholic identity of all health organizations is maintained and strengthened. It is also the diocesan bishop's responsibility to coordinate all apostolic activity within the diocese, with due regard, however, for the particular character of each apostolate,[6] thereby fostering and promoting that unity in diversity which characterizes true ecclesial communion.

Recent developments in health care delivery, particularly those which involve substantial modifications in the canonical or corporate status of a Catholic health care organization, often give rise to questions concerning the applicability of church laws governing the administration of temporal goods; the alienation of church property; the fulfillment of the intentions of founders, benefactors, and donors; and effective control of a Catholic health care organization. The diocesan bishop, sponsors, and other leaders must assess the applicability of such laws and evaluate proposed arrangements in the light of Catholic identity and the relevant laws of the Church. Dialogue in such matters is most fruitful and should occur at the earliest stages of considering any venture, affiliation, or relationship that has the potential substantially to affect the mission, Catholic identity, or canonical or corporate status of a Catholic health care organization.

Fostering Collaboration

Collaboration among all involved in the Catholic health care ministry, including Catholic social agencies such as Catholic Charities, is essential because bishops, sponsors, and other leaders approach the ministry from complementary perspectives which result from various levels of their involvement in the ministry and their differing responsibilities for the apostolates in the local church. The diocesan bishop is in a unique position to foster this collaboration and has a canonical duty to do so. As the recent ad hoc committee statement, "The Responsibility of the Diocesan Bishop for Strengthening the Health Ministry," asserted in its opening paragraph:

> Throughout Catholic health care ministry today, there is a renewed commitment to cooperation and collaboration among bishops, sponsors, and health care leaders. They are seizing the moment to pool the immense spiritual and material resources invested in this ministry in order to ensure its future viability and effectiveness. Indeed, recent developments—especially the new covenant initiatives which have brought together bishops, sponsors, and leaders in an unprecedented effort to encourage greater collaboration among Catholic health care providers on a national level— have created a particularly auspicious environment for the exercise of episcopal leadership in this area.

The leadership of the diocesan bishop is best exercised in collaboration with sponsors and other leaders who have devoted their energies to the health care ministry with exemplary consistency and vigor and who, together with the bishop, seek to ensure the continuance of this vital ministry in a rapidly changing environment.

The religious superiors, sponsors, and other leaders of our Catholic health care systems have initiated a series of creative ventures in response to developments in the national health care industry that have a direct impact on the institutional provision of Catholic health care in the United States. In exercising their pastoral role in the Catholic health care ministry, diocesan bishops are encouraged to invite religious sponsors and other leaders to join in the effort to support and stimulate initiatives that will preserve and extend the health care ministry and ensure its Catholic identity. An important initiative, designed to foster this collaboration, is the National Coalition on Catholic Health Care Ministry, which brings together representatives of the bishops, sponsors, and other health care leadership to develop a common vision for Catholic health care in the United States.

Practical Issues of Collaboration and Coordination

Given the complexity of the new developments in the health care field that need to be addressed and the intersecting competencies that need to be respected, the effective exercise of the diocesan bishop's pastoral responsibility in the health care ministry presupposes communication and dialogue among all those involved in the ministry. Such an approach will both strengthen the Catholic presence in health care as well as contribute to the ecclesial communion of the local church.

The apostolic activity of religious institutes in particular reflects an important element of this communion.[7] The *Code of Canon Law* provides direction for the relation of the diocesan bishop and religious superiors in the coordination of such apostolic activity: "Religious are subject to the authority of bishops, whom they are obliged to follow with devoted humility and respect, in those matters which involve the care of souls, the public exercise of divine worship and other works of the apostolate."[8] At the same time, "in exercising an external apostolate, religious are also subject to their own superiors and must remain faithful to the discipline of the institute, which obligation bishops themselves should not fail to insist upon in cases which warrant it."[9] For this reason, in coordinating "the works of the apostolate of religious, it is necessary that diocesan bishops and religious superiors proceed after consultation with each other."[10]

The diocesan bishop's responsibility encompasses not only the health care apostolates conducted by religious of diocesan and pontifical right but also those initiated and conducted by the Catholic laity as well. Thus the diocesan bishop can foster the kind of collaboration among these apostolates that will strengthen the health care ministry overall and guarantee that they are conducted in accord with the moral teaching of the Church. In this way the diocesan bishop will fulfill his responsibility to be vigilant about the Catholic identity of any individual or group operating within his diocese.

In order to provide a common basis for collaboration and dialogue, the diocesan bishop and his staff should strive to become informed about the complexities of the current health care environment, while sponsors, administrators, and board members need to develop a fundamental grasp of the doctrinal, pastoral, and canonical principles that have a bearing on Catholic health care delivery.

An important subject for dialogue among bishops, sponsors, and other leaders is, as the *Ethical and Religious Directives for Catholic Health Care Services* state, the assessment of partnerships "that will affect the mission or religious and ethical identity of Catholic health care institutional services."[11] Sponsors and other leaders make an important contribution to the diocesan bishop's exercise of this responsibility by providing adequate and timely information about developing partnerships. As directive 68 of the ethical and religious directives goes on to affirm, "Diocesan bishops and other church authorities should be involved when such partnerships are developed, and the diocesan bishop should give the appropriate authorization before they are completed."

The bishop, sponsors, and other leaders of Catholic health care should give the highest priority to ventures, alliances, mergers, or other associations among Catholic health ministry organizations within the diocese or in conjunction with other dioceses. Such collaboration could serve to protect and strengthen the individual and collective well-being of the ministry as well as contribute to the fuller realization of ecclesial communion. When collaboration with other than Catholic providers is considered necessary or opportune for sustaining and enhancing the ministry, the bishop should be consulted and, when necessary, appropriate approval should be obtained according to the principles of canon law.

In today's national health care market, where collaboration is often seen as essential to vitality and survival, cooperative arrangements often transcend diocesan territorial boundaries. The needed dialogue will often have to draw together bishops, sponsors, and other leaders from across diocesan and state boundaries. In pursuit of the common good, it is desirable for diocesan bishops, in consultation with sponsors and other leaders, especially in neighboring dioceses or where local health care organizations belong to systems that cross diocesan boundaries, to strive to cooperate in fostering consistent diocesan policies in their supervision of the health care apostolates of their dioceses, insofar as this is possible. Consultation and collaboration by diocesan bishops at the provincial and regional levels would improve chances for success among new ventures in the apostolate. Contrary or contradictory policies among neighboring bishops can mislead people and do a disservice to the ministry of the whole Church. On the other hand, when two or more particular churches unite in a common effort, they witness to the catholicity of the whole Church.[12]

Diocesan Guidelines and Procedures

Particular diocesan guidelines or procedures, often called diocesan protocols, developed in dialogue with religious sponsors, other health care leaders, and with consultants possessing the requisite legal, canonical, and theological expertise, would be helpful to evaluate new forms of health ministry. Procedures should be in place to ensure that there will be a consistent approach to the challenges and opportunities posed by the current health care environment. The form such procedures or guidelines take will vary depending on several factors, among them the size of the diocese, the diversity of sponsoring bodies, the level of the Church's involvement in health care provision in the local area, and the extent to which multistate and multidiocesan interests converge in the provision of this health care. Normally, such procedures would provide guidance for a generally consistent approach to the variety of circumstances that might arise as new collaborative arrangements affecting the Catholic identity of the providers in question are pursued and developed.

Such guidelines or procedures—designed to meet local circumstances and respect legitimate local competencies and interests—may be seen as further specifying the general direction provided by Part VI of the ethical and religious directives in this area. In this way bishops, sponsors, and other leaders can pursue together their common objective of ensuring the future of the Catholic health care ministry by fostering the thorough review of proposed affiliations, partnerships, mergers, ventures, and any other relationships that affect the Catholic identity and institutional integrity of the health care provider as well as the Catholic presence in the health care field.[13]

Conclusion

As Catholic bishops, we seek to exercise our pastoral leadership in an ever-changing health care environment. Already in many parts of the country on a regional or local level dialogues are underway to enhance the capacities of bishops, sponsors, administrators, and board members to exercise their distinctive roles of leadership in sustaining and revitalizing the health care ministry of the Church. Following the first new covenant national gathering under the auspices of the National Coalition on Catholic Health Care Ministry, the Catholic Health Association and Consolidated Catholic Health Care local gatherings have provided forums for all the involved parties to come together and from various perspectives to address a plan for future ministry in the Church. Such forums should help to create an atmosphere of mutual understanding and fruitful collaboration in which creative initiatives can emerge to meet the needs of our communities.

This call for the exercise of the bishop's pastoral office is issued to make this collaboration more effective. Out of such cooperation and with the pastoral direction of the diocesan bishop, Catholic health care organizations will continue to manifest the teaching and love of Christ through their caring ministry that serves the whole person—body, mind, and spirit—embracing that person with all of the compassion and love which says to the sick, the infirm, and all those in need of health care, "As Christ would reach out to touch and heal you, so too do we."

Notes

1. "Health Care: Ministry in Transition," *Origins* 17:17 (October 8, 1987): 292.
2. See, for example, Second Vatican Council, *Dogmatic Constitution on the Church (Lumen Gentium)*, no. 20; *Decree on the Pastoral Office of Bishops in the Church (Christus Dominus)*, no. 11; and canons 394.1, 216, 223.2, 375, 381.1, 391.1, 392, 678, and 680.
3. *Lumen Gentium,* no. 23; canons 753, 756; see also John Paul II, *The Splendor of Truth (Veritatis Splendor)* (Washington, D.C.: United States Catholic Conference, 1993), no. 4.
4. Second Vatican Council, *Constitution on the Sacred Liturgy (Sacrosanctum Concilium)*, no. 22; canons 835, 771.1.
5. Canons 394.1, 223.2.
6. Canon 394.1.
7. *Lumen Gentium,* no. 44; *Christus Dominus,* no. 35; canons 675, 681.1; see also John Paul II, *The Consecrated Life (Vita Consecrata)* (Washington D.C.: United States Catholic Conference, 1996), nos. 48-49.
8. Canon 678.1.
9. Canon 678.2.
10. Canon 678.3.
11. National Conference of Catholic Bishops, *Ethical and Religious Directives for Catholic Health Care Services* (Washington, D.C.: United States Catholic Conference, 1995), directive 68.
12. *Lumen Gentium,* no. 23; *Christus Dominus,* no. 37.
13. *Ethical and Religious Directives,* Introduction.

Source: *Origins* 26:43 (April 17, 1997): 700-704.

Open Wide the Doors to Christ:
A Framework for Action to Implement
Tertio Millennio Adveniente

A Document of the NCCB Subcommittee on the Third Millennium

June 1997

Part One: Introduction

As the Third Millennium of the Redemption draws near, God is preparing a great springtime for Christianity, and we can already see its first signs.[1]

A Message from the NCCB Subcommittee on the Third Millennium

On December 24, 1999, on his way to celebrate midnight Mass, Pope John Paul II will open the Holy Year Door in St. Peter's Basilica and inaugurate the Great Jubilee of the Year 2000—a jubilee that commemorates the coming of Jesus Christ as a child in the womb of a young Jewish woman and his birth in Bethlehem two thousand years ago, which propelled world history in an irreversible forward direction; a jubilee that also prepares us to enter the next millennium of Christianity as a renewed people. Let us now prepare for this celebration of celebrations.

This preparation, which John Paul II invites us to undertake, is a three-year journey or pilgrimage towards the celebration of the Great Jubilee of the Year 2000 and the new millennium. It is an opportunity to deepen our spiritual lives and become holy people. As with any journey, it is important that we know the destination: *life with Jesus Christ.* This time is also an extended *Advent season,*[2] which begins with Vatican II[3] and leads us "to the threshold of the third millennium."[4] It is a season of self-examination, expectation, and intense prayer; a season of hope, rooted in the presence of the Holy Spirit.[5] During this time, we not only examine what changes need to be made but also celebrate the good already present in our Church and in our world though often hidden from our eyes.[6]

The guideposts for this spiritual journey are the papal exhortation *Tertio Millennio Adveniente,* the rich biblical tradition of "jubilee," and the renewed study and application of the teachings of the Second Vatican Council. We begin by proclaiming that *Jesus Christ is our Savior and Redeemer* and seeking to deepen our relationship with Jesus Christ, the fulfillment of jubilee (Lk 4:19). Secondly, we seek to examine our conscience in light of the Gospel and the teachings of the Church. This provides us an opportunity for repentance, forgiveness, and reconciliation—to enter the new millennium as a new people: a people who are healed by the love of Jesus Christ and strengthened by the power of the Holy Spirit. In Jesus Christ we see that the "joy of every jubilee is, above all, a joy based on the forgiveness of sins, the joy of conversion . . . the pre-condition for reconciliation with God on the part of both individuals and communities."[7]

This journey also calls us to pay attention to the care of future generations.[8] Throughout his pontificate, John Paul II has consistently called upon the Church to reach out to young people since "the future of the world and the Church belongs to the younger generation, to those who, born in this century, will reach maturity in the next, the first century of the millennium."[9] It is important that the adult community provide them with guidance and love. It is in this way that we "bring our Catholic tradition to life in the hearts, minds, and spirits of new generations."[10]

Therefore, let us view these last years of the twentieth century as an opportunity to reconfirm our faith, sustain our hope, and rekindle our charity.[11] It is our hope that this framework will provide you with some strategies for your journey to the Great Jubilee of the Year 2000, so that our crossing into the new millennium may truly be a new springtime of Christianity where we go forth and bear fruit (Jn 15:16).

> One generation praises your deeds to the next
>   and proclaims your mighty works.
> They speak of the splendor of your majestic glory,
>   tell of your wonderful deeds. (Ps 145:4-5)

Reasons to Celebrate the Jubilee Year 2000

As we draw near to the year 2000 there is growing discussion about the impact and meaning this time will have for us personally, as women and men of faith, and as a country. Some fear these years, believing that 2000 will usher in an end time—the second coming of Christ to establish one thousand years of Christ's rule before the end of time. Others view this time as an occasion for a party to celebrate the new millennium. Many Christians will commemorate the jubilee as a moment to remember and celebrate two thousand years of Christ's presence in human history. Others will find little significance in this passage of time—just another day or another year. Even within our own Church, many fear that initiatives being planned will bring additional tasks and programs to already burdened workloads and distract us from our true ministry.

We wish to say loudly and clearly that these years are meant to help people deepen their faith and strengthen their Christian witness[12] through personal and communal conversion. We also wish to say that the most effective way to prepare for the jubilee year is to weave the themes from *Tertio Millennio Adveniente* into the yearly rhythm of church life. Let these years be an opportunity to renew our spirits, strengthen our ministry, and further our evangelizing outreach, so our churches can be communities of salt and light. We begin by offering five compelling reasons why we should pay attention to this time in our history.

1. The Holy Father has invited us to do so. For John Paul II, the Great Jubilee of the Year 2000 is an extraordinary event in the life of the Church and the world. He asks us to "do as much as possible to ensure that the great challenge of the year 2000 is not overlooked, for this challenge certainly involves a special grace of the Lord for the Church and for the whole of humanity."[13] He invites us to prepare by listening carefully to what the Holy Spirit is saying to the Church, to the churches, and to individuals through different charisms.[14]

2. As a jubilee year, it is "a year of favor from the Lord"—an opportunity to begin anew. The "two thousand years which have passed since the birth of Christ (prescinding from the question of its precise chronology) represent an extraordinarily great jubilee, not only for Christians but indirectly for the whole of humanity."[15] We celebrate both Christ's birth two thousand years ago and the fact that Christ's Church "has endured for 2000 years. Like the mustard seed in the Gospel, the Church has grown and become a great tree, able to cover the whole of humanity with her branches (cf. Mt 13:31-32)."[16]

This Great Jubilee of the Year 2000 will be the first holy year that marks the turn of a millennium since the first was proclaimed by Pope Boniface VIII in 1300. A holy year is held to encourage holiness of life through repentance and conversion, works of charity, and participation in community (*www.vatican.va/jubilee_2000*). Today, in contemporary society, we especially sense a need for healing and reconciliation where we have the opportunity to begin anew and to acknowledge, as an act of honesty and courage, the weaknesses of our past. In this way our faith is strengthened, so we are able to face the present temptations and challenges and are prepared to give a more mature Christian response to the world.[17]

3. Since a new millennium only comes once every thousand years, it is a unique moment in history that calls for an engaging message of faith. One in every fifty generations experiences the change of a millennium. This opening the door into the third millennium is a unique moment in history. Pope John Paul II asks us to pay attention to this time when he says, "Humanity, upon reaching this goal (the twenty-first century), will leave behind not just a century but a millennium."[18] We urge you to discern the signs of the time that point out new challenges and new opportunities: "There is a need for a better appreciation and understanding of the signs of hope present in the last part of this century, even though they often remain hidden from our eyes."[19]

In order to take advantage of this "historical moment," we must preach and witness to the gospel message in ways that are clear, engaging, and appealing. The Church can provide leadership within society by calling all men and women to a deeper reflection on the meaning of life and a desire to work together for the common good. By renewing our commitment to Jesus Christ and the Church, we work to transform the communities in which we live: our family, our neighborhood, our workplaces, the civic community, and society in general.

4. *These years provide a special opportunity for evangelization.* If we believe these years to be a unique time in history, we must also believe that the "presence of the Holy Spirit will be more deeply experienced, impelling Christians to preach the Gospel with new power, giving hope of liberation to the marginalized and the oppressed."[20] Our witness must reflect love and zeal for the Gospel in our own lives. This task, to bring the good news of God's love and mercy into the world, is the work of all baptized women and men. It takes place in the everyday dynamics of life, especially in the family, in the workplace, in schools and universities, within our neighborhoods, and during moments of recreation and leisure. The eucharist, the source and summit of Christian life, strengthens us for this witness and nourishes our zeal for the Gospel.

5. *It can be a moment to re-energize ourselves and celebrate the good that is already present in our lives, our Church, and society.* Through its members, the Church does wonderful work throughout the world. There are many excellent examples of this, including initiatives such as small Christian communities and faith sharing groups; the catechumenate; the renewal of liturgical life; social action initiatives that work to feed the poor, care for the homeless, and advocate for the sanctity of life and for justice and peace; a renewed interest in spirituality; the participation of the laity, especially women, in many and varied roles in church and civic life; the formation of youth; and the continuing dialogue among Christians and with those of other faiths. Other examples include the richness in our diversity, the witness of faithful men and women in the workplace, and the wonderful sense of compassion and commitment present within so many people.

John Paul II calls us to once again embrace the spirit and teachings of Vatican II to strengthen Christian unity and deepen Catholic identity. As we prepare for the Great Jubilee of the Year 2000, our focus should not be triumphant but a desire to proclaim that in Jesus Christ God loves us and that Christ came for us.[21] Above all, the Great Jubilee of the Year 2000 is "a great prayer of praise and thanksgiving."[22]

> For I know well the plans I have in mind for you, says the Lord, plans for your welfare, not for woe! plans to give you a future full of hope. (Jer 29:11)

Part Two: A Vision for the Journey

"Open Wide the Doors to Christ"

The Holy Year Door of the jubilee of the year 2000 should be symbolically wider than those of previous jubilees, because humanity, upon reaching this goal, will leave behind not just a century but a millennium.[23]

Introduction

In their document *Called and Gifted for the Third Millennium*, the conference of bishops begin their reflection by asking the question, "What is the Spirit saying to the world today through the Church in the United States, particularly through the lives of lay men and women?" Today, we wish to echo this question by asking: "What is the Spirit saying to us today as we approach this unique historical time, this *kairos* moment, of the Great Jubilee of the Year 2000 and the crossing into the third millennium?"

Pope John Paul II, in the beginning of his apostolic exhortation *Tertio Millennio Adveniente*, provides a first glimpse to the answer. He says, "As the third millennium of the new era draws near, our thoughts turn spontaneously to the words of the Apostle Paul: 'When the fullness of time had come, God sent forth his Son, born of a woman'" (Gal 4:4).[24] The whole Church is invited, through three years of preparation, to open the door to the third millennium by opening the doors of our hearts to the trinity and especially to Jesus Christ. Therefore, this preparation is primarily a *journey to deepen our spiritual life*—to be the holy people God calls us to be.

Being a holy person "requires effort and commitment to live the beatitudes" daily in our lives[25] and to undertake *repentance and forgiveness*. It means practicing the theological virtues of faith, hope, and charity; the cardinal virtues of patience, justice, fortitude, and temperance; and the gifts and fruits of the Holy Spirit.[26] It means understanding the call to holiness as a gift from the Holy Spirit and our response as a gift to the Church and to the world.[27]

A slogan we invite you to embrace for this journey is *Open Wide the Doors to Christ*. When we open the doors of our hearts to Christ we seek a relationship with Jesus Christ, who is the way, the truth, and the life (cf. Jn 14:6). This phrase calls us to action and speaks of what we need to do and how we should respond to God's gift of love if we are to be holy. The image invites us, as Jesus himself did, to make the words of the prophet Isaiah our own:

> The spirit of the Lord God is upon me,
>   because the Lord has anointed me;
> He has sent me to bring glad tidings to the lowly,
>   to heal the brokenhearted,
> To proclaim liberty to the captives
>   and release to the prisoners,
> To announce a year of favor from the Lord
>   and a day of vindication by our God,
>   to comfort all who mourn. (Is 61:1-2)

Doors are a powerful symbol that evokes strong images. Open doors speak of welcome, hospitality, openness; closed doors convey isolation, discrimination, being shut off from community and love. The incarnation itself is a powerful reality whereby God opened the doors to the kingdom through the life, death, and resurrection of his son, Jesus Christ.

Our goal for these years is to open the door to the year 2000 by celebrating jubilee. Therefore, we propose an image of four doors to pass through to reach the Great Jubilee and the new millennium. First, we open the door through Jesus Christ. Once we have passed through this door our hearts are opened to pass through the doors of conversion and reconciliation, community and unity, and peace and justice. A personal examination of conscience begins the process of opening each of these doors.

Open Wide the Doors Through Jesus Christ

The preparation for the third millennium provides us with a privileged historical opportunity—to proclaim anew to the world a profound faith that in Christ the Lord "can be found the key, the focal point, and the goal of all human history."[28] We are invited to renew and deepen our faith in God by deepening our relationship with Jesus Christ, a relationship sustained and nurtured through the presence of the Holy Spirit in our world today.

These preparations provide us with the opportunity to usher in a "new evangelization" of holiness and service. "God is opening before the Church the horizons of a humanity more fully prepared for the sowing of the Gospel. . . . The moment has come to commit all of the Church's energies to a new evangelization. . . . No believer in Christ, no institution of the Church can avoid this supreme duty: *To proclaim Christ to all peoples.*"[29]

Open Wide the Doors Through Conversion and Reconciliation

To deepen one's spiritual life, Pope John Paul II invites the Church to enter into a kind of worldwide retreat, an intense period of prayer, a "journey of authentic *conversion.*" This begins with an *examination of conscience*—the personal space and time to pause and be quiet, to listen to God speaking to us, an opportunity to let the land of our own lives lie fallow for a time. The "joy of every jubilee is above all a joy based upon the forgiveness of sins, the joy of conversion," which "takes place in the heart of each person, extends to the believing community, and then reaches to the whole of humanity."[30] This spirit of repentance and conversion leads us to be people of reconciliation. We, individually and as a Church, are also called in a spirit of repentance to ask God's forgiveness for those times in our history when we have fallen short of serving his kingdom through our own negligence and sin.[31]

Open Wide the Doors Through Community and Unity

This journey also calls us to examine how we participate in the community of believers and to look, in a special way, at how we have been instruments of Christian unity: to restore the bonds of faith between Christians and even among Catholic communities. We are created by God and brought into community through our baptism. We are all God's children and belong to God. It is through this community that we are enriched in faith and grow in the knowledge and love of God. And, the family is the first community to which we belong.

A significant goal in *Tertio Millennio Adveniente* is Christian unity. How can we embrace the pope's wishes to "celebrate the great jubilee, if not completely united, at least much closer to overcoming the divisions of the second millennium? . . . It is essential to not only continue along the path of dialogue on doctrinal matters, but above all to be more committed to prayer for Christian unity."[32] Let us work to further Christian unity, realizing that this "unity is a gift of the Holy Spirit."[33] Consider our ecumenical prayer to be that which our Lord taught us, "Our Father, who art in heaven. . . ." It is important to remember that that which unites us, Jesus Christ, is far greater than anything that divides us.

Open Wide the Doors Through Peace and Justice

The Great Jubilee of the Year 2000 should be seen as a time of the Lord's favor (Lk 4:18-19; Is 61:2; and Lv 25:10), in which "the presence of the Holy Spirit will be more deeply experienced, impelling Christians to preach the Gospel with new power, giving hope of liberation to the marginalized and the oppressed."[34] Jesus, the teacher, is anointed by the Spirit of the Lord to proclaim good news to the poor and to everyone a year of jubilee—a time of freedom from bondage, restoration, forgiveness of debts, and favor from the Lord (cf. Lk 4:18-19).

Today, we are called to imitate the great followers of Christ who have cooperated with God's grace in the transformation of the world in such social justice movements as the abolition of slavery and the death penalty; the promotion of civil rights, the rights of workers, and women's rights; the expansion of higher education opportunities; and respect for life from conception to natural death. The jubilee tradition reminds us that all the earth is God's and we are stewards of that earth. Being "jubilee" people, we must not be afraid "to build in the next century a civilization worthy of the human person, a true culture of freedom. . . . In doing so, we shall see that the tears of this century have prepared the ground of a new springtime of the human spirit."[35]

Mary, the Model of Faith and Hope for the Twenty-First Century

As we open these doors we look to Mary as a model of faith and hope. These years are compared to an extended Advent season, and Mary is the primary patroness of this new Advent. Just as the Blessed Virgin carried the Christ child in her womb before his birth, "so the present millennium, in its final years, bears within itself the seeds of the millennium now waiting to be born."[36]

Mary, in fact, constantly points to her Son. She is the *"model of faith"* put into practice.[37] Mary is "a woman of hope" who gives "full expression to the longing of the poor of Yahweh and is a radiant model for those who entrust themselves with all their hearts to the promises of God."[38] Mary becomes for us the "perfect model of love towards both God and neighbor."[39]

The Journey: Guided by Vatican II and the *Catechism of the Catholic Church*

As Catholics, we are compelled to examine our conscience according to the challenges of renewal of the Second Vatican Council, the "Advent Liturgy" for the Great Jubilee of the Year 2000, and the sacred Scriptures. The best preparation for the jubilee year will be a "renewed commitment to apply, as faithfully as possible, the teachings of Vatican II to the life of every individual and of the whole Church."[40] We are challenged to strengthen our commitment to deeper pursuit of holiness, wider community participation, and a stronger witness of faith. Aided by the *Catechism of the Catholic Church*,[41] we are invited to grow in our Catholic identity and knowledge of and enthusiasm for the faith. Through prayer and dialogue, we are to seek deeper unity within the Catholic family and to continue our ecumenical pursuit of full communion with fellow Christians.

Goals and Objectives for the Journey

We suggest one goal with four objectives, along with several pastoral strategies, to implement the vision contained in *Tertio Millennio Adveniente* and this framework. These are offered to help the Church in the United States prepare for and celebrate the Great Jubilee of the Year 2000.

The Goal: To Open the Doors to the Third Millennium by Celebrating Jubilee

To develop appropriate efforts for the celebration of the Great Jubilee of the Year 2000, so that this *privileged historical moment* is an opportunity to open wide the doors to Christ. In doing so, provide individuals, families, and communities a clear and engaging vision of faith for the twenty-first century.

Objective One: Open Wide the Doors Through Jesus Christ

To make the preparation and celebration of the jubilee year a "new springtime of Christianity" through a deepening of our personal relationship with Jesus Christ who is the "key, focus, and goal of all human history."[42]

Pastoral response:

1. Help those who already know Jesus Christ to strengthen their faith through a deepened relationship with him and to "proclaim Jesus Christ" with zeal to those who do not yet know him.
2. Encourage the celebration of the eucharist, on a regular basis, as the source and summit of all Christian life and as the key moment to give praise and thanks to God.
3. Study the Scriptures, the documents of the Second Vatican Council, and the *Catechism of the Catholic Church*.
4. Promote a greater appreciation of Mary, the Mother of God, as the model of faith, hope, and love.
5. Effectively utilize modern communications to make known the profound impact of Jesus Christ on world history.

Objective Two: Open Wide the Doors Through Conversion and Reconciliation

To make these "Advent years" a time of personal conversion and spiritual renewal in preparation for celebrating the jubilee year through an examination of conscience leading to conversion and reconciliation with God and community.

Pastoral response:

1. Encourage all Catholics to use these years of preparation as an opportunity for an *examination of conscience* based on the Gospel of Jesus Christ and the teachings of the Church.
2. Help individuals, families, and communities move from an examination of conscience to a *conversion of hearts* and a reconciliation of relationships.
3. Strongly encourage people to celebrate the sacrament of reconciliation on a regular basis.
4. Encourage the Church in the United States to prepare for the new millennium by identifying situations where repentance and forgiveness are necessary.

Objective Three: Open Wide the Doors Through Community and Unity

To answer the prayer of Christ "that all may be one" (Jn 17:21) by working to nourish community and strengthen the unity among all Christians.

Pastoral response:

1. Support the family as the domestic church, the first community and church for each person.
2. Work for Christian unity through continued study, common dialogue, and constant prayer.
3. Foster the development of small Christian communities.
4. Identify specific pastoral initiatives that can be undertaken ecumenically and with a family perspective for the celebration of the jubilee year 2000.
5. Seek opportunities for all women and men who believe in God to work together for the common good.
6. Pray for and work together to overcome divisions and misunderstandings that cause pain and disunity within the Catholic Church today.

Objective Four: Open Wide the Doors Through Peace and Justice

To work towards creating a more just and peaceful world by proclaiming in word and deed the good news of Jesus Christ.

Pastoral response:

1. Work for justice and peace by praying and promoting cooperation and unity among the nations and regions of the world, so as to seek forgiveness of past wrongs and affirm the dignity and worth of each person.
2. Make a covenant with one's neighbors, especially with the poor, the marginalized, and those who experience injustice, prejudice, discrimination, rejection, or are "held captive" in any way.
3. Be good stewards of God's earth and all creation.
4. Work towards the reduction of debts, both spiritual and economic, among all people and nations.
5. Teach peacemaking and strengthen efforts at reconciling communities in conflict or those experiencing the pain and division of violence, including families, neighborhoods, and nations.

A Yearly Schema (1997-2001) to Celebrate the Jubilee and to Open the Doors to the New Millennium

(Dioceses, parishes, organizations, and movements may wish to use these slogans as themes for the years of preparation. These are based on the outline presented by John Paul II in Tertio Millennio Adveniente *and the objectives contained in this framework.)*

As we open the doors to the new millennium by opening wide the doors of our hearts to Jesus Christ, we become

- *A people of faith* in Jesus Christ
- *A people of hope* through the Holy Spirit
- *A people of forgiveness and justice* on a journey to the Father
- *A eucharistic people* opening the door to the new millennium

Themes: Preparing for the Jubilee Year 2000 and the Third Millennium

Year 1–1997
General Theme: A People of Faith in Jesus Christ
Trinitarian Theme: Christ the Son
Virtue Highlighted: Faith

Sacramental Focus:	Baptism
Mariological Theme:	Model of Faith
Ecumenical Goal:	Sharing of Faith

Year 2–1998

General Theme:	A People of Hope Through the Holy Spirit
Trinitarian Theme:	Holy Spirit
Virtue Highlighted:	Hope
Sacramental Focus:	Confirmation, Charisms
Mariological Theme:	Model of Hope
Ecumenical Goal:	Christian Unity

Year 3–1999

General Theme:	A People of Forgiveness and Justice on a Journey to the Father
Trinitarian Theme:	Father
Virtue Highlighted:	Charity
Sacramental Focus:	Penance
Mariological Theme:	Model of Charity
Ecumenical Goal:	Dialogue with World Religions and Cultures

1997: A People of Faith in Jesus Christ

What is it that gives meaning and purpose to our lives? For us as Christians, these questions point to the person of Jesus Christ, the incarnated Son of God. Faith in Jesus Christ allows us to see life in a new and engaging way. Faith in Jesus Christ gives meaning to the varied experiences of life from the joys of married life, new birth, graduations, and accomplishments, to the suffering and pain of sickness, death, loss, and failure. Faith in Jesus Christ, lived within a community of believers, helps to make sense out of life.

Some specific nationwide strategies can include designating a door of the diocesan cathedral as a Holy Year Door, inviting people to designate a door of their home as their family Holy Year Door, and inviting Catholic institutions to display a jubilee banner.

1998: A People of Hope Through the Holy Spirit

What is the source of our hope for the future? It is the Holy Spirit in the world today, the promise of God's love for us and his presence among us. The Spirit, alive in our world, gives us hope that in opening the doors to Christ we can achieve great things. The role of the Holy Spirit in Church and society is to strengthen us for the journey and our mission—the transformation of the world. Our hope for ourselves and the world is also manifested, through the power of the Holy Spirit, in raising up great women and men. We look to these people to give us hope: Mary, the Mother of God, and especially the saints and martyrs. This hope compels us to move forward on our own journey of faith, our own pilgrimage to God. The presence of the Holy Spirit and these holy men and women gives us the courage to open wide the doors to Christ as we walk into a new millennium.

Some specific strategies include designating special days of prayer and action.

1999: A People of Forgiveness and Justice on a Journey to the Father

The Christian life can be viewed as "a great pilgrimage to the house of the Father . . . , which has many doors!"[43] Pilgrimages are journeys of repentance, thanksgiving, healing, and adoration. They provide us the opportunity to examine our conscience, to undertake the "call to conversion as the indispensable condition of Christian love . . . in contemporary society."[44] As each of us is called to examine his or her conscience, we ask forgiveness for those times when we have turned from God or humanity. This examination also calls us to ask, "Who are the people from whom I need to ask pardon?" "What changes must I make in my life?" "How must my life be different?" Our journey to the Father is truly a journey towards justice and peace where we constantly seek to discover who are our sisters and brothers.

This focus on an examination of conscience and forgiveness should highlight, in a special way, the sacrament of reconciliation with individual confession. For it is in "this sacrament that each person can experience mercy in a unique way, that is, the love which is more powerful than sin."[45]

Some suggested strategies include facilitating diocesan and/or parish reconciliation services to prepare for the jubilee year with a focus on an examination of conscience, inviting parishioners to enter into a covenant with the poor, and having a special ritual/celebration to inaugurate the Holy Year and open the Holy Year Door at midnight Mass on December 24, 1999 or some other appropriate time.

2000-2001: A Eucharistic People Opening the Door to the New Millennium

The jubilee year, a year of favor from the Lord, provides an opportunity for a new beginning, to set things right. Only through conversion and reconciliation can this new beginning take place. Christ comes to make all things new. We turn our minds and hearts to praise and thanksgiving as well as petition. We can turn to Christ with grateful hearts. We praise God for the generosity that has been shown to us.

We celebrate the fact that we are a eucharistic people—a people of praise and thanksgiving. This happens when we acknowledge our need for forgiveness, when we experience healing, a change of heart. How wonderful to open the door to the new millennium renewed and ready to be the people God calls us to be, to be the "children of the light."

Some specific suggestions include having a diocesan or parish jubilee celebration of the sacrament of reconciliation; co-sponsoring with a number of ecumenical churches a year 2000 religious festival/pilgrimage on December 31, 1999 and December 31, 2000; participating in a campaign for peace; and convening a diocesan eucharistic congress.

Notes

1. John Paul II, *On the Permanent Validity of the Church's Missionary Mandate (Redemptoris Missio)* (Washington, D.C.: United States Catholic Conference, 1990), no. 86.

2. John Paul II, *Redeemer of Man (Redemptoris Hominis)* (Washington, D.C.: United States Catholic Conference, 1979), no. 1.

3. John Paul II, *On the Coming of the Third Millennium (Tertio Millennio Adveniente)* (Washington, D.C.: United States Catholic Conference, 1994), no. 20.

4. John Paul II, *That They May Be One (Ut Unum Sint)* (Washington, D.C.: United States Catholic Conference, 1995), no. 100.

5. *Tertio Millennio Adveniente*, no. 44.

6. Ibid., no. 46.

7. Ibid., no. 32.

8. National Conference of Catholic Bishops, *Called and Gifted for the Third Millennium* (Washington, D.C.: United States Catholic Conference, 1995), 20.

9. *Tertio Millennio Adveniente*, no. 58.

10. *Called and Gifted for the Third Millennium*, 21.

11. Cf. *Tertio Millennio Adveniente*, no. 31.

12. *Tertio Millennio Adveniente*, no. 31.

13. Ibid., no. 55.

14. Cf. *Tertio Millennio Adveniente*, no. 45.

15. *Tertio Millennio Adveniente*, no. 15.

16. Ibid., no. 56.

17. Cf. *Tertio Millennio Adveniente*, no. 33.

18. *Tertio Millennio Adveniente*, no. 33.

19. Ibid., no. 46.

20. Avery Dulles, "John Paul II and the Advent of the New Millennium," *America* 173:19 (1995): 10-11.

21. Cf. John Paul II, *The Vocation and Mission of the Lay Faithful in the Church and in the World (Christifideles Laici)* (Washington, D.C.: United States Catholic Conference, 1988), no. 34.

22. *Tertio Millennio Adveniente*, no. 32.

23. Ibid., no. 33.

24. Ibid., no. 1.
25. *Called and Gifted for the Third Millennium*, 3.
26. *Catechism of the Catholic Church* (Washington, D.C.: United States Catholic Conference, 1994), nos. 1803-1832.
27. *Called and Gifted for the Third Millennium*, 4.
28. Second Vatican Council, *Pastoral Constitution on the Church in the Modern World (Gaudium et Spes)*, no. 10.
29. *Redemptoris Missio*, no. 3.
30. *Tertio Millennio Adveniente*, no. 32.
31. Ibid., no. 33.
32. Ibid., no. 34.
33. Ibid.
34. Dulles, 11.
35. John Paul II, "Address to the United Nations," October 5, 1995, no. 18.
36. Dulles, 10.
37. *Tertio Millennio Adveniente*, no. 43.
38. Ibid., no. 48.
39. Ibid., no. 54.
40. Ibid., no. 20.
41. *Tertio Millennio Adveniente*, no. 42.
42. *Gaudium et Spes*, no. 10.
43. *Tertio Millennio Adveniente*, no. 49.
44. Ibid., no. 50.
45. John Paul II, *On the Mercy of God (Dives in Misericordia)* (Washington, D.C.: United States Catholic Conference, 1980), no. 13; cf. no. 2.

Source: Washington, D.C.: United States Catholic Conference, 1997.

The Oklahoma City Bombing Case: The Church and the Death Penalty

A Statement of the Chairman of the USCC Committee on Domestic Policy, Bishop William Skylstad, on Behalf of the United States Catholic Conference

June 1997

Together with the rest of the country, the Catholic bishops' conference continues to mourn the horrendous loss of life caused by the bombing of the Alfred P. Murrah building in Oklahoma City. This terrible act still burns in our hearts.

Raw memories of that dreadful day in April 1995 have resurfaced for all of us as the trial of Mr. McVeigh concluded and the guilty verdict was announced. But we can only imagine the magnitude of the agony being felt by the families of the victims and the survivors, and the stories of their losses bring us to tears. Our thoughts and prayers are still with them as they and we relive that painful tragedy.

The jury that found Mr. McVeigh guilty of this horrible crime must now decide whether he should be executed for his offenses. In the face of such massive destruction of human life it is easy to understand why many say yes, he should suffer the same fate as so many of his victims.

However, we as bishops believe that to execute Mr. McVeigh would tragically perpetuate a terrible cycle of violence and further diminish respect for life. Nor could it truly ease the pain of those who have suffered so much loss. No act, including an execution, can fill the void and heal the wounds of the loss of a child, a mother, a father, a brother or sister. Mr. McVeigh's death cannot bring back those who have been lost.

Our passions cry out for vengeance. However, our God calls for justice and mercy, to love our enemies and pray for those who persecute us. We are called to seek justice without vengeance.

We must always seek ways to break the culture of violence that grips our society. Sending Mr. McVeigh to prison for life rather than to death row would be one step in demonstrating that all life is precious, even the life of one who has been found to have so brutally destroyed the lives of others. We do not believe that killing the person who killed so many of our sisters and brothers can teach our society that killing is wrong.

Source: *Origins* 27:6 (June 26, 1997): 84.

Always Our Children:
A Pastoral Message to Parents
of Homosexual Children
and Suggestions for
Pastoral Ministers

A Statement of the NCCB Committee on Marriage and Family
Approved by the Administrative Committee

September 1997

Preface

The purpose of this pastoral message is to reach out to parents trying to cope with the discovery of homosexuality in their adolescent or
adult child. It urges families to draw upon the reservoirs of faith, hope,
and love as they face uncharted futures. It asks them to recognize that
the Church offers enormous spiritual resources to strengthen and support them at this moment in their family's life and in the days to come.

This message draws upon the *Catechism of the Catholic Church*, the
teachings of Pope John Paul II, and statements of the Congregation for
the Doctrine of the Faith and of our own conference. This message is
not a treatise on homosexuality. It is not a systematic presentation of the
Church's moral teaching. It does not break any new ground theologically. Rather, relying on the Church's teaching, as well as our own
pastoral experience, we intend to speak words of faith, hope, and love
to parents who need the Church's loving presence at a time that may be
one of the most challenging in their lives. We also hope this message
will be helpful to priests and pastoral ministers who often are the first
ones parents or their children approach with their struggles and anxieties.

In recent years we have tried to reach out to families in difficult circumstances. Our initiatives took the form of short statements, like this
one, addressed to people who thought they were beyond the Church's
circle of care. *Always Our Children* follows in the same tradition.

This message is not intended for advocacy purposes or to serve a
particular agenda. It is not to be understood as an endorsement of what
some call a "homosexual lifestyle." *Always Our Children* is an outstretched hand of the bishops' Committee on Marriage and Family to

parents and other family members, offering them a fresh look at the grace present in family life and the unfailing mercy of Christ our Lord.

> An even more generous, intelligent and prudent pastoral commitment, modeled on the Good Shepherd, is called for in cases of families which, often independently of their own wishes and through pressures of various other kinds, find themselves faced by situations which are objectively difficult.[1]

A Critical Moment, A Time of Grace

As you begin to read this message you may feel that your life is in turmoil. You and your family might be faced with one of the difficult situations of which our Holy Father speaks:

- You think your adolescent child is experiencing a same-sex attraction and/or you observe attitudes and behaviors that you find confusing or upsetting or with which you disagree.
- Your son or daughter has made it known that he or she has a homosexual orientation.
- You experience a tension between loving your child as God's precious creation and not wanting to endorse any behavior you know the Church teaches is wrong.

You need not face this painful time alone, without human assistance or God's grace. The Church can be an instrument of both help and healing. This is why we bishops, as pastors and teachers, write to you.

In this pastoral message, we draw upon the gift of faith as well as the sound teaching and pastoral practice of the Church to offer loving support, reliable guidance, and recommendations for ministries suited to your needs and to those of your child. Our message speaks of accepting yourself, your beliefs and values, your questions, and all you may be struggling with at this moment; accepting and loving your child as a gift of God; and accepting the full truth of God's revelation about the dignity of the human person and the meaning of human sexuality. Within the Catholic moral vision there is no contradiction among these levels of acceptance, for truth and love are not opposed. They are inseparably joined and rooted in one person, Jesus Christ, who reveals God to be ultimate truth and saving love.

We address our message also to the wider church community, and especially to priests and other pastoral ministers, asking that our words be translated into attitudes and actions that follow the way of love, as Christ has taught. It is through the community of his faithful that Jesus offers you hope, help, and healing, so your whole family might continue to grow into the intimate community of life and love that God intends.

Accepting Yourself

Because some of you might be swept up in a tide of emotions, we focus first on feelings. Although the gift of human sexuality can be a great mystery at times, the Church's teaching on homosexuality is clear. However, because the terms of that teaching have now become very personal in regard to your son or daughter, you may feel confused and conflicted.

You could be experiencing many different emotions, all in varying degrees, such as the following:

Relief: Perhaps you had sensed for some time that your son or daughter was different in some way. Now he or she has come to you and entrusted something very significant. It may be that other siblings learned of this before you and were reluctant to tell you. Regardless, though, a burden has been lifted. Acknowledge the possibility that your child has told you this not to hurt you or create distance, but out of love and trust and with a desire for honesty, intimacy, and closer communication.

Anger: You may be feeling deceived or manipulated by your son or daughter. You could be angry with your spouse, blaming him or her for "making the child this way"—especially if there has been a difficult parent-child relationship. You might be angry with yourself for not recognizing indications of homosexuality. You could be feeling disappointment, along with anger, if family members, and sometimes even siblings, are rejecting their homosexual brother or sister. It is just as possible to feel anger if family members or friends seem overly accepting and encouraging of homosexuality. Also—and not to be discounted—is a possible anger with God that all this is happening.

Mourning: You may now feel that your child is not exactly the same individual you once thought you knew. You envision that your son or daughter may never give you grandchildren. These lost expectations as well as the fact that homosexual persons often encounter discrimination and open hostility can cause you great sadness.

Fear: You may fear for your child's physical safety and general welfare in the face of prejudice against homosexual people. In particular, you may be afraid that others in your community might exclude or treat your child or your family with contempt. The fear of your child contracting HIV/AIDS or another sexually transmitted disease is serious and ever-present. If your child is distraught, you may be concerned about attempted suicide.

Guilt, Shame, and Loneliness: "If only we had . . . or had not . . . "are words with which parents can torture themselves at this stage. Regrets and disappointments rise up like ghosts from the past. A sense of failure can lead you into a valley of shame which, in turn, can isolate you from your children, your family, and other communities of support.

Parental Protectiveness and Pride: Homosexual persons often experience discrimination and acts of violence in our society. As a parent, you naturally want to shield your children from harm, regardless of their age. You may still insist: "You are always my child; nothing can ever change that. You are also a child of God, gifted and called for a purpose in God's design."

There are two important things to keep in mind as you try to sort out your feelings. First, listen to them. They can contain clues that lead to a fuller discovery of God's will for you. Second, because some feelings can be confusing or conflicting, it is not necessary to act upon all of them. Acknowledging them may be sufficient, but it may also be necessary to talk about your feelings. Do not expect that all tensions can or will be resolved. The Christian life is a journey marked by perseverance and prayer. It is a path leading from where we are to where we know God is calling us.

Accepting Your Child

How can you best express your love—itself a reflection of God's unconditional love—for your child? At least two things are necessary.

First, don't break off contact; don't reject your child. A shocking number of homosexual youth end up on the streets because of rejection by their families. This, and other external pressures, can place young people at a greater risk for self-destructive behaviors like substance abuse and suicide.

Your child may need you and the family now more than ever. He or she is still the same person. This child, who has always been God's gift to you, may now be the cause of another gift: your family becoming more honest, respectful, and supportive. Yes, your love can be tested by this reality, but it can also grow stronger through your struggle to respond lovingly.

The second way to communicate love is to seek appropriate help for your child and for yourself. If your son or daughter is an adolescent, it is possible that he or she may be displaying traits which cause you anxiety such as what the child is choosing to read or view in the media, intense friendships, and other such observable characteristics and tendencies. What is called for on the part of parents is an approach which does not presume that your child has developed a homosexual orientation and which will help you maintain a loving relationship while you provide support, information, encouragement, and moral guidance. Parents must always be vigilant about their children's behavior and exercise responsible interventions when necessary.

In many cases, it may be appropriate and necessary that your child receive professional help, including counseling and spiritual direction. It is important, of course, that he or she receive such guidance willingly. Look for a therapist who has an appreciation of religious values and who understands the complex nature of sexuality. Such a person should be experienced at helping people discern the meaning of early sexual behaviors, sexual attractions, and sexual fantasies in ways that lead to more clarity and self-identity. In the course of this, however, it is essential for you to remain open to the possibility that your son or daughter is struggling to understand and accept a basic homosexual orientation.

The meaning and implications of the term homosexual orientation are not universally agreed upon. Church teaching acknowledges a distinction between a homosexual "tendency,"which proves to be "transitory,"and "homosexuals who are definitively such because of some kind of innate instinct."[2]

In light of this possibility, therefore, it seems appropriate to understand sexual orientation (heterosexual or homosexual) as a deep-seated dimension of one's personality and to recognize its relative stability in a person. A homosexual orientation produces a stronger emotional and sexual attraction toward individuals of the same sex, rather than toward those of the opposite sex. It does not totally rule out interest in, care for, and attraction toward members of the opposite sex. Having a homosexual orientation does not necessarily mean a person will engage in homosexual activity.

There seems to be no single cause of a homosexual orientation. A common opinion of experts is that there are multiple factors—genetic, hormonal, psychological—that may give rise to it. Generally, homosexual orientation is experienced as a given, not as something freely chosen. By itself, therefore, a homosexual orientation cannot be considered sinful, for morality presumes the freedom to choose.[3]

Some homosexual persons want to be known publicly as gay or lesbian. These terms often express a person's level of self-awareness and self-acceptance within society. Though you might find the terms offensive because of political or social connotations, it is necessary to be sensitive to how your son or daughter is using them. Language should not be a barrier to building trust and honest communication.

You can help a homosexual person in two general ways. First, encourage him or her to cooperate with God's grace to live a chaste life. Second, concentrate on the person, not on the homosexual orientation itself. This implies respecting a person's freedom to choose or refuse therapy directed toward changing a homosexual orientation. Given the present state of medical and psychological knowledge, there is no guarantee that such therapy will succeed. Thus, there may be no obligation to undertake it, though some may find it helpful.

All in all, it is essential to recall one basic truth. God loves every person as a unique individual. Sexual identity helps to define the unique persons we are, and one component of our sexual identity is sexual orientation. Thus, our total personhood is more encompassing than sexual orientation. Human beings see the appearance, but the Lord looks into the heart (cf. 1 Sm 16:7).

God does not love someone any less simply because he or she is homosexual. God's love is always and everywhere offered to those who are open to receiving it. St. Paul's words offer great hope:

> For I am convinced that neither death, nor life, nor angels, nor principalities, nor present things, nor future things, nor powers, nor height, nor depth, nor any other creature will be able to separate us from the love of God in Christ Jesus our Lord. (Rom 8:38-39)

Accepting God's Plan and the Church's Ministry

For the Christian believer, an acceptance of self and of one's homosexual child must take place within the larger context of accepting divinely revealed truth about the dignity and destiny of human persons. It is the Church's responsibility to believe and teach this truth, presenting it as a comprehensive moral vision and applying this vision in particular situations through its pastoral ministries. We present the main points of that moral teaching here.

Every person has an inherent dignity because he or she is created in God's image. A deep respect for the total person leads the Church to hold and teach that sexuality is a gift from God. Being created a male or female person is an essential part of the divine plan, for it is their sexuality—a mysterious blend of spirit and body—that allows human beings to share in God's own creative love and life.

Like all gifts from God, the power and freedom of sexuality can be channeled toward good or evil. Everyone—the homosexual and the heterosexual person—is called to personal maturity and responsibility. With the help of God's grace, everyone is called to practice the virtue of chastity in relationships. Chastity means integrating one's thoughts, feelings, and actions, in the area of human sexuality, in a way that values and respects one's own dignity and that of others. It is "the spiritual power which frees love from selfishness and aggression."[4]

Christ summons all his followers—whether they are married or living a single celibate life—to a higher standard of loving. This includes not only fidelity, forgiveness, hope, perseverance, and sacrifice, but also chastity, which is expressed in modesty and self-control. The chaste life is possible, though not always easy, for it involves a continual effort to turn toward God and away from sin, especially with the strength of the sacraments of penance and eucharist. Indeed God expects everyone to strive for the perfection of love, but to achieve it gradually through stages of moral growth.[5] To keep our feet on the path of conversion, God's grace is available to and sufficient for everyone open to receiving it.

Furthermore, as homosexual persons "dedicate their lives to understanding the nature of God's personal call to them, they will be able to celebrate the sacrament of penance more faithfully and receive the Lord's grace so freely offered there in order to convert their lives more fully to his way."[6]

To live and love chastely is to understand that "only within marriage does sexual intercourse fully symbolize the Creator's dual design, as an act of covenant love, with the potential of co-creating new human life."[7] This is a fundamental teaching of our Church about sexuality, rooted in the biblical account of man and woman created in the image of God and made for union with one another (Gn 2–3).

Two conclusions follow. First, it is God's plan that sexual intercourse occur only within marriage between a man and a woman. Second, every act of intercourse must be open to the possible creation of human life. Homosexual intercourse cannot fulfill these two conditions. Therefore, the Church teaches that homogenital behavior is objectively immoral, while making the important distinction between this behavior and a homosexual orientation, which is not immoral in itself. It is also important to recognize that neither a homosexual orientation, nor a heterosexual one, leads inevitably to sexual activity. One's total personhood is not reducible to sexual orientation or behavior.

Respect for the God-given dignity of all persons means the recognition of human rights and responsibilities. The teachings of the Church make it clear that the fundamental human rights of homosexual persons must be defended and that all of us must strive to eliminate any forms of injustice, oppression, or violence against them.[8]

It is not sufficient only to avoid unjust discrimination. Homosexual persons "must be accepted with respect, compassion and sensitivity."[9] They, as is true of every human being, need to be nourished at many different levels simultaneously. This includes friendship, which is a way of loving and is essential to healthy human development. It is one of the richest possible human experiences. Friendship can and does thrive outside of genital sexual involvement.

The Christian community should offer its homosexual sisters and brothers understanding and pastoral care. More than twenty years ago we bishops stated that "homosexuals . . . should have an active role in the Christian community."[10] What does this mean in practice? It means that all homosexual persons have a right to be welcomed into the community, to hear the word of God, and to receive pastoral care. Homosexual persons living chaste lives should have opportunities to lead and serve the community. However, the Church has the right to deny public roles of service and leadership to persons, whether homosexual or heterosexual, whose public behavior openly violates its teachings.

The Church also recognizes the importance and urgency of ministering to persons with HIV/AIDS. Though HIV/AIDS is an epidemic affecting the whole human race, not just homosexual persons, it has had a devastating effect upon them and has brought great sorrow to many parents, families, and friends.

Without condoning self-destructive behavior or denying personal responsibility, we reject the idea that HIV/AIDS is a direct punishment from God. Furthermore

> Persons with AIDS are not distant, unfamiliar people, the objects of our mingled pity and aversion. We must keep them present to our consciousness as individuals and a community, and embrace them with unconditional love. . . . Compassion—love—toward persons infected with HIV is the only authentic Gospel response.[11]

Nothing in the Bible or in Catholic teaching can be used to justify prejudicial or discriminatory attitudes and behaviors.[12] We reiterate here what we said in an earlier statement:

> We call on all Christians and citizens of goodwill to confront their own fears about homosexuality and to curb the humor and discrimination that offend homosexual persons. We understand that having a homosexual orientation brings with it enough anxiety, pain, and issues related to self-acceptance without society bringing additional prejudicial treatment.[13]

Pastoral Recommendations

With a view toward overcoming the isolation that you or your son or daughter may be experiencing, we offer these recommendations to you as well as to priests and pastoral ministers.

To Parents

1. Accept and love yourselves as parents in order to accept and love your son or daughter. Do not blame yourselves for a homosexual orientation in your child.

2. Do everything possible to continue demonstrating love for your child. However, accepting his or her homosexual orientation does not have to include approving all related attitudes and behavioral choices. In fact, you may need to challenge certain aspects of a lifestyle that you find objectionable.

3. Urge your son or daughter to stay joined to the Catholic faith community. If they have left the Church, urge them to return and be reconciled to the community, especially through the sacrament of penance.

4. Recommend that your son or daughter find a spiritual director/ mentor to offer guidance in prayer and in leading a chaste and virtuous life.

5. Seek help for yourself, perhaps in the form of counseling or spiritual direction, as you strive for understanding, acceptance, and inner peace. Also, consider joining a parents' support group or participating in a retreat designed for Catholic parents of homosexual children. Other people have traveled the same road as you but may have journeyed even further. They can share effective ways of handling delicate family situations such as how to tell family members and friends about your child, how to explain homosexuality to younger children, and how to relate to your son or daughter's friends in a Christian way.

6. Reach out in love and service to other parents struggling with a son or daughter's homosexuality. Contact your parish about organizing a parents' support group. Your diocesan family ministry office, Catholic Charities, or a special diocesan ministry to gay and lesbian persons may be able to offer assistance.

7. As you take advantage of opportunities for education and support, remember that you can only change yourself; you can only be responsible for your own beliefs and actions, not those of your adult children.

8. Put your faith completely in God, who is more powerful, more compassionate, and more forgiving than we are or ever could be.

To Church Ministers

1. Be available to parents and families who ask for your pastoral help, spiritual guidance, and prayer.

2. Welcome homosexual persons into the faith community and seek out those on the margins. Avoid stereotyping and condemning. Strive first to listen. Do not presume that all homosexual persons are sexually active.

3. Learn more about homosexuality and church teaching so that your preaching, teaching, and counseling will be informed and effective.
4. When speaking publicly, use the words "homosexual," "gay," and "lesbian" in honest and accurate ways.
5. Maintain a list of agencies, community groups, and counselors or other experts to whom you can refer homosexual persons or their parents and family members when they ask you for specialized assistance. Recommend agencies that operate in a manner consistent with Catholic teaching.
6. Help to establish or promote support groups for parents and family members.
7. Learn about HIV/AIDS so you will be more informed and compassionate in your ministry. Include prayers in the liturgy for those living with HIV/AIDS, their caregivers, those who have died, and their families, companions, and friends. A special Mass for healing and anointing of the sick might be connected with World AIDS Awareness Day (December 1) or with a local AIDS awareness program.

Conclusion

For St. Paul love is the greatest of spiritual gifts. St. John considers love to be the most certain sign of God's presence. Jesus proposes it as the basis of his two great commandments, which fulfill all the law and the prophets.

Love, too, is the continuing story of every family's life. Love can be shared, nurtured, rejected, and sometimes lost. To follow Christ's way of love is the challenge before every family today. Your family now has an added opportunity to share love and to accept love. Our church communities are likewise called to an exemplary standard of love and justice. Our homosexual sisters and brothers—indeed, all people—are summoned into responsible ways of loving.

To our homosexual brothers and sisters we offer a concluding word. This message has been an outstretched hand to your parents and families inviting them to accept God's grace present in their lives now and to trust in the unfailing mercy of Jesus our Lord. Now we stretch out our hands and invite you to do the same. We are called to become one body, one spirit in Christ. We need one another if we are to " . . . grow in every way into him who is the head, Christ, from whom the whole body, joined and held together by every supporting ligament, with the proper functioning of each part, brings about the body's growth and builds itself up in love" (Eph 4:15-16).

Though at times you may feel discouraged, hurt, or angry, do not walk away from your families, from the Christian community, from all those who love you. In you God's love is revealed. You are always our children.

> There is no fear in love . . . perfect love drives out fear. (1 Jn 4:18)

Notes

1. John Paul II, *On the Family (Familiaris Consortio)* (Washington, D.C.: United States Catholic Conference, 1981), no. 77.
2. Congregation for the Doctrine of the Faith, *Declaration on Certain Questions Concerning Sexual Ethics* (Washington, D.C.: United States Catholic Conference, 1975), no. 8.
3. The *Catechism of the Catholic Church* states also: "This inclination, which is objectively disordered, constitutes for most [persons with the homosexual inclination] a trial" (no. 2358).
4. Pontifical Council for the Family, *The Truth and Meaning of Human Sexuality* (Washington, D.C.: United States Catholic Conference, 1996), no. 16.
5. *Familiaris Consortio*, no. 34.
6. Congregation for the Doctrine of the Faith, *The Pastoral Care of Homosexual Persons* (Washington, D.C.: United States Catholic Conference, 1986), no. 12.
7. United States Catholic Conference, *Human Sexuality: A Catholic Perspective for Education and Lifelong Learning* (Washington, D.C.: United States Catholic Conference, 1991), 55.
8. *The Pastoral Care of Homosexual Persons*, no. 10.
9. *Catechism of the Catholic Church* (Washington, D.C.: United States Catholic Conference, 1994), no. 2358.
10. National Conference of Catholic Bishops, *To Live in Christ Jesus: A Pastoral Reflection on the Moral Life* (Washington, D.C.: United States Catholic Conference, 1976), 19.
11. National Conference of Catholic Bishops, *Called to Compassion and Responsibility: A Response to the HIV/AIDS Crisis* (Washington, D.C.: United States Catholic Conference, 1989).
12. In matters where sexual orientation has a clear relevance, the common good does justify its being taken into account, as noted by the Congregation for the Doctrine of the Faith in *Some Considerations Concerning the Response to Legislative Proposals on the Non-Discrimination of Homosexual Persons*, 1992, no. 11.
13. *Human Sexuality*, 55.

Source: Washington, D.C.: United States Catholic Conference, 1997.

Resolution on Computer Networking

A Statement of the USCC Committee on Communications

September 1997

Pope John Paul II has called the mass media one of the "modern equivalents of the Areopagus" of Athens, one of the "the new sectors in which the Gospel must be proclaimed."[1] A relatively new aspect of the media which is already reshaping the ways in which we interact with one another is computer networking and in particular the Internet. The Committee on Communications of the U.S. Catholic Conference wishes by this resolution to affirm the value of these new means. We also wish to identify some concerns about their potential misuse which can divert them from service to the truth and to the common good.

With regard to their use within the church community, many dioceses, parishes, religious communities, schools, and other church institutions and organizations are already effectively employing these new means. An outstanding example is the Holy See's establishment of its web site. By the convenient and almost instantaneous communications they make possible, these new means help bring about an enhanced sense of working together, whether in a pastoral center, a diocese, or a far-flung religious community. This conquest of time and space offers new ways to gather people together for a common purpose. We encourage an extensive exchange of information and ideas among church leaders and communicators about creative uses of computer networking and the Internet for service to the Church's pastoral mission.

The Church and her institutions (including schools, social service agencies, and health care facilities) and all persons regardless of income should have access to these means of communications. As computer networks become more essential to functioning within society, legislation and regulation regarding them should guarantee that access.

At the same time, we wish to raise up our concerns about the possible abuses of computer networking.

Our principal concern is that what is presented on the Internet and elsewhere as "Catholic" be authentically so and that truly Catholic sites not be linked to sites which contradict church teaching and practice. Among the preventive steps which ought to be considered are

- A review of canon law to determine whether the canons which govern printed matter and the authorization of the use of the name Catholic can be applied by diocesan bishops in this regard
- Development by local dioceses of criteria for establishing web sites and for linking web sites to one another and the designation of appropriate diocesan offices to oversee their application
- Development, maintenance, and promotion by the conference, in consultation with local dioceses, of a list of reliably Catholic sites on the Internet

Related concerns are

- That sites which do not accurately reflect church doctrine or devotion not be presented in existing official or semiofficial guides as Catholic sites
- That the integrity of church documents not be compromised
- That the church community and the general public not be deceived by individuals who use these means to misrepresent their relation to the Church or to use the name Catholic to exploit extremely vulnerable people and lure them into deceptive and even fraudulent schemes which drain their resources

These new means of communications can also make an important contribution to the common good of society. Their use should enhance the unity of the human family rather than increase its divisions.

Thus we urge that the capacity of these new means for the nearly instantaneous dispersal of information worldwide be employed with a commitment to the truth and to the common good.

We also wish to express our profound concern about the immoral uses to which these networks are being put in ways that harm adults and children both, denying them their human dignity and turning them into objects of exploitation. The fact that children are often more "computer literate" than their parents or guardians can place them at special risk.

As these means become necessities for earning one's income or simply going about the activities of daily living, we pledge our support for the poor and vulnerable having access to them.

Computer networking is a rapidly changing reality. This articulation of concerns should not be construed to be exhaustive or final. In order to affirm the importance of these means of communications and to raise up our concerns in a timely fashion, we limit ourselves at present to this brief resolution.

Note

1. Cf. John Paul II, *On the Permanent Validity of the Church's Missionary Mandate (Redemptoris Missio)* (Washington, D.C.: United States Catholic Conference, 1990), no. 37c.

Source: *Origins* 27:17 (October 9, 1997): 300.

Some Observations Concerning the Catholic Theological Society of America Report on Tradition and the Ordination of Women

A Statement of the NCCB Committee on Doctrine

September 1997

In June 1996, the Catholic Theological Society of America received the first draft of a report titled "Tradition and the Ordination of Women,"[1] which raised serious questions with regard to the *Responsum ad dubium* of the Congregation for the Doctrine of the Faith (October 28, 1995) on the reservation of holy orders to men. During the business meeting of the June 1997 CTSA convention in Minneapolis, the membership present voted to endorse the conclusion of the report, which was subsequently published.[2] The conclusion reads as follows:

> There are serious doubts regarding the nature of the authority of this teaching [namely the teaching that the Church's lack of authority to ordain women to the priesthood is a truth that has been infallibly taught and requires the definitive assent of the faithful] and its grounds in tradition. There is serious, widespread disagreement on this question not only among theologians, but also within the larger community of the Church. . . . Further study, discussion, and prayer regarding this question by all the members of the Church in accord with their particular gifts and vocations are necessary if the Church is to be guided by the Spirit in remaining faithful to the authentic tradition of the Gospel in our day.

On June 11, 1997, the president of the CTSA sent copies of the report and the resolution endorsing its conclusion to the president of the National Conference of Catholic Bishops, who in turn asked the Committee on Doctrine to review these materials and develop an appropriate response to them. The following observations were prepared in response to the CTSA's initiative in sending a copy of the report to the national conference of bishops. In addition to transmitting this response to the president and board of the CTSA, the Committee on Doctrine has also determined that, given the public nature of the report, it would be helpful to provide the text of these observations to the bishops and the Catholic community at large. The following observations were prepared by the staff of the Committee on Doctrine and are made public now with the authorization of the committee.

These observations respect the limitations of the CTSA report itself. The report was intentionally limited in scope, presenting not "arguments for or against the ordination of women" but rather questioning "whether the reasons given by the congregation justify the assertion that the definitive assent of the faithful must be given to the teaching that the Church has no authority whatsoever to confer priestly ordination on women."[3]

The scope of the following observations is similarly limited. No attempt has been made here to advance a comprehensive theological argument for the Church's teaching on the reservation of priestly orders to men. Rather, these observations address the scriptural basis for this teaching; the appeal to tradition; and the authority with which the teaching is proposed and the assent it requires.

1. Scriptural Basis

According to the CTSA report, the Congregation for the Doctrine of the Faith was in error in claiming in the *responsum* that the teaching that the Church has no authority to ordain women is "founded on the word of God." In support of this objection, the report appeals both to the work of biblical scholars and in particular to the conclusion of the Pontifical Biblical Commission in 1976 that "it does not seem that the New Testament by itself alone will permit us to settle in a clear way and once and for all the problem of the possible accession of women to the presbyterate."[4]

But in presenting the conclusion of the Pontifical Biblical Commission in this way, the CTSA report appears to misconstrue it. The commission states not that there is no evidence in the New Testament that women are not to be ordained, but that this evidence "by itself alone" is inconclusive as a determinant of the Church's practice concerning the sacrament of orders. Furthermore, when read in a Catholic perspective, the commission's work can be seen as confirming the Church's teaching that priestly ordination is reserved to men.

The appeal to Scripture is an essential element in the Catholic understanding of the faith. But in a properly Catholic understanding of the matter, the Church is recognized as the divinely guided interpreter of the revelation contained in Scripture. In the Catholic approach, the Bible must be read within the broad context of biblical scholarship, the history of exegesis, the tradition of theological reflection and interpretation, its liturgical use in the Lectionary and sacramental settings, and pertinent magisterial interpretations, whether papal or conciliar. In such a communally and doctrinally guided reading, the Church

expounds the teaching contained in the Scripture through evangelization, catechesis, preaching, and official teaching within the framework
of a tradition of interpretation. This is the proper context within which
to assess the results of the work of the Pontifical Biblical Commission.
Read in this perspective, the commission's conclusion can be interpreted to be in harmony with the teaching of the magisterium.

Instead, the CTSA report implies that the Pontifical Biblical Commission found no good reason in the New Testament to support the
reservation of priestly ordination to men. It is not clear how such an
implication can be drawn from what the Pontifical Biblical Commission actually asserted in the following passages, for example:

- "The apostolic group thus established by the Lord appears
  thus, by the testimony of the New Testament, as the basis of a
  community which has continued the work of Christ" (i.e., the
  New Testament associates the institution of the Church with
  the clearly defined apostolic group established by Christ).[5]
- "We see in the Acts of the Apostles and the epistles that the
  first communities were always directed by men exercising the
  apostolic power."[6]
- "The masculine character of the hierarchical order which has
  structured the Church since its beginning thus seems attested
  to by Scripture in an undeniable way."[7]

The biblical evidence thus can be construed as supplying at least a
partial warrant for the reservation of priestly orders to men, especially,
as shall be noted in the next section, when the relevant scriptural passages are read within the context of the Church's living tradition of
interpretation.

In addition to citing the Pontifical Biblical Commission, the CTSA
report claims that "many reputable Catholic biblical scholars have not
found" the argument from Scripture for the reservation of priestly
ordination to men to be "convincing."[8] In a particularly significant
passage, the CTSA report reads as follows:

> Since Jesus left the Church under the guidance of the Holy
> Spirit to make many decisions on its own regarding the
> organization of its ministry, scholars judge it very doubtful
> that he intended to lay down such a particular prescription
> regarding the sex of future candidates for ordination. The
> majority of exegetes hold, instead, that Jesus' choice of only
> men for the Twelve was determined by the nature of their
> symbolic role as "patriarchs" of restored Israel.[9]

The reasoning of this passage is unclear. If being male was necessary for the Twelve to symbolize the patriarchs of restored Israel and if

the priestly ministry in the Church derives from the apostolic ministry of the Twelve, then it seems natural to conclude, not that the gender of the priest is irrelevant, but that it has precisely the relevance that it did for the Twelve. It follows that to construe Christ's choice in this matter as a provisional one is gratuitous.

In summary, the CTSA report advances the misleading conclusion that the Church's practice of reserving priestly ordination to men is without biblical basis. Yet even the brief analysis presented here indicates that the reasoning behind this conclusion reflects neither a careful reading of the actual evidence nor a sound methodological approach to the interpretation of Scripture in the Catholic tradition. While the Church has not claimed that the question of the reservation of priestly orders to men can be settled by appeal to Scripture alone, the biblical record nonetheless confirms the exclusively masculine character of pastoral office in the New Testament and in the early Church.

2. Appeal to Tradition

The CTSA report admits that "it has been the unbroken tradition of the Roman Catholic Church and the Eastern churches to ordain only men to the priesthood. Furthermore, when the question has been raised about the suitability of women for such ordination, a negative answer has been given consistently by early Christian writers, by medieval theologians, and by recent popes."[10] But this tradition must be challenged, according to the report, since the principal reason proposed for the exclusion of women from ordination was their being in a "state of subjection."

It must be stated at the outset that the force of this challenge is unclear. St. Thomas Aquinas, for example, while he holds that, according to Scripture, women are in a "state of subjection," recognizes that women can have civil authority over men, that abbesses have a kind of authority in the Church, and that there are many women who are morally and spiritually superior to many men.[11] Again, it is true that, although some of the church fathers (see the citations in *Inter Insigniores*) speak of a natural weakness in women, they also speak in glowing terms of the holiness of many women (preeminently, of course, the Blessed Virgin Mary).

An interpretation of the historical record that holds as its first principle that a differentiation between women and men reflects a prejudice that can and must be rooted out does not do justice to this record. It is a proper task of theologians, philosophers, and historians to investigate more thoroughly what the Christian understanding of the nature of women and men, and their relations, was at various times in history. But it is clear that earlier ages attributed a fundamental significance to holiness that has tended to be displaced in our day by an ideology of power.

Even more important, the CTSA report admits[12] that, while the alleged "natural inferiority" of women was often cited in the past as a reason why they could not receive ordination, this argument is explicitly rejected in both *Inter Insigniores* and *Ordinatio Sacerdotalis*: "The nonadmission of women to priestly ordination cannot mean that women are of lesser dignity nor can it be construed as discrimination against them."[13]

The CTSA report fails to acknowledge the significance of the rejection of such a "natural inferiority" argument in the overall logic of the case the magisterium has advanced in these documents. In effect, what these documents can be understood to affirm is that, while appeal to the natural inferiority of women played a significant role in theological reflection on the issue in the past, the explicit rejection of this appeal by the magisterium now means that other factors, already present in the tradition, should be accorded greater weight in our current recovery of the doctrinal and theological tradition on ordination and its reservation to men. Prominent among these factors is the iconic or representational character of the priestly office.

What is more, the magisterium has been careful to stress that the finally decisive considerations in determining the reservation of priestly orders to men are the example of Christ and the Spirit-guided recognition that his action in choosing only men for pastoral leadership was normative for the apostles and for the Church. Whatever theological arguments may have been advanced in the past, the appeal to tradition on the part of the magisterium is an appeal to the Church's faithful adherence to Christ's example and will in this matter.

When the CTSA report considers theological explanations of the reservation of ordination to men on the basis of "iconic appropriateness" or "beliefs in a natural gender complementarity," it admits that these are not inconsistent with a belief in the equal personal dignity of men and women.[14] But the report then asserts that such explanations should be contested because "the 'effective history' of the practices supported by these appeals can be shown to involve consistent patterns of superiority and inferiority, domination and subordination rather than of equality."[15] In other words, the CTSA claims that arguments that are not objectionable in themselves may be objectionable in the way they are applied.

To say that arguments of iconic appropriateness and beliefs about a natural gender complementarity have been misused is not to show that they are invalid. Furthermore, it is surely wrong to be suspicious of someone's endeavor to speak and explain a truth in charity because the same truth has at other times been used to support an injustice.

Thus, to cite a pertinent example, Pope John Paul II has spoken again and again of the dignity of women, and he, along with his recent predecessors, has reckoned the emancipation of women as one of the "signs of the times" through which God continues to speak to the Church today. The Holy Father has authored profound reflections on the dignity of the human person and has displayed a rich understanding of the nature of man and woman. Contrary to what the CTSA report implies, there is no reason to suppose that his declaration that the reservation of priestly orders to men as part of the deposit of faith contradicts his teaching on the dignity and equality of women.

Theologians, guided by the magisterium, will continue to explore the reasons for the reservation of priestly orders to men. As noted already, some scholars have explored the iconic or representative nature of the ordained priesthood; others have suggested that there is a connection between the sacrificial act of the priest and the kind of sacrificial act that is appropriate to men. More work, historical and systematic, needs to be done in this area. We will never come to a clear and certain proof of the appropriateness of reserving ordination to men, any more than we will reach such a proof of the appropriateness of water for baptism or bread and wine for the eucharist. Nevertheless, reasons have already been adduced that allow us, employing a properly Catholic theological method, to discover the intelligibility or fittingness of the reservation of holy orders to men.

A basic weakness in the CTSA report's analysis of the appeal to tradition as demonstrative of the intention of Christ for the Church lies in the report's failure adequately to distinguish between ecclesial ministries and sacramental ordination. In claiming that the teaching belongs to the deposit of faith, the magisterium affirms that it belongs to God's plan for the sevenfold sacramental economy which is his gift to the Church. This is a major point of contention—for it is not clear what the CTSA report would allow as evidence for the determination of God's will *in any matter* on the part of the Church. Skeptical fundamental theology regards with suspicion any imputation of a direct intention to the Christ concerning the Church. But this skepticism runs counter to the Church's teaching that, together with her ministry in its current form, she was instituted and willed by Christ.

The Church affirms that it is in the divinely instituted, sacramental character of the priesthood that the reason for its reservation to men is to be found. Many things besides bread and wine feed our bodies, but it was Christ himself who chose to allow the natural signification of bread and wine as food and drink to supply the appropriate basis for the sacrament of the eucharist. While his selection of bread and wine should not be seen as arbitrary—for bread and wine are food and drink, after all—it could have been otherwise. The same can be said of his institution of the sacrament of holy orders where the complex natural significations associated with maleness and paternity are taken up into the sacramental sign which Christ established.

Thus, the distinction between sacramental priesthood and ecclesial ministry (forms of service established by the Church) is critical if the reservation of priestly ordination to men is not in our time to appear to be a violation of justice. Because it neglects this distinction, the CTSA report fails to take proper account of the recent affirmations of Pope John Paul II, the Congregation for the Doctrine of the Faith, and other church authorities of the "equal personal dignity of men and women." Moreover, experience shows that there are very few inherent limitations in a woman's ability to do any job as well or better than a man. If the priestly office were an ecclesial ministry only, one founded simply on baptism and not on a sacrament of holy orders, there would be little reason to reserve it to men and withhold it from women, who would seem to be just as able to carry it out.

However, while the range and structure of ecclesial ministries are, broadly speaking, subject to institution and development by the appropriate ecclesiastical authority, the sacraments are not. The sacraments are not the creation of the Church. By definition, they could not be since, though their celebration depends on human agents, they produce effects that are beyond what human agents can accomplish on their own power: initiation and strengthening of communion with the blessed Trinity in baptism and confirmation; transformation of bread and wine into the body and blood of Christ in the eucharist; the forgiveness of sins in penance and reconciliation; the imaging of Christ's union with the Church in matrimony; conferral of a participation in the saving work of Christ in holy orders; enhancement of physical and spiritual well-being in anointing of the sick.

Only God can establish a sacramental order in which such effects can be counted upon to be produced regularly through created signs and human activities. The seven sacraments have been entrusted to the Church by Christ as part of the economy of salvation and, as part of the deposit of faith, their nature, number, and structure constitute a given that the Church guards and administers but is not authorized to alter in any substantial way.

It has been the constant conviction of the Catholic Church that women cannot validly receive priestly ordination. Given the absolutely vital place of valid episcopal and priestly orders in the entire sacramental economy and liturgical practice of the Church, it would be doctrinally and theologically unthinkable, as well as pastorally irresponsible, for her to depart from the way pointed out by Christ and the apostles in this matter. In the end, the issue turns, not on a decision of the Church, but on her *obedience* to Christ and the apostles.

3. Level of Authority of the Teaching

Finally, the CTSA report challenges the claim of the Congregation for the Doctrine of the Faith *responsum* that the reservation of ordination to men "has been set forth infallibly by the ordinary and universal magisterium." The gist of the report's argument is this: Since the pope did not specifically say that his teaching on this point is infallible and since it cannot be proved that the bishops or the faithful throughout the world are united in the belief that this teaching should be held definitively, it is not clear that it has been infallibly defined. Canon 749.3 of the *Code of Canon Law* says that "no doctrine is understood to be infallibly defined unless this fact is clearly established."

It should be noted in the first place that by understating the degree of episcopal consensus on this issue, the CTSA report gives the misleading impression that the burden of proof for the definitive character of the teaching set forth in *Ordinatio Sacerdotalis* and identified as such in the Congregation for the Doctrine of the Faith *responsum* falls on the magisterium, the appeal to *Lumen Gentium* 25.2 being allegedly unsustainable in this case. But only in the past few decades, and then only because of the initially unauthorized ordination of women in the Episcopal Church in the United States, have any serious questions about the reservation of priestly orders to men been raised in the Catholic Church. The magisterium's appeal to *Lumen Gentium* is legitimate and well founded, and the burden of proof—were there any to be had—surely falls on those who oppose the traditional teaching or question its centrality within the deposit of faith. The CTSA report fails to acknowledge this point and focuses on the narrower question of whether the teaching about the reservation of priestly ordination to men has been infallibly taught.

It is the understanding of the Church that Christ's promise that the Holy Spirit would guide her into all truth means that he will not leave his people in doubt about matters pertaining to the deposit of the faith. Hence, an important question in determining whether something has been infallibly taught is whether it is the sort of thing that *can be known* infallibly by the Church—that is, whether it belongs to the deposit of faith. Many Catholics who assent to the doctrine of the immaculate conception without hesitation, for example, might not be able to show its connection with the central truths of the faith. Their faith, as a truly "theological act," rests in the truthfulness of God revealing and in his promise to guide the Church in teaching his revelation in an authentic and complete manner. The doctrine of the immaculate conception is part of the object of faith which is revealed by God and proposed by the Church. In teaching this and other doctrines, the Church strives to show how the matter in question bears on the deposit of faith that can be known infallibly as part of divine revelation.

With regard to the reservation of ordination to men—while, unlike the dogma of the immaculate conception, it has not been the object of an exercise of the extraordinary magisterium—it is important that teachers in the Church explain how the doctrine concerns something that can be known infallibly. Only a matter proposed as formally revealed or as certainly true can be known infallibly and thus can be the object of infallible teaching, whether extraordinary or ordinary, requiring full and definitive assent on the part of the faithful. The crucial issue then is that, as we have seen, because the origin of the sevenfold sacramental economy lies in the will of Christ, the matter of the proper recipient of ordination is a teaching that pertains to the deposit of faith. Hence, the issue is doctrinal, as the Church has repeatedly insisted, rather than purely disciplinary. The CTSA report neglects this crucial point.

There is, of course, the further question about the level of authority with which the Church has taught on the subject under discussion. The Holy Father has not exercised his extraordinary infallible magisterium in affirming the teaching of the reservation of priestly ordination to men; nor, of course, has any council done so. It therefore belongs to the ordinary, rather than the extraordinary, magisterium, as the Congregation for the Doctrine of the Faith explicitly affirms in its *responsum*. The CTSA report questions how it can be clearly shown that a teaching belongs to the ordinary universal infallible magisterium.

One might well ask what could avail as evidence that "the whole body of Catholic bishops is teaching the same doctrine and obliging the faithful to give it their definitive assent"[16] if the long-standing and undisturbed possession of the teaching concerning the reservation of priestly ordination to men does not constitute an instance of universal ordinary magisterium. The consensus of the pope and bishops, upon which the ordinary magisterium rests, implies not only a contemporary unanimity but a historic one as well, one that encompasses the Church throughout the ages.

As we have already noted above, the CTSA report profoundly understates and undervalues the significance of the consensus already in place in the Church and overrates the doctrinal significance of the *dissent* from that consensus at the present time and in certain quarters. But the existence of such dissent does not in itself constitute grounds for underestimating the force of the consensus that in fact has prevailed in the Church in the past and that continues to prevail now. Scripture provides the basis for the teaching, and the tradition presents a constant witness to it. The magisterium of the popes and bishops throughout the centuries has adhered to the teaching. In our day Pope John Paul II, in communion with the bishops, has explicitly judged it to be part of the deposit of faith.

The Holy Father did not make this judgment an exercise of the extraordinary magisterium. In effect, he vouched for the infallibility of the constant teaching of the universal ordinary magisterium on this matter and thus confirmed, with his own authority as successor of Peter, a teaching that is already part of the faith of the Church.

The very point of affirming that something is taught by the universal ordinary magisterium of the Church, which is the normal form of her infallibility, is to indicate that not everything that the Church teaches requires dogmatic definition in order for it to command full and complete assent on the part of the faithful. The proper action of the pope with respect to the universal ordinary magisterium is not to supplant it with an ex cathedra definition, but to confirm its own infallibility. The infallibility of the universal ordinary magisterium does not derive from the extraordinary magisterium. Rather, it comes from the ordinary magisterium itself, in particular from the magisterium of the pope as head of the episcopal college who gives voice to the entire episcopal body.

Contrary to the complaint of the CTSA report, the Congregation for the Doctrine of the Faith appropriately indicated that it is the definitive assent of the faithful to the universal ordinary magisterium that is required with regard to the teaching of the reservation of priestly ordination to men in its *responsum*. The congregation took this action only after continued questions had arisen about the force of the teaching already affirmed in *Ordinatio Sacerdotalis*.

Theologians in the Church have the responsibility of elucidating the truths of the faith. Sometimes that elucidation will involve the theological community in long and difficult discussion. The understanding of the Church's teaching on the reservation of the sacrament of orders to men will require just such discussion and debate, since the theological arguments for the teaching have not yet been fully explored.

Instead of undertaking this task, the CTSA report raises a series of difficulties about the grounds of the teaching. At one point, the report asserts that the effort to conform one's judgment to the judgment of the pope "may not suffice to overcome a person's doubts and bring one to sincere internal assent."[17] This may well be. But in the present case it should be recognized that the teaching concerning the reservation of holy orders possesses as much of a claim to definitiveness as one might reasonably expect—one that has a basis in Scripture, that is attested by an unbroken tradition in the Church, that has been supported by serious theological work, and that is proposed by the magisterium as requiring the definitive assent of the faithful. It may be hoped that this recognition would aid in overcoming doubts where they persist and in fostering the sincere internal assent that the truths of faith demand of all of us.

Notes

1. Catholic Theological Society of America, draft report "Tradition and the Ordination of Women," *Origins* 26:6 (June 27, 1996): 90-94.
2. Catholic Theological Society of America, "Tradition and the Ordination of Women," *Origins* 27:5 (June 19, 1997): 75-79 (hereinafter CTSA report).
3. CTSA report, 77.
4. *Origins* 6:6 (July 1, 1976): 92-96; in CTSA report, 77.
5. *Origins* 6.6 (July 1, 1976): 95.
6. Ibid.
7. Ibid.
8. CTSA report, 77.
9. Ibid.
10. Ibid.
11. St. Thomas Aquinas, IV *Sent*. d. 25, q. 2, a. 1.
12. CTSA report, 78, 79.
13. Congregation for the Doctrine of the Faith, "Declaration on the Question of the Admission of Women to the Ministerial Priesthood *(Inter Insigniores)" Origins* 6:33 (February 3, 1977): 517-524, nos. 35-39; John Paul II, "Apostolic Letter on Ordination and Women *(Ordinatio Sacerdotalis)" Origins* 24:4 (June 9, 1994): 49-52, no. 3.
14. CTSA report, 79.
15. Ibid.
16. Ibid.
17. Ibid.

Source: *Origins* 27:16 (October 2, 1997): 265-271.

Called to Global Solidarity: International Challenges for U.S. Parishes

A Statement Approved by the National Conference of Catholic Bishops

November 1997

Introduction

At a time of dramatic global changes and challenges, Catholics in the United States face special responsibilities and opportunities. We are members of a universal Church that transcends national boundaries and calls us to live in solidarity and justice with the peoples of the world. We are also citizens of a powerful democracy with enormous influence beyond our borders. As Catholics and Americans we are uniquely called to global solidarity.

One of God's greatest gifts is the universal character of the Church, blessing and calling us to live in solidarity with our sisters and brothers in faith. In many ways our community of faith practices solidarity every day. Missionaries preach the Gospel and celebrate the eucharist. Catholic relief workers feed the hungry and promote development. Our prayers, donations, and volunteers assist the Church in Latin America, Central and Eastern Europe, Asia, and Africa. The United States Catholic Conference and other Catholic groups defend human life and human rights, promote global justice, and pursue peace.

However, these international institutions, programs, and collections have not yet awakened a true sense of solidarity among many Catholics in the United States. The international commitment of the Church in the United States is not all it can and should be. Our parishes often act as islands of local religious activity rather than as parts of the mystical body of Christ. At the parish level, where the Church lives, we need to integrate more fully the international dimensions of Catholic discipleship within a truly universal Church.

While many parishes do build global bridges, the Church's teaching on global solidarity is too often unknown, unheard, or unheeded. The coming jubilee offers U.S. parishes a graced moment to strengthen our international solidarity, since the themes of the millennium call us so clearly to this vital task.

The Church's teaching on international justice and peace is not simply a mandate for a few large agencies, but a challenge for every believer and every Catholic community of faith. The demands of solidarity require not another program, but greater awareness and integration into the ongoing life of the parish. The Church's universal character can be better reflected in how every parish prays, educates, serves, and acts. A parish reaching beyond its own members and beyond national boundaries is a truly "catholic" parish. An important role for the parish is to challenge and encourage every believer to greater global solidarity.

These reflections are intended for pastors, parish leaders, and other involved Catholics. They address the Catholic call to global solidarity in two distinct but related ways. One is the individual responsibility of every Catholic founded in our baptism and expressed in our everyday choices and actions. Another is the essential role of the parish as the spiritual home and religious resource for the Christian faithful, both sacramental and educational, and as a place for common prayer and action in pursuit of global solidarity.

A few years ago we developed and adopted *Communities of Salt and Light*, a modest reflection on the social mission of the parish. We would like to build on the remarkable response to this document and encourage parishes to strengthen ties of solidarity with all the peoples of the world, especially the poor and persecuted. We also wish to provide a framework for parish leaders looking to strengthen or initiate programs of international solidarity.

Signs of the Times

For Catholics in the United States, the call to international solidarity takes on special urgency. We live in the largest of the world's wealthy nations, a global military and political power. Yet all around us are signs of suffering and need:

- 35,000 persons die of hunger and its consequences every day around the world.
- The specter of genocide and ethnic violence has become sadly familiar in Central Africa and other places.
- Christian and other believers are persecuted or harassed in China, Vietnam, Indonesia, parts of the Middle East, and within our own hemisphere.
- Conflicts with religious dimensions divide and destroy people in Bosnia, Sudan, Northern Ireland, East Timor, and too many other places.
- Foreign debt crushes hopes and paralyzes progress in too many poor nations.

- Refugees and displaced persons are overwhelming borders in much of the world.
- 26,000 people, mostly civilians, are maimed or killed every year by antipersonnel landmines.
- Forests, rivers, and other parts of God's creation are being destroyed by environmental neglect and devastation.
- Some nations and nongovernmental organizations resort to attacks on human life, including coerced abortion and sterilization.

These are just some examples of the crisis of solidarity facing our world.

Our world has changed dramatically. Walls have fallen and communism has collapsed. Lech Walensa, Vaclav Havel, and Nelson Mandela have moved from prison cells to presidential offices. The Cold War has ended, but our world is still haunted by too much violence and not enough development for those in need.

During the last decade, the rapid globalization of markets, communication, and transportation has dramatically drawn the world together. Global economic forces empower some and impoverish many. The gulf between rich and poor nations has widened, and the sense of responsibility toward the world's poor and oppressed has grown weaker. The world watched for too long as thousands died in Bosnia, Rwanda, and Zaire.

There is increasing complacency about the defense of human rights. Our country is tempted to turn its back on long traditions of openness and hospitality to immigrants and refugees who have nowhere to turn. The United States ranks first in the world in the weapons we sell to poor nations yet near last in the proportion of our resources we devote to development for the poor.

Our nation is deeply affected by economic, political, and social forces around the globe. The effects of these forces are evident in our economy, the immigrants and refugees among us, the threat of terrorism, dynamics of the drug trade, and pressures on workers. We are tempted by the illusion of isolationism to turn away from global leadership in an understandable but dangerous preoccupation with the problems of our own communities and nation. In the face of these challenges we see divergent paths. One path is that of indifference, even hostility to global engagement. Another path views the world as simply a global market for the goods and services of the United States.

Our faith calls us to a different road—a path of global responsibility and solidarity. The call to solidarity is at the heart of Pope John Paul II's leadership. He has insisted that the test of national leadership is how we reach out to defend and enhance the dignity of the poor and vulnerable, at home and around the world. He calls us to defense of all human life and care for God's creation. In his visits to this country, the Holy Father called on our nation to "spare no effort in advancing authentic freedom and in fostering human rights and solidarity."

Theological Foundations

The Moral Challenge

Cain's question, "Am I my brother's keeper?" (Gn 4:9), has global implications and is a special challenge for our time, touching not one brother but all our sisters and brothers. Are we responsible for the fate of the world's poor? Do we have duties to suffering people in far-off places? Must we respond to the needs of suffering refugees in distant nations? Are we keepers of the creation for future generations?

For the followers of Jesus, the answer is yes. Indeed, we are our brothers' and sisters' keepers. As members of God's one human family, we acknowledge our duties to people in far-off places. We accept God's charge to care for all human life and for all creation.

We have heard the Lord's command, "Love your neighbor as yourself." In our linked and limited world, loving our neighbor has global implications. In faith, we know our neighbors live in Rwanda and Sudan, in East Timor and China, in Bosnia and Central America, as well as across our country and next door. Baptism, confirmation, and continuing participation in the body of Christ call us to action for "the least among us" without regard for boundaries or borders.

One Human Family

Beyond differences of language, race, ethnicity, gender, culture, and nation, we are one human family. Whether at World Youth Day, on World Mission Sunday, or in the daily celebration of the liturgy, the Church gathers people of every nation, uniting them in worship of the one God who is maker and redeemer of all. In so doing, the Church attests to the God-given unity of the human family and the human calling to build community.

Promoting the unity of the human family is the task of the whole Church. It belongs to the Holy Father, but it also belongs to the local parish. In the eucharist the Church prays for the peace of the world and the growth of the Church in love, and it advances these gifts. Readings from Acts and the Letters of Paul tell us of the concern of distant churches for the needy communities in Jerusalem and Macedonia. In faith, the world's hungry and homeless, the victims of injustice and religious persecution, are not mere issues; they are our sisters and brothers.

The Demands of Solidarity

Pope John Paul II has written, "Sacred Scripture continually speaks to us of an active commitment to our neighbor and demands of us a shared responsibility for all of humanity. This duty is not limited to one's own family, nation or state, but extends progressively to all . . . so no one can consider himself extraneous or indifferent to the lot of another member of the human family."[1]

Duties of solidarity and the sacrifices they entail fall not just on individuals but on groups and nations as well.[2] According to Pope John Paul II, solidarity with the human family consists in "a firm and persevering determination to commit oneself to the common good."[3] In pursuit of solidarity, Pope John Paul II calls for a worldwide effort to promote development, an effort that "involves sacrificing the positions of income and of power enjoyed by the more developed economies" in the interest of "an overall human enrichment to the family of nations."[4]

Solidarity is action on behalf of the one human family, calling us to help overcome the divisions in our world. Solidarity binds the rich to the poor. It makes the free zealous for the cause of the oppressed. It drives the comfortable and secure to take risks for the victims of tyranny and war. It calls those who are strong to care for those who are weak and vulnerable across the spectrum of human life. It opens homes and hearts to those in flight from terror and to migrants whose daily toil supports affluent lifestyles. Peacemaking, as Pope John Paul II has told us, is the work of solidarity.

Pope John Paul II sharply challenges the growing gaps between rich and poor nations and between rich and poor within nations. He recognizes important values of market economics but insists that they be guided by the option for the poor and the principle of the global common good. He challenges leaders to respect human life and human rights, to protect workers and the vulnerable. He insists that nations halt the arms trade, ban landmines, promote true development, and relieve the crushing burden of international debt. The Holy Father's call to global responsibility is the core of a Catholic international agenda and the foundation of a Catholic commitment to solidarity.

U.S. Catholic Responses and Responsibilities

Around the United States, parishes, dioceses, and national church agencies strengthen the ties that bind our global family of faith. The U.S. Catholic community is a leader in global missions, relief, and development efforts. Our missionaries and relief workers risk their lives to preach and act on the Gospel.

Catholic Relief Services is our community's international relief and development arm, offering the solidarity of the American Catholic community to people in more than eighty countries. Each year, the United States Catholic Conference's Migration and Refugee Services assists almost a third of the refugees who flee religious and political persecution and immigrants seeking a new life. Through annual collections, the Church in the United States provides financial and other support for the mission and pastoral programs of the Church in Latin America, Central and Eastern Europe, Asia, and Africa. Through the Propagation of the Faith we help preach the Gospel, aid missionaries, and support the development of local churches. Through the work of our International Policy Committee, the U.S. bishops advocate for the needs of the poor and vulnerable around the globe.

The international agencies of the U.S. bishops are working together to strengthen the international witness of the United States Catholic Conference and to help parishes recognize their responsibilities as parts of a universal Church. There are many examples of U.S. Catholic international commitment: the Holy Childhood Association, Catholic Near East Welfare Association, National Council of Catholic Women, mission societies, religious advocacy groups, volunteer programs, exchange programs, and thousands of other ties between our Catholic community and the Church in other lands. These efforts put the Gospel to work and change lives here and abroad.

Across the country parishes are building relationships with sister parishes, especially in Latin America but also in Africa, Eastern Europe, Asia, and Oceania. Parish committees and legislative networks respond to pleas for help and advocate on issues of development, human rights, and peace. Parishes honor the memories of martyrs in Central America and Africa, and they act in defense of the unborn, the hungry, migrants, and refugees. Human rights advocates work for the release of prisoners of conscience and those suffering for their faith. Many parishes work on an ecumenical and interfaith basis to build bridges and act effectively on issues of global solidarity. These commitments transform and enrich U.S. parishes. As bishops, we seek to fan these flames of charity and justice in our parishes, dioceses, and national structures, so that the Church in the United States will be better light for our world.

Our international responsibilities enrich parish life and deepen genuine Catholic identity. Integrating themes of solidarity into the routines of parish life will make for a richer, more Catholic experience of Church. In giving a little, we receive much more.

All these efforts cannot be cause for complacency. Given the size of our community, our response through the years has not fully reflected our capacity or our calling. While much has been given overall, many of us have given little or nothing. The crisis of solidarity in our world demands more attention, more action, and more generosity from Catholics in the United States.

A Strategy of Integration

We have much to learn from those parishes that are leading the way in making global solidarity an integral part of parish ministry. They understand that social mission and solidarity are not a task for the few, and that concern for the Church in foreign lands cannot be confined to an occasional small offering. Christ is calling us to do more. In a sense, our parishes need to be more catholic and less parochial. A suffering world must find a place in the pastoral priorities of every Catholic parish.

Catholic communities of faith should measure their prayer, education, and action by how they serve the life, dignity, and rights of the human person at home *and* abroad. A parish's "catholicity" is illustrated in its willingness to go beyond its own boundaries to extend the Gospel, serve those in need, and work for global justice and peace. This is not a work for a few agencies or one parish committee, but for every believer and every local community of faith. This solidarity is expressed in our prayer and stewardship, how we form our children and invest our resources, and the choices we make at work and in the public arena.

These are matters of fundamental justice. Our nation has special responsibilities. Principled and constructive U.S. leadership is essential to build a safer, more just world. As Pope John Paul II insists again and again, our efforts must begin with fundamental reform of the "structures of violence" that bring suffering and death to the poor. The Catholic community will continue to speak on behalf of increased development assistance, relief from international debt, curbs on the arms trade, and respect for human life and the rights of families. We will continue to oppose population policies that insist on inclusion of abortion among the methods of family planning. Our foreign aid and peacemaking efforts can be reformed and improved, but they cannot be abandoned. Massive cuts in recent years in U.S. assistance for the poor around the world are an evasion of our responsibility as a prosperous nation and world leader. The recent decline in resources for sustainable development must be reversed.

It is not only the poor who need our solidarity and advocacy. Our world is still marked by destruction of human life and denial of human rights and religious liberty in so many places. Genuine solidarity requires active and informed citizenship. It requires common action to address the fundamental causes of injustice and the sources of violence in our world.

Conclusion

The Catholic community in the United States should be proud of the mission, advocacy, humanitarian relief, and development activities of our Church. U.S. Catholics are generous, active, committed, and concerned. But we must recognize that still too many children die, too many weapons are sold, and too many believers are persecuted.

Through the eyes of faith, the starving child, the believer in jail, and the woman without clean water or health care are not issues, but Jesus in disguise. The human and moral costs of the arms trade, international debt, environmental neglect, and ethnic violence are not abstractions, but tests of our faith. Violence in the Holy Land, tribal combat in Africa, religious persecution, and starvation around the world are not just headlines, but a call to action. As Catholics, we are called to renew the earth, not escape its challenge.

Our faith challenges us to reach out to those in need, to take on the global status quo, and to resist the immorality of isolationism. Pope John Paul II reminds us that a turn to "selfish isolation" would not only be a "betrayal of humanity's legitimate expectations . . . but also a real desertion of a moral obligation."

In one sense, we need to move our Church's concern from strong teaching to creative action. Working together, we can continue to help missionaries preach the Gospel, empower poor people in their own development, help the Church live and grow in lands marked by repression and poverty, and assist countries emerging from authoritarian rule. We must help reform and increase development assistance, curb the arms trade, ban landmines, relieve debt, and protect human life and human rights.

Many middle-aged and older Catholics grew up with a keen sense of "mission" and concern for children half a world away. Years ago we raised funds for "pagan babies," cleaned our plates, and prayed after Mass for the conversion of Russia. We didn't have global TV networks or the Internet, but we had a sense of responsibility. Over the years, we have continued this tradition through our missions, our collections for and advocacy on international needs, and our global development programs. We need to acknowledge and renew this traditional Catholic consciousness in a new age of global communications and economic interdependence. We respond very generously when the network news tells us of hurricanes and famines, but how will we help those victimized by the less visible disasters of poverty caused by structural injustice, such as debt, ethnic conflict, and the arms trade?

Our Church and parishes must call us anew to sacrifice and concern for a new generation of children who need food, justice, peace, and the Gospel. A central task for the next century is building families of faith that reach out beyond national boundaries.

As we approach the jubilee, let us rediscover in our time the meaning of the mystical body of Christ. We should mark the new millennium by making our families and local communities of faith signs of genuine solidarity—praying, teaching, preaching, and acting with new urgency and creativity on the international obligations of our faith. As our Holy Father has pointed out, "A commitment to justice and peace in a world like ours, marked by so many conflicts and intolerable social and economic inequalities, is a necessary condition for the preparation and celebration of the Jubilee."[5] This calls us to a new openness, a strategy of integration, and a true commitment to solidarity. In the words of the Apostle Paul, we must strive "to preserve the unity of the spirit through the bond of peace: one body and one Spirit . . . one Lord, one faith, one baptism; one God and Father of all, who is over all and through all and in all" (Eph 4:3-6).

Notes

1. John Paul II, *On the Hundredth Anniversary of Rerum Novarum (Centesimus Annus)* (Washington, D.C.: United States Catholic Conference, 1991), no. 51.
2. Ibid., no. 51; Paul VI, *On the Development of Peoples (Populorum Progressio)* (Washington, D.C.: United States Catholic Conference, 1976), no. 48.
3. John Paul II, *On Social Concern (Sollicitudo Rei Socialis)* (Washington, D.C.: United States Catholic Conference, 1987), no. 38.
4. *Centesimus Annus*, no. 52.
5. John Paul II, *On the Coming of the Third Millennium (Tertio Millennio Adveniente)* (Washington, D.C.: United States Catholic Conference, 1994), no. 51.

Source: Washington, D.C.: United States Catholic Conference, 1998.

Appendix A
Chronological Table of Important Events in the History of the Church in the United States from 1989 to 1997

1989

- Bicentennial of the establishment of the United States Catholic hierarchy.
- Fall of the Iron Curtain.
- Six Jesuits killed in El Salvador.
- U.S. Supreme Court in *Webster* decided that states had some authority to regulate abortions.
- Thomas Melady appointed U.S. ambassador to the Holy See.
- Earthquake in California damaged ecclesiastical properties, especially in the Diocese of Monterey.

1990

- *Ex Corde Ecclesiae* published.
- Special assembly of U.S. bishops at Santa Clara, Calif., on "The Bishop: A Person Called to Be a Priest, Prophet, and Leader."
- Roman synod of bishops on priestly life.
- Oregon Catholic Conference opposed State Health Care Rationing Plan and Oregon Sisters of Providence supported it.

1991

- *Centesimus Annus* published.
- Episcopal consultation in Rome on the pastoral on women's issues.
- Archbishops Roger Mahony of Los Angeles and Anthony Bevilacqua of Philadelphia created cardinals.
- Washington State Catholic Conference campaigned against initiatives 119 (on euthanasia) and 120 (on abortion).

1992

- Quincentenary of the discovery and evangelization of the Americas.
- U.S. Supreme Court upheld and modified Pennsylvania's Abortion Control Act.
- National Black Catholic Congress held in New Orleans.
- Archbishop John Quinn urged defeat of California physician-assisted death initiative (proposition 161), which was defeated.
- Archbishop Weakland and Cardinal John O'Connor exchanged views in *The New York Times* on "Dialogue on Women in the Church."

1993

- Centenary of papal representation in the United States.
- World Youth Day in Denver, Colo., at which Pope John Paul II presided.
- Catholic Relief Services announced its annual budget of $300 million for justice and peace operations in more than eighty countries.
- Michigan Catholic Conference opposed euthanasia and physician-assisted suicide.
- *Veritatis Splendor* published.
- Cardinal Joseph Bernardin named in sexual abuse suit.

1994

- *Ordinatio Sacerdotalis, Tertio Millennio Adveniente,* and the *Catechism of the Catholic Church* published in English.
- Oregon voted 51 to 49 percent to legitimate physician-assisted suicide, the first such law enacted in the United States.
- Dropping of suit vindicates Cardinal Bernardin.
- Cairo International Conference on Population and Development.
- Archbishops William Keeler and Adam Maida created cardinals.

1995

- Convocation '95: The Hispanic Presence in the New Evangelization in the United States held in San Antonio, Tex., to commemorate the fiftieth anniversary of the establishment of a national episcopal office for Hispanic affairs and to discuss issues of evangelization.

- *Evangelium Vitae* and *Ut Unum Sint* published.
- Pope John Paul II visited the United States and addressed the United Nations.

1996

- Seven Trappist monks in Algeria murdered.
- Cardinal Bernardin launched the Catholic Common Ground Project.
- Cardinal Mahony opposed California Proposition 209, which would eliminate, he asserted, affirmative action.
- Cardinal Bernardin of Chicago died.

1997

- Archbishop Francis George appointed to Chicago.
- Synod for America held in Rome.
- Eighth National Black Catholic Congress held in Baltimore.
- Mother Teresa of Calcutta died.
- St. Thérèse of Lisieux declared a doctor of the Church.
- President Bill Clinton vetoed the congressionally approved partial-birth abortion ban.
- First successful cloning of a sheep raised moral issues about human cloning.
- Archbishops Charles Chaput of Denver and Eusebius Beltran of Oklahoma City invited all people of goodwill to turn away from the death penalty.
- U.S. Supreme Court overturned its 1985 ruling in *Aquilar vs. Felton,* thereby allowing federally funded remedial instruction to take place in religious schools, and the court upheld Washington State's ban against assisted suicide.

Appendix B
Significant Statistics of the Church in the United States 1989-1997*

Categories	1989	1997
Population	57,019,948	61,207,914
Archdioceses	34	36
Dioceses	155	164
Priests	53,111	48,097
Seminarians	6233	4655
Parishes	19,860	19,677

*Statistics from the 1990 and 1997 editions of the *Official Catholic Directory,* published by P. J. Kenedy and Sons, New York, N.Y.

The decline in the number of priests (9%) and seminarians (25%) continued a post-1960s trend, but the decline in the number of parishes was a new phenomenon in American Catholicism.

Appendix C
Organization and Purpose
of the NCCB/USCC

The National Conference of Catholic Bishops (NCCB) and the United States Catholic Conference (USCC) are the organizations of the U.S. Catholic hierarchy. Through these distinct but closely related conferences—one a canonical entity, the other a civil corporation—the bishops fulfill their responsibilities of leadership and service to Church and nation, as called for in the Second Vatican Council.

The voting membership of the two conferences consists of approximately 300 active Catholic bishops of the United States. Although they do not have a deliberative vote, retired bishops—numbering around 110—also are invited to all general meetings and may take part in discussions. The two conferences share the same officers—president, vice president, treasurer, and secretary—who serve three-year terms and are elected by their fellow bishops. The conferences function through a general assembly, which meets at least once a year and usually twice, an administrative committee/board of approximately fifty bishop members, four executive-level committees, and some sixty standing and ad hoc committees. The committees deal with issues of pastoral concern that are important to the Church as a whole. The membership of the NCCB committees is exclusively bishops, while the USCC committees include clergy, men and women religious, and lay people.

The NCCB enables the bishops to exchange ideas and information, deliberate on the Church's broad concerns, and respond as a body. The USCC specifically acts as the public policy agency of the U.S. Catholic bishops. It provides an organizational structure and the resources needed to ensure coordination, cooperation, and assistance in the public, educational, social, and communications concerns of the Church at the national or interdiocesan level. Generally, the USCC committees develop policy and programs for approval by the administrative board and the body of bishops.

The General Secretariat, located in Washington, D.C., is staffed principally by the general secretary, who is elected by the body of bishops for a five-year term, and three associate general secretaries. It provides day-to-day administration and direction for the work of both conferences. The NCCB/USCC committees are staffed by individual secretariats and offices also located in Washington and administratively responsible to the General Secretary. Their staffs help the bishops establish and implement policy and pastoral programs on many

878

matters closely connected with Catholic life in the United States. The conferences also offer a multitude of information and consultative services to diocesan offices and other church agencies and institutions.

Presidents of the NCCB/USCC

1966-1971   Cardinal John F. Dearden of Detroit
1971-1974   Cardinal John J. Krol of Philadelphia
1974-1977   Archbishop (later Cardinal) Joseph L. Bernardin of Cincinnati (later Chicago)
1977-1980   Archbishop John R. Quinn of San Francisco
1980-1983   Archbishop John R. Roach of St. Paul
1983-1986   Bishop James W. Malone of Youngstown
1986-1989   Archbishop John L. May of St. Louis
1989-1992   Archbishop Daniel E. Pilarczyk of Cincinnati
1992-1995   Archbishop (later Cardinal) William H. Keeler of Baltimore
1995-1998   Bishop Anthony M. Pilla of Cleveland

Index